DEDICATION

This book is dedicated to the men and women of the Jewish faith who
served in the defense of the United States of America.

Editors
Michelle Beth Spivak
Natioanl Director of Communications
Development and Programs

Robert M. Zweiman, PNC
National Centennial Chairman

TURNER PUBLISHING COMPANY
Paducah, Kentucky

3

TURNER PUBLISHING COMPANY
Publishers of Military History
412 Broadway, P.O. Box 3101
Paducah, KY 42002-3101
Phone: 502-443-0121

Jewish War Veterans of the USA:
National Commander: Neil Goldman
National Centennial Chairman: Robert M. Zweiman, PNC
National Executive Director: Col. Herb Rosenbleeth USA (Ret)
National Director of Communications, Development
and Programs: Michelle Beth Spivak
National Consultant/Senior Fellow: Seymour S. Weisman, Ph.D.
Archivist: Sandor Cohen

Special Photographic Acknowledgement to: The Garrison
Studio, Washington, D.C.
Ed Owen Photography, Washington, D.C.

Turner Publishing Company Staff:
Chief Editor: Robert J. Martin
Designer: Ina F. Morse

Library of Congress Catalog Card No. 95-062445
ISBN: 1-56311-230-2
Limited Edition. Printed in the U.S.A.

Photo: JWV Convention, 1931.

TABLE OF CONTENTS

THE STARS AND STRIPES
MEDITERRANEAN

Vol. 2, No. 27, Saturday, June 10, 1944

For U.S. Armed Forces

TWO P

Bitter Tank Battle In Normand

West Wall Going West

SOUTHAMPTON WINCHESTER DOVER
BOURNEMOUTH PORTSMOUTH HASTINGS
WEYMOUTH NEWPORT EASTBOURNE

ENGLISH CHANNEL

cliffs
DUNKIRK
CALAIS ROULERS
BOULOGNE
DEAVRES LILLE
LE TOUQUE
ARRAS
CAYEUX
DIEPPE AMIENS
FECAMP
HAVRE NEUFCHATEL
HONFLEUR ROUEN
COMPIEGNE
PARIS
Seine R.
Somme R.
Pfc HOFFMAN

CHERBOURG
VALOGNES
CARENTAN BAYEUX
CAEN
COUTANCES
GRANVILLE

0 10 20 30 40 50 60

N TROOPS who landed on the Normandy coast of France Tuesday were engaged
mile front extending east and north from within 12 miles of Cherbourg
g was reported within the city of Caen and tank battles were in prog
southwest of Bayeux, first important town to fall to the Allied
troops.

Allied Troops Pushing Forward Past Bayeu

By Sgt. DON WILLIAMS
(Stars and Stripes Staff Writer)

Fierce fighting raged on a 70-mile front o
Normandy coast of France Friday as Allied
forces, under the personal command of General S
nard L. Montgomery, met with increasingly he
position in efforts to push across the Contentin p
and isolate the great port of Cherbourg.

Heavy tank engagements were reported
ress in the rolling Normandy fields several mi
south and southw
tured Bayeux,
from the coas
important town f
American, British
forces.

The Associated
that Allied troo
five miles south
eux. And the T
News Agency
afternoon tha
driven a wed
ward the Bayeux r
ward St. Lo
miles.

Allied and
reported lo
fighting in
city of C
of Bayeux
said in
Headquar
Force
had
phb

MAAF Plasters Munich In First Blow From Italy

ALLIED FORCE HEADQUAR-
June 9 — Strong forces of
an heavy bombers today
home the first attack on
shrine of Munich from
ases and used, for the
on record in this theater,
for accurate bombing
cast conditions.
e special MAAF an-
onight revealed no
e of more than 750
mbers and their
ings, Thunderbolts
as reported to
considerabl

tures Viterbo
les From R

Normandy and Nurnberg

E STARS AND STRIPE
MEDITERRANEAN
Printed In Italy

OWER IN VIEW

day, August 19, 1944

President Bill Clinton

THE WHITE HOUSE

WASHINGTON

August 15, 1995

Greetings to all those who have gathered for the 100th anniversary of the Jewish War Veterans of the United States of America.

Our nation's veterans have served America valiantly. Their experiences remind all of us of our great debt to those who have risked their lives in defense of liberty. We must always remember the supreme dedication, efficiency, and skill shown by our men and women in uniform, even as they faced daunting adversity. On behalf of a grateful nation, I express our deep appreciation for your selfless service and devotion to our country. I salute you for your important contribution to safeguarding our freedom and democracy.

Best wishes for a wonderful anniversary.

Bill Clinton

John M. Shalikashvili

CHAIRMAN OF THE JOINT CHIEFS OF STAFF
WASHINGTON, D. C. 20318-9999

March 1996

100TH ANNIVERSARY GREETINGS
TO THE
JEWISH WAR VETERANS OF THE U.S.A.

Congratulations to the members of the Jewish War Veterans of the U.S.A. on your centennial anniversary! This milestone recognizes the legacy of Jewish veterans who truly deserve sincere appreciation for devoted service and personal sacrifices in serving our country in peace and war.

Since its establishment in 1896, the JWV members have reached across the spectrum of our society; to our youth, and our retirees, the healthy and the homeless. But the military, and our veterans, have been the greatest beneficiaries of the work done by the JWV.

From the Spanish-American War, through the first and second World Wars and Korea to the jungles of Vietnam and the Gulf War, you were there, helping to set the stage for victory. It was through your determination, fortitude, and courage that you survived very difficult times and circumstances to return home to family and friends. And, we must never forget those who made the ultimate sacrifice in the name of freedom.

On behalf of the Joint Chiefs of Staff and the men and women of the Armed Forces, I salute each member of JWV, past and present. We who wear the uniform today are proud to stand beside you, guarding the wonderful heritage you have entrusted to our care.

Congratulations on your 100th anniversary. Best wishes for continued success in the future.

JOHN M. SHALIKASHVILI
Chairman
of the Joint Chiefs of Staff

9

William J. Perry

THE SECRETARY OF DEFENSE
WASHINGTON, DC 20301-1000

**100TH ANNIVERSARY GREETINGS
TO THE
JEWISH WAR VETERANS OF THE U.S.A.**

It is my great pleasure to congratulate the members of the Jewish War Veterans of the U.S.A. on your centennial anniversary. Few associations have reached this important milestone or have contributed so much to the Nation and its veterans.

Since its inception in 1896, the JWV has been at the forefront of the veterans movement, providing an active forum to discuss and study veterans and national security issues. Your efforts have helped to promote a strong America and to preserve the legacy of the many men and women who have served our Nation bravely in both war and peace.

The Civil War veterans who founded the JWV understood well the price of freedom. Most had emigrated to America to escape oppression, and they fought bravely in a war that claimed the lives of one-sixth of their comrades. Succeeding generations of Jewish War Veterans have demonstrated the same courage, determination, and love of country in every conflict from the Spanish-American War to Desert Storm. Your efforts contributed significantly to the safeguarding of our Nation.

I thank each and every member of the JWV, past and present, for your many efforts and sacrifices on behalf of this Nation. Your organization has done much to protect our heritage, and I know that we can depend upon you in the future.

Congratulations on your 100th anniversary, and best wishes for continued success.

William J. Perry

Jesse Brown

THE SECRETARY OF VETERANS AFFAIRS
WASHINGTON
August 10, 1995

A MESSAGE FROM THE SECRETARY OF VETERANS AFFAIRS

It is a profound honor for me to offer congratulations to the membership of the Jewish War Veterans of the U.S.A. on the occasion of your 100th anniversary.

Jewish War Veterans is the oldest national veterans organization, but the contributions of Jewish veterans go back much further than 1896. From the earliest days of colonial America, your ancestors were there, and when it came time to take up arms against the British, they were among the first to join the ranks of the upstart revolutionaries. In every battle since Lexington, Jewish Americans have been in uniform. No group of Americans seems to have a better understanding of the value and need for individuals to step forward in times of need and put aside their personal lives for the betterment of us all.

The Jewish War Veterans also exemplify the premise that I believe should be at the core of all veterans organizations -- that when service to country ends, service to community begins. For 100 years now, your members have brought that service to their communities all around the nation, and America is definitely richer for it.

You and your predecessors have built an incredibly strong and vibrant organization over the past 100 years. It is the kind of organization that I know will be a solid foundation for the next century for the Jewish War Veterans of the U.S.A.

May God bless you, and God bless the United States of America.

Jesse Brown

Putting Veterans First

O Loving Father, be with us in our tour o
Vietnam. Help us to meet and conquer o
daily temptations, our frustrations and our fea
We know we now live in a world of danger
a world of rocket and mortar, a world
mines and booby traps. Trials come down up
es swiftly and unexpectedly. Lift us at th
es. Pour out upon us Thy mercy and Thy
compassion which Thou hast shown us in
Be with our loved ones, we pray, and l
safe return...Amen.

JOSEF SCHVIMMER
021184

NINTH IN
OLD

Do

U.S. so
illed du
er atta

Carl E. Foley

477 H Street, NW
Washington, DC
20001-2694

202-371-8880
1-800-669-7079
Fax 202-371-8258

August 15, 1995

Mr. David H. Hymes
National Commander
Jewish War Veterans of America
1811 R. Street, Northwest
Washington, D.C. 20009-1659

Dear National Commander Hymes,

On behalf of the members and National Officers of the Blinded Veterans Association (BVA), I'm extremely pleased to offer JWV a hearty congratulations on reaching your 100th anniversary. You and I both know however that the effectiveness of a veterans service organization (vso) isn't solely judged by its longevity. Your past 100 years of service advocating for not only Jewish veterans but veterans of all creeds clearly places JWV at the forefront of today's veterans service organizations.

Just this past year, we, at BVA, celebrated our 50th anniversary. It's comforting to know that as we begin the journey into our second half-century, we're neither lost nor traveling an unexplored trail to some unknown destination. Rather, our quest to 100 years of successfully serving America's blinded veterans begins on an expressway already paved by JWV. Your example, your successes and even your set-backs will guide us. We can only pray that BVA will find the same amount of success in our second 50 years that you did in yours.

Thanks for the example!

Sincerely,

Carl E. Foley

Carl E. Foley
National President

Chartered by the United States Congress

William M. Detweiler

The American Legion

★ NATIONAL HEADQUARTERS ★ P. O. BOX 1055 ★ INDIANAPOLIS, INDIANA 46206 ★
(317) 630-1200 ★ FAX (317) 630-1223 ★

OFFICE OF THE
NATIONAL COMMANDER

July 31, 1995

Jewish War Veterans of the U.S.A.
1811 R Street, NW
Washington, DC 20009-1659

The American Legion is proud to recognize the 100th Anniversary of the Jewish War Veterans of the U.S.A., an organization dedicated to patriotism, Americanism and service.

Your organization's proud history has contributed greatly to the cause of veterans and their families while pushing America forward in the quest for national security and peace.

Jewish men and women have served bravely in the United States Armed Forces and I am proud that many of them are also members of The American Legion. As we work together to build a better America, we consistently devote our efforts to common goals:

- Quality VA health care.
- A strong military.
- Benefits for retired veterans.
- Sufficient pay for active duty GIs so they can raise families.
- Improved processing of VA claims for disabled veterans.

All of these issues require our combined efforts.

Congratulations to the Jewish War Veterans of the U.S.A. on a century of service to veterans, their families and to our country.

With best regards, I remain,

Very truly yours,

William M. Detweiler

WILLIAM M. DETWEILER
National Commander

General Jack N. Merritt

ASSOCIATION OF THE UNITED STATES ARMY

2425 Wilson Boulevard, Arlington, Virginia 22201-3385 • (703) 841-4300

General Jack N. Merritt
United States Army (Ret.)
President

14 August 1995

Jewish War Veterans of the U.S.A.
Attn: Beth Cohn, Editorial Assistant
1811 R Street, N.W.
Washington, D.C. 20009-1659

Dear Commander Hymes:

On behalf of the Association of the United States Army, it is my distinct pleasure to extend greetings as you mark both the centennial anniversary of the Jewish War Veterans of the U.S.A and the publication of the history of your great organization.

Your devotion to country with the individual service and sacrifice of every member of the Jewish War Veterans has shaped and kept the United States a beacon of liberty. This is as true today as it was in 1896 when your organization was founded as living proof to the nation of the valor of Jewish soldiers in the Civil War. For 100 years, Jewish War Veterans have worked selflessly to serve the needs of both our nation's veterans and our communities. This tireless dedication to helping others improves the quality of all our citizens. This is a time to mark your accomplishments.

Among these we would include your charter from Congress, especially recognizing the Jewish War Veterans of the U.S.A. for its work for the men and women who served our nation in World War II and Korea.

We also salute your efforts in educating Congress on the need to establish the Department of Veterans Affairs as a cabinet position.

We share with you a continuing commitment to promoting Americanism and the contributions of those who fought so very hard to preserve the freedoms we all enjoy. This is especially true in your historic defense of the fundamental freedoms contained in the First Amendment to the United States Constitution and your efforts to extend those freedoms to all men and women.

You can take great pride in your organization's strong advocacy in Congress on behalf of all veterans and the entitlements promised the men and women who served in our armed forces.

We wish you continued success as you address the challenges of a new century and serve tomorrow's veterans.

Sincerely,

General Jack N. Merritt
U.S. Army, Retired

JWB JEWISH CHAPLAINS COUNCIL
A service of Jewish Community Centers Association/NA
15 East 26th Street, New York NY 10010-1579
Telephone (212) 532-4949 • Fax (212) 481-4174

Jewish Community Centers Association NA

President
Ann P. Kaufman

Executive Vice-President
Allan B. Finkelstein

Associate Executive Director
Solomon Greenfield

JWB Jewish Chaplains Council

Chairman
Rabbi Frank M. Waldorf

Executive Committee:
Rabbi Mattew H. Simon,
  Chairman
Rabbi Jacob J. Greenberg
Rabbi Barry Hewitt Greene
Rabbi Moshe Samber
Rabbi Victor M. Solomon
Rabbi Frank M. Waldorf

Armed Force and Veterans Services Committee

Chairman
Ronald L. Leibow

Director
Rabbi David Lapp

Deputy Director
Rabbi Nathan M. Landman

ב"ה

July 25, 1995

Jewish War Veterans of the U.S.A.
1811 R Street, NW
Washington, DC 20009-1659

As Director of the Jewish Welfare Board Jewish Chaplains Council, the agency of the Jewish Community Centers Association of North America, which has been serving Jewish Chaplains and Jews in the Armed Forces of the United States, and in Veterans Affairs Medical Centers, I wish to express our heartiest congratulations and warmest greetings on the occasion of the 100th anniversary of the Jewish War Veterans of the U.S.A.

In Pirke Avot, the Chapters of the Sages in the Mishnah, we are admonished, "In a place where there are no men, strive to be a *mentsch*." Throughout its distinguished history the Jewish War Veterans of the U.S. A. has stood up as advocateson on behalf of of Jews who have served the United States in uniform and has been a champion for protecting the rights of all citizens and the cause of religious freedom for all Americans. You have also fought valiantly against those who would spread hatred and distrust in American society.

As we salute you on this notable occasion, we express our prayers that the Almighty will continue to prosper the work of your hands and hearts in the years ahead.

Sincerely,

Rabbi David Lapp
Director

FLEET RESERVE ASSOCIATION

Representing All Active Duty, Reserve, and Retired Personnel of the
U.S. NAVY ☆ U.S. MARINE CORPS ☆ U.S. COAST GUARD

125 N. West Street, Alexandria, Virginia 22314-2754
(703) 683-1400 • (800) FRA-1924 • FAX (703) 549-6610

25 July 1995

GREETINGS TO THE JEWISH WAR VETERANS OF THE U.S.A.

On behalf of the 162,000 "Shipmates" of the Fleet Reserve Association, I am delighted to send greetings to the membership of the Jewish War Veterans of U.S.A. on their 100th Anniversary.

The steady and lasting support provided by the Jewish War Veterans of the U.S.A. since 1896 has contributed directly to the spirit and strength of our Armed Forces over the last 100 years. The result being the finest Armed Forces in the world today.

Your dedication since inception, has served a dual role in America. As a veterans' organization, you have served a patriotic mission by staunchly promoting Americanism and by your significant efforts toward protecting the rights and benefits of our nation's war veterans. As a Jewish organization you have provided a strong voice for religious freedom throughout the world.

It is my honor to salute the Jewish War Veterans of the U.S.A. for your commitment to the well-being and protection of the dedicated people who are serving or have served in our Navy, Marine Corps and Coast Guard.

In Loyalty, Protection and Service,

George P. Hyland

GEORGE P. HYLAND
National President

Valerie May

American Gold Star Mothers, Inc.

ORGANIZED JUNE 4, 1928
INCORPORATED JANUARY 5, 1929
CHARTERED BY CONGRESS - JUNE 12, 1984
FOUNDED BY GRACE DARLING SEIBOLD

NATIONAL PRESIDENT

Valerie May

TELEPHONE 202 – 265-0991
NATIONAL HEADQUARTERS
2128 LEROY PLACE, N.W.
WASHINGTON, D.C. 20008-1893

August 1, 1995

David H. Hymes, National Commander
Jewish War Veterans of the U.S.A.
1811 R. Street, N. W.
Washington, D.C. 20009-1659

Dear Commander Hymes:

Congratulations on the 100th anniversary of the Jewish War Veterans of the United States of America.

It is an honor to send you greetings on behalf of the American Gold Star Mothers, Inc.

Your dedication to service to our country, our Veterans and communities across this great nation has withstood the element of time and your organization is as strong and devoted now as in the past.

The Jewish War Veterans served side by side with men of all heritages as brothers with only one purpose, to preserve the freedom we still enjoy today.

In this year of celebration on your 100th year of commitment to promoting patriotism and the contributions to all who fought for our freedom, be proud as we are proud of you.

American Gold Star Mothers are also committed to the same purposes and offer our support.

We send our appreciation for your efforts and wish you continued success for at least 100 more years.

Sincerely

Valerie May

Valerie May
National President

Richard D. Tex Wandke

LEGION OF VALOR
OF THE UNITED STATES OF AMERICA, INC.

FOUNDED AS MEDAL OF HONOR LEGION-1890
CHARTERED BY ACT OF CONGRESS 1955

National Commander
Jewish War Veterans
1811 R. Street N.W.
Washington, D.C. 20009-1659

Dear Commander Hymes,   5 August 1995

The members of the Legion of Valor extend warm greetings to
the members of the Jewish War Veterans as you celebrate your
100 years of existence. As we all know, War comes at a high
price. Those of us, who have put on a uniform, know that we
must be ready to defend the freedom that our forefathers fought
for to ensure that we remain a strong Democratic Nation. In
order to maintain this freedom we must from time to time go
to War. Wars it seems is the price we have to pay to ensure
that our Democratic ideals are not taken away from us. This
year is significant in that not only are you celebrating your
100th year, but we are remembering the 50th Anniversary of the
end of World War II. Those of us who have spilled our blood
in combat know the sacrifices that have been made in war. Today
it seems that many who have never worn a uniform find it fitting
to change the way our History was made. We have had to pass
an amendment to our constitution in order to protect our flag.
We have had to battle the Smithonian Institute in order to ensure
that how World War II ended is not changed. Now we find that
our evening news has taken up the the sword to assist those
who want to change History. As we look at our elected officials
we find that most have not served a day in the Military. We
as Veterans must work harder than ever before to ensure that
the word Veteran does not turn into a four letter word.
We the members of the Legion of Valor are proud to join hands
with the Jewish War Veterans. We wish you continued success
in the years to come.

Sincerely,

Richard D. Tex Wandke
National Commander 1994-1995
Legion of Valor

Lynn Lyss

NJCRAC 50th Anniversary 1944–1994

August 14, 1995

David H. Hymes
National Commander
Jewish War Veterans
  of the U.S.A.
1811 R Street, N.W.
Washington, D.C. 20009-1659

Dear Commander Hymes:

With the greatest respect, I am writing to offer heartfelt congratulations to the Jewish War Veterans on the occasion of its 100th anniversary. Throughout its history, the JWV has made a unique contribution to the Jewish and general communities. Veterans of our armed forces who happen to be Jewish have played a special role in expressing and transmitting our national and Jewish values. The JWV has embodied these values in its efforts to build the just society we all want to see.

The National Jewish Community Relations Advisory Council appreciates the active role that the JWV has played in our deliberations. Your voice, together with that of our other national and local member agencies, has helped shape the direction of our community relations concerns and activities.

Again, the leadership and staff of the NJCRAC joins me in congratulating the Jewish War Veterans on achieving this momentous milestone.

Sincerely,

Lynn Lyss

Lynn Lyss
Chair

National Jewish Community Relations Advisory Council
443 Park Avenue South, New York, New York 10016.7322 • 212.684.6950 Fax 212.686.1353

Hugh H. Mayberry

HUGH H. MAYBERRY
NATIONAL PRESIDENT

NAVY LEAGUE OF THE UNITED STATES

Serving the Sea Services since 1902

2300 WILSON BOULEVARD
ARLINGTON, VIRGINIA 22201

A Message to the Members of the Jewish War Veterans of the U.S.A.

Congratulations and best wishes on the centennial of the Jewish War Veterans of the U.S.A. and on the publication of *The History of the Jewish War Veterans of the United States of America*. Indeed this is a momentous anniversary commemorating the sacrifices and many contributions of America's Jews to our national security, and the contributions of your outstanding organization.

Our two associations stand together, working to educate the American people on issues affecting our defense, our veterans, and, ultimately, our nation itself. The Jewish War Veterans of the U.S.A. has been an articulate and effective spokesman for the veterans who served in World War I, World War II, Korea, Vietnam, and the Persian Gulf War, and is helping to ensure that we do not forget the lessons of the past in our planning for the future.

This book will provide generations of Americans with important insights and information on the vital contributions of our Jewish citizens to the cause of freedom. The entire membership of the Navy League of the United States joins with me in wishing the Jewish War Veterans of the U.S.A. success in your next 100 years.

Sincerely

Hugh H. Mayberry

HHM/pab

PVA

PARALYZED VETERANS
OF AMERICA
Chartered by the Congress
of the United States

August 11, 1995

David H. Hymes
National Commander
Jewish War Veterans of the U.S.A.
1811 R Street, N.W.
Washington, D.C. 20009-1659

Dear Commander Hymes:

On behalf of the Paralyzed Veterans of America (PVA), I wish to offer our congratulations
to the Jewish War Veterans of the U.S.A. (JWV) on the occasion of your centennial. We await
the publication of the history of the JWV, and look forward to reflecting upon the many
accomplishments of our Country's oldest, continuously active veterans' organization.

During your 100 year history, JWV's dedication to veterans, and to all Americans, has been a
model of service in the cause of freedom and liberty. JWV's vigilance through a century of
strife and turmoil has helped preserve the dignity and rights we all enjoy. Every citizen of this
Republic owes the members of the JWV a debt that cannot be repaid.

The members of PVA honor and salute the Jewish War Veterans of the U.S.A.'s century of
service and dedication to the ideals of this great Nation.

Sincerely,

Richard Grant

Richard Grant
National President

Michael A. Nelson

THE RETIRED OFFICERS ASSOCIATION

201 North Washington Street, Alexandria, VA 22314-2539 (703) 549-2311

Michael A. Nelson, Lieutenant General, USAF (Ret)
President

Greetings to the Jewish War Veterans of the U. S. A.

Congratulations to the officers and the members of the Jewish War Veterans of the United States of America on your 100th Anniversary of service to God and Country!

As our nation's oldest, continuously active national veterans' organization, you and your members have been in the vanguard, supporting the well-earned rights of our veteran population as well as promoting Americanism and the contributions of those who fought to preserve the freedoms of this country. Moreover, Jewish War Veterans has always been one of the strongest voices for religious freedom throughout the world.

For all of us, the Jewish War Veterans of The United States of America has served as an organization to emulate -- solid and steadfast, yet dynamic and forward thinking. As an Association, you have continued to grow in stature as your officers and members continue to serve our great nation.

Our organizations have worked together in the furtherance of our members' mutual interests and goals, and I foresee and look forward to an even more active and closer working relationship with the officers of Jewish War Veterans and The Retired Officers Association in the months and years to come.

I am indeed honored to have the opportunity to address the membership of Jewish War Veterans of The United States within the pages of this historic publication. As you reflect on the many achievements of your organization over this last century and rededicate yourselves to service to all veterans and their families for the next 100 years, I thank you on behalf of the 400,000 members of The Retired Officers Association for what you have done and wish you continued success in all your future endeavors.

Michael A. Nelson

Charles R. Jackson

CHARLES R. JACKSON
FM/C USN (RET)
PRESIDENT/CHIEF EXECUTIVE OFFICER

Non Commissioned Officers Association of the United States of America

225 N. Washington Street · Alexandria, Virginia 22314 · Telephone (703) 549-4579

Dear Commander Hymes,

It is with great pleasure that I extend greetings on behalf of the entire membership of the Non Commissioned Officers Association to you and the members of the Jewish War Veterans Of The U.S.A. as you celebrate 100 years of service to America and it's veterans.

During your distinguished 100 year history the Jewish War Veterans has never wavered from its founding goals of promoting Americanism and protecting the earned entitlements and benefits of those who have served in the nation's armed forces. The commitment the JWV has shown to America and to all of her veterans is commendable and your entire membership can take great pride in the history of dedication which you commemorate this year.

As a voice for religious freedom throughout the world the courage shown by the JWV is only matched by the courage shown on the battle field by its many valiant members. As you move into your second century of supporting Americans who have supported America NCOA salutes you and wishes you every success in the years ahead.

Fraternally,

Charles R. Jackson
President/CEO

Chartered by the United States Congress

Ukrainian American Veterans

National Commander
Dmytro Bodnarczuk, Ph.D.
15 Windmill Lane, New City, NY 10956
Tel: (914) 634-2775 • Fax: (914) 634-5370

Senior Vice Commander
STEVEN SZEWCZUK
151 Cypress Drive
Kings Park, NY 11754
(516) 361-7972 Home
(212) 667-5538 Office

Junior Vice Commander
MATTHEW KOZIAK
411 South 3rd Avenue
Highland Park, NJ
(908) 247-0726

Finance Officer
MICHAEL WENGRYN, PNC
5 Birchwood Terrace
Clifton, NJ 07012
(201) 472-9237

Adjutant
WASYL LUCHKIN, Ph.D., PNC
49 Windmill Lane
New City, NY 10956
(914) 634-9353
Fax: (914) 634-5370

Judge Advocate
MYRON B. KAPUSTIJ, ESQ.
36380 Maas Drive
Sterling Heights, MI 48312
(810) 268-9832 Home
(313) 274-6298 Office

Quartermaster
PETER KAPITANEC
4372 Bernice Avenue
Warren, MI 48091
(810) 757-4018

Chaplain
MYROSLAW PRYJMA
26436 Haverhill Drive
Warren, MI 48091
(810) 755-6855

Historian
VASYL LUCHKIW, Ph.D., PNC
49 Windmill Lane
New City, NY 10956
(914) 634-9353
Fax: (914) 634-5370

Welfare Officer
BOHDAN SAMOKYSZYN
2822 Park Drive
Parma, OH 44134
(216) 843-9943

Scholarship Officer
MICHAEL DEMCHUK
1653 Aspenwood Drive
(216) 642-0802

Immediate Past
National Commander
MIROSLAUS MALANIAK, Lt. Col.
73 Mercer Avenue
Buffalo, NY 14214
(716) 837-7855

Service Officer
WASYL LISCYNESKY
5907 State Road
Parma, OH 44134
(216) 888-4220

Publications Officer
GEORGE MIZIUK
P.O. Box 13
Windsor, NJ 08561
(609) 394-4824

Public Relations Officer
HAROLD BOCHONKO
47-43 47th Street
Woodside, NY 11377
(718) 786-7541

NATIONAL HEADQUARTERS
2 East 79th Street
New York, NY 10021

October 5, 1995

Mr. Warren Dolny
National Commander
Jewish War Veterans of the USA
1811 R. Street N.W.
Washington, DC 20009-1659

Dear Mr. Dolny:

On behalf of the Ukrainian American Veterans I send my greetings to you on the occasion of the 100th anniversary of the establishment of the Jewish War Veterans of the U.S.A..

Jewish-Americans have an outstanding record of courage and loyalty in srving our nation's armed services from the time of American Revolution to the present day.

My sincere best wishes to you and each of your members, and many more successful and rewarding years.

Sincerely,

Dmytro Bodnarczuk
Commander

Vietnam Veterans of America, Inc.

1224 M Street, NW, Washington, DC 20005-5183

Telephone (202) 628-2700 • General Fax (202) 628-5880 • Advocacy Fax (202) 628-6997 • Finance Fax (202) 628-5881

A Not-For-Profit Veterans Service Organization Chartered by the United States Congress

"VVA, At Work in Your Community"

August 8, 1995

David H. Hymes, National Commander
Jewish War Veterans of the U.S.A.
1811 R Street, NW
Washington, DC 20009-1659

Dear Commander Hymes:

Vietnam Veterans of America is pleased to salute the Jewish War Veterans of the U.S.A. on its 100th anniversary, and to acknowledge the contributions of all Jewish-American veterans, who have served our nation with honor and distinction in wartime and with charity and selflessness in peacetime.

As the oldest veterans service organization, JWV set the standards which all others seek to emulate in promoting patriotism and the preservation of the principles of freedom and equality upon which our nation was founded. JWV is widely recognized by all veterans as an organization committed to these goals, and Vietnam Veterans of America has long looked to JWV as the model for service to veterans of all generations and all needy citizens in our communities.

On this occasion, Vietnam Veterans of America is pleased to wish JWV and all of its members peace, unity, and long life.

Sincerely,

James L. Brazee, Jr.
President

Allen F. "Gunner" Kent

VETERANS OF FOREIGN WARS OF THE UNITED STATES

THE COMMANDER-IN-CHIEF

July 26, 1995

David H. Hymes, National Commander
Jewish War Veterans of the
    United States of America
1811 R Street, N.W.
Washington, D.C. 20009-1659

Dear Commander Hymes:

On behalf of the more than 2.8 million members of the Veterans of Foreign Wars of the U. S. and its Ladies Auxiliary, it is a great pleasure to extend greetings as you mark both the 100th anniversary of the Jewish War Veterans of the U.S.A. and the eagerly awaited publication of the history of your great organization.

Your devotion to country coupled with the individual service and sacrifice of every member of the JWV has helped make and keep the United States a beacon of liberty. Throughout your organization's distinguished history, JWV members have worked selflessly to serve the needs of not only our nation's veterans but those of our communities across the nation. Your tireless dedication to helping others has contributed greatly to improving the quality of life for our citizens, our veterans and countless Americans across this great country.

In this centennial year of the founding of the Jewish War Veterans of the U.S.A., we share your continuing commitment to promoting Americanism and the contributions of those who fought to preserve the freedoms of this country. You can take pride in your organization's responsible advocacy on behalf of our veterans and the entitlements promised the men and women who served in our armed forces.

We appreciate your efforts on behalf of our nation's veterans are appreciated and we wish you continued success as you prepare to meet the challenges of a new century.

Sincerely,

Allen F. "Gunner" Kent

ALLEN F. "GUNNER" KENT
Commander-in-Chief

★ WASHINGTON OFFICE ★
VFW MEMORIAL BUILDING ● 200 MARYLAND AVENUE, N.E. ● WASHINGTON, D. C. 20002 - 5799 ● AREA CODE 202-543-2239

30

BENJAMIN L. CARDIN
3D DISTRICT, MARYLAND

COMMITTEE ON WAYS AND MEANS
SUBCOMMITTEE ON HEALTH
SUBCOMMITTEE ON OVERSIGHT

COMMITTEE ON STANDARDS OF
OFFICIAL CONDUCT

Congress of the United States
House of Representatives
Washington, DC 20515–2003

COMMISSIONER
COMMISSION ON SECURITY
AND COOPERATION IN EUROPE

DEMOCRATIC CAUCUS
STEERING COMMITTEE

ASSISTANT DEMOCRATIC WHIP

October 3, 1995

Jewish War Veterans of America
1811 R Street, N.W.
Washington, D.C. 20009

Dear Friends:

Our nation owes the Jewish War Veterans of the U.S.A. an enormous debt that is impossible to repay. On your centennial anniversary I want to take this opportunity to say thank you for all you have done to protect and defend our country.

Your 100-year history has been full of great sacrifice and commitment. From the Spanish-American War through the two World Wars, Korea, Vietnam and the Gulf War, Jewish soldiers have fought with courage and determination. You and your comrades have fought to protect freedom and liberty throughout the world.

I want to thank you for your sacrifice and extend my best wishes to all of you on this very special anniversary.

Sincerely,

Benjamin L. Cardin
Member of Congress

BLC:ss

REPLY TO: ☐ 104 CANNON HOUSE OFFICE BUILDING
WASHINGTON, DC 20515–2003
(202) 225–4016

☐ 540 E. BELVEDERE AVENUE, SUITE 201
BALTIMORE, MD 21212-3750
(410) 433–8886

Bob Dole

BOB DOLE
KANSAS
141 SENATE HART BUILDING
(202) 224-6521

COMMITTEES:
AGRICULTURE, NUTRITION, AND FORESTRY
FINANCE
RULES

United States Senate

WASHINGTON, DC 20510-1601

August 14, 1995

David H. Hymes
National Commander
Jewish War Veterans of
 the United States of America
1811 R Street, N.W.
Washington, D.C. 20009-1659

Dear Commander Hymes:

It is my great pleasure to extend to you my greetings and best wishes as you celebrate the 100th anniversary of the Jewish War Veterans of the United States of America (JWV).

Since 1896, the JWV has been a powerful voice on behalf of the nation's veterans and of religious freedom around the world. The service of the JWV, America's oldest, continuously active national veterans' service organization, is exemplary of the sacrifice and dedication of its members. Not only have the members of the JWV served this nation well in uniform, but like so many veterans of United States military service, they continue to contribute to the greatness of our nation by serving their fellow veterans and their communities.

You and all the members of the JWV can be proud of your work on behalf of this nation and its veterans. America appreciates the contributions made by the JWV, and will continue to benefit from its service well into the next century.

Again, congratulations and best wishes.

Sincerely,

BOB DOLE
United States Senate

Benjamin A. Gilman

BENJAMIN A. GILMAN
20TH DISTRICT, NEW YORK

INTERNATIONAL RELATIONS
COMMITTEE
CHAIRMAN

SUBCOMMITTEE:
INTERNATIONAL OPERATIONS
AND HUMAN RIGHTS

GOVERNMENT REFORM
AND OVERSIGHT COMMITTEE

SUBCOMMITTEES:
POSTAL SERVICE
CIVIL SERVICE

Congress of the United States
House of Representatives
Washington, DC 20515–3220

October 3, 1995

Neil Goldman
National Commander
Jewish War Veterans of the U.S.A.
1811 R Street NW
Washington, DC 20009

Dear Commander Goldman:

The one hundredth anniversary of the founding of the Jewish War Veterans of the United States is an appropriate time both to look back upon the accomplishments of the past century and towards the challenges of the future.

Since 1896, the JWV have reached out to those in need.   The homeless, our youth, and our golden age citizens have all benefitted from the compassion and willingness to help which have been JWV hallmarks.

Our veterans most especially owe much to the tireless efforts of the JWV. Adequate medical care, educational opportunities, and the battle against discrimination are just some of the ways the JWV has been the champion of those who took up arms to defend our way of life.

My personal membership and participation in the activities of the Jewish War Veterans goes back through many years and is one of my proudest associations.

I congratulate the JWV on this milestone occasion, and look forward to working together with all of you for many years to come.

Sincerely,

BENJAMIN A. GILMAN
Member of Congress

PLEASE REPLY TO:

WASHINGTON OFFICE:
2449 RAYBURN BUILDING
WASHINGTON, DC 20515-3220
☒ TELEPHONE: (202) 225-3776

DISTRICT OFFICE:
407 EAST MAIN STREET
SUITE 2
P.O. BOX 358
MIDDLETOWN, NY 10940-0358
☐ TELEPHONE: (914) 343-6666

DISTRICT OFFICE:
377 ROUTE 59
MONSEY, NY 10952-3498
☐ TELEPHONE: (914) 357-9000

DISTRICT OFFICE:
32 MAIN STREET
HASTINGS-UN-HUDSON,
NY 10706-1602
☐ TELEPHONE: (914) 478-5550

THIS STATIONERY PRINTED ON PAPER MADE WITH RECYCLED FIBERS

Tom Lantos

TOM LANTOS
CALIFORNIA

WASHINGTON OFFICE:
2217 RAYBURN BUILDING
WASHINGTON, D.C. 20515
(202) 225-3531

DISTRICT OFFICE
400 EL CAMINO REAL
SUITE 820
SAN MATEO, CA 94402
(415) 342-0300
IN SAN FRANCISCO:
(415) 566-5257

INTERNATIONAL RELATIONS COMMITTEE
Ranking Member
Subcommittee on International Operations
and Human Rights
Subcommittee on Western Hemisphere

GOVERNMENT REFORM AND OVERSIGHT COMMITTEE
Subcommittee on Human Resources and
Intergovernmental Relations
Subcommittee on National Security, International
Affairs, and Criminal Justice

Cochairman, Permanent United States
Congressional Delegation to the
European Parliament
Cochairman, Congressional
Human Rights Caucus

Congress of the United States
House of Representatives
Washington, D.C. 20515

October 3, 1995

Mr. Neil Goldman
National Commander
Jewish War Veterans of the U.S.A.
1811 R Street, N.W.
Washington, D.C. 20009

Dear Commander Goldman:

I wish to extend my heartfelt congratulations to the Jewish War Veterans of the
United States of America (JWV) on the 100th anniversary of the founding of
your outstanding organization. Your century of commitment to our national
security and to honoring all of our veterans serves as a source of pride for all
Americans.

The JWV's steadfast dedication to American values and the defense of freedom
reminds us of own obligations to stay true to our democratic ideals and honor
the memory of those who lost their lives so that we might be free. Through the
JWV's example, future generations will understand the meaning of patriotism,
sacrifice, and honor.

Thank you for your continued service to our nation. May you enjoy the
blessings of a happy and healthy new year.

With all best wishes,

Tom Lantos
Member of Congress

Charles E. Schumer

CHARLES E. SCHUMER
NEW YORK

2211 RAYBURN HOUSE OFFICE BUILDING
WASHINGTON, DC 20515
(202) 225-6616

DISTRICT OFFICES:
1628 KINGS HIGHWAY
BROOKLYN, NY 11229
(718) 627-9700

118-21 QUEENS BLVD.
FOREST HILLS, NY 11375
(718) 268-8200

90-16 ROCKAWAY BEACH BLVD.
ROCKAWAY, NY 11693
(718) 945-9200

Congress of the United States
House of Representatives
Washington, DC 20515

COMMITTEES:

JUDICIARY

BANKING AND
FINANCIAL SERVICES

WHIP-AT-LARGE

September 14, 1995

Mr. David H. Hymes
National Commander
Jewish War Veterans of the U. S. A.
1811 R Street, N. W.
Washington, D. C. 20009

Dear Commander Hymes:

It is with great pleasure that I write to congratulate the Jewish War Veterans of the U. S. A. on the celebration of your centennial year. What an auspicious milestone in the history of your outstanding organization.

Since 1896 the JVW has supported the brave men and women who have served our country so valiantly. As the oldest, continuously active veteran's organization you have lead the way in this cause.

The JWV has been a beacon of dignity and liberty for all the citizens of the United States. I look forward to reading the forthcoming history of your organization. Every citizen owes the JWV a debt of gratitude.

I want to wish you all many more years of good health and prosperity in which to reach the goals you have set for yourselves. Once again, congratulations.

Sincerely,

Charles E. Schumer
Member of Congress

CES/mmv

Neil Goldman

1896-1996

Jewish War Veterans of The United States of America
Chartered By an Act of Congress

Neil Goldman
National Commander

Dear JWV members and friends:

It is indeed an honor for me to serve as National Commander of the Jewish War Veterans of the United States of America during our Centennial Year. As you read the history of JWV and the Bios of those Jews who served our Nation in times of peril, in this our 100th Anniversary Book, you will gain a clearer perspective of the relationship of our service in the military and our continuing service to the Jewish and Veterans Communities, to our Nation and Israel within the framework of our wonderful organization.

Our Centennial Year gives us the opportunity to show our pride in the purposes and accomplishments of JWV throughout its history. It is good to beat our chests, and to let the rest of the world know what we are and what we do.

There are many Centennial celebrations planned throughout our country - Centennial Shabats, Military Balls, Postal Sub-stations, proclamations from States, Counties, and Cities declaring Centennial Years in our various areas. Many posts have had street names changed to JWV Avenue. Media coverage has been and will continue to be outstanding. The Centennial has been the catalyst to make all this Nation aware of our century of service to veterans, our continuing fight against bigotry and Anti-Semitism, our lobbying of Congress for veterans benefits, and our continuing aggressive support of Israel. The entire Centennial celebration will be fittingly climaxed as our organization hosts the 1996 Veteran Day celebration in Arlington Cemetery on November 11, 1996.

Our Centennial Celebration opens windows of opportunity to us to position ourselves to continue on in a posture of strength well into the 21st century. We can assure ourselves a continuing participation in our most important programs: our Museum, Allied Veterans Mission to Israel, our work with the VA hospitals, our Descendants, to mention a few. The centennial also gives us an unparalleled opportunity to achieve the growth necessary to support our programs and projects.

I look forward to sharing, with all members of JWV, a better and brighter future.

Sincerely,

Neil Goldman

Neil Goldman
National Commander *"The Patriotic Voice of American Jewry"*

1811 R Street, N.W. • Washington, D.C. 20009 • (202) 265-6280 FAX (202) 234-5662

Herb Rosenbleeth

1896-1996

JWV

Jewish War Veterans of The United States of America
Chartered By an Act of Congress

Herb Rosenbleeth
Colonel, U.S. Army (Ret)
National Executive Director

March 1996

To Each Member of JWV,

I am extremely gratified and honored to be your National
Executive Director as we enter our Centennial year! I am proud to
be your advocate in Washington at the VA, in the Pentagon and on
Capitol Hill.

JWV leaders have never feared taking a stand. We have been, and
continue to be, an activist organization. During the past 100
years JWV has stood for a strong national defense and for just
recognition and compensation for veterans. JWV prides itself in
being at the forefront of our nation's civic groups in supporting
the well-earned rights of veterans, in promoting American
democratic principles, in defending universal Jewish causes, and
in vigorously opposing bigotry, anti-Semitism and terrorism -
here and abroad. Today, even more than ever before, we stand for
these principles.

I am even more pleased with the accomplishments of our
Departments, Councils and Posts, and, most of all, of each of
you, our members. Your record of war time service, your record
of service to your country and to your communites, and your
fantastic record of volunteer service in VA medical centers makes
each of us justly proud of our organization and our Jewish
heritage.

I see the Centennial not as a culminating event but as a stepping
stone to even greater achievements of which we can be justly
gratified. I see our Centennial as an important milestone, not
as our destination. There will be continued challenges to
veterans and Jews in the years ahead. You can make a difference
in helping us meet these challenges!

My thoughts will be with you on March 15, 1996, and I look
forward to seeing you each at our National Convention in
Washington, DC in November 1996.

Herb Rosenbleeth

"The Patriotic Voice of American Jewry"

1811 R Street, N.W. • Washington, D.C. 20009 • (202) 265-6280 FAX (202) 234-5662

Robert M. Zweiman, PNC

1896-1996

Jewish War Veterans of The United States of America
Chartered By an Act of Congress

Robert M. Zweiman, PNC
National Centennial Chairman
214 Columbia Avenue
Fort Lee, NJ 07024-0948
201-941-2440
201-224-9740 (FAX)

Welcome into the century of accomplishment of the Jewish War Veterans. As you read this book, you will realize JWV's contributions were not mere rhetoric, but were substantive in both activity and accomplishment.

We all have a tendency to remember things which occurred during our lifetime and we all have a tendency to either put it in a best or worst light depending on its impact on our lives. The Centennial gave all of us a pause to reflect upon where we had been and what actually we had done. It was a very rewarding pause because we acknowledged to ourselves, at least, that all in all our presence on the American scene was important to both veterans and to Jews. We stand tall in our accomplishments for veterans and Jews.

With the Centennial celebration of the Jewish War Veterans well on its way, we look forward to our next century of service to our country.

Yours in comradeship,

Robert M. Zweiman, PNC
National Centennial Chairman

"The Patriotic Voice of American Jewry"

1811 R Street, N.W. • Washington, D.C. 20009 • (202) 265-6280 FAX (202) 234-5662

Sophie Ruderman

NATIONAL LADIES AUXILIARY
Jewish War Veterans of the U. S. A., Inc.

1811 R STREET, N.W.
WASHINGTON, D.C. 20009
PHONE: (202) 667-9061

Dear Jewish War Veterans:

On this occasion of the 100th Anniversary of the Jewish War Veterans, I bring greetings and love from the National Ladies Auxiliary.

We are so proud of all of our men and women who served our Country. The Jewish War Veterans have been a part of United States wars since the Revolutionary War. The Jewish War Veterans have held honors in all battles that have been fought for freedom. The Jewish War Veterans have withstood prejudice and hatred. All of you have held your heads up high and made not only your Country proud, your families and loved ones, as well as all Jews over the world. Jewish War Veterans are buried all over the world with honor. Medals from the Good Conduct, Sharpshooter and The Congressional Medal of Honor have been bestowed upon Jewish War Veterans.

The Auxiliary is made of your mothers, sisters, wives, children and grandchildren. The pride we have for all of you, is made up in the letters, love and tears that we shared with you in all walks of life. Your women have always been there while you have served in the boot camps, did basic training, served overseas, on the ships, on the planes, and walking in the infantry, you have never walked alone.

Personally, I am so privileged to be the National President during the 100th Centennial, to be the one to bring you greetings.

All of you are heroes. You served your country with pride and love.

Sophie Ruderman

Sophie Ruderman
National President
National Ladies Auxiliary
Jewish War Veterans of the U.S.A., Inc.

DESCENDANTS OF JEWISH WAR VETERANS
OF THE UNITED STATES OF AMERICA, INC. ®

"If We Forget, Who Will Remember"

Sharon L. Portnoy
National President

November 21, 1995

To the Members of Jewish War Veterans:

We are fortunate because we live in a free society. This was accomplished with the help of Jewish men and women who have served and continue to serve in all branches of the United States Military Service. On behalf of the Descendants of Jewish War Veterans, I take tremendous pleasure in offering our congratulations on this most auspicious occasion in recognizing and celebrating the one hundredth anniversary of the Jewish War Veterans of the United States of America.

To grow up in a JWV family is a very special experience. Descendants of Jewish war veterans are instilled with tremendous pride, not only in our Jewish heritage, but in American patriotism as well. You, our parents, have taught us from a very young age, that we must provide service to our community, to all people equally. You have set an example which is far reaching throughout our lives. It is incumbent upon us to continue your work and tell the story of your deeds and accomplishments to both our children and the children of all people.

Congratulations on reaching your Centennial year. May this be the beginning of a more enlightening era for Jews throughout the world.

Respectfully yours,

Sharon L. Portnoy

National Headquarters • 1811 R Street, N.W. • Washington, D.C. 20009-1659 • (202) 265-6280 • FAX: (202) 234-5662

Edward D. Blatt

National Museum of American Jewish Military History

1811 R Street, NW, Washington, DC 20009
(202) 265-6280   Fax (202) 462-3192

MUSEUM
ARCHIVES
LIBRARY
MEMORIAL

Edward D. Blatt, Past National Commander
President

2941 Jenny Place
Philadelphia PA 19136
Home (215) 934-5439
Fax (610) 640-9863

December 12, 1995

Dear JWV Members, NMAJMH Members and JWV Friends,

It is my pleasure to include my greetings among those of such distinguished stature within the pages of this milestone edition of American Jewish history on the occasion of the 100th anniversary of the Jewish War Veterans of the U.S.A.

I am gratified to know that so many whom I personally, admire, recognize the outstanding accomplishments and patriotism of Jews in service to this nation.

As President of the National Museum of American Jewish Military History, I am honored to have the duty and responsibility of preserving the records of patriotic contributions of Americans of the Jewish faith who have acted in this nation's defense.

Our museum, archives and library protects the evidence of service and will educate future generations as to our proud heritage as Jewish Americans - just as this 100th anniversary volume does.

To you, the men and women of JWV and to those yet to come, I commend you, I support you, and I congratulate you!

Sincerely,

Edward D. Blatt, PNC
President
National Museum of American Jewish Military History

Under the Auspices of the Jewish War Veterans, USA, National Memorial, Inc. chartered 1958 by Act of Congress

PREFACE

Robert M. Zweiman

To just say that the Jewish War Veterans of the United States of America (JWV) is one hundred years old would be an ordinary item of general interest - if that was its primary accomplishment. BUT - and there is always a "but" - the reality is that the men and women of JWV made a difference and a meaningful contribution in its one hundred years of existence to the Nation and to the Jewish Community. This book will hopefully provide you with an insight into that difference.

The logical question for anyone to ask is why is there any need for hyphenated organizations on the American scene. There is probably no area other than the veterans' area which has as many groupings of special interest organizations and all of whom are intensely protective of veteran rights. There are the Catholic War Veterans - the Polish, the Italian, the Paralyzed, the Blinded, the Disabled, those who served outside the United States, those who served in particular wars, such as Korea, Vietnam, Corregidor or in particular divisions such as the 369th and on and on we can go.

JWV was formed for a greater purpose than to merely be a social club of Jews who served in the Armed Forces of the United States. We formed to put the truth to a lie of Jews not having served this Nation. Being Jewish is to be a part of a group easily targeted for hate by segments of a society which may be looking for a scapegoat for its own inadequacies or merely looking to organize like-mindlessness for political control or social or political purpose.

As you read through this book you will realize that JWV has not only fulfilled its purpose, but has made a distinct difference by its accomplishments. We had two strikes against us - first off, we are Jews in a Christian society and secondly, we are veterans in a society which sought to avoid its obligation to those who served in our Nation's defense. And what made it even more difficult was that we found ourselves in a centrist position on many issues, to the occasional dismay of both the Jewish community and the veteran community.

We have refused to accept any specious label to be affixed to our programs and policies directed toward a greater America - to some in the Jewish community, we have been tagged as right-wing, to some in the veteran community, we have been tagged as left wing. You don't make a difference by taking the easy way of following a concensus and fearing to express a contrary opinion lest someone call you out for being either a Jew or a veteran. We don't extoll this as being our rationale for existence, for we have on a number of issues been a creative leader and on others a vocal and intense supporter.

JWV has had a very unique existence as being the only Jewish organization which has worked with the non-Jewish community on a daily basis in hospitals, community relationships, legislatively and elsewhere - and, that has made a meaningful difference, especially when you find that our members are also members and leaders in the other veteran organizations.

So, what difference has the Jewish War Veterans actually made on the America scene?

Proof that Jews were and are an integral ingredient in the defense and maintenance of the American security. JWV made the difference.

We created a repository documenting that proof in the exhibits and archives in our National Museum of American Jewish Military History in Washington, DC. JWV made the difference.

When the American Jewish Community adopted a quarantine approach to Nazi Germany by sticking its head in the sand rather than confronting the dangers, JWV instituted a successful boycott of German goods into the United States and by openly and physically demonstrating against the German American Bund. JWV made the difference - if all of the Jewish organizations had adopted a similar approach, we wonder whether world public opinion would have affected a change in history on the Holocaust.

JWV members visit the forgotten veterans in our VA and state hospitals assuring them that they will not be forgotten by all and providing them with entertainment and support. JWV made the difference together with its brother and sister veteran organizations.

When extremists of both right and left appeared, JWV was out there debating and demonstrating against the John Birch Society, the American Neo-Nazis, the KKK, the Jewish Defense League and involving the veteran community in the fight against hate. JWV made the difference.

When the Brown and Williamson Tobacco Company submitted to the Arab Boycott of Israel, JWV issued a white paper and boycotted their products in the United States until they reversed their policy and commenced sales of their products in Israel; and based on that program got Coca Cola and other companies to avoid the Arab Boycott. JWV made the difference. Of course, whether we did Israel a health favor or not by opening it to further tobacco sales is yet another question.

When JWV became the first veterans' organization to participate in the Civil Rights March in Washington, DC - JWV made the difference.

When JWV organized the largest parade in Jewish history in New York City supporting the establishment of the State of Israel - JWV made the difference.

And, as you read this book, you will find the many other programs and policies of the Jewish War Veterans, where JWV made the difference.

I express here my very sincere thanks and appreciation to my co-editor of this book - Michelle Spivak, our National Director of Communications, Development, and Programs. Her devotion to telling the story of the Jewish War Veterans in this book and in our Centennial exhibit and programming, made the job rewarding and fully allowed an open review of a veterans' organization of Jewish vets for all to see that JWV did, in fact, make a difference in service to and in the development of America. That's what this book is all about - Jewish Pride and American Patriotism...our Centennial slogan.

Robert M. Zweiman
Past National Commander
National Centennial Chairman

Editorial Notes and Acknowledgements

(L to R) Michelle Spivak, JWV National Director of Communications and Programs, and Robert J. Martin, Turner Publishing Company, Chief Editor.

This is the story of the Jewish role in defense of our nation and the organization which stands alone as the "Patriotic Voice of American Jewry" - the Jewish War Veterans of the United States of America (JWV).

As the 100th anniversary of the Jewish War Veterans of the USA approached, the members of JWV realized the publication of a comprehensive history is a fitting way to honor this milestone occasion and the Americans of the Jewish faith whose devotion to democracy translated into military service. Their story parallels the history of the struggle for freedom and democracy in America.

All who have contributed to this volume deserve recognition and praise for their efforts. But, apart from all others, my special appreciation goes to Past National Commander Robert M. Zweiman of New Jersey, a Past President of the National Museum of American Jewish Military History (NMAJMH). His vision gave birth to this book and his spirit brought JWV into a new era of vitality and action. As JWV's National Centennial Chairman, PNC Zweiman has invested this organization with the strength needed to enter the 21st century and to embark on new adventures in support of veterans and Jews in our ever changing world community.

Among the major contributors to this book is Seymour S. Weisman, Ph.D., JWV Consultant and Senior Fellow of the National Museum of American Jewish Military History (NMAJMH), I am deeply grateful to him for his interest in this project. The story which unfolds here relies heavily on exhibit scripts authored by Dr. Weisman. I am grateful for essays of notable American Jews written by Seymour Brody, Past Department Commander of New Jersey, author of *Jewish Heroes of America*. I would also like to acknowledge the fine illustrations by Art Seiden reproduced herein. Without his contribution, it would be difficult for the reader to capture the spirit of the early period of our nation's history.

My thanks also to Paul Hansen, an independent film producer from Denver, CO, who has produced several movies about JWV and the activities of American Jewish war veterans.

The books *Jews In American Wars* by J. George Fredman and Louis A. Falk and *The Jewish War Veterans Story* by Gloria R. Mosesson, both published by the Jewish War Veterans of the USA, formed additional source material for this book.

I am deeply indebted to Beth Cohn, my Editorial Assistant, Sandor Cohen, Archivist/Assistant Museum Director and Laura Willoughby, Museum Assistant, of the National Museum of American Jewish Military History, and Captain Robert E. Adler (USN-Ret), a JWV volunteer, for their research and organizational expertise.

My thanks to Professor Laurence Sharpe of Hagerstown Junior College for his insights into Jewish life in the Colonial period and to Robert J. Rosenthal of Washington, D.C. for his work on Civil War anti-Semitism.

To Herb Rosenbleeth, National Executive Director of JWV and the professional staff at JWV Headquarters in Washington, D.C. my sincere thanks for their indulgence, kind assistance and support during the term of this project.

This book honors all Americans of the Jewish faith who gave of their lives in service to this nation, preserving the freedom we cherish and enjoy today.

Michelle Spivak
Washington, DC

Seven Jews were recipients the Congressional Medal of Honor, the nation's highest military award, in the Civil War. Pictured here are some of the Jewish recipients throughout the years: Leopold Karpeles (Civil War), Sidney Gumpertz (WWI), Raymond Zussman (WWII) and Jack Jacobs (Vietnam).

The story of Jewish American patriotism predates the establishment of the Jewish War Veterans of the USA. It precedes the birth of this nation. It begins with a people who have sought - throughout their five-thousand year history - liberty and equality for all and who possessed the skills, determination, commitment and faith to protect and defend their home - the United States of America.

Throughout our nation's history, Americans of the Jewish faith have fought for the right to serve in uniform, to fulfill their responsibilities as citizens, and to protect America's precious freedoms. The truth is, Jewish-Americans have always served in numbers greater than their representation in the general population. This fact often comes as a surprise, so ingrained in our psyches is the stereotype - fostered by anti-Semites of every generation - of the Jew as completely self-serving or as a cowering victim.

"The Jew is charged with the disinclination patriotically to stand by the flag as a soldier. By his make and ways, he is substantially a foreigner and even the angels dislike foreigners."
Mark Twain

The lie has been promulgated throughout the centuries and became particularly vehement during the Civil War. In December 1891, the *North American Review* printed a letter from a Civil War veteran alleging the veteran never saw a Jew in uniform and claiming, after the war, among the Civil War veterans he knew he could not find anyone who remembered having served with a

Jew. The publication refused to print any of the many letters submitted refuting these false allegations.

The famous satirical writer, Mark Twain, allowed himself to become a participant in the dissemination of this hate when he wrote a scathing article in *Harper's* declaring the Jew "is charged with the disinclination patriotically to stand by the flag as a soldier. By his make and ways, he is substantially a foreigner and even the angels dislike foreigners."

The response to the hateful charges of a man of Twain's stature and notoriety, and an alarming atmosphere of anti-Semitism in America, was the forging of an allegiance of Jewish war veterans.

This was done on Sunday, March 15, 1896 when a group of 63 Union veterans of the Civil War called their first meeting at the Lexington Opera House in New York City, forming the Hebrew Union Veterans Association.

Truly Jewish-Americans have struggled in wars waged on two fronts - battling enemies of America on foreign soil and age-old prejudice and bigotry here at home.

Jewish-American veterans gave birth to an association to protect the interests of the Jewish people by bearing witness to their service. In so doing, the Hebrew Union Veterans Association (Jewish War Veterans of the USA) exemplified the meaning of American citizenship - freedom and opportunity for all paired with the rights and responsibilities of service to the nation.

This history of the Jewish War Veterans of the USA is proof of the Jewish contribution to America's military history and documents the role of Americans of the Jewish faith in shaping that history. This organization is proof. And, each individual biography submitted for inclusion in this book joins in the substantiation of fact and reality.

CHAPTER ONE

The New World

Years before the official establishment of the United States of America as a nation, Jews were fighting for the right to defend themselves and their families in the New World.

Among the earliest settlers, Jews arrived on these shores with others seeking religious freedom and new opportunities. The first came in the 1600's wandering away from second-class citizenship, religious prejudice, ignorance and intolerance.

In other lands, in other ages, Jews were not allowed to practice their faith, were denied the right to own land, and were forbidden to bear arms in defense of their country or themselves.

In this brave New World, religious freedom and property ownership were to be essential rights exercised by all. The privilege and opportunity to share in the defense of these rights was another matter.

An early Jewish-American patriot, Asser Levy, was determined that Jews would be full participants in the democratic process, even to the point of risking life and limb for the fledgling nation.

Asser Levy is recognized as the first American Jew to bear arms, for he successfully petitioned the director of the West India Company in Holland to lift Governor Peter Stuyvesant's edict requiring Jews to pay a tax rather than serve in the militia.

Asser Levy, among the most prominent of New York Jews, became a "freeman" in 1657 (the right of burghership). He was a schochet (Kosher butcher) and owned a tanning shop. Levy loaned the Lutheran community funds to build its American church in 1671. In 1730, the first American synagogue, Shearith Israel, was built on Levy's land on Mill Street in New York.

Jacob Barsimson also fought against restrictions on Jews in the New World, petitioning Stuyvesant for the right to buy a burial plot, to hold public positions and to practice the Jewish religion in large gatherings. Jacob Barsimson, Asser Levy - these men of conviction and courage begin the story of the Jewish defense of America, of full Jewish citizenship, with all its blessings and its risks.

The New Nation

At the time of the Revolutionary War, there were approximately 2,500 Jewish settlers in America. The influence of this small number of early American-Jewish patriots was rewarding to the Nation. The outcome of the war and the history of our great nation could have been far different had it not been for this small and dedicated Jewish population.

Jewish Americans were among the first to call for and demand independence from England, and they offered more than just debate on the subject. They offered of themselves - their homes, their money, and their sons.

The story of Haym Solomon stands out among those of the Revolutionary War. A good friend of General George Washington, Solomon, a financier, reached into his accounts time and time again to support the war effort. Additionally, he organized fundraising campaigns among the Jewish community that proved to be the salvation of the starving, poorly outfitted, ragtag army which General Washington led.

One of the most famous "veterans" of the Revolutionary War never served in the Colonial Army, but spent his time as a foot soldier raising money and gathering contributions for the cause. Haym Solomon, born in Poland, moved to New York after the partition of Poland in the middle 1700's. An educated man, Solomon was a well-known banker. Outspoken, Solomon was arrested by the British several times. First imprisoned as a spy, Solomon was later condemned to be hanged. He narrowly escaped the death penalty, with the help of some friends, and put himself back in the middle of the Revolution. After his escape, he went back into business and used his profits to buy food for the Colonial Army.

Known as the financier of the Colonial War, Solomon had the gift of being able to find money whenever it was necessary. The founding fathers of our country often took advantage of this talent, as Solomon poured a tremendous sum of money, some say in excess of $640,000, into the war effort.

Solomon loved his adopted country so much that, as legend tells it, when he received word from George Washington on Yom Kippur that the Colonial Army was in dire need of money, Solomon in-

Jacob Barsimson doing guard duty.

Haym Solomon

Solomon Bush is honored with a citation.

terrupted religious services on this holiest day of the year, long enough to gather pledges from the congregants to support the Army. After he received enough money, he allowed services to proceed. Solomon was eventually appointed to be the broker to the Office of Finance. Neither Solomon nor any member of his family ever received repayment or any sort of gift from the government of the United States.

Lieutenant Colonel Solomon Bush was the highest-ranking Jewish officer in the Continental Army. He served in the Pennsylvania State Militia. Captain Lewis Bush, the Colonel's brother was mortally wounded in battle during the War of Independence.

Following exemplary service, which included being wounded on the battlefield and imprisoned by the British, Colonel Solomon Bush went on to act as President George Washington's unofficial Ambassador to Britain.

Another Jewish soldier who gained prominence during the Revolutionary War and parlayed it into a political career was Georgian David Emanuel. He was captured by the British and held at a prison known as McBean's Creek. His fighting days were not over, though. In a daring attempt, Emanuel escaped the British prison and rejoined the Colonial forces. He fought until the war's end and following the war was elected Governor of Georgia.

Other important Jewish figures of the Revolutionary War period include Aaron Lopez of Newport, Rhode Island, called the "Merchant-King" for helping to keep the Revolutionary Army supplied and Francis Salvador, who as a delegate to the South Carolina Provincial Congress, became the first Jew elected to public office in the Western hemisphere. Salvador also holds the sad distinction of being the first Jew killed in the War of Independence.

David Salisbury Franks was an aide to Benedict Arnold when Arnold attempted to invade Canada. Franks was exonerated of complicity in Arnold's treason trial, promoted to Lieutenant Colonel and served as an advisor and aide to Benjamin Franklin, Thomas Jefferson and John Adams.

By the 1800's Jews had earned the respect of members of the military in our country, and were entering into careers in service to the nation. In 1807, Samuel Noah became the first Jew to graduate from the United States Military Academy. Research by Professor Laurence Sharpe, an expert on the Colonial Period of our history, confirms that in the War of 1812, the Seminole War, the Mexican War and thereafter, men and women of the Jewish faith answered muster. Despite this, America's Jews were yet to be recognized as full participants in America's efforts at creating its armed forces.

One veteran of the War of 1812 was unique for his leadership and service to the nation. Uriah Phillips Levy has become the stuff of legends for his rise from the most humble of beginnings to the rank of Commodore in the United States Navy. His selfless dedication to improving the treatment of sailors - it was through his efforts that flogging was outlawed in the Navy - and his bravery in battle are well-documented.

In his later years, Levy's unquestionable patriotism was again demonstrated when he saved the property of President Thomas Jefferson in Charlottesville, VA - Monticello - to be protected for generations of Americans to come. When it was evident Jefferson's personally designed estate would be auctioned off without thought to its his-

Commodore Uriah P. Levy rose above the anti-Semitism he faced in the Navy and was a hero of the War of 1812. Levy is credited with abolishing corporal punishment in the U.S. Navy and saving Monticello, the home of President Thomas Jefferson.

toric significance, Commodore Levy purchased Monticello himself and later donated the property to the federal government which preserves it to this day as an historic treasure.

A French Jew who distinguished himself in the War of 1812, Commodore John Ordroneaux was the central figure in a dramatic sea battle. He commanded a privateer, the Prince de Neufchatel that took on a British forty-gun frigate. William Maclay, an historian of the American Navy describes the battle:

"One of the most remarkable actions of the war was between the British forty-gun frigate *Endymion* and the armed ship *Prince de Neufchatel*. The extraordinary feature of this affair lies in the fact that a vessel fitted at private expense actually frustrated the utmost endeavors of an English frigate of vastly superior forces in guns and men. As the commander of the *Endymion* said, he lost as many men in his efforts to seize the *Prince de Neufchatel* as he would have done had his ship engaged a man of war of equal force, and he generously acknowledged that the people in the privateer conducted their defense in the most heroic and skillful manner.

"Captain Ordroneaux himself fired some eighty shots at the enemy. Springing up the sides of the vessel, the British would endeavor to gain her deck but every attempt was met by deadly bows by the sturdy defenders. It was well understood that Captain Ordroneaux had avowed his determination of never being taken alive and that he would blow up his ship with all hands before striking his colors. At one period of the fighting when the British gained the deck and were gradually driving the Americans back, Ordroneaux seized a lighted match, ran to the companionway, directly over the magazine, and called out to his men that he would blow up the ship if they retreated further. The threat had the desired effect. Such a sanguinary fight could not be of long duration and at the end of twenty

minutes the English cried out for quarter, upon which the Americans ceased their fighting."

Judah Touro served as a civilian volunteer in the American Army during the War of 1812, but is well-known for establishing one of the earliest American synagogues, Touro Synagogue of Newport, Rhode Island.

Captain Mordechai Myers of Richmond, Virginia saved the lives of 200 men who were drowning after their vessel had capsized from enemy bombardment.

In Charleston, South Carolina - one of the largest and most active Jewish communities of the time - Captain Levi Myers Harby dreamed of a life at sea. His exciting career in the Navy extended from the War of 1812, to the Seminole Indian War, to Bolivia's struggle for independence, to the Civil War.

Brother Against Brother

By the mid-1800's Americans were in the midst of an industrial and land development boom, while enjoying the most plentiful food supply in history to date. This resource combination would eventually lead the United States to "superpower" status.

The population was growing too, mostly from an influx of immigrants seeking financial opportunity, inexpensive land and, of course, greater freedom. Among the many who sought to claim a stake in this rich and powerful country were German Jews. These German Jews would eventually reap success beyond their dreams, but before that, they would participate in the bloodiest war in our nation's history and pay dearly for their rights as American citizens.

Before the Civil War anti-Semitism was concentrated in the North. The Jews of the South were mostly native born and well-integrated in their communities. Until 1830, there were only a few thou-

Jewish Congressional Medal of Honor Recipients of the Civil War

Leopold Karpeles

Leopold Karpeles, a native of Prague, Czechoslovakia, came to the United States as a child. Although Karpeles was in Texas when the War Between the States began, he joined the army in Springfield, Massachusetts. He served in the 57th Massachusetts Volunteers. Karpeles was awarded the Congressional Medal of Honor for action at the Battle of the Wilderness, May 6, 1864. While color-bearer of his regiment, he rallied the retreating troops and induced them to check the advance of the enemy.

Benjamin B. Levy

Benjamin B. Levy, who enlisted in the First New York Volunteers at sixteen, was aboard a steamship carrying dispatches from General John Mansfield to General John Ellis Wood. The steamboat, which was towing a water schooner, was attacked by a Confederate gunboat. With the Confederate ship threatening capture, Levy cut the tow rope and freed the steamboat from the schooner. Later, at the Battle of the Wilderness in 1864, Levy was severely wounded, but recovered to see General Robert E. Lee surrender at the Appomattox Courthouse. Before rejoining his regiment at Appomattox, Levy was granted the Congressional Medal of Honor.

Abraham Cohn

Abraham Cohn received the Congressional Medal for two heroic acts performed as a Sergeant-Major in the Sixth New Hampshire Volunteers. At the Battle of the Wilderness, Cohn reorganized and rejuvenated the weary, fleeing troops. His new lines held their position against the advancing Confederate troops. At the Battle of Petersburg, Cohn was brave and level-headed carrying orders from commander to commander while under heavy fire.

Henry Heller

Henry Heller, a sergeant in Company A of the 66th Ohio Infantry, broke through enemy lines to rescue a badly wounded Confederate officer at the Battle of Chancellorsville. The officer ultimately became an informer, providing the Union Army with valuable information which saved many lives.

David Orbansky

David Orbansky, a private in Company B of the 58th Ohio Infantry, received the Congressional Medal of Honor for his gallantry in action at the Battle of Shiloh and the Battle of Vicksburg.

Isaac Gause

Isaac Gause, a sergeant in Company E of the Second Ohio Cavalry, received the Congressional Medal of Honor for capturing the colors of the Eighth South Carolina Infantry in hand-to-hand combat while on a reconnaissance mission along the Berryville and Winchester Pike in 1864.

Abraham Gurenwalt

Private Abraham Gurenwalt of the 104th Ohio Infantry won his Congressional Medal of Honor for capturing the Southern Corps Headquarters prize.

Colonel Edward S. Salomon

sand Jews in America. After that date, thousands of Jews migrated from the impoverished German speaking countries of Central Europe. They settled into livelihoods similar to those in Europe - engaging in buying and selling, acting as middlemen and distributors of consumer goods. The stereotype of the "Jew Store" and the Jewish peddler was created.

By 1860, approximately 150,000 Jews were living in America. In drama, literature and art, Jews were depicted as shrewd and untrustworthy. Shylock of the *Merchant of Venice* and the popular dime-store novels of the time *Deadwood Dick* planted the seeds of hate and mistrust.

The hardships of the Civil War intensified this prejudice and it was during this war of brother against brother that the cruelest canard was advanced, the one that described Jews as cowards, unable and unwilling to serve their nation, interested only in enriching themselves through the miseries of others.

However hurtful the words, they belie the truth of the time. The proportion of Jews in the military was higher than that of any other ethnic or religious group, according to Civil War Historian Robert J. Rosenthal. Approximately 8,000 Jews served on the Union side and 2,000 fought for the Confederacy.

It was in this context of hate that unprecedented devotion to country, unparalleled dedication to fellow American citizens, and extraordinary courage was demonstrated by Americans of the Jewish faith. These were truly among the spiritual ancestors of the Jewish War Veterans of the United States of America.

Edward S. Salomon began an illustrious career in the United States Army. Salomon was born in Germany and came to America when he was in his teens. At age 25, he enlisted in the Union Army and rose rapidly through the ranks. Ten years after Salomon came to the United States he found himself commanding a regiment at the Battle of Gettysburg, and later leading his troops down Pennsylvania Avenue in a six-hour congratulatory parade.

After the Civil War, Salomon went back to his home in Chicago and was selected to be the Clerk of Cook County. In 1869, in appreciation for all that Salomon had accomplished for the country, President Grant appointed him Governor of the Territory of Washington.

Six Jews, Union soldiers, won the Congressional Medal of Honor, the country's highest award for bravery, during the Civil War. They were Sergeant Leopold Karpeles, Sergeant Benjamin B. Levy, Sergeant-Major Abraham Cohn, Sergeant Henry Heller, Private David Orbansky, and Corporal Isaac Gause. Some believe there, in fact, were seven recipients of the Congressional Medal of Honor for the Civil War. Private Abraham Gurenwalt was bestowed the medal, but there remains an issue as to the certainty of his Jewish faith.

Harassment of Jewish soldiers in the military was commonplace. But, at the seats of power, the leaders of the Union and the Confederacy did not share the prejudices of their troops. President Abraham Lincoln welcomed Jews to the Republican Party. Two of the three delegates who placed Lincoln's name in nomination were Jews.

President Jefferson Davis of the Confederacy chose Judah P. Benjamin as Attorney General and Secretary of War and State. A political conservative, Judah P. Benjamin, in 1852, was the first Jew elected to the U.S. Senate. He was the leading voice

Judah Philip Benjamin

Michael Allen serves as regimental chaplain.

to advocate the Southern view while Lincoln was campaigning for the presidency. Once Lincoln was elected, Benjamin recommended that the South secede from the Union.

After Louisiana's secession, Judah P. Benjamin resigned his seat in the Senate and was swiftly appointed Attorney General of the Confederacy. Soon after, Confederate President Jefferson Davis changed Benjamin's appointment, making him Secretary of War. Benjamin was then appointed Secretary of State.

With the Confederacy in disarray, the North picked up momentum and swept through the South. President Davis drew his cabinet into seclusion and sent emissaries to negotiate peace with the North. Benjamin and his family escaped to the West Indies, where he boarded a ship for England.

The Halls of Congress were not immune to anti-Semitic sentiment during the Civil War. The Volunteer Act of 1861, required military chaplains be ordained in the Christian Church. Therefore, Jewish soldiers serving in the field could not receive spiritual guidance and were denied Jewish burials.

In July 1861, Congressman Clement Vallandigham submitted a bill to allow ordained rabbis to be commissioned as chaplains. While Vallandigham's bill was being debated, the 5th Pennsylvania Cavalry, either in defiance or ignorance of the law, elected one of its men, Michael Allen, to be the regimental chaplain.

Allen was a Philadelphia Hebrew teacher who at one time wanted to study to become a rabbi. He was well liked by the Christian and Jew-ish soldiers in his regiment and his services and sermons reflected his mixed congregation.

While the 5th Regiment was encamped outside Washington, DC, a YMCA worker visited them and discovered the regimental chaplain was not an ordained minister or a Christian. The YMCA worker considered the appointment of Allen a violation and reported it to army officials.

Allen resigned and the regiment, under command of a Jewish officer, Colonel Max Friedman, tested Vallandigham's bill by nominating Rabbi Arnold Fischel, an ordained rabbi and an experienced lobbyist, as their chaplain.

The Secretary of War was compelled by law to deny the nomination and Rabbi Fischel began a year of lobbying until Congress passed another law allowing rabbis to be commissioned as army chaplains.

This occurred only when President Lincoln was petitioned to redress this injustice. On July 17, 1862, legislation passed permitting ordained rabbis to serve as chaplains. Congress simply changed the wording of the original law to "religious denomination" instead of "Christian denomination", and legal discrimination against Jews in the military "officially" ended.

Rabbi Fischel was finally commissioned to replace Allen as chaplain of the 5th Pennsylvanian Cavalry. But, not until after, Rabbi Jack Frankel, a well known cantor of Congregation Shalom of Philadelphia, was commissioned on September 18, 1862. And so, Rabbi Frankel holds the honor of being the first official Jewish chaplain. Rabbi Frankel attended to military hospitals in the Philadelphia area.

The first regimental chaplain was Ferdinand Leopold Sarner, who was elected by the 54th New York Volunteer Regiment. Most of the soldiers in the regiment were German-speaking. Rabbi Sarner was commissioned on April 10, 1863. He was the first Jewish chaplain to be wounded and the first Jewish chaplain to go AWOL (absent without leave). He was severely wounded in Gettysburg and was hospitalized while awaiting his formal discharge papers. Feeling better, however, he didn't wait for his formal discharge papers to arrive and left on his own to go home.

The career of Jewish military chaplain was created in the Civil War. Thus began the legacy of brave and dedicated Jewish chaplains serving G-d and country.

General Ulysses S. Grant and General George Sherman attempted to restrict Jews from trading during the Civil War. Grant issued Order No. 11 requiring the expulsion of Jews from the Tennessee Department (Mississippi, Kentucky, and Tennessee) without trial or hearing. These Jews were uprooted from their homes and forced to leave their possessions and businesses. President Lincoln later rescinded the order and expressed his regrets to the Jewish community. Grant, who as president was a friend of the Jews, never publicly apologized.

Many years later in July 1938, JWV's national commander and a small delegation of Hebrew Union Veterans, most in their mid-nineties, attended ceremonies marking the 75th anniversary of the Battle of Gettysburg. The old veterans expressed their pride of service and held back tears when recognized at the ceremonies. Approximately one thousand Jewish soldiers participated in the three days of fighting at Gettysburg, a tremendous sacrifice when measured against the anti-Jewish sentiment of the age.

CHAPTER TWO

The Hebrew Union Veterans Association

The founding fathers of the Hebrew Union Veterans Association established a new veterans' organization on March 15, 1896 to commemorate the deeds and actions of Jewish servicepersons who served in America's military, to create a fraternal support group of persons with shared experiences, and to refute anti-Semitism in America.

Upon the establishment of the Hebrew Union Veterans Association, a major effort to rebut false allegations against Americans of the Jewish faith was launched.

Preamble of the Jewish War Veterans' Constitution

We, citizens of the United States of America, of the Jewish faith, who served in the Wars of the United States of America, in order that we may be of greater service to our country and to one another, associate ourselves together for the following purposes:

To maintain true allegiance to the United States of America; to foster and perpetuate true Americanism; to combat whatever tends to impair the efficiency and permanency of our free institutions; to uphold the fair name of the Jew and fight his battles wherever unjustly assailed; to encourage the doctrine of universal liberty, equal rights and full justice to all men; to combat the powers of bigotry and darkness wherever originating and whatever their target; to preserve the spirit of comradeship by mutual helpfulness to comrades and their families; to cooperate with and support existing educational institutions and establish educational institutions and foster the education of ex-servicemen and ex-servicewomen, and our members in the ideals and principles of Americanism; to instill love of country and flag and to promote sound minds and bodies in our members and our youth; to preserve the memories and records of patriotic service performed by the men and women of our faith; to honor their memory and shield from neglect the graves of our heroic dead.

Oath of Obligation

In the presence of the Eternal G-d surrounded by Defenders of the Flag and our Faith I swear to support the Constitution of the United States of America and to respect and protect its Flag and Institutions. I will obey the Constitution and By-Laws of the Jewish War Veterans of the United States of America and obey its orders.

I pledge that I will protect the Jew from persecution by him in order to the best of my ability. I will be true to the high ideals of our ancient Faith. I will do my best to obtain fair treatment for veterans, for their families and dependents.

I will maintain true loyalty to the principles of patriotic citizenship, true comradeship to all veterans, and Judaism.

This obligation I promise to fulfill, ON MY HONOR, and in the presence of the Flag of my Country. So help me G-d.

The key player in this all out attack was the most distinguished leader of the American Jewish community from the Civil War until the end of World War I, Simon Wolf.

Wolf published a book *The American Jew as Patriot, Soldier and Citizen* in June of 1895. Excerpts of the book, in the form of a letter, were published in *The Washington Post*. His words are reflected in the preamble of the current constitution of the Jewish War Veterans of the U.S.A.

> "A country can hardly expect those of its inhabitants to be ardent patriots whom it treats as aliens and outcasts. In spite of the prevalence of anti-Semitism, Jews demonstrated their patriotism as soldiers and citizens."
>
> **Simon Wolf**

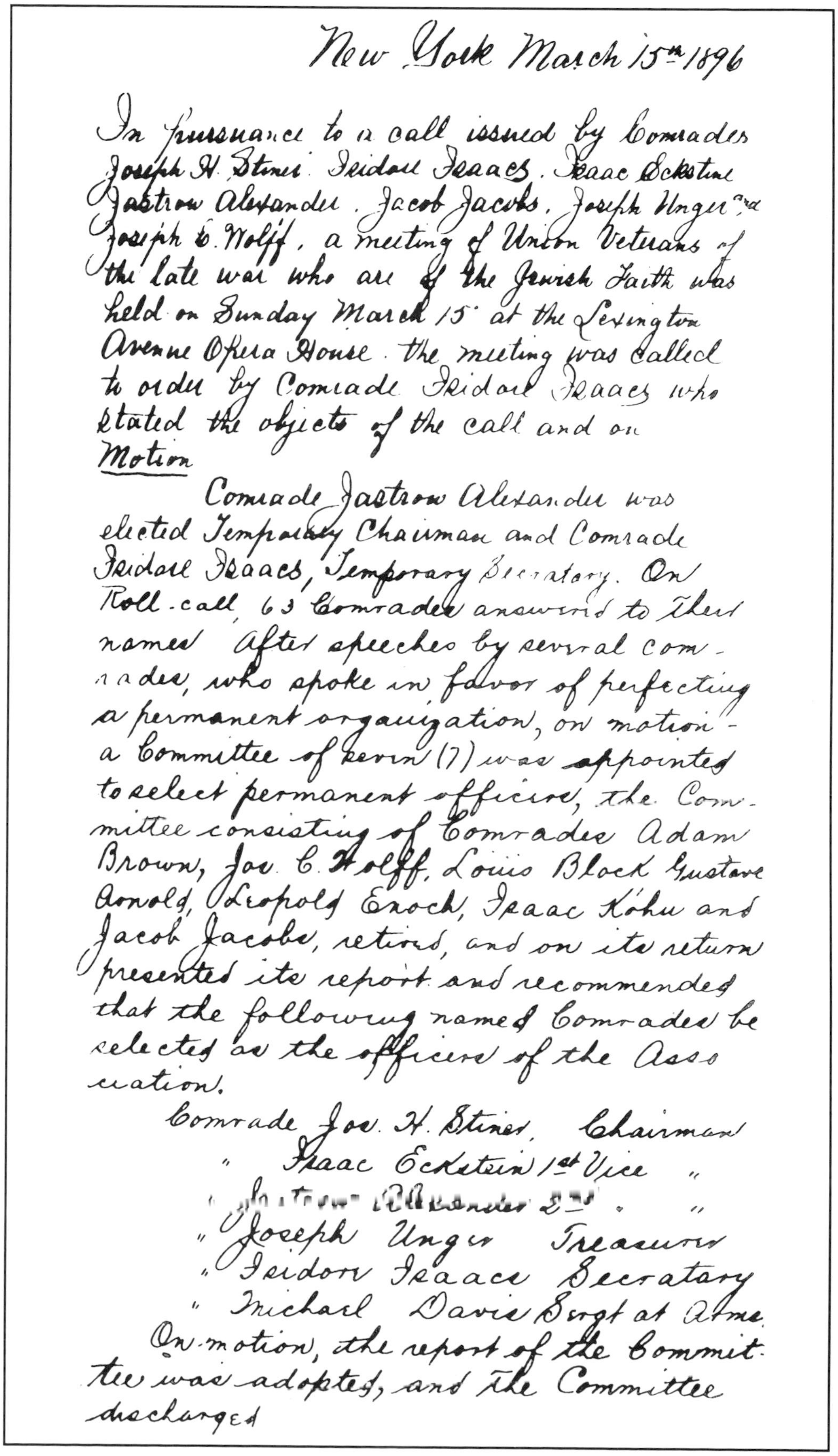

New York March 15th 1896

In pursuance to a call issued by Comrades Joseph H. Stines, Isidore Isaacs, Isaac Eckstine, Jastrow Alexander, Jacob Jacobs, Joseph Unger 3rd, Joseph C. Wolff, a meeting of Union Veterans of the late war who are of the Jewish Faith was held on Sunday March 15 at the Lexington Avenue Opera House. The meeting was called to order by Comrade Isidore Isaacs who stated the objects of the call and on Motion

Comrade Jastrow Alexander was elected Temporary Chairman and Comrade Isidore Isaacs, Temporary Secretary. On Roll-call, 63 Comrades answered to their names. After speeches by several comrades, who spoke in favor of perfecting a permanent organization, on motion a Committee of seven (7) was appointed to select permanent officers, the Committee consisting of Comrades Adam Brown, Jos. C. Wolff, Louis Block, Gustave Arnold, Leopold Enoch, Isaac Kohn and Jacob Jacobs, retired, and on its return presented its report and recommended that the following named Comrades be selected as the officers of the Association.

Comrade Jos. H. Stines, Chairman
  " Isaac Eckstein 1st Vice "
  " Jastrow Alexander 2nd "
  " Joseph Unger Treasurer
  " Isidore Isaacs Secretary
  " Michael Davis Sergt at Arms.
On motion, the report of the Committee was adopted, and the Committee discharged

Minutes of the first meeting.

These men, all Union Civil War veterans, were among the 63 founders of Jewish War Veterans of the United States of America.

One of the Hebrew Union Veterans Association's earliest activities was sponsorship of a Memorial Day parade and observance to honor the sacrifices of fallen veterans of the Jewish faith. Emotions ran high at that first parade and memorial service, held at Temple Emanu-El on May 29, 1896, in the midst of the anti-Semitic tensions of the day.

A recently ordained Rabbi, Stephen S. Wise, conducted the service. Wise's association with Jewish war veterans would continue for the next fifty years. From that warm May day at the end of the 19th century until now, at the edge of the 21st century, Jewish war veterans have repeated this Memorial Day service.

Support of veterans was a paramount concern of the fledgling service organization. Early minutes suggest funds were collected to assist needy Jewish veterans and their family members. Shortly, support programs were extended to encompass all veterans of all faiths, all nationalities and all races.

A tradition maintained — the Memorial Day Parade to Temple Emanu-el on May 21, 1939.

The Spanish American War

In 1898, the United States declared war on Spain following an attack on the U.S.S. Maine in Cuban waters. The Hebrew Union Veterans wrote to then President William McKinley pledging their support for the war effort. Approximately 5,000 Jews volunteered for service in the brief war. This figure is known because of the number of furlough requests received by the Army during the Jewish High Holidays in 1898.

Fifteen Jewish sailors were among those on board the battleship Maine when it was attacked on February 15, 1898. The Maine's Executive Officer was Adolph Marix, a Jew who was later to become a vice-admiral in the U.S. Navy and a member of the board of inquiry assigned to investigate the mysterious sinking of the Maine. Marix was a graduate of the United States Naval Academy and was honored to be appointed a candidate for the Academy by Abraham Lincoln.

Vice Admiral Adolph Marix, United States Navy, Executive Officer of the Maine.

THE

AMERICAN JEW

AS

PATRIOT, SOLDIER AND CITIZEN

BY

SIMON WOLF

EDITED BY

LOUIS EDWARD LEVY

PHILADELPHIA
THE LEVYTYPE COMPANY
PUBLISHERS

NEW YORK—CHICAGO—WASHINGTON
BRENTANO'S
1895

Simon Wolf, one of the first members of JWV, wrote this book in 1895 chronicling the participation of Jews in American wars in response to the allegations that Jews were not patriotic and did not serve in the military.

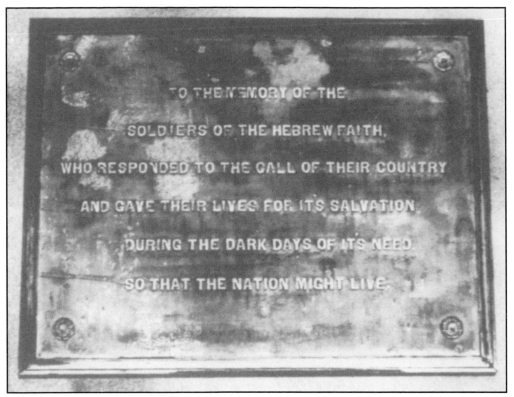

The pedestal of the monument erected at Salem Field by the Hebrew Union Veterans Association.

Himan Levenson of Pennsylvania. Enlisted Nov. 30 1899, discharged Nov. 29, 1903.

When war was declared with Spain on April 21, 1898, the first volunteer was a Jewish physician, Joseph M. Heller. Heller left a thriving medical practice to become acting assistant surgeon of the Army.

Corporal Benjamin Prager was the recipient of the Silver Star medal for his bravery in skirmishes in the Philippines. His citation describes action in 19 engagements during which he faced heavy fire.

A good number of Teddy Roosevelt's famous Rough Riders were Americans of the Jewish faith.

In his book, *Jewish Heroes of America,* author Seymour Brody describes a 16-year-old Jewish boy named Jacob Wilbusky as the first Rough Rider to be killed in action.

Sergeant Maurice Joost of the First California Volunteers, a regiment with over 100 Jewish soldiers, was the first man to fall in the attack on Manila.

The heroism of 19 year-old Samuel Schlesinger, who fought Indians at Arickaree Fork under the command of General Forsyth, was legendary and inspired this poem:

The Little Jew

When the foe charged on the breastworks
With the madness of despair
And the bravest souls were tested,
The little Jew was there.
When the weary dozed on duty
And the wounded needed care,
When another shot was called for,
The Little Jew was there.
With the festering dead around them
Shedding poison in the air,
When the crippled chieftain ordered,
The little Jew was there.

The Hebrew Veterans of the War with Spain

In 1900 the Jewish veterans of the Spanish-American War formed the Junior Hebrew War Veterans, later renamed the Hebrew Veterans of the War with Spain. Theodore Roosevelt became an honorary member. Dr. Samuel Kopetsky was the first commander of the group.

Colonel Maurice Simmons, the second commander of the Hebrew Veterans of the War with Spain, was to become instrumental in the growth of the Jewish War Veterans of the U.S.A. as we

The Science of Light: Naval Officer and Nobel Prize Winner

Albert Abraham Michelson

In 1907 Albert A. Michelson, a Jewish graduate of the U.S. Naval Academy, distinguished himself in the field of physics as winner of the prestigious Nobel prize.

Michelson was born on December 19, 1852 in the Prussian town of Strelno (now Strzelno, Poland) and settled with his parents in 1854 in San Francisco, California.

His extraordinary scientific gifts were discovered during his high school years and at the urging of his teachers he applied and was accepted to the Naval Academy. He was 17 years old when he crossed the country to enter school in Annapolis. He graduated in 1873 and served as a science instructor from 1875 until 1879.

In 1878 he began the work to which his life was dedicated, the accurate measurement of the speed of light. He studied in Europe and it was there he began building an interferometer, a device which would lead him to achieve his goal.

He served as a professor of physics at Case School of Applied Science in Cleveland, Ohio and at Clark University in Worcester, Massachusetts. He headed the physics department at the young University of Chicago in 1892.

Professor Michelson ultimately determined that the speed of light is a fundamental constant and he devised a method of making unprecedentedly accurate distance measurements using the length of light waves.

He was president of many scientific societies and published seventy-nine highly regarded scientific papers. Albert Abraham Michelson died in Pasadena, California of May 9, 1931.

know it today. He was an early advocate of Jewish veterans' rights and is responsible for legislation in 1912 removing restrictions on Jewish service in the New York National Guard.

Support of threatened Jewish communities worldwide became a priority for the two Jewish veterans' groups. They joined forces in 1903 to protest pogroms directed against the Jewish communities of Kishinev, Russia. The Hebrew Union Veterans Association and the Hebrew Veterans of the War with Spain called upon President Roosevelt to exert diplomatic pressure on Tsarist Russia to end the bloodshed.

To honor the memory of their departed comrades, the two Jewish veterans' groups again collaborated in the erection of a monument to Jewish patriotism at the Salem Field Cemetery in Brooklyn, New York. Among the prominent Jews supporting this project were financiers August Belmont and Felix Warburg; merchants Nathan Strauss and Abraham Abrahams; and Simon Wolf.

As America faced the prospect of World War I, Colonel Maurice Simmons supervised the merger of the two Jewish veteran organizations into a singular group which retained the name Hebrew Veterans of the War with Spain.

CHAPTER THREE

World War I

The Jewish population in the United States of America grew to 3.4 million in the years just prior to World War I. Many of these Jews were of Polish and Russian origin. They were among a large influx of Jews that arrived following the terror of the pogroms of 1903-1907. When the United States joined Great Britain and France in the war against Imperial Germany and her Central European allies in April 1917, Jews were anxious to demonstrate loyalty to their new country and its concept of democracy.

The Hebrew War Veterans of the War With Spain offered its assistance too, and in a letter sent to President Woodrow Wilson the Jewish veterans pledged their full support and cooperation in the war effort.

Thousands of young Jews were conscripted to serve in the armed forces when Congress imposed the first national draft of civilians. In combination with the volunteers, Jews constituted five percent of the military while they represented less than three percent of the nation's population at the time.

As in previous wars, Jews distinguished themselves on the battlefield. More than eleven hundred citations for valor were conferred on Jewish soldiers in the Army, including three Congressional Medal of Honor recipients, and 104 Distinguished Service Crosses.

Americans who fought in World War I were recognized for their unparalleled loyalty and courage as soldiers by military leaders of the period. General John Pershing, the Allied Expeditionary Forces Commander-in-Chief, considered the Jewish fighting force exemplary.

"When the time came to serve their country under arms, no class of people served with more patriotism or with higher motives than the young Jews who volunteered or were drafted and who went overseas with other young Americans."

Over ten thousand Jews were commissioned as officers during World War I. The most notable

Jewish Legion Veterans

Some new Americans had joined an allied army just prior to World War I, in an effort to assist in the fight to liberate Palestine from the yoke of Turkish tyranny. These men fought with the British Army forming the redoubtable fighting force known as the Jewish Legion.

They had become British citizens in order to support the fight against the Turks. They returned to America, and as repatriated Americans, formed the Jewish Legion Veterans organization.

Having fought for an allied army, they were allowed associate membership in what was to become the Jewish War Veterans of the USA, and a good number also joined the newly created American Legion.

Memorabilia from World War I shows the many roles played by American Jews, from serving in the infantry overseas to volunteering in a Jewish Welfare Board facility.

Sergeant Sidney Gumpertz, World War I recipient of the Congressional Medal of Honor.

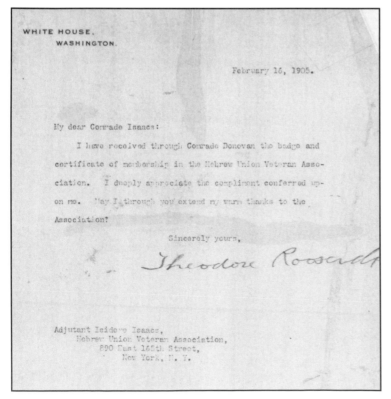

Born with the birth of JWV - 100-year-old Julius Daniels a World War I doughboy and longtime JWV member of the Department of Massachusetts.

was General Milton I. Foreman, who later became the first national commander of the American Legion.

Jewish Congressional Medal of Honor Recipients of World War I

Sergeant Benjamin Kaufman

Among those World War I soldiers Pershing referred to was Brooklyn born Sergeant Benjamin Kaufman. So stellar is his record of service that nine allied governments honored him for his heroism. From the United States, he received the Congressional Medal of Honor for action on October 4, 1918 in Argonne Forest. Severely wounded,

PNC Benjamin Kaufman, WW I Congressional Medal of Honor Recipient

Kaufman succeeded in destroying a German machine gun nest and in so doing saved many lives. Kaufman was a dedicated member of the Jewish War Veterans of the U.S.A. for over fifty years, serving as National Commander for 1941-43 and as its National Executive Director.

Sergeant William Sawelson

Sergeant William Sawelson was awarded the Congressional Medal of Honor posthumously for action at Grand Pre on October 26, 1918. He lost his life ministering to wounded buddies.

Sergeant Sidney Gumpertz

Sergeant Sidney Gumpertz single-handed bravery at Bois de Forges on September 26, 1918 against a heavy barrage of German guns earned him the Congressional Medal of Honor.

"If the great war has proved anything, it is that men of all races and from all climes are brave to a fault, and that heroes may have unfamiliar names: the name of Abraham Krotoshinsky, for instance."

The New York Times

The Fighting Jew: Sergeant Sam Dreben

A heroic Russian refugee joined the American Army upon his immigration to the United States. Sergeant Sam Dreben fought in the Spanish-American War, the Philippine insurrection and the Boxer rebellion in China before distinguishing himself in the First World War.

For many days at St. Etienne, a German machine-gun crew nest had been shooting at the American lines stationed there, including Sam Dreben and his regiment. The artillery troops had attempted desperately to destroy the nest, but they could not reach their equipment. After several days, Dreben rushed the German post, and single-handedly killed 23 of the 40 German soldiers who had been menacing the Americans. For this act, Sergeant Sam Dreben was awarded the Distinguished Service Cross and earned the nickname, "The Fighting Jew".

Brigadier General Abel Davis

A Jewish general was a hero of the first world war. His name was Abel Davis. Davis a veteran of the Spanish American War was a successful Chicago businessman when WW I broke out. He had previously served as a private in the Spanish American War. Davis served in France as a colonel with the 132nd Illinois Infantry. Under fire for six months be-

fore the Armistice, Davis was promoted to General. He led his regiment in the battle at Amiens, the Meuse-Argonne offensive and in the fighting at St. Hilaire. He repulsed an enemy attack at Hilaire and was recognized for this gallantry with the Distinguished Service Medal and the ribbon of an officer of the French Legion of Honor.

Captain Elkan Voorsanger

Captain Elkan Voorsanger is known as the "Fighting Rabbi" of World War One. Rabbi Voorsanger served as senior chaplain of the 77th Division, a unit that saw considerable action in

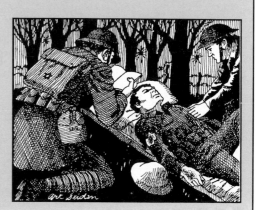

France and Germany. Voorsanger never wavered from service no matter the personal danger. During the Argonne engagement, while tending to a wounded serviceman, Rabbi Voorsanger was himself wounded. He was later awarded a Purple Heart and the French Croix de Guerre. He served all soldiers of all faiths with equal enthusiasm and affection, expanding his role as chaplain to duties as division burial officer and school and entertainment officer.

The exploits of Abraham Krotoshinsky earned him the Distinguished Service Cross. Private Krotoshinsky is credited for rescuing the Lost Battalion (308th Battalion of the 77th Division). The 308th was surrounded by Germans and short of rations. Several men had lost their lives trying to get word of their dire straights to headquarters. The Jewish soldier from the Bronx stepped forward, volunteering for the life-threatening assignment to reach headquarters. Although wounded along the way, Krotoshinsky completed his mission and the 308th was rescued.

"I can only say that when I think of the conduct of the Jewish boys who were entrusted to my guidance, my heart swells with pride that I was their commander. And I am thrilled to think of the fact that the principles of Americanism and the principles of loyalty to our country can so animate human nature and humanity in general to carry them through the trials and dangers and the discomforts to which they were necessarily subjected as triumphantly as they did."

Major General Robert Alexander

On the homefront, Jewish Americans and veterans' groups were busy organizing Liberty Bonds sales and volunteering at all levels to assist in the war effort. The very first attempt to mobilize civilian resources was organized in large part by American Jews.

The nation entrusted the Advisory Council of National Defense (later reorganized into the War Industries Board) with directing government efforts on the civilian front in order to assist the nation in bearing the hardships of the war.

Among the Council's members were Bernard M. Baruch, Council Chairman, Samuel Gompers, Julius Rosenwald, and Felix M. Frankfurter - destined to become the Assistant Secretary of War and an Associate Justice of the U.S. Supreme Court. The War Savings Stamp was conceived by Manny Strauss and the War Risk Insurance System was developed by S. Herbert Wolfe. Eugene Meyer was a member of the War Finance Commission and Albert Lasker served on the Shipping Board.

Julius Stieglitz was responsible for developing war gases in response to the German threat and substitutes for German dyes and chemicals Americans had previously utilized.

Jewish Welfare Board

In 1917, the Jewish Welfare Board was organized to meet the religious needs of Jews in service. Among the WWI chaplains serving on the front lines were 30 rabbis.

A Summary of The War Record of American Jews, WW I

Total population of the
United States in 1917 103,690,473

Jewish population in the
United States in 1917 3,389,000

Total number in the Armed Forces of
the United States 4,355,000

Jews serving in the Armed Forces of the
United States (approximate) 250,000

Percentage of Jews in the total
population 3.27%

Percentage of Jews in the
Armed Forces 5.73%

Distribution among services
Infantry 35.7%
Artillery 11.6%
Cavalry 1.5%
Engineers 4.2%
Signal and Aviation 6.5%
Ordnance 2.4%
Medical 11.6%
Quartermaster 8.9%
Other Branches 17.6%

Casualties
Dead (approximate) 3,500
Wounded (approximate) 12,000

Commissioned Officers
Army-Generals 1
Colonels and lieutenant colonels 94
Majors 404
Captains 1,504
Lieutenants 6,000
Navy - Miscellaneous
(including one admiral) 1,013
Marines - Miscellaneous
(including one general) 161

Total 9,177

Decorations
Congressional Medal of Honor 3

Distinguished Service
Medals and Crosses 147

Other decorations, citations and
awards 982

Total 1,132

Credit: Jews in American Wars

Jewish Families in service to America

The Dodek Family

Mayer Benjamin Dodek of Washington, D.C. served in the Regular Army of the United States in the Spanish American War. He enlisted in 1896 and was honorably discharged in 1899.

During his term of service he took part in the battle of Santiago de Cuba, July 10-11, 1898. He received a citation from the Government of Cuba and a Campaign Medal from the U.S. Following the war, Mr. Dodek was among the founders of the U.S. Spanish War Veterans.

Mayer Benjamin Dodek was the founding father of a dynasty of Jewish war veterans. Two of his sons and a daughter-in-law served during World War I. Harry H. Dodek was a sergeant major in the 2nd Machine Gun Battalion, A.E.F. in France. Oscar A. Dodek was an infantryman, and his wife Esther Dodek was an ambulance driver for the Red Cross. Mayer Dodek's third son, Samuel M. Dodek, was a Captain in the U.S. Medical Corps from 1927-1932.

Mayer Dodek's grandsons continued the legacy. Samuel M. Dodek, 2nd was a 1st Lieutenant in the Infantry, serving in Korea, 1955-1957. Dr. Lloyd Goldstein, Oscar Dodek, Senior's son-in-law was a lieutenant in the Navy Dental Corps

from 1952-1954 and Dr. Oscar Dodek, Jr. was a captain in the Medical Corps between the years 1961-1963.

Mayer Benjamin Dodek began the Dodek family tradition of military service serving in the Spanish-American War. Eight members of Mayer Dodek's immediate family have served in the military since that time. Pictured here are Mayer B. Dodek (center of photo at left) who served in the Spanish American War, Captain Samuel M. Dodek (top photo) who served in the U.S. Army Medical Corps from 1927-1932, pictured with his father, Mayer and Oscar I. Dodek (above) who served with the Coast Guard in WW II.

CHAPTER FOUR

Between World Wars

The Growth of the organization known as JWV

After the Armistice ending World War I was signed on November 11, 1918, the Hebrew Veterans of the War with Spain felt a name change was appropriate and became the Hebrew Veterans of the Wars of the Republic. The organization then launched a nationwide campaign to enroll returning Jewish servicemen and women into its ranks.

Veterans of the Boxer Rebellion in China, the uprising in the Philippines and the 1916 war with Mexico were among those welcomed to the swelling ranks.

It did not take long for these former soldiers to find new action in their own neighborhood. Six months after the end of the war, on May 29, 1919, ten-thousand newly-returned Jewish war veterans took to the streets of New York City to protest against the pogroms inflicted upon their brethren in Poland, Romania and Galicia. The march, overwhelming for its size at the time, was to be the first of many demonstrations sponsored by the Jewish War Veterans of the U.S.A. over the years in support of oppressed people worldwide.

The Hebrew Veterans of the Wars of the Republic continued its unprecedented growth and activity under the guiding hand of Maurice Simmons. Colonel Maurice Simmons was the first in a long line to be selected national commander. He was chosen for this position in 1921.

Chapters, traditionally called posts in veterans' organizations, were chartered from coast to coast. Veterans of the Civil War and the Spanish-American War formed the first posts in New York - Post 1 in Manhattan, Post 2 in Brooklyn, Post 3 in the Bronx, Post 4 in the Lower East Side, Post 6 in Brownsville, and Post 7 in Washington Heights, Post 10 in Jersey City, NJ.

Within the next decade, posts were organized in New Jersey, Pennsylvania, Connecticut, Massachusetts, Rhode Island, Illinois, Chicago, Ohio and Washington, D.C. And so it went, year after year, until the organization reached its present day configuration with 500 posts nationwide.

The Jewish War Veterans of the United States of America (JWV) became the organization's official name on April 10, 1927. At this time, JWV began the practice of electing national commanders on an annual basis at the national convention.

Anyone who enjoys great theater would appreciate the excitement, drama, tension, elation and despair an election for JWV national commander held. Today's JWV members would tell you that old war stories cannot hold a candle to old stories of elections of JWV national commanders!

To reach the burgeoning membership of JWV, the organization began publishing a newsletter. *The Jewish Veteran* has been continuously published since 1925 and to this day serves as the central line of communication in JWV. A national headquarters office was opened at 15 Park Row in Manhattan to administer JWV programs and serve the members.

In the late 1920's, the agenda of Jewish War Veterans reflected the newspaper headlines of the period and the concerns of the national veterans' organizations - which were now a strong, not to be ignored, meaningful force in American society.

As they did from JWV's beginning in 1896, Jewish war veterans continued their primary work to overcome prejudice in the general population.

On veterans' issues, JWV aligned with most major veteran organizations of the time in requesting an amendment to the Veterans Bureau Hospitalization Act to include clinical treatment for all veterans.

The organization successfully petitioned the American Battle Monuments Commission to place Star of David markers on the graves of Jewish soldiers buried in war cemeteries in France. Only Christian crosses were used prior to this request.

Violence against Jews in Central and Eastern Europe led JWV to seek legislation giving preferential consideration to families and immediate relatives of veterans for immigration to the United States. And, JWV appealed to the Government to use its influence among the family of nations to open Palestine to Jewish immigration.

JWV warned of the growing menace of the Ku Klux Klan and the need for combating all racial and religious hate groups in America.

Maurice Simmons

The Jewish War Veteran, April 1926.

To promote American patriotism and democracy in youth JWV became involved in the national scouting movement. JWV sponsors many troops around the country to this day, offering scholarships and sportsman awards. The earliest JWV scout troop, founded in 1920 by Post 76, was Troop 14 of Union City, New Jersey.

By the time of the Great Depression, the Jewish War Veterans of the U.S.A. had emerged as the most proactive of America's Jewish organizations and veterans' organizations. Its operating credo was "Fight Back".

JWV leaders never feared taking a stand. Commencing in the early 1930's and continuing to this day, the JWV national commander has testified annually at Congressional hearings in Washington, D.C. presenting JWV's legislative priorities to members of the House and Senate Veterans Affairs Committees.

JWV continues to be action oriented and to maintain a congruency between its concern for this nation's veterans and its commitment to American Jewry.

The collaboration of JWV and its allied veteran organizations had its greatest impact in the fight to combat Fascism and Communism. These radical ideologies poisoned the domestic and international scene in the 1930's and threatened the peace in our nation and our world.

Veterans' groups monitored the activities of 21 German Bundist camps. These camps were staging grounds for the preparation and dissemination of Hitler's Nazi propaganda in America. The facilities were used to train future American-Nazi leaders and to recruit spies for the German government.

The arrest of the head of the German Bund, Fritz Kuhn, was cause for celebration for veterans' groups and the American Legion and JWV, in particular. These two organizations had united in the fight against German American Bundists. It was not until war was declared, in 1941, that the German Bund camps were closed, once and for all.

Allied veterans' groups united too in denouncing the anti-Semitism that flourished in over one-hundred hate-groups that came to prominence during the thirties. Groups such as the Silver Shirts, the Christian Mobilizers, the Ku Klux Klan and radio hatemongers such as the Rev. Charles E. Coughlin of Detroit, were spewing their hatred without restriction. Efforts by veterans' associations to pass libel laws which would have driven the hatemongers underground failed.

The spread of Communism in America and internationally was of deep concern to America's men and women in uniform. The Jewish War Veterans and the American veterans' community deemed Communism to be a paramount threat to America's security and way of life.

History has proven JWV leadership to have uncanny foresight in international affairs and the courage to stand-up and sometimes stand alone for their beliefs. Today's JWV members are particularly proud of these attributes of organizational action.

Non-Jews recognize and appreciate this characteristic of JWV action, too. While making the film, "Jewish American Patriots: How Jewish-Americans Helped Shape Our Military History," producer, Paul Hansen was impressed with JWV's activities as a forerunner, "Time and time again JWV would be among the first to spot hatred and anti-Americanism and bring it to the attention of Congress and the country. JWV has always been in the vanguard, watching out not only for anti-Semitism, but for Fascism and Communism at home and abroad."

Hansen's admiration of JWV is well-deserved for in the early 1930's few saw the Nazi handwriting on the wall as early as the Jewish War Veterans of the USA. Few were prepared, as was JWV, to face the oncoming darkness.

All attention was on the worst economic crisis to befall our nation, the Great Depression. JWV did what it could to support its members and their families suffering from economic adversity. The organization experienced its most phenomenal growth during these trying times going from 30 posts in 1930 to 277 posts by 1939. The system of departments (regions) was established, with each department electing its own commander.

Another subsidiary of JWV was formed in 1936. The Sons of JWV, was a teenaged membership group affiliated with local JWV posts. Within four years, 120 posts around the country had established Sons of JWV chapters with more than 10,000 members. In 1938, teenagers nationwide converged on a JWV summer camp, a program of Sons of JWV.

Forty Drum and Bugle Corps were created from Sons of JWV chapters. It was quite a sight to see these young men (and women) marching proudly along side their parents in Veterans Day parades, decked out with colorful uniforms and shiny brass instruments provided by JWV.

In 1935, JWV helped another veterans' service organization to establish itself. It was the Catholic War Veterans (CWV). Once this was completed the two organizations applied for Congressional Charters but were turned down on the basis of "religious affiliations." Five decades later, JWV and CWV finally were chartered by Congress.

JWV takes great pride in the diverse programs it created in the 1930's and the support and cooperation it developed domestically and internationally for the veterans' and Jewish agenda.

The JWV National Ladies Auxiliary

By the early 1920's, some of the posts of JWV had organized auxiliaries consisting of wives, mothers, sisters and daughters of Jewish war veterans to "remember the forgotten men" of the First World

1929 Convention of the Jewish War Veterans held in Atlantic City, New Jersey.

Developing a Government Benefit Plan

It was during the thirties that the organized veterans' community called upon Congress to create law which would lay the foundation for future government services for those who risked their lives to preserve our democracy. Among the legislative priorities of the nation's veterans were the following:

- provide pensions for widows and orphans of deceased veterans
- increase compensation for disabled veterans
- distribute a bonus for World War I veterans
- assist unemployed veterans in obtaining jobs
- improve medical care for hospitalized veterans
- provide burial allowances to families of deceased veterans

The variety of JWV's concerns is shown in this 1935 cartoon in The Jewish Veteran.

An early photograph of the members of the Department of New York JWV National Ladies' Auxiliary.

War—the hospitalized veterans. As part of its veterans' service program, the Jewish War Veterans would visit these servicemen in the hospital. Certain posts then began to experiment with auxiliaries which devoted themselves entirely to this sort of work. By 1928, five auxiliaries had been established. Their work was so exemplary that a National Ladies Auxiliary was formed. Today, the JWVA has 260 chapters with an approximate membership of 12,000 women.

At the beginning, the Auxiliary's main responsibility in peace time was to provide social welfare, entertainment and recreational services for disabled veterans. During wartime, JWVA participated in War Bond drives, blood drives, civil defense activities, and provided recreation and canteen facilities for servicemen.

In more recent years, the war support programs have turned into the Aid-to-Cancer-program, and programs addressing the need for education, training and scholarships continue to increase. The Auxiliary has supported Israel since 1947. JWVA is a major contributor to the Chaim Sheba Medical Center, the official hospital of the State of Israel.

In recent years, JWVA has instituted scholarship and child welfare programs, become active on Capitol Hill in order to champion veterans' rights, and has established links with the White House and Pentagon to further the rights and treatment of women in this country and throughout the world. The Jewish War Veterans National Ladies Auxiliary has evolved into an active and respected organization over the past 60 years.

National Presidents of the JWV National Ladies Auxiliary

1929-31	Fannie Davis	1965-66	Sarah Nemon
1931-32	Henrietta L. Kraditor	1966-67	Marcia K. Kantorwitz
1932-35	Ethel J. Cohen	1967-68	Cherie Siegel
1935-36	Ann G. Rubenstein	1968-69	Ellen G. Kaplan
1936-37	Dorothy Kurman Kirchenberg	1969-70	Freda L. Alexander
1937-39	Malvina V. Freeman	1970-71	Frances L. Forman
1939-40	Frances Brams	1971-72	Billie Kern
1940-41	Jennie Silverman	1972-73	Florence K. Vucker
1941-42	Miriam G. Hoffman	1973-74	Anne Teitelbaum
1942-43	Rae K. Schoenberg	1974-75	Anita Gotthoffer
1943-44	Jessie C. Gneshin	1975-76	Elaine Mass
1944-45	Bessie Kronberg	1976-77	Rose L. Toye
1945-46	Alice Gilman	1977-78	Frances S. Wapnick
1946-47	Tina Brill Stein	1978-79	Sylvia Herman
1947-48	Ethyl Novak	1979-80	Eleanor Medoff
1948-49	Mae Weiner	1980-81	Evelyn Mermonstein
1949-50	Anna R. Abelow	1981-82	Bernyce T. Ford
1950-51	Minna D. Levine	1982-83	Jeanette L. Shapiro
1951-52	Jessica Slatis	1983-84	Florence G. Levine
1952-53	Rose Chanin	1984-85	Jeanette Schneider
1953-54	Florence D. Hularman	1985-86	Sharlee F. Friend
1954-55	Sarah Stone	1986-87	Donna S. Green
1955-56	Fannie Bramnick	1987-88	Ceil Steinberg
1956-57	Bertha S. Schwartz	1988-89	Gladys L. Simon
1957-58	Bertha K. Greenberg	1989-90	Rose S. Hurst
1958-59	Sylvia R. Piltch	1990-91	Ethyle K. Bornstein
1959-60	Pearl Goldhagen	1991-92	Charlotte Steinberg
1960-61	Bertha W. Krause	1992-93	Eleanore J. Kolosky
1961-62	Miriam Shor	1993-94	Rosalin Nathan
1962-63	Ceil Schwartz Broder	1994-95	Adele Zucker
1963-64	Miriam Kaplan	1995-96	Sophie Ruderman
1964-65	Rose Schorr		

CHAPTER FIVE

The Approaching Darkness
The JWV Boycott of German Goods

The United States was not alone during the years of the Depression. Many nations struggled similarly with economic crisis and a blanket of darkness began its approach.

This kind of darkness was too great for some to comprehend. It was ignored for too long, by too many, and it grew into a loathsome enemy.

In the beginning, just one American voice spoke out against the evil which gripped control of Germany on January 30, 1933, when Adolph Hitler was made Chancellor. It was the voice of the Jewish War Veterans of the USA.

Perhaps the Jewish people, having suffered under the darkness of old, were more alert to the potential for catastrophe. Perhaps those Jews who served in the military, having experienced the capacity of cruelty man can achieve in war, could better conceive of the destruction to come.

JWV acted early to call the world's attention to the oncoming threat. Just six weeks after Hitler's ascension to power, JWV began a campaign against the German government, starting with a boycott of German goods to the United States.

On March 23, 1933, JWV staged a parade in New York City publicizing its boycott program. More than four thousand veterans participated. The parade terminated at City Hall where Mayor John O'Brien publicly endorsed the boycott and appealed for diplomatic protests of German cruelty by the Roosevelt Administration. The parade captured national and international attention.

To implement the campaign, JWV distributed placards and stamps with anti-boycott slogans for those supporters who picketed retail stores selling German goods and it compiled lists of German import goods and alternative sources for these goods.

Jewish leaders met with representatives of the U.S. State Department to demand government support of the boycott concept. State Department officials downplayed Nazi atrocities and described the boycott as counterproductive, because Germany had initiated its own boycott of American goods.

The 1936 Olympics could be a propaganda coup to the sponsoring country, Germany. JWV and allied veterans' organizations vigorously opposed American participation in the games. According to Dr. Seymour Weisman, JWV Consultant and historian, the veterans accurately predicted that minority members of the American teams would face discrimination.

Research by Weisman indicates that in 1937, the year following the Berlin Olympics, the leaders of the American Athletic Union (AAU) which promoted United States participation in the Berlin games were removed from office in a hotly contested election. American veterans' organizations were pleased by the outcome of the vote.

Again, in the sporting arena - an arena of great public exposure - JWV forcefully opposed the heavyweight boxing championship fight between Jimmy Braddock and Max Schmeling, a member of the Nazi Party. The protest did not succeed, perhaps due in part to the fact that the promoter for the boxing championship was a Jew named Mike Jacobs.

JWV did enjoy success when it forced a quick

JWV organized a nationwide boycott of German goods in response to Hitler's rise to power.

The JWV German Boycott parade, held in New York City, March 23, 1933.

OVER THE FENCE!

end to Schmeling's victory tour following the fight. In each city Schmeling visited, JWV notified the media of the fighter's intention to contribute his fight and tour proceeds to the Nazi led German government. The bad press finally caught up with Schmeling and he cut short his tour returning to Germany without the intended "booty."

The night of shattered glass, "Krystalnacht" was also a night of shattered illusions. On November 9, 1938, Nazi storm troopers desecrated and destroyed synagogues, Jewish owned businesses and Jewish homes throughout Germany. Now the world could not deny the atrocities perpetrated against the Jews of Germany. But, for many Jews it was already too late.

In 1937-38, 55 percent of world imports were from Germany. The best evidence of the effectiveness of the German boycott came from German sources. Records of the period shed light on the

potential success of JWV's boycott of German goods had it garnered the appropriate support. Throughout the 1930's, the German government engaged in massive efforts through various channels to counter the impact of the boycott. Most revealing was the episode on "Blue Monday", July 18, 1938, when prices on the German Stock Exchange plunged.

What triggered the market decline was the announcement that German exports showed a deficit for the first six months of the year of 175,000,000 marks as compared to a surplus of 194,000,000 marks for the first six months of 1937. It is possible that had the United States and its allies taken seriously the Nazi threat, when alerted to it by JWV, Germany's capacity to wage war would have been severely diminished.

JWV did not succeed fully in its early private, little war with Nazi Germany. But, Dr. Weisman believes it did appreciate a moral victory in the struggle for human rights. And, JWV members got further practice in standing up for their beliefs, even when it means standing alone.

JWV continued to pursue its German Boycott Program. When the United States entered World War II in December of 1941, the entire country adopted it.

"With the advent of the adventurer who surrounds himself with a horde of fanatics and desperadoes, and by sheer violence makes himself the ruler of the people, the fate of the Jew has been sealed, unless he recognizes the signs himself and takes the proper precautions to prevent his annihilation."

JWV member and author,
Louis A. Falk, 1936

The Refugee Problem

In November 1933, the Jewish War Veterans of the USA petitioned government leaders to permit Jews seeking to flee Nazi Germany to enter the United States. An article in *The Jewish Veteran* of that date, appealed for support from the League of Nations for such an effort.

The atmosphere of the time was isolationist due to the financial devastation caused by the Great Depression. Jobs were scarce, thousands of businesses had failed, and public opinion leaned toward self-preservation and away from international aid.

When Franklin Delano Roosevelt was elected president hopes were high that the plight of the refugees would be addressed. But, immigration officials refused requests, time and again, to fill available quotas for immigration with refugees from Germany and Austria, denying entry to 100,000 despairing people.

Jewish refugees of World War I camped out at JWV National Headquarters in New York City, seeking information on loved ones in Europe. JWV assembled a volunteer team, fluent in the German language, to assist the families. Fundraising projects were embarked upon by JWV leaders nationwide to provide operating funds for the JWV refugee support program.

The British Consul General was approached by JWV in March of 1937 with the goal of petitioning Great Britain to open the gates of Palestine to German Jews. The effort, sadly, failed.

Jewish American Unity

In 1933, when JWV was unable to garner full support for its boycott of German goods from among its peers in American Jewish associations, JWV determined it was time for direct confrontation. Jewish groups must unify just as veteran groups had, postulated JWV's commanders, if they are to have the strength needed to face the challenges to world Jewry ahead.

They approached major American Jewish groups seeking unity of policy, purpose and efforts. They sought to avoid wasteful duplication of resources and to strengthen the clout of America's Jews through better coordination of activities.

It was a difficult task but, ultimately, the American Jewish Committee, American Jewish Congress and B'nai B'rith agreed to create an advisory council to share information and make policy decisions.

Domestic anti-Semitism and burgeoning Nazi tyranny in Europe led JWV to suggest the establishment of a federation composed of American Jewish organizations committed to fighting anti-Semitism. This federation would act as a clearing house for coordinated community activities both locally and nationally. JWV made this proposition in December of 1938. In 1944, after several false starts, the National Jewish Community Relations Advisory Council was formed.

Personalities and JWV

The importance of forging links with recognized national personalities was not lost on JWV. During the war years, JWV gratefully sought the talents of respected celebrities, educators, politicians, religious and military figures on behalf of our nation's veterans and for Jewish causes.

Leon Blum, premier of France; Eddie Cantor, acclaimed Broadway and film star, Nobel scientist Albert Einstein, Zionist orator, Rabbi Abbe Hillel Silver; Governor and later Senator Herbert H. Lehman (a member of Albany, New York Post 105); all offered their support during the war years.

For many years Americans huddled in their living rooms listening to radio and anxiously awaiting news of the war. JWV produced a 15 minute radio news show in Washington, D.C. that was carried by all three of the national networks. JWV leaders appeared on the program with prominent speakers, entertainers, leading civic and political figures, and military and religious leaders.

Necessarily neutral in matters of politics, JWV has never endorsed a candidate for office. But, no matter the party, JWV has always supported the elected Commander-in-Chief. In 1933 and in 1937, JWV received nationwide publicity as the only Jewish association to carry its colors and march in President Franklin Delano Roosevelt's inaugural parades.

International Jewish War Veterans

French Jewish war veterans sponsored an international conference of Jewish war veterans in Paris during the summer of 1935. An American delegation headed by the JWV National Commander William Berman attended. The agenda included the mounting threat of anti-Semitism; needed havens for Jewish refugees; and relations between the Jewish war veterans and the Jewish community in Palestine.

One year later, the International Conference of Jewish War Veterans was held in Vienna. National Commander Abraham Kraditor represented JWV. Kraditor extended his trip and included visits to Poland and to Paris to participate in Bastille Day activities and pay an official visit to American Ambassador to France, Nathan Strauss.

International Jewish war veterans continue to hold convocations every five years to address joint concerns and formulate programs.

The tradition of each national commander visiting our European allies and world leaders also continues today. Depending upon the political climate, overseas trips might include stopovers in Belgium (NATO headquarters), Eastern Europe, the Soviet Union or Israel. JWV leaders operate in the belief that international contact provides insight into world affairs for the organization's members and leads to greater understanding of the American veterans' agenda among world leaders.

Developing a National Presence

JWV stood solidly behind President Roosevelt's New Deal. With passage of what was to become known as the National Recovery Act (NRA) in 1933, posts nationwide were directed to participate in their local area's NRA programs.

Memorial Day, Veterans Day and Flag Day Observances

Beginning in 1934, JWV promoted the annual celebration of Flag Day, noting in its publicity releases that Ben Altheimer, a German Jewish naturalized citizen and honorary member of JWV was the person most responsible for influencing President Woodrow Wilson to issue the first proclamation to observe Flag Day in 1916.

Memorial Day parades and services took on special significance during the war years. In the 1990's, the Jewish War Veterans of the USA and its subsidiaries, the JWV National Ladies Auxiliary, the National Descendants of JWV and the National Museum of American Jewish Military History are each represented at national Memorial Day and Veterans Day functions.

Preserving WWI Battlefield Monuments in France

JWV representatives were among those appointed to a commission established in 1937 to oversee monuments erected in cemeteries in France after World War I. The commission, led by General John J. Pershing, paid special attention to the graves of Jewish soldiers. Attempts were made to identify all those who were Jewish and to assure grave markers were the Star of David. The commission also developed a plan to expedite the return of remains to the United States for burial in family plots.

New York World's Fair 1939

JWV Day at the 1939 World's Fair in New York provided the association with an opportunity to address its concerns and diverse activities to a large audience. Hundreds of members attended, distributing boycott literature and general organization information.

Boy Scouts of America

At its 1932 national convention JWV resolved to encourage good citizenship in America's youth by expanding post sponsorship of Boy Scout troops. The commitment has spanned nearly seven decades. According to officials of the Boy Scouts of America, JWV posts have sponsored more boy scout troops than any other national Jewish organization. Thousands of Eagle Scouts have been recognized at special JWV ceremonies and presented with JWV certificates of merit for their achievement. Participation of Girl Scout troops is encouraged.

Jewish All-American Football Team

In cooperation with the Seven Arts Feature Syndicate and affiliated anglo-Jewish weeklies, JWV sponsored a collegiate All-American Football Team in 1937.

Planning for the Future

Among the projects JWV postponed for financial reasons were the establishment of an office in Washington D.C. to promote its legislative programs and the purchase of a building to serve as its memorial to the Jewish men and women who served in this nation's armed forces. These aspirations were to be fulfilled in the post World War II period.

JWV fought to have Jewish graves marked by a Star of David, rather than the Christian Crosses used until the 1920s.

JWV came to Paris in 1935 for an international convocation of Jewish ex-servicemen. Seated are National Commander William Berman, a British delegate, a French delegate, and Jack E. Spector, whose idea it was to found JWV Paris Post No. 120. Standing are aides to Commander Berman and two British ex-servicemen.

JWV echelons sponsor hundreds of Scout troops nationwide. Here, members of the Department of Maryland with the boy Scout troop they sponsored.

Chapter 6

World War II

The Fall of 1939 brought war to Europe. President Roosevelt's Administration immediately approached the Congress to provide economic and military aid to Great Britain and France in their fight against Germany and Italy.

This would prove to be a challenging task, for as our national leaders sought to reach out to threatened allies in Europe, here at home isolationist sentiment was mobilized once again. And, once again, the vehicle for transporting this fear was a national hero, the charming and handsome flying ace, Charles Lindbergh. The popular Lindbergh proved to be a most effective spokesman for the group, America First, garnering formidable public support for a neutral American posture.

The Jewish War Veterans of the USA opposed America First in the staunch belief that a German defeat was crucial to Jewish survival in Europe. JWV encouraged its members to give generously to organizations providing humanitarian aid to Great Britain and France, and to the Finnish people who were fending off invading Soviet troops.

The Roosevelt Administration was successful on Capitol Hill in urging Congress to enact legislation establishing a draft of civilians for the armed services. Veterans' groups universally endorsed this policy of war preparedness as well as the industrial rearmament program that was instituted.

The Jewish Veteran featured an article in its December 1940 issue by General George C. Marshall, Chief of Staff, United States Army, describing programs for new inductees. At its mid-year conference in February 1941, JWV adopted a comprehensive program to support these and other mobilization efforts.

The Jewish War Veterans and the Jewish Welfare Board worked cooperatively to provide activities for draftees including support for the United Service Organization (USO).

The JWV-JWB relationship continues to the current day. During the Persian Gulf War, the two joined forces to provide free copies of the Bible for Jewish troops serving in Saudi Arabia.

The handwriting on the wall predicted America would join the fighting forces in due time. The government moved to established a permanent selective service system and began developing support programs to assist draftees during their military service and after their terms of duty as well. For example, free mail service was offered to military personnel in the continental United States, and the G.I. insurance act was amended to provide protection for death or total disability resulting from military service.

At JWV, volunteers were recruited to assist German Jewish refugees wishing to enlist in the U.S. armed forces, civil defense groups were trained nationwide, and preparations were made for the undeniable conflict ahead.

As the defense industry expanded its employment recruitment, JWV called attention to the discrimination in hiring of Jews, Blacks and other ethnic minorities. JWV supported federal legislation to ban unfair hiring practices.

All these efforts to prepare for war brought an outcry from the America First movement claiming Jews were influencing President Roosevelt, encouraging the President to enter World War II to save their brethren in Germany.

When a U.S. senator involved with American First said publicly that leading movie producers in Hollywood were predominantly "foreign born, mostly Jewish", suggesting they had undue influence over the public, President Roosevelt sent the senator a telegram which read "Have just been reading a book called the Holy Bible, has large circulation in this country. Written entirely by foreign born, mostly Jews."

America at War

December 7, 1941 is the day that "lives in infamy". American territory was directly attacked in the surprise Japanese bombing of Pearl Harbor. The following day, President Roosevelt secured Congressional approval to declare war on Japan, Germany and Italy.

For the next four years, until total victory was achieved in August of 1945, members of the Jewish War Veterans ceaselessly devoted their energies to helping win the war.

Jewish Congressional Medal of Honor Recipients of World War II

Sergeant Isadore S. Jachman

Isadore S. Jachman of Baltimore, Maryland was awarded the Congressional Medal of Honor posthumously following a daring defense in which he single-handedly forced two German tanks to retire. At Flamierge, Belgium, Jachman's company was facing a harsh German attack, causing many casualties. Sergeant Jachman, understanding his company's predicament, left his safe location and voluntarily exposed himself to heavy enemy fire to save his company. He took a bazooka from a fallen soldier and fired on the tanks, both of whom were firing at him. Jachman's actions confused the enemy and disrupted their attack. They soon left, and Jachman had saved a large portion of his company.

Lieutenant Raymond Zussman

Lieutenant Raymond Zussman of Detroit, Michigan was killed in action several days after being awarded the Congressional Medal of Honor for his bravery in the battle for the little village of Noroy Le Bourg. The tank in which Zussman was traveling became bogged down in a field. Not willing to settle for watching the action, Zussman jumped out of his tank, grabbed a carbine and preceded another tank on foot. From his vantage point Zussman could direct the tank's fire. This action accounted for the slaying of 17 German soldiers, the capture of 32 German soldiers and the capture of two anti-tank guns and two trucks.

Zussman continued his rampage, destroying a machine gun nest and a German jeep. Zussman's exploits earned him, the son of Russian immigrants and the brother of a World War I soldier wounded

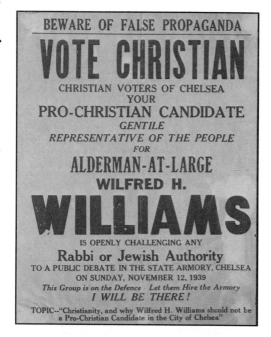

BEWARE OF FALSE PROPAGANDA
VOTE CHRISTIAN
CHRISTIAN VOTERS OF CHELSEA
YOUR
PRO-CHRISTIAN CANDIDATE
GENTILE
REPRESENTATIVE OF THE PEOPLE
FOR
ALDERMAN-AT-LARGE
WILFRED H.
WILLIAMS
IS OPENLY CHALLENGING ANY
Rabbi or Jewish Authority
TO A PUBLIC DEBATE IN THE STATE ARMORY, CHELSEA
ON SUNDAY, NOVEMBER 12, 1939
This Group is on the Defence · Let them Hire the Armory
I WILL BE THERE!
TOPIC--"Christianity, and why Wilfred H. Williams should not be a Pro-Christian Candidate in the City of Chelsea"

World War II was the first American war in which women participated in large numbers. Some women actually joined the military, in units such as the WAACS and WAVES and as nurses, while others worked on the homefront in factories, in hospitials and at USO posts.

Second Lieutenant Raymond Zussman, World War II recipient of the Congressional Medal of Honor

Vice Admiral Hyman George Rickover

in action, the highest medal of bravery that an American soldier can receive.

"**Thousands of Americans of Jewish faith are serving under my command. Many of them have been killed in the service to their country. To American soldiers of Jewish faith go my most sincere thanks for their faithfulness, diligence and bravery in battle. To those who have passed on must go a nation's gratitude.**"

General Mark W. Clark, Commander of 15th Army Group in Italy during WWII

Major General Maurice Rose

Major General Maurice Rose began his Army career in 1916, enlisting as a private in the Colorado National Guard. Selected for officer candidate school, he was commissioned as a second lieutenant. He fought in France during World War I. After a brief return to civilian life, he returned to the Army in 1920.

In the years between the world wars, Rose taught at the Army Industrial College and at Kansas State Agricultural College on the ROTC staff.

In 1942, as a recently promoted Colonel, he participated with the 2nd Armored Division (Hell on Wheels) in the war in North Africa and Italy. During the Italian campaign, Rose was promoted to Brigadier General.

He assumed command of the newest American tank division - the 3rd Armored. He was the first army commander since Napoleon to invade Germany from the West and his was the first division to break the Siegfried line. Additionally, his was the first American unit to capture a German town.

On the evening of March 30, 1945 Rose led his men more than 100 miles in a single thrust. While the small column made its way through wooded terrain, the group was ambushed and Major General Maurice Rose was killed.

Vice Admiral Hyman Rickover

During World War II a young Jewish naval officer was to come to the attention of his superiors

Jewish Families in Service to America

More than 11,000 Jews died defending America. Over 50 Jewish families lost two sons in service and at least one Jewish family endured the tragedy of three losses.

The Wilkof Tragedy

Twin brothers Bernard and Sanford Wilkof of Canton, Ohio made the ultimate sacrifice for their country. Pfc. Bernard Wilkof was mortally wounded on June 3, 1944 while serving in North Africa. Sgt. Sanford Wilkof was killed in action less than four months later, on September 13, in Italy. The Bernard and Sanford Wilkof JWV Post 73 of Canton, Ohio, honors their memories and serves veterans to this day in their names.

The Wilkof Twins

The Schlesinger Brothers: A Chance Meeting

"It was late August 1945. My field artillery company, 27th Division, was camped in northern Okinawa. We'd landed a week earlier, after a month of convoy travel across the Pacific. Along with Americans everywhere, we awaited the Japanese response to the bombings of Hiroshima and Nagasaki.

Word finally came—Japan had surrendered! The 27th Division proceeded to Razor Ridge and Sugar Loaf Hill, areas of bloody tank and infantry battles. Not far from us GIs were doing mopping-up operations, flushing Japanese soldiers out of caves and convincing them Japan had lost.

Burned-out tanks littered the hillsides. Unexploded shells and mines were all around us. Too frequently you'd come across a pair of combat boots with shattered shin bones sticking out of them. I was a green soldier, two months short of 19-years-old. This was a very sobering introduction to the horrors of war.

My unit was among the first occupation troops to land in Japan. We prepared to fly to the island of Honshu after the surrender papers were signed on the battleship *Missouri*. Biding our time on this hot, coral-covered island, I decided to try for a long shot of luck.

I had not seen my brother for almost three years. We'd exchanged an occasional letter. I knew he'd been in New Zealand, Australia, New Guinea and the Philippines. I had a hunch his outfit, the 69th Fighter Squadron of the Fifth Air Force Pacific, might be on the island.

I got the go-ahead from my C.O. and hitched a ride to the Kadena airbase near the

Sgt. Max Schlesinger, left, 69th Fighter Squadron/5th Air Force meets his brother, Pvt. Carl of 105th Field Artillery/27th Division, by chance on Okinawa in August, 1945.

capital of Naha. With the overconfidence of a kid, I felt sure I could locate my brother.

Talk about beginner's luck! My brother's unit was there. Armed with a little camera, I opened his tent flap and there he was—30 pounds lighter then when I'd last seen him, sitting on the edge of his cot, writing a letter home! I'll never forget the expression of shock and surprise on his face when he looked up and saw me. "Where the hell did you come from?" he exclaimed. I couldn't resist. "I just happened to be in the neighborhood and thought I'd drop in," I declared!

---

and make a name for himself in submarine warfare. That name is Hyman Rickover.

Born in Russian Poland, Rickover's family immigrated to the United States and settled in Chicago. At age 18, Rickover received an appointment to the United States Naval Academy. He graduated in 1922 and was commissioned an ensign. Rickover spent five years at sea, before being assigned to the Naval Academy to do graduate work in electrical engineering. He continued his studies at Columbia University where he received his M.S. degree in 1929.

Rickover was assigned, in 1946, to Oak Ridge, the site of the development of the atomic bomb. Rickover visited other nuclear research centers and became convinced ships could be powered by nuclear energy. Almost alone in his belief, he finally convinced the Navy to develop a nuclear submarine in 1947.

Before long he was placed in charge of the project and worked with the Atomic Energy Commission, which was overseeing the construction of nuclear reactors. The reactors were built in Idaho; the submarine in Groton, Connecticut. Finally, in January 1954, the first atomic-powered submarine, the Nautilus, was launched.

Admiral Rickover had a vision of a nuclear Navy. He was, without question, ultimately re-

sponsible for building the most powerful nuclear Navy in the world. He created a major revision in Naval tactics and strategy due to this new technology. Additionally, he instituted a training program that is still in effect today. This training program resulted in the regeneration of Naval officers based on technology that allowed no nuclear incidents. Rickover was instrumental in formulating the nation's nuclear power program, as well.

Despite his success, Rickover faced opposition to his work which often took the form of overt anti-Semitism. After he had been passed over, two times, for promotion to admiral (naval codes require retirement after promotion is denied twice), congressional leaders suspected that he was a victim of foul play. Following an investigation, he was named a rear admiral in 1953. His many plans for nuclear ships were put aside during the Congressional hearings.

In 1982, he was forced into retirement at age 82. When Rickover retired, he expressed regrets about the role he played in nuclear proliferation and called for an international agreement to outlaw nuclear weapons and reactors because of the radiation dangers that they pose.

Throughout the war, *The Jewish Veteran* carried feature articles recording military exploits of

---

Jews. Building on Simon Wolf's monumental work *The American Jew as Patriot, Soldier and Citizen*, published in 1895, J. George Fredman and Louis Falk authored *Jews in American Wars* which was first published in October, 1942.

Fredman and Falk report on the efforts of JWV and the Jewish Welfare Board to compile records of American Jews in WW II. The two organizations determined that over 550,000 men and women of the Jewish faith served in World War II. More than 52,000 awards and medals were conferred on Jewish men and women who served in World War II.

A Summary of the War Record of American Jews, WWII

Total population of the United States	135,000,000
Total Jewish population of the United States	4,500,000
Total number in the Armed Forces of the United States	13,000,000
Jews serving in the Armed Forces of the United States	550,000
Percentage of Jews in the total population	3.33%
Percentage of Jews in the Armed Forces	4.23%

Distribution among services

Army	80%
Infantry	16 2/3%
Other Ground Forces	8 1/2%
Air Corps	33 1/2%
Navy	17%
Marine Corps	2%
Coast Guard	1%

Casualties

Dead (approximate)	11,000
Wounded (approximate)	40,000

Decorations

Congressional Medal of Honor	2
Distinguished Service Medals and Crosses and Navy Crosses	157
Silver Star	1,600
Other decorations, citations and awards	50,242
Total	52,000

About 60% of all Jewish physicians in the United States under 45 years of age were in the service.

Credit: Jews in American Wars by J. George Fredman and Louis A. Falk

Stories of American Jewish military heroes abounded in World War II. Among the most famous, as well as the ones most telling of the patriotism and dedication of American Jewish soldiers, are the stories of Francis Slanger, the first American nurse to die in the European Theater of Operation and a Rabbi Alexander Goode, one of the famed "Four Chaplains".

Frances Slanger

Early one morning, Lt. Francis Slanger, of Roxbury, Massachusetts, wrote a letter home praising the efforts of American soldiers in the European Theater. One of four nurses who participated in the Normandy beach landing on D-Day, Slanger overlooked her own heroism to celebrate her fellow soldiers, all men, about whom she said: "But you— the men driving our tanks, flying our planes, sailing

An hour after writing a letter celebrating the bravery of American soldiers, Nurse Francis Slanger was killed by an enemy bullet. She was the first nurse killed in the European Theatre.

This portable ark and Torah, used by Jewish chaplain, Martin Weitz, is on display in the "I Remember" exhibit at the National Museum of American Jewish Military History in Washington, D.C.

Rabbi Alexander Goode was one of four chaplains who sacrificed their lives following the bombing of the USS Dorchester. The four gave their lifejackets to other servicemen and reportedly sank to the depths of the seas while holding hands in prayer.

our ships, building bridges— it is to you that we doff our helmets. To every GI wearing the American uniform, for you we have the greatest admiration and respect."

Slanger wrote that her hardships were small compared to those of the men. She claimed that she and the other nurses had "... a stove and coal. We even have a laundry line in the tent", while the men were lying in the mud. In truth, the men of whom she wrote depended on her and the dedicated nurses and medics of the front lines to care for the sick, wounded and dying.

The letter was mailed on October 21, 1944. An hour after composing her letter, Francis Slanger was killed by a stray enemy bullet and became the first American nurse killed in action in the European Theater. Her ironic letter declared, "Sure we rough it, but in comparison to the way you men are taking it, we can't complain nor do we feel that bou-

quets are due to us". Nurse Slanger, a Jewish woman, gave her life for her country and for a cause she believed in. Lt. Slanger's letter was published in *The Stars and Stripes*, before the editor knew that she had been killed in action. Her message, passed on posthumously, spoke volumes about the women of World War II and the devotion of all women who have worn or currently wear "the uniform".

Chaplain Alexander D. Goode

On February 3, 1943, the *U.S.S. Dorchester*, carrying 900 American servicemen headed for combat, was working its way through icy, churning waters off Greenland when it was struck by a U-boat torpedo. It was forced to leave the convoy and it didn't take long before a second torpedo scored a direct hit killing 100 men in the hold of the ship.

Throughout the ship there was confusion, ter-

ror, and chaos as men scrambled about to get their life jackets and in many cases to get dressed. Trying to calm the men were four chaplains: Rabbi Alexander D. Goode; John P. Washington, a Roman Catholic priest; George L. Fox, a Methodist minister; and Clark P. Poling, a minister of the Reformed Church in America.

The extra life jackets were handed out but there were still many servicemen without them. Standing in front of the four chaplains were four men without life jackets. They were cold and afraid. The four chaplains took off their jackets and gave them to these men. The ship was quickly sliding into the sea. Many lifeboats filled with men were already in the water and many others were being launched. The four chaplains went about the deck helping men get into lifeboats and comforting those that were terrified. Finally, all lifeboats were on the waters filled with the remaining troops.

The last vision the survivors saw of the *U.S.S. Dorchester* was of the four chaplains. They were clinging to each other on the slanted deck as it slowly went into the sea. Their arms were linked together with their heads bowed in silent prayer.

Rabbi Goode was one of 309 Rabbis to be commissioned in World War II. He was one of many to give his life.

Homefront Activities

Meeting on December 18, 1941, the JWV National Executive Committee drew up an "Emergency Program for Victory." The program called for mobilization for military service, civilian defense activities, volunteer programs for home service (nursing aid, canteen services, youth activities for boy scouts and girl scouts, conservation programs, blood donations), and fundraising for charities such as the America Red Cross and the USO.

The major JWV fundraising campaign was dedicated to the purchase of six fighter planes, costing two-hundred-thousand dollars each. The first two planes donated by JWV were named "The Jewish Veteran" and "The Star of David." The organization also purchased twenty-five ambulances and field kitchens.

Responding to a request from Navy seamen, JWV supplied five gallon urns to be used for coffee breaks while seamen were on watch duty. JWV also initiated a program to send playing cards and various entertainment items to military personnel.

At the request of JWV, the Navy Department commissioned several new ships to honor Jewish naval heroes, most notably the U.S.S. Uriah P. Levy, named for the nineteenth century naval commodore renowned for eliminating the traditional naval punishment of flogging.

The Jewish War Veterans' homefront campaigns also included patriotic events tied in with U.S. saving bond drives. JWV was honored to be commended by the United States Department of the Treasury for its extraordinary achievements in selling war bonds— over two hundred million dollars worth.

JWV posts nationwide sponsored Jewish festival and cultural events, such as Passover seders (elaborate holiday meals including prayers, songs, readings and rituals) for soldiers unable to celebrate with family.

JWV established a nonsectarian "Adopt a Yank" program, which was copied by many organizations across the country. Under this program, posts adopted individual servicemen and sent them boxes of necessities for comfort throughout the war.

There continued to be many battles for JWV on the homefront throughout the war years on issues of anti-Semitism and civil rights. Henry Ford proved to be a surprising new ally in the fight to combat anti-Semitism. Previously linked to paid anti-Jewish propagandists, Ford in a letter dated January 7, 1942 repudiated charges of anti-Semitism and condemned bigotry as "disservice to the United States." He expressed the hope that when peace was achieved after, WW II, hatred against all racial and religious groups would cease.

When bigotry appeared at home during those war years, JWV responded swiftly and aggressively. In October 1943, a police sergeant in Boston, Massachusetts was accused of brutally beating a 17 year-old Jewish youth with a rubber hose. Jewish war veterans spoke out and encouraged friends in allied veterans' groups to do the same. They called upon the governor to order a full investigation into the incident. Subsequently, the governor ordered the removal of Boston's chief of police.

Pro-Nazi German Bundist groups went underground during the war, but the Ku Klux Klan remained visible and active. In its new propaganda

Thousands of packs of cards were given to servicemen en route overseas.

One of a large number of ambulances purchased by JWV and presented to the Army.

Launching of the escort destroyer Uriah P. Levy, sponsored by JWV.

Dedication of the "Star of David," the first fighter plane paid for with funds raised by JWV and presented as a gift to the government.

JWV members, with Eddie Cantor, promoting the gift program for hospitalized veterans.

all Jews were branded as "Commies" but even that inflammatory mantle did not deter JWV in its fight.

A major civil rights advancement came from the Executive Order issued in June 1941 by President Roosevelt establishing the Fair Employment Practices Commission (FEPC). Jewish War Veterans supported this initiative which prevented discrimination in hiring by defense industries supported by the government.

The crowning achievement of America's veterans' groups was securing the passage of the G.I. Bill of Rights by Congress in June 1944. This legislation provided a full range of medical, education, housing, pension, compensation and employment benefits and services for veterans and their dependents.

This far-sighted social legislation was to be the most generous program for assisting veterans since the nation's founding.

Preparing for the Post World War II Era

In March 1943, the Jewish War Veterans National Executive Committee (NEC) announced plans to raise $100,000 (later increased to $250,000) for an Expansion Fund to meet the challenges Jewish War Veterans would face after victory in WW II. The aim of the Expansion Fund was to organize new posts in cities and towns not then served by JWV; to increase membership of existing posts; and to develop programs to serve returning veterans.

To accomplish these goals, JWV leaders hired a professional staff to serve at national headquarters. Further, JWV sought to recruit field staff to organize new posts and increase membership in existing posts.

Several resolutions were passed by the organization that looked toward the peace and returning soldiers needs. For example, the JWV National Executive Committee passed resolutions asking the Congress to extend reinstatement time for discharged veterans by six months following discharge. If the soldier was physically unable to apply within that time, JWV recommended the time be extended another six months. These resolutions were more than words on a page, they served as a call to action for the organization's nationwide membership.

To meet the needs of returning veterans, JWV appealed to the armed forces to undertake orientation programs at discharge centers. The aim was to provide veterans with information regarding their benefits under the new G.I. Bill as well as to alert them to the programs available in their communities sponsored by civilian agencies.

As early as 1943, JWV held meetings with the Jewish Welfare Board to plan for post war collaborative efforts on behalf of returning veterans.

Recognizing that the veteran community would have a more influential role in the post war period with regard to national and international affairs, JWV and its counterparts in the National Council of Veterans' Organizations conferred on future policy issues.

JWV leadership correctly predicted JWV's increased membership in the post war period would strengthen the organization's voice among its peers in the Jewish community and the veterans' community and add to its responsibilities of leadership.

This prescience was confirmed in 1944 when JWV gained admission as one of the five agencies in the National Jewish Community Relations Advisory Council. This new council was created by the

Among the many fundraising efforts of the Jewish War Veterans of the U.S.A. during WW II was the sale of War Bonds. JWV members are credited with selling over $200 million worth of U.S. War Bonds.

A group of Jewish War Veterans discuss the veteran program with President Harry S. Truman. Pictured from L to R: President Truman, J. George Fredman, National Commander 1932, Maxwell Cohen, National Commander 1945, and Al Fleishman, Director of Public Relations.

Council of Jewish Federations to combat anti-Semitism.

JWV sent representatives to the national plenary sessions of the American Jewish Conference which held meetings in 1943, 1944, and 1945. This conference sought to act as a clearing house for cooperative action by Jewish organizations on national and international issues.

After VE Day in May 1945 and VJ Day in August 1945, JWV geared-up to accommodate the avalanche of returning veterans. Its national staff now in place, JWV now hired a legislative director to work in Washington, D.C. The national headquarters was moved to larger space on West 77th Street in Manhattan.

Between 1943 and 1945 JWV organized 118

new posts and its paid membership more than doubled. The growth of the organization gave JWV the clout and resources to offer greater assistance to the veterans it serves.

"As a symbol of patriotic service rendered by our citizens of Jewish faith, your organization is the living answer to those who would confuse our people with the evil doctrines of bigotry and hatred."
President Harry S. Truman
From letter to PNC Archie Greenberg
September 8, 1945

JWV gave enthusiastic support to the *Report*

on *Veterans Programs* submitted to President Harry S. Truman by Bernard M. Baruch in 1946 on the problems facing returning veterans and the programs to meet their personal needs. One of Baruch's key proposals was for each community to establish one place where the returning veteran could go to learn all of his rights and how to obtain them. Baruch commented that veterans were given the "run around" by too many self-serving bureaucratic agencies. He also sought to protect veterans from fraud by "hucksterism."

Baruch said the United States must show that its political and economic system, which met the test of war so magnificently, can be as effective in solving human problems in the return to peace. "How the United States treats the returning veterans," said Baruch, "would be the acid test of democracy." Mr. Baruch was awarded JWV's Medal of Merit and made an honorary member on December 1, 1946.

JWV Administers Veterans' Services

Effective January 1, 1948, the Jewish Welfare Board with the approval of the Veterans Administration transferred to the Jewish War Veterans of the USA the responsibility of administering claims and contracts for veterans.

Both organizations agreed to work cooperatively in serving Jewish military personnel and in providing for recreation and religious activities for hospitalized veterans.

This transfer of responsibility was the impetus for the development of JWV's National Service Officer Program. In fourteen cities nationwide, JWV offers all veterans and their families the expertise of a trained service officer (NSO). NSO's guide their clients through the Department of Veterans Affairs (VA) benefits maze and represent veterans before the VA Board of Appeals.

Later that year, the Ida S. Latz Foundation of Los Angeles, California organized by members of JWV, designated JWV as the operating agency to augment aid and give supplementary assistance to federal, state and local agencies which provide rehabilitation to amputees and other disabled veterans.

Through funding provided by the Latz Foundation, JWV service officers nationwide supervised rehabilitation programs to assist disabled veterans. Many of the pilot programs originally financed by the Latz Foundation were subsequently adopted by the Veterans Administration.

The biggest gripes expressed by returning veterans stemmed from the failure by the federal government to provide for affordable housing. Veterans' groups decried the government's inability to solve the housing shortage problem. Finally, in 1949, Congress approved a housing act responding to this critical shortage.

JWV considers its tradition of guarding and maintaining the graves of the fallen as a sacrosanct responsibility. Maintaining and protecting the gravesites of Jewish servicepersons who lost their lives during World War II became a major project of the organization. Today, families of Jewish veterans can be assured that the graves of their loved ones, located in the United States, will never be neglected as long as JWV remains active and strong.

JWV and Labor Relations

Labor and veterans did not always agree on important public policy issues. JWV understood the importance of developing good relations among labor union leaders and the allied veterans' community. In 1949, JWV established a unit to act as liaison to organized labor. The unit's mission was to ascertain labor's positions on key domestic and foreign policy matters and seek out opportunities where Jewish veterans could support policies of common interest.

Subsequently, JWV joined organized labor in supporting a permanent Federal Employment Practices Commission to ban discrimination in employment practices; in legislation to prevent discrimination in the sale or rental of housing; and in pressing for new laws to deny the use of racial or religious quotas in college admissions. JWV and labor leaders agreed on the need to support the State of Israel.

Jewish Brethren in Europe and Palestine

Two foreign policy issues were of paramount importance to JWV leaders in the post war period. The first was finding havens for refugees living in the displaced persons camps of Europe. The second was the establishment of the Jewish State in Palestine.

In December 1945, JWV petitioned the government to provide special quotas for admitting Jewish war refugees to the U.S. and to urge Great Britain to lift its restrictions on Jewish immigration to Palestine. JWV received only limited support from the other veterans' organizations on these requests.

When the Displaced Persons Act of 1948 was approved by Congress, the legislation limited the number of Jews from the camps who could enter the U.S.

Concurrently, JWV sought to utilize the newly-formed United Nations as an agency to assist the camp refugees. To bring public awareness to the critical refugee problem, JWV mobilized 4000 veterans on July 15, 1946 to march down Constitution Avenue in Washington, D.C. protesting the British delay in admitting one hundred thousand Jewish refugees to Palestine.

In 1946, JWV renewed its contacts with Jewish war veterans in Europe by attending an international conference in Paris. At the conference, the agenda addressed the problems of Jewish refugees and the need to open the gates of Palestine for Jewish immigration.

In August 1947, JWV lauded the decision whereby the United Nations agreed to take responsibility from Great Britain for administering Palestine. After the United Nations voted for partition of Palestine in November 1947, the situation in Palestine became precarious. The fate of the Jewish community was at stake as both Jews and Arabs vied for public support.

The Birth of the Jewish State

On April 4, 1948, with the cooperation of its allied veterans' groups and the financial support of the Jewish community, JWV organized the largest parade in Jewish history to date, to demonstrate the solidarity of the American people in support of a Jewish State. Over 250,000 veterans accompanied by 90 marching bands paraded down Fifth Avenue in New York City. The demonstration was an inspiring manifestation - from the ashes of the Holocaust there would arise a Jewish State in fulfillment of a 2000 year old dream.

When five Arab nations invaded Israel in May 1948, JWV called on its members to donate their uniforms to the new Israeli Army. Over one million uniforms were collected and shipped out.

JWV Growth in the 1940's

At the end of the decade of the 1940's, JWV leadership could look back at several significant accomplishments:

First and foremost, despite the tragic consequences of war, America and its allies were victorious. In the face of unparalleled human losses, a new Jewish unity and strength of purpose had been achieved and the Jewish Nation had been reborn.

As an association, JWV had grown to became one of the largest Jewish organization in the United States. It had successfully integrated WW II veterans with WWI veterans and had expanded, significantly, the number of posts nationwide. In 1949, a WW II veteran was elected National Commander.

In the area of Jewish community relations, JWV established its role through membership in the National Jewish Community Relations Advisory Council. And, its strong and more visible presence in the Halls of Congress was enhanced by the new legislative office in Washington, DC.

JWV became the official agency to represent the interests of Jewish veterans in the Veterans Administration.

In foreign affairs JWV attained official observer status at the United Nations and mobilized public opinion on behalf of refugees and the State of Israel.

JWV had grown in membership and stature and was prepared to meet the challenges of the post war period both domestically and internationally.

JWV members march in solidarity with Israel after nationhood is established.

CHAPTER SEVEN

The Boom Years

The period following World War II reflected an emerging awareness of America's economic and industrial superiority, countered by growing social consciousness and responsibility as the world leader.

With this stature America assumed the duty of aiding in the rebuilding of Europe, creating military alliances to fend-off the spread of Communist aggression (NATO), and developing a framework for future international cooperation (UN).

Large and small military actions around the world kept America's government leaders and defense industry in an "at-the-ready" posture.

At home, American families were reuniting and building new and better lives. The fifties were good to many Americans. A growing middle-class bought homes, cars, and labor saving gadgets which had developed from the technological advances of the war years. And, Americans were having babies. Lots of them!

The major vehicle for the fulfillment of the American dream was a benefit available to veterans known as the G.I. Bill. (Some referred to it as the "great equalizer".) The G.I. Bill put homeownership and a college education within reach of large numbers of Americans. And, for the first time, racial, ethnic, and religious minorities were able to actively participate in "the dream".

Post War Programs and Policies

Before war had ended, JWV with its usual foresight was engaged in establishing programs to assist returning veterans and their families and was actively developing plans with allied veterans' and Jewish organizations in support of America's post war policies.

The G.I. Bill, the Lehman-Ives Fair Employment Practice Bill and others instituted to assist veterans were the direct result of these early efforts.

In international affairs, JWV supported the 1953 convention on Genocide and all Human Rights policies of the United Nations. JWV was given official permanent observer status at the United Nations and appointed an officer to attend regular sessions. Past National Commander Archie Greenberg of Brooklyn, NY was the first JWV UN Liaison.

He was followed by Dr. Seymour Weisman, JWV National Consultant, from Connecticut, and Dr. Martin Dworkis of New Jersey, an expert in International Relations. Stanley Silver of New Jersey is the current liaison, and has for many years represented JWV admirably at the United Nations.

JWV endorsed the joint statement of President Dwight D. Eisenhower, Foreign Ministers, NATO, and Congress of "no retreat from the defense of West Berlin" in 1959. And, whenever the issue arose, JWV was a staunch advocate of military preparedness and favored universal military training.

Minority Rights Following World War II

Despite demonstrable American patriotism, American Jews still had to deal with the stereo-

Stanley Silver (NJ), JWV United Nations Liaison and PNC Albert Cohen (NJ) visit with Israeli soldiers in February 1992. This trip represents one of many made by JWV U.N. Liaisons over the years to support the State of Israel and Middle East peace efforts.

JWV National Commander Malcolm Tarlov and members protesting the Russian invasion of Czechoslovakia in 1968.

types, the quotas, the barriers and the restrictions placed upon them in society. But, the hand American Jews were dealt could in no way compare to the prejudice and hatred foisted upon so many of JWV's Black American brothers and sisters.

This bigotry was particularly distasteful to members of the Jewish War Veterans of the USA who emotionally identified with the plight of Black Americans and who had so recently observed the gallantry of Black Americans during World War II. Jewish war veterans were deeply distressed when Black Americans returned home to the same ignorance and abuse they had experienced prior to the war.

Determined Black Americans would not be left behind in the new boom years for America, Black and Jewish leaders engaged in dialogue and then joined forces in the Civil Rights effort.

In the 1950's, JWV was unique among veter-

ans' organizations in vehemently fighting proponents of the concept of separate but equal, as it applied to Black Americans and Americans of Japanese ancestry.

JWV was, for quite some time, alone as a veterans' organization in speaking out in favor of the Japanese American community's efforts to seek redress for those who were interned during World War II.

The Red Scare

At the conclusion of World War II, an international Cold War developed between the world's two superpowers, the United States of America and the Union of Soviet Socialist Republics. In short order, the elation of the victory over Nazism was overshadowed by the threat of the spread of Communism.

In the U.S., a number of right wing groups

emerged. In addition to the ever present Ku Klux Klan, there were the American Nazi Party, headed by George Lincoln Rockwell, the John Birch Society and Gerald L.K. Smith. These groups and individuals tried to link Judaism with Communism. They were a focal point for anti-Semitism in America and immediately attracted a noble opponent, the Jewish War Veterans of the United States of America.

JWV was also on alert against groups operating outside of the United States in Europe and in Asia. International right wing and anti-Semitic groups, such as neo-Nazis in Germany and Poland were closely monitored.

In the early 1950's, Senator Joseph McCarthy of Wisconsin began his public purge of all suspected communists living in the United States.

Like most patriotic organizations, the Jewish War Veterans pledged to assist the United States government in ridding the country of communists threatening our security. It instituted the All American Conference to Combat Communism in 1950. In September 1951, JWV led other veterans' organizations in implementing a boycott against Russian goods.

In 1968, the JWV representative, Past National Commander Robert M. Zweiman, was elected National Chairman of the All American Conference to Combat Communism, in preference to a John Birch adherent.

Eventually, McCarthyism grew to be a great concern to the Jewish War Veterans. The Senator targeted many Jews and persons of European ancestry. Could JWV become a target? Certainly, it would have been absurd for the Senator to allege a group of Jewish Americans who had served their country in time of war was a Communist front. But, rationalism and bigotry have never been partners and this was most assuredly the case with the Senator from Wisconsin.

JWV began working to convince the U.S. government that the Senator was not practicing law but discrimination. McCarthy was engaged in promoting lies and fear.

McCarthyism did indeed make its way into the U.S. armed forces and JWV was ready for it. Jewish war veterans, nationwide, vowed to help patriotic Jews whose loyalty and service were questioned.

In September, 1953, a graduate student at the University of Michigan, Milo Radulovich, was labeled a security risk and dismissed from the Air Force Reserve. Although Radulovich had never done anything to lead the U.S. government to question his loyalty, his father, born in Siberia, was a Communist and his sister marched in Communist demonstrations. Radulovich's loyalty proved genuine, yet his discharge was upheld.

At the same time, several Jewish employees of Fort Monmouth in New Jersey were dismissed from their jobs without hearing and with no reason given. Upon investigation, it was found these employees had no organizational ties whatsoever, beyond veterans' groups, nor did they display any suspicious behavior. They were discharged, regardless.

In another case assuming a Jewish-Communist connection, Wolfgang Ladejinsky, a native-born Russian living in the United States, was dismissed from his job at the Department of Agriculture in 1954, without reason. When questioned, his employer referred to Ladejinsky's remaining family in Russia, with whom he had not been in touch for years.

At this point, the Jewish War Veterans met with other veterans' organizations to form an investigative group. Two years later, after arguments with national officials and altercations with government bureaucracy, all three of these cases were ultimately settled favorably. Ladejinsky was returned to his position at the Department of Agriculture, Lieutenant Radulovich was reinstated in the Air Force Reserve, and the employees at Fort Monmouth were all cleared.

As many of Senator McCarthy's accusations proved to be false, he was ultimately exposed as an extremist. JWV was among the first to condemn the Senator's actions and support McCarthy's censure by his peers in the U.S. Senate.

In 1956, JWV kicked-off its Americanism Programs which were divided into the following major areas:

Americanism Activities
Community Service Activities
Immigration, Naturalization and Citizenship
   Activities
Legislative Activities
Youth Activities
Publication of an Americanism Manual

A JWV reminder on the privileges and duties of citizenship.

JWV helps to assure healthy minds in healthy bodies by its sponsorship of juvenile sports groups.

JWV caps in the forefront of a rally for Soviet Jews.

JWV National Commander Ralph Plofsky and Catholic War Veterans National Commander Charles Shelley discuss the plight of Soviet Jewry with Pope Paul VI at the Vatican.

JWV, in 1958, requested the House Un-American Activities Committee investigate the financing of hate sheets and hatemongering groups. The Committee complied with this request. In 1964, President Johnson signed the "Controls for Extremist Groups" Bill, which warned extremist groups of the government's interest in closely monitoring their subversive activities.

For many years JWV's Americanism program has been directed by Debra Stern of Florida, JWV's National Americanism Chairman, and a veteran of World War II. Mrs. Stern has made it her personal mission to teach the ideals of American patriotism to as many school age children as possible. During her tenure as chairman, JWV members have visited hundreds of public schools delivering this message.

JWV Spearheads Organization of American Soviet Jewry Movement

Community Conferences to Fight Communism emerged nationwide in the early 1950's. These conference groups were made up of private citizens determined to halt the spread of Communism within the United States. JWV participated in these conferences, but, did not limit its fight against Communism to the borders of our own country.

JWV members sought to retard the spread of Communism in Asia and halt the diminution of human rights under Communism in the Soviet Union and Eastern Europe. Harsh restrictions on people seeking to freely practice their faith had turned a dangerous corner in the USSR. The tools used to restrain freedom were becoming violent and perilous. They included travel limitations, educational restrictions, loss of employment, separation from family, imprisonment and even torture - all tactics abhorrent to the principles upon which JWV was founded.

A 1958, a Soviet dictate denying rights of immigration for all Jews residing in the Soviet Bloc instigated the emergence of a number of associations and campaigns. dedicated to freeing Soviet Jews.

At the 1962 National Convention of JWV, a resolution was passed condemning the treatment of Jews in the Soviet Union and urging the United States to turn its attention toward Jews behind the Iron Curtain.

In the Fall of that year, JWV National Commander Morton London, National Executive Director Joseph Barr and National Consultant Dr. Seymour Weisman helped found the American Jewish Conference on Soviet Jewry, known today as the National Conference on Soviet Jewry (NCSJ). The first official meeting was held in January 1963.

JWV housed the offices of the National Conference on Soviet Jewry, in the decade of the seventies, rent free and provided office services to support the organization. JWV maintains its membership in NCSJ to the present day.

As one of 24 agencies of another Soviet Jewry group - American Council on Soviet Jewry - JWV participated in the National Eternal Light Vigil in Washington, D.C.

In a 1964 meeting of the JWV National Commander Ralph Plofsky, the Commander of the Catholic War Veterans, Charles Shelley, and Pope Paul VI, JWV appreciated a major diplomatic success on behalf of Soviet Jews. At the meeting, the Pope agreed to make a public, humanitarian statement opposing the restriction of freedoms of Jews under the control of the Communist regime.

A planned tour by then-National Commander Milton Waldor to the Soviet Union in 1966 was abruptly cancelled by the Soviets just two days prior to Waldor's scheduled departure.

The Jewish Veteran

November/December 1987

JWV WAS THERE!

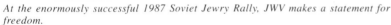

At the enormously successful 1987 Soviet Jewry Rally, JWV makes a statement for freedom.

Julius "Mickey" Cohen (CA) and Manuel Auerbach (DC).

In 1971, National Commander Jerry Cohen made a trip to the Soviet Union. During his visit, Commander Cohen met with Jewish scientists and technicians who had been denied visas. Commander Cohen was briefed by the Soviet Veterans Commissions in Leningrad and Kiev. An official "audience" with Soviet Colonel General Kuznestov and Vice Admiral Boydenka gave Cohen the opportunity to voice JWV's opposition to restrictive emigration policies toward Soviet Jewish veterans.

National Commander Stanley Zwaik of New York visited the Soviet Union in 1972. This was the same year JWV participated in a demonstration known as "Let My People Go". Demonstrations, marches, petition drives, phone-a-thons and all manner of protests were attempted to call public attention to the plight of Soviet Jews. Rallies on the steps of the Capitol, lunchtime gatherings at the gates to the Soviet Embassy, candlelight vigils and prayer services kept the names, faces and stories of imprisoned and persecuted Jews in the minds and hearts of the American Jewish community.

JWV's involvement in rescuing Jews trapped in the Soviet Union continued for over thirty years. Through the many years that the Soviet Union played the "state secrets" card with Soviet Jewish veterans, the Jewish War Veterans kept the flame of hope from extinguishing.

All manner of Judaica, clothing and cigarettes with black market value, office supplies and personal care items were smuggled to JWV's friends in the Soviet Union over the years.

In almost every issue of *The Jewish Veteran* from the late 1950's until the 1980's, JWV dedicated a page to news from the Soviet Jewish community. Many of these pages focused on Project Yachad, the Jewish War Veterans' solidarity project.

JWV's "Project Yachad", meaning unity, matched Jewish-American veterans with Soviet-Jewish veterans. The "adopted" brothers and sisters kept in touch through letters which were often printed in *The Jewish Veteran*.

The most highly decorated Soviet veteran of World War II was a Jew, Colonel Lev Ovisischer. The Colonel was refused a visa numerous times on the grounds that he knew state secrets. In truth, Colonel Ovisischer's desire to depart the country was a great embarrassment to the government, as was the similar desire of so many Soviet World War II veterans.

The names of the so-called "refuseniks" (Jews refused exit visas by Soviet officials) became as familiar as family to JWV. They were frequently included in the famous "Refusenik Roll Calls" sponsored by Jewish groups and supportive members of Congress.

As a letter writing campaign, Project Yachad served to keep American Jews in touch with Colonel Ovisischer and others and gave warning to Soviet and US government officials that the powerful veterans' "lobby" was on guard for Soviet Jews.

JWV's "Matzah of Hope" campaign in the 1980's held great appeal for JWV's members and Soviet refuseniks. During the Festival of Freedom thousands of boxes of the "bread of affliction" were sent to the Soviet Embassy in the U.S. and to Soviet Government officials within the USSR to protest treatment of the Jews of the Soviet Union.

One of the largest rallies in Washington, D.C. history was held in December 1987, when President Mikhail Gorbachev visited Washington to meet with President Ronald Reagan.

Every Jewish organization in the country sent a delegation. JWV was well-represented with several hundred members from around the nation present and accounted for.

With the fall of Communism, hundreds of thousands of Soviet Jews emigrated and now reside in the United States and Israel. The surviving former "refuseniks", adopted by the Jewish War Veterans some ten, twenty and thirty years ago have now joined JWV as patrons of the organization. Many are impoverished, old, frail and ill. JWV has not forgotten and continues its commitment to the well being of its adopted brethren.

JWV remains proud of its role in fighting the Cold War - advocating military preparedness, speaking out against right wing groups, seeking freedom of religion and emigration in Communist strongholds, and monitoring growing threats to the peace in Korea and Southeast Asia.

CHAPTER EIGHT

The Korean Conflict

When North Korean Forces invaded South Korea on June 25, 1950, the United Nations authorized its member nations to support South Korea. Fifteen nations responded, including the United States. General Douglas MacArthur was appointed Commander of the United Nations fighting forces. The Jewish War Veterans staunchly supported United States and United Nations action. As in the past, American Jews responded to the nation's call to arms.

The following policy statement was released by JWV:

"Communist aggression against the free way of life is global in nature and can only be defeated by a total muster of the physical and moral resources of the earth's remaining free peoples. A state of preparedness which permits no more than police action against such localized outbreaks as the Communist invasion of the Republic of Korea is inadequate to safeguard world peace. All who cherish peace and freedom have been heartened by America's prompt action in upholding the dignity and authority of the United Nations. If we are to count on these people to help in meeting new Communist challenges to the free world we must demonstrate our readiness to meet aggression with a military and economic establishment that is prepared to seize the initiative in any new breach of peace."

When the Korean conflict broke-out, there were no reserves of blood available either for the military or civilian population. JWV pledged, as its special wartime project, to do all in its power to rectify this shortage. JWV urged the public to join in supporting American troops in Korea through a blood bank drive.

William Levin, JWV Chairman of the National Blood Donor Committee, sent out an urgent call to JWV posts nationwide. Each post was to pledge an annual donation of three pints for each member. By mid-1951, JWV posts had a 100 percent pledge fulfillment record.

JWV holds the honor of providing the first hundred pints of blood sent to Korea. The blood came from two Washington, D.C. posts which answered the call from the American Red Cross and the Department of Defense.

In connection with the blood drive, the JWV Department of New York sponsored a visit of a contingent of Korean veterans whose lives had been saved by blood plasma. These veterans traveled across the United States in support of blood plasma drives.

The National "Play Ball, America" Blood Drive

In 1952, JWV sponsored National Baseball Blood Month (June 15-July 15) to acquire even greater quantities of blood for our armed forces. JWV coordinated blood donations at major and minor league baseball parks in 53 cities nationwide. This event dubbed "Play Ball, America" was promoted nationwide with publicity emphasizing the support of President Harry Truman and the U.S. Department of Defense. Additionally, the American Red Cross, Commissioner of Baseball Ford Frick,

Thousands of American Jews served their country during the Korean conflict.

Corporal Abraham Geller in Korea.

the presidents of the major and minor leagues, and all the national veterans' groups supported the effort wholeheartedly. Red Cross Bloodmobiles were stationed in baseball parks and blood pledge cards were collected.

Gloria Mosesson describes the enthusiasm for JWV's National Baseball Blood Month, in her book *The Jewish War Veterans Story*. Over 50,000 people contributed blood during the campaign.

Another important JWV project which evolved during the Korean crisis was a U.S. savings bond campaign. JWV speakers traveled the nation encouraging American citizens to support their country and the war effort through the purchase of savings bonds.

JWV's support of service personnel in Korea also included gift packages, holiday programs, and

pressure on Congress for benefits for returning Korean veterans.

Corporal Abraham Geller

Corporal Abraham Geller was a Jewish hero of the Korean conflict. The son of a rabbi from the lower East Side of New York City, Geller was an Orthodox Jew. During enemy action around the Han River on the day after Yom Kipper, the Jewish Day of Atonement, Geller came across a North Korean soldier who was playing dead. Suddenly, the North Korean began moving in an attempt to attack Corporal Geller's platoon leader, George O'Connor. Geller detected the movement and killed the Korean with his bayonet, after taking three bullets meant for his platoon leader. Geller's wounds were not as serious as they could have been for one very important reason, he had fasted the previous day of Yom Kippur and he had virtually no food in his stomach. Geller's steadfast devotion to this Jewish requirement of fasting allowed for a quick recovery and perhaps saved his life.

Colonel Melvin Garten

Colonel Melvin Garten was a highly decorated World War II veteran who was wounded four times in battle. In Korea, Garten was the captain of K Company, 312th Infantry Regiment, U.S. Army. His unit assisted besieged troops on October 30, 1952 near Surang-Ni. The troops were without command, so Garten took charge. Employing the principle of fire and maneuver, Garten and eight men stormed enemy trenches displaying such tenacity and heroism that the enemy was routed and the objective was secured. Garten was awarded the Distinguished Service Cross. While serving in Vietnam, the brave Colonel Garten lost a leg in battle.

Major Joseph I. Gurfein

West Point graduate, Major Joseph I. Gurfein of Brooklyn, was a WW II veteran and a parachute-engineer liaison officer attached to a battalion whose mission was to break through enemy lines. The battalion came upon a booby-trapped mine which exploded, injuring several in the group. Confusion reigned but Gurfein organized and comforted the soldiers and despite snow and below freezing temperatures led them forward to engage the enemy. Gurfein was awarded the Silver Star Medal.

Geller, Garten and Gurfein are just three of the thousands of brave soldiers who exemplify the heroism and love of country demonstrated by Americans of the Jewish faith who served in Korea.

Victims and Victors:
Two Holocaust survivors become American soldiers

Many Jews who fought in the Korean War were veterans of World War II, others were Hitler's victims during World War II. These men were survivors of Nazi concentration camps. Liberated as teenagers by American G.I. Joes, these survivors felt they owed a debt of gratitude to their new home, America.

They joined the American armed forces to become G.I. Joes themselves, and were mobilized during the Korean war. Two JWV members who survived the camps only to utilize those survival skills later as members of the U.S. armed forces are highlighted on pages 73 and 74. They are Tibor Rubin and Mike Cynamon. They represent just two of many, many survivors of Hitler's atrocities who became American citizens and soldiers.

In 1952, JWV reaffirmed its support of the United Nations and its decision to check Communist aggression in Korea by military means. After the armistice, JWV's National Commander, Harry T. Madison, flew to South Korea as a guest of the American Korean Foundation. This community-wide support program, run in conjunction with other veterans' groups, was committed to the rebuilding and rehabilitation of South Korea.

In 1954, a JWV resolution called for a United Nations investigation of Korean atrocities and a delay of the admission of Red China to the United Nations until the investigation was completed. JWV led the way in support of legislation and search efforts for the return of missing American veterans of the Korean War. JWV also urged the State Department to demand Red China account for the 450 American prisoners of war.

JWV was an early supporter of the Korean War Memorial which was dedicated in July of 1995. Several JWV past national commanders, including Ainslee Ferdie of Florida, Edwin Goldwasser of New York and Harvey Friedman of New Jersey - veterans of the Korean Conflict- attended White House ceremonies honoring Korean veterans on this significant occasion.

JWV National Memorial Inc.

The Jewish War Veterans National Memorial Inc. was officially dedicated in May, 1955 by Vice President Richard Nixon at 1712 New Hampshire Avenue, Washington, D.C. On September 2, 1958 President Dwight D. Eisenhower affixed his signature to H.R. 109, the bill granting the new "Shrine to Jewish War Dead" a Congressional Charter.

This charter climaxed a 63-year-old struggle on the part of JWV to irrevocably forge into American history and culture a monument to the glory, courage, and sacrifice of Americans of Jewish faith.

Today, the JWV National Memorial Inc. is composed of the National Museum of American Jewish Military History (NMAJMH), a complete archives and library. The building is also home to the administrative offices of Jewish War Veterans of the USA, the JWV National Ladies Auxiliary, and the Descendants of JWV.

The vision of the museum was first publicly expressed by then National Commander Paul Ginsburg at the JWV National Executive Committee meeting held in October of 1951.

Commander Ginsburg urged JWV leaders gathered at the meeting to move JWV's national headquarters to Washington, D.C. He suggested the new headquarters building include a "Shrine" or memorial to Jewish American veterans. He envisioned the memorial as a sanctuary for valuable records and memorabilia of Jewish service to America, in

PLAY BALL WITH OUR ARMED FORCES

YOUR Blood Will Get Him Home SAFE!

SPONSORED BY
BLOOD DONOR COMMITTEE, AMERICAN RED CROSS AND THE JEWISH WAR VETERANS OF THE U.S.A.

Tibor Rubin

The Tibor Rubin case has been one of the most heartfelt issues addressed by the Jewish War Veterans in the past decade. In the late 1980's, JWV launched an all-out campaign to honor Tibor Rubin, a veteran of the Korean War, with a Congressional Medal of Honor.

Rubin, a Hungarian native, survived the Nazi death camps of the Second World War and immigrated to the United States soon after the war's end.

Within a year of being in the United States, Rubin enlisted in the US Army and was sent to Korea. An action of battlefront bravery occurred which Rubin's commanding field officer neglected— some suggest due to anti-Semitism— to record or submit for commendation.

In November, 1950, Rubin was taken prisoner by the Chinese in Unsan, North Korea. He was a prisoner of war for 2 1/2 years, during which time his heroic actions saved the lives of over thirty of his fellow prisoners.

Several times during his imprisonment Rubin turned down offers to return to his native Hungary. These offers would have certainly saved his life. Suffering from battle wounds and disease, Rubin was finally released in 1953, smuggling out the names of his imprisoned comrades in his leg cast. Years passed and Rubin's fellow prisoners assumed he was dead, as the Chinese told them.

Tibor Rubin was in fact alive. Released to the United States in an exchange of the most severely wounded prisoners of war, Rubin settled in California establishing a career and family.

Decades later, at a veterans' gathering, Rubin was "found" by some of the men imprisoned with Rubin, men who owed their lives to him. The meeting was extraordinarily emotional. His comrades made a commitment, at that meeting, to launch an ambitious campaign to honor Rubin with the Congressional Medal of Honor.

This effort was soon adopted by the Jewish War Veterans of the United States, which worked with Congress to introduce a bill that would make Rubin the first Jewish recipient of the Congressional Medal of Honor from the Korean War by extending the time limit for consideration.

Hundreds of thousands of names were collected in support of the JWV veteran. The majority of the national veterans' organizations and many members of Congress endorsed the bill and JWV's campaign in Rubin's behalf. But, the Army Military Awards Branch remains steadfast in its rejection of all efforts.

Despite long battles with life-threatening illness, Tibor Rubin's indefatigable spirit and zest for life remains an inspiration to his comrades and all those who are lucky enough to come to know him. He resides in Garden Grove, California with his wife, Yvonne. He is the father of two children, Rosie and Frank.

addition to being a living memorial to the patriotism of American Jews.

A search committee was selected to find a suitable building. JWV Post 58 of Washington, D.C. was a key player in the establishment of the "Shrine".

After three years of fund drives the National Executive Committee of JWV voted in February 1954 to authorize a building fund committee to negotiate and sign a contract for a building at 1712 New Hampshire Avenue, N.W. The committee also established a holding corporation with a board of directors of the national "Shrine" which was officially named the JWV National Memorial Inc. The building was purchased in April 1954.

Messrs. Joseph Barr and Bernard Weiter were instrumental in obtaining the federal charter for the National Memorial Inc. The charter was registered as Public Law 85-93, HR 109. The law said, in part, that the National "Shrine" was "to mention and conduct a National Memorial and museum dedicated to and commemorating the service and sacrifice in the Armed Forces of the United States during the period of war by Americans of the Jewish faith. . . and to gather, collect, edit, publish, and exhibit the memorabilia, data, records, military awards, donations, citations. . . for the purpose of preserving the memories and records of patriotic service performed by men and women of the Jewish faith while in the Armed Services."

The by-laws of the National Memorial Inc. were formulated to include sponsorship of memorial services on appropriate holidays to commemorate the contributions to our nation by American Jews.

Colonel S. J. Pomerance was hired as the first archivist of the National Memorial Inc. He began collecting and organizing the archival files. The limitation of space in the building was detrimental to establishing the exhibits hoped for by the board of directors.

A building at 1811 R Street, N.W. was purchased in 1983 and in December 1984 became the new home of the JWV National Memorial Inc. and was officially dedicated by then Vice-President George Bush.

The museum division, the National Museum of American Jewish Military History, initiated a major program to collect information and artifacts related to the service of Jewish military personnel.

Recent exhibits at the museum have included:

(a) GIs Remember: Liberating the Concentration Camp. This project included a major exhibit in the headquarters building at Washington, D.C., a book/catalogue, a film, and a traveling exhibit.
(b) I Remember: Personal Recollections on the end of World War II
(c) A Salute to Jewish Chaplains in the Military - a traveling exhibit.
(d) The Major General Julius Klein Gallery - His Life and Work.
(e) Candid Moments in the Military - a photographic exhibition
(f) Operation Desert Storm
(g) The Captain Joshua L. Goldberg Chapel

In conjunction with JWV 100th anniversary celebrations, the National Museum of American Jewish Military History prepared the exhibit "JWV Celebrates One Hundred Years (1896-1996)" which opened, officially, in March, 1996.

The American troops who liberated Nazi Concentration Camps had no inkling of the destruction and human degradation they were to face. Most servicemen, especially the Jewish soldiers, were so shocked by the sight that they eagerly offered help of food, clothing, shelter and friendship.

Mike Cynamon

Nomick Cynamon was a Holocaust survivor who joined the American Army immediately upon arriving in America. Nomick "Mike" Cynamon was born in Lodz, Poland in 1927. The Germans invaded Poland in September, 1939, and soon after closed off the Jewish ghetto in Warsaw, imprisoning the Jewish population. Cynamon and his family, which included his mother, father and brother, were sent to the ghetto. Cynamon stayed in the Warsaw Ghetto for two years, until he became ill with typhus. While he was in the hospital, the Germans issued a decree of deportation for all young children, the sick and the elderly.

Somehow the Nazis missed Cynamon and he remained in the hospital. Once released, Cynamon returned to the ghetto to find that his family was among the deported. He later learned they were dead. Cynamon was placed in Chaim Rumkowski's orphanage until 1944 when the orphans were sent to Auschwitz.

Cynamon was spared this deportation too. He was sent to work in a German overshoes factory. But, the camps did not escape him. When the factory closed, Cynamon was taken to Birkenau and from there to Auschwitz. He stayed in Auschwitz until late 1944, when the Russians started moving in. At this point, Cynamon was moved from camp to camp before finally participating in the 40 kilometer death march to Dachau. He remained at Dachau until the camp was liberated by Patton's 3rd Army on May 9, 1945.

The Red Cross cared for Cynamon until he chose to go to a displaced persons camp in Italy. He enrolled in school and stayed until 1948, supported by the Joint Distribution Committee (JDC) and the United Nations Relief Organization (UNRO).

Cynamon was also trained by an Israeli brigade in the DP camp. This unit prepared young survivors for life in Israel and arranged for them to be a part of the historical Aliyah Bet. Of the 300 young people who made this trip from Mike Cynamon's orphanage, only 14, by Mr. Cynamon's count, are surviving today. Most were killed in the 1948 Israeli War of Independence.

In 1948, Cynamon left for America, under President Truman's immigration bill, determined to build a new life. Feeling as if he had an obligation as a new citizen, he enlisted in the Army and was called to active duty in 1950. During the Korean War, Mr. Cynamon was sent to Germany with the 4th infantry division. He quickly worked his way up the ranks and eventually attained the rank of Staff Sergeant. Because of his proficiency with many different languages, Cynamon stayed with Army Intelligence in Germany until 1953, when he was discharged. The Cynamon family resides in California, where Mike Cynamon is an active member of JWV.

In 1993 attendance at the museum showed a marked increase. Approximately 10,000 people visited the National Museum of American Jewish Military History that year, as compared to just 1,800 recorded visitors in 1990. Visitor figures continue to reflect growth in attendance.

In February 1995 the Captain Joshua L. Goldberg Chapel was dedicated and concurrently the mortgage on the building at 1811 R Street was symbolically "burned". PNC Harvey S. Friedman of New Jersey was chairman of the successful Burn the Mortgage Campaign.

The National Museum of American Jewish Military History is dedicated to collecting and preserving memorabilia documenting the historically important role Jews have played in the United States military.

The museum is a nationally recognized educational institution which specializes in detailing the history of Jewish participation in the armed forces of the United States.

PNC Herman Moses and Auxiliary Past National President, Florence Levine, Past President of the National Museum of American Jewish Military History, at opening of Major Gen. Julius Klein Gallery.

Presidents of the JWV National Memorial Inc.

Fred Harris, PNC
Meyer J. Abgott
Morris Luck
Frederick R. Tourkow
Ainslee R. Ferdie, PNC
Norman Tilles, PNC
Robert M. Zweiman, PNC
Florence Levine, PNP
Nathan M. Goldberg, PNC
Edward Blatt, PNC
Maj. Gen. Julius Klein, PNC
Harry T. Madison, PNC
Rabbi Joshua L. Goldberg

The Jewish War Veterans National Headquarters in Washington, D.C.

JWV representatives at the dedication of the National Korean War Memorial in Washington, D.C. Left to right: PNC Harvey S. Friedman, PNC Robert M. Zweiman, PDC Martin Greenberg, PNC Edwin Goldwasser, PNC David H. Hymes.

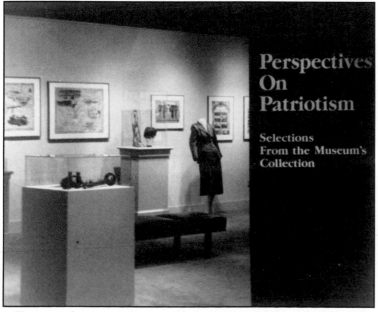

The museum has grown to incorporate both permanent and changing exhibits in three different galleries. Pictured here are parts of the "Perspectives on Patriotism" exhibit.

CHAPTER NINE

War in Southeast Asia and Civil Rights Wars at Home

By the early 1960's a large number of reactionary groups had once again established themselves on the American scene. The John Birch Society continued its aggressive efforts to garner members, as did the American Nazi Party, the Black Muslims and Students for a Democratic Society. Literature produced by each of these organizations condoned violence as the pathway to gain political power in America.

JWV was among the most aggressive Jewish organizations in combating radicals, anti-Semites and political extremists who threatened the well-being of American citizens.

JWV furthered its alliances with minority groups who also opposed this violence. The organization was one of the earliest members of the Leadership Council on Civil Rights, a coordinating body of 90 national organizations, chartered in 1949 to fight discrimination by legal means. JWV assisted Black America's veteran leaders in establishing their own national veterans' groups.

In 1961, Theodore Brooks came to the position of National Commander as a strong advocate of Civil Rights, a strong opponent of anti-Semitism and an organizer of counter-demonstrations against George Medole and Nazi George Lincoln Rockwell.

Brooks was a powerful political force within the organization. He was known for his passionate advocacy on behalf of needy veterans and their families, a staunch patriot in defending human rights and a devoted Zionist.

JWV is proud to have been the only veterans' organization to march alongside the Reverend Martin Luther King, Jr. at the now famous civil rights "March on Washington", demonstrating its solidarity and compassion for the Civil Rights movement and protesting all forms of religious, racial and ethnic bigotry.

Vietnam

In the early days of the Vietnam War, JWV supported the Administration and Congressional view in favor of American involvement in the conflict.

Jewish war veterans immediately set to work to aid our allies and our troops. Care packages consisting of clothing, personal hygiene products and desperately needed medications were sent to the Vietnamese people.

Thousands of packages containing toiletries, treats, games, reading materials and Judaica were forwarded to American troops serving in Southeast Asia by JWV.

A series of educational presentations sponsored by JWV sought support and understanding from the homefront for our troops serving in Vietnam, in light of the growing anti-Vietnam sentiment. JWV denounced the actions of radical groups who sought to support the Viet Cong.

In 1967, JWV declared its support for the continuation of government efforts to improve the pacification program and land reform in the Vietnam countryside in order to promote the stability of the Vietnamese government.

JWV echelons undertook a campaign petitioning world leaders to pressure the government of

Brotherhood meeting: JWV was the only veterans' group to march with the Reverend Martin Luther King, Jr. and was a founding member of the Leadership Council on Civil Rights. Here JWV participates in one of the many Brotherhood gatherings of the 60's with other Civil Rights activists.

Congressional Medal of Honor Recipient, Jack Jacobs

One American of the Jewish faith received the highest award for bravery bestowed by the U.S. Government, the Congressional Medal of Honor. Colonel Jack H. Jacobs received the medal on March 9, 1968.

Jacobs was a first lieutenant serving as assistant battalion advisor, Second Battalion, 16th Division, 9th Army Infantry, in the Kien Phon area of Vietnam. When his unit was attacked by a superior Viet Cong force, Jacobs called for and directed air strikes against the enemy positions. During the action, he suffered a head wound and was bleeding profusely. Under intense fire, Jacobs exposed himself to enemy fire in order to determine the situation of his unit. He took the opportunity, at this time, to rescue two wounded personnel. His first aid saved the men's lives.

Colonel Jacobs also received two Silver Stars, three Bronze Stars and two Purple Heart medals for service in Vietnam.

Jack Jacobs, Congressional Medal of Honor recipient from the Vietnam War.

Jewish American Families in Service

Colonel Jack B. Zimmerman began a tradition of family service to the nation when he selected a career in the military by attending the U.S. Naval Academy. He graduated in 1964, joined the United States Marines, and immediately served two tours of duty in Vietnam. During the Vietnam War, Zimmerman performed with bravery and valor. He received two Bronze Star Medals and a Purple Heart.

Zimmerman resigned his commission in 1978 but remained active in the Marine Corps Reserve until 1994. Colonel Zimmerman retired from the U.S. Marine Corps Reserve in 1994 - but the Zimmerman family did not.

First Lieutenant David Zimmerman, Colonel Zimmerman's son, is a Naval Academy graduate also. He is presently a Naval Flight Officer stationed in Pensacola, Florida. Terri Jacobs, the Zimmerman's daughter, is serving in the Marines as a Judge Advocate stationed currently in El Toro, California.

Colonel Jack B. Zimmerman, his wife Ilene and their children, 1st Lieutenant David Zimmerman and Captain Terri Jacobs at Colonel Zimmerman's retirement ceremony from the Marines.

More than thirty years after the Vietnam Conflict, we are discovering the depth and breadth of Jewish service.

President Lyndon Baines Johnson greets National Commander Milton A. Waldor and presents him with a pen used to sign into law the new GI Bill of rights H.R. 12410.

North Vietnam to adhere to the Geneva Convention for Prisoners of War.

Exact figures as to the number of Jews who served in Vietnam are not available. Servicepersons were not required to identify their religious preference and many chose not to. Estimates are upwards from 10,000 Jews wore the uniform during the Vietnam Conflict.

It is generally and falsely accepted that there was little Jewish participation in Vietnam. Many who believe this are not guilty of anti-Semitism, merely of ignorance. The best kept secrets of Jewish service to America are the stories of those who did wear the uniform, did serve their country and did risk their lives. These men and women struggled, like so many of us at the time, with the issue of the morality of war. But, in the face of this moral dilemma, they chose to do their duty as well.

Many Vietnam veterans are today's JWV leaders. They include Michael Berman of New Jersey, JWV's National Judge Advocate, Daniel Weiss of New Jersey, JWV's Anti-Drug and Anti-Alcohol Abuse Chairman, Barbara Simon of Georgia, Bob Sherman of Virginia, David Magdison of Florida, Leroy Vegotsky of New Jersey - all National Vietnam Veteran Chairpersons.

The current JWV National Executive Director, Col. Herb Rosenbleeth, a former Marine who retired from the U.S. Army, served in Vietnam.

In the National Museum of American Jewish Military History many of the exploits of Jews in service in Vietnam are recorded. Three fighting men included in the museum exhibitions are Roger Steven Briskin, Fred Zedeck and Joseph Ira Goldstein.

Briskin was a corporal in the U.S. Marines. It was in Da Nang Quong Nam Province, on March 31, 1967, when he was in the thick of a fierce battle, that Briskin saw one of his men wounded by mortar. While attempting to rescue him, Briskin himself was killed. He was posthumously recognized for bravery.

Captain Zedeck served with the U.S. Air Force, 388th Tactical Fighter Wing in Korat, Thailand. In the Southeast Asia area of operations, Zedeck flew 165 combat missions and logged more than 450 combat hours. His many decorations include the Air Force Distinguished Flying Cross and the Air Medal with Ten Oak Leaf Clusters.

Lieutenant Joseph Ira Goldstein, U.S. Navy Fighter Squadron VF154, flew 110 combat missions in Vietnam. He received the Navy Unit Commendation Medal and the Vietnam Gallantry Cross among others.

In each American war Jews proved their mettle and despite hardships and prejudice moved up the ranks. Vietnam was no exception. Major Generals Stanley H. Hyman and Robert B. Solomon are among this elite group.

Hyman was a major when he received the Legion of Merit for his outstanding work with the Military Intelligence Branch of the U.S. Army in Vietnam from August 1968 to August 1969. He used his expertise in intelligence to predict the enemy's intentions, thereby assisting American commanders in their battles with the enemy. Major General Hyman hails from Long Branch, New Jersey.

Major General Robert B. Solomon made many notable contributions to the war effort in Vietnam. He served as chief of Command Information Division for the U.S. Military Assistance Command in Vietnam. He was promoted to major general in January of 1982 and resides in Baltimore.

The current Chief of Naval Operations, Admiral Jeremy Michael Boorda, is among the many Jews who served in Vietnam who have dedicated their careers to the U.S. military.

JWV was among the earliest of the veterans' organizations to reconsider American involvement in Vietnam and to urge the government to extricate our fighting men and women from this hopeless conflict. In 1971, JWV passed a resolution to withdraw all troops from Vietnam when the Administration's credibility as to the Conflict was openly challenged while our troops remained in harms way.

As the conflict drew to a close, JWV's platform for returning Vietnam veterans included full government funding of Veterans Administration programs to insure high quality care in fully equipped VA hospitals; encouraging the maximum use of G.I. Educational Benefits— especially for Black and other minority veterans; and renewal of active G.I. housing on a permanent basis.

After the conclusion of the war, JWV took special effort to recognize the contributions of Black American veterans of the Vietnam conflict and initiated projects to support training programs for these veterans. JWV received public acclaim for these activities and for its membership's deep interest in the needs of minority veterans in areas such as housing, employment, health care and education.

In 1974, JWV National Commander Malcolm Tarlov paid a visit to President Lyndon Johnson seeking greater support through Veterans Administration's programs for returning Vietnam veterans. JWV continued these efforts after the war urging legislation which would finance studies by both the Department of Defense and the Veterans Administration into the effects of the defoliant Agent Orange, and the medical/psychological phenomenon that has come to be known as Post Traumatic Stress Disorder (PTSD).

POWs and MIAs

The Jewish War Veterans of the United States of America is concerned for people everywhere who are not free, in particular POWs (prisoners of war) and MIAs (missing in action) which include veterans of the Korean and Vietnam conflicts.

In 1983, the delegates to JWV's annual convention passed the following resolution regarding POWs/MIAs:

"Although the Paris Peace Accords were signed ten years ago, 2,500 Americans remain listed as missing in action in Southeast Asia. The recent transportation of the remains of American servicemen from the Socialist Republic of Vietnam to the U.S. proves that American remains are still being found in Southeast Asia.

The Jewish War Veterans of the USA urges the Administration to pressure Vietnam and Laos to cooperate with the U.S. government in finally and completely resolving the issue of Americans missing in Indochina."

The Jewish War Veterans participates in the National League of Families' public awareness campaign, and continually urges its members and friends to write to the Vietnamese Mission at the United Nations to urge the fulfillment of its pledge to account for the missing soldiers.

In testimony before Congress, JWV's National Commanders always include this crucial issue in their presentations.

Thankfully, the numbers of MIAs unaccounted for is diminishing. Many members of JWV continue to wear the symbolic red ribbons which keep the missing in their hearts and minds.

The Jewish State

From the earliest days of the dream of a Jewish homeland, Jewish War Veterans' members have utilized their considerable clout in support of the fulfillment of the dream, the fledgling state, and the now flourishing democracy.

Boycotts, parades, fundraising drives, bond and blood drives, hospitals, veteran facilities, forests, roads, playgrounds, absorption centers, water reclamation projects have all been included in JWV's extensive agenda on behalf of the State of Israel.

JWV members are frequent visitors to the halls of Congress and the headquarters of America's national veterans' associations to influence U.S. policy on the Middle East. This advocacy takes the form of support for foreign aid to Israel, military and technological exchange and cooperation, protests of the Arab boycott, and public awareness of threats to Israel's security from terrorism.

JWV's programs for Israel include support of the Disabled Israeli Veterans Rest and Recreation Home in Beersheva. Programs designed in cooperation with the Jewish National Fund include; the Jewish War Veterans Forest in Israel, land and water reclamation programs, and ground-preparation for new housing. JWV remains active in Israel Bond programs. The organization provides direct support to a group of elderly Soviet veterans who recently immigrated to Israel.

The fact that members of the Jewish War Veterans of the USA are first, foremost and forever Americans, does not diminish the emotional, theological and ethical link that inexorably binds the organization with its co-religionists in the State of Israel.

Protesting International Cooperation with Arab Nations

Over the years, JWV utilized foresight and its position as a leader on the American scene to disavow nations who seek to harm or destroy the State of Israel. There have been many wars waged against the tiny country. We are all familiar with the War of Independence, the Six-Day War, the Yom Kippur War, etc. War has also been waged against Israel on the political platform and in the economic arena. Whatever the form of aggression perpetrated by Arab nations and other potential enemies of Israel, JWV has responded. JWV led many boycott efforts at the time of the establishment of the State.

In 1970, JWV protested the visit of the French President George Pompidou with PLO leader Yassir Arafat and urged the United States to launch a diplomatic protest of the French for their relationship with Arab terrorists.

In 1973, after the outbreak of the Yom Kippur War and heavy pressure by the Jewish War Veterans of the U.S.A. and other American Jewish organizations, President Richard Nixon and the U.S. Congress appropriated 2.2 billion dollars in aid to the State of Israel.

Immediate retribution by the Arab oil cartel (OPEC), in the form of an embargo, was instituted against the United States and its people. JWV waged a strenuous public relations campaign to urge Americans to hang tough for our democratic ideals and not to "cave-in" to the economic terror tactics of the oil rich Arab nations.

Effective JWV Boycotts

As a lead organizer against the Arab boycott of Israel, JWV conducted many education and action campaigns. In 1959, JWV targeted the Brown and Williamson Tobacco Company for participating in the Arab Boycott of Israel. Other companies identified were Aramco, Shell Oil and Renault.

So successful was the boycott against Brown and Williamson that in 1966, when JWV led a campaign against Coca Cola to protest the beverage company's cooperation with Arab nations, James Farley, CEO and Chairman of Coca Cola met with JWV's representative Past National Commander Abraham Kraditor in an attempt to convince the organization not to boycott the world's largest beverage company.

In 1965, JWV placed advertisements in national newspapers and led demonstrations protesting West German support of the Egyptian war effort. The Germans provided the Egyptians with scientists, Nazis who had formerly plied their trade for the Third Reich. The German government determined that it was justified in its action as the statute

Separation of Church and State: A JWV Victory

In 1966 the United States Marine Corps erected a 65 foot illuminated Latin Cross at Camp H.M. Smith in Hawaii. The Cross was built with federal money for a Easter sunrise service and was left in place as a "non-sectarian symbol of hope" to families of POWs and MIAs who remain in Southeast Asia. There it stood for more than 20 years, prominently displayed and maintained with federal funds. Upon discovering this, JWV turned to its fellow Jewish communal groups and asked for their support in a suit to have the Cross removed. JWV's requests were not answered. The JWV then filed suit on its own to have the Cross removed, claiming that if the Cross should serve only as a memorial, it was still a "religious purpose mixed in with a secular purpose" being supported with public monies on government property.

In briefs filed by JWV member, attorney Ronald Koerner of New York City, JWV stated the illuminated Cross does not honor or respect Jews who died in Vietnam or the several Jewish families who have loved ones missing in action. The case of JWV, pursued during the terms of PNCs Friedman, Goldwasser and Greff, differed from most other separation of church and state cases, because in this case the military, and therefore the federal government, defied an established constitutional principle by endorsing the presence of a permanent religious symbol on government property.

In 1985, the Navy's judge advocate general, Rear Admiral Thomas E. Flynn urged that the Cross be removed as its presence at the base was unconstitutional. Marine commanders ordered this as well, but the Marine commandant, General P.X. Kelley countered the orders, and the Cross, overlooking Pearl Harbor, remained until JWV brought the case to court. The JWV suit in the district court included an individual plaintiff, Maxwell Feuerman, a Jewish war veteran from Hawaii. Feuerman stated that the Cross on base upset him so much that he avoided the base, including the medical facilities located there.

The defendants in the case, former Secretary of the Navy James Webb and former Commandant of the US Marine Corps, General P.X. Kelley, maintained their position that the Cross was simply a "beacon of hope". Later in the summer, a federal court ordered that the 22 year old Cross be removed because it was "too laden with religious meaning to be appropriate for a government memorial." Judge Thomas Hogan's decision was a victory for the Jewish War Veterans, and was the second time the Cross was ordered removed, after protest from the Hawaiian Jewish community. Commander Greff extolled the court's decision, saying he knew that it was possible for the United States to memorialize those missing in Southeast Asia in a more fitting manner. The Jewish War Veterans never called for the removal of a memorial, only for the removal of the Cross.

The Cross was not removed immediately, as the judge's decision allowed for a 60 day grace period in which the government could review the

Latin Cross which stood for 22 years at Camp H.M. Smith.

judge's orders and decide whether it would appeal the case. Two months later, in October 1988, the government chose not to appeal the case, but asked that the Cross remain on base until December 2, a month after the scheduled removal date, in order to have time to erect a "suitable substitute" memorial. The new memorial was to consist of an illuminated flagpole which flew the US and POW/MIA flags 365 days a year. An inscribed plaque at the base of the flagpole dedicates the memorial to recognize the courage, honor and sacrifice of those who served in Vietnam and those who are still missing in action from all branches of the armed forces.

of limitations of the War Criminals Act had expired (20 years).

JWV's advertisements awakened its peers in other Jewish groups and ultimately the West German government removed the scientists from Egypt and dissolved this cooperative program. In future dealings with the United States and Israel, the West German government often inquired as to the position of the Jewish War Veterans on issues of common concern.

In 1971, JWV tackled Japanese car manufacturers- Datsun and Toyota- and Nippon Airlines. In publications throughout the nation, JWV urged consumers not to support these Japanese companies as they cooperated with the Arab economic boycott of Israel.

In 1972, JWV began a boycott of travel to Mexico due to Mexican government actions against Israel in the United Nations.

The United States policy against providing arms to Arab nations was endorsed by JWV. When the French government terminated a long-standing agreement to provide defense systems to Israel, JWV helped to organize a boycott against French exports. In 1988, the boycott was applied to corporations who continued to cooperate with the Arab nations, such as Cadbury-Schweppes and Safeway stores.

Saving the Haifa USO

In March, 1989, United Service Organization (USO) President Charles Hagel announced the closing of the Haifa USO, as well as six other USO facilities, in order to "ensure that management control and day-to-day accountability exist in all our operations worldwide." The Haifa USO was a favorite among United States Navy personnel serving the Sixth Fleet in the Mediterranean. This, coupled with the economic and political repercussions of closing the facility in Israel, convinced the Jewish War Veterans to begin a letter-writing campaign to influence Hagel to keep the port's USO operating.

Upon receiving JWV protest letters and statements from other national veterans' groups, the USO decision was reversed and the Haifa USO is now open and running. Financial support comes from Jewish War Veterans and many private donations. Since that time, a strong relationship has been built between JWV and the Haifa USO. JWV sponsored member trips to Israel and the annual Allied Veterans' Missions to Israel always include a visit to the USO in Haifa in the itinerary.

Allied Veterans' Mission to Israel

In 1956, JWV leaders and six other veterans' organizations traveled to Israel to participate in meetings on the import of the Middle East to American interests. Years passed and similar joint missions to Israel did not materialize.

Then in 1989, JWV's International Liaison, Past National Commander Robert M. Zweiman of New Jersey, reinvigorated the forgotten mission program and created what can easily be called JWV's most successful veterans' outreach program on behalf of the Jewish State.

Since the late 1980's, when PNC Zweiman breathed new life into the JWV Allied Veterans' Mission to Israel, over one-hundred non-Jewish veterans - leaders of America's major veterans' groups - have visited the Jewish homeland.

American Jews in Israel's Defense Forces

Over the many years of conflict in Israel some American Jews have heeded the call to aid the Jewish State by serving in its military. The desire was particularly acute during the 1948 War of Independence and in the early turbulent times. Two Americans highlighted on this page exemplify the many who risked their lives so that threatened Jews will always have a safe haven, a homeland..

Colonel David "Mickey" Marcus

David Daniel Marcus was born February 20, 1902 in New York City's Lower East Side. He was the fifth child of Mordecai and Leah Marcus, a Jewish immigrant couple from Rumania. Marcus excelled in sports as a young boy - boxing, football and baseball.

He took special academic studies at New York City College to prepare himself for West Point and in 1920 received an appointment. In 1923, he was intercollegiate Welterweight Boxing Champion and was nominated as a Rhodes Scholar in 1924. After serving four years in the military, he resigned to pursue the study of law. In 1940, Marcus was appointed New York City Commissioner of Corrections. With war clouds on the horizon, Marcus joined the New York National Guard 27th Infantry Division.

After Pearl Harbor, Marcus' division was sent to Hawaii and he was named the commander of a Ranger training school on the islands. In 1943, he was sent to Washington, D.C. to work in the civil affairs division which had begun planning for the occupation of Europe. While in this position, Marcus was part of the U.S. presidential delegation in Cairo, Teheran, Quebec, Yalta and Potsdam. He was then assigned to the War Crimes Division and helped choose the prosecutors to handle the second echelon trials in Nuremberg.

At the end of the war, Marcus was recruited by Moshe Sharett, Prime Minister David Ben Gurion's representative, to supervise the creation of a shadow Jewish army in Palestine.

He immediately started a training program which bore fruit on May 14, 1948 when Israel declared its independence and its Arab neighbors attacked. Marcus developed fast jeep patrols armed with heavy machine guns which halted the Egyptian forces. He was then promoted to General as Commander of the Central Front. He was charged with defeating the world famous Arab Legion and holding on to Jerusalem.

In order to supply the Jewish defenders, he bulldozed a road to connect Jerusalem with the coastal strip. All the work was done at night to conceal the operation. On June 7, 1948 the "Marcus Road" was completed and the supply trucks rolled into Jerusalem.

On June 11, 1948, the night of a victory party held for General Marcus and his staff, General Marcus was mistakenly shot by one of his own sentries. General Mickey Marcus is buried in the cemetery of his alma mater, the U.S. Military Academy at West Point.

U.S. Naval Academy Graduate Establishes Israeli Navy

Lt. Paul Nathan Shulman

Paul Nathan Shulman was born on March 31, 1922 in Long Island, New York. His parents, Herman and Rebecca Shulman, were active Zionists and his mother was a president of Hadassah. As a youth, Paul Shulman spent time sailing the Long Island Sound, endearing him to sailing and the sea.

Paul Shulman entered the U.S. Naval Academy in 1941, participated in one of the earliest accelerated programs at the academy and graduated in 1944. Lt. Shulman served in the U.S. Navy in the Pacific during World War II. While home on leave in 1941 he met David Ben Gurion. He resigning from the U.S. Navy after the war, Paul Shulman spent two years smuggling refugees and arms into Palestine.

In early 1948, Shulman was invited to Palestine, once again, to become the naval advisor to the naval wing of the Hagannah (Israeli underground army) forces. In November 1948, Ben Gurion, now prime minister, appointed Shulman the first commander of the Israeli Navy.

Within nine months, Shulman formally organized the naval command, initiated the first formal officers' training program and laid the foundation for a professional and modern navy in Israel. Paul Shulman was then all of 26 years old.

Shulman spent three years as naval advisor to Ben Gurion. He resigned to go into private business. Paul Shulman died in Haifa, Israel on May 15, 1994.

Past National Commander Albert Schlossberg is among many JWV leaders to develop close relations with Israeli leaders (pictured here with Prime Minister Yitzhak Rabin to build a bridge of understanding between Israel and America's veterans' community. On Rabin's left is PNC Alfred P. Chavie of the American Legion.

JWV Allied Veterans' Mission participants at the USO in Haifa, Israel. Frank Tucker, Past Department Commander of Massachusetts, Veterans of Foreign Wars, presents a U.S. flag which flew over the U.S. Capitol to the Director of the Haifa USO.

Non-Jewish veteran leaders participating in the JWV Allied Veterans' Mission pray in Jerusalem, Israel. James H. Tanner, Disabled American Veterans, Department of Massachusetts Commander and Joseph Cramens, American Legion, Department of Massachusetts Commander place personal prayers between the stones of the Western Wall of the Temple in Jerusalem.

In London, at the annual Remembrance Day Ceremonies, NC Al Cohen join with members of the British Association of Jewish Ex-Servicemen and Women (AJEX), the Israeli War Veterans League, Brig. Gen. Zvi Shur and the Israel Defense Forces Association, Lt. Col. Shimon Behar. JWV International Liaison, PNC Robert M. Zweiman, at far right, is coordinator of JWV's International Affairs.

Past National Commander Edward D. Blatt, at right, and Congressman Benjamin Gilman, chairman of the House Foreign Relations Committee and JWV's National Legislative Chairman celebrate the signing of the Middle East Peace Accord at White House Ceremonies in 1994.

America's veterans' community has always held the Israeli military in high regard, but without direct consultations with the Israeli military and a personal visit to the country, these non-Jewish veterans could not have a clear picture of the security threat faced by Israel.

JWV takes these veteran leaders to Israel each year, to meet with Israeli government figures and military officials, and ordinary Israeli citizens as well. As representatives of a veterans' community 27 million strong, these officers of veterans' groups can share their Israeli experience with a much larger number of people than JWV could reach on its own. This is a wonderful "diplomatic" program for Israel and a great education program for America's non-Jewish veterans.

Support of the Israel Defense Forces

Veterans of Israel's defense forces are supported by JWV through direct financial contributions and several hands-on projects. Beit Halohem in Tel Aviv is a center developed to provide disabled veterans of Israeli wars and their families with a comfortable and accessible facility for recreation and entertainment.

The center, which opened in 1974, offers physiotherapy and rehabilitative services, but even more importantly, has become a place for families to get away and enjoy swimming, basketball, movies and social events. JWV is a major contributor to Beit Halohem.

JWV also supports disabled Israeli veterans who visit the United States. Israelis love to travel,

and one of their favorite destinations is the United States. Each year groups of disabled Israeli veterans travel to Washington, DC. When they visit, JWV attempts to make their stay meaningful. The organization offers to arrange meetings with government officials and legislators and escorts the Israelis. Private museum tours and screenings of JWV films and other films related to American military history are offered, along with private luncheons and receptions.

JWV's three posts of American veterans in Israel, located in Jerusalem, Haifa and Natanya, are very supportive of Israel's veterans. The JWV members, mostly retirees, socialize with them and keep in touch to gauge their needs and concerns, and they keep JWV National Headquarters informed.

The Israeli War Veterans League and "Tsevet," the Israel Defense Forces Association, are two of the Israeli military associations with close ties to JWV. Tsvi Shur, Chairman of "Tsevet" and Meir De Shalit, Chairman of the Israel War Veterans League, and their staffs, are in frequent contact with JWV and regularly attend JWV's annual national conventions.

The "Roof for Demobilized Israeli Veterans" is another project of JWV's. This residential facility, located in Haifa, was established to provide inexpensive rooming to young Israeli veterans attending college. The Israeli government offers financial aid to veterans seeking a college education, but not enough funds are available for young Israelis from families of limited means to cover all of their expenses. JWV solicits contributions from its members to support this worthwhile cause.

Israeli POWs and MIAs

Just as JWV is concerned with American POWs and MIAs it seeks to assist the Israeli government in the safe return of its POWs and MIAs.

For more than ten years, JWV has followed the cases of Zachary Shlomo Baumel, Ron Arad, Yehuda Yekutiel Katz, Zvi Feldman, Joseph Fink, Samir Assad and Rachamim Levi Alsheikh.

The case of Zachary Baumel is particularly close to the hearts of JWV members. Zachary's family is American. They made aliyah (immigrated to Israel) when Zachary was a child. His parents Yonah and Miriam Baumel have traveled around the globe urging world leaders to remember the forgotten young men and to use diplomatic means to attain information about their status.

CHAPTER TEN

The Cold War Ends: Mopping Up and Moving On

Berlin Wall

The destruction of the Berlin Wall, a vivid symbol of the Communist nemesis and the Cold War built in August of 1961 and brought down on November 9, 1989, the 51st anniversary of Kristalnacht, was a long awaited event by JWV members. Our JWV National Commanders, on official tours of Europe, made certain to visit our troops in Berlin.

That November 1989, the American Military took National Commander Murray Rosen to the Wall and what had been "Checkpoint Charlie" for discussions with Berliners and to confer with East Berlin Jewish community leaders on the needs of united German Jews just relieved from the yoke of Communism. All of JWV celebrated the demise of the Wall — a divisive symbol of oppression.

Helping New Immigrants

When Communism began to crumble, metropolitan areas of the U.S. attracted large numbers of Russian immigrants - many of whom were aging World War II veterans. JWV offered living assistance to these new emigres. The Jewish-Russian veterans were given free patron status in the organization, which allows them to participate in every aspect of JWV, except they may not vote in a JWV election or hold office.

New Needs, New Projects: A Nation Makes Peace with Vietnam Vets

The Jewish War Veterans supported the establishment of a National Vietnam Veterans Memorial and upon dedication of the monument established a Vietnam Veterans Memorial Committee in Washington, DC to assist veterans in wreath laying ceremonies, name rubbings and escorted visits to the "Wall", as it has been dubbed.

JWV's membership includes women who served in Vietnam. Recognizing their contributions is important to the Jewish War Veterans of the USA. That is why when the organization was approached by Diane Carlson Evans, a nurse who served in Viet-

nam and dreamt of a monument honoring others like her, JWV did not hesitate to offer its support. The Vietnam Women's Memorial now stands in its deserving location near the National Vietnam Veterans Memorial in Washington, D.C. as a testament to the courage and dedication of women who served.

Homeless Vets and the Poor

JWV recognized the problem of homeless Vietnam veterans early on and created a "Lend the Hand" project, to assist them and other impoverished people. Project volunteers collect winter coats, used eye glasses, non-perishable food, boots, shoes, first aid kits and toiletries for the poor and homeless. JWV National Service Officers assists those who are veterans to determine what benefits are available to them that could set them on the path toward independence and good health. A member of JWV who sells hearing aids, offers used hearing aids for impoverished elderly veterans.

A unique program created by JWV mainstreams homeless veterans at national veterans' memorial services and events. JWV coordinates with homeless shelters and social service agencies, arranges for transportation, picnic lunches and even purchases wreaths to be presented by the homeless veterans so that they can participate in Veterans Day and Memorial Day events, take pride in their service, and be recognized and appreciated for their contributions to America.

Battling Drug Abuse

In the early 1970's, JWV recommended the formation of a committee to combat drug use within the armed forces. JWV supported the Department of Defense National Drug Control Strategy favoring the use of U.S. military forces to bolster coastline and border patrols attempting to impede drug traffic. JWV recommended under-utilized military bases with hospital facilities be used as drug treatment centers.

JWV continues its commitment to assist in the rehabilitation of veterans who have abused drugs or become addicted to drugs. The organization was an early supporter of Vet Centers. These centers were established throughout the nation, following the Vietnam conflict, in an attempt to provide support systems such as job retraining, psychological counseling, and drug rehabilitation for returning veterans.

Drugs and the Elderly

Another important program relating to drug abuse has put JWV at the cutting edge of a contemporary problem facing our nation's growing elderly population. Prescription drug abuse and misuse costs our nation millions of dollars in insurance and medical fees, and costs thousands of lost lives. JWV was one of the first American organizations to identify the problem and recognize its severity.

JWV produced a film, which has been distributed nationwide, explaining the importance of using prescription drugs, as well as over-the counter medications, responsibly and following directions carefully. The film, "The Other Drug Problem: Medication Misuse Among Older Americans", explains how essential it is to follow usage instructions carefully and to inform health providers of all prescriptions and medications taken.

The homeless veteran depicted in this drawing is a symbol of our proud, down-trodden comrades in need. This drawing was commissioned by JWV to be used on a brochure distributed to JWV supporters who are not members, but who believe in our projects and goals. The drawing is not meant to represent any one individual or any particular branch or unit of the American armed forces.

Dr. Seymour S. Weisman and PNC Benjamin Kaufman, then JWV National Executive Director, receive Jewish Community Service Leadership Awards at Department of MA Brotherhood luncheon in 1956. L to R, seated: Oscar Toye, PNC Albert Schlossberg. L to R, standing: Seymour S. Weisman, PNC Benjamin Kaufman. At podium: then National Commander William Carmen.

Then National Commander Herbert D. Greff with wife, Francine (L) and National Executive Director Herb Rosenbleeth with wife, Sandy (R) at Brandenburg Gate, the Berlin Wall, 1989.

Homes and Havens

The organization has purchased and reconstructed several older homes that serve as halfway houses for veterans who have completed drug rehabilitation through the VA system, but are not yet ready to be on their own.

In Monroeville, Pennsylvania, JWV maintains a home for senior citizens of limited means.

Taking A Position: JWV and the Domestic Agenda

Throughout the years, JWV has been a proponent of legislation to promote the well-being of fellow Americans. Among the bills it supported were the Humphrey-Hawkins Bill advocating full employment, and President Jimmy Carter's Federal Housing Law to provide housing for senior citizens, disabled persons and minorities.

JWV has also supported the Violence Against Women Act, providing for increased criminal penalties for individuals charged with violent acts against women and for increased support services for women.

JWV has long supported groups advocating federal legislation to assist in protecting children against abuse. The organization has, for the last ten years, assisted the Center for Missing and Exploited Children by printing and distributing flyers and publishing photos and information on missing children for nationwide distribution.

Public Education

As early as 1959 and as recently as 1995, JWV has expressed concern about the public education system and encouraged all of its members and echelons to work with their community leaders to en-

sure that every child in America has access to free, good quality, public education.

National Defense, Civil Defense and Gun Control

JWV took stands on major issues of concern to the American public during the seventies. The organization opposes the all-volunteer Army. It is unique among veterans' organizations in its support of gun control legislation, including the well-known Brady Bill. JWV first stood up for gun control following the assassinations of President John Kennedy, Martin Luther King, Jr. and Robert Kennedy. JWV disavows the activities of the Jewish Defense League (JDL).

JWV and the Nation of Islam

One of the more disturbing phenomenon of the 1980's and 1990's has been the emergence of the Nation of Islam (NOI), an African-American group which while promoting black power and self-reliance based upon the principles found in the Koran, also preaches anti-Semitism, racism, bigotry and separatism.

Its charismatic leader, Minister Louis Farrakhan, is an outspoken agitator. His diatribes against the Jewish faith, "a gutter religion", according to the Minister and against Jews, "bloodsuckers", have put the American Jewish community on alert.

JWV has confronted the Nation of Islam (NOI) head-on, decrying its racism and bigotry by sending representatives to attend NOI official speaking engagements.

Many of Farrakhan's followers use college campuses as the platforms for their hateful presentations and finance these engagements by solicit-

ing college students for funds. JWV took exception to the notion that Jewish students were forced to finance addresses by individuals or groups which explicitly call for the destruction of the Jewish people. In a plea to university presidents and administrators, JWV urged that no student funds be used to finance speaking engagements by representatives of the Nation of Islam and other hate groups.

JWV's consistent battle against NOI anti-Semitism was seen by millions on the syndicated talk-show, <u>Donahue</u>. Appearing on the program was Khalid Abdul Muhammad, an NOI spokesman well known for his virulent anti-Semitic writings. Members of the American Jewish community were invited to sit in the audience and challenge Mr. Muhammad. The Jewish War Veterans of the USA was the only group to accept the invitation.

In a hostile audience, comprised primarily of followers of NOI, then National Commander Edward D. Blatt, Past National Commanders Robert M. Zweiman, Warren S. Dolny, Albert Schlossberg and JWV National Action Chairman Melvin Hurwitz, challenged Mr. Muhammad's assertions that Jews financed the slave trade and unmasked his bigotry by vociferously refuting Mohammad's claim that Americans who served in the armed forces were "murderers."

JWV is a leader in supporting legislation which denies federal funding to groups preaching racial division and hatred. In concert with Representative Peter King of New York, JWV supported the "Hate Group Public Funding Exclusion Act", which permits the Department of Housing and Urban Development, or any federal agency, to deny granting funds to the Nation of Islam for group housing, security patrols and medical facilities, if these organizations promote prejudice, racial intolerance, anti-Semitism or racism.

In October of 1995, Louis Farrakhan announced a "Million Man March" on Washington, DC, which would bring a million African-American men, only men, to the nation's capital for a day of atonement and forgiveness. While the goals of the march were admirable, JWV was concerned that Farrakhan and the Nation of Islam would use the march to promote the message of separatism and hate.

JWV was the first Jewish organization to protest the march. At its 100th National Convention in August 1995, JWV released a statement opposing the march because of its exclusion of African-American women and because of Farrakhan's history of hate toward the Jewish people. JWV called upon the African-American community to refute Farrakhan's statements which counteract the positive message of the march. Unfortunately, Minister Farrakhan's hateful rhetoric continued to the moment of the march.

JWV will continue to refute Farrakhan's incendiary comments against the Jewish culture and his call for a separate Black and White America.

America's Service Academies

The national organization is in regular communication with chaplains at the major military academies and urges its local posts to do the same. Many local posts sponsor regular "onegs," small receptions which follow religious services on campus. Some members "adopt" cadets and provide them with friendship and a local "family".

The national publication of JWV, *The Jewish Veteran,* is distributed to all of the nation's military

Hurricane Relief

National Commander Warren S. Dolny
Jewish War Veterans of the United States
1811 R Street, N.W.
Washington, D.C. 20009

Dear Commander Dolny,

My family was quite suprised and delighted at the check forwarded and given to us by the Jewish War Veterans.

Enclosed please find a photograph of our house after the hurricane so that you and all of the Jewish War Vets will understand that your gift was not in vain.

Thank you and best wishes.

Sincerely,
David L. Magidson

academies and free membership in the organization is offered to all students and to all in-service personnel. Graduation gifts, usually in the form of silver kiddush cups, are presented each year to the Jewish graduating class by the various JWV liaisons around the country.

ROTC programs on college campuses are supported by JWV through small educational scholarships offered to high school and college participants.

The JWV Disaster Relief Fund

When natural disasters such as floods, hurricanes, fires and earthquakes threaten JWV members specifically and Americans in general, JWV is ready to assist through its National Disaster Relief Fund. JWV raises money for the fund directly from its membership and dips into the fund regularly to help victims of these catastrophes. The fund is supervised by the JWV Emergency Management Team.

When Hurricane Andrew hit South Florida in 1992, the JWV National Disaster Relief fund enabled then National Commander Warren S. Dolny to bring money, materials and manpower to the area in order to assist needy victims. Financial assistance was provided to victims of the most recent northern California earthquake from the JWV National Disaster Relief Fund also.

Granada

American troops have skirmished in various locales in the 1980's and Granada was one of them. JWV supported U.S. action in Granada in 1983. National Commander Joseph Zoldan of Ohio sent a telegram to President Ronald Reagan on behalf of the Jewish War Veterans stating, "We believe it was necessary to take military action to protect the approximately 500 Americans on the island."

Chaplain Jacob Goldstein of the Army Reserves served in Granada and celebrated Hanukkah with the Jewish troops there. Rabbi Goldstein considers it one of the most memorable experiences of his career.

Operation Desert Storm

Jewish-American patriotism was never more prominent in the the 1990's then during Operation Desert Storm, when an estimated 5000-plus people

of the Jewish faith served in the Gulf Region. Pinpointing the number is difficult as servicepersons are not required to identify themselves by faith, and during the Gulf War, Jews were not encouraged to practice their faith openly or to display the Star of David - although many did anyway.

JWV supported Jewish and non-Jewish troops serving in the Gulf. The Jewish War Veterans established a contact desk at the Pentagon to gather and disseminate the most current news of troop activity to posts and Jewish communities nationwide.

All echelons and subsidiaries (auxiliaries and Descendants of JWV chapters) were encouraged to participate in blood drives, creating kosher care packages for the troops, and keeping "In-Touch" programs.

JWV was in frequent contact with the Jewish Welfare Board (JWB) and Jewish chaplains stationed in Saudi Arabia and Israel. Items for Jewish troops were distributed through the Jewish Chaplains and also through contacts with Protestant and Catholic chaplains serving Jewish troops aboard ships in the Mediterranean.

The Jewish Veteran - which has been distributed to Jewish servicepersons worldwide since the mid-1920's - was once again shipped overseas to keep Jewish men and women up to date and in contact with activities and friends at home. Despite the publication's long and varied history, shipping *The Jewish Veteran* to Saudi Arabia was indeed a first.

Another first for JWV - and most likely for the

Operation Desert Storm saw American Jews fighting in Saudi Arabia to save the lives of a people who, in peacetime, restrict their entry into the country.

JWV Services America's Military Academies

At the nation's military academies, JWV developed a liaison system to provide friendship and respond to the needs of Jewish cadets. JWV sought to assist in the establishment of Jewish chapels at each of the academies and was intimately involved with and a major contributor to the West Point Jewish Chapel.

Past National Commander Stanley Zwaik at groundbreaking ceremonies for West Point Jewish Chapel.

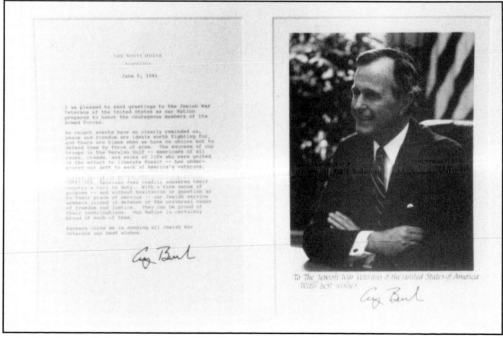

President George Bush wrote to the Jewish War Veterans recognizing Jewish service in Operation Desert Storm.

Saudi Arabian's too - was a shipment of hundreds of copies of the Jewish Bible to Jewish troops serving in Operation Desert Storm. Approached by Senior Army Chaplains about the shortage of Jewish Bibles and funds to reprint them, JWV came up with the money and coordinated the printing. The Jewish Welfare Board shipped and distributed the Bibles.

The sheer joy of helping Jewish military personnel serving in an Arab land brought out the humor and generosity in JWV members. Who got more pleasure was indistinguishable, the guy who sent the kosher salamis to Saudi Arabia or the guys who ate them there!

After Desert Storm, hundreds of returning servicepersons complained of joint aches, lethargy and other mysterious health problems. JWV urged the Congress and the Veterans Administration to commit dollars to research into what had caused this Persian Gulf Syndrome, and what possible treatments could cure it.

No End to the Volunteer Spirit

Back at home, JWV increased its support services in VA hospitals following Operation Desert Storm. With thousands of hospital volunteers serving in hundreds of VA hospitals nationwide, JWV has one of the top records in the Veterans Administration Voluntary Service program (VAVS) in the entire VA system. Millions of volunteer hours have been contributed to VA hospitals by JWV members.

No program reflects the true meaning of brotherhood or is as deeply appreciated as the holiday service exchange program. It is most rewarding for its participants. Each year at Christmas time, throughout the country, members of the Jewish War Veterans trade places with volunteers and selected staff so that their Christian counterparts can practice their faith and enjoy the day. This program extends into peacetime the many acts of brotherly support shared by active duty personnel during the Christian and Jewish holidays in wartime, acts which forged friendships that exist to this day.

Organizing and supervising this expansive network of JWV hospital volunteers is no small job. Making sure Jewish patients are properly attended to and that Jewish religious requirements are met is a daunting task. This duty has been handled with concern and professionalism for many years now by World War II veteran and longtime member Miriam P. Jaffee of New York who serves as JWV's National VAVS Chairman.

International Terrorism

In the Summer of 1972 Americans were preoccupied with the Olympic Games being played in Munich, Germany. Television sets throughout the nation were tuned-in to the spectacle of international competitive sport. Then the horror began and the games turned ugly. Americans watched in disbelief as an act of televised terrorism unfolded.

The hateful attack on Israeli athletes at the 1972 Olympics in Munich was the impetus for a JWV program, by Shaldon Miller, PCC, to alert Jewish students on college campuses to the vulnerability of American and Israeli Jews to these heinous acts. The campus program took the form of small informal meetings offering discussions of bias in the media, protecting threatened and dwindling European Jewish communities, and reinvigorating Jewish life on college campuses. An important aspect of the campus program was JWV's financial sponsorship of the distribution of a film on bias against Israel in the American and world media. The film advised college students to be cautious about believing what they read, to do their own research, and to come to their decisions based upon independent information, reason, and their own personal beliefs. The film was distributed to many Hillel Centers nationwide.

JWV established an Olympiad Award program in memory of the fallen Israeli athletes. Each year, educational scholarships and awards are presented to youth exemplifying the ideals of JWV through outstanding academic and sports achievement. Any high school student may apply for the award, regardless of race, religious preference, or national origin.

JWV issued public statements condemning the murder of Leon Klinghoffer on the Achille Lauro and urging nations of the world to offer no safe haven for perpetrators of such heinous acts.

Largely through the efforts of JWV, the U.S. Congress passed the Export Administration Act of 1979 which prohibits the transfer of U.S. aid to any country that condones terrorism.

In light of intensified terrorist attacks around the world, the Jewish War Veterans, in 1985, called on the United States government to establish a training center in the Department of the Treasury to combat terrorism, both in this country and abroad.

In 1987, JWV condemned any deal which would extricate suspected terrorist Mohammed Ali Hamede from incarceration and punishment. Hamede was under suspicion of being the ring-

leader in the bombing of a Rome synagogue that year.

In 1988, at JWV's national convention, the organization commended the U.S. government decision to close the PLO office in Washington, D.C. and at the United Nations. The convention body also recommended that the State Department spotlight acts of terrorism connected with Fidel Castro's Cuban government.

When terrorism continued, JWV publicly condemned the American Jews who met with Yasser Arafat, the leader of the Palestinian Liberation Organization, in Stockholm in 1988. Following that meeting, the Jewish War Veterans sent a telegram to then Secretary of State George Schultz praising his decision to deny Arafat a visa to the United States.

In 1992, JWV established Entebbe Rescue Day to honor the memories of slain Israelis, Americans and all victims of terrorism throughout the world.

Fighting Nazis

In a 1985 public statement, JWV reconfirmed its demands for prosecution and deportation of Nazi war criminals residing in the United States of

PNC Jerome Cohen visits with hospitalized veteran, MSgt. Winfield H. Ball (USMC-Ret) in November of 1971.

The David J. Hirsch Post 490 was honored for outstanding volunteer service by the Helen Hayes Hospital in West Haverstraw, New York.

The JWV delegation to the Fifth World Assembly of Jewish war veterans. Among those pictured: past National Commanders Jack Litz (PA), Joseph Zoldan (OH), Murray Rosen (CA)-deceased, Samuel Greenberg (PA), and Herbert Greff (OH).

JWV Past National Commander Samuel Greenberg's home was targeted by anti-Semitic vandals in 1993.

Members of the Oklahoma City Fire Department accept donation and recognition plaque from JWV leaders (second from left) Maj. Gen. Stanley Newman, then National Commander David H. Hymes of Illinois and Past National Commander Samuel Greenberg of Pennsylvania (second from right).

has helped to establish many neighborhood watch programs and school alert programs.

JWV fights terrorism at home through its National Action Committee and its National Reward Fund. When Jews or Jewish institutions are the targets of anti-Semitic vandalism, JWV works with the local police authorities to educate the community and apprehend the perpetrator. JWV publicizes its reward through flyers and in local newspapers and sends trained members of the organization to speak to students of public schools about the hurtful and destructive nature of these crimes.

JWV was recognized by the Montgomery County, Maryland Police Department for offering a reward which led to the arrest of Nazi skin-head Jeffrey Lee Eskew, who vandalized a school in the community.

In the Spring of 1990, Eskew and two associates broke into the Yeshiva School of Greater Washington, located in Silver Spring, MD, and caused over $20,000 (twenty-thousand) worth of damage. JWV offered a reward of $2,000 (two-thousand) for information which would assist police in solving the case. An informant came forward and the reward was delivered to him by police.

Rewards have also been offered in cases of synagogue and home vandalism in Pennsylvania. In the Summer of 1993, Congregation Ohav Zedek of Wilkes Barre, Pennsylvania was targeted. JWV offered to assist in the investigation and put up a reward. Editorials expressing concern about increases in anti-Semitic vandalism were placed in the local papers by Past National Commander Samuel Greenberg. To date, the perpetrator of this hate crime has not been identified.

New Style Hatemongers: The Oklahoma City Bombing

Racism and anti-Semitism continue to thrive in the United States. Desperation, poverty, illiteracy, abuse generate hatred. In the final decade of the 20th century, human kind continues to destroy one another in the name of religion, ethnic origin, color and political ideology.

Hatemongers of the ilk of Thomas Metzger, a White Supremacist, and Louis Farrakhan, leader of the Nation of Islam, continue the time worn tactic of tearing down one people in order to lift up another.

Whether it relates to Jewish Americans or not, JWV and its membership will vigilantly combat prejudice, bigotry and evil acts perpetrated upon the innocent.

Following the bombing of the World Trade Center and the Murrah Federal Building, JWV became one of the leading proponents of the Omnibus Terrorism Act, which classified terrorism as a federal offense punishable by severe penalties. JWV urged Congress to pass legislation to deal with the rise of nationalistic, citizen militias which spread violence and hatred of the government.

JWV sent its top leadership to Oklahoma City on a mission to honor the memories of the people slain in the bombing of the Murrah Federal Building on April 19, 1995. Past National Commanders David Hymes of Illinois and Samuel Greenberg of Pennsylvania presented a plaque and a donation in the amount of $2,000 (two-thousand) dollars to representatives of the Oklahoma City Fire and Rescue Department.

America. No compromise measures would be acceptable to JWV. This was not news, JWV has a long history and close association with government agencies, particularly the U.S. Justice Department, Office of Special Investigations (OSI) in detection of war criminals. In conjunction with with the Justice Department, JWV also supports the concept of FBI pursuance and surveillance of neo-Nazi groups.

The Bitburg Disgrace

While participating in ceremonies marking the 40th anniversary of the end of World War II, in May of 1985, President Ronald Reagan made an ill-advised visit to the German cemetery of Bitburg where members of the Nazi's infamous SS troops are buried.

Despite President Reagan's high popularity rating at the time, and his strong record of support for Jewish causes, the Bitburg gesture with all of its symbolism was an extraordinary insult to the memories of Jewish victims of the Holocaust and the brave men and women who fought the Nazis.

When JWV learned of the planned visit, it vehemently protested and urged President Reagan to cancel the wreath laying ceremony at Bitburg. JWV Past National Commander Samuel Greenberg and representatives of many other Jewish groups joined in the protest at Bitburg.

Mr. Reagan was unswayed and followed-through on his original plan. He spent many weeks justifying his action in the media. JWV, on the other hand, was deluged with praise for its challenge of the President, and appreciated overwhelming support for its position by the American people.

Domestic Terrorism

The Jewish War Veterans also recognized the threat of terrorism here in the United States. At the National Convention in 1983, JWV passed a resolution entitled "Domestic Hate Activity", which calls the Ku Klux Klan, the neo-Nazi movement and paramilitary vigilante groups to be threats to the socio-political health of society. In this resolution, the Jewish War Veterans urged that legal penalties for religious and ethnic-related crimes be strengthened.

Through its National Action Committee, JWV

Veterans Get a Seat in the President's Cabinet

The number one domestic priority for JWV throughout the 1980's was the enactment of legislation to create a position in the president's cabinet for Veterans' Affairs.

Elevating the Veterans Administration to cabinet level status would give veterans' issues a higher level of import and greater attention, on par with other functions of the government.

JWV and its friends in allied veterans' organizations who worked so diligently for so many years to establish a Department of Veterans Affairs, had their efforts rewarded on March 15, 1989 with the creation of the new office of Secretary of Veterans Affairs. Ironically, this date is the 93rd anniversary of the establishment of JWV.

The first Secretary of Veterans Affairs, appointed by President George Bush, was Edward Derwinski, a former Congressman from Illinois. JWV has maintained a close association with the Secretary of Veterans Affairs since Mr. Derwinski's term and regularly invites the Secretary to speak at JWV functions, including the annual national convention.

Capitol Hill Action Day/JWV Congressional Reception

Each year the National Commander of JWV is invited to present testimony on Capitol Hill to a joint session of the House-Senate Veterans' Affairs Committee. This is an important opportunity for Jewish veterans to present their concerns to our government leaders.

On Capitol Hill Action Day, JWV members from around the nation visit their legislators to discuss the organization's current activities and policies on a wide range of political, military and social issues. The date of Capitol Hill Action Day is selected, each year, to coincide with the National Commander's testimony.

Well in advance of the date, members schedule visits with their legislators. When they arrive in Washington, D.C., their first objective is to participate in briefings on domestic, veteran, and international affairs so they are well informed, with up-to-the-minute information, before embarking on the appointments with members of Congress.

Capitol Hill Action Day provides JWV with a platform to present its concerns, gives members valuable experience and opportunity to voice their points of view and develop their leadership potential. Members of Congress appreciate meeting representatives of America's Jewish and veterans' communities and learning of their constituencies views.

Concurrent with Capitol Hill Action Day, JWV sponsors its annual Congressional Reception. The guest of honor is a member of Congress who has, through action, demonstrated support for veterans' causes. Honorees receive the prestigious JWV Medal of Merit. Past honorees have included Congressmen Benjamin Gilman, Sonny Montgomery and James Talent, Senators John Warner, Daniel Inouye, Barbara Mikulski, Jay Rockefeller and Phil Gramm, and the late Secretary of Defense Les Aspin.

NED Herb Rosenbleeth with current Secretary of VA, Jesse Brown.

Building Americanism in New Generations

The Sons of JWV, a JWV youth group that once numbered over 10,000 members, no longer exists. The majority of those boys, now men, became veterans themselves, and joined the ranks of the Jewish War Veterans of the USA.

A new subsidiary group, made up of young professionals, continues in the mission of the original Sons of JWV - but now includes daughters, granddaughters and sisters, as well.

Descendants of Jewish War Veterans, established in 1987 under Past National Commander Jack Litz of Pennsylvania, is active and growing around the nation. There are currently 40 officially chartered chapters of Descendants of JWV nationwide with programs ranging from assisting troops abroad, caring for hospitalized veterans, and exclusively social functions.

Descendants of JWV is playing a crucial role in the planning and implementation of JWV programs for veterans in the twenty-first century. Members of Descendants are important to the future

At a 1989 NEC meeting, a dinner was held to honor past NEC Chmn. Pictured are from L -R: PNC Nate Goldberg, PNC Herman Moses, PNC Robert Shor, PNC Ainslee Ferdie PNC Robert Zweiman, PNC Ralph Plofsky and PNC Norman Tilles. Seated are PNC William Carmen and PNC Benjamin Chasin. Those past NEC Chmn. who were unable to make the testimonial included Lt. Col. Joseph Solomonow, PNC Harry Madison and PNC Paul Ribner.

Shown after the presentation of JWV flags for display in Congressional Committee hearing rooms are (L-R): Al Lyman, Post #791); Sen. Alan Cranston Chairman-Senate Veterans' affairs Committee; Willy Herbst, Post #83; Rep. Sonny Montgomery, Chairman-House Veterans' Affairs Committee; and National Commander Jack Litz.

Descendants of JWV Past President Steve Elfman at National Vietnam Veterans Memorial.

PNC Alfred Schwartz ctr. presents testimony on behalf of JWV to the joint House-Senate Veterans Affairs Committee. On his left is JWV Legislative Officer Benjamin Gilman (R-NY) now the chairman of the House International Relations committee. On his right is JWV National Executive Director Herb Rosenbleeth.

At JWV Congressional Reception on Capitol Hill. L to R: JWV National Supply Officer Paul Luterman, JWV National Controller Manuel Auerbach, JWV National Centennial Chairman, PNC Robert M. Zweiman.

growth of the National Memorial Inc. and its museum, the National Museum of American Jewish Military History.

National Presidents of Descendants of JWV

Michael Friedman of New Jersey
Steven Elfman of Massachusetts
Sharon Portnoy of New York

Citizenship Starts Early

JWV continues its Americanism activities today, through programs in our public schools and the scouting program. Starting with one troop in 1920, JWV now sponsors scores of troops nationwide and has honored thousands of young people who have attained the title of Eagle Scout. In 1988, JWV received the prestigious Mortimer Schiff award for its work with youth. Mortimer Schiff was President of the National Boy Scouts of America

in 1931. JWV was the first Jewish organization to be honored with this award, presented by the National Jewish Committee on Scouting of the Boy Scouts of America.

Trained JWV members visit public schools nationwide, teaching about the tradition of patriotism in American Jewry and encouraging all children of all faiths, races, and nationality to be proud American citizens. Hundreds of flags and history lessons have been distributed through the JWV Americanism program.

A Stamp for JWV

Among the many projects undertaken to honor JWV and its members on the occasion of the organization's 100th anniversary, was a campaign to be recognized by the U.S. Postal Service with a 100th anniversary stamp.

For several years, through thousands of letters, postcards and petition campaigns, JWV lobbied for a 100th anniversary stamp. The decision making body, the Citizens' Stamp Advisory Committee, continually turned the organization down. The Committee advised that it did not feel it appropriate to recognize a religious organization.

At two rallies, one on the steps of the Capitol and one in front of U.S. Postal Service Headquarters, JWV protested the decision of the Postal Service and declared that it would not give up the fight.

In meetings with Postmaster General Marvin Runyon, JWV Centennial Chairman, PNC Robert M. Zweiman, has reiterated a long litany of precedent for honoring veterans' organization with stamps. The Veterans of Foreign Wars was honored, as were Buffalo Soldiers, POWs/MIAs and many others. Additionally, with regard to the religious issue, PNC Zweiman has pointed out that

JWV 100th Anniversary Stamp Rally, February 1995. Foreground PNC Robert M. Zweiman, JWV National Centennial Chmn., at his right PNC Edward Blatt.

PNC David Hymes of Illinois meets with President Bill Clinton (1994) to discuss issues of veterans' concern.

the Postal Service does not hesitate to issue a Madonna and Child and a Christmas Tree stamp every year. Recently the Postal Service honored Chinese Americans with a Chinese New Year stamp.

As we go to press for this book, JWV and its members remain hopeful that the U.S. Postal Service will recognize the validity of JWV's request and issue an official stamp recognizing the Jewish War Veterans of the U.S.A. 100th anniversary.

The Smithsonian Institution and the Enola Gay

As the fiftieth anniversary of the end of World War II approached, JWV learned that the Smithsonian Institution's National Air and Space Museum in Washington, DC was preparing an exhibition entitled The Last Act: The Atomic Bomb and the End of World War II. In its original script, the Smithsonian chose to engage in historical revisionism and factual corruption by centering the exhibit on the suffering of the Japanese after the atomic bomb was dropped. The exhibition portrayed Americans as racist and described the act as revenge for the Japanese attack on Pearl Harbor. The centerpiece of the exhibition was the Enola Gay, the plane that carried and dropped the atomic bombs.

JWV members believed that the exhibit desecrated the memories of the soldiers, sailors, marines, and airmen who gave their lives in the Pacific to defeat Japanese imperialism. The exhibit neglected to chronicle aggression and atrocities perpetrated by the Japanese military, and failed to include Japan's brutal violation of the human rights of POWs and the rape of Nanking.

Long before American veterans' organizations made this issue their own concern, JWV was speaking out against the exhibition and demanding it be revised or removed. In a resolution passed at JWV's 99th annual convention in August 1994, and in a subsequent letter to Dr. Martin Harwit, Director of the National Air and Space Museum, JWV demanded the exhibit be modified to present an accurate picture of the reasons behind the dropping of the bombs within the context of the times.

Soon disagreements between the Smithsonian and veterans' organizations escalated endangering the spirit of the 50th anniversary of World War II commemoration. In November 1994, JWV National Commander David H. Hymes wrote to President Bill Clinton asking that the entire exhibit be canceled and funding withdrawn.

Script revisions were attempted but did not satisfy either side. In May 1995, the exhibit was cancelled and Martin Harwit resigned. The Smithsonian exhibited the Enola Gay only, with some perfunctory photographs describing how the plane was restored.

However, the controversy was far from over. The American University in Washington, DC announced it would exhibit those items stricken from the original Smithsonian exhibit. JWV contacted the university's Department of History and requested the script be reviewed by credible historians or that the exhibit be canceled. Dr. Peter Kuznick of the American University wrote to National Commander David H. Hymes to assure JWV the university's exhibit "would not demean the contribution or diminish the heroism of American troops in World War II".

Caps and Salutes

Jewish War Veterans' greet 1995 convention speaker General William Westmoreland. (L-R) Joe Kraut (GA), PNC David Hymes (IL), National Commander Neil Goldman (TX), General Westmoreland, PNC Robert M. Zweiman (NJ), National Judge Advocate Michael Berman (NJ).

JWV's efforts in this entire controversy were commended by President Bill Clinton in an Oval Office meeting with representatives of American veterans' groups. President Clinton thanked JWV for taking the lead and said the government would be more mindful of future exhibits displayed at the federally-funded Smithsonian Institution to ensure they represent accurately the history of this nation.

Veterans Continue Fighting

First and foremost, the Jewish War Veterans of the USA is committed to protecting the rights and entitlements of the men and women who served in our nation's armed forces.

"...Let the hand of history tear the fangs of slander from the throat of anti-Semitism. No forged protocols with Old World venom, no poltroonery nor buffoonery...can tarnish the achievements of our Jewish boys overseas."

Colonel Maurice Simmons, 1922

As one of the major players in the American veterans' community, which represents over 27

million men and women, JWV doggedly looks out for America's in-service personnel and cares for the families of servicepersons.

JWV battles those who would threaten our nation's security, and demands freedom and equality for all Americans.

Americans of the Jewish faith have answered the call to duty from the time of the earliest settlers in 1654. They have served their country honorably. No doubt JWV will be forced to continue the fight to prove that fact. The world we share is dangerous, but it would be less so if bigotry could be buried, forever.

Jewish War Veterans continue to seek that day. This was the guiding vision of the founders when they met in 1896. This is what JWV has done for over 100 years. This is what it will continue to do as long as peace remains a dream to attain.

"For devotion to peace, for devotion in war, Jewish citizenship - as I know it - is a shining example to all the world."

Franklin Delano Roosevelt

PAST NATIONAL COMMANDERS OF JEWISH WAR VETERANS

Maurice Simmons

David Solomon

Morris Mendelsohn

Julius Berg

Harold Seidenberg

J. George Fredman

William Berman

MAURICE SIMMONS, 1921-22. The first Commander of the modern Jewish War Veterans, Simmons worked diligently to combine several Jewish veterans' groups into one.

DAVID SOLOMON, 1923

MORRIS MENDELSOHN, 1924-1927. PNC Mendelsohn lied about his age in order to fight in the Spanish American War. Mendelsohn served as the editor of the JWV national publication, as well as its business manager from 1925 to 1930. During his tenure as National Commander, the organization selected its current name as an attempt by PNC Mendelsohn to bring together the United Spanish War Veterans, the Hebrew Veterans of the Civil War and the Jewish Veterans of the Wars of the Republic.

JULIUS BERG, 1928-1930. PNC Berg served with Company I, 308th Infantry, 77th Division during World War I. He was severely wounded on the front line in Arras, France. He was honorably discharged in 1920 as a Sergeant. PNC Berg served as a board member of several veterans' organizations including the American Legion and Veterans of Foreign Wars. A lawyer by profession, Berg was very active in politics, serving as a New York State Assemblyman and a State Senator.

HAROLD SEIDENBERG, 1930-31

J. GEORGE FREDMAN, 1932-1933. Fredman rejuvenated the Jewish War Veterans in many ways. During his administration *The Jewish Veteran*, the official publication of the organization, was expanded and published every month. Fredman also organized four new posts, as well as the Department of New Jersey and the Kings County Council of Brooklyn, both of which came into being during his year as National Commander. PNC Fredman also called for and organized a community-wide boycott of German goods when Hitler came to power in early 1933.

WILLIAM BERMAN, 1933-1935. Berman left Harvard Law School to enroll in the Officers' Training school at Plattsburg, New York. During World War I, Berman spent 18 months in France. Upon returning to the United States, PNC Berman resumed his studies at Harvard and was admitted to the Massachusetts Bar in 1919. Berman was a member of many organizations, but chose to concentrate most of his efforts on JWV.

ABRAHAM KRADITOR, 1935-1936. Kraditor's membership in JWV spanned 50 years, characterized by his devotion and enthusiasm towards the organization. PNC Kraditor served in two wars— as a doughboy in the First World War and as a Paymaster performing special assignments in the Second World War. At the Jewish War Veterans' convention in Los Angeles, 1958, PNC Kraditor received the Gold Medal of Merit, the highest award granted by the organization. Kraditor originated the concept of the JWV National Foreign Affairs Committee and served as its chairman for many years.

HARRY SCHAFFER, 1936-1938. Schaffer was dedicated to increasing membership and the number of JWV Posts in the United States. PNC Schaffer was instrumental in founding posts in the Chicago and Indianapolis areas. Schaffer also served JWV as Chair of the Olympics Committee.

ISIDORE WORTH, 1938-1939. PNC Worth included goals of increasing membership as well as increasing the amount and quality of programming in the Americanism and patriotism arenas into his year as Commander. PNC Worth will also be remembered as the man who put the Jewish War Veterans finances in order.

EDGAR BURMAN, 1939-1940. During a very difficult year for Jews around the world, Burman focussed his term on Americanism and patriotism.

FRED HARRIS, 1940-1942. Since the U.S. entered the war during his term of office he was permitted, under the by-laws, to run for a second term. PNC Harris was a World War I veteran and founded Meridan, Connecticut Post 92 in the early 1930's. Following his term as National Commander, Harris continued to work for the organization, playing a crucial role in the passage of the Displaced Persons Act. PNC Harris served as the president of the National Shrine for the Jewish War Dead for approximately 25 years. PNC Harris passed away in 1985.

BEN KAUFMAN, 1941-1943. Kaufman served during World War I in the famed Company "K" of the 308th Infantry, 77th Division. During the war, PNC Kaufman was injured, but refused to remain in the hospital while his company continued fighting. He was decorated for bravery by all allied governments, and the United States, which awarded him the Congressional Medal of Honor. Because of the Second World War, Kaufman was permitted to hold the position of National Commander for two consecutive terms. He belonged to nearly every veterans' organization and eventually became the National Executive Director of the Jewish War Veterans of the United States of America.

ARCHIE GREENBERG, 1943-1945. A World War I veteran, served as JWV's National Service Chair and then took on the position of National Commander in 1943, holding the position for two terms. PNC Greenberg was also active in his community and Jewish community, holding positions in several other veterans' groups and serving as President of his synagogue.

MAXWELL COHEN, 1945-1946. A founder of the Boston Post as well as the Commander of an American Legion Post, Cohen also participated in the organizing of the Department of Massachusetts, later serving two consecutive terms as its Commander. Before serving as National Commander, PNC Cohen was PNC Seidenberg's Chief-of-Staff, Associate Editor of *The Jewish Veteran*, and the Adjutant General of the organization.

MILTON RICHMAN, 1946-1947. A native of Hartford, Connecticut, a veteran of two wars, and a charter member of Hartford Post 45, PNC Richman worked his way up the ranks of JWV. Taking office in a difficult time for both the American and World Jewish communities, Richman focussed his term in office on fighting

Abraham Kraditor

Harry Schaffer

Isidore Worth

Edgar Burman

Fred Harris

Ben Kaufman

Archie Greenberg

Maxwell Cohen

Milton Richman

Julius Klein

Myer Dorfman

Jackson Holtz

Henry Albert

Paul Ginsberg

anti-Semitism, having been a militant leader in the campaign to drive the Nazi Bund out of Connecticut. PNC Richman was active in Jewish communal organizations and other veterans' groups and served on the executive staff of the Hartford Jewish Ledger, a leading Anglo-Jewish newspaper.

JULIUS KLEIN, 1947-1948. A prominent Chicago Jew. In the midst of political tension both in the Middle East and among American Jews, PNC Klein brought dynamic leadership to JWV. During the war he had been Gen. Dwight D. Eisenhower's Public Affairs aide and through this prestigious position had developed many influential friends. Klein organized a large rally in support of Israel, held in New York City on April 4, 1948, one month before Israel declared her independence. Klein, a conservative, cared deeply for the Jewish War Veterans, even going so far as to resign his membership when his own controversial ideas opposed JWV's, and most of the country's, so as not to cause the organization any embarrassment. Upon his death, Klein left all of his valuable military memorabilia to JWV. In his honor, JWV created the General Julius Klein Gallery in the National Museum of American Jewish Military History.

MYER DORFMAN, 1948-1949. During a very turbulent time for both the United States and Israel, PNC Dorfman, an ardent Zionist, sympathized with the State of Israel and struggled in the United States for her freedom. His persistency paid off in the form of conferences with President Truman and close friendships with cabinet members. A former World War I Naval officer, Dorfman led JWV out of tight financial times and laid the groundwork to move the headquarters from New York to Washington, DC. After completing his term as National Commander, Dorfman continued using his fundraising skills for JWV and was appointed chairman of the building fund.

JACKSON HOLTZ, 1949-1950. Holtz was very active in his local community. A politician at heart, PNC Holtz sought the 10th Congressional District seat in Brookline, Massachusetts in both 1954 and 1956.

HENRY ALBERT, 1950-1951. Having been a member of JWV for 13 years prior to assuming the Commandership, PNC Albert also served as the National Editor of *The Jewish Veteran*. An activist in both the Jewish and secular communities, in his hometown of Jamaica, Long Island, Albert chose to focus his term in office on such issues as civil rights, services to veterans and their dependents.

PAUL GINSBERG, 1951-1952. During his time in the service, PNC Ginsberg was awarded 3 Bronze Star Medals and a Purple Heart. Ginsberg served two terms as National Judge Advocate before he was elected to the Commandership. PNC Ginsberg was active in other veterans' groups, as well as JWV.

JESSE MOSS, 1952-1953. A former special government prosecutor, PNC Moss served in the ETA with the Army Signal Corps during the Second World War. PNC Moss believed strongly in the non-partisan aspect of JWV, and remarked immediately upon assuming responsibilities about the injunction in the JWV constitution against partisan political activities.

HARRY MADISON, 1953-1954. PNC Madison enlisted in the Army during World War I at the age of 16, which made him one of the country's youngest veterans of World War I. Madison joined the Jewish War Veterans in 1937 and founded the Jewish War Veterans Memorial Home Association of Detroit, which erected a building which is now one of America's most outstanding memorials to American Jewish servicemen who lost their lives fighting in the First World War. PNC Madison was involved in community service, both Jewish and secular and was cited in 1951 by the mayor and city council in Detroit for his contribution to communal and veterans' activities.

JOSEPH BARR, 1954-1955. A veteran of the United States Army in the First World War, Barr's term as National Commander followed many years of dedication to the Jewish War Veterans, including serving as a National Judge Advocate from 1934-1945 and on the National Committee of Observance of Veterans Day. The level of Barr's participation in the Jewish War Veterans over many years earned him the honor of having the longest continuity of service as an elected member. Barr

was also active in the greater American Jewish community serving as an elected member of the Executive Committee of the National Jewish Community Relations Advisory Council.

REUBIN KAMINSKY,1955-1956. Kaminsky, of Hartford, Connecticut, served in the US Army in an Anti-Aircraft Battalion and in the European Theatre until his discharge in 1945. After his discharge, PNC Kaminsky devoted much of his time to veterans' affairs. In 1954, PNC Kaminsky was appointed National Public Relations Officer of JWV, and was a member of the National Executive Committee and the National Policy Committee for many years.

WILLIAM CARMEN, 1956-1957. PNC Carmen held several national positions in the Jewish War Veterans over the years while balancing a very active life in the Boston Jewish community. A World War II veteran, Carmen was an active fundraiser for JWV's museum, then called the National Shrine, and believed in training local and national leaders. As National Commander, Carmen addressed such issues as the nuclear threat, the principles of the Korean War and the security of Israel.

BENJAMIN CHASIN, 1957-1958. PNC Chasin received the Bronze Star Medal as a member of the 33rd Infantry Division during the Second World War. After separating from active duty in 1946, Chasin remained a member of the active reserve and became a member of the Jewish War Veterans. Chasin proceeded to become active in JWV and held every office available in the lower echelons. Chasin also served on JWV's Foreign Affairs Committee and many other subcommittees on major issues which faced the organization. Following his term as National Commander, Chasin was appointed Chairman of the National Executive Committee.

SAM SHAIKEWITZ, 1958-1959. PNC Shaikewitz, a former Marine, is the founder and first commander of the Allied Veterans Americanism Commission of St. Louis and is also a past commander, Post 6510, Veterans of Foreign Wars. Along with his many communal activities, PNC Shaikewitz was also Post, Department, and Regional Commander, and a member of the Shrine.

Jesse Moss

Harry Madison

Joseph Barr

Reubin Kaminsky

William Carmen

Benjamin Chasin

Sam Shaikewitz

Bernard Abrams

I.L. Feuer

Theodore Brooks

Morton London

Daniel Neal Heller

Ralph Plofsky

PNC Shaikewitz has received citations from the Marine Corps, the AMVETS, the Catholic War Veterans, the VFW, and various other groups as well as from the Jewish War Veterans.

BERNARD ABRAMS, 1959-1960. Abrams hails from Jersey City, New Jersey. PNC Abrams served during World War II. As National Commander, Abrams oversaw JWV's first national conference in Israel. As a Post Commander, he worked to join various veterans' groups against McCarthyism. After Abrams' term as National Commander, he continued to be active in the Department of New Jersey and the Grover Post by attending almost every event and conducting Post Commanders' Seminars.

I.L. FEUER, 1960-1961. A veteran of World War I, Feuer organized a Youngstown (Ohio) Jewish War Veterans Club in 1928, which was the forerunner of the Jewish War Veterans Post 59. PNC Feuer served as Post Commander, Department Commander, Regional Commander and as a member of the National Executive Committee. He also committed his spare time to the YMHA, B'nai Brith, the Jewish Welfare Board and the Jewish Community Relations Council as well as several other veterans' groups.

THEODORE BROOKS, 1961-1962. During World War II PNC Brooks of Roslyn, New York served in the Army as a Sergeant in the Military Police. Brooks was an active member of the JWV, serving at every level of the organization. Brooks held the position of National Judge Advocate before being elected National Commander, was chairman of the Personnel Committee and also served as the International Liaison Officer. Toward the end of his life, PNC Brooks dedicated himself to establishing a JWV memorial commemorating the "service and sacrifice of the Jews who fought in America's wars." This institution is now the National Museum of American Jewish Military History.

MORTON LONDON, 1962-1963. PNC London was in the US Army for five and one- half years, serving in the field artillery overseas in Guadalcanal and France. Before assuming the responsibilities of National Commander, London was the first Commander of the West New York, New Jersey Post 467, Hudson County Commander and eventually became a National Vice Commander. PNC London

was the Permanent Observer at the United Nations for the Jewish War Veterans and also served on the Board of Directors of the National Shrine to the Jewish War Dead.

DANIEL NEAL HELLER, 1963-1964. On the Civil Rights front, Heller called on all JWV posts to support the racial equality goals advocated by the Kennedy administration. PNC Heller believed strongly in peace, saying that it was "patriotic to be for peace", yet was against deep cuts in foreign aid, considering it to be a "reckless act of unilateral disarmament, and a victory for Communists". PNC Heller was President of the first men's ORT, and received the 1963 President's Award as the outstanding young man in the Combined Jewish Appeal.

RALPH PLOFSKY, 1964-1965. PNC Plofsky was an infantry officer during World War II and was recalled to active duty during the Korean War. A lawyer active in community affairs, PNC Plofsky was a Past President of the Hebrew Institute of White Plains, New York and a member of the Jewish Community Council and American Legion Post 135, White Plains, New York. Plofsky currently lives in Port St. Lucie, Fla.

MILTON WALDOR, 1965-1966. A much decorated World War II veteran, discharged as a First Lieutenant, PNC Waldor held every elective post in JWV and served two terms as the National Judge Advocate, before being elected to the National Commander position. PNC Waldor was also the JWV National Civil Rights Officer and the National Recruiting Officer.

MALCOLM TARLOV, 1966-1967. PNC Tarlov, of Norwalk, Connecticut, a World War Two veteran, joined the Jewish War Veterans immediately after his military discharge in 1946. Tarlov served three years in the military as a staff sergeant, including with the 79th Infantry Division overseas. Before his election to the highest position in JWV, PNC Tarlov served as a Post, Department and Regional Commander. Tarlov was the Chairman of the JWV National Insurance Committee, tripling the gross premium collected from the program. PNC Tarlov was also involved with his community, both Jewish and secular, serving as the President of the Norwalk Jewish Community Council and as the secretary of the Norwalk Little League.

SAMUEL SAMUELS, 1967-1968. A graduate of the Naval Reserve Officers' School, PNC Samuels served as a Communications Officer with the Pacific Fleet and retired as a full Commander in the US Navy. Before being elected National Commander, Samuels held positions as the Department of Massachusetts Commander, Regional Commander, on the National Executive Committee and as the National Scholarship Chairman and the National Youth Chairman. PNC Samuels was active in other veterans' organizations including AMVETS and is a Past Commander of Post 940 of the Veterans of Foreign Wars.

CHARLES FEUEREISEN, 1968-1969. Charles Feuereisen was elected National Commander following an already distinguished career with the Jewish War Veterans. Immediately after World War II, in which Feuereisen served in the 511th Parachute Infantry Regiment and was severely injured, PNC Feuereisen returned home and organized the Ascher Post 226 of the Bronx. Following his marriage and relocation, Feuereisen organized yet another post, Post 773 in New Milford, New Jersey. As the chair of the JWV Foreign Affairs Committee, Feuereisen represented JWV as an Observer at the 5th Plenary session of the World Jewish Congress in 1966 in Brussels and was a delegate to the International Conference of Jewish War Veterans held in London in 1967. For many years, PNC Feuereisen represented JWV at the American Jewish Conference on Soviet Jewry and the NCRAC Commission on International Community Relations.

BERNARD DIRENFELD, 1969-1970. Prior to his election, Direnfeld was active at the Post, County, Department, Region, and National Levels of JWV as well as being a member of the American Legion and the Veterans of Foreign Wars. In 1967, Direnfeld was awarded the Joint Veterans Commission Plaque after being voted the "outstanding veteran of the year". PNC Direnfeld served with distinction in the U.S. Army Air Force and was decorated by both the U.S. government and the government of Belgium.

ALBERT SCHLOSSBERG, 1970-1971. Al Schlossberg joined JWV Post 22, the oldest Jewish War Veterans' post in New England, immediately after his discharge from the US Navy after World War II. While Department Commander, PNC Schlossberg initiated the formation of the Mattapan,

Milton Waldor

Malcolm Tarlov

Samuel Samuels

Charles Feuereisen

Bernard Direnfeld

Albert Schlossberg

Jerome Cohen

Norman Tilles

Ainslee Ferdie

Paul Ribner

Dr. Robert Shor

Herman Moses

Dorchester, Roxbury (Massachusetts) District Council and served as the Commander of the Council. Before his election as National Commander, PNC Schlossberg served the national organization in many ways, including as a member of the National Executive Committee, and the National Policy Committee. PNC Schlossberg, a funeral home director, was well-known in his hometown of Boston for his deep involvement in community affairs and his frequent articles and commentaries in the local media. Before his death, PNC Schlossberg was the National Editor of *The Jewish Veteran*.

JEROME COHEN, 1971-1972. Jerome Cohen began his affiliation with the Jewish War Veterans as a young child, with membership in the Sons of the Jewish War Veterans. After discharge from the Navy, Cohen joined Brooklyn Post 50 and eventually was named the first National Action Chairman. As an attorney in his native New York, Cohen led the legal battles against the Nazi Rockwell, teamed with Edward R. Murrow to expose McCarthyism, and set in motion the anti-Walter-McCarran Immigration Act rallies and petitions.

NORMAN TILLES, 1972-1973. PNC Tilles began his affiliation with the Jewish War Veterans after his service in World War Two, in which he served in the Air Force as a first lieutenant in the European Theatre. After returning to the U.S., he joined the Providence, R.I. Fineman-Trinkel Post 439, named after his wife's twin brother who was killed in Iwo Jima. PNC Tilles served as Department Commander of Rhode Island and then assumed many positions on the national level, including the Chair of the National Insurance Committee and the Chair of the National Budget Committee. Currently, PNC Tilles is president of the Hebrew Immigrant Aid Society.

AINSLEE FERDIE, 1973-1974. A veteran of the U.S. Army Transportation Corps, PNC Ferdie was one of the youngest veterans ever elected National Commander of JWV. After retiring from the military, Ferdie became a lawyer in Florida. He was active in the Murray Solomon Post 243, and served as Post Commander and Department Commander. As National Commander, Ferdie traveled to Israel during the Yom Kippur War. Ferdie received the Julius Deutsch award as the outstanding Jewish veteran of Florida, and served as chairman of the Conference of Department Commanders of Veterans and Allied

organizations of the State of Florida. During PNC Ferdie's tenure as President of JWV's National Museum of American Jewish Military History, the institution had unprecedented growth.

PAUL RIBNER, 1974-1976. PNC Ribner served as a captain in the US Air Force during the Korean War. Along with JWV, PNC Ribner was involved in a multitude of communal activities including the American Legion, the Law Enforcement Square Club, the George Washington Consistory. In addition, PNC Ribner was a 32nd degree Mason and was President of the 21 Jewel Square Club the same year he was National Commander of the Jewish War Veterans.

DR. ROBERT SHOR, 1976-1977. A JWV member since 1948, and a highly regarded surgeon in Los Angeles, PNC Shor is a former National President of the American Podiatry Association. During his term as National Commander, PNC Shor was concerned with the "eroding legislative priority of veterans programs" and US support of Israel. Prior to his election to the position of National Commander, PNC Shor held positions on the National Executive Committee, National Policy and Budget Committees. Shor resides in California. His wife, Miriam Shor is also a veteran of WWII and is a Past President of the JWV National Ladies' Auxiliary.

HERMAN MOSES, 1977-1978. PNC Moses served in the US Navy during the Second World War and was released in 1946 as a Lieutenant. He stayed active in the Reserve until the mid-fifties when he retired from the US Navy Reserve. Before serving as National Commander, PNC Moses was the State and Regional Commander of the Jewish War Veterans, the National Judge Advocate, and the Director of the National Shrine of the Jewish War Dead. Among PNC Moses' achievements is his role as plaintiff in the landmark JWV, Department of Illinois, and Herman Moses, Commander -vs- The American Nazi Party case. PNC Moses was named Department Commander of the Year in 1967 and was named Man of the Year by the Department of Illinois in 1968.

NATHAN S. GOLDBERG, 1978-1979. A second generation Jewish war veteran, PNC Goldberg served in the U.S. Navy as an enlisted man and officer and was released from active duty in 1945 with the rank of Ensign. After being discharged from the Navy in 1955, he joined Albany Post 105, of which

his father had been an early member. Goldberg became Commander of the Albany Post in 1958, and then of the Department in the following years. Among PNC Goldberg's achievements in JWV have been his initiation of a Vietnam Veterans' program in the Department of New York and his selection as a recipient of the Ed Nappan Trophy, awarded to the Department Commander of the Year. PNC Goldberg had held positions of National Personnel Chairman and President of the National Museum of American Jewish Military History. During his term as President of the Museum, visitor attendance increased dramatically and the Chaplain Joshua Goldberg chapel was dedicated.

HARRIS B. STONE, 1979-1980. A recipient of the US Navy's highest honor— the Distinguished Civilian Service Award, PNC Stone served as the Chairman of the National Executive Committee for 2 years and, after his tenure as National Commander, went on to be the National Executive Director of JWV from 1981-1985. A veteran of World War II and the Korean War, PNC Stone rose through the enlisted ranks to commissioned officer status.

IRVIN STEINBERG, 1980-1981. A World War II Army veteran decorated with the Purple Heart and the Bronze Star Medal, Steinberg was the three time Post Commander of the Abe Horriwitz Post 681 of North Miami Beach, Fla, which he helped to organize in 1953. In 1955, PNC Steinberg was named Outstanding Post Commander of the U.S.A., and was Department Commander and Regional Commander, as well as serving on the National Convention Committee. During his time in office, PNC Steinberg strived to keep "the members more involved and better informed as to what is taking place in their local communities, in the nation and throughout the world." PNC Steinberg resided in Florida until his death in 1995.

ROBERT M. ZWEIMAN, 1981-1982. PNC Zweiman joined JWV in 1948 after serving in the Second World War. Zweiman has served the organization at every level, beginning with two terms as the Commander of the North-Hudson-J. George Fredman Post 76 in New Jersey. He continued up the ranks serving as the Commander of the Hudson County Council and later as the Department of New Jersey Commander. After finishing his term as National Commander, PNC Zweiman served as the

Nathan S. Goldberg

Harris B. Stone

Irvin Steinberg

Robert M. Zweiman

Stanley Zwaik

Joseph Zoldan

Samuel Greenberg *Harvey S. Friedman* *Edwin Goldwasser* *Jack Litz* *Herbert D. Greff* *Murray Rosen*

JWV International Liaison Officer, as the Chairman of the JWV Centennial Committee, and as JWV Development Chairman. In these capacities, PNC Zweiman created JWV's most successful fundraising programs and the Allied Veterans' Missions to Israel. PNC Zweiman currently resides in Fort Lee, NJ with wife, Jeri.

STANLEY ZWAIK, 1982-1983. PNC Zwaik, as JWV Action Chairman for the Department of New York, led the New York delegation in demonstrating against French premier Pompidou and in boycotts of French goods when the French refused to fulfill their contracts to sell Mirage planes to Israel. Zwaik was voted JWV's Outstanding Department Commander at the National Convention in 1969. Currently PNC Zwaik resides in Holliswood, New York.

JOSEPH ZOLDAN, 1983-1984. A veteran of the Korean War, Zoldan joined JWV immediately after his discharge from active duty. PNC Zoldan served the organization for over 35 years both locally and on the national level. The positions that PNC Zoldan held for the Jewish War Veterans include National Program Chairman, National Foreign Affairs Chairman, National Finance Board Chairman, Department of Ohio Commander and Canton, Ohio Post 73 Commander. PNC Zoldan was also involved in many community activities including the Agudas Achim Congregation, the Canton Jewish Community Center and the Canton Veterans Council.

SAMUEL GREENBERG, 1984-1985. A veteran of World War II, PNC Greenberg held the editorship of *The Jewish Veteran* and was a member of the National Executive Committee. He was also the National Public Affairs Officer, Central District Commander, Department of Pennsylvania Commander and the Commander of Wilkes-Barre Post 212. A civic and Jewish communal organizer, PNC Greenberg, in 1976, received the Tapper Award which honored him as Man of the Year, from the Greater Wyoming Valley Jewish Community Center. PNC Greenberg is also a sculptor, and a picture of him beside his steel-sculpture memorial to the Israeli athletes murdered at the 1973 Olympics is displayed at the Diaspora Museum in Tel Aviv. PNC Greenberg is currently JWV's National Disaster Relief Chairman. Greenberg resides in Kingston, PA.

HARVEY S. FRIEDMAN, 1985-1986. Harvey Friedman served as National Commander during the 90th anniversary of the organization. A Navy veteran of the Korean war, Friedman traveled around the country and world during his tour of duty. PNC Friedman has been awarded the Jewish War Veteran Man of the Year award three times, each by a different echelon of the organization. In 1962, he was honored by the Ein-Unger Post, in

1968 by the JWV Department of New Jersey and in 1976 by the Essex County Council. In 1984 Friedman received the prestigious Moe Lazarus and Louis Saiewitz Memorial Award, presented by Bayonne Post 18. Friedman was the three-term chairman of the National Action Committee, leading the JWV campaign against racism and anti-Semitism. PNC Friedman conceived and successfully directed the "Burn the Mortgage" fundraising campaign of 1994. PNC Friedman is also involved in secular veterans' groups and communal activities, such as the Governor's Task Force to help Vietnam era veterans adjust to civilian life, and on the Liberty Park Monument Committee, which erected a statue in Liberty Park commemorating the liberation of Nazi-occupied Europe by the Allies.

EDWIN GOLDWASSER, 1986-1987. PNC Goldwasser, a Korean War veteran, held local, state and national JWV positions before being elected National Commander. He was the National Editor of *The Jewish Veteran* and served as Chief of Staff to NC Nathan M. Goldberg. PNC Goldwasser chaired the 90th Anniversary Celebration activities of the Jewish War Veterans of the USA. During his tenure as National Commander, Goldwasser met with then-President Reagan to discuss some of the more pressing needs of U.S. veterans, and with Pope John Paul to discuss the fate of the American-Israeli MIA Zachary Baumel. PNC Goldwasser was also proud of his close involvement with the Jewish cadets at West Point. Goldwasser represented the Jewish War Veterans on the West Point Jewish Chapel Advisory Board, responsible for the erection of the chapel. PNC Goldwasser is now living in Delray Beach, Fla.

JACK LITZ, 1987-1988. Jack Litz, of Philadelphia, was a member of the Jewish War Veterans for 36 years before his election to the National Commander position, Litz was the National Judge Advocate, as well as serving in several other national capacities. While in the military, PNC Litz served in the USAF 8th Bomber group. Besides his involvement in JWV, Litz was a member of AMVETS. He leads an active life as an attorney. PNC Litz will long be recognized for his outstanding effort and commitment to the birth and growth of the Descendants of JWV organization.

HERBERT D. GREFF, 1989-1990. Greff was a Personnel Administrative Specialist in the United States Military from 1962 to 1963. Before assuming the position of National Commander, Greff served as his Post Commander and the Department of Ohio Commander. He was also, for many years, JWV Insurance Chairman. Greff is the first Vietnam era veteran elected National Commander of JWV. During his tenure as National Commander, Greff successfully urged the USO not to close its facility in Haifa, Israel, citing the "mutually beneficial arrangement between those serving in the U.S. Navy and

the Haifa Community." PNC Greff also served in various communal leadership positions in his hometown of Columbus, Ohio.

MURRAY ROSEN, 1989-1990. Murray Rosen served in the Army during World War II and joined the Jewish War Veterans in 1949. For the next forty years, PNC Rosen was a well-respected leader at all levels of the organization. PNC Rosen served as the JWV National Convention Co-Chair and sat on the National Executive Committee, among other committees. PNC Rosen served as a Post and County Commander in his native New York and then relocated and served as the California State Commander and the Los Angeles County Commander. PNC Rosen's commitment to the United States' military and soldiers was illustrated by his Chairmanship of the Vietnam Servicemen's Package Committee in New York.

ALFRED SCHWARTZ, 1990-1991. A veteran of the Second World War, PNC Schwartz has held many leadership positions in the Jewish War Veterans, including Department Commander and National Supply Officer. In 1960, PNC Schwartz was voted Department Commander of the Year and in 1980, JWV Man of the Year. PNC Schwartz was also active in civic activities, including serving on the Selective Service Board of Georgia and on the Georgia Department Commander's Conference. As National Commander, Schwartz was devoted to caring for hospitalized, disabled and needy veterans. Schwartz is a native of Atlanta, GA where he ran a successful retail business before retiring.

ALBERT COHEN, 1991-1992. A practicing attorney from West Orange, New Jersey, Cohen served in the US Army during the Second World War as a weather observer. He was elected on a platform of combatting anti-Semitism and racism, supporting America's veterans and "eradicating the scourge of drugs among youth in our country." Along with his dedication to the Jewish War Veterans, which Cohen has demonstrated by holding many leadership positions, including Post, County and Department Commander, he is also a member of the JWV National Museum of American Jewish Military History.

WARREN S. DOLNY, 1992-1993. Warren Dolny of Monsey, New York previously held several positions within the Jewish War Veterans, including Chief of Staff to NC Stanley Zwaik in 1982, member of the National Executive Committee and Policy Committee for many years, Insurance Chairman, and National Editor of *The Jewish Veteran*. Dolny has also been occupied with communal activities, such as serving as the chairman of the Selective Service Board in Rockland County and as a commissioner on the Board of Directors of the Metropolitan Transportation Authority of New York, appointed by Governor Mario Cuomo.

Alfred Schwartz

Albert Cohen

Warren S. Dolny

Edward Blatt

David Hymes

Neil Goldman

EDWARD BLATT, 1993-1994. A Philadelphia native, PNC Blatt served in the US Navy at Camp Perry, Williamsburg, Va, attended service school at Great Lakes, IL and served aboard the USS Iowa during WWII. As JWV Chief of Staff, PNC Blatt represented the organization as a Special Representative in South Vietnam in support of American troops stationed there. Blatt now serves as President of the National Museum of American Jewish Military History and as a Commissioner of Veterans Affairs for the City of Philadelphia, a position to which he was appointed by Philadelphia's mayor, Edward Rendell.

DAVID HYMES, 1994-1995. David Hymes was in the Army in Panama and England. PNC Hymes was among those who landed at Omaha Beach to furnish all APO's with their supplies. Soon after he was injured and spent 9 months hospitalized. Hymes founded the Dr. Samuel Perlman Post 800 (Chicago) and was subsequently elected Illinois Department Commander and National Executive Committee Secretary. Prior to becoming National Commander, Hymes was the National Civil Rights Officer, National Public Affairs Officer, and currently serves on the Board of Directors of the National Museum of American Jewish Military History.

NEIL GOLDMAN, 1996. A member of Dallas Post 256, Goldman enlisted in the U.S. Air Corps as an aviation cadet. He served as a celestial navigation trainer operator and instructor, and was honorably discharged in February 1946. Commander Goldman was born in St. Louis, MO and attended Washington University. He was a buyer and merchandiser for the Mays department store chain, and also operated his own wholesale business for several years. Goldman initiated the Days of Remembrance program on the Holocaust at Carswell Air Base and the Dallas Naval Air Station, held all major leadership positions at the department level and was elected Department Commander of the Department of Texas, Arkansas and Louisiana for two terms. At the national level, Mr. Goldman chaired the National Insurance Committee, was Vice-Chairman of the National Centennial Committee, and served on the NMAJMH's Board of Directors, the NEC, and the National Court. Goldman is a member of DAV, the Dallas Holocaust Center, the Yad V'Shem Holocaust Museum, and the North Texas Cemetery Commission.

Lt. Philip W. Carroll, Lt. Joseph Brunner, Lt. Hatcher, Lt. Bob Bryans, Sgt. Bednarski, Sgt. Bosserman, Sgt. Pung, Sgt. Brosey, Sgt. Edward Whaley, Sgt. Karatkiewicz, 8th Air Force, 466th Bomb Group, 784th Squadron. (Courtesy of Ed Carroll)

Dave Turner - President, Turner Publishing Company

It is a great privilege to publish a century of America's Military History. The Jewish War Veterans of the U.S.A. is the oldest Veteran organization in the Nation, celebrating one hundred years of defense of the freedom the United States.

With origins dating to Sunday, March 15, 1896, when 63 Jewish Civil War Veterans assembled in their first meeting at the Lexington Opera House in New York City resulting in the formation of the Hebrew Union Veterans Organization, through today, the cause of freedom has been proudly represented by Jewish War Veterans of the U.S.A.

These Veterans have stood strong, fought hard, and triumphed in the face of the adversity that war brings, but sometimes under the unfair adversity of the warfare of prejudice. The Jewish men and women who have served our Nation from the 1600s and the Revolutionary War, the Civil War, the Spanish American War, World War I, World War II, Korea, Vietnam, Grenada, and Desert Shield/Desert Storm have distinguished themselves as deserving a place of honor in the annals of American history.

It is my hope that the families and future generations who read this book will realize that the adage is very true "freedom is not free." The liberty that Americans enjoy comes with a price. Certainly the Jewish Veterans have paid the price for Jewish freedom, but every American enjoys the liberty that they bought.

A special thank you for the valuable assistance provided by Ms. Michelle Spivak, National Director of Communications, Development and Programs, who spent many extra hours even on a weekend while reviewing the manuscript in our Paducah Office, as well as proof reading the biographies. Also, thank you for the support and help given by Mr. Neil Goldman, National Commander, Mr. Robert M. Zweiman, PNC, National Centennial Chairman, Col. Herb Rosenbleeth, USA (Ret), National Executive Director, Ms. Inez Bunte, Communications Secretary, and Mr. Sandor Cohen, Assistant Museum Director/Archivist. Most of all thank you to the more than 1,100 individual Jewish War Veterans and families who chose to send in their biographies and photographs to be included in your 100th Anniversary history book.

I am very thankful for the sacrifice of Jewish Veterans. I salute all of you. In the years to come may all of us as Americans have peace. may our children's children not have to defend liberty. However, if it is necessary, may they fight the good fight that the heroes that have gone before have left as an example.

Sincerely yours,

Dave Turner

Dave Turner
President

JEWISH WAR VETERANS BIOGRAPHIES

Editor's Note: All members of the Jewish War Veterans Association were invited to write and submit biographies for inclusion in this publication. The following are from those who chose to participate. The biographies were printed as received, with a minimum of editing. As such the Publisher is not responsible for errors, omissions or inaccuracies contained herein.

World War I Jewish War Veterans. Left to right: Norman Levin, Charles Cohn, and Solly Cornell. (Courtesy of Edwin H.J. Cornell)

ERMA E. MEYERS AARONS, born April 21, 1916, Cleveland, OH. Joined the Army Nurse Corps Regular Army, May 7, 1941; 2nd lieutenant; Walter Reed Hospital 1941; Australia 1942; New Guinea-Finchaven and Good Enough Island; Halloren General Hospital USA 1945; 28th Surgical Hospital and 360th Station Hospital, SWPA; 1st lieutenant given at discharge.

Memorable experiences: Shipping out from Walter Reed Hospital eight weeks after Pearl Harbor; having no uniforms and medical equipment was dated 1918; sailing through Panama Canal into the Pacific; when distillers broke down and there was no water; stopping at Bora Bora where Navy ship pumped water to their ship; arriving at New Zealand in May and then going to Australia.

Among first American nurses in the Pacific Theater and sent to New Guinea at time of Buna Battle; took care of 1st Marine Corps right after Guadalcanal. Did ship duty on Dutch ship from Australia to San Francisco, then went back to New Guinea. Suffered with malaria, jungle rot and dysentery. Her worst memory was the many snakes and living on Spam.

Discharged July 7, 1945, she received the pre-Pearl Harbor Medal, American Theater Medal, Asiatic-Pacific Medal with two Battle Stars and the Victory Medal.

ASHER BENJAMIN ABELOW, the son of David Abelow. Enlisted in WWII ASN 12141766. Served in an advanced Replacement-Depot on the Meuse River at the edge of the Battle of the Bulge.

After surrender of Germany, he was stationed in Munich for six months. He earned combat medals for Ardennes, Central Europe and Rhineland, among others.

DAVID ABELOW, born Oct. 18, 1892, and died in 1966. Enlisted somewhere in Texas at the age of 15 (claimed to be 17) and said his birth certificate was home in Brooklyn. Being large for his age, the enlisting officer believed him and he was enlisted.

Served six years in the Army Cavalry from 1907-1913. He was stationed in Yellowstone National Park during 1907-1910, then served three years in the Philippines during the Aguinaldo Insurrection.

IRA L. ABELOW, was twice reported missing in action. In addition to other medals and a Bronze Star, he was awarded the Purple Heart with three stars for war injuries. He was troop transport commander on ship torpedoed and sunk off North Africa in March 1944. His plane was shot down while carrying him to a North Africa Army hospital. He was treated in a British field hospital until he recovered sufficiently to be transferred to the U.S. Army 79th Station Hosp. in North Africa.

He had a varied series of difficult assignments of unusual nature and his file contains many letters of commendation and appreciation.

Abelow attended the Army's Military Government School and the Civil Affairs Training School taking courses in oriental languages. After the surrender of Japan, while en route for duty in Korea, he stopped in Manila, the transfer point, for a brief reunion with his brother Lt. Joseph Abelow, on duty with the 855th Engr. Avn. Bn. He directed and coordinated administration of civil affairs in an occupied territory (Korea) at national level, with the economics section, department of domestic commerce and assisted in the re-establishment of industry and trade.

In 1946 the CIA invited Lt. Abelow to undertake important missions. He requested discharge from the Army and joined the CIA, but still honors his pledge of silence and will not discuss his CIA work.

IRA M. ABELOW, born June 19, 1920. Enlisted in WWII, January 1942 and assigned to the infantry. Subsequently, commissioned first lieutenant in the Chemical Corps and served in a special research unit for the balance of the war.

He received his Certificate of Service in March/April 1946 as well as the second highest civilian medal award, the Decoration for Meritorious Civilian Service.

After WWII, 1st Lt. Ira Abelow joined the Reserves. He was called back for active duty in the Korean War, from July 1951-July 1953, to again serve in the Chemical Corps.

IRVING ABELOW, a graduate medical doctor, volunteered to serve in the Army during the summer of 1941. He was called to active duty Sept. 20, 1941, and commissioned first lieutenant. Duty in Ft. Knox, KY followed by a course in the Army Field Service Training School at Carlisle, PA and various assignments. He served in the 220th Armd. Med. Bn. in the 20th Armd. Div. and was promoted through the ranks to major.

In March 1945 in Germany, the 220th Armd Med. Bn. was advancing rapidly at night to give close medical support for the 20th Armd. Div. which was advancing deep in Germany when Maj. Abelow's jeep crashed into a roadblock that was not visible under blackout conditions. He suffered two broken teeth, several fractured ribs and other injuries. Nevertheless, within one day, with a strong sense of duty, he insisted upon rejoining his battalion because the advance of the 20th Armd. Div. was critical and played an important role in helping to win the war against the Nazis.

JOSEPH ABELOW, volunteered in the U.S. Army in 1942. He has a bachelor's and master's degree in accounting, business administration and education and has several years experience in public accounting and in teaching business subjects in the high schools of New York City. After basic training and graduating from OCS at Carlisle, PA, he was commissioned 2nd Lt. and assigned to a station hospital unit being formed at Ft. Dix, NJ.

Transferred to the 855th Engr. Avn. Bn. in Finschhafen, New Guinea where, in addition to his duties as MAC commander of the Med. Detach., he served as education and information officer. Seeing an opportunity to help the Negro soldiers improve their education and prepare for their eventual return to civilian life, he organized the GI Jungle College of New Guinea. The Jungle College was an immediate success and was extensively described in the SWPA newspaper for September 1944.

HQ in Hollandia temporarily assigned Lt. Abelow as liaison officer to the USNH on Manus Island in preparation for the invasion of the Philippines. After establishing procedures for Army soldiers being treated at the Navy hospital, he was called back to New Guinea when the 855th was alerted for forward movement and was transferred to Manila, Philippines. It was there that the 855th EAB rebuilt Nichols Airfield. The 855th was in the "black book" slated for the invasion of Japan when the atom bomb ended the war.

The only synagogue on American soil that was destroyed during WWII was in Manila. Lt. Abelow started the drive to rebuild it. He took his discharge in Manila and remained there to establish a business. He made a hurried two-week trip back to New York to marry the girl waiting for him, Ruth Moed, then the newlyweds flew back to Manila where their first two children were born. In 1953 they returned to the States and settled in Miami Beach, FL.

SANFORD CYRUS ABELOW, born Nov. 26, 1922, tried to enlist in WWII but was rejected for medical reasons because he had asthma. However, he persisted and was finally accepted. Among other places, he served in Finschhafen, New Guinea, in the South Pacific, where 1st Lt. Joseph Abelow visited him several times.

Lt. Abelow was also serving in Finschhafen at that time with the 855th Engr. Avn. Bn. Sanford Abelow was reported to have contracted malaria in New Guinea. His death on Oct. 19, 1976, was caused by asthma.

SOLOMON ABELOW, born July 22, 1894, and enlisted in WWI as a private. He was assigned to field artillery, served in the 77th Div. and was commissioned 1st lieutenant in France.

Veteran affiliations: JWV of the U.S., 1st commander Boro Park Post (Brooklyn); 1st commander, Kings County Council (Brooklyn); State Commander of New York, 1935-36; American Legion, 106th Inf. Post; and VFW, Pvt. Bud Alben Post.

His wife, Anna, is deceased. She was national president of JWV's Ladies Auxiliary in 1949. Their only child, Sanford, served in WWII.

ARNOLD ABRAHAM, born June 24, 1964, Westchester, NY. Received BS in physics from Rensselaer Polytechnic Institute May 1986; MS, International Relations, Troy State University July 1992; Commissioned OTS, USAF an Intelligence Officer April 1987.

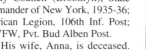

Tours of duty in Japan, Korea, Germany, and the Pentagon. Combat deployments to Saudi Arabia, Mogadishu and supporting operations in Bosnia. Conducted strategic targeting and mission planning from Taif during Operation Desert Storm. Interrogated prisoners, planned psychological warfare ops, and ate the military's first Kosher MREs while serving in Somalia as Chief of NATO's first operational Battle Damage Assessment cell, HQ 5ATAF, Vicenza, Italy. Left active duty from Defense Intelligence Agency to take position as private consultant on Information Warfare for Dept. of Defense and support Joint Staff/J2 Targeting Div. as Captain, USAF Reserves. Lives in Lakeridge, VA with his beautiful wife, Tamyla and son Jacob.

Awards: Joint Service Commendation Medal x 3, Air Force Commendation Medal x 4, Joint Service & Air Force Achievement, National Defense, Southwest Asia Service, Armed Forces Expeditionary and Kuwait Liberation Medals.

ABRAMOWITZ FAMILY (REUBEN, BENJAMIN, SID), On a cold November day in 1906 the SS *Gregory Mark* docked in New York carrying Reuben, age 5, four siblings and his mother Yetta. Their start point, Yekaterinoslav, the Ukraine, Russia. Benjamin Abramowitz, Reuben's father, was in New York where he worked as a cap maker and union organizer. Arrived in the States two years before his family joined him. Life was tough in the "Golden Medina," especially in 1908 when Benjamin was killed while organizing workers. Reuben's home was on the Lower East Side where living was no picnic. He was a street kid, always working for a buck or whatever the traffic would bear. It was an age where there was no welfare or food stamps. Everyone worked to put bread on the table.

Reuben's formal education ended at fourth grade. One Spring day in 1916 when he was 15, Reuben came home and found five chairs around the kitchen table with six people present. The next day he went to Whitehall Street, told the enlistment sergeant he was 18 and enlisted, with no questions asked. Previously, he belonged to the New York National Guard.

Assigned to Ft. Hancock, the first recruit in that Coast Artillery regiment in five years. It was not an easy life, but there was plenty of guard duty and KP to keep him busy. After participating in the Mexican Punitive Expedition, he was off to Europe in 1917 where he served with the First Trench Mortar Bn. of the "Big Red One." Later, he was assigned to the 37th AA Btry. in the grade of sergeant. After the war, Reuben participated in the occupation of Germany with the 1st Field

Signal Bn. He was the only enlisted member of the All-Army Rugby Team and also boxed. He was a member of the Army contingent to the 1920 Olympics.

Reuben continued to serve at Ft. Monmouth, NJ from the early 1920s until WWII with the exception of a three year tour of duty with the 9th Sig. Svc. Co. in Hawaii. In Hawaii he played on several championship basketball teams. "Abe" was known as the pride of Hester Street. During the summer months he was often detached from duty at Ft. Monmouth to teach communications to cadets at the USMA. He often joined the New York Celtic's basketball team as an extra player when needed. It was a way to make a few extra dollars. In 1933 he married the late Olga Holtz of Long Branch, NJ.

"Abe3" gained the nickname "Dean of Hanger One" from his long years of teaching code and radio operations in the old WWI hanger which once stood at Ft. Monmouth. In 1942 M/SGT Abramowitz traded his stripes for gold bars. His innovative teaching methods helped speed up the training of radio operators so desperately needed. He was a key player in breaking the Japanese code. In 1944, Maj. Abramowitz became OIC, Sig. Ctr. of the USA HQ ETO. As a lieutenant colonel in 1945, he activated and organized the European Cmd. Sig. School where he served as commandant until 1948 when he was reassigned to Ft. Monmouth.

Col. Abramowitz retired in 1949 after 33 years of active duty. In retirement he continued to support the USA by active participation in TROA, National Sojourners, JWV and the Long Branch USO-Jewish Welfare Board Armed Services Committee. Reuben Abramowitz died in 1967. On June 7, 1985, the Abramowitz Field House was dedicated to his memory at Ft. Monmouth. His military decorations included the Legion of Merit with OLC, Bronze Star, Army Commendation Medal as well as the French Legion of Honor and the Croix de Guerre.

Ben Abramowitz was born at Ft. Monmouth, NJ, a Jewish Army brat. In fact his bris was the first conducted at an Army post, or so he has been told. Everything went well until Dec. 7, 1941, a few days before his father was commissioned. Then the moves began. First to Long Branch, his mother's home town, then back to Ft. Monmouth. In early 1944 Ben's father went overseas, then it was back to Long Branch for Ben and his mother. In 1946 Ben and his mother rejoined his father in Ansbach, Germany, where his father was Commandant of the European Signal School. In 1947 Ben had his Bar Mitzvah in the Ansbach Synagogue that was completely reconstructed by the German Government, with the "encouragement" of Ben's father. The Bar Mitzvah was the first in Germany after the war. The synagogue stands today and looks the same as it did in the 1730s.

In 1955 Ben graduated from Virginia Polytechnic Institute and State University with a degree in business and a RA Commission as a 2nd lieutenant of Infantry. Through the years he served in every capacity from platoon to battalion commander. For eight years Ben served in Army Avn. assignments having completed his training in both fixed and rotary wing aircraft by 1959. Served as Chief of International Standardization for the Army, as a member of the Faculty of the US Army Command and General Staff College and commanded a brigade in the 3rd ROTC Region. He served in Germany, Korea and two tours in Vietnam, the first as executive officer 1st Bn.5th Cav., and the second in 1971-72 as senior advisor to the 8th ARVN Regt. Ben's awards and decorations include the Legion of Merit with OLC, Bronze Star with "V" device and OLC, Air Medal with five OLCs, Meritorious Service Medal, Commendation Medal, Combat Infantry Badge, Senior Army Aviator Badge, General Staff Identification badge and the Vietnamese Cross of Gallantry with star and Palm.

In 1958 while serving at Ft. Riley, KS, Ben met his future wife, Irene Miller, at a Community Seder. They were married soon after and had three sons. David is an AF Academy graduate, but saw the light and was commissioned in the Army. Dave is presently a major, promotable to lieutenant colonel, serving as a staff officer at Forces Command, Ft. McPherson, GA. David has commanded units in the US, Germany and Korea. During Desert Storm he commanded HQ&HQ Co of the 4/229 Attack Bn. (Flying Tigers). Later he assumed command of an Apache Co. in the same battalion. Prior to his present assignment he served as operations officer 4/6 Cav., an Apache unit. Dave's awards include the senior Army Aviator Badge, Ranger Tab, Airborne Wings, Air Assault Badge, Air Medal, Meritorious Service Medal, Army Commendation Medal and Army Achievement Medal. David is married to the former Gloria Carpenter. They have three children, Leah, Jacob and Kaila Rose. While overseas David and Gloria served as Jewish lay leaders for their military community. David is a member of the JWV.

Sid graduated from Tulsa University in 1982. While at Tulsa he was a two-time All-American offensive tackle. After graduating and receiving his commission through ROTC, Sid was drafted and played four years in the NFL. During his time in the Reserves, Sid commanded a postal detachment and a replacement company. Sid's unit was called up for Desert Storm. He deployed to Ft. Sill, OK where he served as a captain with the 381st Repl. Bn. until the end of the emergency. Sid is married to the former Sherri McElfresh of Tulsa, OK. They have three children: Emily, Adam and Alex. Sid is packaging sales manager for Meade-Zellerbach in Tulsa, OK.

Alan received his undergraduate and graduate degrees from Kansas State University and also played football. Received his commission in the Signal Corps through ROTC. In 1989 Alan graduated from the Florida State School of Law. After passing the Florida Bar Examination, he served as an English instructor at a small village. Upon his return to the US, Alan married the former Jodi Katzin, a classmate of his at law school. Both Alan and Jodi have been public defenders in Polk County, FL. In 1994 Alan and Jodi took a leave of absence from the Public Defender's Office and did volunteer work for the UN Commission on Refugees in Kenya. He is presently a captain (JAG Corps), FLARNG. He works with the Florida Dept. of Juvenile Justice as a senior attorney.

Since retiring from the Army in the grade of colonel, Ben has taught full time at the University of Central Florida. He teaches business ethics and society and other courses in the Dept. of Management. Ben and Irene have been involved in Jewish activities since arriving in Brevard. They are members of Temple Israel where Ben served as President for four years. Additionally, Ben has served on the Jewish Federation Board and co-chaired the Combined Jewish Campaign for two years. Additionally, Ben coordinated the Volunteers for Israel Program locally and is a member of the JWV.

MORRIS A. ABRAMOWITZ, MSG, USAAC, born in Bridgeport, CT, Feb. 11, 1919. Received his degree in accounting from Junior College of Connecticut, University of Bridgeport in 1938. Enlisted in the 242nd CAC, CTNG on Oct. 10, 1939. Trained with the NG at Camp Niantic, CT and at Ft. Wright, Fishers Island, NY.

The 242nd CAC was activated into federal service Sept. 16, 1940, assigned to 2nd Bn. HQ, 242nd CAC. Transferred to AAC cadet training, Class 43-C, San Antonio, TX. Resigned from flight training and was assigned as sergeant major, 314th AB Sqdn. Air Svc. Cmd., Charleston, SC.

Arrived in the ETO on Nov. 27, 1944, and assigned to the security of the bases of the 1411 Air Trans. Cmd. at Istres and Marignane, France. On May 8, 1945, he was assigned as administrative chief, Post Exchange, and supervisor of the VIP Lounge at Marignane. Requested assignment to an intense six week French language and culture course at Sorbonne University, Paris, then requested return to the US.

Memorable experience was attending Passover service in Marseilles with congregates who had escaped the Nazis campaign of extermination.

Discharged Nov. 1, 1945, Ft. Devens, MA. Awarded the Bronze Star (Rhineland Campaign), Good Conduct Medal, American Defense Service Medal, American Campaign Medal, EAME Campaign Medal and WWII Victory Medal.

Married Lillian Linet in 1940 and they live in Orlando, FL area. Their daughter Mrs. Elaine Sarah Goldberg lives in Massachusetts and son Robert lives in Connecticut. He is employed on the staff of *Heritage Florida Jewish News*, Fern Park, FL.

ALFRED ABRAMS, born Dec. 18, 1917, Brooklyn, NY. Joined the U.S. Army in November 1940, and was stationed in Australia, New Guinea and Philippines.

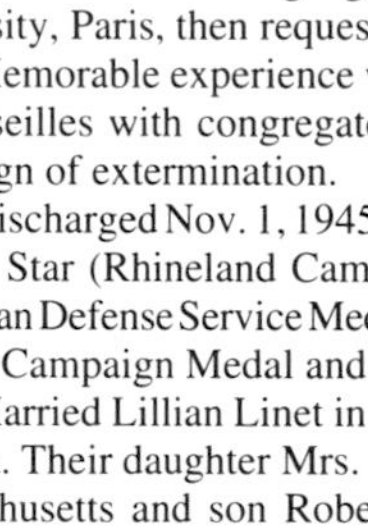

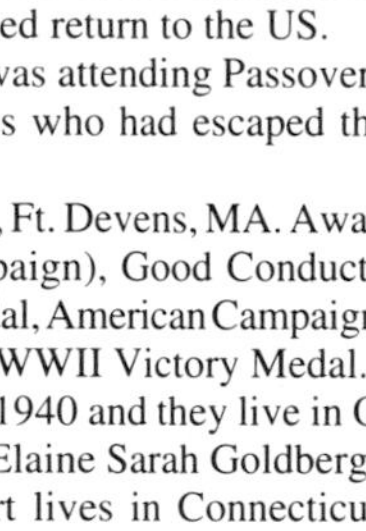

Memorable experience was participating in the re-capture of the Philippine Islands attached to Headquarters Base M.

Awards/Medals: Philippine Liberation Medal with four Bronze Battle Stars, Asiatic-Pacific Medal, Good Conduct, American Campaign Victory Medal and the Philippine Presidential Unit Citation. Discharged in November 1945 as sergeant.

He graduated from Textile High, New York City. He is currently retired in Florida.

BERNARD W. ABRAMS, born 1925 West Palm Beach, FL. He attended Boys' High School, Georgia Tech and graduated from the USMA, West Point in 1947. He served in the Army of Occupation Germany and fought in Korea in 1950-53.

Awards/Medals: Silver Star, Bronze Star with V, Purple Heart with OLC and Combat Infantry Badge. He retired as a result of wounds in 1953 with rank of captain of infantry.

He joined Abrams Industries, Inc. Abrams was civilian aide to the Secretary of Army; founder and past-president of West Point Society of Atlanta; past-president of Atlanta Chapter Assoc. of the U.S. Army; a founding trustee of West Point Cadet Jewish Chapel; liaison officer to White House for Jewish War Veterans and a member of Military Order of World Wars.

Awards include multiple USO awards, Honorary Cadet Colonel Georgia Tech Cadet Battalion, AUSA Creighton Abrams Award, Secretary of Army's Outstanding Civilian Service Award; president of Atlanta Area Council Boy Scouts, president of Gate City Lodge B'nai Brith, general chairman of Metro-Atlanta United Way Campaign, trustee Hank Aaron Scholarship Fund and on Advisory Board of College of Industrial Management, Georgia Tech.

He has three grown children: David, Janet and Judy, and lives in Atlanta, GA.

SEYMOUR C. ABRAMS, born in Russia near Odessa, Feb. 12, 1914. After the Czar was overthrown in Russia in 1917, there was no government, no jobs and no food. When his aunt and uncle in America learned that Seymour's mother, father, sister and two brothers had perished from starvation, they immediately made arrangements to have what remained of the family (Seymour-age 9, one brother and two sisters) brought to America to be adopted as their own.

He volunteered in the Army on Aug. 4, 1943; received basic training at Camp Upton, NY; was sent to Camp Clairborne, LA and Camp Shelby, MS; transferred to Lathrope Engineering Depot in California and had special assignments to Brea, CA, Santa Anita, CA (POW) and Ft. McArthur. From there he was sent to New York to be shipped overseas with the 69th Div., 269th Engr. Cbt. Bn., Co. C.

His unit departed on Dec. 1, 1944, on the liberty ship *Lejeune* for Southampton, England. After a short stay in Northwood Park, Winchester, Plymouth and Portland, they left for Le Havre, France to Leipzig, Germany. The first Ukrainian Army of Russia that the 69th Div. met was from the same area where Abrams was born.

Abrams was separated on Feb. 23, 1946, at Camp Atterbury, IN, as tech sergeant. Battles/Campaigns: American Theater, Rhineland and Central Europe. Decorations and citations include the American Theater Ribbon and Medal, EAME Theater Ribbon with two Bronze Stars, Good Conduct Medal, WWII Victory Medal, Army of Occupation Medal and Meritorious Unit Emblem.

Retired, after owning a real estate office for over 30 years. He is an active member of the VFW and participates in community and civic activities. He has one daughter, a grandson and a granddaughter.

JACK ABRAMSKY, born Oct. 13, 1923, in Newark, NJ. Reported active duty 1943 to USNTS, Newport, RI. Attended

Hospital Corps School, Portsmouth, VA, followed by duty at Memphis, TN Naval Hospital for additional training. Transferred Fleet Marine Force, USMC at Field Med. School San Diego, CA.

Sent overseas to New Caledonia and thereafter to Guadalcanal for assignment to their 1st Prov. Mar. Bde., 4th Mar. Regt., 6th Mar. Div. He participated in initial waves in Guam invasion, was hospitalized just prior to outfit's participation in invasion of Iwo Jima.

Returned to the States to Oakland Naval Hospital, then to Sampson Naval Hospital New York prior to discharge in 1945. He married Ruth Salamon (holocaust survivor) in 1949 and has two sons. Retired after 40 years service with U.S. Treasury Dept. A member of the JWV and treasury post of the American Legion. Presently participates in volunteer work for charitable organizations.

CARL ABRAMSOM, born in Philadelphia, PA, Sept. 17, 1922, of immigrant parents from Russia and Rumania. Inducted U.S. Army February 1943 and trained at Camp Robinson, AR and Camp Ellis, IL.

Promoted to sergeant, arrived in Liverpool, England, April 1944 and Normandy, France, June 1944. He joined Gen. George Patton's 3rd Army in Normandy for the battle of St. Lo and remained in the 3rd Army until the end of battle for Europe, including France, Luxembourg, Belgium, Germany and Austria. Was in Patton's 100 mile march from Strasburg, France through Luxembourg into Bastogne, Belgium to save the 101st Abn. at the height of the Battle of the Bulge, December 1944. Invasion of Germany in January 1945 and part of the liberation team of Buchenwald Concentration Camp and several other camps.

Decorated with five Bronze Battle Stars for valor in combat. He remained in the occupation force with the 79th Inf. Div. hunting Nazi's and contraband. Received an honorable discharge in December 1945.

Post-war college professor with BS, MS and Ph.D., author and lecturer on infectious diseases. Married with four children and four grandchildren. Presently, national and international lecturer on AIDS and related diseases.

ROBERT S. ABRAMSON, born March 13, 1925, Syracuse, NY. He attended Charles Andrews School, graduated from Nottingham High School and attended Syracuse Univ.

Service History: He died June 12, 1945 at the age of 20. He is survived by his father, Moses; mother, Lillian; sister, Hollis Yaritysky; and brother, Arthur.

LORRAINE W. ADDELSTON, born July 4, 1913, New York City. Enlisted Oct. 6, 1942, in the USNR, WR - coding officer. Stationed in New York and participated in Second Front.

Memorable experience was her night duty protecting convoys to Second Front.

She was discharged Jan. 7, 1945, as lieutenant junior grade.

Married to Aaron Addelston, they have one son, Jonathan, and two granddaughters, Miriam and Rachel. She is a retired New York City junior high school principal.

NATHAN B. ADELMAN, born Feb. 3, 1919, Baltimore, MD; graduated Northeast High School, Philadelphia, PA inducted March 19, 1942. Basic training at Ft. Dix, NJ. Sent to Camp Shelby, MS for 11 months training; maneuvers in Louisiana and California. Shipped overseas to North Africa for two months of additional training then on to Italy with the 85th Inf. Div., May 11, 1944. The 85th Div. attacked the German Gustav Line in the vicinity of Minturno, 40 miles north of Naples. The 85th was among the first to reach Rome.

As a front line MP, he kept the thousands of men and vehicles moving forward over a limited number of roads that were being constantly shelled; assisted in enforcing military laws in Africa and Italy; guarded prisoners and government property; and patrolled streets to maintain law and order.

Awards/Medals: EAME Campaign Medal with three Bronze Stars, American Campaign Service Medal, Meritorious Unit Badge and WWII Victory Medal. Served 19 months continental service and 23 months in Africa and Italy.

Married to Zena for 50 years, two sons (one deceased), daughter and three grandchildren. Was senior lecturer at the technion in Israel. Retired in 1985, he owned Greynolds Art and Frame Gallery.

ALEXANDER ADLER, born Dec. 20, 1919, New York City. He was pre-med major, City College of New York, George Washington University. Entered the Army Aug. 8, 1942, was discharged on March 13, 1946, as corporal.

Assigned by the Army Surgeon General to work in research laboratories (staffed by medical researchers) to find causes and cures for tropical diseases that were killing troops in the Pacific Islands. Research was conducted at the Respiratory Diseases Commission Laboratory at Ft. Bragg, Walter Reed Tropical Medicine Laboratory, Washington, DC and Ft. Knox Medical Laboratory in Kentucky. At Ft. Knox, researchers determined the daily, prophylactic dose of atabrine needed to prevent malaria. Became severely ill from an unknown viral pneumonia being studied at Ft. Bragg.

He was discharged March 13, 1946, as corporal; received American Theater Ribbon, WWII Victory Medal and the Good Conduct Medal.

At war's end worked as pharmaceutical advertising executive. In 1957 worked at the National Institutes of Health and the Health Resources Administration, agencies of the U.S. Public Health Service. Started the NIH Record, the first and ongoing report on NIH research activities and served on the National Diabetes Advisory Board; Federal Advisory Committee, U.S. Science Exhibit, Seattle World's Fair; and the HRA Task Force to develop research initiatives for United Nations 1979 International Year of the Child.

Adler retired from USPHS, April 1984, as Deputy Chief, Division of Student Assistance. Married to Ruth, daughters, Alison and Linda, grandchildren, Jonathan and Jocelyn. Member of Post 59 and past department commander.

LEONARD DAVID ADLER, born Sept. 5, 1925. Joined U.S. Army Ft. Sheridan, IL in December 1943. Camp Campbell, KY, 1944, 110th Gen. Hosp., Univ. of Tennessee Medical School, Memphis, 1944 as X-ray tech. Sailed for England from Camp Miles Standish in June 1944 on USS *America*.

Military locations: 110th Gen. Hosp., Cheltenham, England, June 1944-March 1945, X-ray tech; sailed to France, 12th Reinf. Depot, Le Havre in infantry; March-May 1945, 28th Div., rifleman, France, Belgium, Luxembourg, Ger-

many; June 1945, 2nd Repl. Depot, Marseilles; July 1945, sailed to Panama, Ulithia, Atoll, Manila (USS *Monterey*), 305th Gen. Hosp., X-ray; October-November 1945, sailed to Japan, 27th Gen. Hosp., Tokyo and Japan, USS *Comfort*, hospital ship; November-May 1945, 5th Station Hosp., Iramagawa Japan (assigned to 5th AF) in charge of X-ray Dept.; May 1946 sailed from Japan to Seattle, Ft. Lewis, WA on USS *Swallow*).

Discharged May 11, 1946, Camp McCoy, WI, rank tech sergeant. Awards: Good Conduct, Presidential Emblem, Meritorious Unit Emblem with star, American Campaign Medal with star, Asiatic-Pacific Medal with star, EAME Campaign Medal with star, WWII Victory Medal, Army of Occupation Medal, Philippine Liberation Medal, Combat Infantry Badge and four Overseas Bars.

MANFRED ADLER, born Kelsterbach, Germany on Feb. 17, 1928. Immigrated to USA (Connecticut) in June 1937. Upon graduating from Hillyer College, University of Hartford, enlisted in Army. Basic training Fort Knox, KY. Commissioned 1952. Served with 3rd Armd. Cav. Regt. 7th Army, Regensburg, Germany and 411th Civil Affairs, West Hartford, CT. Awards: Meritorious Service Medal, European Occupation, National Defense, American Defense, Army Reserve Comp. Graduate of Command and General Staff College, Ft. Leavenworth. Retired as lieutenant colonel.

Civilian Career: 34 years manufacturing, research and development engineering management, Pratt & Whitney aircraft Div. of United Tech. responsible for new manufacturing process. Have consulted, manufacturing tech. precision forging for several firms in the States and Europe. Chairman building committee of new synagogue; president (three years) synagogue; chairman, Boy Scout Committee; University Alumni Committee, past chairman, homecoming/reunion. Committees: Indian Guides, Indian Princess

Has three children and three grandsons.

HOWARD M. AISON, born in Amsterdam, NY, Oct. 12, 1945. Graduated with a BA degree in liberal arts at Syracuse University in 1967 and with a JD degree at Brooklyn Law School in 1970. Entered the U.S. Army in 1970 as a first lieutenant; schooled at Ft. Gordon, GA; Ft. Sill, OK; and Ft. Hood, TX. Was promoted to captain and served at the 52nd Avn. Bn. (Combat) in Pleiku, Vietnam.

Awards/Medals: Bronze Star for meritorious service. Was Montgomery County's Legal Aid Society Attorney from 1973-1975; Montgomery County, NY District Attorney from 1979-1985; and Montgomery County, NY, Judge from 1986 to present.

Past Capital District Council Commander, Jewish War Veterans 1989-1990; past Old Tyron Counties Council Commander VFW, 1991-1992; member of Jewish War Veterans Post 401; VFW Post 55; American Legion Post 39; and AMVETS Post 21.

Married to Margaret Havey Aison since 1979, they have two children, Jacob born in 1986 and Sarah born in 1981.

HARRY N. AIZENSTAT, born April 1, 1916, Springfield, MA. Graduated West Springfield, MA High School; BA, American International College; and MA from Clark University. Employed as a DOD buyer, Springfield Armory, 1937-1966; Westover AFB, 1966-1973; retired from Federal Civil Service in June 1973.

Entered the U.S. Army, December 1942; basic training, Camp Pickett, VA; assigned May 1943, 210th General Hospital, later 368th Station Hospital, Ft. Gulick, CZ. Discharged as tech 4 in November 1945. Recalled to active duty for the Korean War in September 1950 with 915th Mobile Army Surgical Hosp. and assigned to Camp Pickett, VA. Subsequently, transferred to 2114th ASU, Camp Pickett, VA as POM NCO. Assignment to French Indo-China in March 1951 was canceled.

Released in April 1952 as master sergeant. Awards/Medals: Good Conduct Medal, American Theater Victory Medal, WWII Victory Medal, National Defense Service Medal and Unit Citation.

He is married to Sarah Freedman. Member of JWV Post #26, Springfield, MA, since 1945, adjutant since 1952.

EDGAR ALEXANDER, born July 2, 1921, in Hamburg, Germany. Attended school in Altona, Germany; ejected from school at age 16 due to Nazi persecution. Escaped to England, 1938; emigrated to the U.S. in 1940 to Newark, NJ.

Drafted into the Army in 1942; assigned to 94th Inf. Div. at Camp Phillips, KS. Became U.S. citizen in 1943 at Salina, KS. Served with Co. G, 376th Regt. from basic training through battles in Brittany, Siegfried Line, Germany, Battle of the Bulge and the occupation in Germany and Czechoslovakia. At Camp Phillips won division light weight boxing title. Served G Co. as a 60mm mortar gunner and later as a section leader. Acted as interrogator and interpreter for his company commander during hostilities and occupation of Germany. Recipient of Bronze Star. Transferred October 1945 to 90th Inf. Div. for rotation to States.

Joined International Transportation and became a licensed ICC practitioner and traffic manager and worked in International Freight Forwarding companies until retirement in 1984. Active in US Army Reserve Transportation until 1965, retired as M/Sgt. (E-8).

Married Miriam Katz, 1951. Father of one set of twins, Audrey Ruth and Robert Alan. There are five grandchildren. Member of JWV Posts: W. Elin Unger #273, Newark, NJ, Sheldon Sheinfeld #311, South River, NJ and until his death in 1995, #133 New Brunswick. He held office as county commander and National Reparation and Memorial Officer.

Founded Kayak and Canoe Club of New York, a whitewater boat club in 1958. President, newsletter chairman and at time of his death, executive board member.

Served as President on NJ Chapter, 94th Inf. Div., Assoc., when national reunion was held in Atlantic City in 1975, served on the 94th Div. Assoc. Executive Council from 1974 until his death. Headed the Constitution and By Laws Committee from 1979-1985 and updated constitution in 1985. Served as National President of 94th Inf. Assoc. 1987-1988.

Assisted in establishing 94th Inf. Div. Peace Monument in the Saar-Moselle Triangle area in Germany, the only US Peace Monument on foreign soil. Participated in the ecumenical peace mass, in a Catholic Church in Germany in 1991 and 1994. Assisted in obtaining a Memorial Plaque for the division in Arlington National Cemetery, 1995.

Alexander died on March 17, 1995, in Israel, attending an Elderhostel.

SIDNEY ALINIKOFF, born Nov. 30, 1915, Wilkes-Barre, PA. Joined the U.S. Army April 11, 1944; received basic training at Camp Wheeler, GA; served with the 2nd Armd. Div. in Germany.

Awards/Medals: Combat Infantry Badge. Discharged April 11, 1945, as a private.

Married Aug. 6, 1939, he has three sons and three grandchildren. Semi-retired, he works in an athletic store.

ARTHUR ALPERT, born March 9, 1911, Lakewood, NJ. Earned BS and MBA degrees NYU. Entered military Oct. 5, 1942.

Served as assistant finance officer, Fousa Ft. Gulick and Rio Hata AB, Panama until June 1946.

Recalled to active duty August 1950. Assigned to Selective Service System. Became Deputy Director, NYC HQ. Retired as colonel Aug. 31, 1969. Awarded Legion of Merit for service, September 1959-August 1969.

Lives with his wife, Florence, at St. Pete Beach, FL.

ROBERT M. ALPERT (BOB), born on July 19, 1932, in Boston, MA. Enlisted in the USN in April 1952. Attended boot camp, Bainbridge, MD and elected "Honor Man" of the company. Completed *Electronic* School and assigned to aircraft carrier USS *Hornet* (CVA-12), 1953. Made two world cruises operating primarily in the Far East in the waters surrounding Korea and Formosa.

Awards/Medals: Good Conduct Medal, Navy Occupation Service Medal (Europe), National Defense Medal and China Service Medal. Discharged April 1956.

Attended Northeastern University, AE, BBA in engineering/management and MBA. Married Abby Schiff, have five children. Served as Brotherhood president, executive vice-president, board of directors, Tiferet Israel Synagogue (Dallas, TX) many civic rolls and currently commander of JWV Post #256.

WILLIAM I. ALTMAN, born Nov. 4, 1916, Holyoke, MA. Joined the USAAF in June 1942 with duties as flight radio operator. Stationed at Ft. Devens, Scott Field, IL; Avon Park, FL; Lake Charles, LA; Europe; Africa; and ETO.

Participated in the Battle of the Bulge and flew in supplies for battles in Europe and Great Britain.

Awards/Medals: three Battle Stars for Europe. Discharged Dec. 5, 1945, as staff sergeant.

He and his wife, Melba, have two children, Mark and Linda. He is currently semi-retired.

CHARLES ALTSMAN, born Sept. 16, 1923, Bronx, NY. Inducted in U.S. Army March 12, 1943. In Battle of Bulge Co. formed road block against German units in Monschau Forest. First Ord. Co. to cross the Rhine River. Reached Plauen, Germany near Czech border.

Awards/Medals: ETO Medal with three Bronze Stars. Was T/5 in 135th MM Ord. Co. from his induction to discharge Nov. 10, 1945.

Life member JWV and Museum. Served in every elected office of Post 603, LA District Council, Dept. of California including National Executive and Policy Committees. Currently, Dept. of California Centennial Chm. Received Man of the Year awards from Post, County, Department and outstanding Dept. Commander of the Year from National, special National Commander's award for years of service.

Married Mary, June 15, 1946. Has two married daughters, one grandson and two granddaughters. BBA degree from Pace College, NY. Retired after 50 years working as accountant, controller, treasurer, financial vice president and president of various corporations.

ED ANDISMAN, was drafted in September 1943, Philadelphia, PA. Had basic training in Indiantown Gap, PA. Shipped to Camp Van Dorn, MS, joined the newly formed 63rd Div. and put in HQ Btry of the 861st FA laying wire and working switchboard.

Shipped overseas, landed at Marseilles, France and then up to the front lines at Alsace-Lorraine (border of France and Germany). On line for about six-eight months, crossed the Danube River near Munich, Germany. Was right in front of Dachau Prison Camp and fed quite a few of the released people that were coming out of the camp.

Shipped back to the States June 1945 from Camp Lucky Strike, Le Havre and assigned to 2nd Div. for the invasion of Japan. After bombing of Japan, when war was over, was discharged as corporal T/5 and sent home in February 1946.

ABRAHAM ANSON, inducted on March 30, 1943, at New York City, Sent to Ft. Belvoir, VA and assigned to 949th Topographic Engr. Co. (Avn.) Attached to 3rd Tactical AD (USAAF) at Ft. Leonard Wood, MO as geodetic computer and aerial photo interpreter. In November 1943 moved to Esler Field, Bogalusa, LA, for training in swamp areas. Six months later moved to Ft. Carson, CO in Rocky Mountains. The 949th was sent to Guam November 1944 to prepare bombardment charts for Japan. Ordered to Ft. Belvoir, VA for OCS. March 1945 was commissioned a 2nd lieutenant, Engr. Cbt. Plt. leader.

Volunteered on V-E Day to remain in service to train engineer replacement troops. Transferred to the USAR in February 1946. During the ensuing 20 years, completed extensive extension courses, taught classes in engineering subjects and took two weeks active duty every year while carrying on a career of Topographic Engineer and Photogrammetrist for the U.S. Geological Survey for 11 years, transferred to the U.S. Army Topographic Engr. Ctr. in research and development for 17 years.

Last Reserve assignment, Lt. Col., Chief Planning Branch, TD MOS 07915, Directorate of Topography and Military Engrs., Chief of Engr., Washington, DC. Transferred to USAR Control Group (MOBDES), March 29, 1966, Retired Reserve.

JOSEPHINE L. JERUM ANTON, born Brooklyn, Feb. 19, 1916. Received BA from Brooklyn College; MA from Columbia Teachers College; three years night school at Brooklyn Law School. Left law school to join first WAAC recruits in Des Moines, IA. Married PFC Irving Anton in Des Moines. Accepted first OCS class from the ranks and remained there training new recruits until March 1943.

In Ft. Devens served temporary commands including a Black company. June 1943 transferred to HQ, 2nd AF as commander, WAAC Co., Colorado Springs; 98% of her command re-enlisted in WAC, one of the highest in the country. She became first lieutenant.

In 1945 opened an office equipment outlet in Richmond Hill Queens with her husband. They retired to Florida in 1971. Mother of three children and grandmother of six. After husband's death in 1980, moved to Boca Raton and joined Post 459. First woman commander of the Post from 1988-1989. In 1992 received the Harry Mazey Hospital Award from Dept. of Florida, mainly for work with multiple sclerosis wheelchair veterans. In June 1993 became first woman commander, Department of Florida.

ROSE HELIG APPLEBAUM, born June 14, 1914, Vineland, NJ. Alliance Grammar School, Vineland HS, Bridgeton Hospital, Bridgeton, NJ School of Nursing and Charity Hospital School of Anesthesia, New Orleans, LA. Enlisted, Atlanta, GA in the ANC, Oct. 1, 1942.

Awards/Medals: Bronze Star. Discharged Dec. 21, 1945, as captain.

Served in the 1st Army, unit awards for Normandy, Northern France, Central Europe, Ardennes and Rhineland Campaigns. Unit mobilized at Camp Shelby, arrived July 26, 1943 for desert maneuvers at Camp Pilot Knob, CA until Dec. 12, 1943. Departed for England in convoy, Dec. 29, 1943.

Their were 10 evacuation hospitals in the first Army that leap frogged. Patients were transferred to England as they were in a new set-up every 10 days. Helped treat 3,964 patients, 258 deaths. Experiences: seasick coming and going; horrors of Buchenwald; making gallons of penthohal for anesthesia; tarp falling on nurses during a sandstorm on desert maneuvers (quite often); all nurses from evacuation units "stranded in Marseilles" as captains would not let them on ships for fear they would fraternize with servicemen. Arrived in States Oct. 12, 1945. Retired in all ways.

IRVING W. ARKIN, born in December 1899. Attended Putman School and graduated from Central High School and Central City Business School. Employed as a salesman at Philips Jones Corp. Also worked at the New York State unemployment Ins. office. Was in the U.S. Army. He died in May 1953 at the age of 53.

NAT D. ARLAN, born April 9, 1917, New York City, NY; entered the U.S. Army Sept. 10, 1943, as light tank driver. Military stations include Camp Upton, Ft. Knox; battles and campaigns in Central Europe, Normandy, Northern France and Rhineland.

Memorable experiences were crossing into Germany with the 3rd Armd. Div. during the High Holiday of October 1944; on special assignment in Antwerp and hit by V-2 rocket; and when a V-I landed about a mile away, harmless, but made a big crater in the field. Another memorable experience was returning home after 18 months overseas; his son was three months old when he left and nearly three years old when he returned and asked, "Mommy who is that man?"

Awards/Medals: Good Conduct Medal, American Service Medal, EAME Service Medal and the WWII Victory Medal. Discharged Dec. 18, 1945.

Married with two children and seven grandchildren, he is retired and lives in Brooklyn, NY.

HYMIE ARNESTY, spent most of civilian life in Los Angeles, CA. Graduated Fairfax HS in 1942. Was a two year varsity letterman in gymnastics and set long standing world intersholastic record in rope climbing. Elected to Ephebian Society, scholastic honorary organization. Joined U.S. Army, Feb. 11, 1943. Basic training at Camp Polk, LA with 6th Armd. Div.

Shipped out from Northern California for New Guinea and assigned to 25th Inf. Div. Received special TDY assignment to HQ DET 1st Corps for invasion of the Philippines, then occupation of Japan.

Awards/Medals: American Campaign Medal, Asiatic-Pacific Medal, Philippine Liberation Ribbon, Good Conduct,

Bronze Star Medal and WWII Victory Medal. Discharged from WWII, enlisted in the USAR, March 21, 1946, discharged, Feb. 13, 1949, enlisted Feb. 14, 1949, in the Army-Korean War.

Joined the Reception Center at Ft. Ord, classification and assignment. Last six months of tour, he trained to be an escort officer, representing the U.S. Government, bringing back the war dead to their families for their final resting place. The Army needed master sergeants to volunteer for this special assignment. Discharged Sept. 16, 1952, as master sergeant.

Worked in toy industry for 36 years as an outside salesman, for Pensick & Gordon. Received salesman of the year award five times. Inducted in Toy Hall of Fame, by Western Toy & Hobby Representative Assoc., March 5, 1995, at Pomona Toy Show.

Retired in 1984 and does volunteer work. Active member of the JWV, Myron B. Sutton, Hollywood Post since 1946.

HERBERT ARON, born May 4, 1933, in New York City, NY. Drafted June 1953 into the U.S. Army. Stationed at Camp Polk, LA and Ft. Riley, KS.

Discharged in April 1955 as a sergeant (only five draftees made sergeant in entire corps of which two were Jewish and he was one of them).

Awards/Medals: National Defense Medal, Good Conduct Medal and Sharp Shooter Medal.

A financial consultant and college instructor, he is married to the former Doris Wald and they have four children.

STANLEY E. ARONOFF, born Dec. 30, 1923, Baltimore, MD. After attending schools in Baltimore, he entered Union College, Schenectady, NY in 1941. After volunteering for the Navy, he was called to active duty in the V-12 Program on July 1, 1943; returned to Union College where he graduated with a BS in EE in February 1944; attended Midshipman's School, Columbia University and was commissioned an ensign, USNR in June 1944. He went to Anti-Submarine Warfare School in Miami and the West Coast Sound School in San Diego.

Assigned to the USS *Eaton* (DD-510), participated in action in the South Pacific, Philippines and Borneo. After V-J Day, the *Eaton* was sent to Shanghai and Aronoff was prize master of Japanese LST-144 for several weeks.

Memorable experiences include being in first American convoy up Yangtze River in 1945 and meeting a Jewish woman in Hanrow who owned a restaurant and made Shabbos dinner for the servicemen.

Was granted emergency leave in November 1945 because of his father's heart attack. Returning home he married the former Millie Kellman. Aronoff was released to inactive duty on Dec. 22, 1945, and discharged as lieutenant jg on Oct. 5, 1953.

Awards/Medals: Asiatic-Pacific, two Battle Stars and the Victory Medal.

He joined his father in the Southern Plate Glass Co. After completing a career in Baltimore and Washington, he and Millie moved to Tampa, FL in March 1994 to start new career. He and Millie have five children and four grandchildren.

WILLIAM ARONSON, served in the U.S. Army from Oct. 12, 1943-Nov. 12, 1945. He entered the service in Boston, MA with the rank of PFC.

He received his basic training in the infantry at Camp Devens, MA and Camp Croft, SC.

He sailed overseas on the USS *Stephen Douglas* from Newport News, VA; arrived at Oran, North Africa and served with the 34th Div. in Africa, Italy, France and Germany.

Awards/Medals: Bronze Star, Silver Star, Good Conduct Medal and Combat Infantryman's Badge. He visited Paris, Rome, Naples and Edinburgh, Scotland. *Submitted by Max Sigal.*

ALBERT ASCHER, born March 23, 1912, in Poland. Enlisted Dec. 30, 1942, the USAAF; served with the 13th Air TF, 42nd Med. BG, 75th BS. Stationed in Banika Island, Solomons, Palawan Island, Philippines and New Guinea.

Battles/Campaigns: Bismark Archipelago, Luzon, New Guinea, Northern Solomons, Western Pacific and Southern Philippines.

Memorable Experiences: selected crew including group commander; returning from a mission and finding it necessary to ditch in enemy territory; engineer obtains food in jungle as per information during intelligence briefing; engineer suggested engraving commander's name on beach, resulting in recon personnel being lead to location of lost crew.

Awards/Medals: Asiatic-Pacific Service Medal, Good Conduct Medal, Philippines Liberation Medal and WWII Victory Medal. Discharged Dec. 22, 1945, as sergeant, bomb-sight specialist.

Retired with wife, Ruth, to Palm Beach County from Long Beach, NY. He currently does volunteer work at the Veterans Administration Clinic at the local hospital.

THEODORE ASNER (TED), born Aug. 4, 1916, Detroit, MI, son of Jacob and Sarah. Schooled in NYC through high school. Did army service from 1941-1945. Served as demolition specialist and later as staff sergeant in the QM Corps in England.

Married Sylvia Shapiro, Nov. 18, 1939, in New York. Had three children, Barry, Cheryl and Batley (Bart), and five grandchildren: Jodi 27, Alicia 25, Lara 17, Brian 15, Michael 13 and great-grandson Trevor (as of Sept. 1, 1995). He died

Dec. 4, 1985, and is buried in Costa Mesa, CA. *Submitted by Henrietta Henderstein.*

SAM AUERBACH, born in Akron, OH in 1915. Married wife, Rebecca in 1939. Their son was born in June, 1943 and Sam was drafted into the Army in August, 1943. Sent to Camp Wolters, TX for basic training as a rifleman replacement.. He was shipped overseas to England, Oct. 1944 crossed over to France Jan. 1, 1945. Auerback participated in the Battle of the Bulge with the 78th "Lightning" Infantry Division. He was assigned as a runner to Co. G, 309th Regiment.

He was discharged in Oct. 1945 with rank of Tech. 5. He was awarded the Combat Infantry Badge, Purple Heart, Bronze Star, European Campaign Medal and Good Conduct Medal.

Auerback worked for Goodyear Tire & Rubber Co. and began a regular practice of donating blood to the Red Cross, giving 11 gallons. He joined the JWV Post #62 in Akron in 1950. He has been Post Adjutant and Post Commander and also Dept. of Ohio Quartermaster. He also belongs to Veterans of the Battle of the Bulge, 78th "Lightning" Infantry Division Veterans Associations. After retirement in 1980, he and his wife moved to Arizona. He is now a member of Friedman-Paul Post #201 JWV in Tucson.

MORITZ AUGENSTEIN, born 1823, Old Buda, Hungary. Enlisted August 1861 in the U.S. Army; served with Co. D, 52nd Regt., New York Volunteers Inf. Stationed in Fairfax, VA in the winter of 1861-1862.

He suffered from rheumatism and paralysis from exposure to winter weather. Discharged Sept. 12, 1862, as second master sergeant quartermasters.

After the war he lived in Washington, DC and married Teresia. Augenstein passed away in 1892. *Submitted by his great-great-granddaughter Therese C. Wertheimer.*

MEYER P. AVERS, born Chicago, IL, Jan. 28, 1928. BA in history from DePaul University in 1949 and MA in history from Northwestern University in 1950. A teacher, counselor and assistant principal with the Chicago Public Schools, he retired in 1992 after 38 years of service. He married Revelle in 1951.

Drafted into the U.S. Army in 1952; basic training at Ft. Leonard Wood, MO. Overseas service in Korea with the 8th Army Machine Records Unit, 1953-1954.

Awards/Medals: National Defense Medal, Korean Service Medal with two Battle Stars and the United Nations Medal. He was discharged in 1954 as sergeant.

He is a member of the Jewish War Veterans Private Sam Neivelt Post 407; life member of the American Legion; past commander, 1st District, Illinois; and past commander, Board of Education Post 471; life member of VFW; and past commander of Louis D. David Post 235.

MAURICE AVIDAN, M.D., joined the U.S. Army and served in WWI with the Medical Corps as a surgeon. Discharged with the rank of captain. His brother, Samuel, also served in the U.S. Army, WWI and his sister, Rose, served as yeoman first class, 3rd Naval District.

ROSE AVIDAN, born Oct. 25, 1892, Newark, NJ. Joined the U.S. Navy on Aug. 23, 1918, New York City. Served with 3rd Naval District, Great Lakes. Discharged July 15, 1919, as yeoman first class. Brother, Maurice served in the Army Medical Corps and brother, Samuel, served in the U.S. Army, both during WWI.

Married William H. Hasburg, Veteran of WWI, 2nd Lieutenant, Corps of Engineers. She passed away Dec. 15, 1989.

SAMUEL AVIDAN, born on Aug. 25, 1895. Joined the U.S. Army July 4, 1917, serving during WWI. Discharged on June 17, 1919. He passed away Oct. 14, 1973. He was an attorney. His brother, Maurice, a renowned surgeon, served in WWI in the Medical Corps with rank of captain. His sister, Rose, served in WWI as yeoman first class, 3rd Naval District.

SAMUEL BABISCHKIN, inducted in USN on Feb. 12, 1943. Arrived at Sampson Naval Station, NY on Feb. 13, 1943. Sent to Cooking School in Charleston, SC for 16 week course as a chef. Promoted to 3rd class petty officer, volunteered for PT boat duty and trained in Melville, RI for three months.

Assigned PT No. 217 Squadron 15, the Red Falcon, in the Mediterranean Theater off the coast of Africa with bases in Tunisia, Bizerte, Bastia, Corsica. Experienced numerous missions with ship's dog Parad Musket. He remembers the invasion of Southern France when he asked his skipper if he should leave Musket behind. He looked him square in the face and said, "Of course not! That dog goes wherever we go." Shortly afterwards, he got his orders to return to the States and received permission for Musket to accompany him.

The war ended and his PT boat was sent to Chicago for Navy Day. Discharged on Nov. 25, 1945, Lido Beach, Long Island.

Married Ann on Oct. 15, 1944.

MILTON BACKAL, born Jan. 13, 1929. He was drafted April 17, 1951, into the U.S. Army, serving with Co.G, 27th Inf. APO 25. Stations included Fort Hood, TX, and Korea, where he participated in battle on the front line.

Awards/Medals: KSM "/iBBSS, CIB, and UNSM.

He was discharged Jan. 19, 1953, with the rank of private first class.

He is married and has one daughter. Today he is retired.

JOE BACKFIELD, born on Feb. 12, 1923. He enlisted in the Marines in 1942 and was shipped to Bougainville in 1943. He participate in reconnaissance and light combat patrols as part of Company B, First Battalion, Third Marine Division. Backfield also served in Guadalcanal, New Caledonia and Guam.

It was on Guam, he remembers, when the Marines had begun a sweep of the island. "It was a Bonzai moon - a full moon when the Japs usually attack. We ran into crack Imperial Japanese Marines. There was one Jap who just kept coming. So I just kept firing until he dropped."

Backfield remembers about a dozen kills. "Plenty of times I had to open fire. I never had a problem with that. They were the enemy ... no face, no family. Just the enemy." For Joe, proving he was the toughest soldier was his way of standing up to anti-Jewish sentiment.

After his discharge in 1945, Backfield re-enlisted in the 1950s and made the military his career. He received a Bronze Star during the Vietnam War.

SIMON S. BACOLA, born in New York City in 1922, and grew up in Astoria, LA. He enlisted in 1943 and did training with the 12th Armored Div. 56th Infantry, at Ft. Knox, KY. After training he transferred to the 17th Armored Div. and went overseas to E.T.O. and was killed.

He was awarded the Silver Star, for gallantry in action on Dec. 10, 1944, where his platoon was pinned down by the fire of eight machine guns, leaving his cover he crawled to several wounded men to render them first aid, even pulling another wounded man back to cover with him. He also received an Oak-leaf Cluster for gallantry in action on Jan. 16, 1945, when in a similar situation he left his fox hole and made his way to the side of his squad leader who had been wounded, (who was later evacuated). Private First Class Bacola was last seen rendering aid to his friend. *Submitted by Isaac Bacola, his brother.*

ROBERT "T" BAER, (S1C SK), USNR, born in Newark, NJ, Nov. 9, 1925. Graduated Arts High School, Newark, June 1943. Entered U.S. Navy Feb. 21, 1944. Honorably discharged at Camp Shelton, VA, June 1, 1946.

After completing boot camp at NTS Sampson, NY, graduated Storekeeper School upon completing 16-week course.

Assigned to U.S. Navbarracks, NSD, Norfolk, VA. Later assigned to Cub 16, USNABPD, San Bruno, CA.

After serving approximately six months as administration office clerk in San Bruno the war ended, he was then assigned to a group headed for CBI Theatre, but orders were changed and he was headed back to Norfolk.

Graduated Thomas A. Edison College in 1977 with a BA after having attended Rutgers U. some 30 years earlier on the G.I. Bill.

Now retired, living at the Jersey Shore some 44 years. Keeps busy being a Lifetime JWV member; JWV Post #125 Publicity Chairman; U.S. Navy League; Sampson WWII Navy Vets; F&AM Lodge #247; "200" Club; Thomas A. Edison Alumni, et al.

ALAN M. BAGULLY, born in Brooklyn, NY, on Oct. 6, 1940. Moved to Charlotte, NC, at age 13. Commissioned second lieutenant in Army Intelligence and Security from North Carolina State ROTC. Entered Active Duty August 1963. Initial Infantry training at Ft. Benning followed by Crypto School at Ft. Devens. Highly classified assignments included CONUS, Panama, and Argentina with a lot of TDY to worldwide field teams.

Southeast Asia and Combat Intelligence Schools the summer of 1968 were followed by a year in Vietnam as OIC of an Engineer Tech Intel Section with theater-wide responsibility for enemy mines, booby traps, tunnels, and bunkers. Wounded with shrapnel in both hands while disarming a booby trap.

Served last two years at the National Security Agency at Fort Meade. Released from Active Duty with permanent grade of captain in July 1971.

Decorations include the Bronze Star, National Defense Service Medal, Vietnam Service Medal, Vietnam Campaign Medal, Vietnam Technical Service Award 1st Class, and the RVN Engineer Badge.

Married to Rachel since 1970. Daughter Miriam graduates high school in 1995; son Michael is a West Point Cadet, class of 1996. Self-employed in sales. Member JWV Post 112.

STANLEY B. BALBACH, born in Normal, IL, on Dec. 26, 1919. Resided in Chenoa, Chicago and Champaign/Urbana, IL. Service commenced in the Cavalry ROTC, at the University of Illinois in 1936, commissioned as a second lieutenant in 1940, and called into active duty at Ft. Riley, KS, April 30, 1942. He taught horse cavalry riding and tactics until August 1942, when horse cavalry training was terminated and cavalry officers were assigned to teach infantry replacements for about 90 days. His next assignment in August of 1942, was to Camp Gordon, GA, to serve with 692nd Tank Destroyer Battalion. This tour ended, after Balbach was sent to explosives school in Texas, with a transfer to pilot training in Montgomery, AL; Jackson, MS; Greenville, MS; and Dothan, AL. The rest of the war Balbach taught flying at Newport, AR; Moultrie, GA, and Bryan, TX, which was the Central Instrument Instructors School for the Air Force.

Balbach left active duty in December of 1945 and continued training on a reserve basis for approximately 10 years, while stationed at Chanute Air Force Base in Illinois.

Balbach was married on May 22, 1944, to Sarah Troutt Witherspoon of Jonesboro, AR, and five children were born of that marriage. The first, Stanley Byron Balbach Jr., at Bryan, TX, and the others - Nancy Ann Fehr, Barbara C. Balbach, Edith Balbach and Jacob Balbach, were all born in Urbana, as were his six grandchildren.

Balbach was licensed as an attorney April 30, 1942, and practiced law in Hoopeston from 1945-48, and in Urbana from 1948 to date. He is a member of the Local Reserve Officers Association, which is a social organization and his main activity, other than the practice of law, is as a community supporter through the Chamber of Commerce and life long service to the Champaign County, Chicago, IL, and American Bar Associations.

HERMAN K. BALDINGER, born Sept. 29, 1918, in Passaic, NJ. He graduated in Passaic. He enlisted in the U.S. Army on April 15, 1941. Service included: Ft. Dix, NJ; Ft. Bragg, NC; Ashchurch, England; Utah Beach Caen, France; Marseilles, France; Krupp Factory, Germany. He participated in battles in Europe.

Memorable experience is delivering and leading convoy of loaded half tracks from North France to Gen. Patton at his HQ Fontainebleau (Paris).

Awards/Medals: Good Conduct and Europe VE Day.

He was discharged Oct. 21, 1945, with the rank of tech. sergeant.

He married Jean (Nee Goodman) and has two married daughters and four grandchildren. He has served as Post Department Commander, NJ JWV; member of American Legion; VFW serving on County Veteran Service Advisory Council. Presently he is hosting a radio program.

JOSEPH LOUIS BALE AND JOSEPH LOUIS BALE, (BIG JOE & LITTLE JOE) were born in Detroit, MI. Big Joe in August 1923 and Little Joe in January 1924, both named after their paternal grandfather. Famous for their athletic abilities. All City and championship teams in baseball and basketball. Their sports feats consistently made sports page headlines. They were inseparable. While roommates at Michigan State College in 1942, World War II separated them. Little Joe joined the Army. The week of his 21st birthday in Southern France, while heroically destroying enemy tanks with his bazooka, was mortally wounded. For this heroism, Little Joe was awarded the Distinguished Service Cross posthumously.

At the same time in 1942, Big Joe joined the Navy, V-12 program; then Columbia University Midshipmen's School (NY); amphibious training base Coronado, CA; USS *Dickens* (APA 161) boat officer and first division officer. Philippines, Tinian, Iwo Jima, Okinawa. Beachmaster on V-J Day at Yokohama, Japan. Beachmaster post-war (September 1945) Kure-Hiroshima. Magic Carpet. Senior watch officer (3rd officer) of *Dickens* last few months before decommissioning of vessel.

In memory of Little Joe dormitory building at Michigan State College; playground in Detroit, MI; Pfc. Joseph L. Bale Post #474, JWV, which became largest Post in Department of Michigan.

Big Joe served in many capacities in Bale Post. Commander a few different years. Department of Michigan Man of the Year, Editor of Department publications, many times. Commander of Department of Michigan 1973-74 and 1974-75. NEC, "Top Commander" Fifth Region. Awarded honors by Allied Veterans organizations for spear heading Vietnam Veterans Michigan bonus successfully. Life Member of JWV for 50 years. Now consultant to Post 101, where he resides in Ventura, CA, since 1981. *Submitted by Mr. Joseph Bale.*

MARTIN BALICK, born Sept. 17, 1917, in Wilmington, DE. Joined the service in 1940, serving in the Army Infantry at Ft. Pitt; Ft. Bragg, NC; African Campaign; and ending in Hattiesburg, MS. He fought in five major battles.
Awards/Medals: Bronze Star and Silver Star.

He was discharged in February 1945, with the rank of sergeant.

Married Nov. 25, 1943, and has two daughters, one son, and six grandchildren. Retired from state of Delaware as a Purchasing Agent in 1982. He died in February 1993.

LEWIS BALNICK

ARTHUR B. BANGEL, born Nov. 16, 1913. Enlisted in the U.S. Army Nov. 21, 1942. Assigned to transportation. Stationed at the Port of New York (MP), England, France, Germany and Austria. Participated in battles of Ardennes, Central Europe, Rhineland, Normandy and Northern France.

Memorable experience was operating a Welfare Program and Refugee Camp.

Awards/Medals: American Service Metal, WWII Victory, Good Conduct, and EAME. Discharged on Dec. 5, 1945, with rank of sergeant.

Married, has son, daughter and five grandchildren. Retired as a sculptor, teacher and counselor.

HARRY D. BARAZ, born March 15, 1920, in New York City, NY. Enlisted in 1937 New York National Guard, and 1941 Regular Army Air Force. He served with the 9th Air Force in Europe. Military locations includes Langley Field, VA; Gander, Newfoundland; England; France; and Holland. Participated in battles in the air over Europe and sub patrol B17s before war and B26s in Europe.

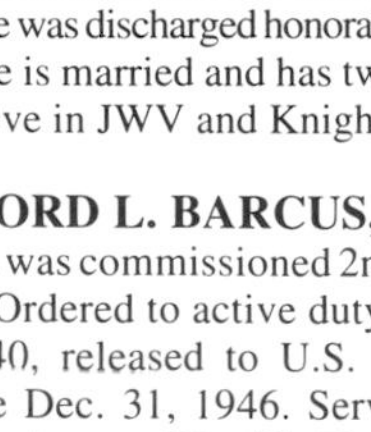
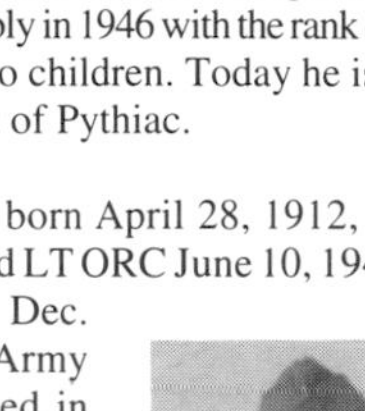

Memorable experiences include three crashes, low level mission over sub pens and flak and air attacks over France in B-26s.

Awards/Medals: Air Medal and Cluster - European Theater.

He was discharged honorably in 1946 with the rank of S/Sgt.

He is married and has two children. Today he is retired and active in JWV and Knight of Pythiac.

SANFORD L. BARCUS, born April 28, 1912, Elmira, NY. He was commissioned 2nd LT ORC June 10, 1940, U.S. Army. Ordered to active duty Dec. 27, 1940, released to U.S. Army Reserve Dec. 31, 1946. Served in the American and Pacific Theaters, commanded units in U.S. Army and U.S. Army Reserve. Graduated from U.S. Army Command and General Staff School.

He retired from the U.S. Army April 28, 1972, with the rank of colonel.

Member of the Southern Tier Post 124 JWV, formerly post commander.

MEYER BARGTEIL (MIKE), born in the Ukranian town of Luber in 1910 and moved to Baltimore, MD, in 1912, with his parents and three siblings.

During his youth, Mike became involved in Zionist activity and joined a Gordonia "garin" where he was in charge of fundraising. In 1932 Gordonia received a limited number of immigration passes to Palestine, so Mike and Hannah - members of the same garin - decided to marry in order to increase the size of the group going to Palestine. Once they were in Palestine, a "get" would take effect. Due to serious family illness, however, their departure was postponed, and they remained a married couple, in time the parents of four children.

Mike served in the U.S. Army during the Second World War, traveling with thirteen other men in his "own" pullman car throughout the United States, instructing troops on how to arm and disarm mines and booby traps. After the War, he established a chain of motels in the Washington D.C. area. The Bargteils settled in Jerusalem in 1971, and immediately became involved in communal affairs, notably the AACI (Association of Americans and Canadians in Israel) and the Moreshet Yisrael Synagogue. In 1973 they established the Jerusalem Scholarship Fund to provide stipends to high-school children who came from families where someone had fallen or been wounded in the War. To date, the Scholarship Fund has distributed over $1,000,000.

It is said that at any given time there are 36 "tzadikkim" (righteous people) in the world. Mike must surely be numbered among them.

IRVING O. BARKER, in September 1942, Irving O. Barker was drafted into the U.S. Army from his hometown of Wilson, NC. Before leaving home, he went to a nearby military installation and bought a complete uniform for a second lieutenant. Private Barker completed basic training at Camp Breckinridge, KY, and was the first soldier in his unit selected for Officer Candidate School. He was sent to OCS at Ft. Benning, GA, was graduated and appointed a second lieutenant and then volunteered for Airborne Training.

His first assignment was as a platoon leader in the newly activated 88th Glider Inf. Regt., 13th Abn. Div. The division was sent into the ETO in late 1944 where Lt. Barker served in a series of organizational assignments to include several assignments in logistical support roles in the combat areas of operation. In 1946 Lt. Barker voluntarily left the Army to attend the University of North Carolina and obtained his BS degree. In 1951 Captain Barker was recalled to active duty (Korean War) and served initially as an instructor at the Infantry School, Ft. Benning, GA.

Volunteered Korean War duty and was assigned to the 2nd Infantry Division, where he was placed in command of Company A, 9th Inf. Regt. Capt. Barker was later assigned as Operations Officer (S-3), 1st Bn., 9th Inf. Regt. On return from Korea Capt. Barker was assigned as ROTC Instructor at Drexel University in Philadelphia. Capt. Barker voluntarily departed the Army in 1954 to engage in a business venture.

Recalled as a major during the Cuban Missile Crisis and was assigned as Commanding Officer, 13th Psychological Operations Battalion. U.S. Army Special Warfare Center, Ft. Bragg, NC In 1962, Major Barker attended the Command and General Staff College. He was promoted to LTC while at C&GSC. Following graduation from C&GSC, LTC Barker was assigned to the 7th PSYOP Group on Okinawa. While on Okinawa, LTC Barker served as president of the local chapter of B'nai B'rith. From Okinawa LTC Barker was assigned to duty on the Army General Staff in the Pentagon, Office of the Deputy Chief of Staff for Operations.

Two years later LTC Barker volunteered for duty in Vietnam and served as commander of the 6th Psyop Battalion in Bien Hoa and later as deputy commander of the 4th Psyop Group. On return from Vietnam, LTC Barker was assigned to Combat Developments Command at Ft. Belvoir, VA. He was promoted to colonel in 1970.

Colonel Barker retired from the Army in 1972 after 30 years of Federal Service. His awards included the Legion of Merit w/Oak Leaf Cluster, Bronze Star Medal, Combat Infantry Badge, Air Medal, Meritorious Service Medal, Army Commendation Medal, Army General Staff Badge, and Campaign Medals. In 1993, Colonel Barker was inducted into the Officer Candidate School Hall of Fame.

Colonel Barker and his wife Helen (of London, England) currently live in Fayetteville, NC.

JAMES W. BARNARD, Captain, USAF, born in Chicago, IL, July 24, 1942. Graduated from Wayland Academy, Beaver Dam, WI; Bradley University, Peoria, IL, 1965; commissioned second lieutenant USAF, June 1965. Served at Malmstrom Air Force Base, Great Falls, MT, 1965-68.

Married to Mirian, two daughters, Deborah and Michelle. Sole proprietor, leather goods business, Littleton, CO.

MORTON JOHN BARNARD, Lt. Col. JAGC Rtd. USA, born Chicago, IL; March 22, 1905; graduated Wayland Academy, Beaver Dam, WI, 1922; University of Chicago, PhB 1926, JD 1927. Commissioned second lieutenant, F.A.Res 1926. Active duty, Jan. 1, 1942; Captain, comdg., Signal Maintenance Co., Borinquen Field, P.R. and Service Battery, 22d FA Bn, P.R.; Div. HQ 42d (Rainbow) Division, June 1943 - August 1945; service in Europe as part of 7th Army Division liberated Dachau 1945. Completed active duty at Ft. Sheridan, IL, June 1946. Subsequent service in Judge Advocate Revenue Unit. Married to Eleanor; one son, James. In practice of law in Chicago. Member, Rainbow Division Veterans; Jewish War Veterans.

KENNETH BARNES, born in Kingston, NY, on June 7, 1934. Volunteered for service, inducted into U.S. Army Oct. 8, 1953. Basic Training at Ft. Dix, NJ, and sent to Ft. Sheridan, IL.

Assigned to 22nd Group, 45th Brigade, 49th AAA Heavy Gun Bn. Skokie, IL, completed training at Brigade Electronics School, Ft. Sheridan, IL, Range Officer and Operations School, Navy Pier Chicago, IL. The 22nd Group was called the "Steel Ring," its mission to protect the northern border of U.S.

Attained rank of corporal and converted to SPC 3, primary MOS, Radar Fire Control Specialist.

Radar instructor at Camp Haven, WI, trained Michigan National Guard for their mission in the "Steel Ring."

Received commendations as instructor, National Defense and Good Conduct Medals. Honorable discharge Oct. 7, 1955.

Graduated Union University, Albany College of Pharmacy under the Korean Bill. Married Elsa in 1958, three children Kirk, Kym and Keri. Retired in Florida, member JWV Post 196.

HAROLD BARON, born Sept. 21, 1922, in Brooklyn, NY. Enlisted in the USAF served as a navigator with the 8th Air Force stationed in Knettishall, England.

As part of the 388 Bomb Group, navigated a B17 for 35 missions. Targets included Berlin, Munich, Frankfort, Dresden, Leipzig and Hamburg. During the Berlin Raid, the plane received 40 flak holes and was forced down in Belgium, landed on English field and later returned to England.

Decorations: E.T.O. Ribbon with three battle stars, Air Medal with four oak leaf clusters and Presidential Citation.

Discharged as a first lieutenant in November 1945.

Married to Esther in July 1945, two children, Steven and Judy and five grandchildren.

Worked as a junior high school principal in New York City. Retired in 1980. Spends winters in West Palm Beach, FL, and summers in Rock Hill, NY.

Member of Post 206 and past commander of Mountain District Council, Department of New York.

JEROME BARON, born Buffalo, NY, Feb. 15, 1920. Joined U.S. Navy, Jan. 27, 1942. Discharged Jan. 23, 1946. Discharged with rank of Pharmacist Mate First Class

Medals: Bronze Star for bravery on Saipan and Tinian Islands; Purple Heart: Wounded on Iwo Jima Feb. 19, 1945; Presidential Unit Citations, two; Navy Commendation, one; Good Conduct Medal; Asiatic Pacific with four battle stars.

After six months training as a hospital corpsman he was transferred to the 3rd Battalion, Twenty-fifth Marines, Fourth Marine Division as a corpsman with an infantry company. Besides the three invasions mentioned above, he also was in on the invasion of Roi-Namur in the Marshall Islands. As a first-aid corpsman with the infantry, he had many close calls treating the wounded where they fell.

After the War he was a postal employee, for 17 years he was supervisor and retired in 1975, after 26 years in the U.S. Postal service, his four years in the Navy counted towards his 30 years for retirement.

His parents had five sons (all served in WWII): Samuel in the Air Force, Robert in Army (Europe), Harry in Army Air Force (Pacific), George in Navy (South America Base).

In retirement they traveled, he did a great deal of volunteer work, and still does…and played golf as much as he could.

HERMAN N. BAROUCH, born Aug. 6, 1916, in New York City. Graduated Class of 1937 (BBA) CCNY School of Business (Baruch College). Drafted Jan. 28, 1942, U.S. Army. Basic Training - Ft. McLellan, AL. Assigned to HQ Infantry School, Ft. Benning, GA. Appointed warrant officer junior grade Oct. 7, 1942. Then assigned to HQ OCS, Australia, assistant adjutant. OCS graduate and commissioned nearly 4,000, second lieutenants who were assigned to units in Southwest Pacific. OCS closed after VE Day in June 1945. Assigned personnel section, Special Troops GHQ in Manila.

He separated from the service in November 1945 as chief warrant officer.

Self-employed in garment industry 1946-1982, presently semi-retired. He is married and has three children (two sons, one daughter) and is a grandfather. Member of JWV Post 550.

SANFORD WILLIAM BARRON, born Jan. 13, 1928, in Cleveland, OH. Joined the U.S. Air Force in February 1946. Service included SAC San Antonia, Andrew Field, Washington D.C., Cleveland, OH, Bomber Plant.

He was discharged Aug. 15, 1947, with the rank of private first class.

SAUL BARRON, was a captain in the Air Force in WWII. His function as a flight test engineer was to develop systems on Air Force aircraft in order to operate at 65 degrees below zero, in Alaska. They experimented on prototype fighters, all the way through the heavy bombers, such as the P-47, P-38, B-24, B-17, etc. Their missions were sometimes costly. Of their group of 11 men, they lost four. They went on missions that he would strictly avoid today, but they were young then. He spent most of five winters in Alaska.

His detachment at Ladd Field, AK, included Allerdice, All American football player from Princeton, and Aubrey, who just died), who was a former president of CBS.

He enclosed a photo typical of himself in Alaska, alongside the wheel of a test bomber. He also served in the Korean Campaign. The second photo of himself is a current one in sunny Florida.

ARTHUR BART, born Aug. 10, 1925, in New York City. He was inducted into the U.S. Army in September 1943, serving with the 4th Infantry Division, Co. E. 8th Regiment, as a private first class.

Memorable experience includes being wounded in Cherbourg, France, on June 25, 1944.

Awards/Medals: Purple Heart and Bronze Star for Normandy Campaign.

He was discharged in September 1945.

He is married to his childhood sweetheart Marilyn Stecher. They have two sons, Michael and Andrew and now have three grandchildren (two boys and one girl) Greg, Justin and Isabel. He retired from accounting and is living part-time in Florida.

HAROLD T. BARTELL, LTC USA-RET., born Jan. 18, 1933, Brooklyn, NY. Distinguished Military Graduate, ROTC Cornell University, Commissioned 2LT 1955. Stateside assignments included: Ft. Hood, TX; Ft. Sill OK; Ft. Lee, VA; Brooklyn, NY; Cameron Station, VA; and the Pentagon. Oversees assignments: Heidelberg and Giessen, Germany; Athens, Greece; Bangkok, Thailand; Yongsan, Korea; Long Binh and Saigon Vietnam. Retired in November 1977 at Ft. Meyer, VA. Decorations: Legion of Merit, Bronze Star; Meritorious Service Medal with OLC and the Joint Service Commendation Medal with OLC. Also numerous service medals, ribbons, unit awards and the Army General Staff Badge.

Married to Leona. Son Arthur, LTC USA and daughter Lisa, DA Civilian. Three grandsons and a granddaughter. Employed by Unisys Corporation. A member of JWV Post 589.

MAX BARTH, born Oct. 23, 1926, in Newark, NJ. Enlisted in Navy at the age of 17, inducted Sept. 15, 1944. Boot training and Navigation & Signal School at Bainbridge, Maryland.

Assigned to the USS *Topeka* CL 67, a light cruiser, which was a flagship for a group of cruisers, part of a large armada of destroyers, cruisers, and battleships whose function were to protect the large carriers that were making air strikes against the Japanese homeland. He was promoted to QM 3/c and his main wartime duties were helmsman and bridge lookout.

When the two atomic bombs were dropped they were off the coast of Japan, and with the sudden end of the war men were taken off their ship to police Tokyo until the Marines and Army could take over. Afterwards they returned to one of the islands to pick up several Jap officers who were responsible for war atrocities against the Americans that were prisoners of war. They were taken by them to Guam for trail and subsequent execution.

After the War he entered Rutgers College of Pharmacy, graduated in 1950, bought his own pharmacy which he owned for 39 years, and after a total of over 42 years practicing his profession he retired in September 1994.

He has been married to his wife Barbara since Sept. 8, 1951, and after their children grew up they worked together as a team in their pharmacy for the last 30 years. They have a daughter, Fern, married to Sterling, who have given them two grandchildren, Rachel and Jason, and they have a son Michael, married to Jodi, who have given them three more grandchildren, Adam, Jonathan and Sara.

ALVIN BASS, born in Buffalo, NY, on March 30, 1917. He entered the Army on May 27, 1943, and separated from the service on April 5, 1946. His first nine months of duty were spent in the States. He was stationed at Camp Hulen for basic, and he participated in maneuvers at Camp Campbell and

Camp Davis. The next two years were spent in England. He saw action in France, Belgium, Holland, and Germany. Their outfit was involved in the Rhineland and Ardennes Campaigns. His rank at the time of discharge was first sergeant.

His most memorable experience was during the Battle of the Bulge. To this day, he can clearly remember the confusion, misdirection, and crazy rumors that were floating around … and repeated.

At the present time, he is a proud father of two wonderful, married daughters, he has four grandchildren and is a widower. He is enjoying life during his retirement.

JULIAN BATLAN (BUD), a direct descendent of Jacob Barsimson, the first historically known North American Jewish settler, and a soldier in the Dutch militia, who arrived at New Amsterdam in 1654. In 1941 enlisted as an infantry volunteer, United States Army. Sent to Officers Candidate School August 1943. Assigned to the "Big Red One" 1st Infantry Division. Awarded 11 medals and decorations including the Silver Star, Bronze Star, Purple Heart with Oak Leaf Cluster, and three battle stars. Served as post adjutant, Fort Huachuca, AZ. Discharged July 1946 with the rank of captain.

Elected 1993-1994 Commander, Monmouth-Ocean County Council, and appointed Department of New Jersey Officer of the Day as well as State Chief Aide for Public Relations and Publicity. Joined Jewish War Veterans Elin-Unger Post 273 in 1946. Elected Junior Vice Commander Oglensky-Jackson Post 359. Founder, Charter Commander and Life Member of the Manalpan-Marlboro Post 972.

Other community service includes: president Eatontown Kiwanis International; chairman Chamber of Commerce; scoutmaster for 10 years, and then served as Police Explorer councilman, Boy Scouts of America.

Married to Shirley. Has three children and two grandchildren. Currently lives in Manalapan, NJ. President of Asset Management Associates.

ABRAHAM J. BAUM, Major DSC, born March 29, 1921, in New York, NY, enlisted as a private in December 1941. Assigned to the Second Armored Division. Graduated Armored Force OCS in November 1942. Assigned to Fourth Armored Division in January 1942, and to 10th Armored Infantry Battalion. Promoted to first lieutenant. March 1, 1944. Promoted to Captain Oct. 1, 1944. Held job as S2. Promoted to Major on April 15, 1945. Then became plans and training officer. Went overseas as second lieutenant in December 1943. Participated in five campaigns in the European Theater of Operations. Participated with Moshe Dayan and Teddy Kollek in the 1948 Israel War of Independence. (See *Warrior States-man, the Life of Moshe Dayan*, written by Robert Slater, published 1991 by St. Martins Press.)Has been awarded in addition to the Distinguished Service Cross the following decorations, etc. Silver Star with cluster, Bronze Star with Cluster, Purple Heart with three clusters, Distinguished Unit Citation and the Combat Infantry Badge.

He is the past president of the 4th Armored Association, Commander Army and Navy, Legion of Valor, Southern

California Chapter, also a life member of the VFW, member of the North County Post #385 Jewish War Veterans.

He now lives in San Diego, CA, is married and has four children and three grandchildren. He was the owner of a blouse manufacturer and retired in 1988.

ABRAHAM R. BAUM, Major, USAF, Ret., born Feb. 26, 1920, in New York, NY, (Manhattan). Education included BSS CCNY 1941, and MBA Baruch, 1961. Inducted into the U.S. Air Force on Feb. 6, 1942. Commissioned Feb. 4, 1943, from Aviation Cadet Program. Served as airborne electronics maintenance officer in England, France, Columbus AFB, MS, Belgium, Germany. Military locations and stations included England, France, Belgium, Holland, Luxembourg, Germany, (WWII) Japan, Korea. Post WWII Newark College of Engineering AFROTC instructor, Johnson Air Base, Japan, Osan AB, Korea.

Memorable experience includes 3rd Air Rescue Group Duty, Johnson AB Japan; 1953-1956, best duty assignment; 1950-1953, AFROTC instructor, Newark College of Engineering; touring Europe at the end of WWII while waiting stateside reassignment.

Awards/Medals: Good Conduct Medal, Victory Medal, American Campaign Medal, European Theater Medal, Presidential Unit Citation (2), (Europe and Japan) seven awards in total. Supported recapture of France, Belgium, Germany, Holland, Luxembourg.

He retired Jan. 31, 1963, with the rank of major.

Married Dec. 27, 1946, Ruth Demb, and has two sons, Richard (with IBM) and Barry (with AT&T). Richard born Ft. Dix, NJ, 1950, and Barry born Johnson AB, Japan, 1955. He is a retired accountant.

RUDOLF BAUM (RUDY), born in Frankfurt, Germany, April 11, 1915. Left Germany in 1936, and arrived in New York City on November 23. Drafted from Dallas, TX, on June 16, 1941. Stationed at Ft. Sill, OK, and Ft. Logan, CO. Graduated QM OCS, Camp Lee, VA, July 16, 1943. Transferred to Military Intelligence and graduated from Military Intelligence School, Camp Ritchie, MD, as foreign language propaganda officer.

Landed in Normandy July 4, 1944, as member of 3rd Mobile Radio Broadcasting Company, assigned to 12th Army Group and attached to XX Corps of Third Army. After the end of the war, served in Military Government as information control officer, stationed in Marburg, Germany.

Most memorable experiences: V-1 attacks on London, Liberation of Paris, return to Frankfurt and Liberation of Buchenwald Concentration Camp. Helped organize taking 5,000 German civilians through the Camp, forcing them to be confronted by the evidence of Nazi atrocities.

Discharged as captain, MI in March 1946. Married to Hannelore since 1943. One son, two daughters, six grandsons.

Retired 1985 after 54 years in the shoe industry. Member of JWV Post #256, Dallas, TX.

Awards: Bronze Star Medal, Good Conduct Medal, ETO Campaign Ribbon with five stars, American Defense Service Ribbon, American Theater Campaign Ribbon and Victory Ribbon.

H. BAUMGARTEN, M.D., born NYC, Mar. 2, 1925. Served in WWII in Co. B, 116th Inf., 29th Div. Landed with first wave on D-day, June 6, 1944, and fought in Normandy until June 7, 1944, when he was evacuated after being wounded five times.

Awards/Medals: Combat Infantry Badge, two Bronze Stars, Purple Heart, Croix de Guerre with Silver Palm, Good Conduct Metal, Presidential Citation, ETO Medal with star and Arrowhead, and Conspicuous Service Cross of the State of New York.

After WWII graduated from the University of Miami School of Medicine. He is a practicing MD in Jacksonville, FL. On the 50th Anniversary of D-day his story was written in *Peoples Magazine* (May 29, 1994), *U.S. News and World Report* (May 23, 1994), and *USA Today* (June 4, 1994) and featured on the front page of the *Florida Times Union*. He is the author of *Eyewitness on Omaha Beach*, a true story of D-day by a survivor.

SIMON L. BAUMGARTEN, DDS-FACD, LT COL. USA RET., born Feb. 5, 1912, St. Louis, MO. Army Reserves 1934 to May 1941 first lieutenant. Active Duty May 27, 1941, 8th Cavalry 1st Cavalry Division. Assigned to 343 Engineer Regiment as part of cadre to form medical detachment. Temporary duty, Carlyle Barracks and Walter Reed Hospital. Served three years, five months in European Theater Operations. Served in four invasions and eight battles: Rhineland, Central Europe, Tussisia, Sicily, Naples-Foggia, Rome-Arno, Southern France, Algeria-Morroco.

Citations: Campaign Ribbon with eight Bronze Stars, American Defense Service, Meritorious Unit Citation with Bronze Arrowhead.

Discharged Feb. 10, 1946, back to Reserves hospital unit until retired from duty with rank of lieutenant colonel.

Graduated Washington University Dental School 1934. Staff member St. Louis County Hospital 1934 to May 1941. Staff member Jewish Hospital 1947 to present emeritus. Dentist for professional athletic teams: Hawks, basketball Cardinals, baseball Stars, soccer Steamers, indoor soccer Spirit, basketball Blues, hockey (part-time). Predominantly active in developing dental clinic at Jewish Hospital. Geriatric Dental Clinic at Jewish Center for Aged, the Lasky Cleft Palate Center now at Barnes Children Hospital.

Retired from private practice March 1986. Volunteering services for Bellevue and Tamm Pharmacies.

Divorced 1956. Married Feb. 1, 1968 to Doris Boos Lazare. Stepchildren: Gayle, John, and Paul. Four grandchildren and one great-grandchild.

BERNARD BECKER, born April 5, 1930, Boston, MA. He enlisted Nov. 1, 1950, Air Force. Stations included Sheppard AFB.

Awards/Medals: Good Conduct Medal, Korean War Service Medal.

He was discharged Oct. 31, 1954, with the rank of staff sergeant.

Today he is import traffic manager. Joined JWV in 1955 as member of Robert A. Carpenter Post #485 Past Post Commander, Past Department of Massachusetts Commander, Past Regional Commander 1967-68,1973-74. Serving member National Executive Committee.

DOUGLAS H. BECKER, born April 24, 1948, San Francisco, CA, USA June 30, 1970, Captain DED Special Representative, Thailand. Ft. Knox, KY; Ft. Benning, GA; Bamberg, Germany; 2/2 ACR, Vietnam 153rd MACV; Ft. George Mead, MD NSA; Thailand. Airborne Ranger, Air Medal, Bronze Star, Vietnam Campaign Ribbons.

One of his most memorable experiences was watching boys grow to men. Discharge date 1982. Wife Tammy, children Christina, Laura and Geoffrey. 1995-96 Commander Post 688, senior vice. Certified Financial Planner. Currently resides Daly City, CA.

EMANUEL BECKER, born in New York, NY, on Feb. 22, 1896. Entered Army on Oct. 8, 1917, at Riverhead, NY. Training was at Camp Upton, Long Island, NY. December 1917 left for overseas duty with AEF. Served in 164th Infantry Machine Gun Company, 41st Division in France. Honorable discharge from Army on March 7, 1919, at Camp Dix, NJ, as PFC.

Married to Lena since June 17, 1923. Son Seymour; daughter Ruth, two grandchildren (Bruce and Joyce); two great-grandchildren (Jennifer and Jacqueline). Went to work for the Post Office as letter carrier in 1920, retired from Post Office in 1960 from West Farms Station, Bronx, NY.

On April 1, 1966, moved from New York to Randallstown, MD, Died in Randallstown, MD, Nov. 1, 1993, at the age of 97.

HENRY W. BECKER, born March 3, 1926, in Berlin, Germany, both of his parents were Jewish. He left Germany July 1939 for England in a "kinder transport." Received his high school education in England and some university. Came to USA August 1943. He was drafted at 18 years, June 1944. After basic training (infantry) arrived as a rifleman replacement, Christmas 1944, in Marche Belgium for Battle of the Bulge. Went with Co. A, 334th Inf., 84th Div. All the way to Elbe River. At end of war transferred to Military Government Det. E3 Darmstadt.

Awards/Medals: Army Commendation Ribbon, Bronze Star Medal, Bronze Star Medal Citation.

He was discharged May 1945, stayed in inactive reserve. Recalled October 1950, sent to Korea, platoon sergeant 23rd Regt. 2nd Div. Returned and discharged August 1951. Retired to Florida in December 1990, after 45 years with same company (1947-1990 plus 1 1/2 years consulting, mid 1992).

ISIDORE BECKERMAN (AL), born Oct. 30, 1919, in New York City. Basic training was at Ft. Jackson, SC, with the 77th Infantry Division. Commissioned second lieutenant after completing OCS at Camp Davis, NC, as anti-aircraft officer. Reassigned to the infantry and sent as replacement officer to join the 80th Infantry Division in Europe. Platoon leader for the 2nd Platoon, Company F, 317th Regiment. Led first patrol to cross the Our River into Germany so that our engineers could establish a pontoon bridge across the river.

Wounded in action Dec. 27, 1944, and March 15, 1945. Flown to England and hospitalized there for two months. When war ended in Europe was assigned as liaison officer between the Army and UNRA with the duty of requisitioning supplies for Polish refugees in the displaced camp at Bad Richenhall Germany. Discharged February 1946, with the rank of first lieutenant.

Decorations: Combat Infantry Badge, Purple Heart with cluster, Bronze Star, American Theater Ribbon, African Middle-East Campaign Medal.

Presently resides in Marlboro, NJ, with his wife Anne. They have two sons and four grandchildren. Is a past commander of the JWV Post #972 in Marlboro, and past commander of the VFW Post #59 in Brooklyn, NY. Also member of DAV and Military Order of the Purple Heart.

MICHAEL J. BEGAB, PhD, 1st LT, USAF RET, born in Chicago, IL, Nov. 12, 1918. Enlisted U.S. Army Air Force as Aviation Cadet in April 1942. Completed navigation training, commissioned 2nd lieutenant, February 1943. Deployed to England, ETO, 8th Air Force Flying Fortress Unit. Ten combat missions over Germany before plane was shot down by fighters. Blinded by cannon fire, parachuted, and later captured and hospitalized in Paris. After six months, transferred to POW camp in Barth. Returned to US, September 1944, one year after capture, via prisoner exchange. Discharged from Valley Forge Hospital for disability, December 1946.

Attended University of Chicago as blind student unde PL 16, and earned BA, Liberal Arts and MA Social Work PhD in Sociology, 1968, at Catholic University. Served 2 years in federal employment with Children's Bureau, Whit House, and National Institutes of Health.

Awards/Medals: ETO Campaign, Air Medal with Oa Leaf Cluster, Purple Heart, POW Medal.

Married to Estelle since 1942, three children, thre grandchildren. Past Commander, Post 381, Washington, DC

DAVID M. BEHAR, In early February 1963, received hi draft notice. It was not unexpected and he looked forward t military service. All his brothers were drafted years earlier an

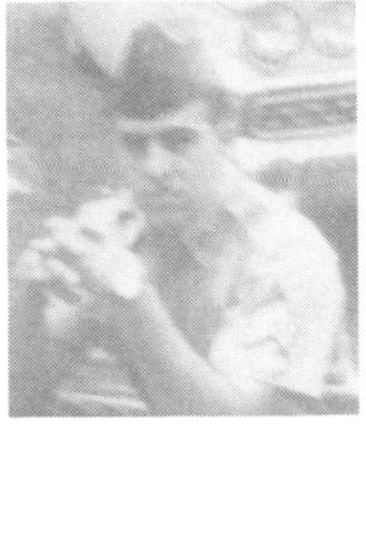

some of his friends were then in service. He also wanted part of this adventure.

His adventure started on a cold morning in Paterson, NJ, where he was sworn in. He and about 50 others were bussed to Ft. Dix, NJ, where they were gassed, yelled at, made to do mindless chores, and learned how to be soldiers. The ultimate weapon!

After basic training most of his company went back home to their National Guard or Reserve Unit and he never saw them again. He was trained at Aberdeen Proving grounds in Maryland to repair tanks and artillery pieces. After 16 weeks he was assigned to the 20th Ord Co. in Ft. Lewis, WA, and worked on 104, 155 mm and 8" howitzers in the Mojave and Yakima deserts.

JOSEPH BEHAR, born Oct. 19, 1930. On Nov. 21, 1951, he was inducted into the U.S. Marine Corps. From Newark, NJ, with many inductees traveled by train to Yemassee, SC, and then onward to the Marine Corp base at Parris Island. In his platoon were men from New Jersey and New York. Inside of 10 weeks their drill instructor Sergeant Day made Marines out of all of them! The Korean War was on at this time and some of the men in his platoon were sent further for combat training and then on to Korea.

He was sent to Camp Lejeune in North Carolina for training in plumbing. Upon graduation he was transferred to Camp Pendleton in California. He was stationed at this base for about 1 1/2 years. From there he was sent to Quantico Marine Base in Virginia till he was discharged on Nov. 5, 1953.

On Sept. 29, 1959, he was commissioned a second lieutenant in the U.S. Air Force National Guard as a nurse officer. His unit was at McGuire Air Force Base and would meet on Saturday and Sunday once a month. Also they would have to go on two weeks of active duty for annual training. For annual training he served at the following Air Forces Bases, Wright-Patterson, Otis, Andrews, Homestead, Savannah and Torrejon in Spain.

When he was discharged from the Marines Corps he had a rank of private first class and when he retired from the USAF in June of 1980, he had a grade of major.

LOUIS BEHAR, enlisted in the Air Force Cadet Program September 1943, took their test and was accepted. A week after he was accepted, he had severe stomach pains. His doctor (Saberese of Garfield) said his appendix was bad and may burst very soon. He took him to the Passaic General Hospital. The appendix burst on the way to the hospital it took two months to recuperate. When he went to the Air Force, they said that they did not need any more pilots.

He was then drafted into the Army Engineers. He took basic training at Ft. Belvoir, VA. He went by train to San Diego Naval Base.

From San Diego his ship (the HB *Freeman*) took soldiers to Calcutta, India. On that trip, the motor stopped below the Fiji Islands for 20 hours. They were lucky there was not any Japanese subs nearby.

Stopped in Frementel, Australia for three days to pick up supplies.

From Calcutta they went to New Delhi by train.

They went to the Assam Valley where the Ledo, Burma Road started. Was there until the Atom bomb was dropped. Went back to Calcutta to Camp Shopiero. From there he was shipped to Shanghai, China. He was living in the Race Course Hotel (rough duty) for a month.

From Shanghai he flew to Peking, China, nearly cracked up when plane finished one tank of gas. The gas line to the other tank was clogged. They were going down like a stone with about 1,000 feet to go, when the pilot got the motors going. Plane was a C46 or E46.

At Peking he was assigned to the air field in engineer and aircraft supply. On the 4th of July 1946, a friend of his, Samuel Russummy and he were invited to the U.S. Embassy to celebrate the 4th of July.

On the way to the Embassy, they crossed the Marco Polo bridge. When they got across Russummy and he noticed a man carrying a boy out of the lake. Behar knew how to administer artificial respiration. They jumped over the fence. Pushed their way to the child and gave the boy artificial respiration. After about three to five minutes the boy threw-up. He took one look at Behar and ran away into the crowd. The crowd cheered and gave them a big hand.

When they got to the Embassy, one of the diplomats criticized him for having mud all over his pants.

When he told him how they got muddy, he brought Russummy and Behar a gin and tonic. He then announced to the other diplomats and other branches of the armed force the good public relations they accomplished.

He always considered those 10 minutes were the best he gave the U.S. Armed Forces during his time in service.

The next day, an English-Chinese newspaper said a Chinese Policeman gave the child artificial respiration. He paid no attention to it. He was never in any danger and wanted the satisfaction of doing the right thing.

Chinese Proverb: "When you save a life, you save the world."

SABETAY BEHAR, November 1950 - November 1952, inducted U.S. Army Nov. 11, 1950, went to Ft. Hood, TX, (2nd Armored Division). Finished basic training then sent to Ft. Belvoir for Surveying School, graduated and rejoined his outfit (1402 Engineering Combat Battalion). During the Korean War their division was sent to protect Europe.

They were sent to Baumhower near Kiaserslauten in Germany. He learned his brother Joseph was drafted into the Marines. Many of the November draftees were shipped with him to the 3rd Army at Gerzewski Barracks in Karlsrvhe, he was battalion surveyor. They had a few projects there. He did topography for a soccer field in Germersheim. They bridged the Rhine with the floating treadway widened for new tanks. He had furloughs and passes to Paris, Copenhagen, Antwerp, Heidelberg, Munich, Frankfurt, Wiesbaden, and Aabenra Denmark.

They went home in a troop ship. Coming in, they saw New York skyline and the Statue of Liberty from New Jersey.

He was discharged in November 1952, at Ft. Dix, NJ.

MORRIS I. BENATOR, born March 11, 1924, in Atlanta, GA. Enlisted in the U.S. Navy on Feb. 12, 1943, serving as storekeeper first class. Attended boot camp in San Diego; stationed in Farragut, ID, and Norfolk, VA.

He was discharged April 1946, but in August 1946 reenlisted for four years until August 1950. In June the Korean War started and he was called back to active duty. As luck would have it stationed again in Norfolk. So over all 12 years in Norfolk, no sea duty, although several times he was scheduled for ship duty, but pulled off draft. The only sea or overseas duty he served was when he went from Norfolk, to Portsmouth, VA, to see his son Barry born (for only five cents by ferry).

Awards/Medals: Good Conduct Medal

He moved to Atlanta 37 years ago. Married and has five children, one girl and four sons. His oldest son Barry (50) retired from the Navy as captain, with 28 years service time. Mr. Benator's three brothers also served, Asher and Johnny in the Army and Max in the Navy.

Today he is retired and active in his synagogue, JWV and other organized units.

KENNETH M. BENDER, was the first volunteer under selective service of McPherson County, Eureka, SD, to join the U.S. Army after he graduated from the University of Minnesota Law School on Nov. 26, 1940.

First assignment was to the 3rd Inf. Regt., Ft. Snelling, MN, where he was promoted to PFC, buck sergeant, and selected to attend Infantry School at Ft. Benning, GA. Commissioned a 2nd lieutenant on Nov. 6, 1941, assigned to the 2nd Inf. Div. at Ft. Sam Houston, TX. Promoted to captain on Jan. 3, 1943, assuming command of Co. B, 38th Inf. Regt. His unit landed on Omaha Beach on D+1 (June 7, 1944).

After hospitalization in England, he was transferred to HQ Co., 9th U.S. Army on Jan. 1, 1945.

Awards/Medals: Silver Star, Combat Infantry Badge, Bronze Star, two Purple Hearts and three Bronze Stars. He was separated from the service on Jan. 2, 1946, with the rank of major.

MORRIS BENDER, M.D., born June 8, 1904, Uman, Ukraine. Was one of the most erudite neurologists in the world. Military service as commander in Medical Corps of USN with special honors.

His bibliography covers extensive writings from 1935-1974, some 325 publications-up to 1974 and after that wrote some 100 more articles of major importance. Wrote *The Ocular Motor System*, the only book of its kind in the world, published by Hoeber Medical Division of Harper & Row, NY, since sold to other companies, now a Dutch firm in 1964 and currently out of print. *Submitted by Milton J. Freiwald, M.D., Philadelphia, PA.*

ROBERT BENYAS (BOB), born Oct. 12, 1923, in Omaha, NE. Enlisted in the Air Force May 26, 1943, stationed in China, Burma, India.

Memorable experience was spending Jewish holidays with Indian Jews.

He was discharged April 2, 1946, with the rank of sergeant.

Married Shirley and has sons Ed and Mark (Dorothy), grandchildren, Jordan and Dana. Today he is a photographer.

HAROLD T. BERC, born in Chicago, IL, Aug. 12, 1914. He was educated at Northwestern and DePaul Universities and entered the practice of law in 1937. When World War II commenced he applied for and early in 1942 was given a commission in the United States Navy Reserve. He first saw service aboard the USS *Washington,* a battleship which participated in the major sea action at Guadalcanal in November 1942. Later he commissioned the USS *Reno,* a light cruiser and served as her fighter direction officer during many engagements in the Central Pacific. He was awarded the Combat Bronze Star Medal for fighter direction services which precluded the sinking of the cruiser *Princeton* by Japanese air attack after that vessel was bombed earlier on. The *Reno* was torpedoed by Japanese submarine action in November 1944 during the Leyte Gulf action. He was then assigned to be training officer of the Naval Officers Tactical Radar School in Hollywood, FL. He left active duty in December 1945, but continued in the Reserves until 1953, attaining rank of lieutenant commander. He was in 10 qualified naval engagements.

He became active in veterans affairs and in 1959 became National Commander of AMVETS. In that role he was material in obtaining a congressional appropriation needed to complete the USS *Arizona* Memorial at Pearl Harbor. He has also been instrumental in establishing an anchor exhibit at

Navy Pier in Chicago memorializing the service of American war ships Parad USS *Chicago*.

He has been a member of JWV Post 800 in the Department of Illinois for many years. He continues to reside in and to practice law in Chicago, IL.

MAX BERG, M.D., 1942 enlisted to serve in the U.S. Military with an MD degree in medicine, a PhD in pathology and fluency in German and French. He was appointed a first lieutenant in a service company in the Air Corps and promoted to captain. After three years, they were ordered to the Pacific theater of the war via San Francisco. Arriving in San Francisco, he was transferred to a station hospital as a pathologist. The following week came orders to report to the Adjutant General in Washington, D.C., he was appointed to be the Pathologist and Medical Legal Consultant to the War Crimes Branch in Europe. In Germany, he investigated the extensive war crimes records for the Nuremberg trials which he attended, and other war crimes; he performed autopsies and testified at the Darmstadt trials. He was promoted to major, then returned to the USA and discharged.

HERBERT BERGEN, born Baltimore, Nov. 17, 1916. Married to Binnie 1944; two daughters, Mira and Sally. Enlisted U.S. Army 1942. Commissioned second lieutenant 1943. Retired Major 1963. Ordnance logistician 18 years. Ordnance supply and maintenance assignments domestically and overseas.

Accomplished hands-on development and management of three annual U.S. Ordnance Military Assistance Programs (MAP) to provide logistics materiel to Taiwan, 1956-59. Developed and managed the only formal in-country All Services Map for Laos, 1961-62. Consolidated all organic maintenance and supply services within Second Infantry Division, Ft. Benning, 1962-63.

Plans and Projects Officer, Columbus General Depot. Collaborated with U.S. Postal Service in developing a new procedure to express ship small supplies consolidated in mail bags to military addresses throughout the world.

Federal employee with 31 Air Defense Artillery Brigade (Hawk and Nike Hercules) in South Florida, 1964-79. Upon brigade deactivation, appointed Executive Officer, 915 Tactical Fighter Group. Retired January 1981.

Military Awards: three Army Commendation Medals, 1959, 61, 63. Special Achievement Certificate, LAOS, 1962.

Federal Civilian Awards: Sustained Superior Performance, 1977 and 1979. Outstanding Performance, 1971 and 1975. Outstanding Federal Service, Supervisory and Administrative, by Miami Federal Executive Board, 1975.

Attended seven colleges. Bachelor of Business Administration, University of Miami, 1969. Master of Science in Management, Florida International University, 1974.

Member of Institute of Management Science. Life Member Jewish War Veterans and Retired Officers Association. Raised in Masonic Sun Lodge No. 6, Taipei, Taiwan.

JOSEPH WALLACE BERGER, volunteered for service one year before World War II broke out. He served four years in the continental U.S. and was sent overseas in December of 1943. He shipped out on the *Queen Elizabeth* to Wales and subsequently was stationed with the Quartermaster Corp in LeHavre, France. One of his many duties was guarding the German POW. He was in one of the first contingents to return when peace with Japan was attained. He returned home to his wife and small son in November 1945. Sgt. Berger passed away on June 21, 1988.

JULIUS BERGER, born July 6, 1921, in New York City. Enlisted Nov. 4, 1942, Army, sawmill foreman 459. Stations included Ardennes, Central Europe, Normandy, North France, Rhineland.

Awards/Medals: European African Middle Eastern Service Medal, Good Conduct Medal, World War II Victory Medal.

He was discharged Nov. 25, 1945, with Tech. 5.

Married and had a son and daughter. Deceased Nov. 22, 1966.

RUTH BERGER, enlisted in U.S. Army as a nurse in 1944. Assigned to the 34th Hospital Train, 14th Army, stationed in Paris, France, 1944-45. Train was actually made up of converted cattle cars containing bunks three levels high as well as one ambulatory car. It followed the American Army as it advanced into Germany, riding four miles behind the front, taking in casualties from the battles, and when it reached its capacity of 300, evacuating them to hospitals in Paris or the hospital ships waiting off Cherbourg or Le Havre.

She also helped evacuate German POWs and concentration inmates. There were the usual wartime hardships. Many times the train operated without heat on its way to the front in order to preserve the coal. Showers and clean clothes were scarce.

After V-E Day she worked in many Army Hospitals until discharged in 1945 with the rank of 1st lieutenant.

Currently she is adjutant of the Fem-Vets Post #192, JWV.

SIDNEY BERGER, born Dec. 12, 1920, in Baltimore, MD. Entered active duty June 1, 1942, Corps of Engineers, MOS 1363 Small unit commander, 1st Engineer Special Brigade. Military locations and stations: Camp Edwards, MA; Northern Ireland; Rosneath, Scotland; Arzew, Geroit, Zerelda, Algeria, Monaco; Gela, Sicily; Salerno, Naples; Exmouth, Badmia, England. Participated in battles in D-Day landings at Gela, Sicily; Salerno, Italy; and Utah Beach, Normandy.

Memorable experiences include preparing bridges for demolition at Maastricht, Holland, during Ardennes Campaign.

Awards/Medals: Silver Star.

He was discharged March 1946, with the rank of captain, Armor Reserve.

Married Mary C. Berger (Army Nurse Corps, service in Normandy, France; etc., Israel Def. Army, 1948-49). Today he is an independent consulting engineer, presently writing a book on engineer troops in Normandy Invasion, to be published by Society of American Military Engineers.

ALVIN L. BERKOWITZ, went into the service Jan. 1, 1943, at Camp Upton Long Island, NY. Took basic in Atlantic City, NJ, 989 Sq. AAF. Learned all the intricacies of the B-17 in Amarillo AAF Texas and then to Aerial Gunnery School in Las Vegas, NV. Crew training at Alexandria AAF Louisiana. Then to Ridgewell, England, 8th Air Force, 553rd Bomb Squadron, 381st Group, 1st Division. He was the flight engineer and top turret gunner for 35 missions and was separated Sept. 3, 1945.

He married his first wife Shirley and had two children, Gary and Debra and four grandchildren. She passed away in 1979 and he married his present wife, Muriel.

DAVID BERKOWITZ, born in Poland, April 2, 1922. Arrived in the USA in 1923. He entered the Army on March 17, 1943, at Camp Custer, MI. Then transferred to the Army Air Corps at Seymour Johnson Field, NC. After basic, sent to

Army Ordinance School at Brookings, SD, after which he arrived at the 55th Bomb Wing at Tampa, FL.

On Feb. 22, 1944, he embarked at Newport News for the ETO. Arrived at Oran, North Africa on March 12, 1944. Left Oran on March 26, for Italy where he disembarked at Bari on April 5, 1944. Their base was established at Spinnazola and later north at Foggia. His MOS at HQ SQ was dispatcher.

Awards/Medals: EAME theater ribbon, Good Conduct Medal and the World War II Victory Medal. Also a battle star for the Rome-Arno Battle.

He returned to the USA on Jan. 2, 1946, and discharged Jan. 6, 1946, with the rank of sergeant.

Retired in 1985, after 40 years as an auto parts distributor in Detroit and then moved to Carlsbad, CA.

His wife, Shirley and he have been married 40 years. They have a son and two daughters and three grandchildren.

HERBERT BERKOWITZ, born Aug. 7, 1929. Drafted November 1950, Army, 48th Anti-Aircraft Bn. (HQ Co.). Stations included Ft. Bliss and Ft. Sam Houston.

Memorable experience was forming first Jewish congregation called Cong. Bnai Bliss at Ft. Bliss.

He was discharged in November 1953, with the rank of sergeant.

Married Fay Berkowitz and has three children and five grandchildren. Joined JWV in 1994 and formed a new post in Ft. Worth, TX; Post 755 and as Post Commander has now recruited 75 members.

IRVING H. BERKOWITZ, enlisted in the U.S. Signal Corps on Dec. 9, 1942. He shipped to the ETO in January 1944, joined the 3252nd Signal Company, a radio intelligence unit of the First Army. After invasion training, landed in Normandy on D plus 4, and participated in five campaigns in France, Belgium, Holland and Germany. After the Nazi surrender his platoon was detached and shipped to the Philippines prior to the Japanese surrender. He served in the occupation of Japan and was mustered out as a staff sergeant in January 1946.

Berkowitz was born in Belleville, NJ, in 1924, graduated from Rutgers University and took graduate studies in Mexico. His wife Frieda and he owned two retail businesses before retirement in 1991. He is president of his synagogue, volunteers at the Clara Maass Hospital, loves fishing, tennis, gardening and visiting his grandson in Oregon.

JULIUS J. BERKOWITZ, born on April 2, 1919. Enlisted in U.S. Army on June 21, 1941. Reported to Camp Custer and transferred to Recon Co. 32nd Armd. Regt., 3rd Armd. Div. Transferred to Ft. Knox, KY, then to 45th Armd. Regt., Camp Beale, CA, 8th Armd. Div., then to the 13th Armd. Div. Promoted to master sergeant, regimental sergeant major.

Transferred to 780th Tank Bn. and back to the 135th Armd. Ord. Bn. at Camp Bowie, TX. Fought in the European Theater arriving in February 1944. Served through Germany to Austria. Memorable experience was visiting Hitler's Berchesgaden.

Discharged Nov. 15, 1945, with the rank of technical sergeant.

Married Ruth and has five children and five grandchildren. Currently retired from the Auto Parts business in Detroit, MI to Leisure World, Laguna Hills, CA in 1987. An active member of JWV, VFW, American Legion, Masons and Shriners.

MELVIN J. BERKOWITZ, born March 3, 1927, Brooklyn, NY. Enlisted Feb. 28, 1945, USCG, seaman first class. Stations included Manhattan Beach Training Center, USS *Alacrity* PG87, USS *Calaterra* DF390.

Awards/Medals: America Area Campaign, Victory Medal, Asiatic Pacific Area Campaign.

He was discharged May 15, 1946.

Has been married to Claire since October 1949. They have two sons and three grandsons. Retired, working part-time for McDonalds, Delray Beach, FL.

JEROME BERLINER, born Brooklyn, NY, Sept. 22, 1919. Raised in Astoria, Queens. Brooklyn College and St. John's University in New York. George Washington University, Washington, D.C. Foreign Liaison Officer, Economic Specialist, U.S. State Department.

Basic training Little Rock, AR, trained for invasion in South Wales, United Kingdom, with 28th Infantry Div. 112th Regt., Committed at battle of St. Lo, fought in Normandy, Northern France, Belgium, Luxembourg, and wounded in Germany Sept. 19, 1944. Three battle stars, Combat Infantry Badge, Purple Heart, Bronze Star for leading reconnaissance squad behind German lines prior to crossing of Sauer River into Germany. Croix de Guerre, with Bronze Star. Entered Paris as infantry support with Liberation Army, under command of French Gen. LeClerc, Commanding General of French 2nd Armored Div.

After hospital stay joined Information and Education Division, SHAEP HQ, Paris, December 1944. Wrote and lectured for field Division. Left Army December 1945, as staff sergeant.

December 1992 celebrated 50 years of marriage to Pauline. Two sons, Mitchell and Guy. Four grandchildren.

For 30 years operated, with wife, a company specializing in the international marketing of high technology electronics. Moved company in 1971 to Florida, and later retired. A member of Snyder-Tokson Post #459 JWV.

JEFFREY A. BERMAN, Major, Medical Corps, U.S. Army Reserve, active service includes Operations Desert Shield and Desert Storm, serving as Battalion Surgeon Patriot Task Force (4th/43rd Air Defense Artillery), Israel.

Jeff has served in the U.S. Army Reserve since 1983. In 1988 he and his family moved to Israel and were living in Raanana when the Gulf War started. Jeff was activated for command training at Ft. Sam Houston in early January 1991. He volunteered for service with the Patriot Task Force, which became operational on January 17, 1991.

During the course of the war, including Scud bombardment, wife Bonnie and sons Yonah and Yosef continued to reside in Raanana. Jeff as Battalion surgeon, commanded medical support for the Patriot Missile Forces in Israel. Medical care provided by Dr. Berman ranged from daily routine problems to psychiatric, orthopedic and acute surgical illnesses.

Following the war, Jeff resumed his role with the USAR association with the American Embassy.

The Berman family currently resides in Teaneck, NJ. Jeff is actively practicing medicine and Yonah and Yosef are attending yeshiva.

JACK BERMAN, born Dec. 19, 1922, in Sharon, PA. Entered the Army Engineers March 1943. Served in the Philippines and South Pacific.

Awards/Medals: Pacific Theater.

He was discharged May 1946, with the rank of T/4.

Today he is retired from General Insurance Agency (35 years) Hollywood, FL. Joined JWV in 1958 Post 613, Hollywood, FL, Past Post Cmdr., Past Department Commander, State of Florida, Past Regional Cmdr., 4th Region; Past NEC, National Insurance Committee, Past National Chairman Soviet Jewery, Centennial Chairman Dept. of Florida, Vice President National Museum of American Jewish Military History.

MICHAEL B. BERMAN, born April 10, 1942, Flushing, NY. Graduated Jamaica High School, 1959. BA (history and political science) Iowa Wesleyan College, 1964. MAT (elementary education) Trenton State College, 1973. MA (industrial relations) Rutgers University, 1978. JD Cardozo School of Law (Yeshiva University) 1984.

Enlisted U.S. Army 1968. Served at the Finance Center-United States Army (FCUSA), Indianapolis, IN, 1968-69; 8th FASCOM, Seoul, Korea 1969-70. Established first clerical quality control procedure to be implemented at FCUSA. Received Certificate of Achievement in recognition of outstanding work. Transferred to 8th FASCOM as an auditor, auditing non-appropriate funds throughout the command. Obtained the rank of Specialist Fifth Class. Awarded Good Conduct Medal, Armed Forces Expedition Medal, and the National Defense Medal. Honorably discharged January 1970.

Life Member JWV, Past Department Commander of New Jersey, National Judge Advocate, Life member Vietnam Veterans of America and former General Counsel and State Council Vice President-VVA of New Jersey. Married to Shelly Holland Berman, father of Michele, grandfather of Raiana.

Attorney-at-Law with offices in Toms River and Lakewood, NJ.

PHILIP I. BERMAN, born June 28, 1915, Pennsburg, PA. Attended Pennsburg HS; graduated Ursinus College, Doctor of Laws, 1968; Lehigh University, Doctor of Humane Letters, 1969; Hebrew University, Doctor of Philosophy, Honoris Causa, 1979; Beta Gamma Sigma, Honorary Business Fraternity Delta Chapter, 1968; and Honorary Fellow, Hebrew University, Jerusalem, Israel, 1975.

Was in the USMC for 3 1/2 years in WWII as a Marine gunner, CWO.

Awards/Medals: Citation for Business and Humanitarian Activities, Senate of Pennsylvania, Nov. 22, 1968; Citation for Business and Humanitarian Activities, House of Representatives, State of Pennsylvania, Nov. 10, 1968; Citation for Civic and Humanitarian Activities, U.S. Congress and William Harber Agency Award, B'nai B'rith Hillel, May 1992.

Honors/Awards: First Annual Pennsylvania, Delaware, Maryland Region Award, American Jewish Committee, Distinguished work in the area of human rights, 1983, and the Distinguished Leadership Award, American Jewish Committee, 1983.

Married Muriel, a Doctor of Optometry, has children: Nancy, Nina and Stephen.

PHILIP M. BERMAN, born Aug. 24, 1926, Pittsburgh, PA. Enlisted January 1944, U.S. Army, Infantry, 9th Inf. Div. 60th Regt., Co. F. Military stations include Camp Wheeler, GA; Camp Campbell, KY; Europe; France; Belgium; Germany. Participated in battles at Rhineland, Ardennes Central Europe, three battle stars.

Memorable experience was crossing Remargen Bridge.

Awards/Medals: Good Conduct Medal, ETO Ribbon, Combat Infantryman Badge, Bronze Star, and three Presidential Unit Citations.

He was discharged June 26, 1946, with the rank of private first class.

He has been married 44 years to Barbara, and has four children, six grandchildren, and four great-grandchildren. He owns a small business and is in the process of retiring and selling the business. His wife is employed as food services director of a high school. Member of JWV Post 300.

MURRAY BERNS, born in Bronx, NY, landed in Italy at age 18 and entered combat as a 1st Class Radio Operator for the 1st Battalion HQ, Radio SQ., Communications Platoon, 361st Infantry Regiment, 91st Division. Entered combat as part of the 1st Armored Division at Anzio, 1944. When remaining regiments arrived went from Rome to the Arrow River, the Gothic Line and Po River Campaign. Received a Presidential Citation, two Bronze stars with oak leaf cluster, Victory Medal, and other commendations. Active combat radio operator at observation posts and in the Battle of Livergnano, Italy, October 1944. One of the few survivors of that battle. Berns holds four Combat Stars. While occupying a Yogolav town at wars end had the unusual experience of being tracked down by his brother Robert, in the Merchant Marines.

Married Muriel, now deceased and has two children, and two grandchildren. Past president of the New York Metropolitan Insurance Agents and Brokers Assistant and presently semi-retired as a mortgage broker in Ormond Beach, FL.

Member of the 361st Infantry Association of WWII.

DONALD IRVING BERNSTEIN, born Bronx, New York City, NY. Distinguished Military Graduate; Cadet Colonel Commissioned June 12, 1957, CCNY RA Infantry. U.S. Army Infantry and Aviator Officer, Education and Training/Management Specialties. Military stations included Ft. Benning, Ft. Campbell, Ft. Dix, Ft. Lewis, Ft. Rucker. West Point/USMA, Germany and Vietnam. Participated in battle for two years in Vietnam, 1967-68 and 1969-70.

Memorable experiences include Grumman OV-1 Mohawk Surveillance aircraft staff/aviator, 1,000 hours plaque. Conceived of RECONDO School; Deputy Post Commander, West Point/Jewish Lay Leader.

Awards/Medals: Distinguished Flying Cross with one Oak Leaf Cluster and Air Medal with 17 awards.

He retired May 31, 1984, with the rank of colonel.

He is married to Ronnie Bernstein and has son Steven Bernstein, and daughter Laurie Bernstein. Today he administers High School Army Junior ROTC Program in NYS. Conduct JROTC Summer Camp, Ft. Dix, NJ.

JOSEPH E. BERNSTEIN, born April 25, 1920, NYC, NY. Entered active duty with the U.S. Army on Jan. 15, 1942, assigned to the Field Artillery Officer Replacement Pool attaining the rank of captain.

Participated in battles and campaigns at Sicily and Naples-Foggia. Assigned to the 320th Glider FA Unit, a part of the 82nd Abn. Div., and became the adjutant to Gen. Maxwell Taylor.

Wounded in action June 6, 1944, at Normandy. Landed in glider, with 33 other men and a jeep, behind the German lines at St. Mere Eglise—right smack on a land mine which killed 11 men.

Awards/Medals: two Overseas Service Medals, Purple Heart, Victory Medal, EAME with three Bronze Battle Stars and one Bronze Arrowhead, American Theatre Medal and the Distinguished Unit Citation. Honorably discharged on Jan. 29, 1946, at the Army & Navy General Hospital, Hot Springs Nat'l Park, AR.

WILLIAM SIMON BERNSTEIN, born Nov. 28, 1898, in New York City. His parents were Louis Bernstein and Fanny Bernstein. He moved to Montreal with his family as a teenager. Joined Canadian Army in Montreal, April 1917. Service Training at Val Cartier Camp in Province of Quebec July 1917. Medic and stretcher bearer in Canadian Army Medical Corps. Became seriously ill in France and was transported to a convalescent hospital at Folkstone, England

January 1919. Transported back to Canada June 3, 1919.

Met and married Sarah Moehler in Montreal and had second ceremony of marriage in New York in January 1923. Sired one living child, Fern Helen Bernstein Feinman, moved to Los Angeles, CA, 1938. Later to Laguna Hills (Leisure World) 1983.

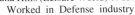

Worked in Defense industry during World War II. Hired and remained with the Los Angeles County Sheriffs Department until his retirement in 1967.

Became active member of American Legion, Chanters Post #534, 1940, Los Angeles; American Legion Post #253, 1951, Beverly Hills; LA Sheriff Star Post #809, 1959, until his death, April 3, 1986.

Philanthropic and humanitarian with sense of humor and wit. Life member of City of Hope.

MAURICE BERRY, entered the Army in March 1943, and, after sojourns at the Brooklyn Army Base in the Medical Corps removing wounded vets from hospital ships and the University of Maine (Army Specialized Training program) he was assigned to Company C, 104 Infantry Regiment, 26 Infantry Division, as an assistant Browning Automatic Rifleman.

They landed in Cherbourg harbor on Sept. 7, 1944, and entered combat in the Third Army on October 7, relieving the 4th Armored Division. He was wounded on October 22, but returned to his company five weeks later, promoted to buck sergeant, and participated in a total of four battles. In April 1945, he was transferred to the Division's M.P. Platoon to guard prisoners of war.

In addition to his Bronze Star and Purple Heart, his regiment was decorated with the French Croix de Guerre with Palm embroidered "Lorraine" and the Fourragere for "...liberating the last parcel of French territory then held by the enemy in this sector."

ERIC J. BERRYMAN, born Aug. 3, 1940, in Berlin, Germany. Raised in England and Wales. Emigrated to the U.S. in May 1958, arriving aboard the freighter SS *Zoella Lykes* and landing in the port of Mobile, AL. Enlisted in the Army (1958) and served on active duty for six years as a military policeman in the 8th Inf. Div. in Germany, on occupation duty in Berlin, at posts in the U.S., and with the Military Assistance Command, Vietnam, 1962-63. Vietnam helicopter gunner, Mekong Delta area, 1963.

BA (1966) Hofstra University; MA (1968) and PhD (1971) University of New Mexico. Commissioned in the Naval Reserve in 1969, served on active duty for another eight years in assignments with NATO, the Pentagon, Mayport, FL, and at sea. Continuous Reserve service to date. Rank of commander.

Decorations: Air Medal with Oak Leaf Cluster, Navy Commendation Medal with Gold Star, Navy Achievement Medal, Purple Heart, Gallantry Cross with palm, Army of the Republic of Vietnam.

Wife, Roberta "Bobbie." Six children, four girls and two boys. Federal civil service public affairs officer/spokesman, Department of the Navy, Washington, DC. At home in Falls Church, VA. Member of JWV Post 154, Norfolk, VA.

SIDNEY BICK, born March 20, 1913, Philadelphia, PA. Joined the USN during WWII; went to boot camp at Great Lakes Naval Training Station, June-August 1943, and participated in the Drum and Bugle Corps. Graduated West Coast Sound School as ST3/c; assigned to the USS *Morrison* (DD-560) at commissioning Dec. 18, 1943; promoted to PO2/c just

prior to his ship being hit by four Japanese kamikaze aircraft and downed on May 4, 1945. Hospitalized, then discharged at Great Lakes. He received the Purple Heart for shrapnel wounds.

Active member and officer in DAV, MOPH, JWV, VFW, AMVETS, AL and Cook County Veterans Assistance Commission. His wife Edith is a past department president of the Ladies Auxiliary of the MOPH.

Employed by CNA Ins. Co. for over 41 years and retired in 1972. During next 10 years he was engaged in partial employment and volunteer service at West Side Dept of Veteran's Affairs Medical Center. Began working as veterans service officer in 1982 for the Illinois Dept. of Veterans Affairs and is still employed full-time. Worked with draft board from 1971-76 and in 1983 was appointed to the Northern Illinois Appeal Board where he still serves.

THEODORE BIERSTEIN, born in Newark, NJ. Inducted into the service Aug. 21, 1942, Army Air Force. He was radio-gunner on B-26 airplanes. He served in air offensive in Europe (Rhineland, Normandy, Northern France, Belgium, Battle of the Bulge).

Memorable experiences include flying 68 missions over France, Belgium and Germany. He remembers being strafed by a German plane while he was writing a letter in his tent on Dec. 23, 1944. Also one particular bombing mission over Paris was scary. Their plane was zeroed in by an ack-ack gun (anti-aircraft). Fortunately his pilot, Lt. Helbock evaded the bombardment with evasive tactics. As he went back and forth he saw puffs of smoke where they had just been. After many missions they would see damage to the plane and realize they had made it back to base one more time.

Awards/Medals: Air Medal Co. 12, 1X BC 1944 with one Silver and four Bronze Oak Leaf Clusters, European-African-Middle Eastern Service Medal.

He was discharged with the rank of tech sergeant.

Today, he is retired with his wife of 50 years (Gloria) and he enjoys their six grandchildren, three boys and three girls, ages 21 months to 24 years of age.

IVAN W. BILLET, enlisted Sept. 29, 1942, first month, private AAF basic training; 17 months, A/c flight student; 14 months, first lieutenant navigator. Served in WWII, 828 Bomb Squadron, 485th Bomb Group, 15th Air Force. Stationed in Venosa, Italy. Served from Aug. 28, 1944 to Nov. 18, 1945. Promoted to captain in Reserves.

HYMAN BINSTOCK, born March 7, 1921, Brooklyn, NY. Enlisted April 1944, U.S. Navy, M2C ship repair unit. Military stations included Bainbridge, MD; San Diego Naval Base; San Bruno, CA; Okinawa. Was to be in invasion force for Japan, did repairs on ships coming in to San Diego. Built quarters on Okinawa, endured two typhoons, met many good friends.

Awards/Medals: Asiatic-Pacific, American Theater - WWII Victory Medal.

He was discharged Feb. 11, 1946, with the rank of M1C.

Married Eva Laskin and has two children, Shelton M. and Brenda. Retired from Internal Revenue Service in 1977.

RAYMOND V. BIONDO, M.D., born in the Bronx, NY, on June 13, 1936, and grew up in Atlantic City, NJ. He enlisted in the Air Force on Sept. 16, 1954. After basic training at Sampson AFB at Geneva, NY, he served as the assistant

management analyst at the 3450th USAF Hospital (ATC) which became the 389th USAF Hospital (SAC) at Francis E. Warren AFB in Cheyenne, Wyoming. Ray was an airman of the month at Warren and held the *Air Force Times* 90650 (Medical Administrative Specialist) Award. After his discharge as an A/1C (E-4) on June 2, 1958, he graduated from the University of Northern Colorado (BA-60) and the University of Arkansas for Medical Sciences (MS-63, BSM and MD-67).

He was the founder and past post commander of JWV Arkansas Post 436. His activities are listed in *Who's Who in the South and Southwest* 1993-94 and *Who's Who in Science and Engineering,* 1994-95. He retired from the solo private practice of dermatology in 1990. National Surgeon, 1993-94. National Assistant Boy Scout Officer, 1993-94.

JULIUS M. BLACK, born Nov. 8, 1920, Syracuse, NY. Attended Hebrew School and Sunday School at Temple Adath Yeshurun. Graduated from Nottingham High School in 1937. Active in basketball, citizenship, and other activities. Entered Syracuse University, College of Business Administration in 1937. Majored in accounting and graduate Magna Cum Laude in 1941, with a degree of bachelor of science in accounting.

Entered service Oct. 26, 1942. Basic training at Camp Campbell, KY, Artillery Division. July 18, 1943, sent to Syracuse University as a Russian language student under ASTP program. This program was discontinued in April 1944. Transferred to infantry at Camp Shelby, MS. Went overseas to ETO in November 1944, as a staff sergeant with the 69th Infantry Division. Killed in action Feb. 22, 1945, at the age of 24.

He was returned to the States and rests in Temple Adath Yeshurun Cemetery. Survived by mother Mary, father Jacob, brother Leonard, sister Lillian.

HERMAN BLACKMAN, born on March 11, 1917, Bergenfield, NJ. Graduated Newark College of Engineering 1938. Drafted into Army Infantry Camp Breckinridge, KY. Released from Army, assigned Naval OTC, Commissioned Ensign (Eng.) USNR. Assigned to minesweeper AMC84 Panama Canal, then to Portland, OR, Engineer in charge construction USS PCE 894 (patrol craft), ship assigned Aleutian Island for patrol and escorting U.S., Lend Lease ships to Russians. Transferred to USS *Tacloban* in Pacific as executive officer. After VJ ship returned to west coast for decommissioning, discharged 1946 as lieutenant (S.G.) USNR.

Various engineering jobs in industry. Left to star hardware and insulation supply business in New Jersey. Sti at it after 48 years, married Anne Klompus, three childrer five granddaughters, live in Springfield, NJ, and West Pal Beach, FL.

Awards/Medals: Atlantic Theater, Pacific Theater Good Conduct.

MILTON BLACKMAN, born Oct. 22, 1923, New Yor NY. Enlisted Dec. 7, 1942, inducted June 21, 1943, U.S Army, rifleman, infantry. Stations included Parachute Schoc Camp Ashwell, England.

Memorable experiences include participating in t Ardennes Campaign with the 507th Parachute Infantry, 17 Airborne Division. Wounded Jan. 5, 1945, at the Battle the Bulge.

Awards/Medals: Combat Infantryman's Badge, Pa chute Wings, American Service Medal, ETO Service Med World War II Victory Medal, Good Conduct Medal, Pur Heart Medal.

He was discharged Dec. 22, 1945, with the rank private first class.

He and his wife Ruth have one daughter Sally. He is retired.

JACK BLANE, born Sept. 1, 1908. Enlisted May 24, 1943, Dental Corps U.S. Army. He was inducted as a first lieutenant in Ft. McCellan in Ala-

bama. He practiced dentistry for several months and was shipped to Ft. Benning in Georgia.

Several months later he was sent to New York to prepare for an overseas trip. He was seasick for 11 days and recovered when they reached Scotland. He was assigned to the 53rd General Hospital in England. There he stayed for about one and a half years. He was promoted to captain.

Jack Dempsey visited our hospital and he posed with him in a boxing pose. Then he was shipped to France for a trip to the Pacific. The war ended before he boarded the ship.

Memorable experiences include buzz bombs when he was in London.

He was discharged in December 1945, with the rank of captain.

He has a son and daughter, five grandchildren and one great-granddaughter. Retired.

ALEX BLANK, born New York City, May 28, 1918. Lived mostly in the Bronx and Monticello. Married April 8, 1943, inducted July 15, 1943, discharged Dec. 24, 1945. Departed for the Pacific March 21, 1945. Returned to the U.S.A. Oct. 21, 1945, motor sergeant 880 Airborne Engineers. Active in New Guinea and the Philippines. Received Asiatic Pacific Service Medal, Philippine Liberation Ribbon, Bronze Star, WWII Victory Medal.

Lived on Long Island, NY, until 1977, then moved to Florida. He has two married children and three grandchildren.

DANIEL BLANK, born in the Bronx, Feb. 17, 1927. Graduated DeWitt Clinton High School June 1945, followed by entry in the Marine Corps. Trained at Parris Island, SC, and Camp Lejeune, NC. Saved by "The" bomb and war's end in August.

Left for North China on the "Wakefield," serving in the 1st Marine Division, HQ., 1st Signal, in Tientsin. Was billeted Japanese Girls School Temple building, where he slept on the alter next to his carbine. They repatriated occupying Japanese military and civilians. They drew fire from the Chinese Communists, who wanted them out of the country.

Returned to the states on the "Breckinridge," discharged at Quantico. Lived in L.A., met an married former Woman Marine Elaine Sevel of York, PA, where they now reside. In October 1992 they joined a "Return to China Tour" with other China Marines (and two civilian women POW's), visiting many areas where Marines had been stationed.

ELAINE (SEVEL) BLANK, USMC-WR, born in York, PA, Aug. 25, 1923. Secretarial major at Webster College, Washington, D.C., graduating June 1943. Enlisted in the Marines October 1943, attending boot camp, 22nd Battalion, and Quartermaster School at Camp Lejeune, NC. Stationed at Quantico, Va. Marine Corps Base from May 1944, till discharge as a corporal in December 1945.

Was in charge of the book storeroom in the Marine Corps Schools Bldg. for the Command and Staff and Advanced Field Artillery Schools. Later on transferred to the base commissary. Met husband, Daniel, also a Marine, at an American Legion Dance in Hollywood, CA.

Married in 1948 and lived in the Bronx and Mt. Vernon, NY, for eight years. Have been back in York since 1956, where son Stephen and daughter Linda grew up. Now have three grandsons. For 20 years was secretary-bookkeeper in husband's real estate firm. Happily semi-retired and love to travel.

ERWIN M. BLANT, born July 17, 1924, Port Chester, NY. Entered U.S. Army on Feb. 23, 1943. Infantry training Camp Wheeler, Georgia Rank PFC. Postal Clerk Bizerte, North Africa, Bari, Italy and Marseilles, France, after landing in Casablanca, Africa on July 17, 1943. Combat Infantryman in Co. E 8th Infantry Regiment Fourth Division, U.S. Army participating in combat in France, Luxemburgh, Belgium, Italy and Germany.

Participated in the North African Campaign, Invasion of Southern France, Battles of the Bulge, Rhine and Central Europe.

First memorable experience was "seeing the destruction at Kasserine Pass, North Africa after the defeat of General Rommel and the Africa Corps. The liberation of the siege at Bastone Belgium and freeing the entrapment of the 101st Airborne Division. The entry into Dachau the day it was liberated and viewing of the camp's horrors, with dead bodies piled as logs of wood, ready to be placed into the ovens. My volunteering as the only German speaking in the company, to act as decoy and lead the company in a night attack therein, I was to be 100 yards in front of the company, with a sergeant and when and if challenged tell the Germans, that I was a lost German soldier, giving the company time to ambush them and overcome the pill box location and dug in German Infantry Company. Lead the company through those lines resulting in the capture of the complete German Company without firing a shot. Gave Danny Cohen, (a 14 year old Jew liberated from Belsen concentration camp, whose whole family was killed there) enough supplies to sustain him before getting additional help, as a fellow Jew and hope for his future, by stating the American Jewish veterans would not forget him, his dead family and others in the future, with continued aid. Worked on the Nuremberg War Criminal Trial, when Goering took poison."

African and European Campaign Medal with four campaign stars Combat Infantryman's Badge, Bronze Star, Purple Heart, Good Conduct Medal, Unit Presidential Citation with two clusters, Victory Medal, New York State Conspicuous Service Medal.

Discharge Dec. 5, 1945, PFC, with 29 months overseas time. Married Pearl Blant with son Ian L. Blant attorney and son Stuart L. Blant deceased. Grandchildren Corey and Jesse Blant.

Past commander and member Post #67 Jew War Veterans, Past Commander of Jewish War Veterans Westchester County and member D.A.V. Port Chester, NY.

Retired Justice of the Justice Court, Port Chester, NY. Past Corporation Counsel of Port Chester, NY, and Mediator and Fact Finder New York State Public Relations Board. Presently engaged in the practice of law.

EDWARD D. BLATT, PNC, born Oct. 29, 1928, Philadelphia, PA. Enlisted Oct. 7, 1945, U.S. Navy, fireman. Military stations included Camp Perry, VA; Great Lakes, IL; and USS *Iowa* BB61.

Memorable experience was serving in the U.S. Navy Awards/Medals: Good Conduct Medal and Victory Medal. He was discharged Nov. 4, 1947.

He married Katherine and has two daughters, two sons, 12 grandchildren, and one great-grandchild. Today he spends his time serving JWV, director of Jewish cemetery, and representing a Jewish funeral director.

KARL BLAUSTEIN, born May 10, 1895, Rumania. Served in the Army during World War I, in France. Participated in three major battles including Argonne Campaign. He was wounded in action and received citations. He was discharged with the rank of sergeant. Deceased Oct. 26, 1965.

SHELDON E. BLAUSTEIN, born in New York City on Aug. 22, 1923, and spent his childhood there. His attendance

at City College was interrupted in 1944, when he was drafted into the U.S. Navy.

After lengthy training in electronics, he was assigned to China until his discharge in 1946. He returned to City College and received a BA degree of electrical engineering in February 1947. During the next few years he undertook graduate studies. In 1950, he was recalled and was assigned to the National Security Agency. Until his discharge from active duty in 1952, he was stationed in Europe and Washington, DC.

After his discharge in 1952, he worked at the Picattiny Arsenal as an engineer and project leader until his retirement in 1981. His projects dealt with nuclear and conventional munitions for the U.S. Army.

Sheldon married Ruth Schlein with whom he raised three sons.

ALEXANDER A. BLEIMANN, born Jan. 28, 1918, New York. Enlisted Feb. 4, 1940. Service includes Infantry, Coast Artillery Anti-Aircraft, Chemical Warfare Service, and U.S. Army Air Force. Military stations were 7th Regiment NYNG; Ft. Stewart, GA; Edgewood Arsenal Chemical Warfare Center, MD; Westover Air Force Field, MA. Participated in Naples-Foggia, Rome-Arno, Sicily, Tunisia, and European Air Offensive.

Memorable experiences were assisting in the formation of the 15th Air Force in five months for which he was awarded the Air Force Commendation Ribbon and Medal by the Secretary of the Air Force.

Awards/Medals: Air Force Commendation Medal, American Defense Medal, Victory Medal WWII, European-African-Middle Eastern Campaign Medal with five battle stars, American Campaign Medal, New York State Conspicuous Service Medal.

He was discharged Sept. 5, 1945, with the rank of staff sergeant.

Attended Columbia University, graduating with a bachelor of science degree. Also attended Wagner College and University of South Carolina. Started own chemical manufacturing business, selling out after 35 years, and retiring. Currently in Publishing business and in writing. Member JWV for 43 years; Life Member DAV; American Legion; Life Member 7th Regiment New York; Masonic War Veterans; Member Masonic Fraternity; Rotary Intern '1; ran for the State Senate 1952, but lost. Two years as President of Synagogue Temple Emanuel, S.I. Recipient of many awards and honors from State of Israel, Jewish Theological Seminary, Bnai Brith, etc.

He has been married for 52 years to Jeanne. They have three sons and five grandchildren.

HAROLD BLOCK (HAL), (BMG3) USNR,, born Nov. 6, 1925, Scranton, PA. Graduated Central High School June 1943. Enlisted U.S. Navy Seabees Nov. 6, 1943.

Basics at Camp Perry, Williamsburg, VA. Assigned to 32nd SPEC. NCB. Participated Liberation of Philippine Islands (Samar) and China (Tsingtao). Honorably discharged May 6, 1946.

Awards/Medals: WWII Victory Medal, American Theater Ribbon, Pacific Theater Ribbon, Philippine Liberation Ribbon (one star).

Graduated 1950 Kutztown State Teachers College (PA) - BS education. Married to Pearle in 1951, and has three sons and a daughter, ten grandchildren. Founded Block Insurance

Agency, Inc. in 1952. Retired 1990. Member JWV since 1946. Joined Lehigh Valley Post 239 in 1960. Post Commander 1963, 64, 65 and 1971, 72, 73, 74. Department PA Commander 1975-76. Also National Chief of Staff 1984-85 and National Action Chairman 1989, 90, 91. Life member JWV and AMVETS.

HERMAN BLOCK, born Jan. 2, 1924, Scranton, PA. Enlisted March 23, 1943, U.S. Air Force, 574 Signal Air Warning Bn., radar operator. Stations included New Guinea and Leyte Islands. Participated in battles in Leyte Gulf, Wake Island, Hollandia Island.

Memorable experiences includes being shot by friendly fire while crossing a rice field.

Awards/Medals: three Bronze Stars, Arrowhead.

He was discharged Jan. 5, 1946.

Married to Zelda, three children and two grandchildren. Retired Insurance Executive. JWV: Past Post Commander, 1989-90, Post 153, Illinois; Past Department Commander, 1993-94, Illinois; and NEC, 1994-95.

IRVING J. BLOCK, RABBI, born March 17, 1923, Bridgeport, CT. Enlisted Nov. 17, 1942, called to active duty on March 9, 1943, Army (ROTC University of Connecticut, Class of 1947). Military locations and stations: inducted Ft. Devens, MA; trained Ft. Benjamin Harrison, IN; served Ft. Gulick, Canal Zone. Later served with the Haganah Defense Force 1947/48 in the defense of Jerusalem in the War of Independence.

Memorable experience: Ot Aleh Medal for service in the Haganah to establish the State of Israel.

Awards/Medals: American Theater Campaign, Unit Meritorious Service Award, Victory Medal WWII, Good Conduct Medal.

He was discharged Dec. 11, 1945, with the rank of technician 4th grade.

Married Phyllis Susan Robinove in 1964, a niece of U.S. Army Brig. Gen. Irving Bersoff. They have a son Herbert. He is an ordained Rabbi from Hebrew Union College Jewish Institute of Religion. Twice appointed National Chaplain Jewish War Vets 1982-83 and 1992-93. Also National Jewish Chaplain 369th Veterans Association. Two honorary degrees: Hebrew Union College, Jewish Institute of Religion and General Theological Seminary (Episcopal). Ordained in June 1953, Hebrew Union College Jewish Institute of Religion. Founding Rabbi of the Brotherhood Synagogue in New York City, 1954. Honored by countless civic and religious groups for achievements in the field of inter-religious and inter-group relations.

HARVEY J. BLOOM, Captain, USN, born Feb. 2, 1918, Minneapolis, MN. Graduated North High School, Minneapolis, MN, June 1936. Entered Naval H-V (P) Program as Ensign, June 1939. Graduated University of Minnesota, DDS degree, June 1942. Entered regular Navy as Lt. Jg., (DC), June 1942. Retired as captain, (DC) USN December 1963.

Stateside Assignments: U.S. Naval Training Center, San Diego, CA, Fleet Marine Training Center, San Diego, CA, Great Lakes Naval Station, Great Lakes, IL, NAS Minneapolis, MN, NAS Dallas, TX, NAS, Willow Grove, PA, NAS, South Weymouth, MA, Boston Ship Yard, Boston, MA, Chelsea Naval Hospital, Boston, MA.

Overseas assignments: Goodenough Island, New Guinea, New Britain Island, Russel Island, Palau Island, and Okinawa.

Memorable experience: "As a junior officer of Medical Co. D, 1st Marine Division FMF, I was assigned the duties of combat loading officer on the Cape Gloucester, New Britain landing on Xmas Day 1944, and I was figuring my dental service wouldn't be needed.

The initial landing was in operation, and I was busy directing the unloading of our medical equipment and vehicles when his Dental Corpsman, James Small, came calling me. "Doc," he said we have an emergency.

Looking beyond Small, I saw a grungy, dirty Marine who informed me he was a member of a machine gun platoon, but for three days had been suffering with an abscessed tooth. Small handed me my emergency dental kit and directed me to a bombarded palm tree where my dispensable duty did the indispensable dental extraction to relieve the uncomfortable Marine of his problem by removing the tooth so a indispensable member of a platoon could get back to his assigned place.

Decorations: Presidential Citation with star, Navy Unit Commendation Ribbon, Naval Reserve Medal, American Campaign Medal, Asiatic-Pacific Medal with three stars, World War II Victory Medal, National Defense Medal and Naval Expert Pistol Medal.

Community: Practiced dentistry in Dallas, 1963-75. Retired from practice in 1975. Assistant Professor at Baylor Dental College of Dentistry, 1975-78. Served as a Boy Scout Leader, Council Member and was awarded the Order of the Arrow for outstanding service to the Boy Scouts. Post Commander of Dallas Post 256, 1985-87. Held Post Quartermaster position, 1976-85 and 1985 to present. Also held numerous other positions in JWV. Was chairman of the Dallas Dental Society Judicial and Peer Review Committee, 1975-77, Life member of JWV, DAV, Masonic Blue Lodge 323, Minneapolis, MN, Alpha Omega Fraternity, ROA-Reserve Officers Association, TROA-The Retired Officers Association, OKU-The Honorary Dental Fraternity. Member of the Dallas County Dental Society, Texas Dental Association, American Dental Association and a fellow of the Academy of General Dentistry. Married to Sylvia. Children: Myron E. Bloom, M.D., and Nola Bloom DVM, (deceased). Two grandchildren.

SAMUEL MICHAEL BLOOM, M.D., born Portland, ME, 1908. New York University, BS, 1932 cum laud; MD, 1935. Alpha Omega Alpha (Honor Medical Society). Internship: The Mount Sinai Hospital, New York. Residency: Chesapeake and Ohio Hospital, Clifton Forge, VA. Residency: MSH, Otolaryngology. Diplomat: American Board of Otolaryngology, 1940.

Commissioned 1st Lt. Med-Res, April 1936. Active duty, Captain, Med. Corps AUS. May 1, 1941. Assigned to Station Hospital, Camp Lee, VA, Chief EENT. Transferred to Ft. Stotsenburg, Philippine Islands, August, to Fort Mills (Corregidor) December 1941; to Ft. Drum, March 23, 1942.

All U.S. Forces were surrendered to Japanese Army, May 7, 1942. To Bilibid Prison, Manila. To Military Prison Camp #1, Cabanatuan. We experienced Dengue fever, Amebic and Bacillary Dysentery, Malaria, Starvation, and various manifestations of Vitamin Deficiency: Amblyopia (visual impairment) Beri Beri, Pellagra and Scurvy. Of ten thousand prisoners, three thousand died in the first year, (Memorial Day May 1942 to May 1943). Many were shipped to Taiwan and Japan. Diphtheria appeared, of 300 cases, 100 died.

The Japanese established a farm which enabled us to grow food in 1943. I worked on the farm along with the other prisoners.

On Feb. 29, 1944, I was transferred, along with Captains Pope Noel and Garnet Francis, to Santo Tomas (University) Internment Camp in Manila. I was appointed Chief EENT and Public Health Officer. We cared for 3,800 allied civilian men, women and children. The Army nurses and the Jesuit priests did a magnificent job. Malnutrition was our prime problem. There was an epidemic of Bacillary Dysentery which was brought under control by eliminating infected food handlers. Diphtheria appeared. The cases were promptly identified and treated with Diphtheria antitoxin. We were liberated by the U.S. First Cavalry (tanks) on Saturday, Feb. 3, 1945, 8 p.m. Received letter of commendation from the allied Internee Committee. Promoted to Major. Evacuated to Leyte, February 23.

Transferred to Valley Forge General Hospital Phoenixville, PA, July 1945. Assigned to ENT and Plastic Surgery Services. Encountered three soldiers with visual impairment, who had been my patients in Cabanatuan. In collaboration with two ophthalmologists, Doctors Earl Merz and William Taylor, we wrote the article on *Nutritional Amblyopia in American Prisoners of War Liberated from the Japanese.*

At my request I was relieved from active duty Sept. 17, 1946, and separated from the Service Nov. 15, 1946.

Decorations/Awards: Bronze Star Medal, Asiatic-Pacific Campaign with three battle stars, Meritorious Unit, Distinguished Unit, Philippine Defense, Philippine Liberation, WWII Victory, American Defense Service and POW Medals.

Resumed practice in New York in 1947. On staff of the Mount Sinai Hospital for 58 years. Retired as consultant 1982. On faculty at Mount Sinai School of Medicine, taught rhinoplasty and otoplasty for over 30 years. Retired as Associate Clinical Professor of Otolaryngology Emeritus in 1977. Staff Physician VAMC New York, 1980-1990. Published 21 articles, including chapter on *Cosmetic Rhinoplasty.*

Member Jewish War Veterans, U.S.A. since 1946. Appointed Post, County and Department Surgeon. American Defenders Bataan and Corregidor since 1951.

Married Zita S. Greene, son Lloyd, daughter Betty, and grandsons Michael and Benjamin Berson. Retired. Interests: Studying of Talmud and Nature.

LEONARD J. BLOOMENTHAL, born Aug. 26, 1913. Capt. Inf. Syracuse University 1937, BA Temple University DPM Armored Force 1942. Combat Military Police HQ and HQ Commandant. Omaha Beach D-Day, 3rd Wave. Decorations Bronze Star, Seven Battle Stars, Arrowhead, all Combat Victory Medals. Refused Purple Hearts. National, Massachusetts Deputy Surgeon. 1970-71-72-73, Man of Year Unsung Hero 1972. Managed ETO Heavy Weight Champion. Vince Kozak and Tommy Lemmon Middleweight. Honorably discharged 1946. Terminated Reserve Apt (Major) 1953. Trustee Post 556.

Holds certificates London School Economics, Baliol College, Oxford, Paris Sorbonne, American-Israeli Physicians Fellowship, Jewish Big Brother, Federation of Temple Brotherhoods. Fellow American Academy Human Services. United Garden City Masonic Lodges, Allepo Temple Shrine. Married to former Honine Odza of Syracuse and Long Island, NY Daughter Lisa Moreno of Caracas, grandchildren David and Shari Moreno. Retired after 50 years as podiatrist.

ZACHARIAH BLOOMFIELD, was born in Cleveland, OH and raised in Brooklyn, NY. Inducted in Service June 3, 1952 and sent to Camp Kilmer, NJ. Served in 9th Division, USA and did Basic Training at Ft. Dix, NJ. He served in Korea from April 1953 to May 1954 in the 55th QM Division. He was discharged May 8, 1954.

His most memorable experience was facing anti-Semitism in his own barracks. He was attacked and ended u[p] with a broken nose.

Bloomfield was discharged as PFC and awarded th[e] Korean Service Star w/2 Bronze Stars, United Nations Se[r]vice Medal, and National Defense Service Medal.

He came back to his wife, Leila, and raised a daught[er] Caryn. He has been married 43 years and has 3 Grandsons. H[e] is retired from the New York Post, where he worked for [] years. He is a member of T/Sgt. Murray H. Lebowitz/ M[a] Reismen Post #129 JWV of the USA.

SHELDON E. BLOUSTEIN

ED BLUM, born Feb. 2, 1926. U.S. Navy June 1943-Ju[ne] 1946, RM3/C, honorable discharge.

Most memorable experience of WWII was being at I[wo] Jima for 10 days, five days prior to the invasion, and five d[ays] after with the experience of having seen the flag raising on M[t.] Suribachi on Feb. 23, 1945.

Awards/Medals: two battle stars of the Asiatic-Pacific Ribbon, plus the following awarded ribbons: American Theater of Operations, Philippine Theater/Occupation, China Service Victory or VJ Medal. (all ribbons are medals) Amphib. Patch.

Married Aug. 28, 1949, two children and five grandchildren. Retired since 1983 due to illness, but active as a Docent for seven years at Reid Park Zoo in Tucson and founder and participant in The Sage Society (Seniors Achieving Growth Through Education) at the University of Arizona Extended University. Life Member of the Jewish War Veterans of the USA, Friedman-Paul Post 201, Tucson, AZ.

SIMON (SZEINBLUM) BLUM, born Aug. 24, 1924, Was a refugee from a Nazi camp in France in 1941 and a native of Warsaw, Poland where he attended school. He spoke seven languages, learning English in Peterson Night School.

Entered the U.S. Army in 1943, serving in the infantry. Inducted in 1943 and sent to Ft. Dix, NJ, Camp Wheeler, GA, and Camp Blanding, FL.

Left for overseas in November 1943. Was with the first American troops to hit the beach at Okinawa, Co. K, 32nd Inf. Regt. Survived the landing, but was wounded while driving the Japanese back into the hills and died April 8, 1945. He was buried with military honors accorded by members of the Preiskel-Miller-Glassberg Post, JWV in Adas Israel Cemetery Passaic Junction, NJ. He is survived by his parents Mr. and Mrs. Benzion Szeinblum and his sister, Regina Brenner.

RONALD BLUMBERG, born near Milwaukee, WI. Drafted November 1952, U.S. Army Infantry, 45th Division and 5th RCT. Ft. Ord. Alameda Naval Air Station and Korea. Participated in battles in Chrismass Hill North Korea.

Memorable experience include members in his platoon, KIA.

Awards/Medals: Bronze Star, Korea Service Medal, Good Conduct Medal, CIB.

He was discharged October 1954.

Married since 1960, with two children. Retired from Civil Service (Federal) Corp of Engineer and Air Force. All pertinent photos were lost in a home fire!

I. RALPH S. BLUMENTHAL, born April 19, 1923, in Hamburg, Germany. Arrived in USA May 1941. Joined U.S. Army in April 1943. Replacement in 3rd Infantry Division in Corte Africa, Naples, Italy, Monte Cassino, First Wave Auzio Beachhead.

Wounded on Feb. 29, 1944, taking to seas captured German prisoners. Second time wounded in forward observation, farmhouse on March 8, 1943. Discharged after nine months and 11 days from hospital and recovered from wounds. To this day 100% disabled.

Awards/Medals: two battle stars and two Purple Hearts.

Married 48 years, beautiful wife, two lovely daughters and three grandchildren. Entire family outside of myself and sister annihilated by the Nazis.

MORRIS A. BLUMSTEIN, born May 15, 1910, in Poland, stationed in Camp Forrest, TN; Ft. Brady, MI; Ft. Ord, CA. ETC. Enlisted February 1942, went to OCS and spoke to my friend Col. Burstein who was my doctor. He was stationed there. From Ft. Ord we went to Hollandia, the infantry and para-troopers were together. I met Trooper Anderson who was a Golden Glove Heavyweight Champ. In Texas we boxed an exhibition. Also boxed in Sieux St. Marie, MI. Arrived in Hollandia and joined the 32nd Division as a sergeant. I went on patrol with my squad the first day. I was resented by my men, as I was taking the place of a regular man.

Went to the Philippines and saw a lot of action in Leyte. Lt. May gave me a detail of five men to help unload a ship. First three men loaded the net and the other two were next. One of them asked me to help them. As a sergeant I was not allowed and I told him so. This man [illegible], a big coal miner from Pennsylvania. He said I was yellow, all Jews were yellow. He found out it's not true. I stopped the net from coming down, and we put our hands up. I only hit him twice and he was finished. The next day Lt. May sent for me. He said sergeant I hear you were fighting with a private. "Yes sir," I said. He never asked why.

He said take a bust or a court marital. I took a bust. The next day they were going on higher ground. The lieutenant called me and told me to take the point, had to obey an order and walked in front of the company. As I walked, I felt that I was being watched. I glanced down to my right and saw eyes looking out of a slit. I turned and fired a few rounds. Five Japs ran out, and I killed four, and someone in the back killed one. I never found out if others were killed in the hole, Lt. May came over to me, and said, "Good job, Blumstein."

I was entitled to a promotion, or at least my stripes back. I saved American lives by killing the ones I killed. I refused to take the point and told the lieutenant to get someone else. He did, once you kill you fear no one.

Was in Hospital with jungle rot, still have it, get ointment from VA. While on top of a hill the earth started to shake, scary as hell, don't know where to run.

His memorable experience was not being able to get food while in Leyte. Planes dropped Hershey chocolate bars and some dropped in river. Some Japs got some. He received one and one-half pieces and found a banana about two inches long in three days time.

They were finally told to stop as they were to be relieved there. Most of them took off most of their clothes, as they stopped on a hill and the sun was bright. Did not take their clothes or shoes off for a long time.

He was in his shorts and enjoying the sun when firing from across the water started. He hit the ground and was lucky to have a mound of dirt to protect him. As the machine gun bullets went over him they hit the dirt and some of the dirt on him. The large insects were also on him and he moved to get rid of them. First Sgt. Richard Pieh was below him and yelled up to him to stop moving around as they may stop shooting, thinking they hit him. This lasted about an hour.

When they were relieved shortly after the trucks rolled up not far from them. They had turkey and white bread. Everyone grabbed the food and took a few bites, they cried like babies. Not having food for a few days, one doesn't start with heavy food. Hasn't eaten turkey since.

He was awarded the Combat Badge, American Service Medal, Asiatic Service Medal, with three stars, World War Victory and the Good Conduct Medal.

Married, has three children and six grandchildren. Plays golf, enjoying family.

EDWIN H. BOCK, born in New York City, March 20, 1925. Entered U.S. Army in June 1943, as draftee. Trained at Ft. McClellan, Alabama, Camp Breckinridge, Kentucky as infantryman. Sent overseas to Wales in October 1944, and then to France in early December 1944. Served in defense against German attack in Belgium in December 1944 "Battle of the Bulge" and in counter attacks in Ardennes in January 1945. Wounded during attack and taken prisoner of war on January 15, 1945. Liberated by Americans on April 15, 1945. Returned to USA in June 1945 and discharged in November 1945, as corporal after treatment for wounds at Hallman Hospital. Decorations: Purple Heart, Infantry Badge, European Theater Medal, etc. Completed education at New York University in August 1948 and commenced career in public accounting Retired as CPA in 1988, moving to Rockville, Maryland. Married to Estelle in 1947, three children, Glenn, Andrea and Steven.

CHARLES BODOW (CHUCK), was a private in the US Army during World War II. He was drafted in October 1942 into the First Army and the 49th Combat Engineers. He had his basic training at Camp Carson, CO and was shipped [illegible] in December 1943. He was part of the "D" Day Invasion when his ship was torpedoed and sank. He was rescued by a Navy ship. There were many casualties. He was in the Battle of the Bulge. Belgium was his rest period for several months before he was discharged in October 1945. He met Fred, his brother-in-law in Paris during a rest period. He was a member of Post 131, JWV, Syracuse, NY.

LEWIS BOLNICK, born Elmer, NJ. I was drafted as a private on March 21, 1941. At the time I had opened my office after graduating dental school.

After spending a few weeks at Camp Dix, I was sent to Camp Grant in Rockford, IL. I was there for a month in Replacement Medical Center and received my commission as a first lieutenant. My next post was at the Officer Training Center at the Carlisle Barrack in Carlisle, PA. After completing my office training I became a platoon leader for training enlisted men in the Medical Replacement Center. Next I went to Camp Robinson in Little Rock, AR. I was company commander. This also was a medical replacement center. I received my captaincy while at Camp Robinson.

In 1943 I was sent to Camp Hood, TX, with the 404 Field Artillery Group. Worked as a DDS, went with the 404th Field Artillery Group overseas (ETO). Missed D-Day by two weeks. With the 404th I was the dentist. Also had an ambulance and was responsible for evacuating the wounded for our three battalions. Was wounded by a 88mm artillery in Singbush, Germany. I was awarded the Purple Heart and later the Bronze Star. In ETO received four battle stars. Received rank of major. Discharged in January 1946, but stayed in the reserves until 1952.

CLAUDE M. BOLTON, born Canton, MS. Enlisted March 28, 1944, Air Corp, ETO 8th Air Force and 16th Air Force. Participated in battles in Britain, wounded two times.

He was discharged May 16, 1946, with the rank of private first class, and June 21, 1955, with the rank of sergeant.

Married with four boys and two girls. Retired from sales and moved to Canton, MS, to visit 10 grandkids. Member of DAV, AL, VFW, JWV.

JOSEPH L. BONNETT, born in Washington, D.C. on Oct. 23, 1934. Engineering major at George Washington University. Entered Army in February 1954. Training at Ft. Knox, KY. Served with Headquarters and Service Company, 44th Tank Battalion, 82nd Airborne Division, Ft. Bragg, NC, 1954-56. Returned to college 1956.

Married Carolyn Kimball September 1956, three daughters, Wendy Joan Bonnett Bergman, M.D., Doreen Michelle Bonnett, and Marjorie Darlene Bonnett Papier.

Worked in the construction business with his father and subsequently formed his own company from 1956 to 1983. Completed law school education at the University of Baltimore School of Law 1986. Practice law from 1986 - present.

Member of Post 1776 Jewish War Veterans. Date discharged, 1956, rank of SP3.

CLARENCE BOOKBINDER (DUKE), born Jan. 9, 1921, Burlington, NJ. Enlisted Sept. 10, 1942 - Jan. 14, 1946, U.S. Navy Phm 1/c USNR 7th Beach Battalion U.S. Navy. Military location and stations included Naval Hospital Philadelphia, PA; Naval Hospital Sampson, NY; Camp Bradford, Little Creek, VA; Ft. Pierce, FL; Lido Beach, NY; Sulcombe, England; Dogwhite, Omaha Beach, Beach Battalion School, Oceanside, CA; USS *Fillmore* APA 83, Navy Shipyard Philadelphia.

Memorable experiences include D-Day Invasion Normandy June 6, 1944, landed 1st Troop in Aomori Japan.

Awards/Medals: European Medal one battle star, American Theater Medal, Asiatic Pacific Liberation Medal, Asia Occupation Service Medal, WWII Victory Medal, Philippine Liberation Medal.

He was discharged Jan. 14, 1946, Phm 1/c.

Married 49 years Esther Hoffman; Superior Court Judge, Ronald Eric, BA LL.D., and daughter Nancy F., BSN. They have four grandchildren. He is a retired podiatrist.

MORRIS BORDMAN, after graduating from high school in June 1942, he enlisted into the coast artillery. After six weeks of basic training at Ft. Screvens, GA, he was assigned to Btry C, 53rd CA Regt. Harbor Defense of Miami Beach, FL. After six months, a promotion to corporal and assigned to the plotting room bunker. As 1943 ended the Harbor Defense units became passé. The 53rd was shipped to Camp Pendleton, VA, and disbanded.

Next assignment was Btry A, 779th FA Bn., Ft. Bragg, NC, for retraining, then a new job as liaison agent, glorified runner. Shipped to the Pacific Theater ending in the Philippines, also being promoted to sergeant. At the end of the War, there was duty recovering and attending to Allied POWs.

On the way home, he met fellow Clevelander, Sanford Berkowitz on his way to the ship's library for Friday night services. He was not attending. Sanford said, "You must be grateful you are on your way home. Come and give thanks." He never forgot Sanford or that Friday night.

He came home February 1946, for his college degree and eleven more years active reserves.

HARRY Z. BORNSTEIN, born in Berlin in 1925. He left Europe for British Palestine before WWII where he spent the war years. He moved to the USA after WWII and is an American citizen. He studied at CCNY and served in the Army during the Korean conflict. He returned to America in 1983, after 23 years in Japan and the Far East where he represented American and European commercial and industrial interests. He was a member of the board of the Jewish Community of Japan of which he is a honorary life member. He was chairman for many years of the United Israel Appeal in Japan, the founding chairman of the Zionist Federation of Japan and the Jordan is Palestine Committee there. He was a delegate from Japan to the 1980 conference of Asian Jewish Communities in Hong Kong and to the Zionist Congress in Jerusalem in 1982. He made regular contributions on Jewish and Israeli affairs to the Japanese press.

He is now chairman of the "Jordan is Palestine" Committee of New York, member of the International Affairs Committee of the ADL, member of the National Public Affairs Committee of the ZOA, and was on the board of the Westchester Jewish Conference. He contributes, from time to time, to local publications, is married and lives in New York City.

MAX H. BORNSTEIN, born Oct. 15, 1915, the oldest of six children; five boys and one girl. The boys all served in the Armed Services, four in World War II, one in Korea. Max attended Wadsworth Grammar School, Hyde Park High School and Northwestern University. He served six months in the CCC Camp and on June 7, 1942, married Esther Weis. They had one son, Robert and have two grandsons, Paul and Richard. Max worked for the general accounting office in the Navy Payroll section in Washington, D.C. prior to being inducted into the Armed Forces on Nov. 18, 1942. He served in the European Theater of War in the Finance Office of the 104th Infantry Division, better known as the Timberwolf Division. He was returned to the States in July of 1945, to be redeployed to Japan, when two days before sailing, his Division's orders were canceled. Max was honorably discharged on Dec. 3, 1945, as a staff sergeant. Following his return to civilian life, he was a jack of many trades. At various times he owned grocery stores and a shoe store and later in life became a real estate broker. Following the death of his wife, Esther in July 1977, on July 9, 1978, he married Ethyle Katz, at which time he inherited another son and a daughter and five more grandchildren, one girl and four boys. In August of 1990 Ethyle Katz Bornstein was elected National President of the National Ladies Auxiliary of Jewish War Veterans.

Max joined Jewish War Veterans in 1954, and through the years he has held just about every office in chairmanship his Post has to offer. After coming up the ranks of the Department of Illinois JWV, he was elected State Commander at the Annual State Convention in 1981, at the O'Hara Ramada Inn in Rosemont, IL. He has also served as the National Executive Committee Representative from the Department of Illinois. Max is a Life Member of JWV and is at present retired.

GLORIA PRESS BOROCHOFF, was inducted into the U.S. Marine Corps Women Reserves in October 1943, and sent to Camp Lejeune, NC, for boot camp training. The Marine Corps Women were the last of the Women's Service Groups to be formed. There was a big recruitment campaign on in Philadelphia, PA, for 8,000 women to be assigned to Ground Aviation in California. After strenuous training in the cold winter (snow) grounds, she was transferred to Cherry Point Aviation, NC, and then traveled with assignment all the way west by troop train to San Diego. Barracks were ready for hundreds of them in a separate section of the Marine Corps Air Depot in Miramar, San Diego.

Her sister, Eleanore Press joined the Navy WAVES a whole year earlier and was serving her duty at Hunter College, NYC, as a storekeeper, which was a Navy Training Base for women during World War II. Her duties at Miramar Marine Corps Air Depot were to assist in the office of Major Gooding as stenographer. Major Gooding had already seen duty in the South Pacific and realized the urgent need of a training school-Parad the Construction and Maintenance School to engage our Marines to construct fast housing for the troops landing in the jungle islands of the South Pacific, quonset huts with electricity, plumbing, sanitation and netting to restrain the spread of Malaria. Our Marines could not get help from the Navy Seabees and they were hard pressed to get any help result: They assembled their own crew of available personnel at the depot to hurry up this production which was a valuable part of our amphibious landings on the Islands.

The USO favored our barren base quarters with first-run Hollywood shows. A big morale booster. Today, there is a large Naval Air Station, a new facility in place of the Marine Corps Air Depot.

About six weeks before the destructive bomb was exploded over Hiroshima, she married a Navy man, Marvin Borochoff, who had served three years on a minesweeper in the South Pacific, and they were so fortunate that the bloody war ended and all of them could get honorably discharged and begin a new life.

"I know that we were very proud to be part of the war effort. It was a tough one but we were young and brave and will have proud memories of our service years."

Fifty years later, VJ-Day was celebrated very recently and a heartfelt memorial interfaith service was held mid-August 1995, in a Palo Alto, CA, Church, hundreds of Veterans, families and friends attended followed by socializing at their Stage Door Canteen, with big band music (recorded), refreshments and pictures of all the theaters of war (Europe) and South Pacific. Nostalgic conclusion to a miserable World War.

SAMUEL BOSCH, born March 24, 1916, Wilkes-Barre, PA. Enlisted Oct. 25, 1943, Army, 3rd Infantry Division. Participated in battles in Northern France, Alsace-Lorraine, Black Forrest, Germany, Austria.

Memorable experience was surviving.

Awards/Medals: Bronze Star with cluster for heroism in combat.

He was discharged Nov. 11, 1945, with the rank of CPL.

Married to Thelma Kluger Bosch, two children. Today he is retired.

KENNETH C. BRAIDMAN, born March 9, 1924, Chicago, IL. Enlisted in the U.S. Coast Guard at 18 in Chicago. Started active duty on Nov. 25, 1942.

Attended boot camp, Manhattan Beach Training Station, Long Island. Was assigned to the captain of the Port Barracks for duty at NYC docks. Completed Radar School in Virginia Beach, VA, and was rated radarman 3/c. Assigned to the Coast Guard Cutter Dione as radar operator for six months. The Dione did anti-submarine convoy escort duty from New York to Key West.

Transferred to the Amphibious Force ship, USS *Cepheus,* AKA-18, shortly after commission. Promoted to radarman 2/c. Was in charge of the Combat Information Center Radar Control. Served in American, Atlantic and Pacific theaters of operation. Participated in invasions of Southern France and Okinawa. Traveled an estimated distance to circle the globe three and one-half times to England, Scotland, North Africa, Italy, Sicily, France, Panama, Hawaii, Guadalcanal, Ulithi, New Zealand, Philippines, New Hebrides, Saipan, Guam, Japan and China. The *Cepheus* was credited with downing three Japanese aircraft. Saw Hiroshima after the Atom Bomb and the Surrender.

After the war ended, had enough points to be discharged but was classified essential. Made two trips to China.

Discharged March 22, 1946, in Detroit, MI. Moved to Miami, FL.

1950 to 1978: Employed in the field of architecture as project manager, supervisor of construction services. Projects included: missile bases at Cape Canaveral; Trident, Bull Goose, Polaris, Pershing and Saturn. Saturn was the largest moving structure in the world at that time.

1978-1988: Owner and president of his firm, Braidman Associates, Construction Consultants.

1972-1986: Elected four-terms as city of West Miami councilman.

Retired in Miami, 1988.

Married to May since 1946, two children, Steven and Susan and five grandchildren, Jonathan, Michael, Scott, Samantha and Marcy. Member of JWV since 1946.

ERNST F. BRAUN, born Aug. 26, 1914, Weinheim, Germany. Enlisted Jan. 28, 1942, 399th Infantry Regiment, 100th Division. Military stations included Infantry OCS Ft. Benning, GA; Camp Howze, TX, ETO. Participated in the invasion at Normandy, all battles of 3rd and 7th Army in Europe.

Memorable experiences are as follows: Initiated psychological warfare for 399th Regiment. Liberated his hometown of Weinheim, found one Jewish woman alive. Crossed enemy lines, blindfolded and liberated the City of Innsbruck, Austria. He participated in the interrogation of Field Marshal Herman Goering in Augsburg, Germany.

Awards/Medals: Bronze Star, four battle stars, Combat Infantry Badge.

He was discharged Dec. 14, 1945, with the rank of captain.

Married Marjorie Silverstein-Braun, and has one daugh ter and one son.

Retired from the Fruit of the Loom Company. Co-Chai Blood-drive Committee, 13 gallon blood-donor.

IRWIN ZABUSKY BRAUN, Sgt., born in Brooklyn NY, on June 16, 1931. Graduated from New York Technica College, in 1951, with an AAS in Advertising Design Drafted into the Army on Jan. 16, 1952, and served with HC Co., 32nd Regiment, 7th Infantry Division in Korea. Serve with intelligence and operations and awarded Comba Infantryman's Badge, Army Commendation with Meta pendant, Korean Service Medal with three battle stars National Defense Medal, Good Conduct Medal, Unite Nations Medal. Took part in the battle for Triangle Hill as combat artist and sketched enemy positions for G-2. One o his drawings appears in the book, "Porkchop Hill." Dis charged from the Army in Oct. 27, 1953.

Graduated from the City College of New York in 1957, with a BBA president of Braun Advertising, Inc. in New York City from 1964 to 1994. Author of the book, "Building a Successful Professional Practice with Advertising" and the Federal Trade Commission research paper, "Advertising Healthcare Professionals."

Married to Marilyn since 1957, and has one daughter, Karen. Member Jewish War Veterans, DAV, Korean War Veterans.

ALLEN BRAUNSTEIN, served as a Lieutenant Commander, U.S. Navy, Pacific Ocean Area, in the Korean War.

LEONARD BRAVERMAN, as a member of the 724th Field Artillery Battalion attached to the 69th Infantry Division, we were occasionally sent out with our 155mm cannons to back up other Battalions with less firepower. This happened when the 2nd Battalion requested heavy firepower to help in their efforts to dislodge the Germans from a heavily fortified hill near Ramscheid. We were warned that a turn in the road leading to the town, was called dead man's corner, and as we

neared the corner our jeep driver floored the gas pedal and the German 88's missed us. We drove into town under heavy shelling, and then parked the jeep. I put the 610 radio on a sled and heaved it over my shoulders and started walking toward the hill where the Germans were entrenched. We walked down the middle of the road with me in the center, and then I almost died, literally, I stepped on a land mine, and in a few seconds I expected it to jump three feet and disembowel me, but nothing happened. Apparently it had been set for vehicles, and I wasn't quite heavy enough. We continued up the snowy hillside, near the top being unbalanced with the radio, I slipped and fell and was saved by a small tree from falling 300 feet. When I got to the top of the hill, my legs locked and I couldn't move, so I set my radio down and decided to broadcast from that spot. Meanwhile the Germans kept pelting us with machine guns, 88's and 150mm howitzer shells, and then suddenly, I thought the world had come to an end, they started firing "screaming meemies" at us. These were rockets that would kill you if they landed near you, or the sound, similar to flying freight cars could cause you to go crazy. Luckily, I missed on both counts. The next day we were relieved and we returned to our battery to continue our drive across Germany, culminating with our meeting with the Russians at Torgau cutting Germany in half.

JACK BRAWARSKY, born New York City, May 15, 1922. Graduated Seward Park High School 1939. Entered family business, New York Store Fixture Company on Bowery in NYC. Joined Navy February 1943. Boot Camp at Samson Carpenter School Great Lakes. Volunteered for PT Boats. Millville, RI, assigned to Squadron 8 and proceeded to New Guinea, December 1943. Served in New Britain-Biak-Phillipines with Leyte in Australia. Proceeded to Leyte December 1943, under constant kamikaze attack for three days. Cargo ship lost and many DDs damaged. Invaded Mindanao at Zamboango and was on boat ordered to pick up and interrogate Moro Gorilla leader-Chief Charlie. His Para

was Charlie Werbel-had a Jewish father and Filipino mother. Discharged December 1943, CM1/C.

Married Muriel Korn October 1947, lived in Elmont, NY, for 34 years. Have three daughter and four granddaughters. My children are Phyllis and Noah, Diane and William and Sandee. The granddaughters are Erica and Sarah DeVos-Marnina and Emily Cherkin. Retired from New York Store Fixture in 1987, son-in-law William Cherkin took business over. I now live at North Shore Towers, Floral Park, NY, and Indian Spring, Boynton Beach, FL. Not bad for the son of immigrant parents, God Bless the USA.

ADELE BRENNER, (Name in Service Adele B. Joseph) born Sept. 1, 1921, Bronx, NY. Enlisted from Brooklyn Jan. 10, 1943, WAAC/WAC Medical Corps. Basic training, Ft. Des Moines; Camp Monticello, AR; Ft. Dix, NJ; Station Hospital. Remained stateside, working mainly as lab technician in Ft. Dix, NJ. While stationed in Monticello, AR, managed the setting up of the hospital's dental clinic which was eventually used as a camp for enemy aliens.

Awards/Medals: Good Conduct, Women's Army Corps, and American Campaign.

She was discharged August 1945, with the rank of corporal.

Married November 1946, (47 years) to Joe Brenner, two sons, one daughter, two grandsons and four granddaughters. Retired from board of education 1985. Member JWV #57, DAV, AMVETS and Women's Army Corp Vets Association.

"There were seven of us cousins, five served in the military. Three of those serving were women. I was a WAC. My cousin Ruth Kornblum was an Army nurse (deceased). My cousin Betty Kornblum was a woman Marine (deceased). My cousin Frank Wascerman was in the Army. My cousin Edmund Heiman was a Sea Bee."

JESSE H. BRENNER, born Aug. 14, 1924, Brooklyn, NY; raised in Chicago, IL. Entered the U.S. Army in March 1943, training as a rifleman with the 291st Infantry. Stationed in Europe from November 1944 through January 1946, engaging in campaigns in Ardennes, Rhineland and Central Europe. Received American Campaign Medal, European African Middle Eastern Ribbon with three Bronze Battle Stars, Good Conduct Medal, World War II Victory Medal, and the Purple Heart. Honorably discharged January 1946, as PFC.

Completed bachelor's degree at University of Illinois, and received law degree from Columbia University Law School. Member of New York and New Jersey Bar Associations, practiced in New York City until retirement in 1985. Married to Marilyn Alpart since 1960; has two children, Laurence David and Morra Beth.

FRANK BRESLAU, born in Chicago, IL, on May 5, 1944. He graduated from the Hebrew Theological College in 1965. He entered the U.S. Army as a Jewish Chaplain in 1967, and served at Ft. Campbell, KY. He completed Airborne School in July 1965, as the first airborne qualified Jewish Chaplain in the history of the U.S. Army.

He was re-assigned to the 101 Airborne Division and went to Vietnam in December 1967. Then he went to the XXIV Corps in Phubai as the Jewish Chaplain for all U.S. troops in I Corps covering six Army/Marine Divisions, a Marine and AF tactical fighter wing, a Navy construction brigade and two hospitals.

After Vietnam, he was assigned to Ft. Dix, NJ, until his discharge in January 1970.

Awards include the Bronze Star, Army Commendation Medal, NDSM, Vietnam Service Medal with seven stars, Vietnam Medal, and Distinguished Unit Citation.

He lives in Teaneck, NJ, with his wife, Eleanor and daughters, Ilana and Rebecca.

ABRAHAM BREVERMAN, born Sept. 5, 1919, in Pittsburgh, PA. Enlisted in the U.S. Army on March 21, 1942. Sent to Ft. Jackson, SC; assigned to the 77th Inf. Div., Co. D, 307th Inf. as machine gun squad leader. Transferred to the 77th Div. HQ as leader of a defense platoon to guard the commanding general.

Stayed with Ordnance being sent to Aberdeen, MD, for training with a specialty of automatic weapons. Served with the 307th Inf. Div. during the invasion of Guam, then with the 306th Inf. Div. on Leyte, Ryukyus, Karamaritus, Iwo Shimo and Okinawa. After the Japanese surrender, he was sent to Hokido, Sapora with the 77th Inf. Div.

Awards/Medals: American Theater Ribbon, Asiatic-Pacific Theater with three Bronze Stars, Philippine Liberation Ribbon with one Bronze Star, Presidential Meritorious Unit Award, and the Victory Medal.

Honorably discharged at Camp Attebury, IN on Dec. 9, 1945, with the rank of Tech-3rd Grade, 777th Ord. Co., Component AUS.

JULIUS BRICKER (See Weiner Family for write-up)

MAURICE A. BRICKMAN, born Aug. 22, 1920, Worcester, MA. Inducted at Ft. Devens, MA, Sept. 16, 1942. Discharged honorably as staff sergeant, Nov. 16, 1945. Attended Airplane Engine School at Seymour Johnson Field, NC, and Pratt Whitney Engine School at Chevrolet Division of General Motors, Detroit, MI. Assigned to 99th Air Drone Squad, Caspar, WY, May 1943. Left U.S. Aug. 3, 1943, on USS *Uruguay*. Arrived Bombay, India, Sept. 10, 1943, stopping at Hobart, Tasmania and Perth, Australia. In Karachi Staging Area was assigned to 303rd Transport Sq. of ATC at Mohanberry, Assam, as Aerial Engineer. Transferred to 1311th AAF Base, Guya, India, August 1944. Sent home for 45 days TD Aug. 8, 1945. A-bomb dropped on Japan.

Married Libby Gaffin June 27, 1948. Two sons, Steven and Kenneth, two grandchildren, Jean and Jonathan. Medals: Asiatic-Pacific, with two Bronze Stars, Distinguished Unit Badge, WWII Victory, Good Conduct, American Theater, CBI Campaign, Aerial Engineer. Org: Past Commander. JWV Worcester Post 32, Pres. B'nai B'rith 600, Past Master Isaiah Thomas Lodge, 32nd Degree Mason.

DONALD BRODER, born July 14, 1930, Bronx, NY. Entered the U.S. Army Oct. 16, 1951; received basic training in Ordnance Corps at Aberdeen Proving Grounds, MD, with additional training as ordnance supply specialist

Sent to Korea and arrived in Pusan on May 18, 1952. Assigned to the 21st Trans. Port at Inchon. Transferred Feb. 15, 1953, to HQ I Corps to serve as assistant Jewish Chaplain, promoted to corporal. For three months, he served as the I Corps Jewish Chaplain in the absence of a Jewish Chaplain.

Awards/Medals: Commendation Ribbon for Meritorious Service, Korean Service Medal with three Bronze Stars, United Nations Service Medal and National Defense Service Medal. He separated from active duty on Sept. 5, 1953.

A member of JWV for 25 years and a textile salesman in New York's garment center. Married Rita, children Alyssa and Mitchell. Recently became a grandfather for the first time.

SIDNEY BRODER, born Nov. 29, 1918, Brooklyn, NY. Enlisted Aug. 31, 1943, Army, 35th Infantry Division. Participated in battles at St. Lo, France, as of June 30-43, wounded July 16, 1943, hospitalized five months, England

Awards/Medals: Purple Heart, CIB, Good Conduct, ETO and others.

He was discharged Feb. 1, 1946, with the rank of private first class.

Married and has two daughters. Retired now and volunteer in VA Hospitals. Member of JWV Post #519 (Florida) Life member DAV.

ELI BRODIE, born in Bristol, England, on Oct. 12, 1920. At the early age of 1, his family moved to America where he was fortunate to live and make a very full and beautiful life for 71 more years.

Eli enlisted into the United States Air Force on April 18, 1942. Through hard work and diligent training, Eli was promoted to be a sergeant in the Aerial Photography Division. He was in the 13th Battalion of the 13th Air Force, stationed in New Caledonia, New Guinea and Australia from April 1942 to September 1945. He was honorably discharged on Nov. 16, 1945.

Eli was married to Cecilia Barkan on Aug. 11, 1946. They lived in Jamaica Estates, NY, for six years. They were blessed with a son and a daughter. They moved to New Hyde Park, NY, where they lived for 40 more years. Eli worked for 35 years for General Motors.

Eli was a family man and did whatever it took to make his family happy and secure. After a heart attack Eli retired and worked part-time in a doctor's office as a patient liaison, file clerk and a johnny on the spot...

Unfortunately, illness struck Eli once again and he began an arduous battle with cancer. His illness never stopped his dry English humor or his love for people. His stories began and although a very private and frequently a painful time, Eli had the strength to talk and write about his past adventures. Until recently, his Air Force years were a very private time only Eli chose to remember ... or forget ... We found out about his medals: a Bronze Battle Star, a Victory Ribbon and a Good Conduct Medal. Eli started to write some memoirs and one story titled "Tomato Lovers in the Pacific." *In loving memory of my father, Deborah Brown.*

EUGENE BRODSKY, following licensure as a physician and surgeon on Feb. 13, 1945, application was made for a commission as a medical officer in the armed forces of the United States. A commission was issued from the U.S. Public Health Service as an assistant surgeon (Lt. J.G.) and assignment to active duty with the U.S. Coast Guard. Original assignment was to the USCG Training Station in Atlantic City, NJ.

Transfer orders came through at the beginning of June 1945. Reported to the USS *Knoxville* (PF64) on June 10, 1945, as medical officer until the ship was decommissioned on June 10, 1946. At that time, transferred to the U.S. Naval Auxiliary Air Station in Mayport, FL, occurred where service as senior medical officer was rendered until release from active duty in October 1946.

The above Parad officer received the following awards: American Theater of Operations, European Theater of Operations, Victory Medal.

During the Korean Conflict, a commission of Captain in the U.S. Air Force was received on Nov. 14, 1950. Orders to report for active duty were issued on Jan. 3, 1953, with assignment to the 463rd Troop Carrier Squadron, 14th Air Force, with further duty to the School of Aviation Medicine, Randolph Air Force Base on Feb. 12, 1953. The prescribed course of study was completed and was graduated as an Aviation Medical Examiner in May 1953. Following this, reassignment to the 463rd Medical Group, Ardmore AFB, Ardmore, OK, as base flight surgeon. Following separation from active duty on Sept. 4, 1953, was placed on Inactive Reserves until March 1, 1968, at which time transfer was accomplished to the Retired Reserve, United States Air Force.

STUART A. BRODSKY, at the age of 50 decided to try and fulfill a long-held dream, that of serving his country as a member of the military. He was certain that he would be rejected because of his age, but much to his surprise and happiness, he was accepted. Surgeons were needed by the Navy.

His wife, Ilene, and daughters, Donna and Elizabeth, were quite supportive. They were living in Albuquerque, NM, at the time. After graduating from Officer Indoctrination School in Newport, RI, November 1988, he proceeded to Naval Hospital, San Diego, later transferred to Naval Hospital Camp Pendleton.

Deployed to Saudi Arabi in September 1990 with the 1st Marines, 1st Field Svc. Spt. Gp. where he became the senior medical officer. He served in Al Jubail, Manifah Bay and Ras al Mishab during Desert Shield and Desert Storm. His deployment was for seven months.

Awards/Medals: decorated with nine awards including Navy Commendation Medal and Combat Action Ribbon of which he is most proud. Honorably discharged Nov. 18, 1994, with the rank of commander.

Returned to Camp Pendleton and was appointed Department Head of General Surgery.

LEONARD C. BRODY, born Oct. 20, 1935, in Providence, RI. Oldest child of Miriam and the late Albert Brody. Brother, Melvin; sisters, Rochelle, Linda. Graduated from Hope High School, Providence, RI. Married Minnette Laux (April, 1959) Children: Helene, David, Marc.

Military Service: Joined the U.S. Marine Corps Reserve while a senior in high school. Went on Active Duty in the Marine Corps in November 1954. After boot camp at Parris Island, SC, and infantry training at Camp Lejeune, NC, attended and graduated Sea School at Portsmouth, VA, and was assigned to the Marine Detachment aboard the USS *Des Moines,* discharged in November, 1956.

Re-enlisted in December 1956, and was assigned to school at the Great Lake Naval Training Center. Transferred to Camp Lejeune, NC, and went on two Mediterranean Cruises with the 3rd Bn., 6th Marines. This included the landing in Lebanon in 1958.

Arriving back from Lebanon, was transferred to 2nd Marine Air Wing at Cherry Point, NC, where he was in charge of a Squadron Armory. Discharged in December 1959, as a sergeant, E-4.

Service Awards: National Defense Medal, Marine Corps Good Conduct Medal, Naval Occupation Medal, American Expeditionary Forces Medal (Lebanon, 1958).

Organizational Service: Held all offices in the Marsack-Feldman Post #145, JWV. Held numerous offices in the Department of Wisconsin, JWV. State Commander, Department of Wisconsin, JWV, four years. President, Department of Wisconsin Memorial Trustees. Adjutant, 5th Region, JWV, seven years. Delegate at large to the National Executive Committee, JWV. Member of the National Honor Guard, JWV. Life Member, Jewish War Veterans of the USA.

Delegate to the Council on Veterans Programs, State of Wisconsin, 22 years. Delegate to the Allied Veterans Council of Milwaukee County, 1963, to date. President, Allied Veterans Council of Milwaukee County, 1981-1982. Secretary, Allied Veterans Council of Milwaukee County, 1983, to date. Life member, Marine Corps League. Life member, VFW. Member of AMVETS, 1980 to date. Member Army and Navy Union. Life Member 2nd Marine Division Association. Life member USS *Des Moines* Memorial Society. Member National Museum of American Jewish Military History. Member of the National Personnel Committee, JWV, 1994. Member Milwaukee Lodge, F&AM. Scoutmaster, Troop 472, BSA, Milwaukee County Council, 21 years.

IRWIN BROMBERG, entered the U.S. Navy, in September in 1942, as a Pharmacist Mate 3rd Class, advanced to 2nd Class and shortly after applied to officers training school. Upon being accepted to the program in September 1943, he was sent to the University of Notre Dame at South Bend, IN. The course was completed in four months and he was commissioned an Ensign in the U.S. Navy. His orders sent him to Amphibious Training School at Norfolk, VA, to be an officer-in-charge of an LCT (Landingcraft Tank). In time he was went to New Orleans to pick up his LCT where it had been placed on an LST. Their LST took them to the Island of Leyte where the LCT was placed in water and they participated in the invasion of Leyte in the Philippines. He spent 18 months there with his crew operating the LCT. During that time the Philippines were liberated. After being promoted to LTJG, he was sent back to the states for shore duty. In January 1946, he was put on inactive duty.

Awards/Medals: American Theater Ribbon, Pacific Theater Ribbon, Philippine Invasion Ribbon.

MURRAY BROMBERG, born Oct. 30, 1924, in Brooklyn, NY. Reported for active duty in 1943, to USNTS, Newport, RI. Attended Hospital Corps School in Portsmouth, VA, followed by duty at U.S. Naval Hospital, Memphis, TN. Transferred to Fleet Marine Force, USMC and Field Medical School, San Diego, CA, and then to the 1st Marine Division and VMSB 142, 1st Marine Air Wing. Participated in invasion landings with the assault forces in the Solomon Islands, Lingayen Gulf, Luzon and Zamboanga, Mindanao in the Philippines.

Was in the review of Marines by President Roosevelt, Admiral Nimitz and General MacArthur at their historic meeting in Hawaii to plan strategy of the War in the Pacific.

Awards/Medals: Navy Until Commendation with one star, America Theater Campaign Medal, Asiatic-Pacific Campaign Medal with four stars, Victory Medal WWII, Philippine Presidential Unit Commendation, Philippine Liberation Medal with one star and the Solomon Islands Campaign Medal.

He was discharged as pharmacists mate 3rd Class, USNR, April 1946.

Attended Brooklyn College, had Podiatry Medical education and internship in Chicago and has offices in Bloomfield, NJ. Married late Marcia Gilbert and have one son, Daniel. Married Helen Leinkram in 1990 with two children, Mark and Sharon.

A Diplomate of the American Board of Pediatric Orthopedics and a fellow and past president of the America College of Foot and Ankle Orthopedics and Medicine. Dr. Bromberg is on the staff of Beth Israel Hospital in Passaic, NJ, and Roseland Surgical Center. Is listed in Who's Who in the East, Who's Who in Science, Who's Who in the United States, Who's Who in the World and Who's Who in Executive and Professionals. 1992-1995, Commander of Post 146 JWV; member of VFW, and the Marine Corps League. 1993-94, State Commander of the year, Department of New Jersey. 1993-94, Parad County Commander of the Year, JWV. 1995-96, County Commander, Essex Council, JWV.

ROBERT BROMBERG, born in Brooklyn, NY, on Nov. 20, 1921. Entered the U.S. Army in October 1942, and had Infantry Training at Camp Edwards, MA. Additional training was received in North Carolina and San Bernardino, CA. Underwent desert training in Needles, CA, and went over seas on the *Queen Elizabeth* to Scotland Was stationed in Birmingham, England and then Bangor, Northern Ireland. Transferred to Manchester, England and was hospitalized with Pneumonia.

Landed with the U.S. first Army in the invasion of France. Was at the battle of St. Lo and witnessed the 1,000

plane air raid. Fought in the battle of the Bulge in Belgium and then on to Germany. Helped Holocaust survivors upon release from concentration camps. Participated in battles in Normandy, Northern France, the Ardennes, Central Europe and the Rhineland. Awarded the Sharp-shooter Medal, the European-African-Middle Eastern Campaign Medal with five Bronze Stars, the WWII Victory Medal and the Good Conduct Medal. Was discharged in September 1945. Married to Shirley Schnier of Waterbury, CT, and has a daughter, Karen and son-in-law, Robert. Attended the new school in New York after discharge from the U.S. Army.

EDWARD B. BRONSTEIN, born April 25, 1932, Bronx, NY. Drafted November 1953, Army, 519 Engineering Co. (Depot) 29th Battalion. Stations included Engineering School, Ft. Belvoir, VA; Philippines, Okinawa; Sep. Ft. Dix, NJ. Participated in battles with the 30 Eng. Co. in Okinawa, 14 months, served as table of information and education officer and made sure all the enlisted men without a high school education went on to further their education in the service.

Memorable experience was teaching drafting at the Army School in the "Ryukyu" (Okinawa), enjoyed seeing Hong Kong and Japan on vacation trips.

Awards/Medals: Good Conduct Medal.

He was discharged Sept. 1, 1955, with the rank of SP 3(T) July 5, 1955.

His daughter Marcia is a successful fund-raiser for Federation of JWV Philadelphia in Philadelphia. His son Gary is a computer operator for VA in East Orange, NJ. Has one grandchild, Ross. Today Mr. Bronstein is a civil engineer for ENV Protection City of New York, responsible for quality of drinking water. Active as NEC Bronx JWV County Commission.

MELVIN M. BROOK, born July 20, 1927, in Pittsburgh, PA. Enlisted April 1945, Navy. Military stations included Camp Perry, VA; Norfolk Naval Base, USS *Bmareus* AR12.

Awards/Medals: American Theater and Victory Medal.

He was discharged June 1947, with the rank of seaman first class.

He has two daughters and five grandchildren. Today he is a CPA with a public practice.

MIRANDA BLOCH BROOKS (RANDY), I fought World War III, to get into WWII Marines, with my father and I lost! So, I had to wait until I did not need his signature and enlisted Sept. 30, 1943, in Washington, D.C. as we had moved there after I graduated West Philadelphia High School. I was sworn in on Nov. 10, 1943, on the steps of the Library of Congress, on Nov. 10, 1943, 168th Birthday of the USMC. I received orders to report to Camp Lejeune at the end of November 1943, to eight weeks of boot camp.

I tested mechanically inclined, and was sent to an experimental class of Aircraft Radio Repair with 29 other females.

We repaired the radio gear from planes that had ditched in the ocean, or crashed on land, and were repairable. Then we installed that in the planes, and eventually I was one of the few women who were granted flight orders, so that we could fly along in the planes to be sure that the radio gear was working properly. These planes were mostly PBJs, Patrol Bombers by North American (Navy lingo), or the B25 Billy Mitchell Bomber which was the plane that Doolittle flew off the Carrier Hornet, to bomb Japan (Army designation of this plane).

We wore the pilot's alpaca lined leather jacket; a seat parachute; and the "Mae West orange colored vest" which would inflate and keep you on top of the ocean, if you had to ditch the plane for any reason. We wore the same "Boondocker" shoe boots as the men, and I always said that if we had to ditch in the ocean, those Boondockers would carry us right down to the bottom of "Davy Jones Locker." (You had to be of my generation, to know "Mae West" the actress).

"Flight Pay" is 50% of your basic salary. Sergeant was paid $78.00 a month at that time, so I made $78.00 plus $39.00, for a total of $117.00, and I thought I was a millionaire. We had to "enlist" for the Duration of the War, plus six months, so that none of us knew how long we would be in the Corps. But I loved every single minute of it, even though I had never been away from home. Don't forget that life was very different then. I was not allowed to date until I was 16, and then I had to be home by 10 p.m.!

We were 360 females in our barracks, 90 to each of four Wings in the building. Our double-bunks were three and a half feet apart, so you had two females to your left, two to your right, and one over or under you. Your tall lockers were lined up down the middle length of the wing, to provide a very small amount of privacy. Your foot lockers were at the bottom of the bunks.

We had many of the same type of classes during boot camp as the men. We also had two weeks of "Mess Duty" after boot camp was finished, till our classes could be formulated. After our classes we went to Norfolk Naval Air Station Radio-Radar School, then back to Cherry Point, NC. I was discharged Dec. 15, 1945, very sadly, as were most of us. But we were proud to have been "Pioneers" for Women not only going into the military, but also "Rosie the Riveteer" into the Commercial world, and things have never been the same since!!! Incidentally, out of the 360 Women in our Barracks, only five that I know of, were Jewish, and we still keep in touch.

I was born in Jerusalem, Palestine, on 29 Sulieman Road, across from New Gate in Damascus Gate, next door to what was the "Notre Dame De France Convent." When I was back in 1982, it had become the "Notre Dame De France Hotel." My grandfathers' house had only part of the front wall that was standing as it had been rocketed and shelled. My mother and her younger sister were also born in this house. My grandfather, Abraham Solomiac came to Palestine in 1888 with 21 other Belyahudim. There is a book written in Hebrew by Schulamit Yesco with a chapter devoted to each of these men. My grandfather became the Post Master General of Palestine and the Russian Consulate. My mother had gone to school with Golda Meir. We came to this country when I was two years old, and went back for a few years when I was 6.

My father Isaac E. Bloch, came into Palestine with General Allenby as his aide, from England. He met and married my mother. Then he brought his brother Aaron Bloch to Palestine from England and he met and married Dora Feinberg or Feingold (I cannot remember which, and she is the Dora Bloch left behind at Entebbe.) Incidentally, her sons told us that her body as found three years later, in a forest tortured and burned. (My mother's friend, Dora).

SAMUEL H. BROOKS, born Nov. 12, 1895. Enlisted June 9, 1917, Army, Chemical Warfare. Military stations were Washington, D.C. and France.

Awards/Medals: Victory Medal and Purple Heart.

He was discharged Dec. 19, 1918, with the rank of sergeant. He had three children and is now deceased.

SELIG BROOKS, served as a Russian translator in Army Security Agency, 1955-58. Graduated from Army Language School, Monterey, CA. Assigned to Ft. Richardson, AK. His unit was responsible for intercepting Russian Radio Communications. He was discharged as specialist second class.

ISADORE BROSBE, born May 8, 1915, Burlington, NJ. Enlisted March 1943, Army, pharmacist, rank T-3. Stations included Oran, Africa and China/Burma/India Theater. Participated in battle in first convoy in the Mediterranean to go through the Suez Canal, lost one ship in the battle in the area, 1,500 lives were lost.

Memorable experience was near Salween, China, his unit of 30 men were surrounded by the Japanese, another unit broke through and freed his unit.

Awards/Medals: European Theater, CBI Theater cluster.

He was discharged December 1945.

Mr. Brosbe resides in Levittown, PA, with his wife Harriet. He is the father of Rita, Robert, Geri and has six grandchildren.

ALAN S. BROWN, born Oct. 8, 1933, Boston, MA. Enlisted Oct. 30, 1956, U.S. Navy, Supply Corps.

Military Stations: Navy OCS, Newport, RI, January 1957-May 1957; Navy Supply Corps School, Athens, GA, May 1957-November 1957; USS *Mullinnix* DD944, November 1957-October 1958; USS *Claud Jones* DE-1033, October 1958-January 1960; NAVSTA, New Orleans, LA, January 1960-June 1961; Trans. Management School, Oakland, CA, June 1961-November 1961; NAVSTA, Rota, Spain, December 1961-January 1965; Military Traffic Management Service, St. Louis, MO, January 1965-June 1967; NAVSTA, San Juan, P.R., July 1967-June 1969; HQ COM10/CaribSeaFron/Antilles Defense Camp, P.R., June 1969-May 1970; USMACV, Naval Advisory GP, Saigon, RVN, May 1970-December 1970; U.S. Naval Support Activity, Saigon, RVN, December 1970-May 1971; Underwater Systems CTR, Newport, RI, July 1971-July 1976; HQ COMDR U.S. Naval Forces, Carib/ComNavBase, PR, August 1976-June 1978. Participated in four campaigns in RVN, 1970-71.

Awards/Medals: Bronze Star with Combat V; Navy Achievement Medal; RVN Staff Service Honor Medal (1st Class); RVN Civil Action Medal; RVN Meritorious Unit Citation; RVN Gallantry Cross Medal; National Defense Service Medal; Vietnam Service Medal; RVN Campaign Medal; Navy Unit Commendation.

He was discharged June 30, 1978, with the rank of LCDR.

His wife is Marise Alves Pinheiro Brown of Rio de Janeiro, Brazil; son, Henry R. Brown (deceased 1962-92). Retired from U.S. Navy (1978) and General Public Utilities Corp. (1993).

BERNARD B. BROWN, born in Detroit, MI, on Aug. 9, 1919. Business major at The University of Michigan. Enlisted in December 1940, and Commissioned in the U.S. Navy in March 1942. Honorable Discharge, March 1946. Rank of lieutenant commander.

Attended mine warfare school and became specialist in mine sweeping. Commanded ship, sweeping mines throughout South Pacific, including Samoa, Figi Islands, New Caledonia, and Philippines. Served as Naval Pilot for ships coming into harbor including aircraft carrier *Enterprise* (joining Rear Admiral Davis on board), *Saratoga*, and Battleship *Washington*.

Involved in a number of critical strategic operations. Swept in Guadalcanal with the Marines. Involved in the invasion of Treasury Island and the Death March out of Bataan. Caught in typhoon on way to Japan to join invasion forces in 1945, when Japan surrendered. After surrender, swept South China Sea and Yang-Tse River en route to Shanghai.

Married to Dorothy Dunitz since 1944. Three children: Barbara, Connie and Richard, and five grandchildren.

CEO and Chairman of B&U Corporation, a conglomerate corporation.

EDMUND J. BROWN, born in Boston, MA, 1918, entered into the United States Army, 1943, honorably discharged 1946, as a sergeant. Served with the 84th Division European Theater, assigned to the 334th Infantry Regiment. The outfit was in the Battle of the Bulge, Germany, Holland and France. While reconnoitering a German town for billets, he, along with an officer and another soldier engaged in a hand to hand battle in which seven (7) Germans were killed, wounded or captured. Investigation revealed that the enemy force was preparing an ambush with machine guns, small arms and automatic weapons. This encounter prevented their troops from falling into a trap.

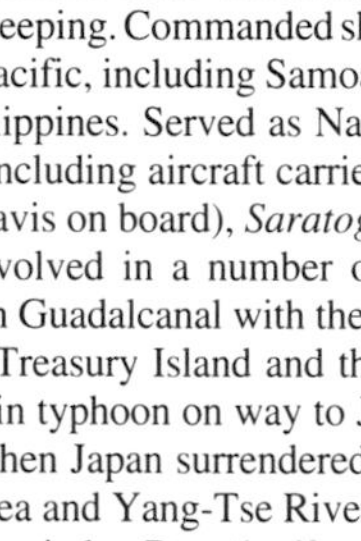 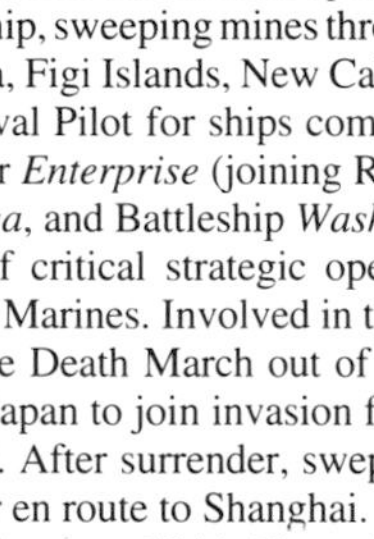

He was instrumental in arranging the first religious service for both the Jewish and Catholic women that were liberated from the concentration camp at Salzwedel, Germany.

Awards/Medals: Silver Star Medal Citation

He has been married to Rose since 1941, two daughters and two grandsons. Member of the Jewish War Veterans, Post 104, Winthrop, MA.

LOTHAR (BROWN) BRAUSCHWEIGER, born in Wuestensachsen, Prussia, Germany. Escaped Nazi-Germany in March 1937, to America. Worked as a carpenter till called for induction. Had a hernia and was classified 4F. However, he felt he had to serve his new country and went for an operation. He was re-classified 1A. After basic training, he was shipped to Great Britain, and joined the 2nd Infantry Division for the invasion of Normandy in June 1944. Swam to Omaha Beach, France, as forward observer for the 12th Battalion Field Artillery due to his knowledge of German. Fought from Normandy to Czechoslovakia, where a car from the German 11th Panzer Division ran over him. There was a special story written about his escapades in the *Stars & Stripes*, and in the 2nd Infantry Division Book. He was flown to France for recuperation. While in Paris, France, he became an American Citizen, and changed his Para to Lothar Brown. Was discharged in Camp Swift, Austin, TX. Received five battle stars and the Good Conduct Medal. He was never issued the Purple Heart.

Married to Ingrid in 1947. Has three children and seven grandchildren. Started Able Woodworking Company in 1948, and still in business in 1993.

MANUEL BROWN, entered the service at Ft. Devens, MA, in October 1942. Transferred to Camp Barkeley, TX, where he trained with the 90th Infantry Division also received training in Louisiana and California. Promoted to sergeant prior to being sent overseas in March 1944. Participated in the now famous D-Day invasion of Normandy on June 6, 1944. Wounded at St. Lo, France, July 24, 1944.

While recuperating at the 192nd General Hospital in England, Manny was visited by two members of the Flaschner family, Jerry Flaschner and Sol Tunis.

Sent back to the States on a hospital ship in November 1944, Ira Flaschner boarded this ship in the harbor at Charleston, SC, to check patients. Both Manny and Ira were pleasantly surprised.

Received the Combat Infantry Badge and Purple Heart Medals. Discharged from the service in October 1945. *Submitted by Max Sigal.*

PHILIP BROWN, born in Los Angeles, CA, on Oct. 16, 1924. Attended Los Angeles City College before entering Army in March 1943. Overseas to England in October 1944. Served in France, Belgium and Germany and left Army in March 1946, as Tech 5, receiving European, African, Middle Eastern Campaign Medal with two battle stars, American Campaign Medal, WWII Victory Medal, and Good Conduct Medal. Operated Army telephone switchboards during Potsdam Conference and helped relay telephone call from President Truman to the Pacific to go ahead with the atomic bombing.

After war, graduated Woodbury College in Los Angeles. Retired in 1988, after working 39 years in the grocery industry. Life member of JWV Post 603 (currently hospital chairman). Also active member of local City of Hope Chapter and active in two Jewish Senior Citizens Organizations. Married to Evelyne since 1949, have three children and five grandchildren.

PHILIP N. BROWN, Lieutenant Colonel, is currently assigned to Headquarters Allied Forces Central Europe, The Netherlands.

Lt. Col. Brown was born Sept. 11, 1949, in Washington, D.C. He graduated from Suitland Senior High School, Suitland,

MD; the University of Miami, FL; and the University of Southern California, CA. He received his commission through Air Force ROTC. Professional military education includes Squadron Officer School, Air Command and Staff College and the Air War College.

He earned his pilot's wings at Vance AFB, OK. Operational assignments include the 33rd Tactical Reconnaissance Training Squadron (TRTS) and 18th Tactical Reconnaissance Squadron (TRS) at Shaw AFB, SC; 15 TRS, Kadena AB, Okinawa; the Pentagon; 62 TRTS, Bergstrom AFB, TX; Pacific Command, Camp Smith, HI; 333rd Tactical Fighter Squadron (TFS), Davis-Monthan AFB, AZ; 76 and 75 TFS, England AFB, LA; and Commander, 75 FS, Pope AFB, NC.

He is a command pilot with almost 3,000 flying hours in the A-10 and RF-4C, including 10 combat missions during Operation Desert Storm.

He is married to the former Lynne Israel. They have two daughters, Rebecca and Jessica.

WILLIAM BRUENNER, born Oct. 11, 1929, Vienna, Austria. Family emigrated to New York City, 1938. BS, CCNY; MS, Brooklyn Polytech. Entered USAF as second lieutenant September 1952. Observer training Ellington AFB, Electronic Warfare Course-Keesler AFB. RB26/RB66C Aircrew member, HQ 9AF Intelligence Officer-Shaw AFB. HQ TAC Intelligence Staff Officer-Langley AFB. HQ USAFE Electronic Warfare Staff Officer-Wiesbaden. Student/Instructor Staff College Maxwell AFB and German Armed Forces Staff College, Hamburg. Flew 60 EB66 combat sorties 1972 from Korat AB, Thailand. HQ USAF Electronic Warfare Staff-Pentagon; Director of Housing and Services, HQ USAFE-Ramstein AB. Saceur Representative MBFR Negotiations with Warsaw Pact-Vienna 1979-82. Legion of Merit, DFC, Airmedal with two OLC, Meritorious Service Medal with two OLC.

Retired March 1982 as colonel. Married with three children. BBA-Georgia Southwestern College 1983, worked as accountant after military retirement. Member Jewish War Veterans Atlanta Post and VFW.

ROSS BRUMMER, born Bronx, NY, June 4, 1928. Graduated Brooklyn College 1956, with MA in Liberal Arts. Taught 38 years, high school English in New York City and English Professor at St. John's University. Published several encyclopedia articles and is continuing professional writing.

Joined the 955 FA Bn, Brooklyn National Guard 1948. Artillery unit activated 1950 and sent to Korea. Disembarked Pusan. Attached 24th Division; entered Seoul across Haan River Pontoon Bridge. Saw immediate action assisting First Marine Division and First Cavalry.

As personnel sergeant, accompanied outfit from Ichon to Inchon; from Yung Dong Po to ASCOM City; from Taegu to 38th parallel and beyond. Most notable engagement was Chinese offensive April 21, 1951. ROK Army guarded flanks. When North Koreans attacked, ROK's fled leaving flanks unguarded. Many outfits were caught including the 555 FA Bn who suffered many casualties. The 955th was the last American outfit to evade the attack.

Returned on Feb. 14, 1952, married Mona, and had two children, Janis and Allan.

Awards/Medals: The Korean Service Medal, Unit Citation, Citation for bravery, FECOM Service Medal.

SAMUEL MAJER BRUMMER, born May 24, 1922, Poland. Joined the service Feb. 24, 1943. Military locations included Central Europe, Northern France, Rhineland, Normandy.

Awards/Medals: Distinguished Unit Badge, European-African Middle Eastern Service Medal with Bronze and Silver Arrowhead. Good Conduct Medal, COM INF Badge Co. 15 HI 115th Inf.

He was discharged Oct. 19, 1945, with the rank of private first class.

Married Rona Feb. 20, 1961, and has sons, Marc and Michael, and a grandson David. Been in restaurant business for 50 years, Hobby's Restaurant, Newark, NJ.

GERALD E. BRUSON, (USA) born Aug. 22, 1921, Cincinnati, OH. Enlisted at Ft. Thomas, KY, June 25, 1942. Served in 5th Armored Division, 71st Infantry Division, both 3rd and 7th Army. Saw action in France, Germany, Alsace Lorraine and Austria. Participated in liberation of Mauthausen Concentration Camp.

Awards/Medals: American Theater, European with two Bronze Stars, WWII Victory and Good Conduct Medal. Discharged at Camp Atterbury, IN, Feb. 22, 1946.

HARRY SOLOMON BURDMAN, born April 13, 1922, Minneapolis, MN. Enlisted in the U.S. Navy in May 1942.

He was given an honorable discharge due to Polio. Married twice, divorced from Gloria, one daughter. Second wife, Del, have son and daughter, also nine grandchildren. Retired.

HERMAN BURDMAN, born Dec. 4, 1929, Minneapolis, MN. Served U.S. Army in Communications. Stations included Korea.

Married and has three children and four grandchildren. Retired.

SAMUEL BURDMAN, born June 1, 1924, Minneapolis, MN. Enlisted June 1942, U.S. Army. Military locations and stations included Assam, India, Sicily, flew the Hump as aerial photographer.

Married twice, first wife and baby son died; divorced from second wife, Shirley. Have a daughter Cheryl and three grandchildren. Deceased 1986, New Years Eve.

JOHN R. BURNETT III, born in Knoxville, TN, on May 15, 1963. Converted to Judaism at nineteen. Received BA in Classics from King College and MA in Classics from University of Southern California. Entered Army in August 1988. Basic Training at Ft. Knox, KY, and AIT as Intelligence Analyst at Ft. Huachuca, AZ. Stationed at Hunter AAF, Savannah, GA, with S-2, Avn Bde, 24 ID(M).

Deployed to Saudi Arabia as part of Desert Shield on August 20, 1990. Personally promoted to sergeant by MG McCaffrey, 24 ID Commander, while in Saudi Arabia. Served as S-2 representative in Avn Bde HQ (FWD) during all offensives of ground war, including final battle at Rumaylah, Iraq. Returned to HAAF in March 1991. Personnel Security NCO for Rotary-Wing Aerial Displays and Aerial Review of the National Victory Celebration in Washington, D.C. Honorably discharged on Aug. 29, 1991.

Awards/Medals: Army Commendation Medal with two Oak Leaf Clusters, AAM, GCM, NDSM, Southwest As-

Service with two BSS, ASR, Saudi Arabian Liberation of Kuwait Medal; Named *Soldier of the Quarter*, 3rd Qtr, and *NCO of the Year*, 1990, Avn Bde, 24 ID.

Currently employed as safety manager for Tennessee Electric Company, Inc., an electrical contracting firm, and serving in S-2, 2-278 ACR (TNARNG) in Kingsport, TN.

Jewish experience: I arrived in Saudi Arabia rather early during the days of Desert Shield. The High Holidays were just around the corner and I was truly concerned as to what I would do about observing the time-honored ceremonies and rituals of those sacred days.

My own chaplain, MAJ Hemingway, was a good-hearted Baptist who looked out for everyone in the brigade. Nonetheless, I was still amazed when he came to me and asked what I had planned for Rosh Hashannah. It turns out that the division Support Battalion's chaplain was a rabbi and he fully intended to have services for all who could get to him. I told MAJ Hemingway to let the rabbi know that I would attend. MAJ Hemingway had arranged for his assistant to drive me the six hours to the rear and to return me the next day. I was truly grateful. I packed the tallis that I had brought with me and headed to the division rear.

Chaplain Ben Romer was the only rabbi in Saudi Arabia at the time. He was serving all Army and Air Force personnel as well as all Marines on the ground. During the services, he made note of the fact that we were probably the first Jewish minyan to celebrate the first day of the Jewish New Year in Saudi Arabia in quite some time. (I remember feeling both proud and terrified by that thought.) He distributed small siddurs to all the service members there, speculating that they were probably the first siddurs newly printed by the armed forces in at least twenty years. We had our first sip of forbidden alcohol during the Kiddush. It tasted even sweeter because of the Saudi prohibition against spirits. It was a day of firsts. By the end of the evening, I felt vindicated in my decision to travel the long distance to the services.

Being a Jewish soldier in Saudi Arabia was not without humor. The 24th Infantry Division printed Christmas cards which it distributed to all the soldiers; then, realizing not all soldiers were Christian, the division printed a small additional run with "Season's Greetings" rather then "Merry Christmas" on the inside of the card. But the cover was still the same silhouetted soldier staring off the same sand dune into the same night sky … a sky dominated by the unmistakable Star of Bethlehem!

PEARL KAUFMAN BURNS, born Sept. 13, 1920, Brooklyn, NY. Enlisted Oct. 10, 1942, WAAC - WAC. Stations included Algiers, NA, Caserta, Italy.

Memorable experience was her contact with Gen. Eisenhower and so many other experiences in both Africa and Italy.

Awards/Medals: Good Conduct Medal, WAAC Service Ribbon, European-African-Middle Easter Service Medal with one Bronze Star.

She was discharged Sept. 30, 1945, with the rank of T/5.

Widow with two surviving children. Today she is a business/office manager for an Environmental Inst.

CANTOR HENRY BUTENSKY, born Aug. 12, 1922, New York City. Inducted October 1942, Infantry, Rifleman, 57mm cannon anti-tank. Service locations included Camp Croft, SC; Camp Van Dorn, MS; Camp Carson, CO; War Maneuvers, CA; Ft. Benning, GA; Camp Lucky Strike, France.

Memorable experience was liberating two concentration camps: Straubing and Gunskirchen Lager in Austria. Liberated one labor camp, Wels Austria. Being the farthest east, 71st Division, 3rd Army met Russians on May 5, 1945.

Awards/Medals: Good Conduct, Victory Medal, American Service Medal, European African Middle Eastern Service Medal, two battle stars.

He was discharged with the rank of first sergeant.

He married Sally Taub. They have a daughter, Helaine Rona Butensky, who married Gerald Lazarus, their children are Mathew Alan and Perry Samuel. They also have sons, Sanford J. Butensky and Jan David Butensky, who married Barbara Gelzer, their children are Tobi Beth and Paige Ilana. He has been Cantor at Temple Beth Shalom, Livingston, NJ, for 36 years.

VICTOR CAHAN, enlisted in the U.S. Coast Guard on June 18, 1942, as a storekeeper, 3rd Class. He received his boot training in Boston and was stationed at Fargo Building, Boston, MA, for four years. He received his honorable discharge on June 30, 1946, with a rating of chief petty officer. *Submitted by Max Sigal.*

FINDLAY CAMERON, born in Ft. Wayne, IN. Enlisted Jan. 8, 1930, U.S. Army, PFC, 5th Army, 10th Div. Military locations and stations Ft. Riley, KS, 1951, Stayburker, Gev. Breman, Gar. Chinon, France.

Memorable experience Chinon, France, waited only a few night alerts, easy worked in Chinon, France depot, seen felt their guilt. Occupied Germany and France 1951-53.

He was discharged Oct. 3, 1953, or Sept. 8, 1953, with the rank of PFC.

Mother's maternal parents' Jewish Chapter. Today he is 63 years old, retired; golfs and takes care of his quarter horses.

ISAAC S. "IKE" CANETTI, born on the lower East Side of New York City on Aug. 29, 1923. Accounting major at CCNY. Enlisted as aviation cadet in the Army Air Force, February 1943. Graduated Pilot School in June 1944, and assigned as B-24 Bomber Pilot to the 15th Air Force in Italy. Forced to bail out over enemy territory on March 19, 1945. Entire crew survived and captured. Sent to Stalag VIIA, POW. Camp at Mooseberg, Germany. Liberated on April 29, 1945, by Patton's Third Army, 13th Armd. Div. Discharged as second lieutenant, Aug. 13, 1945, returned to college then went on to law school. Admitted to New York Bar 1952, and earned CPA Certificate 1954. Represented Julius LaRosa when fired by Arthur Godfrey.

Married to Beverly since 1947. Two daughters Meryl and Robin, one son Samuel "Sandy" and five grandchildren. Decorations: Air Medal, Former POW Medal and NYS Conspicuous Service Medal.

HERMAN "HANK" CARGAN, (at one time "Cohen"), born Trenton, NJ, Feb. 2, 1921. Enlisted in USN December 1941. Basic training at Newport, RI, where later served as building commander, D Barracks. While at Newport, cited to Annapolis by Adm. Edward Kalbfus. Shipped out to Pacific Theater 1943, 1st Echelon, line 4, destination: Admiralty Islands. Commanded LCM dry-dock, Manus Island, rate boatswain's mate 1/c. Most memorable experience: witnessed explosion of USS *Mt. Hood*, ammunition ship.

Discharged January 1946. After discharge served as Cubmaster, Scoutmaster and Explorer Adviser. Also served as Hillel director at Rider and Trenton State Colleges. Received certification from UAHC as religious instructor and taught at local synagogues.

Wife, Florence; two sons, Abba (married Karen Teltsher, daughter of Jane and the late Murray Teltsher) and Jonathan (both sons physicians); and a granddaughter, Madison Rachel. Presently self-employed as fitness/nutrition consultant.

ARTHUR CARL, S/Sgt., served in the 96th Squad, 2nd Bomber Group H. The plane he was on was shot down over Austria on Feb. 24, 1944. He was listed as missing in action until the end of the war in Europe.

The plane was found with his remains and he is buried in our military cemetery in St. Arnold, France.

He received the Purple Heart Medal and the Air Medal with two leaves.

Enclosed is a picture of him in uniform and a picture of his final resting place.

WILLIAM CARMEN, born in Salem, MA, May 27, 1919. Was an instructor, USN, Jacksonville NAS and Memphis NAS, Aviation Machinist Mate's School, 1942-44 and the management engineer, Aircraft Assembly and Repair Department, USN, Pensacola NAS. Received the USMC Aviation Training Unit-Outstanding Instructor Award in 1943.

He is member of the American Legion Post, VFW and JWV. Was the State Commander, Massachusetts, JWV from 1954-55, the National Commander of JWV from 1956-57, the military aide to two governors of Massachusetts, rank of colonel from 1963-70, the chairman of the National Executive Committee, JWV from 1965-67, and chairman of the Past National Commander's Organization for 12 major National U.S. Veterans Organizations from 1987-90.

Awards/Medals: Medal of Merit, 1964, JWVUSA.

Married to Beverly, has three daughters: Jane Davis, Ruby Yolles and Dawn Sibor, and six grandchildren.

EDWARD I CARROLL, Captain, served in Vietnam with the armor, infantry and the corps of engineers, 9th Infantry Division. He was awarded the following medals: Purple Heart, Bronze Star Medal, Army Commendation Medal, Air Medal with V Device, Air Medal with V Device and eighth Oak Leaf Cluster, and the Distinguished Flying Cross.

JACOB AND PHILIP CARROLL

MARIAN CHABAN, served in the WAAC and also in the WAC from Jan. 7, 1943 in September 1943, when she was discharged. She entered the service as an auxiliary and when discharged at Ft. Oglethorpe, GA, she was a private first class. She received her basic training at Ft. De Moines, IA, and was attached to the Officer Candidate School Headquarters, both at Ft. De Moines, IA, and at Ft. Oglethorph, GA. She visited in Chicago, IL, Tennessee, Georgia and the South. *Submitted by Max Sigal.*

MARVIN CHABAN, served in the USN and enlisted on Nov. 26, 1943. He received boot training in the Electrician's School at Sampson, NY, and also in the Naval Training Station at Sampson, NY. He saw considerable action on the USS *Astoria* and the USS *Springfield* (CL 66).

He received several award and decorations. Among them were WWII Victory Medal, the American Theater Medal, the Asiatic-Pacific Theater Medal with two stars, and the Philippine Liberation Medal. He was discharged on Feb. 1, 1946, with the rating of electrician's mate second class. *Submitted by Max Signal.*

HAROLD CHAIET, is proud winner of the Combat Infantry Badge, Bronze Star Medal. The state of New York issued him a medal because of the Bronze Star.

He served with the 5th Div., 11th Regt. Co. F. Serving in England, Scotland, France, Germany, Austria, Luxembourg, Sudetenland and Czechoslovakia. Member of the JWV, life member of Veterans of Foreign Wars and member of the 5th Division Society.

IRVING CHAIMOWITZ, born Jan. 19, 1924, in New York City, NY. Joined the U.S. Army Signal Corps Jan. 4, 1943. Military locations and stations included Ft. Lewis, WA; Oregon State College (ASTP); University California, Davis; Camp Crowder, MO; Hawaii; Okinawa; Korea.

Memorable experience meeting Russian Jewish soldier in Korea and got low-down on Russian General, Army and Staff, all in Yiddish, November 1945. In Korea the Communists shot at him at the 38th Parallel, December 1945, reported and ignored!

Awards/Medals: Good Conduct Medal, Victory Medal, Asiatic-Pacific with one star, and American Theater.

He was discharged March 6, 1946, with the rank of technician 5.

He received his BS from City College of New York in 1948; MA from Columbia in 1956. High school and community college teacher of math, physics, and electronics for 25 years in New York City, and 10 years in Florida. Family lived in Israel four years, 1967-72. Married, three children, three grandchildren, one son was officer in USN Subs for 10 years. Member of JWV Post 177 and DAV. Retired in Florida.

CANTOR KALMAN CHAITOVSKY, born March 10, 1924, in Lithuania, came to U.S. in 1940. Attended Rabbinical Schools in Boston and New York, and voice and Cantorial lessons.

Entered the Army September 1943, basic training at Ft. Bragg, NC, became specialist gunner on 105mm Howitzer. Also served Ft. Mead, MD; England; France; Belgium; Luxembourg; Austria; Czechoslovakia.

Went to England, February 1944, landed in Omaha, France 10 days after D-Day. He was wounded twice once on his shoulder near France, and in his leg, in the Battle of the Bulge, which left him with pieces of metal to this day.

Being a Rabbinical student and Cantor, he was conducting services for Jewish soldiers. He was an assistant to a Catholic Chaplain, as the worked from his office. During this time, he was transferred to the 104th Regt. of the 26th Yankee Div., 2nd Bn. Co. B, his rank S/S.

Memorable experiences were many, Co. B liberated a slave labor camp near Weiden Neuburg, Austria, as they opened the doors of the barn, people were crawling out on their knees, and one girl yelled out "Kalman Vos Tustu Do" What are you doing here, you see this girl, named Esther Paam was at the train in Kaunus, Lithuania when our family was able

to leave for the U.S. in 1940. Also after the war Co. B remained in Czechoslovakia and he was one of the soldiers in charge of a DP Camp, he made contact with a Israeli Group "Brachia." They worked underground stationed in "Salzburg," when he told them, that they have hundreds of displaced persons they showed him a way, how to transport many to "Salzburg" and among them was his friend Esther Paam, who landed in Italy, and to Cyprus. He knew they arrived in Israel, because he received a letter from her.

Awards/Medals: Purple Heart with Cluster, Bronze Star, France Medal, Good Conduct Medal, WWII Victory Medal. (Recommended for a Silver Star, but never received it. He was on the front line, fighting Nazis until the end.)

He was discharged Jan. 5, 1946, with the rank of S/Sgt. Platoon Sgt.

Since 1965 he has been Cantor and teacher in Kesser Israel Syng, Springfield, MA. Member and former Chaplain of Post 26, JWV.

WILLIAM CHARNEY, born Jan. 18, 1918, in St. Petersburg, Russia. Entered Army on April 8, 1942. Stationed at Bouman Field, KY; Ft. Jay, NY; European Theater; Medical Field Service School, Carlisle, VA.

Awards/Medals: Ribbons, Meritorious Service Unit Plaque.

He was discharged Aug. 15, 1945, U.S.A. with the rank of captain. Today he is sick with Parkinson's at nursing home.

HILBERT P. CHASKY, (HC 1/C USNR) born Feb. 8, 1927, in New York, raised in Brooklyn. Attended PS 188, PS 239 (Mark Twain Junior High School) Abraham Lincoln High School, Pharmacy major at Brooklyn College of Pharmacy, Long Island University.

July 1944, completed a trimester before enlisting in USNR at 18 (April 23, 1945). Boot Camp April to June 1945 (seven weeks) U.S. Naval Training Station Great Lakes, IL. R.T. training in Chicago (four weeks) July 1945 Hospital Corps. School at Farragut, ID, (seven weeks) September 1945. Seattle Naval Hospital HC 1/C in charge of Orthopedic Ward. Escorted a train convoy of 200 wounded for R&R, Ithaca New York Naval Hospital and returned to Seattle. Reassignment to Aiea Heights Naval Hospital via troop ship *Burias*, December 1945. Participated in choir, conducted Sabbath Services, separated, July 2, 1946, at Lido Beach, Discharge Center. Re-entered Pharmacy School, graduated June 1949, with a BS in pharmacy degree, passed licenser exams in New York, New Jersey and Florida.

Married High School classmate, Bella Rhine, December 1948. Son Judah (dentist) and Sarah (special Ed teacher) have three children: Moshe, Devorah and Neima and daughter Miriam (speech pathologist) and Mitch (computer consultant) have three children, Deena, Dafna and Yaacov.

Employee pharmacist for many years, finally opened his own store, sold business after 12 years, and is happily retired. Member of the JWV Marcus Smolowitz Post #218, Brooklyn, Fortitude Lodge #19 F&AM, Young Israel of Flatbush, board of directors of the Yeshivah of Flatbush, (chairman of the Red Cross Blood Bank).

JACK R. CHONOLES, born April 17, 1924, New York, NY. Enlisted Feb. 13, 1943, in the Army, 75th Div. 289th Inf. Regt. Co. B. Military locations and stations were ATO, NATO, ETO. Participated in battles in Rhineland and Ardennes.

Awards/Medals: Purple Heart, Combat Infantry Badge, European-African Middle Eastern Theater Ribbons, 2 Bronze Stars.

He was discharged Sept. 26, 1945, with the rank of PFC.

Married Dorothy, three children: Stephen, Cathy and Andrew, grandchildren, Akiba and Rachel. Retired, Delray Beach, FL. Member JWV Post 266.

MILTON E. CIVINS, born Feb. 8, 1916, in Newark, NJ. Entered the Navy on Sept. 21, 1942, in New York. Stationed at Motor Torpedo Boat Sq. Rhode Island., South Pacific Area, Hospital in Australia and San Diego, CA.

Awards/Medals: Purple Heart, Bronze Star, American Campaign, Atlantic Pacific Campaign, Presidential Unit Citation.

He was discharged Mare Island, CA, March 31, 1945, with the rank of SC2C V6 USNR.

He owned a wholesale food distributing firm in Irvington, NJ. During WWII, he served in the South Pacific on P.T. boats and was awarded the Bronze Star, Purple Heart and Presidential Unit Medals from the Naval department. He was past commander of JWV Post 309, Irvington and a life member of Veterans of Foreign Wars Post 1941 past president of Wrater Civic and Social Club and active in many civic and social clubs. Milton passed away on June 4, 1990, leaving his wife, Edith and three sons, Jeff, Arnold and Gary and a sister Ruth Miller. His brother Henry, also a veteran of African and European Theater, died in 1982.

ABRAHAM J. COHEN, born in 1922, New Bedford, MA. Served April 5, 1943, to April 7, 1946. Separated at Ft. Devens, MA.

Attended the Citadel Military College of South Carolina 1943. ROTC (artillery and infantry). Called into service by Army Reserve. Basic training (Atlantic City, NJ) passed aviation cadet exams. Shipped to Jefferson Barracks, MO. (Combat training) then to Butler University, Indianapolis, IN. (Air Crew College Training Detachment) had navigation, flight training-airport etc. Next stop San Antonio, TX (Aviation Classification Center) Next, Lowry Air Force Base (Denver, CO) for Air Force armament training. Overseas duty included 8th and 9th Strategical-Tactical Air Force Group at Base Air Depot #1 AAF 590 Lancashire, England (26 months). Duties were supply clerk handling records and replacement parts for combat-damaged aircraft.

Awards/Medals: Good Conduct, European-African-Middle-Eastern Theater and Foreign Victory Ribbon.

Married for 46 years, two daughters and two grandchildren. He is retired civilian engineering technician (1987) 28 years with Department of Defense-Army, Ft. Monmouth (Electronics Command) New Jersey, living in an adult community (ClearBrook) Cranbury, NJ. Member of their JWV Post #395 of the USA.

ABRAHAM COHEN, born March 23, 1933, Plymouth, PA. Graduated Plymouth High School. All-scholastic player of the year 1950-51. Graduated University of Tennessee/Chattanooga in 1956. Was Southeastern Conference champion in wrestling 1953-54-55.

Drafted in U.S. Army in Miami Oct. 26, 1956, processed at Ft. Jackson, NC, and sent to Ft. Hood, TX, 45th Medical Battalion. Rank Spec. 4th Class, 3rd Armd. Div.

At Ft. Hood, was player-coach of the football team and won the Army championship and played Bolling Air Force at Galveston, TX, in the "Shrimp Bowl."

In 1957, was sent to Frankfurt, Germany and was All-Army wrestling heavyweight champion 1957 and 1958 and a player-coach in football. Entered in the University of Tennessee/Chattanooga Football Hall of Fame in 1990 and Pennsylvania Sports Hall of Fame/Luzerne County in 1992.

After service, played guard-linebacker in 1959 in Canadian football for the Hamilton Tiger Cats. In 1960, qualified for U.S. Olympics in wrestling in Rome but played in the AFL for Boston Patriots as guard. Was player-coach of the Boston Sweepers in the semi-pro Continental League 1961-64.

Has one son, Brad, a teacher and assistant hockey coach in Fairbault, MN, and a daughter, Gaye, a travel consultant in San Jose, CA. Member of Post 212, Wilkes-Barre, PA.

ALBERT L. COHEN, born March 4, 1923, in Newark, NJ. His family moved to Montclair when he was one year old and he continued to be a Montclair resident for 50 years.

Entered the Army Air Force on April 1, 1943, and was stationed at Ft. Dix, NJ, after induction, with basic training at Miami Beach, FL, and Glider Field Training at Shepard Field, TX. He was with Group Carrier Squadrons for one year and then transferred to weather school and weather duty, serving in England, France and Germany. He was discharged on April 1, 1946.

He received the American Campaign Medal, the EME Campaign Medal, Good Conduct Medal and WWII Victory Medal. After discharge from service, he entered college earning a BA degree from Rutgers University in New Jersey, a JDL from Rutgers Law School, in New Jersey, and LLM Masters in Law from New York University Law School.

He served as National Commander of JWV from August 1991 to August 1992, after serving in various national offices including national inspector, and national judge advocate. He is presently a member of the National Museum of American Jewish Military History. He is active in other veterans organizations being a life member of Disabled American Veterans and Veterans of Foreign Wars besides the JWV, USA, and the American Legion. He is presently serving as judge advocate of the Department of New Jersey AMVETS and he is vice-chairman of PANCO, Past National Commanders Organization).

In addition to the above, he is presently active in the practice of law, having completing his 44th year as a practicing attorney.

BERNARD I. COHEN, born March 3, 1917, Baltimore, MD. High school, Baltimore City College, 1931-34. University of Maryland, School of Pharmacy, 1934-38, BS degree.

Volunteered September 1941, USNR. U.S. Naval Academy Jan. 9, 1942-May 1942, Ensign (EVG) Attended Radar schools, designated fighter director, radar watch officer aboard USS *Sangamon* CVE-26, CARDIV-22 (first ever carrier division in any naval history) August 1942.

Served on *Sangamon* 23 months; North Africa Invasion 1942. New Hebrides 1943. Tarawa 1943, Kwajalein 1944, Eniwetok 1944.

Ordered back for reassignment and eventually reported to USS *Springfield* CL-66, that joined task group 38.4 or 58.4 with Admirals Halsey (38) and Spruance (58). Bombarded Japan July 1, 1945. The ship was the first cruiser to enter Sagamiwan Aug. 27, 1945. Separated Dec. 10, 1945, with the rank of lieutenant (S.G) from active duty; remained in Naval Reserve for about six months then resigned. Earned 10 campaign and battle ribbons.

Practiced retail pharmacy as an employee and store owner until 1974. Started working for Food and Drug Administration; still employed there.

Wed Edith Ruth Nordin, May 8, 1942; have three married daughters and five grandchildren.

BRUCE A. COHEN, born Sept. 22, 1953, Brooklyn, NY. Enlisted Feb. 28, 1990, USN, Medical Corps. Military locations included 4th FSSG, OIC DET K FLT HOSP 500 CBTZ20, Philadelphia, PA, Battalion Surgeon, Operation Desert Shield and Storm.

The following is taken from his presentation for the Navy Commendation with Combat V for Valor: "For heroic achievement while serving as battalion surgeon, Headquarters and Service Company, 1st Battalion, 25th Marines, 1st Marine Div., during Operation Desert Storm. On Feb. 24, 1991, 1st Battalion, 25th Marines forward command post advanced through two Iraqi obstacle belts in trace of the assaulting task forces for the purpose of establishing a temporary holding area for an expected large numbers of Iraqi enemy prisoners of war. This location was situated in an area that was still under enemy direct and indirect fire. Lieutenant Commander Cohen was immediately confronted with the dilemma of dealing with large numbers of wounded Iraqi soldiers and some wounded Marines. Undaunted by the indirect fire going on around him, Lieutenant Commander Cohen worked feverishly through the next four days during which he directed the medical evacuation of 300 wounded Iraqi soldiers and treated over 600 others for various types of ailments. His professional, yet compassionate spirit and style inspired all who observe him and contributed significantly to the accomplishment of the unit's mission. Lieutenant Commander Cohen's courage, initiative and selfless devotion to duty reflected great credit upon himself and were in keeping with the highest traditions of the United States Naval Service."

He attained the rank of lieutenant commander.

He has been married to Marjorie for 13 years; daughters: Melissa, Samantha, Marlo. Today he is senior medical officer for COMSUBGRU-9 Silverdale, WA, Naval Sub Base, Bangor.

CHARLES COHEN, born Dec. 25, 1915, Mt. Vernon, NY. Served with the 83rd Chemical Mortar Bn, 5th Army in European Theater, Italy. Participating in battle in the Italian Campaign.

Awards/Medals: Purple Heart with five Battle Stars.

He and his wife Lillian had one son and two daughters. He died Jan. 28, 1976.

CHARLES J. COHEN, inducted July 15, 1942, Ft. Jay, NY. Reported July 29, 1942, Camp Upton, NY. Assigned to Company C, 1st Chemical Warfare Service Training Bn. Camp, Sibert, AL. November 1942, assigned to Div. HQ Chemical Warfare Section. Jan. 10, 1943, made T/5 Div. HQ, 99th Inf. Div., Mississippi Camp Van Dorn. May 1943, ASTP, Brooklyn Poly Tech, Brooklyn, NY. March 1944, assigned to HQ, 2nd Bn, 289 Inf., 75th Inf. Div. Camp Breckinridge, KY. Overseas ETO Oct. 2, 1994 Dec. 17, 1945. Discharged Jan. 12, 1946, Camp Dix, NJ.

Awards/Medals: Bronze Star, Combat Infantry Badge, Good Conduct Medal, Meritorious Unit Award, American Campaign Medal, ETO with three Battle Stars: Battle of the Bulge, Battle of Colmar (Alsace), Battle for the Ruhr (Germany). WWII Victory Medal, Army of Occupation-Germany, Sharp Shooter Badge, M-1 Rifle.

My close call story: towards the end of the Bulge we started pushing the Germans Eastward; we were given the job of lifting an anti-tank mine field. After being shown the mine for the first time and A/10 minute instruction period, we started at early night time and had to be out by 2 a.m., using bayonets we prodded, the snow, and upon finding a mine, separated the top web and fuse from the body of the mine into two separate stacks. At 2 a.m. we had not finished and covering shells started to come in fairly close. But finally they got the word back to the field artillery to stop the shelling.

DANIEL F. COHEN, Commander of Lt. Cmdr. Ben Dobris Post 750, JWV, Palm Springs, CA. Born in St. Louis, MO, on Dec. 30, 1922. One of three brothers who served in the U.S. Army during WWII. Entered Army Infantry training at Camp Roberts, CA, on August 1942.

Served with the 27th Div. in Pacific Theater. Assigned to heavy weapons, 80 mm mortar, squadleader. Participated in the battles of Saipan, Philippines and Okinawa. Honorably discharged Oct. 29, 1945. Awarded Bronze Star, Presidential Citation and others.

Married Mae Honigman, Dec. 9, 1945. Two daughters, four grandchildren. Daniel and Mae now retired and residing in Palm Springs, CA.

Occupation after being discharged … Rancher in California and insurance agent with Prudential Ins. Co. in Los Angeles.

EMANUEL COHEN, born Feb. 1, 1919, in Philadelphia, PA. Entered the U.S. Army on March 11, 1942, at Ft. Meade, MD. Assigned to 10th Field Hospital as an administrative sergeant.

Participated in the following battles and campaigns: Tunisia, Sicily, Naples-Foggia, Rome-Arno, Rhineland, Central Europe, Southern France.

Awards/Medals: Good Conduct Medal, Meritorious Service Unit Plaque, EAME with seven Bronze Stars, Bronze Service with Arrowhead. Honorably discharged on Aug. 1, 1945, at the rank of S/Sgt.

He died on Aug. 26, 1988.

FRANK I. COHEN, born Oct. 1, 1921, St. Louis, MO. Enlisted in U.S. Army June 1942, and honorably discharged on February 1946. Went to Chicago University for one year to study Chinese under Army specialized training program. Trained further at St. Petersburg, FL, and Ft. Riley, KS. Sent to Chunking, China to be interpreter of General Wedemeyer, General Joe Stillman and General George Marshal. Traveled between enemy, Communist and Allied lines to coordinate. Honorably discharged rating of LTG2. Deceased February 1961.

Occupation after discharged … attorney (tax attorney). Graduated Harvard University. Served government as assistant IRS commissioner in Washington, DC, until his demise in 1961.

GEORGE COHEN, born 1921, New York, NY. Enlisted Oct. 29, 1940, U.S. Army Air Corp, 487th Bomb Group (H) 8th Air Force, armament and gun turret specialist. Stationed at nine air bases in the States, plus Cuba, Trinidad and England. The group flew 185 missions over Germany and the occupied countries.

Memorable experiences include frequent buzz bomb attacks in England. Flying many ocean patrols as crew member on sub anti-sub flying prior to England.

Awards/Medals: American Defense Service Medal, American Service Medal, European African Middle Eastern Service Medal with six Bronze Stars, Good Conduct Medal, Victory Medal, Distinguished Unit Citation.

He was discharged Aug. 27, 1945, with the rank of tech. sergeant.

Married twice, first wife died in 1973. Has two daughters from first marriage. Married present wife Lenore in 1976. Retired in 1985, as a supervisor of subway car repair and maintenance New York City Transit Authority.

HENRY L. COHEN, born in Essen, Germany, June 19, 1922. Escaped Holocaust July 1939, for Panama, South America. July 1940, emigrated to USA. Some high school education. Machinist in War Production.

April 12, 1944, entered U.S. Army, trained in Camp Blanding, FL. Joined 65th Infantry Div., Communication Battalion in Camp Shelby, MS. Landed in Northern France, went into action across Germany and Austria. During combat transferred to 430th (later 970th) Counter Intelligence Corp. Involved in capture of Gauleiter of Upper Austria and approximately 1,500 Nazi officials. Liberated Ohrdruf Concentration Camp. Discharged May 1946, sergeant.

Awards/Medals: Bronze Star Medal, Combat Infantry Badge, European-African-Middle Eastern Theater, Good Conduct and WWII Victory Medal.

Interrogator 1946-48, Military War Crimes Tribunal, Nuremberg, Germany. 1948-1953, War Department Civilian, Military Intelligence Service, Vienna, Austria, Civil Censorship Group. 1953 Retail Credit Business, 1958-1991 Investment Real Estate Operation. Now happily retired.

Married 45 years to Rita, have daughter and two sons and five grandchildren. Member of Jewish War Veterans Post Paul D. Savanuck Memorial #888, Baltimore, MD.

IDA NEEDLE COHEN, WAAC, private first class, inducted from Lawrence, MA, in 1943. Assigned to Luke Field in Arizona to maintenance and supplies. Honorably discharged in 1945. Married Jacob M. Cohen, two children … now retired and residing in Petaluma, CA.

IRVING COHEN, 1914-1991, 30th Div. Quartermaster Corp ETO 40 months in service.

JACOB COHEN, inducted into the Medical Corps on Aug. 31, 1945, as a surgeon technician and was discharged on Nov. 16, 1946.

He was stationed at Ft. McClellan, AL. He received several citations and decorations, among which were the Good Conduct Ribbon, American Service Medal and World II Victory Medal. *Submitted by Max Sigal.*

JACOB M. COHEN, Sgt., U.S. Army Medical Corp. Inducted March 1942. Honorable discharge, January 1946. Served together with brother Daniel F. Cohen at Camp Roberts, CA. Jacob served in Australia and New Guinea. Deceased February 1992.

Jake was born Jan. 1, 1919, in St. Louis, MO, brother of Frank and Daniel Cohen. Retired from U.S. Mint in San Francisco, CA. Occupation, accountant. Married, two sons and one grandson.

JEROME D. COHEN, Justice, born in Coney Island into a Jewish War Veteran family, and was a member of the Sons of JWV and a drummer in the band before he was 10 years old.

At age 17 he enlisted in the Navy, served aboard the battle scarred USS *Nashville* (MacArthur's Flagship), was the coxswain of the General's motor whaleboat and a gunner's mate for three years. He was wounded in the Philippines receiving the Purple Heart, Navy Unit commendation, Asiatic Pacific Ribbon with eight Battle Stars, Philippine Liberation Ribbon with two Battle Stars, WWII Victory Medal, China War memorial Medal, Navy Occupation Medal with Asia Clasp, Philippine Liberation Medal, Philippine Independence Medal, Philippine Presidential Unit Citation Badge, and New York State Distinguished Service Cross.

At age 22 he was elected commander of the Abe Cohen-Lehman Post serving three years and married.

He then completed high school, college and law school, supporting his family and at the same time leading the fight against neo-Nazis in Yorkville, appearing as the attorney against flag desecrators, and his briefs were upheld by the Supreme Court of the United States. He was responsible for the arrest of Nazi George Lincoln Rockwell, and wrote the legal brief submitted to the Supreme Court of the State of New York. He served in the echelons of the JWV and of the N.E.C. for 12 years and led a vigorous tri-state action committee before his election as National Commander for 1971-1972. Some highlights include being invited to the Soviet Union for the purpose of reporting the status of anti-Semitism to President Nixon, instituting the "Jewish Veteran" magazine, proposing the presence of the U.S. Fleet in Haifa, which was brought to fruition after a five year struggle, and these were only a few of the "firsts" of an aggressive National Commander.

After 20 years as a successful trial attorney, he was elected a Civil Court Judge and then a Justice of the Supreme Court of the State of New York.

His retirement gives him the opportunity to enjoy his three sons and nine grandchildren (the eldest granddaughter a recent college graduate and a grandson serving with the Marines in Okinawa). He sails his own 35' sailboat, raced from Newport to Bermuda, golfs, travels, is still active in the Jewish War Veteran and the Supreme Court Justices Association, and lives by his credo, "If you want a job done well, give it to a busy person."

JULIUS MICKEY COHEN, born April 21, 1926, Brownside, NY. USA, enlisted June 1944, Pvt. Ft. McClellan, AL, Ft. Benning, GA. Discharged December 1945. Wife, Marjorie, children, Dr. Lawrence J. Cohen, Judy, Jeri, Marty and seven grandchildren. Chief of Staff 1979, Chairman Century Club, PDC 1971-72, National Inspector 1979-85. Board of NNAJMH.

MARC J. COHEN, born Feb. 19, 1960, in New Bedford, MA, and grew up there. He joined the USN Seabees on Nov. 3, 1980, and after boot camp in Orlando, FL, and Steelworker A School in Gulfport, MS, he was assigned to Naval Mobile Construction Battalion one, which was being deployed to the Indian Ocean atoll of Diego Garcia.

After six months, they were relieved by another Seabee battalion and headed back to Gulfport for six months of construction and combat training. Then back to Diego Garcia again for nine months, where he has promoted to steelworker third class.

After several months back in Gulfport, he was honorably discharged from active service and remained in the reserves for two years, while attending Florida Institute of Technology. He was honorably discharged in 1986. He now works and resides in Ft. Lauderdale, FL, and plans to finish college.

MURRAY L. COHEN "MICKEY," Division HQ G-2, was born Oct. 3, 1923, in Manhattan, NYC, and attended New York University before entering the USAAC March 27, 1943. After basic training, completed aerial photography course at Lowry Field, Peterson Field and Will Rogers Field, going overseas February 1944, to the 325th Photo Recon Wing, 8th Army Air Force in England.

After learning of the death of brother-in-law Capt. Lewis S. Mentlik, killed in action June 14, 1944, with the airborne, he put in transfer to the 101st Abn. Div.

Thereafter occurred the unforgettable events of sewing on the Screaming Eagle Patch and Jump School with pinning on Jump Wings.

The worst events of the ETO were losing a beloved brother-in-law and liberating Concentration Camp #5 in a wooded area outside Landsberg, Austria, with Sgt. Russ Engle. The shock and horror of this experience are forever.

Service in G-2 included combat and aerial photography in Division Artillery L-5 Recon airplanes for pre-patrol photos and aerial observation intelligence. Also served in the 506th PIR.

Left ETO December 1945 and discharged January 1946. Received the EAME Campaign Medal with four Battle Stars for Air Offensive (Ardennes, Central Europe and Rhineland), Good Conduct Medal, Bronze Star, WWII Victory Medal, Parachute Badge, Glider Badge, Combat Infantry Badge, Official U.S. Army Photographer Patch, Presidential Unit Citation with OLC and Belgium Croix de Guerre.

Graduated New York University in 1948 with BS. Attended Columbia University, Graduate School of Philosophy three years. Charter member and life member #1 of 101st Abn. Div. Association, served as president, national president and chairman of the board.

Married Priscilla Pinkney Robinson in 1981; they were blessed with daughter Alissa-Rose Moira in 1985. His four sons: Charles, Neal, Kenneth and Roger, from a previous marriage.

NATHAN COHEN, born Aug. 24, 1919, in Portland, ME. Enlisted in the U.S. Army in November 1942, assigned to the infantry with the 71st and 90th Inf. Div. Military locations include Ft. Bragg, NC, Panama, Ft. Dix, NJ, Camp Carson, CO, and the invasion of France.

He was assigned to the 71st Inf. Div. formed at Camp Carson, CO, and sent to Hunter Liggett, CA, as a replacement to the 90th Inf. Div. After a few days at Normandy Beach was wounded and captured. While a POW he lost 100 lbs.

Memorable experience was playing checkers against the Russian champion while a POW.

Awards/Medals: Good Conduct Medal, Purple Heart, Bronze Star and CIB. Honorably discharged in May 1947 with rank of corporal.

He is in the International Checker Hall of Fame and *Guiness Book of Records* for playing 182 players, winning all the games in 4.5 hours. He is a retired postal clerk.

NEILAND COHEN, born Feb. 1, 1927, Milwaukee, WI. Enlisted USN February 1944. Basic training Great Lakes, IL; amphibious training Little Creek, VA. Served on LST 565 as yeoman. Participated in five major invasions Pacific area including D-Day Oct. 20, 1944, Tacloban, Leyte, Philippines. Saw General MacArthur walk ashore. D-Day April 1, 1945, Nanha, Okinawa. Ship bombarded twice, credited with shooting down Japanese plane. Jewish holidays observed Pacific area at Army camps.

Re-enlisted May 1946, in active naval reserve Milwaukee. Recalled to active duty June 1950 for Korean War, stationed at Great Lakes Training Center. Honorable discharge December 1951. Awarded a number of medals for service including five Battle Stars. Was YN2/c WWII and PN 2/c Korean War.

Married to Amelia. Graduated University of Wisconsin, major accounting. Employed by IRS for 35 years as Revenue Agent, Tax Law Specialist and Program Analyst. Is now self-employed tax consultant.

PHILIP M. COHEN, born June 24, 1948, Minnesota, MN. Enlisted Jan. 29, 1968, U.S. Army, TDY D Co. 47th Inf. Bn. 101st AB Div. Military locations included Ft. Dix, Ft. Gordon, Presidio, Firebase Baring RVN, Stuttgart Germany, TET.

Memorable experience included scoring 18 points and 23 points in basketball doubleheader.

Awards/Medals: VN Service Ribbon, Army Commendation Meal, Bronze Star, Air Medal, CIB, Jump Wings.

He was discharged Jan. 30, 1971, with the rank of sergeant E-5.

Married and has four children. Today he is a television/video producer in Tampa, FL.

ROBERT L. COHEN, Colonel, Military Police Corps, U.S. Army, 25 years. Retired 1993. Born Dec. 9, 1945, Waterbury, CT. MA, Criminal Justice; BA, Political Science.

Entered the Army in 1967 from ROTC and served as platoon leader in Vietnam with the 552nd MP Co. at II Field Force north of Bien Hoa; later attached to the 2nd Armd. Cav. Regt. in Quan Loi to provide convoy security. Other assignments: Briefing Officer to the Secretary of the Army; The White House as Assistant to the Vice President and in the Executive Office of the President; Military Assistant to the Assistant Secretary of the Army; Inspector General, the Pentagon; Chief of Staff, U.S. Disciplinary Barracks, Ft. Leavenworth, KS; 21st Support Command, Kaiserslautern, Germany; and Company Commander, 207th MP Co., Ft. Riley, KS.

Awards/Medals: Legion of Merit (three awards), Bronze Star Medal, Meritorious Service Medal, White House Presidential Service Badge, Vietnam Campaign Medal, and Vietnam Cross of Gallantry with Palm (unit citation). Distinguished Military Graduate, University of Connecticut, 1967.

Employed in Washington, DC, as senior associate for public policy research. Member JWV, USA; Life Member - DAV.

RUDOLPH COHEN, born Gelsenkirchen, Germany Oct. 5, 1924. Escaped Holocaust July 1939, came to Baltimore 1940 via Panama. Graduated Polytechnic Institute, attended courses Johns Hopkins University.

Entered Army January 1944, Ft. Geo. G. Meade MD. Training: Basic, Camp Blanding, FL, Infantry I&R Man Convoy from Newport News to Oran, Africa, 1944 then Italy. Invasion of Southern France, Germany and Czechoslovakia. Left Infantry, transferred to 759th Railroad Operating Battalion. Went into Dachau Concentration Camp.

Awards/Medals: European African Middle Eastern Theater Ribbon, Good Conduct, WWII Victory Ribbon, three Battle Stars, Rone-Arno, Rhineland, Central Europe.

He was honorable discharged Army January 1946, with the rank of Corporal.

Married, three children (two sons and one daughter) and seven grandchildren. Owned and operated retail credit business with brother Henry 1953. Went into real estate 1958 operating investment properties. Today, Real Estate Broker, State of Maryland, with own office. Member JWV, Paul Savanuck Post #888 Baltimore, MD.

SEYMOUR COHEN, born April 6, 1922, in Poland. Enlisted Oct. 20, 1942, U.S. Army Veterinary Det. 616 FA Bn. (PK) 10th MT Div. Military locations included Ft. Dix, NJ; Camp Carson, CO; Camp Hale, CO; and Camp Swift, TX. Participated in battle in Northern Apennine Mountains, Po Valley, Italy.

The 10th Mtn. Div. was the only one of its kind in WWII. The infantry were the mountain climbers and skiers. The artillery was 75 mm Howitzers that were carried on the backs of mules. They were called pack artillery. He was a vet technician, and gave aid to a sick mule. He took care of these animals with great care as they cost U.S. Army about $350 a head. The Army brought over to Italy thousands of these

animals and when the War was over the farmers of Italy and Yugoslavia had strong mules to farm the land.

Awards/Medals: WWII Victory Medal, American Theater of Operations Ribbon, Good Conduct Medal, EAME Ribbon.

He was discharged Dec. 13, 1945, Camp Crowder, MO, with the rank of corporal.

Married to Ruth and has two children and four grandsons. Retired Oct. 1, 1988.

SOLOMON COHEN, born April 19, 1916 in Philadelphia, PA and entered the U.S. Army on May 9, 1945. Assigned as rifleman at the rank of private. His awards and decorations include the WW II Victory Ribbon. He was honorably discharged on March 4, 1946 at Ft. Meade, MD.

SYDNEY M. COHEN, USAFR (RET.), Colonel, born in Allentown, PA, on Jan. 17, 1924. Enlisted in the U.S. Army's Enlisted Reserve Corps in December 1942, when a sophomore at Lehigh University, Bethlehem, PA.

Called to active duty on June 8, 1943. Took infantry basic training at Camp Wolters, TX, in summer of 1943. Sent to the Army Specialized Training Program studying mechanical engineering at the University of Delaware, Newark, DE, from September 1943 to March 1944.

At end of March 1944 joined the 104th Infantry Div. (Timberwolf Division) Company K, 415th Infantry Regt. at Camp Carson, CO. Div. went to Europe landed in France in September 1944. Division fought in Holland and Germany. Participated in three campaigns, Northern France, Rhineland and Central Europe.

Awards/Medals: Combat Infantry Badge, Silver Star, Bronze Star Medal with Valor Device and one Bronze OLC, Purple Heart with one Bronze OLC, Meritorious Service Medal, Presidential Unit Citation, Army Good Conduct Medal, American Campaign Medal, European-African-Middle Eastern Campaign Medal with three Bronze Stars (campaigns listed above), WWII Victory Medal, Air Force Longevity Service Award Ribbon with one Silver OLC and three Bronze OLCs (over 36 years of active and reserve military service), and the Armed Forces Reserve Medal with two Hourglass Devices (over 30 years of Reserve Duty).

Discharged from Army on Nov. 26, 1945, as a private first class.

Enlisted in the U.S. Army's Enlisted Reserve Corps on Nov. 26, 1945, for three years.

Received direct commission in the U.S. Air Force Reserve on June 27, 1950, as a second lieutenant. Retied as a colonel on July 26, 1980. Held several mobilization positions in the USAFR, the last being a Research and Development Director in HQ, USAF (Pentagon).

Married to Harriet since 1956, one son and one daughter, and one grandson, two granddaughter and two a member, Commander of JWV Post 589, Arlington, VA, from May 1986 to March 1988. Retired from consulting engineering firm in August 1993, presently do part time consulting.

DAVID S. COHN, inducted October 1942, at Ft. Devens, MA. Basic training with the 10th Armd. Div., Ft. Benning, GA. Attended Armd. Forces Radio School at Ft. Knox, KY, in 1943. While at Ft. Knox was so impressed with the hospitality and fellowship by the Louisville JWV Post and the Jewish Center he signed 93 servicemen to become service members in JWV. Went overseas to Cherbourg, France in August 1994, with the 10th Armd. Div. and after a period of hospitalization in England was re-assigned to the 1056 Port Construction Company that rebuilt destroyed bridges over the Northern

Rhine River at Menzelen. Upon discharge in August 1945, became active in the Hartford Post #45 and was elected post commander in 1951. Became department commander, Department of Connecticut in 1959.

Active in civic affair and politics, served on the Hartford City Council in 1954, and was elected to the state legislature in 1967. Recently retired from his wholesale meat business, he now is a volunteer at the Hebrew Home and Hospital in West Hartford, CT. He is the father of three children and four grandchildren, and still active in Post #45 serving as Judge Advocate.

FRANK COHN, was born in Breslau, Germany, on Aug. 2, 1925. In 1938, he fled Germany with his parents on a visitor's visa to New York, ten days before Kristallnacht. He was drafted into the Army in September 1943, and became a citizen while stationed at Ft. Benning, GA, early the following year. He arrived in Belgium in August 1944, and due to his German language ability, was assigned to an intelligence unit designated as T-Force, 12th Army Group. During the Battle of the Bulge, he was engaged in the hunt of German infiltrators in U.S. uniform. Later, he participated in missions to arrest

Gestapo, SS and Nazi Party members as well as take control of industrial complexes like the Stahlof in Duesseldorf and IG Farben in Frankfurt. By the end of the war he was in Magdeburg where he met the Russians. In December 1944, he went to Berlin where he confirmed that the many relatives he had left behind had died in concentration camps. He was discharged in May 1946, in the rank of staff sergeant and returned to CCNY for his college degree. In 1948, he married Pauline Brimberg from New York and at graduation in 1949, was commissioned as an officer in the Regular Army. He served as a Military Police officer from 1949-1978, to include tours of duty in Europe, Korea and Vietnam, and retired as a colonel, with his last position as chief of staff, Military District of Washington. His awards include the Legion of Merit with OLC, the Bronze Star, the Meritorious Service Medal, the Commendation Medal and the German Grosse Verdienstkreuz. Subsequently he worked as an administrator for the University of Maryland and fully retired in 1992. His daughter Laura is a travel agent who helps plan his trips from his home in Mount Vernon, VA.

RABBI BARUCH J. COHON, born in Chicago, April 1926, he grew up in Cincinnati, where his father taught at the Hebrew Union College. June of 1943, he graduated from Hughes High School, September of that year he held his first High Holiday position as a Cantor in Pontiac, MI. One month later he was in the Navy. He served in the Aleutian Islands, first in a ship repair unit, then on a YMS, the smallest of the minesweepers. He was a soundman, later they called it Sonar, reached second class. He was also the only Jewish enlisted man on his ship.

Discharged in April 1946, he went to college on the GI Bill, first in Cincinnati and later at UCLA where he met his wife Claire. They were married in 1950, and now have four children and three grandchildren. He spent about 12 years of

his working life in the studios, earning 300 credits as a TV writer, production manger, and producer. Then he turned to full-time synagogue work and served several California congregations as Cantor. He received Rabbinical ordination in 1969, and continue functioning as Cantor, or Rabbi, or both. He also turned out a few books, a great deal of music, and four recordings. The current picture is from an album he just made with his son Sam, also a rabbi and cantor.

MAXWELL S. COLON, Colonel, born in the South Bronx, New York City, on June 14, 1941. His initial military service was as an enlisted person on Sept. 1, 1964, in the New York National Guard 42nd Div. Arty. and attended basic and advanced training at Ft. Dix, NJ. He was commissioned second lieutenant in the artillery Aug. 19, 1966, from Officer Candidate School. April 5, 1975, transferred to the 77th Army Reserves at Ft. Totten as a captain and was promoted to full colonel June 13, 1988. He has been eligible for general officer assignment since 1990.

He received a bachelor of science degree from the University of the State of New York in social science in 1980. Holds a masters of professional studies degree from Long Island University in Criminal Justice 1981 and awarded it's Outstanding Graduate Award. Member of Alpha Phi Sigma and Epsilon Beta Criminal Justice Honor Societies. Holds post-graduate certification certificate from Long Island University in security administration 1984 and awarded the Security Administration Award. Recipient three different times of the New York City Certificate of Educational Achievement.

Col. Colon graduate of numerous senior service colleges to include Command and General Staff Officers College, National Security Management University, Army Logistics Executive Management College, and Air War College. Also graduated from DOD Equal Opportunity Institute, Federal Emergency Management Agency, DOD Industrial Security Institute, and multiple number of other military schooling. Col. Colon holds the Army wide record for completion of the most military correspondence courses.

Col. Colon held a wide variety of command and staff positions in the Combat Arms, Combat Support and Combat Service Support Branches of the Army which include service as a forward observer, section commander, executive officer, battery commander, liaison officer, target analysis, commanding officer/S-4, assistant S-3, Adjutant/S-1, project manager, equal opportunity staff advisor and instructor, secretary/S-1, assistant director with the United States Special Operations Command, member of Secretariat for DA Active Selection Promotion Boards and member of Secretariat for Reserves Component Selection Promotion Boards. Presently, Military Police colonel in the Army Reserves, with over 29 years of service time.

During his years of military service he has been the recipient of the Meritorious Service Medal, Army Commendation Medal with two OLCs, Army Achievement Medal with OLC, National Defense Service Medal, Armed Forces Reserve Medal with 10 years device, Army Reserve Component Achievement Medal with three OLCs, and the Army Service Ribbon.

In civilian life, he is a retired New York City Correction Captain. Married for over 27 years and resides with wife Linda Sue and two of their four children in La Costa, CA. Present Commander of North County Post No. 385, and has been a member of the JWV of the USA since 1990.

Memberships in various Associations have included the Correction Captains Association, Gibborim Society, Hispanic Society, Board of Governors, 77th USARCOM Officers Association, Reserve Offices Associations Department of California Reserves Officers Association, Air War College Alumni Association, National War College Alumni Association, University of the State of New York Alumni Association, Long Island University Alumni Association, Alpha Phi Sigma National Criminal Justice Honor Society, Long Island University Epsilon Beta Criminal Justice Honor Society.

SOLOMON COLOW, born Brooklyn, NY, April 5, 1922. Inducted into the Army Nov. 6, 1942. Basic training in Armd. Div. Camp Campbell, KY. Specialized training, radio, International Morse code, cryptology, FM maintenance. Volunteered for the 101st Airborne Paratroops on same base. Rejected because of one bad eye. Transferred to the 4th Armd. Div., Troop D 25th Calvary Recon Squad Mechanized.

Plymouth England to Omaha Beach Invasion from hedgerows to breakout St. Lo. Led Patton's armor from Normandy-Bastogne-Germany.

Awards/Medals: Presidential Citation, Distinguished Unit Badge-Europeans Service Medal. Five Battle Stars for Ardennes, Central Europe, Normandy, Northern France, Rhineland.

Liberator of concentration camp Ohdruff, sub camp of Buchenwald.

Discharged Oct. 20, 1945. Married to Lillie, son and daughter and two grandchildren. Member of JWV Post 569, retired.

MORTON CONFELD, born March 5, 1912, in Minneapolis, MN. Graduated from West High School 1930. Attended University of Minnesota for a short while.

Enlisted Air Corp in 1941. Sent to Ft. Knox for training and became a staff sergeant. Mont was chosen to attend OCS at Harvard. Became second lieutenant in 1943.

Married Shirley, July 1943, in Seattle.

Sent overseas in October 1943, Spent two years as a statistical control officer in Italy. Returned home August 1945, as first lieutenant.

Discharged after war in Europe ended.

Three children, two boys and one girl. There are seven grandchildren with four to carry on family name. Worked at plumbing eight years and then in plumbing supply until retirement.

Mont died Jan. 19, 1989.

ARTHUR E. CONN, Colonel, born in Philadelphia, PA, Nov. 22, 1907. BS Wharton School University of Pennsylvania, 1928. MA in education New York University. Commissioned second lieutenant QMC. USAR 1938. Overseas with Gen. Patton North Africa 1942, Assistant Operations Officer, QM Div. in Armd. Corp; served on Liaison Staff to General Sir Harold Alexander, Commanding General 15th Army Group Invasion of Sicily; Planning Staff Invasion Southern France, Assistant Operations Officer, QM Section, CONAD; QM Section General Eisenhower's staff, Frankfort, Germany, when WWII ended.

Integrated into RA 1945. Helped to reestablish QM School, Camp Lee, VA, 1946. Attended Command and General Staff College 1947, retained as instructor, Editor English Edition Military Review 18 months.

Korea 1951, Operations Officer QM Div. 8th Army. Liaison Officer Kobe, Japan, QM Depot. Pentagon, Property Disposal Officer U.S Army Promoted to full colonel Nov. 1, 1954. Belle Mead General Depot, QM, SO and CO. France 1957, QM BASEC Supply 6th Army Group.

Returned 1960 USA West Coast as IG for the Supply and Maintenance Command.

Retired and took final review May 1, 1963, Presidio, San Francisco.

Awards/Medals: Legion of Merit Bronze Star with OLC, Army Commendation Ribbon with OLC. Eleven Battle Stars all pertinent Theater and Victory ribbons, OBE from Great Britain, since retiring, residing in Miami, FL, with wife Leah.

BENJAMIN D. COOPER, born Dec. 24, 1921, Avon, CT. Inducted into service Sept. 25, 1942, Army, Medical Department, Camp Barkley, TX.

Memorable experience: Medical basic training at Camp Barkley, TX, in 1942, and was sent to a repple depple in Italy in September 1944 where he was assigned to the 45th Infantry Div. also known as the Thunderbird Division, and joined the 179h Infantry Regt. part of the 45th Infantry Div. on Nov. 1, 1944, in Contrexveille, France, as a litter bearer with the forward Battalion Aid Station and later as a medic with various rifle companies and an anti-tank company.

Upon joining the rifle company, he was told to keep his dog-tags in his pocket and not around his neck, because the dog tags designated whether you were Hebrew, Protestant or Catholic, and if he was ever captured, he probably would be tortured. On April 29, 1945, part of his outfit the 45th Infantry Div., namely, the 157th Infantry Regt. liberated Dachau Concentration Camp and a couple of days later several of the medics were taken to Dachau Concentration Camp. He remembers vividly meeting and talking to hundreds of inmates in one large open area and restricted from the rest of the camp because Typhus and other diseases were rampant. They were told emphatically not to give the inmates any water or food and they had to wear a make shift mask because of the stench of hundreds of corpses and other horrible conditions of the camp. That traumatic incident as well as other incidents left him with a knot in his chest and he could never discuss his experiences with anyone at home until 1990, when a high school teacher asked him about his experiences during WWII. Since then he has been talking to high school students about his experiences as a combat medic, Dachau, liberating a Russian slave factory in Germany, liberating two persons who had been living in their house in Germany surrounded by barbed wire and he found that one was a doctor one a lawyer and one was Jewish and the other a German. They were husband and wife. He also saw in Munich hundreds of German prisoners being marched through one of the main streets and among them was Herman Goering, stripped of all his medal and many German residents trying to give him flowers, etc. but the American guards forbid them.

Another memorable experience was coming home on a ship named the *Acquitania* with 7,000 troops aboard and as they passed the Statue of Liberty, the ship was listing badly because they were all on one side facing the Statue with tears in their eyes.

In February 1945, the rifle company he was with was taken off the front lines and in Germany and taken to France for a short rest. They stopped in Luneville, France, and there he found a synagogue that had been decimated. He made the acquaintance of a Frenchman and his three young daughters and he gave him his Star of David which he treasures to this day. He has been trying to locate the Frenchman and his daughters but with no luck even though he has sent a picture of them that he had taken at the time they met to the Mayor of Luneville.

He was awarded the Bronze Star and took part in three combat campaigns, namely the Rhineland Campaign, the Ardennes-Alsace Campaign and the Central Europe Campaign. He was awarded the Combat Medical Badge in 1945. His wife, Dorothy and he have been married for 51 years and have four children and four grandchildren.

At the present time he is junior vice-commander of Post 45 JWV, Laurel Post, West Hartford, CT.

He was discharged Nov. 25, 1945, with the rank of tech 5.

ROBERT COOPER (KOOPERSTEIN), born Brooklyn, NY, July 27, 1940. Graduating from Erasmus Hall High School in 1958, he attended Polytechnic Institute of Brooklyn where he received his ROTC Commission as a second lieutenant upon completing requirements for the BSEE and MSEE degree. His first assignment was a maintenance and communications officer in the 522nd BARC Platoon, Camp Leroy Johnson, New Orleans, LA. Following a commercial airline crash into Lake Pontchartrain in 1963, Lt. Cooper participated in amphibious search and rescue operations. In 1964, Lt. Cooper was transferred to Ft. Eustis, VA, where he served as

adjutant in the 394th Transportation BN. He was honorably discharged as a first lieutenant in July 1965.

He is currently employed as an engineer for GEC-Marcony Systems in Wayne, NJ, where he develops communications equipment used by the U.S. and NATO armed forces.

Mr. Cooper has two adult children and resides in Edison, NJ, with his wife of 31 years, Carol.

JERRY COPPERSMITH, born Oct. 31, 1921, in Bronx, NY, entered the USAAF on Nov. 11, 1942. Trained as a radio operator in Chicago, IL; in gunnery in Boca Raton, FL and as Link Trainer instructor in Wilshire, England. Was an automatic pilot instructor for the B-26 Marauder, 386th BG in Bishop Stratford, England.

Awards/Medals: Distinguished Unit Badge, EAME, WWII Victory Medal, Air Offensive, Europe-Ardennes, Normandy, France and Rhineland.

Married Gloria, 51 years, with two sons, one daughter, three grandsons, and two granddaughters. Retired from the position of sales manager L'Oreal of Paris on Dec. 31, 1987, after 25 years of service. Head football referee for 30 years, Section 1-9 New York State. Did Olympic Trials as a track official and currently does high school and college baseball umpiring. A member of the Nauset, NY, JWV. He resides in Pearl River, NY.

EDWIN H. J. CORNELL, born on Oct. 20, 1922, in Rochester, NY. Graduated from the University of Rochester in 1943, as pre-med with a BA degree. After the war, in 1949 graduated from the University of Buffalo with a BS (cum laude) in pharmacy.

Entered service in the Army in October 1943. Received infantry basic training in Army Specialized Training Program at Ft. Benning, GA. Was scheduled for medical school, but program was discontinued. Transferred to 86th Infantry Div. at Camp Livingston, LA. Sent overseas as a rifleman and a replacement in 28th Div., 110th Regt. Fought in Battle of Hurtgen Forest and Ardennes among others. Earned Combat Infantryman Badge, ETO Medal with three Battle Stars, Bronze Star Medal, POW Medal and WWII Victory Medal.

Captured in Battle of Bulge in Luxembourg. served four months in German POW Camp. Discharged in November 1945.

Married Lorraine in July 1945. 48th Anniversary this year. Has son and daughter and five grandchildren. Retired as pharmacist five years ago. Belong to American ex-POWs, the DAV, JWV and is a member of a Masonic Lodge. Have lived in Scottsdale, AZ, for the past 20 years.

'REDERIC CORNELL, born in Springfield, MA, Jan. 24, 1915. Lived in New York since August 1924. BS in chemical engineering 1935, New York University. MS in chemical engineering 1936, University of Michigan, Ed. D 1976, Teachers' College/Columbia University.

Commissioned second lieutenant, Chemical Warfare Service Sept. , 1939. Retired as lieutenant colonel, Chemical Corps Nov. 8, 1967.

Active duty July 7, 1940, to Nov. 13, 1946. Served at Edgewood Arsenal, MD, and Huntsville Arsenal, AL. Oct. 14, 1950, to Jan. 31, 1957, served at Edgewood Arsenal, MD, and Gifu, Japan.

Awards/Medals: Pre-Pearl Harbor, American Theater, WWII Victory, Korea, UN, National Service, 20 years in the reserve.

Taught chemistry at Brooklyn Technical High School. Retired 1977. Married and has three children. Member Post No. 2, Brooklyn, NY.

'ULES M. COWEN, born in Clarksburg, WV, on Jan. 23, 1921, but most of his youth and adult life was spent in Pittsburgh, PA.

During WWII he enlisted in the USN and served in the South Pacific aboard the USS *Palmyra* ARST-3 of which he was part of the original commissioning crew. He obtained the permanent rank (rate) of SF3/c. He did his boots at Samson, NY, and was discharged from the very same camp.

He has been married 54 years to Alice Kaufman, born and raised in Pittsburgh, PA, they have four grown children and eight grandchildren.

In 1977 they left the north and moved to Pompano, FL, where they still live as full-time Floridians. They spend their retirement years doing the usual, golf, cards, theater, travel and general socializing.

Presently he belong to JWV Post 196, which meets on a regular basis at Temple Shalom here in Pompano.

He enjoys retirement, but feel sorry that he's been unable to contact any of his old shipmates, there were only three Jews aboard, two enlisted men and one officer.

RABBI JON EDWARD CUTLER, born May 30, 1956, Philadelphia, PA. He is a graduate of the Reconstructionist Rabbinical College in Wyncote, PA. He served as a Navy chaplain for five years on active duty. His tours of duty included two years at Subic Bay Naval Station, Philippines, eighteen months at Camp Lejeune, North Carolina, and one year on Okinawa with the Marines. He also served as circuit rabbi for the Seventh Fleet in the Indian and Pacific Oceans and as chaplain for the School of Infantry at Camp Lejeune. During Desert Storm, he served as the sole Jewish chaplain for all Navy and Marine land forces stationed in the Persian Gulf. He has received two Navy Commendation medals for meritorious service in Desert Storm as well as in Southwest Pacific. He presently holds the rank of lieutenant in the Naval Reserves and is the rabbi for a congregation in Flemington, NJ.

SAMUEL CUTLER, born Samuel Cutler, served in the U.S. Army with the Military Police Detachment and entered service at Ft. Devens, MA, in April 1944, and when discharged in January 1946, was stationed at Ft. Logan, CO. He entered the service with the rank of private and was discharged as a private first class. His training consisted of medical training at Camp Grant, IL, from March 1944 to July 1944, and Ft. Custer, MI, with the Military Police from August 1944 to Oct. 12, 1944. He was guarding prisoners for a great deal of the time while in the service.

IRVING CYMBLER, born in a small town in Zawierci Poland, on Nov. 22, 1927. On September 1939, the German's invaded his town. He was 11 years old. Soon after that they put him and his family into the ghetto. After three years in ghetto they shipped them to Auschwitz. Later he was sent to Warsaw to clean up after the Jewish ghetto uprising. One year later they send him to Dachau. They marched one week without food and water who couldn't make it, was shot on the road. On May 1, 1945, he was lucky and he was liberated by the American Army. He was in a DP Camp till he was able to come to America. On Aug. 9, 1949, he arrived in New York City alone. He lost his parents and three sisters and all the families close to him in Auschwitz. He worked in New York as a jeweler. On April 6, 1951, he was drafted into the

Army, during the Korean War. Because he knew a few languages Polish, German and others he was lucky and was shipped to Germany. He served in the 14th Ordnance Company. After two years he was discharged but was still in the reserve for five years. He got married and has a son, Jeffrey. He is a lawyer in New York City.

Retired and lives in Florida. He is a holocaust survivor and a Jewish War Veteran of the USA. His authorized medals are Honorable Discharge, Army of Occupation and National Defense.

EDWARD M. DANIELS, M.D., born March 7, 1921, in Paterson, NJ. Entered the Army in June 1943, serving at New Haven, CT (Yale Medical School) and Cushing VA Hospital, Framingham, MA.

He was discharged July 7, 1948, with the rank of captain.

Today he is retired from 50 years of psychiatry and psychoanalysis. Now consult in non-medical areas like business and education.

JEROME DANENBERG, born in 1924, in Brooklyn, NY. He was a sergeant in the U.S. Army Air Force and served as an aerial gunner. He was killed in action in the Pacific Theater in 1944.

Irwin Goss was born in Bloomfield, NJ, and was killed in action in World War II.

REUEL DANKNER, born in Ardsley, NY, father of a SABRA from Petach Tickva Palestine, Reuel and family at the age of nine migrated to Palestine. After his Bar Mitzvah he was recruited into the haganah and later during the riots of 1936-69, he served in the "special Nite Squads" under British Capt. Wingate at Kvar Yonah. Then went to Egypt with the British. Was wounded and returned to Palestine at which time the family decided to return to the United States. Left to Egypt New Years 1941. Boarded one of their small ships for the trip through the canal south to Kenya then on to Capetown South Africa dodging enemy ships and U-boats crossed the south Atlantic to Recipe Brazil, from there up the coast line to New York. The same boat (ZAM-Zam) leaving New York for the return trip was sunk by U-boat three days out. He joined the U.S. Army in 1942, and after training was attached to an Armored Artillery Bn. They sailed out for the Casablanca landing NA.

After that campaign they went east to Algeria, with the surrender of the Africa Corp they prepared for the invasion of Sicily, he flew to the beaches of Sicily from the deck of a LCT in a piper cub as he was a forward observer directing the fire of their BN Artillery guns landing on the beach, they joined the BN and moved south to Palermo after the capture of Palermo they turned east towards Italy. They ran into stiff resistance and took part in what was called two leap frog landings behind the retreating German lines, he received the Silver Star and the Purple Heart from General Patton after the second landing. They moved on to Italy from Sicily, but only stayed about two weeks as they were loaded on a ship for the trip to England as they were to take part in the D-day Landing in France. After a short training period they were loaded for the trip to France. He went in about 10 minutes before H-hour with the advance units of the Infantry Division that they were attached to. He was again wounded at the battle for St. Lo and was sent back to a hospital in England only to return to his unit in time to take part in the Battle of the Bulge. Returning to the states in February 1945, on a rotation furlough he was lucky and received his discharge on May 10, as #120 in the Army too get discharged on Points.

Pictures included: 1) Second from left in back row at a camp for the Special Nite Squads Kvar Jonah; 2) Himself taken in England before D-Day invasion; 3) Xerox copy of original picture taken with General Patton 1943; 4) Taken May 1994.

LEONARD S. DANZIG, M.D., born Dec. 30, 1925, in Newark, NJ. Joined the service Oct. 30, 1944, Inf., Military Intelligence Services, wireman and interpreter. Military locations included ETO Interrogator-Prisoner of War Camp.

Awards/Medals: Combat Infantry Badge, Good Conduct Medal, Victory Medal, WWII with two Battle Stars. ETO.

He was discharged Aug. 8, 1946, with the rank of technical sergeant.

Today he is a cardiologist in Red Bank, NJ. He has four children and four grandchildren.

BERNARD DARROW, served in the Army Air Forces from June 11, 1942, to date of discharge in 1945. He trained at Ft. Meade, MD, and entered the service there with the rank of private and was discharged with the rank of corporal at Pawling Convalescent Hospital for the AAF. His basic training was had at Keesler Field, MS. *Submitted by Max Sigal.*

OSCAR DASHEF, served in the U.S. Army from Jan. 16, 1941, to September 1945. He entered the Medical Corps with the rank of first lieutenant at Boston, MA, and was discharged at Indian Town Gap, PA, with the rank of major. He had field medical training at Camp Edwards, MA, from Jan. 16, 1941, to Jan. 19, 1942, with the 101st Medical Regt., 26th Div..

He went overseas from New York City on the SS *Santa Elena* and arrived at Melbourne, Australia, and sailed from Melbourne on the SS *John Ericksson* to Nouhea, New Caledonia, leaving there on the SS *Crescent City* and landing in Guadalcanal. He served in the South Pacific Theater from Jan. 23, 1942 to April 21, 1945, and saw action at Guadalcanal, Northern Solomon's and the Philippines; all campaigns as an Americal Division. He was in the Fiji Islands, Bougainvillea, Leyte, Philippine Islands and from there he sailed to San Francisco, CA.

He received many citations, decoration and promotions including the Legion of Merit, Asiatic-Pacific Ribbon with three Battle Stars, the American Defense, Philippine Liberation, American Theater Citation and the Victory Ribbon. He was promoted to captain and major. He visited Panama, Melbourne, Ballarat, Australia, New Caledonia, Guadalcanal, Fiji Islands, New Guinea, Leyte and Bougainville and states the most outstanding place of all visited was the United States of America. Most of his service was as Commanding Officer of Divisional Hospital Company but was also Division Malariologist for approximately one year, consultant pediatrician for the natives of all South Pacific islands visited and town physician for Capoocan, Leyte Philippine Islands. *Submitted by Max Sigal.*

MAURICE I. DASHEVSKY, member of the JWV. Now retired and a volunteer at the elderly meal site at the Jewish Community Center. He served with Co. G, 87th Mtn. Inf. Regt..

Awards/Medals: Purple Heart, Bronze Star Medal, Good Conduct Medal, Asiatic-Pacific Theater of Operations, European-Middle-Eastern Theater of Operations.

ABRAHAM DATTNER, born April 20, 1923, in Bronx, NYC. Entered the Army, Jan. 4, 1943, 335 Inf., 84th Div. Stationed at Camp Clairborne, LA, landed in France Nov. 4, 1944, went all the way to the Elbe River Germany, took art in the Battle of the Bulge start to end.

Awards/Medals: Ardennes Central Europe Rhineland GO 33, American Service Medal, European AME Service Medal, Good Conduct Medal and Victory Medal.

He was discharged Jan. 23, 1946, with the rank of private first class.

His sister Malvina served three years in the WACS. Both his uncles, (Colonel Med. Corp, Philippines and Japan and Staff Sgt. Translator, Germany HQ) served. Today he is retired.

ERWIN B. DAVIDSON, born Dec. 15, 1922, Bronx, NY. Inducted April 5, 1943. Med. Det. 263, Inf. 66 Div. Military stations include Camp Blanding, FL; Camp Robinson, AR; Camp Rucker, AL. Overseas to England, November 1944. St. Nazaire, France, January 1945.

Awards/Medals: one Battle Star Battle of Northern France. EAME Campaign Medal, WWII Victory Medal.

Separated April 8, 1946, with the rank of T/5.

Worked as cartographer, artist. Married Shirley Schechter 1959, son Len.

Member of to 297, JWV. Member The Battle of Normandy Foundation. Member 66 Division Veteran Organization. Member Untied States Holocaust Museum. Member Simon Wiesenthal Center.

Now devotes all of his time to preserve the record of sacrifices made by members of the armed forces that led to the defeat of Nazism in World War II.

LOUIS DAVIDSON, born in Romania in 1882. The family emigrated to Canada and about 1890 and settled in Lipton Colony, a small Jewish farming community near Regina, Saskatchewan, Canada. He was the oldest of six children, five boys and one girl. At 13 years of age, he ran away from home to New York City. At 15 he attempted to join the U.S. Army but was refused because he was too young. He left New York City and ended up in Missouri, where he was befriended by a local Rabbi. The Rabbi vouched for him that he was older than his real age and he was able to join the Army. After training, he was sent to the Philippine Islands and fought in the Spanish-American War with Company I, 11th Infantry. He was wounded in battle, recovered and returned to active duty. After the war was over he continued as a career military man. He was transferred to Ft. McPherson, GA, about 1908, and in about 1909, he met and fell in love with Rae Finkelstein. She agreed to marry him only if he left military service. He did so and they were married in 1911.

He lived in Atlanta with his wife and three children Annette, Haskell and Jonas. He died in 1923 in Atlanta, GA, of a burst appendix and is buried in Greenwood Cemetery.

MARIAN B. DAVIDSON, born Aug. 31, 1921, in Atlantic City, NJ. Enlisted February 1943, active service May 10, 1943. Served with WAAC first then, WAC ACorps. Commissioned Des Moines, IA, second lieutenant. Stationed postal office Lincoln, near Ft. Logan, CO; special duty in Atlantic City, NJ (recruiting); administrative officer, Ft. Logan.

Memorable experiences include all men under her command (very cooperative).

Separated March 23, 1945, with the rank of second lieutenant. Her father was a WWI hero.

She has three children and three grandchildren. Retired.

MELVIN DAVIDSON, born in 1925. Immigrated by himself from Kybartai, Lithuania to Olean, NY, in 1936. Inducted 1944. Infantry-basic at Camp Wheeler, GA. Served with 380th Combat Engineer Battalion in Northern Luzon and Japan. Technical Corporal. Discharged 1946.

University of Buffalo graduate, psychology. Holds Certificate with Distinction in Hebrew. Licensed Religious Instructor. Conducted research in Kibbutz Lehavot Habashan 1949. Counselor, Ben Shemen Children's Village 1950. Probation officer in Tel Aviv 1951. Returned to Buffalo, 1952. Now semi-retired. Held simultaneous positions as college professor, school psychologist, Hebrew teacher, and acting Rabbi. Active with Israel Bonds, ZOA, Jewish Federation. JWV member. Israel Army volunteer 1987. Published. Married Miriam Ginsburg, sabra, psychiatric social worker, U.B. graduate. Three children, college graduates One granddaughter.

JOSHUA V. DAVIDOW, born in South Rosenhayn, NJ, on Dec. 23, 1909. Graduated with bachelor of arts degree from University of Pennsylvania in June 1931, and commissioned a second lieutenant in Infantry from University of Pennsylvania ROTC, and from Rutgers University as a lawyer in 1935. Entered U.S. Army in October 1940. Was assigned to command an infantry camp company at Ft. Hancock, NJ, and transferred to the Infantry School at Ft. Benning, GA, in December 1941, for refresher in heavy weapons and training officer candidates. Was promoted to captain and transferred to Camp Plauche, LA, to assist in formation of the Army Transportation Corp. supervising basic training. Promoted to major and served as a battalion commander until transfer to the South Pacific Theater following attack on the Philippines, with the 6th Army Div. under General Douglas MacArthur. Following the Japanese surrendered on VJ Day served in Japan and was active as a Law Member, Defense Counsel and Trial Judge Advocate in military courts martial trails. In November 1945, was appointed by General MacArthur as his chief war crimes prosecutor in Tokyo, Japan and tried the first Japanese prisoner of war Commander, Kei Yuri, as a war criminal for torturing our American prisoners of war, at the first opening war crimes trials beginning on Dec. 18, 1945, obtaining the first conviction of a Japanese prison camp commander. Discharged as a lieutenant colonel on Oct. 15, 1946, and placed in charge of the newly organized Reserve Infantry School in Camden, NJ. Elected president of the New Jersey Department of the Reserve Officers Association of the United States in 1948.

Awards/Medals: Asiatic-Pacific Medal, Army Commendation Medal, Philippine Liberation Medal, American Theater Medal, WWII Victory Medal.

Married to Marion since 1938, have two daughters, Rosalie and Joan, and two grandchildren.

Retired after 50 years of law practice and Municipal Judge in Bridgeton, NJ. Member of Post 601 JWV, Life Member of American Legion and Veterans of Foreign Wars. Active in B'nai Brith and Zionist Organization of America.

Also active the Boy Scouts of America. For the past 60 years, as Scoutmaster, Scout Commissioner a president of the Southern New Jersey Council of the Boy Scout of America, and a recipient of the Prestigious awards of Silver Beaver and Silver Antelope. He also continues to serve on the National Executive Body of this important youth organization. He was the first Reserve Officer to voluntary enter the Army shortly after Hitler entered Poland in 1939, and is still a member of the inactive Reserve of our U.S. Army since WWII when he was honorably discharged as with the rank of lieutenant colonel of Infantry. He is proud of having been the first Jewish officer to enter WWII.

ALBERT DAVIS, born July 30, 1918, Boston, MA. Enlisted Feb. 20, 1941, 2nd LT ORD Dept. Nov. 7, 1942. Served with Med. 4th Evac Hospital, Ft. Devens, NS ORD Officer HQ SOS ETO. Military locations included Ft. Devens, Walter Reed Hospital, Ordnance OCS Maryland; Frankfurt, Germany; Cheltenham, England.

Memorable experience include meeting some very fine people as personnel officer for chief of ORD HQ ETO.

Awards/Medals: Bronze Star.

He was discharged Jan. 14, 1946, with the rank of captain.

Married Edith Wainhouse, 1942, two sons, four grand children, two wonderful daughters-in-law. He is a retired optometrist.

DAVID DAVIS, born July 22, 1914, Syracuse, NY. Attended Central High School. Graduated from Manlius Military Academy in 1931. Worked as a clothing salesman for Kings Stores and liquor salesman for Schenley's and Poppe Morrison Co.

Inducted in the service March 16, 1942. Held rank of staff sergeant in the Air Force. Served as flight chief, in the China-Burma-India Theater of Operations.

Awards/Medals: American Service Medal, Asiatic Pacific Service Medal, Good Conduct Medal, and the WWI Victory Medal.

He was honorably discharged on Jan. 8, 1946.

Killed in an automobile accident on Feb. 20, 1952, at the age of 38. Buried with full military honors at the Poiley Tzedeck Cemetery. Survived by father, Samuel and brother, Nathan L.

RICHARD N. DAVIS, born in Brooklyn, NY, Jan. 19, 1922. He was Pre-Med Major at St. Johns UN, NY, and was later graduated with DVM degree from Middlesex University in 1945, at which time entered the U.S. Army. Received basic training at Ft. Leonard Wood, MO. Following basic training left for New York City for post as foodstuff and meat inspector. Promoted to corporal and ordered next to Quartermaster Purchasing Center in New York City, and remained there until discharged in 1947.

At wars end entered family retail business. He was married to Rosaling in 1947, two daughter and three sons plus 11 grandchildren followed. Following a term in family retail business received National Institute of Health Training Grant to prepare for a career in science. Now happily retired. He is commander of Major Gary Grant Post 680, which bears the side name he created; the "Energizer Post." For 1995 Community Service to beleaguered school children in need of supplies and learning tools was honored by two school systems (80 schools). He was made "California Angel" for May 1995 by Cal. Angel Baseball Club and American Airlines.

1995-96 Commander Post 680 and Senior Vice Commander South Coast District Council.

BERNARD DELITSKY, served in the European Theater and was wounded in France. He was awarded the Purple Heart Medal and was discharged in 1944, due to his wounds. Unfortunately he died in 1972. In 1945, he moved to California, was married and had two daughters, Maria and Carol.

RALPH DELITSKY, born in Brooklyn, NY, on Oct. 27, 1922. He graduated from Thomas Jefferson High School in 1941. He went to work as a floor covering installer. On March 14, 1943, he entered the USN. After boot camp he was assigned to a PT Boat Squadron #31. After shake down in the Miami area, they sailed through the Panama Canal and were loaded aboard ships for transfer to the southwest Pacific. They were unloaded and proceeded to New Guinea, Palau, the Philippines and then to the island called Okinawa which was several hundred miles from Japan.

While in the Philippine Islands he met a Jewish man that was born in the Philippines and who did shoe repairs.

During their stay in Okinawa, they ran sea rescue missions, saving many pilots who had to ditch in the sea because of damaged aircraft. They also experienced many Kamikaze raids.

He was separated from the Navy Dec. 6, 1945.

In December 1950, he married Ida Sharick and had three children, Mona who is a space scientist, working with NASA in Pasadena, CA. Robert and his wife Laurie, and a son Evan and daughter Fara. They live in Merrick, Long Island. His son works as a finance officer.

Their daughter Carrie and her husband Harvey live in Connecticut and have two daughters. Their names are Carly and Abby. Harvey has a law practice in Connecticut.

He is presently retired and also has a second home in the Catskills.

ALEXANDER DEMBY, born Jan. 5, 1905. Enlisted in the USN on Oct. 2, 1942, and assigned to the Seabees for three years. Stationed at Norfolk, VA, he participated in the battles of Pearl Harbor and Midway.

Served with the National Guard for three years, 1923-26. Became sick when his boat was sunk on the way to Kodiak, AK. Honorably discharged in October 1945, having achieved the rank of EM1/c.

Married with two children and three grandchildren. He is retired.

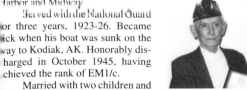

CARL DENEFF, MD, born Aug. 22, 1909, in Brooklyn, NY. Entered the U.S. Army on April 30, 1941, and assigned as a medical officer. Attended Medical Field Service School at Carlisle Barracks, PA, and Shrivenham, England.

Served during the Pearl Harbor attack receiving a commendation for "the brave and excellent manner in which ... you performed your duties in caring for and evacuating the wounded of this Station Hospital, Hickam Field, T.H. on morning of Sunday, Dec. 7, 1941, while under the attach of enemy airplanes."

Awards/Medals: American Campaign Medal, Asiatic-Pacific Theater Ribbon with one Bronze Service Star, EAME Service Ribbon, American Defense Service Ribbon with Metal Clasp, WWII Victory Medal. Honorably discharged on March 12, 1946, with the rank of captain.

Currently retired. His wife passed away in February 1991. He has three children.

SIDNEY ROBERT DESSAUER, born Oct. 9, 1936, Chicago, IL. Put one year in the 33rd Inf. Div., Illinois National Guard before entering the US Army, taking basic training at Camp Leonardwood, MO, and artillery training at Camp Chaffee, AK, then on to Korea, via Ft. Lewis, WA and Japan. Assigned to the 25th Div., 69th Field Arty. Bn. Co. A and B in 1954 through 1956. He was discharged November 1956 with the rank of staff sergeant.

Awards/Medals: six ribbons and two Presidential Unit Citations.

When the 25th moved to Hawaii, he moved with them and stayed for two fun filled years before rotating to the States and getting out of the Army at Ft. Ord, CA, as his parents had moved to San Francisco, CA, while he was in the Army. He has been living in San Jose, CA for the last 25 years. He married Sandra Kay Masters May 12, 1963, and they have one daughter Helen Victoria. She is now married and he has one grandson. He also took in four teenagers, two boys and two girls that were not welcome in their own homes anymore. He's very active in several Veterans organizations in the San Jose, CA area.

Dessaur is a taxi cab company executive; received AA in business administration College of San Mateo 1960. 1977-Chairman No. California Vets. Employment Co., 1976. Sergeant, US Army. 1953-1956, Korea. Member VFW (life, Dist. 12 Allstate Commander 1980-1981); AMVETS (life), American Legion (life), Mil. Order Cooties (life), Jewish War Vets. (life, district commander 1976-1977, State Man of Year Award 1976), United Veteran Council Santa Clara County (president, 1976, Man of Year Award 1981), Hole in One Club. Avocations: stamp and coin collecting, golf. He was selected and was in the 22nd Volume of Marquis "Who's Who of the West."

WARREN L. DEUTSCH, born March 8, 1945, Passaic, NJ. Enlisted June 17, 1966, U.S. Army, Spec. E-4, ORD, 626 Repair Parts. Stationed Ft. Dix, NJ; Hawaii; West Germany.

Memorable experience includes setting up perimeter for Israel 6 Day War.

Awards/Medals: Good Conduct, Army Europe, Sharpshooter.

He was discharged June 1968, with the rank of spec. 4.

Married Norma in 1965, and has two daughters, Robyn and Stacy. Owner of a retail furniture store.

BERNARD DEVACK, entered Army March 1943, after basic training he studied at Manhattan College, NY (AATP) until he joined the 69th Div. Co. D 271st Camp Shelby, MS, in March 1944. Overseas in November 1944. Entered combat Malmedy, on Feb. 12, 1945, with Co. D 271st Regt. until wars end. May 1945 with division capture of Leipzig, Germany; then with Army of Occupation in Germany with the 685th Ord.

Ammunition Co. and other units until discharge in March 1946. His unit awarded Combat Infantry Badge and Bronze Star for Meritorious Service under enemy fire.

Attended Hunter college in New York City (first male Class) September 1946 - January 1950. Earned business degree in accounting. Completed 23 years of Tax Auditing work with New York State Tax Department retiring in 1988. He and wife Muriel have two daughters, one married with two grandsons. Enjoys contacts with Army buddies and outdoor exercise to keep fit.

MAURICE DIAMOND, born Dec. 7, 1925, Worcester, MA. Graduated Classical High 1944. Entered Army March 1944. Discharged March 1946.

Served in 347th Inf. Regt. Of 87th Div. as rifleman and scout. Received three Battle Stars for the Battle of the Rhineland, Central Germany, and the Belgium Bulge. Also received Purple Heart Medal.

Married to Anne and has two daughters. Member JWV, Veterans of Battle of Bulge and DAV. Retired 1992 from FAA.

ROBERT IRVING DIAMOND, inducted into the U.S. Army on Dec. 14, 1942. He was stationed at New Guinea, in the South Philippines. Robert was in the Army for a period of four

plus years; he was honorably discharged on January 6, 1946. At time of discharge Robert reached the ranks of staff sergeant. As well, he received four overseas service bars, one Service Stripe American Campaign Medal, an Asiatic-Pacific Theater Ribbon with two Bronze Battle Stars, a Campaign Good Conduct Medal and a WWII Victory Medal. His duration in the Army included a battle with Malaria and Dinghy Fever.

SAUL DIAMOND, born Brooklyn, NY, (USA). Enlisted Nov. 12, 1941, U.S. Army training at Camp Upton, NY, and then to Ft. Eustis, VA. Military locations include Ft. Eustis, Harbor Defenses of New York; Ft. Hancock, NJ; Ft. Tilden, NY; Ft. Wadsworth, NY. Served as an aide to Commanding General, Ft. Hancock, NJ HDNY and Chief Clerk of personnel Department.

Memorable experience include Commendation by Commanding General CDY OSTROM, HDNY, Ft. Hancock, NJ.

Awards/Medals: American Service Medal, Good Conduct Medal, Sharpshooter, WWII Victory Medal.

He was discharged Dec. 12, 1945, with the rank of corporal.

He has been married to Dorothy since Jan. 2, 1944. They have two daughters, Nancy and Ellin; two grandchildren, Erica and Seth. Member of the American Legion. He is self-employed. Vice president, American Credit Associates, Red Bank, NJ; and chairman, Board of Adjustment, Red Bank, NJ.

TERRY "ESTHER" SOLOMON DIMARCO, was always petite and skinny, so waivers had to be granted to facilitate her enlistment in the WAAC on Aug. 19, 1943. The Army knew that her experience in finance would far outweigh any limits in physical stature. On Aug. 31, 1943, while in basic training at Daytona Beach, FL, Terry reenlisted in the newly formed WAC. Her skills as a financial clerk typist were put to work at ports of embarkation on both US coasts, at Ft. Kilmer, NJ, and at Camp Stoneman, CA. Many soldiers left for Europe and the Pacific wearing the "Good Luck" rings given them by Terry.

After being honorably discharged as a technician third grade from Ft. Dix on March 20, 1946, Terry studied accounting under the GI Bill. Subsequently Terry has worked as an accountant, both in Los Angeles, CA, and Baltimore, MD, for over 30 years.

Back in her native Baltimore, Terry met Albert DiMarco at a Jewish nursing home where both of their mothers were patients. Terry and Albert were married on Aug. 21, 1973, by a Reformed Rabbi; they were remarried by an Orthodox Rabbi when Albert later converted to Judaism.

Though they have no children of their own, many a young person has known their love and caring over the years.

Terry is a lifetime member of the JWV, Post 113, in Los Angeles. Terry proudly treasures the honors she received in service to her country: The American Service Medal, WWII Victory Medal, Good Conduct Medal, a Meritorious Service Plaque, and the WAAC Service Medal.

"God bless our country; God bless our veterans," this is Terry's constant prayer.

MARTIN DINOWITZ,

born Oct. 9, 1913, Brooklyn, NY. Enlisted May 8, 1941, Survey and Instrument man, 228 Forward Observer, Field Artillery, 977 Field Artillery, 155 Long-Tom VI Corp. Military stations included Camp Blanding, FL; Camp Shelby, MS. Battles: Central Europe; Naples; Foggia; Rhineland; North Africa; Rome; Arno; Southern France.

Memorable experience was Anzio, Casino Invasion of Southern France, Dachau Concentration Camp.

Awards/Medals: American Defense Service Medal, EAME Service Medal, Good Conduct Medal with Clasp.

He was discharged Sept. 26, 1945, with the rank of corporal.

Married and has two daughters and three grandchildren. Retired.

JACQUE DOLGOFF, born in Omaha, NE, Jan. 23, 1916.
Enlisted Dec. 4, 1940, U.S. Army, 35th Inf. Div. Medical Dept. 205 Hospital Ship Complement. Stations include Camp Robinson, AR; Camp Hahn, CA; Camp Anza, Ca; USS *Comfort*, Hospital ship. Participated in battles in Southern Philippines, Luzon, Central Pacific, GO 33 WD 45, Okinawa, Ryukyu, GO 40 WD 45, Kamikaze attack April 28, 1945.

Awards/Medals: Good Conduct Medal, Asiatic-Pacific Campaign Medal, Philippine Liberation Ribbon with one Bronze Star, American Campaign Medal.

He was discharged Oct. 4, 1945, with the rank of private first class.

Married Nov. 23, 1947, widowed in 1971, Adele Dimenstein Dolgoff, Holocaust Victim, three sons (one deceased). Retired living Omaha, NE. Active JWV Post #260. Life member Brookline Post #72, Commander 1981-82.

WILLIAM DONATH, born Feb. 22, 1911, in Chicago,
IL. Recalled to active service Dec. 28, 1942, being assigned to 287th Engrs., Co. C, 3rd Army. Stations included Ft. McClellan, AL, Charleston Naval Base, Camp Rucker, AL. Landed in Cherbourg, France, crossed the channel for more basic training in England.

Participated in the Battle of the Bulge, the 18th day relieving the 94th Inf. Div. The 69th Inf. Div. came across, lost

---

men and WACS. They gave the Germans hell. He was supposed to receive two Bronze Stars, being discharged on Feb. 7, 1946, at the rank of PFC, T-5 Temp.

Married to Fay for 50 years. She was a crossing guard for 18 years. They have a son who is a biology teacher, and two grandchildren. Retired, and life member of JWV Post 169 and DAV Chapter 78.

NORMAN DORFF, served in AUS during WWII.

ALVIN M. DORFMAN, born April 12, 1926, Brooklyn,
NY. Joined the service August 1944, was assigned to 32nd Inf. Div. in August. 1945 Served with 32nd Signal Co.

Signal Corp Camp Crowder, MO, ARITAO Philippines, Fukuoka Japan. Achieved the rank of technician 4th grade at time of discharge.

Memorable experience included establishing and maintaining communications, viewing Hiroshima late in 1945.

Awards/Medals: Asiatic-Pacific Campaign Medal, Philippine Republic Unit Citation, WWII Victory Medal, Army Occupation (Japan Medal) Good Conduct Medal.

Married Miriam, have three children(one deceased) two grandchildren. Retired government employee DOD.

JULIUS DORFMAN, born Jan. 19, 1929, East Manhat-
tan, NY. Drafted Feb. 21, 1951, AUS INF ERC INF, SECOND ARMY AREA. Stations include Camp Rucker, AL, Korea and Okinawa.

Memorable experience was being assigned to CO K 5th CAV REGT (Korea), Engaged in combat against North Koreans in October 1951, beyond the 38th parallel (Mingore and Chingore) reassigned to Okinawa after being wounded twice October 16, and October 30.

Awards/Medals: Purple Heart with OLC, Bronze Star, Korean Service Medal, Occupation Medal (Japan).

Discharged Feb. 13, 1953, with the rank of corporal.

Married Sylvia G. Kahansky June 29, 1958. They have two sons, Harold Henry and Beryl Benjamin, daughter-in-law Mechal, grandson Jonathan E. Today he is an electronic technician with Walter Reed Army Medical Center.

RAYMOND DORFMAN, Sgt. AAF, born June 3, 1923,
Newark, NJ. Graduated High School June 1941, enlisted Army June 10, 1942. Ft. Dix, Schooled Engines, and propellers. Assigned Oklahoma City AB. Overseas to England October 1943, by convoy. Lost engine and convoy half way to destination, aboard WWI prize, German Tub with worlds largest upright steam engine. Engine repaired, caught up with convoy many hours later, whew!

Maintained planes, major overhaul. Volunteered for secret mission, which turned out to be in Russia. Built base in Ukraine, purpose; Triangle Bombing of German ball bearing factories, by B17s, from England to Russia, across Germany, Russia to Italy via Germany, Italy to England, again across Germany. Factories decimated.

Our base in Russia was destroyed by Germans in a two hour raid, horrendous! Honorable discharge Nov. 29, 1945!

Married to the former Rose Malcman, Holocaust survivor, have two sons, two daughters, nine grandchildren. Happily retired in Florida. Member North Essex Post 146.

ROBERT DORFMAN, born Feb. 27, 1920, Newark, NJ.
Enlisted March 13, 1942, 7th Armored Div. 77th Medical Bn. Stations included Ft. Dix; Camp Polk, LA; Ft. Benning, GA; Mojave Desert, CA; France, Belgium, Holland, Germany, Battle of Bulge, Verdun, Prisoner Camp Liberation.

Awards/Medals: Verdun Medal from Mayor of Verdun for liberalization, four Battle Stars and regular medals.

He was discharged Sept. 15, 1945, with the rank of technician 5.

Married, two children, five grandchildren, one greatgrandchild. Retired happily.

SAM DORFMAN, born Nov. 12, 1918, Manhattan, NYC.
High school graduate. One year of college. Basic training, Sheppard Field, TX. Enlisted Feb. 1, 1943, AAF ATC. Military locations included Bermuda and Pesquil, Maine. Spent 18 months Bermuda AB.

Memorable experience included supplying the Air Force Bombing Squads to and from Europe.

Awards/Medals: American Service Medal and Good Conduct Medal.

He was discharged Nov. 4, 1945, with the rank of corporal. Hardship discharge at Armistice signing.

Married Frances and has two sons Jay and Ted, and three grandchildren. His youngest son Jay Dorfman is the inventor of the battery tester on the face of all Duracell batteries. Reentered the retail business. Retired 1990. Member of Abraham Kraditor Brooklyn. Post #2.

SAM DORSHOW, St. Paul, MN, Post #354. We all take
pride in all our service people in all Wars but once in a while a special story is found and should be conveyed to all of us about a certain place in time, about a brave person or whatever. This is about a JWV who fought for his country, his dedication, his bravery, his wounds, his medals and his luck to have survived and can still talk about this particular time in his life

Sam Dorshow was a native of St. Paul who grew up on East Isabel Street. He graduated Humboldt High School and attended the University of Minnesota. The day after Pearl Harbor, Sam enlisted in the Army … his first choice was the Marines but they thought he was too old and over-the-hill. Sam was 33 years old. He was sent to the Artillery and at 34 years old he was a forward observer, who is a man who goes up with the infantry and gets into the tallest place he can find and spots enemy movements for the artillery back of the foxholes. Potential suicide is what the forward observers called it.

During these war years he received many medals and citations for his bravery and many bumps and bruises, serious wounds to the head, eye, leg, back and was told he would never walk again. He fought in France and Germany. One time somewhere near Huertgen Forest, Germany, during a brief breather, he was asked to step forward out of a formation by his unit and a general stepped up and pinned the bars of a second lieutenant on his collar, a battlefield commission.

Sam never forgot the words of the general, "I wish I could do more for you, son," said General George S. Patton.

Sam Dorshow has received three Silver Stars, three Purple Hearts, a Bronze Star, The Croix de Guerre, assorted ribbon and citations and this was a man "too old to fight for the Marines."

Sam died two years ago. He specified in his Will that all his service medals and articles, citations, ribbons, maps, guns, flags, etc. be donated to the JWV Shrine in Washington, D.C. This has been done.

ISRAEL DRAZIN, BRIGADIER GENERAL has
been successful in several fields. He was ordained as a Rabbi in 1957, and entered on Army active duty, at the age of 21, as the youngest U.S. Chaplain ever to serve on active duty. After leaving active duty in 1960, he officiated as a Rabbi at several synagogues, including being the first Rabbi in the planned city of Columbia, MD. He is a member of the

Rabbinical Council of America and is on the board of directors of the National Committee for Furtherance of Jewish Education and JWBs Commission on Jewish Chaplains. He was honored with the RCA 1985 Joseph Hoenig Memorial Award and the JWB 1986 Distinguished Service Award. Mayor Kurt Schmoke, of Baltimore, MD, named Feb. 8, 1988, "Israel Drazin Day." He was named "Man of the Year' by Shaarei Zion Congregation, in Baltimore, MD, in 1990.

In addition to several rabbinical degrees, he has a BA in theology, M.Ed. in psychology, an MA in Hebrew Literature, a JD in Law, and a Ph.D. with honors in Aramaic Literature. He has also done two year of post-graduate study in philosophy, and is a graduate of the Army's Command and General Staff College and the Army War College for Reservists. He is admitted to practice law in Maryland and before the U.S. Supreme Court. He is the author of more than 100 popular articles, edited a book on legends and wrote four scholarly books on the Aramaic translation of the Bible. *Targumic Studies*, was published by University Microfilm International in 1982. *Targum Onkelos to Deuteronomy*, published by Ktav Publishing House in 1983, was praised by biblical scholars as being copious and excellent. *Targum Onkelos to Exodus*, was published by Ktav in 1990. *Targum Onkelos to Leviticus* was published by Ktav in 1993. He was awarded a grant by the University of Denver to write one additional scholarly book. He is the senior attorney of a law office and president of the Society for Targumic Studies, Incorporated. STS is a non-profit corporation that publishes scholarly studies on the Aramaic translation of the Bible. He is included in the recent edition of *Who's Who in World Jewry, Who's Who in American Law* and *Who's Who In Biblical Studies and Archaeology*.

Dr. Drazin served on Army active duty as a first lieutenant from 1957 to 1960 in Louisiana and Germany. Returning to the active reserve in 1960, he served, in increasing grades, with about half a dozen units. From 1978 until 1981, he was a lecturer at the U.S. Army Chaplains School. In March 1981, he was requested by the Army to return to active duty to handle special constitutional issues. Dr. Drazin was responsible for preparing the defense for the suit challenging the constitutionality of the Army Chaplaincy which the Government won in 1984. He returned to civilian life and the active reserves in 1984 as assistant chief of Chaplains, the highest reserve officer position in the Army Chaplaincy, with the rank of Brigadier General. He completed this four year tour of duty with honors in March 1988 and is now in the inactive reserve.

The General's wife Dina is the office manager of the Drazin Law Firm and an artist. The two have four children and 11 grandchildren.

MURRAY DRONSKY, born in Boro Park, Brooklyn, Sept. 27, 1925. Studied aeronautics at Haaren High School of Aviation, in Manhattan, NY Inducted into the Army on Nov. 15, 1943. Took 13 weeks of Infantry Basic Training at Ft. Benning, GA, as a member of the ASTP, A-12 (Army Specialized Training program). After basic training he was to go to college and study aeronautics. Instead three infantry division were stripped and their troops sent to Europe as replacements. The ASTP Program and many others were closed and all the troops were went to the infantry. That was his introduction to Co. E 341st Inf. Regt., of the 86th Inf. Div., (The Black Hawk's). This all took place at Camp Livingston, LA, at Alexandria. There he received his infantry training and became a bugler of the Guard, due to six years training as a trumpet player.

The division then transferred to Camp Callan, near San Diego, CA, for amphibious training. Went on a two week cruise, making landings from the ship, to LCVP's, to Santa Catalina Island. Transferred to Camp San Luis Obispo, CA, for additional amphibious training and shipped across the U.S. by train to a POE near Boston, MA.

The division arrived at LE Harve, on March 2, 1945. Was trucked to Ourville, France for a few week and then joined Gen. Hodges 1st Army on the Rhine River south of Cologne. After facing the Germans for a week, they crossed the Rhine at Remagen Bridge, to split the Rhur pocket by joining up with General Montgomeries British 9th Army coming south from Holland. He was wounded in a battle at Priorei on Friday the 13th of April, 1945. Fought their way north to Hagen, near Essen and then were ordered to join Gen. Patton's 3rd Army.

After a 24 hour forced march to the South, they joined up with and lead the 3rd Army over the Danube River into Austria, capturing the Quisling minister of Hungary, a Hungarian Division, and the Crown Jewels of Hungary. Wound up the War in Europe at Hitler's Berchtesgaden mountain retreat on VE Day. Did occupation duty in Mannheim, Germany, and then went home for 30 day furlough on June 17, 1945.

Reported to the 86th Div. July 20, 1945, at Camp Gruber, Muskogee, OK, for one month, shipped out to San Francisco POE arriving in Battangas, Luzon, PI. The voyage was from Aug. 20, 1945 to Sept. 12, 1945, across Pacific Ocean. After rounding up Japanese hold-outs for several months he was transferred on detached service to the Philippine Scout Replacement Depot, at Clark Field, north of Manila, as a form 20 expert. His job was to assign new Philippine enlistees to their appropriate MOS in what was to become the new Philippine Army. Spent home for discharge on April 24, 1946, at Ft. Dix, NJ.

Awards/Medals: American Campaign Medal, Asiatic-Pacific Campaign Medal, EAME Campaign Medal, Good Conduct Medal, Purple Heart Medal, WWII Victory Medal, Bronze Star Medal, Combat Infantryman's Badge.

Married Dec. 31, 1950, to Marion and have three children, Debra, Robin and Richard. Have five grandchildren: Shayna, Deena and Esther and Avi and Sharon. Retired from Prudential Insurance Company of America Jan. 2, 1981. Hope to hear from Army buddies, who may read this.

HERMAN DROOKS, was drafted from Brooklyn, NY, and his point of entry was Camp Upton, NY. After being assigned to the Army Air Corps he was trained as a radio operator for a fighter direction team and was assigned to an admiral staff. He took part in the campaigns of Sicily, Salerno, North Africa and was on USS Ancon at the Normandy invasion. He was sent to the Philippines after the European Victory.

After four and one-half year he was discharged as a corporal. He attended Columbia University where he earned an MA in education. He stated as a housing assistant for the NYC Housing Authority in 1947 and rose to become a project manager from where he retired in 1979. He made number one of the Civil service managers list.

He was married to Evelyn and there are three children, Lawrence, Rhonda and Mark. He was a founding member of the JWV Post 769 in Pelham Pkway, Bx NY. He died Aug. 24, 1988.

CLIFFORD DROPKIN, served in the U.S. Army, Corps of Engineers, from March 4, 1942 to 1946. He entered the service March 4, 1942, with the rank of private at Ft. Dix, NJ, and was discharged with the rank of first lieutenant. He had his basic training at Camp Polk, LA, March 17, 1942 to Aug. 14, 1942. His officer's training at the Officers Candidate School, Belvoir, VA, from Aug. 22, 1942 to Nov. 11, 1942, and was assigned to the 379th Engineer Battalion for training at Camp Shelby, MS, on Nov. 25, 1942, and continued his training in the 244th Engineer Combat Battalion and the 1287th Engineer Battalion at Camp Rucker, AL, from November 1943 to December 1944. He shipped overseas on the U.S. Army Transport Borinquin, out of New York and arrived at Le Havre, France, sailed on the Oceanmall for Marseilles, France and arrived at Okinawa, Ryukyus Islands, and the shipped on LST 1975 from Okinawa to Inchow, Korea. He saw considerable active service in the ETO with the 1287th Engineering Combat Battalion and the 1408th Engineer Base depot from January 1945 to June 24, 1945, and in the Pacific Theater of Operations with the 1408th Engineer Base Depot from Sept. 9, 1945 to Oct. 10, 1945, when he sailed for the United States. He participated in the Rhineland Campaign in Germany and his unit also participated in supplying engineering equipment for the crossing of the Rhine from Feb. 15, 1945 to May 26, 1945. He received as citations the authorized Bronze Star for Rhineland Campaign on ETO Ribbon, EAME Ribbon, Asiatic-Pacific Ribbon, American Theater Ribbon and WWII Victory Medal. He visited France, Belgium, Holland, Germany, Panama Canal, Okinawa, Marshall Islands, Carolina Islands and Korea in the Pacific area.

EDMUND I. DUBAN, because of his knowledge of languages, was assigned to the Office of Information and Education, Headquarters Command, London, from which he was transferred to France in October 1944 to work on the terms of capitulation in French, German, Russian and English. While still in England, he was briefly a patient at the Seventh General Hospital where I was serving as a nurse.

We first met when I made the rounds of Jewish patients to inquire who would be interested in attending Kol Nidrei services in the nearby town. Even after his hospital release, he continued to return to the Seventh General for Sabbath Services. Friends surmised that his interest was not entirely limited to Sabbath Services. We were married in June 1948. Between the end of the war and our marriage, he stayed on in occupied Germany, with the rank of second lieutenant, to help found and run the American University in Berlin.

In June 1952, he became one of the first Americans to receive the degree of Doctorat d'Etat from the Sorbonne (in French Literature). He died in California in 1956, survived by his wife and two children, of whom James is a Professor of English and Jeffrey is a practicing attorney. *Submitted by Sylvia Mould Duban.*

HAROLD R. DUBERSTEIN, born Nov. 20, 1922, in Bronx, NY. Received armored basic training at Ft. Knox, KY. Sent to Vehicle Maintenance School. Due to the Battle of the Bulge he was rushed overseas arriving in Europe and assigned to the 702nd Tank Bn., 80th Inf. Div., 3rd Army, when the major offensive began to cross the Rhine River and finally crush the Germans. He "won the lottery" and became a crew member of the lead tank.

On Mar. 15, 1945, his tank was hit by an armor piercing shell, two crew members were killed, one was wounded and he was moderately burned helping the wounded man climb out, the driver got out O.K. Later the driver and Harold's brother Herman, who had entered the service with him, trained with him, and was in the same unit, were given the job of moving the disabled tank to the rear lines for salvage. This was when the brothers parted. Harold was flown to the 99th Gen. Hospital for a 10 week stay. After his recovery he attended Intelligence School at Ft. Riley, KS with the rank of T/3.

Married with children. Civilian career was in the family business.

HERMAN DUBERSTEIN, born Aug. 15, 1918, in Malden, MA. He and his brother, Harold, both had occupational deferments. Herman was the manager in the family metal parts manufacturing company and Harold a junior scientist for the Manhattan project. Both enlisted in the U.S. Army the same day, May 31, 1944, and being taken for twins were kept together for most of the service.

Herman received basic training at Ft. Knox, KY; attended Vehicle Maintenance School, Luxembourg City until assignment to the 702nd Tank Bn., 80th Inf. Div., 3rd Army in Europe. Arrived in February 1945 as an armored replacement.

When his tank was hit by a armored piercing shell, wounding one and killing two crew members, he helped move the disabled tank to the rear lines for salvage. After this incident, Herman and his brother, Harold, parted. Herman continued on with the 702nd crossing the Rhine River and reached Buchenwald where he was chosen as a Yiddish interpreter processing concentration camp survivors. He brought comfort to many, especially teenagers.

Married, had children, and continued his career with the family business. He died on Jun. 30, 1991. *Submitted by Harold R. Duberstein.*

STEPHEN J. DUNCHESKIE, born May 9, 1952, Ft. Campbell. Entered USAF, April 1971, as an avionics technician for the F111 fighter/bomber. Assignment at Nellis AFB involved the bombing of North Vietnam (Linebacker II) through Thailand. Deployed to Turkey with the F111's to cover an option during the Iranian Hostage situation. Discharged, SSGT, April 1981, with an AS degree in electronics from Arapaho Community College, a BS degree from the University of the State of New York and the Master in Aviation Management from Embry Riddle Aeronautical University.

Entered Naval Reserves, October 1981. Deployed aboard the carrier *America* CV 66 as an aircraft maintenance officer. Certified "Order of the Blue Nose" and "Shellback."

Promoted to lieutenant and departed the USNR in October 1987; to join the Army as an aircraft maintenance warrant officer. Deployed to Korea during Desert Storm. Now an instructor of avionics for Army Armament Maintenance Officers. Life member of Old Dominion Post 158.

SYDNEY S. DWORKIN, born in Brooklyn, New York City, U.S.A. Enlisted Aug. 12, 1914, Army of United States, Inf. 5th Div., 10th Regt., 3rd Plt. 1st Sq. Served as a quartermaster, Salvage Depot Rheins France. Reassigned April 1945. Military locations included France and Metz, Germany. Participated in European Theater and Germany.

Awards/Medals: WWII Victory Medal, American Defense Service Medal, Combat Infantry Medal, Bronze Star, Purple Heart Medal, ETO with two Battle Stars, Unit Presidential Citation.

He was discharged Oct. 15, 1945, with the rank of private first class.

Married Lillian in 1936, and had two sons. Today he is retired and golfing, traveling with his wife, Lillian.

AARON EDELMAN, born Sept. 28, 1925, Wheeling, WV. Drafted Aug. 12, 1944, U.S. Army, HQ. Military locations and stations included Camp Atterbury, IN; Joseph T Robinson, AR; Ft. Bragg, NC; Ft. Meade, MD. Participated at Rhine, Germany. Transferred from Infantry Replacement to (don't know why) Clerk's School.

Awards/Medals: Good Conduct Medal, Army Commendation, one Battle Star - Rhine, Germany.

He was discharged July 8, 1946, Honorable, with the rank of tech. 5.

Married and has three daughters. Partner in local CPA firm.

ELLIS S. EDELMAN, O.D., born entered the U.S. Army in March 1943. Completed basic training at Camp Barkeley, TX; assigned to the 6th Inf. Div. in California. Stationed at Schofield Barracks in Oahu, HI, where he received jungle training which included identification of poisonous snakes and tropical diseases.

Assigned to the 32nd Inf. Regt., 7th Div., he fought in Tarawa and Leyte in October 1944, as well as part of the first day landings on Okinawa in 1945 where his platoon was hit with mortars. "Ashcan Charlie" bombed and strafed them every three hours around the clock.

Awards/decorations: Asiatic-Pacific Campaign Medal with three Bronze Stars, Philippine Liberation with three Bronze Stars, WWII Victory Medal and the Presidential Unit Emblem.

He is an optometrist. Has wife, two boys, one girl and six grandchildren. He is a member of JWV Post 0148.

IRWIN HENRY EDELMAN, born on Dec. 9, 1921, in Newark, NJ, and enlisted in the U.S. Marine Corps Aug. 7, 1942. He served in the Pacific Theater of Operations from January 1943, to February 1945. Participated in the battles for Cape Gloucester, the Northern Solomon Islands, New Guinea and Peleliu Island.

Awards/Medals: American Theater Medal, Asiatic-Pacific Campaign Medal with three Bronze Stars, WWII Victory Medal, Rifle Sharpshooter Medal.

He was discharged as private first class in October 1945. Married Sylvia Sine in 1946 and have two children, Stuart and Bobbi and four grandchildren. He was in trucking business for 40 years. He was president of the Wet Orange Bnai Brith Chapter, honored by the State of Israel Bonds and was a member of the board of Temple B'nai Shalom in West Orange, NJ. He was shot and died in an attempted burglary in 1994.

ALFRED A. EDELSOHN, born Nov. 20, 1925, Scranton, PA. Enlisted June 24, 1944, U.S. Navy. Military stations included USNTC Bainbridge, Radioman School Bainbridge, Newport, RI; USS *Sylvania* AKA 44, NAS Cape May. He was part of magic carpet, took troops from Asia to USA; and from Europe to Asia.

Memorable experience include the peaceful invasion of Japan, August - September 1945.

Awards/Medals: American Theater, Asiatic Theater, WWII Victory Medal, Good Conduct Medal.

He was discharged May 30, 1946, radioman third class.

Married to Nitzi, daughters Gail and Carol, grandson Jesse. He has been a public school teacher for 34 years, now P/T sales. PC Post 165, Scranton, PA.

RICHARD EDGAR, born June 1, 1919, in New York. Entered the USAAF on February 1943. Served the 43rd HBG, stationed at Debach, U.K.; Stalan Luft, #1 (Jewish Barracks) Barth.

Memorable experiences include being shot down Nov. 21, 1944.

Awards/Medals: Air Medal, DOW, Unit Citation, Purple Heart Medal, DFC.

He was discharged February 1946, with the rank of lieutenant. Today he is retired.

GEORGE EDLIN, born in Brooklyn, NY, on Nov. 12, 1925. Graduated Brooklyn College in 1949. MA Columbia University 1950. Enlisted in the Army in August 1943. Served from December 1943 to May 1946. Basic training Ft. Benning, GA. Assigned to 488th Engineer Light Ponton Company at Ft. Jackson, SC. Served in ETO from January 1945 to May 1946. Married to Carolyn R. Rosenberg in December 1950. Two children, Ilene Samuel and Steven Edlin, one grandchild, Emily Lauren.

Joined JWV in 1946, Past Commander Hoffman Post No. 94. Now charter member of Post 303 Sun Cities, AZ. Retired NYC school supervisor residing in AZ.

LOUIS EDLIN, born in New York City on May 11, 1893, and died in January 1969. Was drafted into U.S. Army in 1918, and served with the 1st Div. at Battles of St. Mihiel Offensive, Meuse Argonne Offensive and German Occupation.

Married Rose Toister in July 1924. Two children, George and Phyllis Dunayer. Five grandchildren. Was past commander and life member of JWV.

Had a brother, Samuel Edlin, who also served with the Army in Europe during WWI.

JULIUS EICHENBAUM, one of three brothers who served in the Armed Forces, Commander Leo in the Navy and Dr. Louis in the Army, was originally sent to 9th Inf. 2nd Div. in San Antonio in 1941. Sent to OCS September 1942, graduated as second lieutenant. Sent to Europe for 24 months, served with Infantry, Air Force and English Navy.

Awarded six medals including the Soldiers Medal and Bronze Star. Also awarded Presidential Citation and six battle stars. Left the Army in February 1946, as a lieutenant colonel, to marry Sylvia. They have two sons, Terry and Gary and a grandson Max. Served for 3 years as a member of the West Point Council, member of Post 68 JWV. Now retired and still serving the West Point Council.

JULIUS J. EINGOREN, born in Bronx, NY, Jan. 21, 1920. Drafted into Army November 1942, Camp Upton, NY. Assigned afterward to Induction Station in NYC; then to Greenhaven Prison, Stormville, NY. From there to Ft. Dix, NJ, and then to Camp Grant, IL. Finally to Camp Beale, CA. Suffered an injury, excluded from Pacific Theater and assigned to hospital thereat as a medic.

Discharged in California as private first class, February 1946. No decorations.

Memorable experience, scant, however in NYC he took chest x-rays of Danny Kaye and other entertainment personalities. Also met and spoke to Joe Louis at an exhibition bout in Camp Beale.

Married June 1946 to Ruth Lillian (nee Jaffe) of Philly PA. No children. Past Commander of Post 209 in Jackson Heights, NY. Also active with the Masonic Order and Order of Elks. An attorney since 1947 and 27 years with the Legal Aid Society (Criminal Division) NYC.

KURT EISEN, born Sept. 12, 1926, Vienna, Austria. Entered the U.S. Army Jan. 22, 1945, serving Engineers, in Florida, Tokyo, Yong Dong Po.

Awards/Medals: Good Conduct Medal, American Campaign Medal, Atlantic Pacific, Army of Occupation, WWII Victory Medal.

He was discharged Dec. 6, 1946.

His family includes wife Muriel, (son) Stanley and Gail; (daughter) Sharon and Bruce; four grandchildren. Today he is in the fur business.

SAM EISEN, was left without parents at an early age. Our family was the only other Jewish people on the block. My mom took him in and raised him. He had many illnesses and for years wore a back brace. When he reached his teens he was healthy, and tall. He enlisted in the service when he was 10 years old. He served in the Red Arrow Division and was killed on his 21st birthday in New Guinea. After the notification of his death, a letter arrived, thanking my mom for the years she gave him. He must have felt he would not be back.

Allen Zaslow, my nephew served in Vietnam in the fields for over a year. When he came home he was often depressed. At one family gathering someone made a racist remark. He stormed out of the room. He later told us that his Army buddy was black young man. They were under heavy fire, it was coming at Allen; the black friend threw himself, knocking Allen down; he took the fire and died. It took Allen many years to let go of the pain of that experience. *Submitted by Gert Left - POP Michigan.*

THEODORE M. EISENBERG, born Avon, NY. Drafted Feb. 13, 1941, from Jersey City, NJ, U.S. Army, 337th Engineer Combat Bn. Basic training Ft. Dix, NJ, and Camp Upton, NY. Joined his first outfit at Camp Edwards, MA, the 198th CA Unit. Served on Bora Bora for seven months and then was sent to OCS at Camp Davis, NC. Stations included Mediterranean Theater and Asiatic-Pacific Theater; Naples, Foggia, North Apennines, Rome, Arno, Po Valley.

Upon receiving his commission he joined his unit at Oran, North Africa where he served eight months and then joined the 5th Army at Bari, Italy. After the German Air Force was captured, he joined a combat engineer battalion and served a little over two years till VJ Day in Europe. Then was trooped shipped to the Philippines, enroute the Atomic Bob was dropped. "Thank God, Coming home!"

Awards/Medals: American Service Medal, Asiatic-Pacific Service Medal, EAME Service Medal, Distinguished Unit Badge, WWII Victory Medal.

He was discharged Feb. 17, 1946, with the rank of captain.

Married Jessie Kreps, sadly she passed away in August 1991. Have a lovely daughter HeLain, hubby Lenny and two granddaughters Blake and Alanna. Today he is retired and member Post #10 Jersey City, NJ.

EDWARD ELBAUM, born Nov. 18, 1921. Entered the USN Aug. 7, 1942. Boot camp and Hospital Corps School, Great Lakes, IL. Hospital Duty, Brooklyn, NY. Attached to CB's, Williamsburg, VA, January 1943, with 93 CB Battalion in South Pacific for 25 months (Guadalcanal to Philippines)

Memorable experience: "almost lost right arm thusly: invaded Green Island (off Bougainvillea). Vowed to sleep during daylight and be awake at night. The fourth night in foxhole I felt an irritation on my right side, I reach down with my left hand to examine. All I felt was the wall of the shallow foxhole, where was my right arm? The irritation must be the result of bleeding! I've been wounded! I'm going to die! I raised my head in panic and in so doing the blood flowed through my right arm again, I had fallen asleep with my arm under my head, "it" had fallen asleep! I was not dying; I had not lost my arm."

He was discharged Dec. 5, 1945, with the rate of PHM1/c.

MARTIN ELFENBEIN, served as a lieutenant (procurement) in the Army Air Force. Italian campaign.

JACK ELKIN, his parents were both born in Russia. He was born in Brooklyn, NY, Sept. 1, 1922. He attended public and high school in Brooklyn, and after graduation enlisted in the Army Nov. 8, 1940. He went to the ETO via the *Queen Elizabeth*, reached England, was in Scotland, then was sent to North Africa. It was near Kasserine Pass that he was captured and was then a buck-sergeant in Co. A., 18th Inf. 1st Div.

He was in a prison camp in Italy with other American soldiers and some British soldiers (treatment was not good). When the American Army approached the camp, the guards fled and some prisoners who were physically able, took to the hills. After some weeks of freedom they were recaptured by German soldiers coming back to that area. The escapees live off farm produce as long as they, according to the Italian farmers, did not show themselves during the day. Otherwise, the Italian farmers feared being shot by the Germans. They were then sent to Germany as laborers. They were in East Germany and the Russian Army started to come close to the camp, which had Russians soldiers, also prisoners, near-by. In the confusion, Jack and a friend escaped and were picked up by some Russian soldiers. Making their way back they finally reached the American lines. His time as a POW was characterized by poor rations and general care.

After returning home, he studied cabinet making under the GI bill and has a good career as a cabinet maker. He and his wife, Eleanor, came to Rio Rancho in 1972, after he retired in 1965. They have three children. In Rio Ranch (N.M.), he has joined several veteran organizations and is active with them. He has spoken before many organizations on his wartime experiences.

MORTON A. ENOWITZ, born March 30, 1916, Jersey City, NJ. Enlisted May 10, 1943, USNR, Storekeeper 3c SV6 of rate. Military locations included NRS Newark, NJ; NTS Newport, RI; OL A GR(L) SK School; NTS Newport, RI; NRB Shoemaker, CA; USNAB Esparto Santos, NH; USD Navy 926; RS NOB Navy 926; NSD Guam, M.I., PSC Lido Beach, NY. Participated in battles in the Pacific and American Theaters.

Memorable experience include 28 days zigzagging on the USJ *Mintaka* bound west for New Caledonia, living with natives, three days burning tall grass on Guadalcanal to flush out remaining Japanese.

Awards/Medals: Pacific Theater, American Theater, WWII Victory Medal.

He was discharged Nov. 25, 1945, with the rank of SK3/c.

Married to Laura Sklaren, two children, Evan, and Ann Ruth Enowitz, two grandchildren, Leah and Benjamin. Member of JWV Geo. Fredman Post #076 Nobergem, NJ.

HENRY I. EPSTEIN, born Oct. 20, 1921. Enlisted in the U.S. Army on July 31, 1942, at Ft. Dix, NJ. Transported to Ft. Ontario at Oswego, NY, where he received basic training. Assigned to 717th Military Police Bn. in NYC. His Town Patrol Unit was ordered to duty in the 1943 Harlem Riots.

Accepted into the ASTP but the Army canceled the program. Assigned to the Elite Ordnance School at Aberdeen Proving Grounds. Went to NCO and Instructors Schools becoming an instructor at the Elite Ordnance School.

Married Geraldine Hannes during a furlough on Jan. 28, 1945. Sent to Oahu, HI, where he was assigned to the Signal Corp HQ Office. When the war ended the commanding general formed a unit to record the activities of the Pacific Ocean Areas Armed Forces, he was the NCO in charge at the rank of master sergeant.

A CPA. He is Fourth District Vice Commander of Post 125 Budget and Finance Committee.

HYMIE EPSTEIN, "medic" was killed in action in the southwest Pacific on Dec. 1, 1942. He was the son of Mr. and Mrs. Morris Epstein and had been a member of Aleph Zadek Aleph in Omaha and the Round Table of Jewish Youth which sponsored a "buy-a-bomber" campaign in his memory.

According to an article by George Weller of the Chicago Daily News Foreign Service "Epstein was a medical aide with the American Troops near Sanananda in the South Pacific. His group was sent out to carry rations to one of the units cut off in the forest. The Japs opened fire on the group. Suddenly a man about eight feet ahead of Epstein was hit in the neck by a machine gun bullet." "And this little kid crawls right from the mud to the wounded man. He gets out his sulfanilamide powered and bandages, and lying on his back also, binds the wounded man's neck. Then he crawled back with bullets all around him," according to Maj. Bert Zeeff who had already fought in two wars.

"A second time when another man was hit Epstein crawled out, dressed the man's wounds, and with fire all around him, got back. However, at dawn when the Japanese became more accurate with their machine guns, Epstein crawled out again to help a man who was hit. Five minutes later word was passed up the line that Epstein was dead. He had stayed a little too long."

The Epstein-Morgan JWV of Omaha is named for Hymie Epstein and Samuel Morgan who was also killed in the war.

JACK EPSTEIN, born in Brooklyn, NY, Feb. 16, 1920. Entered Army, Friday, Feb. 13, 1942. Basic training, Ft. Bragg, NC. Assigned to an artillery outfit, Camp Shelby, MS. Then to a Task Force #5889 specially designed to serve in Liberia, West Africa. Next, to the Army Air Transport command in Lagos, Nigeria. Completed service with Air Transport command at Presque Isle, Maine. Discharged November 1945.

Returned to Brooklyn College for one semester and received BA degree. Completed Post Grad degrees at Columbia and G. Washington Universities. Was a social studies teacher, NYC High Schools; Vocational Counselor; personnel specialist, training officer and retired from Federal Service as Chief, Civilian Career Programs and Training and Development, Air Force Systems Command. Consulted in areas of Human Resource Management and Development. Currently a volunteer Career Planning, Educational Counselor at Northern Virginia Community College, Alexandria, VA.

A very touching memory during service in Liberia, HQ Co., of which he was one, had a contingent of 176 folks. When his mother died in 1944 the 10 other Jewish soldiers joined him for a minyon to say Kadish for his mother.

Battles: Malarial Mosquitoes; Jungle Rot and Fungi; Elephantiasis and similar non-battle star actions.

Married to Evelyn since 1947. Two sons, one grandson. Formerly with Brooklyn Post #2. Past Commander Post #676, his current affiliation.

LAWRENCE S. EPSTEIN, born April 1, 1949, Brooklyn, NY. Graduated from New Utrecht High School, Long Island University and was commissioned from ROTC at Pratt Institute, all in Brooklyn, NY. He served on active duty from 1969-77 as an counterintelligence special agent with the 110th MI Det., 500th MI group and continued to serve in the Army Reserve to eventually attend the Army War College Resident Class of 1992 and graduate with the Bristol Oral History Award from the Military History Institute. Called for duty by the Presidential Callup for Desert Shield and Storm he was

alleged to be an Israeli spy while serving as the Deputy Commander of Special Security Command Forces, Command as a result of anti-Semitism by members of that command. LT COL Epstein has continued his career in the USAR with the complete support of the Jewish War Veterans USA. His brother, LT COL Edward P. Epstein also proudly continues to serve.

WILLIAM H. EPSTEIN, born Oct. 24, 1915, in Neptune, NJ. He was inducted into the Army on Jan. 28, 1943, at Ft. Dix, NJ. Three days later he was shipped to Miami Beach, FL, for two months of basic training. His next stop was Ft. Custer, MI, for two months of investigator training. Next stop was a bivouac area in the vicinity of New Orleans, for one month; next on his itinerary was Ft. Shanks, NY, for one week and then to New York for overseas. He left in June 1943, and landed in the United Kingdom. He stayed overseas for 31 months, 29 months in England and two months in France. He was sent to France at the height of the Battle of the Bulge.

He was discharged on Jan. 28, 1946, at Ft. Monmouth, NJ, completing exactly three years of duty.

Memorable experience: B Bomb, Air Raid and Bomb damage in London. Friday Night religious service in the dark during an air raid.

HERMAN ERDMAN, married to Beatrice, and has two children and one granddaughter. Now employed Atlantic Steel Corp., NY, as salesman. Living in Delray Beach, FL. Inducted Nov. 30, 1940, discharged May 12, 1945. Combat Central Europe, Northern France.

Awards/Medals: Good Conduct Medal, Purple Heart Medal with OLC, American Defense Service Medal, Bronze Star, Distinguished Service Cross, EAME Service Medal, Conspicuous Service Medal New York State. 44th Inf. Div. 71st Inf.

SAM ERLICK, born in Philadelphia, PA, on April 24, 1924. Enlisted in Army on Dec. 8, 1942. Discharged Oct. 27, 1945. After basic training, served as a rifleman with the 104th Inf. Regt., 26th Yankee Division. Onto Tennessee Maneuvers, then training at Ft. Jackson, SC. Fought through France, Germany and Luxembourg with Patton's 3rd Army. Left Army as PFC. Decorated with Bronze Star Medal, Purple Heart Medal, plus OLC, Good Conduct Medal, American Campaign Medal, EAME Campaign Medal with four Battle Stars, WWII Victory Medal, Army of Occupation Medal, combat Infantryman Badge, Expert Infantryman Badge, Expert Badge with Rifle Bar.

Memorable experience was being rushed by truck to Luxembourg to fight in the Ardennes Offensive.

Married Sandra B. and have daughter Carynelisa and son Eliot. Member of JWV, American Legion, and 104th Inf. Reg. Association presently employed as an auditor with the federal government.

MORRIS E. ESON, born Montreal, Canada, April 18, 1921. Came to Chicago in 1937. Studied at the Hebrew

Theological College. BA from Illinois Institution of Technology and MA from the University of Chicago. Ordained in 1945 and enlisted in U.S. Army as chaplain. Served with 4th Inf. Div., Camp Butner, NC, Post Jewish Chaplain at Fort Lee, VA. Served in Panama and then discharged at the rank of captain in 1947 at Ft. Knox, KY. Continued graduate education at University of C., earning Ph.D. in psychology in 1951. Joined faculty at the University at Albany, State University of NY. Was Fulbright Scholar in Israel, 1957-58, and visiting professor, University of Haifa, 1970-71. Active in Temple Israel, Albany, NY. Retired from faculty at SUNY in 1993. Married to Joy Platt, 1943. One daughter, three sons and five grandchildren. Member of JWV Albany Post.

DR. MILDRED ESTES, born in Brooklyn, NY. The first in Washington, D.C., to join the newly organized WAAC in 1942. Mildred was then placed on military furlough from her permanent civil service professional job as a junior economist for OPA. Mildred had been graduated from Brooklyn College, cum laude, in 1939, and had almost completed two years of graduate work toward a master's in public administration when she was hired by the federal government via a civil service exam. Though she had a great career job, the call to serve in the Armed Forces was irresistible. She was trained in Des Moines, IA, and became the first acting first sergeant of a WAC Regt. that went to Ft. Sam Houston, TX. A year later she volunteered for a special overseas assignment without rank and on May 18, 1944, she left Newport News, VA, with a special WAC regiment in a convoy of the 82nd Airborne. They landed in Naples, Italy on May 28, 1944. The troopers went on to the Battle in Rome and later France. The WACs went to Headquarters, Middle Eastern Theater, Cairo, Egypt. In March 1945, Mildred married an American soldier in Cairo, Egypt. She had met Gordon at Camp Tel Litvinsky in Tel Aviv now Israel. He was stationed in the Persian Gulf. After the war, the Estes lived in Pacific Grove, CA, for a few years and then Los Angeles. Mildred obtained an MS in educational psychology from USC in 1952, and a Ph.D. in clinical psychology from the California Graduate Institute. She worked as a school psychologist and counselor for 25 year and later as a clinical psychologist for 2 years in the field of developmental disabilities. She has four children and two grandchildren and a mother she takes care of who is over 100 years of age.

HARRY ETTLINGER, born on Jan. 28, 1926, in Germany. He and his family left Germany one day after his Bar Mizwa for the USA in fall 1938.

He was drafted into the U.S. Army in August 1944, after graduating from a Newark, NJ, High School. In January 1945, he landed in Europe, but never saw front-line action. In May 1945, he started his assignment as a member of the U.S. Army Military Government to recover and return works of art stolen by the Nazis. In July 1946, he was discharged in the rank of sergeant.

Harry had a career in engineering and management. During his working life, he obtained a MS in mechanical engineering and an MBA. Before his retirement in 1992, he was a program manger on the Navy's Trident Missile Guidance Program.

Harry married Mimi Goldman in 1951; They have three and two grandchildren. He is currently commander of Post 689 and chief of staff to Dept. Cdr. Department of NJ. Mr. Ettlinger is a past county and district commander in JWV.

MORT ETTINGER, (Y1C) USNR, born May 6, 1924, Chelsea, MA. Graduated high school June 1942. Entered USN March 2, 1943. Discharged, honorable, April 10, 1946.

Basic at NTS, Newport, RI. Yeoman School at NTS, Newport, RI. Assigned to ARGUS 17 at USNABD, Port Hueneme, CA. Shipped overseas to NAS Maui and NAS Barbers Point in the Hawaiian Islands for training and assignment to the U.S. Marine Corps. Participated in the invasion of Guam with the Third Marine Division. Transferred to

ComAirPac Staff on Ford Island. Transferred to Coronado Heights where he was the Yeoman in Charge of the Discharge Center. Competed for and received a principal fleet appointment to the Naval Academy at Annapolis. Transferred to NAPS at Camp Perry, VA. Failed Annapolis physical and was transferred to the Fargo Building in Boston, MA, for discharge.

Decorations: Asiatic-Pacific Medal with a battle star, American Theater Medal, Good Conduct Medal, WWII Victory Medal.

Married to Charlotte Kahn and had two sons and a daughter. His daughter, Linda Joyce, died in 1976. His two sons are Steven Alan and Jonathan Mark Ettinger. Member of JWV and Veterans of Foreign Wars. Presently a Professor at Salem State College, Salem, MA, after a career of 36 years as an industry executive.

JACK H. EVERS, born Aug. 1, 1913, in Jersey City, NJ. He was drafted in April 1942. The officer-in-charge said, "You can be excused from serving, as you are the last of five siblings to be called into the military." He said, "Oh, no!" and off he went to the 474th Transportation Co.

Spent two years in the States at Camp Lee, Camp Shelby, Ft. Henry Harrison and then two and one-half years in Oahu and Okinawa. After 20 years in the Reserves, he was discharged as a lieutenant colonel.

Awards/Medals: American Campaign Medal, Asiatic-Pacific Campaign Medal with one Battle Star, WWII Victory Medal and Meritorious Service Unit Plaque.

Married 52 years to Malvina with two daughters, Jane and Ruth, and three grandsons, Seth, Arin, and David. Retired after 20 years from traffic management positions. He is a charter member and past-commander of JWV Post 666.

MARTIN FALK, born June 2, 1925, graduated New York School of Printing, June 1943. Drafted October 1943. Served his boot training at Sampson, NY, sent to Electrical School at the same place. Sent to Brooklyn Navy Yard, served as electrician aboard the USS *Evarts* DE #5. Escorted convoys to the Mediterranean. It took 22 days to get to a port on the Met. Made five crossings first to Oran, second Algiers, third Birzerte Tunis, fourth Palamo Sicily. They engaged German Junkers 88's who came off Southern France where he got their first Battle Star. They hunted German subs off Halifax. They dropped depth charges but never sank any subs. The last year of his service was served aboard a subchaser in Miami. Training new officers, 90 day wonders. Was discharged April 1946, with the rank of second class petty officer, EM2/c. Lived 1766 Park Place Brooklyn, NY. Married 1947, has two children boy and girl and one grandchild.

Bronze Star and Commendation from Truman for action of Gibraltar. Wife Marilyn and Larry David and Helene Audry. Reside in San Fernando Valley.

SHELDON H. FAST, born Feb. 28, 1924. Enlisted in the Army Infantry on Nov. 16, 1942, at Lafayette College, Easton, PA, where he was a sophomore. Tried to enlist on Friday November 13, but the colonel was away so he had to wait for Monday. Basic training IRTC at Ft. McClellan, AL. ASTP at North Carolina State College of A&E, Raleigh, NC. Joined Co. L. 347th Inf., 87th Div. at Ft. Jackson, SC. Shipped to England as infantry replacement and then to France. Joined Co. E., 328th Inf., 26th (Yankee) Div. in eastern France. I combat he served as rifleman and scout (although he was als trained as a flame thrower.) Hospitalized with trench foot.

Spent time from late November 1944, in various hospi tals in France, England, Scotland and the US until discharge from Camp Butner Convalescent Hospital, NC, on July 12

1945. Arrived home on Friday, July 13, 1945. Rank at discharge private first class. Awards: American Campaign Medal, WWII Victory Medal, Presidential Unit Citation, Good Conduct Medal, ETO Medal with Battle Star, Combat Infantryman Badge and Bronze Star Medal. Under Public Law 16 for disabled veterans he finished Lafayette College in 1947 and was graduated from Cornell Law School, Ithaca, NY, in 1950. Today he is retired after 43 year of practicing law and as president of two title insurance agencies he founded. Life today is wonderful. His wife and he travel often particularly to Israel where they go almost every year. And of course they spend time with their children and grandchildren who all live nearby.

War experience, "nothing unusual for an infantryman, except that he was lucky not to have been wounded or killed. On admission to trench foot hospital ward in England, the soldier in the next bed (a milk man in civilian life) stated rather boldly to the effect that he couldn't be Jewish because there were no Jews in the infantry. Jews always get out of dangerous service. I think I ruined his knowledge of life as he thought it was, not as it is. I certainly hope so."

SELMA KING FAUER, born Baltimore, MD, Sept. 21, 1921. Raised Washington, D.C. Graduated R.N. Sinai Hospital, Baltimore, 1942. Enlisted as second lieutenant Army Air Force Nurse Corps, Sept. 1, 1943. Stationed Brookley Field, Mobile, AL. Volunteered for overseas service and assigned to 98th General Hospital (Army) to ETO February 1944, Southern England to Munich, Germany June 1945 as Occupation Hospital until December 1945. Separated from service as first lieutenant February 1946.

Married New Jersian Marvin Fauer (also WWII Vet.) 1948, two great children, Lauren (now Patten) and Charles who provided super twin grandsons, Adam and Ben.

Past president West Orange, NJ, Chapter and No. NJ Council of B'nai Brith Women. Marv and Selma both members of JWV Post 146, Bloomfield, NJ. Marvin died 1981. Selma retired from North Jersey Blood Center 1988 after 40 years service and now lives with second mate, David Niren, in Dunwoody, GA.

Most memorable experience was 1945, War with Germany had just ended. Yom Kippor Service for allied Jewish personnel was held at the Opera House in Munich, Germany. Full to capacity the Kolnidre was sung by a cantor who had just been liberated from Dachau. It was heartrending! A most poignant memory in a full and exiting career.

FREDERICK B. FEIGENOFF, born Sept. 22, 1918, Paterson, NJ. Served in the US Army, platoon leader, Inf. at Camp Stewart, GA; Camp Edwards, MA; Camp Picket, VA; European Theater, 1944-45. Participated in battles in Ardennes (Bulge) Central Europe, Rhineland.

Memorable experience include being one of the first troops hit in the Bulge only a few of them survived, but they slowed the German advance; and crossing the bridge at Remagen a week after it was found intact under heavy shell fire.

Awards/Medals: three Battle Stars, ETO, American Theater Medal, WWII Victory Medal.

He was discharged January 1946, with the rank of staff sergeant.

Married Phyllis in 1947, have a son and daughter and two grandchildren. Retired. Member of Post 210 JWV.

HARRY E. FEIN, born in Chicago, IL, Nov. 28, 1918, married March 15, 1941. Entered into the Marine Corps Aug. 3, 1943. Boot Camp in San Diego. Overseas to Guadalcanal, became part of the 1st Provisional Brigade,

took part in the invasion of Guam on D Day. While on Guam he saved a native young man from being shot. They became good friends. Before entering the corps he worked for a dress manufacturer and wrote them to send dresses or material for his sisters which they did. While on Guam he was put in charge of the company mail and remained in the post office the rest of his tour in the corps. Was in Japan when the peace treaty was signed. Was discharged Feb. 1, 1946. His oldest brother, Frank was in the cavalry in WWI. His sister Mae Fein retired from the Army as a major. His brother Cpl. Arthur Fein was killed in action in the Battle of Leyte. He now has a son, daughter, son-in-law, grandson and a granddaughter. His wife of 54 years and he are now retired and live in an adult retirement area in Palm Springs.

BERNARD S. FEINBERG, D.D.S., born July 17, 1912, West Hoboken, NJ. Enlisted Jan. 31, 1941, Ft. Dix, NJ. Dental Corps, captain, 104th Med Bn. 29th Div. 116th Inf. Regt. Stationed at Ft. Dix, Ft. McClelland, England, France and Holland. Participated in battles in European Theater, Normandy, Northern France.

Enlisted as private Jan. 31, 1941, age 29, left dental practice because he was first, a patriotic American and second, a Jew. Commissioned first lieutenant August 1944. Volunteered for combat April 1944 when in England. Joined 29th Div. 116th. Inf. 104th Med. Bn. April 1944. Became Regt. Dental Surgeon After D Day invasion. Regt. Awarded Presidential Citation for holding Beachhead so that troops could land etc. (Omaha Beach) wounded battle for St. Lo, July 12, 1944. Bronze Star for action in combat.

Memorable experience being first wave Normandy, Omaha Beach June 6, 1944. First Liberated Rosh Shoshana, Sept. 20, 1944; first troops to brake through Siegfried Like.

Awards/Medals: Presidential Unit Citation, American Theater, Good Conduct Medal, WWII Victory Medal, American Defense Service Medal, ETO, Arrowhead, three Battle Stars, Bronze Star, Purple Heart Medal.

He was discharged Feb. 5, 1946, with the rank of captain AVS Dental Corp.

He has three children and five grandchildren: Barbara Sue Nehmad, David S. Feinberg, Judi McGregor, Laura Jnehman, Jacob, Arlene Feinberg, Matthew, Allison McGregor. Retired dentist.

BERNARD S. FEINBERG, born in New York City, on Sept. 3, 1913. Attended NVHS and LIU where he earned letters for track and lacrosse.

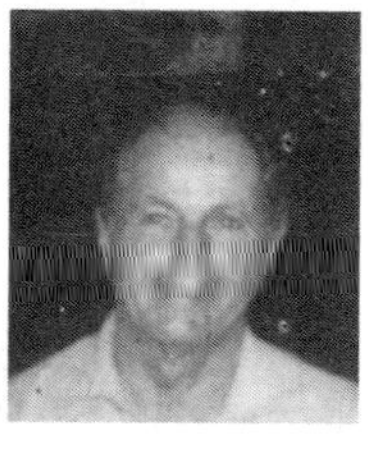

Drafted into Army Feb. 3, 1941. Honorably discharged Aug. 24, 1942, to accept appointment as second lieutenant AUS. Retired as captain, May 25, 1946, due to combat injuries in WWII.

Serving as assistant battalion surgeon in 23rd Tank Bn. Of 12th A.D. was awarded Bronze Star and Purple Heart Medals for heroic action in combat near Bohl, Germany. Also received Colmar Fr. Coat-of-Arms, Presidential Unit Citation, Meritorious Service Unit Plaque, American Campaign Medal, EAME Campaign Medal, WWII Victory Medal.

Married to Julianee Weinstock, 50 years. Three married daughters, Madelyn, Helaine and Terez, sons-in-law, Dr. Robert Kent and Malcolm Harris, and four grandchildren Eli, Rebecca, David and Sallie. Member of the JWV Post 258.

Memorable experience was temporary assignment to General George Patton as he raced across Europe.

JOSEPH L. FEINBERG, born Feb. 6, 1927, Fall River, MA. Joined USN December 1944. Served on destroyer escorts in Norfork, Philadelphia, Key West, FL- Marshall Islands, Pacific.

Memorable experiences include during a ship convoy trip to England a German submarine surfaced and surrendered upon learning of Germany's surrender May 9, 1945.

Awards/Medals: Atlantic and Pacific Combat Bars.

He was discharged September 1949, with the rank of lieutenant (JG).

Married in 1952 and has three sons. He has been president of a manufacturing company for past 35 years.

RAYMOND LEON FEINSTEIN, the late second lieutenant was flying a single engine plane when it crashed on June 5, 1944, over Passage Key Florida in the Gulf of Mexico because it had not been inspected in nine days.

June 27, 1944, Mitchell E. Simms, Major, Air Corps Commanding, Squadron Sarasota Army Air Field, Florida wrote: "I had rather not put in a letter all of the details concerning your husband's death. The things I am able to tell you where that he crashed on a routine training flight. The medical officer says that there was evidence of flame being taken into the lungs. This within itself would be sufficient to cause death. It is not known whether the flames or the crash caused death. The explanation that I gave you while you were here still holds true. For security reasons I had rather not repeat it in a letter."

The night before his death my 28 year old husband told me that he couldn't wait until he would be sent to California. He told me that you "redneck" mechanics were calling him "Yankee Jew Boy."

Ray was a textile engineer who had received a sports scholarship from his college in Philadelphia. Ray was working for the government as a duck cloth inspector when he enlisted in the Air Corps to serve his country in wartime.

I was pregnant when his coffin, which my father and I brought back by train from Florida to NYC was lowered into cemetery earth to a stirring tribute of taps being blown by fellow servicemen whose bugles glistened in the June sunshine.

Ray died because southern American boys were still fighting the Civil War and were imbued with anti-Semitism ideology. Naomi Rae was eight years old when he remarried and became the wife of a Holocaust survivor. Naomi became Naomi Rae Gombinski when she was nine years old. The following year Steve Joseph Gombinski was born and named after Mendel's parents Sarah and Joseph who were Holocaust victims in Poland. Steven's birth and the births of his two young sons are living proof that Nazi genocide was a failure.

I write this in memory of Raymond Leon Feinstein. The story of his death was hushed up by the USA Air Corp because of "Security Reasons."

Naomi Rae is now the mother of two young women. This Passover holiday in was in NYC and Jordana, Naomi's younger daughter age 23, asked me to tell her about "Ray." I recounted the story and cried. She wept with me and we bonded in the present out of a past half century when the war of hate left death in its wake.

WILLIAM H. FELBURG, enlisted in the U.S. Army on June 17, 1942. He was attached to the Army Air Force, Air Transport Command Ferrying Division. He received his basic training at Ft. Dix, NJ, and also at Miami Beach, FL. He attended airplane mechanics' school at Seymour, Johnson Field, NC, also instructor school C-46, specialist school Buffalo, NY, and engine mechanics' school at La Guardia Airport, NY. He served as a technical instructor in Tennessee, Wisconsin, North Carolina and California. He was discharged on May 3, 1945. *Submitted by Max Sigal.*

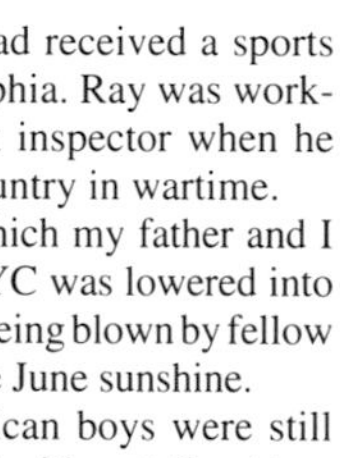

ARTHUR FELDMAN, born July 25, 1918, Bronx, NY. Joined service Feb. 21, 1944, U.S. Marine Corps, Parris Island, Camp Lejeune, Camp Pendleton, Guadalcanal, Okinawa, April 1, 1945. Ryukyu Islands, two landings.

He was discharged May 17, 1946. Married 53 years, two children and six grandchildren. Retired and seeing the world.

CHARLES FELDMAN, born Nov. 12, 1924, died Dec. 10, 1977. Enlisted in Army Infantry in November or December 1942, while a freshman at Lafayette College, Easton, PA. Basic training IRTC Ft. McClellan, AL. ASTP at North Carolina State College of A&E, Raleigh, NC. Joined 346th Inf., 87th Div. at Ft. Jackson, SC. Stayed with that outfit and served as rifleman and MP in Europe until end of war in Europe. Discharged, in late 1945, or early 1946.

Awards/Medals: Combat Infantryman's Badge, Good Conduct Medal.

He was discharged with the rank of private or private first class. Finished Lafayette College under GI Bill. Married in 1948, one son. Became chief operation officer of general insurance agency. Died of heart attack.

DONALD E. FELDMAN, born June 14, 1936, Philadelphia, served in the Marine Reserves and U.S. Army. Enlisted Jan. 31, 1954. Served in Hanau, Germany, with 3rd Armd. Div. 23rd Comb. Engr.

Mr. Feldman lives in Sewell, NJ, and is married to the former Edith A. Price. He has seven children and 11 grandchildren.

IRVING FELDMAN, born Dec. 19, 1918, Amsterdam, NY. Enlisted in December 1941, Navy. Military stationed included Norfolk, Newfoundland and Quonset Point. Participated in battles of the New England Forest Fires.

Memorable experience fighting forest fires with a broom.

He was discharged in 1945, with the rank of seaman second class.

His wife Annette died in 1968. He died in November 1984. He developed a film wrapping machine used in the laundry business.

JACK A. FELDMAN, Third Class Pharmacist Mate, USNR, born Dec. 19, 1923, Amsterdam, NY. Graduated Wilbur H. Lynch Senior High School on June 1943. Moved to Los Angeles, CA, July 1943. Worked for a few months at the National Reeder Aircraft Company.

He entered the Navy in Los Angels, CA, on Jan. 25, 1944. He took boot training at Camp Decatur, in San Diego, CA. Then he took training at Balboa Park U.S. Naval Hospital and studied Anatomy, Materia Medical, First Aid, Hygiene and Sanitation, Nursing, Chemical Warfare, and Metrology. From there he went to U.S. Naval Hospital at Long Beach, CA, where he trained in nursing and took care of 120 orthopedic patients in the orthopedic ward for a few months. Then he was sent to Port Hueneme, where he took care of a contagious ward for a few months.

They sent him to Oceanside, CA, where he trained in the Amphibians, Platoon 7, Bn. D. They were trained in making landings as a landing and beach hospital. They took calisthenics in the sand and learned how to set up medical stations on the beach for taking care of casualties.

Then they went to Astoria, OR, where he caught his first ship, the USS *Lenawee,* APA-195. They went to several ports along the West Coast, and then finally went to the Hawaiian Islands. They practiced and prepared for battle and then went into the invasion of Iwo Jima, Okinawa, and finally, the surrender of Japan.

His duties during this time were to give first aid to emergency victims during wartime, take care of the Main Sick Bay, the Mental Ward, the Isolation Ward, and fill prescriptions in the ship's pharmacy. Also, his duties included keeping the facilities, for medical care, clean.

During their invasion into Okinawa, their ship was attacked by Japanese Kamikaze, suicide planes. He was doing sick call duty for the marines at the time of the attack, when he heard the warning. He was up all night taking care of patients during the Iwo Jima invasion and also he was up all night taking care of patients during the Okinawa invasion He took care of one man who had his face blown off by a mortar shell and another who had his liver torn apart by a grenade, along with other men with head and brain injuries, and many other patients with other injuries, who were wounded in battle.

On Sept. 2, 1945, Sunday, their ship, the USS *Lenawee,* APA-195, was next to the Missouri in Tokyo Bay. At 9:00 a.m., they heard the entire ceremony, when the Japanese Admirals singed the surrender papers, while Gen. Douglas MacArthur was in charge of this historic event. The plaque, from the deck of the Missouri, marking where this great moment in history took place, along with the surrenders papers, are now on display at the Gen. MacArthur Memorial in Norfolk, VA.

During his tour of duty, he was sent to the Philippines, Tokyo, Hiroshima, Yokohama, Japan, New Hebrides, Ulithi, Eniwetok, Pearl Harbor, Honolulu, the Solomon Islands, the New Hebrides and Saipan, Subic Bay, Manilla, Guam, Sidney, Australia and other ports and places.

He served on the USS *Lenawee,* APA-195, the USS *Valaria,* AKA-48, and the USS *Oxford,* APA-189.

He was awarded two Battle Stars, Asiatic-Pacific Area Ribbon, American Area Ribbon, Philippine Liberation Ribbon.

He was honorably discharged at U.S. Naval Base, Terminal Island, San Pedro, CA, on May 1, 1946.

He moved to Norfolk, VA, May 1946. Started work at U.S. Naval Air Station, June 1946. Married Margaret Alice Waldman July 19, 1946. They had two children, Robert Louis Feldman and Diane Lynn Feldman. He retired from the U.S. Naval Air Station, Standards Laboratory, as an electrical engineering technician, Jan. 12 1979, after 32 years. His duties in the Electronic Standards Laboratory were calibrating electronic standards for the Navy all over the world, including the U.S. He calibrated the primary standards for not only the Navy and foreign ports, but for large civilian companies and corporations as well. He also did research and gave technical engineering assistance upon request from other technical facilities. His other jobs were training members of the armed forces as well as civilian engineers in the art of setting up primary calibration standards and performing calibrations to accuracies as high as seven parts over ten to the twelfth.

His total time working for the U.S. Navy, as a uniformed member as well as a civilian, was 35 and one-half years.

MELVIN FELDMAN, served in the U.S. Army from April 25, 1944, to Jan. 20, 1946, when he was discharged from the Army of the U.S. for the purpose of re-enlistment in the Regular Army. He entered the infantry branch of the Army with the rank of private at Boston, MA, and trained at Camp Blanding, FL, from July 12, 1945, to Nov. 1, 1945. He received ASTRP at the University of Maine from July 5, 1944 to Oct. 5, 1944, and also at the University of Minnesota from Oct. 10, 1944 until June 26, 1945. He was promoted to private first class upon his enlistment in the Regular Army on Jan. 21, 1945 and was again promoted to T-5 under assignment to the First Army at Ft. Bragg, NC, on March 1, 1946, and again received a promotion to T-4 on April 9, 1946.

At the age of 17 he enlisted in the U.S. Army in the ERC and spent three moths studying Japanese and was at the University of Minnesota when he turned 18. He took his basic training and was sent to Yale University to continue Japanese but reenlisted in the Regular Army for a period of 18 months thereafter. *Submitted by Max Sigal.*

MEYER I. FELDMAN "MIKE," born in Brooklyn, NY, on Aug. 7, 1922. Graduated from the Manhattan School of Aviation in 1940.

Worked at Wright Paterson as an airplane mechanic and was transferred to Sebring, FL, at which time he married his childhood sweetheart, Ruth Greenberg.

After one and one-half years, he was transferred to Granada, MS, and then went into the service.

Mike took his basic training at Ft. Sill OK, until he was sent overseas to the European Theater (joined the 177th FA Bn.) as an airplane mechanic.

The enclosed picture is Mike Feldman (sitting, right) with his three brothers.

Isaac Feldman (standing right) was in the 4th Marine Div. and is now living in Tucson, AZ.

Jack Feldman (Standing, left) was in the 66th Div., European theater, and is now living in Brooklyn, NY.

Sol Feldman (sitting, left) was in the Italian theater and is now living in Florida.

Mike Feldman currently lives in New City (Rockland County), NY.

MORTON M. FELDMAN, RT3/c, born Sept. 3, 1921, Syracuse, NY, graduated May 1943, Syracuse University, degree in mechanical engineering. Employed May 1943 to May 1944, at Brooklyn Navy Yard as a mechanical engineer.

Enlisted in the Navy, May 1944, Buffalo, NY. Six weeks Pre-Radio, Chicago, IL. Twelve weeks USN Training School (EE&RM) University of Houston. Twenty-eight weeks Radar Training, Navy Pier, Chicago, COM School, Oceanside, CA.

Boarded USS *Spangler* (destroyer escort). Served as radar operator and technician in the Pacific. Witnessed War's devastation to people and property in Hong Kong, Shanghai and ports.

Discharged May 1946, electronic technician mate third class.

Married to Florence since 1950, two sons, David and Joel, one daughter, Ann Merle and four grandchildren: Philip, Amy, Kate and Andy.

Member of JWV, Post 131. Heating and air-conditioning contractor since 1946.

PEARL FELDMAN, born Jan. 22, 1916, Detroit, MI. Enlisted August 1942 in WAC, taking basic training in Ft. Des Moines, IA. Other duty stations include Daytona Beach, FL, to train recruits in Tent City; Norfolk, VA; Ft. Oglethorpe, GA, for overseas training; Camp Shanks, NY, POE.

Sent to ETO and London in the midst of buzz bombs from Germany. Shortly after D-day, left for France through Valogne, mud, minefields and the perils of war. Arrived in Paris and worked in offices spattered with blood. Their outfit worked in motor pool, communications and the Signal Corps. She remembers being restricted to quarters during the Battle of the Bulge when the Germans were trying to get back into Paris.

They were in touch with a Jewish family, whose menfolks had been taken by the Germans and not seen again. Her mother's sister and children were taken to Auschwitz. One daughter was spared when she escaped with a friend and made it to Detroit, MI.

Awards/Medals: Good Conduct, WAAC Service Ribbon, WWII Victory Medal, EAME Service Medal with one Bronze Star and American Campaign Medal. Discharged September 1945 with the rank sergeant major.

Belongs to JWV, VFW and AMVETS.

RICHARD L. FELDMAN, born May 23, 1937, Philadelphia, served in the U.S. Army during the Vietnam conflict He resided in Clementon, NJ. He was married to Agnes Kine and had four children and seven grandchildren. He died i January 1991.

ROBERT W. FELDMAN, born March 18, 1932, Detroit, MI. Enlisted in the U.S. Army April 26, 1952. After basic training was sent to Austria and served in the 518th Engr. Co in St. Johann Im Pongau Austria during the Korean War.

The 518th Engr. Co. duty was to protect the Army in the Austrian Alps if the USSR were to try to take over Europ while the U.S. was at war in Korea.

Awards/Medals: National Defense Medal and Good Conduct Medal. Discharged April 1, 1954.

Married Sandra Sept. 26, 1954, and has two sons, Marc (medical doctor) and Howard. Worked at the Detroit Free Press for 41 years, retired June 1, 1992. Joined the JWV in 1990, elected vice commander in 1992 and commander of Silverman Post 135 of Detroit, MI, in 1995.

STEVEN ALLAN FELDMAN, born Feb. 8, 1948, Flint, MI. Enlisted May 22, 1968, U.S. Army, Signal Corps. Military locations included Ft. Bragg, Ft. Jackson, Ft. Gordon, DaNang, Dalat Buprang. Participated in battle in Vietnam.

Awards/Medals: Bronze Star Medal.

He was discharged Dec. 5, 1970, with the rank of sergeant E-5.

Father, Charles Feldman, T-5, served WWII, Aug. 5, 1941 to Oct. 28, 1945, military occupational specialty, MP.

Steven married Reta Schafer and has one son, Daniel William Feldman, born Sept. 30, 1987. Both Charles and Steven own a tire and car repair facility, well known as C&B Tire Company in Flint, MI. Charles, Steven and mother Bessie are member of JWV and Detroit, MI, Charles Shapero Auxiliary #510.

THEODORE FELDMAN, born Dec. 20, 1915, Philadelphia, PA. Enlisted Dec. 22, 1943, U.S. Army, 101st AB, Glider Inf. 401/327, as staff sergeant, platoon sergeant and guide. Military locations include Rallying, Ft. Redding, England, Holland, Normandy, Bastogne.

Awards/Medals: Purple Heart Medal, Bronze Star Medal, Good Conduct Medal, Distinguished Unit Badge, EAME Service Medal with three Bronze Stars and one Bronze Arrowhead.

He was discharged Sept. 27, 1945, with the rank of staff sergeant.

KENNETH H. FENIGSTEIN (NOW KENNETH STONE), born March 10, 1924, Philadelphia, PA. Graduated Erasmus Hall HS, Brooklyn in January 1942, first class after Pearl Harbor. Volunteered Oct. 26, 1942 in USAAF 1942-43); U.S. Army Signal Corps (1944-46) and Reserve Recall to USAF, 1951-52.

Military Stations: Reception at Ft. Dix airplane mechanic training at Chicago; Flight Engineer Air Transport Command, Romulus AFB; ASTP Engineering, Ripon, WI; Signal Corps School, Camp Crowder; 1944-46 AFWESPAC/Finschhafen and Hollandia, New Guinea; Leyte and Luzon, Philippine Islands.

Memorable Experience was transporting B-24 to England and visiting New Guinea, Tacloban, Manila and meeting the people.

Awards/Medals: Air Crew Wings, Infantry Badge, Expert Rifle, American Theater Ribbon, Pacific Theater Ribbon, Philippine Campaign, Victory Ribbon and Korean Era. Final discharge in January 1952 as tech sergeant.

Married Myra Gold, June 1, 1947, has three children: Richard, Hilary and Jonathan. and five grandchildren: Brian, Erik, Jared, Samantha and Taylor.

Self-employed sales agent for Paymaster Corp. He intends to work as long as possible.

AINSLEE R. FERDIE, born Oak Park IL, July 18, 1930, graduated SENN H.S. 1948, Jr. ROTC; Lawrence College (Wisconsin); University of Miami, BBA; J.D.; entered Army Reserve 1948 Arm-CAV, 85th Div. Recon Co; Active Duty, 5th Army HGs. 1949; Commissioned ROTC DMS, 1953; US Trans Corp., North East Air Command Newfoundland 373rd Major Port, 1954-55; Patient/ Walter Reed Army Hosp; Ft. Eustis, VA, 1955-56; C.O. WAC Co.; Acting C.O. HQ Co., Reserves DUKW Co. platoon leader to 1961. Wife Roslyn Frost, children Marshall

1967, Meredith 1970; Deborah 1973, are life members of descendants: mother Evelyn was department president JWVA; life member, Korean War Veterans; JWV Post 243 Coral Gables, Florida Department Commander 1964-65; National Judge Advocate 1972-73; National Commander 1973-74; Chairman NEC 1976-78; President JWV USA National Memorial Inc. (JWV Museum) 1980-86, negotiated purchase of New museum and National HQ Building; led JWV group into Israel during Yom Kippur War; president Florida Veterans Department Commanders Conference 1964-65; was chairman, Dade County Urban Renewal Agency; Associate Judge West Miami; Dade County Traffic Magistrate. As vice-chairman NEC chaired historic meeting in Israel in 1971.

CHARLES FEUEREISEN, born May 18, 1918, New York City. Enlisted Jan. 22, 1942, Airborne, 11th Airborne Div., 511th Parachute Inf. Military locations included Camp MacKall, NC; Camp Polk, LA; New Guinea; Leyte; Mindoro; Luzon, PI. Participated in battles in Leyte and Luzon.

Memorable experience was meeting with Gen. MacArthur for 27 minutes.

Awards/Medals: Purple Heart Medal, Silver Star, Bronze Star, Distinguished Unit Citation.

He was discharged Nov. 25, 1945, with the rank of private first class.

Married May 3, 1953, two children, Patti and Henry, one grandchild, Aviva. Retired.

GEORGE A. FICHTENBAUM, born New York City, Sept. 6, 1921. Enlisted June 12, 1942, Army, Inf. 5th Regt. 71st Div. Military locations included Ft. Totten, NY; Ft. Devens, MA; Ft. Benning, GA. Saw action along western front, crossing Rhine and Danube River.

Memorable experience was liberating Gunskirchen Lager Concentration Camp.

Awards/Medals: Bronze Star, Combat Infantryman's Badge, EAME Service Medal, Army of Occupation Medal with German Clasp, Good Conduct Medal, American Campaign Medal, member of JWV Post 209, Farthest East Outfit in ETO.

He was discharged Feb. 12, 1946, with the rank of corporal.

He is a widower with no children. Former court clerk in criminal court, retired after 39 years in 1988.

MORRIS FIELSTEIN, selected Marine Corps May 1942, boot camp in Parris Island, SC. Then to Philadelphia Navy Yard.

To Camp Pendleton, CA, for formation of 5th Marine Div. Assigned 5th Pioneer Bn. HQ. Sailed to Hawaii. Next Iwo Jima Battle. Witnessed flag raising on Mt. Suribachi.

Attended Jewish services on Iwo Jima, back to Hawaii for rehabilitation. He was a sergeant.

Morris dreamed of big explosion, later read the atomic bomb was dropped on Japan. Occupation of Japan at Sasebo Fortress. Back to U.S. and honorably discharged May 1945.

Graduated New York University. Morris married Helen in 1950; celebrated 43 years of marriage in 1993. A girl and boy were born, son is married and has a daughter.

Morris was an accountant and retired after 27 years. Has been studying musical theory and piano, as a hobby.

He is in VFW Harry Green Post 150 in Starrett City, Brooklyn, NY.

CHARLES J. FIENBERG, born in Boston, Dec. 31, 1918. Married Nov. 10, 1940, to Rita Rudnick, daughter Phyllis, born 1942. Inducted into Navy December 1943. After boot camp in upstate New York, attended Fire Control School in Newport, RI, followed by amphibious training in Bradford, VA. Assigned to LST 208 in East Boston, MA, to be based at Pearl Harbor, joining a huge task force 650 ships, ferrying men and supplies to Guam, Saipan and Okinawa. Promoted to Fire Control 3rd class, at sea. Returned to Philippines after last mission to China during the Great Typhoon. Assigned to a converted LCI for return to the States. Honorable discharge Dec. 24, 1945. Son Harold, born in 1947. Helped Milton Post #696 get started and became commander. Still a member though not active. Now lives in Boynton Beach, FL, and has seven grandchildren and two great-grandchildren.

Memorable experience was great typhoon.
Awards/Medals: WWII Victory Medal.

REUBEN FIER, born Feb. 19, 1923, Bronx, NY. Enlisted in the Army Air Corps in NYC, Jan. 10, 1942. Attended Aircraft Mechanics School, Biloxi, MS. Left AM School for Aviation Cadet Training. Graduated Big Springs, TX. Bombardier School April, 1943, class 43-5.

Formed crew and trained on B-17 at Blythe, CA, and Dyersburg, TN, prior to picking up new B-17 at Grand Island, NE, for flight to European Theater of Operations (8th Air Force).

Assigned to 94th BG, 332nd BS, 8th AF, Bury St. Edmunds, England (Station 468) flying first mission Nov. 5, 1943. Shot down on 10th mission by flak on Dec. 31, 1943, over Cognac, France. Parachuted from burning plane and with Marquis/Resistance assistance evaded until captured on March 15, 1944, prisoner of Gestapo for two months before imprisonment at Stalag Luft III, Sagan, Germany, on May 14, 1944. Subsequently liberated at Stalag VII-A, Moosburg, Germany on April 29, 1945. Left active duty as first lieutenant on Feb. 10, 1947. Retired from Air Force Reserve as lieutenant colonel on April 28, 1971. Served as New York City Police Officer 22. Retired to become a special agent with Department of Health and Human Services, Office of Inspector General, retiring after 20 years service. Military Awards: Presidential Unit Citation and Air Medal with cluster.

Married wife Elinore and three children, Robert, Caryon and Eric.

BENJAMIN FIERING, WWI, Army, 28th Inf. Div., France. Awards/Medals: Purple Heart Medal. Married to Dora and has two sons and two daughters, and three grandchildren. He died May 6, 1953.

SAM S. FIERSTEIN, born Oct. 2, 1921, New York City. Joined the U.S. Air Corps Ferrying Cmd., July 28, 1942. Stationed at Truax Field, Madison, WI, Rosecrans Field, St. Joseph, MO, Love Field, Dallas, TX and Calcutta, India.

Some of his memorable experiences include speaking personally with Eleanor Roosevelt in Natal, Brazil; participating in a musical comedy revue in Madison, WI; visiting the Taj Mahal twice; flying overseas and back eight times; and when interned for 24 hours in Azores.

Awards/Medals: India-Burma, Air Offensive Europe, China Central Burma, Philippine Liberation, Luzon, EAME Medal, WWII Victory Medal, Good Conduct Medal, Air Medal with Bronze Cluster, Meritorious Unit Award, Radio Operator and Mech. 2756, AAF Air Crew Member Badge and AAF Tech Badge. Discharged Nov. 29, 1945, with the rank staff sergeant.

Married, wife deceased, has two sons. One handicapped with spina bifida and one married with daughter and son. President of Bikly Hebrew School for retarded children; past president of the Spina Bifida Assoc. of Greater New York and is one of the founders of Spina Bifida Assoc. of America. In tech sales almost 48 years with Seagrave Coatings Corp.

THEODOR FINDER, born Vienna, Austria, Feb. 23, 1920. Emigrated to U.S., 1938, after escaping from capture by Gestapo. Drafted U.S. Army, January 1941, became first NCO, as corporal to receive superior instructor for teaching German Military Tactics. Volunteered for four times before landing on Omaha Beach June 6, 1944, D-Day, as sergeant Inf., 29th Div. Received five Bronze Stars in as many combat missions as acting platoon leader. Received two Purple Heart Medals for being badly wounded rear-guarding retreat and captured by Germans in Brest France. Later recaptured by Allies, hospitalized for numerous surgeries. Discharged September 1945 as staff sergeant, 100% disabled. Married his Army nurse, Bess, three children and six grandchildren. Retired as fur buyer age 63.

FREDDY IRVIN FINE, born and raised in the deep south during the Great 1930s Depression, the sole surviving son of Russian and Polish Immigrant parents, Fine grew up in rural Alabama, in a very distinct minority, the only Jewish family in the Lamar County, AL area. Enlisting in the Air National Guard in 1942, Fine honorably served in the Guard and Reserves as well as Active Air Force and Army in and during the Korean Conflict, Vietnam Conflict, Intergrations of both the Universities of Alabama and Mississippi and local and County Alabama Schools, the Selma-to-Montgomery March, the Bay of Pigs Invasion, the Cuban Missile Crisis and numerous natural disasters (tornadoes, floods and hurricanes) in the Southeast. In 1967, while on active duty at Ft. Belvoir, VA, completing the Engineers Officers Advanced Course, Fines volunteered and was on stand-by call for deployment before and during the six-day war in Israel. He is an honor graduate and graduate of the U.S. Army Command & General Staff College, the Air War College, the Industrial College of the Armed Forces and the University of Alabama. Fine is proficient and school-trained in six enlisted MOS's and five officer branches serving at Command & General Staff positions in the Combat Arms, Combat and Combat Service Support at Platoon, Company (Squadron), Battalion, Group, Brigade and Corps Level Commands. He has completed Active Duty service schools in Terrorism and Espionage, Psychological Operations, Civil-Military Operations, Logistical Executive Management and Personnel Management and Missile Munitions Ordnance. Retired in 1986 after tour in Federal Republic of Germany. Volunteered and ordered to active duty in 1990 and 1991 in Desert Shield/ Storm and since has served tours in Germany, El Salvador and Panama. From 1942 until 1989 Fine worked in family retail business retiring as president/CEO. He served on town council for 12 year and state legislature, and still remains active in local and state political life. Serves as public affairs director, Alabama Employer's Support of the Guard and Reserves. Fine is a life member of the JWV of the USA, the American Legion and the Paralyzed Veterans of America and a colonel in the Alabama State Defense Force. Anticipated retirement from the Reserves in 1996 to coincide with the 1996 Olympics and Paralympics Games and the 100 Years Anniversary of the JWV of the USA.

JOSEPH FINE, born Jan. 3, 1914, in Bloomfield, NJ. Entered the USN on June 25, 1943, active duty July 2, 1943. Served with Co. 962, Newport, RI, Naval and Section Base Staten Island, NY; sea duty on PC1246.

Memorable experience was their ship being one of the escorts for the cruiser that brought Pres. Roosevelt to Yalta.

He was discharged Nov. 28, 1945, with the rank of SK1/c.

Resided in Montclair, NJ, until retired Jan. 1, 1979, now live in retirement in Lakehurst, NJ. Member of Post 146 JWV for 51 years.

SOLOMON FINEBLUM, born April 21, 1925, Baltimore, MD. Inducted August 1943, U.S. Army, rifleman, Co. A, 301st Inf. Reg., 94th Inf. Div. Military locations included Ft. Benning, GA; Camp Croft, SC; England; Brittany; Normandy; Germany, Northern France, Ardennes, Rhineland.

Memorable experience included patrols with free French, battles being captured, prison, MIA, POW Liberation from prison April 21, 1945.

Awards/Medals: WWII Victory Medal, Combat Infantry Badge, Bronze Star.

He was discharged Nov. 30, 1945, with the rank of private first class.

Married since 1946 to Dr. Carol Fineblum. Has five children and three grandchildren. Retired from AT&T Bell Labs. Active on own engineering projects. Was active in JWV Post 689; now Post 41.

HARRY FINGERROTH, born New York City, March 26, 1918. Attended Tilden High School and Brooklyn College. Drafted into Army February 1941. After basic training assigned to 22nd Inf. Med. Det., 5th Inf. Div. Ft. Benning, GA. Trained in all phases of military preparedness including amphibious training, Camp Gordon Johnson, FL. Arrived Liverpool, England, February 1944. Landed on Utah Beach D-Day morning at H hour plus three June 6, 1944. Served with 4th Div. through entire European Theater, including Campaigns of Ardennes, Central Europe, Normandy, Northern France and Rhineland.

Awarded Bronze Arrowhead for D-Day, Presidential Unit Citation for Breakthrough at St. Lo with Patton's 3rd Army, EAME Campaign Medal with five Battle Stars, three Bronze Stars including two battlefield Citations for heroism under heavy enemy fire, American Defense Service Medal, American Campaign Medal, WWII Victory Medal, Combat Medical Badge and Good Conduct Medal. As surgical technician third grade, set-up and guided the operation of battalion forward first-aid station in close proximity to combat infantrymen so that walking wounded and wounded carried on liters could be given first aid quickly, then transported to rear for follow-up treatment. As a high-pointer after V-E Day sent home and discharged August 1945.

Married to Ann while in Service, for 52 years now, raised two beautiful daughters, Carol and Marla, who gave them two wonderful sons-in-law, Joel and Lenny and a lovable grandson, David. Past Commander of JWV San Fernando Valley Post 603 in California and very active as volunteer in two Veterans Administration Hospitals.

On June 1, 1994, awarded D-Day Plus 50, French Commemorative Medallion, and on Jan. 1, 1995, awarded Gold Medal of Liberation from French Consul General. *Submitted by Harry Fingerroth.*

IRWIN L. FINKEL, born July 20, 1925, New York City. Joined the service Oct. 2, 1943, U.S. Army, Cadet Air Corp, 13th Armed Div., forward observer. Military stations included Ft. Bragg, NC; Ft. Sill, OK; Ft. Bowie, TX; Pope Field, OK; Germany; France; Liechtenstein; Austria.

Memorable experience was being first vehicle to enter Dachau Prison Camp May 1945.

Awards/Medals: Bronze Star Medal, Distinguished Service Cross, America Theater Medal, ETO with two Bronze Stars, Good Conduct Medal, WWII Victory Medal.

He was discharged Feb. 6, 1946, with the rank of private first class.

Married to Hana, and has four children, Hal, Ken, Deb, Glen. Six grandchildren: Keith, Jeffrey, Andrew, Lindsey, Adam and Timmy. Retired after 41 years in garment industry.

MURRAY FINKEL, born on Yom Kippur, Oct. 2, 1922. In 1943, he was assigned to 3rd Bn., 15th Regt., 3rd Div. He landed at Anzio as part of the first wave in 1944. "After a week on a British ship, the bagpipes were driving us crazy. We couldn't wait for the landing to start. It was 0600 and the temperature was about 20 degrees. The British dropped us about 100 yards from the beach and we were up to our necks in water. There was no opposition but it wasn't long till the Germans counterattacked."

Believing in miracles was not unique to Jewish soldiers but Finkel recalls more than a few life-saving coincidences. "I was one of a few soldiers guarding the medics. The Germans had been infiltrating and capturing them. Their quarters were in an old barn. When I wasn't walking guard I tried to sleep in a nearby haystack. I had just gone back to the barn when a shell landed in the middle of the haystack."

Luck ran out on Oct. 25, 1944, on a hill in the Vosges Mountains. "The Germans were on an adjacent hill and we had just moved out of our foxholes. They spotted us a and fired a barrage of mortar shells. I was hit by a "screaming memmie." The shrapnel hit me in the back, both legs and hand. If it had been a conventional shell, which has metal fragments inside the casing, they would have picked me up with a shovel."

E. NEAL FINKELMAN, born Maywood, IL, Aug. 3, 1934. Senn High School graduate, Chicago, February 1952. Military and Air Science ROTC Cadet, two years, BA journalism, June 1955, University of Wisconsin, Madison. Attended John Marshall Law School, Chicago, evenings,, from September 1958 to January 1959.

Enlisted in U.S. Army Sep. 23, 1955. Trained in infantry and heavy weapons with "The Big Red One," 1st Inf. Div., Ft. Riley, KS, and Ft. Ord, CA. Assigned to the Public Information Office of "The Golden Arrow," 8th Inf. Div., Ft. Carson, CO. Arrived in Germany just before the Hungarian Revolution, Thanksgiving, 1956.

Being stationed at the Cooke Barracks, Goeppingen, American Sector, was proud and grateful to bless the post chapel for High Holidays as the first soldiers of the Status of Forces Agreement, guests of the West German Republic, to replace the Army of Occupation. Early medical evacuation in January 1957, to Walter Reed Army Medical Center, Washington, DC. Returned to duty at 2nd Army HQ, Ft. Meade MD, May 1957. Transferred to Active Reserve with honorable discharge Sept. 20, 1957. Awarded 100 per cent service connected disability, May 1959. Reenlisted Naval Air Reserve, August 1979.

Starting as an apprentice in business, performed general clerical, sales and executive services. Was appointed Township Precinct Committeeman, 1985. A student pilot, athletic and condominium owner in rural Gurnee, IL, pursue interests in very many philanthropic and civic enterprises.

DAVID FIRESTONE, T/4, Signal Corps, born Sept. 15, 1923, NYC, NY. Chemistry major, CCNY. Enlisted Reserve January -July 1943. Entered Army (FT. Dix) July 28, 1943. Training, Camp Crowder, MO; Ft Monmouth, NJ, Signal Engineer School, Chicago, IL. Sailed for New Guinea Nov. 1[illegible] 1944, with 4025 Signal Service Group. Arrived at Hollandi[illegible]

Dec. 15, 1944. January 1945 battling amebic dysentery. February 1945 to the Philippines. August 1945 to Japan. At Yokohama on Sept. 2, 1945, when Japan formally surrendered. In Tokyo serviced telephone central office equipment, supervised switchboard in Dai-Ichi Bldg. (Gen. MacArthur's HQ). Honorable discharge Feb. 12, 1946. Joined Food and Drug Administration June 1948. Senior Research Chemist with FDA to 1994. Happily married to Berdie Flegenheimer; children, Richard, Michael, Janice. Member of Post 58, JWV.

MILTON FIRTEL, born in New York City, in 1913. In 1929 at the age of 15 and a half, he began his studies at NYU and received a BS degree in 1932. Attended NYU Law School and received JD degree in 1934. Practiced as a law clerk for the large sum of $7.50 per week for a few years.

In 1941 he was inducted into the U.S. Army and sent to Aberdeen, MD, where his duties included drill sergeant and instructor in the handling of ammunition and it's components.

He was staff sergeant when sent overseas and stationed at ammunition headquarters in Cheltenham, England. Was then sent to London on detached service and collaborated with the British Movement Control to insure ammunition and various components were loaded properly on outgoing vessels for the D-Day invasion. During his time in London, Germany buzz bombings were frequent with one occurring only two blocks from where he was billeted, hitting Victoria Station. Damage was extensive, yet no one was harmed.

After serving overseas, he was returned to the U.S. and assigned as personal affairs/rehabilitation officer at Miami Beach, FL. Was then sent to Washington Lee University for further training, and returned to Miami Beach serving in an advisory capacity. Shortly thereafter, he received his discharge from service.

In 1945, married Pearl Baker and opened own business in Miami Beach, in 1947. Retired in 1977. Had daughter, Helaine, born in 1955, and now have one wonderful grandson named Brian.

HAROLD FISHER, born Jan. 25, 1925, Philadelphia, PA. Inducted May 15, 1943, assigned to 163rd Engr. Comb. Bn. and stationed at Camp Van Dorn, MS. Spec was personnel sergeant major.

Military service locations: Arrived Swansea Wales, England February 1944; ... on Salisbury Plains Wales; stationed outside Oxford, England until debarking from Southampton, England; landed Utah Beach, D+4. Advanced with 1st, 3rd, and 7th Armies, through France, St. Mere Eglise, Cherbourg, St. Lo, Le Mans, Paris, Troyes, Nancy, Metz. Through Germany, Mannheim, Nuremberg, Augsburg, Munich. Through Austria, Salzburg, Berchtesgaden, Linz. Temporary occupation from May 1945 - to December 1945, Munich, Germany. Repatriated to States from Le Havre, France and discharged from Indiantown Gap, Dec. 31, 1945, as sergeant first class. Joined Inactive Reserves Jan. 1, 1946, reenlisted in inactive Reserves January 1949. Recalled to Active Duty September 1950 during Korean Conflict. Released September 1951 as master sergeant.

Memorable experience: Construction of longest bridge (floating Bailey - 635 ft. long) at Rhines, France, over Seine River in ETO. Meeting Russians in Metz, Austria and shaking hands with Gen. George Patton.

Medals: Good Conduct Medal, American Campaign Medal, Middle Easter Campaign (four Bronze Stars), WWII Victory Medal, Korean Campaign Medal.

Family data: Married 49 years to Harriet, three sons, four grandsons. Retired since 1986. Presently National Adjutant for JWV, editor of Post #697 Newsletter, Board of Directors NMAJMH, Delegate, Deputy Rep VAVS, Executive Board DVA Medical Center - Philadelphia VAVS, Past Post and Philadelphia County Council Commander.

LAWRENCE H. FISHER, born in Worcester, MA, on Oct. 15, 1914. He graduated from Commerce High School and Northeastern University.

December 15, 1942, he enlisted in the U.S. Army and was stationed at Camp Crowder, MO, and stationed at Ft. Custer, MI, as an MP.

He was a corporal at time of discharge May 1945.

He was a draft board member for 20 years following WWII, commander of the Worcester Veterans' Council; member of Worcester Housing Authority.

1953 after the tornado struck Worcester causing loss of life and injury, he was commissioned by the Governor to embark upon a mission of mercy. The Purple Heart Veterans Organization presented him with a special Humanitarian Award.

May 3, 1989, a testimonial was held in his honor as a Founding Father of the Genesis Club, which serves people with psychiatric illness.

He is a disabled veteran and a retired attorney.

PAUL FISHERMAN, born in the Brownsville section of Brooklyn, NY, on Dec. 12, 1924. He was an electrician's helper at the time of his induction in the U.S. Army on April 30, 1943. After 30 days at Camp Upton, NY. He was sent to Camp Stewart, GA, where he was assigned to section 3 D-Battery 789 Anti-Aircraft Artillery (automatic weapons) Bn., which consisted of a 40mm gun and 4-50cal. machine guns on a trailer. After duty outside of the Richmond Army AB, VA, additional training at Camp Pickett, VA, he shipped overseas

in May 1944, arrived in Liverpool Eng., took a train to Blackshire Moor in the Midlands where they slept on real straw mattress. In September 1944 he arrived in France then Belgium and Germany. He has four Battle Stars, Ardennes, Alsace, Central Europe, Northern France, and Rhineland. He received the Belgium Faurragere, Good Conduct Medal, WWII Victory Medal, Army of Occupation WWII and American Campaign. He was discharged Oct. 9, 1945. He is a Past Commander of Post #2, New York. Now a member of Post #459 Boca Raton, FL.

MICHAEL M. FISHKIN, LTC, served as platoon commander with the 172nd Medical Cleaning Company. This unit provided medical support for the 1st Inf. and 3rd Armored Div. They treated over 300 American, British, and Iraqi injured in the 100 hours of hostility.

HERMAN L. FISHMAN, born July 4, 1918, Grand Forks, ND. Enlisted 1942, Ski Troop, Camp Hale, CO.

Memorable experiences include drafted from Ft. Snelling, MN, all soldiers dressed in uniform with gun over shoulder etc. marched to trains, family send off - good-bye. His mother, sister, and brother were there, mother fainted, he left group to revive mother, then rejoined group and said good-bye!

He was discharged 1943. Married for 17 years then, divorced had one daughter Cindy. Founder and owner of Watertown, SD, Iron and Steel Company for 35 years. After a tough battle with heart problems, cancer, diabetic, passed away Aug. 1, 1993. His mother passed away three months before on May 12, 1993, at age 101.

NATHAN FISHMAN, born Boston, MA. Enlisted Oct. 5, 1941, USAAF. Military locations included Alaska, Aleutian Island, Europe NPTO, ETO, USA, Germany.

Memorable experience included meeting his brother, Pete in Germany.

Awards/Medals: American Service Medal, Asiatic-Pacific Campaign Medal, EAME Service Medal.

He was discharged Nov. 12, 1945, with the rank of sergeant.

Married and has a son and daughter, and eight grandchildren. Retired.

MILTON FIXEL, born July 14, 1918, New York City. Entered the service Feb. 12, 1942, at Camp Dix, NJ, serving with Cbt. Engrs. (1186). Their trucking group delivered supplies to Russia and traveled throughout the western section of Iran.

As WO(jg) he was able to arrange a trip to Palestine in 1943. Also had the opportunity to go to Western Wall where no Jew was allowed.

Went through Suez Canal, landed in Marseilles, moved north through France and over the Remagen Bridgehead. Stopped at Erfort, 70 miles SW of Berlin, Eisenhower and Zhukov were discussing who would take Berlin. Fortunately Russia won the toss. While in Anthop V-2 missiles were coming in from Germany while they were sleeping in the cabs of trucks loaded with ammo.

Received European/Middle East medals. Discharged Feb. 22, 1946.

Married since May 29, 1949, to Helen, they have three children: Francine, Judith and Loren, and 14 grandchildren. He is in real estate management.

LAWRENCE M. FLAMBERG, born Brooklyn, NY, April 16, 1923. Enlisted January 1943, U.S. Army, Medical Corp. Trained at Camp Pickett, ETO, attached to 29th Div. (TDY) D-Day plus 6.

Memorable experiences include giving Joe Lewis the boxer, a booster shot.

Awards/Medals: American Defense Service Medal, ETO, Army of Occupation, Good Conduct Medal.

He was discharged Jan. 24, 1943, with the rank of private first class.

Married Hannah Ruth Flamberg, children: Daniel S. Flamberg, Zachary C. Flamberg and Nancy R. Flamberg.

ABRAHAM FLASCHNER, first served in the U.S. Army from January 1924, when he entered as a reserve officer, until Feb. 8, 1945, when he was retired with the rank of lieutenant colonel. He received SOS training at Ft. Devens, MA, from Sept. 29, 1942, and the Station Hospital there until Dec. 22, 1942. He sailed from New York City overseas on the SS *Largo Bay* and arrived in Europe and France January 1943. He set up the dental units in the European Theater and France from February 1943, and in the 10th Regional Depot from March 1944 to June 1944, and in the 313th Station Hospital there from June 1944 to September 1944. He saw action in 1943 during the Germany blitz attacks on London and the United Kingdom. He received several citations and decorations, among which was the Award Certificate of Merit. He criss-crossed the United Kingdom and had a short stay in France in 1944. He was a "student" at the University of Edinburgh, Scotland. He also took a special course at Aldershot, England, with the British forces. *Submitted by Max Sigal.*

ESTHER FLASCHNER, served with the American Red Cross from April 15, 1945 to September 1946. She left New York for Washington, DC, for a training period on April 15, 1945, as a secretary with the American Red Cross and on June

5, 1945, left for overseas from Camp Stoneman, Pittsburgh, California, and arrived in Manila, Philippine Islands. On July 3, 1945, she arrived at Hollandia, New Guinea (Base G), on assignment to American Red cross Area Office there by place with stopovers at Tacloban, Morotai and Biak. She served there until Sept. 10, 1945, when she left New Guinea by air for assignment in Manila. Stopovers at Biak, Peleliu and Samar. On Sept. 30, 1945, she flew to San Fernando, La Union, Luzon (Base M), on assignment and she was promoted from secretary to junior accountant in the area office there.

On Jan. 4, 1946, she flew back to Manila for assignment north and on Jan. 8, 1946, she left Manila by plane for assignment at American Red Cross Area Office XXIV Corps, Seoul, Korea, with stopovers at Okinawa. She spent about a week in Japan at Tachikawa, Atsugi, Yokohama, Osaka and Kyoto. On Jan. 15, 1946, she arrived at Seoul, Korea. Her service has continued to when she was discharged with honors. *Submitted by Max Sigal.*

FRANKLIN FLASCHNER, served in the United States Navy from Feb. 29, 1944, to May 14, 1946. He entered the Naval Service as an ensign and when discharged to inactive duty was a lieutenant, junior grade. His training consisted of two months' indoctrination duty at the Naval Training School, three months communications at the Naval Training School and was communications officer attached to the staff of the commander operational training of the Atlantic fleet for 10 months. He also was communications officer attached to the staff of the Commander-in-Chief of the Atlantic Fleet for 10 months.

He was awarded the Atlantic Theater and Victory Ribbons and has a personal letter of citation from Admiral Ingram, Commander-in-Chief of the Atlantic Fleet. He had 20 months' duty as a flag communication first officer on the staff of a 4-Star Admiral and then on the staff of a 2-Star Admiral. He did not see much of the war or any of the combat in WWII, but he did have a chance to see how the Navy is run by the "High Brass" and this experience afforded him many beneficial lessons. *Submitted by Max Sigal.*

GEORGE FLASCHNER, served in the USN from Jan. 19, 1943 to Sept. 27, 1945. He entered the service at Boston, MA, with the rank of apprentice seaman and was discharged at Memphis, TN, with the rank of aviation radioman second class. He received his boot training at Great Lakes, Chicago, IL. Attended Aviation Radio School at Memphis, TN; attended Gunnery School at Hollywood, FL, and received operations training at Daytona Beach, FL. He sailed from the Philippines on the USS *White Plains* on July 17, 1945, and arrived at Alameda Air Station Oakland, CA, on July 9, 1945. Was stationed on board a CV20 with the USS *Bennington.*

He saw considerable action and was on the first aircraft carrier which struck over Tokyo on Feb. 25, 1945, hitting the Japanese fleet and the Kure Naval Base on March 19, 1945. He had many missions over Japan, Okinawa and Iwo Jima, East China Sea area participating in sinking much Japanese shipping. He received two Battle Stars in the Asiatic-Pacific Theater for Iwo Jima and Okinawa engagements and Distinguished Flying Cross and four air medals. He visited the Hawaiian Islands, the southern portion of Japan the Philippine Islands and Guam. Saw considerable action among which was a mid-air collision over Iwo Jima and was forced down after his plane was hit by a 75 mm shell over Okinawa. *Submitted by Max Sigal.*

HAROLD FLASCHNER, served in the U.S. Army from Feb. 8, 1943, and was discharged at Ft. Dix, NJ, Oct. 27, 1945. He enlisted in Boston in February 1943 and went to Ft. Devens, MA, on June 25, 1943, with the rank of private and when discharged on Oct. 27, 1945, held the rank of private first class. He trained with the Coast Artillery Corps, Anti-Aircraft Unit at Ft. Eustis, VA, and also at Camp Pickett, VA.

He sailed for overseas on the Queen Elizabeth from New York and arrived at Gourrch. Scotland, and returned on the USS *West Point,* sailing from La Havre, France, and arriving at Newport News, VA, in October 1945. He saw action in the European Theater of Operations with the 197th Anti-Aircraft Artillery AW Bn. From Jan. 2, 1944, until he left from France for the U.S. on Oct. 16, 1945. He participated in the D-Day Invasion and landed on Omaha Beach, France, on June 6, 1944, at 9:30 a.m. and saw active action in the Battle of the Bulge in Belgium, and saw much more action in France, Luxembourg, Belgium and Germany. He received the Good Conduct Medal, the ETO Ribbon with five Battle Stars and Arrowhead for D-Day invasion in Northern France He visited London, Paris, Nuremberg and Munich. *Submitted by Max Sigal.*

IRA FLASCHNER, served in the U.S. Army from Jan. 16, 1941 to Feb. 19, 1946. He entered the service at Boston, MA, with the rank of first lieutenant and was discharged at North Carolina with the rank of captain. He was battalion surgeon with the 26th Div. and marched along the Eastern Coast from Camp Edwards, MA, to North Carolina then returned to Camp Edwards from where he went to Maine, then to A.P. Hill Virginia, to Ft. Meade, MD, to Ft. Jackson, SC, to Washington, DC, and then to Camp Gordon, GA.

He became chief anesthesia and operating section of Station Hospital, Camp Davis NC, and later at the Stark General Hospital, SC. His most pleasant memories of the five years which he spent in the Armed Forces are the meetings which he had with Capt. "Jessie" Flaschner in Georgia who later went overseas, Sgt. Manny Brown in South Carolina, who after being wounded in action in France returned to the U.S. and the first person who met him was his own cousin Ira. Also Capt. Lou and Bea Raverby in North Carolina. *Submitted by Max Sigal.*

JESSE FLASCHNER, served in the United States Army from Feb. 6, 1944, to December 1946. He entered the service in the Dental Corps with the rank of first lieutenant on Feb. 6, 1944, at the Carlisle Barracks, PA, and remained there until April 1944. From Carlisle he went to Ft. Bragg Station Hospital and remained there until October 1944. He sailed on the SS *George Washington* from New York and arrived at Marseilles, France.

He served in the European Theater of Operations with the 100th Inf. Div. He remained overseas until 1946 when he returned to Texas to be reassigned. He saw action as regimental dental surgeon and served in Aid Stations both forward an the rear. He was present at the 100th Div. entry in Roan L'Etape in November 1944, which was one of the high points in the history of this division. He was promoted to the rank of captain on June 1, 1945, and was awarded combat medical badge in March 1945 and also received two Battle Stars for the Rhineland and Central Germany activities. Some of the outstanding places which he visited were Paris and the Riviera "on passes" in January and September 1945. *Submitted by Max Sigal.*

MILTON FLASCHNER, first served in the Merchant Marine Maritime Service from July 1941, until June 1943. He spent considerable time at Hoffman's Island, NY, and entered the regular Merchant Marine Service aboard a taker and while en route to Murmansk, Russia, on his second ship he was torpedoed on March 16, 1943, receiving wounds.

After a short recuperation he joined the Navy in June 1943, and was stationed at the Philadelphia Navy Yard and sent from there to Camp May, NJ, and while there did crash-boat duty pulling targets for planes and rescue work. From Camp May, NJ, he was shipped to Camp Bradford, VA, and was placed in the 8th Beach Battalion and from there he went to Miami, FL, where he did duty as dockmaster, small boatman, and finally ended up as a tugboat captain. He was discharged at Bainbridge, MD, on Dec. 21, 1945, and was rated a boatswain, second class. When he left the Merchant Marine he was a fireman. He had many thrills during his extended service. *Submitted by Max Sigal.*

MORTON FLASCHNER, served in the U.S. Army Cavalry Division from June 18, 1941, to Sept. 14, 1945. He entered the service with the rank of private at Ft. George E. Meade and was discharged with the rank of technician 5, at Indiantown, PA. His basic training was had at Ft. Riley, KS, in the Cavalry from June 23, 1941 to Sept. 19, 1941, and at Ft. Bliss in the cavalry from Sept. 21, 1941 to June 26, 1943. He shipped overseas on the George Washington, sailing from San Francisco on July 3, 1943, and arrived on July 24, at Brisbane, Australia. He served in Australia, New Guinea, Bismarck Archipelago and Philippine Islands.

He saw action against the Japanese with the 5th Cavalry which is an element of the First Cavalry Division on the Admiralty Islands about March 1, 1944. Also saw considerable action on Leite Islands about Oct. 20, 1944, and was with the first troops to land on Philippines and again the first to enter Manila, Philippine Islands on Feb. 3, 1945. He received the Good Conduct Medal, the American Defense Service Medal, Philippine Liberation Ribbon with two Bronze Stars, Asiatic-Pacific Campaign Medal with two Bronze Stars and arrowhead for initial landing and Combat Infantryman's Badge. His service as divided between the band when he was not in combat an letter bearer and worked on supplies while in combat. He was discharged on Sept. 14, 1945. *Submitted by Max Sigal.*

JOSEPH J. FLASHMAN, USAR, Ret., Life member as of July 31, 1995. American Legion, Zachary Taylor Post #180; AMVETS, Post #9, Louisville; Association of the Century, 100th Div. Louisville; Adopted alumnus University of Louisville; Boston Public Latin School, graduated 1934, School founded 1634; DAV, Post 89, Louisville, KY; Heroes of 76, Ft. Knox, KY, MIP; Louisville Memorial Society, Louisville, KY, director; Military Order of World Wars, Louisville Chapter; NAACP, Louisville, KY; National Sojourns, #134, Ft. Knox, KY, 1st VP The Retired Officers Association of U.S. Louisville Chapter; Reserve Officers Association of U.S. 100th Div. Chapter Louisville, KY; VFW Post #170, Middletown, KY; ZOA.

Bates College Alumnus, 1934-35, Lewiston, Maine. Wesleyan University, 1935-36, Middletown, CT. U.S. Army (Reg. Army), September 1940-42, USA Sig. Corps AW. U.S. Army (AUS) January 1941-June 1943, Sig C OCS Ft. Mon. NJ. U.S. Army (AUS), July 1943 to December 1945, North Africa, Italy, Corsica, Northern Italy, USA. U.S. Army Reserve, Active, Boston, MA, 1945-54, Captain USAR. U.S. Army Reserve. Retired, 1954 to date USAR Ret.

Also yearly memberships include AARP; Kosair Temple Shrine, Odom Foundation, Odom Club, Scottish Rite Foundation, St. George Lodge #239 F&AM, Louisville, Valley of Louisville Scottish Rite, Citizens Flag Alliance. Louisville Flag Committee, Louisville, KY, Coordinator.

MARTIN FLAUM, born June 26, 1923, in Syracuse, NY. Attended Croton, Central Schools. Enlisted on Dec. 8, 1941, the first to enlist in Syracuse after the bombing of Pearl Harbor. He was a private first class in Co. C of the 1st Marine Raider Bn. Killed in action July 3, 1943, at the age of 20. Survived by father Edward who saw action in WWI, mother Eva, brothers Norman and Milton, and grandmother Mrs. Rosen.

HENRY FLEISCHER, born Nov. 20, 1923, Paris, France. Enlisted Nov. 19, 1942, U.S. Army Corps of Engineers. Military locations included ETO, Asiatic-Pacific Theater of Operations.

He was discharged Feb. 23, 1946, with the rank of sergeant. Married to Rhoda for 44 years, son Niles received Ph.D. Weizmann Inst-Rehovot Israel and son, Bruce received Ph.D. Stanford University, CA. V.P. R&D Fox Numatics Inc. a Multinational Corp.

By the end of 1942 he finished two years of Engineering School and had a deferment to conclude his studies. He decided at this moment in his life to enlist rather than continue his education. He felt he had a duty to his county and had to make his little contribution to the war effort.

After circulating around the country at various camps he wound up at Camp Chafee, AR, in the 1273rd Combat Engineers Bn. Much to his dismay he ended up next to a vehement, out spoken and belligerent ant-Semite. The irony was that he had a bunk-mate five feet away that exhibited the same hatred and spewed the same venom of a demagogue 5,000 miles away that was the cause of his volunteering in the first place.

He just had to step outof bed to be embroiled in a bottle, without going overseas, with an individual who was a citizen of his country, in the same Army, wearing the same uniform, that was supposed to be reserved for the enemy across the Atlantic.

He tried logic, discussions and reasoning but all to no avail. It came to a head one morning in the mess hall amidst the entire company where he challenged him to a boxing match that evening in the battalion gym. He willingly immediately accepted the challenge. He asked the company sergeant to referee the bout. He felt he had to finally call his bluff for he did not want to back down.

That evening as he was nervously waiting in his corner, primed for action, he viewed what appeared to be the entire battalion eagerly waiting for the fight to begin. The referee called them into the middle of the ring, gave them instructions and directed them to their respective corners to await the bell. The bell rang and they both came to the center of the ring, where upon the other man dropped his hands to his side. He didn't want to hit him with his guard down and told him and motioned him to put up his dukes to defend himself. He refused, looked at Henry and said, "Go ahead and wipe the floor with me, I deserve it." He couldn't believe what he heard. He quipped back, "Do you mean it?" He said, "Absolutely." Upon hearing this remark he instantly removed his gloves and pulled his off as well. This was his first contact with him. He apologized, they shook hands and walked out with their arms around each others shoulders.

After that they had no further confrontations. In fact, he turned out to be an excellent buddy. They lost contact once they went overseas. He feels strongly that he remained a fair and democratic citizen of our country after that episode.

JOSEPH M. FLEISCHER, born May 22, 1925, in Chicago, IL. He attended Lane Technical High School, where he was in the ROTC and earned many medals and stars for rifle marksmanship.

On July 12, 1943, Joe entered the U.S. Navy and was sent to boot camp in Farragut, ID. He picked up his first ship duty at Mare Island where he joined the crew of the USS *Morris,* DD417. While serving on the this ship he earned a Battle Star for the Makin Island capture in the Gilbert and Ellis Island Archipelago Campaign.

A seasoned "tar" now, he was transferred to Treasure Island and as part of the new crew helped to commission one of the newest and largest destroyers, the USS *Stockham,* DD683, which was part of the greatest Naval Armada in History - Admiral "Bull" Halsey's Third and Fifth Fleet.

With the USS *Stockham* Joe earned the Asiatic Pacific Area Campaign Medal with seven Battle Stars; American Area Campaign Medal; WWII Victory Medal; Philippine Liberation Medal with two Battle Stars for action during the Marianas Islands (Guam and Saipan) "Turkey Shoot" in which the fleet downed 540 Japanese aircraft and the USS *Stockham* downed six planes as well [illegible] Japanese destroyer, the ship was awarded the Bronze Star.

At Honshu, Japan a Japanese officer was taken aboard the ship and he guided the USS *Stockham* through mined waters of Tokyo Bay, with the fleet following into Yokosuka Naval Base. The war was won and Joe was able to witness the surrender of the Japanese Empire to General Douglas MacArthur aboard the battleship *Missouri.* He returned to Bremerton, WA, where he was honorably discharged and joined the Naval Reserves. When he arrived home in Chicago, IL, he enrolled in college under the GI Bill and received a BSC degree. He also married Regina Lewin, a Holocaust survivor and they had two children, Janice, born in 1952, and Marc, born in 1955.

When the Korean War broke out, Joe was recalled to active service and on Jan. 29, 1951, he was back in the Navy at Great Lakes, IL. After tours of duty on USS *Osberg,* DE538, and USS *Rizzi,* DE537 he received his second honorable discharge on April 23, 1954.

Upon Joe's return home he went into the insurance business and spent 37 years as an agent-broker, 33 of which he spent representing New York Life Insurance Company.

He retired in January of 1991 to spend time with his wife Regina and their three grandsons. Regina and Joe are involved in many senior citizen activities and are learning new skills.

EDWARD FLEISCHMAN, born in Chicago, IL, March 22, 1916, MA University of Wisconsin, trained for diplomatic service married to Reva Ganansky 49 years (deceased July 24, 1991). Elected to board of trustees Village of Skokie, served eight years, also acting mayor.

Entered service Sept. 24, 1942, as private: attended Adjutant General OCS at Grinnell, IA; graduated second lieutenant. Sent to 796th Bomb Sq. as adjutant. February 24, 1944, as first lieutenant, assigned to XII Air Force Service Command General Staff Assistant Chief of Staff Al in charge of military and civilian personnel in Italy, including replacements for combat casualties of 12th AF in Mediterranean Theater of Combat; in charge of 6,000 Italian and 2,000 German POWs.

Adjutant for 88th Depot Repair Sq. and commander of a Fire Fighting Platoon. Greatest accomplishment ... created and set up a Sedar and Services for 1,500 Jewish AF personnel in Mussolini's Forum in Rome, which resulted in opening the doors of the great Synagogue of Rome for its first service in eight years.

He has a daughter, Suzanne, professor at University of California, Berkeley, author and world lecturer. Honorably discharged captain AF Feb. 19, 1946.

As a JWV held virtually every appointive national office and elective-Post, State and Regional Commander and 20 years on the NEC. Also was state newspaper editor, chaired National Resolutions and Co-Chaired Constitutional Committees. Fought the Nazi bigots in Chicago with club and pen and on television.

Represented JWV at AF Academy Graduation Exercises, at NCRAC as delegate, at United Jewish Fund for funding and presented plaques from JWV to Prime Minister Golda Meier, Mayor Teddy Kollak of Jerusalem and Moishe Dayan in Israel. Also met with prime Mister Menachim Began and, among other things, discussed several items of interest to JWV.

JACOB S. FLEISHMAN, born Oct. 5, 1919, Brooklyn, NY. Graduated Dewitt Clinton HS, Bronx, NY; CCNY with degree in business administration. Joined the service July 23, 1942, served with QM, Ordnance, Engineers. Military locations and stations include Ft. Dix, NJ; Camp Lee, VA; Camp Bowie, TX; Ft. Knox, KY; Camp Pickett, VA; Ft. Belvoir, VA; Camp Ellis, IL; Columbus Ohio Army Depot; Jersey City Army Depot; Camp Shanks, NY; Aschurch and Southampton, England; Paris (where he witnessed V-E Day) and Marseilles, France; Manila, Philippines and Nagoya, Japan.

Moved to Atlantic City, NJ in 1952. Practiced as CPA and senior partner (now retired) of Silverman, Fleishman, Rimm, et al, Ventnor, NJ for 30 years. Past VP and past president of Temple Emeth Shalom; past president, Congregation Beth Judah; and JWV, Greenstein Garr #39 and several civilian organizations.

Awards/Medals: Good Conduct Medal, American Campaign Medal, Asiatic-Pacific Campaign Medal, EAME Campaign Medal, WWII Victory Medal, Philippine Liberation. Discharged February 1946 with rank captain.

Has wife Mary Marsha; three children: Ilene, Rhoni and Joel; seven grandchildren: Lisa, Robyn, Jennie, Julie, Mindy, Joshua and Jonathan.

STANLEY ROBERT "BOB" FLESHIN, born Oct. 16, 1919, in Cleveland, OH. Spent childhood and teens in New Jersey and attended St. John's University in Brooklyn, NY. Returned to Ohio and entered the U.S. Army June 18, 1941. Became a qualified parachutist in February 1942. Graduated Officer Candidate School December 1942.

Parachuted into the Southern Philippine and participated in the liberation of Leyte Island and New Guinea.

Received the Combat Infantryman's Badge, Paratroopers Badge, WWII Victory Medal, American Campaign Medal, Asiatic-Pacific Campaign Medal, and Philippine Liberation Ribbon.

Discharged March 24, 1946, as first lieutenant.

Married to Frances Hoffman in 1948 and had a son, Richard and daughter, Terry. (Rick is currently a lieutenant colonel on active duty in the Army Nurse Corps.)

Moved to Dallas, TX, during the 1950s and became a factory representative for a major merchandising company. Well known for his love of music, he sang with several opera companies and collected rare operatic records. In addition, he studied and collected tropical fish and became president of the Dallas Aquarium Society.

Bob died following a massive heart attack at the age of 44 on Sept. 26, 1964.

JEROME L. FLUSTER, born Dec. 28, 1914, Schenectady, NY; BS and MS in education, University of Southern California. Entered the Army April 3, 1942, Camp Upton, Long Island. Basic training Camp Croft, SC. OCS Ft. Benning, GA. Commissioned second lieutenant Nov. 3, 1942.

Assigned to 100th Div. 399 Inf. HQ Co. Reassigned, arrived in North Africa April 1942, 34th Div. 133rd Inf. Co. K Platoon Leader. HQ 5th Army 14th course Mine Warfare and Demolitions. In Italy, 133rd Inf. 2nd and 3rd Bn. HQ Co., P&A Platoon Leader and S-1. Promoted first lieutenant while serving with 3rd Bn. HQ Co., 133rd Inf. After reclassified in hospital as limited duty, 910th ABS, H&S Co. Platoon Leader. Back in States, 2nd Div., 9th Inf., Regt. supply officer. Discharged August 1947. First Lieutenant USAR 1947-53.

Awards/Medals: Bronze Star Medal with V device with one OLC; Purple Heart Medal with three OLC, WWII Victory Medal, Combat Infantryman's Badge, Army of Occupation Medal, EAME Theater Ribbon with four Bronze Stars (Tunisian Campaign, Naples-Foggia Campaign, Rome-Arno Campaign and two other Italian Campaigns.)

Married Henrietta 1947, have two daughters and one son, six grandchildren. Teacher and administrator in public schools and private foundation of mentally handicapped. [illegible] president two years Retired. Life member of DAV and MOPH.

FRANKLIN FOOSANER, born July 31, 1928, Floral Park, NY. Joined the USN, FMF, June 1948, New Port Hospital, Camp Lejeune.

Memorable experience was receiving the Bronze Star Combat V, and the Military Cross New York State.

Awards/Medals: Bronze Star Combat V, Korean Medal Military Cross, Presidential Korean Medal Japanese Occupation Medal, Good Conduct Medal.

He was discharged June 1952, the rank of HM2.

Married Ruth and has son Craig and daughter Barbara. Retired from the NYC schools, special education. Now sculpting ceramic, porcelain and leather.

HERSCHEL W. FORNER, born Aug. 3, 1921, York, PA. Enlisted September 1942, Army Ordnance Corps. Military stations included Aberdeen Proving Ground, MD (1942-44; 1947-53); Germany (1944-47; 1953-55); Redstone, AR (1955-59); C&GSC (1959-60); Korea (1960-61); USMR (1961-64); Detroit Arsenal (1964-65); Washington (1965-66); Israel (1966-69). Participated in battles in WWII, Central Europe, Rhineland Campaigns.

Memorable experience includes three years as Army Attaché at American Embassy, Tel Aviv, Israel highlight of military career.

Awards/Medals: Army of Occupation Medal (Germany with three overseas bars); Armed Forces Reserve Medal, National Defense Service Medal with one OLC; Joint Service Commendation Medal.

He retired in October 1969, with the rank of lieutenant colonel.

Married to Betty 1942, son Stephen, two daughters Nancy and Michelle; and two grandchildren, Sara and Geoffrey. Subsequent to retirement from Army spent 20 years in office furniture business. Fully retired in 1991. Member Alexander D. Goode Post 205, JWV.

ETHA BEATRICE FOX, born Feb. 1, 1914, Chicago, IL. Enlisted May 1944, USCGR. During WWII served in Norfolk, VA, and Baltimore, MD. Since WWII short periods of extended active duty various places.

Awards/Medals: WWII Victory Medal, American Theater, Reserve Ribbons.

Ended extended active duty in WWII December 1945, remained in reserve as "week-end warrior" 30 years, till age 60 in 1944, at which time was four striper, captain.

Today, retired lawyer still very active in bar association and temple activities and charitable projects, e.g. just celebrated 38 years as volunteer for Recording for the Blind and am hoping to make it an even 40 in 1995.

PAUL FOX, born in the Bronx, NY, on Feb. 17 1930. He graduated from Bronx High School of Science in 1948. In April 1951, Fox was inducted into the Army and served his basic training at Ft. Breckinridge, KY. In the autumn he sailed for Korea from Seattle, WA.

Upon entering the Army, Fox was a private first class. He then became a corporal when he arrived overseas, and eventually became platoon sergeant when his platoon sergeant was killed. He served in the 2nd Inf. Div., and as part of the UN effort fought alongside Thailanders, Australians and Dutch.

After serving overseas for one year, he remembered the bitter cold weather and the warmth and gratitude of the South Korean people. He also recalled being many miles from the nearest Jewish service during the High Holy Days and being

encouraged by the Catholic Chaplain to sit in on his services during that lonely time.

He received numerous medals and badges for his service, including the Bronze Service Star, the Purple Heart Medal the Korean Service Medal, Combat Infantryman's Badge, and the United Nations Service Medal. He was discharged from the Army on Feb. 3, 1953, at Camp Kilmer, NJ. That summer he met Lauren Burres of Hartford, CT, and they were married Dec. 24, 1953. They had three sons: Jason and his wife Joan of Harrington Park, NJ; David and his wife Sandy of Wayne, NJ; and Carter of Tenafly, NJ.

Following the war Fox went to college on the G.I. Bill, and graduated from NYU in January 1957 with a BS degree in business management. He eventually settled in Northern New Jersey and formed Paul A. Fox and Associates, a firm of manufacturers representatives marketing roofing and waterproofing materials.

He became a member of the JWV, joining the Gold-Moses Post 654 of Bergenfield-Dumont, NJ. On March 9, 1992, he passed away after fighting a year and a half battle with leukemia.

RUDOLPH B. FOX, born in St. Louis on March 27, 1921. Following his graduation from Soldan High School, he enrolled at National Farm School, in Daylestown, PA. He was inducted into Air Force in 1942. Following basic training, he was assigned to the Weather Station on his base, in Texas.

The following year he was transferred to Antiqua. Here he learned all about "Rum and Coke." In June 1944, he returned to the States for 30 day leave, to his family in St. Louis. Here he met his "dream girl" Selma. Although he wanted to marry, she did not say yes, she was enroute to basic training in Des Moines, IA; as she had enlisted in the Army. They enjoyed and shared many dates until each went back to serve Uncle Sam.

Sgt. Rudy Fox was enroute to Alaska, again assigned to a weather station. The romance continued via mail; often letters came by pilots flying into Long Beach, CA, where Selma was stationed, Rudy was honorably discharged in 1946.

He enrolled at University of Missouri, was a charter member of AETT fraternity; received his BS in 1948. Rudy married Selma in 1947. They have two daughters and one son. Rudy taught high school for 22 years, until his death in 1973. He was a member of Post 346, JWV.

SELMA MASHBEIN FOX, born in St. Louis, MO. Her career in retailing was going well, until 1944; being patriotic, she and a very close friend made their decision to join the Army.

July 1944 her basic training began at Ft. Des Moines, IA. It was tough, but six weeks later, Pvt. Mashbein was enroute to Long Beach, CA. Hoping to full-fill her ambition to enter the nursing profession, She had to get through to personnel and pull many strings, other wise she had no reason to join! Recruitment offices had stated "I would be trained for Medical Technician," as they were badly needed to replace the shortage of GI males, who were being shipped overseas.

She feels that this GI learned quickly and promotion followed. She was the first WAC to be placed in their base hospital, working 12 hour shifts.

As a sergeant she was officially "in charge" of sick call, working closely with physicians and nurses. Work hours became shorter, week ends off, allowed her to explore southern California. She went to the Hollywood Canteen, Catalina Island and the studios.

Even met Gen. Ike Eisenhower, when he toured their base hospital and WAC medical barracks. She achieved great

satisfaction helping the cause, hated to witness the causalities that were flown into their base before going to their homes.

After Europe and Japan fighting ended, she selected to take an honorable discharge for serving two years. Now she was free to resume her romance with Rudy and married June 1947. They met and had the pleasure of shaking hands with President Harry Truman in Independence, MO.

They have three children, Trudy, Sanford and Charlotte and two grandson.

She is now retired as a widow. She keeps busy with several groups as a volunteer for young and aged. Traveling to the children and few hobbies keep her active. Member of JWV Post 346.

BERNARD FRANK, born Feb. 8, 1897, New York, NY. Enlisted USN, WWI. Served North Atlantic sea duty and anti-sub duty.

Memorable experience was being wounded when ship was torpedoed.

Awards/Medals: WWII Victory Medal and Purple Heart Medal.

Family includes mother, father, three sons and a daughter. Died July 28, 1965.

ERWIN FRANK, born in St. Paul, MN. Enlisted December 1940, Inf. staff sergeant, 63rd Inf. Services included Hawaii, New Guinea and wounded in Philippines.

Awards/Medals: Purple Heart Medal and Bronze Star with clusters.

He was discharged in 1945, with the rank of staff sergeant.

Married Evelyn, children: Jeffrey, Peter and Wendy. Died in 1965 from service connected problems.

HARRY H. FRANK, born Dec. 24, 1887, Pittsburgh, PA. Died Oct. 26, 1982, Ft. Myers, FL, at the age of 94. He graduated from Cornell University in 1912 with a BA degree in civil engineering. Inducted into the U.S. Army April 19, 1918, Philadelphia, PA. Stations included H&M College, College Station, TX, May 24, 1918; 32nd Service CO., July 19, 1918; C.G. Camp, Merritt, NJ; MAT'L DET., APO 731, Sept. 25, 1918; 44 Service Co., Jan. 5, 1919; 44 Service Co., May 29, 1919; and France.

Memorable experience "November 11 will always be a memorable day for me. In WWI, I was a member of the first Meteorological Section of the Signal Corps sent to France and stationed at Gieveres. We inflated para rubber balloons and followed them every six hours day and night with a theodolite to obtain the speed and prediction of the upper winds. This information was very necessary to the field artillery for adjusting their range for shrapnel and high explosive charges.

Our source of balloons was at our headquarters located at Colombes LaBelle, where I was sent for a supply. After receiving it, I routed my trip back through Paris. I arrived in Paris Nov. 9, 1918, and made arrangements to locate at the YMCA Hote Pavilion ... I was fortunate to become friendly with English-speaking priest (of Cathedral St. Genevev) who told me of the armistice being signed on the morrow and induced me to stay, even though my pass expired. The unforgettable day was, by far, the most interesting one as a veteran."

He was discharged June 27, 1919, with the rank of corporal, at Mitchel Field, LI, NY.

LEON FRANKEL, born Sept. 5, 1923, St. Paul, MN. Enlisted USNR Sept. 8, 1942, as seaman second class, V-5 Aviation Cadet Training Program leading to commission as ensign. Duty with torpedo Sq. 9, 15 months.

Memorable experience includes aboard USS *Lexington* CV-16 first Navy raid on Japan, February 1945, received DFC for fighting a running battle with enemy fighter aircraft across 80 miles of Japanese home island, while flying at a reduced speed in order to protect two crippled planes. April 1945 flying from USS *Yorktown* CV10, won the Navy Cross while flying by instruments through a heavy overcast attacked a Japanese Cruiser and screening destroyer. Torpedoed the cruiser which sank less than a minute later. In May 1948 volunteered for the Israel Defense Forces. Helped start the first fighter unit (101 SQDN) and participated in 25 missions. Flying ME109s, spitfires and other aircraft.

Awards/Medals: Navy Cross, DFC with one star; Air Medal with two stars; American Theater; WWII Victory Medal; Presidential Citation Lexington, Yorktown.

He was discharged Dec. 10, 1958, with the rank of lieutenant.

Married 42 years to Ruth, and has two children. Retired.

MAX G. FRANKEL, born in Bridgeport, CT, on Jan. 24, 1914. Attended New York University, majoring in business administration. Entered U.S. Army Feb. 24, 1944. Basic training and electronic schooling at Ft. Monmouth, NJ, followed by being assigned on the Signal Corp. Had intensive training in specialized electronic equipment at the Philadelphia Signal Depot. Served with the 324th Signal Base Maintenance Company for 12 months in the European and Asiatic Pacific Theaters of Operation. Was also attached to Gen. Patton's 3rd Army during his march on Berlin. Also served in the Philippines and Japan.

Received awards medals from both theaters of operation; namely, American Theater Campaign, Asiatic Pacific Theater Campaign, EAME Theater Campaign, Philippine Liberation Ribbon, WWII Victory Medal, Expert Rifleman Medal.

He was honorable discharged May 9, 1946, with rank of technical sergeant.

Married to Molly since 1940. Has one son, Robert, two grandchildren, Lauren and Jane. Past Sr. Vice Commander of JWV, Laurel Post 45.

Founded electronics company, Frankel Enterprises Inc. sold business in 1981 and retired to Florida. Spends winters in Florida and summers in Connecticut.

THEODORE FRANKEL, Captain, U.S. Army, born in the Bronx, NY, on May 18, 1918, graduated from high school in 1935, and continued extended education after discharge from the Army in 1948. Entered as a private in November 1940 and was discharged in February 1948 as a captain. Basic training at Ft. Dix, NJ, then to Camp Claibourne, LA, and Ft. Lewis, WA. Commissioned lieutenant at Ft Benning on Dec. 22, 1942, assigned 20th Inf., 6th Inf. Div. Served in Far East invasion of New Guinea and Philippines.

Awards/Medals: Distinguished Service Cross, Silver Star with cluster, Bronze Star, Purple Heart Medal with cluster, Combat Infantryman's Badge, American Defense Service Medal, American Campaign Medal, Asiatic-Pacific Campaign Medal, WWII Victory Medal, Philippine Liberation Ribbon, Honorable Service Button.

Married to Marcia since 1946. Have son, Michael, and daughter Sandi, and six grandchildren. Presently retired but was in the retail business. Member of the JWV, MOPH 669 and Retired Officers Association.

ROBERT FREED, born Feb. 4, 1927, Buffalo, NY. Joined the service June 28, 1945, serving with Corps of Engr. 8th Div. Co. A 15th Engr. Bn. Service included Germany Army of Occupation.

Memorable experience was Dachau detail.

Awards/Medals: Army of Occupation Medal, WWII Victory Medal, Lapel Button issued.

He was discharged March 1, 1947, with the rank of staff sergeant.

Son of Joseph and Frances Cohen Freed, grandson of Joseph Cohen, founder of Cohen's Rye Bread Bakery in Buffalo, NY. He is a Clerk of Erie County, board of elections. Life Member of JWV of USA, 9th Inf. Div. Association, NRA, Buffalo Revolver and Rifle Club, Alumni of Kappa Nu Fraternity, University of Buffalo.

CHARLES FREEDMAN, born on Aug. 27, 1920 to Benjamin and Molly. In a family of seven children, Charles had three brother; William, Irving and Harris and three sisters; Edith, Anne and Sophie.

After graduating high school Charles entered the Army and was assigned to artillery. He soon transferred to the Air Force where he was a bombardier-navigator on a B-24 Liberator called the *Merchant of Menace*. After flying on 25 missions, he reupped for an additional 25. On his 47th mission his plane blew up at Bari, Italy and all aboard were killed in what was suspected as sabotage. There was a group burial at Jefferson Barracks in St. Louis, MO.

During a bombing mission over the Ploesti oil fields in Hungary the bombs were stuck in a bay and Charles walked out on the catwalk and pushed them through. He was awarded several Air Medal Oak Leaf Clusters and a Purple Heart.

After World War II some veterans joined a Bustleton Post 706. In 1956 a group of three from that Post were requested to investigate a change of the post's name. Mel Israel, "Chuck" Atchick and Fred Greenberg met with Irving Freedman, brother of the late Charles Freedman, and agreed that the new post name would be Lt. Charles Freedman Post 706 of Philadephia, PA.

DAVID FREEDMAN, born Aug. 9, 1922, Bronx, NY. Inducted March 5, 1943, and sent to Camp Patchogue, NY. Early training in Camp Hood, TX, then shipped to Camp Shelby, MS.

Shipped to England in 1943; went into France D+6 as a replacement. First with Patton's 3rd Army, then with Simpson's 9th Army. While in France was stationed near French guerrillas, FFI and became very friendly with them.

Awards/Medals: Purple Heart, Good Conduct and ETO. Served as a medic. He was wounded in Holland by shrapnel during air raid. Discharged December 1945 as PFC.

Went to school three years on the GI Bill. Worked for a bank in customer service until retiring. Now works at home as telemarketer. Married to Ceil and has two grown sons. Belongs to Post 148 in Philadelphia.

HAROLD FREEDMAN, born Dec. 26, 1919, Brooklyn, NY. Graduated Dickinson HS, Jersey City, NJ. Enlisted Nov. 17, 1942, in U.S. Army, was stationed in Ft. Belvoir, VA and discharged March 7, 1946, as tech sergeant.

He attended New York University and has been associated with Muriel's Dress Shop for the past 49 years. Was instrumental in shaping the lives of many OHS students. An avid sports fan, he has so far helped to send 30-35 students to basketball, football, soccer and wrestling camps.

Member of Bloomfield Post #10. Semi-retired he still helps out at Muriel's, which is currently being run by his nephew, Robert Schachtel.

Married to Flora Walsky and resides in W. Orange, NJ.

HENRY E. "HANK" FREEDMAN, born Sept. 21, 1921, Boston, MA. Entered U.S. Army Oct. 13, 1942. Ser-

---

geant 313th Inf. 79th Inf. Div. Weapons Plt. October 1942-April 1943; ASTP University Alabama/Auburn University May 1943-March 1944; program ended-reassigned to Regt. HQ Co. 422nd Inf. 106th Div. Shipped to ETO October 1944. Participated in Battle of the Bulge, captured in action Dec. 19 1944, in Bleialf, Germany. Sent to Stalag 9B, BAD ORB where Jewish Soldiers were segregated, moved to Stalag 9A, Zeigenhain. Lost 55 lb., during confinement. Liberated by 6th Armored Div. Returned to States May 9, 1945.

Memorable experiences: being attacked by Tiger Tanks w/o Artillery to counter, being bombed x-mas eve. While locked up in box car, starvation diet at both Stalags, when first captured, listening to German officer and NCO arguing that they should be shot (a La Malmedy). Thank God, the officer won! Flying over Boston on a flight back to the States!

Awards/Medals: Bronze Star, Combat Infantryman's Badge, POW Medal and other appropriate service and theater of operation ribbons.

He was discharged Ft. Meade, MD, Nov. 24, 1945, as a technician 4th grade (sergeant).

Married Betty, have sons Robert and Alan, and three beautiful granddaughters, Jennifer, Haley and Tori. Retired 1987 after over 40 years merchandising consumer electronics for a large department store group. Life member American Ex-POW's, 106th Inf. div. Assoc., JWV, VBOB. Leading active life enjoying family, travel. Survivor of lymphoma cancer, so he's going to enjoy life every golden minute of it! Making their home in Roswell, 30 miles north of Atlanta.

MYRON I. FREEDMAN, born in Syracuse, NY. Attended Syracuse schools and graduated from Syracuse University. Associated with the *Syracuse Herald Journal* as district manager.

Had charge of maintenance and building supplies at Ft. Hamilton during WWI. He was one of the first members of the JWV. Was a member of Temple of Society Concord.

SAMUEL A. FREEDMAN, born June 27, 1917, Canton, OH. Graduate of Canton McKinley High School. Joined the USN Dec. 4, 1940, and sent to U.S. Naval Radio and Training Center in Los Angeles, CA. Continued at the USNB Treasure Island, CA. Bunked on board SS *Delta Queen*. After Pearl Harbor assigned to Compat 12 to Ireland and then reassigned British Corvette to USS *Fury* (PG69). Sub Patrol North Atlantic and Eastern North America. Transferred to USS *AnCon* AGC-4 (first USN Communication ship) HQ for the EAME Amphibious Focus, participated in invasion of Casablanca, North Africa, Sicily, Salerno, Anzio and France. Appointed as chief traffic checker aboard USS *AnCon*. Received Captains Merit Award and appointed chief radioman. Aboard ship at various times with King George of England, General Montgomery, Admiral Mark Clark and General Patton. Quenton Reynolds wrote two books, *The Curtain Rises* and *Amphibious Adventure* while aboard; Douglas Fairbanks Jr. served aboard. Transferred to USS *Alamance* AKA-75 for Pacific Amphibious duty, Asiatic Pacific duty with Reoccupation of Philippines, duty at Sasebo, Japan at signing of treaty with Japan. Returned to U.S. and discharged in Seattle, WA, on Nov. 28, 1945. Decorations: WWII Victory Medal, Good Conduct Medal and EAME with three stars, American Defense Service Medal, Philippine Liberation Ribbon, American Theater.

Married to Janice E. Freedman and had three boys and two girls. Life member of JWV Post 73 and VFW 693. Established Freco Chemical Company and later served as a broker with Samuel A. Freedman & Assoc., both in Northeastern Ohio. Retired, but still serves as consultant to SJF,

Inc., parent company of Samuel A. Freedman & Associates, Joliet, IL.

DAVID FREEMAN, born Feb. 12, 1894, in Romania. Came to America in 1903, with his parents the late Levi and Rebecca Freeman. Attended Croton and Jackson Schools. Member of Ilion Lodge #400 IOOF. Entered service in 1917, wounded in action during the St. Meheil Drive. Member of 310th Inf., 82nd Div. Died in France on Dec. 23, 1918, at the age of 24. Buried in Ahavath Achim Cemetery, Jamesville Avenue, Syracuse.

Employed as a sheet metal worker, by the Library Bureau and Cabinet Works of Ilion, NY.

Survived by brothers, Albert and Myer of Syracuse, Hyman B. of Rochester; sisters, Mrs. Dora Simons, Mrs. Sarah Shimberg, Rochester, Srul Fraiman, Mrs. Feiga Gorenstein, Bessarabia, Romania; nieces and nephews, Ruth and Arthur Freeman, Leonard and Benjamin Shimberg, Reva Shimberg Arman, Shoil and David Fraiman of Israel, Bluma and David Gorenstein of Uruguay.

LAWRENCE I. FREEMAN, born March 28, 1917, Worcester, MA. Joined U.S. Navy Dec. 3, 1939. Discharged honorably as chief machinists mate, April 24, 1946. Basic NTS Newport, RI. Completed MM School, Norfolk, VA. Arrived Long Beach, CA, via Panama Canal. Sailed for Pacific, assigned to USS Canopus in Manila Bay, Oct. 19, 1940. Learned December 8 that Japs bombed Pearl Harbor. Two days later while docked at Army Pier, Japs bombed Manila. Moved to Mariveles Bay when Manila evacuated. Bombed twice while there. Left Bataan April 9, 1941, for Corregidor. Taken prisoner May 1941. POW at several prison sites. Stevedore for 1 and a half years. Became ill, sent to Bilibid Prison Hospital. July 4, 1944, sailed for 62 days from Manila to Moji, Japan on old scow crammed with 1,000 POW for Omuta, Fukuoka, Camp 17. Worked coal mines about one and a half years until surrender. Suffered many health problems due to lack of sanitation and malnutrition. Endured inhuman treatment for three and half ears. Left Japan through Nagasaki after A-bomb was dropped August 1945. Returned U.S. October 1945, five years to the day he reported aboard the USS Canopus.

Awards/Medals: Army Presidential Unit Citation with OLC, Pre-Pearl Harbor with fleet bar, Asiatic-Pacific Campaign Medal with two stars, American Theater, WWII Victory Medal, Good Conduct Medal, Defense of Philippines with two stars, POW, Bronze Star. Org: JWV, DAV, AMDBC, AM Legion, AM Ex-POW.

ROBERT FREEMAN, born April 1, 1921, New York City. Graduated St. John's U., BA in mathematics; New York U., BS in mechanical engineering; City College of New York, Baruch School of business administration.

Entered the military in October 1941; attended Air Force Cadet School System for engineering and pilot training. Group leader, squadron leader, 56 combat missions, 465th (H) BG. Shot down four times, held and interrogated by the SS twice, escaped both times, returned to base with the aid of the Partisan underground in Yugoslavia and in Italy.

Awards/Medals: Silver Star, Distinguished Flying Cross with cluster, Air Medal with three OLCs, Conspicuous Service Cross, Purple Heart with two OLCs, plus other decorations.

Participated in the invasion of France, the Italian Campaign, the Air Battle for Germany, Eastern Europe, the Balkans and North Africa. A memorable experience was printing and dropping leaflets of hope to the hopeless in the death camps. Discharged as captain, June 29, 1945.

National Grand Master of Brith Abraham and vice president of Bnai Zion. Serves on the board of directors of many organizations and has been a stalwart of the Zionist movement. Member of the JWV, DAV, Air Force Escape and Evasion Society and Military Order of the Purple Heart.

President and CEO of Freeman Research Inc. Innovator, inventor, industrial trouble shooter, experimental engineer. Presently working on solar cell technology for amplified voltage output, storage and transfer. His work has been published in many scientific and technical journals.

Married to Millie over 49 years and has two sons, Michael Freeman and Dr. Denny Freeman.

BERNICE SAINS FREID, born in St. Paul, MN, graduated Mechanic Arts High School, and worked as a stenographer at the St. Paul Police Department.

Entered the USN (WR) on Sept. 18, 1944. Duty stations: Hunter College, Bronx, NY, basic training Yeoman Training School, Oklahoma A&M College, Stillwater, Fleet Post Office and District Passenger Transportation Office, 12th NAVDIST, San Francisco, CA. Discharged on April 19, 1946, as Y2/c. After discharge, Naval Reserve duty 1949-58, COM 3, NYC and Naval Reserve Training Center, Brooklyn, NY. Presently member of Waves National, organization of ex-WAVES.

After discharge moved to New York to study under GI Bill. Graduated New York University, BS and Teachers College, Columbia University, MS Nutrition.

Taught nutrition and home economics. Worked as a registered dietitian in hospital and various institutions. Past President of Hadassah and B'Nai Brith Women. Have visited Israel five times. Currently retired. Member of JWV Post #169 in Brooklyn. Two children and two granddaughters.

MILTON J. FREIWALD, M.D., born Jan. 12, 1910, Philadelphia, PA. Military Service: Major, U.S. Army Medical Corp, WWII. Medical School and Year of Graduation: New York University College of Medicine, 1943. Type of Practice: general ophthalmology; Diplomat, American Board of Ophthalmology, Hospital Affiliations: Emeritus staff member, Albert Einstein Medical Center; Philadelphia and Woman's Hospital of Philadelphia; former attending staff member, Thomas Jefferson University Hospital. Medical Society Activities: Member, PCMS, PMS, AMA; Fellow, International College of Surgeons; life member, American College of Eye Surgeons; Fellow, military surgeons of the U.S.; former Medical Director and Chief Medical Liaison Department of Health, Education and Welfare, Region III.

Awards/Medals: Distinguished Service Award, U.S. Army Medical Corp, given by the Surgeon General of the Army; entered in "Ripley's Believe It or Not" for saving the life and sight of a soldier during WWII by removing a bar machine gun rod and spring, which passed through the orbit and emerged in the back of the throat; medical emissary of President John F. Kennedy, was the first ophthalmologist to lecture at the Helholtz Institute in Moscow, USSR, and the Filatov Institute in Odessa on Prevention of blindness.

BERNARD I. FRIEDENBERG, born in Philadelphia, PA, Oct. 20, 1921. Enlisted March 13, 1942, Medic, Ft. Hancock, served in England, Africa, Sicily, France, Belgium, Germany and Czechoslovakia. Tech. 3, Staff Sergeant, Sept. 24, 1945, discharged.

Memorable experience was during the Battle of the Bulge, under exposure to heavy machine gun, small arms fire and artillery fire. (Direct fire from a Mark Six tank) he crawled out ahead of their line and carried five wounded men to a place of relative cover. He was wounded by tank fire when carrying the fifth man in.

When he became member of the JWV, he learned that one of the wounded he carried in was Phil Kahan, a present neighbor and member of his post.

He landed on Omaha Beach in the fourth wave. Needless to say that was also a very memorable experience. He was awarded his first Silver Star for action on that day.

Awards/Medals: Silver Star with OLC, Bronze Star with OLC, Purple Heart with OLC, Presidential Citation, ETO Ribbon with five Battle Stars, N.J. Distinguished Medal.

IRVING L. FRIEDLAND, born Feb. 2, 1919, Brooklyn, NY. Active duty, Sept. 6, 1942, Carlisle Barracks, PA. Basic training: Wright-Patterson Field, OH. School: Armament School, Lowry Field, Denver, CO. Assigned to 550th SQ, 385th Bomb Group Heavy (B17s) Spokane, WA. Overseas duty: July 8, 1943, 3rd Div. 8th Air Force, Great Ashfield, England. Additional schooling: Power Gun Turret School, RAF Kirkham, Eng. Reassigned 548th SQ, 385th Bomb Group Heavy. Discharged honorably Sept. 30, 1945, Ft. Dix, NJ.

Awards/Medals: ETO Ribbon, Good Conduct Medal, two Presidential Unit Citations. The 548th SQ also received Letter of Commendation from General Castle for sending every plane they had (19) out on missions every day for a full 30 days during the month of November 1944 with no planes aborting.

STANLEY FRIEDLAND, born Feb. 1, 1923, Brooklyn, NY. Joined the AAF Dec. 7, 1942, 5th. Military stations included Townsville, Australia, Gusap, New Guinea, Biak NEI, Lingayen Gulf AI, I.E. Shima, Kanoya, Japan, Okinawa.

Memorable experience: "Jewish service men were invited to Rosh Hashanah services on Biak, Netherland East India's Island, north of New Guinea. On my way saw atop a hill two Japanese soldiers holding a white flag of surrender. I took my camera, and began climbing motioning for them to descend. One offered me a camera pin as a gift, which I declined and instead turned them over to an infantry officer. I was on Ie Shima, where war correspondent Ernie Pyle was killed AWD on Aug. 2, 1945, when Major McLure escorted three white Japanese planes with green crosses to the air strip when Lt. General Kawabe Vice-Chief of Staff of Imerial General Guar lead 16 officials for transfer to C-54's, enroute to Manil for the official surrender."

Awards/Medals: WWII Victory Medal, Good Conduct Medal, Asiatic Pacific Ribbon, Philippine Liberation Ribbon and Japanese Occupation.

He was discharged Dec. 24, 1945, with the rank of staff sergeant.

Married to Ruth for 47 years, three sons and two grandchildren. Allan a physician, Gene, manager of a drug store, and Scott a lawyer, and two grandchildren Brandon and Brittany. Sold uniforms and supplies to police, correction officers, EMTS, firemen, and postal employees several hours per week.

MAX FRIEDLANDER, born and raised in New York City. Now retired and living in the Bronx, NY. Enlisted the Navy on June 24, 1942. Assigned to the USS Columbia in the 12th Fleet. Spent the entire three years aboard the USS Columbia in the Pacific War Zone. Discharged Oct. 31, 1945, Water Tender 1st Class.

MEYER FRIEDLANDER, born and raised in New York City has lived in California for the past 48 years. Retired and now living in Leisure World, Laguna Hills, CA.

Inducted into the Army Aug. 31, 1943, basic training at Ft. Belvoir, VA Shipped overseas July 1, 1944. Assigned to 12th Armored Div. 714th Tank Bn, as an assistant driver and machine gunner. Left England for France and was in combat with the 4th Army in the Rhineland of Germany was in heavy combat with the enemy.

Wounded twice in battle, received WWII Victory Medal, Bronze Star, Purple Heart Medal with OLC. Also received President Roosevelt's Citation for Bravery above and beyond the call of duty for saving many lives. Discharged Feb. 3, 1946, at Ft. Dix, NJ.

MURRAY FRIEDLANDER, born and raised in New York City now retired and living in Sunrise, FL. Started out at Camp Upton, NY, did basic training at Camp Wholters, TX. Served with 530th MP Bn. HQ Det. At rank of T-5, in the Philippine Islands and Japan. Separated at Ft. Dix, NJ, Aug. 18, 1946.

PAUL FRIEDLANDER, born and raised in New York City now retired and living in Spring Valley, NY. Volunteered June 3, 1942, Ft. Jay, NY. Assigned to Medical Corp Camp Adair, OR, spent two years there. Transferred to Presidio of Monterey, CA. Transferred to Camp Beale, CA, Separation Center. Discharged Jan. 4, 1946, as tech. 5.

SIDNEY FRIEDLANDER, Sergeant, U.S. Army, May 5, 1941-Nov. 6, 1945. Inducted into the Army in 1941, prior to Pearl Harbor. After basic training he was sent to a combat infantry division, then transferred to the Air Force and later entered into the ASTP at Rutgers, where he studied French. He was transferred to the Army Military Government program and shipped to England for training as an interpreter in military government and civil affairs.

On D-Day Plus One he landed at Omaha Beach in Normandy, attached to an infantry division. Their detachment served as a combat unit and then was dropped off in various captured towns in order to organize municipal affairs, he served in Mauberge, Belgium; Eupen, Belgium; Friedberg, Germany and Frankfort.

Their unit was involved I the campaign near Malmedy and Bastogne. Later they ran displaced persons camps. He had the unique opportunity to see combat, civilian life and Nazi death camps.

VICTOR FRIEDLANDER, born and raised in New York City. Lived most of his life in New Jersey. He died Oct. 4, 1978. He was stationed at Ft. Dix, NJ, for two years.

BERNARD FRIEDMAN, born Oct. 19, 1919, Snino, Czechoslovakia. Inducted July 17, 1942, at Ft. Dix, NJ, into the AAF. Graduated AAF Radio School Sioux Falls, SD, as radio operator-mechanic in December 1942. Worked in a control tower at Northern Field in Tulahoma, TN. Went to Radar School in Boca Raton, FL, to learn how to operate homing beacons.

In March 1944 was sent from the U.S. by boat and train to North Africa and then through the Suez Canal to India and over the Hump to China where he served for 18 months and helped the B29s in the Bombing of Japan. He witnessed the return of the planes from the first B29 raid on Tokyo. Also he went through some air raids from the Japanese His primary duty was with the 129th AACS operating and servicing homing beacons for the 20th Bomber Command in China.

With the help of a non-Jewish Chaplain he would lead Friday night services for the Jewish Airmen at their base in Chenghtu, China.

Received Meritorious Unit Award from the USAF and order of the Flying Cloud from the Chinese Government. Discharged Jan. 8, 1946, at Ft. Monmouth with the rank of sergeant.

For most of his life he has worked as an electronic technician in the aerospace field until he retired. He has a wife, three daughters and two grandchildren. He is a member of Post 651 JWV.

DAVID FRIEDMAN, born Nov. 22, 1908, Perecin, Czechoslovakia. Enlisted USN May 1, 1943. Military stations included NRS Cleveland, OH; NTS Great Lakes, Chicago, IL; RS Washington, D.C.; RS San Francisco CA; USS *Mustin* (413); S/M Base Navy #128; USS *Apollo* (AS-25).

Memorable experience: "David loved his country and was proud to be in the USN. David was stationed Hawaii for two years at a submarine base. David repaired instruments in the submarines. During the war time, many parts of the instruments were not available and the need was immediate. David had the knowledge, capacity and skill to design and make the missing pieces. *Submitted by Ruth Mills Friedman"*

Awards/Medals: American Theater Medal and Asiatic-Pacific Campaign Medal.

He was discharged Sept. 27, 1945, with the rank of special artificer (WR) first class, V6 USNA.

Married Ruth Mills June 14, 1936, and has two daughters Joen and Helen. Member JWV Post #14, Cleveland, OH.

ERNEST FRIEDMAN, born Dec. 9, 1924, Leechburg, PA. Enlisted Sept. 13, 1943, Inf. rifleman T/5, 45th Div. Basic training at Camp Croft, SC, stationed include Rome ARNO, Southern France, Rhineland, Central Europe.

Memorable experience includes being among early troops entering Dachau Concentration Camp and seeing first hand the survivors and the ovens and hearing first hand their stories. He can still see the horrible conditions.

Awards/Medals: Bronze Star and cluster, Purple Heart Medal with cluster, Good Conduct Medal, EAME with four Bronze Stars.

He was discharged Oct. 13, 1945, with the rank of technician 5.

Retired Real Estate Insurance Broker, married to Marie 34 years, working part-time in real estate management.

GILBERT R. FRIEDMAN, basic training Camp Blanding, FL; advanced radio training, Inf. Sch. Ft. Benning, GA. Rifleman radio operator with Co. A, 143rd Inf. Regt., 36th Div. From Southampton, England to LeHavre, France, through France and Germany to Bavaria at War's end. Prior to being shipped home on points played in the 7th Army band. Served 1944-46.

Awards/Medals: Bronze Star with cluster, Purple Heart Medal, Good Conduct Medal, Presidential Until Emblem, American Campaign Medal, EAME Campaign Medal, WWII Victory Medal, Army of Occupation Medal with Clasp, Combat Infantry Badge, Marksman Badge with Rifle Bar, Croix de Guerre Unit Citation.

Married Trudy January 1952, two children Laura and Larry, two grandchildren Aaron and Rachelle. President of M&G Sales Company, Inc. a family-operated Army-Navy Surplus store, 48 years in business in Norfolk, VA. Born in Norfolk, now residing in Virginia Beach, VA.

HARRY FRIEDMAN, M.D., born March 21, 1939, Memphis, TN. Enlisted April 1956, USAR, staff sergeant; and November 1986, USNR Medical Corps. Stationed included Operation Desert Storm, Bahrain January -March 1991. He is active reserve now with the rank of commander. His father, Abe Friedman, was born in Memphis, and mother Miriam Weber Friedman was born in Zezmera, Lithuania. Today he is a neurosurgeon.

HERMAN FRIEDMAN, born May 3, 1925, Brooklyn, NY. Enlisted July 30, 1943, U.S. Army, Co. G, 175th Inf. Regt., 29th Div. Blue and Gray from ML. Stationed at Camp Adair, OR.

Memorable experience was sitting on ship prior to invasion, sky black with planes, Ocean covered with ships as far as you could see.

Awards/Medals: European Eastern Campaign with two service stars, St. Leo and Brittany Pen. Purple Heart Medal with OLC, Good Conduct Medal, Expert Rifleman.

He was discharged May 23, 1945, with the rank of sergeant.

Married Sylvia, two sons, four daughters, and three grandchildren. Employed by national ship shops from 1957-82, retired in Florida since 1989. Member JWV and VFW.

MARTIN M. FRIEDMAN, inducted Dec. 1941, as a private. Trained and then entered officers training at Ft. Benning, GA. Joined the 31st Div. and Camp Shelby, MS. Trained in Co. I, 155th Inf. Regt. as a lieutenant and captain.

His division landed at Buna in New Guinea and took over the patrolling and securing and area and the fighting at Sawar Airdome. He received the Combat Infantryman's Badge and the Bronze Star Medal. His company made the initial landing on Moratai Island. Their division defended and secured the air installations from frequent Japanese attacks. Their regiment then landed at Cotobato Mindanao. His company was the first to secure Malaybaly, the capitol. They fought through the interior to the north coast. He was then given command of the Army base at Butuan where they supported and supplied their other regiments in the upper Agusan Valley until the Japanese surrender.

MILTON FRIEDMAN, born Nov. 20, 1923, Pittsburgh, PA. Enlisted Feb. 10, 1943, U.S. Army Air Corps. Basic training Atlantic City, NJ; Signal Corps Training Camp Crowder, MO; ASTP University of Missouri; Lincoln Air Base, NE; overseas to CBI Theater. Served with the 14th Air Force in China with the 3rd Air Base Comm. Det. Sp.

Memorable experience was seeing Bombay and Calcutta Inora, served in Kinming, Chungking and Shanghai, China.

Awards/Medals: CBI Theater with two Battle Stars, Good Conduct Medal, WWII Victory Medal.

He was discharged Jan. 13, 1946, with the rank of corporal.

Married for 43 years with three children an three grandchildren. Retired. Member of JWV Post #49.

SAM FRIEDMAN, born Dec. 3, 1922, K.C., MO. U.S. Army Infantry, Feb. 13, 1943. Camp Stout, IL; England,; France; Ft. Robinson, AR; Germany; Russia. Discharged with the rank of captain. Retired.

Memorable experience "Of the 197 in my company (Co. A) 10 minutes after landing 189 were either dead or injured. Friedman said a comrade pulled him aside and using the saltwater for the ocean wiped the blood out of his eyes. He late climbed up the cliff at the beach watching the action unfold below him. He survived the invasion and received a Purple Heart Medal for his efforts. However, he was not as lucky later on in the war. He was severely injured when a bridge he was on was blown up. By the end of WWII, Friedman had received two more Purple Heart Medal plus the Silver and Bronze Stars for his bravery.

SAMPSON LESTER FRIEDMAN, born in Brooklyn, NY on Nov. 5, 1923. Enlisted in the Air Corps December 1942, and inducted February 1943. Graduated Bombardier School in Deming, NM, and was assigned to B-29 training, 20th AF, 9th BG, 5th BS in McCook, NE. In January 1945, he went overseas to Tinian Island in the Pacific. He flew 24 missions some with Capt. Bill Dolan, commander of the "Tokyo K.O.," then with Capt. Carl Donica on #40. July 28, 1945, on the Uji-Yamada mission, the #40 was frontally

attacked by a Kamikaze plane. Lt. Friedman fired his six remote-controlled 50-caliber machine guns into the Kamikaze cockpit while the Japanese pilot fired into the #40. Capt. Donica's control cables were cut but co-pilot Lt. Conrow banked the B-29 to the right in time to avoid the head-on collision. The enemy aircraft passed under the left wing and went down and exploded. After dropping the bombs on the target, the damaged B-29 went to Iwo Jima for repairs. He continued on bombing missions over Japan until the end of the War, September 1945, and then dropped POW supplies to camps in Japan for several missions. He was discharged a second lieutenant in February 1946, and was awarded the Air Medal with two OLC and the Distinguished Flying Cross. He married his childhood sweetheart, Lila Ritter, soon after being discharged. They have three children and three grandchildren. He received a BS degree from NYU, and worked in the jewelry industry at David Friedman and Sons manufacturing company and is now retired living in Bellerose, NY. He is a member of JWV Post #552.

SAMUEL FRIEDMAN, born March 25, 1919, New York, NY. Inducted Active Service July 9, 1942, Ft. Dix, NJ. Assigned to AAF, basic training Atlantic City, NJ. Attended radio/operator and Mechanic School, Scott Field, IL. Control Tower Operator School, Chanute Field, IL, assigned to Army Airways Communication System as control tower operator. Served as control tower operator at Blvethenthal Field, Wilmington, NC; Moody Field, Valdosta, GA; Warner Robins AFB, Macon, GA.

Awards/Medals: AAF Technical Badge, American Theater Medal, Good Conduct Medal, WWII Victory Medal.

He was discharged honorably Jan. 24, 1946, with the rank of sergeant. After discharge returned to job with Federal Service as Federal Credit Union Examiner until retirement July 31, 1983. Now retired, living with his wife of 46 years, Sylvia. Have two daughters, Jeanne Friedman Boston, MA and Linda Thomas, Montreal, Canada.

SOL L. FRIEDMAN, born in Long Branch, NJ, Sept. 1, 1925. He entered the Army Air Force as an air cadet in December 1943, and was honorably discharged in April 1946. He graduated from Rutgers University in 1953, with a BA in political science and history. He then attended Seton Hall Law School.

Married for 42 years, Sol and his wife Virginia have three children, Shayna Ann, Marc and Danny, and two grandchildren, Heather and Matthew.

He is CEO of Delta Security Bureau in Long Branch, NJ. He has served 10 terms as commander of Long Branch Post 316 and is a life member of the JWV. He is a member of the JWV National Museum in Washington, D.C. and a charter member of the Holocaust Museum in Washington, D.C. He is currently commander of the Department of New Jersey, JWV.

WALTER J. FRISCH, born on Dec. 6, 1914, and enlisted in the U.S. Army on June 24, 1940. On Dec. 6, 1941, their unit left San Francisco for the South Pacific.

The next day, Sunday the seventh of December, was peaceful and no one had any idea that it would be the turning point of their lives. When they received word that Pearl Harbor had been attacked they made a U-turn and returned to the States.

Their unit spent the next 10 months preparing for combat; in October 1942 they sailed for Australia and spent the next three years there, the Dutch East India and the Philippines.

In 1945 they were stationed in Manila preparing for the invasion of Japan when he was awarded the Bronze Star which counted five points towards being returned to the States. During the trip home the atomic bombs were dropped on Japan and when he arrived home, the war was over.

MARTHA METTER FRITZ, born in Boston, MA. Inducted June 1, 1943, Army Nurse Corp, Maxwell Field, AL, CBI Assam, Okinawa. Rank first lieutenant.

She was part of a general hospital working in a jungle cleaning at Mile O of the Lido Road in Assam, India. They cared for Merrall's Marauders and the truckers going over the Hump to China. Her specialty was contagion and dermatology, medical when necessary the hospital and staff were fine but the heat, monsoons, and limited but made it difficult. They were at the end of the mail line. While one R&R in Danpceling they received orders to report to Calcutta and soon were on high seas to set up a hospital on an island to prepare for invasion of Japan. The atom bomb was dropped, the War ended, and they put off in Okinawa. After a time, typhoon 500 nurses were sent back to the States on the SS *Brerchner*.

Awards/Medals: Bronze Service Star, American Campaign Medal, WWII Victory Medal, three Overseas Bars.

Today she is retired from school licensing. In earlier years she worked for Planned Parenthood. Her time is spent volunteering for Planned Parenthood classes, Trustee Temple Ne Tamied, board member of Sisterhood and various committees. She is a board member of Hadassah and also belong to other religious and secular organizations. Hobbies: bridge and traveling and her children and grandchildren.

BENJAMIN FROST, born April 25, 1892. Enlisted Oct. 12, 1917, Div. 77-307, 305th MG Bn. Co. C. Stationed at Camp Upton, NY. He was discharged Feb. 11, 1918, with the rank of private. Has a daughter, Thelma Frost Mann. He is deceased.

HENRY S. GAFFIN, USNR, Y2/c, born Jan. 4, 1925, Worcester, MA. Graduated high school February 1943. Entered U.S. navy May 19, 1943. Discharged honorably, April 21, 1946. Boot Camp: Naval Training Station, Newport, RI. Assigned to USS *Colahan* DD658. Participated in ship's commissioning in Brooklyn Navy Yard, Aug. 23, 1943. Underwent shakedown exercises along east coast of U.S. and Bermuda. After shakedown departed Norfolk, VA, for San Francisco, CA, via Panama Canal. Arrived San Francisco Dec. 4, 1943. Left San Francisco for Pearl Harbor, HI, Dec. 7, 1943. Arrived Pearl Harbor Dec. 11, 1943. Joined rapidly growing Pacific Fleet. First combat action was invasion of the Marshall Islands. Our next action against the Japanese was the bombardment, invasion and occupation of Guam. The ship played key roles in the invasion of southern Palau and Leyte in the Philippines. The *Colahan* became radar picket ship of the Third Fleet and joined in the raids of Formosa, Luzon, Camranh Bay, Hong Kong, and Hainan Island. Participated in the last great series of air raids on Okinawa, Iwo Jima and Japan itself. Survived the Great Typhoon off the Philippines December 1944, with severe damage to fleet. Three destroyers ran out of fuel and capsized with heavy loss of life. In January 1945, while coming out of the South China as radar picket ship to rejoin fleet during Kamikaze air attack, was hit by shrapnel while serving at battle station on bridge as telephone talker for Captain. Treated for shrapnel wound by ship's doctor in sick bay.

Decorations: Asiatic-Pacific Campaign Medal with eight Battle Stars, Philippine Liberation Ribbon with two Battle Stars, American Theater Medal, Navy Occupation Medal (Asia clasp), Purple Heart Medal, WWII Victory Medal.

Married to Ethel and has a son and daughter. Member of JWV of USA, Post 32; Life member of Military Order of Purple Heart; life member of DAV; member of USN Memorial (plank owner). Employed by the Department of the Army from July 1955 to February 1982. Retired from Federal Service, February 1982. Attended Clark University Evening College while employed by Department of Army, Natick Laboratories.

Currently serve as a volunteer of the Caring Committee of Temple Emanuel and member of Temple Adult Volunteer Choir. Serve on Temple Worship Committee. Participate in Annual Memorial Day Sabbath Service and Veterans Day Sabbath Service as a member of JWV by being involved as a Lay reader and deliver sermon. Hobbies: writing poetry, golf

MURRAY GAILE, born Brooklyn, NY. Enlisted April 7 1943, Army 83rd Chem. Mortar Bn. 54th AIB. Military station Camp Upton, NY; Camp Landing, FL; Camp Jos. T Robinson, AR; Camp Patrick Henry, VA, POE; Algiers, Alg. Oran, Alg.; Tunis and Matur, Tunisia, Bizerte, Tunisia; Naples Capua, Venafro, San Pietro, Anzio, Rome, etc. Italy; Southern France; Louxenberg; Belgium; Germany; Austria; Czechoslovakia. Returned to Ft. Dix, NJ, USA approximate Oct. 14 1945, for discharge.

Battles participated in Ardennes, Central Europe, Naple Foggia, Rhineland, Rome Arno, Southern France, Anzio.

Memorable experience: Member of Honor Battalic representing entire 3rd U.S. Army to greet its Command Gen. George S. Patton Jr. on his return to Holzkirchen Fiel Bavaria, Germany, Approximately July 5, 1945.

Awards/Medals: Bronze Star; Good Conduct Meda American Campaign; EAME with seven Battle Stars ar Bronze Arrowhead for Invasion of South France; WWII Vi tory Medal; Occupation WWII with Germany Clasp; Belgi Croix De Guerre WWII with palm for Bastogne; Comb Infantryman's Badge; Presidential Unit Citation with OLC; Mark man M-1 Rifle; New York State Conspicuous Service Medal.

He was discharged Oct. 19, 1945, with the rank priva first class.

Married 1949, wife Sydney, son Harlan, daughter Robi grandson William. Business major CCNY on GI Bill. Ser retired account executive.

HERMAN GAINES, born in Lynn, MA, on Nov. 2 1909. Graduated from Northeastern University Law Scho and was admitted to the Massachusetts Bar in 1932. Practic law in Boston until 1942, when enlisted in the U.S. Co Guard. He was assigned to a Coast Guard unit on detach service with the U.S. Army Engr. Amph. Cmd. at Ca Edwards, MA. They were to instruct Army personnel in operation of landing craft for invading hostile territory by s

Later he attended Pay Clerk School at Curtis Bay, MD, and was promoted to pay clerk and transferred to the Coast Guard Training Station in Groton, CT, where he served as assistant supply officer and legal assistance officer.

He was then transferred to a USN troop transport, the *Gen. Grealey*, AP 141, which was being commissioned in California and was to be manned entirely by Coast Guard personnel. The *Grealey* accomplished an extraordinary feat; they sailed out of San Pedro on a shakedown cruise which turned into a trip around the world, serving as a troop transport.

He was discharged on Jan. 11, 1946, with the rank of chief warrant officer. He was awarded the following medals: American Campaign, EAME Campaign Medal, Asiatic-Pacific Campaign Medal, WWII Victory Medal.

His wife Edith and he have two children and five grandchildren. He is presently employed in the office of the Commissioner of Veterans' Services of Massachusetts.

HARRY GALPIRIN, born, Oct. 20, 1920, Buffalo, NY. Joined the service Oct. 13, 1942, and served in the Medics. Stationed at Camp Barkeley, TX; Camp Harahan, LA; Milne Bay, New Guinea; Tacloban; Leyte; Philippine Islands; Manila and Luzon as member of 49th General Hospital. Previous to that he was member of the 182nd General Hospital that went to England.

Memorable experiences include February 1944 as a passenger on the ship, *President Grant*, 10 miles from their overseas destination, Milne Bay, the ship hit a reef and they had to abandon it. Xmas Day 1944 he was in the middle of an air raid while a passenger on the U.S. Army hospital ship, the *Marigold*. March 2, 1945, while disembarking from LST-924, he saw Gen. MacArthur returning from Corregidor.

Awards/Medals: Good Conduct, five Battle Stars, Asiatic-Pacific and Philippine Liberation. Discharged Dec. 30, 1945, as PFC.

He is retired.

GLADYS LONSTEIN GAMAN, born June 28, 1917, Worcester, MA. Entered active duty Feb. 8, 1943, in the Army Nurse Corps as a 2nd lieutenant. Her major assignment was in the ETO in Braintree, England with the 121st Station Hospital which was surrounded by B-26 and B-17 air fields. Later transferred to the 112th General Hospital also in southern England. Worked in operating room, central supply, ward and charge duties.

Memorable experience was when on night duty covering three wards and they had direct hit. Fortunately very close to a Nissen hut ward that had been emptied the day before. She still recalls the scream of the bomb and the terror of realizing they would be hit. There was much damage, some casualties, but luckily no deaths.

Discharged Feb. 6, 1946, Ft. Ord. CA. Member of JWV Post 0220 Peabody, MA.

Married Manuel Gaman in June 1947, he passed away in February 1991, and has two sons, Steve and Philip. Would love to hear from the five Jewish nurses she served with at the 121st Station Hospital.

MANUEL H. GAMAN, born Oct. 3, 1914, Boston, MA. He was one of four brothers from Chelsea, MA who all served in the Infantry during WWII in ETO. Two brothers were injured, shrapnel and trench foot. Enlisted in the NG Nov. 10, 1940. Later joined the 6th Armd. Div. as a band clarinet player.

Saw active duty in battles of Northern France, Rhineland, Ardennes and Central Europe.

Awards/Medals: Good Conduct Medal, Bronze Star Medal and EAME Campaign Ribbon. Separated from the service Sept. 30, 1945, with the rank staff sergeant.

Married Gladys Lonstein in June 1947 and had two sons, Steve and Philip. Was member of JWV Post 0220 Peabody, MA. He passed away in February 1991.

MARTIN L. GANDERSON, USA, Ret., Colonel, born Richmond, VA, May 20, 1939; parents deceased; Lillian Price (1978), Maurice (1968); brother Victor, sister Sharon (Fink); daughters Celeste and Nora; six uncles served in WWII. Graduated Richmond Public Schools; USMA, 1961; commissioned Signal Corps; transferred Infantry 1964; Attended language schools, Armed Forces Staff Coll, Inf. Sch., Abn.

Sch., Med. William and Mary, 82nd Abn. 1961-63; Adv. Tm. 54, RVN, 1963-64; Inf. Sch. 1965-66; CoCO, January 1958-67; 1st Inf. Div. (Co. CO, BN S3, 2-2 and 1-16) 1968-69 RVN; HQ CONARC 1969-71; District Sr. Adv. 1972-73, RVN. HQ TRADOC 1973-76; Assist Army Attaché, Tel Aviv, 1977-81; USREDCOM, MacDill AFB 1981-84; Army War Coll 1984-87; U.S. Military Delegation to the United Nations 1988-89. Currently professor of military studies and national strategy, Army Management Staff Coll, Ft. Belvoir, VA. Scribe for USMA class; supporter of USMA Jewish Chapel; volunteer for local organizations. Served as military observer for the Vietnam Peace Treaty; took part in U.S. Embassy work for Camp David Accords; advisor to U.S. Ambassador to UN on U.S. military role in UN peacekeeping operations.

SIDNEY GANTMAN, as an aviation cadet was transferred into the Infantry when there were too many pilots waiting in the training pools. His final unit was the 103rd Div., 409th Inf. Wounded in France, he returned to duty after V-E Day. Transferred to the Corps of Engrs. Received a direct commission as a 2nd lieutenant and continued in the Reserves, retiring as lieutenant colonel.

His sister, Edna, was in the U.S. Nurse Cadet Corps. She was a student nurse at Beth Israel Hospital in Boston.

Brother Milton served with the Marines in the South Pacific in the 7th and 12th AA Bns. attached to the 1st Mar. Div. He was involved in the invasions of Peleliu and New Britain Islands and other lesser islands.

His father owned a "det." He cut the fat from the briskets (corned beef) which his mother rendered and gave to the war effort. Mother was also a regular blood donor to the Red Cross.

EDWARD GARBER, born in Poland on Aug. 19, 1915. He came with his family to the United States as a young boy and grew up in the Bronx. He entered the Army in March 1941 and was a member of the 165th Combat Engineers. He attained the rank of sergeant and was discharged in November 1945.

Fighting in Europe from France through Austria and Germany, his unit was surrounded during the Battle of the Bulge for several days. He always remembered the prejudice he encountered against Jews and Blacks while in basic train-

ing down South; the horror of Dachau, and his pride as a Jewish American taking part in victory over the Nazis.

Married to Ray; daughter, Pauline and son, Mark (USN 1972-76) with granddaughters, Elise and Lara. He worked in sales until his retirement and died in April 1993. We miss you, Dad.

JULIUS GARBER, born June 3, 1923, Milwaukee, WI. Joined the service April 29, 1943, with MOS Military Policeman 677. Assigned to Co. A, 141st Inf., 36th Div. Stationed in the States, North Africa, Italy, France and Germany.

Participated in Battle of Cassino, Naples-Foggia Campaign, Rome-Arno Campaign, Southern France Campaign and Rhineland Campaign. Wounded twice, Velletri, Italy and Alsace, France.

His memorable experiences include meeting President Truman at the White House, when freed from POW camp, having survived and coming home.

Awards/Medals: four Bronze Battle Stars, EAME Medal, Good Conduct Medal, Purple Heart with OLC, Combat Infantry Badge and POW Medal. Discharged Oct. 14, 1945, with rank of corporal.

Married and has one son and two grandsons. He is retired.

ROBERT D. GARDNER, born in Cleveland, OH, April 13, 1916. Entered the Army in February 1942, Ft. Knox, KY. He spent six months on the Mojave Desert in the 5th Armd. Div.

In 1943 he entered the Air Force to train for pilot training but could not complete the flight training as he was too old when they accepted by application as he was 26 years old and they did not catch his age until he was half through the course.

He then transferred to the AATC and became a radio operator on the DC 6 transport plane. He flew from Florida to South America and then on to North Africa. For 17 months he flew all over Africa and India to Italy, Greece and France. He was discharged in February 1945 and returned to Cleveland, OH.

He has been married since December 1941 and has two daughters. He retired from his business in 1987 and retired to Florida. He belonged to the JWV in Canton, OH, Post #073.

His mother wrote him while he was in Cairo, Egypt to see if he could go to Paris as she received a letter from her brother that just got out of a concentration camp and living outside Paris. He flew up to Paris on leave and brought them two large suit cases of cigarettes and coffee beans and clothing. They lived on the mdse. he gave them for two years trading the mdse. for food.

JEANETTE E. GARFINKEL, WAAC, enlisted in Buffalo, NY, where she was born on May 12, 1918. Enlisted right away in the WAAC on July 29, 1942, and stayed in when it became WAC, part of the Army until March 22, 1945.

Her most memorable experiences were when she met her husband, a second lieutenant and they dodged MP's for fraternization.

She also had many a laugh as she was one of the first WAACs and the Army didn't really know how to treat women. They had men officers!

Her late husband and she retired to Jerusalem and she is a member of JWV of USA, Post 180 and a national member too.

JACQUELINE GARRICK, when she joined the Army, it was several years after she had gotten her master's degree in social works. She had also been counseling combat Vietnam Veterans, and decided to see what it would be like to work with soldiers who had experienced more recent combat and other military related trauma.

She has spent the last few years at Walter Reed Army Medical Center covering various wards from neurology, the ICU, and now she is chief, in-patient psychiatry, social work service. In this capacity she has gotten to deal with a variety of veterans from WWII, Korea, Vietnam, Desert Storm, Somalia, and most recent, Croatia. Through these experiences, she has come to see that the effects of combat trauma do not just pertain to our Vietnam Veterans, but in every generation of combat survivor there are long lasting effects. The memories of a war zone do not go away, whether it is 50 years later or a few weeks ago. Images of liberating concentration camps in Eastern Europe, holding a dying buddy in An Hoa, or delivering food to the starving in Haiti are forever imprinted in the memories of those who bared witness. In sum, she can only hope that in her professional capacity, she can help some of these veterans make an easier transition to returning home.

MELVIN MOISH GART, born March 17, 1920, Denver, CO. His father was born in Brest Litoskt Russia and mother in Austria, Hungary area. Enlisted Dec. 5, 1941, served in the Infantry. Basic training was at Camp Roberts, CA. Stayed there until March 1945 when sent to the Philippines as a 2nd lieutenant. Assigned to the 32nd Inf. Div., 26th Inf. Bn., Co. G.

Memorable experience was being overrun by Japanese one night.

Awards/Medals: Asiatic-Pacific Service Medal, American Service Medal, Combat Infantry Medal, WWII Victory Medal, Philippine Liberation Medal with one Bronze Star. Discharged March 5, 1946, as 1st lieutenant.

Retired as VP of 52-chain sporting goods company, Gart Bros., SPTC Gas Co. He is married.

ARTHUR GEDULDIG, term of service 1956-58, U.S. Army, stationed in the Republic of Panama, MOS jungle expert training troops from Korea.

Presently married with two children; wife Claudine, son Paul with the Israel consulate and continuing studies with the University of Georgia masters program and daughter Monique attending the University of Miami. President of Dynamic Metals, Inc., President of Atlanta Men's ORT and previous President of ZOA.

LOUIS GEFFEN, born in New York City on Nov. 1, 1904, son of Rabbi and Mrs. Tobias Geffen. He was educated in Elementary and High School Systems of Atlanta, attended Emory University. Graduated in June 1920, with bachelor of arts degree with honors. Continued education at Columbia University, receiving doctor of laws degree in 1926. Practiced law in Atlanta from 1927, as general practitioner. Appointed captain, U.S. Army Reserve, Judge Advocate General's Corp. Ordered to active duty by President

Roosevelt in 1940, to report to Camp Shelby, MS, on Jan. 14, 1941, where he served as Post Judge Advocate for two years, continuing at Camp McCain, MS, and Camp McKall, NC.

Ordered to San Francisco there received orders sending him to the Philippines, assigned to the War Crimes section there. While in Manila, together with other Jewish Military Personal, he served as chairman to raise funds to rebuild the Jewish Synagogue there, which the Japanese had destroyed. Happily, he later learned in Japan, the money had been raised and the synagogue rebuilt!

He was later sent to Tokyo, Japan, to set up and organize the War Crimes Section. He personal served as chief prosecutor of the first War Crimes trial held in Japan. The nick-name of the accused was "Little Glass Eye." After a lengthy trial with the use of interpreters, he was convicted by a court of military officers, appointed by Gen. Douglas MacArthur. The accused was found guilty and given a life sentence.

After his military service, he returned to Atlanta to be with his family. He resumed civilian law practice here and renewed his civilian life. Participating in the activities of the community, he became interested in the JWV, serving in various offices and then was commander of Atlanta Post JWV 112.

Has now retired from his law practice, and resides in Atlanta together with his wife. Their son, Rabbi David Geffen, Ph.D. was a chaplain in the Army for two years at Ft. Sill, OK. Then he accepted the pulpit in Wilmington, DE, for 10 years, where he served successfully. Decided to go on Aliyah with his wife, two sons and a daughter in 1977. They reside in Jerusalem. Their granddaughter, Elissa, is happily married, has two sons, Ori and Leron. They are the proud great-grandparents.

MELVIN W. GELBER, USNR, Lt.(JG), born Aug. 14, 1923, Hackensack, NJ. Enlisted April 1942; active duty September 1942 in V-12. Graduated BS in mechanical engineering, University of Notre Dame, February 1944, Prairie State Midshipman School, NY, June 1944; General Motors Diesel School, Flint, MI, July 1944. Engineering officer, LST 621; boarded ship at Norfolk, VA, August 1944; served in Pacific Theater. Returned to San Francisco, August 1946.

Awards/Medals: Philippine Liberation Ribbon, Asiatic-Pacific Campaign Medal, Okinawa with one star, WWII Victory Medal.

Married Beverly Gilman, August 1948; five children (three girls and two boys); one grandchild.

Earned doctor of engineering science degree, May 1981, New Jersey Institute of Technology. Owner of Consulting Engineering firm, 1950 to present.

MAX GELFAND, trained at Camp Croft, Infantry Replacement Camp in South Carolina after 16 weeks basic training, including a short furlough, visiting wife and new baby at hospital in Bord Park, Brooklyn December 1943, embarked by ship from Virginia, with a convoy on a 30 day trip to Brindisi, Italy off Adriatic Coast.

Then joined up with Co. B, 142 Inf. Regt., 36th Inf. Div. with Gen. Mark Clark 5th Army. Fought through Caserta, Naples, Cassino, Rome, Anzio up to Pisa. Then training off Anzio, joined with a huge armada from Naples, Invaded Southern France Aug. 15, 1944.

Moving up north, past Remiremont, Grenoble, Lyons, Vosges Mountains, was hospitalized in Besancon near Swiss border. Then was reclassified into quartermaster in Paris with a QM Railroad Co. for 12 months. Was in-charge of warehouse, serving Army units with dot, soap, mops, brooms, brushes, prophylactics. Was billeted on Blvd. Diderot near the Bastille.

Left France December 1945 for discharge at Ft. Meade, MD, near his new home in Washington, D.C.

SANFORD JOSEPH GELFAND, born Dec. 4, 1913, Cleveland, OH. Entered the service Feb. 20, 1942; basic training at Ft. McClellan, AL. Sent to California to POE and arrived on one of the Cook Islands in the South Pacific. Assigned to 702nd Signal Air Warning Bn. in the ground forces where he became a supply clerk. His leg was burned in a fire while on the island.

His memorable experience was carrying radar system down a mountain during a hurricane. His company was cited for their achievement in disconnecting the radar.

Awards/Medals: After the war he received a Commendation from Gen. Richardson and later received the Asiatic-Pacific Medal and Good Conduct Medal. Was selected Veteran of the Year by his JWV Post in 1944. Discharged Sept. 15, 1945, as corporal.

Married March 16, 1947, wife died one month short of 30 years together. There are no children. Worked as a dry cleaning driver salesman for 25 years before retiring.

Chaplain for post, state and county, JWV, Paul A. Rosenblum Post 44 and also chaplain of Chap. 127, DAV in Maple Hts., OH.

JEROME H. GELLER (JERRY), born Pittsfield, MA, Oct. 19, 1923. His father, Arthur, was a WWI veteran. Jerry enlisted in the Army December 1942. He was stationed at various Army and Air Corps Camps: Camp Picket, VA, Greensboro, NC, Miami Beach, FL, and Rockford, IL. He served overseas in France and Germany with the 185th Medical Section and later the 388th Med. Collecting and Aerial Evacuation Co.

Jerry's authorized awards are: Good Conduct Medal; American Campaign Medal; EAME Theater Campaign Medal; Army of Occupation of Germany Medal and WWII Victory Medal; two Bronze Stars for Rhineland and Central European Campaigns. His highest rank was corporal T/5 awarded in Germany. Honorably discharged April 1946.

Graduated University of Massachusetts 1948. Married Diana Pines, Philadelphia, PA, Oct. 18, 1953. Jerry taught science at Herberg Middle School for 32 years, retiring at age 67. Diana works for Pittsfield School Department (24 years).

Their elder son, Nate, graduated Brandeis University, married Marilyn Light. Their daughter is Aliza age 8 and son Jaacov (Koby) is age 5. Nate directs Manhattan office of National Conf. On Soviet Jewry. Lyn works for Manhattan Jewish Federation. They live in Teaneck, NJ.

Their younger son, Andy, graduated University Massachusetts, lives in Manhattan, and has been employed by the Jewish Theological Seminary.

Jerry is active in KI Shul and is a member in good standing of Louis Green Post 140, JWV, Pittsfield, MA.

IRWIN D. GERECHOFF, born Dec. 26, 1931, in Asbury Park, NJ. Enlisted Sept. 9, 1952, U.S. Army, Combat

Medic, 7th Div. assigned to Combat Engr. Stationed in Korea and Chorwon Valley. Participated in battles at Old Baldy and Pork Chop Hill.

Memorable experience " I was a combat medic attached to a engineer company. One day I was helping carry a wounded soldier down a hill at the 38th parallel. When I came down to the bottom of the hill, a jeep with a stretcher was waiting. Upon putting the wounded soldier on the stretcher I asked the driver, "What happens to the wounded?" The driver explained that they are driven to a medical sorting station. From there they are assigned to different hospitals or hospital ships to be sent home. Those who were more seriously wounded would be put on helicopters for another destination. I didn't understand what the driver meant until I saw the T.V. series "Mash" years later. Then I realized I was part of the medical chain in helping our wounded.

Awards/Medals: Korean Service Medal with two Bronze Service Stars. United Nations Service Medal, National Defense Service Medal.

He was discharged July 31, 1954, with the rank of private first class.

Married to Nancy, two children, son Russell and daughter Abbey. Real estate broker, he owns his own agency, G&G Realtors, Deal, NJ, Monmouth County.

SAMUEL R. GERSH, born in Brooklyn, NY, Oct. 8, 1930. Studied physics and mathematics at Brooklyn College. Entered U.S. Army of Engineers July 15, 1951. Assigned to various pre-OCS duties at Ft. Dix, NJ, and the Pentagon, Washington, D.C. Designated lead NCO at the 13th Artillery Park, Ascom City, Korea. Subsequent to POW Repatriation Oct. 20, 1993, was assigned to personnel administration 8th Army HQ Seoul, Korea. Beginning December 1953, they gathered several members of the Jewish persuasion to build a brick-enclosed synagogue building on the main road inside the 8th Army HQ, Young-Dong-Po, Korea, which was dedicated the first Sabbath services in April 1954. Those persons working with Gersh were Albert Chernick, Victor Sklar, Bill Magliaro, and a team of 10 Korean-indigenous persons. Relieved of active duty July 3, 1960. Presently retired from U.S. Defense Logistics Agency volunteering most of spare time as adjutant of the JWV and executive board director for service and membership of the DAV in "Big-D" Dallas, TX.

LOUIS GERSHMAN, born Grand Forks, ND. Enlisted Oct. 24, 1941, U.S. Army, Engineers. Stationed all over the U.S. Participated in battles in Normandy and beyond.

Memorable experience includes landing Omaha Beach D-day.

Received eight medals.

He was discharged Dec. 30, 1945, with the rank of staff sergeant.

He is married and has six children and eight grandchildren. Today he is consulting.

LEWIS GERSHOWITZ

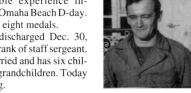

GORDON M. GERSON SR., born Oct. 2, 1936, New York City. Commissioned June 4, 1958. Graduated from the USNA in 1958. Commissioned in the USAF, served for 21 years. Received master's degree in electrical engineering from University of Michigan (1965); Ph.D. in computer science from University of Texas (1971); taught computer science at AFIT for six years. Served as chief of quality control, 505th Tac. Control Group, RVN 1966-67.

Awards/Medals: Bronze Star, Meritorious Service Medal, Defense Meritorious Service Medal, campaign service awards.

He retired May 31, 1979, with the rank of lieutenant colonel, USAF.

His son is a USAF captain, M.D. at Lackland AFB, TX. Today he is an independent computer consultant.

EMANUEL GERSTERN, born Bronx, NYC, June 10, 1916. Inducted April 10, 1942, Ft. Jay, NY, 362nd MP Escort Guard. Stations include Camp Upton, Long Island; Camp Bowie, Basic Texas; OCS North Dakota State College, Fargo, ND January 1943; POW Camp, Scottsbluff, NE (Guard). Left

Ft. Hamilton, NY, April 1, 1943; arrived Oran, North Africa, April 13, 1943. Departed Oran April 18, 1943, with Italian POW. Arrived in USA April 30, 1943.

Awards/Medals: American Service Medal, EAME Service Medal, Good Conduct Medal, WWII Victory Medal.

Married 46 years, one son married and one granddaughter 10 years old. At this writing he is working in a greenhouse garden center, part-time 30 hours per week.

BEATRICE ESTHER GIBBS, born Oct. 16, 1918. Inducted Nov. 10, 1942, USNR WAVES, Aer M 1/c. Stations include Pensacola, FL, after boot training at Cedar Falls IO and primary aerographers training at Lakewood, NJ.

Memorable experience is friendships with sailors and WAVES. Finding Jewish services and holiday experiences in unfamiliar places. Serious study for advancement. Financial management on $30 a month.

She was discharged Sept. 15, 1945.

She is a librarian, traveler and grandmother. Her children are Paula, Bonnie, Marian, Ben.

DAVID B. GOLDBERG/AKA DAVID B. GILBERT, born Sept. 3, 1931, Chicago, IL. Enlisted Jan. 15, 1952, USCG, Aviation. Military stations include Cape May, NJ, basic; Groton, CT, Radio School; Elizabeth City, NC, aviation electronics; St. Petersburg, FL, Air Station.

Memorable experiences include being crew member on mercy flight to save life of severely injured doctor, off the southwest tip of Cuba. Landed at sea and successfully transferred the injured man to the Coast Guard PBM plane and flew to Miami Hospital (and innumerable other search and rescue missions).

Awards/Medals: National Defense Service Medal.

He was discharged Jan. 14, 1955, with the rank of aviation electronicsman third class.

Married to the late Judy Lee Schwartz, loving wife of 28 years. Three children, Mitch, Melody and Cliff Gilbert, brother of Norman J. Goldberg, USAF. Real estate broker, D.B. Gilbert Realty, Washington, D.C. Also, he and wife are well known artists, with paintings in the collections of Pres. Jimmy Carter and Prime Minister Margaret Thatcher.

PAUL N. GILBERT, a bomber pilot in the 8th Air Force during WWII. They were shot down once and had to ditch in the North Sea. They completed 35 bombing missions in which their entire crew of 10 survived.

After the War, he completed his education under the GI Bill at UCLA and received his BA degree in business administration. He is a CPA and has been active as a tax accountant in Los Angeles and now in Palm Springs. He was married and divorced and has one child who wants to be a pilot.

Awards/Medals: Distinguished Flying Cross

JEROME J. GILDEN, M.D. born in St. Louis, MO. Joined the Army Infantry Jan. 20, 1944. Assigned to 253rd Regt., Co. F and HQ Co. 253rd Regt., 63rd Inf. Div. Stationed at Ft. Benning, GA for basic training (ASTP); Camp Van Dorn, MS, basic and advanced including Ranger Plt. and ETO.

Participated in action at Battle of the Bulge, Rhineland, Central Europe Campaign, from Saareguemines across the Rhine to Munich.

Memorable experiences include special battle patrol activities co-ordinated by regiment S-2. Numerous patrols were made in squads of 2-5, crossing the Saar River in rubber boats. Missions were accomplished under small arms fire and crossing mine fields. Movements were slow and extremely hazardous. This work aided in securing valuable troop information on enemy troop dispositions with 16 prisoners captured by their patrol.

Awards/Medals: Combat Infantry Badge, WWII Victory Ribbon, Bronze Star with two OLCs, EAME Theater, two Overseas Bars and Good Conduct Medal. Discharged March 16, 1946, with the rank staff sergeant.

M.D. with specialty orthopedic surgery; chief, Division of Ortho Surgery Jewish Hospital of St. Louis, Washington University Medical Center. Married 45 years to former Annette Londe, has four children and two grandchildren.

GERALD GILLMAN, born in Brooklyn, NY, on Nov. 27, 1921. Graduated high school. Inducted on July 31, 1945, Quartermaster Corps. Inducted at Ft. Meade, MD, and had basic training at Camp Blanding, FL, then shipped overseas to occupied West Germany. In Amberg, West Germany he processed incoming and outgoing enlisted men, supervised laundry and dry-cleaning facilities for battalion, kept supply records and books and procured clothing and equipment to supply troops. Subsequently he transferred to Frankfort, West Germany at U.S. HQ and worked for a major in his office.

Memorable experience is on the way home to the U.S. on a troop ship he guarded official secret German documents.

Awards/Medals: Army of Occupation Medal and WWII Victory Medal.

He was discharged Dec. 21, 1946, with the rank of private first class.

Married to Trudy and have a son and a daughter, with five grandchildren. Today he is retired from the U.S. Government after 40 years at the Interstate Commerce Commission and the U.S. Customs Service. After retirement from the government, he became active with the National Association of Retired Federal Employees (NARFE) serving as financial secretary and president of Chapter 260 Silver Spring, MD. Also became active with the JWV of the USA. He is a life member of Joseph F. Barr Post #58, serving as post commander for three year and as commander of the District of Columbia Department for one year. He was awarded Post Commander of the Year plaque and a Career Achievement Award plaque.

BERNARD A. GILMAN, Major, Hartford, CT, served in the U.S. Army for 22 years and retired in 1974. A younger brother, Leon Gilman retired from the U.S. Navy Reserves in 1977, after serving in WWII and the Korean War.

Major Gilman is a graduate of the University of Richmond and received a master's degree from Trinity College and the University of Hartford. He served in the Pacific area in WWII, as well as in Korea immediately following WWII.

Decorations include the Asiatic-Pacific Campaign Medal with one Battle Star, Philippine Liberation Ribbon, American Defense, American Theater Medal, WWII Victory Medal,

Armed Forces Reserve Medal, Defense Service Medal, four overseas bars. Attended the Command and General Staff College at Ft. Leavenworth.

Married to Eleanor Goldberg (deceased 1980), two step-children and seven grandchildren, Member Post 045, West Hartford, CT.

Employed as a guidance counselor at Hartford Public High School. Served on various military bases in the United States, including Panama, Alaska and Hawaii.

KURT GIMSON, born and brought up in the city of Krefeld, Germany and shortly after his 14th birthday Hitler and the Nazis took over the government. During the next five years the pressure and privations on all citizens who resisted Nazi policies in particular upon Jews was ever increasing culminating in the horror of "Kristallnacht" (Nov. 9-10, 1938) which he experienced in its full impact until leaving the country in January 1939.

Emigrated to the U.S. in February 1939, and settled in Paterson, NJ. Exactly two years later, entered the U.S. Army and after basic training was assigned to the 161st Signal Photo Co. at Ft. Benning, GA, where he spent the next two years as photographic laboratory technician.

In March 1943 the entire company went overseas to the South Pacific Theater of War. He became supervisor of a movable photo processing laboratory in an especially designed trailer unit to be set up in combat areas to serve military processing needs of films and prints. Participated in the Solomon Islands campaign with a crew of five men starting on Guadalcanal, then was in the front wave of the invasion of Rendova Island from the flagship *McCauley* (under Adm. William Halsey), where they set up lab operations 24 hours later under extremely trying conditions while suffering relatively large casualties. After operating on Rendova for two months they got ready to transfer everything to the next island, New Georgia with its only "Munda" Air Strip north of Guadalcanal, where they set up the processing lab and operated same for two months under XIV Corps Commander Gen. Griswold. Then on to Bougainville Island amidst bombing attacks and survived one severe earthquake. Their unique laboratory activities in the jungles of Bougainville are documented in National Geographic, Vol. 86, #3 September 1944, pages 264, 272.

He was discharged Nov. 19, 1945, staff sergeant.

Many months after his discharge, he learned that 14 members of his family perished in concentration camps and death camps in Eastern Europe.

JACK GINN, born Aug. 24, 1918, Brooklyn, NY. Enlisted July 21, 1941, 47th Inf., 9th Div. Stationed at Camp Croft, Spartenberg, SC; Ft. Bragg, NC; Morocco, North Africa.

Participated in action in Tunisia, Germany, Battle of the Bulge, Sicily, liberation of Normandy. His memorable experience was D-day, Normandy.

Awards/Medals: EAME Campaign Ribbon with seven Bronze Stars, Purple Heart, Combat Infantry Badge, Bronze Star, Distinguished Unit Citation and WWII Victory Medal. Was discharged March 31, 1946, with rank of sergeant.

Has wife Sarah; two daughters, Francine and Michelle; five grandchildren and two great-grandchildren. Retired and now living in Century Village, Boca Raton.

IRVING GINSBURG, born Jan. 19, 1921, Syracuse, NY. Graduated from Central High School in June 1939. Played quarterback on high school football team. Enlisted in USCGR in 1942. Killed when the boat he was in capsized at Lighthouse Station, Oswego, NY, on Dec. 2, 1942, at the age of 21.

NATHAN GISCHE, entered the service Feb. 16, 1943, at Ft. Dix, NJ, after which he was sent to Camp Wheeler, GA, for basic training. Then assigned to 35th General Hospital Camp Harahan, New Orleans, LA, and trained to be a dental technician. On to Camp Barkley, Abilene, TX, and then to Ft. Lawton, OK, until February 1944, after which shipped to New Guinea, and transferred to special services office new assignment and made technician T/5.

After serving in New Guinea for one year, shipped to Philippines to Base M Sore Fernando in Northern Philippines and spent 10 months there. Then shipped to Tacloborn, Leyte to 710th Tank Bn. for a couple of months, after which returned to U.S. in January 1946. Finally arriving at Ft. Dix, NJ, and honorably separated Jan. 22, 1946.

Along the way received the following awards and decorations: American Theater of Operations Ribbon, Asiatic-Pacific Theater of Operations Ribbon, Philippine Liberation Ribbon, three Battle Stars (New Guinea, Luzon) Philippine Liberation Medal, Good Conduct Medal of Service 710th Tank Bn.

ARMAND GISSIN, born Aug. 28, 1928, Rochester, NY. USMC, stations: Tsingtao, China HDQ CO QM Section 3rd Bn. 4th Marines. Participated in the occupation of China 1945 to 1947.

Memorable experience: "From Paris Island after only two months of training I left for China with the 96th Replacement on the USS W*akefield* from all the experience I had from growing up and working at Busch & Lomb and being a member of NY State Guards, my second day in China my company commander only a lieutenant picked me to be acting supply sergeant. This I did for all the time that I was in Tsingtao. I did a real good job and thanks to the Navy, I was able to board their ships for supplies and manage to keep every one happy in the 3rd Bn.

Awards/Medals: Good Conduct Medal.

He was discharged March 27, 1947, with the rank of private first class.

Married Ruth Narzissfeld April 15, 1951, two sons Bernard and Steven. Manager of Gissin Electric, Rochester, NY, until 1964. In 1965 moved to Miami, FL, now he owns Trail Lighting and Electrical Products, he is the president.

HARRY M. GLASS, born New York, NY. Commissioned in 1935, active duty 1942-46, veterinary officer, MOS3200, 56th QM Base Depot.

Awards/Medals: German Occupation, American Campaign, EAME with two Battle Stars, WWII Victory Medal.

He was discharged May 1946, with the rank captain. Today he is Professor Emeritus and involved in community actives.

RICHARD GLASS, born Aug. 16, 1924. Enlisted May 27, 1943. Died Nov. 10, 1944, at the age of 20.

ARNOLD J. GLASSER, born Oct. 5, 1917, in Brooklyn, NY. Entered the Army on Jan. 11, 1943. Stationed at Massachusetts, Canada, Florida, Georgia and Okinawa.

Awards/Medals: Asiatic-Pacific Campaign Medal, Central Command Expert Rifleman.

He was discharged April 15, 1946, with the rank of second lieutenant.

Today he is very much alive and in the textile business.

SHIRLEY LEFF GLASSMAN, Delray Beach, FL, the Medical Corps of the Women's Army Corps (WAC) veterans, Shirley Leff Glassman of Delray Beach, FL, and Thelma Ash-Moskowitz of Westwood, NJ, were reunited 45 years after they met in basic training during WWII. The emotional moment occurred at the home of Shirley's son and his wife, Ron and Meryl Glassman of Edison, NJ, on May 7, just a few hours before the start of VE Day.

"We trained in Ft. Ogelthorp, GA, and were transferred to Kennedy Gen. Hosp. In Memphis, TN, and later went on the Army and Navy Hospital in Hot Springs, AR," Shirley explained to the 50+ friends and relatives gathered to witness their meeting.

Born in Bayonne and Passaic, respectfully, Thelma and Shirley spent 14 months in the service. Shirley is married to Paul, a realtor, and Thelma's husband is a retired teacher. The Army pals were honorably discharged at Ft. Dix, NJ, never to see each other again until May 7. Thelma studied art in college and Shirley practiced (registered) nursing for over 40 years.

After getting involved in Florida's Gold Coast Women's Veteran's Group in 1994, Shirley got to thinking more about Thelma's whereabouts. "Shirley picked up the phone and called me out of the blue at a number she had for over 30 years. I answered and it was if no time had passed between us. It was old times all over again," says Thelma. "I recognized Thelma's soft voice immediately. All it took was a short hello and I knew it was her," says Shirley.

"We spent most of the day looking over old pictures, talking about our Army days and, of course, our grandchildren," says Shirley. "I am so thankful that Ron and Meryl made this moment possible."

The two friends agreed to meet again soon ... this time on the sunny shores of Florida.

SAUL GLASSMAN, born in Brooklyn, NY, on June 4, 1922. Attended PS 128, Seth Low Jr. High School, New Utrecht High School and Pre-Law at St. John's University. While studying at St. John's, he was drafted into the Army and

traded his law books for a Browning Automatic Rifle. He performed his basic training at Camp Upton. He was subsequently assigned to the 243rd Coast Artillery Bn. He was honorably discharged from the service in February 1946. He started law school all over again at New York Law School from where he graduated in 1950. He maintained a private law practice until 1975, at which time he became an administrative law judge. He is currently senior administrative law judge, branch manager and branch legal director for the New York City Environmental Control Board. He married Rose Roskin in 1949. They have two children, Iris and Kenneth, and four grandchildren. Member of Post 2 JWV.

NORMAN GLASSMAN, D.D.S., born June 1, 1929, in Newark, NJ. Entered the USAF on July 1955, Medical Unit, 3550th USAF Hosp., Moody AFB, Valdosta, GA. He was discharged July 1957, with the rank of captain. Today he is a retired dentist.

IRVING GLAZER, born Sept. 29, 1921, Bridgeport, CT. Entered U.S. Army, August 1943, Ft. Devens, MA. Basic training, Ft. Belvoir, VA, Corp of Engineers. Shipped overseas to England March 14, 1944. Assigned to 1st Engr. Amph. (Special) Brig. 531st Engr Shore Regt., demolition specialist.

Embarked for the Normandy invasion June 2, 1944, landing on Utah Beach, D-day, H-Hour (June 6, 1944, 0630). Squad assignment: destroy enemy water obstacles, clear beach and sand dunes of minefields (while under enemy fire) to secure the beach for assault forces.

Battles and Campaigns: Normandy, Northern France, Rhineland and Central Europe.

Decorations: EAME Theater Campaign Ribbon with Bronze Service Arrowhead and four Battle Stars, French Croix DeGuerre with palm, WWII Victory Medal with service star. Discharged Jan. 5, 1946.

Married Visselle Gold June 8, 1952, three children, four grandchildren. Graduated 1975 Bridgeport Engineering Institute, BS electrical engineering. Retired 1987 as a senior test engineer. Member JWV Post 88.

NATHAN B. GLAZER, born Nov. 23, 1919. Served from January 1942 to October 1945 in USAAC, flew in the European Theater during war in France and received the Air Medal with two OLCs.

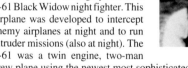

He flew in the highly secretive P-61 Black Widow night fighter. This airplane was developed to intercept enemy airplanes at night and to run intruder missions (also at night). The P-61 was a twin engine, two-man crew plane using the newest most sophisticated secretive airborne radar during WWII.

Married to Roslyn Feb. 12, 1944, and they have four children and seven grandchildren.

SHERWIN I. GLAZER, born in Syracuse, NY, in 1924. He enlisted in the Army Air Corps in January 1943, at the age of 18. He was commissioned a second lieutenant on Sept. 30, 1944. As an 8th AF B-17 Flying Fortress navigator based in England, he participated in bombing missions over Germany. Decorated with the Air Medal and OLC, his 385th Heavy Bombardment Group received a Presidential Unit Citation. After Germany surrendered, he participated in mercy missions dropping food to the starving people of the Netherlands and flew displaced persons from Austria back to France.

He returned to Syracuse University in 1945, and completed his studies to earn a bachelors degree in business administration in 1949. He married Lillian Biberberg, of Newark, NJ, in 1952, and has a son, Bradley, of Beachwood, OH, and a daughter, Julia, of Somerville, NJ, and five grandchildren. He owned and operated a furniture business in Syracuse for 40 years, retiring in 1989 at the age of 64. He now does various volunteer work, including reading to the visually handicapped over public radio.

SAUL H. GLOSSER, born Wilkes-Barre, PA. Enlisted June 3, 1943, USAF. Military station included Ft. Sill, OK; Amarillo, TX; Fairmont, NE; Wendover, UT; Tinian Island, Marianas; Roswell, NM; Santa Ana, CA.

Memorable experience: Member of 393rd, 509th Composite Group (first atomic bombardment).

Awards/Medals: Asiatic-Pacific Campaign Medal, Good Conduct Medal, WWII Victory Medal.

He was discharged Feb. 14, 1946, with the rank of corporal.

He is married to Faye and has a daughter Sharon. Retired Detroit school teacher.

ROBERT GLUCK, born Springfield, MA. Enlisted Jan. 20, 1942, Army Air Corps. Stationed Ridgewell, England. Schweinfort August 1943, Kiel 1943, heavy water plant Norway.

Memorable experience being shot down on Oct. 8, 1943, POW 19 months in Germany.

Awards/Medals: Distinguished Flying Cross, Air Medal with three clusters, P.H. POW Medal, etc.

He retired as lieutenant colonel.

Married Sylvia Graiver Baston, three sons, Paul Stewart, and Ronald. Retired and enjoying life.

IRVING GLUCOFT, born July 16, 1920, Chicago, IL, and eventually became a business and psychology major at New York University in 1940. In August 1942 entered U.S. Army during WWII, served in ETO and honorably discharged in November 1945 at Ft. Monmouth, NJ.

Participated in basic training at Camp Gordon, Augusta, GA. Spent three and a half years as HQ clerk (Corporal) with the 1st Army 45th Evacuation (Mobile) Hospital in the USA, in England, France, Belgium and Germany.

Awards/Medals: American Campaign Medal, EAME Campaign Medal with Silver Star (for Omaha Beach Normandy landing and for Battle of Bulge), Army of Occupation Medal (for Liberation of Buchenwald Concentration Camp, Germany), WWII Victory Medal, Good Conduct Medal, Meritorious Service Unit Plaque awarded to hospital staff as citation by U.S. Surgeon General for performing the highest standards in military medical and surgical service in WWII.

Married to Iris Neuberg Glucoft, artist and fiction writer, since January 1962. Family includes son Gary, daughter Amy and son-in-law Fred with grandsons Jesse and Steven.

While in Germany in 1945, as unit historian edited and published book, *Medical Service in Combat,* which is presently included in the library of Congress Collection in Washington.

Retired since 1990 a salesman and purchasing agent from Lockheed Aircraft Corp., world-wide exporter of aviation equipment. Presently member of Bronx, NY Post #107 JWV, also serving as volunteer at the Bronx Veterans Administration Medical Center.

BENJAMIN GNESHIN, (Greshin) Army, Panama Defense Command, 1944-1946, Technician 4th Class.

JACOB GNESHIN, 82nd (All American) Div., 1917-19. Battles stars: Argonne Forest, St. Mihiel, Meuse Argonne, Belleau Woods, Chateau Thiery. Served in Sahe Regt. as Sergeant Alvin York.

JESSIE COHEN GNESHIN, (Past National President Ladies Auxiliary JWV) Brooklyn Navy Yard, Yeoman (F) 1st Class (Yeomanette), 1917-19.

STANLEY GNESHIN, (Greshin) Army, Chemical Warfare Branch, 1951-53, private.

CARL GOCHMAN, S.M., born Dec. 2, 1925, in Philadelphia, PA. Educated in South Philadelphia High School and Temple University as chemistry major. Enlisted in U.S. Army Air Corp on Dec. 2, 1943. Basic training in Ft. Benning, GA. Due to color blindness was transferred to 87th Inf. Div. at Ft. Jackson, SC. Trained as a 60mm mortar gunner of the Co. I 4th Plt., 3rd Bn. 347th Inf. Regt. went overseas on the *Queen Elizabeth,* docked in Scotland Firth or Fourth and was billeted in Knutsford, England. First combat engagement helped capture forts in Southern France, Metz. Division moved on to Saar Valley became squad leader and won Bronze Star for directing mortar fire on German machine gun nest which had pinned down entire battalion's move forward. Destroyed nest under adverse murderous fire. Helped crush Germany's Siegfried line, pill boxes with heavy loses to their regiment. Division brought back to Rheins, France for rest of two days. Shipped via truck to battle position outside of St. Vith, Belgium. They were now part of Patton's Third Army to crush the Battle of the Bulge.

Knocked out two tiger tanks while guarding crossroads with bazooka shells. Division shipped to make Rhine River Crossing on Easter Sunday. Hoping to surprise Germans. They were waiting for them. Under smoke screen from Air Force. Crossing to initial landing, they took a heavy toll in lives. After taking beach and Remagen Bridge and Coblenz going through Germany was fairly easy. Germans were surrendering to them rather than be captured by Russians.

They linked up with Russians outside of Plauene, in Czechoslovakia. Stayed in Army of Occupation. The division was shipped back to U.S. for 30 day leave. The 87th Div. was to be refitted and geared up to go to Pacific Theater of Operation for the invasion of Japan Homeland. But the war ended and he was discharged on March 16, 1946. Returned to work as a research chemist for Wyeth Labs. Retired from there after 40 years. He married Shirley in 1949, has two sons, Alan and Larry, one granddaughter Pamela Staci.

Still live in Philadelphia. He was past president of Overbrook Park Bnai Brith, past president of Wolfe Baron Lodge #56. Active board of trustee of Congregation Beth T'Fillah. Very active as scoutmaster of Troop 218 Boy Scouts of America for 53 years. Eagle Scout, plus many other awards. Belong to veteran groups, JWV, American Legion, VFW. Enjoy collecting scouting stamps, going camping and photography and he still stays in tough with his buddies of the Army through his membership in the 87th Div. Assoc.

SAMUEL GOLD, born Nov. 12, 1915, Rocky Hill, CT. Enlisted Feb. 4, 1942, inducted at Ft. Devens, MA, 7th Air Force, 98 SQ., airplane maintenance technician, B-17s - B-24s. Keesler Field, MS, five and a half months at Aeronautical University, Chicago, IL; Hickham Field, Air Offensive; Japan; Central Pacific; Eastern Mandates; Western Pacific. Discharged Nov. 15, 1945, technician sergeant. Serviced the B-29 that dropped the first Atomic Bomb on Japan. American Medal, Asiatic-Pacific Campaign Medal, Bronze Star, WWII Victory Medal.

Married Beatrice Sigal, 1946, three sons, Jerrold (CPA) Leonard (P.E.) Barry (D.Sc.). Four grandchildren: Leah, Abby, Jessie and Andrew. Life member of 11th Bombardment Group (H) Association. Member JWV since 1945. Retired and enjoying life.

PAUL GOLDBAND, born July 4, 1916, New York City. Volunteered Nov. 29, 1940, U.S. Army, 82nd Airborne paratrooper (20 jumps). Military stations included Ft. Dix, Ft. Lewis, Camp Upton, Ft. Bragg. Participated in Ardennes Central Europe, Normandy, Rhineland.

Memorable experience is being present at D-day at Normandy, liberation of death camp of Ludwiglust.

Awards/Medals: Bronze Star, Presidential Unit Citation, American Campaign Medal, EAME Campaign Medal, Parachute Badge with Rifle Bar, Good Conduct Medal, Combat Infantry Medal.

He was discharged honorably Sept. 20, 1945, with the rank of corporal.

He and his wife Pauline have three children and six grandchildren. Retired manager community store, mental health unit. Now living in Deerfield Beach, FL. Member JWV #196 Pompano, FL.

AVROME DAVID GOLDBERG, born March 12, 1925, Little Rock, AR. Enlisted June 12, 1943, U.S. Army, Finance Department, trained at Ft. Benjamin Harrison, IN. Military locations included ODB, Newark, NJ; Finschhafen, New Guinea; Camp Chaffee, AR. Participated in battle in the New Guinea Campaign.

Memorable experiences include crossing equator and debarking at Espirto Santo for recreation.

Awards/Medals: Good Conduct Medal, Asiatic-Pacific Theater Ribbon with one star, American Theater Ribbon, Victory Ribbon.

He was discharged March 6, 1946, with the rank of technician 3.

Married to Jean, one daughter, Ellen, one son, Louis. Still working for Sysco Food Service and predecessors since 1950.

BEATRICE ZOLITKOFSKY GOLDBERG, born

in Brooklyn, NY, on June 3, 1920. Graduated Bellevue School of Nursing, February 1944. Entered ANC Feb. 1, 1944, Discharged March 1946, as first lieutenant. Basic training Atlantic City, MO Worked as neuro-psycbiatec and general duty nurse in Utica, also England, France and Germany.

Awards/Medals: ETO Ribbon, WWII Victory Medal.

Married to Seymour for 45 years, two daughters and three grandchildren. Worked as school nurse at Queenboro Community College for 13 years before retirement to Liberty, NY.

HARRY GOLDBERG, born in New York City, the oldest

son in the family of eight children and was one of three brothers and two brothers-in-law to serve in WWII. Inducted into the Army on March 3, 1942, at Camp Upton and served in the U.S. Pacific Northwest guarding the U.S. coastline. Volunteered for Parachute Training School at Ft. Benning, GA, in early 1944, and was assigned to the 82nd Airborne Div. as a combat infantry paratrooper 517th Regt. A then reassigned to the 504th due to

heavy casualties. Participated in the following battles and campaigns earning five Battle Stars: Ardennes (Battle of the Bulge), Central Europe, Naples-Foggia, Rhineland and Rome-Arno. Injured while he and another paratrooper carried a severely wounded comrade down a mountainside in the dark of night. Combat conditions removed a lot of formalities and while rank was that of private first class, best friends in Co. G were Lt. Herman Lang and Aaron Shore the only two other Jewish soldiers in this company of the 517th. Served one year eight months in Europe and quoting from the 517th calendar date of June 18, 1944, "met first Germans (on business, not socially)," engaging the enemy many times. Discharged Nov. 18, 1945. Received invitation from Col. "Mickey" Marcus to serve as trainer of troops in Israeli War of Independence but declined to do so because of family responsibilities by this time. Passed away 1990 survived by wife, Rose, son, daughter-in-law and one grandson.

HERBERT S. GOLDBERG, born Oct. 30, 1925,

Asheville, NC. Enlisted Sept. 18, 1943, U.S. Navy, RM 3/c, USS *Menifee* (APA202) The *Menifee* carried troops and cargo to many islands in the South Pacific. Participated in battle in the invasion of Okinawa.

Memorable experience being the first troopship to bring occupation troops to Nagasaki; one month after the atomic bomb blasted the city. Kamikaze plane just missed their super-structure and crashed into the sea off their fantail, just off Okinawa.

Awards/Medals: Battle Star of Okinawa.

He was discharged April 16, 1946, with the rank of RM 2/c.

Married Helen Lipman Oct. 15, 1950. Have three grown children and six grandchildren. After retiring from Charleston Naval Shipyard in 1984 as an electronics engineer for 34 years he is now with Century 21 selling residential real estate.

HOWARD I. GOLDBERG, born March 8, 1922,

Brooklyn, NY. Enlisted Sept. 12, 1942, Signal Corps. Military locations included Camp Crowder, MO, and Camp Reynolds, PA. Participated in battles in Normandy, France, Belgium, Ardennes, Germany.

Memorable experience: "The whole damn thing, from Camp Upton to the victory ship which brought me home."

Awards/Medals: five Battle Stars and the Good Conduct Medal, American Service Medal, EAME Service Medal, WWII Victory Medal.

He was discharged Dec. 31, 1945, with the rank of staff sergeant.

Married 50 years in December 1993. Three children, two grandchildren and at this writing one on the way. Licensed electrician in New York City.

HYMAN GOLDBERG, summary of act for which Lt.

Hyman Goldberg was awarded Distinguished Service Cross.

On April 6, 1943, 2nd Lt. Hyman Goldberg, while engaging in high altitude bombardment mission against enemy shipping, distinguished himself above and beyond the call of duty.

Just prior to beginning the bombing run on the target, Lt. Goldberg's B-17 was attacked by enemy fighters. During this attack, a 20mm cannon struck and exploded in Lt. Goldberg's back, blowing his parachute and inflicting critical wounds with such violence as to throw him from his bombardiers' seat to the floor of the aircraft. One hole four inches in diameter was ripped from the right lumbar region of his back with two smaller wounds two inches in diameter adjacent. In addition, shell fragments pierced and lodged in the peritoneal cavity.

Because of lacerated muscles, he was unable to move, but despite his acute pain, loss of vast quantities of blood, and the high altitude, Lt. Goldberg refused first aid offered by Lt. B. Aikens, Royal Navy Volunteer Reserve who was present in the bombardiers compartment as an observer. Lt. Goldberg demanded to be lifted back to his bombsight, at the same time appealing to Lt. Aikens to man the nose machine guns. Mindful only of his responsibility as lead bombardier for his element, he then proceeded to synchronize his sights on the target, even though he had to be held upright on his seat, drop his bombs, report "Bombs Away," and close the bomb bay doors.

His actions were not futile, since these and other bombs of the flight caused immense damage to the target through his unerring skill. Furthermore, upon return to the become so intensely painful that medical officers were unable to remove him from his seat at the bomb sight and had to administer an intravenous anesthetic before they could remove him to the ambulance.

Through the whole of his action, Lt. Goldberg thought and acted with supreme devotion to his duty and responsibility and with no regard whatsoever for his own perilous position. He carried out a difficult task under extreme hazards in a manner of extraordinary heroism, which through his gallantry, endurance, courage and absolute devotion to duty, reflects the highest credit to himself and to the military."
Reported by Carl Spaatz, Major General, USA Commanding, Hyman Goldberg, Cohen-Bokoff Post 93, Dept. of CT Scottsdale, AZ.

J. ELLIOT GOLDBERG, enlisted in the Army at Ft.

McPherson, GA on May 15, 1942. He was assigned to USA Quartermaster Corps and completed Basic Training at Camp Lee, VA. On Feb. 25, 1943, he accepted appointment as 2nd LT., AUS, at Camp Lee, VA and assigned to 102nd QM Co., 102nd Inf. Div at Camp Maxey, TX. Promoted to 1st LT.

On Sept. 12, 1944 departed with unit to European-African-Middle Eastern Theater. Awarded 2 Bronze

Stars, Victory Medal, American Theater Medal, Meritorious Service Medal w/1 star. Late in 1945, he was assigned to British 18th Airborne Corps and stationed in Northern Germany. He returned to US April 15, 1946 and was separated from active duty July 1, 1946. He was then a member of the Active Reserves until May 7, 1952.

Goldberg joined JWV and elected to: Commander, Atlanta (GA) Post 112 (3 terms); Comander of Dept. of GA and SC; Commander of 4th Region; National Executive Committee; and now serves on Board of Directors of the National Museum of American Jewish Military History. He is married to former Sarah Spiegelman and has two children and five grandchildren. He is a successful real estate broker and owns Elliott Goldberg Realty Co., in Atlanta, GA.

JACK E. GOLDBERG, O.D., born in Chester, PA, Jan.

20, 1920, graduated Atlantic City High School in 1938, and Pennsylvania College of Optometry in October 1943. The Aviation Cadet Communication School at Yale University, from which he graduated in May 1944, enhanced his interest in electronic and was a useful skill in his civilian life. He was a first lieutenant in the 11th Air Communications Service Squadron 58, ACS, Group 5 ACS wing from May 4, 1944 to Sept. 11, 1946. He served in Rome, Italy at La Senia Airfield in Oran, North Africa, Algiers, Casablanca, Marrakech and Orly Airfield, Paris.

While in North Africa he participated in Passover Seder with the local Jewish citizens.

Upon his return stateside, he married Bernice Goldblum of Philadelphia, PA, and opened his practice of Optometry in Atlantic City, NJ, which he continued actively for over 40 years.

He joined the JWV Post #39 of Atlantic City, and never missed decorating veteran's graves each year. He served for many years as quartermaster, and then was post commander.

He died Nov. 10, 1992, after a dedicated and happy life, devoted to his country, his ideals and his beloved family. He is survived by his wife, Bernice, a son, Robert M. Goldberg, M.D., a daughter, Judith Goldberg Berman, M.D., Ph.D., and four granddaughters.

JOSEPH GOLDBERG, born in 1886 in Russian occu-

pied Poland, tailor by occupation. Immigrated to U.S. in early 1900s and settled in Albany, NY. Served in Cavalry Unit of Army during WWI. Active member in Workman's Circle, Albany Hebrew Tailors. Joined Albany Post 105, JWV in 1935. Father of PNC Nathan Goldberg.

NATHAN M. GOLDBERG, served in the Naval Air

Corps, 1942-45, where he taught aerial gunney to Navy pilots. He was released from active duty following WWII with the rank of ensign.

He earned a bachelor of business administration degree from Siena College and Juris Doctor designation from Albany Law School of Union University. Since graduation he has conducted full-time practices as a certified public accountant and as an attorney. He is also a trustee in bankruptcy.

Besides positions on local boards, he served as president of his synagogue, executive committee of NJCRAC and Presidents' Conference. Within JWV, his activity included Post, County, Department of New York and National Commander Chairman of NEC and president of National Museum of American Jewish Military History. Nate also served JWV as foreign affairs, budget and personnel chairman.

Introduced to JWV at age 12 accompanying his father, a WWI veteran and member of Albany Post #105, Nate continues to reside in Albany with his wife, Selma, who served in the Cadet Nurse Corps. They have two children, Janet and Larry, and three grandchildren.

NORMAN J. GOLDBERG, A3/c, born Dec. 25, 1932, Chicago, IL. Moved to Philadelphia as a boy and graduated South Philadelphia HS, January 1951. Worked as a clerk/typist for the U.S. Army Signal Corps.

Enlisted in the USAF September 1952. Basic training at Sampson AFB, Geneva, NY. Assigned to the Comptroller's Office at Lawson AFB, Ft. Benning, GA in 1953.

Awards/Medals: Korean Service Ribbon and Good Conduct Medal. Discharged from USARR in 1960.

Attended classes at U. of Georgia and Temple University. Currently operates a wholesale food business. In January 1953 he was the first person to receive a new operation that preserves original body function in certain instances of rectal cancer at Fox Chase Cancer Center, Philadelphia.

Married to Phyllis since Aug. 26, 1956. Has three daughters: Julie, Rochelle and Ellen.

NORMAN N. GOLDBERG, born Nov. 5, 1920, Denver, CO. Enlisted USN Air ARM VPB 21. Military locations included Coeur d'Alene, ID; Alameda, CA; Corpus Christi, TX; Santiago, Cuba; San Diego, CA; Kaneohe, HI; Okinawa. Participated in battle in Okinawa.

Memorable experiences include while on an air patrol, his aircraft was subjected to a 45 minute running battle attack by several Japanese fighters. Subjected to Kamikaze attacks while based aboard the Chandeleur Sea Tender.

Awards/Medals: Distinguished Flying Cross, Air Medal with clusters, Good Conduct Medal, Asiatic-Pacific Campaign Medal.

He was discharged Nov. 26, 1993, with the rank of ARM3/c.

He has one brother (an Army veteran). Involuntarily retired.

PAUL GOLDBERG, born Jan. 8, 1917, Pittsburgh, PA. Drafted Feb. 4, 1942, AAF 8th, photo lab technician. Inducted at New Cumberland, PA, sent to Ft. McClellan, AL, for basic training transferred to Tucson, AZ, to 901st Engr. AF HQ Co. as cadre, went to Pendleton Field, OR, then sent to Ft. Dix, NJ, for shipment overseas. Arrived in Liverpool, England on Aug. 18, 1942, and was sent directly to Bushey Park in Kinston. In 1945 Headquarters moved to St. Germain, France, from where after three weeks he was transferred back to Bushey Park. When the war ended he was separated at Indiantown Gap, PA, on Nov. 10, 1945, with the rank of technician third grade.

Memorable experience includes coming face to face with Gen. Eisenhower and giving him a big salute.

Awards/Medals: Good Conduct Medal, Meritorious Unit Award, EAME through Service Medal with one Bronze Star, WWII Victory Medal.

Widower with one daughter, son-in-law and two boys. Wife served in Navy for two and a half years. Officially he is retired but he still put in six days a week. Overseas three years, three months six days.

SAM GOLDBERG, born June 13, 1916, Toronto, Canada. Joined the USAF in September 1942, radio operator. Basic training Atlantic City, Radio School, Madison, WI.

Memorable experience includes serving as a crew member of Search and Rescue SQ.; helped bring downed crews out of the jungle foot hills of the Himalayans in the CBI Theater. Also aided infiltrating allied troops by dropping supplies to assist their operation in taking on the Japs in Burma. Was shot down by three Jap Zeros on Dec. 10, 1943. Returned to the U.S. April 1945, and reassigned as radio

instructor at Homestead AFB until discharged as staff sergeant.

Awards/Medals: Distinguished Flying Cross with OLC, Air Medal, Purple Heart Medal, Asiatic-Pacific Campaign Medal, Presidential Unit Citation.

He was discharged Oct. 3, 1945. He had three brothers in the service during WWII. Today he is retired.

SEYMOUR GOLDBERG, born April 15, 1919, Brooklyn, NY. Graduated DeWitt Clinton High School in 1939. Enlisted May 29, 1942, USAF. Served in U.S. only, inducted at Camp Upton, NY; basic training Miami Beach, FL. Worked as a lithographer at air bases in Asheville, NC; Sioux Falls, SD; Madison, WI; and in Harlegen, TX.

Awards/Medals: American Theater, Good Conduct Medal, American Campaign Medal, WWII Victory Medal.

He was discharged Dec. 11, 1945, with the rank of sergeant.

Married Beatrice, March 27, 1948, two daughters and three grandchildren. Had a printing business for 35 years. Retired 1982 to Liberty, NY. Member of JWV.

SHELDON A. GOLDBERG, Lt. Col., USAF (Ret.) enlisted in the Air Force in 1956 as a clarinetist, was accepted to OCS in 1960 and commissioned in 1961; earned navigator wings and flew C-124 and C-141 transports at McChord AFB. After receiving his MA on a graduate

scholarship in 1968, he became an F-4 WSO and flew 214 combat missions in Southeast Asia with 497th TFS (Nite Owls). A brief stint flying F-111s at Cannon AFB NM was followed by three consecutive overseas tours: F-111E WSO, RAF Upper Heyford UK; USAF Liaison Officer, German Command and General Staff College, Hamburg, GE; and Air Policy Staff Officer, Headquarters Allied Forces Central Europe (AFCENT), Brunnsum, NL. His final assignment was on the faculty of both Air Command and Staff College and Air War College, Maxwell AFB AL. He retired as a lieutenant colonel on Aug. 1, 1985, and moved with his wife, Waltruad, to the Washington, D.C. area and a PhD program at the University of Maryland.

LOUIS B. GOLDBLATT, D.D.S., born May 2, 1920, Norwich, CT. Enlisted 1942, Res. Off., Army Dental Corps. Military locations included ETO, Ft. Rucker, Grant, Stewart, Banks, Devens, Gordon.

Memorable experience includes visiting Dachau one day after liberation, served during Korean.

Awards/Medals: ETO with two Battle Stars, U.S. Forces in Austria, Occupation Medal, WWII Victory Medal, Korean War.

He retired from National Guard with 21 years active service in 1968, as a major.

He has three sons, one daughter, one stepson, one stepdaughter, and numerous grandchildren. Today he is engaged in dentistry.

ALEXANDER GOLDENBERG, DDS, FICD, born March 13, 1914, Brooklyn, NY. Enlisted May 1953, Army Dental Corps. Stationed at Ft. Eustis, VA Hospital.

Memorable experience was 1953, polio epidemic with entire hospital complement, inoculating children, men and women.

He was discharged June 1954, with the rank of major, D.C.

Married 53 years to Sylvia, two sons (Dr. Jeff, deceased) five grandchildren. Chairman Advisory Board Broward County, FL. Board of Care of Elderly Services,

Past Commissioner, South Broward Hospital District, Hollywood, FL. Post surgeon for the state of Florida, JWV; assistant professor, Cranio-Facial Birth Defects, University of Miami, School of Medicine. Active member: JWV, Masons, B'nai Brith. Director, Retired Physicians Dentist Association, Memorial Hospital Hollywood, FL.

ALLEN B. GOLDE, born Nov. 10, 1920, Syracuse, NY. Attended Croton and Central High Schools. Enlisted in May 1942, second lieutenant in 155th Inf., 31st Div. Awarded Soldiers Combat Medal. Killed in line of duty on Morotai Island, South Pacific, on Feb. 3, 1945, at the age of 24. Lies at rest in the family plot, Temple of Concord Section, Woodlawn Cemetery. Survived by brother, Irving, Newark, NJ; sisters: Mrs. Celia Tompkins, Syracuse; Mrs. Sally Sorin, Clifton, NJ; Miss Fay Golde, Miami Beach, FL.

ARNOLD I. GOLDEN, born Jan. 2, 1928, in Syracuse, NY. Attended Nottingham High School. Active in football, baseball. Competed in Golden Gloves Boxing Tournament. Bowled in YMHA League. Received "The Most Improved Bowler" Trophy. Worked at the Indian Novelty Company. Served in the Pacific Theater. Died March 31, 1951, at the gave of 23 years. Survived by parents, Mr. and Mrs. Louis Golden; sister, Mrs. Carl Mendelson; nephews, Richard and Andrew.

GILBERT GOLDENBERG, born June 19, 1926. Enlisted in the U.S. Army Sept. 11, 1943, in Newark, NJ. Basic engineering at Alfred University and Virginia Military Institute. Infantry basic training at Camp Wheeler, GA.

Sent overseas, disembarking at Grennock, Scotland on Jan. 14, 1945. Crossed English Channel on LCI, landing in Le Havre, France. Assigned as a replacement to I Co., 180th Inf., 45th Div. Served as a scout in a rifle company.

Participated in the liberation of several satellite concentration camps of the infamous Dachau Camp. Combat in France and Germany; frozen feet in the Vosges Mountains and airlifted, May 1945, from the 93rd Evac. Hosp. in Munich to a general hospital in France.

Reassigned to the 864th Ord. HAM Co. and placed on detached service with the Inspector General Bremen Port Command Area.

Awards/Medals: Combat Infantry Badge, Bronze Star, EAME Campaign Medal with two Battle Stars, Good Conduct, WWII Victory, Army of Occupation with Germany Clasp and from the state of New Jersey the Distinguished Service Medal. Discharged from service April 23, 1946.

Married Aug. 26, 1951, to Gwendolyn Shefkowitz, has two children, Judith and Steven, and two grandchildren, Kira and Jeremy. He is a retired optometrist who was a low vision practitioner.

SOLOMON GOLDFARB, a private in the 803rd Tank Destroyer Battalion. Served in Great Britain at the invasion staging area.

LEE GOLDFARB, born April 12, 1920, in Jersey City, NJ. Went to school in Jersey City and then in Nov. 1, 1940, enlisted in the USN. Was sent to radio school in Norton Heights, CT, and graduated with the rate of radioman 3/c. Was sent to Pearl Harbor and was assigned to the Flagship of the Mineforce the USS *Oglala*. Was aboard the *Oglala* on Dec. 7, 1941, when she was sunk during the Japanese attack. Spent most of the war in the Pacific and returned home Nov. 4, 1945.

Sometime late 1946 became a charter member of the Grover Post in Jersey City and is still a member to this day.

In addition to belonging to JWV became active in the Pearl Harbor Survivors Association and served as a chapter president rose to state chairman and later 7th district director, national vice president and is currently serving as national president.

Married to his lovely wife Molly, has four children as well as four grandchildren. Lee and Molly reside in East Hanover, NJ.

IRVING GOLDFEDER, born in New York City, NY, on Oct. 12, 1889. Enlisted in the Navy in 1907, trained in Newport, RI. Assigned to the USS *Kentucky* which was part of the Great White Fleet. Sailed around the world with the Great White Fleet from 1907-09. Among the ports visited were Japan, China, Italy (where they gave assistance due to a volcano explosion), North Africa, Australia, New Zealand, and many others. Was a light weight boxing champ in the fleet division.

WWI enlisted in Navy again in 1917 and served as armed guard for merchant vessel escort on active duty 1917-19. During the flu epidemic remained on duty several 24 hour shifts until coming down with the flu and transferred to the hospital ship *Comfort*. Was returned to active duty. After WWI ended placed in reserves. Received honorable discharge in 1923.

Married to Sarah, and had three sons and one daughter, grandchildren and great-grandchildren. Was employed by the Savannah line of the Ocean Steamship Company and later became an insurance broker in New York City.

During WWII was employed by the Navy department as civilian police in Philadelphia, PA, at lend lease Depot, attained rank of sergeant.

Upon retirement moved to Essex, MD, and later to Delray Hospital, Miami, FL, died April 16, 1984, at age 94.

BEN GOLDFELLER, enlisted Sept. 22, 1942 into the 27th Evac. Hosp. which as a medical unit formed at the University of Illinois Medical School. The unit was activated on Oct. 15, 1942, at Camp Brechenridge, KY. The unit consisted of 42 doctors, 52 nurses and 37 enlisted personnel. The unit operated as a fixed tent hospital in Tennessee Maneuvers under bivouac conditions. They were sent overseas at the end of March 1943, landing in Oran, North Africa, where they re-assembled their effects before moving up near the battle area in Italy. They arrived in the battle scarred area of Naples on May 12, which gave them their first view of the devastation of war. They were assigned to the 7th Army which began its offensive which was to push the line from Cassino to Pisa. The night of their arrival the Germans started an air raid over Naples and through the night they experienced the flash of bombs, anti-aircraft, missiles etc. A week after the invasions of South France they were ordered to join the 7th Army in the vicinity of Marseilles. From that time on, until the collapse of Germany the unit played "leap frog" with their advancing troops, seldom being out of earshot of battle and never out of personal danger. During the Battle of the Bulge, shells continued to be in the vicinity of the tent hospital. At the peak of the battle the unit was treating about 1,100 men. Since arriving in South France the 27th Evac. Hosp. Unit treated approximately 21,000 patients. He was discharged on Dec. 18, 1945.

DAVID H. GOLDIN, enlisted in Signal Corps June 1942 in Philadelphia. After basic training he was sent to Mississippi State College for advanced Signal Corps training.

Upon completing this course, he requested a transfer to the Air Corps for pilot training, Washed out as a pilot, and was sent to Scott Field for Air Crop radio training. Was then transferred to Reno Air Force Base for air transport radio training.

Then shipped to the China-Burma-India Theater as a radio operator and mechanic, and was based in India. He operated and maintained a transmitter and receiver on a C-46 type transport aircraft. Contacted other planes or ground stations for weather reports and operational instructions. Flew over hazardous terrain and under adverse weather conditions over the Himalayas to transport equipment for a period of more than 15 months. Attained the rank of staff sergeant. Total years of service, three.

Awards/Medals: Distinguished Flying Cross, Air Medal with OLC, Good Conduct Medal, American Campaign Medal, Asiatic-Pacific Campaign Medal with three Bronze Star, WWII Victory Medal.

AARON H. GOLDMAN, born in New York City on Aug. 26, 1924. Upon graduation from Morris High School in the Bronx at the age of 16, he went to work for uniform cap manufacturer as a bookkeeper. He entered the U.S. Army on April 3, 1943, and took medical basic training at Camp Grant, IL, graduating at the top of his class as a medic. He was then sent to Trinidad, BWI, where troops were being trained for jungle warfare. Having studied court reporting and being a skilled shorthand writer and stenotype operator, Goldman was assigned to the Inspector General's Department when the need for someone who could take classified testimony was required.

His duties in the I.G. Department expanded to administrative inspector and investigator and he was recognized as an expert in Administrative Regulations and War Department directives. He authored a Manual of Inspection and his inspection and investigations through out the Caribbean Defense Command resulted in substantial monetary savings for the U.S. Army. He was awarded the Legion of Merit by direction of the president for "exceptionally meritorious conduct in the performance of outstanding services above and beyond the call of duty." He was also awarded the American Campaign Medal and Good Conduct Medal. He was honorably discharged as a technical sergeant on Jan. 25, 1946.

A particularly memorable experience occurred in 1944, when while on assignment in Puerto Rico, and in the absence of a Jewish Chaplain, then Sergeant Goldman conducted Jewish High Holy Day services in a building supplied by the Army, not only for the Jewish military personnel stationed there, but also for all the Jewish civilians on the island who were invited to attend.

Upon discharge from the Army, Goldman worked his way through college and graduate school at night while working full time first as a legal secretary for a prominent New York law firm and then as a sales executive with a New York textile firm with which he is still associated.

Mr. Goldman holds a bachelor's degree in accounting from New York University where he was on the Dean's List and a master's degree in business administration, cum laude, from Long Island University where he won departmental honors in business administration and was the only straight "A" student in this graduating class. He is also a New York State licensed insurance broker and for the past 35 years has been teaching business subjects in night school.

In addition to his membership in JWV Post 769, he is past vice-president of a B'nai Brith lodge, a member of the Law and Legislation Committee of the Bronx County Grand Juror's Association and a member of the board of directors of his orthodox synagogue.

Mr. Goldman is single and resides in the Pelham Parkway section of the Bronx.

HECTOR GOLDMAN, born Antwerp, Belgium, Sept. 9, 1924. Arrived in New York from Cuba in June 1943. Inducted at Camp Upton in November 1943. Trained at Ft. McClellan, AL, shipped to England in June 1944. Joined 102nd Inf. Div. (OZARKS), HQ. Co., 1st BN, 407th Inf., anti-tank squad. Combat duty in North Germany, around Roer River. Pulled out of foxhole to serve as interpreter to Maj. Gen. Frank Keating, Commander of the 102nd. Witnessed surrender of the remnant of an entire German Army Group, stood by the General for the purpose of interpreting.

Present at Gardelegen, when troops came across a barn in which civilian prisoners had been herded and put on fire after being doused with gasoline. Has pictures of this sordid event, with General Simpson, Commander of the 9th Army, and other General's present.

Court martialled for "fraternizing with enemy civilians," who were actually Jews freed from various camps. Returned to unit, found guilty, reduced in rank, confined to quarters. Story appeared in *PM*, a New York daily. Promoted to sergeant not long afterwards. Taught French in Army of Occupation. Discharged May 1946.

Awards/Medals: Bronze Star, past Commander Post #264 JWV, life member.

Married to Gisele in 1948, three children and five grandchildren. Joined family firm, importing diamonds and gems.

IKE H. GOLDMAN, born Nov. 4, 1892, Syracuse, NY. Attended Andrew Jackson, Putnam and Washington Irving Schools. At the age of 13, he started to learn to be a barber. At 15, he had his own barber shop.

Enlisted in Detroit in April 1917. He was rejected because he was underweight and too short. When 20 other Jewish enlistees refused to join unless he was accepted, they waived his lack of physical standards and let him join the Army.

Served with the 1st Div. was gassed and wounded. Received a decoration for being one of 11 runners to get through the front lines from Headquarters. He was honorably discharged. He came home for a short while to be the best man at his twin brother, Joseph's wedding. Re-enlisted in the Army. He was sent to Schofield barracks in the Hawaiian Islands, where he did on March 22, 1921, at the age of 28.

Body was brought back to Syracuse for one of the largest military funerals seen in Syracuse. Taps were blown by Jacob Erlick, a lifelong friend.

NEIL GOLDMAN, a native of St. Louis, enlisted in the Army Air Force as an aviation cadet in July 1942. He served his country as a celestial navigation trainer operator/instructor, and was honorably discharged on Feb. 22, 1946. He completed his education at Washington University in St. Louis and subsequently earned his living as a merchandising executive with a May Co. Div. He moved to Dallas in 1967 as an executive with a subsidiary of Zale Corp.

He then joined Jewish War Veterans, and rose rapidly through the ranks to post Commander, Department of Texas Commander, and is currently running for National Commander of JWV for 1995-96, our Centennial year. He has been an active membership recruiter, and has been instrumental in creating new posts in the Department of Texas. He is National Insurance Chairman, Vice Chairman of the National Centennial Committee; he inaugurated Allied Veterans Mission to Israel in the Department of Texas. With his wife, Maxine, he led the mission in 1994.

Neil also has been active in scouting and B'nai Brith He is a member of the Dallas Holocaust Center Yad V'Shem and the North Texas Cemetery Commission.

ROBERT GOLDMAN, born Nov. 18, 1919, New York, NY. Enlisted as apprentice seaman Oct. 10, 1942. Completed PHM course, Columbia University and Navy Training Course for PHM2/c.

Stations/Ships served on: R.O., Philadelphia; CGTS, Curtis Bay; COTP, Norfolk; DCGO5ND; DCGO3ND; Man. Beach Tra. Sta.; CGTS, Alameda; USS LST-66; CG Rep. Pool; USN #17, Navy 3115; USNH, Portsmouth, VA; USS LST 68; CG Bks. New Chambers St. NY; USCG PerSepCtr.

Participated in the Eastern New Guinea Operation, Bismarck Archipelago Operation, Admiralty Islands Landings, Western New Guinea Operations, Leyte Landings, Lingayen Gulf Landings and Borneo Operations.

Awards/Medals: Among his awards are the Purple Heart, Navy Unit Commendation and Bronze Star Medal w/ Combat V. Received honorable discharge Sept. 15, 1945, PHM2/c

SIDNEY GOLDMAN, born in the Bronx, NY, on April 30, 1926. Graduated James Monroe High School January 1943, and entered CCNY. Inducted into the Army July 11, 1944, and took field artillery basic training in Ft. Bragg, NC. Overseas to Asiatic-Pacific Theater to join the 81st Div. in New Caledonia. Served as forward observer in the HQ Bn of the 318th FA Bn. Served in the Philippines and the Army of Occupation (Japan). Discharged Aug. 10, 1946, as a technician 4.

Awards/Medals: Army of Occupation, Asiatic-Pacific Campaign Medal, Philippine Liberation Ribbon with one Battle Star, WWII Victory Medal and Good Conduct Medal.

Returned to CCNY and earned an engineering degree. Presently principle in an architectural engineering firm.

Married to Fay Lupu since 1950, three sons Howard, Roy and Lance and five grandchildren. Erica, Samantha, Joshua, Joel and Jonathan. Member of sons of JWV prior to WWII and member of JWV Post #82 since 1944.

KENNETH G. GOLDSHER, USAF, 1960 50FF, served proudly Nov. 22, 1957 to Nov. 21, 1961.

LUDWIG MICHAEL GOLDSMITH, born Oct. 17, 1950, New Brunswick, NJ. Enlisted May 25, 1973, USN Regular Navy Surface-Atlantic Fleet. Military stations included Norfolk, VA.

Memorable experiences include commissioning crew as main propulsion officer for USS *Peterson* DD969.

Awards/Medals: National Defense Service Medal.

He was discharged Aug. 5, 1977, with the rank of lieutenant.

His father Karl (sergeant in the U.S. Army) and mother were German refugees. His bother Jonathan is a lieutenant colonel in U.S. Army Medical Service Corp. Today he is an architect in New York City.

BENJAMIN GOLDSTEIN, born in Hartford, CT, attended local schools and after his military service graduated from the University of Hartford.

Entered military service February 1943, sent to City College of New York to study engineering and later sent overseas (Europe) where he served with the 75th Inf. Div.

and the 528th FA as an artillery observer. At the conclusion of WWII he returned home joined the Hartford Police Department and also the Connecticut Army National Guard.

While serving in the police department in July 1950, he was called to active duty and served in the 24th Inf. Div. in Korea. He returned to the police in May 1952, after receiving the Bronze Star for bravery in action. He retired from the police as assistant chief and from the military as a lieutenant colonel.

In 1969 he was appointed to serve as deputy director of the Connecticut Justice Commission until 1983. Presently he serves as a member of the Connecticut Board of Arbitration and as a member of his synagogues board of directors. He has been an active JWV member has served as the Post 45 Commander from Hartford, CT. He is married to Kayleen Goldstein and has three children and four grandchildren.

BERNARD GOLDSTEIN, served in U.S. Army from March 6, 1943 to Nov. 9, 1945. He entered the service at Camp Upton, NY, as a private on March 6, 1943, and was discharged at Ft Dix, NJ, with the rank of corporal on Nov. 9, 1945. His basic and artillery training was had at Ft. Bragg from March 15, 1943 to June 1943 and at Camp Shenango with the infantry from June 1943 to July 1943. He also served at Camp Patrick Henry with the 88th Inf. Div. from July 1943 to November 1943. He was shipped overseas on the Liberty Ship *Sherman* which sailed from Newport News, VA, to Oran, Africa and returned to the U.S. on the USS *Monticella* from Naples, Italy, debarking at Newport News, VA.

He served in Africa with the 88th Inf. Div. from November 1943 to January. 1944 and in Italy, Mediterranean Theater of Operations from January 1944 to November 1945. He saw a great deal of action throughout the entire Italian Campaign Naples Foggia Campaign through the Gothic Line, Rome, Brenner Pass, crossing the Po River and ceased fire in the Alps. He received the Bronze Star Medal for meritorious service in combat, from May 2, 1944 to May 2, 1945, Rome Arno Battle Star, Po Valley and North Apennines Battle Stars and Good Conduct Medal, July 1944. Among the outstanding places visited was a tour of Switzerland in September 1945, which taught him that a country can be run just like one happy family. His service totaled 365 days at the front. His unit was so far ahead of communications, that they fought on eight hours after the fighting was over. Coming home was the best of all. *Submitted by Max Sigal.*

DAVE GOLDSTEIN, born April 20, 1922. Enlisted in the U.S. Army on April 20, 1942, After serving in SCCC in Oregon worked Sawmill, CA, ordnance bomb disposal in Panama transferred to Inf. Co. # 347th Inf. Regt., 87th Div. with outfit across Germany. Military stations included Panama, England, France and Germany.

Memorable experience includes exchanging boots with officer, frost bitten toes. "Thank God I was in right place at right time."

Awards/Medals: Rifleman's Badge.

He was discharged 1945. Today he is lecturing senior.

DAVID GOLDSTEIN, born April 1, 1917, Hightstown, NJ. Graduated Hightstown HS, Columbia College of Pharmacy. Earned BS in Pharmacy, 1939 and MA from Teachers College, Columbia, 1941. Left Walgreen Drug Co. in NYC January 1942 to join the U.S. Army at Ft. Dix.

Basic training in Florida, received his 2nd lieutenant rank at Carlisle, PA Training Center. Assigned to field

hospital and sent to Hawaii, reassigned to the 24th Inf. as medical supply officer. Sent to Australia, New Guinea and participated in the invasion of Leyte, Philippines. As a casualty of the invasion, he was air lifted to the States. After six months in three hospitals, he was given a medical discharge on May 24, 1945.

Married Helen June 15, 1947, has three married children: Larry, head of Matawan English Dept. of the high school; Joyce, a speech therapist; and Marion, a registered dietitian of elementary schools. Has three grandchildren: Ryan, Sarah and Jay.

For 32 years he operated the Hights Pharmacy in Hightstown, NJ. He formed the Hights Pharmaceutical, a consulting corporation. Retired in 1986. A member of American Legion Post 148, JWV Post 444, TROA, Hightstown Elks Lodge and Legion of Honor, Chapel of Four Chaplains.

HARRY E. GOLDSTEIN, born Sept. 15, 1917. He joined the Army November 1943. He served with 65th Inf. Div. 261st Regt. 3rd Bn. He was stationed at Ft. Dix and Camp Shelby. He participated in battles and campaigns from Normandy to Austria.

Memorable experience was Struth, Germany, April 1945.

Awards/Medals: Silver Star and Gallantry in Action.

He was discharged in 1946 with the rank of T5.

He has been married for 54 years and has two sons and seven grandchildren. He is retired.

IRA GOLDSTEIN, born in the Bronx, NY, on Dec. 26, 1925, served in the 78th Div., 310th Inf. from 1944-1946, and remained together, being separated only when one deposited the other to the medics. Ira was wounded three times.

He married in 1949, has two married children and four grandchildren. He is a retired printing plate-maker. Married 44 years, Ira and his wife Doris reside in Delray Beach, FL.

MORTON GOLDSTEIN, born in the Bronx, NY, on Dec. 26, 1925, served in the 78th Div., 310th Inf. from 1944-1946, and remained together, being separated only when one deposited the other to the medics. Morton was wounded twice.

Morton married in 1952, has three married children and seven grandchildren. He recently retired from electrical sales. Married 41 years, Morton and his wife Barbara live in Randolph, MA.

SID GOLDSTEIN, born in the Bronx June 11, 1920, Ament Ave, Long Island, NY. Entered service Jan. 11, 1941 to Feb. 28, 1961, 1941 Panama - 1944 Italy - 1949 Pentagon - 1951 Korea - 1953 Japan - 1955 Governors Island - 1961 California.

Awards/Medals: Army Distinguished Service Cross.

Infantry Platoon Leader, Co. A, 133rd Inf. Regt., 34th Inf. Div. Italy, WWII, Sept. 19, 1944. 2nd Lt. Goldstein attacked enemy held hill in the Gothic Line with 24 men. Assaulted enemy dugout and captured four German soldiers. Then Lt. Goldstein with two men assaulted second enemy dugout capturing a German officer and two enlisted men.

The German officer offered to surrender the remainder of his force only upon the condition that only Lt. Goldstein accompany him. There two more German officer and approximately 40 enlisted men surrendered. When the German officer volunteered to lead Lt. Goldstein to other German position and they returned with 16 more prisoners. Lt. Goldstein's bravery and aggressiveness resulted in the capture of 67 Germans and effected a break-through in sector of the strong enemy Gothic Line. The DSC was personally pinned on by 5 Star Gen. George C. Marshall in February 1945.

Past National Commander Legion of Valor, 1990-91. Personally decorated by Gov. Thomas E. Dewey with the New York State Conspicuous Service Cross. Awarded the Cross of Valor for combat heroism by the Italian Government. Enlisted as a private in the Regular Army on Jan. 11, 1941 at $21.00 per month. Retired in grade of major February 1961. Graduated Ft. Benning, GA, on Aug. 2, 1943, in grade of second lieutenant infantry. Served on the Orange County Veterans Advisory Council as the Second District Repr. since Nov. 19, 1985.

Married to Syd Goldstein, children: Larry Wayne (Hava) - Jonathan, Etyan; Debra I (Jay) Johnson - Jessica and Daniel; Steve C. (Becky) - Scott, Aaron, Amanda; Mitchell Jay; Gayle I. (Stan) Surdam - Emily and Jared.

STANLEY GOLDSTEIN, in 1954 volunteered for the draft because, having concluded that he would serve two years at sometime, he preferred to chose his own schedule. After basic training at Ft. Dix and quartermaster training at Ft. Lee, VA, he was sent to Hohenfels, Germany, a training ground for the various combat units stationed there.

The two years in the Army are among his most proud achievements. That is strange considering that his top rank was corporal, served at a time when no active war was in process and accomplished far less than a vast majority of America veterans. He did succeed, however, in maintaining a family tradition whereby his two older brothers served as officers in the Army Air Corps. during WWII. His parents were immigrants from Europe who encouraged their five children to be patriotic Americans and to always do their share, or even a bit more.

All three Goldstein boys were able to return to civilian life and make up for time spent in the service. They may be a bit more grateful for the bounties of their wonderful nation having served in the armed forces which forces one to recognize the possibility that America might not have survived had fortune turned the wrong way.

EDWIN GOLDWASSER, PNC, Sgt. U.S. Army, Feb. 12, 1953 to Feb. 3, 1955. Born and educated in the city of New York, Edwin Goldwasser entered the U.S. Army upon graduation from Long Island University. After basic training at Ft. Campbell, KY, and a short tour of duty at Ft. Monroe, VA, Korea was his next assignment with the 336th EDU attached to 8th Army HQ, as the unit's supply sergeant.

While in Korea, the highlight of that tour was spending the High Holy Days in Seoul. Services were attended by the United Nations Troops from all over the world. All did not speak the same language, but gathered to pray in Hebrew.

Upon discharge in 1955 Goldwasser married Iris Weinstein, also of Brooklyn. They have two children, son David married to Anita Levine, and daughter Reina married to Marc Greenbaum, and five grandchildren, Ashley, Michael, Arielle, Alexis and Perri.

In 1960 both Iris and Ed joined JWV/JWVA and in 1986 Ed was elected National Commander in Honolulu, HI.

GERALD GOLDWASSER, born in New York City on May 2, 1924, entered the Army in January 1943. Took basic training at Camp Lee, VA, and also graduated Non-Commissioned Officers School at Camp Lee, VA.

Served overseas for over 25 months in the ETO as a Tech. Fourth Grade in various posts, among which were HQ Advanced Section Communications Zone in England, France and Belgium. After the Battle of the Bulge, "K" Co. 409th Inf. Regt. of the 103rd Div. in France, Germany and Austria. Discharged in September 1945.

Worked as a district supervisor in New York for large men's clothing chain. Went into business with relatives in Florida (men's' clothing chain) in 1957 and then merged with National Clothing Chain in 1979. Retired in 1990 only to be asked to do public relations work for national funeral homes where he is currently employed by Levitt/Weinstein Chapels in Florida.

While in the Army received five Battle Stars in the ETO and most memorable experiences in the Army overseas were being one of only two Jewish soldiers in his company and the freeing of survivors of death camps in Germany and his only regret not knowing Yiddish as these survivors were enthralled by meeting an American Jewish soldier who came to free them.

Married Marilyn Sennet September 1947 Marilyn passed away in 1975 and is now married to Joan Bazelon Sirkin for past 17 years. Have three sons from first marriage and two stepdaughters. Have six grandchildren, three grandsons and triplet granddaughters. Member of JWV Post 223 in South Miami, FL.

JACK GOLOMB, born in Washington, DC, March 27, 1921, to Saul and Ethel, the second of four children. Earned Scholastic Scholarship to Wilson Teachers College and Boxing Scholarship to Columbus University. Lost only to inter-collegiate champ. Enlisted USNR Sept. 25, 1943. Won all seven bouts on Boots Battalion Boxing Team. Awarded Outstanding Athletic Achievement Award at Bainbridge, MD.

Served as SK(V) 3c, NAS Miami, FL; VTB-3; VSB-5; VFOTV-10, NB4 OTV-3, and NAAS Whiting Field, FL. Supervised issue of aviation parts and supplies. Recommended synchronization of Navy, Air Force and Marine aviation parts nos. Turned down by base skipper. Adopted after WWII.

Boxed on MNAS 20 match undefeated team. Lost two of 36 bouts in Navy. Won all three invitational tournaments. Awarded Golden Glove, Navy Blue and Gold Robe and an 8-day Clock. Also participated on Navy fast pitch champion softball team. Ran track and baseball. Contributed all awards, pictures, printed articles, etc. to JWV museum. Boxed professionally as Jackie Greenberg, 16-51. Honorable discharge on May 23, 1946.

Spent several holidays with area residents who were interested in his career.

Earned BS degree in business administration at American University, 1949. Retired as financial analyst, 1977, Federal Government. Re-elected commander of the JWV Post 692; elected Veteran of the Year May 16, 1993, elected Commander-of-the-Year June 13, 1993, by Department of Maryland. Member of JWV Museum, 32 degree Mason, B'nai Brith, FUDDA NABI, Past Commanders Association, Boxing Hall of Fame, etc.

RALPH GOLUBOCK, born Nov 18, 1921, Buffalo, NY. Enlisted Feb. 15, 1942, Army Air Corps, aviation cadet.

Prior to the war he was a salesman, selling to the Ladies Garment market. He enlisted immediately after Pearl Harbor.

He took his pilot training in the West Coast training command, graduating as a second lieutenant pilot from Douglas Army AB on April 12, 1943.

He began his training in B-24s immediately after graduation and left for overseas in September 1943, arriving in England shortly thereafter. He had additional training in England and joined the 506th BS, 44th BG, of the 8th Air Force in November 1943. He began combat flying in December and was on operations continually until May 29, 1944. On that date he was on his 30th and last mission. The target was Politz. He was hit by fighters and spent the next six months as an internee in Sweden.

Back to the U.S. November 1944. He finished as a captain stationed at Scott Field in Illinois. Went on inactive reserve duty Sept. 21, 1945.

He participated in the air battle of Germany and the pre-invasion of France battle.

He received the Distinguished Flying Cross, Air Medal with five OLC, European Theater Medal with two Battle Stars and the American Theater Medal.

He was married while a cadet to Thelma Eviaiff on Dec. 31, 1942. They are still married. They have two sons Marc Barry and Bruce Alan, and two grandchildren, Wendy and Andrew.

CLARENCE GOMBERG, served in the U.S. Army Feb. 7, 1943-March 27, 1946. Assigned to the 3rd Army, 3116 SCU, 1st Service Command, 78th Hospital Train. Served in the ETO Dec. 27, 1944-March 27, 1946.

Awards/Medals: Army Commendation, Purple Heart with OLC, Good Conduct, American Defense, American Campaign, EAME with three Campaign Stars, WWII Victory, Occupational Service, National Defense, Army Service, Army Overseas and Combat Medic Badge.

Member of JWV, DAV, Federation of the Four Chaplains of Allegheny County, National Order of Trench Rats. Was Officer of the Day; post commander; Western District Commander, Department of Pennsylvania; Allegheny County Council Commander; Commander of the Federation of War Veterans' Societies of Allegheny County; Chairman of the Board of Commissioners' Veterans Advisory Council and Commander of Department of Pennsylvania, JWV.

He served on numerous Department and National committees. Recipient of Department Commanders Award, Certificate of Appreciation and others.

ALLEN D. GOODMAN, born Dec. 26, 1952, El Paso, TX. Enlisted Feb. 5, 1973, USAF, aircraft mechanic, tactical fighter. Military locations 460 FIS Grandforks, 84 FIS, Castle, CA, 64OMS Reese, Vietnam.

He was discharged April 28, 1978, with the rank of E4.

Married to Stephanie Goodman, he has two daughters and two sons, work for Department for the Army Civil Service. Joined JWV in 1985, Post #749 El Paso, Past Post Comdr. And presently Commander Department of Texas.

IRVIN H. GOODMAN, born in Norfolk, VA, Dec. 25 1917. Inducted Aug. 22, 1942, in Newark, NJ, to U.S. Army Basic training at Ft. Riley, KS. Transferred to 524 MP Bn. in LA, went next to Ft. Ord, 110 Engr. Bn. Amphibian Tank Force. Left Frisco July 29, 1943, arrived Adak Alaska Aug. 5 1943, Left Adak Sept. for Oahu, T.H. arrived Oct. 2, 1943 Left Oahu Oct. 22, 1944, arrived Leyte Island, P.I., Feb. 1 1945. Left Leyte P.I. March 27, 1945, arrived Okinawa Islane on April 1, 1945. Left Okinawa Oct. 5, 1945, arriving Kore Oct. 10, 1945. Discharged as T/4 and Dec. 15, 1945.

Memorable experience includes making an assault landing on Okinawa, carrying a flame thrower will always remain in his mind. He'll never forget the screams as he rolled the flame into the caves.

Awards/Medals: Philippine Liberation Ribbon with one Bronze Star, Asiatic-Pacific Campaign Medal, WWII Victory Medal, one Bronze Service Arrowhead, Asiatic-Pacific Ribbon with one Bronze Star, one Bronze star for Ryukyu Campaign, six overseas service bars, Good Conduct Medal.

His wife Sylvia and he recently celebrated their 53rd wedding anniversary. They are the parents of David 47, Andrea 44, Ira 35, Jeri 28. All of the kids are college graduates and married. Before he entered service, he managed one of first supermarkets on the east coast, Jersey City.

While he was in service he received a letter saying his family had moved to Elizabeth, NJ. They stayed with them until he went in business with his father-in-law in Norfolk, VA. They returned to Elizabeth in 1947 where his brother Julius (a veteran) and he opened a restaurant (Goodman's of Elmora). They both retired in 1980.

In 1955 they bought a large house in Elizabeth which had five bedrooms. This house became a meeting place for his kids friends and any one who needed a place to stay. There was a very large rec. room where kids spent hours. These days he stays occupied working around the house, painting, repairing, building, lawn work and everything else. He stays busy and as a result he's in good health. He will be 77 years old.

JEANETTE GOODMAN, born Sept. 4, 1913, Bradford, PA. Joined the USCG Dec. 13, 1943, and served in Communications.

She was the first female assigned to the communications engineering section (radar, sonar, loran) and was not welcomed.

Awards/Medals: Good Conduct and European Theater. Discharged Feb. 7, 1946, as specialist second class, draftsman.

Went to the University of Miami, graduating with degree in sociology. Now retired from social work.

Her brother served five years in Europe with the 5th Army.

MUNROE GOODMAN, joined the U.S. Army with the rank of private on March 13, 1942, at Ft. Dix, NJ. He received his basic training at Camp Polk, LA, Camp Coxcomb, CA, and also Ft. Benning, GA.

He went overseas on Feb. 28, 1944, with the 7th Armd. Div., 709th Tank Bn., sailing on the H.M. *Brittanica* out of Boston and arrived at Liverpool, England. He served in the European Theater of Operations including the Ardennes, Central Europe, Normandy, Northern France and Rhineland sectors. He received many citations and decorations among which were the American Service Medal, European, African Medal, Eastern Service Medal, five stars and French Coat of Arms.

He visited London, England; Paris, France; Holland, Czechoslovakia; Luxembourg, Germany and the French Riviera. He was discharged on Oct. 31, 1945, with the rank of sergeant at Ft. Dix, NJ. *Submitted by Max Sigal.*

JOEL S. GOPEN, born April 11, 1931, Malden, MA. Enlisted March 14, 1951, USN, radarman, OI Div. He served three years four months on USS *Wasp* (North Atlantic Operations world cruise, med cruise, far east duty)

Memorable experience includes on first cruise after shakedown hit their own destroyer USS *Hobson* and sunk it over 150 *Hobson* sailors drowned, biggest sea accident at time. He was up in bow of carrier and nearly crushed by sinking *Hobson* bow.

Awards/Medals: National Defense, Good Conduct Medal, Korean Service Medal, United Nations, Navy Occupation, China Service, European Clasp.

He was discharged April 15, 1955, with the rank of radarman first class.

Married three grown children and three grandchildren. Social worker in public schools and work with delinquents for 30 years. Now retired. Recent member of JWV.

SIDNEY J. GOPIN, born June 21, 1922, Chelse, MA. Entered April 26, 1943, Air Corps, private first class, airplane and engine mechanic, 62nd Bombardment SQ. Military stations include IPS Lanti, MI; Keesler Field, MS; Mariana Islands, Guam. Participated in battle in air offensive Japan and Western Pacific.

Memorable experience was receiving a certificate of appreciation from Rabbi de Sola Pool for assisting Army personnel of the Jewish Faith with their religious endeavors.

Awards/Medals: Asiatic-Pacific Campaign Medal, American Theater Campaign Ribbon, Good Conduct Medal, WWII Victory Medal.

He was discharged Jan. 6, 1946, with the rank of private first class.

Married to Pauline 51 years, children, grandchildren and great-grandchildren. Today he is working hard to recover from a stroke. Hopes to get back into real estate brokerage business. Recently was transferred as a member of Post 100 and has been accepted as a transfer member to Post 72.

ALFRED G. GORDON, born June 19, 1926, in Syracuse, NY. Attended Croton School and graduated from Vocational High School in June 1944. Entered the U.S. Army in September 1944. Killed in action in March 1945, at the age of 19. Buried at the Henri Chapel Cemetery II in Belgium. He was a member of the Phi Alpha Sigma Fraternity. Because he was an ardent amateur photographer, a room has been dedicated in his memory by his fraternity at the Jewish Community Center.

HARRY GORDON, born in Houston, TX, on Oct. 15, 1922. Attended University of Houston, studied electronics. Enlisted Oct. 20, 1942, U.S. Army Signal Branch, HQ Eighth Service Command 318th Signal Bn. Sent to the University of Texas for war training in engineering science and management, completing March 1943.

April 28, 1943, went to Ft. Sam Houston, San Antonio, TX, and May 1943 to Camp Kolher, CA, for basic training and other training as private first class. January 1944 at Camp Crowder, MO, attached to Co. D, 800th Signal Regt. for technical training as a telegraph, telephone installer, repairman and communications. After completing course given rank technician 5th grade. In June 1944 was assigned to 4025th Signal Bn. July 1944 went back to Camp Kohler, and on Sept. 27 1944, left for overseas to the Pacific by ship. October 1944 arrived at Hollandia, New Guinea attached to the 8th Army.

November 1944 boarded on an Australian troopship with supplies. Left with a 40-ship convoy of destroyers and battleships for the invasion of Leyte in the Philippines. Attacked on the Pacific Ocean by Japanese planes dropping torpedoes, firing and diving on our convoy for three days and nights until they received air protection. Landed under heavy attack by the Japanese.

Their battalion handled communications between the 6th and 8th Army on Leyte. The great typhoon of December 1944 struck and capsized three destroyers with heavy loss of life. In September 1944 they were airlifted to the battle of Manila, Luzon, there until war ended December 1945. Departed to the United States, separated at Camp Fannin, TX, and discharged, honorable, Jan. 21, 1946.

Decorations: Asiatic-Pacific Campaign Medal with four Bronze Stars, Philippine Liberation Ribbon with one Bronze Star, American Theater Campaign Medal, WWII Victory Medal and Good Conduct Medal.

Married to Helen since 1944, and has two daughters and three grandchildren. Member Post 574 Jewish War Veterans. Life member DAV and AMVETS. Retired from lumber business, December 1992.

HENRY N. GORDON, born Jan. 18, 1926, Louisville, KY. Enlisted June 5, 1943, U.S. Army, 285th Combat Engr. Bn., Co. C. Military stations included Ft. Dix, NJ; Camp Crowder, MO; and Camp Shelby, MS.

Memorable experience serving with Gen. Patton's 3rd Army, "Battle of the Bulge."

Awards/Medals: Good Conduct Medal, ETO with three battles stars (Ardennes, Rhineland, Central Europe), American Campaign Medal, WWII Victory Medal, Army of Occupation (Germany) Medal.

He was discharged April 26, 1946, with the rank of technician 4.

His mother, age 92 resides at a Florida retirement home, his brother Ted in California, also an Army Vet. A nephew in Canada, a cousin on Long Island. He is a lifelong bachelor. Retired from work, residing at a Patchogue, L.I., NY Veterans Home (27 years). Life member Sgt. Morgan Lander Liblit Post #251, JWV of USA.

ISIDORE GORDON, born Dec. 15, 1906, in Russia. Attended Grammar School in Linden, NJ. Attended Central High School in Syracuse. President of Gordon Tobacco Company. Served in Armed Services from January 1944 to November 1944. Honorably discharged. Died Feb. 2, 1948, at the age of 41. Survived by wife, Esther, sons Hillard Stephen and Martin Neil.

JOSEPH GORDON, charter member JWV Post 377, NVW Post 10 Comd. 1948-1949. Drafted July 15, 1941, Basic Training Camp Croft. Joined 34th Inf. Regt. on Carolina Maneuvers, October 1941.

Left Presidio San Francisco Dec. 16, 1941. Served as Assistant Regimental Communications Officer WOJG with 34th Inf. Regt., 24th Div. in combat at Hollandia, New Guinea, 49 days; Biak Island, New Guinea, 20 days and Leyte, Philippines 79 days, landed in 3rd wave at Red Beach, Leyte.

Awarded Combat Infantry Badge, Bronze Star Medal, Regimental Commendation, Asiatic Pacific Ribbon with two Battle Stars with arrowhead for Leyte Beachhead; also Philippine Liberation Ribbon with Battle Star.

34th Infantry Regiment awarded Presidential Unit Citation for Philippine Campaigns.

Overseas 40 months and reassigned to Staff and Faculty, Cavalry School, Communication Department, Ft. Riley, KS. Discharged October 1945.

MARK W. GORDON, born in Hartford, CT; lived and attended schools in New Britain, CT, and was graduated from New Britain High School, Teachers College of Connecticut, and the Hartford School of Accounting. Mark entered the U.S. Marine Corps in 1953 and underwent basic training at Parris Island, SC. He was then sent to Camp Pendleton, CA, enroute to a stint of one and a half years in Japan with the 3rd Marine Div. where he served at Atsugi Naval Air Station and Tachikawa Air Force Base.

In 1956, Mark was honorably discharged from the USMC at the Groton Navy Base in Groton, CT, having attained the rank of sergeant. After service, Mark returned to Connecticut where he continued his education and subsequently took a position with the Bostonian Fishery, Inc., a wholesale/retail seafood market, which he now owns with his wife, Barbara and their son, Andrew, Mark and Barbara also have a daughter, Tracy and five grandchildren.

MONROE GORDON, born Feb. 23, 1923, New York City, NY. Enlisted in the USAAC Oct. 27, 1942. Assigned initially to Camp Lee, VA, then trained as an aerial engineer at Sheppard Field, TX and elsewhere at specialized training schools. Assigned to the 315th BS, 21st BG at MacDill Field, FL

Subsequently reassigned as an aircraft and engine mechanic on P-47s at Abilene AFB and Sweetwater AFB in Texas. Shipped to Camp Stoneman, WA in July 1945, reissued new gear and were told that they were part of a task force for the Invasion of Japan.

Shipped out on a concrete troop ship in early August 1945. The atomic bomb was dropped on Hiroshima and Nagasaki, and the Japanese surrendered. The task force was stopped and re-routed to Guam where he was assigned to the 52nd BS, 29th BG and involved with maintenance.

Awards/Medals: American Service Medal, Asiatic-Pacific Service Medal, WWII Victory Medal and the Good Conduct Medal. Received honorable discharge Feb. 16, 1946, and resumed his civilian life.

TOBIAS GORDON, born Oct. 19, 1931, in Shenandoah, PA. Entered U.S. Navy on May 21, 1951. Stationed at Bainbridge Naval Training Newport Naval Hospital and USS *Noble* APA218; USS *Estes*; Camp McGill Army Base Japan.

Memorable experience being at evacuation of prisoners at Ko-Gi-Do and bringing Catholic Refuges from Hifong to Sigong in Vietnam.

Awards/Medals: Korean Theater and United Nations Ribbon.

He was discharged May 16, 1955, with the rank of DT2. Today he is an insurance agent.

NEAL D. GOSMAN, born March 2, 1947, Philadelphia, PA; raised in Bridgeton, Vineland and Margate, NJ. Attended Atlantic City High School, University of Pennsylvania, MacMurray College. Active in civil rights and anti-war movement. Served in VISTA anti-poverty program 1970-71. Joined U.S. Army October 1971. Trained at Ft. Dix and Ft. Gordon. Served as military policeman in Vietnam and Ft. Bragg. Assigned to 504th MP Bn. in Danang, then 560th MP Co. in Pleiku and Qui Nhon. Left Vietnam in March 1973; left the Army in September 1973 as SP4.

Lives in St. Paul, MN. Involved in community organizing, First Amendment (neighborhood press and cable access TV), educational (inner-city and adult), peace, justice, political, veterans, and Jewish activities. Four years at IRS. Founding member of Shir Tikvah Congregation. Contributing artist to the first "Vietnam and the Arts" exhibit 1980 (St. Paul and New York). JWV Chapter 354; VVA Chapter 62. Married to Sandra Pappas in 1976; three daughters Merissa, Nicolea and Cassarah.

SOL D. GOSMAN, born June 18, 1913, Philadelphia, PA. Graduated from initial Overbook High School class 1930; from University of Pennsylvania Dental School 1936. Commissioned 1st Lt. U.S. Army Dental Corps February 1938. Was Dental officer in the Southern Sector of the ALCAN Highway with the 95th Engr. Gen. Serv. Regt. (colored) from June 1942 to May 1943. Shipped to England in 1943 and reassigned to the 50th Field Hospital for D-day and European Campaign.

Married Bernice Weinberg in 1942. Nearly died from bad inoculation in Louisiana in 1942. On the ALCAN Highway, 1,600 mile and 200 bridges were built in eight months and 15 days. Landed at Normandy at D-Day plus 3. In Namur during the Battle of the Bulge. Earned five Battle Stars. Left Army in January 1946 as a major.

Practiced orthodontics in Bridgeton, Vineland and Margate, NJ, for 33 years. Operated Camp Caribou, Waterville, Maine, 10 years. Active leader in synagogue, professional and civic activities. Died Philadelphia, Sept. 18, 1978. Survived by wife, two sons (Neal and Howard) three granddaughters.

JULIUS H. GOTTESMAN, served in the U.S. Army from December 1953 - September 1955. During basic training he suggested to some fellow Jewish soldiers that they volunteer for K.P. duty on Christmas Day. Their offer was accepted

and since it was his idea he volunteered for the hardest job as pot washer. However the soldier who was assigned with him refused to put his hands in the water claiming he was an artist. So he was left with all the pots.

After one year of medical training at Ft. Sam Houston, TX, and Fitzsimons Army Hospital he was assigned to Camp Gordon, GA.

He still has fond memories of the kindness shown to the Jewish soldiers by the members of the Augusta Community, where they were offered home hospitality and a warm welcome in the synagogue.

Currently he is a member of many National Jewish organizations but he is the most proud of his affiliation with the JWV.

He has taught for over 30 year in the New York City Public School System and is now retired.

HENRY GOTTFRIED, born Dec. 25, 1919, in Vienna, Austria. Immigrated to the U.S. in 1938 prior to the deportation of Viennese Jews to the death camps. Entered the service Nov. 13, 1941, at Camp Upton, NY. Sent to Camp Monmouth and Camp Crowder for training.

Attended Sig. Corps Radio Repair School. Overseas he participated in battles and campaigns in Central Europe, Libya, Egypt, Rhineland, Germany, France and Battle of the Bulge.

Awards/Medals: American Defense Medal, American Service Medal, EAME Service Medal and Good Conduct Medal. Discharged Nov. 10, 1945, with the rank of staff sergeant.

Married and has two daughters. He is retired.

LUDWIG GOTTLIEB, born Fulda, Germany. Inducted Aug. 14, 1921, U.S. Army. Stations included Ft. Riley, KS, November 1942 - March 1943; ETO November 1945. Reenlist June 1946. Participated in battles in Sicily, South Italy, Anzio, South France, Germany, Korea.

Memorable experience was being forced to leave school in 8th grade; attended Yeshiva, Fulda one year. Immigrated to USA April 1937 on children's non-quota Visa under Auspices of Hias together with younger sister; entered 4th grade due to lack of English, transferred 6th grade after two weeks for two weeks studied English intensively during summer vacation also worked when available; entered high school as senior September 1937 left. October 1937 for job to be able to make affidavit of support to get parents and youngest sister out of Germany father arrested Crystal night and confined to Buchenwald Concentration Camp. Finally allowed to leave Germany June 1939. Family of four lived on his income of $15.00 week until parents found work. Declared enemy alien thus could not enlist after Dec. 7, 1941 transferred to highly classified assignment in North Africa March 1943, Already on truck for trip to Tunisia pulled of because still German National. Sworn in as U.S. citizen in Canstel, Algeria and then sent to Tunisia.

Awards/Medals: Good Conduct Medal, ETO, WWII Victory Medal, American Defense Service Medal.

Retired Feb. 28, 1965, with the rank of CWO.

Married, three children, three grandchildren, and two great-grandchildren. Jewish lay leader, Stuttgart Germany Military Community.

Member of Kreis County of Ludwigsburg Senior Citizen's Council; active in local German seniors club; member Post 753, San Antonio, TX.

SHEPHERD L. GOTTLIEB, born in Bronx, NY, April 2, 1925. Left DeWitt Clinton High School, November 1942, to join U.S. Navy, age 17. Boot Camp, Newport, RI; Diesel School, Richmond, VA. Assigned to USS *Electra* KA4 cargo ship converted for amphibious operations. Went through Panama Canal to Pearl Harbor, then island hopped with crew of 50' tank lighter. Part of invasion of Eniwetok, Kwajalein, Saipan, Leyte, Luzon and Palau. Back to Pearl, loading troops and supplies for invasion of Japan when war ended. Brought troops to Japan for occupation. Returned to Pearl, then San Francisco, and home for discharge, with rank of motor machinist's mate second class. Married Rita Siegel in 1952, had daughter Beth and son David, who died at age 2. Beth lives in Glen Cove, NY, with husband and three children. Had own business; also began teaching in 1971. Married Louella Hanson 1978. Lives in Suffern, NY, near wife's daughter Liisa, her husband, and two children. Conduct Medal, Asiatic-Pacific Campaign Medal with six stars, Philippine Liberation Ribbon with two stars, WWII Victory Medal.

HY G. GOWSEIOW, born April 27, 1916, in Chicago, IL. Graduated high school (Soldan) in St. Louis, MO, on June 1933. Inducted into service on June 6, 1941, at Jefferson Barracks, MO. Reported for duty at McClellan Field in Sacramento, CA, on June 13, 1941. Assigned to 7th Transport Sqdn. which was redesignated 7th Troop Carrier Sqdn., and made part of the 62nd Troop Carrier Group on July 4, 1942. Assigned overseas duty on Sept. 15, 1942; operations included airborne drops on North Africa, Sicily, Italy, Southern France and paratroops training in Egypt - Palestine.

Received campaign ribbons for Tunisia; Sicily; Napels-Foggia; Rome-Arno; Southern France; North Apennines; Po Valley; Air Combat and EAME Theater. Returned from overseas in June 1945 after 34 months of overseas duty and was discharged June 26, 1945. After 36 years on the road as a sales representative he retired in 1982. Currently active with the St. Louis Senior Olympics and a member of JWV of USA, St. Louis Heritage Post 644, St. Louis, MO.

MAX GRABER, born Bronx, NY, Feb. 13, 1920, enlisted Oct. 9, 1941, Army Air Corps. Graduated Air Corps Radio School, Scott Field, IL, as radio operator mechanic February 1942. Made private first class. Aerial gunnery school, Harlingen, TX, but transferred to Army Airways Communication System, Albuquerque, NM. Made Corporal. Six months at Southampton Island, Northwest Territories, Canada below Arctic Circle, handling coded radio traffic. Made sergeant. Ten day delay enroute through New York, then off to air base at tip of Greenland.

Boarded wooden steamer loaded with building materials, food and fuel, sailed north along east coast of Greenland, through area of the "Dorchester" calamity and drowning of the four chaplains. Landed on island "Kulusuk" just south of Arctic Circle and helped build quarters and radio weather station. Made staff sergeant. For 14 months, 13 men isolated from world, supplied by air drops with food and necessities directed planes over the ten thousand foot ice caps towards Iceland and England.

The radio station, call letters WZO, became the ancho station of the renowned Distant Early Warning or Dew Line Made technical sergeant. Returned to U.S. as station chief a Ford Dix and "Ruptured Duck," Aug. 15, 1945.

Married Thelma Jacobs Aug. 18, 1945. Daughter Renee born first anniversary. Advanced radio-T.V. school. Specia assignment as civilian-in-charge to overhaul Caribbean Ai Command radio station, Albrook Field Canal Zone. Year late returned to U.S., bought home Wantagh, Long Island, and entered electronic service field.

Past 25 years co-owner Sono-Vision Electronic Service Daughter Renee, mother of Dawn, daughter Eden, mother o Cassal and Alex, daughter Robyn and son David both Dr.'s o chiropractic. Member Post 724 for 30 years, commander eigh years, VAVS Representative 25 years, Nassau-Suffolk District Council Man-of-Year 1985, inducted Chapel of Fou Chaplains 1990.

IRVING GRALNICK, born April 10, 1921, in Newark NJ. Entered the Army on Oct. 15, 1942, and was discharge

Feb. 21, 1946. He was stationed in the USA for the first two years. He served with Medical Basic Training, Camp Kilmer, NJ. Army Specialized Training Program at the University of Maine for nine months. When the ASTP was disbanded he served with the 26th Inf. Div. (Yankee Division) in Tennessee Maneuvers and Ft. Jackson, SC. He was transferred to Ft. Rucker, AL, and joined the 123rd Evacuation Hospital semi-mobile. He went to Europe with the 123rd Evacuation Hospital as a medical technician. They received Battle Stars for two major campaigns, the Rhineland and Central Europe. They then became alerted for direct shipment to the Philippines, when the atomic bomb was dropped and they didn't go.

Awards/Medals: American Service Medal, EAME Service Medal, Good Conduct Medal, WWII Victory Medal, Battle Stars for Rhineland and Central Europe.

He was discharged Feb. 21, 1946, with the rank of corporal. After discharge he received a bachelor of science degree from Rutgers University and became a certified public accountant. Semi-retired.

Member of Post #309, Irvington, Union, NJ, JWV. Married for over 49 years to Rita, have one daughter and one granddaughter.

EDWARD GRYN GREEN, born March 28, 1925, Philadelphia, PA, of Polish parentage. Inducted Army June 16, 1943, Camden, NJ. Basic Training Camp Croft, SC. Left NY on the *Ile De France,* Jan. 17, 1944, arrived Greenock, Scotland, Jan. 25, 1944. Landed Omaha Beach June 16, 1945. Assigned to 2nd Div. 9th Regt. Anti-tank. Entered Germany Oct. 4, 10 miles east of St. Vith, Belgium. During Battle of Bulge went north to Elsenborn. Crossed Rhine River March 21, near Remagen. Then to Glessen, Gottingen, Leipzig, Bayreuth, Rotz, VE-Day in Rokycany, Czechoslovakia.

Returning to USA: boarded 40 and 8 at Regensburg. Departed LeHavre, France, July 12, 1945, on the General Richardson. Arrived Boston July 19, 1945. VJ-Day at home in Moorestown, NJ, while on furlough. Discharged Oct. 23, 1945, at Camp Swift, TX.

Re-enlisted March 17, 1949, sent to Ord. Sch. at Aberdeen Proving Ground, MD. Then to 84 Ord. Serv. Det., Ft. Buchanna, PR. Transferred to 408th Ord. MM Co., Corozal, CZ, 113 Ord. MM Co., Camp Pickett, VA. Discharged Oct. 5, 1952, highest rank staff sergeant.

Decorations: Combat Infantryman Badge, Bronze Star, ETO with five Campaign Stars, Good Conduct Medal, American Campaign Medal, WWII Victory Medal, National Defense Service Medal.

Member JWV Post 502 No. Palm Beach, FL, life member, twice Cmdr. VFW 4143, Riviera Bch., FL, Past 3rd Dist. Cmdr. VFW of FL, Charter and Life member Loyal Order of Moose Lodge 2010, Palm Bch. Gardens, FL, Life member Palm Bch. County Genealogical Society, Life member Veterans of the Battle of the Bulge.

Retired from 25 years at Pratt & Whitney Aircraft division United Technologies near West Palm Bch., FL, as metallurgist technician.

Resides now in West Palm Beach, FL.

ROBERT E. GREEN, born June 30, 1919, Boston, MA. Enlisted in the V-7 Program in 1940. Served in the Amphibious Service, USNR as deck officer. Stations include USS ABSD #4 (floating dry dock), USS *Zeilin,* USS *Arlington* (both assault transports).

Participated in Guadalcanal Campaign (1942) Attu Island (May 1943), Kiska Island (August 1943) and was assistant beachmaster on Tarawa (Nov. 22-25, 1943). These four days were the most dangerous, frightening and memorable days of his Navy duty.

Awards/Medals: Silver Star, four Battle Stars, Unit Citation and WWII Victory Medal. Discharged October 1945 with the rank of Commander, USNR (RET).

Graduated from Occidental College with BA in economics (1947). Became a life insurance professional, retiring in 1988.

Married to Bette and has five children. Member JWV, Friendship Post #794, Los Angles and B'nai B'rith.

ROBERT L. GREEN, entered service September 1942. Basic training September 1942 - December 1942. Aviation Mechanic School, January 1943 - April 1943. Attached to 389th Ftr Sqd. 366th Ftr Group. May 1943 - August 1945. Six Battle Stars French Fourragiere - Belgian. Fourragiere - Presidential Citation. Involved in Battle of the Bulge, transferred to 531 Ftr. Squad for return home. Arrived USA at Camp Shanks, October 1945. Received honorable discharge Nov. 11, 1945 at Ft. Dix.

BERNARD MICHAEL GREENBERG, born Sept. 5, 1923, in Brooklyn, NY. ROTC Unit called June 1943. Accepted as a cadet July 1944. Corps of Engineers after graduation. Graduated class of 1947 USMA, Army appointment. Military stations include Ft. Belvoir, VA, Eng. Aviation Bn.; Ft. Elmendorf, Anchorage, AL; Ft. Leonard Wood, MO; Eng. Supply Depot, Okinawa.

Awards/Medals: CCNY, USMA, Texas A&M, Masters USC 1957. Graduated #25 in class of 264.

He resigned in 1954, with the rank of captain.

Married Goldie Breslow in 1948, has son Arthur, daughters Myra (Glassman) and Joni (Marine) currently six granddaughters and one grandson. Licensed civil engineer, State of California, formerly in construction. Currently mortgage broker.

DANIEL N. GREENBERG, born June 30, 1925, Chicago, IL. Enlisted March 8, 1944, U.S. Army, 4th Armored Div.. Stationed at Ft. Knox, KY, Camp Chafee, AR. Bastogne European Theater.

Awards/Medals: Purple Heart Medal, Silver Star, ETO.

He was discharged Feb. 18, 1947, with the rank of corporal.

Married, three children (Ruth, Aaron, Joseph); three grandchildren (Rachel, Adam, Lisa). Retired 1988, Administrator of Public Psychiatric Hospital, Chicago, IL.

EMANUEL GREENBERG, born May 3, 1916, Birmingham, AL. Enlisted November 1942, DEML. Stations included Ft. McPherson, GA (Rec. Center); Linz, Austria; Garmisch Partinkerchen and Munich, Germany. Participated in battles in Central Europe.

Memorable experience was working with DPS in Munich and Garmisch Partinkerchen.

Awards/Medals: one Battle Star.

He was discharged in 1946 with the rank of staff sergeant.

He and his wife Ruth have children: Carol, Lee, Alan and Robert. Today he is retired.

HERBERT L. GREENBERG, born Jan. 19, 1924, New York. Enlisted Feb. 22, 1943, Infantry, radio operator, 75th Div. Military location Ft. Riley, Camp Breckinridge. Europe, Ardennes, Central Europe, Rhineland.

Awards/Medals: American Campaign Medal, EAME Service Medal, WWII Victory Medal.

He was discharged Feb. 21, 1946, as private first class.

He and his wife Renita had three children and three grandchildren. Columbia University BS 1948. Today he is chairman Union Benefit Life Insurance Company.

HY GREENBERG, born 80 years ago, Nov. 24, 1914, the good Lord has seen me through the great war and still experiencing good health. The preeminent birth took place in Brooklyn, NY.

Greetings! September 1943, my naval career was an auspicious beginning through Sampson, NY, three month training period. From Norfolk, VA, staging area to Brooklyn,

NY Shipyard, my new destroyer, USS *Monssen,* was commissioned Feb. 14, 1944. The rest is history. My date of discharge Nov. 20, 1945, as radarman third class. During my tenure of service aboard the *Monssen,* I was awarded six medals with 10 Battle Stars, Good Conduct Medal, American Campaign Medal, Asiatic-Pacific Campaign Medal, Philippine Liberation Ribbon, WWII Occupation, WWII Victory Medal.

August 29, 1995, my wife Sylvia and I will be celebrating our 55th Anniversary. We were blessed with a daughter and two grandsons, 25 and 22, residing in Birmingham, AL. A son with a four and half year granddaughter, living in Oakland, CA. Our son, Sheldon, as an associated engineer, involved with a long range artificial heart program in conjunction with Baxter Corp. here in Oakland.

Since my retirement 1979, I've written a book, detailing the exploits of the *Monssen* in the third person. After two and a half years writing the manuscript, contacting a number of publishers, received three contracts with one problem, they required more than $10,000 to publish. Needless to say, that's beyond my financial means. In the interim, I've had articles appearing in the *Modern Maturity* and local newspapers, all relating to WWII; the Enola Gay, Smithsonian contrariness; Hiroshima and Nagasaki detailing why President Truman was right and proper in dropping the bombs.

In conclusion, I am enjoying my retirement to the fullest and above all with continued good health for my wife and myself.

IRVING GREENBERG, born May 11, 1923, Chicago, IL. Enlisted February 1943, U.S. Army, 877th Airborne Engr. Military stations included Darmstadt, Germany, Frankfurt, Germany and Munich, Germany, Sheppard Field, TX; England, Normandy, Paris. Participated in battles in Normandy and Northern France.

Memorable experiences include V-E Day in Paris.

Awards/Medals: EAME Theater with two Bronze Battle Stars, American Campaign Medal, WWII Victory Medal, three Overseas Service Bars, Good Conduct Medal, Glider Badge and MM, MI Rifle Carbine.

He was discharged February 1946, with the rank of corporal.

Married to Marlene, two sons (Kenneth and David), one daughter (Joanne), two grandchildren (Jacob and Sarah). Retired member JWV Post 800.

JOEL M. GREENBERG, a Grant High School, North Hollywood, CA, graduate, received his BA at Cal State, Northridge, his MBA from Virginia. He was commissioned a Naval line officer in 1968. Stationed in San Diego, he served on USS *Segundo* SS398, and in the final crew of both USS *Seafox* SS402, which became Turkish Submarine Burak Reis, and USS *Catfish* SS339, which became Argentine submarine Santa Fe, sunk by the British during the Falklands War. He saw Vietnam action, conducted a special operation and qualified in submarines while on *Seafox.*

Becoming a supply corps officer in 1971 h served on USS *Francis Hammond* FF1067 where he saw extensive

Vietnam action. Next, he was material director, supervisor of shipbuilding, Long Beach, CA, and subsequently at Supply Depot, Yokosuka, Japan. In Washington, D.C. he was assistant project manager, Deep Submergence Program and completed his career as executive assistant to the Navy's first competition advocate general. He retired at the rank of commander (0-5) after 20 years of service. His decorations include the Sea Service and Hostile Fire ribbons and the National Defense, Expert Pistol, Vietnam Campaign, Vietnam Service with three stars, Navy Expeditionary, Navy Achievement and Meritorious Service Medal.

A long-standing member of JWV, he also devotes considerable time to the VFW, Old Crows, Submarine League, the Bay Area Council of Military and Veterans Organizations, Kiwanis and Alumni Groups. He operates his own marketing and consulting business. He, his wife Michelle and their two teenage daughters live in Cameron Park, CA, in the Sierra, NV, foothills above Sacramento, on the way to Lake Tahoe.

LOUIS GREENBERG, born in Brooklyn, NY, Aug. 18, 1922. Entered Army, Dec. 23, 1942, Ft. Dix, NJ. Trained at Ft. Leonard Wood, MO, Camp Atterbury, IN, Ft. Hood, TX, and Camp Gruber, OK. Overseas August 1944, to France. Fought in the Battle of the Bulge with the tank destroyers. Was in Holland, Belgium and Germany. Received three Battle Stars. Returned to the States in June 1945 and was discharged Dec. 7, 1945, in California.

Marketing and Advertising Major at Pace Institute, NY.

Married Barbara in 1948, two children, Janine and Ronald. Barbara died in 1980, married Evelyn in 1989, gained two daughters, Audrey and Barbara and a son Michael. Have six grandchildren. Now happily retired.

Member of Post 651, Fair Lawn, NJ, for 38 years. Life member of JWV, Disabled American Veterans, Veterans Battle of the Bulge, Veterans of Foreign Wars and member of the American Legion.

Post Commander five times, County Commander, First District Vice Commander, Department Chief of Staff, Department Chief Aide and National Executive Committeeman, NJ.

MARTIN GREENBERG, S/Sgt., U.S. Army-Combat Medic, 7th Div., 31st Inf., 2nd Bn., G Co. Trained at Brooks Army Medical Hospital, Ft. Sam Houston, TX, and the 1st Armored Div., Ft. Hood, TX. He receive a retirement discharge due to injuries received Nov. 30, 1953. His decorations include: three Purple Heart Medal, Silver Star, Bronze Star, Good Conduct Medal and multiple service ribbons.

He is a life member of the JWV, VFW, and Disabled American Veterans, as well as a member of the Korean War Veterans. He has held the positions of Senior Vice Commander Korean War Veterans, Wyoming Valley, PA; State Commander, Department of Pennsylvania, JWV; Central District Commander, Department of Pennsylvania, JWV (two terms), Post 212 Commander, Wilkes-Barre, PA, JWV (ten years).

His awards and honors include: Outstanding State Department Commander, awarded by JWV USA (1990); Pennsylvania State Distinguished Service Award (1990); Pennsylvania State, Man of the Year Award, JWV (1986); U.S. Congressional Citation (1990); Philadelphia County Council Brotherhood Award(1991); JWV of USA National Membership Award (five times); Distinguished Service Award, Luzerne County, PA (1989); Distinguished Service Award, City of Wilkes-Barre, PA (1989); Humanitarian and Legion of Honor Awards. Chapel of Four Chaplains, Valley Forge, PA (1987 and 1990); and Korean War Veterans Citation, Wyoming Valley, PA (1990-91).

He and his wife, Sondra, have been married 38 years currently residing in Wilkes-Barre, PA. They have three sons, Mark, Allan, Kevin, and three grandchildren.

MURRAY GREENBERG, enlisted USAF September 1948, discharged honorably as staff sergeant August 1952. Fourteen months Guam, 20th AF HQ; Japan Occupation 1950, Korea 1950-51, 5th AF HQ, helped prepare news releases of air war; got near fatal dysentery; threat of sniper attack while taken to field hospital; spent five days/nights in freight train boxcar during retreat from Seoul. Korean Service Medal with five Battle Stars; UN Service Medal; Occupation of Japan Service Medal; Republic of Korea Presidential Unit Citation.

While in Japan, attended celebration in Tokyo, sponsored by Japan-Israel Cultural Association, honoring Jewish chaplains. Met Japanese who spoke of Col. Yasui, only Japanese cited in Golden Book of Zionism. Met Ambassador Nomura who was in Washington at time of Pearl Harbor attack. He spoke of not knowing of the attack in advance and that he lived many years in America, was educated there, that he loved America and opposed the war.

PERRY GREENBERG, born Dec. 4, 1920, Minneapolis, MN. Enlisted in the USN Jan. 18, 1938. Served on many vessels, but notably on USS *Northampton* (CA-36) at Hawaiian Detachment, Pacific Fleet. The ship was 100 miles at sea when Pearl Harbor was attacked.

Notable events were as screen for the carrier *Hornet*, when Doolittle's planes took off to bomb Tokyo, and the sinking of the *Northampton* the night of Nov. 30 and Dec. 1, 1942, off of Guadalcanal by torpedoes from Japanese destroyers. He survived, swam away and was rescued by the destroyer USS *Fletcher*. (The ship has annual reunions at different places each year.) Left the USN May 18, 1954 with the rank Chief QM E-7.

Re-enlisted in the U.S. Army at Ft. MacArthur, San Pedro, CA. Served 18 months in Inchon, Korea; Kobe and Hiroshima, Japan; Ft. Ord, CA; Ft. Bliss, TX; and Germany for three years as a AJAX, HERCULES and HAWK guided missile technician and instructor. After 14 years in the Army, he retired July 31, 1968 as SFC (E-7) at El Paso, TX.

Awards/Medals: American Defense Service Medal with Fleet Clasp, four Navy Good Conduct Medals, four Army Good Conduct Medals, National Defense Service Medal, American Theater of War, Pacific Theater with eight Battle Stars, Navy Commendation Medal, Army Commendation Medal, WWII Victory Medal, USNR 10 years Service, UN Medal and Korean Service Medal plus a Presidential Unit Citation. He is a plankowner of the USN Memorial at Washington, DC. Belongs to the JWV, American Legion, VFW, DAV and is a 32° Scottish Rite Mason.

Worked for the USPS for 17 years, retiring in March 1986. Married his high school sweetheart, Marian Markowitz, and they recently celebrated their 50th anniversary. Daughter Eileen Drachman passed away Nov. 6, 1991, at age 47; son Harvey is a registered nurse in El Paso, TX; granddaughter Sara is in her second year of Law School at Arizona State University; grandson Tommy attends University of Texas at El Paso.

RUBIN GREENBERG, born Jan. 19, 1924, Brooklyn, NY. Entered the Air Force, March 1943 as an Air Cadet. Attended the Glider training program at Sheppard Field, TX.

He was assigned to the European Theater of Operations in November 1943, as a co-pilot engineer on a CG4-A Combat Glider in the 441st Troop Carrier Command, 100th Squadron as a sergeant, flying status.

Earned four Battle Stars in the ETO with a Presidential Citation and Silver Cluster for services rendered. He survived three Glider crashes and parachuted to safety over France with the 82nd and 101st Airborne Divisions.

Credited with service involvement in Normandy, Southern France, Eindhoven, Holland and Rhine Crossing in Germany as well as the occupation Army. Honorably discharged in November 1945. Presently semi-retired living in New York City and Southampton, NY. The father of Alex, Bruce and Jesse and grandfather of Daniel.

JOSEPH M. GREENE, born New York City 1931. Graduated DeWitt Clinton High School and CCNY. Enlisted in Air Force 1951. After basic training, attended Aircraft Observer School, Ellington Field, TX. Graduated as second lieutenant with certification as navigator, radar observer and bombardier. Assigned to 56th Strategic Recon. Sq., Yokota AFB, Japan. Navigator on RB-29. Completed 153 missions, accumulating 1830 flying hours. Primary missions were locating and tracking typhoons and collecting air samples to detect Soviet atomic bomb testing in Siberia. The flights covered the Pacific area from Formosa, north over Korea, Japan, the Kurile Islands and the Kamchatka Penninsula. Lt. Greene also served as paymaster, assistant trial counsel and flying supply officer. Released from active duty Oct. 13, 1955.

Active reserve with 336th Troop Carrier Sq. where as navigator participated in paratrooper drops with 101st Airborne Div. Ordered to active duty for 10 months Electronics School, Keesler AFB 1956. Resigned active reserve April 1964. Attained rank of captain, senior navigator with 2,900+ flying hours. Received the following commendations: MATS Award for Safety in Military Aviation, National Defense Medal, Korean Service Medal, Air Force Service Medal, United Nations Medal including two Battle Stars, two arrowheads, and OLC.

MARVIN B. GREENFELD, born in Eden Center, NY, March 5, 1925. Graduated high school May 1943, during three month draft deferment. Entered Army July 17, 1943. Reception Center Camp Upon, NY. Basic training Keesler Field, MS. Assigned 88th Army Air Corps Band at Hunter Field, GA. Reassigned Infantry at Camp Livingston, LA, during "Belgian Bulge." Reassigned Army Air Corps at Sheppard Field, TX. Assigned technical school at Lowry Field, CO. Then assigned Unit Personnel Office at Lowry Field. Honorably discharged at Ft. Monroe, CO, Feb. 28, 1946, as corporal.

Good Conduct Medal, WWII Victory Medal, American Theater Medal. Married Renee Aug. 24, 1950, after college. Have two sons and a daughter. Member JWV and two professional societies. Employed as electrical engineer for 40 years. Retired March 1990. Grateful for invitations from families in Biloxi, Savannah and Denver for Jewish Holidays during military service.

ABRAHAM GREENFIELD, born in New York City, Feb. 1, 1920. Entered the Army in March 1943. Basic training at Camp Croft, Spartanburg, SC, with the 65th Inf. Div. Rated technician third class with specialties in light and heavy weaponry and communications.

Sent to Philippines as a replacement troop with the 164 Regt. American Div. was a field radio operator with

158

infiltration and reconnaissance platoon that scouted enemy positions. Engaged in the Battles for Cebu, Dumagetti, and Leyte. After Japanese surrender, sent to Japan with 1st Cavalry Div. as part of the Army of Occupation. Awarded Bronze Star Medal, Asiatic-Pacific Campaign Medal with three Battle Stars, Philippine Liberation Ribbon with Battle Star and Army of Occupation Medal. Discharged from the service in March 1946 at Ft. Dix, NJ.

Married Ruth Halborn, October 1947. Retired as president/business manager of IBEW. Local 1783, White Plains, NY, on Nov. 1, 1988. Has three children, Linda, Debra and Robert and two grandchildren, Elana and Leland. Resides in Spring Valley, NY, North Lauderdale, FL, and on a farm in Belmont, MA.

DAVID M. GREENHUT, born Feb. 10, 1972. Enlisted private, Inf. Maryland Army National Guard, 1989. Promoted sergeant, 1994. Army Achievement Medal. Son of LTC Jeffrey Greenhut.

FREDERICK W. GREENHUT, born Brooklyn, NY, Nov. 5, 1897. Commissioned second lieutenant, FA, AUS, 1918. Discharged, 1918. Commissioned second lieutenant, AUS, 1924. Recalled to active duty, major, Signal Corps, AUS, 1940. Chief signal officer, Port of Oran, 1942-43. Medically retired, 1943. WWI Victory Medal, EAME Campaign Medal with one CS, WWII Victory Medal. Father of LTC Jeffrey Greenhut.

IRA L GREENHUT (LOU), born 1895. Enlisted, private, AUS, 1917. Sergeant, Co. C, 307th Ammunition Train, 82nd Inf. Div. WWI Victory Medal with St. Mihiel, Meuse Argonne, and Defensive Sector clasps. Honorably discharged, 1919. Lt. Col. And ADC, Governor's Staff, Georgia State Militia, 1971. Died 1987. Brother of Maj. Frederick W. Greenhut and Sidney D. Greenhut.

JEFFREY GREENHUT, born New York, NY, March 1, 1942. Commissioned ROTC 2LT, Military Intelligence, USAR, May 25, 1964. Entered active duty, July 1964. Principle assignments; psychological warfare officer, 3rd SFG(ABN), Ft. Bragg, 1965, Order of Battle Specialist, 519th MI Bn, Vietnam, 1965-66. Released from active duty, July 14, 1966. Commanding officer, HHC, 98th Div., USAR, 1972-3, instructor, USAR schools, 1973-84, deputy G-3, 352nd CA Command, 1988-1992, Public Service Team Chief, Kuwait Task Force, 352nd Civil Affairs Command, Operation Desert Shield/Storm. Entered Kuwait City March 2, 1991 and participated in reconstitution of Kuwait Government functions. Retired, LTC, USAR, 1992.

Bronze Star, Meritorious Service Medal, Army Commendation Medal with OLC, Army Achievement Medal, Army Reserve Components Achievement Medal with four OLC, National Defense Medal with BS, Vietnam Service Medal with three CS, Southwest Asia Service Medal with two CS, Humanitarian Service Medal, Armed Forces Reserve Medal with TYD, Government of Vietnam Service Medal, Defense of Saudi Arabia Service Medal. Ph.D., History, Kansas State University, 1978. Currently, Command Historian, Naval Security Group Command, Washington, D.C. Son of Major Frederick W. Greenhut, AUS. Father of SGT David Greenhut, MDARNG, born Feb. 10, 1972; Wendy R. Greenhut, born Sept. 18, 1970; Abigail S. Greenhut, born April 17, 1984; Jennifer R. Greenhut, born Feb. 11, 1987.

JOSEPH B. GREENHUT, born Feb. 28, 1843, Teinitz, Austria. Enlisted, April 17, 1861, as private, Co. A, 12th Illinois Volunteer Infantry. Promoted sergeant, July 1861. Wounded at the battle of Ft. Donnelson, Feb. 15, 1862. Discharged, April 22, 1862, at Pittsburg Landing, TN. Enrolled, Captain, Co. K., 82nd Illinois Volunteer Infantry, July 22, 1862. Served with that regiment at the Battle of Gettysburg. Resigned, Feb. 24, 1864. Married Clara Wolfner, born April 9, 1850, Ayest, Bohemia, on Oct. 24, 1866. Children, Fanny V. Greenhut, born Feb. 26, 1868; Benedict J. Greenhut, born June 24, 1870; Walter Greenhut, born April 1878, died age four; Nelson W. Greenhut, born July 10, 1891. Died Nov. 17, 1918. Cousin of Maj. Frederick W. Greenhut, Sgt. Ira L. Greenhut, and Capt. Sidney D. Greenhut.

SIDNEY D. GREENHUT, born Sept. 15, 1903. Enlisted, AUS, March 30, 1942. Promoted corporal, Sept. 12, 1942. Graduate, Army Air Forces Officer Candidate School, Miami Beach, FL. Commissioned 2nd LT, U.S. Army Air Corps, Dec. 8, 1942. Captain, July 20, 1946. Relieved from active duty, Oct. 2, 1946. Transferred to retired service, 1959. American Campaign Medal, European, African, Mediterranean Campaign Medal, WWII Victory Medal. Died Feb. 20, 1969. Brother of Maj. Frederick W. Greenhut and Sgt. Ira L. Greenhut.

HOWARD F. GREENSPAN, born Dec. 18, 1925, in New York City. Entered U.S. Navy Dec. 13, 1943. Stationed at Samara, Philippines; Tubabao, Philippines; LST 1942; California; Pennsylvania; Illinois; Rhode Island. Discharged on June 10, 1946, with the rank of PHM3/c.

Awards/Medals: Asiatic-Pacific Campaign Medal, North American Medal, WWII Victory Medal.

Today he is a professional engineer and land surveyor.

IRVING A. GREENSPAN, born Jan. 14, 1919, Manhattan, NY. Enlisted Jan. 4, 1942, HQ&HQ Sq. 1st Mapping Group, Bolling Field, Washington, DC, detached service to *Life Magazine* April 1942. Appointed to Aviation Cadet School, Lowry Field, CO, August 1942. Graduated Dec. 4, 1942, 2nd lieutenant, USAF. Graduated 1st Photo Intelligence Officer School, Peterson AFB, Colorado Springs attached to 2nd Photo Gp.

Transferred Jan. 14, 1943, to 1st Motion Picture Unit, Culver City, CA to founding cadre 10th AF Cbt. Camera Unit. Shipped to CBI July 1943 and assigned to 10th AF. Served two and a half years on detached service with various flying units, most notably 1st Air Commandos (gliders), 2nd Air Commandos (paratroopers), 7th BG, 25th Fighter Sq. Assam, ATC "flying the Hump" and every medium bomb group in the theater.

Awards/Medals: Presidential Unit Citation, WWII Victory Medal, Asiatic-Pacific Theater Ribbon with three stars, American Theater Ribbon and Bronze Star Medal. Returned home Nov. 8, 1945, separated from service Jan. 14, 1946, rank captain, USAC, rated Flying Combat Observer.

Retired from family business, Greenspan's Kosher Restaurant and Caterers, and moved to Royal Palm Beach, FL in 1981. Has two sons, Jeffrey and Robert; two step-sons, George and Benji; five grandchildren: Lori, Jaimie, Max, Alex and Jessica.

Charter member of JWV Post Lt. Robert P. Grover #10, B'Nai B'rith member since 1940, F&AM since 1951. Involved with Temple and keeps busy with golf and photo hobbies. Wife, May, was in Medical Corps as a nurse (1LT) and served in England and France following invasion.

MARTIN B. GREENSPAN, born in Brooklyn, NY, on Feb. 16, 1923. He was called to service Feb. 3, 1943. Took basic training at Camp Bowie, TX, for 13 weeks. Transferred to Camp Hood, TX, for advanced training. After advanced training was put into the 820th Tank Destroyer Div. and sent to Camp Breckinridge, KY. At Camp Breckinridge he was reassigned to the 825th Tank Destroyer BN Co. C. Remained with them until the end of the war. Was on Tennessee Maneuvers in September and October 1943 and then sent to Camp Atterbury, IN, to Artillery School Specializing in indirect firing.

In May 1944 shipped overseas to Glasgow, Scotland arrived there June 5, 1944. Spent six weeks in Scotland and England for further training and then went to France July 15, 1944. Took part in the campaign of Northern France, Battle of the Bulge. Also took part in the campaign of Rhineland and Central Europe. At wars end May 8, 1945, was called to Wiesbaden, Germany and stationed there until December 1945.

Honorable discharge Jan. 1, 1946.

When he came back home he got his job back at the U.S. post office. Married Frances Ostrowsky in November 1949. From 1950 until his retirement in 1988 he was in business for himself.

Has four children and five grandchildren.

Joined the JWV in 1958 and went up the ranks to department commander of the DC department and also NEC.

Now doing volunteer work for the Jewish Social Service.

SEYMOUR GREENSPAN (SY), RT2/c, USNR, born June 13, 1925, Brooklyn, NY. Boys H.S. (1937-41); CCNY (1941-43) (1946-49) BSEE; NCE (1949-53) MSEE. Enlisted USN January 1943. Honorable discharge April 1946. Lived in Brooklyn; Long Branch, NJ, and Boca Raton, FL.

Boot Camp, USNTC Sampson, NY (January 1943-April 1943); Radio Technician Schools (April 1943-January 1944); assigned to Destroyer USS *Purdy* DD734, January 1944. Served with 5th Fleet Pacific (Task Force 58) during Iwo-Jima and Okinawa invasions (November 1944-May 1945). Ship was damaged by Kamikaze (suicide bombers) air attack at Okinawa, and returned to Pearl Harbor for repair.

Decoration/Medals: WWII Victory Medal, American Theater Medal, Asiatic-Pacific Campaign Medal with two Battle Stars, 5th Fleet Naval Commendation.

Married Helen Miler Greenspan. Daughter/son-in-law Anise/David Kaplan; grandchildren: Talia, Daniel, Jonathan, Pamela. Son/daughter-in-law - Marc/ Jan Greenspan, grandchildren: Drew, Brian, Dale.

Employed by Department of the Army and RCA (1949-80). Self-employed engineering consultant (1980-1995). Member Board of Education, Long Branch (12 years) and City Council (four years), JWV, VFW, Bnai Brith, IEEE, Army Aviation Association of America, Cong. Bros. of Israel (Long Branch), Old Guard (Long Branch), Knights of Pythias, Cong. Torah Ohr (Boca Raton).

SAUL GREENSPOON, 1st LT, inducted into Army Jan. 23, 1943, at Ft. Snelling, MN. Ordered to QM Truck Company 86th Inf. Div. at Camp Howze, TX. Took basic and went on maneuvers in Louisiana. Shipped to Star Unit at College Station, TX, and then to OCS at Camp Lee, VA. Shipped overseas as a replacement to 3454 Truck Company attached to 8th Armored Div. in France. Stayed with outfit through Belgium and France and ended in the Harz Mountains in Germany.

War in Europe ended and they were shipped to Slovitz, Czechoslovakia (near Pilsen). They (the Division) paraded in Pilsen for Edward Benes, president of Czechoslovakia before he was killed. There were some ex-German prisoners (Russians) hanging around their company so before they left Slovitz to go to a Tent City in France, he took about 30 Russians to Prague in the Russian Zone.

Shipped out of Marseilles, France for Japan and war ended so they went to Patrick Henry, VA. Shipped to Ft. Leonard Wood, MO, to deactivate company, then to Camp Campbell, KY. Picked up by Army Service Forces and shipped to Camp Lee, VA. Trained QM replacements until discharged Aug. 10, 1946, at Ft. Meade, MD.

Awards/Medals: Good Conduct Medal, American Campaign Medal, EAME Campaign Medal with two stars, WWII Victory Medal with two stars, Army of Occupation Germany.

Married and has two children and four grandchildren. Retired. Has been a member of JWV since 1947.

ROLAND GREENWALD, Sgt. Maj. U.S. Army. Born Dec. 10, 1925, New York, NY. BBA, Dallas Baptist University, Dallas, TX. Entered Army March 20, 1944. Basic training, Ft. McClellan, AL.

Stateside assignments: Ordnance Corps Ft. Meade, MD; Camp Pickett, VA; Washington, D.C.; and Ft. Dix, NJ. Sgt. Maj. Ft. Sam Houston, TX; and Adm. Asst., Armed Forces Exam. Station, Dallas, TX.

Overseas assignments: 94th Inf. Div. under General Patton's Third Army, during the Battle of the Bulge. Later assigned to the 1st Inf. Div. to guard the top 10 Nazi War criminals during the Nuremberg trials. Additional assignments include Military Missions in Thailand and Taiwan for five years. Later assigned to the Military Attaché in Mexico City for two years. Then to HQ USAREUR and 7th Army, Heidelberg, Germany, and finally to the 16th Combat Aviation Gp., Vietnam.

Decorations: Combat Infantry Badge with one star, Bronze Star with OLC, Distinguished Service Medal, Commendation Medal with two OLC, Conspicuous Service Medal from New York State, Good Conduct Medal with nine awards, European Campaign Medal with two stars, National Defense Medal with OLC, WWII Victory Medal, Army of Occupation Medal, Vietnam Campaign Medal with 60 Device and two certificates of achievement.

Retired U.S. Army, June 30, 1972, as sergeant major.

Married to Shirley Saville Fleshin, a former captain in the Army Nurse Corps. Retired from Federal Service July 1989.

Life memberships: JWV, DAV, NCOA, Masons, Scottish Rite, Shriners. Past Post Commander of JWV Post 256, Dallas, TX. Currently, Junior Vice Commander of Department of Texas and member board of directors NMAJMH, Washington, D.C.

SHIRLEY S. FLESHIN GREENWALD, Captain, U.S. Army Nurse Corps. Born May 17, 1927, in Morristown, NJ. Raised in Cleveland, OH. Graduated from Cleveland's Mount Sinai Hospital School of Nursing and became a registered nurse.

Joined the Army Nurse Corps in 1961 as a first lieutenant and assigned to Brooke General Hospital, San Antonio, TX. During the Cuban Missile Crisis of 1962 took part in assembling a field hospital on a deserted airstrip in Opalocka, FL. Promoted to captain in 1964. Spent the next two years at the USAH Verdun, France and returned to serve at Beach Army Hospital, Ft. Walters, TX. Left the service in 1968. Received the National Defense Medal.

Obtained a BS degree in nursing from the University of Texas, Austin, TX, and in 1970, was hired by the Dallas County Health Department. Became director of nursing in 1980.

Joined JWV Post 256 in 1983 and the following year met Roland Greenwald at Memorial Day services in a Dallas Cemetery. They were married in June 1987. Retired from nursing.

Life member JWV, associate member of Retired Army Nurse Corps Association, (RANCA), Charter Member of Women in Military Service, (WIMS), and member of the Texas Public Health Association, (TPHA).

HERBERT D. GREFF, born Columbus, OH, on March 23, 1938. Drafted into U.S. Army on Oct. 5, 1961. Served at Ft. Gordon, GA, entire length of service Rank at discharge: private first class. Married to the former Francine Wolpert of Charleston, WV. Have two sons ages 26 and 28. Oldest son married to Amanda Jacobson formerly of Dallas, TX.

He was inducted into basic training at Ft. Knox, KY, and was sent to Ft. Gordon for advanced training. Upon arrival at Ft. Gordon he was assigned to the Military Police Personnel Classification Unit.

While at Ft. Gordon, the Jewish Chaplain was being discharged and a replacement was going to be 3-4 months in coming. Realizing a need, he served as unofficial Jewish Post Chaplain until a replacement was sent. As a result, they were able to have services everyday and went into Atlanta, GA, for the major holidays.

In the Personnel Department, he implemented a more modern processing process through the use of computerization which was available to the base but not being utilized to is fullest capacity.

Today he is a semi-retired consulting actuary. He previously was president of a consulting firm in the area of employee benefits with a staff of 32 employees and an annual budget in excess of $2 million dollars.

Joined the JWV in 1965 and served in all offices at the post and state level. Was appointed national insurance chairman in 1978 and held that position until 1994. On the National Level, he served on the National Court, National Executive Committee and other various positions becoming National Commander in 1988.

He is proud of having served the JWV and becoming a part of its 100 year history.

HERBERT DAVID GRESSER, born Aug. 2, 1930, in Pittsburgh, PA. He moved to New York City in 1938. He attended Bayside High School graduating in 1948. He then attended Queens College of the city of New York where he received a degree in physic and the Polytechnic Institute of Brooklyn where he studied electrical engineering. He was involved in development of early computer devices until he was inducted into the U.S. Army in 1953.

His basic training was at Ft. Dix in the 364th Inf. Regt. He then was assigned as a physicist (enlisted scientific and professional program) to the U.S. Army Chemical Corps, Army Chemical Center at Edgewood Arsenal, MD. The group that he was assigned was to provide theoretical and experimental backup for the development of various Fission and Fusion Bombs. His task was to develop instrument and test devices for the analysis of the various components and yields of the first thermonuclear (Hydrogen Fusion Bomb) device and several other atmospheric tests conducted in the Pacific. He was assigned to the 9710 Technical Service Unit and the Civilian Staff of the Radiological Laboratories of the Army Chemical Corps. While doing these projects he invented several devices used in the analysis of nuclear bombs.

After separation he was employed as a physicist at several companies. He holds many patents. He retired in 1994.

He is a member of the JWV, Gieir Levitt Post 655 at Plainview, NY. He is the senior vice commander of the Nassau-Suffolk District council JWV. He is also a member of the National Association of Atomic Veterans and the Disabled American Veterans.

Married to Adele Davidson Gresser, children: Dr. Mark Geoffrey Gresser, Nina Suddenly Gresser Tacetta, RN. Daniel Stuart Gresser.

PHILLIP FREDERICK GRESSER, born Dec. 27, 1922, Pittsburgh, PA. Entered the U.S. Maritime Training School, Hoffman Island, NY in 1941. Graduated January 1942, as fireman/watertender. Went to sea on SS *Independence Hall*, where his father, Samuel Gresser, was assistant engineer. In March 1942 the ship was split in half due to enemy action. The captain, first and second mate and 10 crewmembers were drowned. After one day in the freezing North Atlantic, they were spotted by a coastal patrol plane and HMS *Witch*, a British destroyer, was sent to retrieve the remaining crew on *Independence Hall*.

He was admitted as a cadet-midshipman to the U.S. Merchant Marine Academy in Kings Point, NY. Training cruise was on the SS *Brazil*. He made many trips as engineer to England, Caribbean, Panama and the islands in the Pacific. Was ensign and engineering officer on DD-717, USS *T.E. Chandler* during the hectic period of the Chinese Revolution.

Attended New York University and graduated as a mechanical engineer. Pursued a career as professional marine engineer until retirement in 1980. Active in Kings Point Merchant Marine Academy Alumni Association. Currently resides at Palm Beach, FL.

Married Phyllis Bierholtz, has two children, David and Dianne.

SAMUEL MARCUS GRESSER, born Jan. 15, 1887, Minsk, Russia. Emigrated to the U.S. around 1900. At the outbreak of WWI he applied for a commission with the USN. Trained in marine engineering, graduated and was commissioned ensign. Became engineering officer on the USS *Kittery* and made many trips to Europe and West Africa.

Continued sailing after WWI as marine engineer in the U.S. Merchant Marines for several years. Went into the monument business until 1938 when he rejoined the U.S. Merchant Marines, serving throughout WWII. In March 1942 he sailed as second assistant engineer on SS *Independence Hall*. Son, Phillip, was also on this ship. Due to enemy action the ship was split half. The captain, second mate, third mate and 10 crewmen were killed. HMS *Witch*, a British destroyer, was able to rescue the remaining crew.

Commander Gresser retired shortly after WWII. Was active in the JWV post in Pittsburgh, PA and the Louis Blum Post in Flushing, NY. He passed away in 1960. Was married to Marion Bialo (also deceased) had children: Phillip, Maxine and Herbert; grandchildren: Michael, Judy, Amy, David, Dianne, Mark, Nina and Daniel; great-grandchildren: Joshua, Tamar, Rebecca, Ariel and Danielle.

SEYMOUR GRITZ, born in Manhattan, NY, on Jan. 29, 1924. Business major Brooklyn College, Pace University (Nee Institute). Drafted March 6, 1943, basic training Ft. Jackson, SC, Camp Atterbury, IN. "I am alive today because I am Jewish. After repple-deppling to Europe in was sent to a

heavy weapons company in the 26th Inf. Div. All the guy were saying they never expected to return home but the wanted the protection of the heavy machine guns, sort of dyin with their boots on. Struck up conversation with few soldie and discovered they were Jewish. They counseled me to g into the mortar section. Always behind the nearest hill and lo the shells onto the enemy. During the months long siege in th Bulge we were pinned down unable to move and all th infantry men and machine gunners were killed or froze death. I wouldn't be here today if the Jewishness did n manifest itself." Married to Frances 1953, two children mem ber JWV Post 116 New York."

RAYMOND GRODEN, spent his youth in Bedfo Stuyvesant in Brooklyn. When he was drafted, he was in th family's mirror manufacturing business, married and settl down with a young daughter. He was the only Jewish soldi assigned to Co. C, 30th Inf. Regt.

In combat he was a wild crazy man and called "Grode the Kraut Killer." Continuously on the front line for the la seven months of the war, he became a legend for his explo as a combat infantryman in Germany. In his company he w one of six men left from an original group of over 200. Ma times he was the highest rank, as sergeant, to lead company.

Awards/Medals: Bronze Star with two OLCs, Silver Star with OLC, Distinguished Service Cross, New York State Conspicuous Service Cross and the Purple Heart. He reached the quarter finals at Wimbledon, competing there in the 7th Army Sports Tournament. Much later at age 51 he won the Senior Men's NYC Championship.

Today he is semi-retired in West Palm Beach working in real estate. He takes pleasure in the accomplishments of his son and daughter and dotes on his five grandchildren.

JACK GROSKIN, born March 23, 1925, in Syracuse, NY. Attended Syracuse Public Schools and played football at Central High. Enlisted in the USMC December 1942; boot camp training at Parris Island, SC and was a guard at NAS, Norfolk, VA. After Saipan he joined G Co., 2nd Bn., 23rd Marines at Maui and fought on Iwo Jima.

His worst day was D+3, each man was running one at a time across the airfield. He was the only Marine that the Japanese laid in with mortars, all landing behind him. Honorably discharged with the rank of corporal on Feb. 18, 1946, he earned many medals.

After the war, he became a self-employed food distributor for 25 years. Today he owns a monument business and lives in Syracuse with his wife Hannah. They have two children Dr. Mark Groskin of Rochester and Debbie King of Lysander, and three grandchildren. Hobbies are jogging, physical fitness and viewing sports.

MURRAY M. GROSS, born March 15, 1916, Bronx, NY. Enlisted in National Guard 1939; assigned to Btry. B, 244th Coast Arty., NYNG. Battery was honored as best 155 Gun Btry. just prior to induction into federal service September 1940. Their regiment was funneled into Americal Div. and sent overseas one month after Pearl Harbor, Dec. 7, 1941.

Moving across the Pacific from Australia, to New Caledonia in the Coral Seas, the Jewish Btry. was assigned to construct Panama mounts to protect the entrance to Noumea Harbor. Shipped to Guadalcanal in 1942, attached to the 1st Mar. Div.

Returned Stateside; attended Coast Artillery School, Ft. Monroe, VA. Served at various posts, then sent to Seacoast Arty. HQ, Ft. Rodman, MA, where, while experimenting with defusing mines, booby traps and infiltration courses, he blew himself up. After months of hospitalization for injuries and for recurring attacks of malaria, he was assigned to inactive duty as XO at Ft. Meade, MD, where he was retired on disability January 1945 with rank of acting 1st Lt. and XO.

Married Ann Weishaus prior to going overseas. Has two children, Irwin and Barbara, five grandchildren. Retired in 1990 from his own insurance agency and now does insurance consulting.

SIDNEY M. GROSS, drafted into the U.S. Army in 1942, after Pearl Harbor and was shipped immediately overseas after basic training at Ft. Bragg, NC.

Assigned to a MP (Aviation) Sq with the 26th [illegible] Group, 9th Air Force, in time to participate in the Egypt-Libya Campaign and the subsequent defeat of Gen. Erwin Rommel and the Deutsche Afrika Corps.

He was then selected as cadre to organize an air transport command air base at the RAF Airfield at Castel Benito, Tripoli, Libya, achieving position of base sergeant major.

Completed tour of duty as first sergeant and provost sergeant at Rosecrans AAB, St. Joseph, MO, and was honorably discharged at the end of 1945 under the point system.

He was married at the end of 1946 and completed his education with a BA from City College and an MBA from New York University and realized his dream of being a small business man as an air conditioning and heating contractor in the New York Metropolitan Area, while raising three children with the help of his wonderful wife, Fanny.

They retired in 1990 and they presently spend six months as Florida residents and six months in upstate New York with their four grandchildren.

IRVING GROSSMAN, PhM2/c, USNR, born July 4, 1921, Newark, NJ. Enlisted in the USN December 1941. After basic training at Newport, RI, Naval Station and Brooklyn Navy Yard he was transferred to the USMC and joined the newly formed 4th Marine Div. at Camp Lejeune, NC.

After extensive training he was shipped with the 23rd Regt. to Camp Pendleton, CA, to complete formation of the 4th Marine Div., and after further training he was sent directly into combat for the invasion and securing of the Marshall Islands on January 1944.

After the successful military operation he was sent to Maui with the division for reforming and to prepare for the invasions of Saipan and Tinian in the Mariana Island group which took place June and July 1944. He was slightly wounded on Saipan with grenade fragments.

Again he went back to Maui to prepare for the big one-Iwo Jima Feb. 19, 1945.

He landed early in the morning and after being pinned down for some hours he advanced toward the air field objective where he was severely wounded by heavy machine gun fire. Due to the seriousness of the situation he was not evacuated until the next morning.

He spent 11 months in treatment and rehabilitation and was discharged January 1946.

He received the Purple Heart, Presidential Unit Citation with two stars, and the Asian Pacific Medal with four Battle Stars.

He has been married to Jean for 43 years, and they have a daughter and a son. He is a member of the JWV, the VFW, Disabled American Veterans, the military Order of the Purple Heart, and the 4th Marine Div. Iwo Jima Survivors Association.

He retired in 1983 and manages to keep busy.

LEONARD GROSSMAN, born in Brooklyn, NY, and graduated from Thomas Jefferson High School in June 1941.

Although he was awarded a scholarship to New York University, he could not accept because he had to help support the family and went to work until he was inducted in the USN in February 1943.

After boot camp at Great Lakes, IL, he was sent to the U.S. Naval Hospital in San Diego, where he was trained as a medical corpsman and later became a physical therapist.

In addition to his physical therapy chores, he volunteered and became the assistant Rabbi, and performed as the cantor at services.

After his Rabbi was shipped overseas, he requested overseas duty as well, and was scheduled to go overseas with the 5th Marines as a medical corpsman. However, because of a severe dental emergency, he could not go with his unit and therefore remained as a physical therapist at San Diego Naval Hospital.

He was discharged August 1945 and went into the insurance business. Today he is retired and living in Bayside, NY. He and his wife just celebrated 50 years of marriage and proud of their two children and two grandchildren, Lindsey and Jonathan Mellen of Scottsdale, AZ.

SAM GROVEMAN, born in Newark, NJ, Jan. 1, 1916. Moved to Cleveland, OH, at age of 3. After graduating high school in Cleveland and several odd jobs, began work at Picker & Pay Company.

Enlisted in U.S. Coast Guard November 1941. Took basic training in Algiers, LA. Served aboard sub-chaser SC528, based out of Greenland. Served on destroyer escort #252, *H.D. Crow*, taking convoys to Preland and Casablanca. Stationed aboard U.S. Coast Guard Cutter *Campbell* to Palermo, Sicily. Served as seaman on the above ships. Also served on USS *C.S. Spar* in Bristol, CT. At time of discharge in November 1946 rank was SOM3/c.

Returned to work at Picker after discharge from Coast Guard. Married Zetta in 1948. Member of JWV Post #33 Cleveland since 1950. Retired from Picker in 1981. Does volunteer work delivering "Meals on Wheels" and sings with a volunteer choral group at local nursing homes.

ALBERT GRUBER, born in Manhallen, NY, on June 27, 1921. Graduate of Stuynescent High School in CCNY School of Business with a BBA where he served as student government president and president of all his classes in evening session. Selected to Who's Who Among Students in American Colleges and Universities in 1948.

Entered Army duty February 1943, arrived in ETO June 1943 and discharged March 1946. Served as an NCO with 339th Combat QM Co. in England, France, Holland, Belgium, Luxembourg and Germany. Last four months was mayor coordinator in touring France. Awarded five Battle Stars, Presidential Unit Citation, Meritorious Citation, ETO Medal, American Theater Medal, WWII Victory Medal. Served as commander Metropolitan Post 164 and on other county and department of New York Committees National Deputy Aide for over 25 years. Member of JWV for over 50 years. Life member of JWV and DAV.

Retired in 1895 as health planer for Montgomery County, MD, after having served many years as program analyst and assistant to the county health officer and a deputy elections administrator for the county. Have been a board member of Jewish Welfare Board, Jewish Community Council and the Seabourn Region United Synagogue of America.

Served six years as chair of Montgomery County Commission for Ethnic officers and now chair emeritus. Appointed by M.C. Council as a commissioner for the humanities serving on the Commission for the Humanities. Former vice president and trustee and a member of the board of Congr. Howtzeon Azudluth Achim for over 30 years.

Married to Lareldn, three sons and a daughter-in-law. Resides in Silver Spring, MD.

ABE MICHAEL GUBERMAN, was drafted into the U.S. Army on Feb. 8, 1943. Subsequently his brothers: Nathan, Sol, Joseph and Isidore, followed him into the military. Due to a bad eye and a scarred hand he was classified "limited service." During his first two years he served in an automatic weapons unit on the West coast, sleeping in an underground bunker and eating field rations.

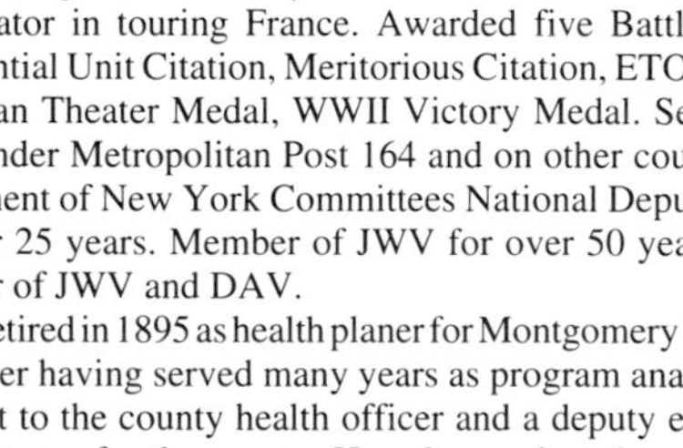

Eventually when there was a need for infantrymen for the planned invasion of Japan, he was selected for advance infantry training at Camp Howge, TX. After completion of the 10 weeks of intense training he was told he could not qualify as a rifleman due to his injured left eye. He was then transferred to Camp Maxey, TX. For the next six months he was given machine gun and mortar weapon training primarily.

When he got on the boat in Oakland, Ca, they were told they were headed for the Philippines. There was, however, a delay of several hours and they were advised they were heading straight for Tokyo, the first boat to go directly from the USA to Japan since the war started. Apparently the Japanese had capitulated due to the detonation of the two atomic bombs.

When they debarked in Yokohama they were loaded on trucks and sent to Atsugi. On the way, thousands of Japanese greeted them like conquering heroes. Japanese soldiers guarded the route and had their backs facing them as a mark of respect.

Soon he was on his way to Hakodate where he was assigned to the 77th Inf. Div., Artillery HQ, where he was stationed the next few months to work with the adjutant to the general. Died on Nov. 2, 1994.

NELSON GUDEMA, born 1912 in the Netherlands, the youngest of a large family. He had three brothers and three sisters who gave him the nickname Nanny. They lived in Stadskanal in the north of Holland, 15 kilometers from the German border.

Nelson emigrated to the U.S. in 1940. Holland was invaded by the Nazis on May 10 of that year and Nelson luckily got passage on the last vessel to leave Rotterdam. He lived with his older brother, Dan, in the Bronx until he was drafted into the Army in 1942. After basic training he was assigned as a tech sergeant to a medical until serving in the New Guinea campaign. He served in the U.S. Medical Corps in the South Pacific Theater from 1943 to 1945. After discharge in 1945, Nelson teamed up with an Army buddy, Gerry LaBelle, to start-up a highly successful burlap importing and distribution business in Elizabeth, NJ. Nelson Gudema passed away unexpectedly in 1977.

JOSEPH GUIDERA, served in the Army Air Forces. He entered the service on May 28, 1942, at Ft. Dix, NJ, with the rank of private and was discharged on Nov. 6, 1945, at Ft. Dix, NJ, with the rank of staff sergeant.

His basic training was had at Miami Beach, FL, from June 7, 1942 to July 3, 1942. His radio training was at Sioux Falls, SC, from July 6, 1942 to Nov. 17, 1942. He also served with the 50th AB Sq. at Hammer Field, Fresno, Ca, from November 1942 to November 1943. He shipped overseas on the SS *Thomas Cresad*, sailing from Newport News and arriving at Oran, North Africa. He also shipped on HMS *Lancashire* British from Oran N.A. arriving at Bombay, India. He served in the Arabian Theater with the AAF from Feb. 1, 1944 to Feb. 29, 1944, and in the China, Burma, India Theater with the 14th and 10th Air Force from March 21, 1944 to Oct. 6, 1945.

He visited the famed Taj Mahal in Agra-India on Dec. 28, 1944. Flew over the Hump into China, staying at Kunming, October 1944. He was the line chief of a group of fighter-bomber planes. His job was to train American and Chinese men for aerial gunnery and they also taught pilot training. All of these fighter pilots received 30 hours of combat training before they were sent into Burma or China for combat duty. The P-51 Mustang on which he served was named after his son, Neil Joseph, on Sept. 10, 1945, of which distinction he is extremely proud. *Submitted by Max Sigal.*

JOSEPH I. GURFEIN, born May 28, 1918, New York City, NY. U.S. Military Academy West Point New York 2nd LT CE 1941. Retired colonel June 30, 1967. Commanded Platoon Co. Bn., Inf. Regt. (in combat) Silver Star with OLC; Legion of Merit with OLC,; Parachute Wings; Presidential Citation (Navy); Combat Infantry Badge; seven French decorations and Korean, 12 campaign stars U.S. Army. (See *Chosin* by Hummel and other Korean Histories for reports on his combat actions.)

BS USMA, MSC Harvard University, Ph.D. Pacific Western. Dean at Federal City College three years. Associate professor emeritus, still teaching civil engineering George Mason University, VA. Professional Engineer Registrars New York, MD, D.C.

Married 52 years to Marion Reh, daughter Marjorie Lowry; son Albert; grandsons, Dr. Daniel and Dr. Jack Lowry, granddaughter Valerie; great-grandchildren, Adina and Raphael.

Memorable experience: In the vicinity of Suim-myon, Korea, during the period of September 14 to Oct. 13, 1951, he served as Regt. EO of the unit, engaged in combat operations against a fanatically determined and numerically superior enemy force. Throughout the bitter struggle for the Heartbreak Ridge, Col. Gurfein supervised the administration of supplies from the rear up to the breach of the rifle units. He made frequent trips through the rifle companies, under the intense enemy artillery, mortar, small arms and automatic weapons fire, to ascertain their conditions and morale. He walked every foot of the front lines in daylight, under hostile fire, as an example to the men. Although his duties as EO did not include such actions his voluntary and frequent front line reconnaissance was an inspiration to the men of the unit and contributed greatly to the success of their mission. The gallantry and selfless devotion to the welfare of his men displayed by Col. Gurfein on this occasion reflect great credit upon himself and the military service.

IRVING GURIAN, born Oct. 15, 1924, New York, NY. Joined USN May 10, 1943 and stationed at USNTS Samson, NY, 8th Beach Bn., USS Sanborn (APA-193).

Participated in invasion of Southern France, August 1944; in replacing naval casualties, Iwo Jima, 1945, Pacific in USS *Sanborn* (APA-193); in invasion of Okinawa, 1945.

Memorable experience was visiting a French Foreign Legion Post in Arzeu, North Africa and finding many Jews who escaped Nazi terrorism in France.

Awards/Medals: Commendation Medal and Unit Citation. Discharged March 15, 1946, as pharmacist mate second class.

1951-88 institutional supervisor salesman, frozen food MFG; 1959-64 scoutmaster of Boys Scouts; 1976 member of Knight of Pythias and B'Nai B'rith Harvest Food Lodge; 1990 JWV commander, Post 68; 1992 JWV West Chester County commander; 1993 JWV, DEC; 1993-94 member, Review Committee U.S. Military Academies; 1993 2nd VP Northeast Jewish Center Yonkers, NY.

Married Vera Kay in October 1946, has two children and five grandchildren.

IRVING L. GUSS, born Oct. 16, 1918, in New York City. Graduated from CCNY; BS January 1938, NYU Engineering, BCE; July 1954, Brooklyn Polytechnic Institute, MCE May 1959. Licensed professional engineer New York State, 1961. Worked for Port Authority 1948-56. Consulting engineering 1956-60, NYC, Traffic/Transportation Dept. 1960-88.

Took leave of absence to work as consulting engineer advisor to the Ministry of Transport in Israel, 1970-71. Adjunct professor from 1962-86 variously at New York University, New York Institute of Technology, Stevens Institute, Fairleigh Dickinson College of Engineering Science.

Member of Institute of Transportation Engineers, New York Academy of Sciences, Air Force Assoc., 15th AF Assoc., 301st BG, Selman Field Navigation Historical Assoc. and AF Navigators Assoc.

Enlisted as private in 1942. Appointed Aviation Cadet 1943, Selman Field Navigation School, LA. Awarded Gunners Wings from Flexible Gunnery School Buckingham AB, FL, 1943. Commissioned 2nd lieutenant navigator March 1944 at Selman Field.

Received combat training at Dalhart, TX, and Gulfport, MS, in B-17 Flying Fortress. Flew B-17 to Europe from Hunters Field, GA, via Presque Isle, ME; Gander, Newfoundland; Azores; Marrakech, Morocco, Tunis AFB, Tunisia to Gioia, Italy. Assigned to 301st BG, 15th AF. Flew 47 combat missions. Appointed 352nd Squadron Navigator after 12th mission. Flew 35 missions with 301st BG as AF lead, wing lead and group lead in rotation.

Awarded Distinguished Flying Cross, four Air Medals, nine Battle Stars on EAME Campaign Medal, two Presidential Unit Citations for 301st BG, WWII Victory Medal, American Campaign Medal, Good Conduct Medal, etc.

Participated in missions on the invasion of the southern coast of France, Ploesti, Vienna, Munich, Berlin, Bleckhammer, Mossebier Baum, Brux, Salsberg, etc. Survived seven crash landings. Encountered the jet stream on Nov. 17, 1944, over the Alps at 30,000 feet on mission to Bleckhammer Oil Refineries, Poland. After bucking prevailing head winds of 400 mph for over an hour, they decided to hit the secondary target, Salsberg. An initial point was set at 50 miles north of target to start the bomb run because of prevailing tail winds at estimated speed of 400 mph with bomb bay doors open. The 301st BG hit the target while other bomb groups were directed to tertiary target when bombs were held up. Luckily the 301st did not sustain heavy wind damage. On the longest mission to Berlin, Daimler-Benz Tank Works, their plane was hit by flak and the largest concentration of German jet fighters used during the war. They hit the target and took evasive action and managed to bring back the crippled aircraft 800 miles with one good engine. Hydraulics and oxygen were shot out and they crash landed with empty tanks.

Retired from USAFR July 1968 as lieutenant colonel.

Married Jeanette (deceased November 1988), has two children, Ava and Jonathan, and granddaughter, Sonia.

LEON K. GUTMANN, born June 26, 1913, Ridgefield Port, NJ. Inducted Camp Croft, SC, Spring 1942. Basic training Camp Sibert, AL. Attended Officers School Chemical Warfare, MD and Officers School G-2. Since Germany did not use chemical warfare, the USA did not and all officers were transferred to other branches. Served in Belgium, Germany, France, reaching captain 1945.

Memorable experience was taking a huge convoy of trucks from Belgium to Cologne, Germany to retrieve U.S. materiel stolen from Belgium.

Lived in Bergen and Hudson counties, NJ. His parents were jewelers. Had three brothers and two sisters. Erwin, eldest brother, major Medical Air Corps. Julius next brother, Reform rabbi, bad eyes no Army. Harry next brother, director American Red Cross, Italy.

In 1946 established with his late wife Dorothy an elegant antiques and diversified gifts. Retired 1970. Active in various cultural and multi-cultural activities. Frequent lecturer. Volunteer Red Cross, etc.

JACK DAVID GUTTENPLAN, born in Baton Rouge, LA, Oct. 10, 1925. He enlisted in the Navy, V-12 program Dec. 2, 1942, at age 17. Received BS degree from Case Institute of Technology, attended Columbia University Midshipman School, and became one of the youngest ensigns in the Navy at 19.

During WWII, he served aboard USS *Athanasia* AF41, USS *Crockett* APA148, and USS *Nespelen* AOG55, remained in the Ready Reserve, and became commanding officer of Santa Anna, CA, Naval Reserve Surface Div. 11-28(L), commanding 300 men and officers. Retired from the Navy after 30 years in rank of commander.

After WWII, he returned to Case, earned MS degree and completed all coursework for a Ph.D. in chemical engineering

Worked for Chrysler Corporation and Rockwell International before retiring in 1990.

Jack helped organize and was commander of Oak Park, MI, Post 716, in 1960, moved to Santa Ana and became a charter member of Orange County Post 760, serving four terms as commander. Was charter commander (two terms) of Southern Coast District council, and served two terms as Department of California commander. Organized and instituted California Posts 385, 595 and 680 during this period. He was co-winner of the Ed Nappen "Outstanding Department Commander" award in 1973, "California Man of the Year" in 1977, and again Ed Nappen awarded in 1982. Served 22 years as NEC or on various national committees, at present vice-chairman of National Action Committee and co-chairman of National Americanism Committee.

Jack is married to Shirley. They have three children and six grandchildren.

HYMAN HAAS, born in Brooklyn, NY, Aug. 14, 1915. Left high school because of the Depression. Entered Army March 27, 1942. Basic in Fort Eustis, VA. In October 1942 assigned as cadre Battery A, 467th AAA. AW. Battalion (SP), Camp Stewart, GA. Trained new recruits as anti-aircraft gunners in Camp Stewart and California desert.

Overseas to England, December 1943. On June 6, 1944, 8:30 a.m., attached to 1st Inf. Div. and as chief of Section 3 of the 1st Platoon, 467 AAA, landed on Omaha Beach in Normandy, France. Within minutes his section engaged a German gun in a bunker and put the gun out of action. The beach landings, the fighting, the terrible sights are never to be forgotten memories.

Fought in Normandy (St. Lo), Northern France, (Mortain, Argentan - Falaise Gap), Ardennes (Battle of the Bulge, Bastogne), Rhineland (Remagen Bridge), Central Europe. Separated October 27, 1945. Earned five battle stars and Arrowhead.

After separation worked in the needle trades and postal service. He married Esther in 1946. they have two daughters, Janet and Deena. Retired from the postal service, returned to school. Graduated from Lehman College (CUNY) in June 1989 with a BA degree (Cum Laude). Member Neuman-Goldman Post 69 JWV.

SAMUEL HABER, born in Buffalo, NY on April 5, 1919. He enlisted in the US Merchant Marines in 1937. Stations included Tonnege, North and South Atlantic, Indian Ocean, East and West Coast of South America, Central America where he received 2nd Mates License. Participated in battles in Atlantic and Pacific oceans. Ship shot down seven Kamikazes over Okinawa.

Memorable experiences being on watch in charge on bridge, riding out the typhoon in Okinawa, and transporting military provisions, soldiers and supplies.

Awards/Medals: Asiatic/Pacific Medal, Merchant Marine Emblem, Pacific War Zone Bar, Defense Bar, Victory Medal, Presidential Testimonial Letter, Atlantic War Zone Bar, Mediterranean Middle East War Zone Bar, Combat Bar and Honorable Service Button.

He was discharged in 1951.

He serves as mashgiach for several kosher companies. He has two sons, the Rabbi Yaacou Haber and David, and one daughter Chana Kass.

HENRY H. HAFT, born January 18, 1892 in Chester Island. Went to Cornell and Syracuse University. Graduated in 1913, the first class to graduate in Forestry College. Entered Syracuse Medical School and graduated in 1917. Interned at Mt. Sinai Hospital in New York City. Associated with Dr. Held in New York and Dr. Harris Levy of Syracuse. Practiced internal medicine.

Went into active service in WWI before his internship was completed. Was a first lieutenant with an air squadron which was sent overseas in January 1918. When he landed in England, he was detached from the air squadron and sent to the US hospital in Winchester, England. Was made chief of medicine there.

Joined the Hospital Unit 52 when WWII broke out. Became a major as head of the Department of Gastroenterol-

ogy. Spent about one year in England. Returned to the United States and was sent to Cushing General Hospital in Framingham, MA.

Married Freda Silverman in 1920. Died in 1952 at age 60. Survived by wife Freda, daughter Mrs. Melvin Estroff of Lakeland, FL and son Dr. David E. Haft of Rochester.

ARNOLD W. HALE, born Sept. 2, 1934 in Colome, SD. He began active duty with the Army as an infantryman in 1953; then commissioned in 1959. He advanced through the ranks to major by 1973 and retired in 1977 after gaining 17 military decorations, including the Bronze Star (1968), two Meritorious Service Medals (1975 and 1977), Army Commendation Medal (1973) and Vietnam Honors Medal First Class (1968). He held various staff and command positions as a Army Medical Service Corps officer. From September 1967 through August 1968, he was a medical advisor to 21st Division, IV Corps, Military Assistance Command, Bac Lieu, Vietnam; participating in four battle campaigns. Served in the TET Counter Offensive in 1968. Captain Hale served as medical training advisor and coordinated medical evacuations in Vietnam.

Earned several college degrees, to include a doctorate.

His career after military service was three years as school librarian, two years as community college instructor of psychology, one year as adult probation officer and from 1983 to present he serves as a licensed marriage and family therapist (psychotherapist) and educator.

Married to Mary Alice, three sons, two daughters and eight grandchildren. Life member of JWV.

GEORGE HALLEMAN, born in Germany. Served in Army Medical Corps as radiologist. Stationed at Fort Sam Houston, TX.

Did pioneer research in the functions of the pituitary gland having an article published in *American Journal of Gastroenterology*. Died March 2, 1957. Survived by wife Esther, daughter, mother and father.

BENJAMIN HAMMERMAN, son of Louis and Rose Hammerman, was born in New York City. Graduate of Stuyvesant High School and Brooklyn College. Served in US Army, April 1941-October 1945 as message center chief, forward observer technician 4th grade. Overseas service April 1942-November 1943 with 576th F.A. Battalion, Americal Division, 1st Marine Division Reinforces.

Battles/Campaigns: East Indies, Guadalcanal, Papuan, New Guinea and Coral Sea.

Decorations: Presidential Unit Citation with Bronze Star, Asiatic/Pacific Theater with four stars, American Defense Service Ribbon, Good Conduct Medal and World War II Victory Medal.

Graduate Officers Candidate School, Ft. Sill, OK, May 1944, 2nd Lieutenant Field Artillery -S-3 Operations and training staff officer.

Married Lorelei Krohn. Children: Judith, Hillel and Deborah.

Post war occupation: Self employed partner with brothers Hyman and Benjamin in jewelry business.

BERNARD HAMMERMAN, son of Louis and Rose Hammerman, was born in New York City. Graduate of Seward Park High School. Served in US Army, March 1943-

December 1945 as radio operator, marksman M, rifle technician 5th grade. Overseas service, January 1944- December 1945 with 991st F.A. Battalion.

Battles/Campaigns: Arvennes, Central Europe, Northern France, Rhineland and Normandy.

Decorations: European/African/Middle Eastern Service Medal, Good Conduct Medal, Purple Heart and WWII Victory Medal.

Married Joan Schwartz; children: Darcy, Brett and Robert.

Post war occupation: employed as partner with brothers Hyman and Benjamin in jewelry business.

HYMAN J. HAMMERMAN, son of Louis and Rose Hammerman, was born in New York City. Graduate of Seward Park High School and attended City College of New York. Served in Army Air Force, July 1942- December 1945 as radio operator. Served as sergeant during overseas service, May 1943- November 1945 with the 48 TC Squadron, 313th TC Group.

Battles/Campaigns: Central Europe, Naples Foggia, Normandy, Northern France, Rhineland, Rome, Arno and Sicily.

Decorations: Distinguished Unit Badge, European/African/Middle Eastern Service Medal, Good Conduct Medal and WWII Victory Medal.

Married Florence Shapiro; sons Stuart, Michael and Herbert. Self-employed partner with brothers Benjamin and Bernard in jewelry business. Hyman died in 1985.

MILTON J. HAMPLE, born July 10, 1916 in Elmira, NY. Enlisted on May 26, 1942 with Army 1146 Quartermaster, 12th Air Force. Stations included Egypt, North Africa, Sicily, Italy and Corsica. Battles participated in included Egypt-Libya, Sicily, Rome-Arne and Naples-Foggia.

Awards/Medals: Good Conduct Medal, American Campaign Medal, European/African/Middle Eastern Victory Medal and WWII Campaign Medal.

He was discharged on Oct. 13, 1945 with rank of private first class.

Worked in men's retail clothing business and also has a real estate broker's license. He is presently retired. Member of American Legion (life membership), DAV, JWV (life membership), Elks (life membership), Eagles, Masons, Consistory and Shriners as well as Sigma Alpha Mu Fraternity (life membership), Sigma Phi Chapter at Bucknell University.

KEITH C. HANCOCK, born March 31, 1920. Graduated high school in 1939 and business college in 1940. Volunteered for Regular Navy on March 3, 1941. Served as platoon leader at Navy Training Center and section leader at Navy Service School. Graduated Naval Engineering School in Dearborn, MI, 1941. Aboard USS *Medusa*, 1941-1943 while in Pearl Harbor. The Hebrides; 1943 *CUB Three*, in VitiLevu, Fiji and 1944 *S R U ADAO* in Hollam, New Caledonia, Canship at Naval Air Station, Pasco, WA 1945-1946, and Naval Air Station, Seattle, WA, 1946-1947.

Awards/Medals: American Defense with Fleet Clasp, Pacific/Asiatic, Commendation, American Theater, Allied Victory and Good Conduct Medal.

Honorably discharged on Feb. 22, 1947 with ranks of AS, S2/c, F3/c, F2/c, F1/c, MM2/c, MM1/c and CMM(AA)(T).

Did best I could wherever I served and met some special individuals, Ehad Amenu and Adam Ehad."

With a WWII GI Education Bill, graduated from University of Washington; carried a double major. Retired as facilitator from Safeco Corporation on Dec. 31, 1985.

HELMUT HANNES, was born in Germany near Breslau, the youngest of two brothers. His father was a prosperous merchant who had fought for his country with distinction during World War I. This no longer mattered in the 1930s, as the anti-Jewish climate made life unbearable in Germany. Against his parents' wishes, Helmut decided to leave. A cousin who lived with his wife and children in Richmond, VA sponsored him for residency in the United States. While awaiting a US visa, he resided in Paris and studied clothing design. In 1937, he arrived in Richmond.

For the next few years, he diligently learned the new language while continuing to work in the clothing industry. When he moved from Richmond to New York some time later, he was a true professional in the business.

Soon afterward, he was drafted into the Army and shipped off to North Africa to fight for his new country. This he did with great pride. The fact that he spoke several languages found him a place with the 88th Division, more commonly known as the "Blue Devils". He was part of the Anzio Landing in Italy and it was in this country that he was wounded. As a reminder, he still has a piece of shrapnel embedded in his leg. After this incident, he was reassigned to a non-combat outfit for the remainder of his three year duty. When it was time for him to return, he reenlisted for one more year so that someone else who had a family might come home in his place. It was his way of saying "thanks" to America for allowing him to live here.

After he left the Army, Helmut moved to the DC area. After several years rebuilding his business, he finally opened "Hannes Formal Wear" in 1955 with a great deal of flair and pizzazz. His clientele ranged from members of the diplomatic circle, congressman and foreign service people to the high school senior hoping to impress a date on prom night. This was his labor of love and it prospered for nearly 30 years.

Helmut Hannes overcame loss and adversity. He found acceptance, enduring friendships and success far from the place he used to call home. We admire his courage and his warmth.

MICHAEL HARAC, born in Brooklyn, NY on May 21, 1945. Entered US Marine Corp in July 1963. Served in 2nd Marine Div. while in the States and the 3rd Marine Div. in Vietnam. Stations include Camp Leveune, NC and Danang, Vietnam. Participated in various operations in northern provinces of Vietnam.

Lived in South America as a boy; learned Spanish. Joined Marines at 18, right after high school, and became Spanish interpreter. Sent to Vietnam, 1966-1967.

Awards/Medals: National Defense with two stars, Vietnam Service, Presidential Unit Citation, etc.

Discharged July 17, 1967 with rank of corporal. After discharge received counseling and education benefits from Veteran's Administration.

Worked as architectural draftsman in New York. Studied tropical architecture in Puerto Rico and Miami and practiced commercial and residential architecture in Florida, Puerto Rico and Panama.

Married to Mati Mitrani; two children, Lani Sara and Seth Morris. Presently he works as a medical facilities architect and is one of the featured writers of Sold*iers Heart, Survivors' Views of Combat Trauma* and author of *Shore Party and Other Tales of War*, Dorrance Publishing Co., Inc. Working on another book of collected short stories.

MYRON J. HARBAND, member of Bill Bauer Post, Redwood City, CA. Served in WWII from November 1942 to November 1945. Staff sergeant of 34th Inf., 24th Div. While serving 30 months overseas, had beach landings on Hollandia, New Guinea; Biak Island, New Guinea; Leyte Island, Philippines; Mindanao, Philippines and Mindoro, Philippines.

Awards: Bronze Star Medal, Combat Infantry Badge, Asiatic/Pacific Campaign Medal, Philippine Liberation Ribbon with two stars, Republic of the Philippines and Presidential Unit Citation Badge.

Married to Eileen for 42 years with three children and two grandchildren.

LEO HARMATZ, born May 26, 1919 in New York City, NY. US Army Medical Service, Mess Sgt. Drafted Aug. 15, 1842, Camp Arlington, Riverside, CA; Aboline, TX for basic training. Ft. Campbell, KY; Camp Killmore, NJ staging area. Took *Queen Mary* to Goric, Scotland. Swindox, England for two years. Departed for France - served in Omaha Beach. La Visinet, France took over a maternity hospital previously held by Germans and spent three years there. Participated in Battle of Bulge - arrived in hospital train moments after medical train left Germans took town of Bistox.

Hobby during this period was performing in five piece band. Band performed at Moulin Rouge. Discharged April 13, 1947.

Married Sylvia; two sons Richard and Harvey, two grandchildren. Reside at Laguna Hills. Junior Vice-Commander, Department CA 1995-96.

SAMUEL H. HARRINGTON, born in Philadelphia, PA, Nov. 7, 1918. Enlisted in the Army, November 1936 and served in Schofield Barracks, HI. Returned to the US and served in the 16th Inf., Governors Island, NY and the 18th Inf., Fort Hamilton, Brooklyn, NY. Was selected to serve in the Honor Detail at the 1939 New York World's Fair, Flushing, NY. Served in Puerto Rico 1940 to 1941 in the Coast Artillery as a Sgt. Reassigned to the US as a Recruiting Sgt., Trenton, NJ.

July 6, 1942 went to OCS, Class #8, Fort Lee, VA. Commissioned as a 2nd Lt. and assigned to the 10th Port of Embarkation, Camp Stoneman, CA. Went overseas to North Africa in 1943. Made the invasion of Sicily. Served in Italy. Returned as a captain to the US after 28 months overseas.

Assigned to 39 Whitehall St. as a recruiting and induction officer. In 1950 was assigned to duty in the Army of Occupation accompanied by wife, Florence and children.

Served in Giessen, Obersdorf and Bremen as the commanding officer, HQs Co., 320th Replacement Bn. Returned to the US in 1953; assigned to Post QM, Fort Dix; served there until retirement as a major with 20 years service, July 1957.

Awards earned: Bronze Star Medal, American Campaign Medal, Defense Medal, EAME Campaign Medal, WWII Victory Medal and Army of Occupation- Germany.

Member of JWV Post 215.

BENJAMIN HARRISON, joined the US Medical Corps as a dental laboratory technician on Feb. 11, 1943 and was discharged on Nov. 28, 1945. He saw active service in England, France, Holland and Germany. He received several citations, decorations and awards, among them being the Good Conduct Medal, the ETO Medal, the American Theater Defense Medal and the Victory Medal. He also received three battle stars for the Campaigns in Northern France, Rhineland and Central Europe. *Submitted by Max Sigal.*

MARTIN HARTH, never told his wife that he had left Hawaii. Under the OPA mailing system, he was able to conceal his location while serving with the 96th Inf. Div. in Leyte in the Philippines and later while invading Okinawa April 1, 1945, Easter Sunday. He wanted to spare her the worry and the mental suffering of knowing where her husband was stationed during WWII. She had enough on her mind because she had not heard from her mother and two sisters back in Lithuania. After the war they learned they were all murdered by the Nazis.

He met Homer Bigart, a reporter from the *Herald Tribune*, newspaper on a 6x6 Army truck going somewhere in Okinawa. Homer asked them about the passing of President Roosevelt. Harth only gave him his name. He knew of nobody in his family or his friends who would be reading the *Herald Tribune*.

However, a member of the America Legion went to see Harth's wife and their 1 1/2 year old son and showed her the newspaper article. The moral of this story is, if you have a secret, don't talk to the press.

SEYMOUR HARTMAN, born Aug. 17, 1918 in Brooklyn, NY. Enlisted in the US Army on Jan. 22, 1942. Attended O.C.S. at Fort Benning, GA, Oct. 26, 1942- Jan. 22, 1943.

Seymour Hartman served as a second lieutenant commanding a heavy weapons platoon in the Third Infantry Division. He served in Sicily, Anzio throughout the Italian Campaign and the Invasion of Southern France.

After 18 months as an infantry officer, he was promoted to first lieutenant and transferred to Italy as a civil affairs officer in the Military Government. As a civil affairs officer he was responsible for the rehabilitation of the entire textile industry in Italy.

Decorations: E.A.M.E. Ribbon with five Battle Stars plus Arrowhead, American Campaign Medal, WWII Victory Medal, Distinguished Unit Medal, Meritorious Service Unit Plaque, French Fourgerre, Italian Knight of Honor and two Purple Hearts.

He was discharged April 14, 1946.

Seymour's favorite memory of the war was of sneaking a patrol into Messina ahead of Gen. Patton's entry and getting fined by the general personally when found out.

Seymour Hartman passed away April 11, 1992.

NORMAN HARTSTONE, born in Boston, MA on Feb. 9, 1920. Enlisted in the Army January 1942. Took basic training at Fort Knox, KY and then was sent to the 1st Armored Division, 47th Medical Bn. Left the country from Fort Dix in May 1942 and landed in Northern Ireland. Was in the North African invasion and was in the entire North African Campaign.

Most memorable sights was their retreat at Kasserine Pass and the surrender of the German/African army. Landed in Southern Italy in fall of 1943 and was there until he went home on furlough in 1945 from Florence. Most memorable sight was the bombing of the Abbey below Casino.

He received five battle stars and a Soldier's Medal for saving the life of a member of their company. He was discharged in June 1945 with the rank of P.F.S.

Married to Esther and have two children and four grandchildren. He is a retired general contractor.

HARRY J. HARTZ, was born and raised in Philadelphia, PA. During his late teens, he attended the University of Pennsylvania, beginning in September 1942. As a chemical engineering student he was deferred, but ultimately enlisted in the US Navy in May 1994.

He served on the light cruiser USS *Reno (CL96)* in the capacity of electronic technician mate 2/c on North Atlantic patrol duty experiencing the severe winter of 1945 including riding out a number of record-setting killer hurricanes. He was discharged in June 1946 having been saved from further duty in the South Pacific by the bombing of Hiroshima and Nagasaki.

He then returned to the University of Pennsylvania and graduated with his chemical engineering degree in June 1948, practicing engineering until his career path took a financial turn.

After a number of years in the corporate world, he started his own company 12 years ago and is now a business consultant specializing in mergers and acquisitions.

During the early part of his career, he vacationed in Europe and in 1957 met a young Parisian who became his wife the following year. It turned out that his wife, Ruth, was a Holocaust survivor having been a hidden child in Southern

France (age 46). Her memoir of that period was published last year under the title, You*r Name is Renee.* In addition to having been a French teacher for many years, she has now become a recognized speaker on the Holocaust and the need for tolerance.

They have now been married 36 years and have two children and two grandchildren.

Their daughter, Diane, lives in Salt Lake City, UT with her husband Arthur and two children where she is an assistant vice-president with the First Interstate Bank.

Their son Eric lives in Atlanta, GA with his wife Jennifer and is a business consultant with McKinsey & Company.

WILLIAM H. HASBURG, born on Feb. 25, 1895 in Meridan, CT. Entered the Army on Sept. 30, 1917. Served with the Corps of Engineers.

Discharged on Jan. 11, 1919 with rank of second lieutenant.

Married Rose Avidan while fighting in WWI as a yeoman (F) first class with the Third Naval District, New York City.

Worked for US Engineer Office, First Districty, New York City, Room 710 Army Building, 39 Whitehall St., New York, NY. Worked for New Jersey State Highway Department. Retired as principal engineer.

Member of JWV Post, Union, NJ.

William died on May 22, 1979.

DAVID HAUPTMAN, brother of Irving Hauptman, born July 9, 1925 in New York City. Drafted into the Navy in October 1943. Served as 3rd class petty officer on board the USS Cincinnati.

Memorable experience convoy duty and patrol duty in the South Atlantic between Brazil, Africa and Ireland.

Discharged on Dec. 24, 1945.

Has two sons and two grandsons. He is presently retired from the New York City Housing Authority.

EDWARD R. HAUPTMAN, son of Mary and Irving Hauptman, served in the US Navy on board the USS Thorn destroyer as a 2nd class petty officer for four years.

While in Barcelona, Spain sailors from his ship were in an NCO club which was bombed by terrorists, as a result one sailor was killed.

He remembers the chaplain arranging for an audience with the Pope. Sailors from the *T*horn went to the Vatican. Being the only Jew aboard ship, Edward volunteered and as a result he is the proud owner of a color photo with the Pope.

IRVING HAUPTMAN, born June 13, 1931, New York, NY. Inducted Nov. 19, 1951, in U.S. Army. Stationed at Camp Kilmer, NJ; Ft. Dix, NJ; Korea, Inchon, Seoul, Pusan, Kunsan and places with no names.

Since he was the company clerk of Co. B, 453rd Engrs. Construction Bn., he did all the paper work and record keeping of all four platoons assigned throughout Korea.

Memorable experience was catching a small naked Korean boy crawling under their compound fence and going through the garbage cans looking for food. Hauptman took him under his care, fed him, clothed him, and took him to an orphanage.

Awards/Medals: National Defense Service Medal, Korean Service Medal with two Bronze Service Stars and United

Nations Service Medal. Honorably discharged Dec. 15, 1959, with the rank corporal.

Married Mary (WAVES veteran) June 8, 1957, has five children: Alice, Bernice, Carol, Diane and Edward (Navy veteran), and nine grandchildren.

Semi-retired, food equipment, engineering and administrative executive for over 30 years. Presently self-employed on a part-time basis as an engineering consultant, designer, draftsman and patent draftsman. Member of JWV, VFW, American Legion and Korean War Vets. Does a lot of volunteer work, such as cooking for the homeless.

MARY CARNEY HAUPTMAN, born Sept. 20, 1935 in Ft. Worth, TX. Entered the Navy as a high school hospital recruit on Sept. 17, 1955 in Dallas, TX. Stations include the Naval Training Center in Bainbridge, MD and US Naval Hospital in Philadelphia, PA.

Memorable experience in class one day, their instructor asked them what they would do if they were told to jump out the window. (They were on the third floor.) No one answered so she got out of her seat and went to the window and looked out. She returned to her seat and responded, "I would jump." The class was startled until she informed them there was a roof just below the window. "I don't know if I made points with the instructor, but the class loved it."

Discharged on Feb. 1, 1955 with rank of HSHR.

Has a husband, five children and nine grandchildren. She is presently a massage therapist.

MORRIS LEWIS HAUPTMAN, born in New York, NY on Feb. 7, 1924. Enlisted Dec. 15, 1942 into the US Marine Corps. Served as radio operator in HQ Co. and "B" Co., 1st Bn., 3rd Regt., 3rd Marine Division. Military locations include Parris Island, SC; New River, NC; Camp Pendelton, CA; New Caledonia; Guadalcanal; Guam; Iwo Jima; San Diego, CA; Bainbridge, MD. Battles in Guam, Marianas Islands, Iwo Jima and Volcano Islands.

Memorable experience "As a result of being in life threatening situation, I realized that prayers are answered and I acquired a profound faith in God."

Awards/Medals: Asiatic/Pacific with Battle Stars, Presidential Unit Citation and Navy Unit Commendation.

Discharged on Dec. 28, 1945 with rank of corporal.

Brother of Irving Hauptman, is retired and glad he has more time with the family and grandchildren.

SEYMOUR HAUSTHOR, born April 25, 1930, New York City. Graduated high school and was drafted into the Army June 27, 1951; training at Ft. Dix.

Sent overseas Dec. 29, 1951, landing at Pusan, Korea. Was sent into the mountains to a training camp called "United Nations Reception Center," running a mess hall for six months. Was then asked to take over the "Post Exchange," P.X. for one year. Their closest neighbors was a North Korean POW camp, which kept them on alert.

Decorations: Korean Service Medal, three Bronze Service Stars and UN Service Medal.

Married Harriet (sweetheart) from Brooklyn, NY and had three children, two boys and one girl.

[illegible] in the food business after two years in the service, joined the JWV, and stayed in the food business (supermarkets) for almost 40 years. At 58, decided to retire.

"My three children, my daughter-in-law and two grandchildren are my pride and joy. Harriet is still my sweetheart."

HYMAN H. HAVES, born Feb. 15, 1916, New York, NY. Graduated Hillhouse High (1932) and USAAF Navigation School (January 1944). Served in the 5th AF in the South Pacific, completing 480 hours of combat. Was acting Jewish Chaplain at overseas bases where 380th BG was stationed.

Awards/Medals: Air Medal with four OLCs and Distinguished Flying Medal with OLC. Left the service with the rank of 1st lieutenant.

Retired at age 62 from B'nai B'rith with 33 years of service. Civilian honors include AZA Legion of Honor, Communication Award for TV show *Rumors*, named honorary mayor of the Pacific Palisades Highlands, B'nai B'rith's Outstanding Volunteer, Honorary life member of the National ADL Commission; Outstanding Senior Citizen (1992).

Ethel Linn; children: Jerri Linn Sozanaski, Laurie Linn Ball, children of the late Morris Linn; Maeera Haves Mougin, Randy Haves whose mother, Sara Jane Ostrowsky Haves, died in 1960. Grandchildren: Solange, Zoe and Jean Ettiene Mougin (father, Claude Mougin); Sam and Max Haves (mother, Barbra Gustafson). Married Ethel Lieberman on June 24, 1966.

Memorable experience was visiting Vietnam Christmas-Chanukah, 1967, at the invitation of the president.

JACK R. HAYNE, born Brooklyn, NY in January 1924. Graduated New Utrecht High School, 1941. Small Arms R&D, Aberdeen Proving Grounds and machine operator at Glenn L. Martin Company. Drafted in May 1943. Field Arty. of 95th and 89th Divisions; Infantry, Ft. Benning.

US Military Academy, West Point, graduating June 1949. Regular Army, 1949-1964. Korea August 1950 to March 1952. Guided missile staff officer, Ft. Totten, NY and Ent. AFB, Colorado. Instructor, Electronic, Air Defense Systems and Nuclear Weapons; retired February 1964.

Decorations: Army Commendation, Good Conduct, American Campaign, WWII Service, National Defense, Korean Service with seven Battle Stars and United Nations.

Grumman Aerospace, project engineer, training devices and simulators for Navy aircraft, 1964-88. Retired.

Married Pearl Anderman of Mountaindale, NY at West Point on graduation day. Daughter Nancy, mother of their grandson Matthew. Son Mitchell married and opting for Boulder, CO. Member JWV Gieir-Levitt Post 655.

HERMAN L. HAZEN, was born in New Brunswick, NJ on March 19, 1918. Graduated with Bachelor of Business degree from Emory University, Atlanta, GA in 1948 and also graduated from Woodrow Wilson College of Law in Atlanta, GA in 1953 with a Jurist Doctor degree in law. Passed the bar examination the same year.

[illegible] training in Camp Wheeler, GA and trained further in Fort Benning, GA; Fort Leonard Wood, MO and Camp San Luis Obispo, CA, in 20th Inf. Regt., 6th Inf. Div. and was honorably discharged on Oct. 14, 1945 as corporal.

Overseas on Sept. 20, 1943 to Oahu, HI; British New Guinea; Dutch New Guinea and Luzon, Philippine Islands.

Received Philippine Liberation Ribbon with one Bronze Star, Asiatic/Pacific Service Medal with two Bronze Stars, Combat Infantry Badge; American Defense Service Medal and the WWII Victory Medal.

As infantry man saw combat in New Guinea and Philippine Islands and made beach landings in both countries receiving an Arrowhead Badge for both landings.

"My most memorable experience was seeing our troop ships attached by Japanese Kamikaze airplanes and seeing some of ships receiving direct hits while making beach landings in Luzon."

Married to Rachel and have a son, daughter and three grandchildren and is presently in the practice of law in Atlanta, GA.

ALFRED D. HEBER "AL", born Nov. 23, 1919 in Kalisz, Poland. Inducted on Jan. 16, 1942 into US Army, QM Corps as supply sergeant. Military locations include Fort Dix, NJ; Camp Lee, VA; Fort Lewis, WA; Philippine Islands; Kyushu, Japan and Seoul, Korea.

Awards: Asiatic/Pacific Campaign Medal, Philippine Liberation Ribbon, American Campaign Medal, WWII Victory Medal and Good Conduct Medal.

Discharged on Jan. 7, 1946 with rank of sergeant.

Married Ruth in November 1942 and they have one son Carey, two daughters, Bonnie and Sandy and five grandchildren: Renee, Jeffrey, Shana, Sarah and Melissa.

Still active as a manufacturer of Schiffli Embroideries. Member of JWV Post 741.

MARK HECHLER, born June 20, 1926 in Detroit, MI. Drafted on Oct. 13, 1944 into the Army. Heavy weapons training at Camp Blanding, FL. Went overseas Easter of 1945 as a replacement to 12th Armored Div., 17th AIB, Co. B. He considers himself lucky to have not participated in any battles. After the war he was put into MP unit to guard government supplies on trains.

Awards/Medals: Combat Infantry Badge and Army of Occupation- Europe.

Discharged on Aug. 23, 1946 with rank of private first class.

Married Rose Rifken on April 13, 1948 and they have two daughters, Andria and Ellen. Three grandchildren: Kevin, Kenny and Scott. Was in the printing trade and retired on 60th birthday.

DR. JOSEPH C. HECHT, born Aug. 26, 1925. Inducted on Sept. 4,1943 into the US Army Airborne as an infantry glider trooper. Served in European Theater of Operations. Rank at discharge was private first class.

Awards: Bronze Star Medal, 82nd Airborne Glider Wings, Combat Infantry Badge, EAME Theater Campaign for Holland Invasion and Battle of the Bulge, Good Conduct Medal, WWII Victory Medal and American Campaign Medal.

Memorable experiences "During Paris Liberation, I met Jewish survivors. We spoke of home, friends, religion and the future. I shall never forget their attitude that tomorrow will be better and the Jews will survive and multiply.

'During an attack by German flame throwing tanks at the Battle of the Bulge, we were over run. I was given the heavy load of leading my squad to safety. No one dare say that Jews did not serve.

'During at patrol we captured a prisoner and I had the pleasure of telling him that I was a Jew and that the future will show the defeat of the Nazis and the growth of the Jewish people. He had to keep his feeling to himself.

'On the initial Israel Independence Day, I marched down Fifth Avenue wearing my Army uniform, my decorations and holding the Israel flag. An important dream was realized during that parade. I knew the future would be better for the Jews, although many more battles would have to be won."

He is a professor of marketing at Montclair State University, an author and editor of many texts, published 25 articles in important journals and have lectured to and consulted for some of the largest retail organizations in America.

LT. COLONEL GEORGE L. HECKER, born in Chicago, IL in September 1909. Graduate of University of Chicago and its Law School, 1933. Entered military service in WWII on May 11, 1942 as First Lt. Field Artillery. Released with grade of Lieutenant Colonel General Staff Corps G-1 Section SHAEF European Theater. Served as Chief of the US Military Personnel Subsection in SHAEF. Served as Chief of Operations 15th United States Army in Germany under then Colonel Robert V. Lee who became TAG United States Army. Served as Chief of Enlisted Personnel Section, 4th United States Army in Ft. Sam Houston, TX.

Married to Janet Hecker for 58 years. One son, Ronald Hecker, served in the Coast Guard. Two brothers, Colonel Robert Hecker and Major Melvin Hecker served in the Second Bomb Division in Europe. One brother-in-law, Charles Field, served as a PFC in infantry overseas.

While with the 15th United States Army as Chief of Operations, prepared and coordinated plans for the demobilization of the German army, repatriation of Allied and enemy prisoners of war. Also set up the War Crimes Investigative Teams; sat as a member of the first Military War Crimes Commission in Germany in May 1945 (see *Life Magazine* July 16, 1945).

Received Bronze Star Medal for preparing the plans relating to G-1 activities for Overlord. Supervised and coordinated plans for the apprehension, detention and preparation for trial of wanted Nazis for war crimes.

Member of the Illinois and California Bars. Member of the American Legion, Jewish War Veterans, Veterans of Foreign Wars, Disabled American Veterans. Active with the City of Hope, Jewish National Fund, ZOA, American Friends of the Hebrew and Tel Aviv Universities. Also helped invigorate and develop in Los Angeles Israel's Red Cross service - Magan David Adom.

Retired with rank of Lt. Colonel. His last assignment being Chief of the U.S. Military Personnel Subsection in Europe (SHAEF). Still an active trial lawyer.

LOUIS HEIDELBERGER, born in Germany on June 8, 1918. Entered the Army in November 1942. Military stations include Oregon; Arizona; Colorado; Cherbourg, France and Elbe, CA.

Memorable experience meeting Russians in Germany and liberating a slave labor camp, "Nordhauseu"; took pictures.

Awards/Medals: Bronze Star, American Service Medal and EAME Service Medal.

Discharged in November 1945 with rank of T/SGT.

His two brothers were in the infantry in the South Pacific, the oldest being killed during the Invasion of Saipan.

He owned and operated a motel in Colorado and worked for the US Government for 15 years. He is presently retired.

ARTHUR HEIFETZ, Lt. Col., born March 12, 1908, Lawrence, MA. Attended the Andover, MA School System, graduated from Massachusetts Institution of technology, Class of 1930. He was a U.S. Army major during WWII with the 87th Inf. Div. A medical inspector, it was his duty to inspect the concentration camp, Ohrdruff, on April 4, 1945.

He arrived at Camp Ohrdruf shortly after it was taken by the Americans. The sights were indescribable. Bodies stacked like cord

wood and persons lying on wooden bunks lined with straw and so weak that they could not get up to take care of their bodily functions The sallow dirty look of these people, the stench, the conditions so terrible it is almost unimaginative.

Awards/Medals: Bronze Star Medal, EAME Service Medal, American Defense Medal

He passed away Nov. 12, 1987.

KARL HEIMAN, is a descendant of a very old and large German Jewish family, whose roots can be traced back well over four centuries. In 1933, when Hitler acceded to power, Karl Heiman was eight years old. Within a few short years, very methodically, his family was relegated from well-to-do Germans to subhuman outcasts. They lost their homes, businesses, property and their human dignity. His father, a political activist, survived Dachau concentration camp. Because of a little known clause in the anti-Semitic Nuremberg Laws, Karl Heiman was allowed to remain in the German (Nazi) school system. This particular paragraph stipulated that children of Jewish World War I Combat soldiers may remain in German schools. His father was not only a combat soldier, as were his father's four brothers, but he was a genuine hero who received among his many decorations the Iron Cross.

After the 1938 Kristallnacht (Crystal Night) pogrom, even the few remaining Jewish students were prohibited from returning to German public schools, ending six years of thorough Nazi indoctrination. His extended family lost 22 children, women and men during the Holocaust.

Karl Heiman fought World War II in the American Army, returning as a much decorated combat veteran. Among his many awards are the Purple Heart, Bronze Star, Presidential Unit Citation, Combat Infantry Badge, Bronze Arrowheads, battlefield promotion and numerous campaign and battle ribbons. After Japan's surrender, he was among the first Americans in Hiroshima.

He frequently speaks to audiences, young and old, students and parents, Christian and Jewish congregations, schools and university about his horrible and fascinating experiences and life before, during and after the Nazi tyranny. Significantly, he also spoke with great success to today's young Germans and parents.

Karl Heiman recently retired after almost 30 years on the staff of the world's largest merchandise retailer.

He is proud to be 20th century living history.

ABE HELFER, was born in Dolina, Poland on Aug. 8, 1923. Entered Army on June 4, 1943 and received basic training at Camp Croft, SC.

Departed from Fort Meade, MD, Nov. 18, 1943 to Casablanca, Morocco and a month later, transferred to Oran, Algeria Replacement Depot until Jan. 5, 1944. Departed to Anzio Netuno, Italy where he was assigned to Company D, 7th Regt., 3rd Infantry Div. Spent four months on Anzio Netuno Beachhead until early May when their unit advanced to liberate Rome, Italy. Spent a few weeks in Rome on occupation duty.

Sometime the end of July 1944, went to Naples area where they trained for the invasion of Southern France which took place Aug. 15, 1944. At the time, he was blown out of Higgins boat near the port of St. Tropez, France. He was wounded and was taken to the island of Corsica, to a field hospital where he recuperated from his wounds and was awarded the Purple Heart Medal.

After a month in the hospital, he rejoined his unit in Southern France, where they advanced towards the Vosges Mountains and saw action in the Kolmar Pocket and Strasbourg, France. At the Rhine River the unit crossed into Germany.

On March 15, 1945 their squad set up 81 mm mortars near Guiderkurch, Germany. At the time, overheard German woman state that their soldiers were in the barn, evidently getting ready to ambush their squad. He, immediately, alerted the squad and they surrounded the barn and captured three enlisted men and one officer. After interrogation, they were transported to Battalion headquarters. For the above action, he was awarded the Bronze Star Medal.

He saw further action in the following areas: Wurtenberg, Ausburg, Nurenberg, Munich and finally Bershtersgarden, German and Saltzburg, Austria, where the war ended May 8, 1945.

Served in Occupation of Germany until Sept. 30, 1945 and was sent home on points. Came home on the ship, Queen *Elizabeth* and discharged at Fort Meade, MD, Oct. 31, 1945 as a PFC.

Received the following decorations and citations: EAME Service Ribbons with Bronze Arrowhead, Good Conduct Medal, Purple Heart Medal, Bronze Star Medal, Distinguished Unit Badge and Croix De Quarre.

After Army service, worked for the post office department from 1947-1985. Married to Anna and have a daughter Rochelle and a son Michael and five grandchildren.

He is a member of JWV, Fred Hecht Post #425, Spring Valley, NY.

HAROLD MARK HELFER, born in Birmingham, AL on Oct. 24, 1942. Joined US Navy Aug. 20, 1960. Served as US Navy photographer's mate. Military locations included: boot camp, San Diego; Photo School, Pensacola, FL; Naval Air Station, Norfolk, VA. Rank achieved at time of discharge was photographer's mate 3rd class. Discharged Sept. 15, 1963.

Memorable experiences: 1. Photo School. 2. Cuban Missile Crisis; developed and printed photos from air flights over Cuba. 3. 26 months of duty at photo lab at Naval Air Station, Norfolk, VA.

Harold has been a photographer ever since his Navy days and has worked commercially in the Washington, DC area as well as a photographer for the federal government. He co-authored a book, *Woodsong*, published in 1969 by the American Forestry Association. He has had several showings of his photography work. He has lectured at local camera clubs and also judged some photography exhibitions in Frederick and Gaithersburg, MD. Currently, he is the senior photographer at the National Institute of Standards and Technology. He has been with NIST for 27 years. Due for early retirement this spring and hopes to venture out on his own, in photography and maybe in some of his other interests such as gardening. He enjoys riding his Harley.

Wife's name is Linda Helfer. They have been married for eight years. They have four sons. Adam is 25 years old and has a restaurant in Washington, DC called "Govinda's". Joe is 23 years old and works as a shift manager for Pizza Hut. Matt is 20 years old and is attending Carson-Newman College in Jefferson City, TN on a baseball scholarship. Andy is 14 and a freshman at Middletown High School in Maryland.

ROBERT M. HELLER, born in 1923 and educated in Philadelphia, PA. T/SGT Army Air Force. Served from April 1943 to July 1945. Fifty-nine missions and five belly-landings as radio gunner in 17th BG, 95th Squadron. Gunnery School, Tyndall Field. Radio School, Scott Field. Crewed up, Barksdale Field.

Bombed ahead of General Clark in Italy and General Patton in Germany. Destroyed bridges leading to Brenner Pass, trapping Germans in Italy. Invasion of Southern France; Battle of the Bulge; breakthrough of the Maginot and Sigfried lines. Sank two cruisers in Leghorn Harbor.

Awarded the Air Medal with 17 clusters, Croix de Guerre Avec Palms for supporting the French Army in Italy and Presidential Citation for pinpoint bombing.

Successful manufacturer from 1945 to 1977. Consultant from 1977 to Happy Retirement.

Married to Jean since 1947. Three children. One grandson and twin granddaughters.

Lifetime member of JWV and DAV as well as member of VFW.

IRWIN S. HENDERSTEIN, was born as grandson of Rabbi Cooperberg and son of WWI Army corpsman Benjamin and Army nurse Frances in Bronx, NY on Jan. 27, 1925.

Entered Navy at age 17 1/2. Did boot training at Camp Sampson, NY (1942). Was in the V 12 Officers Candidate Program at Cornell University and Baldwin Wallace College which he completed with rank of Quartermaster 3rd Class. Engaged in the Pacific Fleet Service until his discharge in 1946. Awarded the Victory Medal, the American Theater Medal and the Asiatic/Pacific Theater Medal.

After discharge he completed BA degree in accounting at City College of New York. Was married to Henrietta Lefkowitz in New York (1949). They had two daughters, Nadine and Francine, and three grandchildren: Brian, 15; Michael, 13 and Renee, 9 (as of 9/1/55).

Irwin died June 9, 1988. He is buried in Costa Mesa, CA. *Submitted by Henrietta Henderstein, President of Ladies Auxiliary, Major Gary Grant Post 680.*

MANNY HENDLER, born July 9, 1923 in Hudson, NY. Drafted into Army on March 15, 1943. Member of 1890th Avn. Engr. Bn. Stations included Ft. Leonard Wood, MO; Madison, WI; ASTP and South Pacific. Participated in battles at Luzon, New Guinea, Southern Philippines and Japan.

Memorable experience involvement in rebuilding of Manila and Environs.

Awards/Medals: Philippine Liberation Ribbon, WWII Victory Medal, American Service Medal and Asiatic/Pacific Service Medal.

Discharged Jan. 18, 1946 with rank of Tech 4.

Married to Laura and have daughter Debra, son Jeffrey and grandchildren, Robert and Shaina. He is presently semi-retired from accounting practice.

NATHAN W. HENDLER, born July 18, 1896. Enlisted in the US Army during WWI. He served in Company B, Development Battalion, Camp Dix, NJ and in the 320th Co., Tank Corps, Gettysburg, PA. He was honorably discharged from the service of the United States in December 1918.

Nathan W. Hendler was the husband of the late Lena G. Hendler, a father, the father-in-law of two WWII veterans and a grandfather. He was a member of the JWV in Brooklyn, NY.

BURT H. HERMAN, born April 20, 1931 in Newark, NJ. Enlisted Jan. 14, 1952. USAF, A/1c, Air Weather Service, Andrews Air Force Base, Washington, DC, also at Sampson AFB, Geneva, NY and Kelly AFB, San Antonio, TX.

Korean Defense Medal. Discharged Jan. 13, 1956. JWV Department of CA Commander, National Controller, National Executive Committeeman.

Married Irma, children Debra and Lori. Three granddaughters. Reside in Northridge, CA.

DR. EARL HERRON, born in Chicago, IL on Jan. 12, 1904. Enlisted in AVS on Aug. 24, 1942 at age 38. Enlisted in US Army Reserve, Nov. 5, 1945. Member of MC AVS.

Military locations include Texas, Louisiana, Scotland, England, Wales, France and Germany. Was general service engineer until France and then with 180th General Hospital. Served in reserves in Chicago, IL, Co. 350 Convalescent Center.

Awards/Medals: five ribbons and three battle stars.

Discharged from AVS in 1945 and US Reserves on June 12, 1964.

Married for 57 years to Frances who died in 1986. Has daughter Joan H. Kastel, a speech therapist, and son Richard I. Herron, a psychoanalyst who was in US Air Corps. Three grandsons: Mark A. Kastel, Jeffrye L. Kastel and Michael C. Herron who was also in US Air Corp. There is one granddaughter, Alana Herron and two great-grandchildren, Ohad E. Kastel and Carly F. Kastel.

Retired to Florida, 1969.

LESLIE NORMAN HERSHCOWITZ, name was legally shortened in 1947 to Hersh. Born Dec. 25, 1919, Newark, NJ. Enlisted July 15, 1942. Closed his butcher shop to enlist and after 10 days basic training was sent to the Flamingo Hotel in Miami, FL. Next to Gulfport, MS; Welding School, Chanute Field, Champlain, IL; San Antonio, TX, where he joined the new group, 3rd Air Commando, 601st Air Engrs., 385th Air Service Group; Ft. Myers, FL, then to POE Oakland, CA, where he boarded the SS *Alcoa*.

On voyage to Leyte they saw the prow of the *Arizona* sticking above the water in Pearl Harbor. The Marines who secured Pearl Harbor hung Japanese soldiers from the exposed parts of the ship, creating quite a stench. They reached Leyte 56 days later. Made sergeant while on Leyte.

Next stop was Luzon, then Ie Shima, the invasion of Japan, back to Ie Shima.

Awards/Medals: American Theater Ribbon, Asiatic-Pacific Theater Ribbon, Philippine Liberation Ribbon, Good Conduct Medal, Victory Medal. Discharged Dec. 12, 1945.

Married Nov. 19, 1944, to Claire and has three children. Their oldest daughter, Phyllis, is married and has one daughter, Amanda; other daughter has two boys, Jonathan and Philip and a girl, Melinda; their son is self-employed.

MAX H. HERSHKOWITZ, born June 22, 1910 in New York City. Entered service on April 6, 1944 (VOC) after serving in New York State Guard in 1941. Served in the infantry in such locations as Dix Reception Center, Co. D; Camp Croft; Camp Blanding; Ft. Benning, Jan. 15, 1945-March 15, 1945; Meade, March 22, 1945; Naples, April 15, 1945 and 6677th M Tousa DTC, April 27, 1945.

Memorable experience was training and defending our soldiers as an attorney at OTC for AWOL, desertion, etc.. Pisa, Italy.

Awards/Medals: EAME Medal, Meritorious Service. Discharged on Sept. 7, 1945 with rank of first lieutenant. In January 1946 joined National Guard, 105th Regt., 27th Div. and retired as major in 1950.

Max married in 1944 and has two children. He is an attorney.

ABRAHAM HARRY HERZEL, born Oct. 21, 1911. Entered service January 1943. Studied at USN Japanese Language School. Served as intelligence officer in Pacific Ocean areas until December 1945.

Discharged April 1944.

Received AB and A.M. at the University of Denver and Ed. D. at University of California, Los Angeles. Spent 38 years in education as teacher, counselor and school psychologist.

Married Lillie Scher Robiczek on Dec. 22, 1984. He has daughter Michelle, 52 and son Joel, 47.

Brother-in-law Murray Scher is a member of US Army with three years service in Europe.

HARRY HEYMAN, was born May 9, 1917 in Old Forge, PA. He enlisted in the Navy Dept. 24, 1938 and received his boot training in Norfolk, VA. He saw action in the North Atlantic from the beginning of WWII until 1942. Assigned gun captain on gun #5 on the USS *Roper*. He was given credit for sinking the first German submarine of WWII, the 85.

He received the Silver Star Medal and citation by Secretary of the Navy Frank Knox, for his action. After four and a half years of sea duty, he was given shore duty at Lakehurst, NJ Naval Air Station.

It was then he met his wife Martha, a refugee from Vienna, Austria. They married in 1943 and have three children and four grandchildren.

Heyman remained in the Navy Reserve four years. His name is noted in many books about WWII battles in the North Atlantic.

SIDNEY HEYMAN, born Jan. 28, 1928 in New York City. Drafted in October 1950 into US Army. Arrived in Japan November 1950 for basic and advanced infantry training. Sent to Pusan Repple Depple, Korea, January 1951 and assigned to Co. F, 31st Inf. Regt., 7th Div. as a rifleman, then BAR man and then 60 mm mortar gunner. Re-assigned to Co. I, 224th Inf. Regt., 40th Div., February 1952 as rifle squad leader. Later transferred to Heavy Mortar Co. as forward observer. Transferred to Regt. HQ I&R platoon. Honorably separated at Ft. Ord, CA, October 1942.

Most memorable experience was saying kaddish with Catholic chaplain over poncho-covered body of his best friend, Larry Gold, KIA. Larry and he helped conduct Yom Kippur services in 1952, taking turns blowing the shofar. "I will never forget him."

Awards/Medals: Bronze Star w/V, Purple Heart, Combat Infantry Badge, Good Conduct Medal, Korean Service Medal with three stars, National Defense Service Medal, United Nations Service Medal and Army Occupation Medal.

Married 40 years to Deborah Beth with three children and two grandchildren. Retired aerospace engineer. Commander of JWV Post 724 since 1991. Charter member of US Holocaust Museum and West Point Jewish Chapel. Member of KWVA, Military Order of the Purple Heart and Museum of American Jewish Military History.

EMANUEL M. HIRSCH (SGT) USAAF, attended City College. Entered service Dec. 24, 1942; discharged Dec. 24, 1945. Entered at Ft. Dix, NJ; basic training at Miami Beach, FL and Ft. Collins, CO. Trained at Alliance, NE. Joined 66th Troop Carrier Sqdn., part of 346th Troop Carrier Group, 54th Troop Carrier Wing. Trained at Pope Field, NC and Ft. Wayne, IN. Shipped out overseas to Townsville, Australia, to Port Morsby and Nadsab, New Guinea. Stationed on the island of Biak. Bombed at New Guinea, strafed at Nadsab, outfit moved to Morati, Philippines.

Received the Asiatic/Pacific, Philippine Liberation, American Theater and WWII Victory decorations.

Lived in New City, New York and married to Marylin. Sons Jeffrey and Alan and daughter Madelyn. Self-employed and now semi-retired as mortgage broker in Boca Raton, FL. Volunteer work, member of JWV and Lions International.

ERNEST HIRSCH, served in the Military Intelligence in the US Army from Dec. 20, 1943 to April 26, 1946. He entered the service with the rank of private at Ft. Devens, MA and at discharge held the rank of technical 4. He received his basic training at Camp Grant, IL. He also received comprehensive military intelligence training at Le Vassinet, France. He shipped overseas on the HMS *Queen Elizabeth* from New York and landed at Glasgow, Scotland. He saw service in England, France, Holland, Belgium and Germany with the 13th

Airborne Military Intelligence. He saw action in the European Theater and helped prepare military intelligence for crossing into Germany from Holland with the 9th Army.

Among the outstanding places which he visited were London, England; Glasgow, Scotland; Paris, France; Brussels, Belgium and Berlin, Frankfort, Wiesbaden, Germany. He also engaged in special service in interrogating prisoners of war and later in the denazification of German personnel engaged by the US Military Government of Intelligence. *Submitted by Max Sigal.*

LEE HIRSCH, born in Brooklyn, NY on Oct. 20, 1918. Enlisted in the USAAF on Dec. 8, 1941. He served in the European Theater of Operations until October 1945. He attained the rank of master sergeant. He recently returned to Valognes, France and to Tottington, England for the 50th anniversary of D-day.

Ted Hirsch, born in Brooklyn, NY on July 9, 1921, served in the USN on the USS *Philadelphia* "The Galloping Ghost of the Sicilian Coast." He passed away on Sept. 30, 1991.

ISIDORE HIRSCHENFANG, born June 19, 1920 on New York City's lower east side. Graduated from City College in 1940 and was drafted in July 1942 following a stint with the Federal Civil Service Commission.

Served in various positions with the Corps of Military Police and for a short time with the Corps of Engineers. Went overseas in April 1945 and for his entire stay in the ETO he served as the police sergeant in charge of a German POW stockade on the outskirts of Brussels, Belgium. "As a Jew, you can imagine the respect and obedience I commanded from the prisoners!"

Before leaving the States, he had married Florence Safier in November 1943 and has been blessed with two children and four grandchildren.

He retired in 1989 and shares his days between Florida and New Jersey. He is a member of Post 536 and has served as adjutant, judge advocate and senior vice-commander.

ANITA CLAIRE GOLD HIRSCHHORN, born Jan. 18, 1919 in Brockton, MA. Entered service on Sept. 1, 1941, called in Dec. 15, 1941. Served in US Army Nurse Corp as second lieutenant. Stations include Melbourne, Australia, April 10, 1942- Jan. 12, 1943 and New Guinea, Jan. 13, 1943- March 16, 1945.

Memorable experience is for 26 months she worked as nurse in front line hospitals in New Guinea. Almost every day her hospital was under enemy attack by plane or artillery.

Awards/Medals: Bronze Star for New Guinea Campaign, 26 months; American Defense Ribbon; American Theater Ribbon and Asiatic/Pacific Ribbon.

Discharged on Jan. 7, 1946 with rank of first lieutenant.

Married 42 years to Fred Hirschhorn. Sister of Stanley Gold, Leonard Gold, Herbert Gold and the late Rosamond Fletcher. Mother of the late Elaine Hirschhorn.

Mrs. Hirschhorn passed away after long illness at VA nursing home, March 2, 1994.

SIDNEY HIRSCHHORN, born in Brooklyn, NY on July 23, 1924. Enlisted in Army on Dec. 12, 1942. Arrived at Camp Gatacre, England on April 4, 1944 with the 357th Inf. Regt., 90th Inf. Div. Had intensive training until June 8 when they went ashore on Utah Beach. Their division was part of Patton's Third Army. They fought through the Maginot and Siegfried Lines. They also were engaged in the battles of Mayenne, Ardennes and Battle of the Bulge to name a few.

In Merkers they located a major portion of the Reich's finances located in a salt mine. It was considered one of the largest legitimate looting jobs in history. They removed tons of gold bullion, German marks, millions of US currency and art works all removed by his battalion.

Received Good Conduct Medal, WWII Victory Medal, EAME Service Medal with Silver Star for five battles, Combat Infantry Badge.

He was honorably discharged from service Dec. 23, 1945 with the rank of sergeant technician 4. After V-E Day, their division was temporarily part of Army of Occupation. He was located in Waldsassen and had the title of mayor. They had a displaced person camp under his control plus a civilian switchboard.

Married to Adele in 1950. Have three children, two daughters, Cheryl and Terry and a son Martin. Retired from business in 1986 and is a charter member of Post 665.

LAWRENCE HOCHFELD (LARRY), born in Brooklyn, NY, Aug. 11, 1932. Enlisted in the U.S. Army at Whitehall Street Recruiting Depot in NYC. Sent to Ft. Devens, MA; then by troop train to Ft. Bragg, NC. Assigned to 420th Engr. Dump Truck Co. and basic training. Ordered to Camp Stoneman, CA, September 1951.

Boarded troop ship, USS *General William Wiegel*, landed first in Osaka, Japan, then Inchon, Korea, then by train to Wonju. Assigned to 504th Trans. Truck Co. as truck driver. Eventually became company clerk for HQ Co. of the 504th.

Awards/Medals: Meritorious Unit Emblem, Good Conduct Medal, National Defense Service Medal, Korean Service Medal with four Bronze Stars, United Nations Service Medal, and Republic of Korea Presidential Unit Citation Badge. Rotated home on Jan. 3, 1953. Reached the grade of PFC.

Member of JWV; past commander of Co-op City Post 1871, American Legion; VFW; Korean War Veterans Association; Franklin D. Roosevelt Lodge 613 and University Co-op City Lodge, 720 Knights of Pythias, past Chancellor.

Employed by ProGraphics Supplies, Inc., Long Island City, NY and lives in Co-op City, Bronx, NY. Married Irene and has two children, Helene Saffer and Steven, and two granddaughters, Kristen and Jennifer Saffer.

ANNE B. BODIAN HODES, enlisted in New York City, 1944-1946. Anne trained at Des Moines, IA. Was stationed at Washington till the end of war.

Anne died Nov. 13, 1989.

DR. MORTON HODES, was born in Brooklyn, NJ on July 14, 1918. Attended James Madison High School, Brooklyn College and Pennsylvania College of Optometry for three years.

WWII interrupted his education and he was drafted into the Army in February 1942. He had one and a half years of Optometry School to finish on his return from the Army.

At Officers Candidates School he was accepted into the Signal Corps, as there were no vacancies in the Medical Corps. He graduated as a second lieutenant on Dec. 31, 1942 and was assigned to the 213th Signal Bn. at Hattiesburg, MS. He was plans and training officer of his company.

On April 22, 1943 he was married to the former Sylvia Milberg and in 1944 was shipped to Hawaii; then on to the invasion of Okinawa.

He received his Army discharge on Feb. 8, 1946 and joined the Medical Service Corps as a captain in the Army Reserve Optometric Corps.

He is the father of two children, Donna Appleton and Dr. Robert Hodes. He also has five grandchildren.

MYER SOLOMAN HODES, 8065915, enlisted in the Navy in 1944. Training at Great Lakes, IL, 515th Co. In 1945 went to Hawaiian Islands. Then sent to Adak in the Alutian chain.

MYER S. HODISH, born Aug. 16, 1918 in Syracuse, NY. Graduate of Central High School. Enlisted in the AF on Jan. 29, 1941. He was attached to the 621st AAF Base Unit and held the rank of staff sergeant. He was discharged November 1945.

Married the former Lila F. Raphael of Brooklyn, NY. Moved back to Syracuse in 1948. Conducted his own businesses under the name of Mal's Heating Company. Died May 1, 1953, age 34. Survived by wife, sons Alan Bruce and Richard Leslie, parents, a sister and a brother.

JACOB HODISS, attended Jackson, Washington Irving, Madison Junior High and graduated from Central High School. Was a sophomore at Syracuse University. Member of the Culture Society, Boys' Club Band, Central High School Band, Syracuse University Band. Enjoyed photography and music.

Was a corporal in the topographical engineer unit of the Army. Died in England.

MYER HODISS, attended Jackson, Washington Irving, Madison Junior High and graduated from Central High School. Was active in the Marvel Society. Enjoyed horseback riding and fishing.

Was a member of a B-29 Group. Second lieutenant in the USAAF.

Died in an explosion of a B-29 at Alamagordo, NM.

IRVING HOFFMAN, born Sept. 8, 1924 in Chicago, IL. Entered AF in 1942. Served with the 13th AF in Pacific tour of duty.

Awards/Medals: Air Medal, seven Battle Stars, 53 missions. Discharged in May 1945 with rank of tech/sergeant. He is married with four children and presently retired.

STANLEY HOFFMAN, was born in Brooklyn, NY in 1932. After graduating from New York University in 1953 he applied for the draft and was inducted into the US Army in August 1953. After infantry basic training at Ft. Dix, NJ, he was sent to Military Police School at Ft. Gordon, GA. Upon completion of his military police training, he received orders to go overseas to S.H.A.P.E. (Supreme Headquarters Allied Powers Europe) which was then in Paris, France. His 520th MP Co. had its quarters in Versailles, France, some 10 miles east of Paris.

He completed his tour of duty in the rank of corporal and was discharged from service in 1955.

Mr. Hoffman spent the greater part of his business career with Citicorp, retiring in 1991 as assistant vice-president. He currently resides in Teaneck, NJ and has three sons, one daughter and two granddaughters.

Member of Post 498, Teaneck, NJ.

LEONARD HOLLAND, (MG), enlisted as a private on April 16, 1941, US Army Inf. Received basic training at Camp Croft, SC and remained as part of the cadre until May 15, 1942. Attended Officer Candidate School, Ft. Benning, GA and commissioned a second lieutenant, infantry, Aug. 6, 1942, assigned to the 40th Inf. Div. Proceeded immediately to the Pacific Theater and re-assigned to the 43rd Inf. Div. in Guadalcanal and for the next 26 months saw action in the Solomons and New Guinea islands. September 1943 commanded Co. H, 103rd Inf. Regt. and then assigned as S-3, 1st Bn., 103rd Inf. Regt. Returned to the United States in October 1944 and was assigned as battalion executive officer, 1st Regt. IRTC, Ft. McClellan, AL. Reassigned battalion commander September 1945. Released from active duty and entered the Officers Reserve Corps in February 1946. Promoted to first lieutenant in December 1943 and to captain in September 1944. Promoted to major in November 1945 and to lieutenant colonel in 1946. Commanded the 385th Inf. Regt., 76th Inf. Div. and in 1959 was promoted to colonel. On Jan. 3, 1961 appointed the adjutant general of the state of Rhode Island and effective March 16, 1961 was federally recognized as major general.

Was first appointed the adjutant general of Rhode Island on Jan. 3, 1961. Continued to serve under five different governors (four democrats; one republican) until retirement on Aug. 6, 1983. At a special session of the legislature, a resolution was passed and signed into law by the governor awarding the life-long title of adjutant general emeritus. Was senior adjutant general in the United States; no other adjutant general served the position for 22 1/2 years.

A native Rhode Islander, Maj. Gen. Leonard Holland presently resides in Pawtucket, RI with his wife, Bernice. They have three children and six grandchildren.

ALBERT HOLTZ, born Sept. 21, 1927 in Pittsburgh, PA. Entered military service on Sept. 25, 1950 as one of the first draftees from the Los Angeles area during the Korean War. With his background in electronics, the Army sent him to the Ft. Monmouth, NJ Signal School where he studied the operation and repair of the current radar systems. After his schooling, he was assigned to the 15th Signal Radar Maintenance Unit stationed at Ft. Totten, New York City. He and his team of five plus one WO-3, serviced the anti-aircraft radar in and around New York City. Al was discharged as private first class on Sept. 25, 1952.

After service, Al worked as an electronic tester and inspector in the aircraft industry. In 1958 he joined DIT-MCO International, Kansas City, MO where he specialized in testing complex wiring systems as used in aircraft, telephone, traffic control and computers. In 1969 he opened the European market for DIT-MCO and in 1966 he was promoted to the manager of the European Operation.

Al took early retirement in 1984 and has been working with hospitalized veterans. In 1993 Al was elected junior vice-commander of the JWV. Department of California. His work with veterans has brought Al a number of honors, 1989 "Man of the Year", Department of California, "Man of the Month"; 1990, National JWV; "Award for Working with Veterans", 1989, Jewish Federation of Orange County. He was recognized by the supervisor of Orange County for his work with veterans. Al is the editor of Post 680's Bulletin and has won a number of Department and State awards and National Twi a newspaper awards.

Al is married to the former Lorraine Feldman of Amsterdam, New York and they have four daughters and one son all living in California. They now enjoy their six grandchildren, all boys.

GERALD I. "JERRY" HOLTZ, was drafted into the Army at Pittsburgh, PA in April 1945. Sent to Ft. Meade, MA for induction, then to Ft. Knox for basic training on the 105 Howizer. Then to Camp Carson, CO for advance training in the Pack Artillery (Mule Pack). When this outfit was disbanded, he was transferred to the Cavalry School at Ft. Riley, KS. He was discharged at Ft. Riley on Oct. 3, 1947 as a tech 5 grade. Received the WWII Victory Medal.

Settled in Los Angeles, CA for a while then to Bakersfield, CA where he presently lives.

ABE HOMAR, was born in Hartford, CT and inducted into the service June 1942. Basic training at Atlantic City and on to Lincoln, NE Mechanic School. Then to Specialist School, Patterson, NJ and Kingman A-2 Gunnery School.

Next to Geiger Field, Spokane, WA for crew training. Flew overseas to join the 91st BG, 323rd BS based in Bassing Bourne, England. Flew 18 missions and shot down Feb. 22, 1944 over Oschersleben, Germany. Fighters came down and upset parachute which reopened shortly before he hit the ground. Wounded and ended up in hospital. Then to Dulag Luft in Frankfurt.

Six days in boxcar, they came to Stalag VII, Lithuania. Almost liberated by the Russians, they were marched to the seaport of Memel, put on a coal boat, and spent a week in the Baltic Sea, embarking at the seaport of Stettlu. they were forced to run to Stalag IV and many were injured.

On Feb. 6, 1945 they marched out and spent 86 days on the road in horrible conditions and were liberated April 18 at Stalag #11, falling Bostel.

He is married and has two daughters and four grandchildren. He is presently employed as a sales representative.

KURT HOMBURGER, was born on Jan. 26, 1909 in Gcolern, Hessen, Germany. After high school education, he was an apprentice for three years in the banking business and 12 years a member of the Boerse (stock exchange) in Frankfurt afm. Germany. He emigrated to the US in May 1938, worked as an accountant and traveling auditor.

Volunteered for military service on July 14, 1943. Received citizenship before being shipped to England. Served in Army Finance with six months of Finance School at Ft. Benjamin Harrison. Stations included 10th Replacement, Midlands, England.

Memorable experience is invasions on beaches in France.

Awards/Medals: Good Conduct Medal, WWII Victory Medal, American Service Medal, EAME Service Medal.

Discharged Dec. 2, 1945 with rank of technician 5 ... After his return to civilian life in 1945, he resumed his old position. Married in 1948 and was widowed in 1990. Married again in 1992 to Mildred Kingloff of Atlanta, GA.

FRANCES WALSHIN HONEYMAN, born in New York City on Oct. 30, 1920. Entered Army Nurse Corps in December 1942. Stations included Tilton General Hospital, New Jersey and Kennedy General Hospital, Memphis, TN.

Memorable experience is nighttime admissions of 200 plus fellows still covered in mildew and mud from Bougainville.

Discharged in January 1944 with rank of first lieutenant.

Her brother Paul was a POW in Germany; his papers are in archives.

Frances just retired from Veterans Administration Medical Center in Connecticut.

SAM AND ALVIN HORN, father Sam enlisted in the Navy at the same time his son Alvin did. He was the oldest enlistee in the Navy. Both have died.

Alvin Horn *Sam Horn*

ALBERT HORNBLASS, born July 5, 1939, New York City. Joined the U.S. Army, Medical Corps in July 1965. Stationed at Walter Reed Hospital, Washington, DC; taught at Kimbough Army Hospital, Ft. Meade, MD; and was an ophthalmic surgeon at 71st Evac. Hospital, Pleiku, South Vietnam.

Memorable experience was acting as Jewish Chaplain, 1969-70, and organizing and arranging High Holiday service in Nha Trang, SVN for 600 Jewish servicemen. Also taught bible classes in Pleiku. He had a $10,000 price on his head by the Viet Cong for the work he did with the civilian population.

Awards/Medals: Bronze Star, two Vietnam Battle Ribbons and Vietnam Medal of Honor.

Married to Bernice Brooks and has three children. Currently employed as chief of ophthalmic surgery at the Manhatten Eye, Ear and Throat Hospital.

EDWIN C. HORNE, graduate of University of Pittsburgh in 1939 with BS degree. Enlisted USAAF for cadet training Dec. 7, 1941, Maxwell Field, Montgomery, AL. Graduate of Navigation Training School, Sept. 1, 1942, Turner Field, Albany, GA. Rank second lieutenant. Assigned as navigation instructor at Ft. Myers AAB, Ft. Myers, FL. Promoted to first lieutenant. Graduated Celestial Navigation Training School, Chanute Field, Champagne, IL, 1943. Assigned to Lake Charles AAF, Lake Charles, LA. Set up navigation training unit simulating all night and day flying conditions and reducing flying training time 35 percent for pilots, bombardiers, navigators and radio operators. Promoted to captain, 1943.

Joined instructor crew training at MacDill Field, Tampa, FL. Led crew on North Atlantic crossing, Labrador, Greenland, Ireland to Knettisball, England, January 1945. Joined 388th BG, 8th AF. Flew 30 missions on B-17 bombers over Europe. Targets included: Cologne, Frankfurt, Hamburg, Linz and Munich.

Awarded Air Medal with two OLCs, ETO Medal with two stars. Promoted to rank of major, USAAC, Oct. 28, 1945.

SAMUEL HORNSTEIN, born in Baltimore, MD, Dec. 8, 1894. Sold his retail store to enter the U.S. Army, serving in WWI in the 71st Inf. He was honorably discharged in 1919 at Ft. Meade.

Married Memorial Day 1920 to Goldie Jacobson, his childhood sweetheart. Operated Haberdashery, Sam the Shirt Man, with his devoted helpmate and four children: Stanley, Calvin, Bernice Paper and Florine Waxman until his retirement due to heart ailment in 1946.

In 1938 when the JWV formed the Maryland Freestate Post, he officiated as chaplain and later as commander, as well as department chaplain of the state of Maryland and national deputy chaplain. He was a charter member of Maccabean Post 32, American Legion, a Noble Grand of the Independent Order of the Oddfellows and a member of Cassia Lodge, Masonic Order.

As VAVs representative to Ft Howard Hospital, he received the Certificate of Devotion for Volunteer Duty 1,000 Hour Award. He was a constant cheerful visitor and secured radios, TVs, electric shavers, drapes, etc for the veterans hospitals.

Personally secured food and Matza for the needy on Passover and other holidays and made sure that anyone in need was helped. His commitment to help the needy was remarkable. With the help of his good friend, Jack Rashbaum, there now exists a beautiful JWV Cemetery owned by the Maryland Free State Post, where both of these hard-working, sincere and fine veterans lie in peace in their final resting place in neighboring plots.

BERTHOLD HORNUNG, born Oct. 13, 1924 in Vienna, Austria. Left Vienna at age 15 in October 1939 for the USA. Went to public school for one year and at the age of 16 years was offered a job as a stock clerk in Westfield, MA.

On May 10, 1943 entered the US Army. From Camp Upton, NY, went to Camp Shelby, MS for basic/advanced military training. In May 1944 arrived in England to join the 82nd Airborne Div. As a rifleman in the 325th Glider Inf., battles took him through the Ardennes, Central Europe, Normandy, the Rhineland and finally a three month occupation of Berlin.

Authorized awards: Presidential Unit Citation, American Service Medal, Combat Badge, EAME Service Medal, Good Conduct Medal, Belgian/Vourragere, Netherlands Orange Lenyard.

Presently retired from store ownership and marketing manager. Living with his wife Betty (married 46 years). Have two children, Felicia and Michael and five grandchildren: Scot, Keith, Brian, Milissa and Gina.

Member in good standing of the JWV Post 717.

ALEX C. HOROWITZ, born Aug. 11, 1919, Vienna, Austria. Has BBA from City College, New York, 1948. Entered the U.S. Army Aug. 4, 1942, Ft. Dix, NJ. Graduated from Military Intelligence Training Center, Camp Ritchie, MD Class 2.

Flew across Atlantic Ocean to Dakar and from there to Casablanca and Algiers. Assigned to the 1st Inf. Div. at Tunisia and after reporting to Gen. Allen at Division HQ was found to be the only American Army soldier certified to interrogate German POWs. He was immediately detached to join Regimental HQ.

Participated in D-day landing at Gela, Sicily, after victory was sent to England to prepare for the Normandy invasion. Was given a jeep with orders to join HQ Co. of the 36th Inf. Div. at Caserta, Italy on detached service. Was wounded at Tunisia and Monte Cassino, Italy.

Awards/Medals: American Defense Service Medal with Foreign Clasp, EAME Theater Medal with four Bronze Stars, Presidential Unit Citation and French Fourragere. Discharged totally disabled from Camp Ritchie, MD with the rank of tech sergeant on May 19, 1945. He taught "enemy armies" at MITC, Maryland after return from the front.

Married 50 years to Toni and has one son, two grandchildren and great-grandchild. He is listed in *Who's Who in America* and received the L.A. County Humanitarian Award in 1983.

IRVIN M. HOROWITZ, born Oct. 24, 1924 in Elizabeth, NJ. Entered the Army on July 31, 1943. Served with the 413th Inf. at Camp Carson, Northern France and Rhineland Campaign.

Awards/Medals: American Service Medal, Purple Heart, EAME Service Medal and WWII Victory Medal.

Discharged on March 25, 1946 with rank of tech/5.

He was a newspaper editor of the *New York Times*. He died on Aug. 20, 1994. *Submitted by widow, Marjorie B. Horowitz.*

JULIUS HOROWITZ, was born in New York City on Oct. 8, 1921. He enlisted in the Army on Dec. 8, 1941 and was appointed an aviation cadet. His first stop was at Maxwell Field, AL where he had pre-flight training. His Primary Flight School was at Camden, SC; basic at Shaw Field, Sumpter, SC and advanced at Moody Field, Valdosta, GA. He received his pilots wings Dec. 12, 1942. Then he went to Sebring, FL to B-17 Transition School. About February or March he was sent to Salt Lake City as airplane commander; he got nine additional crew members. They trained as a crew at Boise, ID then to Rapid City, SD. Following their crew training, they had a five day delay enroute to Salina, KS where he signed for a new B-17 plane and prepared to depart for overseas.

They flew to Palm Beach, Puerto Rico, Georgetown, Br. Guinea, Belem and Natal Brazil. Then across to Dakar, Africa, Marrakech and then to Rabat, Morocco. Their crew was assigned to the 99th BG. He flew his first combat mission July 19 and his 50th on Feb. 12, 1944. Most of his flights were from Tunis, after which they moved to Foggia, Italy. He was awarded 10 Air Medals and two Presidential Unit Citations. One, among many interesting experiences, was while still a novice. He was flying right plane in a V. They had very heavy flak over the target, the plane on the left had several men killed. The lead plane's controls were shot away and they bailed out. After landing he discovered that they had 100 plus holes in their plane.

He returned to the U.S. and requested assignment to B-29 but was made a B-17 instructor. He eventually went to Navigation School at Hondo, TX from where he was eventually discharged. He stayed in Reserves and retired as major.

Married in 1947, one son, both of whom passed away. He was in various businesses and retired to Florida 16 years ago.

MARTIN J. HORWITZ, born April 30, 1921, Newark, NJ. Drafted into the U.S. Army in July 1942 and sent to Ft. Dix then to Pine Camp at Watertown, NY. Assigned to the 186th FA BN, HQ Btry. and spent the winter of 1942-43 at Ft. Ethan Allen, VT. Went to A.P. Hill, VA in Spring 1943 then to Tennessee for 2nd Army maneuvers. Prepared for shipment overseas at Ft. Dix and Camp Kilmer.

Shipped overseas Oct. 20, 1943 in convoy. Arrived in England and spent eight months training at a town near Watchet. Moved May 1944 to Bournmouth and trained for the invasion of Europe. Guarded the dam at Aachin; sent to St. Vith, Stavelot and Bastogne. Assigned to 695th Armd. FA, C Btry. and with them was over the Ruhr, the Rhine and on to the Elbe.

Awards/Medals: American Service Medal, Good Conduct Medal, EAME Service Medal and four Battle Stars. Discharged Nov. 12, 1945 with the rank Tech 5.

Married Carolyn Sept. 16, 1943. Retired from the U.S. Postal Service on Jan. 1, 1987.

MORTON HURWITZ, was a life-long resident of the city of Syracuse, NY and was educated in Madison Street School and Central High School. He attended Syracuse University and received his BA degree in 1934. He continued his education at Syracuse College of Law and graduated in 1937 with an LL.B. degree.

Morton Hurwitz was a practicing attorney in the city of Syracuse from the time he graduated from Syracuse College of Law until his passing on Jan. 4, 1960. Was a member of the Onondaga County Bar Association, the New York State Bar Association and the American Bar Association.

In November 1943 he entered active duty with the USN and served as a storekeeper first class and completed technical training in the Naval Air Technical Training School and was subsequently assigned to California. On Jan. 20, 1946 he received his honorable discharge from the USN.

Morton Hurwitz was a widely known and well liked practicing attorney up to the time of his passing. He was one of the outstanding members of the JWV, both on a local and statewide level. Was well known and respected by post members throughout the state of New York. He served as post commander of Onondaga Post 131 and in 1958 was elected department junior vice-commander of the Department of New York. The following year at the department convention, he was unanimously elected to the post of department senior vice-commander and was expected to undertake the position of department commander of the state of New York the following year.

In 1959 he was also elected president of the Liberty Republican Club, Syracuse, NY and served as committeeman for the Republican Party. He was also a long time member of the Knights of Pythias.

He was survived by his wife Lillian Hurwitz, his son Elliot and a daughter Barbara Dee. Also by his mother Jennie Hurwitz, a brother Jack Hurwitz and two sisters, Ida Lowitz and Cecil Serling.

IRVING ALBERT HYATT, born Dec. 2, 1924. Entered the Navy, USNR on April 9, 1943. Stations included Naval Operation Base, BWI, USS *Core*, USNAS Trinidad, USNTS Bainbridge, MD and USNH Annapolis, MD.

Memorable experiences was on PT boat after Germany surrendered and sinking of mines between Trinidad and Venezuela.

Awards/Medals: ETO, two Bronze Stars, American Theater Ribbon, WWII Victory Medal.

Discharged Feb. 11, 1946 with rank of pharmacist second class.

Married to Minnie (Becker). Two children, Phyllis and Philip and two grandchildren. Retired from retail business.

ALBERT A. HYMAN, born March 13, 1918 in Troy, NY. Entered Army on May 13, 1942. Served with 151st. Com. Eng. BN. Stations included Aberdeen, MD; London, England and Paris, France. Participated in European Theater of Operations.

Memorable experience was meeting brother Joseph (also in Army) in France.

Awards/Medals: American Service Medal, EAME Service Medal, Good Conduct and WWII Victory Medal.

Discharged Jan. 1, 1996 with rank of tech 3.

Married Naomi Ruth and has daughter Elaine, son Bruce and four grandchildren: Kurt, Michelle, Shari and Scott.

He is a retired business man.

BENJAMIN HYMAN, born 1893 in New York, NY. Served in WWI with the Army's Field Arty., 82nd Inf. Div. Stationed in France. Achieved the rank of sergeant.

Benjamin died on Feb. 18, 1954.

MELFORD HYMAN, born in Wilkes-Barre, PA on Sept. 7, 1919. Attended Wilkes College for two years. Joined the AAC on Sept. 11, 1940. Graduated Chanute Field, IL as a crew chief. Was sent to Stockton AF, California and worked on AT-6s for three years. Volunteered for ASTP in 1943 and attended North Carolina University, Chapel Hill for nine months in the German area and language. He was transferred to Camp Crowder, MO to attend the Message Center School. He [illegible]

After spending two weeks in Oro Bay, New Guinea they joined the 11th Airborne in Leyte, Philippines. They invaded Southern Luzon and after a month or so was sent to Batangas to join the 6th Army. They went from there to Kyoto, Japan where he ran the message center for 14th Corps.

Awards/Medals: Good Conduct Medal with clasp, Meritorious Unit Award, Philippine Liberation with Bronze Star, American Defense Service Medal, Asiatic/Pacific Service Medal with two Bronze Stars, WWII Victory Medal and American Theater Service Medal.

Discharged Dec. 2, 1945 with rank of staff sergeant.

Married Ethel Dvorin in 1949. She passed away in 1982. Have one child Sheila Rodgers.

Retired from the post office in 1983 and living in Florida.

DR. MORRIS HYMAN, was born in Cincinnati, OH on July 10, 1902. His parents Elizabeth Wolfson and Jacob Hyman immigrated to the US from Ratno and Rozhishche, Poland (now Ukraine). He graduated from Highland High School in Ft. Thomas, KY, University of Cincinnati and Eclectic Medical College in Cincinnati. He did graduate work in ENT and plastic surgery in Vienna, Austria.

He interrupted his private medical practice in Cincinnati to enlist in the US Army Medical Corp on Jan. 4, 1944. After indoctrination at Camp Barkley, TX, he served as chief of section as otorhinolaryngologist at several posts in the US: Ft. Sheridan, IL; Stark General Hospital, Charleston, SC; Camp Croft, Spartanburg, SC. He completed his service at England General Hospital, Atlantic City, NJ in 1947 with the rank of major.

He resumed his practice in Cincinnati and took an active role in the Jewish community, serving as chairman of Bonds for Israel, ZOA and Jewish National Fund.

His life ended abruptly on May 19, 1966 from a heart attack. Dr. Hyman is survived by his widow, Anita Emmerich Hyman, daughters Judith H. Darsky, Susan H. Shmalo (both of New York) and Barbara H. Rabkin of Cincinnati; seven grandchildren and three great-grandchildren.

STANLEY H. HYMAN, MAJOR GENERAL, (RET), US ARMY, born June 25, 1936, Long Branch, NJ. BA, Temple University, 1957; MLA, The Johns Hopkins University, 1965; MS in Mil Sci, US Army Command and Gen. Staff College, 1968; postgrad MIT, 1969-1971; Nat. War College, 1976. Served through a career of 35 years in Europe, Latin America and Asia as well as the US.

Decorations include the Joint Distinguished Service Medal, Army Distinguished Service Medal, the Legion of Merit with three OLCs, Defense Meritorious Service Medal, Army Meritorious Service Medal with two OLCs, Vietnam Service Ribbon with four Campaign Stars.

Married to Rosalea since 1958, two sons, David and Eliot, and two daughters, Avra and Michel.

Member of JWV Post 316.

DAVID H. HYMES, NATIONAL COMMANDER, after graduating Northwestern University in June 1941, he entered the US Army in September 1941, prior to Pearl Harbor.

He had his basic training at Ft. Warren, WY and served his first overseas duty in Panama starting in January 1942. After 10 months in Panama, he applied for OCS and returned to the States to attend the OCS at Camp Lee, VA. Upon being commissioned a 2nd Lt. in the QM Corps, he was assigned to a new transportation battalion being formed at Camp Ellis, IL.

[illegible] company grade officers were transferred out and replaced by black officers and he found himself in the officers pool in Camp Lee, VA. To his total surprise, he received War Department orders transferring him to the A.G.D. and assigned to temporary duty at the Main Post Office in New York City for 30 days.

His next assignment was a transfer to Sheaf Headquarters in England where he was informed that he would be the postal finance officer for the invasion of Europe. Nine enlisted men and he landed on Omaha Beach and a week later they set up a distribution facility to supply all the APOs in France and then Europe with the postal supplies, V-mail forms, postage and blank money order forms. They were attached to a base post office for quarters, rations and their personnel for guard duty of their valuable inventory.

Shortly thereafter, he was promoted to first lieutenant and on Feb. 29, 1945 he was wounded and spent nine months in hospitals in France, England and in the States. After his accumulated leave expired, he was discharged in February 1946 and returned to civilian life.

MILTON IGLOWITZ, (SSG), entered the service in December 1942. Immediately after entering the service he was inducted into Co. F, 399th Inf. of the 100th Div. Served in the European Theater in Southern France, (Allsace Lourraine). Wounded in the capture of the Maginot Fortification.

Received the Purple Heart Medal, the Bronze Star, Expert Infantry Badge and the Combat Infantry Badge.

JULIUS INGBER, born May 13, 1931, Brooklyn, NY. Entered active service Nov. 5, 1953, Charlotte, NC. Attended Engineer School, Ft. Belvoir, VA. Assigned to 984th Engr. Co. (field maintenance).

Awards/Medals: OCC MED GER and National Defense Service Medal. He was discharged Oct. 21, 1955, at Ft. Dix, NJ, with the rank SP4, USAR.

MAURICE E. INGBER, born March 14, 1931 in Trenton, NJ. Entered USN on Sept. 21, 1953. Stations include USS *Keppler* (DDE-765) as a gunnery and weapons department head.

Awards/Medals: National Defense Service Ribbon and European Occupation Service Ribbon.

Discharged Feb. 25, 1963 with rank of lieutenant.

Married with three children. He is presently retired.

MORRIS INSLEY, USMC, 1942-1945, served as navigator aboard C-35 transport (Curtis Commando) on Hawaii to China flights.

IRVING ISAACSON, born Aug. 7, 1919 in Boston, MA. Entered US Army Inf., Americal Div. in March 1941. Stationed at Camp Edwards, MA. Participated in battles at Guadalcanal, Bougainville and Philippines.

Memorable experience was after 39 months overseas, seeing the United States as he passed under the Golden Gate Bridge.

Awards/Medals: PUC, Combat Infantry Badge, Bronze Star and Good Conduct Medal.

Discharged October 1945 with rank of corporal tech.

Married with three children and three grandchildren. He is a retired jewelry salesman that is active in veterans and community work.

IRVING M. ISAACSON, born Feb. 19, 1919, Plainfield, NJ. Inducted Feb. 19, 1941, in the U.S. Army at Ft. Dix, NJ. Basic training at Raritan Arsenal. Other stations included Ft. Knox, KY; Louisiana maneuvers in 1941; Iceland, 1943-1945; ETO, 1945. Assigned to Antitank Co., 317th Inf. in Germany. Participated in Ardennes, Central Europe, and Rhineland [illegible]

Memorable experience was as a member of the post guard on May 18, 1941, when he apprehended three men of long criminal record and turned them over to the proper authorities. For this he received a Letter of Commendation.

Awards/Medals: American Defense Service Medal, American Service Medal, EAME Service Medal and Good Conduct Medal.

Discharged No. 13, 1945 with the rank master sergeant.

Married to Hilda Lazarus, has three married daughters, two grandsons and three granddaughters. He is retired. Still active, he is a past commander of JWV Post 119, Plainfield, NJ and past commander of JWV Willingboro Post 763, NJ.

HERMAN JACKLER, born Feb. 22, 1918 in Union City, NJ. Entered AC on Aug. 4, 1941 at Trenton, NJ. Departed on Sept. 20, 1943 for EAME Theater, arriving on Sept. 25, 1943. Left for US on Aug. 19, 1945, arriving on Sept. 1, 1945. Attended QM Clerical School, Turner Field, Albany, GA. Served as QM supply tech.

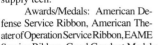

Awards/Medals: American Defense Service Ribbon, American Theater of Operation Service Ribbon, EAME Service Ribbon, Good Conduct Medal and Victory Medal.

Discharged on Oct. 31, 1945 with rank of staff sergeant.

ANDREW R. JACOBS, born in Newark NJ. Served in the Army's Adjutant General's Corps. Stationed at Ft. Benjamin Harrison, IN.

Discharged in 1976 with rank of captain.

Married Yardana and has a daughter Suzanne. He presently is a partner and practices law for Fitzsimmons, Ringle & Jacobs in Newark, NJ.

DAVID S. JACOBS, born Atlanta, GA, Oct. 9, 1922. Entered service Jan. 13, 1943 at Ft. McPherson, GA. Basic training at Keesler Field, MS. After basic training was sent to Air Force Training School at Chillicothe Business College, Chillicothe, MO. Upon graduation was stationed with 22nd Anti-submarine Patrol at Wilmington AAB, Wilmington, NC until October 1943. Reassigned to 467th BG (H) at Wendover Field, UT as clerk in the Operations office. Went overseas with this group in February 1943 remaining at the Rackheath AFB in Norwich, England until the end of the war in Europe. Returned to States in June 1945. As sergeant was honorably discharged at Sioux Falls, SD in October 1945, having earned six Battle Stars for the ETO Ribbon while in England.

After discharge returned to school, graduating in 1950 from the Parsons School of Design in New York City. Have been engaged in the interior design profession in Atlanta, GA since 1950 and still pursues an active business career.

ELI JACOBS, was born in the Bronx, Sept. 18, 1919. Attended DeWitt Clinton High School and graduated from New York University in 1941. Immediately entered the US Army in September 1941 before the advent of Pearl Harbor.

Did basic training at Ft. Mommoth, NJ and joined the 37th Inf. Div. in the Southwest Pacific as part of the advanced group that landed in the Fiji Islands. Their entire company replaced the Marines in Guadalcanal.

He remained in the area for over a year and was sent back to the United States to Camp Irwin where he remained for one and one half years, part of which he was hospitalized for a severe fungus infection.

At the onset of the Battle of the Bulge, he was shipped overseas to Europe and landed n France, then sent to Ramagen where the battle for the control of the Ramagen Bridge was happening. He remained there for six months and became part of the occupation forces which defeated Germany.

EUGENE JACOBS

JEROME B. JACOBS, was born in Pueblo, CO, Nov. 30, 1924, moved to Washington, DC in 1942, and was drafted into the Army July 1943.

He trained at Ft. Knox, KY, departed for England in February 1944, and later joined the 3rd Armd. Div. at St Lo, France. He was assigned to the 33rd Armd. Regt. Recon. Co. They were the first American unit to cross into Germany at Rotgen. Lt. Richard Burrows was killed at that spot and Jerome was wounded. The "Third" was commanded by Gen. Maurice Rose, a Jew, who was killed in combat.

He was awarded the Purple Heart and Bronze Star for bravery. He was also awarded five Battle Stars for European War. He was discharged from the Army, December 1945.

He has been marred for 48 years and has three daughters and nine grandchildren. He has been a member of JWV since 1948.

SEYMOUR B. JACOBS, was born in Newark, NJ on Dec. 25, 1913. He studied at Dana College and received a law degree from the University of Newark, later Rutgers Law School, in 1937. He enlisted in the US Army in 1942 and graduated from Field Artillery School and was sent to Officer Candidate School in Ft. Sill, OK. He served with the 88th Field Arty. in Sicily, Italy and North Africa during WWII and saw combat at the Anzio Beach and Monte Casino. He was a first lieutenant and received the Bronze Star for heroic service and battle stars.

After leaving the Army he returned to civilian life as an attorney in Newark, NJ where he practiced until his death in 1975. Jacobs was a senior partner in the firm of Balk, Jacobs, Goldberger, Selligson & O'Connor. He was married to Pearle Flachen Jacobs and had two sons, Andrew Robert Jacobs and Roger Bruce Jacobs, both attorneys presently practicing in Newark, NJ.

He lived in Union, NJ for the balance of his life and was active in the Jewish community and was a member of Temple Beth Shalom in Union. He was honored posthumously in 1975 by the Trial Attorneys of New Jersey as the Outstanding Lawyer of the Year in 1975. A scholarship in his memory was established at Rutgers Law School in Newark in 1980.

JEANNETTE (GIBIAN) JACOBSON, born New York City. WAAC August 1942: 1st Co., 1st WAAC Training Regt., Ft. Des Moines, IA. WAC 1943. England 1943; France 1944-45. Secretary to deputy general for Operations 8th AF, US Strategic Air Forces in Europe. After cessation of hostilities in Europe, assigned to Intelligence, Captured Enemy Personnel & Equipment. Discharged October 1945.

Decorations: Bronze Star Medal, Good Conduct Medal, WAAC Service Medal, American Theater Medal, European Theater Medal, WWII Victory Medal.

Worked as legal secretary/paralegal in Manhattan. Married 1960; now widowed.

Life member JWV; life member National Museum of American Jewish Military History; past national executive committeeman; Adjutant Department of Florida; past commander Post 682, North Miami Beach; Hadassah; Women's American ORT; member, Temple Sinai of North Dade.

Resides in North Miami Beach, FL.

MIRIAM P. JAFFEE, born Nov. 6, 1924 in Albany, NY. Entered USNR on June 14, 1945. Stationed at US Naval Hospital, Philadelphia, drawing blood.

Memorable experience was caring for patients who survived the Bataan March.

Discharged Aug. 22, 1974 with rank of PhM2/c. National VAVS officer.

WILLIAM I. JAFFE "BILL", (LCDR), USNR, born Aug. 9, 1914 in Birmingham, AL. University of Alabama AB, 1936, JD, 1938. Practiced law in Birmingham. In 1940 received commission as ensign USN. Assigned to USS *New York* convoy duty North Atlantic. 1943 assigned USS *Iowa* as assistant communications officer. Ship's liaison to White House

for FDR, Gen. George Marshall, Gen. Hap Arnold, Gen. Sumerall, Adm. Ernest King, Adm. William Leahy for meeting with Churchill, Stalin and Chang Kai Shek in Teheran.

Awards/Medals: nine campaign ribbons, eight Battle Stars, Fleet Clasp- American Defense, American Campaign, Asiatic/Pacific Campaign Medal, EAME Campaign Medal, WWII Victory Medal, Philippine Liberation Medal with two stars, Naval Reserve, National Defense and Navy Occupation.

Discharged Sept. 19, 1945 with rank of lieutenant commander.

Married with one son, a Vietnam veteran and retired.

ADAH STRAUS JAFFER, was born in Richmond, VA on May 9, 1914. Bachelor of music education from Northwestern University 1935 and MA in music education from Teachers College, Columbia University, 1940. Entered WAAC in June 1943; sworn into WAC August 1943. Basic training at Ft. Ogelthorpe and into 403rd ASF Band (WAC) at same post. Band moved to Stark General Hospital in Charleston, SC where they remained one and a half years. Assistant conductor of military band; conductor of dance band; administrative NCO. Attained rank of T/Sgt. The band performed regular post duties, playing parades, flag up and down, unloading of hospital ships from Europe, departure of hospital trains. She was assigned to produce and participate in a 30 minute show which they took through the wards and from this came her group, "Sgt. Straus and her Hungry Five." The military band and her group entertained troops in hospital auditorium and on tour throughout the 4th Service Command.

At age 31 met her first anti-Semitism. Warrant officer had given her the duties, but not the rank of top NCO. Staff sergeant said, "No ——— Jew is gonna boss me."

After discharge Jan. 14, 1946, went into show business; finally returned to directing bands and orchestras in public schools. Married Harold Jaffer in 1953 and moved to Miami; two sons and a grandson and granddaughter. Is still playing French horn in two community bands, violin in orchestra. Post bugler for JWV 243.

CARL JANOW, born Aug. 11, 1923 in Rhinebeck, NY. Enlisted in the Air corps, Nov. 4, 1942. Honorably discharged as corporal, Nov. 1, 1945. Basic training December 1942, Miami Beach, FL. Radio Operator School (Keystone School) April 1943, Pittsburgh, PA. Assigned to the 344th BG, 495th BS as ground station radio operator at MacDill Field, Tampa, FL. Left for the ETO in January 1944 and stationed at Bishops-Stortford, England. Moved to France in July 1944 and subsequently to Belgium and Germany.

Six battle stars: Air Offensive Europe, Normandy, Ardennes (Battle of the Bulge), Central Europe, Northern France and Rhineland. Decorations and citations: American Service Medal, Presidential Distinguished Unit Badge, EAME Service Medal and Good Conduct Medal.

Graduated Clarkson College of Technology, BEE, October 1948. Vice-commander and commander JWV Post 589, 1966-1967. NASA Engineering Program manager- remote manipulator system for space shuttle. Retired from NASA, April 1981, after 28 years service. Over 10 years as electrical engineer in industry (Melpar, Litton and General Electric). Amateur radio operator (NO4I).

Married Irene Katz, March 2, 1952. Two daughters, Marcia Hillary Kay and Leora Janow Drory. Four granddaughters: Jennifer Beth and Sara Rebecca Kay and Erika Yael and Danit Gabrielle Drory.

DAVID JARVIS, (MAJ), USAF, (RET), enlisted in the AAC on Oct. 24, 1942. He went through basic training and Technical School, becoming a bombsight repair mechanic. He was stationed at several airbases in mid-USA when he received an Army appointment to West Point, entering on July 1, 1944 and graduated as a second lieutenant June 3, 1947. He went directly to pilot training and received his military pilots wings as a multi-engine pilot on Feb. 29, 1949. He then flew troop carrier aircraft until entering the University of Illinois in June 1950 where he earned a masters degree in electrical engineering in June 1952.

He went to the USAF Systems Command as an avionic test project engineer. In 1953 he was sent as an exchange officer for training in the US Army Ordnance Department in Washington, DC. In 1955 he returned to the AF Systems Command as a weapons development engineer. In 1959 he was sent to USAF in Europe HQs in Wiesbaden, Germany as a technical intelligence officer, returning to the AF Systems Command as a technical intelligence analyst in 1962. He retired as a major on Dec. 31, 1965.

After retirement he worked at Lockheed Aircraft Corporation, Burbank, CA for 17 years as an electronic systems engineer, working on the intelligence gathering aircraft U-2 and SR-71 and the anti-submarine aircraft P-3 and S-3A. On Dec. 31, 1982 he retired permanently and moved to Avila Beach, near San Luis Obispo, CA. In November 1989 he moved to Sun City, Las Vegas, NV where he now resides with his wife Evelyn.

His grandson received an appointment to West Point and entered in June 1994 to join the Class of 1998.

WILLIAM J. JASPER, (CDR. DC), USN (RET), born May 7, 1925 in Wilkinsburg, PA. Graduated high school in Pittsburgh, June 1943. Entered active naval service in July 1943 as apprentice seaman, at Navy V-12 Unit, Bucknell University, Lewisburg, PA.

After completion of pre-dental studies and six months assignment at Bainbridge, MD, NTC, was transferred to Navy V-12 Unit, School of Dentistry, University of Pittsburgh, in September 1945. Placed on inactive duty January 1946. In December 1948 while a senior dental student, received active duty appointment as ensign USNR, and on graduation was commissioned LTJG, Dental Corps, USN.

Served on continuous active duty as dental officer (two ships, USS *Antietam* (1951-52) and USS .... (1956-57) his other shore stations including Taipei, Taiwan) until retirement in June 1966 as commander.

Throughout his naval service, was an active Jewish lay leader. Received Hillel Leadership Key (1945) and a Letter of Commendation from Commander, Fifth Naval District (Norfolk), in 1958. Proposed name of Commodore Uriah Levy for Jewish Chapel at Norfolk's naval station. Levy Chapel was dedicated in December 1959. While in Portugal following 1956 Suez Crisis, arranged for Temple Sinai, Newport News, VA to acquire its first Sefer Torah as a gift from Sha'are Tikva synagogue of Lisbon.

Naval decorations include following medals: American Theater, WWII Victory, National Defense Service, Korean

Service with two stars, UN Service and the Korean Presidential Unit Citation.

Member JWV, DAV, TROA, FRA (Fleet Reserve Association) and AMSUS (Association of Military Surgeons of US).

Following final retirement in 1980 in Dallas, TX, moved to North Carolina for permanent residence. Current veterans and naval activities include volunteering at Durham, NC, VA Medical Center, FRA representative to Wake County (NC) Veterans Council and members Navy's Recruiting District Advisory Council.

Wife's name is Retha and they have two children, Noreen Berger and Dr. Warren Jasper.

JACK G. JAY, born Columbus, OH on April 27, 1921. Entered service on July 30, 1942. Member of 98th Finance Disbursing Section, FD, AUS. Stations included Ft. Benjamin Harrison and ETO. Participated in battles of Northern France, Rhineland, Central Europe and Ardennes.

Memorable experience was the fall of 1944 having Rosh Hashanah and Yom Kippur services in Nancy, France in a synagogue that the Nazis desecrated and used as a hospital.

Awards/Medals: EAME Theater Ribbon with four Bronze Stars, American Theater Ribbon and Good Conduct Ribbon.

Discharged Nov. 2, 1945 with rank of tech 4.

Married Betty in 1945 after return from ETO. Three children: Susan, Steven and Lauri. Five grandchildren. Retired from a career as sales representative and sales manager.

DANIEL A. JOSEPH (JOE), born June 30, 1948, Worcester, MA. Joined the U.S. Army Feb. 26, 1969, at Springfield, MA. Stationed at Ft. Jackson, Ft. Leonard Wood, MO, and Vietnam as a technician.

Awards/Medals: National Defense Service Medal, Vietnam Service Medal, Vietnam Commendation Medal with Device 60, two Overseas Bars, Army Commendation Medal, Expert M-16, Bronze Star.

Instrumental in keeping the JWV Menorah Post 368 alive and vital, he and his comrades set out in 1993 to raise money for a JWV Memorial. It was completed and dedicated at the gates of the Fitchburg Jewish Cemetery one year later. Active for many years in Vietnam Veterans, he played an important role in the design and completion of Leominister Vietnam Veterans Memorial, and as a charter member, continues to oversee the yearly 8th grade essay contest on Vietnam. He is president of the JWV.

Married to Gail, has three sons and one daughter. He owns a furniture refinishing business.

MAIER P. JOSEPH, born May 8, 1917 in El Paso, TX. Entered Army on Oct. 4, 1943. Member of HQ IX Air Defense Command, 9th AF, US Army. Stations included London, Normandy, Paris, Bad Neustadt Auf de Seale, Germany.

Memorable experience was attending the Yom Kippur services at the famous Rothschild Synagogue after the liberation of Paris and a desecrated synagogue being found in Bad Neustadt by their command chaplain, a Methodist minister. He charged Maier with seeing the synagogue restored, or he would do it himself. With the help of a former member of the congregation, Cpl. Walter Bunin of Chicago, the synagogue was restored and rededicated on Nov. 2, 1945. Rabbi David Lefkowitz Jr. (9th AF chaplain), Cong. B'nai Zion, Shreveport, LA conducted the rededication service.

Awards/Medals: Bronze Star for meritorious service.

Discharged Jan. 4, 1946 with rank of sergeant.

Married Marian K. on March 21, 1942. Have son, daughter and three grandchildren. Presently a retired federal civilian employee. Member of JWV Chapter 574.

RUTH ZINKOFSKY SPILKY JOTKOWITZ, born June 26, 1922 in Russia. Entered Army Nurse Corp on Jan. 1, 1945. Stations included Atlantic City, NJ; Ft. Bragg, NC; Tinian; South Sea Island and Japan. Served as ward nurse taking care of amputees and supervised medical technicians at a field hospital in Hiro, Japan.

Memorable experience was atomic bomb flown in 1945; saw Hiroshima flattened out.

Awards/Medals: Asiatic/Pacific Campaign Medal and WWII Victory Medal.

Discharged April 1946 with rank of second lieutenant.

Lost mother, father, two sisters, one brother and two wonderful husbands. She is a mother and grandmother with step-children, step-grandchildren and step-great-grandchildren. She makes everyone happy by doing charity work.

HARRY KABLER, born in Boston, MA, July 8, 1921. Enlisted in the USAAC in WWII, serving overseas in New Guinea, Philippines and Okinawa in 822nd BS, 38th BG. Attained the rank lieutenant Colonel, USAFR, RET.

Attended University of Texas, graduated Summa Cum Laude. Went to work for Texas Turnpike Authority June 16, 1955 as chief accountant, became secretary/treasure Jan. 1, 1974, and retired after 39 years June 30, 1994.

A life member of JWV (past commander Dallas Post 256), DAV (current commander of Big D Chapter 57, Dallas), ROA, Air Force Association, TROA, and National Association of Uniformed Services.

Jewish Activities: Served as member of Board of Directors and as chairman or member of several committees. Still active in temple activities such as being in charge of High Holy Days ushering for past 20 years and running two blood drives each year since May 1986. A member of AIPAC, American Jewish Committee, American Jewish Congress, B'nai B'rith, Dallas Jewish Historical Society and others. He is also involved in several civic activities and supports numerous local and national charitable organizations.

Divorced after 17 years of marriage. Nine years later remarried to Beatrice Broneman for 21 wonderful years until her death Aug. 29, 1993. Has a son Karl, his wife Cheryl and two children, Kelly and Joshua; stepdaughter Carol Dochen, her husband Sandy and two children, Katie and Andrew; stepson Steve Broneman, his wife Belinda and twin children, Haley and Chad.

BENJAMIN KAGAN, was drafted from Chicago in 1942 and went into the Army Ord. Corps because he had worked for the Ord. Department before being drafted. After several other assignments, he went overseas as a member of the 89th Ord. Bomb Disposal Squad.

They spent a short time in England, then went to France. One of their first assignments was the removal of unexploded artillery shells from a partially destroyed German ammunition dump. The danger here was that explosives which have been shocked are very sensitive to any further disturbance.

While they were engaged in this work, they were called upon to remove a bomb which had fallen near Gen. Patton's headquarters in Normandy. The general watched them at work and then said that he would recommend the squad for Bronze Stars, but they never materialized. Another time, they were called upon to remove a bomb in a cemetery.

He was discharged in December 1945, having earned a Purple Heart and two campaign stars for his ETO Ribbon.

MORRIS KAHANA, was born in Poland, May 1, 1912. He is an American citizen that went to college for one and a half years in New York. Entered Army on March 25, 1944; training at Ft. Dix. Shipped out to England with 4th Div., 12th Inf. to the Moors England to do training for OD landing in Normandy, France.

They made history being the front Army always moving and shoving the Germans back. "I can honestly say God was walking and guarding me every footstep after a few days in hand to hand combat." He was wounded in his left arm by bombs exploding all around and bullets flying all around. On this occasion he had his wallet and GI prayer book in front pocket covering his heart. The bullet stopped in center on page "Hear O Israel the Lord our God, the Lord is one." It saved his life.

Taken to the rear and emergency operation performed. Sent back to England to recuperate with his two brothers who were serving in the US Army. Discharged from Holloren G.H.S.I.N.Y. 1946.

Married to Anne Oaks who waited for him seven years. They have two sons and three grandchildren. Retired from Bakery Drivers' Union.

Member JWV Post 409 and 542 and lifetime member of DAV.

WILLIAM KAHANE, born Sept. 7, 1945 in Rimalev, Poland. Entered the US Army Signal Corps in November 1969. Stations included Ft. Monmouth, NJ, Pentagon and Long Binh, Vietnam.

Memorable experiences were being interviewed by 6:00 p.m. news on the Gen. Westmoreland rule of uniforms to be worn on Wednesdays. He was invited to Thanksgiving dinner at a church in Berkely on his way to Vietnam. Cameraman for Hubert Humphrey's '72 campaign. Attended a Seder at USO in Saigon.

Discharged June 1971 with rank of first lieutenant.

Married Nancy Shapiro and they have five boys, age 4-11. Owns and operates the Blue Amber Motel in Cape May, NJ.

FRED A. KAHN, born in 1932. His parents left for Belgium shortly after his birth, leaving him behind in Germany to be reared by a childless aunt. In 1938 he escaped from Germany (leaving his aunt and uncle who had reared him) and rejoined his parents. Had he not escaped he undoubtedly would have been killed along with his aunt and uncle who were Holocaust victims.

Although not a U.S. citizen at the time, he volunteered for the U.S. Army during the Korean War period. Entered the service on March 17, 1955, shortly after his immigration from Belgium. He had survived the Holocaust, living hidden throughout in southern Belgium.

After basic training, he was assigned to the 525th Military Intelligence Service at Ft. Bragg, NC. Was naturalized Nov. 24, 1953, while with the All American 82nd Abn. Div. Early in 1954, he was reassigned as an intelligence analyst to the U.S. Army Occupying Forces in Germany.

After discharge, he earned both a BA and MA, the latter from Johns Hopkins University. He taught at Howard University in Washington, DC. Then had a career as an economist with the U.S. Federal Government. His work was recognized with the Secretary of Labor's Distinguished Career Service Award.

Married Rita, has daughter Anna and grandson Jacob Kahn Hogenkamp.

STEVEN S. KAHN, born Oct. 23, 1914, in Germany. Escaped the Nazis and after a short stay in France, America gave him refuge. He was alone, no money and no English, but he worked at menial jobs and went to school at night to learn English. Registered in the first draft and was called up and inducted in the U.S. Army March 7, 1941.

Assigned to 34th Inf., 24th Div., Ft. Jackson, SC for training. Sent to Presidio in San Francisco to get ready for shipment to a place unknown when war was declared Dec. 7, 1941. He was shipped to Hawaii and his company helped to clean up Pearl Harbor. Stationed at Schofield Barracks, he trained as radio operator and repairman.

Shipped to Australia and went into combat Aug. 25, 1943, at Hollandia. Finally came home on rotation October 1944, and was discharged Aug. 17, 1945, at Ft. Dix. Had a bad case of jungle rot which damaged his hearing and for which he receives a small pension.

Awards/Medals: Defense and Asiatic-Pacific Service Medals.

Married Oct. 28, 1944, and had 49 years together before his death on Nov. 16, 1993. Had two daughters, one son and six grandchildren. He was a leather chemist and a farmer. At the time of his death he was owner of S.S.K. Associates. *Submitted by his wife, Inge Kahn.*

LUDWIG KAHN, (SSG), born in Germany, Jan. 26, 1920. Escaped the German Holocaust December 1936 to Milwaukee, WI. Entered US Army on Dec. 9, 1941 and discharged honorably in December 1945. After basic training assigned to 2nd Armd. Div., Ft. Benning, GA. Then cadre to activate the 10th Armd. Div. Transferred to Medical Administrative OCS; reassigned to rejoin 10th Armd. Div.; instead assigned to 37th Inf. Div., Bougainville, Solomon Islands; invasion of Luzon at Lingayen Gulf; Battle of Baguio, Northern Luzon; Liberation of Manila.

Awarded Purple Heart, Asiatic/Pacific Medal with four Battle Stars, Philippine Liberation Medal, American Theater Medal, etc..

In Luzon while checking through casualty lists, he recognized the name of Eric Adler, a friend he had known in Germany. Not having knowledge of his escape from Germany, it was a joyous reunion to find that his friend had also escaped the Nazis and was alive and well.

Married to Blanche Bein for 42 years. Two daughters, Diana and Heidi. Three grandsons. He is a real estate developer.

MAX KAHN (COHEN), born Aug. 15, 1915 in Cleveland, OH. Joined USAF on Oct. 15, 1941. Served as air gunner while stationed at Sheppard AB, Wichita Falls, TX; Geiger Field, Spokane, WA; Muroc AB, CA; Chelveston AB, England; Grafton Underwood AB, England; Casper, WY AB; Galveston AB, Texas and Wright Field AB, Dayton, OH.

Flew first missions over Germany with 305th BG, 422nd SG. Flew 25 missions, 20 without fighter escort. Flew first USAF night mission over Europe. His plane was *Target for Tonight*.

Decorations: DFC, Air Medal with OLCs, EAME Theater Ribbon with one Bronze Star, Good Conduct Medal and American Defense Medal.

He also volunteered and fought in the Israel War of Independence, 1947 to 1949 with Israel air force. Received "Fighter for Israel Medal."

Discharged Sept. 6, 1945 with rank of tech sergeant.

Married to Jacqueline, an artist. One daughter, Heather, an attorney and assistant prosecutor for state of Illinois.

Member of JWV, American Veterans of Israel, 305th BGMA and AFA. Retired furniture manufacturing representative.

JEROME KAISER, born in Bronx, NY. Served in Naval Air Service as a pilot.

Awards/Medals: Navy Cross.

Died on June 2, 1969. Survivors include his wife Rose, father, mother, son and two daughters.

AARON E. KALIN, born April 27, 1909 in Syracuse, NY. Attended Croton School and Central High School. Attached to 1878 Unit, Medical Det., Camp Claiborne, LA.

Discharged in June 1944.

Left Syracuse while in his teens to go into show business in New York City. Was a member of the National Showmen's Association of America and the JWV in the Bronx.

Died on Feb. 2, 1946 at the age of 36 from illness incurred in service.

SAUL KALIN, inducted on Sept. 10, 1943. Basic training at Camp Roberts, CA. Killed in action on July 26, 1944 in France. Body brought back to Syracuse on May 10, 1949. Is at rest in Poiley Tzedech Cemetery.

SOL KALINSKY, born in New York City on Oct. 5, 1919. Inducted on April 1, 1942. Was in Ft. Jackson, SC and Hyder, AZ. Served with 306th Inf. Regt., 77th Div. Was in on invasion and recapture of Grieu in 1944. Went to Leyte, Philippines in 1944.

Memorable experience was his company caught in heavy fire. After several hours they were rescued by two cannon tanks. They kept firing as they who were wounded were carried out. Spent three years in Army hospitals.

Awards/Medals: Purple Heart, Bronze Star, Combat Infantry Badge, WWII Victory Medal, Good Conduct, American Campaign, APO Campaign with two Bronze Stars and Philippine Liberation Medal with one Bronze Star.

Discharged as a corporal on Nov. 10, 1947 at Valley Forge General Hospital.

Married Doris on Oct. 22, 1949. Two children, Marcie and Howard and grandchild Neal. Retired from US Treasury.

HYMAN J. KALISON, who served in the Navy in WWI was born in Russia in 1891 and came to the US at age 13. He became a citizen in 1912.

He went to Europe on the *Leviathan* (have hiss pass) and was stationed in Cork, Ireland. He became an electricians mate c/C. Discharged in 1918 or 1919.

He became an electrical contractor in New Haven, CT after his discharge. He was well-known in the Jewish and business community. He and Ethel were extremely charitable and he was proud he served his country.

He died in New Haven, CT at the age of 95.

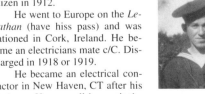

SIDNEY L. KALISON, served in the Navy in WWII. He was born in 1926 and nagged his parents until they signed for him at age 17. He spent the war in the Pacific in small boats up and down the coast of New Guinea. He wa wounded in action and came home on a hospital ship.

Discharged in 1945 and worked as an electrician in New Haven, CT.

Married Mildred, settled in West Haven, CT, and has three daughters and three grandchildren.

Five years ago Sidney was stricken with post-polio syndrome and lives at home, but is completely paralyzed and on a respirator. He is happy watching his grandchildren grow up.

SYLVIA "SCHOP" KAMINSKY, enlisted in the WACS in February 1944. Trained in Ft. Ogelthorpe, GA and was transferred to Aberdeen Proving Grounds, MD. They helped engineers assemble large guns and tanks.

From there she went to Indian Town Gap and worked as an embosograf operator in the printing department.

She was discharged from Ft. Dix on Feb. 13, 1946. She is still in touch with some of the girls from Aberdeen Barracks T4008.

Married in October 1948 and has a son and daughter. Also two lovely grandchildren.

She is active with the Pennsylvania Shandler Berman Ladies Auxiliary 305, JWV.

DANIEL KANEFSKY, born Philadelphia, PA on April 13, 1924. Inducted into Army on Feb. 19, 1943. Basic training at Jefferson Barracks, MO; specialized training University of Kentucky; advanced training Geiger Field and Ft. George Wright, WA.

Assigned Army Corps of Engineers, 1884th Engineer Aviation Bn. Honorable discharge at Indiantown Gap, PA, Jan. 19, 1946 with rank of sergeant.

Left Seattle on July 7, 1944 for Honolulu. Jungle training Hickam Field and Schofield Barracks. Departed in Task Force August 1944 with battalion attached to 322nd Regt. Combat Team, 81st Inf. Div.

Participated Palau Invasion. Battalion built air field on Angaur Island under heavy enemy fire; won Unit Meritorious Service Award.

Palau secure, battalion sent to Guam to "rest." While resting", built entire air base, which became the first forward B-29 operating base with mission to bomb Japan.

Battalion next participated battle of Okinawa. Built airfield under enemy fire, sniper attacks and Kamikaze actions.

Okinawa secure; war ended soon after; was returned to Tacoma, WA on Jan. 11, 1946.

Decorations: Asiatic/Pacific Medal with two Battle Stars, American Theater Medal, WWII Victory Medal, Good Conduct Medal and Unit Meritorious Service Award.

Married to Diane; have three son (two of whom are in the Air National Guard); one daughter, one step-son, one step-daughter and seven grandchildren.

Employed Naval Shipyard September 1951- December 1988; supervisor radar field engineering unit; retired December 1988. Also a teacher in Philadelphia Evening School system December 1956- June 1987. Took engineering studies in DeForest Training in Chicago and Drexel University, Philadelphia.

Presently retired. Member of JWV Post 706, Brith Sholom Lodge No. 8, Knights of Pythias Lodge No. 113 and president of local Civic Association.

WALTER KANER, born in Corona, NY on May 5, 1920. He graduated from Stuyvesant High School in 1938 and attended City College. Inducted in Army in 1943, assigned

to 97th Inf. Div. Served in Germany, Holland, France and Czechoslovakia, then Japan. Joined Armed Forces Radio Service in Tokyo serving as "Tokyo Mose", a disc jockey heard over 18 stations in Japan and Korea. Honorable discharge in March 1946. Holds Combat Infantry Badge and has Good Conduct Medal. Discharged as sergeant.

Three-time commander of Long Island City Post 110, Astoria. Past president Col. David Marcus Lodge, B'Nai B'rith, Astoria, past president of Queens Multiple Sclerosis Society, past president Lifeline Center for Child Development, board chairman of Walter Kaner's Children's Foundation which has entertained 130,000 handicapped children at parties over past 42 years.

President Walter Kaner Associates in Manhattan, a public relations firm. Simultaneously served as columnist for Long Island Press, 1953-1977. Also served as columnist for *New York Daily News*, 1977-1991. Now columnist for *Queens Gazette* and *Western Queens Gazette* and semi-retired. Married wife Billie in 1991 and now living in Port Washington, NY. Recipient of some 50 awards for philanthropic endeavors with children.

Former editor of the *Jewish Veteran* and national radio and television officer of the JWV, 1964-65, also public relations director of Department of New York, JWV.

GEROLD KANENGISER, born Nov. 23, 1917 at Jersey City, NJ. Inducted into the US Army on Jan. 14, 1943 and discharged on Oct. 29, 1945.

His service duties were confined for a brief period in the Internal Securities Division, thereafter in the administration of the ASTP Program at Rutgers University. He was transferred to Camp Chaffee in Arkansas and to Camp Fannin, TX to be a finance officer at a separation center. No memorable awards except for contribution to an Off Duty Educational Program.

JEFFREY S. KANNER, born June 27, 1946, Brooklyn, NY. Graduated high school June 1963. Construction major at NYC Community College. Entered Marines Jan. 17, 1966. Training at Parris Island, Camp Geiger and Camp Pendleton, CA. Traveled to Vietnam via USNS *Eltinge* (AP-154); arrived Danang Dec. 28, 1966.

Served 1st Marine Div. Post Office: Chu-Lai, December 1966- March 1967; Danang, April- December 1967. Company driver/postal clerk. Survived rocket attack, July 14/15, 1967. Walked away from auto accident northwest of Danang, Sept. 7, 1967. Left Vietnam Dec. 3, 1967. Discharged Dec. 17, 1967; corporal.

Decorations: Vietnamese Cross of Gallantry with Palm; Vietnamese Civil Action; Vietnam Service, P.U.C. (2), National Defense Service Ribbon; Vietnam Campaign and Combat Action Ribbon.

Married to Arlene Barbara; son Ivan and daughter-in-law Courtney.

Two architecture degrees, CCNY. Moved to North Carolina in 1973. Architect, N.C. Chief, Building Accessibility Section, Engineering Divisions, North Carolina Department of Insurance.

IRVING M. KANTER, born Feb. 13, 1918, Bronx, NY. Attended New York City public school and St. John's University. Inducted June 29, 1943, and called to active service July 13, 1943. Stationed at Ft. Eustis, VA, basic training; Camp Edwards, MA; Camp Hood, TX; Camp Maxey, TX; and the

Philippines. Assigned to 40th Div. HQ, 115th Med. Bn. in clerical administration.

Awards/Medals: American Campaign Medal, Asiatic-Pacific Campaign Medal, Good Conduct Medal, Philippines Liberation Ribbon and WWII Victory Medal. He was discharged March 16, 1946 as tech sergeant.

Married Gladys and has two children, Lynne and Marshall.

JACK C. KANTER, DDS, born Nov. 29, 1916 in Norfolk, VA. Entered service in November 1942. Commissioned in Dental Corps as lieutenant jg. Stations included: NOB Norfolk, VA; Parris Island; North Africa; Southern France; Mediterranean Theater. Participated in invasion of Southern France.

Memorable experiences was eight days after landing in the invasion of Southern France, he attended Yom Kippur services in a synagogue in Marseilles. He also supervised construction of the first mobile dental unit in the USN by converting a captured Italian communications trailer. It was self-supporting with its own gasoline powered electric generator. He and another dentist operated the unit in Bizerte, Algeria and Palermo, Sicily.

Awards/Medals: Atlantic, North African and European Theaters with one Battle Star.

Discharged June 12 ,1946 with rank of lieutenant commander (DC), USNR.

Married for 47 years. Retired after 50 years of dental practice.

MORRIS KANTOR, born Dec. 4, 1915 in Syracuse, NY. Attended Putnam and Washington Irving Schools. Graduated from Central High School and Syracuse University College of Law. Entered service Dec. 7, 1942 in the USAAF. Graduated as a navigator on a B-17 on Aug. 5, 1943. Arrived in England on Nov. 9, 1943.

Received the Purple Heart, Air Medal with five OLCs and the DFC.

Killed in action on April 13, 1944 at the age of 28. Buried in St. Avold Military Cemetery, Metz, France. Survived by father, Jacob; brothers: David, Sol, Harry and Edward; sister, Mrs. Esther Reisiger.

Married Helen Schreiber on June 21, 1941. Practiced law in Syracuse.

MITCHELL L. KAPHAN, born in Bronx, NY on May 3, 1952. An orthopedic surgeon in private practice in NYC, entered the USAR in 1979. Former OIC of the 309th Medical Det., called into Desert Shield/Storm with the 300th Field Hospital, Ashley, PA, December 1990. After 45 days in Ft. Indiantown Gap, arrived in Dharhan the night of the air attack.

Later on the unit was sent to Sarrar, Saudi Arabia as the hospital taking care of the EPWs at Camp Bronx. Organized and performed a Seder under the stars for 30 plus members of the unit and made fresh bagels out of pita dough. The most memorable moment was when the local Emir and his priest asked him and found out his religious denomination.

Returned to civilian life on May 8, 1991, to the USAR and received the Army Commendation Medal, the Desert Storm Medal with three stars, the Liberation of Kuwait Medal and the Army Lapel Button.

Married to Robin since 1975, have two sons and one daughter: Mark, Adam and Alison. Returned to and reopened his office June 1991 in the Bronx. Member of Post 68- JWV.

B.R.G. KAPLAN, (LTC), USAR, after graduating from Special Forces Training Group (Airborne), he served with the 1st Special Forces Group (Airborne) on an "A" team in the Central Highlands of Vietnam. He had short range plans, live, train Rhode/Mnong and one day become an officer. That was 1963.

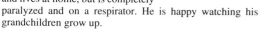

In 1995 still alive, training Reserves in special weapons. He graduated from many special forces schools, Officers Candidate School and went to Medical School.

"I am still proud to serve my country as a soldier."

BEN KAPLAN, born Aug. 1, 1930, Newark, NJ. Entered active service Jan. 9, 1953, Newark. Attended Signal School, April 1953 to December 1953.

Awards/Medals: National Defense Service Medal and Good Conduct Medal. He was honorably discharged Jan. 7, 1955, at Redstone Arsenal, Huntsville, AL.

BERNARD M. KAPLAN, (CW3), born April 20, 1940, New York City. BS at City University of New York, political science major. Joined the Army Reserves in New York City, December 1957. Took basic and advanced training at Fort Dix, NJ. Upon completion of active duty, continued to be a member of the AAR. Rose through the enlisted ranks to the rank of master sergeant and in 1979 was appointed as warrant officer. Branches include personnel and quartermaster. He is presently still in the Active Reserves. His unit, the 318th Transportation Agency (MC) was one of the first Army Reserve units to be mobilized during Operation Desert Shield/Storm. He spent 10 months on active duty, nine months in the Gulf.

Memorable experiences: 1-Getting off the C-5A in Saudi Arabia with full field pack at a remote air base in 137 degree temperature. 2-Survived a number of Scud attacks on their position and watching the first Patriot Missile intercept a Scud. 3-As an officer, being saluted by Arab soldiers of the Multi National Forces. "I guess that they were unaware that my dog tags said Jewish and I was wearing a Chai."

Awards/Medals: Meritorious Service Medal with two OLCs, Army Commendation Medal with three OLCs, Army Achievement Medal with one OLC, National Defense Service Medal, Southwest Asia Service Medal with three Battle Stars, Armed Forces Reserve Medal, Army Reserve Components Achievement Medal with three OLCs, Kuwait LIberation Medal with Gold Palm, Army Service Ribbon and the Meritorious Unit Citation.

Single parent of three daughters: Deborah, Karen and Michelle and Debbie's husband Michael. Retired highway patrol officer, New York City Police Department. Presently employed as a personnel manager for the Department of the Army.

Member of Post 24- JWV.

EARL KAPLAN, born in Omaha, NE on July 9, 1919 from grandparents who homesteaded in Dakota. Graduated with a chemical degree from Nebraska University in Lincoln and Omaha.

Worked for two years as an explosive chemist for DuPont then for 40 years with American Cyanamid in research, development and production. Awarded 15 US Patents in dyes and rubber chemicals.

Served in the 85th Regt., 10th Mountain Div. in US and Italy as a combat medic. Wounded while evacuating wounded in the battle for Mount Belvedere. Awarded the Purple Heart, Bronze Star, Combat Medic Badge, ETO with two stars, American Campaign, National Defense and Victory medals. Member JWV and DAV.

Married for 53 years to Sylvia with one son. Retired in Metuchen, NJ with hobbies in Civil War memorabilia, Palestine Postal History, Holocaust, Judaica in Revolution, Civil War and modern times.

FELIX KAPLAN, (MSG), born July 15, 1922 in Plainfield, NJ. Graduated high school, 1940. Entered Air Corps on Feb. 5, 1941. Attended Air Corps Technical School, Ft. Logan, CO, July 1941. Assigned as permanent cadre at Sheppard Field, Wichita Falls, TX. Served at various air bases prior to assignment to Secret Code Mission in the South Pacific, code name "Ivory Soap." Departed July 17, 1944 on special fitted liberty ship to Biak Island, off coast of New Guinea. Served with 5th Aircraft Repair Unit (floating). Served in Philippine Islands, Leyte and Manila.

Decorations: American Defense Service, Southern Philippines Liberation (Luzon) with Battle Stars, American Defense Ribbon, American Theater Ribbon, Asiatic/Pacific Theater Ribbon, Philippine Liberation Ribbon, Victory Medal and Good Conduct Medal.

Discharged Dec. 31, 1945 with rank of master sergeant.

Married to Fayette Morvay, Oct. 5,1946 in Vineland, NJ. Attended college, BS in accounting. Retired.

Founding member of Post 601, Vineland, NJ.

GILBERT KAPLAN, born March 14, 1914, New York City, NY. He was the first one from his city to enlist in the USN Feb. 14, 1942 and the last one to come home from overseas. Stationed at Naval Training Station, New Port, RI; RCA, NYC; Algiers, LA; Port Director; Shoemaker, CA; San Francisco; Camp Elliot, San Diego, CA; Lido Beach, NY and Pacific.

Memorable Experiences: His travels over the United States; the time spent on various parts of the Pacific Ocean; and the blast of the A bomb.

Awards/Medals: Good Conduct, WWII Victory Medal, American Campaign, Asiatic-Pacific Campaign. Discharged as seaman first class, Fleet Post Office.

Married to Jane, has two sons, Harris and Arnold. Retired after 35 years of delivering mail.

HARRY KAPLAN, was born April 25, 1925 in New York City. He went into the Air Corps on July 5, 1943 and received radio operator and flight operational training at Sioux Falls, SD; Yuma, AZ and Reno, NV.

He arrived in the China Burma India theater of operations in September 1944 and was attached to the 1332nd AAFB unit in the Assam Valley in Northeastern India. His unit flew the C-46 cargo aircraft "over the Hump" (the Himalayan Mountains) providing the entire supplies for the American and Chinese armies and air forces in China as a part of the first air lift ever.

What stands out most in his memory is that the flights were incessant during the monsoons in January and February of 1945. More than one third of his 93 round trips over the Hump were flown during that period — a time when many of his buddies did not return.

He was awarded the DFC with OLC, Air Medal with OLC, Asiatic-Pacific Service Medal with three Battle Stars and the China War Memorial Medal and Wings.

Retired and living in San Diego with his wife Carol. He enjoys traveling and visiting his seven grandchildren.

HARVEY T. KAPLAN, was born in the Bronx, NY on Jan. 26, 1942. Graduated from the Bronx High School of Science (1958) and the City College of New York (1963). As an ROTC and Distinguished Military Graduate, commissioned as a second lieutenant in the Regular Army, Corps of Engineers. Received Master of Arts (in teaching) from Harvard University in 1964 and Ph.D. (in higher/adult education) from New York University in 1976.

Served two tours in Vietnam, one as a company commander and staff officer with the 19th Engineer Bn. (Combat)(Army) in the Qui Nhon area and the second as S-4/ supply officer with both the 168th Engr. Bn. (Combat) and the 159th Engr. Group (Construction). Completed three-year tour in Frankfurt, Germany as engineer staff officer for the 3rd Support Command of V Corps. Other engineer and training assignments included ROTC duty at the City College of New York, tours at the Engineer School (Fort Belvoir, VA), within the office of the chief of engineers (Washington, DC), and duty with the Reserve Components in 1st US Army at Forts Hamilton/Wadsworth and West Point, New York. Joint duty tours included four years as Patrick AFB, FL at the Defense Equal Opportunity Management Institute and as a colonel, as executive director of the DEOC within the office of the Secretary of Defense.

Retired as a colonel in 1989 after more than 26 years of active duty. Recalled to active duty for seven months in 1991 in support of Operation Desert Storm (Persian Gulf War). Awards include the Defense Superior Service Medal, Bronze Star Medal, Defense Meritorious Service Medal, Army Meritorious Service Medal with three OLCs and Army Commendation Medal with one OLC.

Married to the former Naomi M. Smolar of New York in 1966. The family lives in Rockville, MD (since 1983). Three daughters and one son. Member of the JWV Post 567.

HERMAN KAPLAN (HY), born Feb. 22, 1923 in Newburgh, NY. Entered US Army on Dec. 4, 1942. Member of Co. A, 16th Sign. OPNS Bn. Stations included Hollandia, New Guinea; Philippine Islands and Japan. Participated in battles at New Guinea, Philippine Islands, Southern Philippines, Ft. Monmouth, Hollandia, Leyte, Mindoro, Luzon, Manila and Kyoto, Japan.

Memorable experiences were first beach landings on Leyte, Mindoro, Luzon in the Philippines and landing in Japan with the occupation troops.

Awards/Medals: American Service Medal, Asiatic/Pacific Service Medal, Good Conduct Medal, Philippine Liberation Ribbon with one star and WWII Victory Medal.

Discharged Jan. 24, 1946 with rank of tech 4.

Has wife Sara, daughter Janis, son Leonard, two grandsons and one granddaughter. He is presently retired, volunteering, driving senior citizen transport, and traveling. Participated in Volunteer for Israel program.

LAWRENCE J. KAPLAN, was inducted into the Army on Dec. 3, 1942 and discharged honorably on Nov. 18, 1945 Served in the Military Intelligence Service as a techniciar third grade attached to the G-2 Section of the 6th Armd. Div Overseas 16 months.

Selected for intelligence training after serving in th 100th Inf. Div. and in the Army Specialized Training Pro gram at Lafayette College, Easton, PA. Trained at Cam Ritchie, MD and British Intelligence in London as an aeri photo interpreter, responsible for locating enemy concentra tions of guns, equipment and men in the path of the divisio Joined the 6th Armd. Div. in England. Participated in th Normandy Invasion shortly after establishment of a bridge head enabling the landing of tanks. Earned five campaig stars.

Received BA degree, Brooklyn College; MA and Ph.I degrees, Columbia University. Married Jeanne Leon, 194 three children: Harriet, Sanford and Marcia and 10 grandchi dren. Retired as professor emeritus of economics, John J College of Criminal Justice, the City University of New Yor Member Post 504, JWV; American Legion and 6th Armore Division Association.

LOIS J. KAPLAN, born Feb. 6, 1932, in Chicago, I Direct commission appointment, AUS, August 1963; A September 1963 to October 1973; USAR, February 1974 1986. Military schools included WOBC in 1964; WOAC 1968, Ft. McClellan; SSOC in 1965, Ft. Benjamin Harriso CGSC in 1981, Ft. Leavenworth.

AD assignments: HQ 5th Army (Chicago), 1964 1965; HQ 8th Army Rear (Taegu) and Pusan Base Cm 1965-1966; HQ 4th Army (San Antonio) 1966 to 1967; H 7th Army USAREUR (Heidelburg) 1968 to 1970; McClellan, 1970 to 1973.

USAR assignments: 87th MAC (Birmingham) 1974 to 1979; 400th MP POW Cp. (Tallahassee) 1981 to 1983. AD: 1983 to 1986. Retired, USA, Aug. 12, 1986. Awards include the Meritorious Service Medal, ARCOM, AFEM, RFM, RCAM, National Defense Medal, AAM; Expert Badge (45mm and 38 cal.) and Sharpshooter (M-16 and M2 carbines).

Married and divorced; a life member of JWV Post 112, Atlanta, VFW, DAV and ROA; writer, composer, sculptor, recreation consultant and lecturer in the arts and humanities; Fellow, WLA and IAP, Cambridge, England; FCSSI, Rome, Italy.

MELVIN KAPLAN, born in Newark, NJ. Served in the Navy. Discharged Nov. 23, 1958. Deceased.

MILTON KAPLAN, died on the battleship *Arizona* at Pearl Harbor.

MORRIS KAPLAN, born Brooklyn, NY on March 20, 1925. Entered USN November 1942. Stations included Great Lakes Boot Camp; Navy Pier, Chicago; USS *Wolverine*, Lake Michigan and USS *Bataan* (CVL-29). Participated in battles at Japan, Okinawa, Asia and Philippines.

Memorable experience was atomic bomb dropping on Japan while he was on ship near Japan.

Awards/Medals: Asiatic/Pacific with five Battle Stars, Philippine LIberation Medal and European Medal.

Discharged November 1945 with rank of seaman first class (AMM).

Married in 1947. Today he is a semi-retired watchmaker.

SANFORD KAPLAN, born Jan. 6, 1929. Inducted into Army on Sept. 3, 1950. Member of NGHS, 187th FA Obsn. Bn., the old 14th Inf. from Brooklyn. Stationed at Ft. Sill, OK.

Memorable experience was being called a "Jew" by a cowardly Irishman.

Discharged May 1, 1952 with rank of corporal.

Married to Rita and has daughter Pamela Goldberg and sons, Henry and Ben. Today he is retired from New York City Fire Department.

SEYMOUR KAPLAN, born April 7, 1921 in Newark, NJ. Entered service Jan. 15, 1944. Member of HQ Co., 319th Inf. Div. Stations included Northern France, Ardennes, Rhineland and Central Europe.

Awards/Medals: EAME Ribbon, Good Conduct, Purple Heart and WWII Victory Medal.

Discharged Jan. 8, 1946 with rank of private first class.

SOLOMON KAPLAN (TECH 5), born Oct. 15, 1920 in Poland. Entered service on June 11, 1942. Member of 230th QM, 5th Army. Stations included Camp Lee, VA; Camp Claiborne, LA; Oran, North Africa and Italy. Participated in battles at Naples, Foggia, North Appennines, Po Valley and Rome Arno.

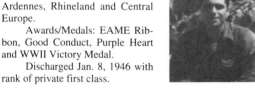

Memorable experience was invasion of Italy and being bombed upon landing.

Awards/Medals: EAME Service Medal, Good Conduct Medal and four Battle Stars.

Discharged Nov. 1, 1945 with rank of tech 5.

Married with five children and nine grandchildren. Today he is retired and does volunteer work.

SOLOMON KAPLAN, born New York City, NY, Sept. 14, 1923. Enlisted USAAC, Dec. 26, 1942. Airplane Mechanics School, Goldsboro, NC. Gunnery School, Ft. Myers, FL. As an engineer gunner with 839th BS, 487th BG, 8th AF, based in Lavenham, England, he flew 224 combat hours in B-17 and B-24 aircraft on 30 missions in 1944, attaining the rank of staff sergeant. Saw action over Germany and France,

including D-day invasion. One of only 10 Jewish members of his AAC flying squadron.

Awarded the DFC, Air Medal with three clusters, EAME Medal with four stars, Good Conduct Medal, American Campaign Medal, WWII Victory Medal.

Honorably discharged September 1945.

Married to Beatrice since 1952. Reside in Silver Spring, MD. Four children: Debra, Leslie, David and Michele and grandson Michael.

Member of Washington, DC Metropolitan Police, 1949-1969. Awarded four commendations. Member of JWV Post 567.

SUMNER KAPLAN (SUNNY), born June 28, 1926 in Boston, MA. Entered Navy in April 1944. Stations included Boston; Norfolk, VA; Sampson, NY where he had boot camp. Participated in battles at Okinawa and Iwo Jima.

Awards/Medals: Service medals for Okinawa and Japan and the Good Conduct Medal.

Discharged May 26, 1946 with rank of seaman first class. Married with three children and six grandchildren. Retired. JWV past post commander, 1971-72, Southshore Post 302, Milton, MA. PDC for state of Massachusetts, 1992-93 and past NEC, 1993-95.

ABRAHAM KAPLON, drafted into the service at Ft. MacArthur, San Pedro, CA. Transferred to Camp Roberts, CA (infantry training camp) where he stayed until war broke out; then to Camp Haan, CA (radar training camp); to Kissimmee, FL and assigned to the 417th Night Ftr. Sqdn. and assigned to communications.

Left Kissimmee in May 1943 on the *Queen Elizabeth* for European service. After a short time in England for training, they were shipped to Oran, North Africa, then to Corsica where they stayed for eight months. Transferred to South France then to Germany. He contacted yellow jaundice and was hospitalized in Reims, France. Returned to his squadron a month later and had enough points to be sent home.

Discharged at Ft. Dix, NJ; visited his brother and family in Brooklyn, NY and reached Los Angeles, CA on Thanksgiving Day.

ALFRED KARCHEM, born in Baltimore, MD, Feb. 22, 1922. Enlisted in the Marine Corps, October 1949. Joined fighter squadron VMF 513 at Itami AB, Japan, October 1950. Boarded the USS *Bataan* with VMF 212, December 1950. Also stationed at Pusan AB, Pohang Bay, Korea. Battles: Communist China Aggression, December 1950-January 1951; first UN counter offensive, January - April 1951; Communist China Spring Offensive, April- July 1951; UN Summer-Fall Offensive, July 1951.

Honorable discharge in November 1953. Awarded National Defense Service Medal, Korean Service Medal, United Nations Service Medal, Presidential Unit Citation, Republic of Korea PVC.

Have two granddaughters, Amy and Stephanie.

HAROLD KARMIN, was born in Brooklyn on Dec. 15, 1919. He graduated Eastern District High School in July 1937 and went to work for the New York Merchandise Company. Enlisted in the Navy April 1943 and was sent to Samson Training Station near Syracuse, NY. Completed boot camp and was sent to Store Keeper School also at Samson. Graduated and became a storekeeper first class. Then was sent to the Shoemaker Base in California, then on a carrier to Brisbain, Australia where he was assigned to the patrol craft PC-477. Then took part in several invasions of New Guinea. Then in the invasions of the Philippines. They remained on patrol around the Philippines until Japan surrendered.

Discharged Jan. 6, 1946.

Authorized awards: Letter of Commendation, Asiatic/Pacific Ribbon with one star, Philippine Liberation Ribbon, American Theater Ribbon and WWII Victory Ribbon.

Married Rhoda Check in March 1949. Have two children. His daughter Sharon married to Bob and has two boys, Brian and Eric and is a housewife. His son Ira is married to Linda, had two children, a girl Jaime and a boy Brandon. Ira is a medical doctor at Mt. Sinai Medical Center.

When discharged he started a restaurant supply business and sold out January 1992. Now retired.

JEROME KARNOFF, born Oct. 22, 1921 in Philadelphia, PA. Graduated from Girard College in Philadelphia, January 1940. From 1940-1943 attended and graduated from Machinist Aircraft Apprentice Course at the Aircraft Div., Philadelphia Navy Yard. Enlisted in USAF in 1943. Trained in B-17, B-24 and B-29s. Flew out of Tinian Island. Completed tour of duty with 505th BG, 20th AF.

Awarded a number of ribbons including Asiatic/Pacific Service Medal with three Bronze Stars, with two OLCs, DFC, etc.

Honorably discharged in 1945.

Back in Philadelphia, attended Temple University. Settled in Scranton, PA. Married Ruth Rubin in 1950. They have two sons, one daughter and two grandchildren.

Owned and operated appliance distributorship business for 41 years. Retired in 1990. Today he is helping his son in the business and just enjoying life.

Member of JWV and Bnai Brith.

HARRIETT KALISON KARP, born in New Haven, CT and inducted from there into the WAVES in Dec. 28, 1944. Her father was in the USN in WWI and her brother served in the USN in WWII. She has a BS in Zoology from the Univ. of Connecticut and was working on a research project when she enlisted.

Served primarily at Great Lakes Naval Station in the laboratory as head of Pathology Section, a type of work she had done in civilian life. She served there until April 24, 1946, when she was discharged with rank of PhM2/c.

Worked in Boston on a Navy Atomic Energy Research project at Harvard Medical School until she married Martin Karp, CPA, now a retired Army Reserve colonel. They first settled in Newark, NJ and now live in Springfield, NJ. They have two children and three grandchildren. She is active in B'nai B'rith Women, Temple Sha'arey Shalom, feeding the hungry and Women's causes.

HYMAN S. KARP, emigrated to the U.S. from Poland in 1929, inducted into the Army Infantry Division Aug. 5, 1943, and honorably discharged Nov. 10, 1945. He served in the QM

foreign service division in northern France, the Rhineland and Normandy and was stationed in Belgium.

He was issued the EAME Service Medal and Good Conduct Medal. Karp was proud to have served his country. He passed away May 10, 1993.

JOSEPH KARP, inducted into the Army May 1, 1942. Basic training in Ft. Jay, NY and Camp Gordon, GA. He was attached to Co. B, 102nd Sig. Corps. His company was awarded the service award of merit.

Shipped overseas in July 1943 and took part in North Africa, Naples-Foggia, North Apennines, Rome-Arno and Anzio campaigns.

Honorably discharged on Oct. 7, 1945, with the following medals: EAME Service Medal and Good Conduct Medal. He was always a staunch member of the JWV, Fleischman Post in Brighton Beach, Brooklyn, NY.

MARTIN KARP, born in Newark, NJ; attended Weequahic High School; graduated from New York Univ. with a BS in accounting; passed the CPA exam and entered the Army as enlisted man. Went to Officers Training School, commissioned as a lieutenant and went to Algeria by convoy. A month later, also in convoy, was bombed heavily in the Mediterranean Sea. They spent almost three years in India.

Stayed in the Reserves for an additional 35 years and graduated from Command and General Staff College, Army Intelligence School, Army Logistics Center as a certified logistician, Industrial College of the Armed Forces. He taught economics to a reserve class of senior officers for many years. Retired as a full colonel.

Attended New York Univ. Graduate School of Business Administration, graduated with a MBA and became a self-employed CPA. Married Harriett and has two children and three grandchildren. They are active in feeding homeless and in travel.

ALBERT KASDEN, was born in Brooklyn, New York on April 26, 1909. When he entered the 102nd Inf. Div. 407th Service Co., he used his trigger finger to earn a Bronze Star at the typewriter as their company clerk.

Like other Jewish servicemen he felt the pain of anti-Semitism. His best friend, Carmine, was a fellow Brooklyn boy who used rosaries instead of tefillin. After surviving the Battle of the Bulge, the two were waiting to be re-deployed by truck. Their sergeant, who resented the friendship between Al and Carmine, had them load into separate vehicles. Carmine's overturned and he was killed.

When Al Kasden passed away on Lincoln's birthday in 1985, he was offered a veteran's honor guard. With the guns of war long silenced, a man's religion was a point of honor, not scorn.

ROBERT KASSE, entered the Army in 1943 at Akron, OH. Member of 36th Inf. Div. Stationed at France. Participated in the battle of Alsace Lorraine (French-German border). He was killed in action at Mittlewehr, France, Dec. 10, 1944. He was a private. He was survived by wife Helaine. Awards/Medals: Purple Heart.

DANIEL K. KAST, born Nov. 15, 1919, in Philadelphia, PA. Served in the USN from May 1943 to April 1946. Sea duty in LST-611, USS *Oneida*, APA-221, ATR (ocean going

tug boat) in Panama, Panama Canal, Hawaii (Oahu and Maui), Ulithi, Enwetok, Kwajalein, New Guinea (Hollandia), Okinawa, Philippine Islands, Guam, Korea (Jinsen), China (Tientsin, Tsingtao and Shanghai).

Active Reserve from 1954-66: Naval Reserve Law Co. 3-3 designator changed from line to judge advocate general (JAG). Inactive Reserve: 1966 to present.

Received six medals, USN American Campaign, USN Occupation Service (China), USN Naval Reserve, USA WWII. Achieved the rank of LT (Line). He is life member of the Naval Reserve Association and member of the JWV.

Civilian occupation: professor (Emeritus) Iona College; attorney and counselor at Law; certified public accountant.

MARVIN A. KASTENBAUM, was the youngest of Harry Kastenbaum's five sons who served their country in WWII. His brother, Jimmie (Sam) was with the 78th Div. in New Guinea and the Philippines. Dutch (Abe), Leon and Jack served in the ETO. Leon, a lieutenant with the 106th Div., was captured in the early hours of the German Ardennes Offensive in December 1944. He was still a POW on April 5, 1945 when he was killed by "friendly fire" in an American bombing raid on the rail yards of Nuremberg, Germany.

In 1944, shortly after he turned 18, he was inducted into the Army. His basic training at Ft. Riley, KS was in horse cavalry, a truly unique experience for anyone and especially for a kid from the Bronx. By that fall, he had reached the jungles of Burma, where he served as "mule-skinner" in both a cavalry regiment (dismounted) and in a field artillery battalion (mountain-pack). These combat units reopened the Burma Road to China. The campaign in Burma ended in the spring of 1945 and he was flown "over the hump" to Kunming, China where he remained until after the Japanese surrender. He spent the remaining months of his service as a MP in Shanghai and was discharged in February 1946.

NATHAN KATKIN, born in New York City in 1915. Entered active duty on July 1942, having completed all the requirements, except writing a thesis for an MBA degree. His civilian work experience was accountant/auditor. No matter, he was sent to AAF Aircraft Mechanic and then to Electrical Specialist schools.

Then it was on to an AAF Pilot Training Base for hands-on experience. In August 1943 he was one of 10,000 troops who boarded two former tourist-trade ships, converted to troop carriers, for transport to India. They had no Navy escort.

After two months at sea and another by train and riverboat, he ended up at an AAF Base near Sookerating, in the province of Assam, the northeastern tip of India. Its mission: to transport material over the Himalayan peaks (the Hump) to Chinese military forces fighting the Japanese. He worked on the ground maintenance crew of the C-46.

In August 1944, he was transferred to an AAF Pilot Training Base in Gaya, Central India. The aircraft were B-17s and C-110Is. His job was also changed to administrative clerk in the flight operations office. After a few months, he contracted dengue (DEN-gee) fever, spent a month in the base hospital, was released, not completely cured, and flown home on emergency leave. His father had suffered a stroke. (10 months prior to that, so had his mother. She died within 24 hours and efforts to fly him home were abandoned.) Though he had now been in the service for two and a half years, his orders were to return to Gaya after a month. "And so I did."

Altogether, he served three years and five months; all except one of which were enroute to, in or return from India. His honorable discharge, with the rank of sergeant, is dated Dec. 8, 1945.

The reverse side of his discharge certificate entitles him to wear the following decorations: Asiatic/Pacific Service Medal, Distinguished Unit Badge, Good Conduct Medal, Presidential Unit Citation, WWII Victory Medal and American Service Medal.

ABE KATZ

ELY J. KATZ, born in Kenosha, WI. Entered Army in September 1940. Stationed at Aluetian Island. Participated in battles in Japan.

Memorable experience was spending one year in Russia, 1942.

Discharged November 1945 with rank of corporal. Married with six grandchildren. Retired.

FRED R. KATZ, born May 8, 1920 in Manhattan, New York. Entered US Army on Jan. 21, 1942 at Camp Upton, NY. Served in field artillery and stationed at Ft. Sill, OK and Camp Bowie, TX as buck sergeant. Served with military police guarding German POWs. Served in supply at post headquarters at Ft. Sill, OK.

Worked in automobile business for 30 years; presently real estate investments.

Married 49 years to Ethel. They have three girls, two boys and five grandchildren.

GERALD KATZ, born Brooklyn, NY on Nov. 21, 1922. Enlisted US Army Signal Corps Reserve while student at Brooklyn College. Upon graduation with BS degree in physics, called to active duty March 1944. Completed basic training Signal Corps, Camp Crowder, MO. After completing OCS at Ft. Monmouth, NJ, commissioned second lieutenant, Signal Corps, Dec. 28, 1944. Joined Signal Bn. which provided Gen. D.D. Eisenhower, theater commander, S.H.A.E.F. all communications within the ETO and to the War Department in Washington, DC. He served as officer in charge of radio teletype station which handled traffic to the War Department.

Awards: American Theater of Operations Medal, Victory Medal, Army of Occupation Medal (Germany). He saw service in France, Belgium and Germany. Discharged with rank of first lieutenant and Officer's Certificate of Service, Sept. 27, 1946.

Profession: Ph.D. in solid state science, Pennsylvania State University, 1965. Research studies of the atomic arrangement in crystalline solids. Presently retired.

Gerald has a wife Tova, sons David and Michael and daughter Judith. All served in Israel army. His father, Moe Katz, served in US Army, WWI as a private at Camp Dix, NJ April 3, 1918- November 28, 1918.

HARRY KATZ, born March 17, 1905, in Syracuse, NJ Enlisted in the USMC and sent to Guadalcanal. Wounded in action and was given honorable discharge.

Re-enlisted in the Marines and sent to Iwo Jima with 1st Prcht. Bn. of the 11th Marines, 5th Div. He was again wounded in action and honorably discharged with the rank of sergeant.

Currently lives in Los Angeles, CA.

JACOB H. KATZ, born Dec. 20, 1924, New York City. Inducted June 24, 1943 in USAAF. Camp Upton was his first military camp and after two weeks was assigned to Keesler Field, MS for basic training; Scott Field, IL for training as radio operator; Yuma, AZ for gunnery training, then met his pilot and crew at Chatham Field, GA.

Flew to Italy and bombed targets in all parts of southern Europe as lead plane for the group. After 45 missions he was sent home and separated from service from the convalescence hospital in Plattsburg, NY on Oct. 22, 1945, as tech sergeant. Received the Air Medal with four clusters, EAME Theater Medal, WWII Victory Medal, American Campaign Medal, Good Conduct Medal and Presidential Citation. Participated in North Apennines, Central Europe, Po Valley, Rome-Arno, Air Combat Balkans and Rhineland.

Graduated from RCA Institute after a two-year electronic course and went to work in the field of radio broadcasting in West Virginia, then for CBS Radio and TV in New York where he worked with Edward Murrow, Lowell Thomas, Walter Cronkite and big bands like Tommy and Jimmy Dorsey. Famous shows he put on the air include Captain Kangaroo and 60 minutes.

Married Roda and they have two children and one grandchild. He is now retired.

MORRIS KATZ, born in Philadelphia, PA, March 28, 1918. Entered the U.S. Army February 18, 1942, stationed at Camp Forrest, TN, 33rd Div., Co. D, Heavy Weapons. Went overseas with Anti Tank Co., 33rd Div., landed in Fiji Islands Sept. 19, 1942 and sent to Guadalcanal, Emirau Island, and Iwo Jima relieving Marines.

Awards include the Expert Infantry Badge, Combat Infantryman Badge, Bronze Star, Navy Unit Citation w/ Battle Star, and Occupation of Japan Medal. Honorably discharged October 26, 1945 at the rank of sergeant.

He has a wife, Anne, and daughter, Robin. He is a retired Federal Employee.

MORRIS KATZ, born in New York City, June 22, 1913. Entered the US Army January 1942 and sent to Camp Claiborne, LA. Upon completion of his training with the 344th Engineer, Co. B, he became staff sergeant of the supply unit. He remained with this unit until his departure in 1945; back to the United States on rotation.

Served the entire time in EAME Campaign, which included time in Great Britain, Algiers, Tinian, Italy, France and Germany. Was able to visit with Jewish family for the Jewish holidays in charge of a group of Jewish men in Chetham, England and Oran, Algiers, which was a memorable experience.

Received the following awards: WWII Victory Medal, Army of Occupation with four stars and one arrow and Good Conduct Medal.

Married to lovely Marrin and one precious daughter Elya.

Served for nearly 25 years with the UN as bookstore manager where he was fortunate to meet notable personages such as former President Carter, Abba Eban and many diplomats and celebrities such as Audrey Hepburn and Anthony Quinn.

PHILIP KATZ, born Dec. 24, 1914, in New York City, NY. Inducted Jan. 7, 1943, in the Army and served with the 428th Tire Repair Ord. Co. as a tire rebuilder. Stationed at Aberdeen Proving Grounds, Sand Island, Oahu, Hawaii and Saipan.

The company he was in and the work they did was most important to the war effort because of the scarcity of tires. The top brass who visited their outfit had never seen anything like their operation and were very impressed. He believes there were only two outfits like his, one in Europe and one in the Pacific.

Each man in his company received the Meritorious Service Unit Insignia from the Western Pacific Base Cmd. APO #244 dated Aug. 15, 1945. He also received the Asiatic-Pacific Service Medal with additional star, Good Conduct Medal and WWII Victory Medal.

Married 57 years to Eleanor and has one son Paul and three grandchildren. His last employment was in the automotive business for 28 years. He is retired.

SAMUEL KATZ, born July 22, 1915 in Boston, MA. Entered Army on Feb. 23, 1942. Served with Inf., 80th Div. Stationed at Camp Croft, SC, part of Gen. Patton's 3rd Army. Participated in Battle of Bulge and Augimtin.

Memorable experience was capture of German infantry men.

Awards/Medals: Bronze Star and two Purple Hearts.

Discharged Nov. 10, 1945 with rank of staff sergeant but stayed in Reserves until 1950. Was called up during Korean War but was given a full medical discharge.

Married with three children. Retired from post office in 1980. Spends winter in Florida. Has four grandchildren.

Joined JWV Post 630 in 1946 as charter member.

SIDNEY KATZ, was born June 22, 1923. He was raised on the west side of Chicago. Attended Penn Grammar School, Marshall High School and Ray School of Advertising. In April 1943 he entered the US Army. Having been a professional trumpet player in civilian life, he was immediately made an Army bugler. In between he drove a Jeep and a half-track

In 1945 he married his school sweetheart, Ethyle Goldstein and they had a son and a daughter. Ethyle later served as national president of JWVA in 1990/1991.

Sidney suffered from service connected illness during the 31 years of their marriage and passed away June 16, 1976. He served as commander of the Austin Post 372, JWV in 1954/55.

WERNER KATZENSTEIN, born April 29, 1922 in [illegible] and fortunate to leave Holland in 1939 for USA. Worked with parents on farm in Blackwood, NJ until drafted into Army as an "Enemy Alien" on March 27, 1944. Had infantry basic at Camp Blanding, FL where he became a US citizen. Joined 100th Inf. Div., Ft. Bragg, NC and went into European combat in November 1944. Was wounded and returned to unit in January 1945. Fought with division until end of war. Applied for and was granted transfer to Military Government until discharged in April 1946.

Medals received: Purple Heart, European Theater Combat Medal with three Battle Stars and Unit Citation. Member of JWV. Owned own business and was also active in real estate sales.

Married to Inge in 1951, two sons, one daughter and eight grandchildren.

BERNARD M. KAUDERER, (VICE ADMIRAL), USN (RET), was born in Philadelphia, PA, July 21, 1931. A 1953 graduate of the US Naval Academy, he first served in the destroyer USS *The Sullivans* (DD-537) and then as executive officer in the minesweeper USS *Hummingbird* (MSC-192). He attended Submarine School in 1957.

Following qualification in the radar picket submarine USS *Raton* (SSR-270), he was selected by Adm. Rickover for the nuclear power program and attended a year of training. He then served in the commissioning crew of the Polaris missile submarine USS *Robert E. Lee* (SSBN-601); as engineer officer in the attack submarine USS *Skipjack* (SSN-585); and then as executive officer in the commissioning crew of the Poseidon missile submarine USS *Ulysses S. Grant* (SSBN-631).

He served as commanding officer of the nuclear attack submarine USS *Barb* (SSN-596) from 1966 to 1970. Command of the Nuclear Power Training Unit, Idaho Falls, ID was followed by command of the submarine tender USS *Dixon* (AS-37). In 1977, while serving as chief of staff for Commander Submarine Force, US Atlantic Fleet, he was selected for rear admiral and assigned commander Submarine Group Five in San Diego. In 1979 he was ordered to Washington, DC as the deputy director, Research, Development, Test and Evaluation on the staff of the Chief of Naval Operations. In June 1981 he assumed command of the Submarine Force, US Pacific Fleet in Pearl Harbor, serving there until June 1983 at which time he was promoted to vice admiral and assigned as Commander Submarine Force, US Atlantic Fleet. He served concurrently in NATO posts as Commander Submarines, Allied Command Atlantic and as Commander, Submarine Forces, Western Atlantic.

Vice Admiral Kauderer is married to the former Myra Frances Weissman of Brooklyn, NY. They have three married children and eight grandchildren.

In addition to the Distinguished Service Medal, the Legion of Merit (three awards), the Meritorious Service Medal and the Navy Commendation Medal, he holds the Navy Expeditionary Medal, the Navy Occupation Service Medal, the National Defense Service Medal and the Vietnam Service Medal.

MARVIN KAUFFMAN, born May 10, 1918 in Columbus, OH. Attended Ohio State University, 1939-40, 1945-46. Member of ROTC, Field Arty. Entered US Army November 1941. Infantry training at Camp Wheeler, GA and Ft. Lewis, WA. Overseas from February 1942- August 1945. Stations in South Pacific area included New Guinea, Bismarck, Archipelago (island hopping) and Luzon, Philippine Islands. Parttime medic but main job was OP (Recon.) radio operator. Served in 98th Chemical Mortar Bn. (4.2" mortars).

Experiences with several close encounters with extinction. (Snipers, mortars and artillery fire.) Crawled under "fire" to give aid to a wounded comrade. (Not on his record.) Contracted severe case of malaria, hospitalized twice.

Awards/Medals: All Asiatic/Pacific Ribbons with Battle Stars, including Bronze Arrowhead.

Discharged September 1945 with rank of corporal. Turned down field commission of second lieutenant.

Last occupation when retired in 1988 was flight instrument tech at Sperry Honeywell Flight Systems.

Served three times as commander of Westwood Post 658 of the JWV of the USA.

HERMAN L. KAUFMAN, born Dec. 31, 1921 in Chicago, IL. Joined USMC in April 1942 as a private. Ten weeks of boot camp in San Diego, CA. Sent to Camp Elliot, CA. Assigned to the KCO 6th Marine, 2nd Div. leaving San Diego in August 1942; arriving in Wellington, New Zealand where he stayed two months. They were then sent to Guadalcanal, replacing the Army who had left, then taking the island over from the Japanese.

They again stayed seven months in New Zealand and then made the invasion of the Gilbert Islands, called Torowa. They had further training in Hilo, HI and then shipped to Saipan and Tinian. Wounded at Tinian and was shipped to the States.

Discharged August 1945 as a private.

Awards/Medals: Purple Heart and Sharp Shooter.

Married 49 years with three children and five grandchildren. Retired.

HENRY KAUFMAN, in 1943 went into combat in North Africa. From there he invaded Sicily, then Salerno, Italy. He fought all the way up until they were stalemated at the Monte Abbey in Cassino.

"Finally my number was up." He invaded Anzio, Italy and was captured on Feb. 22, 1944 during the historic Battle of the Caves. He was held prisoner in four POW camps in Italy; two in Stalags in Southwest Germany and one in Arbeits Kommando (663B); two farm labor details; two German hospitals and five unforgettable days at the infamous concentration camp at Dachau. He later escaped from a farm detail in Ketters Hausen, Germany and made it all the way home before the war ended.

He has now been married 50 years and has two sons. Went into business in Los Angeles, CA in 1958 and have successfully operated three of his own corporations for the past 35 years. He recently retired and has tried to keep busy, writing and lecturing about WWII and the Holocaust.

ROBERT KAUFMAN, born March 10, 1932 in Newark, NJ. Joined USN in June 1952. Boot camp in Bainbridge, MD after which assigned to USS *Smalley* (DD-565), destroyer stationed in Newport, RI. Went to Machinist's Mate School and eventually attained rank of machinist's mate second class petty officer at time of discharge. Served aboard *Smalley* entire four years.

Served in the Korean Theater of war aboard the USS *Smalley* in the Far East and after end of hostilities, ship continued on a cruise around the world which was the highlight of his four years in the Navy. Medals received were: National Defense Service Medal, Good Conduct Medal, Korean Service Medal, United Nations Service Medal, Navy Occupation Medal and Korean Presidential Unit Citation. Discharged in June 1956.

Married for 40 years, two children, four grandchildren. Employed as a sheriff's officer for the Essex County, NJ Sheriff's Office in Newark, NJ.

Joined JWV in 1958. Was active all these years and presently been serving as post commander for the past seven years. Served in all echelons of JWV.

STANLEY KAUFMAN, (SGT), of Newington, CT served in the 20th AF in the Pacific Campaign in WWII. He enlisted in the Signal Corps in October 1942 and later became attached to the Air Corps and was discharged in January 1946.

The 20th AF developed a repair and maintenance depot on a converted Liberty ship operated by Merchant Marine. Navy gun crews were responsible for operating the guns.

There were over 300 AF specialists providing parts and repairs for the B-29 offensive on Japan. The 2nd Aircraft Repair Unit (Floating) was equipped to build and repair parts for

airplanes. Two helicopters were assigned to the flight deck to provide immediate ship to shore movement of emergency parts and accessories. The 2nd ARU (F) dropped anchor in the harbors of Saipan and Iwo Jima shortly after these islands were secured.

There were repair shops for sheet metal, ordnance, welding, instruments, radio, radar and many others. Oxygen was manufactured for the use of airborne flight personnel.

Kaufman served as a radio and radar repair technician during the Saipan and Iwo Jima campaigns.

MELVIN S. KAYE, born April 18, 1924 in New York City. Entered AF in September 1943. Served with 24th Combat Mapping Sqdn. while stationed at Gushkara, India; Clark Field, Luzon and Philippines.

Awards/Medals: Battle Star, Battle of Central Burma and Philippine Liberation Medal.

Discharged in September 1946 with the rank of first lieutenant.

Today is a chemical engineering consultant and grandfather.

SIDNEY A. KEGELES was the son of Mr. and Mrs. Frank Kegeles of Derby, CT. He graduated from Derby High School in 1932 and joined the USAAC. In 1935 he joined the USAF and built a reputation as a decorated war hero in Europe and Korea. He flew more than 200 missions in the European Theater during WWII and received many medals including the Silver Star and Distinguished Flying Cross with OLC.

Served as a military attaché in Israel in 1954; worked as an Air Force Intelligence officer at the Pentagon; was a diplomat in Paris and knighted by the President of Bolivia for saving the lives of more than 1,000 citizens in civilian rescue missions.

Col. Kegeles became deputy base commander at Little Rock AFB in Jacksonville in 1958 and was again sent to Paris in 1964, after which he retired from the AF and returned to live with his family in Little Rock as a civilian.

Was made state purchasing director by Gov. Rockerfeller in 1967-68, and left Little Rock when he became vice-president of Better Business Bureau's International Assoc. in New York. He passed away Oct. 12, 1988, in Little Rock.

HARRY KELLER, a buck sergeant who served in Ft. Belvoir, VA, was part of the honor guard in Franklin Roosevelt's funeral.

IRVING KELLER, entered AAC on Sept. 12, 1942 at Ft. Jay, NY. Served as chief clerk for HQ, Military Administration Section, Base Air Depot 1, US Strategic Air Forces stationed in Warrington, England. Overseas to ETO and England from Aug. 8, 1943- Jan. 5, 1946.

Medals/Awards: EAME Service Medal, Good Conduct Medal and WWII Victory Medal.

Discharged Jan. 10, 1946 at Ft. Dix, NY with rank of sergeant.

National service officer in Michigan for JWV since 1988.

ARMIN KERN, reported for induction on Dec. 31, 1943 and much to his surprise found himself in the Navy. After boot training at Sampson, NY, he was transferred to the Seabees. The reason, being born in Germany and not a US citizen, classified him as "Special Assignment" that limited serving aboard ship.

After becoming a US citizen, he volunteered for overseas duty and joined the newly formed CBMU 615. This small outfit of 250 men, 12 were Jewish and seven were refugees from Europe like himself, happy to serve to protect the freedom of the Free World. They shipped out May 17, 1945 for destination unknown— Okinawa. Crossing the Pacific started out with the failure of the ship's boiler that left them adrift for a few days, until they were towed into Pearl Harbor for repairs.

At Okinawa their duties were to maintain the seaplane base Katchin Hanto NAB with Navy units ACORN 44 and CASU 3. Around Aug. 1, 1945 they were put on a 24 hour gas

and paratroop invasion alert that ended shortly after the nuclear attack on Hiroshima and Nagasaki.

After the war a typhoon hit the island and their base was heavily damaged.

BERNARD KESSLER, served from Feb. 1, 1943- May 13, 1943 after badgering draft board. Was included in quota group at age 19 1/2. Vision bad but memorized eye chart. Drafted into USN but volunteered for USMC. Number 56 out of 60 accepted first day in history of USMC that Corps accepted draftees. Discharged from USMC after visual defect discovered and combat status withdrawn.

June 26, 1943- Nov. 13, 1945 voluntarily "re-drafted" into US Army. Private first class for Medical Corp, hospital training clerk and Ord. Corp as training cadre.

Married Feb. 7, 1944 and has GI baby Robin Susan, born Feb. 21, 1946. Civilian babies Honey April, born 1949, and Gary Craig, born 1953.

Nov. 14, 1945- May 22, 1946, OCS commissioned second lieutenant, Trans. Corps as train commander. Separated May 22.

From 1945- September 1950, active in USAR Program. Voluntarily assigned to NG Truck Bn. and promoted to first lieutenant.

From Sept. 3, 1950- July 24, 1952 voluntarily returned to active duty with 373d TC Major Port. (HQ Commandant, CG Staff); served as liaison officer with Admirals Staff, Operation Bluejay (Thule, Greenland, 1951) DEW Line; admin. officer, Operation Pine Tree (Newfoundland, Labrador, 1952). Separated July 24.

(IRVING) MURRAY KESSLER, born March 6, 1925 in Bronx, NY. Entered USN on March 1, 1943. Stations included Great Lakes, IL; Gulfport, MS; California; Manila and Australia. Was armed guard gunner on troop transports between Philippine and Australia.

Memorable experience was being in several Kamikaze attacks; shrapnel wounds twice.

Awards/Medals: Asiatic/Pacific with one star, Philippine Liberation, American Theater and WWII Victory Medal.

Discharged Jan. 27, 1946 with rank of seaman first class, USNR.

Married Terry May 19, 1946. Two daughters, Jodie Ann and Stephanie Leah. Two granddaughters, Rachel and Sarah.

Member of JWV Lubin Linett Steinman Post 317. Past post commander and state commander. Member of DAV and American Legion.

Retired from AON Insurance Company in 1988. Started new career as insurance agent in 1979 after 30 years as pattern maker of Slim Fit Dress Company in Shelto, CT.

Died April 20, 1993.

MORRIS KIEL was located after a national search was brought about by Max Garcia, a German concentration camp survivor, who was trying to locate the men who were at the CIC office in Nurnberg, Germany between June-September 1946 and especially the person who was in charge. NCICA members were recruited to help in the search.

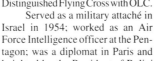

Meanwhile Kiel, a New Yorker who transplanted to North Carolina after the war to become a furniture manufacturer's sales rep. in Greensboro, NC, was unaware of the national search for his whereabouts. He was reading a publication called *Holocaust Survivor Quarterly* when the name Max Garcia popped out of the pages. He had often wondered what happened to him and contacted Garcia in San Francisco. And so it was Morris Kiel, the old commanding officer of the CIC unit in Nurnberg was located.

CHARLES KIMMEL, (MD), born in Newark, NJ on May 28, 1907. Medial degree from University of Maryland, Baltimore, 1933. Practical medicine and surgery, Bloomfield, NJ. Was associate medical director of New Jersey Blue Shield, 25 years. Enlisted USAAC Oct. 15, 1942 as captain. One month at Officers' Training School, Warner Robbins, GA.

Served as medical officer at Harding Field, Baton Rouge; AAB Dalhart, TX; DSGTS Woodward, OK. Departed Norfolk, VA on Oct. 6, 1943 on troop ship *General Pope* with 5,000 troops for Southwest Pacific: New Guinea, Leyte, Philippines, Luzon. Served as squadron surgeon with 96th Service Sqdn., 2nd Airborne Sqdn., 51st Fighter Group, 8th Fighter Control Sqdn.

Returned to US on Oct. 19, 1945. Honorably discharged Jan. 8, 1946 at Ft. Dix, NJ.

Decorations: Asiatic/Pacific with three stars, Philippine Liberation with one star, American Theater Medal and WWII Victory Medal.

Married Minna on May 10, 1936. Three daughters and four grandchildren.

Member, Emeritus AMA JWV North Essex Post 146. Retired in 1981.

JACK D. KIRSHBAUM, MS, MD, born Dec. 31, 1902 in Chicago. Entered Medical Corps, 31st Gen. Hospital on Sept. 12, 1942 as major. Stationed at hospital in Ft. Mead, PA. Spent one year at Shenango, PA and transferred to 31st Gen. Hospital for 18 months in New Hebrides. Promoted to lieutenant colonel. Moved to Philippines in May 1945 for six months. Served as War CO for three months (hospital).

Awards/Medals: Asiatic/Pacific with Battle Star. Discharged in 1945 with rank of full colonel.

Married to Florence and has three sons: Gerald, Robert and Richard.

Retired from medicine in 1972.

JULES KLAUSNER JR., born March 12, 1894 in New York, NY. Served in Army's 307th Inf. Regt. during WWI. Stationed in Europe- France.

Awarded the Purple Heart.

Died Nov. 24, 1972. Had wife Rae, daughter and two grandchildren.

1932 first commander, Mt. Vernon Post 42, JWV. 1934 state commander, JWV. First president of Mt. Vernon Jewish Community Council.

EUGENE KLEIN entered the USAAF on Feb. 24, 1942. Ft. Dix, NJ. He qualified for pilot training and trained in Nashville, TN; Montgomery, AL, Americus, GA; Scott Field, IL, graduating as radio operator. Assigned for combat training to Colorado Springs on a B-24 bomber, graduating in June 1944.

Left for England on the *Queen Elizabeth* with 18,000 men aboard including Glenn Miller and his band. Trained in North Ireland and assigned to the 2nd AD, 453rd BG, 735th BS at old Buckingham AB, England. Flew 38 bombing missions over France, Netherlands and mostly over Germany. He was on two missions with Jimmy Stewart who later became their operations officer.

Received the five Air Medals, EAME Service Medal and the Good Conduct. Retired June 6, 1945, as tech sergeant.

IRVIN I. KLEIN, "Received "Greetings from President Roosevelt" in April 1941 for one year active duty." Spent three months training at Ft. Belvoir, VA before being shipped to Panama to joined the 805th Engineer Aviation Bn. as a platoon leader building air fields in the jungle. Took a platoon to the Galapagos Islands in 1942 to help build an airfield from which bombers could patrol the Pacific Ocean looking for submarines.

Returned to Richmond, VA in 1943 where the 805th supplied cadres for new engineer units. Promoted to captain and battalion supply officer when the 805th was ordered to the Pacific Theater to build airfield on Oahu, a bomber field on Saipan from which the B-29s dropped the A-bombs on Japan, and an airfield on Ie Shima where Ernie Pyle died. Spent three months, February- April 1945 in Seattle, responsible for the procurement and loading engineer equipment onto LSTs for the anticipated invasion of Japan.

Discharged March 1946 as lieutenant colonel, Corps of Engineers.

JACK J. KLEIN, is present commander of JWV of the USA Post 709, East Meadows, Levittown, NY. Twice wounded during six campaigns in ETO. Proud to have served in the command of Gen. Omar Bradley.

Division commander of 28th Inf. of Pennsylvania, the latter was assigned Deputy Corps CO under Gen. D.D. Eisenhower and honored the 28th to follow in successful battles through France, Belgium, Luxembourg and Germany.

"History is glorious because of what we did there and I am proud to have been a part thereof."

LEONARD KLEIN, born in Newark, NJ on June 23, 1918. Graduating from the Wharton School in 1939, he entered NYU Law School. Upon completion of Law School in May 1942, he went into Navy officers' training (V7) program. As an ensign, he was ordered on board the submarine chaser SC-667. They operated in the Caribbean area.

In July 1943 they went through the Panama Canal to the Solomon Islands and operated through the area. In March 1944 he became lieutenant junior grade and in August 1945, lieutenant senior grade.

He took command of the sub chaser in the summer of 1944. Their first battle engagement was in the invasion of Guam, directing part of the invasion crafts.

Subsequently, being relieved of command he went on the destroyer escort USS *Price*, eventually becoming the executive officer.

He was released from active duty in March 1946.

He is married. His wife's name is Barbara. He has two married children and two granddaughters. He is still active as a CPA and attorney.

He is a member of the JWV Post 758.

MARSHALL KLEIN, was born in Elizabeth, NJ on June 3, 1925. Entered the Army October 1943 at Ft. Dix, NJ. Served overseas in Europe as a radio operator with the 229th Field Arty. Group HQ from October 1944- May 1946.

Married Annette Sept. 7, 1947. They have three married children: Sharon, Shelly and Jeffrey, plus seven grandchildren.

Graduated from Seton Hall University in January 1949. Followed by a brief career in insurance, a manufacturer of school uniforms and 20 years as a residential builder/developer.

Active in veteran and community affairs: past commander Post 125, Asbury Park-Ocean, JWV; past deputy commander of New Jersey, JWV and national executive committeeman, JWV; past commander American Legion Post 346 and life member VFW Post 1398.

Appointed to the Veterans Service Council by Gov. Whitman. Served on the E. Orange VA Medical Center Advisory and Bio-Medical Research Boards, Board of the Central NJ Jewish Home for the Aged and the Monmouth County Human Relations Commission; the state of New Jersey 59th Anniversary Commemoration of WWII Committee.

MELVIN KLEIN, born Oct. 31, 1916 in Chicago, IL and graduated in the top 10 percent of his high school class. Entered Wright Jr. College in hopes of becoming an aeronautical engineer but work and school didn't work out.

They married Dec. 5,1937 and in 1941 learned about the Civilian Pilot Training Program under the Civil Aeronautical Administration. He did so well that he was given a scholarship for advanced flying. WWII erupted and all planes were grounded. In 1942 he enlisted in the AAC and received his wings in Chandler, AZ.

In practicing formation flying, two planes collided in mid-air. He was blown out and the sole survivor. Flew tow target to overcome fright only to go to England to fly 35 missions over Germany receiving 11 OLCs. He refused to fly one mission because he felt the plane wasn't safe and was reprimanded. That plane never returned. He always knew as much as the engineer of any plane he flew.

Being a reservist, came home after WWII was over only to be recalled when the Korean War started.

In 1953 his wife and children joined him in Kwajalein where he flew scientists in the SA-16 testing the A-bomb. One day he got too close and his clothes had to be burned. From there it was Orlando, FL where he was an instructor/pilot and later chief pilot of the 57th Rescue Sqdn. and supervised a standardization program for air crews, pilots, co-pilots, navigators, flight engineers, radio operators and para-rescue men. The helicopter people were also under his supervision. It was his direct responsibility to assure that crewmen were qualified to perform rescue missions. He was also involved in the Space Program relating to the recovery of astronauts. During this period unknown to his family, he helped work out the problem of how to refuel planes in mid-air.

Disturbed by the loss of young men in Vietnam, he chose to go there. His group was called "Crown" and it was his responsibility to figure out how to best rescue a downed pilot or crew. After many missions, he was awarded the DFC.

He was forced out in 1971 being a Reservist, not a Regular, as he had no college degree.

After a time, joined the JWV. Post 603 of North Hollywood, CA. Did volunteer work for the VA for eight years until his illness (ALS, Lou Gehrig's Disease) took over and took him on Sept. 3, 1993.

At the funeral services Rabbi Benjamin Elsant said, "Had he not been Jewish, he would have been a general."

MILTON KLEIN, born Nov. 2, 1934 in Detroit, MI. Drafted into Army on Aug. 10, 1954. Member of 22nd Inf. Regt. Stationed at Kirch Gons, Germany.

Memorable experience was being a field medic he was able to treat wounded soldiers.

Awards/Medals: Occupation of Germany, Good Conduct and National Service.

Discharged July 6, 1956 with rank of corporal.

Has wife Ruth, sons, Mitchell and Sheldon and daughter Mindy. Today he is an insurance agent.

NORMAN P. KLEIN, was born in New York, NY on May 3, 1917. Graduated New York University with a BS degree in 1937. Entered Army, Jan. 17, 1941 and assigned to 114th Inf. Regt., 44th Div., Ft. Dix, NJ.

Selected for Officers' Candidate School, Chemical Warfare Service in October 1942. Graduated and received a commission as second lieutenant, January 1943. Served as a staff chemical officer with the 13th AF in the South Pacific from July 1943- November 1945. Relieved for active duty in March 1946. Retained reserve commission and retired in grade of lieutenant colonel in 1977.

After WWII, attended NYU School of Law and received degrees of Jurist Doctor and Master of Laws. Served many years as an attorney for the US Government- last 15 years as chief counsel of the Federal Aviation Administrations' Technical Center, and now retired.

Decorations: Asiatic/Pacific Medal with four Battle Stars, American Defense Medal, American Campaign Medal, Philippine Liberation Medal, WWII Victory Medal, Meritorious Service Unit Plaque and Armed Forces Reserve Medal.

Married July 11, 1948 to Suzanne (Kadou) and has a son Tuvia and a daughter Leah. Member JWV Post 604 (previous member of JWV Post 550).

SEYMOUR KLEIN, (SSG), born in Brooklyn, NY on Oct. 15, 1921. Enlisted in AF on Aug. 12, 1942. Shipped to 8th AF, England, December 1943. Staff sergeant of 467th Service Sqdn. at Station F-375 in Honington, England. In charge of all airplane parts, P-38s and then P-51s.

Good Conduct Medal, European Theater Medal, Battle Star, Unit Presidential Citation, American Service Medal, WWII Victory Medal, Army Citation for work accomplished keeping combat planes on missions.

Nephew of Col. Morris J. Mendelsohn, 3rd National Commander, 1924-1927, four consecutive terms. He changed the name from Union of Hebrew Veterans to the JWV.

P.P.C. No. 459 Boca Raton, FL. On April 18, 1988 received warrant from Department of Florida Commander, appoint him as colonel in Department of Florida, as chief historian.

Married to Jean A. Charmack, July 18, 1943. Sons: Howard, Alan and Jack. Four grandchildren.

ABE J. KLEINER, born in New York City in 1920 and entered the US Army in January 1942. Was discharged in January 1946. Received basic training at Camp Croft, SC and then became a member of the 42nd "Rainbow" Div. at Ft. Gruber, OK. Went overseas in 1944 and served in France, Germany and Austria. Participated in battles in Alsace-Lorraine and Germany. The most memorable and terrible experiences of many were seeing thousands of corpses in box cars and inside of the Dachau concentration camp in Munich, Germany.

Received the Good Conduct Medal, European Theater with two Battle Stars, Bronze Star and Combat Award Badges and unit citation. He was a corporal in rank.

After leaving the Army went to college under the GI Bill and was a high school teacher for 31 years. Married to Anne, a retired chemistry teacher for 46 years, and have two children, both physicians.

Have been active in JWV and elected post commander of the Levitan-Maspeth Post 673 five times and am a lifetime member. At the present time he is retired and enjoying the grandchildren, as well as traveling. Is now a resident of Queens, NY.

JULIUS KLEINER, (MSG), born July 6, 1917. Entered the service on Oct. 3, 1941. Received training as a weather forecaster. In 1943 assigned to 11th AF- Aleutian Islands. There while serving at Cold Bay, a plane crashed on Mt. Pavlov. Rescue team headed by Col. Grossmith was unable to reach the survivors. He sent the colonel a note advising him to use a ski plane and to contact Al Schoutte, ice pilot. Advice was followed and rescue easily made.

Received a commendation for his "resourcefulness and initiative" and a promotion for writing a paper showing how fog which closed down Anchorage airport could be predicted. His forecasts were rated highly by pilots who flew the Aleutians. When the Russians came to his base after the Yalta Pact to receive training in their landing craft, he made the forecast for the DC-3 which flew Pres. Roosevelt's representative to report to him on the mission.

HARRY KLEINHART, born July 4, 1920, Cleveland, OH. Attended Morris HS, Bronx, NY. Enlisted in the U.S. Army June 27, 1942, New Orleans, LA, as marksman/gunner/ mortarman with the 119th Inf., 30th Div. Basic training at Camp Wolters, TX.

Participated in Normandy invasion, France, ETO, Co. H, 30th Div., Sept. 25, 1944. Wounded in enemy action on July 10, 1944 at St. Lo, France.

Awards/Medals: Purple Heart, ETO Medal, Campaign Medal and WWII Victory Medal. Discharged Dec. 23, 1944, with rank private.

Currently living in VA supervised foster home, Newman Community Care Home, Brooklyn, NY.

MILTON S. KLEINMAN, flying career started with model making in his early teens. Flight training and piloting Piper Cubs 1938-41 at the Univ. of Mississippi. Enlisted in the Air Corps on Aug. 29, 1942. Served as a flight engineer between August 1943 and December 1944, making approximately 79-80 round trips over the "Hump." There were thousands of American Jews in the service who served valiantly.

He was classified as Class 3 Engineer. Received the Distinguished Flying Cross with OLC, Air Medal with OLC, Presidential Unit Citation, Good Conduct Medal, American Theater Medal, Asiatic Theater Medal with two Battle Stars, European-African Theater, Victory Medal, Chinese War Memorial Medal, New York State Conspicuous Service Medal, Burma Star Campaign Medal, Flight Wings, American AF,

Flight Wings Chinese AF. He wears his awards proudly at the annual Hump Pilots reunions.

HARRY KLINE, (YNC), USCGR (RET), born Nov. 1, 1919 in Wilkes-Barre, PA. One of three brothers who served. Enlisted in USNR, February 1939. Overseas during WWII. Discharged March 1946. Re-enlisted USNR in 1946, Korean War service. Discharged November 1951. Enlisted USCGR and retired as chief petty officer in 1967. Served aboard ship and at bases/units of USN/USCG.

Memorable experience: Assigned to enlisted staff Adm. Harold F. Stark, Commander, US Naval Forces in Europe (Connaveu) 1944-45.

Employed by and retired from Veterans Administration as assistant field director, Area 4 DVB, Washington, DC. Received agencies highest distinguished career award.

Married to Lillian. Two sons, Herbert who served in both USN and USAF and retired as lieutenant colonel and Allan. Three grandchildren: Richard, Holly and Adam. Member of Coast Guard Reserves Association and JWV.

BEN KLINGER, was in service July 1, 1944- Sept. 23, 1945. Inducted April 29, 1943; no blood pressure! Stations included Ellington Field, Houston, TX where he got navigator wings; San Antonio, TX for boot camp; Sheppard Field, TX for death row; University of Cincinnati, Sept. 15, 1943, officer and a gentleman; Laredo Army Aifield, Laredo, TX; San Marcos Army Airfield, San Antonio, TX for Navigator School; Tampa, FL for who knows and Gulfport, MS where he met crew. While in New York and Savannah, GA he was navigator of B-17 flying north to Iceland, Greenland, then to England and on to North Africa and into Italy. While in Foggia, Italy was navigator of B-17 for 414th BS, 97th BG, 15th AF. Rest camp in Capri. Targets in Northern Italy, Austria and Southern Germany. A week in Naples where they bought their staples!

Awards/Medals: Air Medal with four OLCs, 2,000 lollipops and five million Golden-gaboons.

Discharged in summer of 1945— Hi ho, Hi ho, it's off to work we go!

Married 49 years to one wife, two kids, five grandchildren and one cat. Have old fashioned dime store for 44 years. Worked in parents dry goods store in growing up years.

A member of Congregation Emanu El, Houston since 1954. Attended Rice University two years.

A strong believer and promoter of meaningful work as the best therapy. Can crawl on his belly like a reptile. True love is long green onions. Have written first ever Mexican/Jewish folk dance- Hav a nagela, Hav a tequilla. Have truest Jewish nose— people come from all over the world to gaze at it in utter amazement- touch it- and try to squeeze some of the blackheads out.

CHARLES KLUGLOSE, born June 12, 1915, Little Rock, AR. Entered active service Oct. 8, 1941. Assigned to Infantry, 1st Bn., 186th Regt., 41st Inf. Div. Basic training was at Camp Wolters, TX. Attended Infantry Technical School (general clerk).

Shipped out of San Francisco April 22, 1942. Flew over Owen Stanley Range into combat. Made landing at Biak Island and Mindoro, Philippines. Participated in action in Papuan Southern Philippines and New Guinea.

Awards/Medals: Asiatic-Pacific Service Ribbon and three Bronze Service Stars, American Defense Service Ribbon, Good Conduct Medal, Philippine Liberation Ribbon and one Bronze Star. Discharged June 13, 1945, as T-5.

Married and has three married daughters and three granddaughters. He is retired.

STANLEY L. KNOPFLER, born Sept. 4, 1920 in Bronx, NYC. Entered service on Nov. 11, 1942. Served with Army's 486th Ord.-Evacuation Co. Stations included Great Britain, November 1943-August 1944 and France, August 1944- April 1945.

Memorable experience was sleeping in tents in France, watching a dog fight between Americans and German planes; rooting for the Americans. The captain saw what was going on and shouted for them to get back into the tents before they got shot at.

Awards/Medals: Good Conduct Medal, WWII Victory Medal, EAME Medal with one Silver Service Star, Meritorious Service Plaque, Most Efficient Company for giving service to all trucks, vehicles on fire or disabled on road from Cherbough to Paris, "Red Ball Express".

Discharged Nov. 29, 1945 with rank of tech fifth grade.

Married to Beatrice Losberg. Three children: Gail Knopfler, Dr. Susan Knopfler and Phyllis Berkowitz. Three grandchildren: Leah, Ilan and Danielle.

RUDOLF KOGAN, (COL), was born in Russia and immigrated to China, where he grew up. He came to the US in 1940 and enlisted in Army in 1942. As a lieutenant commanding a platoon of tanks in the 782nd Tank Bn., he was sent to Europe where he saw a great deal of action.

He was almost killed by a Nazi sniper; he participated in the liberation of a concentration camp; and at war's end he personally accepted the surrender of a Germany infantry battalion. He had to deal with problems of Soviet army deserters and German civilians fleeing from the advancing Red Army.

He stayed in the Army and started advancing through the ranks. Toward the end of his military career, he commanded an armored battalion in Korea (1963). He was then promoted to full colonel and appointed chief of staff of the Military Aid and Advisory Group in Taiwan. a job with some political and diplomatic undertones.

His next appointment was to be the Army's attaché to the US Embassy in Singapore, where he stayed until his retirement in 1972, after 30 years of service.

Rudy died in 1986 and was buried with full military honors at the Arlington National Cemetery.

KURT KOLBEN, born in Austria in 1922. His family immigrated to the USA in 1938. Inducted into the Army in 1943 with basic training at Camp Croft, SC. As a replacement he was sent to Oran, Algeria, thence to Naples, Italy and joined the 34th Inf. Div., Co. L, 168th Inf.

Participated at Anzio and broke through to the Gothic Line. With a comrade he was captured by Nazi officers and enlisted men in the Po Valley. Transferred to Intelligence because of language proficiency in German. Orders to Japan were canceled on V-J Day and he separated from the service as a T/3.

Continued to study in electronics under the GI Bill and opened his own shop in New York. Established a book distribution center in Boston, sold out to Interstate Distributors and was employed by them for 15 years when he retired.

Presently in good health and with his wife Edith, he is traveling around the world.

HENRY KOLDIN, born in New York City. Twin brother of Leo Koldin. Served in the Armed Forces for two years.

Employed by Greenway Brewery. Died of a heart attack on Jan. 20, 1953.

LEO KOLDIN, born in New York City. Moved to Syracuse at the age of seven. Graduated from University of Buffalo in June 1924.

Worked in Buffalo for a few years. Also was affiliated with the Daw Drug Company. Married in 1945, had two children. Member of Knights of Pythias, JWV Onondaga Post 131, American Legion Post 41 and YMHA.

Inducted on Aug. 17, 1942. On Jan. 13, 1943 sailed from San Francisco for Pearl Harbor. Traveled nearly all around the world working in different hospitals. Discharged from the service on March 16, 1944.

Died in August 1951. Survived by wife Frieda, two children, mother, brother Hyman and two sisters.

SAMUEL L. KOLINER, born Aug. 30, 1919, in Woonsocket, RI and grew up in New York City. Called into service on Feb. 11, 1941, and after two weeks at Ft. Dix, NJ, was assigned to the 21st Coast Arty. at Ft. Dupont, DE. Attended Coast Artillery School at Ft. Monroe, VA and was assigned to the 246th Coast Arty. in Virginia.

Sent overseas as a stenographer in October 1943 and was part of the Artillery Section of 1st Army HQ. Participated in five campaigns, including Normandy, Ardennes, Central Europe, Northern France, etc. When the armistice was signed, their unit was returned to the States ostensibly to be sent to Japan; however, with 124 points, he was sent home with the rank of sergeant.

Awards include the American Defense Service Medal, Good Conduct Medal, EAME Service Medal and Marksman on the Springfield Rifle, M-1 Rifle and on the carbine.

After discharge he had a wholesale auto parts company and recently retired. Married Elaine Dec. 6, 1942, and they have three sons, three daughters and 10 grandchildren. He is member of JWV Group, Bookbinder Polsky Post 763 for several years.

EDWARD KONIGSBERG, was born Jan. 1, 1910 in Bayonne, NJ. Sworn into Army on April 20, 1943. Served in Medical and Chemical Warfare Supplies Depot. Stations included Ft. Dix, NJ; Camp Pickett, WA; Camp Siebert, AL; England, France; Holland and Germany.

Awards/Medals: Good Conduct, two Battle Stars. Honorably discharged on Oct. 29, 1945 with rank of tech 5. He is presently married and retired.

HERMAN KONIKOFF, born Jan. 20, 1916, in New York City, NY. Graduated from Union Hill High School, Union City, NJ in 1936; worked as shoe machine operator, electrician's helper and machinist helper in New Jersey. Entered active duty military service with the USAAC, Camp Upton, NY, in 1942. Retired as T/Sgt. from the USAF, Air Trng. Cmd. at Robins AFB, GA in November 1962.

Assigned to the ETO in 1945 and participated in the Berlin Airlift. Overseas tours included Germany, England and Puerto Rico. Zone of Interior duties were at Greensboro AFB, NC; Norton AFB, CA; Douglas AFB, AZ; Biggs AFB, TX; Carswell AFB, TX; Ellsworth AFB, SD; Loring AFB, ME;

Fairchild AFB, WA; Beale AFB, CA; Chanute AFB, IL and Robins AFB, GA.

Awarded the Good Conduct Medal with Silver Loop, American Defense Service Medal, American Campaign Medal, WWII Victory Medal, Occupation Medal (Germany) with Airlift Device, National Defense Service medal, AF Longevity Service Award with four OLCs.

Served 25 years as loan officer for Robins Federal Credit Union, Warner Robins, GA, retiring Nov. 24, 1987. Married to Willie Mae Kelly in 1963 until her death in 1981. Married Lura Head Bell in 1987 and lived with her until his death March 14, 1993. Survived by his wife Lura; daughter Bonnie Bell Davis; granddaughters, Teresa and Tamara Grooms.

HARRY KOOPERSTEIN, born in Manhattan on Feb. 10, 1912. Attended George Washington and Commerce High schools. He was a good athlete excelling in wrestling, baseball and four wall handball. Was close friends with several of the great handball champions, Vick Hershkowitz and Angelo Trullio, and participated in open handball tournaments through the US. Became a member of the NYC Fire Department in 1937. Son Robert (See Cooper, Robert, Lt.) was born in 1940.

Joined the Navy in 1944 where he attended boot camp in Sampson, NY and Bainbridge, MD. He served in the 3rd Naval Div. in the Canal Zone as a gunners mate and worked in the ammo dumps.

After being honorably discharged in 1945, he resumed his career with the NYC Fire Department, retiring in 1967 with the rank of Bn. Chief.

He currently lives in Brooklyn, NY with his wife of over 55 years, Nina, with whom he still enjoys ballroom, line and round and western dancing.

IRVING KOPEL, born April 13, 1916. Portland, ME High School graduate. Education included courses in electrical and mechanical engineering at the Lowell Institute School at M.I.T., alternating currents at Harvard University extension; electrical code at Franklin Union; fire control instruments and optics inspector course at Frankford Arsenal. Civilian occupation was as inspector of ordinance materials in private plants.

Entered active service July 8, 1943. Trained at Aberdeen Proving Ground, Philadelphia. Director repairman, electrical heavy AA artillery. Left Camp Miles Standish January 18, 1944 for Liverpool, England. Assigned to 900th Ord. H.A.M. Co. Wargrave, England as electrician to install wiring and electrical apparatus in vans prior to invasion. Left Southampton, England with convoy and landed on Omaha Beach, Normandy with the US 1st Army. Installed telephone wires and maintained communication from Normandy Beach, often utilizing recovered Germany equipment.

Sent on special assignment to an automobile factory in Aachen to see if it could be useable for parts. Went to Burdinne, Belgium for regrouping after the German breakthrough in the Ardennes and their murder of the captured American prisoners. This trip almost ended in darkness at the Meuse River in Belgium because the bridge where they were crossing was blown up. Afterwards, there was a long cold ride to Dombasle, France, and nights spent on concrete floor in the fortress at Metz. He crossed the Rhine at Koblenz and witness the terrible sights of the Buchenwald concentration camp.

Memories: Headgerows. A gas alarm at Falais Gap, Paris. A meeting with a Jewish man and his family in Liege, who had been hiding. Later on a furlough to London, was able to purchase needed medicine for his son. He was alarmed by the ignorance and bigotry of many of the men in the company toward Jews. "At first, I was the only Jew until a mechanic was killed by a mine. His replacements were Jewish."

After the war was over, was employed by the VA as a veterans benefits counselor. Married to Jeanette and has a son, a daughter and two grandchildren. Member of Sharon JWV, DAV and past master of Sharon Lodge of Masons.

HAROLD M. KOPLAN, USAAF, enlisted in the AAF in March 1942 and received training as an aerial photographer and gunner in medium bombers. Participated in battles of the Coral Sea and Bismarck Sea. Was one of the original members of HQ Sqdn. of the 3rd BG.

Participated in daring low-level strafing and bombing attacks on Jap airfields, troop concentrations and shipping in the New Guinea area.

On June 6, 1944, on his 25th and final mission before rotation home, his plane was hit by AA fire over Biak Island and crashed at sea. His body was never recovered.

- and that unrest which men miscall delight, can touch him not, and harm him not again, from the contagion of the world's slow stairs. He is secure...

ROBERT KOPLAN, (CPT), enlisted in the Army in July 1943 upon graduation from University of Illinois College of Dentistry. Was assigned to the 743rd AAA Gun Bn and served in Australia, New Guinea and the Philippines.

Now retired in Lincolnwood, IL. He and Lila have one son and three grandchildren.

Member of Post 800, JWV.

AARON B. KORAN, (DDS, FICD) (CPT, DC, AUS), born in New York, NY on April 23, 1913. Graduated LA High School, June 1929. Worked as bank teller for two years and then entered University of So. California College of Dentistry, graduating June 1936. Residency in oral surgery at LA County General hospital, 1936-37.

Entered US Army November 1943 and discharged December 1945. Assigned to Ft. Ord, CA and later assigned to the ETO in the 1st Armd. Group serving six different tank and tank destroyer battalions, then later supporting the southern (lower) flank of the Battle of the Bulge. Then transferred to the 36th (Texas) Inf., 111th Medical Bn. and then later to the Army of Occupation in Germany.

Decoration: Central Europe, Rhineland, Rome-Arno with five Battle Stars and two letters of commendation. Combat Medical Badge, German Occupation and WWII Victory Medal.

Married to Shirley and has two sons, a daughter and four grandchildren. Retired from practice September 1981.

MILTON KOSEN, born Jan. 12, 1918, New York, NY. Volunteered for the service Jan. 22, 1941; trained in the infantry at Ft. Bragg, then in gliders of the 82nd Abn. Served in campaigns in North Africa; Sicily, Italy; first wave in gliders on D-day landing at Omaha Beach June 6, 1945; Holland; and Western Europe.

Wounded in Holland and returned to the States, spending 18 months in the Army hospitals due to shrapnel in his left arm and leg.

Received a battlefield commission to second lieutenant and when he was discharged on July 16, 1946, he was a first lieutenant. Awards include the Silver Star, Victory

Medal, American Theater Ribbon, EAME Ribbon with four Bronze Stars.

Kosen passed away of cancer on Oct. 31, 1988. *Submitted by his wife, Muriel Kosen.*

MILTON S. KOSTER, was born March 2, 1908 in New London, CT. Entered USCG on Jan. 30, 1942.

Memorable experience was capturing secret Germany weather station in Northern Greenland.

Awards/Medals: Good Conduct, WWII Victory Medal, American and EAME Theater. Discharged Nov. 23, 1945 with rank of chief pharmacist mate.

Married to Rose Koster. Today he is retired.

JEROME KOUNITZ, born July 20, 1917 in New York City. Inducted into Army March 27, 1941 at Ft. Dix, NJ. Basic training at Ft. Eustis, VA and put in Btry. D, 57th Mobile Coast Arty. with 155 mm guns. Unit moved to Camp Pendclton, Virginia Beach, VA and were among the first troops to leave the States after Pearl Harbor attack. Landed in Hawaii Dec. 24, 1941.

Returned to States March 1943 to Infantry Officers' Candidate School, Ft. Benning, GA. Reassigned and went to Co. B, 48th Armd. Inf. Bn., 7th Armd. Div. Sailed June 6, 1944 on *Queen Mary* to Scotland then to Tidsworth Barracks, near Salsbury, England. Division committed to combat Aug. 14, 1944 with Gen. Patton's 3rd Army. Wounded near Metz, France. Rejoined division in 10 days and moved to Holland fighting with British 2nd army. Ordered to Battle of the Bulge Dec. 16, 1944 fighting in vicinity of St. Vith, Belgium. "Missing in action" telegram sent home.

In Germany on March 31, 1945, was sent to Officer's Candidate School at Fontainebleau, France. War in Europe ended while at OCS. Decorations: Purple Heart, Bronze Star, Combat Infantry Badge, four Campaign Stars for Northern France, Rhineland, Ardennes-Alsace and Central Europe, Belgium Fourragere and Netherlands Resistance Cross.

Married to Neomi who passed away in 1956. Remarried to Carolyn in 1958. Have four sons and step-son: Jon, Lance, Martin, Josh and Mike.

Discharged Aug. 9, 1945. Member of JWV Post 156, commander for three years.

LEONARD KOVEL, according to relatives, several 1945 newspaper stories and official records, Kovel tricked the draft board into believing that he was 18 by concocting a story that he was born in New York and had no parents or birth certificate. In October of that year at age 15, he was drafted and went through basic training at Camp Blanding, FL.

Shipped out in March 1945 to Europe where he grew up quickly, racing across Germany and Austria and picking up two Battle Stars for his service. He received an honorable discharge in September 1945. At age 16 he joined the Merchant Marine.

Later in life, Kovel, who never married, worked as a machinist and ran a dental sales and service business out of his home in Bellwood. He passed away at the age of 66 and is perhaps Chicago's youngest WWII veteran.

NORMAN I. KRAITSIK, formerly Isadore Kraitsik, was inducted into the Army on Dec. 31, 1941 at Ft. Sheridan, IL. Since he had a degree in electrical engineering, he requested assignment to the Signal Corps and after three weeks was sent to Camp Crowder, MO. Completed basic training there and was assigned to advanced training as a radio repairman.

Upon completion of his training, he was sent to a staging are and then overseas to a replacement depot in Manila. He was assigned to HQ in the Signal Section where he worked his way up to chief clerk with a rank of staff sergeant.

While there, the Japanese surrendered. He was sent to Tokyo as part of the occupation forces. He completed his tour of duty in 1946 and returned to the United States for mustering out of the Army.

ED KRAMER, USAF, enlisted October 1950. Discharged October 1954 as airman first class. Flew on medical evacuation flights from front line medical hospitals to Japanese and stateside facilities.

GERSON KRAMER, born in Philadelphia, PA Nov. 4, 1919. Still resides there. Had several jobs before being drafted into service before Pearl Harbor, Oct. 29, 1941. This was supposed to be for one year. Pearl Harbor was two months later. War was declared. He was in for four years. He was in four Army camps in Virginia: Camp Lee, Camp Bradford, Camp Pickett and Ft. Belvior where he was trained as an Army engineer.

After training he was sent to Plattsburgh, NY near Canada. In January 942 he was attached to the 36th Engineers Regt. Combat. On March 11, 1942 he was sent to Ft. Bragg, NC attached to the 9th Inf. Div. as part of the Atlantic Fleet Amphibious Corps. He was in five invasions in Europe: North Africa, Nov. 8, 1942; Licata, Sicily, July 10, 1943; Salerno, Italy, Sept. 9, 1943; Anzio, Italy, Jan. 22, 1944 and South France, Aug. 22, 1944.

The battles he participated in were Algeria-French Morocco, Tunisia, Sicily, Naples-Foggia, Anzio, Rome-Arno, Southern France, Rhineland, Ardennes-Alsace and Central Europe.

He received several awards: Unit Citation, Infantry Badge and Marksman Rifle Badge.

His medals included pre-Pearl Harbor American Defense, EAME with Arrowhead and eight Battle Stars, WWII Victory Medal, Purple Heart, Good Conduct and American Campaign.

He was wounded in Italy. He had malaria four times. He was in Austria when the war was over; May 1945. His discharge was on Sept. 14, 1945 with rank of corporal.

His occupation was window display decorator, interior decoration and merchant. His wife's name is Mollie. He has three daughters: Lorraine, Barbara and Roberta, a son Jules and 10 grandchildren. He will be married 50 years on May 18, 1996.

He is retired. Member of JWV Post 98.

STANLEY KRAMER, born Aug. 2, 1930 in Brooklyn, NY. Entered US Army on Aug. 11, 1952. Served as legal clerk for HQ Co., 45th Engineer Group, Yongdong Po, Korea.

Memorable experience was landing in Inchon, Korea. Disembarked via Jacob's Ladder onto floating barge, into an LST, onto the beach of Inchon.

Awards/Medals: Korean Service Medal with one Service Star, United Nations Service Medal, National Defense Service Medal, Merit Unit Commendation for 884th Co., 8th Army.

Married to Elaine L. Kramer. Two children, Ruth and Bruce. Self-employed certified public accountant.

NORMAN KRAUSE, born Aug. 3, 1920 in Pittsburgh, PA. Enlisted in AF on Jan. 19, 1942. Served as plane mechanic. Stations included Ft. Campbell, KY; Charlotte, NC; Ft. Myers, FL; Keesler Field, MS and Hunter Field, GA.

Memorable experiences being first medium bomber unit to occupy Henderson Field on Guadalcanal. His first earth tremors on Bougainville Island. Fighting boa snakes and tolerating kangaroos as well as Kamikazes on Sansiron, New Guinea.

Awards/Medals: Anti-Submarine Patrol Awards, New Guinea Award, Northern Solomon, Bismarck Archipelago and West Pacific Awards, Southern Philippines Medal, Luzon Awards, Victory Medal, Good Conduct Medal, Philippine Liberation Medal with one Bronze Star, Asiatic/Pacific Medal with six Bronze Stars, American Theater Medal with one Bronze Star.

Discharged Nov. 20, 1945 with rank of sergeant.

Retired six years ago. Was a gemologist and horologist jeweler. Married 47 years. Have three fine boys, two of which were professional baseball players and six grandchildren. Member JWV Post 49.

JOSEPH W. KRAUT, born Bronx, NY on May 9, 1925. Graduated Townsend Harris High School, January 1942. Attended CNNY one semester. Drafted Sept. 21, 1943, US Army. Took ASTP (Army Specialized Training Program); basic at Ft. Benning, Columbus, GA. Program discontinued and shipped to 86th Div., Camp Livingston, Alexandria, LA. Sent overseas on *Queen Elizabeth* for a three and a half day crossing to England. Went through Replacement Depots as infantry replacement, joining 1st Inf. Div. in Aachen, Germany. Assigned to Weapons Platoon G Co., 26th Inf. Regt. with 60 mm mortar firing high trajectory over two platoons of riflemen.

Went through Hurtgen Forest, Battle of the Bulge, Harts Mountains, ending in Czechoslovakia. Guarded SS prisoners in compound outside Nurenburg during war trials.

Sent home and discharged March 5, 1945.

American Theater, European Theater, Purple Heart ribbons. 1st Div. wears French and Belgium Fort de Guerres braids, one on each shoulder.

Married to Bonnie, live on cattle ranch in Georgia.

Post commander of JWV 112, 1987-1990. Department commander, Southeast 1991, NEC, 1992.

HYMAN KRAWITZ, during WWI was appointed as an observer and was sent overseas with an advance party of the 82nd Div. He went through the drives at Chateau Theirry, St. Mihiel and the Argonne.

Was a painting contractor. A member of VFW, JWV, ZOA, Temple Adath Yeshurun and the Men's Club of the Temple, past vice-president of Young Men's and Women's Benevolent Association.

Died at the age of 52. Survived by his wife Ella, son Theodore and daughters, Mrs. Meyer Spector and Miss Arlene Krawitz.

WILLIAM KRAY, born in Chicago, IL, Jan. 1, 1914. Civil engineer at University of Illinois, Champaign, IL. Commissioned a 2nd lieutenant in the Corp of Engineers.

Ordered to active duty on Aug. 10, 1940 at Ft. Belvoir, VA. After a one month refresher course, was transferred to Langley Field, VA and assigned to the 21st Aviation Engineer Regt., 3rd Bn. 3rd Bn. was alerted for a secret mission in April 1941. The secret mission was to construct an airbase in Greenland to protect the North Atlantic convoy lanes. This was per agreement between Churchill and Roosevelt at Argentia, Newfoundland in 1940.

In June 1942 the battalion was redesignated the 825th Aviation Engineer Bn. and ordered to England to build an airbase for the 8th AF at Stansted. This has recently been designated as a third airport for London.

Ordered on detached service to American Section, School of Military Engineering as director of training. Attached to the Royal Engineers initially for this training. Their function was to prepare young engineer officers and NCOs upon their entry from the States in training in three courses: Mines and Booby Traps, Construction of the Bailey Bridge, and Airfield Recon.

Was recommended by the school commander for the Bronze Star for this work.

Transferred to the 833rd Engr. Avn. Bn. for the invasion of Normandy. Built the first air strip on the Normandy Beachhead. Participated in all of the battles thereafter: Battle of France, crossing of the Rhine and Battle of Germany (four Battle Stars).

Discharged February 1946. Rank achieved was major, battalion commander. Awards: European, American Defense, American Campaign, WWII and Army of Occupation.

Married college sweetheart, Audrey. Have three children: two girls and one boy, and six grandchildren: five boys and one girl. His son Jeffrey served in Vietnam with the 9th Div., US Army.

ZENITH KREMEN, M.D., Captain in U.S. Army Dental Corps, born April 24, 1924, at Tuttle, ND. Graduated Tuttle HS in June 1942 and the University of Minnesota Dental School in June 1947 with a DDS degree. Practiced dentistry in Minneapolis, MN, for four years before enlisting in the Army Dental Corps in March 1951. Received Army medical officers basic training at Ft. Sam Houston, TX, then was stationed at Camp Stoneman, CA for a few months and then on to Korea.

Received a great deal of personal satisfaction in arranging religious services for Jewish troops aboard a troopship to Japan and Korea. Somehow commanding personnel of the troop ship had made no arrangements. The men really appreciated the opportunity for community prayers since they were very tense and fearful as they headed into a war theater.

In Korea he was assigned as battalion dentist to the 987th Armd. FA BN which participated in most major battles along the central front in Korea. Returned to the States and finished his tour of duty at Ft. Leonard Wood, MO. Discharged March 1953.

Married Merle Anne in 1950. Has two daughters and their spouses: Kathy and David Cooper, Bette Jane and Simon Goldman; and three beautiful grandchildren: Abby Cooper and Isaac and Bronia Goldman.

At this time he is retired after 36 years of individual dental practice in Minneapolis, MN. Resides in Lauderhill, FL, and in Minneapolis.

SEYMOUR KREVSKY, born July 2, 1920, Elizabeth, NJ. Enlisted September 1944 in the U.S. Army and served in the Air Technical Service Command (ATSC), Wright Field, Dayton, OH, in the Special Projects Lab. He was an ECM test and evaluation officer for classified electronic warfare equipment from December 1944 to June 1946.

Awards/Medals: American Theater, WWII Victory Medal and Good Conduct. Discharged June 30, 1946, with the rank of sergeant.

BSEE in 1942 and MSEE in 1950 from Newark College of Engineering. Was principal staff member of the NATO Architectural Assessment Task Group, BDM 90-91. He is the author and co-author of 24 technical publications.

Commander JWV Post 515 in 1972 and in 1995; past county commander, Monmouth Ocean County Council; past 4th District vice commander, Dept. of New Jersey, 1980-87; past national civil defense then emergency management officer 1981-88. He is retired.

Married Gladys Welt Jan. 9, 1944, has two daughters, Ell and Joan.

HARRY S. KRIEGER, born Jan. 7, 1922 in Munich, Germany. Enlisted Nov. 24, 1942. Served with HQ Btry., 100th Inf. Div. Arty. Stations included Ft. Jackson, Ft. Bragg,

Northern France, Central Europe, Rhineland G033 WD 45 as amended. Landed in Marseilles and went through France, Alsace Loraine into Germany. He was a weather observer until Alsace. Then he was put up front to clear out villages, so their units could occupy houses to sleep in. "I threw them out immediately until our chaplain said to me, "Harry, two wrongs don't make a right, give them 20 minutes."

Awards: American Service Medal, Bronze Star, EAME Service Medal, WWII Victory Medal.

Discharged Jan. 10, 1946 with rank of staff sergeant.

Married to Ellen, have one daughter and three grandchildren. He had his own business, retired in 1990 and joined JWV at that time. He belongs to Post 655.

He was arrested by the Nazis at the Chrystal Nacht in 1938. Was released because he was under 16. Went with a children transport to England and came to the USA, October 1940.

LIONEL KRONBERG, born July 14, 1922 in Jersey City, NJ. Entered Army Nov. 24, 1942, Ft. Dix, NJ. Trained at Camp Wheeler, Macon, GA, infantry. To Canastel, North Africa March 1943 as replacement for Co. B, 39th Combat Engineers. Front line combat 28 months, including invasion into Gela, Sicily, Salerno, Italy, both D-day H-hour and Anzio. Assault on Monte Cassini, Balzano to the Brenner Pass and police action near Trieste. Left Italy Oct. 1, 1945. Discharged at Ft. Dix as T-4 radio operator, Oct. 23, 1945.

Married May 24, 1942 to Miriam Kook of Jersey City. Son David was born just before he went overseas. After the war he returned to his plumbing and heating contracting business. They had two daughters, Hazel and Ellen, and a son Howard.

His parents were Jules Kronberg, PFC of Post 10 was born in Brooklyn, Aug. 21, 1895. He served in the Navy during WWI, wounded aboard a destroyer, and discharged in 1918. He also belonged to DAV and VFW.

His mother, Bessie Briefer Kronberg, was P.N.P. Women's Auxiliary, JWV from 1944-1946. She was born in Jersey City, July 9, 1896.

His brother Jerome was tech sergeant with 15h AAF serving in Italy. His sister was Helen Faigen. Both are now deceased.

His brother's son, Stuart Kronberg, served during the Vietnam War, which makes him the third generation of Kronbergs to serve their country in war.

Lionel retired in 1981.

MACEY KRONSBERG, born Tilghman, MD, Aug. 11, 1911. Graduated with BA from John Hopkins University, 1933; MBA from University of Miami, FL, 1954.

Inducted USN, April 29, 1944. Trained boot camp, Perry, VA. Thereafter, assigned to Aerography School (meteorology), Lakewood, NJ. Then transferred to CASU #24, Wildwood, NJ, NAS. Studied thereafter at Aviation Storekeeper School, Jacksonville, FL, NATTC. Last assignment NAS, New York, CASU 21. Honorable discharge on March 5, 1946 at Personnel Separation Center, Shelton, VA. Rating SKV3/c. Even though possessed enough points for earlier discharge, was retained because was in the Supply Corps. After induction, two weeks later older recruits not drafted. In January 1942 sought commission USN without success.

Medals: American Area, WWII Victory.

Married Adele Jules 1935, now have three daughters: Rose, Peggy and Sandra. Also grandchildren and one great-grandson. Retired as a stockbroker in 1974, Ft. Lee, NJ and moved to Jerusalem, Israel, 1975-86. Reunited with family again in Rockville, MD where he is retired.

Following relatives served in US Armed Forces: cousins in WWI; Edwin Fleishman, Arbert and Isaac Jacobson; others in WWII; Bro. Milton W. Kronsberg, cousins: Dr.

Moses Jacobson, Meyer Jacobson, Saul B. Jacobson, William Jacobson, Melvin Jacobson and G. Vernon Horowitz.

After ending Navy service in WWII, joined JWV Post in Charleston, SC and been a loyal member of JWV since then. In 1947 in that city, chaired committee of about 15 WWII Jewish war vets and with others formed Synagoguc Emanue-El there. They acquired a surplus Army chapel, which was the first home of the congregation and he became its first president.

In Jerusalem in 1982 as a member of Post 83 in the US, with Post 180 P.C. Mike Volpin and small number of Jewish war vets re-organized State of Israel Post 180. It had been chartered February 1972. Later in a visit to Jerusalem, the national executive director of the JWV and officials of the JWV approved formation of six local Israeli Membership Committees, in six cities, under the authority of Post 180. He served as first chairman of the new Jerusalem Membership Committee and now continues as a member of Post 180, and attend meetings of Post 692, Rockville.

After his return to the US, he located the personal archives in 1992 of Rear Adm. Solomon S. Isquith, USN. "I met him and his wife in 1936 when I lived in Charleston, SC and he was in the Navy." The files of the admiral were held by his sister-in-law and brother-in-law in Kingstree, SC, whom he also knew. "I negotiated with them to turn over all the files to the National Museum of American Jewish Military History of JWV, Washington." The Isquith memorabilia included Adm. Isquith's USN Cross for heroism at Pearl Harbor, Dec. 7, 1942. He evacuated most of the Navy personnel as officer of the day, from the US *Utah* which had been hit. He passed on to the museum his personal recollections of Adm. Isquith and his wife, since he knew him in his Navy career and retirement.

BENJAMIN KRONICK, born Aug. 15, 1909 in Minsk, Russia. Member of Army, Signal Corp as a private. Served in W. Lafayette, IN (Purdue University). Served from July 1918-November 1918.

Married Molly Kahn Kronick, two children, Naomi and David. Employed by Hatfield Wire Company, NJ and Dubois Uniform Company, NY as manager. Resided in Scobey, MT and West Orange, NJ. Died May 21, 1970.

DAVID C. KRONICK, born Sept. 4,1932 in New York City, NY. Served in Army's QM Corp as private first class. Basic training at Ft. Dix, NJ. Tour of duty- Idar-Oberstein, Germany (Nabollenbach QM Depot).

Medals: Marksman, German Occupation, Good Conduct and National Defense Service.

Married Jeanette Siedband Kronick, Dallas, TX; no children.

Graduated New York University, BS 1956 and MBA 1964 (management). Businessman and president of Dynamics Group, Inc., advertising specialties, printing distributor.

Served six years in the New Jersey Legislature as assemblyman for the 32nd AD and presently serves as executive director of economic development for the township of North Bergen. Also serves on a number of boards including the American Heart Association, Hudson Liberty Council of Boy Scouts, Temple Beth-El of North Bergen, P.E.R.C. (shelter for the homeless).

HERBERT C. KRUPP, was born in Bayonne, NJ on Dec. 8 ,1923. Enlisted in USN, Dec. 1, 1942. Did boot camp at Great Lakes, IL, December 1942- February 1943. Then to Aviation Metalsmith School at NTS Navy Pier, Chicago, IL. Assigned to Quonset Pt., RI as seaman first class. Trained as

ABATU at Quonset Pt., then transferred to CASU- six: VR-2, San Francisco, CA as second class A.M. Transferred to VR-10 VR-12 NAS, Honolulu, HI. Then discharged from Lido Beach, LI on Feb. 20, 1946 as first class A.M.

Graduated University of Illinois, February 1949. Married Sheila in April 1952. Have daughter Ellen, two sons, Steven and Jeffrey and five grandchildren.

Retired from self employment in wholesale meat and provision business after 38 years. Member of Post 18, JWV, Bayonne, NJ.

HARRIET KUHN, born Nov. 25, 1924 in Brooklyn. Entered Coast Guard on Nov. 24, 1944. Served as storekeeper third class. Stations included Palm Beach, Sheepshead Bay, Boston and New York City.

Awards/Medals: Honorable Discharge Button and Service Lapel Emblem.

Discharged May 7, 1946 as storekeeper third class.

She and her husband had two children, both married, and two grandchildren. Her husband passed away.

PHILIP KULE, went into the service with the name Philip Kulichefsky. Born in Brooklyn, Oct. 9, 1923. Graduated high school 1942.

Entered USAF April 1943. Had basic training in Greensboro, NC. Volunteered for Gunnery School and became a flight engineer on a B-17 as a tech sergeant. Served with the 8th AF, 487th BG, 389th BS. Flew 19 missions over Germany. On the 9th mission was shot down, parachuted out and captured by the Germans. Was in a prison camp until Gen. Patton's 3rd Army liberated them.

Decorations: Purple Heart, Air Medal with two OLCs, POW Medal and New York State Distinguished Service Cross.

Participated in Ardennes, Central Europe, Rhineland (Battle of the Bulge).

Married 45 years, three children and six grandchildren. Owned a restaurant for many years and is now retired.

DONALD SANFORD KULKIN, born March 20, 1932 in New Castle, PA, graduated from New Castle High in 1949 and drafted into the Army (Korean War) January 1953.

Being in the meat business, was sent to Food Service School after 16 weeks of basic training at Camp Breckinridge, KY in the 101st Airborne.

Sent to Linz, Austria to the 124th Mobile Surgical Hospital as a medical veterinary meat and food inspector.

He earned Good Conduct, Overseas and Expert Marksmanship medals; received several commendation letters from company commander.

"Looking back, I was the only Jewish boy who served in the Korean War from New Castle."

After his tour of duty overseas, he was transferred to the Boston AB in late 1954. Was honorably discharged January 1955.

Met and married Myra Lita Brayman of Boston and have lived in Framingham, MA for 37 years. They have a son Matthew who is married to Carol and has two children, Justin

and Mariah. A daughter Joni Rose who is married to David Lebov and has one child, Harrison Louis Lebov.

He has been a member of JWV Post 157, Framingham for 35 years.

He was the president and owner of the Brothers Supermarket.

ABNER KUPERSMITH, was a member of the 127th Evacuation Hospital attached to the 3rd Army. He was stationed in Camp Bowie, TX in 1943. He was one of the soldiers that took Dachou Concentration Camp in April 1945.

LEO J. KURLAND, born April 11, 1920 in New York City. Inducted into Army Feb. 12, 1943. Served in Ft. Bragg, NC; Ft. Benning, GA and Camp Chaffee, AK. Shipped to Philippines and finally to Japan where he was chief file clerk (Tech IV) for XIV Corps HQ. Discharged March 12, 1946. Member Post #218.

"As an observant Jew who put on T'filin every day, I found that in most instances I was respected for my observance." An interesting episode was as follows: Passover came out during the basic training period. Several of the other Jewish trainees in the barracks were loudly boasting how they were going to town the following night (for the Seder) to get drunk and have a good time. This riled one of the Gentiles who yelled out "You guys don't deserve to go to town- I don't see you getting up before reveille to put the straps on like Kurland does." "This indeed was a gratifying reaction to my observance."

MORRIS H. KURTZER, born April 15, 1923, Elizabeth, NJ. Enlisted Dec. 8, 1942, and served in the USAF as radar mechanic with the 306th BG(H), HQ, 8th AF. Stationed at Truax Field, WI; Boca Raton Radar School, FL; Thurleigh, England; Normandy; Northern France; Ardennes; Rhineland and Central Europe.

Memorable experience was serving during Battle of Bulge getting B-17 bombers ready to fly support.

Discharged Dec. 28, 1945, as sergeant. Received the American Theater Ribbon, EAME Ribbon, Good Conduct Medal and WWII Victory Medal.

Married Doris Calman Nov. 19, 1950; they have two sons, Charles and William, and four grandchildren: Richard, Allison, Sarah and Aaron. Member of JWV, post commander, county commander. Retired podiatrist, he was in active practice 45 years.

Older brother, Nathan, was a sergeant in Patton's 3rd Army; served in European Theater and was wounded in Aachen, Germany. His younger brother, Edward, served in the Merchant Marine with the rank of ensign and he had some memorable moments traveling the Atlantic Ocean.

JERRY KUSHNER, (SSG), USMC, was a member of 14th Signal Co., USMCR, Brooklyn, NY, 1947-1950. Called to active duty and sent to Camp Pendleton, CA, July 1950. Fleet Marine Force, Pacific Pearl Harbor, HI, August- November 1950. 1st Amph. Tractor Bn., Korea, December 1950-November 1951. Operation against enemy forces in south and central Korea receiving the Korean Service Medal with one Battle Star and the United Nations Service Medal. Left Korea by directive of Anna Rosenberg, secretary of war, that anyone who had served one Christmas in Korea would not spend a second. Left Korea on USS *Noble* on Nov. 28, 1951, arrived Kobe, Japan, Dec. 7, 1951. Boarded the USNS *Gen. John Pope*, Dec. 8, 1951 and arrived in San Francisco off of Alcatraz Island on Dec. 21, 1951. Final duty was at Marine Corps Supply Depot in Philadelphia, PA and was released from active duty Feb. 28, 1952.

Memorable experience: Was able to leave the war behind when it came to the high holidays. They were flown to Pusan from Teagu along with people from other branches of service. The total number of Marines was three. The total number at the service was about 80 people including nurses from the Navy Hospital Ship and the land hospital. "These were the first American women we had seen in a year. The service was inspiring and we had a special time."

Presently he is self employed.

SEYMOUR FLEISHFARB KUVIN, born Nov. 30, 1924 in Newark, NJ. Enlisted April 15, 1942 with US Army, 69th Div., 271st Inf., Co. H. Served as mortar gunner while participating in Battle of the Bulge; crossed to Remagen Bridgehead, Europe and met Russians at Leipzig. The unit disbanded after the war in Europe. Rank at discharge, corporal.

Recipient of Bronze Star, Purple Heart, Combat Infantry Badge and theater ribbons.

Widower with one son, one daughter and two grandchildren.

MD- first a pediatrician, now a forensic psychiatrist. Past president Morris Co., NJ Medical Society.

Past commander VFW Post 2608, member JWV.

HERBERT J. KWART, was a staff sergeant bombardier stationed in England during WWII with the USAAF. He was a member of a B-17 flight crew attached to the 534th BS of the 381st BG, 8th AF. He flew 35 bombing missions over enemy occupied territory and Germany during 1944-45. Four of the missions were to Berlin, Germany. He and his flying crew members had their aircraft attacked by German fighters and endured heavy flock concentrations, however no crew members were injured, but their B-17 aircraft was heavily battle damaged during several missions, but managed to return to England to fly again.

Decorations awarded were the DFC and the Air Medal with six OLCs.

After the war, graduated from the University of Miami and pursued an occupation as an engineer. He is currently retired and living in San Jose, CA. Married to Roslyn S. Kwart for 45 years, has a son Steven who lives in San Francisco and a daughter Debora who lives in Austin, TX.

LOUIS KWART born in 1891 at Hazleton, Pennsylvania. Enlisted US Army in September 1917. Served with Rainbow Div., AEF. Stations included Ft. Hood, TX and France. Participated in battles of Bellow Woods, Ardennes. Wounded at Bellow Woods.

Awards/Medals: Purple Heart and Bronze Star.

Discharged in 1918 at Camp Dix, NJ with rank of sergeant.

Son Herbert lives in California and two daughters, Harriet and Renee lives in Florida.

Occupation was master electrician. Deceased.

SAUL W. LAKIER, (COL) AUS, (RET), born Nov. 27, 1931. Master's degree from Temple University; advanced work University of Pennsylvania and US Army Command and General Staff College.

Served with 3rd Armd. Div. and 6th Armd. Cav. Regt. on border patrol in Germany, 1954-56. Active duty 1961-62 for Berlin Crisis and afterwards reservist on staffs of 79th Div., 157th Separate Inf. Bde. and 358th Civil Affairs Group. Awarded Meritorious Service Medal upon retirement as colonel in 1984. Continuing military connections as volunteer with the Employers Support for the Guard and Reserve (ESGR) and at military bases in Israel.

Civilian career: personnel officer for Philadelphia Recreation Department and administrative services director, Revenue Department until retirement in 1988.

Active as volunteer for Israel (Sar-El Program), JWV, Reserve Officers' Association, Military Order of the World Wars.

Married with two children. Both he and wife Rose served as volunteers at Israeli military bases each year from 1989-93.

EMANUEL LAMB, born New York City, Oct. 16, 1925, entered Army on Jan. 6, 1944. Basic training at Camp Wheeler, GA, then joined 89th Inf. Div. at Camp Butner, NC. Arrived overseas in December 1944, joined 83rd Inf. Div. Fought in Battle of Bulge, received Bronze Star, then fought all the way to the Rhine River and then across the central part of Germany, across the Elbe River, 65 miles from Berlin and met the Russians there.

After the war transferred to the 4th Armd. Div. in Passau, Germany and did occupation work; spoke a little German, became an interpreter. Transferred to the 102nd Inf. Div. at the POW camp at Flossenberg, Germany where they held SS prisoners for interrogation for the Nuremberg Trials.

Left Germany in April 1946, discharged at Ft. Dix, NJ, May 4, 1946. Most of his working years in the men's clothing and apparel field, in sales.

Married to Ruth with three children: Marc, Ronald and Kate and grandchildren Barry Wacholder, Jessica and Joshuah.

Member of JWV since 1946. Past commander, Post 478, 1952-1953.

WILLIAM LANDEY, born Chicago, IL, Feb. 15, 1913. Entered service April 23, 1943. Served in field artillery, Sound and Flash Unit. Stationed with 770th FAB Bn., B Btry. at Camp Bowie, TX, 292nd FA Obsn. Bn., B Btry. at Camp Bowie, TX and 7th Army in France and Germany. Participated in the end of the Battle of the Bulge, Rhineland and Central Europe.

Memorable experiences was breakthrough of Siegfried Line and release of Holocaust victims from Daucha.

Awards/Medals: American Theater Campaign, EAME Theater with two Bronze Stars.

Discharged Nov. 29, 1945 with rank of technician fourth grade.

He is a widower with two daughters in DC area and one in Palo, West Point graduate, served in Korea.

Today he is retired and volunteers at JWV Museum Headquarters building.

GARY LANDMAN, born and raised in Wyoming. Called up with the Wyoming National Guard, the 115th Mechanized Cav. in early 1941. Became company's first sergeant. Discharged in 1946.

Got married and raised family in California. Died in Los Angeles.

JACK LANDMAN, born and raised in Wyoming. Moved to Chicago, IL where he enlisted in the Army, being over 30 years old. Fought in the battle for Saipan.

Had wife and daughter. Died in Phoenix, AZ.

JOSEPH LANDMAN, born and raised in Wyoming. Enlisted with the AAC in February 1941. Served with the 8th AF in England. Discharged in 1945.

Married had one daughter living in California. Maybe still alive.

ABRAHAM LANDSMAN, born and lived in the Bronx, New York City till he was drafted June 1942, at age 28. Assigned to 368th AAA Bn. of the 701st AAA Regt., Ft. Totten, New York City. Was made a company clerk. Since the majority of the men wore glasses, Walter Winchell called us the "Cockeyed Commandos."

Eventually transferred to 1024th Eng. Treadway Bridge Co., Camp Gordon, GA. Company consisted of 134 men, five officers and probably 80 trucks.

Arrived Germany, via Camp Lucky Strike, France, February 1945. Company assigned to many outfits: Eng. Combat Bn., Corps, Armd. Div., etc.

Dismantled and loaded treadway bridge equipment. Constructed bridges over bomb craters, small rivers. The largest bridge was over the Danube River, 1,100 feet, built in conjunction with another bridge company. Most bridges built under enemy fire. Many time the company had to remove 500 pound bombs. One man killed, one man wounded.

On May 6 arrived in Czechoslovakia. The people threw flowers, kissed many of them, and threw packages of food at them. Next day they were "forced" to dance with women for many hours while they were fed fresh eggs, scrambled eggs, milk and beer. Slept that night on a goose down feather bed in a citizen's home.

Returned to the States July 2, 1945 and went to Camp Patrick Henry, VA for additional training prior to going to the Pacific. Discharged as staff sergeant, December 1945.

ESTHER RUDOLPH LANG, born in New York City, brought up in Wilkes-Barre, PA. Enlisted in the Navy Waves, Aug. 9, 1943. Went to Hunter College in the Bronx for boot camp, then to Stillwater, OK for yeoman training.

Was then stationed in Washington, DC and fought the Battle of the Potomac. Actually, she was assigned to BuOrd in the old Navy Department Building.

"On the train to Stillwater they pulled up alongside another train filled with men, we waved, flirted, when we suddenly realized they were German prisoners."

Discharged from the Navy Dec. 11, 1945 with rank of yeoman second class. Received American Campaign Ribbon and Victory Medal. Returned to Wilkes-Barre and married Saul Lang. They are both retired and now live in Media, PA.

While in Stillwater the Jewish community from Tulsa, OK brought in food and had a party for Jewish service people, Army, Navy, Waves. It was great!

SAUL LANG, (SSG), Post 134, born April 5, 1915 in Wilkes-Barre, PA. Inducted in the Army May 2, 1942. Basic training at Camp Shelby, MS, then desert training in California and Louisiana. Then to Ft. Dix to Newport News, VA and shipped out to French Morocco with the 85th Div. of the 5th Army. Then to Italy.

Fought through the Poe Valley, helped free Rome, and on up to the Alps when Germany surrendered. Saw Mussolini hanging upside down in Milan. "One time we were so close behind the Germanys when we went into a house the food was still warm on the table."

The chaplain assigned to their unit was Rabbi Kazis the rabbi from Temple Israel in Wilkes-Barre.

Received the Bronze Star, Good Conduct Medal, EAME Medal.

When the war ended in Europe, they were assigned to go to the Pacific through the United States. The day they boarded ship the war in Japan ended.

Discharged Sept. 30, 1945, returned to Wilkes-Barre, married Esther Rudolph after her discharge from the Navy. They now reside in Media and are retired.

MICHAEL U. LANGENDORFF, born Feb. 26, 1923 in Berlin, Germany. Became US citizen April 1943. Inducted into the US Army, May 1943. Military service was with Medical Corps. Stations included South Carolina, Iceland and England.

Memorable experience was an incident of racial hatred. "At a poker game in England an argument broke out. I was called a Jew b———. Needless to say that didn't sit very well with me. A fight broke out which resulted into my having to leave the platoon. I was transferred to Iceland."

Awards/Medals: ETO Medal, 18 months Overseas Stripes and Good Conduct Medal.

Discharged as private first class.

Married in 1957 and have three children and four grandchildren.

Today he is retired from having his own commercial printing business. In spare time he works as a hospital volunteer.

LEO LANSKY, born Dec. 30, 1918 in Milwaukee, WI. Entered Army July 1942. Served in Adjutant General's Dept. Stations included Camp Roberts, Camp Chaffee and New Delhi, India.

Memorable experience was the anti-Semitism.

Awards/Medals: Good Conduct and Asiatic/Pacific Medal.

Discharged May 1946 with rank of first lieutenant.

Married 50 years with two daughters and four grandchildren. Today he is retired.

ARNOLD J. LAPINER, (MAJ) AUS, (RET), WWII; Inf., ETO, CIB, US Military Government- Denazification Specialist; OIC Civilian Internment Enclosures (for second rank Nazis, Nuremberg rejects), 1948-1963 Counter Intelligence Corps. WIA Korea, Purple Heart plus other thoracic adornments.

Social studies teacher, 1964-84. ("The Army was easier.") EAM Post 724. Freelance writer.

Married to Golda. Daughters Linda and Judy. Grandchildren: Marc, lawyer for Madison Square Gardens; Sharon, national education supervisor, Young Judea; Lauri (secretary, cablevision).

GOLDA E. LAPINER, born 1930 in Newark, NJ. BS in education, New Jersey State Teachers College. 1950s WAC. Training: basic officers at Ft. McClellan, AL; Army Intelligence Center at Ft. Holabird, MD. Duty, Counter Intelligence Corps.

Life member Post 724. Past commander Nassau-Suffolk District Council. Past DEC, past NEC.

Married to Arnold. Daughters Linda and Judy. Grandchildren: Marc, Sharon and Lauri.

SEYMOUR S. LAPPEN, (SSG), born in Hartford, CT, Feb. 3, 1920. With only one semester remaining to received BS, BA degree at Boston University, was drafted and inducted into the Army on Jan. 16, 1942. Basic training at Camp Lee, VA. Then placed in the Finance Department, 3rd AF.

June 4, 1942 sailed on the *Queen Elizabeth* to be one of the first American troops to come to England. October 1942 participated in the invasion of North Africa. Stationed near Oran and Constantine for one and a half years. Enjoyed the hospitality of local Jewish families and their synagogues. Spent over one year in Corsica with 8th AF. Returned to US February 1945 and discharged Oct. 10, 1945.

Completed last semester at Boston University and received degree in 1946. In 1947 married Phyllis Rosenberg, daughter of Mabelle and Louis H. Rosenberg of Lawrence, MA, a former national vice-commander of JWV.

Member of JWV Post 45 since 1946. Continued with the family fireplace business in Hartford. (Established in 1892.) Retired in 1992 and enjoying four granddaughters.

HOWARD J. LASKER, National Boy Scout Committee chairman, entered service Sept. 9, 1941 and was commissioned in the USAAF in April 1943. He was assigned to the 317th Fighter Control Sqdn. which was dispatched to China to join the 14th AF, "Flying Tigers." In August 1944 he was sent with a small detachment to Hsian to organize and operate a Fighter Control Network for the northern part of China. The original mission was to direct fighter control air defense and to provide fighter protection for the B-29 operation from China. This was later extended to include fighter sweeps over enemy held territory.

For his successful organization, operation and command of the unit, he was awarded the Bronze Star Medal by direct order of Gen. Claire Chennault and the Chinese Medal of Honor by the Chinese government.

Since leaving the service, he has lived in Albany, NY with his wife Shirley. They have two children and three grandsons. He is a past commander of Albany Post 105 and has served as National Scouting chairman since 1979.

SOLOMON LASKY, (TECH 5), born March 11, 1913 in New York City. Military service Dec. 11, 1943- Jan. 16, 1946. Basic training at Camp Shelby with the 65th Inf. Div. Overseas to Italy, France and Germany and assigned to 7th Army, 45th Inf. Div., 157th Inf. Regt., Anti-Tank Co.

Fought hard battles at Siegfried Line, Aschaffenburg, Rhine Crossing and Nurnberg, all in Germany. "We were the first American troops to enter Dachau, April 29, 1945 and received the shock of our lives. The sight of the load of death in the box cars, crematorium and the stack of naked bodies drove us wild." After liberating Dachau they took Munich and the war ended.

He was a private first class in the infantry and received his T/5 when he was transferred to Military Intelligence Service (MIS) after the war.

Decorations: Combat Infantryman Badge, Bronze Star Medal with OLC, EAME Service with three Bronze Service Stars, WWII Victory Medal and Army of Occupation Medal with Germany Clasp.

Married to Jean, April 15, 1937 and have two sons and five grandchildren. Retired from Department of Army, 1974. Member of JWV Post 125, New Jersey, 47 years.

IRVING LAUTMAN, was inducted on Sept. 2, 1943 at Camp Upton, NY. Discharged on Nov. 29, 1945. After basic training he joined the 36th Armd. Inf. which was already in Normandy on June 19, his 19th birthday. Fought the entire hedgerow campaign until the breakout in France on July 26. In this campaign he won the Bronze Star Medal for valor. He also received the EAME Medal with four Campaign Stars, Victory and American Campaign Medals.

Then they engaged the Germans through all of France, Belgium and up to the Siegfried line. Because of their rapid movement, they outran the supply trains and stalled. On a patrol on or about Sept. 2, 1944, they were overrun by an enemy attack and eventually surrendered to become a POW.

"I did hard physical labor until they found out I was Jewish. Then I was segregated from the regular prisoners and put together with an all Jewish group. As it turns out, we were lucky that it was close to the end of the war, seeing what they did in the camps. Now we were given work in the forest, cutting down, and cutting up the logs into one meter lengths. This was tougher work as we were all from the big cities and had never seen an axe or a two-man saw."

Before he retired, he managed a clothing factory for most of his working life. He and his wife have three children and seven grandchildren. Born in Brooklyn, NY in 1925. At discharge, he was a corporal.

HARRY LAVINE, born March 11, 1915 in Syracuse, NY. Graduated from Central High School and attended Syracuse University. Was in the livestock and meat business. Entered the service in June 1942. Trained at gunnery schools and was assigned to a crew, training in various parts of the country. Received the rank of staff sergeant. Left for Africa in March 1943 and while there met his brother Sanford.

On Aug. 4, 1943 he was on his 35th mission from Africa to the Ploesti oil fields in Rumania. The mission was accomplished, but on the return trip the plane was struck in the Bombay area. Harry was fatally injured. He was buried by civilians in a cemetery in Caserta, Italy. He was 28 years old.

Awarded the Air Medal with seven OLCs. The plane and its crew were chosen to tour the United States in a bond drive because of the record they had achieved.

In January 1949 the body was returned to the United States. He lies at rest in Temple Adath Yeshurun Cemetery with his brother Sanford, also killed in action. Survived by father Morris, brothers, Bernard and Abe and sisters: Miss Sadie Lavine, Mrs. Anne L. Pearlman and Mrs. Emily L. Goldman.

SANFORD V. LAVINE, born Aug. 8, 1918 in Syracuse, NY. Attended Syracuse schools. Graduated pre-medicine at Syracuse University in 1940. Enlisted in January 1941. Was a member of Co. G, 108th Inf. Transferred to the Air Corps in November 1941. He graduated as a bombardier at Kirkland Field, Albuquerque, NM with the rank of lieutenant. He left for Africa in April 1943 with the 12th AF. Later was transferred to the 15th AF.

Lt. Lavine returned from a mission over Sicily on July 4, 1943. On July 5, 1943 a bombardier was taken ill. Sanford volunteered to take his place on that mission. The squadron was attacked by a large number of planes over Catanis-Syracuse, Sicily. Five bodies from the crew were recovered. Killed in action on July 5, 1943 at the age of 24.

Awarded the Air Medal with four OLCs.

In September 1949 the body was returned to the United States. He lies at rest in the Temple Adath Yeshurun Cemetery with his brother Harry, also killed in action. Survived by father Morris, brothers, Bernard and Abe and sisters: Miss Sadie Lavine, Mrs. Anne L. Pearlman and Mrs. Emily L. Goldman.

NATHAN LAZAROWITZ, born Jan. 7, 1916 in Brooklyn, NY. Inducted US Army May 1941. Basic training in Pine Camp, NY. Assigned to 4th Armd. Div. One and a half years later, after serving as tank technician, was recommended to attend the Armored Force Officers' Technician School. After graduation was assigned warrant officer and attached to 11th Armd. Div.

During the Battle of the Bulge was awarded the Bronze Star Medal for heroic conduct against an armed enemy. A tank was disabled by mortar fire and with disregard of personal safety, he made necessary repairs to this as well as several other vehicles while under heavy enemy mortar fire.

Other decorations: Bronze Star Medal, American Campaign Medal, EAME Campaign Medal, WWII Victory Medal, Meritorious Service Unit Plaque.

Discharged March 27, 1946.

Joined JWV and has been and still is an active member, having been commander four times and served in every echelon in JWV. Life member of Post 50, Brooklyn, NY and presently with Post 265 CVE, Deerfield Beach.

Married to Helen and has one son Barry and daughter Sharyn and five grandchildren: Brian, Russell, Justin, Lauren and Jakie. Happily retired in Florida.

EMANUEL LAZARE, born April 30, 1918 in New York, NY. Entered US Army July 8, 1943. Served in field artillery-2nd Armd. Div., Btry. B, 957th FA Bn. Stations included Ft. Dix, Ft. Bragg, England, Normandy, Omaha Beach, Berlin, Ardennes, Central Europe, Northern France and Rhineland. Participated in battles in Normandy Beach, Omaha Beach and Battle of the Bulge.

Memorable experience was being highly impressed at Carentown with airborne troops and manner in which they were dug in. Also, upon entering German villages all Germans denied being Nazis as the Nazi uniforms were found buried in the yards.

Awards/Medals: Bronze Star Medal, Distinguished Unit Badge, EAME Service Medal, Good Conduct Medal, Purple Heart, five Battle Stars, Bronze Star with cluster.

Discharged Nov. 3, 1945 with rank of staff sergeant.

Has two daughters and four grandchildren.

Today he is retired from many years in retail shoe business and enjoying grandchildren.

MARTIN LAZAROFF, born Nov. 14, 1924 in Syracuse, NY. Attended Croton, Madison and Central High schools. Member of YMHA. Worked at General Electric.

Died March 8, 1945 at the age of 20. Survived by parents, Esther and Louis Lazaroff; sisters, Mrs. Sam Teckler and Mrs. Perry Morgan; brother Yale Lazaroff. Cousins, Harry and Sanford Lavine also died in service.

MILTON LAZARUS, born in Elizabeth, NJ on Sept. 1, 1916. Graduated Union College. Entered Army February 1942. Trained Camp Croft, SC, then Ft. Benning OCS, graduated as second lieutenant. Assigned to 111th Inf. organization. Did guard duty on eastern shore. From there went to Pacific. Regiment involved in mop-up operations on islands Saipan, Tinian, Pelilieu.

Their most harrowing experience involved a mop-up after invasion. Spent the last few months of service on Iwo Jima until his honorable discharge as a first lieutenant in April 1946.

Married to dear wife Rose. They have four children and six grandchildren. He now lives in Paramus, NJ and is retired since 1983, having spent 38 years with an import/export firm where he was assistant to the president; being involved in every day operations.

_____, "While my military service was undistinguished and uninspiring, I did enlist in the Marines and volunteered for overseas service." He joined the Marine Reserve before finishing high school in 1947 and was called to active service at the outbreak of Korea. Receiving a deferment till graduation from American University in 1951, he entered officer candidates course. Although he didn't graduate, he finished the course and remained in the Marines.

While at Camp Lejeune, NC, he volunteered for Korea. Although he was a sharpshooter, he could type; so was assigned as personnel clerk in the 7th Marines and made buck sergeant. He stayed seven months, then sent to Treasure Island, CA for release in March 1953.

"I enjoyed my military experience: It was there that I became a man. In retrospect, I believe that I should have made the Marines my career."

HAROLD J. LEBETKIN, born Aug. 24, 1911. Entered Army on Jan. 4, 1943. Stations included Ft. Campbell, KY; Ft. Ord, CA; Mare Island; Navy Yard; Ft. Custer, MI; Ft. Wadsworth; Staten Island; Ft. Dix, NJ; Bridgton, NJ; Indiantown Gap, PA and Howard Field, Panama.

Awards/Medals: American Theater and WWII Victory Medal.

Discharged Feb. 3, 1946 with rank of private first class at Ft. Deven, MA.

Married Beverly Wald on Jan. 5, 1947. Had two daughters; lost one to cancer. Retired June 30, 1975.

Member of JWV Post 45, Hartford, CT.

SHERWIN LEBEWITZ, born July 8, 1929 in Minneapolis, MN. Entered USAF in August 1950. Member of 7110th Support Wing stationed in Wiesbaden, Germany.

Awards/Medals: European Occupation Medal and Good Conduct.

Discharged August 1953 with rank of sergeant.

Married with son Joel, 39 and daughter Roselynn, 37. Owns a furniture store.

MEYER LEDERMAN, born Oct. 13, 1924, Brooklyn, NY. Graduated Kings Park Central, June 1942. Gave up a farm deferment to enlist May 14, 1943, processed at Camp Upton; basic at Ft. Riley, KS; served in U.S. Horse Cav., 29th Regt. until transfer to Mecz. Cav., 23rd Cav. Recon Sqdn., 16th Armd. Div. Other stations include Ft. Riley, KS; Camp Chaffee, AR; POE New York and overseas.

Detached to Patton's 3rd Army as recon. 1st unit on scene of Flossenberg concentration camp in Czechoslovakia. German camp guards were seen fleeing up into the hills. They were ordered to continue on to Pilsen, Czech and leave camp to rear units (were never mentioned in its liberation in May of 1945). As they left they were almost blown to bits by a German ambush left behind for this purpose and eliminated the threat.

Memorable experiences: being at Ft. Riley while Mickey Rooney was there for his basic; meeting and talking to Lt. Dan Dailey also at Ft. Riley; observing German Armistice team taking off for meeting in France; having lunch in Czech. with Ingrid Bergman and supper with Jack Benny who were on tour with Larry Adzer, Martha Tilton and Dave DeWinter.

Awards/Medals: American Campaign Medal, WWII Victory Medal, EAME Campaign, Central Europe, with one Battle Star and Good Conduct Medal. Discharged April 29, 1946, as T/SGT, radio operator, gunner and first aid tech.

Married Audrey and has three children and six grandchildren. Presently member of Rabbi Lief JWV Post 488 in Huntington, NY.

RONALD L. LEDWITZ, (LTC), an infantry officer spent much of his service in the Army Reserve and retired in 1983. Ron came out of retirement to volunteer for Operation Desert Shield/Desert Storm. He retired again in June 1993.

Prior to Operation Desert Shield/Desert Storm, Ron worked for Macy's Data and Credit Services as the controller of banking and mailing services.

Ron, who is now retired, and his wife Rhoda, a nurse, live in Ocean Township, NJ. Ron and Rhoda between them have five children and Rhoda is expecting her first grandchild in July.

HERBERT LEE (NEE LEPAVSKY), born June 9, 1926, in Chicago, IL. At the time of WWII and while in his senior year in high school, he took and passed the Air Corps mental exam. When he went to take the physical exam for the Air Corps he was told he needed an operation, but to continue the physical and if he passed it and had the surgery he would be accepted into the Air Corps. He had the operation (which was successful), turned 18 and registered for the draft.

When he was called for his Army physical he told the OIC he had been accepted by the Air Corps. His exact words were "once you get the letter from the President, you're ours." Entered the Army on Nov. 8, 1944, at Ft. Sheridan, IL. Two or three days later he was aboard a train on his way to Ft. McClellan, AL and was told by the OIC that they were in the Infantry which meant "we had a strong back and a weak mind."

Went through 16 weeks of infantry basic training at Ft. McClellan, then to Ft. Ord, CA. On April 28, 1945, he was shipped to the Philippine Theater of Operations, arriving there on May 17, 1945. After six months of combat the war with Japan was over and they were shipped to Japan as occupational troops.

At the time he was a private first class and had been awarded the Good Conduct Medal, Army of Occupation/Japan Medal, Combat Badge, Asiatic-Pacific Theater Ribbon with one Battle Star, Philippine Liberation Ribbon with one Battle Star and the Victory Medal. Made sergeant major of the 1st Bn., 27th Inf. Regt., 25th Div., returned to the States on Sept. 23, 1946 and was discharged Nov. 25, 1946.

NORTON L. LEFF, born in Bronx, New York City. Member of infantry, 36th Div., 143rd Regt., Co. E. Stations included Camp Blanding, FL and Camp Edwards, MA. Participated in battles in Africa and Salerno, Italy.

Memorable experience was being captured in Salerno, June 9, 1943- March 12, 1945. Mr. Leff's unit worked its way up the beach and dug in. The next day the unit was attacked by a German tank division. Mr. Leff aided two injured comrades by escorting them from their foxholes to a safe location. This house was later hit by German artillery and Mr. Leff was captured along with his buddies and became a POW for 20 months.

Awards/Medals: Bronze Star, American Ex-POW and campaign medals from Africa, Italy and Europe.

Discharged September 1945 with rank of corporal.

Married Beatrice, 1942-1980; deceased. Married Rea H. in 1982. Have six children: Susan, David, Roger, Eugene, Alan and Jill. They have six grandchildren.

Today he is retired and resides in Pembroke Pines, FL. He is an active JWV member. Held five terms as post commander of Posts 682 and 451. Was department commander of Florida and member of the National Executive Committee (NEC) and secretary of the NEC.

RACHEL ROSEN LEHMANN, born June 1, 1903 in New York City. Entered WAC in January 1943. Member of 1229th SCSU. Stations included Ft. Dix, NJ; Camp Upton; Patehogue and basic at Daytona Beach, FL. Stayed at Ft. Dix and was at Camp Upton for six months to close reception center. He always attended Jewish services.

Discharged January 1946 with rank of technician 4.

He is single with no children. Volunteers with Atlanta Opera. Appears on stage as a super.

MEYER J. LEHRER, was with the 924th Aviation Engineer Regt. in the ETO. Their job was to build air fields under any and all kinds of conditions. Through England, France, Belgium, Holland and Germany. To enable the fighter bombers and medium bombers of the 9th AF and to operate bases always within effective range of their targets.

He was trained as a mechanic in repairing and maintaining all types of equipment. Was also assigned to a 50 mm anticraft machine gun whenever needed. He was in the armed services over three years.

He received five Battle Stars for campaigns: Ardennes, Central Europe, Normandy, Northern France and the Rhineland.

MAX I. LEHR, (DDS), born Aug. 25, 1908 in Tiraspol, Russia. Enlisted Oct. 15, 1942. Served as dental officer, 11th BG, 7th AF. Stations included Bolling Field, Washington, DC; Langley Field, VA; Hickham Field, HI and Central Pacific area. Participated in battles at Gilbert Island, Marshall Islands, Marianas Islands and Air Offensive of Japan.

Memorable experience was when asked to conduct Sabbath services for the enlisted Jewish personnel aboard the freighter *President Tyler* and witnessing the Magen David emblem waving atop the ship's mast.

Awards/Medals: Asiatic/Pacific Theater of Operations Campaign Ribbon with three Bronze Stars, Bronze Star Medal, American Theater Campaign Ribbons, Meritorious Citation and WWII Victory Medal.

Discharged March 3, 1946 with rank of major.

Married to Nannette since 1947, daughter Judy, son Les and four grandchildren.

Today he is practicing general dentistry.

Member of the JWV Post 347 and a life member of the American Legion.

"For meritorious service in connection with military operations against the enemy from 1 September 1943 to 1 November 1944. During this period, Captain LEHR, as dental officer of a heavy bombardment group, performed his duties in an exceptionally meritorious and outstanding manner. Captain LEHR fabricated a compact mobile dental unit which enabled him to carry on his dental services with minimum disruption when the unit moved to four different forward bases. As a result of his foresight and extreme devotion to duty in the construction of this mobile unit, he was able to render complete dental treatments in the combat zone in a rapid and definite manner, and also to provide prosthetic appliances which would have otherwise required hospitalization or evacuation of the patient. Captain LEHR's outstanding professional ability, patience, loyalty and untiring devotion to duty reflects highest credit upon himself and the military service."

RAYMOND LEHRER, was born in Rochester, NY on May 18, 1925. He enlisted in the Army March 1943. Basic training was at Ft. Knox, KY. He was transferred into Anti-Tank Co., 339th Inf. Regt. of the 85th Inf. Div. Enroute to the Mediterranean Theater of Operations (North Africa) December 1943. Trained in landings and mountain climbing while in North Africa. Enroute to Italy March 1944. While in Italy participated in three battle campaigns. Received the following awards: Combat Infantryman Badge, Bronze Star, EAME Campaign Medal with three Bronze Service Stars, Good Conduct Medal, Presidential Unit Citation, American Campaign Medal, Army of Occupation Medal (Italy), WWII Victory Medal and the Blue Fourragere.

At war's end and after returning to the States December 1945, as a private first class, he re-involved himself in the Boy Scout movement. He is an Eagle Scout and this past year received the highest award a local council could present, which is the Silver Beaver Award.

For the past 16 years he has been involved with the New York Guard, a voluntary outfit. He is a LTC in charge of the S1 section. They meet at a local armory. Their function includes providing assistance wherever and whenever either the Army Reserves or the National Guard is called up to active duty as in the case of Operation Desert Storm.

He is married to Phyllis W. since June 1947 and has one daughter and one son. His daughter is married to Michael Karpoff and his son is married to Eve Etta. They have three grandchildren, two girls and a boy.

He was employed with the Defense Logistics Agency as a quality assurance representative until his retirement November 1991.

He is a past commander of the David J. Kauffman Post 41, Rochester, NY; past president of Beth Joseph Center; past commander of the Veterans Memorial and Executive Council of Rochester, NY; member of DAV and VFW. Very active in synagogue activities both in New York and Florida.

DAVID LEIBOWITZ, (SSG), 180th Inf. Regt., 45th Div., was born Oct. 10, 1916. Entered Army Dec. 11, 1942. Received basic training as infantry rifleman. Was assigned as platoon guide handling distribution of rations and equipment for a 47-man platoon. Had responsibility for all heavy weapons and led platoon and battalion scouts in patrolling enemy terrain. Was in charge of defensive field fortifications, land mines and barbed wire fences. Promoted to assistant squad leader with administrative duties in regards to a 12-man squad. Took command if squad leader became incapacitated.

Served in battle campaigns at Anzio, Naples, Rome, Southern France, Rhineland and Central Europe.

In April 1945 was wounded by mortar shell burst to right side of body in Germany. Lost sight in right eye and hearing in right ear.

Decorations: EAME Theater Ribbon with five Bronze Stars, Purple Heart with OLC and Combat Infantryman Badge.

Discharged Oct. 19, 1945. Past commander of Cohen-Lurie Post 129, JWV; member of Temple Emanuel of Canarsie, Brooklyn, NY. Worked in own custom merchandise business.

Married to Sarah 47 years. Three children: Phyllis, Adele and Martin. Three grandchildren: Stuart, Rennie and Michael.

Died Jan. 19, 1993.

HARRY B. LEIDER, born Philadelphia, PA, May 19, 1918. Valedictorian West Philadelphia High School Class of 1936. Attended Temple University Evening School and elected president of the Jewish Student Association. Elected director of the North Philadelphia Realty Board and later president of West Philadelphia Realty Board.

Married Harriet Fink on Sept. 14, 1941. Drafted July 21, 1943 and graduated the Infantry School, Ft. Benning, GA as a high speed radio operator. Assigned to Co. C, 36th Armd. Inf. Regt., 3rd Armd. Div. on June 17, 1944. Participated in all battles through France, Belgium and Germany and wounded in action at the beginning of the Battle of the Bulge. Flown back to England for treatment. Reassigned to AF as a radio operator.

Later attended Biarritz American University in France and appeared in William Saroyan's play *The Time of Your Life* in Biarritz and Paris.

He is currently a vice-president of Yentis Realtors in Philadelphia and a member of the Main Line Board of Realtors. His hobby is singing bass with the Mainliners Barbershop Chorus and Elder Statesmen Quartet.

He is a Mason and a member of the DAV MOPH VBOB and 3rd Armd. Div. Association. A past commander of the Haim Parnes Post JWV.

Lives in Broomall, PA with wife Harriet. Has two sons, one a fellow realtor and the other a stock broker.

HOWARD H. LEINER, inducted into Army ASTP Program in June 1943 in Camp Upton, NY. Basic infantry training in Ft. McClellan, Birmingham, AL. Army Specialized Training Program, Manhattan College, Bronx, NY in fall of 1943. Shipped to Camp Shelby, MS, 81st US Inf. Div. in Spring 1944. Served as small mortar man in weapons squad. Entered Officer Training Program in Spring 1945 in Ft. Benning, GA before the division was shipped to Germany in time for Battle of the Bulge. Most of his training non-coms were killed in that battle as well as several friends. Graduated as second lieutenant in June 1945. Duty as second lieutenant in infantry training program in Florida. Sent to Tokyo, Japan in Fall 1945 after Japan capitulated. Served in QM Corps in a service company in the Naval Paymaster's establishment in Tokyo.

Returned to US in June 1946. Discharged from Ft. Dix which terminated his Army life. Completed his BS degree in chemistry from City College of NY, in February 1947. Married his Atlanta sweetheart in April 1947.

MICHAEL DAVID LEINKRAM, was born March 30, 1925 in Port Chester, NY. Entered the USN Oct. 3, 1943 and reported to the NTS in Sampson, NY. Attended Electrician Mates' School in Sampson, NY.

Served on the USS *Griffin* and the USS *Vogelgesang* in the American and European Theaters of war.

He was awarded the American Theater Medal, the European Theater Medal with one star and WWII Victory Medal.

Discharged as fireman first class on April 20, 1946.

Married Helen Sarah Pechanick on Oct. 10, 1954. They have two children, Mark Irwin Leinkram, born Jan. 31,1958 and Sharon Ruth Leinkram, born April 18, 1959.

He worked in several areas of engineering including electrical and bio-medical. His hobbies were tennis and golf. Michael died July 25, 1986.

HAROLD LEITSTEIN, born Dec. 4, 1918 in Brooklyn, NY. Entered NY National Guard, Sept. 30, 1939. Activated Oct. 15, 1940. Served in Army's field artillery, D Btry., 104th FA, 27th Div. Stations included Ft. McClellan, AL, Ft. Ord, CA and Hawaiian Islands on March 15, 1942 where he built beach and other fortifications. Participated in battles of Gilbert and Marshall Islands and Battle of Okinawa.

Memorable experience was in landing of Eniwetok Atoll. Landing craft got caught on reef. They were dropped off about 100 yards from shore. He slipped on coral reef and got blood poisoning.

Awards/Medals: Navy Commendation for Eniwetok, WWII Victory Medal, Asiatic/Pacific Medal with three stars, American Defense, American Campaign and Good Conduct.

Discharged Aug. 15, 1945 with rank of corporal.

Married to Cecelia in 1948 and have two daughters, Bette and Iris, and six grandchildren.

Retired from New York City Fire Department. Member of Hempstead Post 312.

MARTIN H. LEITZES, was born in Brooklyn, NY on April 27, 1919. He graduated West Orange High School 1938, went on to Casey Jones School of Aviation. Subsequently, enlisted in 1939 in the AAC. However he wasn't sworn in until 1940. Originally planned to make a career in the military. Took basic training at Mitchell Field, NY, soon after went on maneuvers, and then back to Mitchell Field where

Pearl Harbor was bombed. They shipped out to Hamilton Field, CA and then out to the Pacific destination unknown at the time. Winding up in Australia and then New Guinea.

In Australia he made his first flight and from then on he was hooked. His primary job was flight mechanic/flight engineer. He received the Asiatic/Pacific Medal with three stars, American Defense, Freedom Medal, Good Conduct, two Presidential Unit Citations with two palms.

Married to Dorothy Picarsky. Have three sons, one daughter, four grandchildren and one great-grandchild. Due to a serious illness, he was forced to go into semi-retirement from the insurance business. Now he works with his stamp collection and does volunteer work with the North Miami Beach Police Department as a handicapped specialist and do mobile patrol work as the eyes and ears of the police department.

STANLEY LENGA, born Oct. 5, 1927 in Bronx, NY. USN, FASRON-3, USS *Siboney*, service medals. Aerial photographer - 3rd Class (AF3c).

While on photographic mission over Middle East, the pilot of his escort plane did a low pass over an Arab gunnery position. Upon return to carrier, pilot and photographer were called to captain for reprimand. During reprimand the captain stated he received a message complaining about the incident. The captain answered the message "Please inform your gunners of the difference between a five pointed star and a six pointed star." This occurred in 1948.

Discharged Oct. 5, 1948.

Married to Ida, three sons: Charles, Richard and Arthur. Resides in Escondido, CA. Was in photography and management. Photography hobby for JWV and Citizens Patrol of Escondido.

DR. MAXWELL JEROME LEON, was born in New York City, July 8, 1909. Entered Fleet Marines (Seabees) Bn. 125, July 19, 1943. On Guam helped construct Fleet Hospital #3, stood guard duty, laboratory specialist pharmacist second class, nursed paralyzed sailors. Personal citation by Navy Secretary James Forrestal. Honorable discharge Dec. 11, 1945.

Members of his family also participated in the war effort: father Solomon J. Leon, WWI, offered free tailoring service- Army; mother Adele Rose Leon, WWI, free meals and board- Army; father-in-law A.M. Brissman, WWII, machine inspector for labor department- Army; mother-in-law Ida Pearl Brissman, WWII, financed wives of servicemen; brother-in-law Leo Brissman, sergeant, Coast Arty., Germany- WWII; brother-in-law Meyer H. Brissman, ESQ., sergeant, Army Adj. General- WWII; brother-in-law Gerald Brissman, AF machinist, tech sergeant- WWII; cousin Robert K. Leon, killed in action, Germany- WWII; cousin Leon Holster, communications officer, Coast Guard- WWII and cousin Murray Gottlieb, sergeant, US Army, France and Germany- WWII.

Married Rebecca I. Brissman 1939, daughter Roberta [illegible] physician and son Stuart Jay, attorney.

Graduated City College and New York College of [illegible]odiatric Medicine, licensed in 1953.

Taught applied science in New York with license (biology, chemistry and mathematics). New York State certificate for principal of high school. Have 50 Year Gold Award as member of United Federation of Teacher, 47 years as member of American Medical Technologists and 40 years as member of the New York State Podiatric Medical Association and 40 years as member of the American Public Health Association.

DR. MILTON J. LERNER, was born in Newark, NJ on April 15, 1922. Graduated Kearny High, June 1940. Entered service Nov. 10, 1942, Ft. Dix, NJ. Assigned to 102nd Inf. Div., Camp Maxey, TX. Finished basic training early April and transferred to A.S.T.P. at Carnegie Tech, PA. Finished two years engineering course in one year- May 1944. Assigned to Air Corps at Truax Field, WI for radio operator training. Completed training at Scott Field, IL. Shipped overseas from Newport News, VA on the USS *Billy Mitchell*, October 1944 and 49 days later arrived in Bombay, India. After one week train ride across India to Calcutta, flown by C-87s to base unit 1330- Jorhat, Assane, India. Made first familiarization flight Dec. 6, 1944 and by June 6 made 88 round trip "Hump" flights to China.

Awarded DFC, Air Medal with Bronze OLC, Good Conduct Medal, Distinguished Unit Citation Badge, American Defense Ribbon, Asiatic/Pacific Ribbon with three battle stars, China War Memorial Medal, by the Government Republic of China, New Jersey Distinguished Service Medal.

Discharged Nov. 10, 1945.

Graduated Rutgers University with BS in June 1948 and Temple University Dental School, June 1952.

Married Beverly December 1946, two daughters, Judith and Vicki, one son Terry and five grandchildren.

Charter member of JWV Post 538. Held all post offices including quartermaster since 1963. Retired from private practice, June 1992, but continued as Kearny school district's dentist.

PHILIP LE SHAY, was born in Easton, PA on Dec. 16, 1917. Inducted on April 24, 1941 at Wilkes-Barre, PA. Served at Infantry Replacement Center from April 29, 1941- Aug. 5, 1941. Transferred to Co. M, 110th Inf., Aug. 6, 1941. Discharged May 9, 1942.

He was reassigned on Dec. 5, 1942 to Camp Barkeley, Abilene, TX, 90th Inf. Div., Co. I, 357th Inf.

He was married on April 10, 1943 to Cecile Rubin from Eaton, PA at the Army post in Abilene, TX. Went to Ft. Dix and Port of Embarkation. Sailed to Southampton, England on March 23, 1944. In convoy on the English Channel, June 4, 1944. Landed by LCIs on Utah Beach, D plus 2. Wounded three times. Received the Bronze Star "For Heroism in ground combat", Aug. 8, 1944. Returned to Battle of Bulge. Participated in Hedgerow fighting in Normandy, Battle of St. Lo and St. Mere Engles, Battle of Bulge.

Discharged Sept. 16, 1945 as private first class.

Authorized medals and badges: Sharpshooter Badge with Machine Gun, Sharpshooter M-1 Rifle, Marksman Badge with Carbine Bars, Combat Infantry Badge, Purple Heart with two OLCs, Bronze Star with OLC, EAME Campaign with five Battle Stars; WWII Victory Medal, Army of Occupation WWII, American Defense Service, Good Conduct Medal and Honorable Service Lapel Button, WWII.

Went back to school and graduated from Illinois College of Podiatry and Foot Surgery in 1949. Practiced podiatry for 36 years in Allentown, PA.

Married 50 years to wife Cecile, have one daughter, Debbie and two grandchildren, Katie and Greg.

Retired and life member of JWV Post 239, life member Military Order of Purple Heart Chapter 90, life member of AMVETS Chapter 7, American Legion Post 576 and attended Co. D, 357th Inf. reunions for the past 20 years.

EDWARD LETTICK, born Sept. 10, 1895. Entered Army Aug. 2, 1942. Served in Finance Department. Stations included Camp Edwards and Ft. Devens, MS.

Awards/Medals: WWII Victory and American Defense.

Discharged May 29, 1946 with rank of tech 5.

Married Helen L. Baylin who is now deceased.

Today he is retired.

HERMAN LEVENSON, was one of the Jewish veterans that served with 392,000 veterans in the Spanish-American War, 1898-1902, in the Philippines. He enlisted Nov. 30, 1899 and served with Co. F, 26th US Inf. Discharged Nov. 29, 1903.

IRVING M. LEVENSON, born July 13, 1916 in St. Paul, MN. Entered Air Force, Sept. 16, 1942. Served as airplane and engine mechanic on 747s. Stations included Europe, England and France.

Discharged March 2, 1946 with rank of sergeant.

Married in 1950 and has two children. Now a widower.

Today he is retired.

SONIA HOFFMAN LEVENSON, born Minneapolis, MN on Nov. 22, 1917. Entered WACS on Nov. 10, 1943 as general clerk. Stations included Europe and France.

Discharged March 2, 1946 with rank of tech 5.

Married March 18, 1950 and had two children.

Died Feb. 5, 1988.

HERBERT LEVICK, served in Australia during WWII.

SHIRLEY WALLACE LEVICK, served as a foreign correspondent with the Office of War Information, stationed in Italy.

DAVID BERNARD LEVIN, born in Philadelphia, PA on Nov. 23, 1922. Graduated Penn State University, February 1944 with BS in industrial engineering. Enlisted in AAC and entered March 22, 1944.

Graduated AF Navigation Course with an appointment as flight officer. Went to radar training and was assigned to B-29s as a radar navigator.

He served overseas in the 20th AF in the Marianas for 14 months. He participated in the Air Offensive of Japan and received the Distinguished Unit Badge and two Bronze Battle Stars.

Presently he is working as in industrial engineer and has been married 45 years to Rita in Hazleton, PA. They have three daughters: Leah, Ilene and Paula, and eight grandchildren.

He has been a member of Conn Kase Post 287, Hazleton, PA and has served in many capacities including commander. He was also commander of the Central District of Penna.

JOSEPH LEVIN, born Minsk, Russia on Dec. 5, 1895. Arrived in America, 1905, settling in New Britain, CT and later moving to Hartford. Entered Army Sept. 19, 1917. Sent to Camp Devens, MA; helped build the base. Landed Cardiff, Wales, 1918. U-boat activity very heavy. Transport ship rocked many times by torpedoes, but never hit. Served in Co. B First Machine Gun Bn. Saw action at St. Mihiel and Muese-Argonne Offensives.

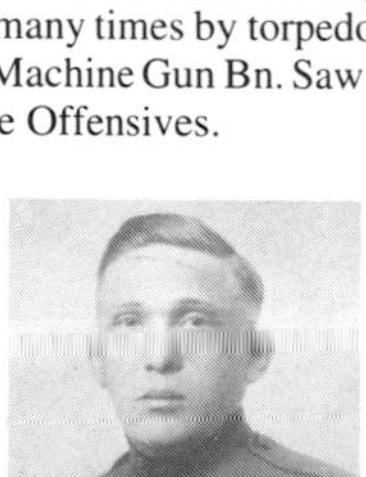

Returned home aboard USS *Von Steuben* called the "Devil Dog" of transports, one of the USN's best known ships, 1919.

"The young Orthodox Rabbi counseling the Jewish boys shipping out told them there would be times when they would have to eat 'treyf.' "Eat it," he said, "but don't enjoy it."

"In Cardiff, the people held a grand reception in a huge hall. They served kippers with all the trimmings. The Jewish boys were delighted."

The war was horrible. Once the troops were moving through the French countryside. It was cold, raining, mud up to their knees, knapsacks like dead weights, exhausted and starved. Coming to a potato field, they devoured the potatoes, mud and all."

"The most profound moment came in the middle of battle. Suddenly, silence... so deep so penetrating, it hurt our ears... Faintly, then louder, the cheers began. The war was over. The armistice declared."

During duties in Army of Occupation, Joseph, deeply disturbed by the plight of starving children, against regulations, took them in and fed them.

He was awed by the Palace of Versailles, especially the hall of mirrors.

Joseph married his childhood sweetheart, Frances Sosin in 1922. Two children, Norman and Thelma; three grandchildren. Did not retire until he was 86.

MEYER LEVIN, born June 5, 1916 in Rochester, NY. Entered AAC on June 6, 1939. Stations included Wheeler Field, HI and Clark Field. Participated in Coral Sea Battle.

Memorable experiences were 60 missions and three bailouts. Awards/Medals: DFC, two Silver Stars, two OLCs, Purple Heart and many others. Killed in action on Jan. 7, 1943. Achieved rank of sergeant.

RAPHAEL A. LEVIN, born July 25, 1914 in Philadelphia, PA, the youngest of six brothers. Graduated from the University of Pennsylvania in 1935 and Jefferson Medical College in 1939. Enlisted Aug. 3, 1942 as first lieutenant Medical Corps. After a year as a psychiatrist at Indiantown Gap General Hospital, sent overseas to join up with the 3rd Div. in Licata, Sicily as Bn. surgeon, 15th Inf. Regt. During rest period after Sicilian Campaign, attended Gen. Patton's formal apology. Landed at Salerno, Italy, waded across Volturno River under fire with the water neck high. Reached Monte Cassino. "Here I survived a direct bomb hit on my aide station at Mignano, but lost most of my men."

After hospitalization in North Africa, reassigned to 105 Station Hospital in Ferryville and promoted to captain. Returned to the USA on June 9, 1944 and assigned to Stark General Hospital, Charleston, SC serving as hospital train commander. Discharged from the service as of June 23, 1946.

Was in private practice of general medicine from 1947-1987. Married Evelyn Jacobs in December 1947. They have two children. son Robert is a psychiatrist in private practice and on staff at Harvard Medical School in Cambridge, MS. Daughter Mina Lea is an internist and professor of medicine at University of North Carolina. Her husband Ronald Schwarz is a gastroenterologist. They have one son Jonathan L.

Now retired and reside at Raleigh, NC.

Decorations: Purple Heart, Medical Badge, American Theater Ribbon, WWII Victory Medal, EAME Ribbon with two stars for Sicilian and Naples Foggia Campaigns.

STANLEY LEVIN, was born on March 7, 1929 in New York City. He attended Evander Childs High School, Bronx, NY and Yeshiva University, New York City. He received BA degree, teachers certificate and Rabbinical Ordination.

He enlisted in US Army Chaplain Corps, June 27, 1955 and took the basic officer Chaplain Course at Ft. Slocum, New Rochelle, NY, July- August 1955. He was assigned to Brooke Army Medical Center, Ft. Sam Houston, TX and served till June 1957 when discharged.

He married Janet Weiss, Crown Heights, New York City, June 27, 1954. Their eldest son was born at Ft. Sam. They organized post wide in 1956 and spent a month at Ft. Polk, LA

organizing a seder in 1957. Janet and three month old son came along (not according to orders).

He then served as rabbi in Cumberland, MD, 1957-58, where their daughter was born. They moved to Baltimore, MD in July 1958. He was a supervisor of Orthodox schools affiliated with the Board of Jewish Education and a lecturer at the Baltimore Hebrew College until 1970. He also served as librarian. Dr. Louis L. Kaplan, president of the college, kindly made it possible for him to work part-time and attend the University of Maryland Law School. He graduated in 1963 and was admitted to the Bar in 1963.

He served as an assistant city solicitor in Baltimore for a year and then engaged in private practice. Their second daughter and second son were born in Baltimore.

They came to Israel in 1970 and have lived there since then. He is on the faculty of Tel Aviv Law School and engaged in private practice. Janet passed away in November 1993. Their four children and 22 grandchildren live in Israel.

He is a recent member of Israel's JWV Post and just joined the USA JWV.

ABEL LEVINE, served in Army-Infantry during WWI with 107th Inf. Regt., 27th Div. Stations included Europe and France. Participated in Hindenburg Line Offensive, September 1918.

Memorable experience was when he took command and reorganized his platoon when higher ranks were wounded and continued the attack. He was severely wounded.

Awards/Medals: DSC (US), Distinguished Conduct Medal (ENG.), Croix deGuerre (FR.), three Battle Stars, Purple Heart with clusters.

Discharged May 12, 1919 with rank of corporal.

Had wife Ann, daughter, two step-sons, five grandchildren and four great-grandchildren. Died June 13, 1963.

BENJAMIN LEVINE, was born and raised in Nashua, NH, Nov. 39, 1907. After high school he managed several jewelry, automotive and department stores in Maine and New Hampshire.

Deeply affected by the news of Pearl Harbor, he enlisted in the Army Jan. 27, 1942 at age 34. He served three years as sergeant in the Medical Corps, helping to build fine station hospitals in primitive jungle conditions. He was in the East Indies and New Guinea Campaigns. While stationed in Australia at the 2nd Station Hospital, he took care of "the boys" who flew on the *Suzy Q* B-17.

Honorably discharged April 4, 1945 as a tech 4 medical technician.

In 1947 Ben married and settled in Maine. He operated one of the first soft-serve ice-milk stands in Maine for 23 years and also had a laundromat business at two colleges in and near Portland.

In 1949 while attending a synagogue service in Houston, TX, he recognized the voice of the cantor. He was thrilled to hear again the voice of the cantor who had conducted services in New Guinea.

Ben and his wife Esther had two daughters, Tobey and Garrie. Tobey, a film location scout and coordinator, works on many Rescue 911 television shows. Garrie is owner/broker of a Re/MAX office in N. Dartmouth, MA.

Ben died June 25, 1993 at 85.

GARY B. LEVINE, born July 15, 1946 in Brooklyn, NY. Drafted into Army on July 20, 1966. Served with 199th Lt. Inf. Stations included Vietnam and Ft. Meade, MD. Served in Vietnam, January 1967- January 1968. Then served at Ft. Meade, MD and was in first unit sent into Washington, DC to stop the Martin Luther King riots in April 1968.

Awards/Medals: CIB, Purple Heart, Vietnam Service, Good Conduct Medal, etc.

Discharged July 19, 1968 with rank of sergeant E-5.

Married to Myra with one son Jeff. Today he is driving a limousine.

GEORGE LEVINE, born Aug. 18, 1920 in Worcester, MA. Enlisted in Signal Corp Aug. 20, 1942 at Boston, MA. Served with Army's 581st Anti-aircraft Arty., Automatic Weapons Bn. Stations included Ft. Devens, MA; Ft. Monmouth, NJ; Camp Davis, NC; Ft. Eustis, VA; Camp Stewart, GA; European Theater while attached with 1st Army. Participated in Battle of the Bulge, Rhineland, Central Europe, Battle Remagen.

Memorable experience was entering Buchenwald concentration camp, third day of liberation and visiting aunt and uncle in Stoke, England.

Awards/Medals: WWII Victory Medal, Good Conduct Medal, American Theater Campaign, EAME Theater Campaign, Army of Occupation, Germany.

Discharged April 5, 1946 with rank of corporal.

Married to Beverly who is presently Department of MA Auxiliary president. Three children: Mark, Barry and Wendy.

Past commander of Department of MA, 1990-91; post commander of Worcester Post 32 at present (also 1984, 85, 86). Semi-retired after being self-employed for 32 years. Life member of JWV, Beverly Life, past president of Commonwealth Lodge B'nai B'rith, 1969 and 1981. Also member of JWVA.

GERALD B. LEVINE, born April 21, 1931 in Long Branch, NJ. Received BA in economics in 1952 from Muhlenberg College. Drafted into Army Sept. 9, 1952. Sixteen weeks basic training at Ft. Knox, KY, Tank Div., 32nd medium military occupation specialty, tank commander. Twelve weeks Finance School at Ft. Benjamin Harrison, IN. August 1953 transferred overseas to Europe. Stationed in center of France Poitier to finance control, paying the troops on the supply run known as "Red Ball Express" from La Rochelle on the coast of France to Verdun on the German border.

Memorable experience was being honor guard at 1953 Kentucky Derby.

Awards/Medals: Overseas Medal.

Discharged in August 1954 with rank of E4, came home on the *Private El Johnson*, the smallest ship allowed to cross the Atlantic, during Hurricane Carol, 40 feet waves. Ship arrived five days late to find no berth open.

Married to former Florence Goldberg (PNP) in 1987. Together they have three sons, one daughter and nine and a half grandchildren.

Former owner of Levine Motor Corporation, 1954-1987. Now happily retired and currently director of Ocean Independent Bank, Ocean, NJ.

HAROLD LEVINE, born in Bronx, NY on Aug. 21, 1919. Investigator for an insurance company. Drafted into Army March 11, 1941 to Ft. Dix, NJ. Trained in various stations and finally assigned to Tank Destroyer Bn., Camp Hood, TX Winter maneuvers in Louisiana and Otto National Forest, M. to test tank destroyer equipment.

Overseas to England August 1944. Served with Patton's 3rd Army through France, Battle of the Bulge in Belgium Rhineland and Germany proper. Discharged after four and half years of service.

Married to Elaine in June 1944, a New York City school teacher. Two children, Iris (d.) and Jesse. Three grandchildren: Janine, Beau and Jedd.

Head of nationwide adjusting firm. Retired 1985 to East Hampton, NY.

IRVING LEVINE (AL), born May 26, 1910 in Nashua, NH. Entered the Army on Feb. 8, 1942. Served overseas in Europe and in the Pacific Theater. Never would talk about the war. Had shrapnel wound in leg but never received Purple Heart.

Discharged Nov. 10, 1945 with rank of technician 5.

Married Ruth Bentson in 1948, had two children, Melissa and Robert and one grandchild at time of death. Managed shoe stores in Houston, TX. Died in 1980.

JOSEPH E. LEVINE, born in Pittsburgh, PA on June 7, 1917. Entered US Army Nov. 28, 1941. Received honorable discharge Sept. 13, 1945, corporal. Member of the 36th and 517th Field Arty. Units known as "Long Toms". Served in North Africa, Italy and South Pacific. Arrived in England 1942. North African campaign, 1942-1943. "Had to read Hebrew Prayer Book to convince Jewish children that I was Jewish." Invasion of Sicily, July 1943. Injured by shrapnel August 1943, awarded Purple Heart Medal. Invasion of Salerno, Italy September 1943. Participated in Naples-Foggia Campaigns. Rotated to United States November 1943.

Arrived in Bougainville November 1944. Participated in invasion of Luzon and Battle for Manila starting January 1945. Decorations: European Theater with three Bronze Stars, Asiatic/Pacific with two Bronze Stars and Bronze Arrowhead, Philippine Liberation Ribbon with one Bronze Star.

Charter member of Parkway Jewish Center and member of Board of Directors, chairman of Cemetery Committee.

Charter and life member, JWV Post 718, Monroeville, PA.

Retired from Westinghouse Electric as corporate manager of Materials Transportation Compliance.

Married to Syma, 45 years - three children, seven grandchildren.

SAMUEL S. LEVINE, born Oct. 9, 1921 in Brooklyn, NY. Attended NYU, 1940-1942. Enlisted in the US Army July 1943, Camp Upton, NY. Sent to radar schools in Madison, WI; Chanute Field, IL and Boca Raton, FL. Served in Italy in the 347th BS as a radar counter measures mechanic during 1944 and 1945. Discharged at AAF ORD Greensboro, NC in December 1945.

Prior to enlisting in the service, Sam Levine was a mechanical draftsman in the ordinance department of the Brooklyn Navy Yard from 1942 to the above enlistment date.

After his period of service, he completed his MA in education and taught in the New York City high schools from 1940 until he retired in 1980.

Married to Maxine G. and they have children Judy Nachlas, Amy Koehler and Michael Levine (deceased). Grandchildren: Joshua Nachlas, Rebecca Nachlas, Tamar Levine, Ariel Levine and Danielle Koehler.

Samuel has lived in Brooklyn, NY; New Britain, CT; Woodside, NY and East Meadow, NY.

ALBERT S. LEVINSON, born June 14, 1919 in Norfolk, VA, the oldest son of Samuel and Rose Levinson.

He entered the Navy in 1941, the day after Pearl Harbor was bombed. He was assigned to Norfolk NB Commissary N.O.B. until 1943 when he was assigned to the LCI *813* and proceeded to Pearl Harbor, HI. From there, his ship was sent to participate in the battle for Okinawa.

Two weeks after the atomic bomb fell on Nagasaki, Levinson and other crew members witnessed first hand the devastation caused by the bomb and vividly remembers that sight to this day.

Mr. Levinson is retired now and was married to the former Renee Goldstein from Brooklyn, NY for 46 years until her untimely death in 1992. They had three sons: Larry, Stanley and Marty; six grandchildren and two great-grandchildren.

Mr. Levinson received five war time decorations before his discharge in 1945.

He was a member of the JWV Post 158 in Norfolk, VA and Brith Sholom Lodge.

GARY M. LEVINSON, was born in Trenton, NJ on Jan. 26, 1944, inducted into the Army on April 5, 1966, basic and AIT training at Ft. Riley, KS. Served with units of the 9th Inf. Div. in Vietnam. Participated in several of the largest campaigns of the war including Operations Manhattan and Junction City. Assigned to 18th Airborne Arty. Corps after returning home from RVN, discharged in April 1968.

A graduate of the Bordentown Military Institute and the Pennsylvania State University. Worked for the Pennsylvania Department of Labor and Industry developing job training programs for veterans and disabled veterans. Currently is chief of the Division of Recruitment, Pennsylvania State Civil Service Commission, Harrisburg, PA.

Received Army Commendation Medal, Vietnam Service and Campaign Medals, NDSM, PUC. Member and past officer of JWV, member of VFW, life member of DAV, co-founder of Vietnam Veterans Organization, Lancaster.

Married to Toni Dana Levinson, four children, resides in Mount Joy, Lancaster County, PA.

PAUL LEVINSON, born in Manhattan, New York City on the lower east side, Nov. 27, 1926. Graduated Samuel Gomper's V.H.S., the Bronx, NYC. Served in the US Army Infantry, 4th Armd. Div., 54th Signal Co. Is a Korean veteran.

His father and mother, Harry and Mary Levinson, arrived as immigrants from Poland in 1906 at Ellis Island, NYC. They raised four boys: Jay, Julius, Sol and Paul. Jay served as a sergeant in the US Army and was assigned as a lawyer at the Nuhrenburg Trials. Julius served in the USAF, Sol served in the US Army Inf., 45th Div. and was in the invasion of North Africa, Sicily, Anzio, Palermo, Rome and Southern France.

All four brothers received US service medals and Sol received the Combat Infantry Badge and the Purple Heart and was wounded twice during the invasions.

Had not their father and mother, Harry and Mary, immigrated to the beloved USA, all would have died in the Holocaust instead of serving in the US Army and helping to defeat the Nazis and the Axis Nations and North Korea. "Rest in peace Mom and Dad. Only in America. The good Lord bless it always."

STANLEY D. LEVINSON, born May 16, 1948 to Albert and Renee Levinson in Norfolk, VA. He left Norview High School in 1967 to enter the AF and volunteered to be sent to Vietnam in 1968. After completing a four month combat security police course at Schofield Barracks, HI, he was sent to Binh Thuey, Vietnam. After his tour of duty for his country, he returned to Langley AB, VA and received an early out to become a Norfolk, VA police officer in 1971.

In 1980 he joined the Army Reserves after graduating from college with a bachelor's in criminal justice. He served with the 80th Inf. Div. and the 88th Military Police Co. until 1993 when he was accepted to the Old Dominion University's ROTC Program as a military science instructor for the freshmen students assigned there.

He is married to the former Cheryl Castello from Powellsville, NC and has a daughter Tanya, 16 and son Sam, 12.

Mr. Levinson plans to retire from the Norfolk, VA Police Department and Army Reserves in 1997.

During his military career which spans the Vietnam, Granada, Panama and Desert Wars, he earned a total of 17 decorations and awards. He has been a member of the JWV Post 158 in Norfolk, VA since 1970 and the Brith Sholom Lodge.

CHARLES LEVY, born in Philadelphia, PA. Entered the Army, 103rd Div. on Feb. 1, 1941 and then transferred to AF. Stations included Ft. Meade, MD; Camp Hood; Big Spring AB; Harlingen AB, Fairmount and Wendover, UT. Then to Tinion in the Marianas.

Memorable experience was being in plane two in the dropping of the atomic bombs over Nagasaki as a part of 509th Comp. Group.

Awards/Medals: Air Medals, etc.

Discharged April 3, 1952 with rank of first lieutenant.

Has wife Frances, daughters, Sharon, 50 and Sandy, 45, who is married to Jeff. Granddaughter Jodi is married to Ed and is the daughter of Sharon. Josh, son of Sandy, goes to Bucks County Community College.

Today he is retired and makes ladies hat pins.

JACK LEVY, ESQ., 1922-1992, (Posthumous Tribute by his children), "There's no such thing as a good war" Jack Levy told *Riverdale Press* reporters in a front-page interview commemorating D-day's 40th Anniversary (enclosed). Jack's insight came after fighting WWII. Jack patriotically flew the US flag over his top floor terrace every national holiday. Thrice Riverdale JWV Post 267 commander; delegate to National JWV conventions (1983-5); decorated with the Bronze Star, Purple Heart and several other medals, Sgt. Jack Levy's Jewish-American heritage antedated the Civil War on his father's side, (Leo Levy, German-Jewish). Jack's history also reflected the struggles of his mother, (Celia Knapper Levy) who arrived from Odessa knowing Yiddish and Russian, but not English that she eventually mastered without accent.

During WWII, Celia sent Jack another uniform, from Macy's, disliking the inferior quality of government issue cloth. Hearing accurate reports about the shortage of disposable paper goods for US soldiers in Europe, she sent Jack toilet paper, (he often chuckled, "the guys threw it across the room" like streamers).

Jack contracted malaria during basic in Georgia but, enthusiastic to go to the front, Jack faked a "normal" temperature, (immersing the thermometer into ice cubes in a glass of Coca-Cola), to get out of the hospital.

Describing his wound, he said, "I looked behind me to bawl someone out for hitting me when I fell down. I knew I was hit because it felt like a hot rock hit me. I called for medics and drew more fire." Jack knew enough French to find out that a German command post was in an old castle; Frenchmen helped his squad over a wall with ladders, providing directions while under fire, "like an audience giving the hero clues to the plot in a movie house."

Jack was proud of his service but angry about it too. He was decorated for valor in D-day landing on Utah Beach the afternoon of June 6; twice wounded outside of Cherbourg while leading his troops. Jack participated in five major battles and had vivid memories of cold snowy days, "We lost ground every day and finally on Christmas the sun came out and we saw tracks of vapor in the sky," meaning the Allies would soon arrived. In civilian life the Army *Field Manual* remained near him, because "it has everything" anyone needed to know. But, he spoke with profound bitterness about the rampant anti-Semitism in the US military which blocked promotions and opportunities for him and other Jews, starting from Officer's Candidate School (OCS). He nonetheless remained sympathetic to US military involvements— until Vietnam. Consistent with then-official JWV position, he un-controversially stated "support our boys in Vietnam" in public speeches. Yet in his heart he knew it was wrong; he regretted not speaking against it. Subsequently, he questioned "the good war"; the so-called "Big Show" of WWII. He spoke often of one time when he was on night patrol and a German soldier passed beneath the tree where he was stationed. He was certain that they saw each other clearly, although neither one fired a shot; two enemies who, for one moment, held each other's lives in their hands. That moment, made more poignant by televised images of Vietnam, led him to tell the *Riverdale Press*, recalling battles as well as glory, wounds and sadness underlying heroic deeds, "There is a tremendous thrill in combat, this is a danger and that's why it's hard to eradicate war... There's no such thing as a good war."

Armistice Day 1945, returned to NYC. College: NYU; Graduated NYU Law in 1948. Member NY Bar and Bar of US Supreme Court. In 1952 married Sylvia Feelus Levy, loving and devoted wife until his death. Children: Fred Levy and Ilise Levy Feitshans, Esq. Grandchildren: Jay and Emalyn Levy Feitshans.

MARVIN WILLIAM LEVY, born Feb. 21, 1925 in Albany, GA. In 1933 family moved to Brooklyn, NY. Graduated from the High School of Music and Art in June 1943. As an aspiring cartoonist worked in comic books until inducted in the Army, Sept. 21, 1943.

Trained at Ft. McClellan, AL as an infantry replacement. At age 19 fought with the 9th Inf. Div. in the Battle of Normandy, June 1944. Wounded June 23 attacking Cherbourg and subsequently received a medical discharge from the Army on Jan. 6, 1945.

Entered Pratt Institute in September 1945 and continued career as cartoonist and commercial artist. Recently produced a documentary video based on his WWII drawings. Also writing a book on the Cherbourg Campaign. Decorations: Purple Heart, Bronze Star and Combat Infantry Badge.

Married to Barbara. Have three children and two grandchildren. Brother Murray fought in WWII and brother Daniel served in the Korean War.

ROBERT M. LEVY

MARTIN LEWENSTEIN, born Oct. 10, 1921 in New York City. Entered AF on Aug. 13, 1942. Served with 463rd BG at Foggia, Italy, March 1944- September 1944 on 50 missions.

Awards/Medals: European Theater, Air Medal, Presidential Unit Citation and five Battle Stars.

Discharged on Oct. 1, 1945 with rank of tech sergeant.

Married Marie on Nov. 21, 1951. They have daughter Lisa Stockbridge and two grandchildren, Christopher and Melissa.

Served three years as director of guidance. Former teacher of social studies and English. Today he is a retired guidance counselor. Sub*mitted by Jack E. Shames.*

CAROL MARTIN LEWIN, in July 1943 WAAC Training Center, Ft. Devens, MA was the beginning of a 13 year adventure that led her to a 30 year civilian career. From Massachusetts, she spent seven years at seven bases in the South during which she graduated from Army Navy Gen. Hospital for medical tech. Just before going to Panama in 1946 for three and a half years, she graduated from QM School.

Her final year in the Canal Zone, the Army gave her a home at Ft. Clayton and her mother was the first WAC mother to live with her daughter in the Caribbean command.

Returning stateside in 1950 to Fitzsimmons Army Hospital, CO to Murphy AH Massachusetts to Medical Field Service School, Brooke Army Medical Center for Electroencephalography Procedure Course. Back to Murphy, then Ft. Bragg, Ft. Bliss, Ft. Sheridan and back east to Ft. Jay, NY. Put on TDY for 20 days to St. Albans Navy Hospital, NY where she ended up for 16 months as chief instructor of their EEG Procedure Course. While taking her Navy students on a field trip to Columbia-Neurological Institute where she met her husband-to-be. They were the first Jewish couple to be married in St. Albans Naval Chapel, a WAC sergeant first class to a civilian. From there to West Point Military Academy, where she was honorably discharged awaiting the birth of her daughter, who was born at St. Albans Naval Hospital.

In civilian life she stayed in the field of neurodiagnostics and went from technician to registered certified technologist to administrator of one of the 20 accredited EEG schools nationwide under the AMA. She was also president of a regional EEG Society, NY, NJ and CT, for 16 years, and then vice-president of a National Society to executive director of that society starting 10 pre-board classes in seven states.

"I have my military career to thank for my successful civilian career." She has been a member of JWV for over 30 years and am adjutant of post 303, Sun Cities, AZ for the past six years.

GOLDIE BOUID LEWIS, born Aug. 8, 1917, Chicago, IL. Joined the WAAC Feb. 22, 1943, Chicago, IL until August 1943, then became WAC AF with duty as clerk/typist. Basic at Ft. Oglethorpe, GA and from there was sent to Eastern State College, Commerce, TX for six weeks. Went to Albuquerque, NM, Kirkland Field for 21 months where she held several different positions.

Sent to Tucson, AZ and worked in the General Office Sect; attended Personal Affairs Consultant Crs. at New York; then sent to San Angelo, TX. Discharged as a sergeant Nov. 22, 1945, from Des Moines, IA. Received the WAAC Service Medal, American Campaign, WWII Victory Medal and Good Conduct Medal.

Went to work for the Chicago Milwaukee Railroad, Marshall Field and the U.S. government in Cleveland, OH. Retired at the age of 76 after working at a flower shop as manager and phone order clerk. Joined the JWV in Maywood in 1946 for a short time as it was to far to travel. Rejoined Skokie Auxiliary 328 in 1962 and has been president three times, state dept. president one term and she helped form the FEM VET Post 192 and has been post commander three times, hospital chairperson and serviceman chairperson.

Married and widowed, she has three children, two daughters-in-law and four grandchildren.

SIMON LEWIS, born Feb. 28, 1918, Beacon, NY. Entered the service Sept. 18, 1942, serving in the Dental Corps, 87th Div. Stationed in England, France, Germany, Camp Grant, Camp McCain and Ft. Jackson.

Memorable experiences: visiting Buchenwald in May 1946; a seder in Katzenelenbogen, Germany; meeting wonderful Jewish people in Rockford, IL.

Received the Bronze Star Medal; discharged May 7, 1946, with the rank of major.

Opened his private practice in Beacon one month after his discharge. He sold the practice in 1981 and now fills his time with volunteer work, operating the Medicaid dental clinic at Vassar Brothers Hospital in Poughkeepsie.

Resides with his wife, Florence, in Beacon. Has two daughters, a son-in-law, Nick, and two grandchildren.

ILSE LEWY, was born in Wuppertal, Germany. She was forced to flee Nazi persecution, arriving in America in 1938 along with her parents, Herman and Margaret, as well as her sister Martha.

Ilse began a new life, finishing high school and achieving her nursing degree in San Francisco. She joined the US Army Nurse Corp on April 24, 1945. One poignant and heroic chapter from her time in the Philippine Islands: Although Ilse was persecuted for her Jewish identity and remains committed to it, she heroically and selflessly baptized a dying Christian serviceman who requested this sacrament in a time and place when there was no minister or chaplain available. Perhaps the fact that she has been persecuted allowed her to always view others without discrimination.

In the Philippines she met John K. Lewy, whom she married in 1947. They had three children: Leonard, James and Deborah. Ilse continues to live today in the house she bought with John in San Francisco.

Ilse is grateful for the life she has had in America. She is proud of the service she saw in the US Army which helped insure democracy for future generations. Because of the terrible days in Nazi Germany, more than many Americans, she knows the value of her citizenship in and service to this democracy. *Submitted by Leonard J. Lewy.*

SIDNEY H. LICHTER, born Brooklyn, NY on May 16, 1943. Enlisted in USAF on Aug. 31, 1966. Basic training at Amarillo AFB, TX; technical training in computer programming at Sheppard AFB, TX. Duty at HQ USAF, the Pentagon (1967-1971); Ching Chuan Kang (CCK) AB, Taiwan (1971-1972); Maxwell AFB, AL (1972-1975); Schierstein ADM, Germany (1975-1980) and Gunter AFS, AL (1980-1986).

Meritorious Service Medal, AF Commendation Medal with OLC, AF Good Conduct Medal with five OLCs, National Defense Service Medal, Vietnam Service Medal with four Battle Stars, AF Longevity Service Awards Ribbon with three OLCs, NCO PME Grad Ribbon with OLC; Republic of Vietnam Campaign Medal; Overseas Short and Long Tour Ribbons; Republic of Vietnam Gallantry Cross with Device. Graduated from USAFE NCO Academy and USAF Senior NCO Academy.

Retired Sept. 1, 1986 in the grade of master sergeant (E-7).

Married the former Vivien A. Toulson of Endicott, NY; two daughters, Valerie and Ruth.

Today he is working as a computer programmer in the private sector.

DANIEL S. LICHTENSTEIN, born Sept. 14, 1916 in New York City. Served in the AF while stationed in Montgomery, AL.

Married first wife Ruth and had three children: Judith, David and Naomi. Second wife was Rita. His brother Harold served in the Army's Engineer Corps.

Daniel is now deceased.

HAROLD LICHTENSTEIN, born Oct. 20, 1921 in Brooklyn, NY. Enlisted in the Army on Sept. 11, 1942 and entered active duty on June 30, 1943. Served as an information and education specialist. Stations included basic training for infantry at Ft. McClellan, AL, ASTP Civil Engineering, Clemson College, SC, Pacific Theater, Okinawa and Okinawa Base Command I & E.

Memorable experience was the Okinawa typhoon, October 1945.

Awards/Medals: Asiatic/Pacific Theater Ribbon and WWII Victory Ribbon.

Discharged March 17, 1946 with rank of private first class.

Married to Betty and has three children: Sally, Michael and Joyce. Brother Daniel served in AF, now deceased.

Received pharmacy degree and worked for Veterans Hospital, Washington, DC. Today he is retired.

ERICK LIEBENSTEIN, immigrated to the USA in April 1937 from Germany, together with his parents and one sister. He is a Holocaust survivor from Nazi Germany. He entered the US Army in the spring of 1943. He was in military intelligence attached to Patton's 3rd Army as a German interpreter. He was wounded in the Battle of the Bulge. He was discharged from the Army in the end of 1945.

He was married in April 1946. He has three children and seven grandchildren. In 1950 he opened a hardware supply business in Forest Hills, NY. Today he is retired and his children are running the hardware business.

In 1986 he was instrumental in building a handicap elevator which is a Shabbos elevator. He was a big boost for the temple in Forest Hills, NY.

IRWIN LIEBERMAN, on Feb. 6, 1945 was a rifleman with the 63rd Inf. Div., 255th Regt., Co. L. They were in Alsace, France, near the Rhine River. A railroad track ran through the woods- the Germans on one side, and they on the other. Their command post, a quarter mile from his fox hole, was an old farmhouse with a wall blown out.

The weather was bitterly cold and snow covered everything. "I was ill with chills and fever when my buddy and I were relieved from the 12 hour shift in our foxhole. A medic took my temperature, said it was high, but no one could go on sick call because 'something was brewing.'"

That morning they attacked the Germans, crossed the tracks, gained ground, and tried to dig in but the grounds was frozen solid. "The Germans counter attacked and I was wounded and evacuated to a temporary hospital. Because of my high temperature, I could not be moved out for almost a week."

"The shrapnel wound in my left arm was a blessing in disguise; because continuing in action with pneumonia could have been much more serious."

SAMUEL Z. LIEBERMAN (DDS), born in 1907 in Pinsk, Russia. Entered Dental Corps in December 1942. Stations included Ft. McClellan, AL; Karachi and Calcutta, India.

Memorable experience was in Calcutta, visited Lady Ezras USO and saw turtles 300 years old. English Officers Club with all privileges. Walked on famous Chiarengee St., a meeting place of American, English and Indian soldiers. At Fespao famous restaurant. "I visited American ships and a bombed out one at the harbor. I had terrible two weeks of Danghe, fever up to 104 degrees.

After practicing general dentistry in the city of Chicago for 12 years, he enlisted and was accepted as first lieutenant in the Dental Corps of the US Army. He was assigned to the Ft. McClellan, AL Soldiers Training Center. They had about 35 dental officers there in two dental clinics in two sections of the camp. He was given the surgery and prosthetic part of dentistry due to his years of private practice. Recent graduate worked on fillings and prophylaxis.

In 1945 after two years, he got orders to report to New York Airport. There he met 17 other officers from all parts of the United States, their destination a secret. After two weeks they got their individual orders as captains, destinations Karachi, that was then India. Their trip on a B-15, unexpectedly was fair. During the three days they had four changeovers.

From there some went to Calcutta where he went and others Berma China to do dentistry.

Discharged in 1946. Awards/Medals: Overseas Medal, Presidential and Governor's Citations. Discharged June 1946 with rank of captain. Joined the JWV the same day.

Practiced with son in Chicago. He retired in 1991.

He has a wife Annette. Son Jack has been a dentist for 30 years and Richard is a special education teacher in high school.

SIDNEY LIEBERMAN, sergeant in the Pacific Theater. Enlisted on Oct. 2, 1942. He covered all island bombing sites prior to invasions. Received a Silver Star for protecting our infantry at the Gulf of Lady in the Philippines.

WILLIAM A. LIEBERMAN (BILL), born Oct. 28, 1918 in New York, NY. Entered USAAC Aviation Cadet Program on Oct. 12, 1942. On Jan. 30, 1943 was at BTC #9, Miami Beach, FL. Stations included 303 College Training Det., Jamestown, ND; Pre-flight School, Santa Ana, CA; Primary Flight School, Thunderbird, AZ; Photographer, Wendover AF, UT. Member of 330th BG (VH) B-29, Walker AAB, KS. In January 1944 was photographer at 330th BG, North Field, Guam. Discharged January 1945 at Ft. Dix, NJ.

ALBERT LIEBOWITZ

WALTER LIEBOWITZ

ARTHUR W. LIGHT, (Y2/C), USNR, (formerly Lichtenstein), born Jan. 9, 1920 in Bronx, NY. Moved to White Plains, NY, graduated White Plains High School. Entered the USN the day after Pearl Harbor. Served in WWII and Korean War and was honorably discharged after the Korean War.

Met Estelle Herzog when she was in the WACS stationed at Ft. McClellan. They married and had four children and five grandchildren. His oldest son enlisted in the AF during the Vietnam War and honorably discharged.

Member of Post 112, Atlanta, GA.

Arthur passed away Nov. 21, 1991, 71 years young.

ESTELLE H. LIGHT, was born in Bronx, NY on Jan. 7 ,1922. Majored in business, graduated from Times Square Business School in Manhattan. Entered the WAACS in 1943 and then rejoined into the WACS in late 1943. After basic training was sent to Ft. McClellan, AL and assigned into the Discharge Department doing office work. Was sent to Ft. McPherson for photography course for three months, then back to Alabama.

Met husband at a WAC dance, he was in the Navy on recruiting duty. They married in June 1944 and she was discharged in August. They have four children and five grandchildren.

Her husband passed away in November 1991, married 48 years. Very successful business which now belongs to four children.

PAUL LILLING, was born in Brooklyn, NY on Jan. 11, 1934. Graduated from Brooklyn College in June 1955 and commissioned second lieutenant, USAF through the AFROTC Det #555. Worked as a bio-chem research assistant at the NY Botanical Gardens prior to Flight Training School at Harlingen AFB, TX in March 1956. After basic and advanced training went operational, flying with the 310th B-47 SAC Bomb Wing at Schilling AFB, KS. Discharged in March 1956 and subsequently recalled to active duty in February 1960 assigned to the 321st BW B-47 at McCoy AFB, Orlando, FL. Participated in operational activities during the Cuban crisis, 1962-63. Assigned to the Pentagon in 1966 working with the assistant secretary of the AF for Manpower and Reserve Affairs and then with the Defense Language Institute as chief, Research and Development Staff Office. Subsequently assigned as senior advisor to the ARVN Joint General Staff, Training Directorate with MACVN US Army. Served in staff and ground combat situations in 1972-1973. Upon return from Vietnam, assigned to Air University, Montgomery, AL from 1973 to and retired in March 1977, rank major-regular.

Staffed the policy change to permit women to be commissioned through the AFROTC Program. Surviving combat patrol actions with Vietnamese ground force units operating from the demilitarized zone to the delta area.

Decorations: Bronze Star, Meritorious Service Medal with OLC, AF Commendation Medal, Army Commendation

Medal, National Defense Service Medal, Vietnam Service Medal, Honor Medal First Class and Staff Service Medal First Class Republic of Vietnam.

Married to Irene and has a son Terry. Life member of JWV, DAV, VFW and the USDR. Work as an independent investment advisor and involved in local municipal affairs.

CHET LINDEN, SGT, was attached to the 14th AF which flew over the Himalayas Mountains Headquarters group and flew supplies into China.

MURRAY LIPNER, born May 30, 1923 in the lower east side of New York City. Entered Signal Corp on March 22, 1943. Served as ASTP (German language) for the 386th Inf. Regt. Stations included Camp Crowder, Carlton College, Ft. Bragg and Camp Cooke for amphibious training. Participated in battles at Rhineland and Czechoslovakia, near Pilson, with Patton's 3rd Army.

Memorable experiences were getting home alive and on the troop ship he fasted on the wrong day for Yom Kippur. Also crossing date lines.

Awards/Medals: American Service Medal, Asiatic/Pacific Service Medal, EAME Service Medal, Good Conduct Medal and WWII Victory Medal.

Discharged March 12, 1946 with rank of private first class.

Married Sara on June 10, 1946 and still loves her. Has five children: a dentist, lawyer, Ph.D., psychologist and Ph.D.

Today he is a CPA and is trying to slow down.

JOSEPH LIPSIUS, born Forsyth, GA Jan. 8, 1918. Family moved to Atlanta, GA 1928. He moved to Montgomery, AL 1940.

Inducted Army at Ft. McClellan, AL as private Oct. 23, 1941. Discharged as major, Feb. 19, 1946.

Basic infantry training, Camp Croft, SC; Officer Candidate School, Ft. Benning, GA. Commissioned 2nd lieutenant, July 2, 1942. Assigned to 96th Inf. Div., Camp Adair, OR. Cadre as Regimental S-2, 272nd Inf., 69th Div., Camp Shelby, MS. Became S-3 shortly after start of basic training. Assigned Cannon Co. commander just prior to overseas movement. Became Regimental S-2 on movement to Siegfried Line. Assigned again as S-3 after VE Day. Transferred to 78th Inf. Div. on 69th redeployment home. Discharged Feb. 19, 1946.

Established and operated chemical business known as Empire Laboratories with his brother for 30 years, until selling in 1976. Continue now in part-time independent contractor sales of chemicals.

Married to the former Anne Davis with three step-daughters and six grandchildren by them. One son from a previous marriage.

Actively pursue hobby of metal detecting for coins and other lost items.

Member of Post 112.

HARRIET BIEBER LIPSON, born March 22, 1920 in Chicago, IL. Enlisted in WAAC on Oct. 26, 1942 in Chicago. In September 1943 she joined the WAC and became recruiting officer in Oklahoma and Texas for two years, then was placed in a detachment to Rordon Center Hospital, Chickaska, OK for one year.

Was discharged as a first lieutenant. "The opportunity to serve and the training I received as an officer was a wonderful opportunity I could never get anywhere. Was able to see the country and to be proud to wear the uniform."

Awards/Medals: American Theater Ribbon, WAAC Service and WWII Victory Medal.

Have two daughters and five grandchildren. Is now a widow and retired after working for the Federal Service in the Veterans Administration for 30 years.

She joined the JWV 29 years ago, belonging to various posts and finally 18 years ago helped organize the FEM VETS Post 192 and became a charter member. Held the office of commander two different terms and also was elected to the NEC in National for one year. Is now the bulletin editor for her post.

TRUDY ABELOW (GERTRUDE) LIPSON, sister to the five brothers, was the sixth sibling in the family's military history. She was married in 1938 to Dr. Henry Lipson who rose to the rank of LTC Henry Ibsen Lipson, MC.

HENRY IBSEN LIPSON, (LTC), MC, joined the Medical Corps of the US Army as a first lieutenant in 1935. He joined the US Army VA in 1938 and served the VA continuously until his retirement.

When WWII broke out, Lt. Lipson was reactivated in the Army as a captain in the Army.

CPT Lipson was promoted to major in 1944. He separated from the Army in 1946. He joined the USAR in 1957. Major Lipson was promoted to rank of lieutenant colonel in 1963.

EUGENE J. LIPSTEIN, was born in the Bronx, NY on Aug. 18, 1918. BS in chemical engineering from University of Delaware, 1939. Commissioned second lieutenant from ROTC same year. Assigned War Department Reserve Pool as essential industry until February 1942. Assigned to a 90 mm AA unit at Ft. Bliss, TX but volunteered for Airborne AA. Unit formed and shipped to Karachi in May 1942. Transferred in the CBI theater to AF to utilize engineering skills. One Battle Star for Assam Valley Campaign on Asiatic/Pacific Ribbon. Upon rotation to continental US in November 1944, was assigned to the NACA Aircraft Engine Lab at the convenience of the government.

Separated administratively and remained in Reserves retiring in 1968 as lieutenant colonel.

Married Leona Feld in 1944. Four children: Freddi, Sanford, Sheri and Robert. Seven grandchildren.

Was president of retail ladies apparel chain and data processing service, both sold in March 1987.

Life member of Reserve Officers' Association, member JWV, B'nai Brith, Congregation Beth Emeth in Wilmington, DE.

JULIUS LIPTON, was born May 1, 1914 in Newark, NJ. Enlisted in the US Army in 1942. He was ranked as corporal with the 914th FA Bn., 89th Div. from 1942 until March 1943. Graduated Field Artillery OCS June 1943 as a second lieutenant. Stationed at the replacement depot in Italy, April 1944. Volunteered for combat duty May 1944 and was attached to the 68th FA Bn., 1st Armd. Div. as forward observer from Anzio to Leghorn, May to August 1944. Attached to the 36th Div. for Southern France invasion, August 1944 until October 1944. He was assigned to B Btry., 338th FA Bn., 88th Div. as forward observer October 1944 until July 1945. Attached to the 91st Div. for Japanese Theater, but the war ended before he left Italy. He received four Battle Stars in Italy, one in France. Promoted to first lieutenant February 1945 in lieu of Bronze Star Medal.

Served with the Army Reserves from 1953 until 1967. Graduated Command and General Staff College in 1962. Was instructor at Command and General Staff College at Army Reserve Schools. Asst. S-3, Kearny, NJ Army Reserve School. Retired from Army Reserves as major in 1967.

After WWII was an US Internal Revenue agent. Promoted to group chief, then assistant branch chief. Retired in 1975. He was assistant director of audits, Board of Public Utilities for state of New Jersey, June 1976 until May 1981.

Married, two daughters and one grandchild. He was the New Jersey four wall handball champ in 1951.

LEONARD H. LIT, born Dec. 18, 1932 in Beverly, MA. Entered USAF on Aug. 18, 1950. Stations included Lackland AFB, TX; Keesler AFB, MI and Erding Depot, Germany.

Awards/Medals: Good Conduct Medal, Occupation Medal (Germany) and WWII Victory Medal.

Discharged Sept. 17, 1954 with rank of A1/c.

Married to Barbara and has son Barry Jay who is married to Susan and has son Isaac Joseph. Daughter Nancy D. married to Brian.

Today he is a retired electronics teacher for a vocational high school.

GEORGE LITSKY, served in the US Army. Served 12 months and 21 days in Korea from July 1952 through August 1953. Member of 2nd Inf. Div., 82nd AAA. Served on a half track 4-50 caliber machine guns. "Our close support to the infantry provided anti-aircraft defense for artillery."

Received four Battle Stars plus other decorations.

RALPH LITTMAN, was born in Chicago, IL on Feb. 1, 1921. Attended Herzl Jr. College in Chicago for two years and the Illinois Institute of Technology for a summer session before going to work for the Army Ordnance Dept. in Chicago.

Entered the US Army in April 1943 as a private in Chicago. Basic training took place in Biloxi, MS. Screening took place in Memphis, TN. He was assigned to pilot training with the AAC and did his flight training in Alabama, Kentucky, Georgia and Mississippi. Received his wings and commission June 27, 1944. Was assigned to B-24s and sent to Italy on Oct. 5 ,1944.

Assigned to the 15th AF, 376th BG, 513th Sqdn. in Sanpancrazia, Italy. Flew 11 missions before being shot down. Was captured by Hungarian troops and turned over to the Germans in Vienna. Spent the remainder of the war as a POW.

Air combat in Balkans and No. Apennines.

Awards: Air Medal, Purple Heart, EAME Theater Ribbon, WWII Victory Medal and POW Medal.

Discharged Dec. 14, 1945 in San Antonio, TX as a lieutenant. Remained in AFR for 23 years. Retired as a major.

Married to Georgia and have three daughters and five grandchildren.

Member of JWV, VFW, DAV and ex-POW organizations. Worked for DOD and HEW after the war. Retired from federal service in 1989.

Most memorable experience: "Meeting my brother on the march from Nuremberg to Mooseburg, Germany while we were both POWs."

LESTER LITVIN

CLIFFORD LOBEL, born in Ridgewood, NY on May 29, 1916. Entered US Army Oct. 16, 1942. Honorable discharge Dec. 15, 1945. Basic training at Camp Crowder, MO and Camp Pendelton, CA.

Served with the 592nd Joint Assault Signal Co. (JASCO) as a radio operator. Sent to Schofield Barracks in the Hawaiian Islands for jungle training.

After amphibious exercises at Guadalcanal, they were assigned to the 81st Wildcat Div. and attached Anguar and Peklien Island in the Philippines. Thereafter JASCO was attached to the Americal Div. which participated in many more amphibious landings in the South Pacific.

Awards/Medals: Asiatic/Pacific Service Medal, Good Conduct Medal, WWII Victory Medal and Philippine Liberation Ribbon.

Life member of DAV and member of Post 115, JWV.

Married to Blanch and has a son, daughter and two grandchildren.

Returning to civilian life, was in the family's retail children's wear business. Retired in 1977.

LOUIS LOEVSKY, born March 8, 1920. Enlisted USAAC Dec. 26, 1941. Graduated Aviation Mechanic School, Keesler Field, Biloxi, MS and B-26 Specialist School, Baltimore, MD. Graduated Navigation School, Hondo, TX, November 1943. Joined 8th AF, 466th BG, 786th BS, Clovis, NM. Stationed at Attlebridge, England.

On March 22, 1944, the 466th BG flew its first mission to Berlin. His B-24, *Terry and the Pirates*, was hit by flak over Berlin and lost #1 propeller. A mid-air collision ensued with *Terry* losing props #2 and #3, and the B-24 *Brand* lost its tail, causing it to go into a tight spin. Thirteen of 20 crew members were KIA, five *Terry* and eight *Brand*. Loevsky bailed out and was immediately captured. Became POW at Stalag Luft III, Sagan, Germany until Russians got close in January 1945. They were evacuated at 2:00 a.m. in a freezing blizzard. Reached Stalag VIIA, Moosburg by marching in sub-zero weather and were crammed into 40 and 8 boxcars. They were improperly clothed and fed; conditions were unsanitary and inhumane. They were liberated by Gen. Patton's troops on April 29, 1945.

He lives in North Caldwell, NJ with his lovely wife, Molly.

MORTON L. LONDON, born Sept. 28, 1917. Graduated Brooklyn College with BA; Brooklyn Law School with LLB; Officer Communication Crs. at Ft. Sill, OK, 1944; OCS Field Arty. School, Ft. Sill, OK and commissioned 2nd lieutenant May 1942. Served in the Pacific Theater 1942-43 in Hawaii and Guadalcanal with the 89th FA BN, 25th Div. and in the ETO from December 1944 to July 1945 with the 293rd FA Observation Bn. (supporting the 66th Div. in France).

Served as national commander of the JWV and as its national chairman for Foreign Affairs and Action Committees, as well as its representative to the UN as a permanent observer. When the National Conference on Soviet Jewry was formed, he was the JWV rep. He was also the JWV member on the Conference of Presidents of major Jewish organizations, an executive committee member of the National Jewish Community Relations Council, and helped found the World Conference of Jewish Veterans in Israel in 1962. Later he was chairman of the International Conference.

Honors: Silver Shofar Award, National Council of Young Israel; Medal of Merit, JWV; Chapel of Four Chaplains; Baccalaureate address, AF Academy 1963. Missions: conference with President Kennedy, July 26, 1963, White House; Civil Rights Conference, White House, June 17, 1963; Chancellor of Austria on Material Claims Mission, 1967; NATO; Israel.

Married to Shirley Kohan London and has two sons, Henry of Randolph, NJ who with his wife Fran are parents of Eryn, Gabriella, Uriah and Torrey; and son Jan of London.

GLADYS LONSTEIN

WILLIAM LOPATIN, born in Russia, Sept. 6, 1910. Arrived Feehold, NJ September 1920. Graduated Freehold High School 1928. Attended NYU and University of Pennsylvania, one year each. Dropped out due to 1930s depression. Worked in father's construction company.

Entered Army May 22, 1942. Assigned to AAC. Attended Radio School, Scott Field, IL and Gunnery School, Cunningham Field, FL.

January 1943 assigned as radio gunner on B-26 crew at Barksdale, LA. Arrived in England June 1943. Their crew was assigned to 449th Sqdn., 322nd BG and later to 584th Sqdn., 594th BG, 9th AF. Flew 72 combat missions over Holland, Belgium, France and Western Germany. Seventeen of these missions flown on D-day and after. Rotated back July 1944 to Barksdale Field, LA as radio instructor. Honorable discharge July 28, 1945, rating tech sergeant.

Decorations: DFC, Air Medal with two Silver and three Bronze Clusters, ETO, Invasion of Europe and Unit Citation Ribbons.

As civilian continued in father's construction business. Retired September 1975. Returned to college, received BA degree in 1981 and MA degree in 1992.

Married Selma June 1945. Have one daughter. Selma died August 1985. Married Joan May 1991.

Charter member of Oglensky-Jackson JWV Post 359 and VFW Post 4374.

GENE LOPOTEN, born Nov. 6, 1925 in Philadelphia, PA. Enlisted in Army February 1943. First soldier selected from Military Police to attend Army Specialized Training Program at Georgetown University. Discovered to be a minor and honorably discharged. Reenlisted on 18th birthday. Served with 256th Engineer Combat Bn. through European Campaign. Three Battle Stars, American Theater, European Theater and WWII Victory Medals. Awarded French Fourragere and commendation for Liberation of Colmar. Participated in liberation of concentration camps at Dachau and Wolfratshausen. Fought in Alsace-Lorraine through Germany and Austria. Sent to Biarritz American University after VE Day.

After war's end, kept contact with British, French and German children he had befriended and now has second generation exchanging visits back and forth. Only GI known to have returned to certain villages in Alsace.

Discharged April 1946 as tech sergeant.

Married to Charlotte. Lives in Lower Gwynedd, PA. Two sons, four step-daughters, three grandsons and one granddaughter. Retired after 35 years as military marketing specialist. Member JWV Post 148.

RAY LOURIE, born Dec. 24, 1915 in Philadelphia, PA. Volunteered in 1940. In 1941 was with 176th Inf., Co. D, 29th Div. at Ft. Meade, MD, moving from private to corporal. In 1942 with 176th Inf. transferred to Washington, DC and HQs Co., US Army where he became sergeant. Transferred to Pentagon, Arlington, VA on G-4 Staff, master sergeant. In 1943 transferred to HQs Co., North African Theater of Operations as first sergeant, Canestell Repeldepo. Also with HQs, G-4, Natuso as master sergeant, Logistic Section, which planned the invasions. Went in on invasion of Italy, up to Rome, then Caserta Southern. In 1944 went in on invasion of France, Dijon and Lyons. Earned a Bronze Star Medal in France. On through Strasbourg, Germany. "Everyone was in at the Battle of the Bulge."

In 1945 after war ended, assigned to G-4 and G-5 SHAEF HQs, Paris, France. Accounting for ship loads of supplies for occupied countries.

Medals: three Battle Stars, Bronze Star Medal and Presidential Unit Citation.

Discharged Oct. 24, 1945 with rank of master sergeant and sergeant major.

He was a Wharton School graduate, University of Pennsylvania before entering service. Major was accounting and finance. Today he is a retired merchant.

DAVID D. LOVITZ, born March 16, 1920 in Chicago, IL. Entered service July 17, 1943. Served with the infantry's M Co., 362nd Bn., 91st Div. Stations included Camp Adair, OR; North Camp Hood, TX and tank destroyers.

Memorable experience was being wounded and buried alive while seeking observation position to direct 81 mm mortar fire with 300 radio.

Awards/Medals: Purple Heart, Bronze Star with cluster, Combat Infantry Badge, EAME Medal, WWII Victory Medal and two Overseas Bars.

Discharged Nov. 10, 1945 with rank of private first class.

Has wife Florence, two children, Sandra and Dr. Fred and four grandchildren: Alison, Andrew, Lauren and Daniel.

Today he is the chairman of the Hartz Mountain Corporation.

GERTRUDE TAUF-LOWENSTEIN, born May 10, 1918, Chicago, IL. Employed by the Department of the Army, Washington, DC 1940-1942. Enlisted in WAAC, Oct.7, 1942, WAC Sept. 1, 1943. Received basic training at Ft. Des Moines, IA then Ft. Oglethorpe, GA; Norfolk, VA; Langley Field, VA and Mitchell Field, NY. Separated Ft. Sheridan, IL, Dec. 5, 1945, with the rank of sergeant.

Eight weeks Cooks and Bakers; four weeks mess sergeant; five weeks personal affairs consultant training, (his occupational specialty).

She'll never forget the day she overhead the girl who was assigned as her roommate in Norfolk tell the commanding officer, she refused to share a room with Gertrude, because she was a Jew. The girl didn't get her way and she and Gertrude became good friends.

Married Herbert Lowenstein in 1948, and had a son, a daughter, and two grandchildren. She is now retired and widowed. Gertrude is active in volunteer work involving children. She is a member of I. A. H. VFW Post 111 (W.V.)

H. ZUSSMAN LUBEL, received his notice for induction in April 1944 and was sent to Ft. Bragg and assigned to the USAAF and sent to Biloxi, MS for training at Keesler Field.

After basic training he was sent to San Antonia for assignment; to a specialized school at Brookley Field, Mobile, AL; training at Tinker Field, OK; at Pratt, KS he was assigned to the 73rd Air Svc. Gp. which was part of the 315th BW which had the Enola Gay and dropped the first bomb on Japan.

Went by troop train to POE at Seattle and arrived on Guam in February 1945 where he ran the laundry until he was sent home and discharged.

MORRIS LUCK, enlisted into the AAC on Nov. 2, 1942. He took tests at Ft. Sheridan, IL; Tinker Field, Oklahoma City, OK and Honda Navigation School at Honda, TX. "I conformed to my mother's wishes not to fly and so I became a cryptographic technician instead." He went overseas and found himself a cryptographer on the island of Saipan. Had short visits on the islands of Tinian, Eniwetok and Kwajalein and also spent several months on the island of Iwo Jima including a Jeep ride on Mount Surabachi also known as "Mount SOB".

After about three and half years, he came back to Milwaukee and has been there ever since. I had an AGCT of 141 and earned two stripes. "Participating in Friday night services on the island of Saipan was one of my more exciting moments."

"My total service was almost equally divided between stateside and overseas duty."

PHILIP LUCKERMAN, enlisted in Chicago, IL, in May 1941. Was assigned to the 3rd Armd. Div. at Camp Polk, LA. Received Commendation for solution of chemical warfare problems June 18, 1942, and because of that, was selected for Officer Candidate School, Chemical Engineering College, Ft. Belvoir, VA, in the summer of 1942. Graduated as a commissioned officer, 2nd lieutenant in October 1942.

His unit, 846th Engr. Avn. Bn., crossed the Atlantic and landed at Perth, Scotland on his birthday, Jan. 14, 1993. Their mission was to build the Birch Air Base, Colchester, England. The facility was operational in May 1944. Crossed the Channel on July 1, 1944. and was honorably discharged with the rank of captain in March 1946.

MAYER LUDEN, born in Poland on Dec. 26, 1926. Holocaust survivor- arrived in US on May 29, 1949. Drafted into US Army on June 2, 1952. Basic training at Ft. Dix, NJ. Member of HQ and HQ Co., 60th Inf. Rcgt., Inf. Div., Ft. Dix, NJ. In charge of communication equipment for training troops; achieved rank of corporal. Became US citizen while in the Army at Ft. Dix, NJ in October 1953. Transferred to Governors Island, HQ 1st Army, Ft. Jay, NY in charge of all refrigeration and heating.

Honorable discharge in June 1954.

Married to Holocaust survivor, Helga Schmitz while in the Army, February 1954. Have three children and five grandchildren. Member of J W V. Presently retired.

"Was very proud to be in the US Army."

CHARLES LUGER, born May 24, 1918 in New York, NY. Inducted April 7, 1941, Los Angles, CA. Discharged Dec. 28, 1945, Davis-Monthan Field, Tucson, AZ. Pvt. Spec. 3rd Class, surgical technician, 7th Surgical Hospital, Ft. Ord, CA. Transferred to USAAC, March 1941. Aerial navigator, USAAC after aviation cadet training. Naval instructor at Mather Field, CA and Ellington Field, TX. Aerial navigator, 1st Emergency Rescue Sqdn., 12th AF, operating in the Adriatic Sea.

PAUL LUTERMAN, born April 18, 1916 in Pittsburgh, PA. Enlisted December 1940 in USAAF. Highest rank attained, staff sergeant.

Mr. Luterman served as instructor in chemical warfare at Langley Field, VA for 18 months. He was sent to England in the 301st BG, 419th BS. This was the first B-17 bomb group to bomb Europe. First target was Rouen, France. Then on October 1 the group invaded North Africa, target Port of Oran, Algeria. This group served as air support for Gen. George S. Patton's 3rd Army. The 301st invasion activity progressed from Tunisia onward to Sicily. Returned to States in September 1945 as cadre unit of B-29s, preparing for the invasion of Japan.

Awards: Six Unit Citations, five Presidential Citations, European Theater, African Campaign, Sicilian and Italian Campaigns, WWII Victory Medal and Good Conduct.

Retired merchant now residing in Richmond, VA with wife Rose. Father of Michele and grandfather of Jennifer and Jodi.

EDWARD O. LUTZ, born July 31, 1919 in Brooklyn, NY. Entered US Army Signal Corp on June 1, 1942. Commissioned July 1, 1943. Stations included Ft. Monmouth, NJ; Signal Corps School, Aberdeen Proving Grounds; Officer Training School; Tom's River, NJ; Weather Station School, San Francisco Ordinance District.

Discharged June 1, 1946 with rank of first lieutenant.

Married Alice Lessem on Jan. 3, 1943. Three children: Terry Jane Goldring, Richard and William.

Today he is professor emeritus, Brooklyn College, a retired CPA and investment counselor.

WILLIAM LYONS (TIGER), fighter pilot, US 8th AF, ETO, 355th Fighter Group, 64 missions, 300 plus combat hours flying P-51 Mustangs. Shot down two Messerschmitt 109s, damaged one ME-262 jet. Flew long-range escort missions protecting B-17s, B-24s, plus Nazi airfield strafing, etc. First lieutenant, flight commander.

Born June 20, 1924, Bay Shore, NY. Raised in Brooklyn. Schooling: PS 185, Brooklyn Tech High School. Enlisted at 18 as aviation cadet. Graduated pilot, Class 44-B, Spence Field, GA. After war, graduated from MIT on GI Bill. (Could never have afforded it otherwise.)

Memorable experiences: "The daily acts of courage of fellow fighter pilots that I took for granted then, but not now. The conscientious work of ground crew chiefs, armorers, etc. that I also took for granted then. I've since realized that my comrades— almost all in our late teens, early 20s— were good guys due to their parents and education, normal for that time. I miss their quality of character today. Five out of my six cousins eligible to serve in WWII, did so, four by enlisting. The loss of my cousin, Maj. Sylvan Feld, fighter pilot, US 9th AF, shot down July 1944, only increased my determination to do my part to destroy Hitler and his bigots."

Daughter Pam and two grandchildren, Gudrun and Rachel. Married to Carol (nee Kinzelberg), daughter Lisa. Retired in 1986 as chairman of marketing company. Enjoy being with family and friends and reunions with 355th Fighter Group.

DAVID MACK, U.S. Army Med. Corp., was engaged in action against the enemy on Saipan from June 17 to July 12, 1944, during which his unit was engaged with the enemy. Left covered positions in numerous instances, crossed open terrain under heavy enemy fire, and succeeded in administering first aid and evacuating casualties under tremen-

dously hazardous conditions, frequently covering the victim's withdrawal with small arms fire until the wounded man reached safety. During the entire Saipan operation his actions were of almost incredible bravery and his devoted care to the men of the unit to which he was attached was far beyond the call of duty.

Technician Mack received the Distinguished service cross for his bravery during this period.

LESTER MACKTEZ, served in the USAAF. Entered in Philadelphia, PA, Aug. 15, 1942, and discharged at Ft Devens, MA, March 6, 1946, with the rank of 1st lieutenant. Trained at Boca Raton, Philadelphia, from Aug. 15, 1942 to March 15, 1943 and at Yale University from March 15, 1943 to June 10, 1943, specializing in aerial photography. Transferred to Peterson Field, Colorado Springs, CO and was trained at Will Rogers Field, Oklahoma City, OK, during 1943. He sailed overseas on the USS Uruguay from Los Angeles, CA and arrived at Bombay, India.

He returned from Overseas on the USS *Rutland* sailing from Okinawa and returning to Los Angeles, CA. He saw considerable service in the CBI area and also in the Philippines, Netherland East Indies, Okinawa and Japan. He flew 22 missions in B-24s as an aerial photographer. Among the outstanding places that he visited were Australia, India, China, Manila and Tokyo, Japan.

Awards/Medals: Air Medal, Presidential Unit Citation, and six battle stars. *Submitted by: Max Sigal*

JOHN MACY, born March 28, 1910. He enlisted with Sig. Corps, U.S. Army, on April 6, 1942. Stations included Camp Crowder, Mo; Ft. Hancock, NJ; Japan; and Australia. Served with the 26th Radio Intelligence Co. (replacement company) which was captured by the Japanese in the Philippines. His HQ was in Japan, where he had his first piece of overseas.

Memorable experiences include being deaf in his right ear and still being accepted; serving in Darwin, Australia, Philippines, and Japan as an intercept operator, Kana Code.

Awards/Medals: Good Conduct Medal and Asia-Pacific Medal.

He is a retired accountant from the Office of Comptroller in New York City.

SAMUEL ROBERT MAGNUS, born Feb. 15, 1923, Newark, NJ. Enlisted in the USAF, Feb. 23, 1945. Served during WWII at Furman University, SC; Maxwell Field, AL; Selma Field, AL; Ellington Field, TX; and during the Korean Conflict at Ellington Field, TX, Randolph Field, TX and Victorville, CA. He was based in Japan and flew bombing missions over Korea as a radar navigator.

Awards/Medals: American Campaign Medal, WWII Victory Medal, Air Medal with two OLCs and Korean Service Medal.

Discharged after WWII on Oct. 10, 1946, and after the Korean Conflict on April 3, 1952.

Married to Shirley and has three children and three grandchildren. He is deceased.

MILTON MAISELL, joined Gen. Patton's 3rd Army at the tail end of the Battle of the Bulge. Was with the 377th Inf., Co. I, 95th Div.

They were on a spearhead without a moment's rest and while in this town in Belgium, they helped liberate a labor camp. The majority of people running out of the barracks were women. With the help of his squad, they pulled down the Nazi flag. Was also on the Ziegfried line and given a special mission. His sergeant, Ed Crabtree, a young private and himself, who only in the front line a

short time, were pinned down by machine gun fire from a cement bunker. Crabtree ran around to see how the young private was doing. His name was Soto and he was being the cement bunker. When the sergeant came back he asked him how the kid was doing and all he would say was the he was okay. In the meantime they were being fired upon with small arms fire, mortars and some heavy stuff. They still had the machine gun to contend with and being he was outranked, he had to knock out the machine gun nest. He did his job successfully and returned to the sergeant. They were at a loss as to what to do next. In front of them was all open terrain. He suggested to the sergeant that he yelled out to the Krauts and see what will happen. He yelled out real loud for the Germans to surrender and in about thirty or forty seconds the sergeant and he saw a short pole with a white cloth coming out from under the ground. Then he started screaming at the top of his lungs and to their surprise, the Germans started coming out in numbers. All told, they captured 27 and there were four dead in the machine gun nest. When they got back to their area, he found out from the medic that Soto had been killed, and this made him very sad. They were all awarded the Silver Star Medal.

They also took part in the liberation of Paris. While he was walking in the middle of the road, a man sprang toward him and asked in Yiddish if he was a Jew. He told him he most certainly was and they began to converse. He told Maisell his wife had been killed by the Nazis and his beautiful daughter had been taken to a brothel. They continued talking and he was choked up by his story. His name was Alexis Zamietoff and he asked Maisell if he could get in touch with his nephew who lived in Brooklyn. Maisell promised him that he would and they embraced and he had to catch up to his unit. As soon as he had the time, he wrote to his wife in the Bronx, gave her the name and address of Mr. Zamietoff's nephew and she wrote to him and told him of the survival of his uncle and his whereabouts. He was very appreciative and for his wife and him it was very satisfying to know that they had been able to help a fellow Jew.

Maisell is presently serving Fred Hecht Post No. 425 in Spring Valley, NY as junior vice commander.

MARVIN I. MALK, born March 13, 1925, New York City, NY and grew up in Hackensack, NJ. Attended Rutgers University. Entered U.S. Army at Ft. Dix on June 6, 1943. Infantry basic at Camp Hood, TX; then ASTP at NYU-Upton for six months. Sent to Camp Carson, CO to E Co., 415th Inf., 104th Div. as barman; October 1944, sent to engineers and went overseas in November 1944 to South Pacific, New Guinea, Leyte and the Philippines. Left the Army in March 1946 as buck sergeant.

Awards/Medals: Asiatic, Pacific and Philippine Liberation Medals.

Married Ruth in 1947 and has two daughters and two granddaughters. Went into headwear manufacturing in Denver in 1950. Sold out and retired in 1987. Now does consulting in sewing plant startup and embroidery. Enjoys ball room dancing and playing clarinet in jazz group. Member of Masonic Lodge and JWV Post, Denver, CO.

MARTIN MALZMAN, born Oct. 11, 1916, Brooklyn, NY. Enlisted April 15, 1941, with 3rd Army, 71st Inf., 271st Eng. Combat Bn. and did basic training at Ft. Bragg, NC. Went overseas to England, France, Germany and Austria in WWII.

His most memorable experience was achieving rank of master sergeant

Awards/Medals: Good Conduct Medal.

Discharged on Oct. 31, 1945.

Married Helen in 1943, has one daughter, Myra, and one grandson, Jeffrey. Malzman passed away in 1987.

MATTHEW MALTZ, born in Chicago, IL, married Edith Goldfein. Volunteered for service in the USN in WWII. Went through boot camp and service school at USN training base, Farragut, ID and attended National Naval Medical School, Bethesda, MD where he was certified as a field epidemiologist specialist. As a petty officer he served with the 4th Marines in Okinawa in the closing days of WWII. Later assigned to staff headquarters, Yokosuka, Japan.

Currently doing labor relations work for an international union. Has been post commander for three consecutive years and is the recipient of the post "ARTY" award for service to his post. Represents the department on the annual Purple Heart Cruise for hospitalized veterans and looks forward to commemorating JWV's 100 years of service.

ARTHUR MANDELL, born May 27, 1930, Winthrop, MA, and moved with his family to Medway, MA where he graduated from Medway High School in 1948. Attended Suffolk University and Burdett College in Boston, MA which resulted in a large accounting practice founded in 1954 with his brother in Franklin, MA. Placed on active duty with the USAF during the Korean War in May 1951 with the 89th Trp Carrier Wing stationed at the Bedford AFB, Bedford, MA. Transferred to the 131st Fighter Wing at Bergstrom AFB in Austin, TX and months later transferred to George AFB at Victorville, CA.

Discharged from USAF in September 1952 due to a truce agreement signed by North and South Korea.

Married Rhoda L. Goldstein Feb. 14, 1954, and have three lovely children, Lois, employed with Harvard Medical Health plan and lives in Watertown, MA; Larry, who has estate consulting and pension firm and lives in Marblehead, MA; and Heidi, employed at Mandell's former accounting firm and lives in Franklin, MA. Also has two lovely grandchildren, Carly and Douglas and his mother Rose who resides in Brookline, MA.

Member in good standing of the JWV Kennedy Post, Director of Ben Franklin Savings Bank in Franklin, MA and was on many committees at the Dean Academy in Franklin and a member of the Franklin Planning Board and other civic organizations. Before his death in 1993, he and his wife resided in Norfolk, MA. He passed away on Aug. 30, 1993, after a lengthy illness. He was a devoted and loved husband, father, son, brother and friend.

LAWRENCE H. MANDELL, born Feb. 29, 1936, Newark, NJ. Photographer in USN from February 1954 to February 1957, a Korean War Veteran. Served with JWV as commander at El Paso Post #749, 1972-1973; commander,

Dept. Of Southwest, 1974-1975; first commander, Dept. of Texas, 1975-1976; and JWV Americanism Award, 1990. Education includes BS degree in communications, 1962, from the New York University.

Career federal employee in Dept. of Army, 1962-1992; chief, visual information, White Sands Missile Range, NM.

Married to Sheila Bernknoph June 27, 1963, and have three children, David, accountant with FDIC in Dallas, graduate of UTEP in 1988 and Cpt Artillery, TANG; Robert, graduate UTEP 1992 in finance, 1st lieutenant Sig Corps, U.S. Army in Germany; and Lesli, senior at UTEP and a social worker. Mandell is retired in El Paso, TX.

BERTRAM MANN, born July 20, 1921, Roselle Park, NJ. Graduated in 1940 from Plainfield High School and attended Chamberlain School of Aeronautical Design. Enlisted in the AAF after passing test requirements for cadet status. Commissioned as 2nd lieutenant in late 1943 and assigned to sub patrol at Langley Field, VA, waiting for embarkation to Europe. Married Doris Lieberman on Jan. 8, 1944, in Newport News, VA before leaving.

Flew 52 accredited combat missions as a bombardier navigator in B24s doing altitude precision bombing using the Norden and Sperry bombsights. Flew the Mediterranean Theater battle area of Rome-Arno (Anzio Beachhead), air offensive over Europe including the bombing of Vienna and Munich, air offensive of Southern France and the round-the-clock bombing in preparation of the invasion of Southern France (the second front), bombing the retreat of the enemy in the Po Valley. Participated in six bombings of the Ploesti oil fields of Romania. Many negligible and skin deep wounds from anti aircraft fire with pieces of flak and shrapnel, five of them were significant.

Awards/Medals: Distinguished Flying Cross, Air Medal with three OLCs, Commendation Ribbon, Presidential Unit Citation with One OLC, Purple Heart with OLC, European Campaign Ribbon with five Battle Stars, African Middle Eastern Theater Campaign Ribbon, Mediterranean Theater Ribbon and American Campaign Ribbon. His highest attained rank was major.

After the war Doris gave birth to a wonderful son, Jeffrey in 1948; then in 1954 a darling daughter, Amy. Amy has two adorable daughters, Sarah and Naomi. He and Doris reside in Margate, NJ and he is a life member of the DAV Post 10, a life member of the Military Order of the Purple Heart Chapter 155 and a member of the JWV Post 39.

HAROLD MANN (NEE MANEVITCH), born April 18, 1921, Boston, MA. Enlisted in the U.S. Army Nov. 20, 1939, Boston, MA. Attended Airplane and Engine Mechanic School, Aircraft and Engine Electrical Specialist School, B-17 School, Aviation Cadet and pilot training, F-86D School; Auto-Pilot School; Management School; NCO Academy; B-47 School; Academic Instructor School; Tech. Instructor School; Aerial Gunnery School.

Stationed at Langley AFB, VA; Mitchell Field, NY; Grenier Field, NH; Maxwell Field; Decatur, AL; Roosevelt Field, NY; Sewart AFB, TN; Tyndall Field, FL; Podington, England; Sebring Field; Lowry Field, CO; Shaw AFB, SC; Landstuhl AFB, Germany; Forbes AFB, KS.

Most of his service was with aircraft maintenance, He was mechanic, electrician, inspector, crew chief flight engineer and flight chief. Flew 30 missions with the 8th AF, 92nd BG. Stationed at Podington, England. He was top turret gunner and flight engineer on B-17s.

Awards/Medals: Presidential Unit Citation, Air Medal with four clusters, three Battle Stars and lots of campaign ribbons. Discharged in October 1945.

Enrolled in New England Aircraft School, graduating in 1947. Hired by MAANG in 1947 as air tech. Bought a service station in 1950. Recalled to active duty in February 1951, re-enlisted and remained on active duty until retirement in June 1965. Worked for TWA, retiring in 1984.

Has wife, Sylvia; three children; and two grandchildren. Currently commander of JWV Post 605.

SAUL MANN, born June 8, 1925, in Minneapolis, MN. Enlisted in the U.S. Army in March 1944 as a private with the 3rd Army. Stations included Camp Hood, TX and the European Theater of Operations. Participated in the Battle of the Bulge in France.

His most memorable experience included almost being killed by a German 88 shelling.

Awards/Medals: Purple Cross with Battle Star.

Discharged in July 1945 as a private.

Married Thelma and has three children: Linda, Robert and Elaine; eight grandchildren: Nicole, Erin, Jason, Michael, Emily, Benjamin, Amey and Joseph. Mann is now a salesman of insurance and investments.

HERBERT MARCUS, entered the armed services in the U.S. Army with the rank of private at Ft. Devens, MA on Nov. 21, 1942. Received his basic training at Ft. Devens in the infantry and was shipped overseas, arriving at Liverpool, England on Jan. 8, 1944. Saw active service in the Normandy, Northern France and Ardennes, Rhineland sectors from June 6, 1944, to Oct. 18, 1945, with the Med. Det. of the 16th Inf. The action that he saw commenced on D-Day, June 6, 1944.

Awards/Medals: EAME Ribbon, four Bronze Stars, Bronze Service Arrowhead, Good Conduct Medal, Distinguished Unit Badge, Silver Star Medal, Combat Medical Badge and several French and Belgian decorations. Discharged from the Lovell General Hospital at Ft. Devens, MA on Jan. 11, 1946. *Submitted by Max Sigal.*

NATHAN MARCUS, passed away on June 29, 1994. He was the JWV Nebr.-Iowa regional post commander and active in JWV Epstein-Morgan Post 260. We remember him as standing tall with his JWV cap at a rather jaunty angle, and great beaming demeanor in events like operating Annual Latke parties for the Post.

ARTHUR MARGOLIS, born Oct. 5, 1910, in Russia. Attended Central High School. Served in Trans. Corps in Italy. He was killed in action on Sept. 15, 1943, at the age of 33.

Awards/Medals: Purple Heart which was awarded posthumously.

He is survived by his brother, Irving.

DONALD D. MARGOLIS, born June 30, 1918, in Milwaukee, WI. Attended Carroll College on a football scholarship and finished undergraduate work at the University of Wisconsin. Volunteered in the U.S. Army in October 1942 and served four years before returning home in January 1946. Served in the 9th Armd. Div. under Gen. Patton overseas. Fought in Germany, Luxembourg, Belgium, and was one of the units that opened Buchenwald Concentration Camp. Served in Adjutant General HQ.

Awards/Medals: Bronze Medal for bravery in action.

On his return to civilian life he finished Law School at Marquette University and now resides in Milwaukee with wife Blanche. He is president of Villard Realty Co. and Land Development. He has two sons, a daughter and four granddaughters.

MYRON B. MARGOLIS, born in Kansas City, MO, July 24, 1937. In October 1954 he enlisted in the USMCR. Graduated from the University of Kansas in 1959 with a BS degree in mechanical engineering; OCS, September 1959 and called to active duty from September 1959-September 1966. Served in Vietnam at Da Nang, 1965, and Chu Lai, 1966, as A-4 Skyhawk pilot.

Awards/Medals: five Air Medals, Navy Commendation Medal with Combat V, Marine Corps Reserve Medal, Presidential Unit Citation, Navy Unit Commendation, National Defense Service Medal, Vietnam Service Medal, RVN Campaign Medal and Vietnam Cross of Gallantry. Joined USMCR, 1966-1978, retired Jan. 1, 1979, with the rank lieutenant colonel.

JoAnn, his wife of 32 years, passed away Nov. 24, 1992. Has one son, one daughter, two grandsons and one granddaughter. He is captain of Continental Airlines, CD-10 (International).

ETHEL MARIAM, enlisted in the USNR on June 16, 1943 (20th birthday), discharged Feb. 1, 1946, as a SKD2c; reenlisted on July 10, 1947 as a DK2, discharged Oct. 28,

1949; commissioned Ensign Supply Corps, USNR Oct. 28, 1949; retired June 16, 1983 as captain, SC, USNR.

Boot camp NTS (WR) Hunter College, NY. Duty stations and schools, Storekeeper School, NTS Indiana University, Bloomington, IN; NTS Bainbridge, MN, in recruit and stewards mate disbursing offices; Demobilization School, NTS Great Lakes, IL; Separation Center, NATTC Memphis, TN, on staff opening this activity, until discharge; Inactive Reserve 1947-1949; NR Units; surface divisions 138 and 139, Reserve training, St. Louis, MO, as mobilization officer and classification officer; Defense Contract Administration Services Region, St. Louis; command officer DCASR 718, 1977-1978; Naval Reserve Officer School; served on selection board for CDRs and CPTs SC.

Awards/Medals: American Theater, WWII Victory Medal, Naval Reserve and Armed Forces Medals.

Civilian career includes member of St Louis accounting firms, administrative assistant for fiscal operations for the Jewish Federation of St. Louis and Consolidated Neighborhood Services Inc.

Retired in 1987 and is a member of the JWV Post 644.

M. WILLIAM MARK, born on the lower east side of New York City, NY, Nov. 5, 1917. Initially drafted into the U.S. Army on Aug. 1, 1941. Later during WWII, he joined the USAF and graduated Navigation School as 2nd lieutenant, at San Marcus, TX. Served in Central Europe, Rome-Arno, Naples, Foggia, Air Combat Balkans and Air Offensive Europe.

Awards/Medals: Air Medal with three OLCs, Purple Heart with two OLCs, Distinguished Unit Badge, American Theater Service Medal, European Theater Service Medal, American Defense Serviced Medal, WWII Victory Medal and New York State Distinguished Service Medal.

Discharged after the war with the rank of captain and became active with the 9212th AF Reserve Sqdn. located in New York City, on Nov. 5, 1977. He was honorably retired from the USAF as a lieutenant colonel.

Married to Selma and has two lovely daughters and seven grandchildren. Member of JWV Post 218 an life membership of JWV, DAV and ROA. Presently manager of the Borough of Queens, NY for the Bureau of Fire Communications.

LEONARD BURTON MARKOWITZ (PFC), born Jan. 4, 1926, Cleveland, OH. Inducted in the Army March 30, 1943, served with Co. L, 2nd Inf. Regt., 5th Inf. Div. with MOS: Artist 296. He drew caricatures of patients in station hospitals, made posters for the American Red Cross and served as staff artist and staff writer for a few Army newspapers.

Treated for battle fatigue and depression, he has been on Army disability since 1946. Received discharge June 1, 1946. Awards include the Good Conduct Medal, three Bronze Stars, EAME Campaign Medal, American Campaign Medal, WWII Victory Medal, Army of Occupation Medal with Germany Clasp. His name, with millions of other GIs, is engraved in Normandy on a wall called "Wall of Liberty."

Attended Cleveland College of Western Reserve University; was on the college newspaper from 1948-1952 as sports writer, editorial and sports cartoonist. Worked for the USPS for 40 years and at present is assistant marketing director and direct mail coordinator for Locum Medal Group.

Married Pauline Stone on Jan. 20, 1946. They have one boy and three girls: Dennis, Sheila, Doreen, Michelle, and five beautiful grandchildren.

RUBIN H. MARKOWITZ, born May 20, 1923. Graduated Nottingham High School and attended Syracuse University. Passed away on Jan. 10, 1950, at the age of 27.

SID MARKOWITZ, graduated Albany High School in 1961; Clarkson University in 1965 (BSEE); and Stevens Institute in 1972 (MMS). Commissioned 2nd lieutenant in June 1965; president of Military Honor Society, 1964-1965; Distinguished Military Graduate.

Officers' basic training at Ft. Gordon, June 3, 1966-Aug. 8, 1966; Maint. officer course at Ft. Monmouth, Aug. 15-Oct. 24, 1966; HHD, 11th Sig Gp., Ft Huachuca, Oct. 31, 1966-June 2, 1967; HHD, 21st Sig. Gp., So. Vietnam, June 3, 1967-May 23, 1968. Was originally assigned to 459th Sig. Bn, Hon Tre Island and transferred to S-3 operation, 21st Gp, in Nha Trang, Vietnam.

Married Eileen Gilbert of Albany in June 1965. He is employed by U.S. Army Picatinny Arsenal Research and Development Centers as staff engineer since 1965. Has his professional engineer's license (state of California) since 1974. Inducted into the Army Acquisition Corps, August 1994; licensed Ham radio operator since 1959; and commercial and ham radio license examiner since 1994.

AARON MARKS enlisted first in the Navy Seabees and was rejected. Later, he was inducted into the Army; sent to Camp Claiborne, LA and put in the 2nd Bn., 110th Inf., 103rd Div. After basic training he joined the 88th Inf. as a replacement radio operator in HQ co., 350th Inf.

Left on liberty ship Dec. 2, 1943, and arrived at Oran, North Africa on Christmas Eve to relieve the British at Mentino on the Grigliano River, then the Beachhead at Anzio and proceeded towards Rome. After six weeks of combat, they were granted R&R. While there he learned that his brother Ed, member of the 34th Div., was nearby and he was granted permission for a two day visit. His brother was later KIA (Sept. 21, 1945).

Hospitalized 10 days for dysentery and malaria, then rejoined his group in the Northern Apennines. Memories of Mt. Bataglia will live with him forever. Wounded on Dec. 8, 1944, and spent a month in the hospital. Returned to his division and was preparing for the crossing of the Po River when the war ended.

Discharged from the service Nov. 28, 1945. Returned home to his wife, the former Natalie Hirsch, and met his 2-year-old son Arthur for the first time.

SIDNEY MARSHALL, born March 22, 1916, in Syracuse, NY. Attended Washington Irving and Vocational High Schools.

Marshall was killed in action at Iwo Jima. He is survived by his parents, Mr. & Mrs. Isadore Lavine, wife, Sally Marshall and brother, Ted Marshall.

RALPH S. MARVIN, born Feb. 25, 1921, in Jersey City, NJ. Graduated from Spring Valley high School in 1939; graduated from Bergen Jr. College. Entered U.S. Army April 27, 1942, and studied radio communication and repair at Scott Field, IL and radar maintenance at Boca Raton, FL. Trained pilots and navigators on flight simulators at Langley Field, VA. Received his AAF discharge Dec. 5, 1945, from Drew Field, FL as a staff sergeant with the American Theater Ribbon, and the Good Conduct and Victory Medals.

Married in 1953. Wife passed away in 1991. He has three married children and six grandchildren. Has lived in Ithaca, NY for 40 years and is now a part time real estate broker. He is a life member of the American Legion Post 221 and a member of JWV Post 100.

MONROE F. MARX, enlisted U.S. Army from Asbury Park, NJ in January 1942. Completed basic training at Ft. Hancock. Was accepted and completed officer's training school, Ft. Lee, VA. Assigned to the 35th General Hospital, stationed at Ft. Sill, OK as quartermaster officer. The 35th was shipped to New Guinea in March 1944. Discharged due to illness in July 1944.

Ruth and Monroe, 1944

Awarded the Pacific Theater of War Ribbon and the Asiatic-Pacific Theater Ribbon.

Military career was shortened by illness, however, his contribution to JWV was most outstanding. In 1945, he joined the Asbury Park-Ocean Post #125, JWV, and immediately became very active. He was a life member and held many chairmanships and offices and served as post commander from 1959-1960 at which time he was awarded commander of the year, department of New Jersey. From 1960-1961 he was Monmouth-Ocean County Commander and also awarded the Commander of the Year.

Married WAAC Corp. Ruth Klompus at Ft. Sill. After almost 48 years of marriage, Marx passed away on Nov. 22, 1992.

RUTH KLOMPUS MARX, enlisted in the Women's Army Auxiliary Corps in January 1943 in Baltimore, MD. The WAAC was organized in 1942 and since she was not yet 21, had to wait to enlist. Basic training at Daytona Beach, FL, assigned to be the company clerk of her company. Promoted to corporal and assigned as the acting first sergeant. In August 1943 the WAAC became the Women's Army Corps. (WAC) and they had the option of re-enlisting or resigning. She chose to re-enlist and remained at Daytona until the camp was closed. Transferred to Ft. Sill, OK, where she was assigned to the 1864th WAC Bn. Assigned to the Post Office, Post Hospital which was very rewarding and she felt that what she was doing was very important; mail is a very important factor in the military and especially to those men who were hospitalized. The smiles on their faces and the appreciation when she delivered the mail to them gave her much satisfaction knowing that she brought them much cheer when they certainly needed a lot of cheering up.

Ruth and Monroe

But it would not be fair to say that the best experience of her military career was the fact that she met a very nice 2nd Lt. Monroe Marx and they immediately became very good friends. They married on Feb. 24, 1944, at the Old Post Chapel at Ft. Sill and remained very good friends for almost 48 years when he passed away suddenly in November 1992. They had two daughters, a son and four grandsons.

Marx joined Asbury Park-Ocean Post #125, JWV, about 1950 and became a life member in 1989. Has been very active in many capacities having served two terms as commander and was very honored to be named county commander of the year in her first term and department commander of the year in her second term as post commander. She has served as editor of the post bulletin since 1984 and still has the job. She has been on just about every committee ever since.

She is very proud to have served her country at a time it needed her help and hopes to be able to continue to serve JWV.

TED MASLANIK, born June 17, 1923, Brooklyn, NY. Enlisted in the USNR on March 29, 1943. Military stations include Detroit, Long Beach, CA, Treasure Island, CA, San Francisco, Portland, OR, and New Haven, CT. Participated in battle at Saipan, Iwo Jima and Okinawa.

Most memorable experience included rescuing Gen. Jonathon "Skinny" Wainwright from Mudken Manchuria Prison Camp.

Awards/Medals: Asiatic-Pacific with one Bronze Star, Victory Medal, American Theater, Occupation Medal and WWII Victory Medal.

Discharged on Dec. 21, 1943, with the rank of MM3/c.

He is married and has four children and five grandchildren. A financial planner and volunteer at a Florida Hospital.

JOSEPH MASLIANSKY, born June 16, 1918, Brooklyn, NY. Entered the U.S. Army on Feb. 14, 1942. Basic training at Camp Forrest, TN assigned first to 33rd Div. and subsequently to Co. I, 320th Inf. Regt., 35th Div. in cadre. Landed on Omaha Beach on July 6th with the 3rd Army, across France to Bliesbruck, Germany; disabled and ZI'd. Led Jewish services at all training camps as well as on troop carrier with no chaplain. Of the 200 original men in the Company only about 20 survived. Discharged on Sept. 1, 1945, as sergeant.

Married Tsippora in 1946 and left for Palestine in March 1946, until after the establishment of the state of Israel. Has one daughter, Sabra, two sons and five grandchildren. Worked in Jewish organizations; retired in 1988 after being director of the council of organizations of the UJA Federation of New York; helped fund almost 300 projects including the Beth Hatefutsoth, the Museum of the Diaspora, Absorption Centers, the Yigal Alon Community Center in Safed, the student dormitory for Holocaust studies at the Ghetto Fighters Kibbutz, etc. Member of the JWV Post No. 250 and the DAV.

IRVING A. MASLOV, born Aug. 6, 1918, Chicago, IL. Enlisted in the USAF on Oct. 10, 1942, with the 100th Bomb Gp. B-17s. Military stations included 12th Armd. Div., Camp Campbell, KY; Thorpe Abbots, Eng., Erlangen, Germany, ASTP, Ann Arbor, MI, and MacDill AFB, Tampa, FL. He participated in the European Theater.

Most memorable experience includes flying in a B-17 over France and Germany on VE Day.

Awards/Medals: Good Conduct Medal, European Theater, American Theater, and Victory Medals.

Discharged on March 30, 1946, with the rank of T/4 cryptographer.

He is a widower with three children and three grandchildren. He retired after 30 years of U.S. Government service.

NATHAN MASS, born 1906 in Busk, Austria and moved to Vienna in 1930. Emigrated to the United States in 1940, after Hitler occupied Austria. Lost his entire family in the Holocaust. Entered the U.S. Army in April 1941, attended basic training at Ft. Eustis and Camp Pendleton, VA. He was due to ship out on the USS *Dorchester* but an injury to the Battalion Commander fortunately delayed their departure.

The Dorchester sank with all hands including the four chaplains. Shortly thereafter he shipped out to Iceland and served as a gunner in the 378th anti-aircraft battalion until his discharge in 1945.

Awards include the European Theater Operation Ribbon and Good Conduct Medal.

Returned to Malden in 1945, married, and had two sons, one a lawyer in New York, the other a physician in San Francisco. His wife passed away in 1982. Mass retired after 31 years in the civil service and remains active in Malden Post #74 (since 1942) and volunteers at Malden Hospital and the Jewish Recuperative Center for the aged.

SOL MASTBAUM, born May 2, 1924, in Minneapolis, MN. Enlisted May 13, 1943, as Army Infantryman, with 27th Inf. Div., Clerk Med. HQ CPBC. Military stations included basic at Ft. Roberts, Ft. Ord and Angel Island (in transit), 27th Div. Hawaii, North Central Base Hospital, Hawaii, and Clerk in Med HQ CPBC, Hawaii. Participated in battle at Marshall Islands and Saipan Mariana.

Memorable experience includes being left for dead on the battlefield June 27, 1944, discovered and saved one day later.

Awards/Medals: Combat Infantry, Pacific Ribbon with two stars and Purple Heart.

Discharged on Nov. 16, 1945, with rank of sergeant.

Married on Dec. 9, 1945, and has one son, age 36, and one daughter, age 32. He is retired after 41 years in education working as a consultant at Metropolitan State University and vice president in charge of sales Twin City Bagels Baking Co.

SEYMOUR MATENKY, born 1921, Detroit, MI. Inducted in U.S. Army in December 1942. Stationed at Keesler Field, MS; Santa Maria, CA; Edwards AFB, Mojave Desert; Malmberg AB, MT and shipped overseas from Camp Stoneman, CA. Assigned to 64th Air Svc. Gp., 5th AF in South Pacific. Debarked at Brisbane, Queensland, Australia and stationed in New Guinea, Biak Island, Mindoro Island, Leyte Island and Luzon Island.

Discharged in November 1945. Attended University of Michigan on GI Bill and finished BS degree in business and MBA.

His memorable experience does not involve hardship, terror, hunger, it is just a loving Jewish experience. He met Elsie Barnbaum while stationed in Brisbane, and for the four months he was stationed there, he escorted her to various social events in the Jewish community.

After WWII, in 1948, he married his wife Marilyn Sasan and has three daughters. He corresponded with Elsie until 1992 when she passed away. She would send him letters, pictures, news articles etc. about herself, family and the Brisbane Jewish community. His wife, Marilyn, kept a scrapbook on the almost 50 years of love and friendship between them two Jews.

Elsie married Kurt Kugelmas, who died in 1982, and had one daughter Dr. Rebecca Mason who is a research doctor and teacher at University of Sydney. Rebecca has visited the Matenkys in Michigan twice and calls almost every Rosh Hashanah and Passover.

EDWARD I. MATES, born May 17, 1919, in New York City, NY. Joined U.S. Army on July 10, 1941. Served with Field Artillery until June 4, 1945 and Military Intelligence until April 1, 1953, followed by Delta Base HQ and Ft. Meade in Military Intelligence. Also with 44th Div and 999th FA BN. Military locations included Ft. Bragg, Camp Dix, Camp Claiborne, Ft. Lewis, Ft. Sill, A.P. Hill, Camp Butner, European Theater of Operations, Camp Upton, Camp Claiborne,

Corvallis and Tennessee Maneuvers. Followed Gen. Patton's tanks across France and Germany, Isle of Orlean Capture.

Memorable experiences include being part of the first Heavy Artillery to cross the Seine River and being under constant bombardment of German artillery for several days while serving as a forward observer at Bitche. Also trained four field artillery survey teams as assistant S-2; served as forward observer and spotter for the 999th FA BN; liason officer of the 999th FA BN to 2nd French Armored BN in Vosges Mountains during the Battle of the Bulge.

Awards/Medals: Good Conduct Medal, Croix de Guerre and five combat medals (ETO).

Discharged on April 1, 1953, with the rank of captain.

Married Ruth Amster on Jan. 29, 1944, and has two children, Michael Amster Mates (9/8/48) and Andrea Paula Mates Landis (2/3/50); and five grandchildren: Sara Lynn Landis (9/9/75), Jonathan Hersh Landis (9/2/77), Eric Feldman Mates (7/7/81), and Rebecca Feldman Mates (9/26/83). He is a member of the Temple Emanuel of South Hills, Pittsburgh, PA; president of brotherhood; board member and life member of the Jewish Chatarua Society; Bower Hill Civic League; American Intellectual Property Law Assn.; past president of Scott TWP, PA School Board; and past member of Chartier Valley School Board. He is now self employed as a patent attorney and a member of the D.C. Bar.

MORRIS M. MATHEWS, RABBI born in Sokolke, Poland, on Sept. 13, 1901, the son of a scholarly rabbi. Came to the United States at the age of 15. A graduate of Columbia University with a BS degree in educational psychology and a MA degree in religious education; received his Ph.D. degree from Webster University in 1943; and his rabbinical ordination at the Rabbinical Seminary of America. Left his post as rabbi of the Community Synagogue Center in New York City and entered the U.S. Army as a 1st lieutenant in March 1944 during the height of WWII. Attended U.S. Army Chaplain's School in 1944 and was assigned to Ft. Monmouth, NJ; was sent on a three month emergency mission to Newfoundland. From December 1944 to 1947 he served in the South Pacific as Post Chaplain to the Hawaiian Ordnance Depot, Central Pacific Base Command, and with the 147th General Hospital. Administered to the spiritual needs of personnel and performed religious services on High Holy Days on Iwo Jima, Saipan, Guam, Kwajalein and Johnston Islands. Other major active duty assignments included service at Ft. Dix, NJ; Frankfurt Military Post, Germany; Ft. Eustis, VA; and in Korea during the Korean War.

Awards/Medals: Bronzed Star Medal for meritorious service in connection with military operations against the enemy from Jan. 6, 1945, to Sept. 2, 1945; 1947, the Army Commendation Medal in the Pacific Command and a second Army Commendation with Leaf Cluster following his service as Post Jewish Chaplain at Camp Drum. These commendations reflected an acknowledgment by others of Rabbi Mathews' devotion to duty and deep sense of responsibilities as Jewish Chaplain. Exhibiting a fine understanding of the problems confronting service, he performed many missions of consolation and cheer, giving solace, comfort and aide to persons of all faiths.

After retirement in 1964, Rabbi Mathews and his wife, Hannah, lived in Bayshore, LI. He served as Jewish Chaplain to the patients of Central Islip State Hospital (psychiatric hospital). In his capacity as chaplain, he ministered to more than 10,000 patients and their families, attempting to facilitate family trials and to soothe their individual family crises as they arose. He is a member of the Rabbinical Council of America and the JWV, Post #682, the Rabbinical Assn. of

Greater Miami, FL, New York Board of Rabbis, American Legion, DAV and Military Chaplains' Assn., as he and his wife continue to impact the American Jewish Community through their affiliations with UJA, Hadassah and Amit.

Upon his retirement from Central Islip State Hospital, Rabbi Mathews and his wife, Hannah, moved to North Miami Beach, FL, where they now reside. Their daughters, Mrs. Miriam Nathan, an interior designer, and Dr. Ruth Katz, a principal of an orthodox Jewish Day School, live in Oceanside, NY, with their respective families. Rabbi and Mrs. Mathews have six grandchildren and five great-grandchildren.

JOSEPH MATLOW, born on July 29, 1911, in Syracuse, NY. Graduated from Central High School and Syracuse University Class of 1935 from School of Journalism and with rank of 1st lieutenant ROTC; played LaCrosse with Championship Central High School and at Syracuse University for three years. In his senior year, he was elected to "All East" LaCrosse Team as defense man.

Upon graduation he worked for two years in New York City for Donnelly Advertising Co. and in 1937, left New York and became vice president and manager of the scrap iron yard for Matlow Co. in Little Falls, NY.

Matlow entered the service in November 1940 and was honorably discharged in December 1945 with the rank of major.

Returned to Little Falls, NY and purchased a business in 1947 under the name of Little Falls Steel and Supply Co. Became active in politics and was a member of the Board of Education, Masonic Order and YMCA.

Matlow passed away on Oct. 22, 1960, at the age of 49. He is survived by his wife, Rose, a daughter, Ruth Ann, and a son, Stephen.

VICTOR W. MAX, born Allentown, PA, March 8, 1917. Enlisted USAAC October 1942 and was honorably discharged October 1945. Basic training in Atlantic City, sent to the USAAC School and assigned to newly activated 404th Fighter Gp. in Meridian, MS. After months of training, they participated in the Louisiana Maneuvers, went to many other stations in the south and was finally shipped to England. Their P-47 Gp. did escort duty to heavy bombers flying over France, prior to and including D-Day, also destroyed enemy armor, bridges, truck convoys, troop concentrations, Rail Head concentrations, and anything that moved! They spent many months in England where Max worked in communications. Then came D-Day the 404th Fighter Gp. was one of the first Air Force Groups. into Normandy, France, a brief time after D-Day, after the beachhead was secured and they had only a little hold inland. Their airfield (A-5) was not too very far from beach and planes took off and landed on wire matting for runways. They moved inland, again and again, and many more airstrips. They were with the 9th Air Force, 29th Tac. Their mission was direct air support to their advancing ground forces, all through France, Belgium and final victory in Germany, V-E Day! They were, as a group, shipped back to the States because they were a high point outfit. The entire group was deactivated shortly thereafter.

404th Fighter Group was awarded six battle stars: Presidential Unit Citation, Distinguished Unit Citation, French Croix de Guerre with Palm (for meritorious action in France), Belgium Croix de Guerre and the Belgium Fourregere (for the Battle of Ardennes Bulge). Each member is entitled to wear all of the above. Max received the ETO Ribbon, Good Conduct Medal, Thompson Expert Marksman Badge, American Campaign Ribbon and Victory Medal.

Married Lillian and they have a daughter, Sharyn. He went into business and retired. He is a member of the JWV and the American Legion.

JUSTIN H. MAY, born Sept. 4, 1916, in New York City, NY. Graduated NYU School of Medicine in 1940. The day after Pearl Harbor he tried to enlist in the USN and then the U.S. Army and was rejected because of torn cartilage in his right knee. Had surgery on his knee and was then accepted by the USN. He entered active duty in October 1942 at Quonsett Point Naval Air Station, RI, then Little Creek, VA. January 1943, assigned to Scouts and Raiders, ATB, Ft. Pierce, FL, as their first and only medical officer, both treating ship's company and training the medics of the Beach Battalions, who were assigned to the ATB for training in invasion tactics. In late 1943 he was temporarily assigned to Bethesda Naval Hospital to write and edit a Navy training film, "Medicine Hits The Beach" as a result of the above experiences. July 1944, transferred to the USS *Talbot*, APD 7, which carried underwater demolition teams who blew up Japanese obstacles to landing craft, all done two days prior to landings by the Marines and Army. Made all the invasions in the Philippines as well as Okinawa. At Okinawa, they had several close calls, when attacked by Kamikazes.

Discharged from the USN in April 1946.

Married to Babette and has three daughters and four grandchildren. Still in active practice of medicine in Florida and a member of the JWV and American Legion.

MONROE E. MAYER, born on Jan. 8, 1928, in New York City. Entered USAAF on April 29, 1946, and sent to Wright Patterson AAF Base after basic. Assigned to PROJECT INDEX, which was charged with collecting, receiving, cataloging, microfilming and distributing German research and development to manufacturers, universities and research centers. Werner Von Braun and other German scientists were part of the program, since they had surrendered to American soldiers, rather than the Russians.

Discharged in 1947, entered the USAFR Wing while attending NYU. Simultaneously with being admitted to Brooklyn Law School, the Korean War began and the 514th Troop Carrier Wing was activated to full duty. The unit participated in troop revolvement and war games in the United States and overseas with MONTE in Special Services as a Recreation Specialist.

Discharged in 1952 and returned to Brooklyn Law School to finish and be admitted to practice in New York.

Married Joan Stringer in 1950, and raised four sons in Nanuet, NY. Served JWV as Post, District, Department Commander, DEC, NEC, National Judge Advocate and National Inspector and numerous other positions.

MARTIN J. MAYERSON, born on April 9, 1920, in New York City. Entered the U.S. Army on April 20, 1942 and was stationed at Turner Field, Albany, GA, with the USAAC, Army Specialized, Army Sig. Corps.

Awards/Medals: American Service Medal, Asiatic Pacific Service Medal, Good Conduct Medal and WWII Victory Medal.

Discharged Jan. 28, 1946, with the rank of T-4.

Mayerson is semi retired and acting as a machinery broker in industrial equipment.

NATHAN HERSCHEL MAZER, born March 11, 1911. Entered active duty on Dec. 12, 1942, and attended Ordnance School, APG, MD. Served with 544th Bomb Sq. from Jan. 6, 1943 to May 21, 1945. Participated in 51 missions, seven aerial combat missions with 47 combat hours volunteered. Stations included: England, Japan, Turkey, Guam and Norway. Completed bomb recon course, B-17 armament, boresighting and Harmonization, and Aerial Gunnery School.

Awards/Medals: Air Force Commendation Medal and the Bronze Star Medal.

Retired on June 1, 1964, with the rank of colonel, with over 22 years of service.

MEYER I. MAZON, born in Brooklyn, NY, Jan. 25, 1922. Enlisted NYNG on March 20, 1939, Battery C 245th Coast Arty; federalized Sept. 16, 1940, and stationed at Ft. Hancock, NJ. Went to Auto Mechanic and Coast Arty Schools. Battery mission changed from time to time and was in range section of 10" gun battery; 90 mm AA and 50 cal machine guns; was electrician and mechanic AA searchlight highest rank obtained was T/5. Sent to ASTP at Brooklyn College as a cadet, rank of private in 1943 and then assigned to Anti Tank Co, 289th Inf., 75th Div, then on Louisiana maneuvers. Was awarded Expert Infantry Badge after examination and promoted to private first class in Camp Breckinridge, KY.

Division moved to Wales in 1944 and then to France. Near Aachen when the Battle of the Bulge started; moved to Belgium and joined the fray; knocked down by a shell burst which damaged his spine. He didn't know, and refused aid. Three other men were injured and they evacuated during this barrage. Served as platoon runner, aid to platoon leader, took care of communications, carried a bazooka when required, assigned to rifle troops as bazooka man, etc. Moved to Alsace to fight in Colmar Pocket after Battle of Bulge, then to Holland, finally into Germany; and fought in Rhineland. Did occupation duty in Germany; moved to Camp Detroit, France to prepare to go to Japan. War ended with Japan and they went home.

Awards/Medals: three battle stars: Ardennes, Central Europe and Rhineland; Combat Infantry Badge, Expert Infantry Badge, Bronze Star, American Campaign, Army of Occupation Medal with Germany Clasp, Good Conduct Medal, American Defense Service Medal, EAME Campaign Medal and WWII Victory Medal.

Discharged on Nov. 30, 1945.

After discharge he worked first as a draftsman and eventually became a licensed professional engineer (New York and Ohio). Retired from Grumman Corp in June 1989 and today he is a self employed consulting engineer on a limited basis and taking courses at Queens College. He is a member of the JWV, DAV and other veteran organizations.

Married Sara. He has a son and had a daughter from a previous marriage. His daughter passed away 20 years ago, and his son is a Vietnam Veteran. His wife has two sons from a previous marriage. Both sons are married and have children.

ROBERT A. MAZON, born on March 25, 1951, in New York City, NY. Enlisted in U.S. Army on Aug. 2, 1967. After basic and infantry AIT training, was stationed at Ft. Polk, LA. Awaiting his 18th birthday to be sent to Vietnam (volunteered to go). Received permission and went to Israel on Furlough prior to Vietnam. Stationed at Phubai Vietnam in 1969 with the 596th Sig. Co., 63rd Sig. Bn., 1st Sig. Bde. While in Vietnam he served as combat medic, combat photographer and from time to time was assigned to combat infantry units for ambush patrols.

Awards/Medals: Vietnam Campaign Medal, Vietnam Defense and Vietnam Cross for Gallantry.

Retired from the U.S. Army for a full physical disabilit on June 1, 1975, with the rank of E3.

Mazon was married to the late Incha Mazon. Today, h a free lance photographer on a time to time basis.

MARVIN MEDWAY, enlisted in the USAAC in Augu 1940. Attended basic training and was sent to Radio Operato School at Scott Field, IL. After graduation, he returned to h original duty station at Bolling Field, Washington, D.C. ar was assigned to the 1st Staff Sq. as a flight radio operator. Ju 1941 became a crew member on the plane of the Secretary War, Henry L. Stimson. June 1942 served as radio operator the plane of the Prime Minister Winston Churchill, during o of his visits to the United States. Served a special duty assignment in Alaska. Attended the Air Corps Officer Candidate School in Miami Beach, FL; graduated in October 1942 (Clark Gable was a classmate).

Separated from the service in February 1946, with the rank of captain, after an assignment in the Philippines. He then served five years in the Reserves.

JACK MEHLMAN,

JACK MEHLMAN, second child of Elias Mehlman and Mary Lickerman Mehlman, born March 12, 1921, in Chicago, IL. Both parents immigrated to the United States as minors from Latvia and Poland, respectively, in the great immigration of the 1900s. Family was a member of South Shore Temple in Chicago. Attended public schools; graduated Senn High School in Chicago; was "All City" basketball champion, graduating class president, National Honor Society, ROTC Cadet Major, and valedictorian of the graduating class in 1938.

Graduated Wright Jr. College, Chicago, 1940; Senior Council President, National Honor Society. Attended DePaul University Law School; was nominated outstanding junior citizen and law school student. Gave several radio interviews speaking about responsibilities of citizenship. Graduated from pharmacy school at night (while attending law school) and became a Registered Asst. Pharmacist working for the Walgreen company to provide funds for his legal education and contribute at home to a family still devastated by the great depression.

On Dec. 9, 1941, the Monday following the Japanese attack on Pearl Harbor, he joined the USAAC as an Aviation Cadet and graduated as a 2nd lieutenant and bombardier in a B27 Squadron. He flew to North Africa as part of the 9th AF and "skip-bombed" against Rummel's tanks in the battles against the German elite Africa Corps.

While visiting Tel Aviv, in then Palestine, and in his letters back home, he evidenced great pride in the pre-Jewish state's accomplishments and in the Jewish Brigade of the British Army in North Africa.

For his bravery and accomplishments in the Ploesti Oil Field raids over Romania he received the Air Medal with three OLCs, the Purple Heart and was featured in the Chicago Tribune.

On the day of the invasion of Italy, Sept. 3, 1943, in support of the Allied landings on his fourth sortie, his bomber was shot down by rocket firing German ME 410s, which stayed out of range of our 50 cal. machine guns. Although all the chutes were counted as leaving the aircraft, he was never picked up by the German E Boats, as were all the other members of his crew, in the waters west of Foggia, in the Gulfo di Manfredonia.

LESTER MEHLMAN,

LESTER MEHLMAN, born June 14, 1923, at the University of Chicago's Lying In Hospital. Attended public school and graduated Senn High School, Chicago, 1940. National Champion Drum Major; World Champion Baton Twirling Competition Chicago-land Music Festival, 1936. Graduated Wright Jr. College, 1942. Attended Philco Airborne Radar School, Bell Labs, U of C, ERC Electronics Program, and Graduated Lewis Institute, Chicago, EE., PE, IL.

Joined the U.S. Army Signal Corps in 1942, as a radar specialist. Transferred to Aviation Cadet Corps in 1943 and graduated as a navigator assigned to a flight crew on a B-17 (*Flying Fortress*) Squadron at Alexandria, LA, where he married Janice Schechter of Chicago. Served as navigator instructor, and communications officer on the base commander's staff at Ellington Army AB, Houston, TX.

After WWII he taught television engineering and math at American Television Institute while attending DePaul University Law School under the GI Bill from which he graduated in 1948; LLB; JD. Practiced law 1949 through 1978 as senior partner in Mehlman, Spitzer, Addis, Ticho, Susman, Randal, Horn & Pies in Chicago. Founded MAT Associates, Inc., a real estate development company, specializing in hotel development. From 1968 through 1991, developed major hotel projects in the United States and Mexico operated by many of the largest hotel operators in the world: i.e., Sheraton Grande, Los Angles; Sheraton Bal Harbor, Bal Harbor, FL; Hotel Cortez, San Diego los Angeles Ventura Ul Recidence inn Condesa Del Mar, Acapulco, Mexico; Swisotel, Chicago; Hotel Intercontinental, Chicago.

Now a consultant, guest lecturer, teacher and author in semi retirement living in Chicago and Palm Desert, CA.

LOUIS MEHR,

LOUIS MEHR, born in Brooklyn, NY. Served in WWII from Aug. 10, 1942 - Sept. 2, 1946, with the USAAC. Served as a research scientist at the Air Force Materiel Command, Wright Field, OH for two years; and HQ Allied Commission for Italy, Allied Military Government in Milan and in Trieste (Venezia Giulia) for two years. Overseas experience includes organizing rehabilitation of food processing plants in Allied occupied Italy for civilian and Allied military requirements.

Expertise used by Air Force to find above previously unknown targets in enemy occupied Italy. Received special commendation for latter.

Awards/Medals: U.S. Military Legion of Merit, Knight Cross of Crown of Italy, Meritorious Service Unit Plaque, American Theater Ribbon, EAME Campaign Ribbon, WWII Victory Medal and Italian Occupation Ribbon.

Discharged with the rank of captain.

He is presently retired.

SUSAN H. SCHECHTER MEISNER,

SUSAN H. SCHECHTER MEISNER, born on Aug. 30, 1962, in Jersey City, NJ. Joined the U.S. Army on May 12, 1984, and served with the 2nd Support Command; 2nd Armored Cav. Regt., 4th Inf. Div.; Army and Air Force Exchange Service. A distinguished military graduate of the Reserve Officer Training Corps Program at Syracuse University, she was commissioned as a Regular Army 2nd lieutenant in the Ordnance Corps in May 1984. Honor Graduated of the Ordnance Officer Basic Course and her first assignment was with the 614th Maintenance Co. in  Nuremberg, Germany. Served as the unit's automotive/armament platoon leader and property book officer from November 1984 to January 1987; next assignment, still in Germany, was as Class II/IV accountable and material management center executive officer for the newly formed Regimental Support Squadron, 2nd Armored Cav. Regt. and held this position until November 1987. Stations included Nuremberg, Germany; Ft. Carson, CO, and Dallas, TX.

Commandant's list graduate of the Ordnance Officer Advanced Course in may 1988. Assigned to the 4th Inf. Div. at Ft. Carson, CO. Served in subsequent assignments there, from June 1988 to March 1992, as Division Material Management Center, Armament Combat Material Officer; 704th Support Battalion Maintenance Officer (Support Operations); C Co. (light maintenance) Commander; and Adjutant, 64th Support Battalion. Received MA degree in human communication theory from the University of Northern Colorado during this assignments, graduating in May 1990.

Attended Public Affairs Officer Course from March to May 1992, and graduated with honors. Served as Media Relations Officer, Army and Air Force Exchange Service, from May 1992 to January 1995.

Awards/Medals: Meritorious Service Medal with one OLC, Army Commendation Medal, Army Achievement Medal, Overseas Service Ribbon, National Defense Service Ribbon, AF Organizational Excellence Award and Army Service Ribbon.

Discharged on Jan. 31, 1995, with the rank of captain.

Following release from the active Army, assumed her present position as manager, personnel services, Trinity River Authority, Arlington, TX. Holds a commission in the USAR, with Reserve assignment as a public affairs officer, Fitzsimons Army Medical Center, Aurora, CO.

Married Roland D. Meisner of Gering, NE. She is presently working at Trinity River Authority, Arlington, TX. A 1994 Commandant's List graduate of the Command and General Staff College. Other schools completed are Combined Arms Services Staff School (1989); Logistics Management Development Course (1988); Military Personnel Officer Course (1988); and the Adjutant General Officer Basic Course (1984).

JEROME F. MEISTER (JERRY),

JEROME F. MEISTER (JERRY), born June 8, 1935, Hartford, CT. Enlisted with ROTC University of Connecticut, Jan. 8, 1958, and served in the U.S. Army QM Corps in various units and in a variety of positions.

Stationed at Pusan, Korea; Schenectady, NY; Ft. Benning, GA; Munich, Augsburg, Karlsruhe, Nuremberg, and New Ulm, Germany; Boston, Ft. Devens, MA; Ft. Lee, VA; San Diego, CA; Cam Ranh Bay, Saigon, Cu Chi and Long Binh Vietnam. Credited with serving a combat campaign stars during service in Vietnam, 1965-1966 and 1970-1971.

Memorable experiences: Officer in charge of a two brigade supply point on the Vietnam border supporting 10,000

troops; 1st Log. Cmd. Gen. Staff Briefing officer in 1965 and 1966; company commander of VII Corps designated demonstration company in Germany during 1961; and organized motor convoy from Cam Ranh Bay to Nha Trang and subsequent airlift of Jewish military personnel to Saigon for High Holiday Services in 1965.

Awards/Medals: Bronze Star Medal with three OLCs, Meritorious Service Medal with one OLC, Army Commendation Medal with two OLCs, Humanitarian Service Medal, Meritorious Unit Citation (2 awards), National Defense Service Medal, Vietnam Service Medal with seven OLCs, Vietnam Campaign Medal with 60 Device, Vietnam Cross of Gallantry with Palm, Armed Forces Honor Medal 1st Class and Expert Infantry Badge.

Discharged on Jan. 31, 1980, with the rank of major.

Married Cynthia and they have a daughter and son. He is chief of emergency operations for the Commonwealth of Massachusetts.

MARTIN MELLITZ,

MARTIN MELLITZ, born on Aug. 19, 1914. Joined the USNR on Nov. 1, 1943, as a coxswain mate. Stations include: USN Station, NY; Philippines Transfer Base; Soloman Islands, RS; Naval Station, New Orleans, LA; Light Flotilla Two, USS LST 660; LCT (C) Gp. 42; Flotilla 14; LCT 763, Flotilla 14; LCT Group 41, Flotilla 14; LCT, Flotilla Three FFT; Alex Heights, USN Seattle, WA; and Philadelphia Naval Station.

Awards/Medals: WWII Victory Medal and others unknown. Discharged on Nov. 19, 1945, and achieved the rank of coxswain.

Married Rose Rockstein Mellitz in 1939. Mellitz passed away and is survived by two daughters, one son and four grandchildren. He was a member of the JWV, USA.

BERNIE MELNICK,

BERNIE MELNICK, born Jan. 18, 1924, Bronx, NY. Joined U.S. Army, Jan. 16, 1943, served in the infantry and stationed at Ft. Dix, NJ, and Camp Butner.

Memorable experiences include Cannon Co., 110th Inf., 28th Div., Utah Beach, St. Lo, Liberation of Paris and was captured at Battle of the Bulge. Taken to Stalag 9-B Berga.

Awards/Medals: the European Theater, four campaign stars, POW Medal, Silver Star, Bronze Star and Purple Heart.

Discharged on Jan. 6, 1946, with the rank of corporal.

Married and has four children and four grandchildren. He has been a volunteer lecturer for the past five years. Retired at the end of 1988.

WILLIAM M. MELNICK,

WILLIAM M. MELNICK, born in New York, NY, Nov. 7, 1927. Enlisted July 18, 1945 with the USCG, with the North Atlantic Ice Patrol and stationed at Argentina, Newfoundland.

Awards/Medals: WWII Victory Medal. He was discharged on May 21, 1946, with the rank of seaman 2nd class.

Married Florence in 1956, and they have a son, Matthew. Worked as travel counselor for AAA in New York for nearly 39 years. Now retired and a member of Long Island City Post #110, and is a resident of Long Island City, NY.

IRVING MELTZER,

IRVING MELTZER, Hartford-Laurel Post 45, received a Russian Medal, The 40th Anniversary of the Victory in the Great Patriotic War, in recognition of his participation in Allied convoys to Archangel and Murmansk during WWII, at a ceremony at the Russian Embassy in Washington, DC on Dec. 8, 1992. Recently, he also received a Battle of the Atlantic Commemoration Badge from the British Government.

He says, "No one asked to be born, but it is most important to know who your are and what your are. I was born Jewish and proud of it."

He was in a convoy with Norwegian refugees bound for Scotland. After the war they returned to Norway. He was in Bremerhaven, Germany. He learned of a Jewish Community Center in Bremen and while there met survivors of the Holocaust. Being a ship's radio officer, he was asked by the survivors to help them return home to Palestine, which he did.

Tempered by war and trained in its technology, they ran the British naval blockade with "illegal immigrant ships." They were captured, interrogated, processed and confined to detention camps on Cyprus, only to return with other illegal ships and later serve with the Israeli Armed Forces.

In the 1950s he was employed by a defense contractor as an electronics inspector. He lives in South Windsor, CT.

ROBERT MENDELL, born June 20, 1933, Malden, MA. Joined USAF on Nov. 5, 1952, as forecaster technician (meteorologist). Stationed at the following between November 1952-August 1973: Sampson AFB, NY; Chanute AFB, IL; Kiwapo AFB, Korea; Barksdale AFB, LA; Dow AFB, ME; L.G. Hansgcom Field, MA; Maxwell AFB, AL; Kindley AFB, Bermuda; McGuire AFB, NJ; Travis AFB, CA; Korat AFB, Thailand; and Buckley ANGB, CO.

Awards/Medals: Air Force Commendation Medal, AFOUA with three awards, one with Combat V, United Nations Service Medal, Korean Service Medal, National Defense Service Medal with one Bronze Star, Good Conduct Medal with three Bronze Loops, Air Force Good Conduct Medal with three OLCs, AFLSA with four Bronze OLCs, Vietnam Service Medal with three Bronze Stars and RVCM.

Discharged on Aug. 30, 1973, with the rank of technical sergeant.

Married Eleanor S. Feldman (passed away in February 1984). They had three children: Beth Ann, born Feb. 22, 1958, Cheryl, born April 17, 1959, and Jason S., born on Aug. 17, 1961. Remarried on June 9, 1985, to Freda Levov Zlotnick. Presently working for the USAF (civil service) as a meteorologist at McGuire AFB, NJ.

SAMUEL MENDELSON, was with the 79th Div., Heavy Weapons Co., 313th Regt. and 367th Regt., Co. D. Wounded, hospitalized and returned to his company in Germany. Shortly thereafter, on Nov. 11, 1918, there was a very heavy fog, so bad they could not move or even identify as to where they were. At 11:00 a.m. they heard loud sounds of gongs and bells and with the din of them came a lot of shouting "It is over." Suddenly the fog started to life and they were slowly able to make out the surrounding landscape. When the fog completely lifted, they were horrified to see that they were at the bottom of a hill and at the top of the hill was a German heavy weapons company. If not for the fog, there was a good chance that their company would have suffered very heavy losses.

Later in life, as boss of painting in the Brooklyn Navy Yard, he was decorated for heroism for rescuing several men who had been trapped in a fire control explosion aboard a battleship that was brought in for repair and clean-up. He went in twice to pull his men out from the fire retardent foam that had engulfed them and the last time he himself had to be rescued as the foam had gotten to him.

He died in a Veterans Hosp. in Brooklyn, NY at age 69. They were told that his death was mostly due to the poison gas that had been in his lungs for many years. The gas was in him from the year he spent in the trenches during WWI. He received the Purple Heart and other awards.

JONATHAN DE SOLA MENDES, born in New York City, NY, Nov. 3, 1920. Received high school diploma in New Rochelle, NY in 1938; AB degree from Dartmouth College, Hanover, NH, 1942; MBA degree, Harvard Business School, Boston, MA, 1947.

Enlisted in the USMCR in 1942 as 1st lieutenant scout bomber pilot in the Central Pacific. Served 180 missions patrols, convoys, etc.; 1946-1951, captain in Reserve Squadrons VMF-217, Boston, MA, and VMF-132, Brooklyn, NY; worked in industrial management from 1947 1951; 1951 1953, served as major, operations officer of VMFT-20, Cherry Point, NC, VMF-224, Edenton, NC and VMF-311, Pohang, Korea, 70 missions; 1954-1958; lieutenant colonel, commanding officer of VMF-132, Brooklyn, NY; 1959-1973, colonel, VTU 1-1 New York, NY, staff assignments until retirement.

From 1955-1992, investment banking and corporate financial consultant; 1973-1993, trustee of congregation Shearith Israel in the city of New York (The Spanish and Portuguese Synagogue, founded in 1654); and 1984-1993, president of the Hebrew Relief Society of the city of New York (founded in 1824).

Awards/Medals: Distinguished Flying Cross and 10 Air Medals. Retired from the USMCR on June 30, 1973.

Married Mary Ellen Rosenbluth (passed away in 1988). They had two children, Eliza and Joshua, and one grandchild, Daniel Marks.

JAMES MENDLIN, born in Philadelphia, PA, June 16, 1917. Attended La Salle, Philadelphia and Brooklyn College. Joined Citizens Military Training Camps; trained with 6th Field Arty. Regt., Ft. Hoyle, MD, 1934-1937; awarded Civitan Medal; appointed 2nd lieutenant FA, USAR, January 1940; active duty, Jan. 15, 1942- February 1946, as captain, FA, 77th Inf. Div.; served as Bn. S-2 (combat intelligence) and battery commander in Marianas, Philippines and Ryukyu campaigns.

Participated in combat landing on Guam, Leyte, Kerama Retto and Okinawa. Wounded in action at Leyte, P.I in December 1944. Served with Central Intelligence Agency from 1950-1973, served in Middle East and Far East, including two year assignment to Vietnam.

Awarded Bronze Star, Purple Heart, Chuong-my Boi-Tinh, CIA Award and various country and theater medals.Currently residing in Los Angeles with his wife of 52 years and composing art music for string orchestra.

MICHAEL MENSCHEL, born in Brooklyn, NY, Feb. 26, 1951. Enlisted in the USAF Nov. 9, 1970. Military location included Lakeland AFB, TX; Lowry AFB, CO; Dyess AFB, TX; Raney AFB, Puerto Rico; Loring AFB, ME; and Kessler AFB, MS.

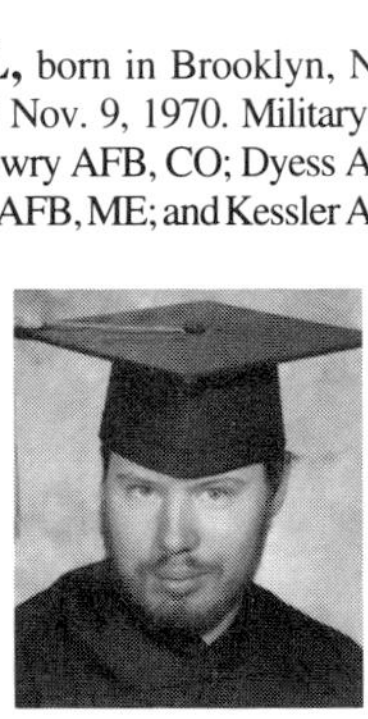

Graduated Inventory Management School in April 1971 and did data processing and also worked material control. Graduated Air Traffic Control School in June 1975; was barracks chief in 1976.

Discharged Aug. 6, 1976, with the rank of sergeant.

Graduated from BMCC, June 1981 in medical records technology. Became a ART September 1992 and presently works at the J.P. ADDABBO FHC. He is member of JWV Post 258.

MARVIN MENTER, born in Syracuse, NY, May 18, 1925. Graduated from Central High School, Sophmore at Syracuse University College of Journalism, member of Phi Epsilon Fraternity.

Served as a lieutentant fighter pilot and at the age of 20 was missing in action off Formosa on Feb. 7, 1945.

He is survived by his parents, Mr. and Mrs. A. Menter.

LEWIS SANFORD MENTLIK, graduated from the University of Wisconsin as the class valedictorian. His various sports letters and writing talents led to screen writing with Warner Bros. WWII found him in the 101st Abn. Div., 401st Glider Inf. Regt. Graduated from Officers Training School at Ft. Benning and selected to attend Brooks Army Corps Field, receiving Aerial Observer Wings upon completion.

Went to ETO on the SS *Strathnaver*. After extensive training at Brock Barracks, Reading, England, he made captain. A few months prior to D-day, his battalion was transferred to the 325th Glider Inf. Regt., 3rd Bn. of the 82nd Abn. Div. in Leicester, England.

As company commander, he landed by glider on June 6, 1944, in Sainte-Mere-Eglise, Normandy and on D+2 engaged in the bridge and causeway key D-day task crossing the Merederet River. The pressure on Gen. Ridgway to seize the causeway was immense. Capt. Mentlik's performance in this critical battle was admirable. He was killed in action June 14, 1944. He was truly airborne.

Awards/Medals: Glider Badge, Combat Infantry Badge, Bronze Star, Aerial Observer Wings, Purple Heart, French Croix de Guerre with palm, Bronze Battle Star and others.

Was married to Helen R. Cohen and daughter, Toby Ann, was born in 1943 at Ft. Bragg, NC just before Lt. Mentlik went to the ETO. *Submitted by his brother-in-law Mickey L. Cohen.*

EDYTHE R. MERMELSTEIN (WOLGEL), was inducted into the WAAC in May 1943. Basic training at Ft. Oglethorpe, GA; assigned to special services as secretary to the head of orientation and education for the Brooklyn Port of Embarkation and stationed at Ft. Hamilton, Brooklyn.

Her section was responsible for the orientation sessions presented to groups of soldiers prior to embarking for overseas duty and to organize and arrange entertainment at the various staging installations in the area.

She made friends who have remained with her to this day. She was discharged in August 1945.

Two points stick in her mind: the resentment at Ft. Oglethorpe towards the Yankee outsider; and the one outbreak of antisemitism at Christmas at Ft. Hamilton. The Jewish girls had all volunteered for duty so that the gentile girls could have their holiday. One of the gentile girls who did not go home for the holiday got drunk and ran through the barracks screaming, "Kill the Jews, they killed Christ".

The best perk in working at the Brooklyn POE was that when her fiancé was coming back to the States in January 1945, she was able to greet him at the dock and arrange for him to get off the ship before the rest of the personnel.

They married in March 1945 and after her husband was discharged in the summer of 1945, she applied for and received discharge at Ft. Sheridan, IL.

MORRIS MESNIK (DOC), born in Bronx, NY, Dec. 14 1918. Enlisted in the USAF in June 1941; served with the 57th Fighter Gp. his entire tour of duty. Went overseas after Pearl Harbor in July 1942, returned after Japanese surrender in 1945 Saw action with the DAF and Gen. Montgomery's British 8th Army from El Alamein to Tunis, Tripoli with the 9th AF through Malta, Corsica, Sicily and Italy Campaigns with the 12 AF

Remembers the great classic Palm Sunday Massacre on Cape Bon when they shot down 74 German planes.

Awards/Medals: Soldiers Medal, Good Conduct Medal, European Medal with seven Battle Stars and three OLCs and WWII Victory Medal.

Married and has three children and two grandchildren. Owns his own business and enjoys having 57th Fighter Gp. reunions and seeing all of his old buddies.

A. MORTON METH, born in Passaic, NJ, on July 27, 1921. Enlisted in the USAAF in October 1942, as a B-29 Flight Engineer. Stations included Walker AAF Base, KS; and Biggs AAF Field, El Paso, TX.

Memorable experiences include airplane flight emergencies; 14 hour flights in B-29s to El Paso, Seattle and other cities in the United States.

Awards/Medals: American Campaign Medal and WWII Victory Medal. Discharged on March 19, 1946, as 1st lieutenant.

Married and has three daughters and six grandchildren. Working as a design engineer for Foster-Wheeler Corp.

BERNARD F. METH, born in Passaic, NJ, Aug. 24, 1917. Entered U.S. Army in September 1941 with the 4th Field Arty. in Ft. Bragg which was a mule pack outfit; shipped to Southwest Pacific N.Z., Australia, New Guinea; spent three years as a medical tech.; wound up in Madigan General Hospital in Tacoma, WA.

Memorable experiences include the bombing raids in New Guinea on Good Enough Island and taking 42 days to get to Australia by way of Panama Canal, Bora Bora, New Zealand.

Awards include the American Defense Medal, Southwest Pacific with one star, Good Conduct Medal and Asiatic Pacific Medal.

Discharged on Sept. 29, 1945, as private first class.

Married with three children. He is presently retired.

BERNARD E. METRICK, enlisted in the U.S. Army after graduating from New York University Dental College in June 1942. Joined the 8th Svc. Cmd. in San Antonio, TX, in July 1942, as lieutenant; assigned to the 8th Armd. Div. in June 1943 at Camp Polk, LA, where they trained other tank divisions as a cadre outfit.

Went to Europe in December 1944 and into combat, Battle of the Bulge, as a liaison officer for the 78th Med. Bn., Co. B, 8th Armd. Div. They were active across France, Belgium, Holland and Germany and were the first Armd. Div. cross the Siegfried Line. At the end of combat they were sent to the border of the Russian army line in Czechoslovakia.

Memorable experiences: Meeting American soldiers who had been on a death march; freeing prisoners from Buckenwald and delousing them; guiding a war crimes investigator, a general for the War Crimes Commission, through a concentration camp and hearing him remark that he never would have believed it if he had not seen it with his own eyes.

Awards/Medals: three Battle Stars for Rhineland, Ardennes and Central Europe, American Campaign Medal, EAME Cam-

paign Medal, WWII Victory Medal and numerous service unit plaques. Was recommended for the Bronze Star on June 22, 1945.

Married Irene in October 1939 and has two daughters, one son and four grandchildren. Still practices medicine, but as a volunteer for the poor in the Department of Health, Delray Beach, FL. He and his wife are charter members of the Holocaust Museum in Washington, DC.

MELVIN METZGER, entered the U.S. Army in 1952 as a first lieutenant in the JAG Corps. Served for two and one half years at Ft. Dix, NJ, handling court martials and other legal matters.

A veteran of the Korean Conflict; member of the JWV; graduate of Baruch College in 1949 with a BBA degree; graduate of Brooklyn Law School in 1951 with JD and a LLM; member of the bar, state of New York; and a CPA. Active in the Democratic Party; president of the young Israel of Windsor Park; president of the Yeshiva High School of Queens in addition to other civic organizations.

Married, has three children and practices law in New York.

LEONARD A. MEYER, born in Atlanta, GA, Feb. 18, 1925. Enlisted in the USAAF on June 3, 1943, with the 374th Troop Carrier Gp., 54th Troop Carrier Wing, 5th AF. Stations included Gulfport Field, MS; Ft. Logan, CO; Kearns Field, UT; Chanute Field, IL; Jefferson Barracks, MO; Lae, New Guinea, Biak, Dutch East Indies; Leyte, Manila, Philippines. Participated in the Paratroop drop at Markaham Valley, New Guinea, the invasion of Leyte and the invasion of Manila.

Memorable experiences include the attack at Biak while the USO show was in progress; 88 were killed.

Awards/Medals: five Battle Stars and a Good Conduct Medal. Discharged on Dec. 31, 1945, with the rank of sergeant.

Married Janet Miller of New York City on March 2, 1946, and they have three children: R. Scott, living in Moscow, Russia in distribution Business; Roger, OB GYN, Carson City, NV; and Richard, recording studio, Atlanta, GA. Sold his business, State Wholesalers, after 44 years to Empire and now works as senior vice president of Empire Distributors, a liquor and wine distributor.

SHERMAN MEYERSON, born in New Haven, CT, Dec. 28, 1921. Enlisted in the USAAF in February 1942 as a bombardier on a B-29, and was stationed at Guam. Formed Guam Zionist Club while in Guam. Participated in 13 bombing missions over Japanese Empire.

Memorable experiences were the night missions; being bombed by radar and bombsight; oil refineries; engine on fire and almost having to bail out over New Orleans on a training flight at 30,000 feet; had 13 holes in plane five miles from Tokyo.

Awards/Medals: Air Medal and Victory Medal, clusters, etc. Discharged in March 1946 as first lieutenant.

Married with three children and three grandchildren. Attended college on GI Bill and received Masters degree from Columbia University. Worked in insurance, accounting, officer manager, and realty.

Served as president of the New Haven District of the Zionist Organization of America for several years; commander of JWV Post 204, 1961-1962, and won award for outstanding post in Connecticut; sang in several operas and enjoys singing Yiddish songs.

HAROLD MICHAELS, born in 1911, enlisted in the USAF at the age of 28 after watching news reels in New York City about Hitler's rise to power. "I would see all these shots of Hitler marching his men into Europe, especially into Germany, and it was very upsetting to me," he remembered. "Not trying to be a hero, or anything like that, I decided to enlist." He was a turret gunner in a B-26 Marauder, flying 67 missions and was shot down three times. The third time, he didn't hear the pilot's order to bail out.

Everyone else bailed out and were killed by the Germans. He bailed out a few minutes later and was hurt when he hit the roof of a French home, but was rescued by the French underground. "It was a job to do and we did it," he said. "We all pretended we were heroes and weren't afraid." But, he said, the young men who pretended to be brave during the day often broke down and cried for their mothers at night.

He is retired as the advertising department supervisor at KVNJ-TV in Fargo, ND.

IRVING W. MICHAELS, served during WWII with the USN. His first action against the enemies, came the second night out, in a 185 ship convoy to England, when several ships were sunk by a Nazi U-boat wolf pack. When his LST reached Plymouth, they loaded up with American Infantry and Sherman tanks for Omaha Beach, D-day plus eight. Two other channel crossings to Omaha and Utah beaches, they carried British and Canadian troops.

They sailed to the Pacific Theater via the Panama Canal and took on the 708th Amphib. Tk. Bn. at Pearl Harbor and made four invasions with them, culminating with Okinawa. They experienced kamikaze attacks day and night at Okinawa April 1, 1945, until the atomic bombing of Nagasaki. They then went to Nagasaki and took back American and British POW's, from the Fukoka prison camp. They were in terrible physical condition. War was indeed hell. To survive is a combination of pluck and luck.

LEONARD S. MICHELMAN, born 1923. Attended Springfield, MA Schools, sports editor of high school newspaper and played football. Undergraduate Brown University BS degree in physics. Joined U.S. Sig. Corps. during WWII, 1943-1945, as a transmitter repairman.

Juris Doctorate degree, Boston University, 1948; Master Patent Law, George Washington University, 1950; U.S. Patent Examiner, 1948-1950; practicing attorney, Springfield, MA. Son, Jay, joined him in Michelman Law Office.

Kodimoh-Israel Bond Chairman, JWV; trustee Springfield Jewish Federation nine years; former chairman, Federation's Collection Committee; campaign chairman, former editor SHOFAR (federation newspaper); Judge Advocate, American Legion Post 175; former member VFW; former director Western Massachusetts Bridge Association; former delegate New England Bridge League and life master of American Contract Bridge League.

Awarded Battle Star at Iwo Jima.

DAN MICHELSON, born in Trenton, NJ, April 9, 1917. Enlisted in October 1942 as private first class in the Army AAA Gun Bn. Stationed in North Africa, Italy, France, Belgium and Germany.

Memorable experience was in July 1938, when he sold his barber Leon Parent a gold cross and chain for his son's Holy Communion. Parent asked Michelson to box it for mailing to Liege, Belgium. In December 1944, Michelson needed a haircut and found a local barber shop. He sat down and noticed the name on the window, M. Parent. When the barber came in, Michelson was aware of a striking resemblance to his barber back home. After a short exchange in French and English, it became apparent that he had walked into Leon Parent's brother's barber shop.

When he told him the story of the cross and chain, Parent became very excited and called his wife and daughter in from the kitchen, and, of course, the daughter was wearing the cross and chain. In 1946, the Parent's from Liege, came to East Orange to visit the brother and all got together for lunch and reminiscence.

Awarded the EAME Campaign Medal, Good Conduct Medal, Victory Medal and American Campaign Medal.

Married and has two children. He is now retired.

JACK MICHELSTEIN, born in New York in 1925. Enlisted on April 15, 1943, with the U.S. Army, 26th Div., 101st Regt., and was stationed in France.

Passed away on Nov. 20, 1944, and is buried in Lorrain Cemetery in St. Avold. *Submitted by George Rosen.*

MAX P. MILIANS, born in New York City, on May 5, 1907, raised in Stamford, CT. Attended YU Talmudical Academy New York City, 1920-1921. Left cartoonist job day after Pearl Harbor to enlist. Medics solved underweight problem while Corps requested my immediate PRO assignment. Pentagon disallowed basic training waiver.

At Upton, waiting to join "This is Army" groups for basic, wrote releases and interviewed inductees to spot talent or possible subversives. Exercising enlisted privilege insisted on Signal, Engineer or AAC for assignment. Landed at QMRTC, creating morale boosting esprit de corps cartoons for Sp Sv, "the Camp Lee Traveller," and several series for Quartermaster General dramatizing achievements of QMC R&D and manufacturers teamwork as industry sponsored ads in major newspapers and magazines.

Commissioned 2nd lieutenant QMC June 1943; assigned School for Special (and Morale) Services as chief, Visual Training Aids; mess officer; chief, handicrafts. TDY Paris, January 1945; assigned to Theater Chief Sp Sv Frankfurt, June 1945; major, chief, handicrafts; chief, control branch; redeployed May 1946 Sp Sv Div. DOD.

Awards/Medals: Legion of Merit, Good Conduct Medal, Meritorious Unit Emblem, American Campaign Medal, EAME Campaign Medal, WWII Victory Medal, Army of Occupation with Germany Clasp.

Discharged December 1946, resuming career as cartoonist and promotion manager national chain and DC newspapers. In Reserves as lieutenant colonel attached to OCINFO; attended Command Gen Staff College Sp Course. Retired June 1967.

With Hearst chain also was Junior Diplomat Director for 17 years escorting outstanding boys on international goodwill trips to all five continents, with State Department and DOD Participation.

Married Ruth Paul Milians and they reside in Teaneck, NJ.

IRWIN J. MILLER, born Feb. 19, 1926, Brooklyn, NY. Entered USN on March 29, 1944. Inducted by JWV as a service member of Post #108 in 1944. Boot training and subsequently Signal School, NTS, Sampson, NY, under the command of Capt. Harry Badt, scion of a pioneer Texas Jewish Family.

Plank owner at commissioning of SS *Kershaw* (APA 176) in Seattle, Dec. 2, 1944. Sailed for Guam, where ship joined 5th Fleet as reserve for initial invasion forces at Iwo Jima. Volunteered for ship's Beach Bn. as a replacement. Received flashing light message of Secretary Forrestal's announcement to the fleet, of the death of FDR, while of Okinawa. Ship's radio transmission had failed. Copy still in his possession.

Awards/Medals: Asiatic-Pacific Medal with two Battle Stars, American Theater Medal and WWII Victory Medal. Discharged at Lido Beach, NY, on May 26, 1946.

Married Vivian and has four children and seven grandchildren. Member Fred Robbins Post #142, Stamford. Former mfrs. rep., now retired. Teaches courses in American Jewish History, at Stamford and Greenwich. A founder and historian of Stamford Jewish Historical Society.

JAY JEFFERSON MILLER II, born in Baltimore, MD, Sept. 14, 1925. Enlisted Sept. 13, 1943, with the U.S. Army, with the 87th Inf. Div. Stations included Ft. Benning, Jackson, England, France, Belgium, Luxembourg, Germany. Participated at Saarland, Ardennes (Battle of the Bulge) and Rhineland.

Awards/Medals: Combat Infantry Badge, Purple Heart and Bronze Star. Discharged on Feb. 2, 1946, with the rank of corporal.

Married Anne and they have six children and eight grandchildren. He is retired and serves as director, Emeritus, MD Historical Society.

MARVIN L. MILLER, born December 1894, Seyny, Poland. Immigrated to United States in 1899; basketball star and graduate of Brooklyn Polytech Institute of Engineering. Commissioned a lieutenant in the Army Sig. Corps., 1917.

Served overseas in France in the Air Service (now USAF) and then under the aegis fo the Sig. Corps. One of the first to operate radio transmission in aircraft. Subsequently served as engineer for Marconi Wireless, Willard Btry., General Motors, and Con Edison. On the morning after Pearl Harbor, Dec. 8, 1941, at the age of 47 he went down to 39 Whitehall St. (Army recruiting) in New York City and volunteered his services.

Was commissioned a captain in the Sig. Corps. and assigned to the base in Orlando, FL. Subsequently promoted to major and in early 1945 sent to Tinian in the Marianas where he was involved in the planning and execution of the flight of the Enola Gay.

Leaving the Army as a lieutenant colonel at the close of the war, he joined Con Edison.

Married to the Edith Landes, they had no children.

SAMUEL L. MILLER, born in Columbus, OH, Aug. 15, 1946. Enlisted in the USAF in 1965, in aircraft maintenance on Jets one and two (4315IC MOS). Stationed at Lackland AFB, TX; Sheppard AFB, Wichita Falls, TX; Shaw AFB, SC; Clark AFB, PI; and Offitt, NE. Participated at Phau Rang AFB, Vietnam, 1967-1968.

Memorable experiences include being sent to Clark and attaching to the 8th Tactical BS. The squadron alternated with the 13th every 59 days. Eventually, the 8th absorbed the 13th. The 8th was the Liberty Squad and the 13th the Grim Reaper. The aircraft was the B-57.

Ironically, the Royal Australian 2nd Squad was positioned next to them. They used the British version, the Canberra. Usually the aircraft was scheduled to fly two missions per 24 hours. For approximately 40 day (Tet), the aircraft flew three missions. Status of maintenance really suffered. As long as the aircraft could fly, it did. One night Miller and three or four others were performing an engine swap, the aircraft was setting on the trim pad, which was located near the perimeter. An SP drove to their location and informed them they had to vacate immediately. They were being sniped at. Because of the noise of the portable flood light, they were oblivious of their precarious situation.

Awards/Medals: Presidential Unit Citation, Outstanding Unit with Valor, Air Force Good Conduct Medal with OLC, National Defense Service Medal, Vietnam Service Medal with two Bronze Stars, Air Force Overseas, Air Force Training, Vietnam Civil Action with Palm, Republic of Vietnam Campaign, Unit Gallantry with Palm, Army Service Medal, Army Achievement Medal, PLDC and Mass Service. He received honorable discharge in 1969.

Currently COC 1-104, 26th Yankee Div., MA Guard, Mortar Plt. 81mm FDC.

SEYMOUR W. MILLER, born in Brooklyn, NY, Dec. 19, 1914. Graduated Brooklyn College (then part of CCNY) in February 1935, with a BS degree in mathematical physics. Attended Columbia University School of Engineering for one semester, then went to NYU Law School at night, working as a law clerk by day. Received JD degree in June 1939, and was admitted to the Bar in December 1939. Save for some four years in the Army in WWII, practiced law continuously since then. After the war, received an LL.M. degree from the Graduate School of Law, NYU in 1948.

Inducted in February 1942. Graduated Infantry, OCS, Ft. Benning, GA, in September 1942, as a 2nd lieutenant. Sent to 8th Div., where the chief signal officer effected his transfer to the Sig. Corps. He gathered, but did not really know, he was to be assigned to a JASCO Co. (Joint Assault Signal Co.), but, not unusually, the orders got mixed up and he was sent to the 17th Sig. Operations Bn., with which he served out WWII. Sent overseas in October 1943; participated in the landing on Omaha Beach. After the European War ended, was sent to Camp Bowie, TX, to prepare for the invasion of Japan, but, with the end of that war, was sent on terminal leave.

Awards/Medals: usual ribbons, plus his ETO Ribbon with Arrowhead for the landing on Omaha Beach, and five Battle Stars. Honorably discharged from active service, with the rank of captain, February 1946. Joined the Active Reserve and, after about 10 years or so, was honorably retired with rank of major. Now, MAJ, USAR, RET.

Life member of the JWV, Reserve Officers Association, and the Armed Forces Communications and Electronics Association. Also, member of the Military Order of the World Wars, the American Legion, and a Gold Leaf Commander of the DAV (honorary). Small but regular contributor to other veterans' associations, as well.

Married the former Claire Glass. Two sons, John and Thomas, and three grandchildren. Mostly retired now, but does pro bono work, principally for the New York County Lawyers' Association, where he chair's the Special Mediation Committee (large scale commercial matters), and co-chair the New York County Lawyer's Association Foundation. About the only thing he did, that was different from that of most other soldiers, was to manage, during campaign lulls, to write a song which, by order, became the official Sig. Corps. song for the ETO.

STANLEY MILLER, born in Brooklyn, NY, Nov. 27, 1931. A licensed pharmacist, he entered the Medical Service Corps., USAFR, September 1955 and served as a medical administrator in military hospitals at Mitchel AFB in NY and at the Thule AFB in Greenland.

At Mitchel Field, he worked with local civilian authorities in the first series of the new polio vaccination program, helping assure that the children of military personnel at the base were included in the program. Other duties included blood drive organizing and updating hospital medical records

At the fairly controlled environment of Thule Air Base he monitored and wrote one of the earliest studies of a Asian Flu outbreak. This was in 1957, and he was release from active duty in November 1957 having attained the ran of captain.

Miller is owner and chief pharmacist at the Prescriptic Center in Williston Park, NY. He also holds a bachelo degree in professional studies in Human Relations and h done counseling in that area. A member of the JWV in Howa Beach, NY, he is also currently the president of the Rockwoo Park Jewish Center there.

Married 38 years, his wife holds a degree in sociolog and their three grown children hold masters degree in phy ics, computer technology, economics, business administr tion, English, and journalism from Polytechnic Institu Princeton University, M.I.T. Brandeis University and Ne York University.

WILLIAM MILLER, born Aug. 30, 1916, Detroit, M Family moved to Norfolk, VA; Washington, DC; Philad phia, PA. Graduated South Philadelphia, HS, June 19 Enlisted in the USCG October 1936, assigned to a CG Champlain, NY; October 1937 assigned to CGC *Unalga*, S Juan, P.R.

Duty Stations/Schools/Ships: QM School, Ellis Isla CG Academy; USS *Everett*, escorting convoys in the Al tians, Bering Sea and North Pacific; USS *Eugene* in N

Atlantic out of Argentia Nfld. on weather patrols. Transferred (1946) to 10th CG District, San Juan, P.R. COTP Operations, CGC *Sagebrush* to establish radio beacon towers in the Panama Canal Zone. Commanding officer (1947) of Patrol Boat CG-83506, St. Thomas, V.I. CGC *Winnebago*, Honolulu, T.H. (1949); CGC *Planetree*, XO, Guam, M.I. (1950); COTP & Group Office, Baltimore, MD (1951); CGC Sassafras, Cape May, NJ (1954); CG Base, Gloucester, NJ as XO (1955); COTP & Group, Baltimore, MD (1959); CGHQ, Washington, DC (1961).

Promoted to commander September 1963, assumed duties of Chief HQ Services Division until retirement September 1965.

Awards/Medals: American Defense, American Theater, Asiatic-Pacific Theater, EAME Theater, WWII Victory, National Defense, Korea and United Nations Medals, Coast Guard Good Conduct Medal (3) Command at Sea Insigne and Commandant Letter of Commendation.

Received BS, John Hopkins University 1973; MLA, 1976; second career in data processing with state of Maryland as Manager II until 1977. Now retired in Florida. Member of JWV Post 503.

Married since 1940.

ARTHUR S. MILNER,
born in Bronx, NY, September 1923. Entered the USN in April 1943; boot training at Great Lakes, IL; served in USS *Gambier Bay* (CVE-73) as a radioman second class.

The *Bambier Bay* (7th Fleet), was in numerous engagements in the Pacific including the Palaus, the Mariana "Turkeyshoot" and finally the Battle of the Philippine Sea where it was sunk on Oct. 25, 1944. After jumping from the flight deck, he was in the water some 48 hours.

After the war he began a broadcasting career until 1966 when he went into public relations and eventually to the Free Library in 1974. As a writer he penned scores of short stories and essays for the the *New York Times, Newsday, Mademoiselle*. etc.

Married to Norma Martin, they had no children. He was a graduate of Journalisn at Syracuse University.

He passed away on June 11, 1989.

EUGENE J. MILNER,
born in Bronx, NJ, in 1916. Graduate of New York University and the Dental School of the University of Pennsylvania in 1942. Was commissioned in the Dental Corps. and assigned to Ft. George Meade, MD. In 1944 he was sent to Italy serving in the field as a dental surgeon.

After the war, practiced in Philadelphia and passed away in Wynnewood, PA in 1982.

Married Jane Rubin Milner and they had two children.

ALVIN MILTON,
born in Bronx, NY, May 8, 1924. Enlisted on July 26, 1943 in the USN, with the Seabees, CBM, 25th and 146th Bn. Stationed at Davisville, RI, Newfoundland and Port Hueneme, CA and participated at Okinawa.

Memorable experience was his 46 days on transport Okinawa.

Awards/Medals: Asiatic-Pacific Medal, Star, American Theater, WWII Victory and Navy Occupation. Discharged on July 26, 1946, with rank of CM3/c.

Married Myrna in 1964 and has two daughters, Susan and Robyn. Retired and spending time with his big band and jazz collection of records. Member of the JWV #569 Toms River.

DAVID MISHKIN,
born in Chicago, IL, July 13, 1928. Graduated from Hyde Park High School, Chicago, IL in June 1946. Enlisted in U.S. Army June 10, 1946, with basic training Ft. McClellan, AL. Served in Korea at 29th Gen. Hosp. and 4th Gen. Hosp, 24th Corps.

Honorable discharge on April 7, 1948, with rank of T/5.

Attended College of Osteopathic Physicians and Surgeons, Los Angeles, CA, 1955; M.D. degree from California College of Medicine, 1962; Diplomat American Board of Anesthesiology, 1968.

Enlisted in USAFR in March 1982; flight surgeon, Aerospace Medicine Primary Course, December 1982; transferred to USAR, 1985. Assigned to 403rd Cbt. Spt. Hosp., Phoenix, AZ. Called to active duty in support of Desert Storm, November 1990-April 1991. Served at Ft. Ord, CA.

Awards/Medals: WWII Victory Ribbon, Occupation Medal (Japan), Army Service Ribbon, National Defense Service Medal, Overseas Service Ribbon, Army Reserve Components Achievement Medal, Air Force Reserve Achievement Medal and Army Commendation Ribbon. Honorably separated in July 1992, age 64, with the rank of LTC MC.

Married Agnes Marie Short of Springfield, MO, February 1985. Has two sons, Aaron Avram and Ari Daniel. Stepchildren are Capt. Keith Brown, USAFR, 2nd Lt. K. Ginger Brown-Castor, NC USAR and Kriss Lani Brown-Carter. He and his wife reside in Bella Vista, AR. Member of JWV, VFW, American Legion and ROA.

JOSEPH J. MITTLEMAN,
born in Brooklyn, NY, Oct. 14, 1923. Joined U.S. Army Sig. Corp as a message center clerk. Stationed at Camp Crowder, MO; New Guinea; Australia; Manila; Philippines; Biak; Milne Bay; Hollandia.

Memorable experience involves surgery on his neck at the 132nd General Hospital, Biak, New Guinea.

Awards/Medals: Asiatic-Pacific Service Medal, Good Conduct Medal and WWII Victory Medal. Discharged on Feb. 12, 1946, with rank of sergeant.

Married Gladys and has a daughter, Susan and son, Randy; two grandchildren, Julie and Matt. Returned to wholesale paper and twine business. Retired and now travels and enjoys seeing the world.

HERMAN MOLLINS,
born in Brooklyn, NJ, July 22, 1926. Entered U.S. Army on Oct. 24, 1944. Basic training at Ft. Knox, TN, then shipped overseas on Aug. 8, 1945. After Germany surrendered, returned to Ft. Knox for jungle training. Landed in Philippines; prepared for invasion of Japan; Japan surrendered and went to Japan with invasion forces; beach landing and stayed for occupation.

Awards/Medals: Army Occupation Medal, Asiatic-Pacific and WWII Victory Medal.

Discharged on Nov. 7, 1946, with rank of technician 3rd grade from the 304th Sig. Operation Bn., as message center chief, Yokohama Base HQ.

Married in 1948, has five daughters and eight grandchildren. Member of JWV, Post 100; past commander of both American Legion Bill Brown Post 507 and Masonic War Veterans Post #3; present commander of VFW; life member of VFW Post #107; member of Military Order of the Cootie. Employed as vice president of a large printing firm for the past 52 years.

MORRIS MONESSON,
born June 4, 1925, Lakewood, NJ. Entered active duty Sept. 21, 1943. Stationed at Camp Wheeler, GA for basic training; Ft. Meade, MD; Hampton Roads, VA; Caserta, Italy; Anzio, Rome, Battipaglia, Italy; Southern France and England. Participated in Anzio Beachhead, Rome-Arno, Southern France and Rhineland campaigns.

Memorable Experiences: cutting lawn grass with a dull bayonet at basic training; encountering fanatical resistance from "Hitler's Youth" at Vosges Mountains where they killed and captured a number of young uniformed German soldiers between the ages of 12-16 (some who surrendered looked like scared wild animals); being wounded by a short round of German artillery while on patrol in the Vosges Mountains. The shell hit Monesson in the lower legs, both feet and left forearm. The same shell blew off his BARman's legs, who later died from loss of blood.

Another unforgettable experience was in Italy while receiving amphibious training. His squad received two new replacements who were rather shy and not at all aggressive. Their squad leader was a combat veteran who persisted in giving them a bad time until one day Monesson couldn't stand it anymore and approached Sgt. Jones and said, "Jones if you don't quit picking on them, I'm gonna shoot you." Jones heeded the warning and from then on became friends and had a mutual respect for one another.

Awards/Medals: Silver Star, Bronze Star, Purple Heart, Combat Infantry Badge, American Campaign, EAME Campaign, WWII Victory Medal, Good Conduct Medal. He was discharged May 20, 1946 as sergeant, infantry squad leader.

Has BS degree from Rutgers University, College of Agriculture, Class 1951. Married and has six children and 10 grandchildren. Retired after 30 years civil service with USDA/FmHA on April 30, 1990. Currently a part-time crop farmer and land developer. He is a member of Robbins-Feldstein Post 178 JWV, Lakewood, NJ.

MARTIN MONDRUS,
joined the U.S. Merchant Marine in 1943 at the age of 18. An act of Congress gave those who served during this period of armed conflict, full veteran status. His teenage years were devoted to becoming an artist, and this has been his calling ever since.

Far away places stirred his imagination and the urge to travel influenced his decision to join the Merchant Marine during WWII. Shipped out on Liberty ships and tankers and reached ports in the Pacific, Asia, Europe and Africa, 1943-1946.

Aboard the ship he made some good friends and has cherished memories of them. He also encountered considerable prejudice, intolerance and anti semitism.

HERMAN F. MONDSCHEIN,
volunteered as a private in the U.S. Army July 1941, in the age of 41, training a weather observer, Bradley Field, CT; then, after five months' training at Chanute Field, IL, became a weather forecaster. Sent to England in April 1943 as a forecaster supporting the 8th AF Combat Fighter Operations; rose to master sergeant and station chief, then to warrant officer.

Awards/Medals: ETO Ribbon with four Battle Stars and Presidential Unit Citation. Separated in December 1945, became a 2nd lieutenant in MOANG, promoted to 1st lieutenant and recalled for 21 months of active duty, 1951-1952.

At Scott AFB, IL, weather lectures to command and staff pilots and operational weather briefings brought several letters of commendation. After separation he joined the Air Weather Service's Active Reserves, rising to lieutenant colonel, 1969.

Retired in 1981 after a 40 year military association.

SIDNEY MONDSCHEIN, born in Bayonne, NJ, on March 22, 1927. Orphaned in 1939 and became a ward of the state from 1939-1945. Graduated Macomb's Junior High School 82, Bronx, New York, 1939-1942; Brooklyn Technical High School, 1942-1945, War Diploma. Enlisted in the UNS February 1945; recruit training, Sampson, NY, 1945.

Stationed at: USNH Corps, 1945-1946; San Diego Naval Hospital; St. Albans Naval Hospital, New York; USN Dental Clinic, Brooklyn, NY; Sampson Naval Training Center; Lido Beach, New York Separation Center. Received honorable discharge as pharmacistmate third class July 3, 1946.

Positions held at Harris Teachers College, St. Louis, MO, 1946-1948; University of Missouri, Columbia, MO, 1948-1949; St. Louis University School fo Dentistry, DDS, 1949-1953; private practice, 1954; USAF Dental Corps (captain), Lincoln AFB, NE, 1955-1957; private practice, St. Louis, MO, 1957-1980; St. Louis University School of Public Health, MPH, 1980-1982; consultant, 1982-1985; dental director HMO, 1985-1987; consultant, 1987-present; commander, St. Louis Heritage Post 644, 1992-1994; commander, Department of Missouri, 1995.

Married Natalie in 1954 and has one married daughter, MD with two children; and two married sons, one an MD and the other a corporate manager.

EUGENE L. MOORE, born in Warsaw, Poland, Jan. 11, 1919. Entered service in April 1942. Infantry training at Ft. McClellan, AL; assigned to Sig. Corps. Radar Unit; entered 5th and 13th AF in battle of New Guinea and Invasion of the Philippines.

Awards/Medals: three Battle Stars and Philippine Liberation Medal. Discharged December 1945 from the 8th Fighter Control Sqdn.

Served four years as commander of VFW Post 4143; Voice of Democracy chairman; district vice commander; district chaplain and other chairs. Obtained charter and started JWV Post 502, North Palm Beach in 1990; current three times commander. Influential in getting the VA Hospital started in Rivera Beach. Every year personally shopping, cooking, purchasing gifts for indigent and homeless children for Chanukah Christmas party. His goal is helping fellow comrades in every way possible.

Married Roslyn Jan. 12, 1946, and has three children: Maxine, Roberta and David; and three grandchildren: Yale, Lisa and Bianca Scarlett.

ROBERT S. MORAY, born in East Orange, NJ, June 26, 1926. Entered USAF on Sept. 18, 1954. Served as dental officer with the 3550th USAF Hospital at Moody AFB, Valdosta, GA.

Discharged on Sept. 17, 1956, with rank of captain.

He passed away on June 1, 1968.

DON MORENO, born Feb. 27, 1931, a Sephardic Jew with Spanish Ancestry. Assigned to the Special Services Branch, Athletic Section of HQ Co., 2nd Bn., 351 Inf. Div.

He was shipped to Hawaii in 1951, the Korean War was in its second year of hostilities. He recalls an incident at Scoffield Barracks, "We were all on the parade grounds. A guy pulls up in a jeep. He says if you want to see a chaplain, get on one of these lines. But there was no line for the other Jewish guy and me. So we walked over to the nearest group. The last GI in line said, 'This ain't your side' and he pushed my buddy to the ground. So I said, 'If you're gonna push somebody, it'd better be me.'" A fist fight followed.

Before long, Moreno was wearing boxing gloves in Trieste (between Yugoslavia and Italy). "The title bout was in the battalion hangar. I was in the latrine before the fight. Some sergeant comes in and says, 'Moreeeno.' Just like that, 'Moreeeno.' He says, 'You gonna fight tonight? I'm gonna watch them knock the crap outta ya. I don't like your dogtag.' But I fooled the SOB I fought my butt off." He compiled a record of 14 and 1 touring Italy, Germany and Austria.

SAMUEL MORGAN, graduated from Creighton University College of Dentistry in the class of 1931. Entered the USAR in 1942 and was sent to North Africa in 1943.

On an August day he and a doctor friend were walking down a street in North Africa, there was a strafing by the German Air Corps and they were shot down among many other.

The Epstein-Morgan JWV of Omaha is named for him and Hymie Epstein who was also killed in the war.

ISADORE MOSCOVITZ, born in Jacksonville, FL, Sept. 15, 1911. Joined the services on Aug. 20, 1941, and went to Ft. Benning, GA for basic training, as captain, in the infantry. Stationed at Camp Van Dorn, MS, and served as a special service officer who helped activate the 99th Inf. Div.

Served one year on the publication section of the Infantry School at Ft. Benning, GA. Fought anti semitism within the division.

Memorable experiences include writing activation speech for Gen. Thompson Lawrence; organized division newspaper, "The Checkerboard"; was in charge of the divisions athletic program; was on general's staff; and served as chaplain for the 800 Jewish personnel in the division.

Discharged in July 1945, with the rank of major.

Retired after 55 years as editor and publisher of the *Southern Jewish Weekly.*

LESTER RAY MOSER, born in New York City, NY, April 27, 1941. Enlisted on April 27, 1941, at Camp Upton, NY, with field artillery and was stationed at Ft. Bragg, NC.

Memorable experience was coming back from Leyte, Philippines on a ship with 3,000 men aboard. They came under the Golden Gate Bridge on Christmas Eve.

Awards/Medals: Good Conduct, American Campaign, Asiatic-Pacific, Philippine Liberation and WWII Victory Medal.

Has two daughters and three grandchildren. Retired and a member of the JWV Post 440, Boynton Beach, FL.

HAROLD MOSES, born March 1, 1929. Enlisted on March 4, 1947, and discharged Aug. 6, 1948. Stationed with 7025th ASU, South Post, Ft. Myer, VA. Attended Service School at Ft. Monmouth, NJ, Radio Operators School.

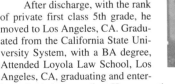

After discharge, with the rank of private first class 5th grade, he moved to Los Angeles, CA. Graduated from the California State University System, with a BA degree, Attended Loyola Law School, Los Angeles, CA, graduating and entering private law practice. He was active within the Jewish community as one of the founders (1956) and active board member of Temple Beth Emet, Anaheim, CA.

Married and the father of three sons. He passed away on April 21, 1975.

HERMAN HERBERT MOSES, born in Chicago, IL, Nov. 1, 1919. Served in the USN on board the USS *Warhawk,* in South Pacific including Philippine, Chinese and Japanese waters. Left the service as lieutenant of the USNR.

Received LL.B and J.D. degrees from Illinois Institute of Technology. Practiced law in Illinois, including service as

attorney for U.S. Government and city of Chicago. Retired to Southern California in 1987.

Served as national commander (1977-1978) and chairman of national executive committee (1982-1984) of JWV of the United States. Member of American, Illinois and Chicago Bar Associations; 32nd degree Mason; life member of JWF, Amvets and VFW.

Married Evelyn and has four children: Marcia Rittenberg, Michael Moses, Ester Gassel and John Moses; and grandfather of 11.

MOE MOSES, born in New York City, and spent his early years in the Bronx, where he attended school and graduated from Evander Childs High School in June 1941. Joined the USAAC in October 1942, for the cadet program and attended Syracuse University with the 65th CTD program. Washed out at San Antonio, TX and ended up at Aerial Gunnery School in Las Vegas.

Was gunnery instructor for a year in both Salt Lake City and Mt. Home, ID. Assigned to a B-24 liberator as a nose gunner with a terrific pilot and a great crew that was like family to him.

Put in 25 missions with the 15th AF stationed in Italy when V-E Day rolled around.

Discharged and moved to California in 1948.

Married to a wonderful wife, and has two children, three grandchildren and two great-grandchildren. They now reside in Cathedral City, CA.

SYLVAN MOSKOWITZ, born Bayonne, NJ, Feb. 5, 1923. Inducted in the U.S. Army May 1943; sent to Reception Center, Ft. Dix, NJ; then to Camp Campbell, KY for basic training with Co. E, 480th Armd. Inf. Regt., 20th Armd. Inf. Div.

Transferred November 1943 to Air Force Reception Center, Jefferson Barracks, MO, then to Washington University in St. Louis to prepare for training as pilot, bombardier navigator in USAAF.

Pre-Air Force training program severely curtailed in June 1944 and sent to Camp Van Dorn, MS, to begin training with Co. L, 255th Inf. Regt., 63rd Inf. Div. Transferred in November 1944 to Camp Shanks, NY to be processed for overseas duty. Landed in Marseilles, France in late November 1944 and traveled in WWI "40&8" freight cars to vicinity of Colmar, France. Served as light mortar gunner in Arienne Alsace Region and in Rhineland.

Awarded Bronze Star Medal for action at Erlach, Germany, April 1945. Armistice in May 1945. Transferred to M Detach., September 1945, when 63rd Div. was inactivated. Embarked for home in February 1946, and separated from service at Camp Kilmer, NJ in March 1946.

Entered Columbia University, September 1946. Married in June 1949 and took up residence at Shanks Village, Orangeburg, NY (formerly Camp Shanks, his port of embarkation for overseas duty). Earned master's degree from Teachers College at Columbia in 1951 and began teaching high school science and mathematics. Retired from teaching in 1989.

Has two children and three grandchildren. Does volunteer work with elderly housebound people at local hospital, and at a small local zoo.

THELMA ASH MOSKOWITZ,
born in Fall River, MA, Aug. 25, 1924. Inducted into U.S. Army at Jersey City, NJ in March 1945. Assembled with others in Newark, NJ. Sent to 3rd WAC Training Center, Ft. Oglethorpe, GA to begin training at Surgical Technicians School.

Transferred to Kennedy General Hospital, Memphis, TN. Worked in out-patients clinic and dispensary. Administered injections, assisted nurses and doctors in physical examinations and emergency out-patient treatment and gave minor first aid treatment.

Promoted to technician 5th class (corporal) in June 1945. Transferred to WAC Det., 9954th TSU Army Navy General Hospital in Hot Springs, AR, June 1945. Served in Medical Records Office typing charts, consultations, retiring board proceedings, etc., using dictaphone and stenography. Separated from the service at Ft. Dix, NJ in October 1946.

Worked as secretary at USN Base in Bayonne, NJ from November 1946-September 1947. Attended Traphagen School for Fashion in New York City from September 1947-May 1949. Turned down offer of work as children's fashion designer in fashion industry to get married in June 1949. Took up residence at Shanks Village, NY, a housing project for veterans who were attending schools in the New York City area (formerly Camp Shanks).

Began at School of Painting and Sculpture at Columbia University in September 1949. Secretarial and art work at American Zionist Youth Commission in September 1950.

Has two children and three grandchildren. Enjoying her husband's retirement as they grow older together.

SOL MOSS,
drafted in the U.S. Army, June 19, 1941; attended basic training at Camp Roberts, CA. Assigned to the 41st Inf. Div., Seattle, WA. The division put him in the 98th Chemical Mortar Bn.

On Dec. 5, 1941, departed by ship to the Philippine Islands from San Francisco. On December 7th when Pearl Harbor was bombed, they returned to San Francisco and returned on December 10. Their outfit was assigned to guard San Francisco. They moved cross country to New York, and sailed on March 4, 1942, and arrived in Australia on April 10, 1942. After a short stay they went into combat in New Guinea for one year and 11 months.

After several island combats they landed in the Philippine Islands, on Luzon. Left the Philippine Islands on June 18, 1945, and arrived in the United States on July 22, 1945.

Positions served in: gunner corporal, one year and three months; section sergeant, four months; staff sergeant, six months; and first sergeant, one year.

Awards/Medals: American Defense Service Ribbon with one Bronze Star, Asiatic-Pacific Theater Ribbon with four Bronze Battle Stars, Philippine Liberation Ribbon with one Bronze Battle Star and six Overseas Service Bars (each represents six months).

Discharged on July 22, 1945. One week later he was taken to Veterans Hospital with malaria.

DAVID MOVSHOW,
born on Feb. 8, 1924. Entered service at Parris Island on Dec. 11, 1942, as a private first class with the USMC, HQ Co., 2nd Bn., 4th Div. as a radio operator. He saw action in Tinian, Saipan and Two Jima.

Awards/Medals: Purple Heart and Bronze Star. He was discharged on Nov. 7, 1945.

Married Rae Sorkin on June 20, 1946. He worked as a purchasing agent with Metro Container Co., Jersey City, until his retirement 12 years ago. He passed away on Aug. 4, 1995.

HERSCHEL E. MOZEN,
born July 24, 1927, Negaunee, MI. Inducted in U.S. Army at Indiantown Gap, PA. Attended Medical Field Svc. School, Ft. Sam Houston, TX. Served in the Medical Corps as surgeon.

Flew out of Travis AFB, CA to Japan. He was a surgeon for six months in 21st Evac. Hosp. in Pusan. Transferred to 7th Div., 17th Regt., 3rd Bn., serving as battalion surgeon. Was also with 74th Tank Co. for several months.

Returned to the States January 1953. Stationed at Ft. Belvoir Hospital until July 1953. Returned to Cleveland, OH to complete training, then practiced chest surgery in Detroit area for 30 years.

Memorable experience was coming face to face with violent death, the crippling wounds and physical trauma to fine, dedicated young men. They did not expect the extreme numbers of enemy troops which were virtually overwhelming. Officers and non-coms were killed way out of proportion. The worst part of the whole thing was going back to identify and classify causes of death of the men in his battalion. It's still like a nightmare.

Awards/Medals: Korea Service Medal and Bronze Star. Discharged November 1953 as captain.

Married twice, unmarried at present. Has two sons, Dr. Paul Mozen and Dr. Neal Mozen; daughter, Sheri; son-in-law Scott Johnson; and two grandchildren, Elena and Noah. Member of PFC Joseph L. Bale Post 474 JWV, Southfield, MI. He is retired and enjoys, golf, travel and meetings.

HERMAN MURANSKY,
entered the U.S. Army in May 1941. Served with the 100th Inf. Div.

Awards/Medals: Combat Infantry Badge and two Bronze Stars. He was discharged in January 1946.

Married to Elaine and lives in Sunrise, FL.

MARVIN MURASKIN,
born in Brooklyn, NY, Jan. 4, 1926, and lived there until he was 40 years old. Served with the U.S. Army during WWII, a year in the States and one year overseas (April 14, 1944-May 7, 1946).

Overseas duty was served with the 1629th Eng. Construction Bn., Co. A, during the battle of Luzon during the Philippines campaign. Also in the initial occupation troops that landed in Japan where he served for about six months until he was sent home to join up with the American army.

Awards/Medals: Philippines Liberation Ribbon, Asiatic-Pacific Campaign Medal and WWII Victory Medal.

Married Ruth on Sept. 3, 1949, and has two daughters, Laura and Janet, one son, Bennett, and three grandchildren, all girls, Andrea, Carolyn and Celina. Worked as a salesman in the lumber and building trade for 40 years, retiring in 1991.

MILTON G. MUTCHNICK,
born in Detroit, MI, March 31, 1942. Graduated from Wayne State University School of Medicine, June 1967; completed internship in Medicine at Yale University, June 1968. Entered the USAF in September 1969 and completed training as a flight surgeon, December 1969.

Served two years active duty, Luke AFB, AZ, accumulating hundreds of hours flying time in fighter aircraft. Re-

turned to Yale and completed a two-year fellowship in Hepatology (liver diseases) before joining the faculty at the University of Michigan, Ann Arbor, MI.

Served as chief of liver disease section, then as acting chief of gastroenterology at Ann Arbor VA Medical Center (1974-1984). Moved to Wayne State University, 1984, and appointed professor and director, Division of Gastroenterology, 1991.

An active clinical investigator and a world lecturer on the treatment of viral hepatitis. He joined the CTANG as clinic commander, continuing to participate in flying fighter aircraft.

Transferred to 180th TAC Clinic OHANG as commander in 1974, flying F-100s and F-16s. Volunteered during Desert Storm and was assigned to Langley AFB in January 1991. Has lectured extensively at active duty AFBs while delivering continuing medical education.

Married Renee in 1983, has four sons and one daughter; oldest son is currently a Peace Corps volunteer in Tanzania.

Member of JWV, USA; Association of Military Surgeons of the United States, Society of Air Force Physicians and the Aerospace Medical Association.

JUDAH NADICH,
born May 13, 1912, Baltimore, MD. Ordained by the Jewish Theological Seminary of America, which also awarded him the degrees of Master of Hebrew Literature, Doctor of Hebrew Literature and Doctor of Divinity (honoris causa). Received his BA from the CCNY and MA from Columbia University.

During WWII he served as an Army Chaplain, spending three and a half years in the ETO as senior Jewish Chaplain with the American Army and Deputy to the Theater Chaplain. After the first German concentration camps were captured, Gen. Eisenhower appointed him his advisor on Jewish affairs.

Awards/Medals: Received several American decorations plus the French Croix de Guerre, Order of the British Empire, Ittur Lohamei Hamedinah from Israel government the Frank L. Weil Award from the Jewish Welfare Board. Retired from active duty in 1946 with the rank of lieutenant colonel.

Following WWII, made extended speaking tour on behalf of the United Jewish Appeal. He has held many offices for numerous Jewish organizations. Served as Rabbi of the Park Avenue Synagogue of NYC since 1957 and as Rabbi Emeritus since 1987. He is the author of numerous books and articles and his biography is listed in several Who's Who books.

Married to the former Martha Hadassah Ribalow and is the father of three daughters: Leah Nessa, Shira Adina and Nommi Nadich, and grandfather of eight.

DAVID A. NAGEL,
born April 5, 1922, New York City, NY. Enlisted in USAAF in 1942. Served with the 305th BG, 422nd Sqdn., 8th AF. Stationed at Randolph Field, TX, Sheppard Field, TX, Tyndall, FL, Poyote AFB, TX and Chelveston, England. Served 35 missions from June 1944-February 1945 in France, Holland, Germany, etc.

Memorable experience was being shot down over Belgium; escaping through Holland; being the first group to spot German jets over Penne Munde Germany.

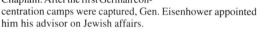

Awards/Medals: Distinguished Flying Cross, Air Medal with five clusters, two Presidential Citations, Purple Heart, Good Conduct Medal, plus other overseas medals. Discharged in June 1945 as technical sergeant and engineer gunner.

Married Norma in 1949, and has daughter, Wendy, and two sons, Bruce and James. He is semi retired.

HENRY I. NAHOUM,
enlisted in the Reserves on July 27, 1942, as 2nd lieutenant, MAC. Went on active duty July 2, 1943, as private first class. Feb. 6, 1944, captain DC AUS through Nov. 21, 1946; served in ETO regimental dental surgeon, 109th Inf. Regt.

Awards/Medals: two Battle Stars.

Brothers who also served in the military are Joseph, 1942-1945, field hospital (Infantry); Albert, 1943-1945, aerial gunner (Air Corps); Isidore, 1950-1952, rifleman (Infantry), Korean War; and Samuel, 1950-1952, sub chaser (Navy), Korean War.

LOUIS NARSON, born in New York City. Joined the U.S. Army in 1916 at the age of 16 and was with Black Jack Pershing chasing Pancho Villa. Went to Germany with K Co., 26th Inf. 1st Div. and fought in five major campaigns of WWI.

Awards/Medals: two Silver Stars, two Purple Hearts, WWI Victory Medal with five Battle Stars, German Occupation Medal, Mexican Service Medal and the New York State Conspicuous Service Medal.

Discharged in 1919 and lived in the Bronx until he passed away in 1966. He left behind his wife Teddye and two sons Paul and Richard. His brother Irving (Bill) Narson served in the same outfit and won a Silver Star and Purple Heart. Louis was active in VFW, JWV and the American Legion.

PAUL NARSON, joined the U.S. Army in September 1959, took basic training at Ft. Dix, NJ; AIT at Ft. Jackson, SC. Shipped out to Germany in March 1960 and served there until September 1962.

Most memorable experience was visiting the museum at Dachua the first time in April 1961. He had trouble getting his body to leave the car and enter the building. He froze and could smell death. He finally entered the building and became very emotional when he realized the price people paid for being Jewish.

Awards/Medals: Good Conduct Medal, Armed Forces Expeditionary Medal, National Defense Medal, Overseas Ribbon and Expert Infantryman's Badge.

Highest rank achieved was specialist first class.

Married Marilyn Ghiotti on March 23, 1980. He has a son, David, a daughter, Maria, and a daughter, Lisa, from a previous marriage. They reside in Flushing, NY. He belongs to the Vietnam Veterans of America, the American Legion, JWV and VFW.

MELVIN L. NASECK, born in Boston, MA, Feb. 2, 1926. Enlisted in September 1944 with the U.S. Army as a combat engineer with Co. A, 2828th Engr. Cbt. Bn., Group 36. Served in Central Europe and Rhineland.

Memorable experiences include assisting survivors of concentration camps; setting up a tailor shop and laundry at battalion HQ to provide survivors with food and a place to stay and work; visiting Dachau Concentration Camp three days after liberation; and being stationed in Berlin, Fall of 1945.

Awards/Medals: Good Conduct Medal, EAME Campaign Medal and WWII Victory Medals. Discharged in July 1946 with the rank of tech sergeant.

Married Barbara and has three children: Barry, Debbie and Bethany, and three grandchildren. He is a semi-retired electrical engineer.

PETER NASH, born Sept. 18, 1917. Enlisted in the U.S. Army April 29, 1941, as a medic. Stationed at Camp Upton

and Ft. Bragg. Went overseas to England and participated in the invasion of North Africa and Italy.

His Jewish best friend was Max Wein. They both grew up on the same street in New York City and were in Italy at the same time. Wein was in the 45th Div. and Nash in the 38th Evac. Hosp. When they were on the Cassino Line, he would stay with Nash's outfit for a couple of days, then go back to his own outfit. Some time later when Nash's outfit went to Anzio Beach, Wein heard on the German radio that Nash's outfit was coming in and was waiting on the beach when they landed.

Awards/Medals: five Battle Stars. Discharged on Aug. 18, 1945, with rank private first class.

Married and has two children and four grandchildren. He is retired.

STANLEY H. NASON, born in Bronx, NY, May 5, 1949. Enlisted Jan. 9, 1942, with the Air Transit Cmd., Air Corps., 59th Ferry Div., Memphis. Stationed at Nashville, Memphis and Fairfield Susson. Served in three combat areas: Rome-Arno, Southern Philippines and Luzon.

Memorable experiences were the 25 round trips outside the continental United States (six Pacific and 19 Atlantic).

Awards/Medals: EAME Service, American Service, Asiatic-Pacific Service. Discharged Nov. 30, 1945, with the rank of captain.

Married Gloria and has two daughters, Andrea and Susan; and three granddaughters: Sarah, Rachel and Kristine. Retired as judge and is a devout fisherman.

NATHAN NATELSON, enlisted in the USN in March 1942. Received boot training, SCTC in Miami, FL. Saw action on submarine, Winifore, on the *Ruben James* and on the USS *Underhill,* which was sunk off Formosa. He was rescued by a USCG ship.

Awards/Medals: received several Navy Commendations, among them the Purple Heart, Cooy, C.M. Received honorable discharge in March 1946 with a rating as a first class machinist mate. *Submitted by Max Sigal.*

OSCAR NATHANS, enlisted in the USAAC in October 1941. Requested aerial photography, but, because of color blindness, was assigned to mechanical schools in Texas and Mississippi. Assigned to the 341st Air Service Sqdn., packed equipment and boarded ship in New York Harbor and departed Sept. 21, 1942.

Spent 42 days at sea on the *Aquitania,* a sister ship of the *Luisitania,* a very high profile four smokestack old ship, easy prey for German subs. There were 5,000 GIs aboard with minimal escort. After 42 days at sea, tacking all the way to avoid torpedoes, first port of call was Rio De Janeiro, next was Capetown, South Africa, Aden, Arabia and on to Suez, Egypt, Oct. 31, 1942. All onboard were warned the ship would not stop if anyone went overboard.

Once landed in Egypt, they settled at British Airdrome named El Kabrit on the Suez. While at El Kabrit, visited the Pyramids, Telaviv and Cairo. Departed El Kabrit May 28,

1943. A truck convoy across Africa for over 2,000 miles to Tunis. LST to Sicily Aug. 2, 1943, to occupy airfields, then on to Italy Nov. 4, 1943. From Italy to Corsica and back to Italy April 1945. Back to the States June 18, 1945, and assigned first to R&R, then to Mitchell Field, NY.

Awards/Medals: five campaign stars. Discharged from Ft. Dix, NJ in August 1945.

MURRAY NEBEL, born in New York City, NY, June 9, 1920. Enlisted July 1943, with the USN Dental Corps. Stationed at Brooklyn Navy Yard, Kings Pt. Merchant Marine Academy, Agana, Guam Naval AB.

Awards/Medals: Pacific Theater. Discharged in April 1946 with the rank of lieutenant (sg).

Married Augusta and has two sons, Cliff and Matt. Retired as attending dentist at New York Medical Center in Queens, NY. Member of JWV Post #90.

ROBERT NEELDEMAN, born in Philadelphia, PA. Inducted in the U.S. Army Sept. 18, 1943, served as radio operator in 908th FA BN of the 83rd Inf. Div. Served in the ETO (landed in France a few days after D-day, fought through France, Belgium, Luxembourg and Germany).

Awards/Medals: Silver Star and Purple Heart. Discharged on Dec. 8, 1945, with rank of T/5 (corporal).

Retired in 1989 from co-ownership of the Juvenile Furniture and Toy Store (Babyland) in Millburn, NJ.

SAMUEL H. NEHEMIAH, born on June 19, 1918. Enlisted in the U.S. Army on June 10, 1942, at Ft. Jay, NY, and served in the Infantry. Stationed in Ft. George Meade, MD and Camp McCoy, WI. Participated in action in Ardennes, Central Europe and Rhineland.

Memorable experience was making staff sergeant in three months.

Awards/Medals: Bronze Star Medal, EAME Service Medal with three Bronze Stars, Good Conduct, Combat Infantry Badge, WWII Victory Medal and American Campaign. Discharged on Oct. 4, 1945, with the rank of staff sergeant.

Married to Irene and has three daughters: Judy, Barbara and Marcia; two granddaughters, Richele and Stacy; and one grandson, Matthew. He is a retired chief aid for Department of New Jersey JWV.

BARNEY NEFF, born 1918, St. Paul, MN. Enlisted in the USN 1942. Boxed and won championships in both heavy and light weight classes. Served as drill and boxing instructor. Became a naval officer cadet in 1942 and appointed naval aviator in 1943. Subsequently served as USMC test pilot for dive bombers and fighter planes. Transferred to the Pacific Theater as fighter pilot.

After war ended in 1945, he was assigned the role of test pilot and also remained actively involved in the boxing program. Supervised training program for flight officers in boxing, self-defense and survival training while serving in Hawaii.

He received a commendation for his outstanding service. Honorably discharged from active service in June 1946, he continued to serve in the USMCR as a fighter pilot with rank of major until Aug. 14, 1967.

As a civilian he continued to participate in boxing as a trainer, referee, cut man and sport administrator. Acted many years as upper Midwest director of Golden Gloves, Deputy Commissioner of Boxing for state of Minnesota and member of the Minnesota Athletic Commission. Received numerous awards for community service. Worked as co-owner of American Tool Supply Co. with his brother and best friend, Elliot Neff. Was an active member of the Fraternal Order of Eagles and the congregation of the Temple of Aaron in St. Paul, MN. He passed away in 1983.

JOHN NEMON, born in Vienna, Austria, on Nov. 28, 1921. Enlisted June 1943 with the USAF, ASTP Drexel University, Sig. Corps. Army. Served in the European Theater, Pacific Theater and at war ends, occupation duty in Japan.

Memorable experiences landing in France; surrender of Germany; landing in Philippines; and Japanese surrender.

Awards/Medals: European Theater, Asiatic-Pacific Medal, WWII Victory Medal, Unit Citation, Victory Medal and Good Conduct Medal. Discharged in March 1946 with the rank T/5.

Married Sarah, PNP Ladies Auxiliary JWVA, has two daughters, two sons and seven grandchildren. Retired and works as a volunteer.

LAWRENCE NESSMAN, born in Brooklyn, NY, Aug. 3, 1931. Graduated New Utrecht High School and attended New York University College of Arts and Science and graduated from the Brooklyn College of Pharmacy (LIU) in 1954. Volunteered for the draft in July 1954, did basic training at Ft. Dix, NJ and Ft. Sam Houston in San Antonio, TX. He was stationed in Germany at Crailsheim and Ludwigsburg until he was separated from the Army in June 1956 as an E-4 and discharged as an E-5 in 1962. Used the GI Bill to go to medical school where he attended the Philadelphia College of Osteopathic Medicine and Surgery. Graduated in 1962 and interned at Cherry Hill Hospital in New Jersey and finished in 1963. Started his practice in Wayne, NJ in 1963.

Enlisted in the USAR in 1977, as a major and rose to the rank of colonel. In 1988, volunteered to serve in Honduras, Central America and was the officer in charge for the American Military Operations at Camp Powderhorn for their reserve increment that year. Engaged in no battles. Was involved in Reforger exercises in Germany and was involved in tamex exercises with NATO.

Memorable experience consisted of being the center commander at Picatinny Arsenal, Dover, NJ and commander of the 322nd General Hospital at Picatinny Arsenal (1,000 bed hospital). He was also the first commander and commander of the year for the JWV Post 695 in 1981-1982.

Member of various Jewish organizations such as B'nai B'rith, Hadassah, been chairman of various Israel bond committees, founding member of the Prime Ministers Club and Ambassadors Club for Israel bonds, chairman on committees and vice chairman of the UJA, on the board of directors of the YMHA. Involved with Boys Town in Jerusalem, belonged to the National Shrine to the Jewish war dead in Washington, D.C. belonged to the American Physicians Fellowship for Medicine in Israel, was involved with the student struggle for Soviet Jewry, involved with the JWV Museum in Washington, D.C. and involved with the West Point Jewish Chapel Fund, and a member of the American Legion and life member in the Army Reserve Officers Association of Military Surgeons of the United States and involved as chairman of the Jewish National Fund in the Wayne area.

On December 1-5, 1973, at the invitation of the Israeli government, he was taken on a tour to inspect the battlegrounds and war casualties of the Yom Kippur War at the Suez Canal, Golan Heights, and Hadassah Hospital. He expects to be discharged from the USAR in January 1995 with the rank of colonel.

Married Leslie Donna Kraut of Brooklyn, NY, has three daughters: Mali, who now lives in Israel and is married to Itimar, an engineer graduate of the Technion University. They have two sons, Matan and Ido. His second daughter, Chari, is married to an Israeli engineering student. His third daughter, Alisa, is now in nursing school. He also has a son, Ravi, just volunteered in the Israeli Army to do basic training for a period of about three months. He will then return to Northwestern University to complete his Bachelor's degree in journalism. His father, Samuel, served in the U.S. Army in WWII. Three of his children speak fluent Hebrew and are Yankees.

His involvement with the New Jersey War Veterans is on the National Defense Committee, the Holocaust Committee and as surgeon. He is still practicing medicine and is still in the Army Reserves.

Two special memories are being a Jew and a veteran. When he was 12 years old, he saw on the lawn of the Kenilworth Hotel in Miami Beach, a sign reading "No Jews or Dogs Allowed." In the 1960s when he moved to Wayne, NJ, a Jew could not buy a house in certain areas, and today, in front of the Town Hall, engraved in granite, is the JWV Star of David. He was also the Grand Marshall in the Memorial Day Parade with the JWV flag flying high.

WALTER NEUBAUER, born in Germany, Feb. 15, 1894. Served in Germany army in WWI and participated in action in France. Was a civilian volunteer in WWII.

Married Heather and had one son and two daughters. He passed away April 17, 1976.

MICHAEL NEULANDER, born in Miami, FL, Dec. 21, 1957. Graduated 1980 from University of Miami with BA degree in political science and commissioned a 2nd lieutenant in the U.S. Army. Graduated helicopter pilot training in 1981 and served with the 9th Inf. Div., Ft. Lewis, WA. Subsequent assignments included the 45th Trans. Co., Camp Humphries, Korea, and the Aviation Logistics School, Ft. Eustis, VA.

During Persian Gulf War, he served with the 1st Cav. Div. as aircraft maint. control officer. Flew into battle the first day of ground war against the Iraqi Republican Guard army. After the war he took early retirement and transferred to the USAR with rank of major.

Awards/Medals: Bronze Star Medal, Meritorious Service Medal, Army Commendation Medal with OLC, Army Achievement Medal, National Defense Service Medal, Southwest Asia Campaign Medal with three Battle Stars, Kuwaiti Liberation Medal and Senior Army Aviators Badge.

Married Sharon and has two daughters, Brandi and Ariel. Worked as the education administrator for the Virginia Peninsula Jewish Community Center.

MELVIN S. NEUMANN, enlisted in the service Oct. 20, 1940, with the Corps of Engineers, 1st Engr. Bn., HQ Co., 1st Inf. Div. Transferred to Air Corps February 1942. Graduated as pilot, Ellington Field, TX. Copilot, Pilot, then flight leader for 81st Sqdn., 12th BG, North Africa, Sicily and Italy.

Completed 37 combat missions from February 1943-March 1944. The plane was damaged innumerable times, including flat tires, engine out, mid-air collision and so many flak holes that they had to use lids from cans in the kitchen because they ran out of aluminum sheets.

Awards/Medals: Air Medal with nine OLCs and all appropriate ribbons for duty areas.

Rose through the ranks to assistant VP of Purchasing and Design where he finished 37 years of service with General Cigar & Tobacco Div. of Culbro Corp.

MORRIS NEWBERG, born in Bronx, NY. Enlisted in the U.S. Army Oct. 15, 1942, and served as rifleman (squad leader) with Co G, 119th Inf., 30th Div. Stationed at Ft. Dix, Colorado Springs, Louisiana and California maneuvers and ETO. Participated in EAME Theater, Normandy, Northern France, Ardennes, Rhineland, Central Europe (Battle of the Bulge).

Memorable experiences: (1) A shelling that resulted with 10 men being hit. He assisted in helping the wounded and didn't realize until they got to the first aid station that he had been hit in the shoulder by shrapnel. Was hospitalized in Paris for 30 days. (2) Relocating from one boat to another, and while crossing the Rhine River, the boat he was originally on was hit, resulting in casualties. (3) Being in on the liberation of a Nazi concentration camp.

Awards/Medals: Purple Heart, American Theater Ribbon, WWII Victory Medal, Good Conduct Medal, EAME Ribbon with five Bronze Battle Stars. Discharged on Oct. 2, 1945, with the rank of staff sergeant.

Married and enjoys his family consisting of wife, son, daughter and grandchild. He works as executive director congregation Brothers of Israel in Long Branch, NJ.

ALBERT NEWMAN, born in Cleveland, OH, Oct. 20, 1926. Enlisted in the U.S. Army May 4, 1944. Served with HQ and was stationed at Base M, Luzon, Philippines and Korea Base Command, Ascom City, Korea.

Awards/Medals: Army of Occupation Medal (Japan), Asiatic-Pacific Theater Ribbon and Victory Medal.

Discharged Nov. 24, 1946, with rank of T/5.

Currently working as a design engineer.

HYMAN NEWMAN, born in New York, NY, Nov. 13, 1922. Enlisted in the U.S. Army Jan. 30, 1943, as a pilot bomber with the 465th BG, 781st BS. Stationed at AFS, Columbia, MS; Maxwell Field, AL; CTD Allegheny (pre-flight) PFS, Maxwell Field, AL; and ETD Americus, GA; BFS, Greenwood, MS. Participated in action in Central Europe, North Apennines, Po Valley, Air Combat Balkans and MTO.

Memorable experiences include his third mission when hit, shot down and bailed out over Lake Balatan, Hungary. Was MIA POW for 30 days when liberated by Russians. He flew 32 more missions.

Awards/Medals: EAME Theater Ribbon and two Air Medals. Discharged Oct. 14, 1945, with the rank of 1st lieutenant.

Passed away on April 28, 1973. Survived by two sons, one daughter and grandchildren.

IRVING NEWMAN, born March 31, 1921, Boston, MA. Enlisted May 2, 1942, stationed at Nashville, TN; Maxwell Field, AL; Jackson, MS; Ellington Field, TX; Big Spring, TX, where he graduated bombardier training as 2nd lieutenant; Hondo, TX, where trained as navigator; then Smoky Hill AAB, KS where he met his crew.

Arrived in Casablanca March 29, 1944, waited for their plane and ended up in Khargpur, India. First mission bombing steel mills at Anshan, Manchuria was a success. Second mission Aug. 20, 1944 [illegible] Japan, was a disaster. On the bomb run they were rammed by a kamikaze and went down in a spin. Three, including Newman, were able to bail out, the others were killed. Captured, he spent a year and 10 days in Japan. Stood trial as war criminal, was found guilty and spent eight months in solitary confinement. Taken to Omori and interned there until liberated. Was never officially registered POW, so never got or was able to send mail and never received a Red Cross food parcel.

Awards/Medals: Presidential Unit Citation, Purple Heart, CBI Theater with two Battle Stars. Discharged March 17, 1947, promoted to 1st lieutenant May 26, 1947, two months after he left the service.

Married Edith Sawyer and has three children and one grandchild. Spent 20 years in retail food business, 15 years in electrical engineering, then went into antique business.

Now unemployed but still looking; at 70, he isn't ready to retire yet.

STANLEY F.H. NEWMAN, graduated from pilot training in March 1944. Completed 57 missions in P-51 with 9th AF in Europe. Credited with one of the last German aircraft shot down. Returned to U. of Illinois where he graduated Magna Cum Laude as an aeronautical engineer. Worked with NASA as an aeronautical research scientist in their pilotless research division.

Joined 185th Ftr. Sqdn., OKANG, June 1948. During Korean conflict, recalled to active duty with that squadron and flew 100 missions over Korea. Returned to OKANG and went from operations officer in 1953 to ANG assistant to CINCMAC, September 1978. Flew several cargo missions into SE Asia during Vietnamese war. Flew over 12,000 hours and awarded the Military Airlift Command's 10,000 Hour Accident Free Pin.

Awards/Medals: AF Distinguished Service Medal, Legion of Merit, Distinguished Flying Cross with one OLC, Meritorious Service Medal and the Air Medal with 13 OLCs. Retired Aug. 16, 1983.

Married Harriette, has three children (son is Lt. Col. George Newman, USAF TAC fighter pilot), and three grandchildren. Charter and life member, AF Assoc.; life member, NGAUS; life member, Enlisted Assoc., NG of U.S.; and life member of MOWW.

MARVIN S. NEWMARK, born in Bronx, NY, Jan. 16, 1926. Enlisted December 1943 with the USN, Amphibious Forces, ship repair unit. Stationed at NTS, Sampson, NY, Fleet Internal Combustion Engine School, San Diego, CA, Amphibious Training Base, Hawaii and Guam, MI. Participated at Guam Campaign, Mariana Islands and Pacific Theater.

Memorable experience was of Guam.

Awards/Medals: Asiatic Pacific Medal, American Theater Medal and WWII Victory Medal. Discharged May 24, 1946, with the rank of motor machinist 2/c USNR.

Married to Sunny and has five children and five grandchildren. Member of the JWV and retired after 40 years of insurance business.

HARVEY P. NEWTON, born in Breslau, Germany, Oct. 4, 1920, as Hermann Neustadt. Emigrated to Holland, Dec. 15, 1938, after one month in Kz. Buchenwald. Immigrated to U.S. Feb. 5, 1940. Joined U.S. Army as volunteer, May 24, 1941. Spent three years with the infantry: 29th Div., Mil. District of Washington, ASTP-Chinese. Direct Commission in MI June 1944. In ETO 3rd Army HQ, 29th Div., 100th Div. Wounded Nov. 20, 1944, Ingwiller, France.

Reassigned to Enemy Prisoner Of War Information Bureau, Ft. Meade.

Awards/Medals: Purple Heart, Good Conduct, American Defense, ETO with three stars, American Theater and WWII Victory Medal. Retired for combat wounds on April 2, 1946, 1st lieutenant.

Received Ph.D. in soil science, Rutgers University, 1951. Major long term assignments: Venezuela, 1953-1957;

Costa Rica, 1958-1960; Somalia, 1961-1967; Ecuador, 1968-1973. Short term: OAS Mission, Barbados, 1970; World Bank Mission, Somalia, 1979; A.I.D. Mission, Bolivia, 1979; Honduras, 1973; Sri Lanak, 1975; Dominican Republic, 1980-1981, 1984; The Gambia, 1981; Bangladesh, 1981-1982.

Lives permanently in Costa Rica. Works as international consultant in agriculture.

WALTER H. NILES (LT COL, USAF, RET), served as deputy commander of WWI Veterans CCC Camp, New Gretna, NJ at tender age of 23, then as 2nd lieutenant. Called to active duty in 1940 as a 1st lieutenant. Served most of WWII career as research engineer at Wright Field, Air Mat. Cmd., Dayton, OH. Received a Legion of Merit for developing and putting into production a test kit for repairing in combat an electronic turbo supercharger regulator to be used on all multi engine aircraft.

Recalled to active duty in 1951 for Korean fracas. Served as lieutenant colonel, as deputy director of production in Eastern Air Procurement District. Among the several assignments he served during WWII was one where he served as chief of the Marine Branch whose responsibility it was to develop and procure sea rescue boats required to save downed pilots who ejected over water. It was said that the Air Force was responsible for more bottoms than the Navy. He also served as a project engineer in the electrical branch of the equipment lab at Wright Field.

Received bachelor's degree in mechanical engineering and a master's in civil engineering.

ALLEN I. NILVA, WO, born in Kiev, in September 1911. Graduated from the University of Minnesota Law School, 1933, where he won feather weight boxing championship. Enlisted in the U.S. Army in August 1942, as a buck private at Ft. Snelling, MN and served as aide to sergeant major. Other duty stations in North Africa, India and Ceylon.

Shipped overseas in Fall of 1943 and met the judge advocate of SE Asia Comd. who recommended him to succeed as judge advocate. Had a radio program called GI Judge.

Awards/Medals: American Theater, African Campaign, WWII Victory Medal and Good Conduct Medal. Discharged in January 1946 as a warrant officer.

Member Jake Henry Nilva JWV Post 722-331, Temple of Aaron Syn., St. Paul; Mason and Shriner; member of American Legion. Two of his brothers were also in the service. He passed away Oct. 25, 1987.

JAKE HENRY NILVA, enlisted Feb. 11, 1942. Served on a Navy bomber plane in the South Pacific. On the night of Nov. 1, 1944, the crew flew out on a bombing run to Kendari, Dutch West Indies. Their plane was shot down after scoring a direct hit on an ammunition dump that had been supplying Japanese troops in the Philippines.

The pilot and navigator died in the crash, and the other nine crew members were taken prisoner. Copilot Kuhlmann, waist gunner Nilva and the other crew members were executed along with two Catholic nuns on Thanksgiving Day 1944.

Awards/Medals: Purple Heart, two Air Medals, American Campaign, Asiatic-Pacific Campaign, WWII Victory Medal and Good Conduct Medal. He was one of three brothers in the service, Army, Navy and Air Corps.

The JWV Post in Minneapolis is named for Jake Nilva, among others, and is known as the Nilva Dansky Neff Post #331.

SAMUEL G. NILVA, born April 29, 1919, St. Paul, MN. Graduated Mechanic Arts High School and attended University of Minnesota until France fell in 1940. Had two years of ROTC, two years CHTC and received pilots license April 1941. Made 1st Sgt. CAP, taught navigation and meteorology at Cretin High School to CAP Cadets. Served in Naval Reserve aboard battleship, *Arkansas*.

After college joined USAAC, graduated primary flight training April 1943. Grounded and was transferred to criminal investigation. Provost Marshall's office, Bolling Field Air Corps HQ.

Awards/Medals: American Theater, Army Good Conduct, Navy Good Conduct and WWII Victory Medal. Discharged Dec. 8, 1945. He was one of three brothers to serve in service, Army, Navy, Air Corps. Brother Jake was POW and executed in 1944.

Life member, past commander of American Legion Post #1; commander JWV Post 722-331 three times; past department commander, NEC 1974; board member variety club 25 years; Mason, Shriner. Member of National Assoc. of Chiefs of Police, National Police Hall of Fame; Adath Jeshuran Synagogue. Helped bring MD Telethon with JWV backing to Minneapolis. Owned national amusement company 35 years.

Married to Harriet Goodman for 49 years, she passed away December 1991. Has three children and seven grandchildren.

RAYMOND NITKIN, born in Bronx, NY, May 16, 1925. Enlisted in USMC, May 16, 1942. Boot camp at Parris Island, SC. Requested Aviation Machinist Mate School; then volunteered as naval air gunner at Jacksonville, FL, Naval Air Station.

Went overseas as turret gunner in December 1944 flying Grumman Avenger Torpedo Bombers. His pilot assumed command of USMC Sqdn., VMTB 232, "The Red Devils" in Western Pacific. Flew bypassed island suppression "Recon/Strikes" and U.S. Pacific Fleet coverage missions.

Wounded in action May 9, 1945, during battle for Okinawa, causing the loss of sight in his left eye, while flying a low level antiradar strike. Flew 46 combat missions.

Awards/Medals: Purple Heart, Presidential Unit Citation with star, Air Medal, Pacific Area Medal with two stars, American Theater Medal and WWII Victory Medal.

Married Ellie in 1947 and has one son, Steve; three daughters: Marsha, Cheryl and Lori; and eight grandchildren. Retired from retail furniture business in 1988. Three times commander of Post 595, Fountain Valley, CA. Writes *Jewish-American, Star Spangled Heroes* columns for Post 595 Sentinel Newspaper, and two articles monthly for The Orange County, CA Jewish Heritage newspaper.

HENRY NORTON, born and raised in Rochester, NY, Jan. 16, 1922. Attended Rochester Institute of Technology. Entered U.S. Army at Ft. Niagara, NY Oct. 20, 1942, with basic training at Ft. Bragg. Graduated Officers Candidate School, Ft. Sill, OK. Graduated Military Intelligence School, and assigned to G-2, 88th Inf. Div. Served in ETO in Italy, France and Germany. Participated in battle which penetrated the Adolf Hitler line from Casino to Anzio and resulted in capture of Rome.

Promoted to serve on staff of G-2, 5th Army HQ as MI officer. Transferred to 7th Army HQ, Naples and participated in invasion of Southern France. Appointed commanding officer, 7th Army Documentation's Center.

Received special appointment to locate leading German rocket scientists, including Werner von Braun, his brother, and numerous other V-1 and V-2 experts, to induce them to continue their research in the States

Awards/Medals: Bronze Star and other decorations. Discharged Oct. 27, 1945, then commanded the 322nd MI Detach. (Reserve) in Miami, FL.

Married the former Jenny Cohen and has two daughters. Graduated from the U. of Miami School of Law. Currently practicing law in Miami. Past JWV Post 223 Commander and Past State of Florida Department Commander.

MORTON NOSENCHUK, born in Bronz, NY, March 10, 1929. Enlisted in the U.S. Army Artillery on Jan. 19, 1951. Stationed at Camp Polk, LA; Hokaido, Japan; and Korea.

Memorable experiences are of the Passover 1952, Seoul, Korea. He was very impressed with the number of GIs that were there for Sedar services. There was not enough wine to go around to all of them.

Awards/Medals: Army Occupation Medal (Japan), Korean Service Medal and United Nations Service Medal. Discharged Nov. 27, 1952, with the rank of corporal.

Married Selma and has two children, Shari and Jeffrey; son-in-law, Chad; three grandchildren: Jaime, Seth, Alex and Kaila. He is retired.

ALLAN NOVICK, drafted at Cheyenne, WY, in the winter of 1942. Took basic training at Ft. F.E. Warren, Cheyenne, WY. Stationed at Camp Hale, CO; Regis College, Denver, CO under ASTP. When that was canceled he ended up with a combat engineer unit. Toured parts of the South Pacific ending up at Manila, Philippines in the Battle of Luzon.

Discharged in 1946. Recalled at the beginning of the Korean War and became a sergeant major of Camp Kobe in the 8th Army. Left the service in the middle 1950s.

Raised family in Cheyenne and moved to Los Angeles.

DAVID NOVICK, raised in Cheyenne, WY. Drafted in senior year of high school, January 1944. Stationed at Camp Polk, LA for basic training and at Camp Cook, CA.

Was youngest man in his outfit when shipped out of Boston for Europe. Assigned to 3rd Army Cbt. Engrs. Ended up at Nuremberg, Germany. Shipped from France to Manila, Philippines where he met up with his brother, Allen.

Raised his family in Cheyenne, WY and still lives there.

JOSEPH NOVICK (J.M.), raised in Cheyenne, WY. Enlisted in USAAF January 1946. Basic at Sheppard Field, TX and Weather School, Chanute, IL. Served as weather observer with the 13th AF, 15th Weather Sqdn., 90th Weather Station, Nichols Field, Manila, P.I., August 1946-April 1947.

Married, raised two daughters and lived in Cheyenne until December 1994. Acquired residency at Indianapolis in January 1995.

LEE A. NOVICK, served from August 1966 to August 1972. Basic training at Ft. Knox, KY. Advanced training at Ft. Dix, NJ.

Served with Detachment A, Co. B, 10th Special Forces Group, Philadelphia, PA and Pedrickstown, NJ. Also served with 11th Special Forces Group, Tulsa, OK and Chicago, IL.

Light weapons specialist, psychological warfare, public information specialist.

IRA NOVOSELSKY, born in Boston, MA, March 2, 1947. Enlisted in the U.S. Army Infantry, Oct. 16, 1968. Assigned to 187th Sep. Inf. Bde. Stationed at Ft. Dix, NJ and Ft. A.P. Hill, VA.

Awards/Medals: American Defense Ribbon. Discharged in October 1974 with the rank of sergeant E-5.

Married Rochelle and has one son, Seth. Member of National Guard part time, 1986-1995; and Operations NCO, E6/SSG.

MAX. M. NOVICH, taught boxing to the enlisted men and organized boxing shows. Unit sent to England to prepare for the invasion of Europe and to fight Hitler's military machine. Requested assault unit and was transferred to the 29th Div. Allies invaded Europe on D-day, and he found himself in France. Was sent to replace a wounded battalion surgeon in the 2nd Bn., 116th Regt. Received a battlefield promotion to captain as his unit fought the Germans through France, Belgium, Holland and into Germany. He was wounded in Julich, Germany.

Awards/Medals: Bronze Star Medal, Purple Heart Medal, Campaign Ribbon with four Battle Stars, Victory Medal, American Theater Medal, German Occupation Ribbon, Army Combat Medical Badge and Croix de Guerre.

Picked up his campaign for safety in contact sports. Served on medical juries for boxing for the Olympic games of 1968, 1972, 1976 and 1984. Was chief physician for the American boxing team for the Maccabiah Games in Israel, 1965, 1969, 1973 and 1977; also the boxing coach for the U.S. team at the 1977 games. Served on medical juries for boxing in the First World Amateur Boxing Cup in Havana, Cuba, in 1974; New York City, 1979; and Montreal in 1981; and the pan Am Games in 1971 and 1975.

He is an honoree of both the New Jersey and the World Boxing Halls of fame.

EDWARD M. OHER, born in Chicago, IL, March 29, 1915. Enlisted with 139th Replacement Bn. as an Army exchange officer Oct. 27, 1943. Stationed at Princeton University, Princeton, NJ; Napier Field, AL, Blytheville, AR; Ft. Benjamin Harrison, Indianapolis, IN; and Japan.

Memorable experience was when he went, before and after WWII, to Northwestern University.

Awards/Medals: American Theater Ribbon, Asiatic-Pacific Theater Ribbon, WWII Victory Medal and Sharp Shooters Medals. Discharged on March 25, 1946.

Married Tobie on Sept. 15, 1940, and has two sons, Joseph and James; one daughter, Kathryn; three grandchildren: Andrea, Samuel and Jacob. Worked as a partner in a CPA firm. He passed away on April 21, 1993.

LEE ORENSTEIN, born in Brooklyn, NY, Sept. 23, 1923. Entered USN January 1941 and USCG in 1947.

Memorable service: USS *Bunker Hill* (CV-17), aircraft carrier; USS General *J.C. Breckinridge,* troop transport; served also on USCG Casco and USCG Mackinac, Greenland to Iceland to Bermuda, weather patrol; USCG Loran Station Catuduanes, Philippines; chief acting executive officer; and Air Sea Rescue Sikorsky with an Air Sea Rescue Certificate.

Awards/Medals: Presidential Unit Citation, Asiatic-Pacific with one Silver Star and five Bronze Stars. Retired from the service in 1961.

Married Helen L. Orenstein. Children are all professionals, Ph.D.'s in education and chemistry. Son is a retired colonel in the U.S. Army. Has five grandchildren. Retired from business in 1987 and is a charter member of JWV Post #336.

ABBOT I. ORENTLICHER, born in Brockton, MA, in 1914. Attended Massachusetts School of Art and took Harvard extension courses in the 1930s. Worked for C.F. Hovey Department Store in Boston and Morse Shoe Corp. in Quincy, MA before entering service in January 1942.

Served in Gen. Patton's famous 4th Armd. Div. Fought from Normandy to the German border. Shot three times. First time was saved by a can of "C" ration beans. Next two times, on Rosh Hashanah, and was flown back to England Erev Yom Kippur. Spent the following two years in Army General Hospitals until discharged in 1946.

Awards/Medals: Received 13 medals and awards including Bronze Star, Purple Heart, Presidential Unit Citation and French Croix de Guerre.

Married Harriet Cotton of Birmingham, AL, whom he met at a Zionist dance after the war. Has three children: George, Joan and Robert.

WALTER ORGEL, drafted into the U.S. Army in December 1942, at the age of 19 1/2. Stateside, he was stationed at Ft. Sll, OK, Camp Hale, CO and Camp Swift, TX.

Was a member of the 10th Mountain Div., 605th FA BN. Served overseas as forward observer in the Northern Italian Campaign.

Awards/Medals: Bronze Star Medal. Honorably discharged after the war ended in 1945.

MORRIS OSBAND, was inducted into the U.S. Army December 1942 from Atlantic City. After basic training at Ft. McClellan, AL and Ft. Washington, MD, he was sent to Ft. Bragg, NC and assigned to 558th Army Postal Unit, being activated at that camp. In March 1943 he married the former Ruth Gurst of Atlantic City and in August was sent to England. APO 558 was set up to service all units of the 2nd Air Div., 8th AF. They were attached to the 446th BG for rations and quarters.

After V-E Day the personnel were attached to a mail distribution point in France until discharged. Command APO 558 received a citation for outstanding performance of duty from August 1943-February 1945.

Sgt. Osband was discharged on Nov. 3, 1945, his wife's birthday. Their first child was born while he served in England.

SOLOMON P. OSTRIN, born in Newark, NJ, on Oct. 28, 1922. Received a BA degree from Montclair State College in 1943. Joined the Enlisted Reserve Corps on Aug. 3, 1942, and called to active duty at Ft. Dix March 5, 1943. Assigned to G-2 section of newly activated 106th Div. at Ft. Jackson. Sent to Army Japanese Language School at University of Michigan in September 1943. After intensive one-year course, assigned to the Army Security Agency in Washington, DC where he participated in breaking of Japanese military codes and translating the deciphered messages.

Memorable experience was learning of the intended Japanese surrender by deciphering the Japanese message to its ambassador in Switzerland for transmission by the Swiss government to the United States and having to remain silent until President Truman made the announcement to the nation.

Discharged on Feb. 27, 1946, at Ft. Meade, MD.

Obtained a BS degree from Rutgers University and an MA from Columbia University. Was a secondary school teacher and department chairman for 39 years.

Married to Lillian since 1949, and has two daughters, Elaine and Lynn, and two grandchildren, Natalie and William. He is a member of the JWV Post 740.

JACK OSTROFSKY, born in Brooklyn, NY Nov. 17, 1917. Enlisted in the USMC April 25, 1945. Stationed at Parris Island, SC and Camp Lejeune, NC.

Memorable experience was V-J Day.

Awards/Medals: Distinguished Flying Cross. Discharged on April 27, 1946.

Married Lena in 1939 and has two sons, one daughter, and nine grandchildren. Retired and active in the JWV and is now serving as district commander of Florida.

VICTOR OSTROW, born in Philadelphia, PA, April 5, 1917. Drafted in 1942 at Ft. Myers, VA. Shipped to USAAF, Mitchell Field, Long Island, NY. Transferred to the Infantry, Camp Gordon, Augusta, GA. After six weeks of intensive training, was shipped out of Boston Harbor on USS *West Point*. Landed in Clydes of Scotland, went by train to Southampton, England. Crossed the English Channel through rough water currents, transferring onto landing craft, Le Havre, France Replacement Center. Assigned to 69th Inf. HQ Co. 273rd Div.; zeroed in their M-1 rifles on firing range; traveled at night by train in 40/8 cattle cars; arrived at forward positions in Belgium; liberated many prison of war camps: Jews, Poles, Russians, etc.

Memorable experiences were with the 69th Div. linkup with the Russian 58th Guard Div. along the Elbe River, Torgau, Germany. Greetings and handshakes where celebrations were in place of the language barrier. Successful conclusion of WWII, April 25, 1945.

Awards/Medals: CIB, Bronze Star, Good Conduct, Meritorious Union Emblem, American Campaign EAME, WWII Victory with two Battle Stars, Army of Occupation with Germany Clasp, Honorable Service Lapel WWII, Marksman Badge with Carbine Sub Machine Gun Bars.

Discharged March 18, 1946.

Married Olga and has two daughters, Susan and Lisa, and five grandchildren. Owner of a gift fruit basket shop. Retired in December 1984. Member of JWV, past commander, Lt. Harold E. Greenberg, Post 692, Silver Spring, MD.

HERBERT OUZER, inducted in the U.S. Army June 30, 1942. Basic training at Camp Charles Wood, Red Bank, NJ. Took specialized training at Ft. Sam Houston in San Antonio, TX. Shipped overseas and landed in Oran, Africa March 19, 1943. The trip overseas was by convoy which took 15 days.

Saw service in Africa, Italy, Corsica, France and Germany. Battles and campaigns were in Central Europe, Naples Foggia, Rhineland, Rome-Arno, Southern France and Tunisia.

Received $100.00 mustering out pay and his decorations.

JOSEPH OZUR, born in Vilna, Lithuania in 1896, one of five children born to Raizel and Mathias Ozur. He was a very inquisitive child. When about six years of age he, and a brother were watching a herd of cattle being driven through town when his brother turned away for a second and hearing loud noises turned to see Joseph on the horns of a bull. Remarkably he was not hurt when thrown. Joseph and his older brother by one year, Nathan, did not want to be conscripted into the Russian army so were smuggled out of Vilna on an underground railroad run by their father and arrived in the U.S. in 1914.

Entrhralled by his new country which he adored and felt could do no wrong, he lied about his age, claiming to be 21, and enlisted in the Army at the beginning of WWI. He was sent to Texas for basic training, then sent to France. Attaining the rank of sergeant, he was ordered to escort a company of men to Paris for a parade after which he was to return to his battalion. After the parade (as told by his daughter) he put his troop back on the train, waved good bye and returned to Paris until his money ran out.

When he returned to his company, now a private, they were ordered to the Argonne Forest where in a fierce battle Ozur was wounded and hospitalized. His father, while visiting in a Black Sea Hotel, was stunned when informed that Joe was in the Army and hospitalized in France, by two men from his company who were recuperating from their injuries. They approached Mathias Ozur after hearing him being paged. After returning to the States on a hospital ship, he was visited by Lillian, whom he had met at a USO dance. In the 1920s, he and his wife, Lillian, moved to Syracuse, NY, settled in, and had two children, Charles and Rosalyn.

Ozur was a successful businessman and respected member of the community. As an active member of the city he was involved in many community activities but especially in JWV. Known affectionately as Papa Joe, he invested a good portion of his life to JWV and was recognized by all as an honest, hard working, philanthropic individual who was loved by all. He passed away at the age of 91, leaving a legacy of many grandchildren, great-grandchildren, and love and devotion to all he encountered.

MORTON A. OZUR, born Feb. 5, 1929 to Rose and Nathan Ozur in Brooklyn, NY. Graduated New York University in 1951 with a BA degree in mathematics. He was married to Shirley B. Berner on Jan. 30, 1949, in New York. Was attending NYU Grad School when drafted in the U.S. Army. Did basic training at Ft. Jackson, SC, Feb. 25, 1952-June 1952. Attended Counter Intelligence Corps School at Ft. Holabird, MD until mid-December 1952 when graduated as an agent and continued assignment at Holabird until discharged Feb. 24, 1954.

Returned to New York City and secured employment as probation officer while attending Grad School, where completed 48 credits. Worked as PO in New York until 1964 and transferred to suburban community nearer home in Syosset, NY, where he continues to live. Retired as assistant deputy director of probation in 1989. Father of three boys: Mark, Gary and Alan. The sons brought home three daughters and now is the grandfather of nine and still counting. Has been active in the JWV since the 1970s in Gieir-Levitt Post 655, Nassau Suffolk District Council, and Department of New York.

SEYMOUR PANFEL, born in New York City, NY, on June 8, 1923. Attended PS 174, PS 109 and TJ High School. Inducted into the U.S. Army on Feb. 3, 1943, with the 3rd Inf. Div. as an infantryman. Served in Africa, Sicily, Italy, France and Germany.

Memorable experiences were of the three invasions in Italy, Anzio and South France; rescuing Jewish families hiding in cellars in Marseilles, France; and liberating towns in Italy and France.

Awards/Medals: Expert Rifle Award, Good Conduct, Purple Heart, ETO Medal, Presidential Unit Citation and Combat Infantry Badge. Discharged on Nov. 5, 1945, with the rank of technical sergeant.

Married Bernice (Bonnie) on Nov. 8, 1958, and has one son, Sandor (Sandy) who is married to Linda, one daughter, Stephanie who is a teacher, and two grandchildren, Brooke and Andrew. Panfel is semi retired and self employed.

MAURICE PAPER (CHIC), born on Nov. 11, 1921. Enlisted Feb. 17, 1943, with the U.S. Army Corps of Engineers. Served at Ft. Belvoir, North Africa, Italy, France and Germany.

Memorable experience is being listed on the present exhibition as one of the GI Liberators, at the JWV Museum; being involved with Task Force Butler that landed 48 hours before the invasion of southern France. His mission was to cut two bridges over the Rhine River at Montelemar (railroad and vehicular bridge) in order to delay the retreat of the 11th Panzer Army stationed in Marseilles. When he landed on the beach he was to be met by the French Marquis Freedom Fighters and the majority of them turned out to be Jewish boys and girls from Pland and Russia so they had no problem with communication since they all spoke in Yiddish. Mission succeeded.

Awards/Medals: six Bronze Stars, two Arrow Heads on ETO Ribbon, Bronze Star Medal and Purple Heart.

Discharged on March 6, 1946, with the rank of captain.

Married Cecile and have two sons and three grandchildren. Retired and working for one of his sons.

THEODORE C. PAPERMASTER (TED), born in St. Cloud, MN, on March 30, 1914. Graduated from medical school in 1938. Enlisted in the USAAF on Feb. 16, 1942, at Gowen Field, Boise, ID, with the Medical Corps as a flight surgeon. Served in the Mediterranean Theater (North Africa, Sicily and Italy), with the 99th BG and the 82nd Ftr. Gp., from April 1943-October 1945. Attended School of Aviation Medicine, San Antonio, TX, August-September 1942.

Awards/Medals: 11 Battle Stars, Presidential Unit Citation with three OLCs and a Soldiers Medal from Gen. Jimmy Doolittle in North Africa in July 1943.

Honorable discharge on Feb. 25, 1946, at Camp McCoy, Sparta, WI, with the rank of captain, MC.

Married Dorothy Feldman in June 1946 and has three children and nine grandchildren. Hobbies are daily religious studies in Tanach, Gemara, Jewish history, gardening, fishing, piano, and watching the grandchildren grow up. Retired pediatrician.

NORMAN PARNASS, born in Brooklyn, NY, Feb. 14, 1923. Enlisted in the U.S. Army Jan. 7, 1943, as an infantryman with the 84th Co. B, 333rd Inf. Div. Attended basic training at Ft. Sheridan and served at Camp Claiborne, ASTP-Lehigh University, England and Germany; and participated in the Battle of the Bulge.

Memorable experience was using his Yiddish to act as battalion interpreter in Germany to clear a small village to use the buildings as Army Billets.

Awards/Medals: Combat Infantry Badge. Honorable discharge on Feb. 17, 1946, with the rank of private first class.

Married Agnes in October 1952, and has two sons who are a doctor and a dentist; two daughters who are a lawyer and a family psychologist; and three grandchildren. Received his BA and MA degree in math and education from Brooklyn College. Retired on May 1, 1992 as vice chairman of the New York City Housing Authority after a 40 year career and is now working as vice president of management for a real estate management corporation.

MORTON J. PARISH, born on Staten Island, NY, Sept. 18, 1918. Enlisted in the NJNG in August 1940 and went on active duty with 122nd CA (AA) Ft. DuPont, DE in January 1941 and in February 1942 with the 71st CA (AA) in Washington, DC protection of the White House as gun commander with the rank of corporal.

In October 1942 from OCS as 2nd lieutenant, was assigned as post ordnance officer at AAF Base, Sioux Falls, SD. Promoted to 1st lieutenant August 1943. From Air Svc. Cmd., Fairfield, OH, in August 1944, went overseas to the 52nd Air Svc. Gp. as ordnance supply officer in India and Central Burma.

At Myitkyina, Burma, he flew to various air strips checking on ordnance supplies, bombs, etc. Returned to the States Dec. 28, 1945, and relieved from active duty March 1, 1946, with the rank of captain. Served in the Reserves until 1952.

Awards/Medals: American Defense Service Medal, WWII Victory Medal, Asiatic-Pacific Theater Campaign Ribbon, American Theater Campaign Ribbon and Meritorious Service Unit Insignia.

Married Rose in May 1946 and has a son, a daughter and one granddaughter. Attended Pace University in New York City and became a CPA in 1952 and maintained a practice until June 1989 when he retired.

MILTON S. PATT, born in New Brunswick, NJ, May 19, 1919. Graduated from Rutgers University in 1939 from Officers Candidate School. Enlisted with the Army Transportation Corps as a 1st lieutenant in September 1942. Stationed at Brooklyn AB, Oakland AB and OCS, Starkville, MS.

Memorable experience was commuting to Brooklyn Base by subway and joking about fighting the battle of the Sea Beach Express.

Discharged on Feb. 22, 1946, with the rank of 1st lieutenant.

Married Ruth and has two sons, Richard (M.D.) in Denver, CO; and Steven (Ph.D.) in Cupertino, CA; and two grandchildren. Retired from Colonial Tank Transport as president. Was involved in Temple Israel Bonds.

BERNARD PAYSON, served as a combat photographer with the 89th Inf. Div. during WWII.

From January 1945 to June 1945, he took aerial and ground photos in the ETO. Included in these photos was the Ohrdauf Concentration Camp in Germany.

Aerial photos were taken from a liaison plane near terrain around rivers the division crossed.

He received the Army Commendation Medal.

JAMES PEARL, born in Philadelphia, PA, May 28, 1913. Self educated as an illustrator and graphic designer. Enlisted in the U.S. Army in April 1941, received basic training at Ft. Belvoir, VA. Became cartographer in the 355th Engr. Bn. and went overseas in October 1943.

Their transport, *Monarch of Bermuda*, was caught up in an North Atlantic ice storm, and Navy vigilance on board prevented them from being swamped by keeping piled up ice to a minimum. It didn't stop the Nazi wolf packs. Trained with British sappers (engineers) on Salisbury Plain, England, when he was suddenly transferred to Supreme Allied Headquarters in London, and placed in G-2 under Gen. Eisenhower's command as a cartographer mapper. Remembers Ike as a no nonsense, compassionate leader, and when speaking had a Clark Gable kind of masculinity in his way. Pearl worked on D-day invasion maps, yet at the time did not realize what their purpose was.

During mission to British HQ on Grosvenor Square in late March 1944, was wounded by a Nazi V-2 missile. Hitler, at the time, realized the war was lost, and so he unleashed his missiles from bases at Peenemunde and Nordhausen on Southern England, with devastating effect.

Awards/Medals: Purple Heart and ETO Certificate of Merit. Discharged in October 1945 with the rank of staff sergeant.

Member of JWV and life member of DAV. At the age of 80, he is still an artist illustrator and enjoying it. He has designed two JWV postage stamps for the 100th anniversary to be submitted to the U.S. Postal Service for their consideration.

ALBERT L. PEIPER, born in Cleveland, Dec. 21, 1916. Entered U.S. Army in September 1943, with basic training at Camp Hood, TX. Joined the 899th Tank Destroyer Bn., on D-day + 6 in France and served through battles in Belgium and Germany. Assigned as radio operator on M-10 tank destroyer and while firing indirect, had a fist fight with their gun loader over his religion. This loader was killed on Nov. 20, 1944, by a direct hit on their destroyer, during which time he was wounded.

Awards/Medals: Purple Heart, Distinguished Unit Badge with OLC, European Theater Service Medal with five Bronze Stars. Discharged in October 1945.

Joined the Cleveland Police Department in August 1946, and retired as a sergeant in October 1972. Selected by department of HEW, as a social security claims examiner and then transferred to the Department of HUD in 1979 as an appraiser, retiring in October 1982. Past commander of Paul A. Rosenblum Post 44, Cleveland, OH, and is currently a member of Harvey M. Albertson, Post 759, Orlando, FL.

Married Florence Jeff Sept. 1, 1940, and has three sons: Howard, a wounded Vietnam veteran, Jeffrey and Brian; and seven grandchildren: David, Jaclyn, Marc, Jodi, Jill, Jamie and Bylli.

JEROME PERLMAN, born in Milwaukee, WI, March 23, 1917. Enlisted in June 1939; boot camp, San Diego, CA; went to Communications School; and then to the Philippines. Served at Bataan and Corregidor; POW from May 1942-September 1945; interned Philippines and Japan. After liberation and Navy hospitals, was stationed at Quantico, VA; Camp Pendleton; Cherry Point; Korea from 1952-1953; Portsmouth, San Diego and Camp Lejeune.

Awards/Medals: Bronze Star with Combat V, Purple Heart, Presidential Unit Citation with star, POW Medal, Army Unit Citation with cluster, USMC Good Conduct with four stars, American Service with star, Asiatic-Pacific with star, Philippine Defense with star, Korean Presidential Unit Citation, Korean Service with three stars, UN Medal, WWII Victory Medal and National Service.

Married Corinne Lehman and has two sons, one daughter and four grandchildren. Member of JWV Post 737 in New Jersey; MC League; American Defenders Bataan and Corregidor. Retired civilian communication field.

SIMEON PERLMAN, born in Brooklyn, NY, in 1918. Drafted as private in the U.S. Army in November 1941. Graduated OCS Ft Belvoir, VA, June 1943. Landed at Utah Beach in July 1944 with the 305th Engr. Cbt. Bn., 80th Div. Participated in Gen. Patton's 3rd Army push through France and Germany. Awarded the Bronze Star Medal. He was discharged January 1946 with rank of captain.

Most memorable experience was finding his uncle and his family during the Battle of the Bulge. They were in hiding in a small village in the Ardennes, Belgium and there had been no contact with them since before the war. No one knew if they were alive or not. When the Army liberated their area, his uncle asked a passing soldier to write his whereabouts to his sister in New York. His mother wrote to his brother, who was with the USAF in France. She did not ask Simeon to try to contact his uncle, knowing he was busy in combat. When Simeon received the address in a letter from his brother, he saw on his map that it was only a few miles from where he was, so he drove over there. He rang the bell at the house of the village mayor and his aunt appeared at the door. Assuming the soldier came to see the mayor, she directed him, in French, to where he could be found. "Aunt Fanny," he said, "It is me, Simeon". It was the happiest of reunions.

Worked as a sporting goods importer and wholesaler, first in New York and for the last 20 years in Chicago. He has two married sons and 12 lovely grandchildren.

HILLEL HYMAN PERLSTEIN (HY), born in Dallas, TX, May 14, 1919. Parents were Max and Dora Perlstein, one brother, Israel and one sister, Eve. Attended John Henry Brown Elementary School and graduated Forest Avenue High School in 1938. After graduation, entered the plumbing industry until he was inducted into the U.S. Army on Feb. 27, 1943. On Nov. 23, 1944, he was shipped to the ETO and assigned to the 346th Inf. Div. as first machine gunner until he was injured in action on March 14, 1945.

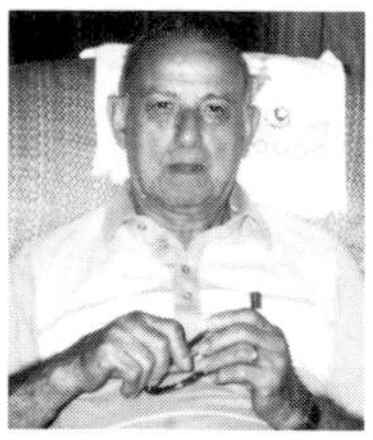

Awards/Medals: Purple Heart and other awards. Returned to the States on Jan. 19, 1946, and was soon discharged in San Antonio, TX.

Returned to Dallas, TX, where he entered into the plumbing industry with Ross Ave. Plumbing Co. and then Milton B. Levy & Son Plumbing Inc. as operations manager.

Married Ann Max of Kansas City, MO on June 30, 1946, and they have two sons and two granddaughters. He is semi retired but still working part time in the plumbing industry.

WILLIAM JAY PETERSON, born in Chicago, IL. Attended high school and community college in Elgin, IL, and Northern Illinois University where he earned his BA degree in history and MS degree geography. In 1982 he completed ROTC as a distinguished military graduate, became a 2nd lieutenant in MI.

First assignment was in Germany as battalion intelligence officer (S2) for a HAWK Air Defense Arty. Bn., and also served in the 3rd Inf. Div. Went to Ft. Bragg, NC in 1986, for duty in the G2, 1st Spec. Ops. Cmd. (airborne). Participated in Operations, Just Cause, Desert Shield and Desert Storm, as part of the psychological operations (PSYOP).

Returned to Germany in 1991 and served in the 701st MI Bde. at Field Station Augsburg. Held the positions of battalion logistics officer (S4), Company Commander, and Battalion Operations Officer (S3). In 1995 he attended the resident Command and General Staff College at Ft. Leavenworth, KS at which time he was a major.

Throughout military career, he has been a Jewish Welfare Board certified lay leader; founder and leader of the military Jewish community in Riyadh, Saudi Arabia called Ivrei Hamidbar Ha'aravi.

Married Sheri Kaplan of Skokie, Illinois and has two sons, H. Jacob and Aaron Sammuel.

SAM PFEFFERBAUM, born in Poland, May 6, 1913. Moved to Vienna, Austria, then to U.S. Nov. 22, 1922. Graduated from City College, 1942, with BBA degree and entered the U.S. Army in June 1942. Basic training at Governors Island, Ft. Totten and Ft. Hamilton. Entered OCS at Grinell University December 1942 and graduated 2nd lieutenant February 1943.

First assignment was New Orleans POE, assignment Fiscal Div., assistant fiscal officer. Promoted to 1st lieutenant and in 1944, after graduating from a Fiscal Directors School, was promoted to captain and became fiscal director of the New Orleans POE. Established the first accounting machine system and was involved in transactions that amounted to billions of dollars.

The most gratifying event in his life was leaving Vienna for the States in 1922.

Left the service in June 1945 and started Reserve duty through 1968. Since he spoke Germany, he was involved in several risky assignments, ending in minor injuries. Graduated from Command And General Staff College.

Married Rose Friedman and has two children and two grandchildren.

HARRY PICKER, born in Chicago, IL, Feb. 16, 1916. Enlisted in the U.S. Army March 10, 1942. Served in Abilene, TX; Hammer Field, Fresno, CA; England; Belgium; France; and Germany. Participated at the Battle of the Bulge, Normandy and Northern France.

Most memorable experience was celebrating V-J Day in Paris and watching Glenn Millers Army Band live.

Awards/Medals: Good Conduct Medal, WWII Victory Medal, EAME and Commendation from the 9th AF Service Command from Brigadier General Myron Wood. Discharged in July 1946 with the rank of corporal.

Married Anita in 1949, and has two daughters, Ellen and Janice; one son, Bruce; and two granddaughters, Arynn and Becky. Retired and enjoying his 500 albums from the 1930s and 1940s. Member of JWV Post 328, Skokie, IL.

ROBERT MILTON PIERSON, born in Syracuse, NY, Sept. 11, 1919. Attended Croton School, graduated from Central High School and attended Syracuse University to study law. Member of Zeta Beta Tau, Temple Adath Yeshurun, Boy Scouts and Louis Marshall Legal Society.

Enlisted in the 411th AAA Gun Bn. with rank of 1st lieutenant at the age of 22. Served in ATO, England and France.

Awards/Medals: Purple Heart.

He was killed in action and is survived by his mother, Hilda.

ART PINANSKY, born in Portland, ME, Aug. 29, 1922. Enlisted Oct. 31, 1942, Air Transport Command, Air Corps. Stationed all through North Africa, Egypt, Palestine and ended up in Abadan, Iran.

Memorable experience was in Abadan, meeting baseball Hall of Fame stars, Carl Hubbell, Harry Heilman and Fred Fitzsimmons, and getting their autographs.

Awards/Medals: Good Conduct Medal, American Theater, EAME and WWII Victory Medal. Discharged on Feb. 5, 1946, with the rank of private first class.

Has been married over 23 years and is a teacher and comedian.

MORRIS PINCUS, born in Brooklyn, NY, Oct. 6, 1919. Enlisted at Camp Upton, NY; attended basic training at Camp Lee, VA, medical technician 409. Served at Camp Lee, VA; transferred to Langely Field, VA, Air Corps; Bradley Field, CT; Westover Field, MA and Grenier Field, NH.

Went overseas to England in 1943 and served with the 356th Ftr. Gp., 8th AF. Participated in Air Offensive Europe, Ardennes, Central Europe, Normandy, Northern France and Rhineland.

Memorable experience was in 1944 when Scotch gliders flew over England to invade Holland. Unfortunately, the Germans were prepared and their mission failed, causing many injuries to the Scotch, who were picked up and treated by Americans in England.

Awards/Medals: American Defense Service Medal, Distinguished Unit Badge, EAME Service Medal, Good Conduct Medal and six Battle Stars. Discharged on Oct. 2, 1945, at Ft. Dix, NJ, with the rank of private first class.

Married Emma in June 1943, and has two daughters, Diane and Debra, and four grandchildren. Was employed as a milk route man and is now retired. Member of JWV Post 550.

IRVING PINKUS, enlisted in the USN in March 1943 and spent six weeks in boot camp at Camp Peory in Williamsburg, VA. Assigned to the Seabees Bn. 1007th. As a S2/c, he was transferred to Port Huenemi, CA. After three weeks he was shipped to the South Pacific. The voyage was rugged and they had to zig zag due to the fact that they were being chased by a submarine. After 30 days at sea they landed in the New Hebrides.

He was baptized the second night. Charlie dropped bombs on their small airport and they were forced to spend many nights in the bomb shelter. After spending 30 months between Guadalcanal, Rabaul and Espirito Santo, they finally saw a little action at Boganville where they followed the 1st Marines ashore.

Duties were mostly to run the commissary. En route to Iwo Jima, he stopped for some R&R. While they were fishing, an ammunition ship blew up about 1/4 mile from them causing them to become temporarily blinded. He spent the next six weeks in the Navy hospital, then sent back home to a hospital in Bainbridge, MD.

He was discharged in June 1945.

ALLAN PLATT, born in Bayonne, NJ, Aug. 24, 1925. Served in WWII and Korean War. Enlisted in the USAC in May 1943; attended basic training at USAAC Aviation Cadet Flight 60C. Sent to the 331st Trng. Detach. at Williamsport, PA; flight training at Maxwell AB, AL, Class 45B; volunteered to be flight engineer in B-29. Finished training at Amarillo, TX and Hondo, TX. When the war ended he was about to be assigned to a B-29 combat crew. Discharged in October 1945.

Went to college on the GI Bill; graduated as a mechanical engineer and commission of 2nd lieutenant, U.S. Army Ord. Corps, June 1950. Called to active duty in May 1951 and

assigned to the 9355th Tech. Unit. Served as research and development officer on the 280mm Atomic Cannon until November 1952 as a captain.

Most memorable experience was being invited to home of Jewish family for a holiday dinner in Williamsport, PA.

Married Ann Hcryla Platt and they have two sons, C.J. and D.G. Platt. Member of the JWV and life member of the American Legion. He is now retired and lives in Richmond, VA.

MANUEL PLOTKIN, born in Pawa, IL, Sept. 6, 1919. Enlisted in the USAACR Dec. 3, 1942. Called to active duty January 1943, graduated pilot training April 1944 and operation training in August 1944 in C-47s.

Flew northern route to Britain where assigned to 91st Sqdn., 439th Troop Carrier Gp. Engaged in Holland Invasion (glider drops), Battle of Bulge with glider drops to Bastogne, and battle front resupply including Patton's 3rd Armor and crossing the Rhine River. Served temporary flight duty at Shaef HQ, ETO. Assigned as senior flight control officer in Paris until his return to the States in February 1945.

Awards/Medals: Air Medal with Palm, ETO Ribbon with four Battle Stars and Presidential Unit Citation. Discharged in April 1946 with the rank of captain.

Married Marlene in December 1948 and has one son, Jerry and one daughter, Barbara. Employed as aerospace engineer and retired from Lockhead Aircraft. Member of JWV Post 595.

WILLIAM PLOTKIN, served in WWII with the 11th Armd. Div. Inducted in the service Feb. 20, 1942, Ft. Dix, NJ. Sent to Ft. Knox, KY, basic training at the Armed Forces Replacement Training Center. Transferred to 80th Armd. Regt. as instructor. Went to Camp Polk, LA in July 1942. Assigned to 42nd Tk. Bn., Co. B. Other stations include Camp Barkley, TX; Camp Ibis in the Mojave Desert; Camp Cook, CA; Camp Kilmer, NJ, where shipped from Staten Island on English troop ship, *Samaria*.

Put on LST, crossed the Channel, landing at Cherbourg Peninsula. Slept in French military barracks on way to Belgium and Battle of the Bulge. Was part of Gen. Patton's 3rd Army. After Bulge, went to St. Vith and built 12 miles of corduroy roads. Used this road to leave there and enter Germany, where 12 days were spent fighting the Mosel-Koblentz Triangle. Crossed the Rhine River, worked way up to Maginot Line and wound up in Czechoslovakia. Went on sick call and was sent to England's 82nd General Hospital where on May 8, 1945 they celebrated V-E Day.

Awards/Medals: EAME Service Medal with three Bronze Stars and Good Conduct Medal. Received honorable discharge Oct. 7, 1945, as sergeant. Active member and past commander of David Blick Post 63 JWV, Elizabeth, NJ.

SEYMOUR POBER, born in Brooklyn, NY, Oct. 7, 1924. Entered service Aug. 19, 1943, as a private at Camp Upton, NY. Sent to Medical Technical School in New Orleans Staging Area. Shipped to England, 106th General Hospital, ETO.

Supervised the requisitioning, storing and issuing of all equipment and medical supplies for the hospital. In charge of consolidating receipts, supplies and inventory and preparation of status reports.

Awards/Medals: American Theater Service Medal, EAME Service Medal, Good Conduct Medal, WWII Victory Medal. Honorably discharged on April 9, 1946, with the rank of technician 5th grade at Ft. Bragg, NC.

Married Rita and has two daughters, Geryl and Karen, one son, Andrew and six grandchildren.

HENRY H. POLITZER, born May 24, 1919, in Vienna (Wien), Austria. Graduated high school in Vienna and joined the Austrian Army in 1937. Was stationed in Pinkafeld, near the Hungarian frontier. After the Anschluss (Hitler's taking of Austria) he was forced to take a soldier's oath to Hitler and the German Reich in spite of his protests. Orders are orders and he had to take that oath as a Jew. He was later dismissed from the Austrian army and put into the Reserves for service without a weapon.

Emigrated to Bogota, Columbia in August 1938 and to the States in August 1944. Sent to Camp Blanding in December 1944 for training; shipped to Manila, August 1945, stationed in Santa Ana (near Clark Field), then sent to Tokyo, where he served in Motor Bn. of General HQ Armed Forces Pacific. Stationed in the Imperial Finance Building, Tokyo, and worked in the old Nissan factory near Yokohama. They took care of the vehicles for Gen. McArthur and all allied officers serving with HQ. In September 1946 he was offered 2nd lieutenant if he re-enlisted, but preferred his discharge as a technical sergeant.

HERMAN POLLACK, born May 13, 1924, Newark, NJ. Entered the U.S. Army Feb. 18, 1943, and served with the 64th and 69th Sig. AW Dets. at New Jersey, North Carolina, Florida, England, France and Germany.

Awards/Medals: EAME Service Medal, Good Conduct Medal and WWII Victory Medal. Discharged on Nov. 1, 1945, with the rank of private first class.

Retired after 40 years with the Veterans Administration.

CLARICE POLLARD, served in the WAAC/WAC from early 1943 to 1946, starting at Ft. Oglethorpe, GA; then to Stephen F. Austin State Teachers College for administration course in Nacogdoches, TX; on to Ft. Lawton/Hotel Stratford POE, Seattle, WA; then to New Orleans Army AB/Transportation Corps at Lake Ponchartrain, LA; followed by School for Personnel Services at Washington and Lee University in VA, touching base again in New Orleans, LA and finishing at Camp Upton, NY.

Author of *Laugh, Cry and Remember* the journal of a GI lady and *Hey Lady, Uncle Sam Needs You* and numerous articles. At the present she is occupied with book signings and speaking engagements.

JOSEPH L. POLLOCK, enlisted in the USA while a sophomore at State Teachers College, West Chester, PA. He was inducted at Ft. Meade and completed his basic training at Camp Wheeler, GA. He was assigned to the cadre of the 63rd Inf. Div., Camp Blanding, FL. The 63rd moved to Camp Van Dorn near Centreville, MS.

The 63rd landed at Marseilles, France and won two Battle Stars for the Ardennes and Central Europe. Pollock's 253rd Inf. Regt. won the Presidential Unit Citation, two Combat Infantry Badges with five Bronze Stars. He co-produced *GI Crunch*, a soldier show which toured Europe for seven months including appearances in Germany, Paris, Rome, Berlin and cigarette camps.

He is leading a campaign to learn of the fate of Samuel Musch who was shot down flying over the Sea of Japan during the Korean Conflict.

Pollock is executive director of the National Clearing House of Public Alumni Assocs.

BERTRAM POLOW, born in Irvington, NJ, April 14, 1918. Enlisted with the USAAF on Dec. 28, 1941, as an intelligence specialist with the 307th Ftr. Sqdn., 31st Ftr. Gp. June 1942-December 1944, stationed in England, North Africa, Sicily, Gela, Palermo, northeast coast, Salerno, Naples, Casino, Anzio, San Severo, and places in between.

Participated in the invasion of North Africa at Oran; Kasserine Pass; invasions of Sicily, Italy, Anzio; and four weeks at Anzio Beach Head.

Memorable experiences were meeting J. Doolittle in North Africa; watching Churchill drive through Tunis after they took it; and seeing Patton in his jeep when they invaded Sicily.

Awards/Medals: 13 battle stars. Discharged on Sept. 5, 1945, with the rank of staff sergeant.

Married Betty; they have three children: David, Sarah and Abby; and five grandchildren living in Vermont, California and Georgia. He is a retired judge of the New Jersey Appellate Court; practices law part time with his son in Vermont and spends five months a year in Palm Desert, CA.

HERBERT B. POPOK, enlisted in the USAAC in early 1943. After basic training became an Air Cadet and graduated as navigator with rank of 2nd lieutenant. Trained with bomber crew in Idaho and assigned to the 451st BG, 15th Air Corp stationed in Italy.

Flew 22 bombardment missions, hitting oil fields, marshaling yards, etc. in Austria and Southern Germany. On their fifth mission two engines went out, they aborted the mission and landed in Zara, Yugoslavia, breaking the nose wheel and crashing off the end of the runway. On last mission, flak hit their engine and they made a forced landing in Vienna on April 25, 1945. The Russians were already there and subsequently they were flown to Kiev, Russia, then by land to Odessa and back to Italy, by which time the war with Germany had ended.

WOLF A. POPPER, born in Vienna, Austria, June 13, 1928, as Baron Wolfgang Alexander Leopold Albert Popper von Podhragy. Holocaust survivor after eight months escaping Austria through Czechoslovakia to Holland on last plane leaving Holland for England. Came to the U.S. via Brazil.

Graduated Forest Hills High School, NY, June 1945. Drafted Oct. 11, 1950, basic training at Camp Cooke, CA, with 40th Inf. Div. AG Section HQ. Completed 6th Army Discussion Leaders School. With division in Sendai, Japan, Certificate of Proficiency for Unit Chemical Defense. Transferred to 2nd T. Major Port by order of Gen. Ridgeway. Chief clerk, North Pier, Yokohama.

Awards/Medals: Korean Service, United Nations and Good Conduct Medals. Honorable discharge Oct. 1, 1952.

Listed in Who's Who in Finance & Industry, president of Wolf A. Popper, Inc., in business nearly 40 years; published in Business Week, Financial World, etc.; interviewed on TV & Radio; was faculty Yeshiva University, Advisory Board Iona College; on Speakers Committee B'nai Brith; Advisory Board Chelsea National Bank; Treasurer of Life Ins. Div. State of Israel Bonds, etc.; Past Commander JWV Post 5; now vice commander American Legion Post 1870. Hobbies: Music, paints, makes toys. Has daughter Cynthia Gayle.

ELLIOTT W. PORTER, born Dec. 2, 1924, Revere, MA. Entered service in 1942 as a member of ROTC unit at Massachusetts State College. Called to active duty by January 1943 as aviation cadet. Commissioned 2nd lieutenant and rated B-17 pilot in May 1944. Completed 21 missions with 8th AF in major targets in Germany.

Discharged as Reserve 1st lieutenant January 1946. Returned to Massachusetts State and continued flying active duty Reserve while attending college. Graduated in 1948 with

BS degree in food technology. Worked as food tech. for General Foods in new product development.

Recalled in 1951, served as pilot, operations officer, staff officer and protocol officer. Appointed to regular Air Force in 1955. Attended AF Institute of Technology, 1961-63. Received BS in aeronautical engineering. Held research and development assignments including range safety officer and chief of instrumentation at Cape Canaveral and Patrick AFB, FL also helicopter commander of squadron in Vietnam, 1967-68. Retired August 1975 as lieutenant colonel. Worked as senior engineer manager at Kennedy Space Center from 1977-89, then became fully retired.

Awards/Medals: Distinguished Flying Cross, Bronze Star, Meritorious Service with OLC, Air Medal with six OLCs, AF Commendation Medal, Army Good Conduct, American Theater, European Theater with three Battle Stars, WWII Victory Medal, WWII Army of Occupation, National Defense Service with one Battle Star, Vietnam Service with two Battle Stars, Armed Forces Reserve Medal, Vietnam Cross of Gallantry with Palm, Vietnam Republic Medal, Presidential Unit Citation, AF Outstanding Unit, Command Pilot Badge, Master Missileman Badge.

Married Ruthe June 1946, has three children: Joel, Susan and Terry (deceased December 1984).

JULES POSNER, of Brooklyn, NY, enlisted in the U.S. Army in March 1941 and trained in Ft. Riley, KS. Shipped overseas in March 1942 on the *Queen Mary* and trained with the British army in Ireland and Scotland. Invaded North Africa Nov. 8, 1942, landing was designated "Operation Torch." Liberated Casablanca, Bizerte, Oran and Tunisia and participated in the El Alamain campaign.

Retrieved a German flag atop a Synagogue in Casablanca. Invaded Sicily on July 10, 1943, and was attached to Maj. Gen. Lucian Truscott's 3rd Div. They liberated Naples with a Jewish Div. from Palestine, attached to the British army. On Jan. 22, 1944, the 3rd Div. made an amphibious landing on Anzio under the code name "Shingle."

Fought side by side with Morris Rosen on Anzio beachhead and throughout Italy and France into Germany. In August 1944, the 3rd Div. was the first Army to liberate Rome from the South. They had an audience with Pope Pius XII. After invading Southern France Aug. 15, 1944, they penetrated into Germany as far as the town of Bischoffinge.

Sent home on rotation and arrived in America on March 12, 1945. Married his childhood sweetheart, Leatrice Shack, March 25, 1945. Received a letter from Morris Rosen written in Germany, sending best wishes on his marriage and apologized for not attending the wedding, but hoped he would be invited to their golden anniversary. March 1995 Posner of New York and Rosen of California, were together to celebrate the Posners 50th Anniversary.

SOLOMON POSNER, born in Syracuse, NY, May 8, 1926. Attended Sumner Grade School and graduated from Central High School.

Entered the service in 1944, receiving training at Ft. Benning, GA and Ft. Lauderdale, FL. Saw action with the 9th Army in the ETO.

He was killed in action in August 1945 at the age of 19.

WILLIAM POSNER, born in Moizaikus, Lithuania and arrived in the United States on July 1, 1927. Was a student at Virginia Polytechnic Institute in Norfolk, VA when he enlisted in the U.S. Army Dec. 11, 1942. Joined the 529th Sig. Ops. Co. at Camp Crowder, MO, Central Sig. Corps School.

Went overseas in the Pacific with the 529th and their primary campaign in Okinawa. Slated to land in Southern

Japan, but President Truman saved their lives by dropping the A Bomb. After Okinawa Occupation duty in Korea, he came home to Norfolk, VA in February 1946.

Married Marjorie Wolfson on Jan. 30, 1944, and has three children: Nancy Becker, Charles and Ira; and six grandchildren. Member of Post 335, Kings County, Brooklyn, NY. Was a county commander and currently a judge advocate for the Department of New York. Has been the executive director fo Kings County and its 20 posts for the past 24 years. Still in active practice as an attorney in New York City.

MILTON POSTER, born in Mt. Pleasant, PA, Aug. 2, 1913. Enlisted Aug. 19, 1941, with the 44th Inf. Div. as a staff sergeant. Stationed at Ft. Meade, MO; Ft. Dix, NJ; Camp Livingston, LA; and Ft. Riley, KS. Participated at Northern France, Rhineland and Central Europe.

Memorable experience was saving the life of two soldiers hit by fire and land mines.

Awards/Medals: Good Conduct Medal, Bronze Star Cluster, American Defense with three Bronze Stars. Discharged on July 15, 1945, with the rank of staff sergeant, (H) Wpns. Co.

Married Vivian and has two daughters. Retired from Chrysler-American Motors dealer after 40 years. Member of JWV Post 718 in Pittsburgh, PA; attended University of Pittsburgh; president of Tree of Life Synagogue for 25 years.

JAMES POWELL, born in Bronz, NY, Aug. 3, 1913. Enlisted in the USMCR Nov. 28, 1938. Original landing with 1st Mar. Div. on Guadalcanal, August 1942. Graduated from Paymaster School as a paymaster sergeant.

Memorable experience was in the heat of battle in Guadalcanal, when the Japanese were shelling them from their ships, he told his fellow Marines, that just in case a bullet had his name on it, he just changed it. The Marines had a good laugh and it helped ease the tension.

Awards/Medals: Presidential Citation, American Defense, WWII Victory Medal, American Campaign, Asiatic-Pacific Campaign and Marine Corps Medal.

Discharged in December 1945 from the Separation Bn., Redistribution Regt., Camp Joseph H. Pendleton, MT&RC, SDA, Oceanside, CA. Paymaster Sergeant.

Married Beatrice Bravin July 2, 1941, and has three children and nine grandchildren (two grandchildren are married). Owned and operated a Union Oil Service Station in Sherman Oaks, CA for 30 years. Retired in 1976 and went to work in the apparel industry, retired again in 1985.

JOSEPH W. PRANE, born in Bronx, NY, June 18, 1923. Drafted into the U.S. Army Feb. 28, 1944. Assigned to Army Corps of Engineers, Special Engrs. Div. Stationed at New York City (Manhattan Project) and Oak Ridge, TN (Atom Bomb).

Memorable experiences involve working on the Atom Bomb and helping prepare material for the first A Bomb test in Los Alamos, NM.

Received the Good Conduct Medal. Discharged May 15, 1946, with the rank of T-3.

Married to Annette Miller Dec. 30, 1945, and has two daughters and two grandchildren. He is semi-retired and still active as a chemical consultant.

ROLAND I. PRITIKIN, born in Chicago, IL, Jan. 9, 1906. Received M.D. from Stritch School of Medicine, Loyola University, Chicago, June 11, 1930. Enlisted in ILNG June 12, 1930. Served several tours of state duty, notably chief medical inspector Illinois Flood Area, for 40 days in January and February 1937 when the Ohio River flooded. Went to Shawneetown with 2,000 Illinois National Guardsmen.

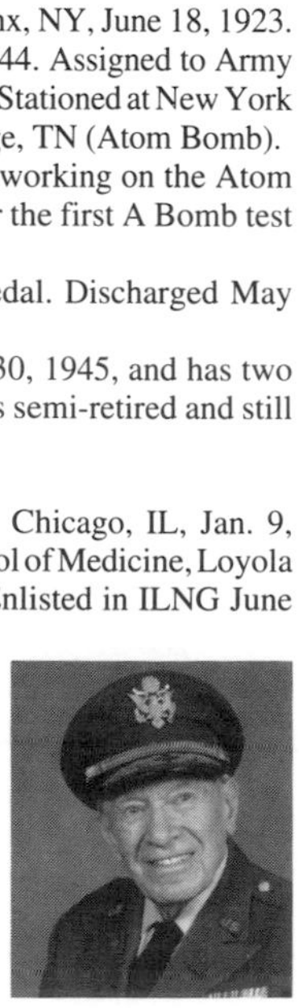

Called to active duty with the 33rd Div. ILNG, March 5, 1941. Went to Camp Forrest, TN; transferred at the request of the Surgeon General of the Army to Stark General Hospital, 125,000 patients went through the Eye Clinic. Remained in Active Reserves until the age of 60. For 25 years was consultant in Ophthalmology, U.S. Army Health Service Command, Ft. Sheridan, IL. When Ft. Sheridan was closed he was given a certificate of appreciation.

Received Army Commendation Medal for a variety of reasons including invention of a method for a removal of non-magnetic introcular foreign bodies from land mine and booby trap accidents. This was called TDY without pay or any other allowances. Served from June 12, 1930-May 29, 1992. Played a prominent role in integration of the Armed Forces and harmonious race relations.

Two consecutive days a month, went from Rockford, IL to Ft. Sheridan for 25 years, first as a consultant in Ophthalmology, 5th Army. When 5th Army moved to San Antonio, TX, title was changed to consultant in ophthalmology, U.S. Army Health Services Command. Served 62 years of service in all.

Order of St. John of Jerusalem given by Queen Elizabeth II in 1970 for 30 years as an intermittent eye surgeon in India, Pakistan and other commonwealth and for her Commonwealth countries. Promoted to commander by Queen Elizabeth II in 1993.

PAUL E. PRITZKER, member of the JWV/USA NEC is national chairman of the descendants of the JWV. Joined the USAAC April 20, 1943. Following Air Corps basic training he was assigned to the Air Corps Specialized Training Program. Member of the 571st Sig. Aircraft Warning Sqdn.; he was involved in the development and improvement of radar systems until his honorable discharge in March 1946.

Graduated Wentworth Institute of Technology in 1948. Awarded the degree doctor of engineering technology (HC) from Wentworth in 1985. He is a Wentworth corporator and chairman of George Slack & Pritzker Forensic Engineers, Weston, MA and Punta Gorda Isles, FL. Was president of the National Society of Professional Engineers, 1985-1986. Licensed as a professional engineer in California, Connecticut, Florida, Massachusetts and Wisconsin. He is a chartered engineer fellow of the Institute of Engineers of Ireland accredited throughout the British Commonwealth and the European Common Market countries. He is an instrument rated aircraft pilot and a USPS navigator.

Married Janice during WWII at Drew/McDill Field, Tampa, FL Feb. 8, 1944. They are parents of three sons: Roger, Bruce and Arthur, and grandparents of three: Morris, Elizabeth and Justina. They celebrated their 50th wedding anniversary by taking their children and grandchildren to Israel. They winter at Punta Gorda Isles, FL and return to Weston, MA each spring.

He is a JWV/USA life member and member of the Robert Kennedy Post #668. Founding charter member and senior vice commander of the Oskar Schindler Post #404, Department of Florida. Past president of the Architects/Engineers Lodge of B'nai B'rith in Massachusetts; served as vice president of the Boston Council of B'nai B'rith where he was active as a public speaker; former trustee of Temple Israel Natick, MA and a member of Temple Shalom, Port Charlotte, FL. He continues to serve as chairman of UJA activities in his community.

LEO M. PROWDA, born in Warsaw Jan. 30, 1895. Connected with Leslie Judge Book Co. of Syracuse, NY. Inducted on May 26, 1918, and served with the 26th Co., 153rd Dept. Brigade.

Passed away on Jan. 24, 1941, at the age of 46.

MANUEL PROWDA, born in 1890 in Syracuse, NY. Worked as a musician at the Strand Theater. Enlisted on April 29, 1918, and sent to Camp Dix. Sailed for France on May 26, 1918, and attached to 307th FA, 78th Div., as a drummer. He saw a great deal of action.

Passed away on Feb. 17, 1919, in France, of pneumonia, at the age of 29.

MITCHELL E. PRUSHANKIN, joined the USAAC/AF from April 1943-April 1946. Convoyed to ETO/England in 1944 and attached to SHAEF, until German surrender, then to U.S. Group Control Council for Germany. One year assignment to American occupied Tempelhof Airdrome, Berlin. Prior to move from London to France, just after D-day, the boys in his outfit were listening to the daily radio propaganda broadcast to American troops. Lord Haw Haw wanted to know "How are you fellows in Sloan Court doing?" This was the day after a V-1 struck, demolishing their billet, and leaving some 20 or more men dead.

Six months after D-day (during the Battle of the Bulge) a call was made for volunteers from the rear echelon for duty at the front. He submitted a letter of compliance. Gen. Patton and his troops had other ideas. Their swift action deprived him of the opportunity of landing his blow and helping to finish off the Third Reich.

Awards/Medals: EAME Campaign Medal, WWII Victory Medal, et al. Discharged with the rank of staff sergeant. Was a member of the 301st Troop Carrier Sqdn., 473rd Aerial Engr. Gp. at time of discharge.

He graduated from the University of Pennsylvania in 1940. Today he is retired from his field of R&D Chemist/Analytical.

JOSEPH L. PULLOCK, enlisted in the U.S. Army while a sophomore at State Teachers College, West Chester, PA. Inducted at Ft. Meade, MD and completed his basic training at Camp Wheeler, GA. Assigned to the cadre of the 63rd Inf. Div., Camp Blanding, FL. The 63rd moved to Camp Van Dorn, MS.

Landed at Marseilles, France and won two Battle Stars for Ardennes and Central Europe. Other awards include the Presidential Unit Citation, two Combat Infantry Badges and five Bronze Stars.

After V-E Day, he co-produced a soldier's show which traveled Europe for seven months, including appearances in Heidelburg, Paris, Rome, Berlin, the cigarette camps.

Currently leading a campaign to learn of the final fate of Maj. Samuel Musch who was shot down over the sea of Japan during the Korean Conflict. He is executive director of the National Clearing House of Public Alumni Associations.

IRWIN PURISCH, enlisted June 29, 1941. Assignments were with the 2nd Tow Target Sqdn, Grenier Field, Manchester, NH, 1941; Hyannis Airport, MA and Cadets, 1942-1943; Psychology and Research Department of Gunnery School, 1943-1944; and the 461st BG (H), 765th BS (H) Cerignola, Italy, 1945.

Attended Rising Sun School of Aeronautics, Philadelphia, PA; graduated as aircraft and engine mechanic, 1941-1942. Pilot training in Montgomery and Decatur, AL, 1943; navigation training, Monroe, LA, 1943; Gunnery School at Tyndall Field, Panama City, FL, 1943. After graduation was instructor until 1944. Combat training with Crew 448, Westover Field, Springfield, MA, 1944-1945; graduated and sent to Italy. Returned home in 1945 for leave and assignments to Ft. Dix, NJ; McDill Field, Tampa, FL; Sioux Field, SD; and Kirtland Field, Albuquerque, NM; then back to Ft. Dix.

Awards/Medals: Good Conduct, Air Medal, WWII Victory, NYS Conspicuous Service, Pre-Pearl Harbor Ribbon, American Theater and ETO with five Battle Stars and two Unit Citations.

Married and have three children, four grandchildren and two great-grandchildren.

ELLEN (NETTIE WEINBERG-HALL) RABELSKIE, born in Brooklyn, NY, Sept. 6, 1924. Attended schools in Brooklyn prior to moving to Jamaica, NY in 1934. Graduated June 1942 from John Adam's High

School, South Ozone Park, NY. Worked for USCG in Washington, DC prior to joining the WAC in December 1944. Went on active duty Jan. 10, 1945, taking basic training at Ft. Oglethorpe, GA.

Sent to Medical Technicians School at William Beaumont General Hospital, El Paso, TX and to Ft. Bragg, NC, for on the ward training. Graduated as a medical technician, promoted to Tech 5th Grade, assigned to hospital at Camp Carson, Colorado Springs, CO. Transferred to Fitzsimmons General Hospital, Denver, CO.

Awards/Medals: Good Conduct, American Service and WWII Victory Medals. Discharged June 6, 1946, Ft. Dix, NJ.

Returned to civilian live and home in Jamaica, NY. Entered Pace Institute, NY in the fall of 1946. Was employed until her retirement, as administrative assistant, in December 1984. live member of the Jesse Brams Post #203 in Monticello, NY.

Married Arthur Rabelskie, has one son, Kevin L. Hall.

ISIDORE RABELSKIE, born in New York City, April 11, 1895. Drafted in U.S. Army Dec. 6, 1917. Became a private in Co. B, 307th Inf, 77th Div. of the AEF. Trained at Camp Upton, Yaphank, Long Island, NY; sailed overseas April 6, 1918. Unit arrived in Liverpool, England April 19, 1918, and went on to Calais, France, April 20, 1918.

Company was involved in campaigns in Picardy and Flanders, Vosges and the Lorraine, Vesle to the Aisne River and the Argonne-Meuse Offensive, all in France. Company aided in reaching and saving the "lost battalion" of the 77th Div. in the Argonne-Meuse Offensive.

Awards/Medals: Purple Heart Medal for having been gassed during his tour of duty. Returned to States at the end of April 1919 and demobilized May 9, 1919.

Married after the war and has one son. Worked in the garment industry in New York City. Passed away in 1980.

BERNARD RABUNSKY, born in Wilmington, NY. Drafted in the U.S. Army May 19, 1953, as sergeant E-5 personnel specialist. Stationed at Ft. Lee, VA and Seoul, Korea.

Memorable experience was when lost north of DMZ, just a few yards from Chinese camp.

Awards/Medals: Army Commendation Medal, Good Conduct Medal and Korean Theater. Discharged on April 29, 1955, with rank sergeant E-5.

Married and has three children and one grandchild. Retired mental health administrator and has worked as a tax preparer and movie extra.

CARL BERLE RADLO, born in Boston, MA, Oct. 18, 1911. Graduated Boston Latin School 1929 and Harvard College 1933. Inducted in U.S. Army at Ft. Devens, MA, May 1942. Spent remainder of 1942 on duty with 14th Gen. Hosp., Camp Livingston, LA. Waived non-combat duty limitations, entered OCS at Ft. Sill, OK January 1943 and commissioned 2nd lieutenant April 1943.

Sent overseas October 1943, served in Africa, Sicily and Italy with the 5th Army as member of the 88th Inf. Div., 913th FA BN. Received his 1st lieutenant bars in June 1944 and was with the first troops to enter Rome and make it the first liberated capitol in WWII. Despite warnings of danger Lt. Radlo set up an observation post in a dangerous building on the crest of Mt. Grande, Italy, successfully directing artillery fire on an area where a counterattack was forming. Nazi shells destroyed the building, instantly killing him.

He was posthumously awarded the Purple Heart and the OLC to Bronze Star Medal. His remains were identified five years later and returned to the U.S., where he was buried Nov. 18, 1949, at the Independent Pride of Boston Montuale Cemetery, Wobur, MA.

EPHRAIM RADNER, born in Springfield, MA Oct. 23, 1921. Enlisted in USAC March 3, 1943, as private then as an air cadet. Trained to become a radar meteorology officer. Established first radar installation demonstrating applicability of radar for military meteorologists and trained bomber crews in use of radar meteorology in hiding behind clouds and storms during their bombing runs. Also established other radar meteorology sites.

Awards/Medals: Commendation Award. Honorably discharged Sept. 16, 1946, with rank 1st lieutenant.

Married Babette Solomon in 1950, has four children and three grandchildren. In 1958 was one of the founders of GCA Corp. Now semi-retired, he does some business consulting and is active in pro bono work.

MAURICE RAFFEL, born in Harrisburg, PA, Dec. 10, 1920. Graduated Temple University, June 1942. Enlisted in Aviation Cadet Program in USAAC June 5, 1942. Received pilot flying training in Eastern Flying Training Command, graduating with Class 43-K. Received pilot's wings and 2nd lieutenant commission Dec. 5, 1943. Assigned to B-17 Training School at Hendricks AFB, Sebring, FL.

Completed crew training and assigned to 483rd BG, 15th AF, Foggia, Italy, arriving July 20, 1944. Completed 50 combat missions by Nov. 20, 1944. Some of the more difficult targets were Ploesti, Munich, Vienna, Budapest. Bombed oil refineries at Ploesti, Romania three times, losing at least one engine to flak each time.

Awards/Medals: Presidential Unit Citation, Distinguished Flying Cross, Distinguished Service Medal, Air Medal with clusters, EAME Theater Ribbon with five Battle Stars.

Separated from service Sept. 18, 1945. Recalled during Korean Conflict March 15, 1951. Served as air research development command personal affairs/Air Force aid society officer until discharge July 14, 1953.

Remained active in Reserve program until honorably retired at age of 60. He was promoted to lieutenant colonel on Dec. 5, 1964.

Served as president 1976-1978 of the Harrisburg, PA Jewish Community Center. Worked as sales representative in the life insurance field, 1948-1951, then from 1953-present. Still active in life insurance business having served as president of the Harrisburg, PA, Life Underwriters Association, the Harrisburg Chartered Life Underwriters Association and the Harrisburg General Agents' and Managers Association.

SAM RAKOFSKY, T-4, born April 18, 1917, Brooklyn, NY. Inducted in the U.S. Army, Camp Upton, NY on April 24, 1941. Stationed at Ft. Eustis, VA for basic training then Camp Stewart, GA. Cruised to South Pacific via Panama Canal with Americal Division in January 1942. While stationed in Noumea (New Caledonia), served as assistant director of musical entitled *Tales of the South Seas. Life* magazine gave it a big spread. (He believes James Michener based his play *South Pacific* on this production.)

Saw action in the Solomon and Society Islands, Guadalcanal, Bougainville, etc. Although he had enough points, after almost 35 months, to be rotated, they were told all rotation had been stopped. They were preparing to go into the

Philippines. There was no Jewish Chaplain in the area and Rosh-Ha-Shanah was approaching. A request was made for anyone capable of conducting High Holiday services and he gladly volunteered. All Jewish personnel from nearby islands were gathered together and he led Rosh-Ha-Shanah and Yom Kippur services. Shortly after, his CO advised him that he was being sent home.

Awards/Medals: Asiatic-Pacific Medal and American Defense Service Medal

Arrived home Dec. 22, 1944 and married Mildred Dec. 31, 1944. Mildred had waited for him since April 1941. Their honeymoon was his R&R in Asheville, NC. He was then sent to Ft. Stevens, OR, then to Camp Ritchie, MD for Intelligence training before being sent overseas again. Fortunately, hostilities ceased and he was honorably discharged from the Army at Ft. Dix, NJ, July 1945.

Circumstances surrounding his rotation filled him with deeper religious feelings. He continued serving Judaism through his Temple, Oceanside Jewish Center, UJA, Federation, Israel Bonds, B'nai B'rith. Youth groups involving their three children: Stanley, Karen and Chaya. They have blessed us with two grandchildren, Jason and Neshama.

After working with the same partner for 40 years, they retired to another tropical island—Florida. Once a year, he and his wife attend a reunion with the Army buddies who were close to him during his Army career.

BERNARD RAPHAN, born in Manhattan, New York City, July 23, 1922. Graduate of all New York Schools - P.S. 4; P.S. 97; Seward Park High School; City College of the city of New York; and the New York Law School. Practiced law in New York City for over 40 years.

Entered U.S. Army in 1943, while still in college, and separated in 1946. His MOS was 245-Rifleman. Served in England, France, Belgium, Luxembourg, Germany and Czechoslovakia.

Awards/Medals: Combat Infantryman, WWII Victory, American Campaign, EAME Campaign and Good Conduct Medal.

Still enjoys the practice of law. Has a wonderful wife, Naomi, two lovely daughters, Melissa and Benita, and two grandchildren.

IRVING RAPPAPORT, born in Brooklyn, NY, June 4, 1916. Enlisted in U.S. Army February 1941, with 4th Div. 22nd Inf. Stationed at Augusta, GA and Columbus, GA.

Memorable experience was being the first outfit to go into France D-day, June 6, 1944. He saved one of his comrades who was in water over his head.

Awards/Medals: Purple Heart, Bronze Star, Combat Infantry Badge and commendations from 83rd General Hospital. Discharged in August 1945 with rank of staff sergeant.

Married for over 51 years and has three children and four grandchildren. Retired and active in several organizations.

MELVIN RAPPORT, born Oct. 29, 1920. Enlisted in Aviation Cadets, January 1942, graduated multi-engine pilot Class 43C. Assigned to 63rd Troop Carrier Gp., flying C-47s. Received orders to fly Col. Richard Ellsworth to India and upon arrival put in for transfer to the 7th BG (H), 10th AAF.

Joined 492nd Sqdn. and flew copilot. Eventually became pilot and got his own crew. Flew 46 missions over Burma, Thailand, Andaman Islands. Bombed to railroad that went to bridge of Kwai. After missions plane was fitted with gas tanks and flew gas over the Hump to Kunming and Luchow China.

Transferred to Karachie India Gunnery School flying B-24s and B-25s. Teaching young gunners to pursuit curve.

Awards/Medals: two Distinguished Flying Crosses, two Air Medals, Asiatic-Pacific Medal with Battle Stars, American Theater Medal, WWII Victory Medal and Presidential Unit Citation.

After separation spent five years in the Reserves and over 25 years in Civil Air Patrol. Highest rank received was major.

Presently semi-retired photographer. Widowed, has two sons and one daughter: Michael, Alex and Wendy; and three grandsons: Ari, Jesse and Jonathan.

ELIOT RASKIN, born Feb. 22, 1925, Detroit, MI. Enlisted U.S. Army, April 18, 1943. Entered service April 30, 1943, Ordnance Branch. Stationed at Ft. Custer, MI; APG, MD; Rossford Ord. Trng. Ctr., Rossford, OH; Camp Young, CA; Camp Shanks, NY; Liverpool, England; Tewksbury, England; Southampton, England; St. Lo; Isigny; Paris; Rue Versies; Liege, Belgium; Aywaie, Belgium; Aachen, Frankfort and Kassel, Germany; plus points in between Normandy, France, Northern France, Holland, Ardennes, Rhineland and Central Europe.

Memorable experiences: Bringing back dead and wounded GIs from the Battle of the Bulge and after the liberation of the concentration camps, running convoys to bring back the survivors to relocation centers for rehabilitation.

Awards/Medals: EAME Ribbon with five Bronze Stars, Good Conduct Medal and WWII Victory Medal. Discharged Dec. 18, 1945 as T-4. He is member of JWV Post 409 in Clearwater, FL.

Remained in the Reserves and recalled to active duty Dec. 11, 1950, to Ft. Sill, OK. Released from active duty Dec. 4, 1951, Ft. Sill, OK. Presently semi-retired and living in Florida with his wife of 47 years. They have two sons and five grandchildren living near them and a daughter and two grandchildren in Michigan. A third son was killed in 1978 in service in the Armored Corps at Schoffield Barracks, HI from a motorcycle accident.

MARTIN RAUCHBERG, born in Poland, April 7, 1918. Educated in Berlin, Germany and came to the U.S. in 1937. Entered the Army in Monterey, CA, December 1942. Trainied in Ft. Warren, WY. Assigned to Quartermaster Corps, where he tried to teach recruits to run sewing machine, without much success.

Later assigned to G-2 at various POW camps with duty of obtaining vital statistics and political opinions, acting as interpreter at court martials, translating official material into German, and censoring incoming printed materials and conversations between prisoners and visitors.

Discharged in March 1946, he started his own successful garment manufacturing business in New York. He is now happily retired. Member of Jesse Brams Post 206 JWV.

Married Ann in January 1943 and has a son, Ronald, born in Camp Forest, TN, January 1944.

LOUIS RAVERBY, served in the U.S. Army from March 31, 1942-Feb. 23, 1946. Entered the Medical Corps with the rank of 1st lieutenant at Ft. Devens, MA. Training consisted of Medical Field Service at Carlisle Barracks, PA, May 1943 to July 1943. Trained for the treatment of gas casualties at the Chemical Warfare School, September and October 1942.

Received medical refresher course at the Walter Reed Hospital, Washington, DC, July-August 1944. Was chest consultant at Ft. Devens Station Hospital; battalion surgeon at Camp Campbell; assistant regimental surgeon from June 1943-April 1945 at Ft. Knox, KY; and train surgeon from April 1945-July 1945 at Ft. Meade, MD.

Member of the medical staff of the VA Hospital at Oteen, NC from July 1945-January 1946. Promoted to captain Nov. 9, 1943, and received Commendation for excellence in instruction on personnel adjustment problems at Ft. Knox, KY and also in Diagnostic School at Ft. Devens, MA as well as a Commendation by GRFD No. I for improvement of medical care of troops while on route.

Attended San Francisco, CA, United Nations Conference as well as the Arizona Maneuver Area and Mammoth Caves, KY.

Besides his medical duties he gave lectures to officers and enlisted men on sanitation Hygiene, Orientation and First Aid. Also flew cross country numerous times in mass transportation of troops as train surgeon and saw much of our country by air. *Submitted by: Max Sigal.*

MARVIN O. REICHMAN, born Nov. 15, 1926. Enlisted September 1944 as Army rifleman, 21st Inf. Regt., 24th Inf. Div. Stationed at Ft. Sheridan, IL; Camp Hood, TX, Philippine Islands, Japan. Participated in Southern Philippines Liberation Campaign and Battle of Mindanao.

Memorable experience was saving the life of a GI in the hole next to his by killing the Japanese soldier who was attacking him.

Awards/Medals: Bronze Star, Purple Heart, Good Conduct, Asiatic-Pacific Campaign Medal, Combat Infantry Badge, Presidential Unit Citation, Philippine Presidential Unit Citation, WWII Victory Medal, Occupation Medal, Philippine Liberation Medal, Philippine Independence Medal and Expert Rifleman.

Married Inez in 1951, and had one daughter, Minda and a son, Ken, who is deceased.

THEODORE REIF, served in the USN, Supply Corps from September 1943-January 1946. Entered service with the rank of apprentice seaman at Great Lakes, IL and discharged at Great Lakes with the rank of SK2/c.

Training at U.S. Training Center under Lt. Lyons in September 1943 and continued until November 1943. Moved to the Clothing Department at Great Lakes in November 1943.

Awards/Medals: Commendation from the Supply Corps for outstanding work done in the Clothing Department at Great Lakes, IL. Discharged at Great Lakes in January 1946. He was in the Supply Corps. *Submitted by Max Sigal.*

LAWRENCE I. REINER, born in New York City, April 26, 1930. Pre-med student at New York University, he sailed on a tanker carrying hi-octane gasoline for the military during the first year of the Korean War.

Inducted in the U.S. Army on Aug. 27, 1951, completed basic training at Ft. Dix, serving there as cadre until volunteering for Korea, (March 1952, FECOM Levy). Due to the need of trained medical technologists, he was transferred from his Infantry Company to the Medical Corps, serving until his honorable discharge Aug. 13, 1953, at the 8162nd AU, Fukuoka, and 8th Army General Hospital, Tokyo, Japan.

Resuming his maritime career as well as completing degrees in geology and gemology, at Arizona Sate University and the Gemological Institute of America, he sailed munition ships during the war in Vietnam and Desert Storm.

Awards/Medals: Korean Service Medal, United Nations Medal, U.S. Merchant Marine Expeditionary Medal, Desert Shield and Desert Storm.

Married April in 1955, lives in Arizona, sails as a merchant seaman and is a published author of several sea novels.

FRANK REINGOLD, born Jan. 5, 1926, Newark, NJ. He was attending Cornell University under the Army Specialized Training Program (ASTP) when his class was disbanded and assigned to basic training at Ft. Jackson, SC.

Assigned to the 87th Div. and shipped overseas in the summer of 1944. After a short stay in England, the division went into combat in France.

While serving as a PFC with Co. K, 347th Inf., 3rd Bn., 3rd Plt. and carrying out assigned duties as a scout rifleman, PFC Reingold was killed in action Dec. 14, 1944, at Petit-Rederching, France.

He was posthumously awarded the Bronze Star for action against the Armed enemy.

SHELDON M. REINHEIMER, born in Philadelphia, PA, May 24, 1940. Enlisted in the U.S. Army June 19, 1957, Armor-Engineers/QM. Stationed at Ft. Jackson, SC; Ft. Benning, GA; Ft. Leonard Wood, MO; SETAF, Vicenza, Italy.

Discharged in July 1959, with the rank of PFC.

Married Judy and has two sons, Alan (member DJWV) and Eric.

Currently, Supports Services Courier Press of Atlantic City. Member of Post 39, Atlantic County, officer of the day, past South Jersey County commander JWV, officer of the day, South Jersey Council, Department of New Jersey officer of the day (south), and member of JWV since October 1967.

NORMAN REISMAN, born in New York City, April 25, 1924, and moved to Kearny, NJ at the age of two. Enlisted Nov. 16, 1942, in the U.S. Army and served in 2nd Plt., Co. K, 410th Inf., 103rd Div. as a rifleman and messenger.

Served in ETO (France, Germany and Austria). Was overseas from October 1944-February 1946.

Awards/Medals: Marksman and Sharpshooter Medals, Purple Heart, Bronze Star and Combat Infantryman Badge. Discharged with the rank of staff sergeant.

Now works as a pharmacist.

LOWELL JAMES RESIG (JIM), born in St. Paul, MN, April 15, 1930. Graduated with BBA degree from University of Minnesota in 1951. Drafted in the U.S. Army in July 1951 with basic training in Ft. Meade, MD. Spent about a year in Bordeaux, France. Traveled all of Southern France to various Army and Air Force Bases, training personnel to ship material to the U.S. Other stations were in Camp Pickett, VA and Camp Bersol, France.

Discharged in July 1953, with the rank of private first class.

Married Audrey in October 1954, and has three children: Martin, Linda and Annette; and four grandchildren. Worked as an accountant and controller for Franklin Mfg. Co. Retired, he now does volunteer work at Methodist Hospital, St. Louis Park, MN.

ARNOLD E. RESNICOFF, CHC, is a USN chaplain on staff of Commanding Officer, Naval Submarine Base New London and the Commander, Naval Submarine Two. Holds bachelor's degree from Dartmouth College and master's degrees from Salve University (International Relations) the Naval War College (NWC), Strategic Studies and National Security Affairs, and the Jewish Theological Seminary of America (Rabbinics), where he was later ordained. He was the President's Honor Graduate at NWC.

A former NROTC graduate and line officer, he has served as chaplain since 1976 and is active in a host of military and civilian efforts. He  worked to create the Vietnam Veterans Memorial and delivered the closing prayer at its dedication. Was present in Beirut, Lebanon during the October 1983 truck-bomb attack and his report was read aloud by President Regan to the 20,000 attendees of the Baptist Fundamentalism 84 Convention. Was the driving force behind military Holocaust observances and served as the USN representative to the DOD days of Remembrance Committee and delivered the closing prayer at the 1987 national convention. He led Yom Kipper services in Iceland during the US-USSR pre-summit talks and helped establish the Haifa USO.

Has lectured widely on pluralism, religious freedom and values at forums. Since 1989 he has been a keynote speaker at every annual NWC conference on Ethics and the Military.

Awards/Medals: four Meritorious Service Medals, two Naval Commendation Medals, Combat Action Ribbon and he is the recipient of numerous civilian honors, including the 1991 Moment Magazine International Community Service Award, and Philadelphia's Chapel of Four Chaplains "Hall of Heroes Gold Medallion" for his work with the wounded and dying in Beirut.

WILLIAM RESNIKOFF,
born in Ukraine, Russia, Sept. 20, 1910. Joined USN in 1942 and worked under Gen. Eisenhower as a naval representative in occupied Germany. Sent to Germany after the war to gather and evaluate information for the Allied Forces. Appointed sub-control officer in charge of all assets of the I.G. Farben Co. in Frankfort-on-Main. Was ordnance officer in 3rd Naval District.

His father was a successful businessman in Russia. He owned two drug stores and was and a graduate pharmacist. He also was in the Russian Army with the rank of lieutenant. Family came to the U.S. to escape from the Bolsheviks after the Russian Revolution in 1924.

At the present he is living in a retirement community. He keeps busy teaching English to Russian immigrants, and playing bridge. He has three children and eight grandchildren. Eldest daughter is a psychotherapist in Austin, TX; another daughter teaches special education in Connecticut; and his son is a radio announcer in New York and Connecticut.

MURRAY RESSLER,
born in Poland, March 5, 1924, and is a Holocaust survivor. Came to the U.S. on May 7, 1947, and legally registered as being born in 1927. Registered with selective service and classified 4F. Was recalled in April 1952 and joined the USMC. Boot camp in Parris Island, SC and advance training at Camp Pendelton, CA.

sent to Korea Dept. 15, 1952, even though he wasn't a U.S. citizen. Requested citizenship before deployment, but was denied because of freeze on citizenship 90 before an election.

Wounded on Oct. 27, 1952 and operated on in field hospital, then hospital ship, Tokyo and air evacuation to St. Albans, NY. Finished his duty at Bayonne Naval Depot.

Awards/Medals: Purple Heart, United Nations Service Medal and Korean Service Medal. Discharged in April 1954 with the rank of corporal.

Married Bella in 1955 and has a son, daughter and two grandchildren. Retired in 1989 and lives in Vineland, NJ.

AROLD W. RETCHIN,
born in Springfield, MA, Dec. 9, 1922. Enlisted as tank destroyer, then USAF navigator.

Trained as message center chief, Camp Hood; Cadet Program, July 1943; pre-cadets, University of North Dakota; Cadets, Santa Ana, CA; advanced navigation, San Marcos, TX, Class 44-9, graduated July 1944. Flight officer, B-24 training, Lincoln, NE and Mountain Home, ID.

Ferried new F-7 from Hunter Field, GA via southern route to Gushkara, India, joining 24th Cbt. Mapping Sqdn., Feb. 15, 1945. First flight in India picking up survivors and bodies of Capt. Kondracki's crew that crashed on takeoff at Cox's Bazaar, Burma. Ten 11 hour mapping missions, invasion of Burma. mapped Assam Valley, Hump and Kunming.

Sent 10 planes of 24th CMS over Hump via Kunming to Clark Field, Philippines, Dec. 18, 1945. Rebuilt Jap basha into "our home." Built NCO Officer's Clubs. Ran USAFI College. Special Services recruiting officer. 13th AF at Manila as budget/fiscal officer HQ.

Awards/Medals: Air Medal, China Defense and China Defense. Discharged Sept. 10, 1946, with the rank of flight officer.

Married Carol Gorden in 1949 and has three sons. Retired furniture dealer. Founder of the USCG Auxiliary Division 9 in western Massachusetts.

DOANLD RETIG,
born in Holland, 1917. Father passed away and mother remarried in Germany. Educated Yeshiva & Engineering School, Berlin. Family forced into Poland in 1938. His immigration visa was refused under open Dutch quota. Made dangerous trip to re-enter Germany. Got visa Berlin. War started and tried to reach Port for Swedish Ferry. Caught at border and locked up temporarily in bunker. Forced door, jumped on passing freight train and onto ferry and freedom.

Inducted into U.S. Army, August 1941; infantry training in Georgia. Assigned to 33rd Inf. Div. TD BN. On special Army Intelligence duty interrogating captured officers.

Received high commendation from Gen. Gaffney for outstanding service. Returned to the USA in 1946 with two Battle Stars.

Happiest day was locating his mother alive in Camp Poland. Saddest day when stepfather was burned alive prior to liberation and kid brother gassed in Auschwitz. Shipped to Israel in 1972, liberated by IDF Yom Kippur war to load tanks. Arrived Suez Canal and returned to Telaviv with bullet holes but never broke down.

Married Lotte in 1951 and has one son, Jeff, (M.D.) and three grandchildren. Established Retig Dist. Inc. in 1946. Founding member of Post 545 in 1947; commander Post 297 since 1983; and chairman of Jewish Affairs, NY County.

ROBERT RIBAKOFF,
born in Kansas City, MO, Oct. 26, 1925. Enlisted on Aug. 15, 1944, and trained at Infantry Replacement School, at Ft. McClellan, AL. He served with the 417th Inf. 76th Div. 3rd Army, in the ETO in France, Luxembourg, Belgium, Germany and Czechoslovakia.

Participated in the Battle of the Bulge, Rhineland and Central Europe.

Clearly remembers when they crossed the Rhine with Gen. Patton in the rapid assault across Germany to Czechoslo-

---

vakia. On the second, of a three day 90 mile forced march in the Rhinish Hills, he suffered a stress fracture in the metartarsais of the left foot, due to short legs and being positioned next to the last man in the column. He marched and fought the rest of the way to the Czechoslovakian border on that broken foot until they met the Russians.

Awards/Medals: Sharpshooter, Good Conduct, WWII Victory, ETO with three stars and Combat Infantry Medal.

Completed service at Ft. McPherson, GA on Jan. 7, 1946, with the rank of private first class.

Earned BS in education in 1953 and MLA degree from University of Southern California. Retired in 1987, after teaching for 36 years. He has been involved in community theater.

Married Diana Gubmann, June 19, 1952, in Montevideo, Uruguay. They have three sons, and eight grandchildren.

ALAN H. RICH,
MAJ, born Nov. 1, 1905, Kovno, Lithuania, and raised on a farm in New Brighton, MN. Attended North High, Minneapolis and graduated with a BS degree, 1927, from the University of Minnesota.

Commissioned a captain, QM Corp, 1942, and following a stint in Washington, was sent to Base HQ, Sydney, Australia. in 1943 reported to Finschhafen, New Guinea. Served in the invasion of Leyte and Luzon, Philippine Islands, 1944-1945.

Memorable experience was in the hinterlands of Luzon, in unceasing heat, air raids, sirens and shelling that his most cherished experience occurred. It was the first night seder for over 200 Army, Air Corps and Navy personnel who could be spared from their duties. Quoting from Chaplain Dudley Weinberg's letter to their families, "It would have cheered you as it did me to see that huge multitude of Jewish soldiers enjoying a real seder-wine, Matzoh, even bitter herbs and charoshes, flown in from Australia, reading the Haggadah together and singing the Pesach songs."

Awards/Medals: Philippines Liberation Ribbon with one Battle Star, Asiatic-Pacific Theater of Operations with three Battle Stars.

Discharged Jan. 3, 1946, with the rank of major.

Married and has two daughters. Retired businessman (president, C.F. Massey Co., Rochester, MN).

LESTER G. RICHMAN,
drafted in the U.S. Army April 20, 1942. After a medical exam by Army doctors, he was put on a train to Camp Grant, IL, where he was outfitted with Army clothing, given a bunch of shots and put on a train, arriving a couple of days later at Camp Forrest, TN a few miles from a small town, Tullahoma.

Classified as rifleman, with the 136th Inf. Regt., of the 33rd Inf. Div. Received basic training there and lived in a tent. September 1942 was selected to attend Air Force Officer Candidate School in Miami Beach, FL, a three month course, which led to his appointment as a 2nd lieutenant Dec. 9, 1919. Advancement was rapid after that. Left Robins Field, GA as a captain for Hickam Field, HI, where he became a major, commanding his own company in the 7th AF.

Left for the States in January 1946, separated from the service Nov. 21, 1946, at Ft. Sheridan, IL.

Member of the Ventura Post of JWV and member of Santa Monica Post in the 1940s. He remembers a visit from Irving Richman, then National Commander, and his executive director, Schottland. He stayed on as a Reserve officer, major, for several years, but resigned his commission when the Korean War broke out. By then he was married and had a child and didn't want to be called up.

LOUIS RICKLER,
an immigrant, enlisted July 9, 1916 in the Mexican Border War for seven years. On Aug. 1, 1916, he

was hospitalized for three weeks, returned to his company and shortly thereafter, suffered a sun stroke aboard his ship and was again hospitalized. On Feb. 23, 1917, he was granted a disability discharge.

On Dec. 8, 1917, he was drafted to serve in WWI. He showed the officers in charge his disability discharge papers, but they completely disregarded them and he was told to serve as a first aid man. He served in several battles, skirmishes and expeditions until the end of the war. He treated the sick, wounded and dying with deep compassion, many times under fire and he himself suffered from shell shock, gas and battle fatigue. He refused to be evacuated and continued carrying for his buddies.

While he and the men of the 77th Div., 308th Inf., 2nd Bn. were caught in a spot called the Pocket in the Argonne Forest, they were known as the Lost Battalion because of advancing so fast, they became separated from the others. For sick days they suffered horrendous agonies. They were without food, water, medical and other supplies; bandages were removed from the dead and placed on the living. The stench of dead bodies was overpowering; 600 men were entrapped, but only 194 were rescued from the Pocket.

He received the Bronze Star.

PHILIP M. RISIK, born in New York City, NY, Jan. 8, 1914. Graduate of NYU University College, 1932 and Law School, 1936. Commissioned 2nd lieutenant in the U.S. Army in 1938, with active duty April 1, 1941. In WWII, stationed staff and faculty QM School, Phila and Camp (Fort) Lee, VA; OCQM-ETO in England and France; Normandy Beach; several HQ, QM Base Depots in Belgium and France, with mission to clear the Ports of Antwerp and Cherbourg.

Awards/Medals: American Defense, ETO with two Battle Stars, Bronze Star, WWII Victory, Korean Service, NY State Conspicuous Service and SecDef Meritorious Civilian Service.

Separated December 1946. Reactivated March 1, 1951. Served on Army General Staff; the Munitions Board; DOD; and OSD. Separated March 1, 1953. Retired as COL, AUS, Jan. 7, 1969.

Employed as civilian procurement specialist OSD; appointed administrative judge, ASBCA, 1962-74. Thereafter private law practice.

Married Natalie Wynn and has three children, seven grandchildren and one great-grandchild. He is a playmate of grandchildren; a tennis buff and umpire emeritus, USTA. Resides in Potomac, MD.

ALBERT ROBBINS, was 30 years old, married for five years to Lea and had a five month old son, Errol, when drafted in the U.S. Army in February 1944. He served basic training at Macon, GA, then shipped overseas, landing on Omaha Beach, France the end of June 1944.

Assigned to the 1st Army, 28th Div. as an infantry rifleman replacement. His division was the first unit to liberate Paris. Served in heavy front line action for four months during the battle of the Hürtgen Forest.

After being trapped for seven days and nights with shrapnel in his lung, he was captured Nov. 7, 1944, and taken prisoner by an SS officer of the Germany Army. Fortunately he had the presence of mind to dispose of his dog tags so that he might survive.

Wife Lea was notified that he was MIA, three long months later she received another telegram stating that he was POW in Germany. For six months he was subjected to forced marches to six different prison camps. He lost 55 pounds before liberation in April 1945.

Awards/Medals: Purple Heart, two Bronze Stars, New York State Medal and POW Medal.

ALLAN ROBBINS, born in Springfield, MA, Dec. 21, 1923. Enlisted in the USN Jan. 11, 1943, Amphibious. Boot camp was at Newport, Rhode Island; USN Radio School, Noroton Heights, CT; ATB, Solomons, MD; LST-49 and NTS Newport, RI as instructor at Radio School.

Memorable experiences are D-Day Omaha Beach landings, Normandy D Day and Southern France Landings; being on duty as radioman during storm off Leghorn, Italy and avoiding mine fields.

Awards/Medals: WWII Victory Medal, American Theater Medal and EAME Ribbon. Discharged Feb. 18, 1946, with the rank of radioman 3rd class petty officer.

Parents are Max and Betty G. Robbins; brothers, David enlisted in the USNAF, and Eugene, graduated from University of Massachusetts; BA sociology, Long Island University MS education.

Public school teacher for 23 years in New York City; Eastern Karate Center master, 1976-1985; and Black Belt Hall of Fame, 1993. He now does substitute teaching for handicapped children.

NORMAN ROBBINS, born in Mt. Vernon, NY, Aug. 28, 1923. Enlisted with the USCG in 1943; spent two years of sea duty in the North Atlantic, and participated in the Antisub Campaign. Highest rank achieved was chief quartermaster.

He passed away on Feb. 10, 1947, and is survived by his father, mother and sister.

PETER ROBERTS, born in Berlin, Germany, 1921. He couldn't join the U.S. Army on foreign soil, but did join the Allied Forces in 1939. First joined the French Foreign Legion and fought in Algeria, North Africa. Joined the British Army Pioneer Corps in 1940.

After the U.S. landed in North Africa, he fought side by side with the USA Forces, and Gen. Montgomery, fighting at El Alamein Tobruk and later landing in Italy. Joining with Gen. Patton's forces, he fought in Monte Casino. He was in this allied campaign for six and one half years. Injured twice, bullet and shrapnel. When the war ended he was in Naples, Italy.

He and his parents were split up by the war in three continents. He went to his mother in Scotland, then to his father in Columbia, South America. Roberts immigrated to the United States in 1949 and settled in Chicago.

Awards/Medals: Croix de Guerre and African Star.

Married a Jewish Girl from Czechoslavakia and has two daughters, Rita and Michelle; and four grandchildren: Eddie, Meagan, Matthew and Courtney. He worked in the food business for 32 years and is now retired.

MANUEL ROGOFF, arrived in England with the 8th AF August 1943 and flew his first mission in November. After several successful missions, he was returning to England by flying over Southern France. Two German fighters fired and hit his plane. Four crew members were killed immediately. A hydraulic accumulator on the plane exploded and put up a wall of flame.

Ran through the flames twice to open the nose-wheeled doors, yelled for his navigator to follow him and bailed out. Rogoff landed hard on his feet about 30 kilometers south of Paris. He was surrounded by French farmers. A 12 year old girl took off his burnt gloves, flying suit and tale-tale dog tags. He was given peasant's clothes and pointed in the direction to walk to avoid the Germans.

Met up with members of the French resistance and taken to the home of one of them. At this point his hands and face were burning badly and he was blind. Was moved to several different homes and finally to home of Pierre Charie, the head of the underground, and where two of the other surviving crew members were. Stayed there. Unable to see a doctor (they were being watched closely by the Germans) Charie turned to a pharmacist friend for medical assistance and eventually Rogoff's sight returned.

After a month in his home Charie put him on a train to Paris where he was met by member of the underground and taken to the home of Maurice and Margot Cavalier. When he left there several weeks later, they promised they would get together again, but never had the chance. The Cavaliers were captured on D-day and shot for their part in his escape. He was taken to Brittany, given work papers and passport that identified him as a French farmer. Crossed three German minefields in total darkness led by a 17 year old girl who knew the placement of the mines, rolled down a 150 foot cliff to wait for the boat that was to take him to freedom.

Resumed his place in the family business, married Irma and had children. Returned to France in 1960 to thank some of the people who sacrificed so much for him. They were met at the airport by Pierre Charie and his family. Rogoff was amazed to find that a museum had been built on the site of his landing. It contains a statue of him wearing the boots, flying suit and dog tags that the 12-year old girl had removed from him years earlier. While he was at the museum the dog tags were returned to him. The six crewmembers who perished in the raid are buried nearby.

DAVID H. ROISTACHER, MAJ, born in Bronx, NY, on March 6, 1912. Graduated from the University of Virginia in 1933 with BS degree from the University of Buffalo in 1937 with DDS.

Trained at Camp Grant, Rockford, IL and served in Northern Solomon's and Philippines, with the 37th Inf. Div. Helped release American prisoners interned by Japanese in Bilibad Prison, Manila.

Awards/Medals: Bronze Star Medal, Asiatic-Pacific Campaign Medal with one Arrowhead, WWII Victory Medal, Meritorious Service Unit Plaque, Philippine Liberation with one star.

Retired in Florida.

DAVID RONIS, 1st LT, born in Detroit, MI, June 6, 1921. Graduated high school in 1939. Volunteered for service in April 1942. Was government major at Wayne University in 1947; MA in international studies at Harvard, 1949. CIA operations officer, 1950-1974.

Taught tank engine maintenance at Armored Force School, Ft. Knox, KY, 1943; served with the 132nd Med. Maint. Co. (Ord.) in close support of combat divisions in the 2nd Army sector in northern Europe, September 1944-May 1945. Participated in the relief of the siege of Bastogne. Saw tens of thousands of liberated slave laborers streaming eastward across Germany in commandeered cars, trucks and tractors, or on foot trying to find their way back home. Many begged for gasoline just to keep their vehicles going a few miles farther.

Real estate management, 1974-1980; part time consultant to CIA, 1983-1994; and volunteer for Jewish Social Service Agency. First wife Geraldine Zendel passed away in 198[illegible] married Barbara Rostov in 1988. He has six children and fiv[e] grandchildren. Member of the JWV Washington Post 58.

MORTON RONSON, born in New York, NY, June 1[illegible] 1924. Enlisted in the USAAC Dec. 12, 1942. Stationed i[n] Sudbury, England as a navigator with the 486th BG, 835th Sqdn. Flew 32 missions, the last 12 as lead crew navigator.

Memorable experience was bombing Berlin, Hambur[g], Karlsruhe and Dresden Cologne.

Awards/Medals: Distinguished Flying Cross and A[ir] Medal with four clusters.

Received honorable separation on June 25, 1945, wi[th] the rank of 2nd lieutenant.

Married Trudy and has three sons: Charles, Joseph a[nd] David; and three grandchildren. Optometrist, SCO in Mem[-]phis, TN, 1950. Had his own practice in New York City f[or] 32 years. Retired in 1987 and lives in Coconut Creek, FL a[nd] Dumont, NJ. Charter member of Memphis, TN JWV, 194[illegible] 1948.

ALVIN ROSE, CPL, born in Poughkeepsie, NY. Af[ter] graduation from Poughkeepsie High School he entered t[he] USMC in January 1944 as radioman forward observer [for] artillery. Served with the 1st Div. in the invasion of Okinaw[a]

Awards/Medals: Unit Naval Citation, Unit Presidential Citation and others. Discharged in April 1946 with the rank of corporal.

After service he graduated from the University of Miami, FL with a BBA. Member of the South Dade Post 778 in Miami, FL. Held all leadership positions with JWV Post, county and department, including commander, seven years; National Executive Committeeman, four years; National Awards Chairman, two years; National Investment Committee, seven years; Executive Committee National Memorial, 10 years; and board of Directors National Memorial.

Married Jackie and has four daughters and eight grandchildren. Co-owner of Rose Realty with his wife, Jackie, in Miami, FL since 1950. Retired at the age of 43 with a large real estate portfolio, including vast acreage's of vacant land. Was voted into the Department of Florida Hall of Fame in charter year.

JOSEPH ROSE, born in Syracuse, NY. Attended Syracuse schools and was in the coal business. Veteran of two world wars; enlisted in the USN as a young boy and saw 20 years of active duty and 15 years of Reserve duty.

During WWII he was stationed at Rensselaer Polytechnic Institutes as an instructor in naval science and tactics and coach of the rifle and pistol teams.

In his long career in the USN, he served with many famous admirals and was on cruises which made history. Also a deep sea diver and called on for assistance when the submarine S-4 sank off Provincetown, MA in 1927.

Charter member of Onondaga Post 131, JWV. Also member of Louis Marshall Lodge, B'nai Brith; Brotherhood of Temple Society of Concord; Post 41, American Legion, Two Timer Veterans Association and Cecil Albright Post 2968, VFWs.

Passed away on Feb. 12, 1951, at the age of 59. Survived by his wife, Gertrude Docter Rose; sons, Bruce and Eric; and daughter, Sondra.

SHELDON ROSEMARIN, born in New York City, Sept. 9, 1930. Enlisted in the U.S. Army Oct. 15, 1951. Trained at Camp Gordon, GA, then sent overseas Sept. 28, 1952.

He was a machine gunner with the 17th Inf. Regt., 7th Div. and participated in actions of Triangle Hill and Pork Chop Hill. His memorable experience was being acknowledged in regimental papers for his participation in Triangle Hill action.

Awards/Medals: United Nations Service Medal, Combat Infantry Badge and Korean Service Medal with three Battle Stars. Discharged Oct. 9, 1953, with the rank of sergeant.

Married Shirley and has two daughters, Deborah and Susan and grandchildren. He is presently retired.

FREDRIC M. ROSEMORE, enlisted in Birmingham, AL, November 1942, as an aviation cadet in the USAAF. Graduated as a navigator and sent to Italy with the 15th AF, 2nd BG, 96th Sqdn.

His aircraft was shot down over Hungary after bombing Germany and trying to return to base. Completed 22 missions and was a prisoner in Budapest, Stalag Luft III, Germany, Nuremberg and finally Stalag VIIA Moosburg.

Awards/Medals: five Battle Stars, Air Medal, OLC, Purple Heart, POW Medal, WWII Victory, Presidential Unit Citation. Licensed as a navigator, pilot, aerial gunner and radio operator.

Discharged with the rank of 1LT, USAF and MAJ, CAP.

Married Marion and has five children and 13 grandchildren. Presently chairman of the board, PMC Capital, Inc. Listed on the American Stock Exchange. (PMC). He and his wife reside in North Miami Beach, FL.

ABE S. ROSEN, had previous experience as a sports writer, copy editor and business page editor which served as background for his military career as editor with China edition, *Stars and Stripes,* and as a military criminal investigator.

While in CID training, he was assigned to the Texas Rangers, where, as an undercover operative, he helped break up illicit gambling dens in San Antonio.

Served two years in China. Writing responsibilities with S&S brought him in contact with CBI Commander Lt. Gen. Albert C. Wedemeyer, Gen. George Marshall, Chang Kai Chek, Gen. Chennault and other American and Chinese leaders.

Prior to discharge in August 1946, he and his partner broke the largest case of its kind in the Far East, The Gold Case, the embezzlement of $200,000 of gold coins from the Chinese government. He presented a complete set of China edition, *Stars and Stripes* to the National Archives in Washington, D.C.

Following WWII, he became a public relations executive; elected to the Philadelphia Public Relations Hall of Fame; and for several years served Philadelphia city government as city representative, director of commerce and president of Philadelphia Convention and Visitors Bureau.

Married to the late Bonnie Mittin, has two daughters, Ellen Coren and Irene Levin and four grandchildren.

BERNARD S. ROSEN, born in Paterson, NJ, Oct. 11, 1932, to Anne and Raymond Rosen the oldest of three boys. After high school he went to work for Sears Roebuck in Paterson for three years before he was drafted in the U.S. Army.

Sent to Camp Kilmer; Ft. Dix; Sasebo, Japan; then Korea. Attached to the 2nd Div. Med. Bn., 44th MASH Unit, as a surgical dental technician during this police action. Was stationed approximately three miles from the line of battle. They took care of all indigenous persons as well as the wounded, both enemy and their own.

Some very interesting things took place and life in Korea was never boring. Listened to Radio Moscow to hear the latest propaganda that Moscow was putting out. Was happy to hear that Gen. Eisenhower and the Congress decided on early releases for those that had the necessary points. He did and was home for the holidays.

Awards/Medals: U.S. Presidential Unit Citation, Korean Service Medal, United Nations Award, Korean Presidential Citation and Good Conduct Medal.

Married Ellen over 35 years ago and has one son, Martin, who served in the MPs. They have one son, Martin, who served in the MPs. Manager in a large offset printing corporation. His wife is past department presiden and he is Department of New Jersey 2nd District Vice Commander.

CHARLOTTE GOLDBERG ROSEN, born in Chicago, IL, and moved to Detroit, MI at the age of 17, where she graduated from Northwestern High. Entered the USN in No-

vember 1943, and sent to Hunter College, Bronx, NY for basic training. Further training at Storekeepers School in Milledgeville, GA. Assigned to Chicago Board of Trade Office and spent the next two years in troop movement and transportation.

Discharged on March 1, 1946, with the rank of storekeeper 2/c.

After discharge returned to Detroit and was employed at the Army Tank Automotive Command, Warren, MI. Received BA degree from University of Oklahoma and MA degree from Central Michigan University. Retired after 25 years. Joined Detroit JWV Auxiliary #420 in 1947. Past Auxiliary president and past department president; joined the Bale Post in the 1970s. Moved to Houston, TX in July 1982 and is past post commander of Houston Post 574 and past auxiliary president of Auxiliary 574.

Married and has one son and five grandchildren.

DAVID ROSEN, born in St. Paul, MN, July 15, 1914. Enlisted in the U.S. Army on Dec. 1, 1943, as a private first class with the 37th Inf Div., Ohio Replacement. Stationed at Camp Blanding, FL; New Guinea; Bougainville; Luzon, Philippines. Served with the Specialty Counter Intelligence Corp. Secret Infantry.

Shipped from Ft. Ord, CA to New Guinea, attached to 148th Inf., 37th Div. Shipped to Bougainville and cut hand on his second scouting mission. Transferred to QM and drove 2 1/2 ton truck delivering ammunition and rations up front. Landed at Luzon (Lingayen Gulf, Jan 9, 1945, D-day), Philippines.

Rested for three weeks after they took Manila, then moved 300 miles into the mountains to Appari Jungle Field Hospital. Returned to the States on a hospital ship and discharged Dec. 14, 1945, as PFC.

Awards/Medals: Philippine Liberation Ribbon with Bronze Service Star and APTC Ribbon with two Bronze Service Stars.

Married and has one son, grandsons and great-granddaughter. He is retired.

EVELYN BAER ROSEN, refers to her enlistment in the WAC in 1945 as 50 pounds ago. In Ft. Knox, KY, at Friday night services, she met New Jersey neighbor, Albert Schutlz. She was three his senior and felt he must meet her sister, Rona. They were married for 47 years when Rona passed away and he followed two weeks later. Albert became the brother she never had and he always kidded her that if she hadn't enlisted, they would never have met.

She was honorably discharged to marry her late husband, Ira, in 1946. She has two daughters, three grandchildren and her sister's only grandchild also refers to her as her as Bubbe. She belongs to JWV of Kearny, NJ and Tamarac, FL and the Florida Gold Coast Women. She is still friends after 70 years, with two girls she knew in WW.

FREDERICK W. ROSEN, born in Brooklyn, NY, Sept. 9, 1917. Graduated from Erasmus Hall Class 1935. Moved to Dalton, GA June 1935 and graduated U. of Georgia Class 1939. Employed in Tufting industry June 1937. Commissioned ensign USNR; reported to port directors officer, Charleston, SC as boarding officer Jan. 4, 1942.

Duty Stations/Schools: Midshipman's School, Northwestern U., MTBC Melville; MTB Ron 14 Nola captain PT-94, MTB Ron 15 Nola captain PT-207, North African waters; MTBSTC Melville as instructor (1944); USS *Randolph* CV-15 as automatic weapons officer operating with Task Force 58 Wester Pacific waters; USS *Noble* as gunnery officer.

Participated in invasions: Sicily July 1943, Salerno September 1943, Anzio January 1944; Okinawa April 1945;

and the initial landing Inchon (Jinsen, Korea). Picked up American POW survivors of Bataan and British POWs survivors of Singapore. In October 1945 participated in accepting last Japanese surrender in Tsingtao, China. Remained as part of Naval Occupation Force, Norhern China Sea.

Awards/Medals: Purple Heart, American Campaign, EAME with four Battle Stars, Asiatic-Pacific Campaign with Battle Star, WWII Victory Medal, Occupation Service Asia and China Service.

Resumed employment in Tufting industry.

Member and past president of Peter Tare; June 1960 made president of Northwick Mills, Inc.; transferred to Retired Reserve Oct. 17, 1955.

GEORGE ROSEN, born in the Bronx, March 23, 1925. Enrolled at City College of New York from 1941-1943. Gave up 3A classification for 1A status. Joined the U.S. Army in April 1943, took basic training at Camp Wheeler, GA; ASTP at the University of New Hampshire; joined the 78th Div. at Camp Butner, NC.

Went overseas with them as a member of a 60mm mortar squad. Contracted trench foot in Germany in December 1944 and was sent home. Received medically discharge on Aug. 15, 1945.

Re-entered City College in September 1945 and graduated as a chemist in 1947. Married Florence Goldenberg and has two daughters, one son, five grandsons, and a sixth grandchild on the way. Retired in January 1992. Member of the JWV, DAV and American Legion.

JACK ROSEN, born in Chicago, IL, 1924; schooling in Chicago Yeshiva. Enlisted as a private in 1942, Solomon Islands, Guadalcanal, Gilbert Islands. Received BA degree from U. of Chicago in mathematics and philosophy; MS degree from the U. of Illinois in physics.

Joined the 24th Inf. Div., Korea. Served as research officer with Signal Corps Labs, Ft. Monmouth; liaison GE R&D semi-conductors; UHF, VHF, microwave communications Signal Corps Co. Commander, Frankfurt am-Main, 5th Army HQ West Germany, helped organize Jewish Services for Noncoms.

Division Of Military Applications, Atomic Energy Commission, Washington, D.C.; Command and General Staff College; nuclear technical advisor Congressional Committee, U.S. Capitol; founding member of Beth Tikva Synagogue; U.S. Delegation, Test Ban Treaty, Geneva, Switzerland; Atoms for Peace Conference with USSR, Vienna and Moscow.

The Legion of Merit was presented to him by President Johnson.

Volunteer leader BSA; trustee, Carl Sandburg School; special assistant to commissioner, AEC; president's council of economic advisors staff.

He was killed at age 46 in a plane crash inspecting Nuclear Facility. Buried at Arlington with full honors. Survived by his wife and four children.

LOUIS ROSEN, born in Little Rock, AR, July 28, 1905. Graduated from Little Rock High School in 1921 at the age of

15. Served three years in ARNG, age 15-18. Graduated from Arkansas Law School, July 10, 1925, at the age of 19.

During WWII, was commissioned from civilian life on May 10, 1942, as 1st lieutenant in the USAAF. Military service locations were 4th ferrying Group, Air Transport Command, Berry Field, Nashville, TN. Group moved to Municipal Airport, Memphis, TN, December 1942. Transferred to 6th Ferrying Group, Long Beach, CA, December 1944. Special Det., Ft. Dix AB, Ft. Dix, NJ.

Discharged Feb. 5, 1946, at Ft. Dix as lieutenant colonel.

Married and has one daughter, one son, six grandchildren and two great-grandchildren. Today he is a private trustee and retired.

ROBERT A. ROSEN, born 1936, Queens, NY. Joined the NYANG in 1959, received commission in 1960 and served in a variety of positions over the following 10 years. Completed 21 years in the ANG and USAFR and transferred in 1980 to USNR.

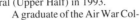

Participated in active Navy operations throughout the world. Tours of duty included missions to Japan, Germany, Beirut, Lebanon, Egypt, England and throughout the States. He retired as a USNR Captain in 1990, was promoted to Rear Admiral (Upper Half) in 1993.

A graduate of the Air War College, Industrial College of the Armed Forces, numerous courses at the USAF University and the Naval War College. Has BBA and MBA degrees.

Awards/Medals: Secretary of the Navy Distinguished Public Service Award, Defense Department Meritorious Service Medal, Navy Meritorious Medal, several Navy Commendations Medals, Navy Achievement Medal, Navy Expeditionary Medal, Navy Meritorious Unit Commendation, Air Force Unit Achievement Citation and numerous other medals, awards and commendations.

He has had a distinguished civilian business career as well as a long history of public service. General partner, investor, manager and developer of shopping centers and industrial. housing, and commercial properties throughout the U.S. Was officer and or member of numerous civilian and military affiliations and activities such as Naval Reserve Assoc., National Guard Assoc. of the U.S., Militia Assoc. of New York, ROA, TROA, MOWW, American Legion, JWV of the USA, etc.

Married Florence Cohen in 1960 and has four children: David, Kenneth, Mark and Emily, and five grandchildren: Chase, Matthew, Justine, Miles and Jacob.

ALAN S. ROSENBERG, enlisted in the USAF on March 26, 1952. Sent to Sampson AFB, NY for basic training. Shipped to Keesler AFB, MS in June 1952 for radio operator training. March 1953 reported to Camp Kilmer, NJ for shipment overseas to Germany.

Arrived Bremerhaven, Germany in April 1953, assigned and transported to the 12th Radio Sqdn. Mobile in Landsberg, Germany. He remained in Germany until October 1953 when he volunteered for a new radio squadron mobile (6952nd) which was forming at Kirknewton

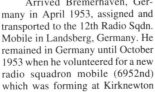

RAF Station, Scotland. Eight of them made the trip from Germany to Scotland and viewed their muddy base with horror. They had left paradise and wound up in "God's Little Acre." He remained there through December 1955.

Discharged from active duty Dec. 29, 1955, with the rank Airman first class. Entered New York University in February 1956 and graduated in August 1958 with a BS degree. Ten years later he received a Master of Social Work Degree from Adelphi University. Presently retired from the city of New York, Human Resources Administration after 30 years of service.

Has resided in Florida since 1991. Divorced, he has two sons, Jonathan and Neal. Member of JWV Post 440, Boynton Beach, FL.

GEORGE ROSENBERG, born in Boston, MA, Aug. 25, 1922. Enlisted in November 1942 with the Flying Tigers, 14th AF, 68th Air Svc. Gp., HQ Sqdn., Finance. Basic training and Finance School at Ft. Benjamin Harrison, IN. Other stations include Thermal AFB, CA; Bombay, Calcutta, Chabua, India; Kunming, Yankai, China. Participated in the China Offensive and China Defensive.

Memorable experience was flying from Chabua, India on a C-46 Commando over the Himalayan Mountains; encountering Japanese fighter planes and with luck landed at Kunming AFB.

Awards/Medals: Asiatic-Pacific Theater, American Theater, WWII Victory Medal, Good Conduct and a special medal from the Chinese Government.

Discharged in January 1946 with the rank of staff sergeant.

Married Marie and has two daughters, Marianne and Sherry, and four grandchildren: Sarah, Philip, Lauren and Aaron. He is presently retired.

GILBERT M. ROSENBERG, born in Chester, PA, June 6, 1922. Entered USN in October 1942; basic training at Bainbridge Naval Station, MD; assigned to ship's company for several months. Further assignment onboard USS *Hannibal* (ARG-8) that took charge of degaussing of ships in the Chesapeake Bay (to neutralize the magnetic field). Decommissioned ship in Philadelphia Navy Yard 1944.

Served onboard USS *Leyte* in 1944 with same captain who was on previous ship. Following battle of Leyte Gulf, Philippines, 1944, Navy changed name of ship to USS *Maui*. Departed Norfolk, VA, via Panama Canal across Pacific Ocean to Finschhafen, New Guinea, on up to Hollandia and continuing on to Philippine Islands. Dropped anchor at Subic Bay to take on job of repairing other ships. Served with 7th Fleet under Admiral Kinkaid. Returned to the States in late 1945 and was assigned to Personnel Div. at Bainbridge, MD, assisting in the discharge of eligible servicemen and servicewomen.

Awards/Medals: Pacific Theater Ribbon, Good Conduct Ribbon, American Theater Ribbon, Victory Medal and Philippine Liberation Ribbon with one star. Honorably discharged on March 21, 1946.

Member of Brown-Sutton Hollywood Post 113, JWV. Employed by National JWV as National Service Officer, Los Angeles, CA.

HENRY B. ROSENBERG, born in Bayonne, NJ, Feb. 8, 1930. Entered the U.S. Army on Dec. 7, 1951, and was stationed at Tageu, Korea, HQ, 392nd Graves Registration Co., 8th Army.

Awards/Medals: Good Conduct Medal and Korean Service Medal. Discharged on Nov. 23, 1953, with the rank of private first class.

Served as commander from 1963-1964 and re-elected commander in October 1993 of Bayonne Post #18, JWV New Jersey.

Previously married to Florence Rosenberg and is now married to Barbara Rand, an elementary school teacher. Has four children: Stuart, CPA, Fairfax, VA; Seena Bulmash, Jewish education teacher, Rockville, MD; Scott, stock broker, Bayonne, NJ; Todd, catering manager, Marriott Hotel, Nashua, NJ. Three grandchildren: Marissa, Gregg and Jacob Michael.

Retired as vice president of marketing of Ever Ready Label Corp. in April 1992; currently manager of Yospin Paint and Wallpaper store, Elizabeth, NJ. Graduated Pace University, 1951 with a BBA in marketing and a minor in advertising and selling. Past president of Bayonne, NJ Jewish Community Center, Jewish Community Council and Temple Beth AM

Current chairman of Bayonne Memorial Day committee (comprised of 12 veterans posts in Bayonne, NJ). Also member of Korean War Veterans Association (Hudson County Chapter)

IDA VIVIAN KEGELES ROSENBERG, born in New Haven, CT, Jan. 19, 1914. Enlisted Jan. 27, 1943, was one of early WAVES. Entered active service Feb. 24, 1943. Stations/Schools: Naval Hospital, Jacksonville, FL (Dental School); Naval Training School, Cedar Falls, IA; Dental School, NNMC, Bethesda, MD; and NAS, Sanford, FL.

Discharged on Oct. 6, 1945, with the rank of PhM2/c.
Has two sisters, Ethel Kegeles and Rose Kegeles (deceased), and one brother, Sidney Kegeles (deceased). Member of JWV Free Sons Israel Post 221, New York City; former adjutant, junior vice commander.

LEONARD Y. ROSENBERG, born in New York City, Nov. 2, 1921. Inducted on March 25, 1943; basic training at Ft. McClellan, AL. Wounded twice, once at Anzio and once at Alsace-Lorraine. Served in Italy (mountains before Cassino, Anzio, liberated Rome. First time in history Rome taken from South). Southern France and Alsace-Lorraine. After second wound was made an instructor in Infantry Corps. Taught classes on Why We Fight. Promoted to Sergeant in France on battlefield.

Awards/Medals: Purple Heart with OLC, Bronze Arrowhead, Combat Rifleman and Combat Medic Badges, French Fourragere Award, L Company Unit Citation, Bronze Star for Bravery, Good Conduct Medal, ETO Award, WWII Victory Medal and six Battle Stars. Discharged on Oct. 25, 1945.

Married and has two children, Amy and Paul; two grandchildren by Amy, Adam and Alexander.

Director of Classification and Compensation, NYC Dept. of Personnel, the city of New York career civil servant. Received BA degree from New York University before enlisting and his Masters degree from Columbia University under the GI Bill. Life member of JWV and DAV. Is permanently disabled from wounds.

LOUIS H. ROSENBERG, of Lawrence, MA, born in 1895. Enlisted in U.S. Army in 1917, served in France. Commander of Lawrence Post #40, State commander of Commonwealth of Massachusetts. Instrumental in founding many posts throughout New England. The first Jewish Mason in Lawrence and actively involved in local and state philanthropies. Discharged in 1918.

Past senior national vice commander of JWV and convention chairman of two national conventions, one during WWII in Atlanta in 1944 and 1948 in Boston. At the Boston National Convention, a host of national dignitaries participated including the later to be President of the United States, John F. Kennedy.

On the occasion of Mabelle and Louis Rosenberg's 45th anniversary, their children established a JWV fund in their honor for a worthy high school senior.

Rosenberg was a political activist, gift of oratory and toastmaster extraordinaire! His 40 year collection of JWV

memorabilia is now part of the archives at the National Museum of Jewish Military History in Washington, DC. JWV was his life.

He passed away in 1973.

HERB ROSENBLEETH, Col., military career began with five years enlisted USMCR service. First served as platoon leader in the 2nd Armd Div. and became a company commander in Germany. Later selected to be assistant chief of staff at Walter Reed Army Medical Center and ultimately, director, Program Review and Evaluation in the office of the Secretary of Defense.

Following that assignment, he joined JWV, representing the organization on Capitol Hill, at the VA and Pentagon, and with national Jewish organizations. He testifies on behalf of JWW before congressional committees and represents JWV at hearings on issues involving human rights, national defense, arms sales and foreign relations. On Feb. 9, 1991, he became the National Executive Director of JWV.

Awards/Medals: Defense Meritorious Service Medal by then Secretary of Defense Frank Carlucci, Bronze Star and Vietnamese Cross of Gallantry for service in Phuoc Long Province near the Cambodian border in Vietnam.

Discharged as a lance corporal, then spent 26 years in world-wide U.S. Army commissioned service. Was elected president of the Combined National Veterans Association (CNVA) for 1990-91 and has been appointed to the President's Committee for the Employment for the Disabled.

Married to the former Sandra Berlack, has three children: Rabbi Aaron, Lynn and Mrs. Alisa Shuman of Baltimore.

DONALD T. ROSENBLOOM, born May 22, 1927, New York City. Enlisted in the U.S. Army Dental Corps, Sept. 1, 1952. Stationed in Ft. Sam Houston; Linz, Austria; Salzburg, Austria; and Governors Island, NY.

Memorable experience was assisting displaced persons left in Austria. Discharged Sept. 1, 1954, as 1st lieutenant.

His wife, an interior designer, worked for HIAS. They have one son (CPA), daughter (MD) and four grandchildren.

Orthodontist, specializing in sleep disorders.

MORRIS ROSENBLUM, born in Baltimore, MD, on Dec. 22, 1921. Entered the USAF on June 6, 1942. Received basic training in Las Vegas, NM and shipped out to the North Atlantic and became a crew chief and waist gunner. Flew all over the North Atlantic going after U boats.

They were hit and he spent the next year in the hospital. Received medical discharge in 1945.

Awards/Medals: Good Conduct Medal, plus others which was lost, WWII Victory Medal, Air Force commendation Medal, Air Medal and National Defense Service Medal.

Discharged in November 1945, with the rank of sergeant.

Married in 1946. Joined JWV Robert P. Grover Post #10 in 1956 and became very active in making hospital visits. 1960 1965 JWV Boy Scouts, 1988 became junior vice; 1989 became senior vice commander; and in 1990-1992, he received the Most Outstanding Award As Commander Of New Jersey.

He is in charge of membership, raffles, making packages for all hospitals and keeps a journal of all the money that he brings in and goes for hospital goodies. Presently retired and is senior vice commander of his post for the past two years. In 1996 he expects to take over as commander again.

DAVID C. ROSENFIELD, born Sept. 12, 1928, Boston, MA. Biology major at Brown University. Further graduate work at Boston University. Entered USNR Sept. 2, 1955. Attended USN OCS, Newport, RI. Commissioned ensign, USNR Jan. 27, 1956.

After further Navy courses, assigned to USS *Merrick* (AKA-97), an attack cargo ship, July 23, 1956-Nov. 17, 1958. During that period, ship participated in search for two U.S. patrol airplanes shot down over the East China Sea. Also was in the Pribilof Islands, AK resupply, brining seal skins back to mainland USA.

Released from active duty to inactive reserve Dec. 2, 1958. Honorably discharged Feb. 23, 1963, as LTJG.

Taught college biology and returned to graduate school, receiving Ph.D in 1967. Studied library science at Southern Connecticut State College and became an academic librarian in 1974. Retired from St. Peter's College Library, NJ, November 1993. Member JWV Post 168.

NORMAN ROSENSHEIN, drafted on Dec. 8, 1964, from Whitehall St. in New York City. Left that day for Ft. Jackson, SC for basic training. Sent to Fort Lee, VA arriving in March of 1965 for on-the-job training (OJT). His MOS was as an electronics technician. At Ft. Lee he was assigned to HQ Co. as a television engineer.

The company grew from 200 men to two companies of 1,000 men each. They were shipping approximately 10,000 troops a month overseas, 9,000 to Vietnam and the rest throughout Europe and Asia. He became a maintenance engineer. During the summer of 1965 a night shift was started for the Quartermaster School and he became the supervisor running the station from 6:00 p.m. until signoff about 2:00 a.m. He stayed in that position until he was separated from active duty on Dec. 7, 1966. He was honorably discharged Dec. 7, 1970, as specialist fourth class.

He continued working in the television industry with CBS for 13 years and Unitel Video for 14 years. Now has his own television system design firm. Married Freda Plotkin in 1967 and has two daughters, Esther and Belle. He is commander of the Department of New Jersey JWV, 1995-1996, and member of David Blick Post #63 Elizabeth, NJ.

GENE ROSENSTEIN, born in McKeesport, PA, March 8, 1928. Enlisted Oct. 1, 1946, in the U.S. Army Infantry, 34th Div.

Stationed in Ft. Knox, KY and Sasebo, Japan. He was discharged March 1, 1948, as private first class.

Presently retired.

HARRY ROSENSTEIN, born in Bronx, NY, July 14, 1928. Was self-employed when he entered the Army in January 1952 at Camp Kilmer, NJ. Basic training at Fort Dix, NJ. After 16 weeks took advanced training in an armored division at Fort Hood, TX.

Went overseas to Korea, January 1953, with the 2nd Inf. Div. Saw action with Tank Co., 38th Inf. Regt., and was on line for the seven months until the war ended.

Awards/Medals: Korean Service Medal with two Bronze Service Stars, National Defense Medal, Combat Infantry Badge and United Nations Service Medal.

Three days after the war ended, he came down with hemorrhagic fever and came down in a med hospital for three weeks. Memorable experience was visiting a close friend, Al Satabsky, with 3rd Inf. Div. and knowing he was safe.

Married Nancy and has four lovely children: Michael, Howard, Heather and Fern, and four grandchildren: Brett, Gabrielle, Jacob and Adam. He is now semi-retired and commander, JWV Post 146.

MORRIS ROSENSTEIN, born in New York City Aug. 13, 1931. Lived in the Bronx, NY until age 16, when the family moved to Pine Brook, NJ. Graduated from Grover Cleveland High School in Caldwell, NJ, June 1950.

Entered the U.S. Army in August, 1954. Took basic training and Food Service School at Fort Dix, NJ. Spent the rest of Army time in Hanau, Germany with the 597th FA BN, except for the last three months at Fort Sill, OK. He was honorably discharged in August 1956.

Married Helene Jacobs on July 4, 1958 and has two children, Beth Joy and Neil Howard, and one grandchild, Dylan Robert.

Living in Monticello, NY since 1966.

BENJAMIN L. ROSENTHAL, born Jan. 23, 1926, in Boston, MA. Entered USAAF Aug. 20, 1943. Stationed 464th AAF Base Unit, 491st BG, Kings Lynn, England. Participated in battles in Rhineland, Northern France and Central Europe.

Awards/Medals: EAME Theater Ribbon with three Bronze Stars, WWII Victory Medal, American Theater Ribbon. He was discharged Dec. 4, 1945, as sergeant.

Married to his childhood sweetheart for 48 years and has three children and four grandchildren.

After 48 years in the furniture business, he is retired but still works two days a week. Does volunteer work at JWV nursing home. J.C.C., commander of Post 26, first vice president Silver Foxes and Belles. He tries to keep active.

MORRIS ROSENTHAL, entered the Army, May 1, 1944, at Ft. Snelling, MN. Basic training at Camp Hood, TX; became a cannoneer on antitank warfare and sent to Camp Shanks in Orangeburg, NY.

Shipped overseas Oct. 14, 1944, arriving in Livorno, Italy, October 29. Trained then transported to Montecatini and joined the 473rd Inf. Regt. First day in combat was almost his last. The Germans opened fire with machine guns and he was the only survivor. Was supposed to have received a medal, but never did get it.

Came through another battle, then sent to rest camp to shower, shave and get clean clothes. He remembered that it was Pesach and he wanted to attend a Seder. He got a pass and hitchhiked to Rome where he found a synagogue, but no one was there. When he returned to his unit, he found they had been shelled and some were killed. It was another Pesach miracle that he had been spared. While pushing north they were shelled again, they abandoned their jeep and ran for cover. He had peanut butter cookies from home and while the Germans were shelling them, they were eating.

Married Gloria Seitz and has three children. Their firstborn, Liz, is married to Stanly Shur; Madeline is a student; and Dan, graduated from Boston University with a degree in biology.

Presently life member and commander of Post 720, life member of Fordham Post VFW 957, which is in the Bronx. He is junior vice commander of the Rockland Orange District Council.

SI ROSENTHAL, former Boston Red Sox outfielder, who lost the use of his legs when a mine blew up off the French coast during the European invasion, wipes the tears from his eyes as taps were sounded for his son killed in the Pacific. Si was honored prior to the Boston-Cleveland game and presented with funds by the Red Sox and fans to build a home.

Pete Carroll was a member of Post JWV 302 when he met Rosenthal on a visit to the VA Hospital. He organized the Si Rosanthal activities, gave up the chairmanship and became co-chairman to get help to achieve their goal of $10,000. With the help of Sam Levine of Roxbury; Col. Dave Eagan, a columnist for the *Daily Record*; JWV and a contribution of $1,000 from the owner of the Red Sox, they raised $10,000.

Rosanthal was on a minesweeper when wounded. His son, a Marine, was an only child and killed during the invasion of an island. *Submitted by Pete Carroll.*

JOSEPH LEON ROSENZWEIG, born in Lake Village, AZ, Oct. 20, 1921. Served in Korean Conflict Dec. 1, 1952-May 23, 1954; WWII May 22, 1942-Aug. 5, 1946.

Served with USNR as medical officer. Stationed USNH, Memphis, TN; *General A.E. Anderson* (AP-111).

Awards/Medals: American Theater, European Theater and WWII Victory Medal. Discharged as lieutenant May 23, 1954.

Has wife and three grown children. Presently a medically retired physician.

THEODORE ROSENWEIG, born in New York, NY, July 22, 1926. Signed his parents name so he could fight, Nov. 11, 1942. He was only 16 years old. Served with U.S. Army as private first class, sergeant with 501st Parachute Inf. Regt., 88th Inf. Div.

Stationed in Africa, Italy and Austria. Participated in battles in Rome, Po Valley, Occupation troops, Trieste. Spent 92 consecutive days on the frontline.

Memorable experience was when surrounded at road block and had to shoot themselves out to get back to their lines.

Awards/Medals: Purple Heart, Bronze Star Medal, Combat Infantry Badge, French Croix de Guerre. Discharged Nov. 5, 1945 as sergeant.

Married and has three children and 10 grandchildren. Now a semi-retired bookkeeper.

AARON ROSIN, born Feb. 10, 1925, in Mt. Vernon, NY. Enlisted in WWII and served in the Army, 69th Inf. Regt.

Awards/Medals: Bronze Star and Purple Heart. Achieved the rank of medical corpsman.

Family consists of his father, mother, wife, Myra and a brother. He died Aug. 16, 1951.

STEVE ROSMARIN, born Oct. 5, 1927, Brooklyn, Sept. 3, 1945, U.S. Army, PFC 17th Inf. Regt., 7th Div., two and half years occupation duty in Korea between 1945-1948. Browning Automatic Rifleman, Military Police. Taujon, Techon, Or Yang.

Medals/Awards: Army of Occupation Korea, Asiatic-Pacific, WWII Victory Medal, Unit received Presidential Unit Citation, July 11, 1948.

Graduate, Pace University 1951. 1961-1962 PDC, Department of California, National Executive Committeeman, National Travel Consultant.

Married Bernice and has two daughters, Judy and Suzie. Currently residing in Los Angeles and running a travel agency.

HERMAN ROSNER, past commander of JWV Post 181 McKeesport, PA was inducted into Army 1942, 68th Cost Arty. They were first American troops to invade North Africa. Went through Italy and wounded on the Anzio Beachhead. He went through seven invasions.

Awards/Medals: seven Battle Stars, Purple Heart and other medals.

Liberated concentration camp near Russian border, survivors were overwhelmed. Those who could, hugged and kissed them. The European war ended in 1945.

They trained in England for the Pacific War. The Atom bomb brought the war to an end and saved many American lives including Rosner's. Met his English wife Lilly at a USO Dance in Bournemouth. It was love at first sight. They will soon celebrate their 50th anniversary. Proud parents of two sons, a lovely daughter-in-law and two grandchildren, Perri and Drew.

Still active in JWV and visiting the hospitalized. His wife is in the auxiliary.

HIRAM (CHAIM) ROSOV, born in Manhattan, July 12, 1929. MS with honors, L.I.U. 1960. Served in Korean War 1951-1954. Served as battalion sergeant major, 179th Inf. at Heartbreak Ridge. Transferred to 10th Corps at conclusion of the war as chaplain's assistant. For two months served as acting chaplain for South Korea until a replacement was available.

Awards/Medals: Combat Infantry Badge, two Bronze Stars, Army Commendation Medal, Korean and Defense Service Medals and ROK Unit Citations.

Taught elementary subjects and high school English for 33 years, was assistant professor at Queens College. Studied Judaic sculpturing with Yehudah Wolpert and Moshe Zabari at the New York Jewish Museum. Created Holocaust Memorials, ceremonial objects and awards for JNF, UJA, Soviet Jewry and for individuals and synagogues throughout the United States.

Married to Reva since 1952, has daughter Sheryl and grandchildren, Daniel and Jillian. Presently living in Boca Raton, FL.

ALBERT ROSS (AL), born Brooklyn, NY, July 9, 1918. Graduated Brooklyn College 1939 and was salesman for two years. Drafted October 1941 and went to basic training at Camp Croft, SC.

Shipped out to Ireland in February 1942. Transferred to 205th MP Co. and underwent HQ training in England. Assigned to AFHQ, 2nd contingent to arrive Algiers in December 1942. Took up guard duty at HQ Hotel St. George, and Eishenhower's residence; also took over town patrol and assigned as French interpreter at the central police station.

Participated in honor guard at Carthage, Tunisia for Mrs. Eleanor Roosevelt and then Prime Minister Churchill who was returning from Teheran conference. In early 1944 moved into the Palazzo, Caserta, Italy and took over guard duty of town. The tremendous pool in back of palace was converted to a recreational pool for GIs and he was assigned as life guard during the swim season of 1944-1945.

He was honorably discharged in August of 1945. After two more years in sales in New York, he moved to Florence, SC where he met and married Rosa. Moved to Atlanta where they operated a food and beverage business until semi-retirement in 1980. Has been blessed with two sons, two daughters, three granddaughters and one grandson. He is still active and piddling around in the specialty food and beverage business and is active in sports, tennis, racquetball and swimming.

ELI I. (ROSOWSKY) ROSS, born July 17, 1918, St. Paul, MN. Entered service and served as Tech 5 (corporal). HQ Btry., 161st FA BN.

Outstanding performance of duty against enemy in France, Luxembourg, Holland, Belgium and and Germany.

Awarded Bronze Star. Discharged as corporal February 1946.

Married to Sybil Harris in 1948 and they have three children and three grandchildren. Was in vending business in Miami, FL. Passed away, April 9, 1993, age 75.

LEONARD ROSS, EM3/c, USNR, born Nov. 18, 1919, in New York City and graduated high school. Served from May 15, 1944. Attended "boot camp" at Sampson, NY and Electrical School at Gulfport, MS. Served aboard two repair ships in the Pacific, until permanently assigned to destroyer escort USS (DE-186) *Swearer.*

Part of a convoy escort to Okinawa, they participated in the entire Okinawa battle from March 26, 1945. At the beginning of this campaign, their fleet and troops captured a group of islands just south of Okinawa, to use as an anchorage and base. Luckily they trapped and captured almost 200 small boats still on land. These boats loaded with explosives were to be used as "suicide" craft to attack their invasion fleet. During this battle, their ship was attacked by kamikaze planes, bombed by aircraft and torpedoes. Fortunately the ship, crew and he came through unharmed.

During this period, after downing one kamikaze, they came to the aid of another DE, which was hit by a kamikaze. They took aboard and treated some 65 badly wounded men while enroute to a hospital ship. Returned to California in July 1945 to be refitted in preparation for the invasion of Japan. Honorably discharged Jan. 2, 1946.

Married Mollie in September 1940. Blessed with daughter Louise Pearl in January 1942. Their son Philip Alan was born August 1946. He worked for the city of New York as an automotive technician until retiring in 1977. They are now blessed with two granddaughters, Elisa and Randi, and two great-granddaughters, Cori and Samantha.

He is a life member and past commander of the Dept. of New York, 1973-1974. Mollie also is a life member and past president of the Dept. of New York Ladies Auxiliary, 1976-1977.

PAULA MEERSAND ROSS, born Aug. 25, 1920 in Vienna, Austria. Joined WAC, Fort Desmoines, IA; Ft. Hamilton, NY; Camp Kilmer, NJ.

Memorable experiences: translator and censor for German prisoners of war (Rommel's Desert Fox Army). As women were not legally allowed to deal with prisoners of war she had to accept to remain a private first class for the duration, there was no one else with her qualifications.

Discharged in 1946 with the rank of private first class.

A retired chiropractor and widow. She has a daughter, Cindy, and one son Norman.

Ross is a NYS and Federal LIC Wildlife Rehabilitator.

ANDREW ROSSI, Andy Rossi, served in the U.S. Army from Jan. 4, 1944-Sept. 17, 1945. First entered the service at Ft. Devens and was discharged with the rank of PFC at Ft. Devens, MA on Sept. 17, 1945. Received basic training at Camp Wheeler, GA with the infantry from Jan. 18, 1944-May 15, 1944.

Sailed overseas on the SS *Queen Elizabeth* from New York arriving at Scotland. Saw active service in the European Theatre of Operations with the 35th Div., 3rd Army, from July 22, 1944-Sept. 11, 1945. Saw action in Northern France [illegible], Luxembourg and Germany.

Awards/Medals: Combat Infantry Badge, Purple Heart, Good Conduct Medal and Presidential Citation. He visited Reims, France, Chateau Thierry, Paris and all of the historical spots in and around Paris, France. *Submitted by Max Sigal*

MEYER ROSSUM (M/SGT, USMC, RET), born June 29, 1919, Buffalo, NY. enlisted in the USMC Nov. 14, 1939. Shipped out to MB Pearl Harbor on Feb. 6, 1940; transferred to MB NAD Luolualu April 1940 to December 1942. Participated in defense of Pearl Harbor on Dec. 7, 1941. Joined 1st Mar. Div. September 1943 at HQ Bn. then to 1st M Trans. Bn. during the New Guinea and Okinawa Campaign.

Stateside from November 1945-August 1950. Stationed at MB Great Lakes, IL and Camp Pendleton. Joined 1sdt Mar. Div. August 1950, HQ Co. HQ Bn. Participated in Inchon Landing, Seoul, Wonsan and Hungnam.

Went to Hagaru-ri Nov. 28, 1950, as first sergeant forward echelon of HQ Co. HQ Bn. commanded by Maj. "Fearless" Freddie Simpson. Wounded in right eye Dec. 7, 1950, but continued to march to Koto-ri. Evacuated by plane to hospital ship and then to Yokosuka Naval Hospital. After two months hospitalization he was transferred to C Co., then to Camp Otsu, then back to division in August 1951. The commanding Gen. G.C. Thomas didn't want anyone that went through the 1950 winter to go through the 1951 winter, so he was sent Stateside in October 1951.

Duty at MC DepSup SF (Motor Pool) SepCo and 3rd MC Recruit Training Bn., MCRD San Diego then to MB NS Long Beach and VMIT El Toro. Overseas to Camp Smedley, Okinawa from December 1957 to May 1959.

Stateside duty with 1st Pioneer Bn., 1st Mar. Div., Camp Pendleton, then to SOES MCAS El Toro where he transferred to the Fleet Reserve on June 1, 1962.

He has a lovely wife Edith, and two daughters from a previous marriage. He retired from Washington National Insurance Co. after over 17 years in 1985.

BEN A. ROTH, born on Aug. 21, 1923, in Brooklyn, NY. Entered the USAR May 1941 and USAAF March 1942. Served with 3rd Armd. at Ft. Knox to Air Transport, Lockhead, Biloxi, MS and 554th ATC Memphis, TN.

He was discharged at Mitchel Field, November 1945 with the rank of acting sergeant (civilian pilot).

Awards/Medals: American Defense, EAME, Good Conduct, etc.

Widower, retired. community, political and veterans activist.

GILBERT ROTH, served in the USN from March 14, 1944-Dec. 12, 1945. Entered the service at Newark, NJ, on March 14, 1944, with the rank of apprentice seaman. Boot training took place at the USN Training Station at Sampson, NY, and from there served at Newport, RI, moved on south to Bainbridge, MD, Portsmouth, VA; St. Albans, NY, and Chelsea, MA.

Assigned to the USS *Benevolence* (AH-13), under Capt. C.C. Laws, with the medical unit on Dec. 13, 1944. Served continually in this unit under senior medical officer, Capt. F. McDaniels, until November 1. The ship on which Gilbert served was attached to Adm. Halsey's 3rd Fleet, and they serviced the fleet, giving medical aid to the sick and wounded.

On Aug. 29, 1945, Gilbert's crew was the first hospital ship to enter Tokyo Bay and all prisoners of war were first screened by them. Admirals Halsey, Nimitz and Capt. Stassen were aboard his ship several times and commended Gilbert and the other members for their fine work. On Dec. 21, 1945, Gilbert was discharged at Lido Beach, NY, with the rank of pharmacist mate third class. He now resides at Newark, NJ, with his wife and family. *Submitted by Max Sigal.*

IRVING ROTH, born June 25, 1917, Brooklyn, NY. Inducted Aug. 8, 1942. Stationed at Ft. Jay, NY for basic training; Ft. Dix; Geiger Field, WA where appointed battalion photographer of the [illegible]

In January 1943, their battalion landed at Casablanca, Africa, then on to Oran. Transferred to a Map Making Unit and from then on belonged to a special tech unit which went on detached service to areas which required photo specialists.

He became ill and was hospitalized two weeks in Sicily. In March 1944 reported to MAAF Cmd. to work in Caserta, Italy. After the fall of Anzio, they moved through Rome. Photo unit was then transferred to the Recon AF and sailed to Marseilles, moving through France and stopped on the west side of the Rhine, near Strasbourgh. They worked day and night filming and preparing photos for analysis and intelligence staff to see where to hit the German army. With the defeat of Germany they moved to Frankfurt Airport where they helped clean-up.

Awards/Medals: EAMF Ribbon, Good Conduct Medal with Bronze Service Star. He was discharged Nov. 11, 1945, with the rank of corporal.

His brother, William, served in the Pacific Campaign and his brother, Nathaniel, served in the ETO.

JERRY ROTH, born July 19, 1932, Brooklyn, NY. Enlisted in the USAF, April 12, 1951. Training achieved at Sampson AFB, Geneva, NY. Spent next three months at Oklahoma A&M College for administrative training, then a short time at Vance AFB, OK.

Processed from Camp Kilmer, NJ to go overseas for special assignment to Germany. Spent a short while in Southern Germany at former SS barracks. From there to Wiesbaden, Germany and an assignment with the 7054th Air Intelligence Sqdn. They screened the escaped personnel from the Iron Curtain countries. Some of them were infiltrators. Reports showed Americans were still prisoners in labor camps as were the Nazis.

Memorable experience was the Iron Curtain and almost crossing through it accidentally.

He received a special accommodation but can't remember the name of it. He was honorably discharged April 12, 1955.

Married in 1955 to Jacqueline Roth and has three children: Joy, Winifred and David, and one grandchild, Jonathan. He is a manufacturers representative and a member of JWV 972.

KENNETH ROTH, served in the U.S. Army Signal Corps. Entered the service at Ft. Dix, NJ, as a private on Aug. 3, 1943, and trained at Camp Crowder, MO, for his basic training, until April 1944. Moved on to Fort Monmouth, NJ, as a power engineer and remained there until March, 1945.

Shipped overseas on the SS *George Washington* out of New York and arrived at Southampton, England. Served in the European Theatre of Operations with the 97th Signal Bn. from July 1944-January 1946. Saw action with intensive fighting at St. Lo, France, crossing the Rhine, Ardennes, Central Europe and in the Rhineland.

Among the outstanding places which he visited was the French Riviera, Paris, London, Brussels, Frankfort, Nuremburg and Leige. Most of his time in Germany was spent working with high frequency radio link transmission between Division and Corps. His work was very dangerous and very interesting. Discharged Jan. 3, 1946. *Submitted by Max Sigal*

MILTON ROTH, served in the U.S. Army Medical Corps from Oct. 5, 1942-Feb. 9, 1946. Entered the service with the grade of private and at the time of discharge held the grade of sergeant. Received his Medical Corps Training at [illegible] Ft. Benjamin Harrison. Also received training with the Quartermaster Corps at Ft. Jay, NY.

Sailed overseas from New York City on the HMS *Queen Elizabeth* and arrived at Scotland. On his return to the States, he sailed from Marseilles in the U.S. Army Transport, *Felix Grundy*, arriving at Newport News, VA. Served in the European Theater of Operations with the Medical Corps and the Transportation Corps and encountered many submarine attacks in the South Atlantic while on transport duty.

Awards/Medals: several citations among which are the Unit Citation Wreath 9222 TSU-TC, American Service Medal,

EAME Medal, World War II Victory Medal and the Good Conduct Medal. *Submitted by Max Sigal.*

PAUL ROTH, entered the military service from New York. He distinguished himself by his outstanding devotion to duty, efficiency and resourcefulness in organizing and training the first all German POW processing companies to handle the tremendous influx of prisoners at the enclosure.

He performed his task in an exceptional manner, personally interviewing and testing each clerk, and conducting the procedures and classes to be followed. Through his resourcefulness the first German POW Mobile Units were established and appropriate equipment made up. Under his guidance the American and German personnel for POW Overhead Detach. 2028 were trained in processing POWs.

Roth assumed great responsibilities in cooperating with Field Interrogation Division and Psychological Warfare Division by choosing cases for special interrogation, checking of Special Nationals, civilians and the regular line. In spite of the shortage of equipment and amount of work to be accomplished daily, he revised the entire line of processing, and as a result it was possible to handle at least 100 prisoners an hour and thus keep up with the constant flow into the enclosure. This enviable record has been made possible through the tireless efforts of this enlisted man. His devotion to duty during this period was a substantial contribution to the establishment of a superior installation.

At the completion of this period, Tech 3rd Grade Roth was supervising a crew of 50 POWs, four mobile platoons and a special unit for a POW Hospital. He received the Bronze Star for his services.

SANFORD ROTH, served in the USN from Feb. 12, 1946, until Nov. 15, 1947. Entered the service with the rate of apprentice seaman, and held a higher rating when discharged.

Received his boot training at Camp Bainbridge, MD, and for four months was stationed at Camp Bainbridge, MD, in the Ships Company as a fire fighter under two year enlistment. *Submitted by Max Sigal*

SAUL ROTH, born in Czechoslovakia, March 1, 1918. Emigrated to U.S. in 1924 with parents and brothers. Settled on outskirts of Wilkes Barre, PA. Enlisted for three years in USAAF Sept. 25, 1940, with cousin Harry Friedman, a four year veteran with Marines. Basic training at Olmstead Field, Harrisburg, PA. Six months at Aeronautical University in Chicago, followed with two-month course on aeroplane instruments at Chanute Field. Assigned to Westover Air Base in Massachusetts. Next orders Pope Field, Fort Bragg, NC, assembling point for overseas duty.

Sailed on SS *Brazil* March 1942 with 1st Air Corps Ferrying Gp. Weeks later troopship arrived Cape Town, South Africa. Directed to the Zionist Hall, a canteen operated by Jewish organization for all Allied troops. Mothers in kitchens preparing food, daughters serving and dancing with troops. An attractive young lady offered him tea and cake. Later that evening invited him and two friends to her home for next night Passover meal. Had dinner a second night and left with a promise to write.

They corresponded five years during which time her father put the "Jewish FBI" on his trail. He had his rabbi write to Rabbi Yung of Yeshiva University, NY, who wrote to Chief Rabbi Davidson of Wilkes Barre for a report on his family. Only then, in March 1947, did he allow his daughter, Dorothy, to come to America. They were married in Wilkes-Barre by Rabbi Davidson November 30 that year.

After leaving Capetown, SS *Brazil* entered Indian Ocean. Weeks later arrived Karachi, India. After living in Sind Desert in barracks vacated by Indian troops they crossed continent to Assam by rail. Arrival of C47 from the States began saga of flying 'the Hump'. Mission to bring supplies to China, destination, Kunming. Also food-search missions for missing crews. For larger pay loads, the C-46 was put into service.

Eventually, because of plane losses, bailouts and crack-ups, a new C-46 piloted by Maj W.T. Arthur was sent to investigate problems. It was on this plane, as crew chief, after 12 prior trips over Himalayas with Maj Arthur at controls, that on return flight from Kunming, first, then second engine failed. Unadjusted hastily-acquired parachute forced him to discard flightsuit and gun. Crew of four safely parachuted. He landed in tree, removed food, medical supplies, group together 10 minutes later. Crew of aeroplane 651 walked along river, stumbled on Chinese village. No one spoke English. Maj Arthur's limited French secured a guide and a jackass which he rode because of injury. Continued walking to next village. On third day rescue team made contact and took them to Kunming.

For tonnage put over the Hump, the unit, part of Air Transport Command, received the Presidential Unit Citation.

After two and a half years in India, back to States and family. Assigned to Brownille Airbase in Texas and then on to Greenwood Air Base in Mississippi. Discharged after five years on Sept. 15, 1945.

Family consists of two daughters, Yolanda an orthopaedic surgeon/oncologyst and Lydia, a doctor of psychology and four fabulous grandsons, two each.

Forty-five years ago, his brother and he started Allentown Bar and Restaurant Supply Company. Now retired.

HAROLD D. ROTHBLATT, born July 26, 1924. Enlisted February 1942. Served in the Army, Antiaircraft Arty. ASTP, Signal Corps, 2101st Sig. Service Bn.

Stationed at Camp Hulen, TX; Rose Polytechnic Inst. Terre Haute, IN; Camp Crowder, MO. Participated in battles North American Defence, Central Burma Campaign.

Awards/Medals: Good Conduct, North American, Central Burma Medals. Discharged May 11, 1946. Achieved the rank of technician fourth grade.

Married and has two children, five grandchildren.

Retired dentist. Volunteer Fountain Valley California Police Department. ADL, Catholic-Jewish Dialogue. Enjoys taking walks and reading.

JIM ROTHBLATT, is a second generation American and a Jew. His father and most of his uncles served in the U.S. Military during WWII. So, in 1965 when the U.S. got itself militarily involved in Vietnam, it seemed natural that he should drop out of college and join the Army.

By the end of 1966 he wound up as a combat medic in the 2nd Platoon of "Charlie" Co., 4th Bn., 12th Inf., 199th LIB. He spent eight and one-half months in the field and another three and one half months as an ambulance driver during his Vietnam tour of duty.

Today he is a school counselor by profession, married 26 years to Susan and has a son, David, and a daughter, Annie. He is proud of his service and is proud to be a member of Post 750 of the JWV of America.

IRVING ROTHMAN, was a skinny guy, 142 pounds, when he enlisted in the USAAC on Oct. 29, 1942.

He was on his eighth mission as engineer on B-17 *Heavenly Daze,* 336th SQ, 95 BG (H), Horham, England, when they were shot down Jan. 11, 1944, on a mission to destroy ball-bearing factories at Brunswick, Germany.

After initial Dulag (Frankfort-am-Main) he was imprisoned at Stalag Luft VI, Heidekrugge, Feb. 2, 1944-July 15, 1944; then Stalag Luft IV, Keifheide (Gross Teichau), July 18, 1944-Feb. 6, 1945.

He was among 5,000-plus prisoners on the Black March, moving under bayonets and attack dogs 638 miles on back roads through villages of northern Germany. Their captors used them as pawns as they sought to evade the Russian Army's advance. In the dead of winter they slept in barns (if they were lucky) or in the open. They lived on roots and scraps; the guards gave them a thin soup once a day. He traded his watch to a farmer for seven loaves of bread and some bacon. They shared everything. The Red Cross found them twice and distributed food parcels. They arrived at Stalag 11B, Fallingbostel, March 29, 1945.

Liberated April 16, 1945, by the British Army and weighed 107 pounds when he entered Camp Lucky Strike, the field hospital in Le Havre.

Awards/Medals: Air Medal, EAME Theater Ribbon with one Bronze Star, Good Conduct Medal and Purple Heart. Discharged Nov. 1, 1945, Patterson Field, OH.

ROBERT A. ROTHMAN, born March 31, 1931, in Bronx, NY. Inducted into the Navy as chaplain May 1957. Stationed in Okinawa and the Great Lakes.

His memorable experiences include being chaplain for the 3rd Marine Div., the 7th Fleet and then at the Great Lakes Naval Training Center.

Awards/Medals: 3rd Marine Division Commendation. Achieved the rank of commander and was discharged June 1980.

Married to the former Miriam Buch of Tel Aviv. and has three children: Dee, Kay and Jessica. Grandfather of Andrea and Kevin. Rabbi of Community Synagogue, Rye, NY. Professor at Fordham University, Touro College and Manhattanville College. Degrees in theology, history and psychotherapy. Deputy National Chaplain of the JWV.

ANDREW ROTHSTEIN, born July 1, 1921, Romania. Volunteered for the U.S. Army and served in HQ Co., 1st Bn., 128th Inf., 32nd Div. (Red Arrow). Stationed at Camp Upton; Camp Croft, SC; Camp Cable, Brisbane, Australia; Saidor; Aitape; New Guinea, Hollandia; Leyte and Luzon, Philippine Islands.

Memorable Experiences: having malaria; when company commander was killed in the Philippines; and meeting his younger brother in Manila.

Awards/Medals: Good Conduct Badge, Asiatic-Pacific Medal, Philippine Liberation Ribbon, Combat Infantry Badge, Bronze Star, three Battle Stars and Presidential Unit Citation. He served 33 months overseas and was discharged Nov. 27, 1945, with the rank tech 5 (radio operator).

Married 45 years and has two daughters and three granddaughters. Retired in 1989 after 25 years of federal service.

MORRIS ROTHSTEIN, born Sept. 16, 1913, Syracuse, NY. Attended Jackson Elementary School and graduated from Central High School.

He was wounded in Germany during WWII and discharged from the Army in 1946.

Associated with Hy;s Super Service Gas Station. He passed away Oct. 16, 1947, at the age of 34. He is survived by his father, Harry; sister, Lillian Hodes; brothers, Hyman and Sam; and nephew, Herbert Hodes.

LEON MORRIS ROTTMAN, born March 12, 1918, Chicago, IL. Had active duty from 1942-1946; Reserves, 1946-1951; and active duty 1951-1968 in the USAAC and USAF. Assigned to the Air Weather Service Unit, stationed in the South Pacific, China-Burma-India, Japan and Germany.

Awards/Medals: two Air Force Commendation Medals, Korean Service Medal, Small Arms Expert Marksmanship Ribbon, United Nations Service Medal, Armed Forces Reserve Medal, Air Force Outstanding Unit Award, National Defense Service Medal, Air Force Longevity Service Award, Philippine Liberation Ribbon, China War Memorial Medal, Good Conduct Medal, WWII Victory Medal (Campaign and Service), Asiatic-Pacific Campaign and Service Medal, American Campaign and Service Medal.

Retired with the rank of lieutenant colonel. Belongs to the Air Force Association, Air Force Academy Quarterback Club, TROA, CBI Vets, 15th and 20th Weather Squadrons, VFW and JWV.

From 1969-1989 he was chief meteorologist, Denver KUSA-TV and from 1989-1992 was "Senior Showcase" host, Denver, KRMA-TV.

Has wife, Leah, and daughter, Vicki.

ARTHUR M. ROWE, (Nee Rosenzweig), born in the Bronx, NY, Sept. 19, 1920. Called up for service Nov. 11, 1942 and entered the Army at Camp Upton, NY. Was shipped to Fort Riley, KS to the 9th Armd. Div., Btry. C. Trained as computer operator converting yardage into millileters based on Forward Observer reports.

Participated in maneuvers in Kansas, Camp Polk, LA and the Mohave Desert in California. Attended Divisional

Supply Sergeant's Course at Fort Riley, KS, Feb. 6, 1943. Sailed overseas 1945 to the European African Middle Eastern Theatre of Operations. Saw action in France, Luxembourg and Belgium. Was wounded at the Ramagen Bridge on Feb. 28, 1945.

Awards/Medals: Good Conduct Medal, Bronze Battle Star, WWII Victory Medal, American Theatre Campaign Medal and Purple Heart. Honorably discharged March 19, 1946.

Married to Doris June 20, 1948. Has daughter Milarie and son Jeffrey. Member JWV Post #24, Past Post Commander and JWV County Council as patriotic instructor.

MORRIS ROZNER, Lt. Col., born Camden, NJ, Sept. 5, 1916. Entered service March 1941. Airplane mechanic, aerial engineer, aviation cadet. Commissioned navigator, June 1943. July 1943, North Africa with 64th Troop Carrier Group. Served in ETO and CBI, 160 combat missions. Navigation instructor, Mather AFB, 1946-1950; Strategic Evaluation Sqdn., MacDill AFB; Command & Staff School; Staff Navigator for training, SAC HQ; training officer, 556th Missile Sqdn. (Snark); Atlas Missile Sector Commander, 578th Strat. Missile Sqdn., Dyess AFB, TX. Retired as lieutenant colonel, Nov. 1, 1963.

Awarded Distinguished Flying Cross with one OLC, Air Medal with three OLC, Commendation Medal.

MA in economics in 1967. Employed by Douglas Aircraft, 1968-1970. Partners with wife, Natalie, in Rayne Water Conditioning Agency in Long Beach, CA. Retired in July 1984. They have three daughters and two grandchildren.

Member of JWV Post 595, Fountain Valley, CA.

BERNARD RUBACK, served in the USAAC from Feb. 2, 1943-October 1943. Entered the service with the rank of private and was discharged with the rank of cadet. Basic training at Atlantic City, NJ, from Feb. 28, 1943-July 17, 1943 and his college training was at Penn State College, PA, from March 31, 1943-July 17, 1943.

Classification training was had at Nashville Army Air Base from July 1943-Aug. 31, 1943 and his pre-flight training was at Maxwell Field, AL, from Aug. 31, 1943-Sept. 15, 1943. Became air cadet on Aug. 31, 1943, and received his discharge in October 1943. *Submitted by Max Sigal*

ALVIN W. RUBEN, Capt, born in Chicago in 1917. Enlisted in the USAAC and inducted at Ft. Sheridan, IL on Nov. 2, 1943. Attended Aviation Cadet School and commissioned a 2nd lieutenant on July 20, 1945. He was a navigator, bombardier and aerial gunner.

Awards/Medals: Good Conduct Medal, American Theatre Ribbon and WWII Victory Medal. He was honorably discharged on Dec. 20, 1916.

Member of the JWV and served in the Retired Reserve where he was promoted to captain. He was married for 52 years, had two children and five grandchildren. He was in the insurance and real estate business for over 55 years.

Ruben died Jan. 3, 1993, and is buried in the JWV section of the Shalom Memorial Cemetery in Palatine, IL.

JACK RUBENFELD, born Feb. 27, 1922, in Scranton, PA. Attended University of Scranton and graduated with a Doctor of Laws degree from Dickinson Law School, Carlisle, PA. Enlisted in the USAAF in May 1943. Served as a radio operator/gunner with the 8th AF, 91st BG., 401st BS from November 1944 until May 1945. Also flew as navigator.

Basic training at Kearns, UT. Studied aviation engineering for four months at Montana State University. Studied code operation and maintenance of radios for five months at Radio School in Scott Field, IL. Attended Gunnery School for six weeks at Yuma, AZ. Studied navigation and radar theory for eight weeks in England.

Traveled overseas on the *Queen Mary* and assigned to Bassinbourne Air Base. Flew 35 combat missions in a B-17G the *Old Battle Axe*. Participated in battles in Central Europe, Rhineland and Ardennes.

Awards/Medals: Air Medal with six OLCs, EAME Theater Campaign Medal with three Bronze Service Stars, WWII Victory Medal, American Theater Campaign Ribbon, Aviation Badge Aerial Gunner, Good Conduct Medal, Sharpshooters-Pistol Badge, Expert Gunner Badge. Honorably discharged from Reserves in May 1953, as a master sergeant.

Admitted to practice law before county, state and federal courts. Practices law in Pennsylvania and is a member of Pennsylvania Bar Association; Lackawanna Bar Association and Trial Lawyers Association.

Married to the former Anne Podrasky. Active member in the following organizations: The JWV; VFW, The 91st BG Memorial Association, The 8th AF Historical Society of Pennsylvania; The Ancient Accepted Scottish Rite of Freemasonry, Valley of Scranton, PA; Keystone Lodge of Perfection, Valley of Scranton, PA; Hyde Park Lodge 339 F&AM Benevolent and Protective Order of Elks; Shrine Club of Scranton, PA; Irem Temple AAONM of Wilkes-Barre, PA; Pennsylvania Society of the State of Pennsylvania.

ARTHUR L. RUBENSTEIN (ART), born Chicago, May 19, 1925, enlisted in the Army at 17. A combat infantryman, he fought in France, Belgium, Holland and Germany.

He was captured in Kesternich during the "Battle of the Bulge." A German tank fired into the cellar of the house his squad holed up in, killing their German prisoners. Accused of killing them, Art was sentenced to die. In solitary for six weeks in Bonn, the day he was to be executed, the RAF bombed the camp and he managed to mix in with other American POWs. Taken to another camp, he remained there until liberated in April 1945.

After many months in hospitals, he was honorably discharged in November 1945. A graduate of Brooklyn College and California State Northridge. Retired after 35 years as a history professor, he lives in Ohio with his wife of 46 years, Ruth. They have four children and seven grandchildren.

Awards/Medals: Combat Infantry Badge, Bronze Star, Purple Heart and European Theater with four Battle Stars.

SAM I. RUBENSTEIN, born London, England. Came to America at the age of two. Graduated from Syracuse University in 1921. Worked as U.S. Internal Revenue agent from 1923 to 1941.

Commissioned as first lieutenant in WWI and honorably discharged. Before WWII, he was asked to give one year of his time and was sent to Savannah Air Base, 3rd BG. World War II broke out and his was the first group to go to Australia, where he joined the 5th Bomb. AF. and commissioned as a major.

Declared missing in action Jan. 7, 1943.

Survived by father, Lewis; wife, Irene K.; son, B. Wm. Rubenstein; daughter, Mrs. Karl Kaye, New York; and brothers, Leon and Maurice.

SEYMOUR RUBENSTEIN, born in Freehold, NJ in 1918. Entered the U.S. Military Academy, West Point, NY on July 1, 1938. Graduated May 29, 1942, commissioned as 2nd lieutenant, Corps of Engineers, U.S. Army. Assigned to the 77th Div.

Wartime experience included D-day invasion of Guam, Leyte and Okinawa; one year in Korea (1952-1953) with engineer units in direct support of front line divisions; one year in Greece (1948) as engineer advisor during Greek Civil War and three years in France (1959-1962).

Memorable Experiences: when his jeep driver, Cpl. L. Blumenkrantz, was fatally wounded by Japanese shell fire as they were relocating with Division HQ on Guam; and when conducting Passover services for the Jewish troops onboard ship just before the April 1, 1945, invasion of Okinawa.

Awards/Medals: Bronze Star Medal wih OLC, Legion of Merit and Greek War Cross Second Class. Retired in 1965 as a colonel while serving as the engineer, 5th Army, Chicago, IL.

He worked 24 years for the New Jersey Dept. of Labor in the field of occupational and public safety. Retired again September 1992 as director, Office of Public Safety Compliance.

Married to the former Lorraine Gene Murman of Minneapolis, MN in 1950. They have one son, Stephen and one grandson, Max.

DAVID S. RUBIN, born in New Haven, CT, Feb. 9, 1918. Married Doris Kessler of Richmond, VA July 22, 1946. Has son and daughter, Martin Rubin and Peggy Borkon, and two grandsons, Andrew and Matthew Borkon.

Received BA in economics, Yale 1939, and MS in accounting, Columbia University Graduate School of Business 1941. Entered U.S. Army, Aug. 9, 1941, at Fort Devens, MA. Basic training at Camp Grant, IL. Medical corpsman at Fort Stevens, OR. Commissioned second lieutenant, Nov. 13, 1942, after graduating from QM OCS at Fort Lee, VA.

Assigned to 1063rd QM Co. Service Gp. (Avn) at Baer Field, IN; Syracuse AAB, NY; Fort Dix AAB, NJ; and Camp Miles Standish, MA. Assigned to 8th AF 2nd Bomb Div., December 1943. In 1217th QM Co Service Gp. (Avn), 392nd BG at Wendling, England, and 1132nd QM Co. Serv Gp. (Avn), 44th BG at Shipdham, England, for about 10 months each as quartermaster and purchasing and contracting officer.

Discharged from service Dec. 13, 1945, as first lieutenant, Air Corps. Recalled to active duty in January, 1951, as chief, Purchasing and Contracting Div., HQ, Continental Air Command, Mitchel AFB, NY. Transferred to Wiesbaden, Germany in October 1953, with various assignments in the 7290th Procurement Sqdn., HQ USAFE. Transferred in July 1956 to the London Air Procurement Office (LAPO) as chief, Production Branch, and deputy chief, LAPO.

One year in training with Industry Program at Republic Aviation and Sperry Rand. From September 1959 to June 1965, in Propulsion Directorate, Ballistic Systems Div., Los Angeles AF Station and Norton AFB, CA. Then in HQ AF Systems Command General, and Chief, Research and Development and Base Procurement Div., DCS Procurement and Production. Retired from active duty as lieutenant colonel, Oct. 11, 1966.

Awards/Medals: Meritorious Service Medal, Air Force Commendation Medal with OLC and 11 other campaign and service medals and ribbons.

HOWARD R. RUBIN, born in New Haven, CT, June 2, 1913. Graduated from Commercial High School in 1931. Enlisted in the Regular Army July 8, 1938, and assigned to the 13th Inf. at Fort Devens, MA. When the Air Corps went on an expansion program in 1940, he passed the necessary exam for acceptance and was assigned to Mitchel Field, NY. His organization the 305th Fighter Control Sqdn. was sent to the Asiatic-Pacific area for setting up Air Ground to Sea Communications with the Marine Corps at Iwo Jima. They did eventual land there after the Marines were about to secure the victory.

Promoted to technical sergeant with a warrant from the Air Corps commanding officer, Washington, DC, Dec. 1, 1941. His total military service exceeded seven years.

Awards/Medals: Good Conduct Medal with two loops, American Defense Medal, American Campaign Medal, Asiatic-Pacific Medal, WWII Victory Medal and two Bronze Stars. He was discharged Nov. 7, 1945.

Resides in Rutherford, NJ with wife Helen. Has five children and five grandchildren. Among other veteran organizations, he is a member of the JWV Post 146 and is an aide-de-camp of the JWV Department of New Jersey.

SEYMOUR RUBIN, born in Brooklyn, NY, April 23, 1931. Enlisted in the U.S. Army, 3rd Div., Automatic Weapons Bn., November 1951. Stationed at Fort Dix, Camp Polk, Korea.

Memorable experience includes seeing dead body floating in Seoul; and the Golden Gate Bridge upon arrival home.

Discharged as corporal in November 1953.

Married to Maxine (Abel), has daughter, Debra, and son, Brian. Received bachelor's degree from Brooklyn College. Retired in 1990 as senior vice president, Penquin USA.

SHERWOOD RUBIN, Past Commander, Abraham Kraditor, Post 2, JWV, born Brooklyn, NY, Oct. 23, 1928. After graduation from Alexander Hamilton High School in 1946, immediately enlisted in the U.S. Army on July 5, 1946. Because he wasn't 18, parents consent was required. The government requested immediate enlistments so that veterans could be discharged.

He reported to Ft. Dix, NJ, July 8, 1946, and one week later was assigned to the Medical Department, Surgeon's General Office and arrived Camp Polk, LA for basic training. Upon completion of training, he was transferred to Tilton General Hospital, Fort Dix, NJ. Being stationed at the hospital was very rewarding, he prepared the x-rays to be reviewed by the radiologists. The amount of suffering endured by the Vets returning was enormous.

Awards/Medals: American Theater Ribbon, WWII Victory Medal and Meritorious Unit Award. Separated from the service as a private first class, Nov. 26, 1947. Today, he and his wife Gloria are retired.

SOLOMON RUBIN (SOL), born in Poland March 13, 1916. Entered service 1942. Served first with antiaircraft, then infantry. Stationed in Tunisia, Algeria, Italy and France.

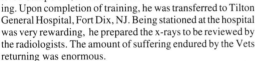

Memorable experiences include submarine attack in the Atlantic, on the way to North Africa; Salerno beach landing; the winter of 1943 at the Cassino front; Anzio beachhead; a few evacuation hospital visits, crutches, cane and home. In Tunisia he heard Hebrew chanting from an open door nearby and walked into a small, old Sepahardic synagogue where nearly everyone was in Arabic attire. He was called to the altar for the Torah reading and a strange custom that followed: The congregation passed by in a single file, put two fingers to their lips and threw a 'kiss' at him.

While digging a foxhole on the Salerno Beach in Italy, he noticed Hebrew letters on the license plates on the British trucks debarking nearby. He jumped over to the newcomers to discover a startling patch on their shoulders: "Palestine Brigade". Heard his ancient tongue spoken among them and soon learned that these 'blokes' came from prominent Kibutzim, volunteers for the war effort.

Awards/Medals: Purple Heart Medal and all the usual. Achieved rank of private and discharged in 1945.

Has two, blue-eyed, talented daughters and one grandchild.

TIBOR RUBIN, born on June 18, 1929, in Hungary. He was held as civilian prisoner in Germany during WWII for 14 months. He enlisted in the U.S. Army on February 1950. Took basic training in Fort Ord, CA and was stationed in Okinawa with the 29th Inf. Regt.

When the Korean War broke out, he was sent to Korea. He became a member of I Co., 8th Cav. Regt., 1st Cav. Div., and was wounded twice. He could have gone back to the USA, but volunteered back to the front lines.

The 8th Cav. Regt. was hit in Unsan, North Korea by the Chinese Reds at the end of October, 1950. He was wounded and on Nov. 3, 1950, was captured by the Chinese army. He was a prisoner of war for two and one half years. Was sent home in April 1953 in Operation Little Switch with the sick and wounded.

Awards/Medals: Army Occupational Medal of Japan, United Nations Service Medal (Korean), Presidential Unit Citation, Korean Service Medal with nine Campaign Stars, Purple Heart Medal with cluster, National Defense Medal, Combat Infantryman Badge, Good Conduct Medal, five Overseas Service Bars, POW Medal, and was recommended for the Congressional Medal of Honor three times plus the Silver Star while he was in the Korean War.

A member of the following organizations: American Legion, VFW, JWV, 4th Infantry Division Association, life member of the DAV and Military Order of Purple Heart, American Ex-Prisoners of War 1st Cav. Div. and The Korean War Veterans Association (also a charter member).

Married to Yvonne and has two children, Frank and Rosalyn.

He is very proud to say that he became a U.S. citizen in 1953, after he came home from the Korean War and the Korean Prisoner of War Camp from North Korea.

BARRY M. RUBINSTEIN, born May 19, 1950, Newark, NJ. Graduate of Husson College, Bangor, Me. He joined the U.S. Army in September 1968. Served with 102nd Armd. Group, NJNG, West Orange, NJ, Co. C, 2nd Bn. and with the 245th Cbt. Engrs. MNG, Bangor, ME. Basic training was at Camp Drum.

Awarded the Marksmanship Medal. He was discharged September 1974 with the rank Spec. 5. He is life member of Cpl. Louis S. Fercinand Post 309, Irvington, NJ. Today, he is a CPA.

His grandfather, William H. Hasburg, served in WWI in the Army Engineering Corps; his grandmother, Rose Hasburg, served in WWI as a yeoman first class; his father, Irving Rubinstein, served in WWII Air Corps; his Uncle, Maurice Avidan, served in WWI as captain in Medical Corps and his uncle, Samuel Avidan, served in the Army during WWI.

IRVING RUBINSTEIN, born on March 22, 1924, New York City. Entered the USAF March 12, 1943.

Served at Morris Field, Moody Field and Mitchel Field. Discharged on Feb. 8, 1946, with the rank of private first class.

Awards/Medals: American Service Medal and Victory Medal.

He is Retired.

HENRY J. RUDELL, born Henry Rubinfeld in Frankfort En Main, Germany, Jan. 24, 1924. Inducted at Ft. Dix, NJ in February 1943 in the USAAC. Basic training was at St. Petersburg, FL. Attended Radio Schools at Truax Field, WI and Sioux Falls, SD.

Shipped to India via Pacific and Indian Ocean with the 69th AACS Gp., a communications unit attached to the 20th Bomber Cmd. of the 20th AF. This unit provided communications support for the first bombing missions by B-29s against the Japanese Mainland from bases in India. It later received a commendation from the 20th AF for its performance.

Later he served with the AACS in ASSAM, Northeast India. They provided communications support for their Air Transport Supply effort to China via the Himalaya's route (also known as "The Hump"). He was discharged December 1945 with rank of sergeant.

Memorable experience was during the voyage overseas when they encountered a severe storm in the Pacific off the coast of Australia. They suffered some damage and were delayed in getting to their destination, Bombay, India. The Japanese were evidently tracking them closely, because "Tokyo Rose" on one of her broadcasts announced that their ship sank during the storm.

Married and has two sons and two grandchildren.

ELLIOTT RUDENSTEIN, born Nov. 27, 1918, Newark, NJ. He joined the USAAF Nov. 5, 1942, and served with the 8th AF. Graduated from AAC Navigation School, San Marcos, TX, August 1944. Ordered to AAC Bombardier School, Roswell, NM, received his Wings and posted to Avon Park, FL to be integrated into crews and checked out on the B-17 Flying Fortress. By the end of March he was a member of Gothard's crew assigned to the 388th BG, 560th BS.

Arrived in the ETO and accumulated 29 combat missions between late May and the end of July.

Awards/Medals: Distinguished Flying Cross, Air Medal with three OLCs, ETO Ribbon with five Campaign Stars and his favorite one, the "Lucky Bastard Club Certificate" which was given by his group to any of its members who had completed at least 25 combat missions. He was discharged in August 1945 with the rank of 1st lieutenant.

The day before he died, Sept. 7, 1944, he wrote about his group's three-legged mission to the Soviet Union. The target was an oil refinery at Ruhland (on the outskirts of Berlin Metropolitan area). Then on to the Soviet Union, where they were to conduct strategic bombing missions in support of the Allied war effort on the Eastern Front. The Luftwaffe decided otherwise. Lined up wing to wing on the Soviet landing field with no attempt at dispersal, the B-17s made excellent targets for even the most erratic German bombardier or gunner. Rudenstein's plane was one of only six of the whole squadron that was able to be flown back to England.

HOWARD RUDERFER, is a JWV who served as a medic during Operations Desert Shield and Desert Storm with the 2nd Plt. (Airborne), 429th Med. Co. (ambulance).

During the conflict in the Gulf, he had the opportunity to attend some of the moral meetings held by Rabbis: Capt. Ben Romer, Capt. Mitchell Ackerson, Lt. Col. Zalis and lay leader, Maj. Cohen, M.D. at various times and places including the High Holy Days. Not one but two Torah Scrolls miraculously came with the participants.

Due to the forbidden nature of the meetings, there was a sense of solidarity among the soldiers that would be hard to describe. During one trip to a field hospital, two of the doctors stationed there invited me to join them in the lighting of the Hanukcah candles, Majs. Richard Andorsky and Jeff Gardner, M.D., made those brief visits to the 28th a special experience that he won't forget.

Currently he is with the 145th Med. Co. (Hel. Amb.), USAR, Dobbins AFB, LA and is enrolled in Life Chiropractic College.

When he looks back at the time in the Gulf, what he remembers most was the incredible support they got from everyone back home. It was truly amazing.

RAYMOND L. RUDOLPH, born June, 1912. Graduated from Central High School and Ohio State University. Employed as buyer in the diamond department of Rudolph's Jewelers.

Basic training at Camp Blanding and Newport News, VA. Was a medical aid man on troopships. In service for five years.

Died Dec. 30, 1948, at the age of 36.

BERNARD RUNIN, was born in New York City Sept. 10, 1919. Drafted Jan. 22, 1942. Served in the U.S. Army, 196th Engrs. Pontoon Bridge Co.

Stationed in England, Africa, Corsica, Italy and Germany. Discharged as corporal in 1945.

He died in 1979.

MURRAY RUNIN, born Oct. 30, 1929, in New York City. Drafted May 14, 1951, into U.S. Army, 430th CounterIntelligence Corps Sub Det "B." Stationed in Linz, Austria.

Served in USN (Inactive Reserve), 1947-1951. Member of American Legion Post 1768. Discharged April 19, 1953, as staff sergeant.

Married to Dorothy and has a son, daughter, and one granddaughter.

Retired and a life member of Post 42. He is actively involved in veteran and community affairs.

SAM RUNIN, drafted in 1918. Served at Fort McClellan, AL. He was discharged in 1919. He passed away in 1990.

HERB SACHS participated in action Dec. 7, 1941, Pearl Harbor. June 1942, 4-F with hernia and had operation in December 1942. Had 40mm antiaircraft training at Camp Haan, CA in March 1943 and infantry basic at Camp McCoy, WI in June 1944.

On Oct. 12, 1944, left for Europe on the *Queen Mary* with 4,200 service men. About Nov. 12, 1944, infantry replacement with 79th Div. near Strasbourg, France and crossed into Germany Dec. 14, 1944.

First day in Battle of Bulge, Dec. 16, 1944, five of his buddies were hit with shell fire. He went for help and was hit in both legs and knocked unconscious. Was awarded the Bronze Star on March 26, 1951.

MELVIN SACHS, born July 16, 1938, Cleveland, OH. Attended Cleveland schools through first grade and in 1945, his family moved to Miami, FL. In 1947 after a successful year at an afternoon Hebrew school, he was transferred to the newly established Hebrew Academy of Greater Miami.

Following graduation from the academy in 8th Grade, he attended Yeshiva University, High School, College and Rabbinic Seminary. He was ordained in 1962 and served as chaplain following training at Ft. Slocum in New Rochelle, NY and at Ft. Polk, LA, ministering to basic trainees from the South.

Following his chaplaincy stint, he served as rabbi in Oil City, PA; Hebrew School principal, Windsor, Ontario; executive director of the Jewish Education Committee of Atlantic City, NJ; principal of Bet Torah Hebrew School, Mt. Kisco,

NY; executive director of the Jewish Education Committee of Scranton, PA; rabbi in Ohev Zedek, Yonkers; rabbi of Shaare Zedek, Hicksville, Long Island and now as rabbi of the Pelham Parkway Jewish Center in Bronx, NY.

While being a pulpit rabbi in Bronx and Yonkers, he served as chaplain at Rikers Island Prison for the Department of Corrections, city of New York. He is a Hebrew School Associate Principal for the Flatbush Park Jewish Center, Mill Basin, Brooklyn.

A divorced father of five children, four of whom live in Israel. The eldest, who is an attorney in Boston, is the mother of his three-year old grandchild. He is a member of various rabbinic and educational associations and is active in the local Jewish Community Council.

CHARLES SADOWSKY served first as a civilian with the Aircraft Warning Svc., then as an enlisted man and as an officer. He designed and invented for fighter pilots and the intercept problem as follows:

Light ray boresighter, an extremely accurate instrument to harmonize plane guns and sight; fighter pilots gunnery handbook, a short explanation of all relevant information; handbook on assessing, explains how to assess gun camera film; apparent lead demonstrator, visually solves changes in apparent lead; angle off estimator, measures angle off while hand assessing; fixed gunnery trainer, first training device to show true resultant of fighter and enemy planes; the timer, gives instant reading of ground speed; the intercept plotter, instantly gives heading and time required to intercept; range finder, gives accurate data on altitude, horizontal range and azimuth; recognition shutter, helps make recognition fast; two training films, these films won high praise; automatic aperture control for gun sight aiming point movie camera and he made it possible to greatly increase amount of usable footage.

Enlisted April 1942, commissioned from the ranks January 1943 and was relieved from active duty January 1946 with the rank of captain.

Awarded the Legion of Merit, the citation reads, "For exceptionally meritorious conduct in the performing of outstanding services."

ALBERT A. SAFERSTEIN, born in Detroit, MI, Jan. 26, 1916. Enlisted Aug. 15, 1942, and served in 98th Malaria Control Detachment.

Military locations and stations included Leyte, Philippines; Hokkaido, Japan; Ft. Custer, MI; Camp Ellis, IL; Camp Plauche, LA and Hollandia, New Guinea.

Memorable experience was assisting in evacuation of Chinese and Korean slave laborers from Japanese Iron Mine in Hokkaido, Japan in October 1945, and dusting them with powder so as to destroy any fleas that might be carrying the bubonic plague germ.

Awards/Medals: WWII Victory Medal, Army of Occupation note this Heal, Battle Diamh Asiatic-Pacific memorial with two Bronze Battle Stars, Philippine Liberation with one Bronze Battle Star, American Theater and the Good Conduct Medal. Tech. Sgt. Saferstein was discharged Jan. 12, 1946.

Married to June for almost 43 years when she passed away. He has two sons, Ben R. and David F.; daughter, Karen R. Altmeyer; granddaughter, Angi Altmeyer and grandson, Brian Altmeyer.

Retired as administrative supervisor after 36 and a half years with the Detroit Personnel Dept.

LOUIS SAFERSTEIN, born May 14, 1914, Detroit, MI. Enlisted January 1941 in the U.S. Army and served with the 5th Inf. Div. as a medic. His military locations included Camp Custer, Iceland and in Europe.

Pfc. Saferstein was discharged in June 1945. Awards/Medals include the Bronze Star for valor.

He passed away in February 1968 and his wife, Sadye, passed away in September 1986. They had one daughter and two grandchildren.

LEON SAGRANSKY, born Philadelphia, PA, Aug. 14, 1920. Graduated Temple University School of Pharmacy with degree of B.Sc. in pharmacy in May 1942. Enlisted in the USN as pharmacist mate 3/c on Sept. 9, 1942.

Served at USNH, Philadelphia, PA; USNTS Hospital, Sampson, NY; CUB 8, Camp Allen, Norfolk, VA; CUB 11, Camp Allen, Norfolk, VA; Unit G-5, Drew 5, Lido Beach, L.I., NY; Med. FSSC, Camp Lejeune, NC and was ship's pharmacist and medical lab technician aboard USS *Montpelier* (CL-57).

Participated in recapture of Philippine Islands, Borneo, Bataan, Corregidor, Okinawa, battles for Japan and in recovery of allied surviving military personnel at Wakayama, Honshu, Japan. He was honorably discharged as PhM2/c on Nov. 7, 1945.

Memorable experience was in 1945 somewhere in the South Pacific when he was summoned to the quarterdeck and was told someone wanted to see him on another boat in the area. His ship's captain arranged for him to go on his personal boat and he was pleasantly and excitedly surprised to see his cousin, Norman Greenspun, 12,000 miles from home in this forsaken area of the world.

Awards/Medals: Good Conduct, American Campaign, Asiatic-Pacific with one Silver and one Bronze Battle Star, Navy Occupation Service Medal with Asia Clasp, Philippine Liberation Medal with two Bronze Stars, Philippine Presidential Unit Citation and the WWII Victory Medal.

Presently retired from his position as director of pharmacy at a local hospital and is living with his wife, Gertude (married 45 years at this writing), in Margate, NJ. They have two children, David and Joan, and two grandchildren, Erin and Matthew.

He is a member in good standing of the JWV Post 39, a member of VFW Post 220 and a member of the JWV Museum.

SEYMOUR SAIFF (DOC), born June 17, 1918, New Brunswick, NJ. Entered the USCG on Nov. 3, 1943 and was stationed at JSIS, Newark, NJ; Man. 3ch. Training Station; Receiving Station, E.I., NY; COTP, NY; Barracks, New Chambers St., NYC and CG PerSepCtr #3, Brooklyn, NY.

He was discharged Feb. 23, 1946 as S2/c. Saiff is deceased.

JULIEN DAVID SAKS, born June 10, 1906, Anniston, AL. Studied chemistry and earned his BS degree from Georgia Tech, graduating with Highest Honors at age 19. In 1933 he passed the Alabama bar exam and began to practice law. Soon afterwards, he entered the real estate business.

He entered WWII as a 1st lieutenant and became chemical warfare officer of the 12th Armd. Div. In Europe, Col. Saks and the 12th Armd. Div. liberated Colmar and 11 of Dachau's satellite concentration camps near Landsberg, Germany. He and his division spearheaded Gen. Patton's drive to the Rhine River, captured a bridge over the Danube River and played a major role in closing the Brenner Pass.

Awards/Medals: Liberation of Colmar Medal from the French government, Bronze Star, ETO Medal with three Campaign Stars, the Pearl Harbor Medal, Occupation of Germany Medal and the WWII Victory Medal.

After the war, he earned his MBA degree in economic statistics from the University of Alabama. He was master of Anniston Lodge AF&AM, president of Congregation Beth-El in Anniston, adjutant of American Legion Post #26 and a member of Posts #40 and #8. Was Regional Holocaust Chairman of the JWV and awarded a commendation by the Jewish Community Council for work done. Author of many publications, his article *Indescribable Horror* puts down his impressions of the labor details of Concentration Camp Kaufering.

Married Lucy-Jane Watson Aug. 6, 1941. They had daughter and son-in-law, Judith-Ann and Haskell I. Rosenthal, and grandson, Brian Julien. Col. Saks passed away March 16, 1993, at the Hermann Hospital Burn Care Center.

SIDNEY D. SALINS, born in Atlantic City, NJ, Oct. 29, 1922, but reared in Washington, DC since 1932, the oldest of 10 children. His mother, Bessie Salins, was cited during WWII for Jewish mother with most sons (6) in the service during that war.

Completed one year at Strayer Business College and in June 1942 attempted to enlist in the Air Corps for pilot training, but failed physical for "color blindness." Drafted and sworn in at Ft. Myer, VA Nov. 16, 1942, and later sent to Air Corp Basic Training Center, BTC 10, Greensboro, NC in February 1943. Became cadre after basic and was promoted to sergeant in July 1943.

September 1943 passed exam and admitted to Sam Houston State Teacher's College, Army Specialized Training Program leading to commission. After completion of equivalent one year college engineering, program curtailed to supply additional needed troops after invasion of Europe. All student cadets sent to nearest infantry divisions, he to 99th Inf. Div., Camp Maxey, TX February 1944. Trained until division was assigned to combat in September 1944.

Shipped overseas with 99th and served seven months on line as 1st gunner 81mm mortar. Division cited for stand at Elsenborn Ridge during "Battle of the Bulge," and received two Bronze Stars during hostilities. In spite of no time missed from combat, never wounded (fortunately) and after several months in occupation duty, he was discharged Feb. 27, 1946, Ft. Geo. G. Meade, MD as sergeant.

Awards/Medals: Bronze Star for repair of communications under heavy shell fire, WWII Victory Medal, American Campaign Medal with two Bronze Stars, EAME Campaign Medal with three Bronze Service Stars, Good Conduct Medal, Army of Occupation Medal with German Clasp and the Belgian Fourragere.

Married Bette Robinson in July 1943 on last stateside furlough, fathered three children on return and has three grandchildren. Bette passed away in 1979.

Forty year, and still ongoing, career selling automobiles. He is ardent golfer, resident of Silver Spring, MD, former president of 99th Inf. Div. Association and representative at Holocaust Museum dedication as member of 99th, designated "liberator Division."

HERBERT SALOMON, born in Walldorf/Baden, Germany, went 4 years to public school then to Ober Real Schule HS, Heidelberg, dismissed in 1937 because of being Jewish. His parents and half-brother perished in concentration camps. He immigrated to the USA in 1938, lived with his aunt and worked various jobs.

Drafted into the U.S. Army in January 1943, Camp Upton, NY. Sent to Vancouver Barracks, WA, then to Mojave Desert in California. Took ASTP test in Pasadena HS, passed with high marks and sent to the University of Syracuse, NY. Eventually sent to Camp Shelby, MS and the 69th Div., FA Svc. Btry.

Stationed in England, France, Battle of the Bulge and crossed the Remagen Bridge. The 69th advanced to the vicinity of Leipzig and the first link up with the Russian army. After the end of the war in Europe, was sent north to Bremerhaven, 29th Div. where he was member of soccer team and played games against European teams and ETO games in Nice, Germany.

Returned to the States and honorably discharged, March 1946, Ft. Dix, NJ. Went back to his last job before service and eventually got a job in the Postal Transportation Service which later merged with PO. Advanced to supervisor of mail in 1952 and retired in January 1985.

Married twice, lost both wives, 1965 and 1986. From first wife has two daughters, one son and seven grandsons.

JOHN HENRY SALOMON, nee Hans H. Salomon, born in Germany on May 2, 1924. He immigrated to this country in 1939, arrived in New York on Feb. 9, 1939, and has lived in Philadelphia, PA since his arrival. Enlisted in the USAAF on July 23, 1942; went to Radio School in Scott Field, IL and then to Control Tower School in Chanute Field, IL.

Shipped to the Texas Panhandle to the 19th BG, 381st BS and before they embarked for overseas duty, he was shipped out because he was not yet a citizen of the USA. He was sent to Dalhart, TX where the 305th Airdrome Sqdn. was formed and became part of that outfit. Changed his name when he received his citizenship papers in the Northern District Court of Texas in Amarillo, TX on Oct. 15, 1943.

His outfit shipped out Feb. 9, 1944, departing from New Orleans. They stopped in Brisbane, Australia; New Guinea; Leyte Island in the Philippines and Okinawa. Returned to the States on the *Sea Flier* and received honorable discharge Jan. 15, 1946, Indiantown Gap, PA.

He and Edna were married 45 years on Nov. 19, 1995. They have a married son and two grandchildren, Eric and Emily.

ROBERT J. SALOMON, graduated from the USN Academy in 1949. Served aboard USS *Coral Sea* from 1949-1951; USS *Gull* (AMS-16) from 1951-1952 during which time they were involved in minesweeping operations in North Korea.

Most significant assignment was serving aboard USS *Flicker* (AMS-9) as executive officer, 1952-1953 and aboard USS *Courser* (AMS-6) as commanding officer, 1953-1954.

Resigned in 1954, honorary retirement as lieutenant senior grade in 1962.

DAVID SALVER, born April 11, 1932, Havana, Cuba. Came to the States in 1949 and graduated from Benjamin Franklin HS, Manhattan, NY. Attended two years in New York State Tech, Brooklyn. Joined the U.S. Army Nov. 16, 1953, went to basic training at Ft. Dix, NJ, QM Cook School, 69th Div., 275th Inf. Regt. When the division was shipped to Germany, assigned to base patrol and drove 3/4 truck to change guards. Later assigned as a cook in Camp Drum, NY, field cooking for National Guard and Reserve units for the summer.

Honorably discharged Nov. 15, 1955. Awards/Medals: Good Conduct Medal and National Service Medal.

After discharge went into business in New York until 1966, moved to Miami where he had stores until 1990 when he retired.

Memberships: JWV, Post 177; Knights of Pythias, Norman Lodge #195; American Numismatic Association R-47188 since 1962; life member of the National Rifle Association; Free and Accepted Masons Lodge Luz de America #255; Worshipful Master in 1973; Scottish Rite, Valley of Miami, Orient of Florida; Mahi Temple, AAONMS of Miami, FL; Past Masters Unit, Hollywood Shrine Club; Florida Group Harmony Association; and Jewish Defense League, rifle and pistol instructor.

His wife, Anna, was born in Poland in 1931 and escaped to Russia until the end of the war. Immigrated to Cuba then to the States and married in 1954. They have two children and six grandchildren.

PHILIP SAMMETH, born in Brooklyn, NY on September 15. Joined the service in January 1942 and served with 39th Ord., 3rd Army.

Memorable experience was having no blankets, mattresses, floor boards or lights.

Discharged in November 1946 as captain.

He is retired.

EGON W. SAMUELS, born Sept. 22, 1921, in Germany. Graduated Franklin and Marshall College in 1943 and was immediately inducted into the Army. Served in North Africa and Italy in Military Intelligence.

Participated in Arno River Campaign with the 88th Inf. Div. and later the Army of Occupation in Trieste Territory. After serving for 28 years in the USAR, he retired in 1975 with the rank LTC, AUS.

Awards/Medals: WWII Victory Medal, Army Commendation Medal and the Meritorious Service Award.

After WWII he received master's degree from Columbia University. Retired as comptroller of large clothing manufacturer. Taught business administration and economics at University of Baltimore, Evening Division for 17 years.

Married to the late Hanna Samuels and since 1984 to Annette. Has two sons, Jeremiah and Dr. David Samuels. He is member of JWV Post 888.

LEONARD SANDEL, spent nearly three years in the Army (19 months was in the States). He was an Army Air Corps mechanic in September 1942 and recommended for the FA OCS in April 1943. He was sent overseas in September 1944 and stationed in England, France, Belgium, Germany and the former Czechoslovakia before being discharged in March 1946. As a field artillery officer, he took part in the Remagen bridge assault and the first crossing of the Rhine into Czechoslovakia, earning the Bronze Star and two Battle Stars.

His fondest memory is his post-war command as a first lieutenant in Btry. A of the 341st FA BN. It was a segregated battalion of black troops, but the majority of the officers were white. He supervised the installation and functioning of wire and radio communications. He and his troops installed a dial telephone system and had their own message center for an area covering five towns in the southern part of Germany.

Sandel begun writing about his war time experiences with the African-American troops and how they influenced his later activities, the black workers he employed in his Lynbrook metal recycling business from 1952-1975 and the efforts he made as trustee and mayor to improve conditions in Rockville Centre's West End, including helping to establish black-owned stores on Centre Ave.

WILLIAM SANDY, born in Germany on March 6, 1917. Joined the U.S. Army Jan. 29, 1941, and served with the Vet. Detachment, 7th Div., Ft. Ord, CA; Vet. Detachment, 44th Div. (1942) and attended FA School in Ft. Sill, OK.

Participated in Philippine Liberation with 24th Inf. Div., Leyte.

Memorable experience was being the official interpreter of POWs from the African Corps in 1943. He was discharged Dec. 31, 1945, as sergeant third class.

Awards/Medals: American Defense, Philippine Liberation with Bronze Star, Asiatic-Pacific and the WWII Victory Medal.

Married Fay in 1946 and they have two sons, one daughter and four grandchildren. Worked for the USDA as a veterinary meat inspector until 1971 when he retired. Travelers aid SFO, a mason and shriner. He volunteers at the Shriners Temple and rides his own horse in parades.

JOSEPH SANES, born in Chicago, IL on April 13, 1922. Graduated Bowen High in June 1940. Enlisted in USN on Nov. 14, 1941 and received honorable discharge Nov. 13, 1947.

Assigned to USS *Hammann* (DD-412) Dec. 17, 1941, at Norfolk. Arrived Pearl Harbor on Jan. 30, 1942, and operated with Task Force 17 with carrier, *Yorktown*. Fought in the Battles of Coral Sea and Midway. At Midway the *Hammann* and *Yorktown* were both sunk.

August 25, 1942, he was assigned to USS *Gansevoort* (DD-608) and participated in its commissioning. They fought in the Solomons and Aleutian Campaign. Assigned Dec. 15, 1943, to the escort carrier, USS *Kitkun Bay* (CVE-71) and put it in commission. With the *Kitkun* he participated in the Marianas Campaign.

His memorable experiences include removing survivors from the exploding and sinking carrier, *Lexington*, during the Battle of the Coral Sea. At the Battle of Midway, the carrier *Yorktown* was severely damaged and her crew was removed. The next morning the destroyer *Hammann* took on key personnel and returned to the *Yorktown* to save the ship. They tied up alongside the carrier to pump out the flooded areas and to cut away guns to remove a port list. For five hours the work proceeded well and headway was made. Late that afternoon a submarine got through the destroyer screen and torpedoed both the *Hammann* and the *Yorktown* fatally. There was a great loss of lives due to underwater explosions. Sanes was lucky to survive.

Awards/Medals: American Area Medal, American Defense Medal, Asiatic-Pacific with five Battle Stars, Good Conduct and WWII Victory medals.

Married to Libby Shipkowitz and they have a son, a daughter and three grandchildren. He retired from Pipe Fitters Union 597 in 1990 and is a member of JWV Post 407.

JULIAN SARACHEK, born in New Brunswick, NJ on Oct. 24, 1926. Was a college student majoring in pre-med when he entered the USN, January 1945, New York. Basic training was at Great Lakes Naval Station, IL; advanced training, pre-radio at Chicago, IL and further advanced training at the Navy Electronics and Radio School at Gulfport, MS.

Stationed in Washington, DC. RS, Shoemaker, CA and USS *Argonar*/PSC, Lido Beach, NY. Awards/Medals: American Theater Medal and Victory Medal. He was honorably discharged from the service July 19, 1946.

Re-entered College and graduated with a degree in business. Worked his way up the business world and rose to vice president for Bank Leumi.

Married Shirley and they have three lovely children: Joseph, Russell and Maggie, and one handsome grandchild, Jacob.

HENRY SATENSTEIN, born Aug. 26, 1911, Providence, RI. Joined the U.S. Army Infantry in March 1941 and served with the 182nd Inf. Americal Div. Military stations/locations: Solomon Islands, Bismark Archipelago and Bougainville.

Memorable experiences: the battle of Guadalcanal, 1942-1943, he was a machine gunner and mortarman in Co. F, 2nd Bn. and had many casualties. On two occasions he carried to safety members of his outfit who were wounded in action by Japanese gunfire. He witnessed the naval battles off Guadalcanal in which both the U.S. and Japan suffered a heavy loss of ships.

Awards/Medals: Received nine awards including the Bronze Star, Combat Infantry Badge and campaign medals. He was discharged in September 1945 as corporal.

Married Judith Daum and they have two children and two grandchildren. He is retired. His two brothers, Jacob and Leon, also served in WWII.

JACOB SATENSTEIN, born in Providence, RI on July 28, 1913. He joined the USN Seabees in April 1942 and served in the Pacific.

He saw action in the Aleutians (Dutch Harbor), Manus Island, New Guinea and Okinawa. The Navy and Seebees suffered heavy loss of ships, equipment and personnel in the Okinawa typhoon of 1945.

Honorable discharge in 1946 as chief petty officer. He received all the usual campaign medals and citations.

Married Frances Talewsky and they have four children and 10 grandchildren. He passed away in 1990.

LEON N. SATENSTEIN, born in Sherborn, MA on Nov. 17, 1917. He enlisted in the service in 1942, served in the Infantry and Military Intelligence Service in the ETO, France, Germany and Austria.

Served in the MI section of the 42nd Inf. Div. in its drive across southern Germany. Their units liberated Dachau April 29, 1945. He witnessed scene of horror of thousands of bodies of Jewish prisoners killed by starvation.

After V-E Day, he joined CIC unit in Kitzbuhel, Austria rounding up suspected Nazi officials and war criminals. He apprehended Von Salomon, one of conspirators in assassination of Rathenau, the key Jewish official in Weimar Republic. He received honorable discharge in May 1946 as first lieutenant.

A bachelor, his two brothers, Henry and Jacob, served in the Pacific Theater of Operations. Co-Chairman of the Brookline Holocaust Memorial Committee, he is a retired government official.

LEONARD S. SATTLER, born in Newark, NJ and enlisted in the Army at age 17. Received orders to report on his 18th birthday and took infantry basic training at Camp Fannin, TX. Spent several months at Texas A&M in the ASTP, then transferred to C Co., 410th Inf. Regt., 103rd Inf. Div. at Camp Howze, TX.

Departed Camp Howze in early September 1944, landed in Marseilles in early October, worked on the docks unloading munitions and supplies for a few weeks and then entered combat as an infantryman at St. Die (Alsace) as part of the 7th Army. Fought mainly in Alsace and the Black Forest during which time two-thirds of the company were casualties (killed, wounded and captured).

Left combat early February, spent three months in hospitals and in rehabilitation. After V-E Day, worked in Army HQ in Versailles; thence to Hoechst-am-Mein where helped to establish and run a large Red Cross Club; and then in the fall of 1945 went to Berlin and co-founded The American Little Theater of Berlin. In early 1946 he toured Paris, Brussels and cigarette-named camps on the USO circuit and worked in Special Services until discharged in May 1946.

Married to Betzi Morris in 1953, has three children and seven grandchildren. Graduated from Seton Hall University and Georgetown Law School and has practiced law in Arlington, VA for 42 years. Member of JWV, DAV, B'Nai B'Rith, Georgetown Synagogue, Holocaust Museum and International Association of Jewish Lawyers and Judges.

EVE (GRAUBART) SATZ, born in Toronto, Ontario, Canada on March 13, 1922. She joined the WAAC, April 3, 1943 and WAC on Aug. 15, 1943, while in Europe. Served with the 169th Co., WAC Detachment, 1st WAAC Separate Bn., 9th AD.

Military locations/stations: Ft. Devens, GA; Ft. Oglethorpe; Camp Shanks, NY; Earlscolne, England; Chartres, Rheims, France; Namur and Belgium. She qualified for OCS but decided against returning to the States for OCS from England.

Memorable experience was trying to find her brother, Ikie, who was a member of Co. E, 346th Regt., 87th Inf. Div., when the division marched out of Belgium on Dec. 28, 1944, to Germany during the Battle of the Bulge. It was a bitter cold, sunny winter day, but no sign of her brother. Finally a jeep passenger told her he carried Ikie out of a skirmish and that he was in a hospital near Paris. Ikie returned to battle and was killed in March of 1945 without her ever seeing him. Later on, she found cousins in Belgium near Brussels.

Awards/Medals: WAAC Service Medal, ETO Service Ribbon, EAME Service Ribbon with six Bronze Service Stars and Good Conduct Medal. She was discharged Oct. 19, 1945 as private first class.

She has a sister and two brothers in the New Jersey/New York area. She is a widow and raised two young sons while working as a legal secretary and real estate sales person in Hollywood, FL.

She is planning to reactivate her real estate license.

MORRIS SAUNDERS, born in Duluth, MN, Nov. 19, 1921. Turned down by draft, March 1942, due to health problems. After obtaining doctor's letter of fitness for service, he enlisted September 1942 in Air Force. Washed out of Pilot's School, Randolph Field, TX; went to Mechanic School, Gulfport, MS; Special B-17 Mechanic School, Boeing Plant, Seattle, WA and gunnery, Kingman, AZ.

Became aerial engineer, top turret gunner with Lt. Maples crew, 388th BG, 563rd BS (H) based at Knettishall, England in 1944. Joined Lucky Bastard Club, a crack lead crew, August 1944 by doing 35 fast and furious missions. They flew and named original B-17 *Gremlins Hideout* (replica can be seen at Eglin AAB Museum, Pensacola, FL).

Participated in shuttle bomb run, June 21, 1944, to loosen up the Eastern Front in Russia [illegible], supplied the Free French Underground hiding in the Alps by Lake Geneva, Albertville, France; participated in invasions of North-Western France and later Southern France. Bombed deep in Germany, their planes were banged up by flak and fighters, but never knocked out. Crash landed four times due to shot-up planes, landing gears, tires and controls.

Awards/Medals: EAME Ribbon with four Bronze Stars, Air Medal with four clusters, Distinguished Flying Cross, Distinguished Unit Badge and Overseas Bars. Gen. De Gaulle promised them the Croix de Guerre, but the French Government backed out. (60 of 320 did get it).

Returned to the States, became aerial engineer and flying instructor. Discharged as tech sergeant from Lincoln, NE, October 1944.

Married Sylvia and has two sons and one daughter. Belongs to Post #354 JWV, life member of VFW, 8th AFHS, 388th BG Association, Minnesota 8th AF Association and Shrine and Masonic groups. Retired after 40 years in dry cleaning related business.

GEORGE M. SAYPOL, born Sept. 4, 1911, New York City. Was 1st lieutenant in Med. Officer's Reserve, June 22, 1935, called to active duty June 26, 1942, MC AUS. Military stations included 7th Evac. Hosp., Ft. Dix, NJ; Tonga, Fiji, Guadalcanal, Luzon, Bismarck Archipelago, New Britain, Central Pacific and Japan.

Awards/Medals: Philippine Liberation Ribbon with Bronze Star, WWII Victory Medal, Asiatic-Pacific Service Medal with Silver Battle Star and the American Campaign Medal. He was discharged Sept. 1, 1947 as lieutenant colonel, MC AUS.

Retired, his family includes wife, Grace; daughter, Marjorie Schoenberg; son-in-law, Edward Schoenberg; son, David; daughter-in-law, Barbara Saypol; and five grandchildren: Deborah, Leah and Jon Schoenberg and Erica and Austin Saypol.

HAROLD I. SCHAFFER enlisted into the service from Los Angeles in 1944. Was a Seabee in the USN as a pharmacist mate.

Served with the 28th Special Seabees and was stationed in Hawaii, the Philippines and Japan.

Schaffer passed away January 1992.

WILLIAM SCHAEFER, born in Manhattan (Beth Israel Hospital) in August 1925. He and his twin sister were the youngest of 13 children. Their mother died 10 days after giving birth and he and his sister became products of orphan asylums and foster homes. He knows the meaning of survival and at the age of 16 was self-supporting. Schooling was at Philip Schuyler High School in Albany where he was then living with his brother and sister-in-law.

Enlisted in the USMC at age 17 1/2. Basic training was at Parris Island, SC, then Artillery School at Quantico, VA. Unhappy with the idea of being in the back line of combat, he requested transfer to the infantry where the real action was. Request granted, he was assigned to the 4th Mar. Div. in Saipan. From there, he saw plenty of action in Iwo Jima and was wounded (shot in the right shoulder and bayoneted in the leg).

Awards/Medals: Purple Heart, Presidential Unit Citation and Navy Commendation Medal.

Memorable experience was being at the bottom of the hill when they raised the flag at Iwo Jima. After the war he did military police duty at the Navy Prison, Portsmith, NH until his discharge, Dec. 8, 1945.

Attended the New York School of Printing under the GI Bill of Rights. From there, he worked his way up the ladder in [illegible] general foreman of La Salle Industries until he retired at the age of 65.

After four days of retirement, he worked at Alexanders. Currently, he is employed in the Bronx Supreme Court as a court aide. He attributes his success to being intensely interested in any work he is currently involved in.

He joined JWV Post 69 in 1972, immediately became active and received the Rookie of the Year Award. He worked Bingo, held many chairmanships and was active through the years. In 1987-1988, he started up the ladder serving Post 69 as junior, senior and commander for two years. As commander he instituted the David Sokol Hospital Service Award which will be an ongoing award. He led Neuman Goldman Post to great heights during his commandership.

Currently married to a wonderful woman, Diane. Between them they have five sons, one daughter, three daughters-in-law, one son-in-law and six granddaughters.

ELLIOTT SCHECHTER,
born July 15, 1917, Brooklyn, NY. Enlisted in the U.S. Army on Sept. 24, 1940, serving as a private with the 165th FA, 44th Div. at Ft. Dix, NJ. Released Sept. 24, 1941 and joined the Enlisted Reserve.

Recalled shortly after Pearl Harbor and became a corporal. Was sent to OCS, 6th Co. TD School and commissioned Nov. 19, 1942. Joined the 607th TD BN and trained at Camp San Luis Obispo, Desert Training Ctr. in the Mojave Desert and at Camp Cooke, CA.

Battalion shipped overseas and landed in England April 21, 1944. They hit Utah Beach D-day plus 11 (June 17, 1944). They landed as part of 90th Div., but supported the 82nd Abn., 6th Cav. Gp., 9th Inf. Div., then rejoined the 90th Div. all the way to the Saarbrücken area. When the Battle of the Bulge broke out, they rushed to Bastogne to help out and joined the 87th Div. War ended at the Czechoslovakia border.

Awards/Medals: American Theater Campaign Ribbon, American Defense Service Medal, WWII Victory Medal, EAME Theater Campaign Ribbon with five Battle Stars and the Bronze Star. He was discharged Dec. 15, 1945 as 1st lieutenant.

He is a retired builder.

HARRY Z. SCHECTMAN,
born on the East Side of Manhattan in New York City. He is a graduate of City College of New York, of Yeshiva University Rabbinic School, a DD from the Jewish Theological Seminary, a Master of Arts in education from Arizona State University and has held many rabbinic positions in various synagogues over the country.

Before overseas duty, he was Jewish Chaplain at Camp Crowder, MO for two years. In April 1945 he was the Jewish Chaplain attached to 10th Army HQ in the invasion of Okinawa. Completed his military duty in May 1946.

After more than 50 years in the rabbinate, he retired and is residing in Phoenix, AZ, where he is chaplain of JWV Post #194 and of the Arizona-Nevada Dept.

Married to Ruth, a daughter of a famous orthodox rabbi in NYC. They have two daughters, one son (a rabbi), six grandchildren (one married to a rabbi) and four great-grandchildren.

HAROLD SCHEER,
born Aug. 26, 1917, Brooklyn, NY. Graduated high school, 1935 and entered USAF March 7, 1941. Military stations/locations: Infantry Staff Sergeant, Mineral Wells, TX; AF Cadet, Navigation, San Marcos, TX, 1943. Navigated Atlantic through Iceland to Great Britain and joined the 8th AF at Molesworth, England.

Flew combat missions until shot down by German fighters over Germany in November 1944. Spent seven months as POW, Stalag Luft #1, Barth, Germany until freed by Russian Infantry in May 1945.

Memorable experiences: marching in review at Ft. Sam Houston as cadet colonial and giving the salute; dogfighting between their B-17 and German fighters; being shot down over Hamburg, Germany; and meeting and sitting next to Gen. Eisenhower at Camp Lucky Strike in France.

Discharged to Ready Reserve December 1945 and served in White Plains, NY until November 1969 when placed in Retired Reserve. Received Air Medal, Purple Heart, American and European Theater and War over Germany POW Medal.

Married Alice Scheer and has three sons: Steven, Andrew and Dana; three granddaughters and four grandsons.

Retired builder and general contractor, he lives in Pompano Beach, FL and is active as commissioner for the Pompano Beach Community Redevelopment Agency.

MILTON R. SCHEIBER,
born Sept. 11, 1916, in NYC. Enlisted September 1938 in NYNG, 244th Regt. and mustered into active duty August 1940. Military stations/locations included Camp Pendleton, VA; Carolina Maneuvers, Pearl Harbor, OCS at Ft. Monroe, VA and Camp Davis, NC, graduating April 1942 as 2nd lieutenant.

Posted to 72nd Regt. of the Atlantic Bde., Panama Canal Dept.; Ft. Amador, Panama as head of Gunnery Dept. in Officers Advanced Artillery School; assigned senior artillery instructor, Camp Davis, NC; assigned to 14th AAA Cmd., South Pacific Area, New Guinea and Philippines. Rotated to States and Camp Davis two weeks before atomic bomb was dropped. Assigned to Army Reserve as captain.

Graduated from Command and General Staff College, Ft. Leavenworth, KS, 1962, as lieutenant colonel and retired in 1965 as colonel.

Awards/Medals: Bronze Star Medal, Meritorious Service, American Theater, American Defense, Asiatic Theater with four Battle Stars, Philippine Liberation, Philippine Unit Citation, Philippine Conspicuous Service, New York State Conspicuous Service and Presidential Unit Citation.

Married Edith Sept. 7, 1940; children: Ruth, Stephen and Carol; grandchildren: Jennifer, Sarah, Rachel, Eva, David, Emily and Jacob.

Belongs to JWV, VFW, ROA, TROA, Albany's Temple Israel, Albany's Jewish Community Center.

ERNEST G. SCHEIN,
born in NYC, NY, March 27, 1915. Entered the Army on April 2, 1942, trained at CRTC Ft. Riley, KS and later joined the 102nd Mech. Cav., Troop C, 2nd Sqdn. at Ft. Jackson, SC. On Sept. 26, 1942, set sail aboard the Dutch steamer *Dempo*.

In 1943 during transport in black out, truck was struck head-on by an armored vehicle, and he was hospitalized in Oxford, England. After release transferred to the 123rd Station Hosp. as medical technician and assigned to special missions in England, France and Belgium.

On July 1, 1945, was attached, unassigned to the flagship of the Merchant Fleet en route to the Philippine Islands via Panama Canal. After 49 days at sea, joined the 123rd Station Hosp. in San Fernando, P.I. Several months later during a typhoon in the South China Sea, lost all his belongings while climbing a Higgins Ladder to board a ship bound for Sasebo, Japan.

Discharged Dec. 3, 1945, Ft. Dix, NJ as Tech 5. Awards/Medals: Good Conduct Medal, WWII Victory Medal, Rhineland Battle Star, ETO Medal and Asiatic-Pacific Medal.

He and wife, Rose, had two daughters, Janice (deceased) and Ronnie. Retired, he is member of JWV Post 651.

ANDRE SCHEINMANN,
born in Munich, Jan. 28, 1915. Enlisted in the service in 1939 and served in the Infantry Intelligence. Military locations included Lille, Rennes and Paris, France.

Memorable Experiences: action in Belgium (1940) where he was wounded, POW evasion. re-enlistment, Free French and trip to England.

Awards/Medals: Legion of Honor, three Croix de Guerre and others. He was discharged in 1946 and attained the rank of lieutenant colonel.

He is retired and a widower.

JACK SHANKER SCHENK,
born Feb. 27, 1920, Chicago, IL. Joined the USAAF on Jan. 12, 1944, and participated in the Japan Air Offensive, China Campaign and India Burma Campaign.

Memorable Experiences: Being wounded in neck, 13,000 feet in the air, while on a raid over the Straits of Rangoon. Ended up in a hospital in Calcutta, India. The remainder of crew went on to forward base in Pacific and were never heard from again.

Awards/Medals: Purple Heart, Asiatic-Pacific Ribbon and Good Conduct Medal. Discharged Oct. 18, 1945, as sergeant.

Married Florence Yager Sept. 20, 1944, and they have two sons, a daughter and five grandchildren. He is retired.

JEROME N. SCHIFF,
born Nov. 8, 1920, Pittsburgh, PA. Graduated Carnegie Tech in 1943 with a BS in printing management. Inducted into the Army May 1943 and assigned to the 949th Topographical Engineers as a photolithographer at Peterson Field, CO. Sent to Camp Maxey, TX in December 1944 for infantry training.

Was shipped to the European Theater in March 1945 as a rifleman and assigned to Gen. Simpson's 16th Corps, 9th Army. Participated in the Battle of the Ruhr and at war's end was reassigned to 667th Topographical Engrs. of Patton's 3rd Army in Pilsen, Czechoslovakia. In July he returned to Munich as Army of Occupation. There he located his mother's cousin, a physician from Lithuania, who survived the death camp, Dachau, and he helped to bring him to the States. The rest of his family, wife and child, perished. While in Paris, he also located other relatives who survived.

In September 1945, he attended Leicester Art & Tech in England for a 4-month printing course. He was honorably discharged in April 1946 as private first class.

Awards/Medals: American Campaign Medal, WWII Victory Medal, EAME Campaign Medal with one Battle Star.

Married Dorothy in 1947; they have three children: Mark, Wendy and Robert, and three grandchildren: Kevin, Aaron and Michael. He retired in 1989 after 44 years in middle management in the printing industry. He is a member of JWV Post 718.

S. GARY SCHILLER,
born Jan. 26, 1917, Brooklyn, NY. Entered military service on Dec. 23, 1943, and completed infantry basic training at Camp Blanding, FL. Served overseas with Co. A, 36th Armd. Inf. Regt., 3rd Armd. Div. Wounded in the hedgerows of Normandy at Mortain, France on Aug. 10, 1944.

Recipient of the Bronze Star Medal, Purple Heart Medal, Combat Infantry Badge, New York State Conspicuous Service Cross with cluster, etc.

He is 47-year member of the JWV of the USA and served as post commander #788, Brooklyn, NY. National Deputy Liaison to the Military Order of the Purple Heart (MOPH), National Deputy Liaison to the Boy Scouts of America (BSA), and presently Commander of Post #504, Queens, NY. Department Commander of MOPH, 1981-1982. Recipient of 7,500 Hour Certificate from St. Albans Extended Care Center for service to the wounded and hospitalized veterans.

Was United Nations Representative for the World Veterans Federation, a 63-year member and international representative for the Boy Scouts of America, he was called "Mr. Hospitality." Was recipient of the Silver Beaver, Silver Antelope Awards, European Recognition Regional Scout Medal and world scouting's highest award, The Bronze Wolf Award

A community mayor of New York State; Master Mason; Shriner and Sojourner; president, Board of Visitors, New York State Veterans Home, Oxford, NY, Honorary member, Honor Legion, New York Police Dept.; honorary member, Honor Legion, New York Fire Dept.; honorary member, New York State Fire Chiefs.

Recipient of Freedoms Foundation Valley Forge Honor Certificate for "Excellence In Individual Achievement." He greeted over 26 flights of returning veterans from Desert Storm. He is member of the American Order of the French Croix de Guerre.

He and his wife, Teddi, have three sons: Justin, Michael and Neil.

GUNTHER GEORGE SCHLOSS, born Feb. 23, 1915, in Germany. Arrived in the USA in 1938 and worked as foreman in an ice cream factory. Drafted into the Army service in March 1941 for one year. America declared war, therefore his service lasted four more years.

Inducted in New York March 1941, he came to Ft. Dix, NJ, then to Ft. Jackson, SC to the 13th Inf., 8th Div. HQ as telephone operator. Became a citizen of the USA in Columbia, SC the same year.

After training in South Carolina, Tennessee and Georgia, he was sent to Ft. Leonard Wood, MO and trained as radio operator with the 8th Sig. Corps. Was sent to Camp Laguna, AZ to help in building comm. facilities. Transferred to Ft. Ord, CA to train for Signal Intelligence.

In January 1944 went to England for Morse Code and Intelligence practice with joint 3251st Sig. Svc. Co., 7th Corps. Was in on the invasion, D-day and landed about 9:00 a.m. in France. His job was to listen to German radio transmissions in either voice or code, working with the 7th Corps HQ.

As interceptor operator went to Cherbourgh through France into Belgium, Hurtgen Forest to Germany, over the Rhein and met the Russians on Elbe River. At the end of war, he was stationed in Leipzig, Germany taking part in Army trials as interpreter and was also involved in moving scientists from Russia into American zones.

Back to the States, October 1945, and discharged as tech 4. Received the American Defense Service Medal, EAME Medal and the Good Conduct Medal.

Married in 1945 to Bertha and has daughter, Peggy Gurock, and son, Rabbi Norman Schloss. Each has four children. A member for many years of JWV Post 209 in Jackson Heights, NY.

MILTON J. SCHLOSS, enlisted as private in Voc. Program on May 27, 1942 at the age of 29. Commissioned 2nd lieutenant, Dec. 9, 1942, and assigned as combat intelligence officer in the XIX Tactical Air Cmd. advance.

Overseas duty from February 1944 to August 1945. Awarded six Battle Stars and Bronze Star in European Theater. Landed in Normandy June 22, 1944 and ended war in Czechoslovakia in May 1945.

He received honorable discharge on Nov. 14, 1945 as captain.

ALBERT SCHLOSSBERG, born Boston, MA, Feb. 22, 1919. Entered the USN April 1944, 1st Naval Air Trng. Cmd., Jacksonville, FL and served at USN Air Station, Jacksonville Municipal Airport and NAS, JAX in Florida.

Participated in the establishment of USN PB4Y training and operations base at USN JAX MUNI which ended threat and damage to ships by German U boats operating in Atlantic Ocean off coast of Florida. In less than one year the unit was fully operative and cleared the waters of German U boats.

He is the author of a weekly column that appears in newspapers across the U.S. An activist in veterans affairs since his discharge in 1946, he was honored by election to JWV Post, District Council, department and regional commandership. In 1970 he was elected National Commander of the JWV of the USA. He is vice president and treasurer of Schlossberg-Solomon Memorial Chapel, Canton, MA.

Married Eleanor Smith and has two children, Bara Post and Bruce, and five grandchildren: Leslie and Adam Post and Benay, Brian and Jonathan Schlossberg.

SAMUEL H. SCHMERLER, born July 10, 1923 in the Bronx. Joined the service Oct. 29, 1942, Ft. Devens, MA. Served in the USAAC as radio operator and machine gunner B-26 with the 9th AF and 8th AF. He flew 50 combat missions in Air Offensive Europe, Normandy, Northern France and Rhineland. Was shot down Aug. 10, 1944, his 38th mission.

Awards include the Purple Heart, Air Medal with eight OLCs, Distinguished Unit Badge, EAME Theater Medal and the Distinguished Flying Cross is pending. He was discharged July 20, 1945 as tech sergeant.

Flew two mission on D-day, June 6, 1944, and was on next to last plane to bomb Utah Beach five minutes before assault troops hit the beach. Their group was picked by Gen. Bradley because of group bombing accuracy.

He and wife, Thelma, have two children, Barry and Susan, and two grandchildren. Retired, he does volunteer work at St. Albans ECC.

MARTIN KURLAND SCHNALL, born Jan. 31, 1931, Brooklyn, NY, raised in Bronx, NY and lived in Deer Park, NY for 30 years. Educated at New York University and Queens College. Drafted with his twin brother, Leonard, and cousin, Sol Reich, he served in the U.S. Army from October 1951-November 1953 in the Ordnance Corps as a track vehicle repairman with the 192nd Ord. Bn. while in Korea. Spent 16 months at Yong Dong Po, Taegu and Pusan in Korea.

Stationed at Camp Kilmer, NJ for basic training, then to Aberdeen Proving Grounds, MD, before shipping out from Ft. Lawton, WA. After brief stay in Yokohama, Japan, he left from Sasebo, Japan for Korea.

Awards/Medals: Republic of Korea Presidential Unit Citation Badge, Korean Service Medal with three Bronze Stars, National Defense Service Medal and the United Nations Service Medal.

Contracted Sarcoma of thigh, hip and lungs 30 years later from Dyoxin injections while stationed at APG, MD. They were used as guinea pigs to develop "Agent Orange" Dyoxin which was later used in Vietnam as the finished product. He is requesting disability, but difficult to get due to fire in St. Louis where his records were destroyed.

Belongs to the American Legion Post 1634, Korean War Veterans (Western Suffolk Branch) and JWV of USA Post 336.

Worked 35 years for the U.S. Postal Service, retiring in July 1985. Presently fighting for issuance of U.S. Postage Stamp commemorating the 100th Anniversary of the JWV of U.S. (1896-1996).

Married Lillian while in basic training and raised four children. Widowed in 1988 after 37 years of marriage, he married Margaret in 1990 and lives in Centereach, NY

HAROLD SCHNEIDERMAN, born June 23, 1919, Revere, MA. Graduated from Middlesex University in June 1942 and enlisted in the USN in September 1942. Basic was at NTS, then transferred to Newport Naval Hospital.

Duty at the following: Seabees at Davisville, RI; Deep Sea Divers, Quonset Point, RI; NAS, Brunswick, ME; Fleet Marines, Stockton, CA; Chelsea Naval Hosp., Chelsea, MA; and the Fargo Building, Boston.

He received honorable discharge September 1944. A charter member of JWV Mattapan Post 302, Randolph, MA.

Married Eva Monsein March 22, 1942, and has three children: Paul, Lois and Stuart, and six grandchildren. Entered active practice of podiatric medicine and foot surgery in Norwood and Sharon November 1944. Continuing education at Temple University, PA; Civic Hospital, Detroit; Pennsylvania College of Podiatric Medicine, earning additional degrees, Doctor of Surgical Chiropody and Doctor of Podiatric Medicine.

Retired in 1979 and has traveled 77,000 miles in his motorhome. Computer literate and Mended Hearts Certified Accredited hospital volunteers.

JESHAIA SCHNITZER, born Jan. 25, 1918, Philadelphia, PA. Enlisted Oct. 22, 1944, and served as Jewish Chaplain in U.S. Army. Stationed at Camp Pickett, Camp Lee, Greenland, Hawaii and Pusan and Seoul in Korea.

Most memorable experience was dropping Pesach supplies by parachute to isolated Jewish soldiers in Greenland. He was discharged in March 1947 as captain.

Attended Columbia Univ., Teachers College, May 1953 Ed.D; Columbia Univ., School of Social Work, May 1949, MS; Jewish Institute of Religion, Hebrew Union College, 1943, Rabbi; University of Delaware, September 1940, BA.

Served as rabbi, coordinator of religious services and programming for Jewish Center and is a licensed New Jersey marriage counselor since 1969. Wrote promotional literature, news releases, newspaper articles, monthly bulletin columns and magazine articles for Jewish and professional magazines. Was consultant and promoter for various committees and programs. He was member, chairman, president of numerous professional and Jewish affiliations. In 1985 he was the coordinator of "The Rabbinic Assembly National Care Line."

Received an award for Meritorious Services, Montclair B'nai Brith in 1955, the Samuel W. and Rose Hurowitz Award in 1976 and the Saul Schwarz Distinguished Service Award in 1990.

Married Hilde Maier in 1947, has two children, Rabbi Jonathan Aaron and Lisa Judith Plavin. At age 75 he still does a full days work as marriage and family therapist.

NORMAN SCHNITZER, born Philadelphia, PA on Dec. 24, 1928. Enlisted November 1951 in the USAF and served as dental lab tech.

Duty stations: Sampson AFB, NY; James Connally AFB, TX; Gunter AFB, AL; Elmendorf AFB, AK; Wright-Patterson AFB, OH; McGuire AFB, NJ.

While stationed at the base hospital in Alaska, a fire broke out and he was involved in the evacuation of over 200 patients. They received a letter of commendation from the Surgeon General of the USAF.

Awards/Medals: Good Conduct Medal with three knots, American Defense Service Medal and the USAF Longevity Ribbon. He was honorably discharged with the rank of staff sergeant in November 1961.

Married with four sons and seven grandchildren. He is semi-retired and very active with Fegelson-Young-Feinberg Post 697. Currently post commander and department Pennsylvania adjutant.

LOUIS SCHNUR, born Warsaw, Poland, Oct. 9, 1919. Entered the U.S. Army May 2, 1941 and trained at Camp Blanding, FL and Camp Shelby, MS. Landed Oran, North Africa, Aug. 2, 1943. Left Tunis/Bezerte for Italian invasion and fought through most of Italian Campaign.

Attached to the 35th FA Group which supported the 3rd, 45th and 36th Divs. They fought at the Monte Casino Area, made the invasion of Anzio Beachhead, entered Rome June 4, 1944, went north about 80 miles to Civitavecchio and pulled out to Naples for invasion of Southern France.

Landed Sept. 2, 1944, in Nice-Toulon-Marseilles area. In combat through France, Alsace-Lorraine and Germany. Numerous experiences were encountered. On Anzio Beach, his bunker was hit, and he was totally buried by debris. His outfit left their positions. Unconscious until the following day, he dug himself out, caught up with his outfit and learned they had believed he was dead and MIA.

After taking Rome, his outfit kept moving with the 6th Corps. While riding on the main radio truck, the first news of the Normandy Invasion was broadcast and he was privileged to shout the news to infantrymen walking on both sides of the highway. They were jubilant, throwing things in the air and happy that they finally had a second front and things looked better for them.

Awards/Medals: American Defense Service Medal, American Service Medal, EAME Service Medal with five Battle Stars (Central Europe, Naples-Foggia, Rome-Arno, Southern France and Germany), Good Conduct Medal and the Purple Heart.

Was in the Army of Occupation, stationed near Munich, Germany close to Dachau Concentration Camp. The Germans in the area denied knowing about the camp. They forced the Germans to go into Dachau to clean up.

Schnur tried to learn of relatives from Warsaw (where he was born) and heard horrible stories. One inmate who had actually known his father, who was a baker when they lived there, told him some bakery owners were considered leaders of the Warsaw Ghetto Uprising and had been shot by the Germans.

Married to Jean and has two sons, Michael and Marvin; daughter, Rhonda; and granddaughter, Andrea. He had a family bakery business and was a builder-developer of apartment buildings in New York City. Member of the JWV, Van Cortlandt-Maccabean Post 107, Bronx, NY.

PHILIP SCHOENBERG, born in New York City, July 22, 1913. He graduated from St. Louis University, School of Dentistry with degree of DDS. Inducted in the USAF June 9, 1942 as 1st lieutenant. First base was Brookley Field, Mobile, AL. From there, he was assigned to Albuquerque Air Depot Training Station, NM. He performed his dental duties on soldiers in groups going overseas.

On Jan. 20, 1943, he was promoted in rank to captain. He was assigned to a few bases doing dental duties. He finally was assigned to Ria Hata in Panama, where he performed his dental duties until the end of the war.

He was honorably discharged March 20, 1946. He received the American Campaign Medal and the WWII Victory Medal.

After the war, he practiced dentistry in Bronx, NY from 1946 to 1968 and from 1968 to 1985 in Long Beach, NY.

Married to Tillie and has two children, Ronald and Carole, and three grandchildren: Justin, Carly and Zachary. Ronald is an assistant district attorney, Carly is a freshman in college and Carole works for a congressman.

HYMAN SCHOENFELD, born Grodno, Poland in June 1906. Was brought up on the lower east side and Harlem area in New York City and at a early age began working in the sign industry. In the late 30s, when Mussolini and Hitler were proudly displayed on some of his neighbors wall, he began to think of what contribution he would make if drafted.

He enlisted Sept. 4, 1940, at the famous 39 Whitehall St. and served with the 3rd Engrs. It just so happened that the colonel of the outfit was looking for a man of Schoenfeld's talents to do some camouflage work. After the completion of the project, the colonel personally told him if he wanted a position in the Engineers office (downtown Honolulu) he would recommend him. He moved on to the engineers office, but was not able to pursue camouflage.

His memorable experience was flying in a Douglas observation aircraft over Schofield Barracks and Pearl Harbor to observe prior to attack. He was discharged June 4, 1941 as private first class.

Retired, he is a member of Morris M. Karpf Post 503 where he does volunteer work.

HAROLD SCHOENHOLTZ, born in Bronx, NY, Aug. 6, 1918. Received a BS from CCNY in 1938 and an MS in chemistry from New York University in 1941. Did chemical warfare research in 1942 at Wesleyan University in Connecticut under the National Defense Research Committee.

Entered the service hoping to get into chemical warfare, but was assigned to the Air Force and became a radio operator gunner on B-25s. Went overseas to Italy November 1944 as part of the 12th AF, 340th BG, 489th BS, flying out of Corsica. Shot down over Northern Italy Feb. 25, 1945, on his 26th mission and was a POW in Germany until liberated by Patton's 4th Armd. Div. April 29, 1945. He was discharged Oct. 12, 1945, as staff sergeant.

Married Evelyn Schneyer of Philadelphia June 22, 1947, and raised three children: Sharon (a doctor in New York) has plans in the near future for engagement to Dr. Lawrence Hanau. Andy (a lawyer in Washington, DC) is married to Janice (a physical therapist), they reside in Bethesda, MD and have three wonderful sons: Ari, David and Noah. Kermit is an economist, currently in London, married to Elvira (also a lawyer). He is extremely proud of all of them.

After 40 years in the industrial paint field, he is retired and lives in Valley Stream, NY. Evelyn is a fine painter. She was a social worker with a BS in community and human services. Both are temple oriented and are past VP's. Evelyn is a life member of Hadassah. He is with JWV Post 770 and is past president of the Five Towns Hebrew High School Board of Directors.

MORRIS SCHORR, joined the U.S. Army on April 16, 1943, and was discharged with the rank of staff sergeant on Oct. 14, 1945. He served in the 440th Troop Carrier Group, 98th Sqdn. as a radio operator and mechanic on a C-47.

He saw considerable active air service and completed 70 missions over Europe. He received several citations, decorations and awards among which was the Good Conduct Medal, ETO Medal, American Theater of Defense Medal, Presidential Citation, Air Medal and Oak Leaf Cluster and the Victory Medal.

Also received seven Battle Stars for Normandy, Ardennes, Northern France, Rhineland, Rome-Arno, Southern France and Central Europe campaigns. He participated in the airborne invasion over France on D-day. *Submitted by Max Sigal.*

DAVID SCHREIER, born in Jersey City, NJ, Feb. 10, 1924. Served in the U.S. Army with the 314th Ord. Bn. and was stationed at Camp McCoy, WI and in the ETO.

Participated in action in Normandy, Northern France, Ardennes, Rhineland and Central Europe. His memorable experience was assisted in welding hedgerow cutters on tanks in Normandy.

Awards/Medals: ETO, Good Conduct, Occupation and WWII Victory Medal. He was discharged Dec. 6, 1944, as tech sergeant.

Married and has a daughter and three grandchildren. He is a retired sewing machine mechanic.

GEORGE SCHRENZEL, born about 1910 and died March 12, 1945. He may have been the only lawyer from Essex County, NJ to be killed in action.

Enlisted early in the war and was a 2nd lieutenant in the Coast Artillery. Some time in 1944, the Coast Artillery was downgraded and he transferred to the infantry.

Was sent to Europe and went straight to France where he was killed by a sniper near the Remagen Bridge.

He had an excellent record as a lawyer and before that he played football on the South Side High School (Newark, NJ) team, and, until his enlistment in the Army, played baseball every Sunday morning with a group of Jewish lawyers and professionals at Cameron Field, South Orange, NJ.

ISRAEL R. SCHULMAN, born Sept. 6, 1922, in New York City. Inducted Feb. 8, 1943 and served with 603rd AAA as a radar operator until disbanded in June 1944. Received five weeks of basic infantry training at Salinas, KS and became a replacement rifleman for the 29th Div., Co. C., 115th Regt., 1st Bn.

Fought in the towns of Kreuzrath, Birgden and Hatterath in Germany. Participated in the successful daring revenge raid on Schierwaldenrath in order to destroy this village because the Germans wiped out Co. K. Wounded in Baesweiler on Nov. 16, 1944, during a major assault.

Awards/Decorations: Combat Infantry Badge, Purple Heart, Bronze Star, EAME, WWII Victory, Germany Army of Occupation, Good Conduct Medal, and the New York State Conspicuous Service Cross. He was discharged from the service on Feb. 12, 1946.

Married Helen Bandel from Brooklyn, NY on Feb. 12, 1949, and has two children, Ilene and Harris, and two grandchildren, Roxanne and Alex. He retired from the USPS, Tampa, FL, April 20, 1990.

MILFORD SCHULMAN, born 1920 in New Jersey. Entered the service in 1943 as USAAF cadet and became a B-17 navigator/bombardier. Based with 463rd BG in Foggia, Italy, he flew 50 missions over Northern Italy, Southern Germany, Yugoslavia and Austria.

Most memorable experience was lone wolf mission at night. Their plane was sent to Germany to bomb a factory. They dropped bombs on target, dodged searchlights and ack-ack, they lost an engine over the Adriatic Sea on their return and he helped to navigate plane back to home base.

Overseas he enjoyed Jewish services conducted by a Jewish Air Force sergeant who was later replaced by a Protestant chaplain who did his best to provide an acceptable service.

Awards/Medals: Air Medal with three OLCs, Distinguished Flying Cross, WWII Victory Medal, ETO Medal with three Battle Stars and the Good Conduct Medal. Received honorable discharge with rank of 1st lieutenant.

Retired from the retail business, he enjoys flying radio controlled models.

SIDNEY G. SCHULMAN, born in New Rochelle, NY. Enlisted in the U.S. Army in 1943, served in the 9th Inf. Div. and was stationed in France, Belgium and Germany. He participated in five major engagements.

After two and a half years service, he was discharged. Awards/Medals: Purple Heart, Bronze Star, Combat Infantry Badge and five Battle Stars.

His family consists of wife, Ethel, son, daughter, parents and three brothers. He passed away June 15, 1948.

ALFRED A. SCHULTZ, born Oct. 6, 1916, Jersey City, NJ. Enlisted Oct. 2, 1942, in the USAF; served with the 434th Troop Carrier, 74th Sqdn. and stationed in Ft. Wayne; Alliance, NE; ETO; England; France; and Germany.

Participated in action in Normandy (D-day); Holland, Arnheim; Bastogne; Wesel, Germany; and Southern France.

Awards include the Presidential Unit Citation, six Battle Stars and Good Conduct Medal. He was discharged Nov. 15, 1946, as sergeant.

He and three brothers were all in the Army, one brother was wounded. Schultz is retired.

MURRAY SCHULTZ, born Jan. 8, 1924, New York City. Enlisted October 1942 in the USAAC and served with the 43rd BG, 63rd BS, 5th AF as bombardier/navigator. Stations included Nashville, TN, Santa Ana, CA; Los Vegas and Carlsbad, NM; March Field, CA; New Guinea; Australia and the Philippines.

Participated in 37 missions in the South Pacific, Philippines, China Sea and Okinawa with the 63rd Sqdn. (Pathfinder Sqdn.). Memorable experiences include being the first land based bomber to hit the Philippines; harassment missions; and invasion of the Philippines and Okinawa.

Awards/Medals: Air Medal with three OLCs, Distinguished Flying Cross and various squadron citations and medals. He was discharged in January 1946 as 1st lieutenant.

Married Elaine in 1955 and has three sons: David, Jonathan and Joshua, and daughter-in-law, Chris. He is a real estate and business broker and a member of Allentown JWV.

PAUL SCHULTZ, born in Jersey City on Sept. 3, 1923. Graduated high school January 1942 and drafted into the U.S. Army February 1943. Spent a year and a half with the tank destroyers at Camp Hood, TX and transferred to Camp Maxie, TX for infantry training when the Battle of the Bulge took place.

Sent overseas to Europe and joined the 100th Div. as a replacement. Went into combat at the Maginot Line in Alsace Lorraine where he was wounded. A memorable experience was when his brother visited him in the hospital in Nancy, France.

Awards/Medals: Purple Heart, Combat Infantry Badge, Presidential Citation, Bronze Star, and European Operations Ribbon. He was discharged in February 1946 as corporal.

Attended Rutgers University under the GI Bill. He has two daughters and four grandchildren; his wife passed away 2 years ago. He is retired.

BARRY H. SCHUMAN, born in Chicago, IL, Feb. 27, 1949, the son of Morton Schuman. Graduated from Birmingham High School in 1967 and joined the U.S. Army, 1969-1971. He served with the 1st Air Cav. Div. in Vietnam for 13 months, achieving the rank of specialist 4th class.

Awarded the Army Commendation Medal with OLC "exceptionally meritorious achievement in support of the U.S. objectives in the counterinsurgency effort in the Republic of Vietnam."

Employed by the federal government and has worked over 18 years at the Veterans administration hospital in Westwood, CA as a supervisor in the Transportation Department. Presently resides in Van Nuys, CA.

His hobbies are railroading, photography and travel. He is a serious railroad buff and has traveled thousands of miles on the train, seeking out the trains making their last trip before being taken out of service. He is an active member of the Pacific Railroad Society.

ELLIS SCHUMAN, born May 25, 1931, Chicago, IL, a brother to Morton Schuman. Served in the U.S. Army from 1956-1958, attaining the rank of corporal. He served with the 34th Inf. Regt., 1st Cav. Div., 7th Cav. Div. in Korea for 14 months.

Presently resides in San Francisco, CA. Retired from the Chicago Public School District in 1981. He received the bachelor of music degree from Chicago Musical College of Roosevelt University and the master of fine arts degree from Ohio University.

He has served on the board of directors of the American Harp Society and was vice president of the Bay Area Chapter. His musical compositions and arrangements have been published and are performed widely. He is very active in the music teaching profession: teaching harp, piano and other string instruments.

MORTON SCHUMAN, born May 29, 1923, Chicago, IL, a brother to Ellis Schuman and father of Barry Schuman. Graduated from Crane Tech High School, Chicago, IL in February 1942. and served in the USN Seabees from 1942-1945. Served with the 84th USN Constr. Bn. for 30 months in the South Pacific, Australia, New Guinea, Dutch East Indies and the Philippines.

After discharge from military service, Schuman's wife Florence, daughter Susan and son Barry, moved to California and settled in Van Nuys for 41 years. In 1990 he moved with his wife to Cathedral City, their present location.

He spent most of his life in the automotive repair field and is a graduate of General Motors Training Center. After selling his interest in an auto repair shop, to his partner, he joined the Los Angeles City Fire Dept. and retired from the department in 1985.

An active fire buff, he is a member of the Box 15 Club of L.A. He and his wife Florence are collectors of fire memorabilia in their home. He is a member of the JWV Post 750 and a member of the DAV Post 73.

SEYMOUR J. SCHUMAN, born in New York City, Oct. 22, 1924, the first of two sons of William and Anna Schuman. Graduated from the NYC school system and NYU from which he received both a bachelor's and master's degree. He served in the U.S. Army from July 5, 1943-April 20, 1946.

Basic training at Camp Roberts, CA, then to Ohio State Univ. to study engineering for three months. Assigned to the 154th Armd. Sig. Co. of the 14th Armd. Div. at Camp Campbell, KY.

Left New York October 1944 for Marseilles, France. The 14th Armd. fought with the 3rd, 36th and 45th Divs. in the 7th Army until February 1945 when they were transferred to the 20th Corps of 3rd Army, Velden, Germany, May 8, 1945. Transferred to the 9th Sig. Co. of the 9th Inf. Div. in June 1945 in the Army of Occupation.

He studied at the University of Basel, Switzerland from January-March 1946 when he was shipped home and honorably discharged in April 1946.

He taught school in New York City for five years, after which he became an electrical contractor, which he is to this date. Married for almost 39 years to Barbara, he has a son who is an attorney. His brother enlisted in the USAAF and spent the entire WWII as an aviation cadet.

JACK SCHUTTE, born in Pittsburgh, PA, July 28, 1920. Graduated high school in June 1938 and entered the U.S. Army in July 1942. Basic training was at Ft. Lee, VA. Had special training in convoy truck driving. Transferred in October 1942 to APG, MD. Left Aberdeen in October 1943 and arrived in England.

Was assigned to be a chauffeur for a colonel in Ordnance from 1st Army. They traveled all over England preparing their troops for the invasion. Several days before D-day they were loading boats, and after a few days they also left for France.

In Normandy he drove the colonel along the front lines where they were losing many tanks. On Aug. 2, 1944 their company was bombed by German planes. He received several shrapnel wounds and was flown to England for surgery. Returned to his duties after many months of recuperation.

Awards/Medals: Normandy, Northern France, Central Europe, Rhineland with four Battle Stars, Purple Heart Medal, WWII Victory Medal and the Good Conduct Medal. Received honorable discharge in October 1945.

Married Bette by a Jewish Army chaplain in October 1942 at Aberdeen. Has two children, Robert and Michele, and two grandsons. He is a member of JWV and a life member of DAV.

SANFORD SCHWABER (SANDY), born Nov. 20, 1914, Brooklyn, NY. Entered the U.S. Army Sept. 23, 1943, Camp Upton, NY, trained at Ft. Bragg, NC and arrived in England May 11, 1944. Joined the 101st Abn. Div. (Screaming Eagles) Prcht. and Glider Divs.

Awards/Medals: Purple Heart, Bronze Arrowhead for Holland Campaign, Belgian Fourragere, Wilhelms Order of Netherlands, EAME Service Medal, Good Conduct Medal, American Service Medal, WWII Victory Medal, Distinguished Unit Citation, Army of Occupation of Germany Medal and four Battle Stars for Normandy, Central Europe, Rhineland and Ardennes-Alsace.

During airborne invasion of Holland, Sept. 17, 1944, his glider was hit by enemy fire and he crash-landed in Ghent Belgium. He was knocked unconscious and received permanent injury to his left eye. Evacuated to Canadian Field Hospital and he pressured medical officers into not evacuating him to England but allowing him to rejoin his outfit fighting in Son, Holland.

Received honorable discharged Dec. 31, 1945 with the rank of corporal.

Founder and president of a food manufacturing company from 1949-1991 and is now retired. Member of Brooklyn Post 2 JWV and past post commander; life member of the JWV of the USA, 101st Abn. Div. Assoc. and life member and charter member of New York Chapter of the 101st Abn. Div. Assoc.

Married to Bernice since 1940, has son, Robert; daughter, Fern; two grandchildren, Michael Brian and Stacey Lynn Schwaber.

ALFRED SCHWARTZ, born in Brooklyn, NY, June 22, 1917. Attended Eastern District HS and Brooklyn College. Enlisted in the U.S. Army February 1941 and served in the 4th and 84th Inf. Divs. Enlisted in the Active Reserves after his discharge in 1945 and rose to the rank of warrant officer.

Elected national commander in 1990 after his service in JWV as national supply officer. Rose through the ranks serving as post, department and regional commander. He was voted the Outstanding Department Commander in 1960 and JWV Man of the Year in Atlanta in 1980. He is a long-time member of the NEC and serves as a member of the board of directors of the National Memorial.

Taught religious school for 25 years at the Ahavath Achim Synagogue and has ushered for 48 years. He is a member of the 11 gallon blood drives, active in hospital visitation for the hospitalized veteran, and a member of the Selective Service Board.

Married to the former Eleanor Ruben and has three daughters and six grandchildren. A retired jewelry store owner, is now devoting his time and efforts to JWV.

BENJAMIN SCHWARTZ, born Aug. 5, 1925, the second of twins. He attended the University of Nebraska prior to enlisting in the USN in June 1943. His active duty training commenced at Duke University and then Midshipman School, Notre Dame, IN, with commissioning March 1945. After brief additional training, he was ordered to the USS *Mt. McKinley* (AGC-7) as CIC and fighter director officer.

Served on the *Mighty Mac* during her occupation of Japan, her mission with the Far Eastern Advisory Commission of the United Nations, and duty as command ship at the Bikini Atomic Bomb tests in 1946.

Returned to the University of Nebraska and graduated with a BS degree in business administration with distinction in January 1948. During the Korean incident, he was recalled and served aboard the USS *Newman K. Perry* (DDR-883), 1951-1952-1953. Later he served as commanding officer of four different reserve units. His final promotion to captain in the Naval Reserve was in September 1966. He retired on July 1, 1976.

The major portion of his business activity was as treasurer and administrative officer of a major frozen food distributor as well as administrative officer of a 250 unit trucking firm. He was a member of Post 318 in South Bend, Department Commander of Indiana, and is now active in Arkansas Post 436 which has earned major national awards in the past two years.

BERTRAM SCHWARTZ, born Brooklyn, NY, 1924. Inducted into the U.S. Army March 3, 1943 and completed 50 missions as radio operator/gunner in B-25s with 14th AF in China, June 1944-April 1945.

Most memorable experiences besides the flak and the fighters, were having the right engine shot out on his first mission, the crash landing on his 23rd mission and his 42nd mission where four planes of his squadron were part of a raid on Hong Kong, Oct. 16, 1944, and they came over the harbor at under 100 feet. In the Hong Kong mission his squadron claimed two ships destroyed, two probably destroyed and two damaged. They were shot up very badly that day.

Awards/Medals: Distinguished Flying Cross, Air Medal, Distinguished Unit Citation, Asiatic-Pacific Ribbon with four Battle Stars, K'ang Chen Nien Medal (Rep. of China), etc.

He was discharged Oct. 27, 1945, as tech. sergeant.

He did undergraduate work (GI Bill) in chemistry at New York University and then graduate studies in physical chemistry and mathematics at Columbia and University of Southern California. He spent two years in polymer chemistry and then 43 years in solid state science and technology (transistors, integrated circuits, lasers, etc.), mostly at AT&T Bell Laboratories. He has published about 80 scientific papers, edited two books and been issued 38 U.S. patents and 126 foreign patents. He retired July 1, 1995.

Married Sylvia Klein in 1948 and has two sons, Warren and Arthur.

DONALD SCHWARTZ, born Feb. 19, 1943, Louisville, KY. Entered AFROTC, Feb. 10, 1966, University of Kentucky. Served in SAC, 308th Strategic Missile Wing and was stationed at Little Rock AFB.

Memorable experience top secret, extra sensitive information, carried nuclear launch codes when B-52 crashed in Greenland.

Awards/Medals: Air Force Commendation Medal and Outstanding Unit.

He was discharged Feb. 11, 1970 with the rank of major. Professor in speech and English; coop ed co-ordinator.

Married Ann Sandra Kikel Aug. 3, 1969 and has one son, Mordy, who is studying religion and Philosophy at University of Nebraska and Israel.

FREDERICK SCHWARTZ, born in Brooklyn, NY, June 23, 1917. Drafted Dec. 7, 1942 in the U.S. Army and served in the Combat Engineers 100th Div., U.S. Army AF 29th TAC 9th AF, 4th Radio Sq. Mobile. Stationed at Ft. Jackson, MacDill Airfield, England, France, Belgium, Holland and Germany.

Participated in Battle of Britain and three more on continent, including the Battle of the Bulge.

A memorable experience was taking a walk with a buddy of his and came to an area about 10 blocks square that had been leveled to the ground by bombs except for one building nearly in the center. It was a Jewish synagogue and as if by some miracle had been spared. Seeing something like that somehow made them feel their effort was worthwhile and meaningful.

Awards/Medals: Presidential Unit Citation, four Battle Stars and Belgian Fourragere. He was discharged in January 1946 as T-5.

Married and has two children. He is retired.

HARRY SCHWARTZ, born Feb. 15, 1930, Belleville, NJ. Entered the U.S. Army June 5, 1942, Ft. Dix, NJ and trained at Ft. McClellan, AL. Joined A Btry., 26th FA, 9th Inf. Div., Ft. Bragg, NC in September 1942.

Overseas to the invasion, Algiers D1 Tunisia, D4 Sicily, D4 Normandy. For three hours the Air Force bombed 1,000 yards in front of troops to break out of Normandy after the capture of Cherbourg for the race across France.

First Jewish service in Germany was conducted by Father Conners because their Chaplain Tepper was killed in action shortly before Battle of the Bulge. Crossed the bridge at Remagen and saw it collapse. Went on to Dessau and met with the Russians at the Elbe River. Liberation of concentration camp Nordhausen, Germany.

Awards/Medals: Good Conduct Medal, EAME Campaign Medal with one Silver Service Star and three Bronze Stars and one Bronze Arrowhead and WWII Victory Medal.

He was honorably discharged Sept. 5, 1945, with the rank private first class.

Married Frances in 1947 and has two daughters and five grandchildren. Still active as account VP Paine Webber, member of JWV Post 146.

JOSEPH H. SCHWARTZ, born Dec. 27, 1899, Minneapolis, MN. Moved to Anaconda, MT, March 1, 1900 and lived there until 1972. Graduated from Anaconda, MT, HS as valedictorian; Wharton School of Business; University of Pennsylvania, BS in economics.

Served in WWI in 1918 and was discharged December 1918. Was in Student Army Training Corps and Officers Training Corps.

Joined the American Legion as a founding charter member of Philadelphia. Served as post commander, district commander, department vice-commander and state officer. Joined JWV in 1978. Presently serving as chaplain Post 303, Sun City, AZ. Joined World War Veterans when founded in 1959 and served as barracks commander and quartermaster, Sun City, AZ. Belonged to and served in various capacities of numerous professional and civic organizations.

Life member of B'nai Israel Temple Butte, MT; member of Beth Shalom Temple, Sun City, AZ; member of Beth Shalom Brotherhood; gold cardmember of SCORE

Received outstanding business man of State, Citizen of the Year, Most Patriotic Citizen

Business was Retail Dept. Store in Anaconda, MT; president since 1932 of Copper City Realty Co. (a family corporation) and vice president of 1st Security Bank, Anaconda.

Retired to Sun City, Az, in 1972. Married Sybila Goggenitem April 30, 1924, she passed away March 8, 1993. Has four children: Joan, Jack Lee, Edgar and Brenda. All deceased except Joan Hirshberg. There are seven grandchildren and seven great-grandchildren.

JULIUS SCHWARTZ, born Newark, NJ, and enlisted in the USNR in 1940, serving as a merchant marine.

Stationed in the North Atlantic for convoy duty; participated in Normandy Beach Operation; was on "China Arrow" when torpedoed in North Atlantic.

Awards/Medals: received numerous citations. He was discharged with the rank of lieutenant, USNR.

Family consists of father, mother and two sisters.

LEO SCHWARTZ, born Sept. 24, 1917, Brooklyn, NY. Family moved to Bronx, NY, then to Coney Island in 1930. Graduated from Lincoln High School in June 1934. Was employed as a metal plater's helper while attending Long Island University evenings as an engineering major.

Met his wife in 1939 and married in 1940. Left school to sell screw machine parts to U.S. companies and our European allies after war was declared in 1939. Became manager of a gear shop and then drafted in 1943, after birth of a son. He was sent to boot camp in Sampson, NY, then to NTS, Dearborn, MI. Graduated as machinist's mate and sent to NAS, Alameda, CA, for duration of the war where he helped to repair aircraft carriers with battle damage. Their outfit did extensive repairs on USS *Intrepid*, now permanently berthed in NYC.

Daughter was born in 1945. Discharged from service in January 1946 as motor machinist's mate third class. Active in local and state affairs for JWV over 20 years.

MILTON SCHWARTZ, born May 12, 1923, Newark, NJ. Inducted in the Army January 1942 and was in the 149th AAA Bde., 8th Army Inf. Stationed at Buzzards Bay, Cape Cod, MA.

Shipped to Scotland and stationed in Berkenfield, England (near Manchester) and later near London. Was in antiaircraft unit and made D-day crossing on D+4. Went through Luxembourg, France, Belgium and Germany and was a liberator of the concentration camps.

After his discharge in October 1945, he became speaker for the United Jewish Appeal as a volunteer. He was in the insurance business until 1970, and, from 1972 until his death Nov. 29, 1977, he worked for Israel Bonds as a manager in Asbury, NJ.

Married to Pearl Fecher of Newark in 1946 and had two children, David and Judith.

MILTON SCHWARTZ, born Aug. 29, 1920, Newark, NJ. Entered US Army Feb. 3, 1943, Newark, NJ; Army cook and rifleman in infantry squad. Did scouting and patrolling, he fought in France and Europe. He drove 3/4 ton truck delivering prisoners of war to work and guarding them.

Awards/Medals: American Theater Ribbon, EAME Ribbon, Good Conduct Medal and Victory Medal. Discharged Dec. 7, 1945, Ft. Monmouth, NJ with the rank PFC.

He is deceased.

WALTER SCHWARZ, born in Vienna, Austria, March 2, 1923. He is a survivor of Kristallnacht. He escaped from Vienna and immigrated to the U.S. in March 1939. Enlisted in the USN in 1943 after initial rejection for non-citizenship.

Attended boot camp at the USNS, Sampson, NY; trained at Hospital Corps School, Portsmouth, VA; qualified for the V-12 Program but was rejected for non-citizenship. He became a U.S. Citizen in June 1944 and proudly wore his Navy uniform.

Assigned as staff member at the Naval Medical Field Research Lab, Camp Lejeune, NC, until his discharge in 1946, acting as chief of staff with rank of PHM2/c.

Awards/Medals: American Area, WWII Victory and the lab received a Letter of Commendation from the Secretary of the Navy.

Married to Phyllis in 1946 and has one daughter, Ruth. He is founding member of the Needle Trades Management Society (1947), an industrial engineer and corporate executive in the Needle Trades industry for most of his working years and served as cost/price analyst at Ft. Monmouth, NJ, from 1980 until his retirement in 1988.

Member of American Legion and JWV; past post commander (125); past county commander; chairman, Dept. of New Jersey Yom Hashoah Program, Liberty State Park, 1990-1996; adjutant, Dept. of New Jersey, 1991-1995; and national co-chairman "Days of Remembrance" 1994, 1995 and 1996.

MARCUS M. SCIARAPPA, born Nov. 3, 1917, Neptune, NJ. Enlisted July 18, 1941, in the U.S. Army. Served with the 26th FA BN, 9th Inf. Div. and stationed at Ft. Dix, NJ; Ft. Bragg, NC; Algiers; French Morocco; Tunisia; Sicily; Normandy; Northern France; Ardennes; Rhineland; Central Europe and the Battle of the Bulge.

Memorable experience was being the first division to cross the Remagen Bridge and it collapsed shortly after.

Awards/Medals: EAME Campaign Medal with eight stars and one spearhead, American Defense, Good Conduct, American Campaign and WWII Victory Medal. He was discharged Sept. 18, 1945 as tech sergeant 4.

Married to Margaret and has one daughter. Returned from and planned to attend the 9th Inf. Div. Reunion in Texas.

MICHAEL STEPHEN SEALFON, born March 2, 1944, Manhattan, NY. Attended Pascack Valley Regional High School, Hillsdale, NJ. Graduated from the Pennsylvania State University and commissioned 2nd lieutenant Med. Svc. Corps, USAR on March 26, 1966. Completed MS Officers Basic and Advanced Courses and graduated from the U.S. Army Medical Technology Fellowship, Walter Reed Army Medical Center as a clinical laboratory officer in 1968.

Commissioned Regular Army June 3, 1969. Served six years of active duty to include a one-year tour in Da Nang, Vietnam as laboratory director of the 95th Evac. Hospital.

Awards/Medals: Bronze Star Medal, Army Commendation Medal, National Defense Medal, Vietnam Service Medal, Meritorious Service Medal, Army Commendation Medal with two clusters, Army Achievement Medal with two clusters, Army Reserve Achievement Medal, Reserve Components Achievement Medal with X Device, Overseas Training Ribbon and RVN Service Medal. He was retired with the rank of colonel.

Received MS and Ph.D. degrees in clinical chemistry while completing 21 years of USAR service to include command of the 363rd Medical Laboratory, Columbus, OH. Received the Office of the Surgeon General "A" prefix in clinical biochemistry. Participated in Reforger 91, Wurzburg, Germany.

Is a board certified clinical chemist (DABCC), and continues to work for Laboratory Corporation of America as a tech director and a member of their Hematology Standardization Committee. Has been a licensed radio amateur for 34 years and is an instrument rated private pilot with over 600 hours.

ALFRED SEGAL, born Nov. 18, 1915, Baltimore, MD. Schooling completed June 1937 when graduated University of Baltimore, law degree; admitted to Maryland Bar September 1937.

Military experience began by attending summer Citizens Military Training camps, 1934-1937, first summer infantry, Ft. Meade, MD, followed by three summers coast artillery, Fortress Monroe, VA, when commissioned 2nd lieutenant, Reserve Corps.

Called to active duty January 1941, Fortress Monroe, platoon leader, 37mm AAA Btry., thence to Ft. Eustice, VA 40mm AAA Btry., 1st lieutenant. After completion Advanced AAA School, Camp Davis, NC, promoted to captain and assigned battery commander, Ft. Sheridan, IL, then Camp Adair, OR. Following maneuvers, Cascade Mountains, headed to Pacific Theater where he commanded 40mm Btry. in two New Guinea landings; then assigned as battalion liaison officer to division headquarters for the Luzon, Philippines invasion. Was staging for invasion of southern Kyushu, Japan when war ended.

Discharged from active duty February 1946 and transferred to active reserve as major. Promoted to lieutenant colonel 1955; served 15 day summer active duty training until 1965 when transferred to Retired Reserve.

Awards/Medals: Asiatic-Pacific Ribbon with two Bronze Stars and Arrowhead, American Theater, American Defense, WWII Victory, and Philippine Victory Medal with Bronze Star.

Married to Hilda; has son, Jimmy; daughter, Bette; grandchildren: Zachary, Harry, Alexis and Michael. He is retired.

Member of JWV, life member of DAV, The Retired Officers Association and Reserve Officers Association.

BLANCHE LIPPMAN SEGAL, born Vitibsk, Russia on Sept. 2, 1902. Enlisted in U.S. Army WACs in 1943 and stationed at Ft. Des Moines, IA; Hamilton AB, NY and Camp Kilmer, NJ.

Memorable experience was being secretary to commander of Hamilton AB, Brooklyn, NY.

Awards/Medals: Good Conduct Medal. She was discharged at a private first class.

She was member of JWV Post 164, Manhattan. She passed away in 1977. *Submitted by her daughter, Marie R. Segal.*

RAYMOND SEGEL, born in Mechanicville, NY, Sept. 26, 1920. Moved to Albany, NY when 12 and after finishing high school, started own business, the Capitol Bag and Burlap Co. Closed business and enlisted in the USN in September 1942. Basic training at Great Lakes Naval Station, reported to Norfolk, VA where ordered to USS *New York* for the duration of enlistment.

Saw action in the invasion of North Africa. Also did sea duty, taking the midshipmen on training cruises from the U.S. to South America (Trinidad). The USS *New York* transferred to the Pacific, where he saw action at Iwo Jima and Okinawa.

Married to Evelyn Dec. 2, 1945. Opened and operated his burlap bag business for 15 years. When plastic replaced burlap and cotton, he switched to non-ferrous scrap metals and moved business to Port of Albany where he is today.

A member of the JWV Post 105, Albany since 1945. Has two married sons, one grandson and three granddaughters. His younger son is now associated in the business with him.

SAMUEL SEIGEL, born in Poland, Aug. 15, 1914. Inducted Feb. 14, 1944, in the U.S. Army, Ft. Dix, NJ. Infantry training at Camp Wheeler, GA, then overseas with 84th Inf. Div.

Dug in outside of Liege, Belgium, November 1944; took St. Vith in France, then to Marche, Belgium. About December 15 Germans broke through their lines in the Ardennes (Battle of the Bulge). Was separated from his division, there was confusion everywhere. Made it back to his outfit, the 335th Regt., about Christmas time.

On Jan. 7, 1945, he was wounded while in the Ardennes near the village of Marche. They took a village (he can't remember the name) and found 10 Germans in the first house they went through. They took them back to their headquarters.

Awards/Medals: Combat Infantry Badge, Purple Heart and two Battle Stars. He was discharged with the rank of sergeant.

Today, he is in the funeral business in Passaic, NJ. Has been married for the past 55 years.

SARA MIRIAM SLUTSKY SEGAL, born June 2 in Russia. Entered the USN on Aug. 9, 1943, Northampton, MA. Was a line officer, Communications. Trained at Smith College and Holyoke College. Stationed at Fleet Office, Brooklyn, Washington, DC and NSD, Oakland, CA.

One of her memories is of Adm. "Bull" Halsey asking her what she was doing on his ship. Guess he didn't recognize Navy Blue on a woman.

Awards/Medals: American Theater Ribbon and WWII Victory Ribbon. Honorable discharge March 26, 1946 with the rank lieutenant jg.

Prior to the USN, she was English and science teacher in the Detroit, MI high school system. In recent years has owned an antique shop and is an active volunteer member of Henry Ford Museum.

She has a daughter, Marilyn, who is an x-ray tech and one granddaughter.

B. NORMAN SEIGENBERG, born Jan. 25, 1924, Brooklyn, NY. Enlisted Nov. 26, 1942, in the USAAF. Assigned to the 5th AF and stationed in Dalhart, TX; New Guinea; Philippines; Okinawa and Japan.

Participated in New Guinea and Okinawa campaigns. Memorable experience was when the Japanese tried to retake Tacloban Air Strip.

Awards/Medals: Bronze Star, Asiatic-Pacific Ribbon and ribbons for all the campaigns he was in. He was discharged Dec. 26, 1945, as corporal.

Married to Edith and has three children and eight grand-children. Also has one sister. He is retired and a past department commander AZ/NV.

MARTIN D. SEILER, born in Brooklyn, NY, Nov. 17, 1916. Graduated from Erasmus Hall High School in 1934. Enlisted December 1942, went to basic training at Camp Hood, TX, Tank Destroyer Bn. Transferred as flying cadet to USAAC in July 1943, graduating as navigator, flight officer, St. Marcus, TX, July 1944. Assigned to Heavy Bombardment B-24s and trained at Mountain Home, ID.

Sent to Italy with 783rd Sqdn., 465th BG, 15th AF. Was credited with 22 missions. Shot down twice, he bailed out over Italy Jan. 20 and Yugoslavia, March 31, 1945. After both bailouts all the crew returned safely to base. Listed as MIA in Yugoslavia, walked out with the aid of partisans and returned to U.S. base via British supply planes.

Awards/Medals: Distinguished Flying Cross and Battlefield Commission to 2nd lieutenant, Feb. 6, 1945.

Promoted to 1st lieutenant in May 1945. War ended in Pacific and he returned to the States for reassignment. Had earned enough points for discharge, so became civilian and reserve officer, October 1945.

Married Mae Gulbin May 25, 1950 (deceased 1984), has daughter Cora Muirhead and granddaughter Molly, Encino, CA.

Served at many levels of JWV in New York area and as a member of the national court.

ISAAC SELDNER, served in the U.S. Army, Co. H, 6th Regt., Virginia Infantry. Participated in action at Chancellorsville and was captured Sept. 14, 1862, exchanged, killed May 3, 1983, at Chancellorsville and is buried in Jewish Cemetery in Richmond, VA. He achieved the rank of lieutenant.

LEO Y. SELESNICK, born IN Bronx, NY, July 16, 1918. Entered the U.S. Army June 5, 1942, and served with the Coast Artillery Corps. Was unit commander, anti-aircraft artillery, Btry. B, Automatic Weapons Bn.

Stationed in the Asiatic-Pacific Theater, Okinawa, Philippines and Hawaii.

Awards/Medals: American Campaign Medal, Asiatic-Pacific Campaign Medal, WWII Victory Medal and Philippine Liberation Medal. He was discharged June 5, 1946 with the rank of captain.

Became a successful dentist; founded and ran a traveling company, Baso Transportation; taught oral surgery at the New York University School of Dentistry; founded the Town and Country Bank; founded the Bet Tikva Synagogue of Flemington, NJ; and was a community leader.

He was an exceptional husband and father to three children. He passed away July 6, 1994.

IRWIN SELIGER, born in New York City, April 6, 1931, grew up in Brooklyn where he graduated from JHS 149. TJHS, Brooklyn College and Brooklyn Law School

Entered the USMC, 3rd Div. in April 1954; trained at Camp Pendleton, CA and went overseas to Japan and then Hawaii. While serving at Camp Kenehoe, Oahu, he acted as legal counsel for non-commissioned personnel.

He was discharged from the service in January 1956 and returned to graduate studies in education and administration.

Married to Sandy since 1952, has two sons (both neurologists) and two adorable grandchildren.

Worked as a school district administrator in several Long Island School Systems. Currently retired and enjoying lifelong learning as well as self-fulfillment from being a really humanistic responsible citizen.

BENJAMIN SELIGMAN, born in 1894 in Russia. Worked first at Dey Bros. then employed at C.E. Chappell's as a furrier for 18 years.

Served in the first World War from 1917 to 1919 and was in France for nine months.

He passed away May 8, 1938.

HENRY W. SELIGMAN, entered the service Jan. 10, 1941. Was sent overseas in March 1942 and stationed in Ireland, England and France. He was wounded in action in the battle around Metz on Nov. 10, 1942.

Awards/Medals: two Bronze Stars, Purple Heart, Infantry Combat Badge, Good Conduct Medal, American Defense, EAME Campaign Medal and the WWII Victory Medal. Discharged with the rank of private first class.

Has one son, David, and two sisters. He is now retired.

JEROME SELINGER, born in New York City, NY, Jan. 1, 1925, and grew up in New Brunswick, NJ. Entered the U.S. Army August 1943, Ft. Dix, NJ. Had 17 weeks infantry basic training at Camp Croft, SC. Initially tapped for ASTP, then to Camp Gordon, GA, the 10th Armd. Div., 61st Armd. Inf. Bn.

Went overseas September 1944 and landed Omaha Beach. Fought with the 10th in battles of Metz, for the Siegfried Line, Battle of the Bulge, Rhineland and crossing the Rhine. Headed south, was surrounded, bombed and strafed for three days by German jets at Crailsheim. To Bavarian Alps and ended up at Garmisch on V-E Day

Awards/Medals: EAME Campaign Medal with three Bronze Battle Stars, Combat Infantry Badge and Bronze Star, American Theater Medal, WWII Victory Medal and Army of Occupation Medal.

Received honorable discharge Nov. 16, 1945 as private first class.

Graduated from Columbia University Dental School in 1951. Solo practice of dentistry for 35 years; dental consultant state of New Jersey, seven years; semi-retired today and consultant with Private Dental Insurance Co. Member of JWV and VFW.

Married to Pearl since 1952 and has one daughter, Janice, and two grandchildren, Howard and Lesley.

STEVEN SELMAN, born in Boston, MA, Feb. 7, 1937. ROTC commission, 1959, USAR Signal Corps and later transferred to Medical Service Corps. Made two Vietnam tours flying bird dogs, forward observer, aerial surveillance and target acquisition.

Was recon pilot, aviation platoon commander, flight safety officer and communications officer throughout the U.S. and Asia. Stationed at Libby AAF, Ft. Huachuca, AZ as operations officer to acting commander. In 1973 he requested and received early release from active duty with rank of major to complete MS in social work (1974) and MBA (1978).

Commanding officer, 383rd Med. Detach. (psychiatry) from 1981-1985. Colonel, USAR, July 1985. Retired August 1990 from USAR.

Awards/Medals: Bronze Star Medal, six Air Medals, RVN Cross of Gallantry with Palm and two Meritorious Service Medals.

From 1985 to present, chief equal employment opportunity counselor for Compliant Processing Program at Hanscom AFB and 140 units in several New England States.

Married to Valerie, has son, Marc, and daughter, Stephanie.

ALVIN SELNICK, born Jan. 13, 1931, Detroit, MI. Enlisted in the USAF April 25, 1951, during the Korean War. His identical twin brother, David Selnick, enlisted in the USAF in December 1950 and died in 1989 of cancer. Basic training was at Sampson AFB, NY, then assigned to Sheppard AFB, TX for A&E training as aircraft mechanic. Transferred to March AFB, CA in 1952 and was assigned to the 302nd Wing HQ.

After four years of service, he received an honorable discharge in 1955.

Auto Repair Shop in 1961, Hawaiian Gardens, CA, where he stayed until late 1988 when he retired. Before and during his retirement he was active in the JWV, Temple Beth David in Orange County, CA and B'nai B'rith organization, working through the ranks to be commander. Was president of B'nai B'rith Lakewood for three years; of Temple Beth David Brotherhood for two years and fireworks chairman for 30 years.

Stayed in California and married in August 1956 to Eva. They have three children and eight grandchildren.

JOSEPH W. SELTZER, born in Philadelphia, PA, March 30, 1926. Enlisted in the USN and entered active service May 12, 1943. After boot camp he was assigned to the light carrier USS *Langley* CVL-27. After shakedown cruise, the *Langley* sailed through the Panama Canal to Pearl Harbor with 1,000 Marines aboard for duty in the Pacific. Served aboard the *Langley* through May 1945.

Participated in the invasions and actions against Marshall Islands, Palau, Hollandia, Marianas, Philippines, Formosa, Luzon, Japan, Battle of China Sea and others.

Returned to the States in 1945 to attend Submarine School, New London, CT; graduated and assigned to the staff of Adm. Styer aboard the USS *Falcon*.

Awards/Medals: Navy Unit Commendation, Pacific Theater with seven stars, Philippine Liberation Ribbon with two stars, American Theater and Victory Medal. Discharged at Bainbridge, MD, March 10, 1946 as RM2/c. Served in the USNR for three years.

Presently retired and living in Jenkintown, PA with his wife, Ruth, and has three grown children and six grandchildren.

SEYMOUR SEROTA, born in Chicago, IL on July 27, 1925. Graduated high school and went into the Army on Jan. 3, 1944. After training, he was stationed in the Philippines. There he worked with the Philippine Army to re-establish their Signal Units. Working at the Signal Center at the war's end. He received the following message from the ship's captain as the ship left Manila Harbor:

Blackout Regulations being observed, but cannot stop the glow that lights to the horizon from the hearts of 200 men freed from the Japanese Prisoner-of-War camp after three years of cruel and inhuman treatment. Discharged May 4, 1946, with the rank T-4.

Married and has three children and eight grandchildren. Today, he is retired and living in Florida.

HARRY SERULNECK, born in Brooklyn, NY, June 19, 1918. Graduated from trade school in 1935 and went to work in his father's restaurant. In 1940 worked in the Brooklyn shipyards. Drafted in the U.S. Army in July 1944, following D-day, and sent to Ft. Dix, NJ for basic training. Infantry training was at Ft. Blanding, FL.

Landed in Le Havre, Normandy on Christmas Day 1944. Was involved in the battles of Central Europe and became part of the famous task force of the 347th Regt. that was involved in the capture and liberation of the Ohrdruf and Buchenwald concentration camps. His division, the 87th Inf. and the 4th Armd. Div. were the first troops to arrive at Ohrdruf in the beginning of April 1945. It contained enough horror to make combat men cry and Gen. Patton himself to vomit when he witnessed the camp. Our soldiers forced the mayor of the town, the Burgomaster, and his wife to come to the camp and witness what he allowed to exist in his community. He and his wife went home and hanged themselves.

A few hundred survivors of the camp surrounded the 17 ton M-18 tank and the prisoners kissed their hands and embraced them. He remembers they were sick, hungry wretches and barely alive. He is proud to have served in WWII and proud that he took part in ending the human suffering that was so evident at Buchenwald and Ohrdruf. He believes it made him a more caring and giving individual, father and husband.

SIDNEY SHACHNOW, Major General, born in Kaunas, Lithuania, Nov. 23, 1934. He imprisoned for three and a half years during WWII in a German concentration camp before being liberated by the Soviet Army. He lived in Europe until he emigrated to the U.S. in 1950.

Enlisted in the Army as an infantryman and attended OCS as a sergeant first class. He was commissioned in Infantry in 1960. Assignments during more than 30 years of commissioned service have been as commander or staff officer with Infantry, Mechanized Infantry, airmobile, airborne and Special Forces units.

Attended Franklin Technical Institute, Boston, MA and graduated from the University of Nebraska. Earned MS from Shippensburg State College; Infantry Officer Basic and Advanced, Special Forces Qualification Course, Army Command and General Staff College and Army War College.

Awards/Medals: Distinguished Service Medal, Silver Star with OLC, Defense Superior Service Medal, Legion of Merit, Bronze Star with two OLCs and V Device, Purple Heart with OLC, Meritorious Service Medal with two OLCs, Air Medal with the numeral 12, Army Commendation Medal with two OLCs and V device, Combat Infantryman Badge, Master Parachutist Badge, Ranger Tab, Special Forces Tab and the Republic of Vietnam Gallantry Cross.

Married to Arlene Armstrong and has four daughters.

MAX SIGAL, served in the U.S. Army from Aug. 11, 1942-Sept. 16, 1945. Entered the USAAF 1942, Ft. Devens, MA. Radio training at Sioux Falls, SD, September 1942-January 1943; advanced radio training with American Air Lines, Chicago, IL; flight training Billings, MT and Memphis, TN; and overseas flight training at Homestead, FL.

Flew overseas on the Army Transport Corps plane C-46 to Assam, India. Served in the Army Transport Cmd. in the China, India-Burma Theater, January 1944-May 1945. Completed 90 round trips over the "Hump" with 700 combat hours.

Awards/Medals: Air Medal with cluster, Presidential Citation, Distinguished Flying Cross with cluster, Bronze Battle Star, India Burma Campaign, China Campaign with Bronze Battle Star, Central Burma Campaign with Bronze Battle Star, Good Conduct Medal, Victory Medal and American Theater Medal.

Discharged Sept. 16, 1945, Battle Creek, MI with the rank corporal.

He visited Puerto Rico, British Guinea, Natal, Brazil, Ascension Island, Accra, Gold Coast, Khartoum, Egyptian Sudan, Aden, Arabia, Karachi, India. Traveled across India to the Assam Valley, Kumming, Chengtu Chanyi, Yuanyi and Chengkung in China and Calcutta, Lucknow in India, Burma. Made frequent trips to the Chengtu Area, China where many air fields were built. They carried among other things gallons of 100 octane gas, bombs and other materials. *Submitted by Max Sigal*

MORTON SHALOWITZ, born Dec. 27, 1923, Chicago, IL. Attended Roosevelt High School, 1937-41; Herzl Jr. College, 1941-43; YMCA College, 1943-45, receiving BA; post-graduate work at University of Chicago, 1945-46. Ordained rabbi in 1949 Hebrew Theological College, receiving Yoreh Yoreh and BHL. All schools in Chicago.

Entered USAR, 1952; graduated chaplain basic, 1952; chaplain advanced officer, 1963; Command and General Staff College, 1972; Air War College, 1974; and Industrial College of the Armed Forces, 1976.

Active duty, 1952-54, Korean War, building Beth Yehee Shalom, 1954, first Korean Synagogue in Seoul. Retired as colonel in 1983.

Rabbi of Minot Hebrew Cong, Minot, ND, 1950-52; associate Kehiloth Israel Synagogue, Kansas City, MO, 1954-57; Heska Amuna Cong, Knoxville, TN, 1957-62; Beth Yehudah Moshe Cong, North Miami, FL, 1962-63; Temple Beth Israel, Fond du Lac, WI, 1963-91. Retired in 1992.

BENJAMIN SHANGOLD, born 1913, Brooklyn, NY. Inducted U.S. Army, July 1942. Assigned to Co. M, 355th Inf. and served at Ft. Jay, NY; England and Northern France.

Awards/Medals: EAME Service Medal with one star, Good Conduct Medal, WWII Victory Medal and American Service Medal.

A nice Jewish boy arriving home on Christmas Eve, 1945. Just in time to miss Christmas in the Ardennes. Discharged as corporal, Dec. 24, 1945.

Married and has two daughters, one son and three grandchildren.

Post-service, Ph.D. clinical psychology. Passed away in 1977.

HAROLD SHANGOLD, born 1908, Brooklyn, NY. Enlisted USN January 1942, Naval Station Rockaway, NY. Served at Lido Beach, NY.

Awards/Medals: American Service Medal and Good Conduct Medal. He was discharged February 1946 as PM1.

Married, has one son, one daughter and two grandchildren.

Was a private accountant. Passed away 1990.

JULES SHANGOLD, born 1916, Brooklyn, NY. Enlisted January 1942 in USN, Naval Station, Rockaway, NY. Served as instructor at Hospital Corps School, Great Lakes, IL and Naval Hospitals at St. Albans, NY; Ft. Lauderdale, FL; Key West, FL; Shang-hi China; and Evac Hospital, Okinawa.

Memorable experience was the assigned work detail Yom Kippur 1945. Huge typhoon came in and not only cancelled work detail but washed away everything to be done.

Awards/Medals: WWII Victory Medal, Asiatic-Pacific Service Medal with two stars, American Service Medal and Occupation Service Medal (Japan). He was discharged Feb. 19, 1946 as PHM1.

Married, two sons, widowed, remarried, step-son, daughter and seven grandchildren. A doctor of podiatric medicine, he passed away 1991.

NEIL SHANGOLD, born 1948, New York. Enlisted in USN Sept. 3, 1968, Ft. Hamilton, NY. Served at Naval Hospital, St. Albans, NY and in USS *Midway* (CVA-41), HM2 (A/C).

Participated in Rolling Thunder, Line backer 1 and 2. General service corpsman assigned to Search and Rescue. Served as Jewish lay leader.

Memorable experience was standing in the helicopter door 60 miles south of Hanoi in a horse collar, under fire, ready to be dropped into the jungle when the copilot realized they were a couple of miles from where they were supposed to be.

Awards/Medals: Presidential Unit Citation, Navy Meritorious Unit Citation, National Defense Service Medal, Vietnam Service Medal with three stars, Armed Forces Expeditionary Medal (Korea), Vietnam Unit Citation with Palm, Vietnam Campaign Medal and Combat Action Ribbon. He was discharged Aug. 24, 1972.

Single and a screenwriter.

COURTNEY SHANKEN, kept his interest in gymnastics by serving on the Men's Gymnastic Olympic Committee and as a board member of the USA Gymnastics, the governing body of the sport. He was elected to the Gymnastic Hall of Fame in 1967.

He is very active in business today as head of a family business involved in marketing used clothing and wiping rags all over the world. He feels blessed and fortunate to have a son, Jeff, who manages the Chicago plant and a daughter, Sandy, who with her husband, Bob Woycke, handle the international operation out of Milwaukee, WI.

No biography of his could be complete without mentioning Edie, his wonderful wife whose picture he had on the wall in the barracks in Manduria. They were married in 1945, have three children (all married) and six grandchildren. What else would a person want out of life?

He serves as secretary of the 47th (?) Association and publisher of the newsletter. He was honored in July 1994 to give the rededication memorial speech in Manduria, Italy at the old airbase.

EARL SHANKEN, has had a long career in business. His entrepreneurial background included, owning his own pharmaceutical and cosmetic businesses in Mexico City, Mexico. His international career also included, working for a multinational corporation as their general manager for all their operations in Latin America.

After living 21 years in Mexico, he returned to the USA and for the past 18 years has lived in Sausalito, CA. He is very active in residential real estate, with over 12 years of experience in that field.

Has been married for over 42 years. Married daughter living in Palo Alto, CA, with two children and another married daughter living in Montreal, Canada. His wife, Flora, is very active as an independent simultaneous conference interpreter in English, Spanish and French.

Despite all the conflicting stories, he is alive and well.

HERBERT SHAPIRO, born June 8, 1924, New York City, NY. Enlisted in USAAF and served with 422nd Night Fighter Sqdn. Basic training at Miami Beach, training at Orlando, FL, then overseas to Belgium, Germany, England and France.

Participated in battles in Ardennes, Central Europe, Normandy, Northern France and Rhineland.

Memorable experience was when told to stand and fight against Germans in Ardennes even though they were not equipped to fight against tanks.

Awards/Medals: Distinguished Unit Badge, EAME Medal and Good Conduct Medal. He was discharged Oct. 5, 1945, with rank of sergeant.

Graduated City College of New York in 1960 and worked for NYS Insurance Fund as accountant for 27 years. Retired in 1987.

Married to Helen since 1950. Has a son, daughter and two grandchildren.

HERSCHEL SHAPIRO, served in the U.S. Marines in the Pacific area. Details of his service history are unknown. *Submitted by a family member, Milton Wallace.*

MONROE SHAPIRO, born Dec. 22, 1924, Newark, NJ. Inducted into military June 26, 1943, 328th Engr. Cbt. Bn. Served in France.

Memorable experience was Jan. 24, 1945. Having finished laying 100 mines, he was returning to the truck, when a buddy asked if he could have his seat. Monroe gladly gave it to him. Shortly later the truck carrying the remaining 400 mines was hit, killing everyone aboard and spraying the area with scrap metal. Monroe lay in the snow and carefully placed the mines he was carrying down beside him. At this point he noticed the snow around him turning red and realized he had been wounded. He spent a year in hospitals (France, England and the U.S.) until his discharge Jan. 10, 1946.

Earned a BS degree from the University of Miami and an MS and an IE degree from Columbia University.

Retired in 1991 from American Airlines after 25 years of service. During this time he had an article published in *Interfaces* - The Institute of Management Sciences.

He was married for almost 40 years to Lois and had two daughters, Linda and Ellen. He passed away Feb. 28, 1995.

MURRAY SHAPIRO, born July 6, 1923, Los Angeles, CA. Two years college ROTC, UCLA, U.C. Berkeley, AA, BA, M.Ed., doctoral program, general sec. teaching credential. Pershing Rifles Drill Team, three years volunteer U.S. Army Infantry with six months combat.

Enlisted in Enlisted Reserve Corps UCLA September 1941; called to active duty Aug. 31, 1942; trained at Ft. MacArthur, CA; Camp Roberts, CA; Ft. Benning, GA; Camp Breckinridge, KY (75th Div.);. Arrived in England, Sept. 17, 1944; landed as combat replacement Omaha Beach, Red/Easy sector; assigned to 28th Div. as sergeant of 1st (H) MG Sq., 1st Section, 1st Plt., M Co., 3rd Bn. In six months was staff sergeant.

Memorable experiences: being one of three to survive at Ouren; climbing Vosges Mts. to trap retreating German army; commanding a town on Patton's flank to guard his Rhine crossing; and crossing the Remagen Bridge before it collapsed.

Awards/Medals: Bronze Star with OLC, Combat Infantryman Badge, Good Conduct Medal, ETO Medal with three Battle Stars (Hurtgen Forest, Battle of the Bulge, Battles of Central Germany), WWII Victory Medal with cluster, Occupation of Germany Medal, American Campaign Medal, Expert Rifle, Bayonet and BAR, Presidential Unit Citation (112th Inf. Regt.), Belgian Liberation, French Victory, Free French, Rhine and Danube Society.

Returned to the States Aug. 3, 1945 and discharged Oct. 25, 1945

Married 45 years to Shirley, four children. Teacher with LAUSD for 41 years.

EMANUEL ABRAHAM SHARLIN (MANNY), born Jan. 17, 1919, Trenton, NJ. Attended Trenton High School and Drexel University where he was on the swim team and received a degree in electrical engineering.

Inducted into the Army in November 1944. Basic training at Ft. Dix, NJ and Biloxi, MS. Stationed in Dayton, OH as an engineer. Discharged from the USAAC as a private first class in April 1945.

Married to Anne Ruth for 52 years, has three daughters: Linda Sharlin Warren, Barbara Sharlin Berkman and Dr. Harriet Sharlin. Has eight grandchildren whom he adores: Mitchell, Amy and Danielle Warren; Lindsay, Douglas and Jillian Berkman; Gabriel Wetmore; and Micole Sharlin.

He took over his father's business, M&M Plating Co., until his retirement in 1983. Then went into real estate until his death on Nov. 30, 1993.

Collected money to build the first Jewish Community Center and pool in Ewing, NJ. Devoted to Israel and made many trips there with his wife. Had his Bar Mitzvah at the Western Wall at the age of 60. Had polio as a baby and later stuttered too much to have a Bar Mitzvah at 13 so had one at 60.

Was a devoted family man, Jew and American all of his life.

IRVING AND ISIDORE SHATTUCK, New York City brothers, Irving and Isidore (Jack), only sons of Bialystock and Warsaw immigrants, Chaim (Herman) and Sara (Sophie) Chertok, both served during WWI: Irving in Army European combat and Jack (originally deferred in 1917 to support his parents and four sisters) on active Navy Yeoman third class duty at Garden City, Long Island, 1918-1919.

Jack Shattuck, Sr.   Jack Shattuck, Jr.

Working all their lives in New York's garment district, Irving died childless (1969); Jack Shattuck (1894-1972) married fashion designer, Jane Engle (1906-1975), raising three children: Jack, George and Lolly Shattuck (Werner), now living in Wilmington, DE; Princeton, NJ; and Scottsdale, AZ.

The eldest, Jack Engel Shattuck, helped National Selective Service System lawyers develop practical, legally acceptable conscientious objector processing during the Vietnam War. A career federal employee since 1974, he's worked full-time obtaining community volunteers supplies and financial donations for Department of Veterans Affairs (VA) Hospitals. In 1986-1987, he helped draft the original National Constitution and By-Laws, personally contributing a special preamble for the Descendants of JWV.

RALPH LEON SHEAR, born Oct. 18, 1923, Brooklyn, NY. Joined the U.S. Army and served with 35th Div., 137th Regt., 2nd Bn., Co. H. Stationed in the States, England, France, Belgium, Holland, Luxembourg, Germany.

Participated in action in Normandy, Northern France, Battle of Bulge, Ardennes, Rhineland and Central Europe.

Memorable experience was opening up concentration camp, Bergen-Belsen in Germany.

Awards/Medals: five Battle Stars, American Campaign, European Campaign, WWII Victory, Combat Infantry Badge, Army of Occupation, Bronze Star and New York Conspicuous Service Cross.

He was discharged Oct. 27, 1945, as staff sergeant.

Married to Florence for 50 years, has three children and five grandchildren.

Retired, was past commander JWV Post 459, Boca Raton, FL (1992-1993). Actively participates in VA Hospitals and general veterans services along with community services.

BEN SHEFREN, enlisted in the Army at the age of 17, Dec. 7, 1942. Basic training at Camp Van Doren, MS. Shipped to Persia in February of 1943 and attached to the 3rd Army, bringing supplies to Russia through Persia.

Because he was a former Golden Gloves champion, he boxed and promoted boxing shows for a year traveling to Italy, Egypt, North Africa, Casablanca while assigned to Special Services.

Also served in India, Australia and New Zealand. He was discharged on Dec. 7, 1945, as a corporal.

While in Persia, he married a Russian Jewish girl who followed him to his home in Rock Island, IL. Later moved to Chicago. After 28 years of marriage, she passed away.

MAX SHENKER, born April 10, 1919. Joined U.S. Army Feb. 13, 1941, sent to Camp Hulen, TX and became attached to 69th AAA Bn. While on special detail in Midland, they learned Pearl Harbor was attacked. Recalled to camp and immediately shipped to North Island NAS, San Diego, CA.

Sent to Camp Hahn, CA in March 1944; while home on furlough, received telegram to report to Camp Howze, TX for infantry training.

Shipped overseas to the European Theater in December 1944 and assigned to the 41st Armd. Inf. Div. and went all the way to the Elbe River in Germany.

Memorable experience was waking up one morning in their foxholes and finding they were surrounded by German tanks. He was a POW for 21 days. Liberated in April by American trucks coming in under white flags. While a prisoner he learned Pres. Roosevelt had died.

Sent home to the States in June for a convalescent furlough. Ended his Army career at Ft. Riley, KS. Discharged at Ft. Dix, NJ with the rank of corporal.

Married Ida Sept. 6, 1942, has three sons and eight grandchildren. After many years of working in the fur industry in New York, he is now retired and lives with his wife in Florida.

LEE M. SHERMAN, Colonel, USA, RET, began his military career in 1943 in the yet to be formed 106th Inf. Div., Ft. Jackson, SC. Served in HQ 2nd Army and XVIII Abn. Corps, ending his WWII service at HQ, Army Ground Forces as master sergeant.

Service in Korea as member of UNPIK, the UN Partisan Forces in Korea assigned to the Far East Liaison Command. Later assigned as an officer of the Combined Command Recon. Activities, Korea. These guerrilla and intelligence activities prepared him for assignment in Vietnam as an operations officer within the J2 Division of MACV.

Served in many world-wide assignments as company commander and assistant G3 in the 101st Abn. Div., assistant

PMS&T, Ohio University; detachment commander and staff secretary, White Sands Missile. White Sands was first assignment in the Ordnance Corps after transferring from the infantry. Assignment in Vietnam as an operations officer within the J2 Division of MACV. Later assignments included the director of Program Management, Advanced Research Projects Agency, Bangkok, Thailand. His last military assignment was as first director of research, development and engineering of the U.S. Army Armament Command.

He retired from the military in 1976 and became a professor of management at the University of North Carolina at Wilmington. He is now a retired Faculty Emeritus from that institution and resides in Wilmington, NC, with his wife, Frances.

Awards/Medals: Legion of Merit, Soldiers Medal for Heroism, Bronze Star Medal with OLC, Meritorious Service Medal, Joint Service Commendation Medal, Army Commendation Medal with three OLCs and the Wharang Military Medal with Gold Star (Korean).

Col. Sherman stems from a military background. His dad, Abe Sherman, was an infantryman in WWI and WWII and won the Silver Star for gallantry in action. His younger brother, Philip, is a retired brigadier general of the MDNG.

NISSON SHERMAN, born Jan. 13, 1932, Malden, MA. Enlisted in U.S. Army Oct. 1, 1952, 1st Army HQ. Stationed at Ft. Dix, NJ; Ft. Benjamin Harrison, IN; Ft. Devens, NJ.

Memorable experience was helping construct and support first and only Kosher Kitchen at Ft. Devens.

Awards/Medals: American Defense Medal. He was discharged Sept. 30, 1954, with the rank of corporal.

An accountant, he is married with four children and six grandchildren.

OSCAR SHERMAN, born Feb. 17, 1932, Bronx, NY. Enlisted February 1951 in USMC. Served in 1st Mar. Div. and 2nd Mar. Div. Stationed at Parris Island, SC; Camp Pendleton, CA; Camp Lejeune, NC; Portsmouth, VA; and Vieqves, P.R.

Participated in operations against enemy forces in South and Central Korea. Memorable experience was the cold in the mountains of North Korea (at the Frozen Chosin).

Awards/Medals: Korean Service Medal with four OLCs, UN Medal, Korean National Defense Ribbon, Good Conduct Medal, Presidential Unit Citation (1st Mar. Div.) and Syngman Rhee Presidential Unit Citation.

He was discharged February 1954 with the rank of sergeant.

Married with two sons, two grandsons and one granddaughter. In the retail sales of shoes. Member of 1st Marine Division, Marine Corps League, Commander of JWV Post 108, Korean War Vets Assoc., American Legion and Knights of Pythias (post chancellor).

IRVING SHINDLER, born Feb. 6, 1916, Manhattan (East Harlem), NY. Graduated from Monroe High School (Bronx), 1934. Inducted into U.S. Army, Camp Upton, NY, Oct. 15, 1941, during WWII. Completed basic training at Ft. Eustis, VA, December 1941. Stationed in Panama Canal Zone, served on staff (Pacific Coast Artillery Brigade HQ). Discharged November 1945 in rank of master sergeant. Four years service, states one year, Panama Canal 2 1/4 years, Germany nine months.

In Panama, from private through various ranks to tech sergeant, September 1943. In October 1943 promoted to master sergeant and transferred to 903rd AAA Separate Battalion stationed along Panama Canal (Pacific side). Mission of battalion and ancillary forces (chemical and barrage balloon units) to defend canal against enemy 5th column groups.

April 1944 in Ft. Jackson, SC for infantry training, completed June 1944. July-December 1944, duty at 1st Army HQ, Ft. Meade, MD. January 1945, replacement in Metz, NE France (very close to Siegfried Line). Assigned to 347th Regt. (87th Inf. Div.). In HQ Svc. Co. during the Rhineland and Central Europe Campaign.

April 1945 (three weeks prior to end of WWII) the 87th Div. located in Plauen at the Czech border and was transferred to military government detachment in Kassel, Germany, as acting 1st sergeant (rank of master sergeant). Detachment (100 enlisted men, five officers) mission to operate complex of warehouses containing food supplies for local population, also for displaced persons in nearby barracks. Detachment responsible for returning displaced persons (older adults, children) to their native countries.

1946-1950, attended Pace College (Evening Division) in June 1951 awarded diploma-accountancy/business administration with gold medal (1st honors). Civil Service (accounting/auditing), federal 16 years (1946-1961); city of New York 17 years (1963-1979).

After retirement 1979, attended college of New Rochelle (School of New Resources in Manhattan). His wife, Ethel, retired 1977 (secretary, city civil service) also attended School of Resources. In 1982, both awarded the bachelor of arts degree.

Joined JWV, 1950, Post 369 through 1971. In Kraditor, Brooklyn Post 2 since 1972; served in all offices, including commander. Involved in virtually all committees and functions. Editor 11 years, membership chairman seven years.

Active in synagogue, trustee-council of Jewish Organizations (Bay Park).

Married to Ethel in 1948. Two married sons, Harold and Brian; daughters-in-law, Gale and Robin; five grandchildren: Melissa, Joshua, Rachel, Adam and Nina.

LARRY SHIFMAN, born Nov. 5, 1918, Poland. Joined the USN, Seabees. Stationed at Sampson, NY and overseas.

He was discharged in October 1945 with the rank seaman second class.

Married 51 years, has three children and seven grandchildren.

ROBERT G. SHINDLER, was in one of two batteries who were guarding the pontoon bridges built by the engineers, April 1945 to May 8 when the war ended.

GILBERT SHMIKLER, born Jan. 4, 1925, Chicago, IL. Spent his life in art. University of Illinois courses to earn a Bachelor of Arts at age 18 on March 20, 1943. Graduated U. of Illinois February 1949 with a BS degree.

Served 16 years as a member of the National Defense Executive Reserve as director of industrial mobilization for the glove industry.

Entire business career was with Illinois Glove Co. Formerly was president and currently on its board of directors.

Married July 24, 1943, to Marian, has four sons: Robert, David, Michael and Samuel.

BARNETT SHOPIRO, born March 15, 1922, Syracuse, NY. Attended Central High School and Syracuse University. Member of Sigma Alpha Mu Fraternity. Served in the Ordnance Corps. He died Nov. 14, 1944, at Leyte at the age of 22.

DOROTHY SHOLIN, with no brothers to serve during WWII and two married sisters raising their children and a younger sister, she resigned as an air raid warden and enlisted in the WAVES in July 1944.

Following boot training in Hunter College, NY, she was sent to Storekeeper Training School in Millidgeville, GA. Rosh Hashana and Yom Kippur was celebrated while there. All Jewish WAVES were sent to Camp Kilmer. They shared barracks with WAACS and attended services.

In November 1944, she was assigned to the Radar Division of the Bureau of Ships in Washington, DC. While there she had the honor of meeting and shaking hands with Eleanor Roosevelt, as well as attending President Roosevelt's 4th Inaugural Ball.

November 1945 she was discharged with the rank of storekeeper third class.

Awards/Medals: Good Conduct Medal.

MIRIAM MILLER SHOR (MIMI), born in Glasgow, Scotland. Moved to Kingston, PA at age 2. Graduated from Wilkes-Barre General Hospital School of Nursing in 1943. Entered the USN Nurse Corps in July 1943, assigned to the McIntire Dispensary, Great Lakes, IL. In 1944 assigned for duty at the San Diego Naval Hospital, Balboa Park. In 1945 sent to Fleet Hospital 111 on Guam during the Iwo Jima and Okinawa campaigns. Discharged from the Naval Nurse Corps in 1946 as a lieutenant (sg).

Awards/Medals: American Theater, Asiatic Theater and Victory Medal.

Married in 1946 to Robert Shor in Los Angeles, CA. Worked in various nursing capacities from hospital, private duty, industrial and office nursing. Proud parent of three sons: Stanley, Michael, Steven, and one daughter, Judy. Grandchildren: Andrea, David and Alyson.

Joined JWV Post 396 in 1948 and JWVA Auxiliary 396. Was auxiliary president, 1953-1955; department president, 1957-1958; and elected national president, 1961-1962. Elected president in 1960 of Women's Auxiliary, American Podiatric Medical Association serving for two terms.

Presently she is legally blind and attends the Braille Institute of America where she is on the Speaker's Bureau and a tour guide. She continues being active in JWV, serving as national liaison officer and on the executive board of the National Museum of American Jewish History.

ROBERT SHOR, Doctor, PNC, born Chicago, IL, April 11, 1921. Pre-med major at University of Illinois. Attending Illinois College of podiatric medicine when enlisted in the USN April 1943. Basic at McIntire Dispensary, Great Lakes, Illinois. Worked in Bacteriology Lab for 11 months.

Shipped out aboard LST 177 in convoy. Armada. Flotilla was attacked by German dive bombers going through the Straits of Gibraltar. Landed in Bizerte, Tunisia and began training for the invasion of Italy. Saw service in Naples, Nisida and then on to the invasion of Anzio.

Prepared for invasion of Southern France, then sent to Palermo, Sicily taking charge of the Port Dispensary. Transferred to Quonset Point, RI and assigned to USS *MacLeish* until decommissioning.

Awards/Medals: American Theater, European Theater with three Battle Stars and Victory Medal.

Finished school at Illinois College of Podiatric Medicine in 1948 Cum Laude.

Married a Navy nurse, Miriam "Mimi" and moved to California. Parents of three sons: Stanley, Michael, Steven; daughter, Judy; grandchildren: Andrea, David and Alyson.

Became president, 1961, of the American Podiatric Medical Assoc. At the same time Mimi was elected National President of the Ladies Auxiliary JWV. He served as department commander, California, 1969-71. Honored in 1976 to be elected National Commander, JWV of the USA, also honored to serve as chairman of National Executive Committee for two years.

MAX SHORT, 1/LT, grew up in Dorchester, MA and practiced law in Boston. During WWII he served with Co. K, 90th Inf. Div. and was killed in action in Europe.

He is survived by his wife, Temma Weinstein Short and three-year-old son, Eli Joseph. The posthumous awards of the Distinguished Service Cross, Silver Star with OLC and Bronze Star with OLC were made to the child by Maj. Ralph A. Conners.

Eli Joseph also became a lawyer and lives in Storrs, CT.

DAVID SHOSS, born in Houston, TX. Two years of college. Drafted Feb. 6, 1941, 36th Inf. Div. Brownwood, TX, master sergeant. Transferred to 8th Air Force, commissioned 2nd lieutenant June 24, 1943, received pilot and navigator wings. Assigned to 100th BG, 418th BS. Stationed at Ellington Field, TX; Childress, TX; San Marcos, TX; England.

Flew 20 missions in B-17 bombing Germany and occupied territory. Shot down June 24, 1944, captured and escaped three months later.

Awards/Medals: three Air Medals, two Purple Hearts, Distinguished Flying Cross and Soldier's Medal. He was discharged July 14, 1945.

Married Doris Mae Levine Dec. 28, 1944, has three daughters: Debbie, Donna and Dori. Member of JWV, DAV, VFW, American Legion, Military Order of World Wars, Air Force Escape and Evasion Society and Caterpillar Club.

Maintains business, Diamond Trade, Inc. and Investments, in Dallas, TX.

GERSHON J. SHUGAR, born June 15, 1918, Tarboro, NC. Attended The Citadel; University of North Carolina, BS chemistry, 1939 and MA chemistry, 1940; University of Florida, Ph.D. in chemistry and chemical engineering, 1943.

Inducted June 16, 1944, Newark, NJ; NTS, Great Lakes, IL; NTS Nav. Armory, Michigan City, IN; NTS College of the Ozarks, Clarksville, AR; RMS Nav. Res. Lab., Washington, DC; USNTS, Noroton Hts., CT; USN Yard, Annex, Tompkinsville, S.I., NY; PSC, Lido Beach, L.I., NY.

Awards/Medals: American Theater and Victory Medal. Discharged Feb. 17, 1946, ETM2/c.

Joined Celanese Corp. as research chemist, then opened up his own chemical manufacturing plant, developing processes for manufacturing synthetic pearl pigments and established a natural pearl essence plant in Maine and Nova Scotia. The company became largest pearl essence manufacturer in the States. Sold his interest in 1967 and became assistant professor at Rutgers University, then employed by Essex County College of Newark, NJ for past 26 years. Author of many reference handbooks.

Married Helen Brauer; son, Ronald; daughter, Rose Bauman; two grandsons and two granddaughters.

HAROLD B. SHUGAR, born April 10, 1923, Tarboro, NC. Enlisted March 18, 1923, USN, PY-20, PYc-16, 1st lieutenant, deck watch officer; USS *Kenneth Whiting* (AV-14) 1st Div. Officer; antisub in North Atlantic and Pacific; participated in operation with killer group of destroyers going after German submarines in the North Atlantic.

Memorable experiences were serving at Bikini Atom Bomb tests; the hurricane in North Atlantic where ship almost capsized in January 1945.

Awards/Medals: American Theater Ribbon, Asiatic-Pacific Theater Ribbon and WWII Victory Medal. Discharged Aug. 29, 1946, as lieutenant jg.

Traveled to Palestine in 1947, joined Haganah and served in defense of Jerusalem during siege; joined Israeli navy as gunnery officer aboard the Eliat.

Returned to the States in 1949. Worked in commercial and industrial construction as chief estimator and project manager for general contractors for over 30 years. Presently semi-retired with his own company, Jodan Construction Consultants.

Married Sally Hope Staier in 1956. Two sons, Joel Kenneth and Daniel Scott. Member of JWV, B'nai B'rith, Temple Israel, American Society of Professional Estimators and Project Management Institute.

LARRY E. SHUGARMAN, was an air raid warden from 1941-1943. Volunteered for Armed Forces and inducted at Ft. Meade, MD. Sent to Camp Grant, IL for basic medical training. Sent to Camp Reynolds, PA and stationed at Dental Laboratory. Moved to Indiantown Gap, PA in January 1945 where he was discharged in April 1946.

Enlisted in Inactive Reserves and recalled in November 1950. Sent to Camp Pickett, VA and put in charge of the dental laboratory there. Discharged in July 1951.

Memorable experience was leading his troops at Indiantown Gap, PA in early 1945.

Married Beatrice June 13, 1945, while on furlough.

Served in PTA and elected president of Baltimore City Council of PTAs for two terms. Upon birth of twins, he co-founded with his wife the Parents of Twins Club of Baltimore. Served on many committees for the Dept. of Education. Rejoined JWV in 1970s and has been commander of Post SZ/NK 493 a number of times. Was commander of Dept. of Maryland from 1991-92 and has been VAVS representative at Ft. Howard VAMC MD for a number of years.

STANLEY SHULKIN, born Aug. 20, 1921, Sioux City, IA. Entered USAAC September 1942, as link trainer instructor. Link Trainer is flight simulator used in training pilots for instrument flying, navigation and instrument approach landings. Learned this craft at Chanute Field, IL.

Stationed at Peterson Field, Colorado Springs, CO where instructed pilots at photo recon base, primarily P-38s, B-17s and B-24s. Next base was Fairmont, NE where instructed pilots of heavy bombardment aircraft, B-29s, which were trained for South Pacific Theater. Discharged at Chanute Field, IL in January 1946.

Married Harriet Mendel of Amarillo, TX. Parents of Dr. Allen Shulkin, Dallas; Dr. Barry Shulkin, Ann Arbor, MI; Craig Shulkin, Lancaster, CA. Has five grandchildren.

Joined JWV Dallas Post 256 and participates in all programs. Post commander in 1993 and 1994. In 1993, Post 256 won Brenner-Jaffe Award. In 1994 post won award for best newsletter. Post hosted 1994 National Convention. Served

as operating chairman of campaign to elect Neil Goldman National Commander. National Vice Chairman of Descendants of JWV. Post-chairman for centennial celebration.

SHERWOOD L. SHULMAN (WOODY), born Watkins Glen, NY, April 24, 1924. Entered USN in March 1943. Following boot camp at Sampson, NY, he was sent to Radio Tech Schools at Michigan City, IN; Stillwater, OK and Treasure Island, CA, graduating as RT2/c.

Was plankowner on LCS(L)3 #75, built in Portland, OR. Saw duty at Eniwetok, Saipan, Philippines and Okinawa. Participated in landings, picket duty and making smoke to protect larger warships during kamikaze raids.

The crew was among the first at Nagasaki after the Japanese surrender. While charting the Yangtse River to Hankow, China, an attack by Chinese Communists was successfully defeated.

Discharged in 1946, he married Esther Ouriel in May 1947. Graduated in 1950 from University of Rochester, aided by the GI Bill. Father of five children. Followed an insurance career.

Moved to Bradenton, FL in 1987. Began writing free-lance art and theater reviews for newspapers, magazines and antique publications.

RAPHAEL SHUSTAK, raised in Newark, NJ. Drafted in 1951. Training at Camp Rucker, AL. Immediately went overseas and spent nine long months in Korea, all the time in a four-point area. When he was there, needed 36 points to rotate. He was, at all times, above the 38th Parallel.

Spent 21 months in the military and 21 long days on a troop ship going to Korea. Was hit in the head and gets very nervous. Now receives 30% disability. Served his country and would do it again if he had to. Korea was a time that our country forgot about.

As a Jew, when he was on the front line, they said Jewish services were being held in Seoul and he went down for one day. In basic training, he went to services on Friday night and had duty on Sunday.

Married, has three children and seven grandchildren.

GILBERT SIEGAL, born May 28, 1920, New York, NY. Left Harvard Law School, Dec. 9, 1941, enlisted January 1942 in the USAAC. Assigned to 565th Sqdn., 389th BG, 8th AF. Stationed at Maxwell Field, AL; Primary Flying School, Ocala, FL; Navigation School, Monroe, LA; crew training, Davis Monthan Field, Tucson, AZ; Hethel AFB, Norwich, England.

Attached 9th AF, Benghazi, Libya, covered invasion of Sicily, July 1943, 12th AF; Tunis, Algeria for Wiener-Newstadt, Austria Air Raid; tour of duty with 8th AF May 1943-April 1944, Air Transport Cmd. April 1944-October 1944; navigation instructor Westover AFB, October 1944-June 1945.

Awards/Medals: Atlantic Theater of Operations, ETO with two Battle Stars, Air Medal with four OLCs, DFC with OLC, Presidential Unit Citation, NYS Conspicuous Service Cross and WWII Victory Medal. Discharged July 1947 as 1st lieutenant.

Has wife, Aranka; daughter, Rise; son, Joseph; brother, Ira and nephew, Glenn.

BA from University Richmond and LLB from Harvard Law School. Still practicing law in New York City.

LEONARD J. SIEGALOVSKY, Corporal, inducted Dec. 26, 1942. Overseas service Dec. 17, 1943-May 15, 1945. Served in the Mediterranean Theater of Operations in Italy with 15th AF, 449th BG(H), 719th BS. Ground crew, armament section. B-24s (Liberators).

A memorable experience was in September 1944 when he and a friend flew to Rome for R&R. They went to the Great

Synagogue near the Tiber for Rosh Hashonah. As American soldiers they were seated in places of honor at the front of the sanctuary. During the service, the names of local Jews who had been taken away by the Germans were read aloud as the congregation lamented. It was one of the most moving moments of his life.

Awards/Medals: 10 Battle Stars, Presidential Unit Citation with OLC. Citation for bombing of Ploesti Oil Fields in Rumania. Oak Leaf Cluster for bombing of Southern France in support of Allied landings. Ribbon for Mediterranean Theater and Good Conduct Medal. Discharged Sept. 8, 1945.

Spent his working career in industrial advertising and public relations.

ALFRED I. SIEGEL, born Nov. 11, 1921, Bronx, NY. Enlisted Aug. 16, 1940 in USAAF. Graduated as aircraft mechanic at Chanute Field, IL, February 1941. Transferred to Air Force group in Langley Field, VA. On Dec. 7, 1941, start of war, his group transferred to California and became the first med. bomb group to patrol the West Coast.

Transferred to Australia and became first med. bomb group to fly in SW Pacific area en masse. Moved with this group and was an aircraft mechanic on B-26s, B-25s and later the B-24s for 35 months in Australia and New Guinea until returning to USA in December 1944.

Awards/Medals: Asiatic-Pacific Campaign Medal and Ribbon with four Bronze Campaign Stars, two Presidential Unit Citations, American Defense Medal, American Campaign Medal, Good Conduct Medal, WWII Medal and AAF Technician Badge. Discharged Aug. 23, 1945, as sergeant.

Worked for National Advisory Committee for Aeronautics in Air Corps Enlisted Reserve in Cleveland, OH from February 1945 to August 1945. Graduated from Syracuse University in June 1949 with BS in accounting. Presently a member of JWV and former officer of JWV. Retired as accountant.

MARTIN J. SIEGEL, born April 3, 1921, Brooklyn, NY. Enlisted USAAF July 9, 1942. Commissioned 2nd lieutenant at Selman Field Advanced Navigational School, Monroe, LA.

Assigned to 453rd BG, 732nd BS in England. While engaged in a bombing run over a military/industrial complex at Magdeburg, his B-24 Liberator was struck by flak. Deep in the heartland of Germany, he guided the plane to the safety of allied lines in France. All crew members parachuted to safety and within a week the reunited crew was back in combat.

Awards/Medals: Air Medal with OLC, EAME Service Medal with two Battle Stars. Separated from active service on Nov. 14, 1945, joined the Reserves and remained a reservist until the end of the Korean conflict.

Graduate of St. John's University School of Law and a member of the Bar, he served for a 1/3 century in various attorney capacities in the New York State Law Dept. including that of assistant attorney general in the administrations of Attorney Generals Jacob Javits and Louis Lefkowitz.

Married to the former Shirley Prager, has five children: Linda, Joanne, Hilary, Carol, Eugene, and nine grandchil-

dren: Jennifer, Jesse, David, Danielle, Jaclyn, Elise, Maxine, Hannah and Cydne.

Past commander of JWV Post 206 and American Legion Post 73, both in Monticello, NY. Now retired and a resident of Las Vegas, NV, he is a member of JWV Post 21 and advocate of VFW Post 8250.

SID SIEGEL, served with Co. K, 410th Inf. Regt., 103rd Div. On or about March 16, 1945, after 40 continuous hours of battle and close contact with the enemy, he was too fatigued to continue and fell out of the advance knowing they were in enemy held territory.

At dusk he came face to face with an enemy soldier who had separated from his squad to search for water. Beating him to the draw, Siegel captured his first prisoner. He was a very large man so Siegel was well hidden behind him in the failing light and so captured the rest of his squad.

They were desperate for water so he passed his full canteen to the squad and it came back still half full. He owes his life to this act because later in the day he came upon an entire company and demanded their surrender. He marched them in the direction he had last seen his company moving and after about an hour their commanding major asked "Veefle zint zee?" Siegal replied "nor ich" just me.

He found his company and rode into HQ astride a horse with over 150 prisoners ahead of him.

THOMAS L. SIEGEL, Colonel, USAF, RET, born Oct. 7, 1939, Teaneck, NJ. Graduate of Rutgers University, Class of 1961 and recipient of its Loyal Son Award, Rutgers' highest bestowed honor. Graduated Cornell University Law School in 1964. Admitted to practice in District of Columbia Bar and Texas.

Served on active duty as a judge advocate at Bolling AFB, Washington, DC, 1965-68. Remained in the USAFR attached for training with the Office of the Judge Advocate General, 1968-80. Reassigned to the SAC in 1980 and trained at Carswell AFB, 1981-85. Appointed to be the Reserve Mobilization Assignee to the Judge Advocate of 8th AF.

Awards/Medals: Legion of Merit and Meritorious Service Medal with OLC. Retired in 1991 after 30 years of commissioned service.

Maintains a private practice of law in Dallas, TX. He is a distinguished mediator and arbitrator and has been listed in *Who's Who in America* since 1979. Member of JWV Post 256.

Married to the former Ruth Rosenthal, has two children, Peter and Karen, and two grandchildren.

ISRAEL SIEV, born New York City, May 29, 1929. Served USN, 1946-48 and USMC, 1951-69. Veteran of Korea and Vietnam. USMC journalist.

Post office employee, 1969-92. Graduated Queens College 1979 at age 50.

Married Yiskfir Mufl a ir a uuumoro, lir a 19'00 hiu two sons. David, born 1964, a New York City Transit Policeman and Kenneth, born 1970, senior at Stoneybrook College.

Was volunteer at Israeli Army camp. Editor of *Crucial Concepts*, a journal dealing with the triple problem of crime, welfare and overpopulation. Is conducting campaign for stamp to commemorate Charles A. Lindbergh, who he maintains was not a Nazi, traitor nor anti-semite. Siev says, "In today's political atmosphere Lindbergh would simply be known as a peace activist. He was not always politically correct, but he was always a patriotic and courageous American."

MAX SIGAL, born Oct. 10, 1923, Bronx, NY. Enlisted Feb. 10, 1943, in the USAF. Basic training at Camp Upton, NY and Miami Beach, FL. Shipped to Lincoln, NE in March 1943 and

received training as an aircraft mechanic. Shipped to Willow Run AAB, Ypsilanti, MI where he received further training as a heavy bomber mechanic. Sent to Salt Lake City, UT and subsequently assigned to Biggs Field, El Paso, TX.

Served as member of ground crew unit and later assigned clerical work at the airbase collaborating upon aircraft historical data where he remained until August 1945. Assigned to Ft. Dix, NJ as a clerk-typist at the Separation Center and served there until his discharge as a staff sergeant on March 7, 1946.

Married to Frieda for 49 years, has two married daughters and one grandson. He is retired.

DAVID D. SILBERBERG, born March 20, 1921, Niedenstein, Germany. Emigrated with his family to Memphis, TN in 1936. He served in the Tennessee State Guard, 1940-42. Entered U.S. Army at Ft. Oglethorpe, GA, 1942. Basic training instructor, Army Air Corps Trng. Cmd., 1943. Commissioned 2nd lieutenant at Camp Ritchie, MD, 1944.

Shipped overseas to England. POW interrogator, 1944-45. Occupation duty in U.S. Zone of Germany, 1945-46. Member of Counter Intelligence Corps Special Projects Board, Ft. Holabird, MD, 1946-48.

Awards/Medals: Combat Infantry Badge, Bronze Star Medal with OLC, Presidential Unit Citation, ETO and various service ribbons, Belgian Fourragere and five Battle Stars for Normandy, Northern France, Ardennes (Battle of Bulge), Rhineland (Remagen Bridgehead) and Central Germany (Harz Mountain Campaign).

Relieved from active duty June 1948. From 1948-70, Active Army Reserve, MI SVC. Retired in 1970 with rank lieutenant colonel.

Graduated Law School and in law practice since 1951. Married Jeanette in 1954, has son, two daughters and one grandchild. Member of JWV Cpl. Harry Washer Post 121, Memphis, TN.

ARNOLD SILBERFARB, entered the U.S. Army in 1944. During WWII his brother, Harry, served in the USN and his brother, Martin, served in the Army.

Left the service in 1945.

HARRY SILBERFARB, born June 13, 1912, Brooklyn, NY. Enlisted Sept. 4, 1934, USN. Called May 2, 1941 to active duty. Assigned as instructor in fire chemistry, fire rescue and damage control duties.

Memorable experience was the morning of D-day and helping people out of the water and off of sinking ships. He pulled one sailor out of the water who turned out to be the son of a New York City Fireman that he had worked with in civilian life.

Awards/Medals: American Defense, EAME Theater, WWII Victory Medal, American Theater Campaign Medal, Navy Good Conduct. Discharged September 1945 as finua iidi a FIA i njin igim ile iii N C Hre Dept. officer. Today he is retired.

Married to Sylvia, has two sons, Stephen and Barry, and five grandchildren: David, Michael, Ross, Daniel and Sharon.

MARTIN W. SILBERFARB, enlisted at Mitchell Field, NY on March 21, 1942. He learned to fly in the USAF and ended up as an instrument instructor.

He left the service in November 1945. His brother, Harry, served in the USN during WWII and his brother, Arnold, served in the Army in 1944-45.

Makes his home in Boca Raton, FL.

signed to the 466th BG as aerial engineer crew chief. Stationed at AAFTS Amarillo Fld., TX; Consolidated B-24 Factory School, San Diego, CA; Attlebridge, England.

Participated in action in Normandy, Northern France, Rhineland, Ardennes, Central Europe and Air Offensive Europe. His memorable experience was meeting Gen. Eisenhower, Jimmy Doolittle and Glen Miller.

Awards/Medals: EAME Ribbon with six Bronze Stars, Presidential Unit Citation and Good Conduct Medal. Discharged Oct. 14, 1945, with rank staff sergeant.

Married, has daughter, son and six grandchildren. Retired and member JWV Post 711.

LOUIS SILVER, born Oct. 31, 1917. BS degree in chemistry, Georgia Tech; MS degree in chemistry, Emory University. Graduated as ensign in the Naval Reserve. Called to active duty May 5, 1941. Assigned to USS *Hornet,* June 10, 1941.

Served as line officer aboard USS *Hornet.* Observed launching of P-25s for attack on Japan by Jimmy Doolittle's boys. Took part in Battle of Midway. Observed demise of the USS *Wasp* in Guadalcanal corridor. Hit by torpedoes from Japanese submarines.

A month later *Hornet* was hit by Japanese carrier planes in the same Guadalcanal corridor. After three attempts to tow her, had to abandon ship.

Transferred and took command of LST-541. After shakedown, joined convoy from New York to England, arriving a month before the invasion of Normandy. Arrived at Normandy D-day night under attack. Made 10 trips across channel carrying troops and supplies.

Transferred back to Little Creek and served on base for three months. When base was shut down, was given LST USS *Okala.* Took her to Pearl Harbor unescorted. Had enough points for discharge. Came back to States in August 1945 and discharged a month later as lieutenant commander.

Married to Margie, has a son, daughter and two grandchildren. Served as technical advisor in the field of specialty chemicals. Retired in 1992. Presently serves as commander of Post 112 and commander of Department of the Southeast.

MILTON SILVER, born Aug. 18, 1918, Long Branch, NJ. Enlisted in the U.S. Army March 17, 1942. Assigned to Btry. A, 443rd Antiaircraft Arty., Automatic Wpns. Bn. Stationed at Ft. Dix and overseas.

Participated in action in European-African-Middle Eastern Theater of Operations.

Awards/Medals: EAME Theater, American Service Medal, Good Conduct Medal and WWII Victory Medal. Discharged Feb. 21, 1946, with the rank of sergeant.

Retired in 1986 from retail liquor store. He had a love for basketball and until his death in 1988 he continued basketball activity with youth groups. Survived by three daughters and four grandchildren.

STANLEY SILVER, born June 28, 1918. A native of Jersey City, NJ, now resides in Hoboken, NJ. A veteran of service in the 898th Ord. Heavy Auto Maint. Co. in the China-Burma-India and Oran-Bizerte operations. His service in the Army during WWII was from March 7, 1941-Nov. 26, 1945, when he was honorably discharged with the rank of master sergeant.

Awards/Medals: American Defense, American Theater, Asiatic-Pacific, EAME Service medals and WWII Victory Medal plus two Battle Stars.

The 898th Ord. was the only company that repaired equipment for the Alaskan Highway and Burma Road. Company was considered the most productive company of the U.S. Army.

STANLEY D. SILVERBERG, born Baltimore, MD, Feb. 10, 1926. Enlisted in the U.S. Army. Stationed at various stateside locations.

Awards/Medals: Good Conduct, American Theater and Rifle Marksmanship. He was discharged in 1947 as private first class.

Wife deceased, has one daughter and two grandchildren.

BEATRICE SILVERMAN, Navy name was Beatrice Silverman Mailer, born March 20, 1922, Chelsea, MA. Active service, April 6, 1944, USNR Midshipmen's School, Northhampton, MA; commissioned May 30, 1944. Attended Naval Training School (Communications) Northhampton. Stationed at NOB Norfolk, VA; USN Berthing Facility, S.I., NY; District Communications Office 3rd ND NY, NY.

Norfolk, VA was culture shock for a young woman from Boston. It was difficult for her to accept the way in which Black Americans were treated in the South and in the Navy (more like servants than military personnel) and she had constant discussions and arguments with friends and other women officers in their BOQ, many of whom were Southerners. She was the only Jewish woman in their quarters, but, luckily, not the only Liberal.

Awards/Medals: American Theater and Victory Medals.

Retired from the practice of psychiatry in August 1991. Has son and daughter, both married with three children each. Her Father, Hyman Silverman, deceased, was awarded Distinguished Service Cross and Croix de Guerre. Her mother, Jennie, deceased, was active in JWV and past national president, Ladies Auxiliary, 1940-41.

DAVID SILVERMAN, born April 24, 1918, New York City. Enlisted March 1, 1944, U.S. Army Infantry, 92nd Div., 362nd Regt. Stationed in Italy, Po Valley and Ft. Devens. Saw action in Po Valley.

Awards/Medals: Combat Infantry. He was discharged June 1, 1946 with the rank corporal.

Married 54 years, has one daughter, Sacramento, CA. He is retired.

HYMAN SILVERMAN, was born in Boston, March 23, 1895. Enlisted Nov. 23, 1917, and discharged Sept. 23, 1919. Inducted as a private, Co. E, 60th Inf., 5th Div. AEF and fought in all their battles. Advanced to corporal in the field at Verdun, where he was wounded and received his decorations.

Awards/Medals: Distinguished Service Cross from the U.S. Government and the Croix de Guerre from the French Government on Oct. 27, 1918.

"When enemy shellfire had ignited an ammunition dump, Pvt. Silverman assisted in removing the ammunition from the blazing dump. Several of his comrades were seriously wounded by exploding shells, and he himself was hit in many places by hand grenade explosions, but he continued until the greater part of the explosives were moved to safety. He then assisted in removing his wounded comrades before submitting to treatment for his wounds."

On his return to the States, he married Jenny Toltz and they had three daughters. Beatrice, the oldest, was a lieutenant in the WAVES during WWII. Jenny became national president of the Ladies Auxiliary, JWV in 1940.

He became a CPA, had his office in Chelsea, MA where he was well-known and admired. He passed away Oct. 23, 1982.

IRVING SILVERMAN, born Aug. 19, 1921, Waterbury, CT. Entered the U.S. Army Aug. 3, 1942, Ft. Devens, MA, then to USAAF, Miami, FL. Graduated with honors from both A/F Radio School and Control Net System.

Overseas with 8th AF to Wrethan, England from September 1943 to November 1945 with the 369th Fighter Sqdn., 359th Fighter Group. His group flew "escort" on many of the bombing runs over France and Germany.

During D-day invasion, he operated group's "CNS Homing Station," assisting pilots in returning to base. Also remembers vividly the "Blitz of London," the "buzz bombs" and the "V-2 rockets" launched by the Germans.

Awards/Medals: European Theater Ribbon with two Battle Stars and Unit Citation Ribbon. Honorably discharged Nov. 13, 1945, Ft. Devens, MA, with the rank of corporal, USAAF.

Served on the JWV Honor Guard Firing Squad for their returning war dead.

Married to Rose since 1950, has two daughters, two sons and six grandchildren. Started his own CPA practice in 1952, retiring in 1990. Member and past president of Post 91, JWV.

IRVING SILVERMAN, M.D., born July 26, 1912, Norwood, MA. Captained undefeated high school-football team and was All-Massachusetts State Tackle, 1930. Later played varsity at Dartmouth College and elected to All-American-Jewish team in 1934.

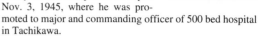

Enlisted in the U.S. Army Sept. 18, 1942. Overseas to England Jan. 2, 1944. Served in European Theater until May 1945, then transferred via the Panama Canal to the Pacific Theater and served in the Philippines and finally in the occupation of Japan Nov. 3, 1945, where he was promoted to major and commanding officer of 500 bed hospital in Tachikawa.

Awards/Medals: American Service Medal, WWII Victory Medal, EAME Service Medal, two Battle Stars, Philippine Liberation Medal with one Bronze Star and Asiatic-Pacific Service Medal. He was discharged May 4, 1946.

Married to Selma Krasnow, son David and grandchildren, Benjamin and Molly. Ended career with professional tank in pediatrics at Harvard Medical School. Member of Post 211, Newton Centre, MA.

LAWRENCE SILVERMAN, born Dec. 19, 1915, Detroit, MI. Enlisted July 29, 1942, in U.S. Army. Served with 5th Amphib. Engrs. Stationed at Aberdeen Proving Ground, Ft. Dix, Omaha Beach, Antwerp, Bremerhaven, Normandy, Northern France, Ardennes and Rhineland.

Memorable experience was participating in one of the most important battles of the century, Omaha Beach.

Awards/Medals: Bronze Arrow Head, EAME Theater Ribbon with four Bronze Stars, Croix de Guerre with one Palm. He was discharged Nov. 30, 1945 with the rank of corporal.

He is retired. Single.

LEWIS K. SILVERMAN, born in Stanhope, NJ, 1914. Attended New York University as a physical education major. Received Ph.D, 1942. Enlisted in U.S. Army in September 1943. Trained and stationed at Camp Crowder, MO. Worked in a Rehabilitation unit with injured and disabled soldiers from local units and with soldiers evacuated to the States because of special injuries.

Awards/Medals: Awarded the Rifle Marksman Awards, Meritorious Unit Award, American Theater Ribbon, Good Conduct Medal and WWII Victory Award. He was discharged in 1946.

Returned to teaching position in the Newark, NJ School System and assigned to the field of Special Education as a physical therapist for orthopedically handicapped children. Retired after nearly 50 years of service.

Married Evelyn Katz Silverman 1941, has two sons, Melvin K. and David Sandford Silverman (both are attorneys); two grandchildren, Josh, a guitarist and song writer, and Annie Laurie, who attends Sarah Lawrence College.

MILTON L. SILVERMAN, born Oct. 27, 1916. Entered the USAAF Jan. 28, 1943. Assigned to 12th AF, 428th BS, 310th BG, 57th BW, as aviation mechanic and top turret gunner. Stationed at Tyndall Field, FL; Sheppard Field, Wichita Falls, TX; Columbia AFB, SC. Flew 70 missions in WWII in B-25, *Billy Mitchell,* in Corsica.

Awards/Medals: Received five Battle Stars (Rome Arno, Naples-Foggia, Southern France, Apennines Campaign and Po Valley), Presidential Unit Citation, Good Conduct Medal, seven Air Medals with six OLCs, WWII Victory Medal and EAME Service Medal. Discharged July 3, 1945, as tech sergeant.

Married to Esther, has son, Keith; daughter-in-law, Alisa Gail; daughter, Alyse; son-in-law, Barry; and three grandchildren: Rhyne, Jacob and Sean. He is retired. Member of DAV, Air Force Association, Eastern Paralyzed Veterans, American Air Museum, American Legion and JWV, Irwin Loetz Post 250.

MORRIS A. SILVERMAN, born Oct. 1, 1918, Buffalo, NY. Enlisted in June 1941 and served with the 76th Inf. Div. Med. Detach. Stationed at Ft. McClellan, AL; A.P. Hill, VA; Ft. McCoy; England; France; Luxembourg, Germany.

Saw action in Ardennes, Central Europe and Rhineland. Was in Germany when the war ended. Memorable experience was Battle of the Bulge.

Awards/Medals: American Service Medal, EAME Theater, Purple Heart, Bronze Star, Good Conduct Medal and Victory Medal. Discharged Jan. 8, 1946, as T-4.

A widower, has one married son and two grandchildren. Semi-retired as a pharmacist, works one day a week.

MICHAEL SILVERS, was inducted in the U.S. Army, Nov. 6, 1941, at the age of 22. Went to Ft. Dix, NJ for 13 weeks of basic training as a tank gunner. Became instructor at Ft. Knox, KY, then sent to Camp Chaffee, AR. Groomed there for the European Theater of Operations and sent to Ft. Lee, NY for embarkation.

Arrived at Le Havre, France and assigned to Gen. Patton's 1st Div.; went from France through Germany and onto Pilsen, Czech., where the American forces met up with the Soviet Army, and ETO war was over.

Spent six weeks in foxholes, on route, saw many American soldiers laying dead, saw mines blowing up tanks, you name it. He lost hearing from the noise of the tanks and developed a skin disease from laying in the foxholes.

On the way back to Le Havre, for home, witnessed the concentration camps and the poor souls who survived. In fact he tried to take two young boys back to the States from the concentration camps, carried them on his back to Le Havre. They were stopped and put in the UNRA Program.

When they got to the States, one of them looked Silvers up and stayed with him and his wife for a couple of weeks, then located some cousins and went there.

Received medical and honorable discharge Jan. 9, 1946, and sent home on the USS *Colby*.

How dare anyone say no Jews fought in the Army; many of his buddies were Jews and didn't survive. They would gather whenever they could with a chaplain on Friday nights and holidays and would pray with the chaplain for the war to be over, liberate the camps and live to see the day to return home.

EVELYN EPSTEIN SILVERSTEIN, born in Chicago. Enlisted in the WAAC June 12, 1943. Trained at Ft. Oglethorpe, GA. September 1943 the WAAC became Women's Army Corps. Sent to Pine Bluff, AR, September 1943 and worked in arsenal office. Trained as a teletype operator, Camp Crowder, MO.

Arrived in Oro Bay, New Guinea Sept. 6, 1944, in first contingent of women assigned to the Signal Corps from U.S. Arrived Manila, P.I., Oct. 16, 1945. Attended trial of Gen. Yamashita and heard witnesses tell tales of horror.

Awards/Medals: WWII Victory Medal, WAAC Service Medal, Philippine Liberation Campaign, American Cam-

paign Medal, Good Conduct Medal, Asiatic-Pacific Campaign Medal with one Bronze Service Star and two Overseas Service Bars. Discharged Nov. 30, 1945.

Attended college under GI Bill. Taught elementary and special education until resigning in 1977. Married Ralph Silverstein Oct. 19, 1957, world champion wrestler and teacher (now deceased). Divides her time between Chicago and Florida. A member of Fem Vets Post 192. Participates in singing groups as a hobby.

RALPH SILVERSTEIN (RUFFY), born in Chicago, March 20, 1914. Physical education major at University of Illinois. Was AAU, Big Ten and National Collegiate Wrestling Champion. Graduated June 1937. Wrestled professionally until 1977. Nationally famous and has two fan clubs named after him, is in the Jewish Sports Hall of Fame in Chicago and the Illinois Sports Hall of Fame.

Was captain in military during the war as athletic director. In counterintelligence in the Pacific Theater. Analyzed intelligence information to determine its value to counter intelligence. Set-up and followed through cases of investigation. Was responsible for handling Ernie Pyle's personal effects when Pyle was killed.

Awards/Medals: American Defense Service Ribbon, WWII Victory Medal, American Theater Ribbon, Asiatic-Pacific Theater Ribbon with one Bronze Battle Star and Overseas Service Bar.

Married October 1957 to Evelyn Epstein, a former WAC and teacher. He taught physical education in high school and continued to wrestle professionally part-time. He passed away April 1980 of Lou Gehrig disease. He was a brother of LCDR Max Silverstein who has a ship, DE-534, named after him.

ALVIN B. SIMON, born Buffalo, NY, Jan. 14, 1931. Graduate of Staunton Military Academy. Member of advanced ROTC at Akron University. Enlisted in USMC Jan. 30, 1951. Boot camp at Parris Island, AIT at Camp Pendelton. Served in Korea 11 months in Antitank Assault Plt., Wpns. Co., 3rd Bn., 7th Mar. Regt., 1st Mar. Div.

Two highlights of his tour were: (1) coming off the line at the "Punchbowl" for services to find his rabbi from Temple Hill in IL in Buffalo, Cdr. Lihu Rickel, USNR, was 1st Mar. Div. chaplain. (2) Meeting Jerry Berkowitz, five house away Buffalo neighbor, coming up as a replacement.

Awards/Medals: Korean Service Medal with three Battle Stars, United Nations Medal, Presidential Unit Citation (for meritorious service while serving as assistant flame thrower operator in Korea, Nov. 3, 1951), USN Commendation Medal with Combat V. Honorably discharged Jan. 31, 1953.

He is divorced, has one daughter and lives in Arizona.

LOUIS CHARLES SIMON, born in Detroit, MI. Drafted in 1942. Basic infantry training at Camp Forrest in Tennessee, where the 80th Div. was activated. Overseas with Patton's 3rd Army, the 80th Div. landed at Omaha Beach long after D-day.

Fought in many battles but a couple stand out in his memory. Crossing the Moselle River, The Battle at Metz and the fighting at Bastogne in the Battle of the Bulge.

The most memorable part of his war experience was being in the first division to liberate Buchenwald Concentration Camp.

After his discharge, he returned to Detroit and worked in his father's hardware store. After the business closed, he worked for Sears, helping to open and working in the hardware department at the Oakland Mall Store for 20 years.

Retired, he is married and enjoys his home, visiting his daughters and traveling.

BETTY J. SINGER, born Oct. 29, 1949. Graduated Clark University, Worcester, MA, 1971. Served on active duty in USNR, 1971-73 as a line officer with Patrol Sqdn. 30, NAS Patuxent River, MD.

Awards/Medals: National Defense Ribbon and the Navy Expert Pistol Ribbon (Marksman).

Editor and publisher of *Options*, The Jewish Resources Newsletter. Has written and published two books, *Friends of the Jews* and *Conversations With My Soul*. Wrote an article in 1976 for *The Jewish Veteran* entitled, *An Unlikely Navy Officer*, (Sept-Oct '76) in which she described her Navy experiences.

Life member of B'nai B'rith Women and the JWV Wayne Post 695 as well as the National Council of Jewish Women and the Coalition for the Advancement of Jewish Education. She resides in Wayne, NJ.

NOBERT D. SINGER, born Sept. 8, 1929, Jersey City, NJ. Drafted in the U.S. Army May 9, 1951. Basic training at Ft. Dix, NJ. Sent by train to San Francisco, then by ship to Japan. Had Infantry MOS and was destined for Korea as a rifleman.

However, his records indicated that he had office experience and two years of college. Luckily, was selected to go to Eta Jima (Japanese Naval Academy) for a month of training as a clerk. After completing course, his MOS was changed to clerk/typist.

Sent to Korea as a replacement. Arrived in Pusan, Korea and sent by truck to a replacement depot in Chun Chon. He was then assigned to B Btry. of the 69th FA, an active combat unit of the 25th Inf. Div. then located in the Punch Bowl.

Awards/Medals: Japan Occupation Medal, Korean Service Medal with two Bronze Service Stars, UN Service Medal. He was discharged April 16, 1953, with the rank of corporal and acting sergeant.

Remarried on July 1, 1984, to Mildred and has one son, Bryan. Retired, he lives with his wife in Lawrenceville, NJ.

SEYMOUR SINUK, born Aug. 22, 1923. Enlisted November 1942 in NYC and assigned to Sig. Corps Reserve. Called to active duty, March 1943, Ft. Monmouth, NJ. Instructor at Eastern OTC in lines, at Monmouth, 15th Sig. Trng. Regt. Transferred November 1943 to AAF, 483rd BG (H).

Group joined the 15th AF in Italy, April 1944. Attained the rank of tech sergeant in Communications Section. Relieved of active duty and assigned to 320th Gp., AAFR at Mitchel Field, NY, October 1945. Received commission in USAF as 2nd lieutenant and assigned to 9214 Volunteer Air Reserve Trng. Unit, June 1948.

Awards/Medals: Distinguished Unit Citation with OLC, WWII Victory Medal, Good Conduct Medal, EAME Campaign Medal with nine Battle Stars (Southern France, Rome-Arno, Air Combat Balkans, Northern France, Northern Apennines, Po Valley, Rhineland, Normandy and Air Offensive Europe).

Received honorable discharge in New Rochelle, NY as 1st lieutenant, USAFR, October 1957. Member of Clearbrook Post 395, JWVUSA.

LOUIS SIROTA, served with the USAAF from May 7, 1941-Sept. 14, 1945. Entered the service in Boston, MA in 1941 with the rank of private and was discharged at Ft. Dix, NJ with the rank of sergeant. His training was had at Ft. Devens and Westover Field, MA with the aeroplane arm and also at Dow Field, Bangor, ME where he had flight combat training.

Sailed for overseas on *Queen Mary* from Boston, MA, Feb. 18, 1942. Landed in Australia March 28, 1942. Served in the Australia, New Guinea Theaters of Operation with the 65th BS and also in Dutch New Guinea with the 43rd BG. Saw considerable action in the Bismark Archipelago on New Guinea and Papoua Islands.

Awards/Medals: Presidential Unit Citation, Good Conduct Medal, American Defense Medal, Asiatic-Pacific Medal with three Battle Stars.

Places of interest which he visited were Sidney, Townsville, Brisbane, Australia, Rio de Janeiro, South America and Capetown, South Africa. Sailed on naval transport from Dutch New Guinea Nov. 15, 1944 and landed at San Francisco Dec. 4, 1944. *Submitted by Max Sigal.*

MURRAY J. SKLAR, born June 11, 1924, Newark, NJ. Reported for active duty with the USMC July 16, 1943. Boot camp at Parris Island, SC where attached to the 11th Air Wing. Trained at Cherry Point as radio/radar operator and went on to AIT at Camp Pendleton, San Diego, CA; El Toro MAS, CA; and Jungle School on Maui, HI.

Awards/Medals: Asiatic-Pacific Medal with two stars, American Victory Medal, American Defense Medal, Good Conduct Medal and Presidential Unit Citation for action in the Pacific. He was discharged as a corporal.

Used GI Bill to become a mechanical engineer with a master's degree. Retired as a staff-mechanical engineer from Lockheed Electronics, Plainfield, NJ in 1990.

Married the girl who never missed a day writing to him during the service. They have two grown children, Charles of Phillipsburg, NJ and Robin Oettle of Livingston, NJ, and two grandchildren.

THEODORE SKLAVER, born April 1, 1930, Boston, MA. Drafted Dec. 11, 1951, in USMC. Trained at Parris Island, NC, Radio-Telegraph Operator School then trained for Korea at Camp Pendleton, CA.

Spent 95% of his time in Korea as radio operator at battalion headquarters until July 1953 when the Chinese Reds tried to overtake the outposts before signing the truce. Spent four days helping to take back Outpost Hills Marilyn Monroe and Jane Russell.

After leaving Korea in May 1954, he spent time at Cherry Point, NC making contact with airplanes and ships at sea with Morse Code.

Awards/Medals: Good Conduct, Presidential Unit Citation, Korean Service Medal, United Nations Medal, Korean Presidential Citation, two Battle Stars and National Defense Service Medal. Discharged Nov. 6, 1956, as sergeant.

Married Edith July 5, 1955, has two wonderful children and two beautiful grandchildren. He retired after 32 years as a salesman.

JAMES I. SKOLNIK, graduated Military Intelliegence Training at Camp Ritchie in 1943. He served in Military Intelligence combat teams during WWII as interrogator and also Order of Combat Specialist.

ARTHUR SKOP, born in St. Louis, MO. Grew up in Cleveland, OH where he was active in many civic and Jewish organizations. Served in U.S. Army Infantry, 1942-1945, with Gen. George Patton and Gen. Mark Clark, 5th and 2nd Corps HQ.

Went to Tampa in 1957 and became active in all Jewish activities. Served as president of Beth Israel Cong., com-

mander of JWV Post 373, national deputy chaplain of JWV. Represented JWV at World Convention in Jerusalem, 1968; active in Jewish Community Center and Tampa Jewish Federation; headed Super Sunday in 1981; serves on board of directors of Congregation Rodeph Shalom.

Works with the Tampa Community Theater Group, taking part in over 35 productions. Has been on television, magazine covers (over 100 TV commercials and 100 ads) and spokesman for many businesses and organizations.

Married to Dorothy over 40 years, has two children, Dennis and Renee. Traveled with his wife the world over, having been to Israel, Paris, Rome, London, Tokyo, Hong Kong, Spain, Morocco, Hwlainki, Finland and Leningrad.

Awarded B'nai B'rith's Outstanding Citizen Award, 1969; a 32nd Degree Mason and member of the Masonic Scottish Rite; and associate member of Hadassah. In Tampa Real Estate for 30 years and has distinguished himself by being a member of the Presidents Club at Tam-Bay Realtors and as a multi-million dollar producer.

BERNARD SKRILOFF, born on lower east side, NYC, March 5, 1924. Resided in the Bronx and presently in Brooklyn. Graduated Morris High School, Bronx. Entered Army in January 1943. Learned American and Japanese Morse Code at Ft. Monmouth, NJ. Taught how to intercept and copy Japanese transmission on a typewriter, then relayed information for translation and decoding. Listened in for Allied aircraft distress signals.

Assigned to the 1724th Sig. Svc. Bn., 8th Radio Sqdn., Mobile AAF. Left Seattle POE in October 1944. Stopped at Pearl Harbor and arrived at Guam November 1944. Helped clear area in jungle for radio direction finders to locate enemy aircraft and set up radio equipment to intercept Japanese transmissions. Harassed by snipers hiding in caves and had casualties.

Awards/Medals: American Service Medal, Asiatic-Pacific Service Medal, WWII Victory Medal. Discharged February 1946 with the rank of sergeant.

Married to Sylvia 47 years, has two sons, Raymond and Michael. Retired from Federal Service in February 1980. Past commander of Cohen-Lurie Post 120, JWV, Brooklyn, NY.

HARRY SKRILOFF, born on lower east side, NYC, June 9, 1920. Lived in Bronx and Brooklyn. Graduated Morris High School, Bronx, NY. Entered U.S. Army in February 1943. Assigned as infantry rifleman.

Sent to Brisbane, Australia and received amphibious training. Was involved in battles of Bismarck-archipelago, New Guinea and Southern Philippines. Landed with troops during invasions of Admiralty Islands and Leyte in the Philippines. Landed at Lingayen, Luzon in January 1945. With the first division to enter Manila in February 1945. After Japan surrendered, was sent to Yokohama and Tokyo. Experienced close combat fighting in villages, mountains, jungles and fields.

Awards/Medals: Asiatic-Pacific Service Medal with Bronze Arrowhead, Philippine Liberation Ribbon, WWII Victory Medal. He was honorably discharged Dec. 14, 1945.

Worked for 30 years with the New York Postal Service. Retired March 31, 1979. Deceased July 15, 1989.

SEYMOUR L. SLAMOWITZ, born in Brooklyn, NY, July 9, 1924. Graduated Thomas Jefferson High School, June 1942. Joined family embroidery business. Entered U.S. Army August 1943. Trained at Camp Edwards, MA, Ft. Bragg, Ft. Fisher, NC with 133rd AAA Gun Bn. (Mobile). Served as instrument observer, ammunition handler, radar

operator, airplane spotter, special assignment with USAAF Weather Station.

Overseas to England, July 1944. Landed France August 1944, Utah Beach, Normandy. Served through France, Luxembourg, Germany and Austria.

Awards/Medals: three Battle Stars (Northern France, Central Europe and Rhineland), EAME Service Medal, Good Conduct Medal, WWII Victory Medal. He was honorably discharged as private in March 1946.

Married Esther Gabay in 1955, has two sons, Mark Nolan (electrical engineer) and Stuart Alan (podiatrist). Member of JWV Post 689 and VFW.

Worked in family embroidery business from 1946-1964. From 1964 to present, is self-employed as an embroidery designer.

HARRY LEO SLATIN, born New York City, May 30, 1919. Enlisted June 3, 1942 in the U.S. Army, Medical Dept., Walter Reed Hospital; Research, Parasitology Dept.; Ft. Sheridan, IL 6th Service Comm. Lab. Serologist; 2nd Malaria Survey Unit, Malariologist.

Overseas on old *Southern Cross* (33 days). They were bait for the Battle of the Coral Sea. Stationed at New Caladonia, New Hebrides, Efate (Roses), Canal, New Zealand, Ataipe, New Guinea (43rd Inf.), Luzon, P.I. (1st Cav.), to end of WWII.

Awards/Medals: Battle of Manila and all the usual WWII medals and ribbons. He was discharged Dec. 25, 1945, Ft. Dix, NJ.

Worked in civilian life in Parasitology, Microbiology, bio-chemist, biologist, patent attorney and industrial hygienist.

LOUIS SLATZKY, born and raised in Omaha, NE. Enlisted in the USAAC.

Served in South Pacific with the 5th AF as traffic control operator.

Married in 1948 and raised family in Cheyenne, had one son, a research doctor in Israel. He passed away in 1980.

NORMAN SLAWSBY, born May 26, 1925, Dorchester, MA. Inducted in U.S. Army at Ft. Devens, MA, July 6, 1943. Completed basic training at Ft. Bragg, NC in field artillery. Assigned to 807th TD BN, Co. B, 3rd Plt. at Camp Pilot Nob, CA for desert training. Went through maneuvers using M-10 TD with mounted 3-inch gun.

Departed States for ETO, Aug. 11, 1944. Arrived Liverpool, Wales Aug. 23, 1944. Crossed the English Channel Sept. 18, 1944, aboard LSTs, landed on Utah Beach, France as towed 3-inch gun battalion and later converted back to self-propelled tank destroyers, proceeded to the front.

First major battle was Battle for Metz, France after crossing the Moselle River Nov. 15, 1944. Metz fell Nov. 19, 1944. Battles and campaigns were Northern France, Rhineland and Central Europe. Duties included serving as field artillery computer in Fire Direction Center of Co. B.

Awards/Medals: Good Conduct Medal, WWII Victory Medal, EAME Theater Campaign Ribbon and American Campaign Ribbon with three Bronze Battle Stars.

Left Europe July 7, 1945, arriving in States, July 16.

President of Jana Brands, Inc., Natick, MA, an international frozen seafood sales and marketing organization. Happily married to Arlene for 44 years, has two married daughters, Debra Bergman and Sharon Hart, and three grandchildren: Allison and Gregory Bergman and Jaison Hart. Presently resides in Needham and Mashpee, MA.

SAMUEL I. SLOANE, born in St. Paul, MN. Attended Lenivard Grade School, Marshall Jr. High, Central High and University of Minnesota. Entered the U.S. Army, Aug. 2, 1942. Sent to Camp Berkeley, TX. Completed training in Medical Replacement Training Corps and assigned to medical unit destined to go overseas December 1942.

Served in Middle East (Africa). Transferred to China-Burma-India Campaign. Before leaving Middle East, had the opportunity to visit the "Wailing Wall" in Jerusalem.

Awards/Medals: EAME Ribbon with Battle Star, Asiatic-Pacific Ribbon with one Battle Star and Presidential Unit Citation. Received a master sergeant rank before leaving the Middle East.

Returned to former position with state of Minnesota as coordinator and supervisor of office and business management for Dept. of Public Welfare and State Institutions. Retired after 41 years of service.

Past president of Ramsey County Allied Veterans Council, past president of the Ramsey County Memorial Day Assoc. Member of JWV since 1954 and past commander of other allied veterans organizations past post commander, past dept. commander and past national executive committeeman. Currently again serving as post commander, St. Paul Post 162.

Married to Sylvia, has three children and four grandchildren.

FRANKLIN GEORGE SLUSSER, born Marlboro, OH 1924. Enlisted in U.S. Army 1942. Served three years in combat engineers, North Africa, Sicily and Italy. Served three years Vietnam as combat intelligence chief and advisor. Participated in combat operations in all four corps areas.

Seriously wounded when his aircraft was shot down approaching landing zone. Wounded and under constant heavy sniper fire, he regrouped his Intelligence Team, destroyed a grenade factory and killed eight enemy agents. He refused personal medical attention until all wounded and dead had been evacuated.

Awards/Medals: five EAME Battle Stars, nine Battle Stars Vietnam. Was in Country with Silver Star for Valor by RVN Gen. Le Nguyen Khanh. Received 24 other decorations including three Bronze Stars, Air Medals, Purple Hearts, Commendation Medals, Combat Infantry Badge and Aircraft Crewman Wings.

Retired in El Paso, TX with wife Rita, a native of Kispest, Hungary. Life member and past commander of Military Order of Purple Heart Chapter 393.

GEORGE SMALL, born Feb. 28, 1908, in Montreal, Canada. The family moved to New York City in 1919. After graduating from the Polytechnic Institute of New York with a bachelor of chemical engineering degree in 1935, he worked for a chemical company in California.

Volunteered for active duty in April 1941 and was assigned to the 19th BG in Albuquerque, NM as chemical officer. Sent to the Philippines, arriving at Clark Field in October 1941. Ordered to Bataan in late December, group was disbanded and he was assigned to Co. F, 31st Inf. After the surrender of Bataan, he was forced to make the Bataan Death March. When he arrived at Camp O'Donnell, the camp commander gave a welcoming speech and shouted, "You are our eternal enemy."

Transferred to Camp Cabanatuan in June and departed from Manila on Nov. 7, 1942 aboard the hell ship *Nagata Maru.* Arrived at Port Mjoi, Japan Nov. 25, 1942, and sent to Camp Tanagawa, Camp Zentsuji, Camp Rokuroski where he was liberated Sept. 8, 1945.

Returned home and learned that one of his brothers, Roland Small, was the first U.S. Army officer killed in the construction of the Alaska Highway, where later a memorial for him was erected. Discharged from the Valley Forge Gen. Hosp. and remained in the Reserves until retiring with the rank of major.

Returned to California and worked for the Dept. of Water Resources. He lives in Reno, NV with his wife Hadessa; they have two daughters, Gail and Wendy. Since there is no JWV Chapter in Reno, he belongs to Post 185 in San Diego, CA.

BERNARD A. SMITH, born July 6, 1923, Brooklyn, NY. Entered the USAAC Jan. 14, 1943. Aerial gunnery training at Lowry Field, CO; Armor School at Las Vegas, NV. Assigned to the 463rd BG, 772nd BS, stationed in Foggia, Italy. Participated in Air Offensive Europe, North Apennines, Po Valley, Rhineland, Rome-Arno and Air Combat.

Was a memorable experience when B-17 was severely damaged over Austria and three men (including pilot and copilot) were wounded. Losing altitude, the aircraft barely cleared mountains tops while being escorted out of enemy territory by P-51s. They finally landed safely even though most of hydraulic system was out.

Awards/Medals: Air Medal with three OLCs, New York Conspicuous Service Medal and EAME Service Medal. Discharged Oct. 17, 1945, as staff sergeant.

Married Irene, has sons, Marc and Larry, and grandchildren: David, Justin, Natalie, Samantha and Lindsey Semiretired from insurance sales and a member of JWV Post 131, Syracuse, NY.

MEYER SMITH, born in New York City, Jan. 17, 1922. Enlisted in the Army Oct. 2, 1942. Served as lineman in the 4th Inf. Stationed at Ft. Dix, Ft. Bragg, Perham Downs, England. Participated in battles: Ardennes, Rhineland, Central Europe.

His memorable experience was Lag Bomer on May 1, 1945, he was guarding German war prisoners in the basement of St. Otilier Hospital near Landsberg. When he got off guard duty he went upstairs and visited the Jewish inmates from the Duchau Concentration Camp. Jews lying in bed were thin as toothpicks. All you could see was skin and bones. He spoke to the inmates in Yiddish and told them who he was. They all

started to cry out "an American Jew." One Jew started to cry to him that he had no wife and child, because the Germans threw them into the crematory. Another Jewish inmate told Smith, his mother and father, brothers and sisters were shot before his eyes, and he started to cry. As he went from one bed to another he greeted the Jewish inmates. Each one told of the trouble they had with the German soldiers.

Awards/Medals: Combat Infantry, EAME Ribbon and three Bronze Battle Stars. He was discharged Oct. 22, 1945, with the rank of private first class.

Married to Clara Spindel in 1952. They have three children and one grandson, Elliot Eric.

Now retired and secretary of synagogue.

WILLIAM S. SMITH, born July 19, 1922, in New York City. Entered the U.S. Army on Dec. 12, 1942. Served with 100th Div., 399th Inf. Regt. and was stationed in Ft. Jackson, Ft. Bragg and Ft. Benning.

Awards/Medals: EAME Campaign Medal, (three stars), Bronze Star, Purple Heart, American Campaign Medal, Victory Medal, Army of Occupation Medal, Good Conduct Medal, Combat Infantry Badge. Discharged March 29, 1946 with the rank of Tech 5.

Smith is now retired.

STANLEY A. SMOLKIN, born March 1, 1943, Brooklyn, NY. Graduated Adelphi University 1964 and Brooklyn Law School 1967. Entered U.S. Army Sept. 20, 1967, training at Ft. Jackson, SC. Arrived South Vietnam, July 25, 1968. Served with Americal Div. Chu Lai area through July 24, 1969. Arriving in Vietnam, he took a steel helmet, that already had a bullet hole in it, believing it would be lucky for him. It was; while wearing it the helmet was hit, but the bullet didn't pass through it.

Awards/Medals: Republic of Vietnam Gallantry Cross, Republic of Vietnam Campaign Medal, Bronze Star Medal, Army Commendation Medal with first OLC, Good Conduct Medal, National Defense Service Medal, Vietnam Service Medal, Republic of Vietnam Campaign Ribbon.

Married to Joyce, two sons, Matthew and Mark. Member of JWV Post 666. Practicing attorney and Associate City Court Judge.

AARON SNYDER, born in Russia Aug. 27, 1914. His family immigrated to Philadelphia, PA in 1923. He served in PANG February 1939-February 1941 and then went active duty. He served in a pre-war horse cavalry unit and spent the war years as an infantry platoon leader, HQ Detachment 111th Inf. He served in Hawaii, Kwajalein, Eniwetok and Palau Islands.

He remembers fondly the unit chaplain, Father Horn, who was knowledgeable about Jewish customs and helped the Jewish men especially at holiday time.

His brother Jack was killed in action May 1945 on Mindanao. His brother Sam served in Europe in a tank unit.

Separated from the Army Nov. 26, 1945. Married Florence Schor, has two children, Alan and Gail, and four grandchildren: Michelle, Scott, Stacey and Ashley. Retired owner of an auto repair shop. He is commander of Sgt. Albert Scolnic Post 242 JWV and resides in Wyndmoor, PA.

RODGER C. SNYDER, born in Baltimore, MD, Jan. 4, 1947. He graduated from Milford Mill High School in June 1965. On Sept. 28, 1965, he and five of his friends patriotically joined the Armed Services, each in a different branch. Snyder chose the paratroopers, and was assigned to the 82nd Abn. Div. Upon graduation from Ft. Bragg in April 1966, he enjoyed a short leave before his unit was shipped to Vietnam. Three weeks before he was to return to the States, his young life was ended on Feb. 7, 1967.

Awards/Medals: Purple Heart Medal, Army Commendation Medal with a V for Valor, Bronze Star Medal and two medals from the government of Vietnam for bravery. The only Jewish young man in his unit, he was highly thought of and respected by the men in his unit. Returned to the States and laid to rest in Arlington Cemetery in Washington, DC. In every letter he wrote home, he encouraged students to complete their education.

Snyder has a very active post and auxiliary named in his memory, as the Rodger C. Snyder Memorial Post #117. This is the first post and auxiliary formed in Maryland after a Vietnam Veteran.

THEODORE SNYDER, born in Brooklyn, NY, Dec. 31, 1922. Studied engineering at Polytechnic Institute of Brooklyn. Enlisted in the U.S. Army and called to duty at Camp Upton, Yaphank, Long Island on June 16, 1943. Infantry basic training at Ft. Hood, TX; ASTP at Newark College of Engineering; 69th Inf. Div. training at Camp Shelby, MS with Co. D, 271st Inf. Regt. in April 1944.

Overseas in November 1944, he entered front lines with his 69th Div. unit Feb. 12, 1945, as a machine gunner at Siegfried Line on Belgian/German border, moving forward to Kassel past the Rhine River. Disabled by jaundice in April, returned to unit in East Germany area of occupation in May 1945. Stayed overseas until honorably discharged at Ft. Dix, April 1946.

Awards/Medals: Combat Infantry Badge and Bronze Star for Meritorious Service under enemy fire.

Completed mechanical engineering degree in 1948 at Polytech and masters degree in industrial engineering in 1951. Served as manufacturing engineer for 20 years with Sealy, Benrus, Fairchild and General Electric Co. including work at Cape Kennedy on the manned space flights (1969) before joining the New York State Department of Environmental Conservation as a senior water pollution control engineer for the past 18 years. Still active enforcing pollution control regulation on Long Island.

Married for 40 years and both his son and daughter received 69th Div. College Scholarships. Steve enroute to a UVA law degree and Leslie at Stanford University as a Ph.D grad. Today, a professor at University of Connecticut in Communications. Wife, Cynthia, is a guidance counsellor at Bethpage High School, NY. He is now retired, doing volunteer work in the community and the JWV Book.

MORTON SOIREF, born in Shumsk, Poland, Dec. 7, 1918. Enlisted June 1942. Served in the USAAF as bombardier with 8th AF, 379th Bomb Gp. Stationed in Childress, TX; Pyot, TX; Alexandra, LA; 379th Bomb Gp., England.

Participated in 30 bombing missions over Europe. On their second bombing mission they were going to Frankfort, Germany and as they started on their bombing run they got hit by flak. It knocked out their oxygen at 25,000 ft. Their pilot let down to 10,000 feet and they started back to the base at 10,000 feet. They were very lucky because they had cloud cover all the way to the English Channel and made it back safely.

Awards/Medals: Air Medal with three OLCs and Distinguished Flying Cross. Discharged June 8, 1945, with the rank of 1st lieutenant.

Married to Helen in February 1941 and has two sons, Brian and Gary, and two grandchildren.

Retired and does volunteer work, plays golf and takes trips with his wife.

MARTIN SOKOLOFF, born Nov. 6, 1923, Brooklyn, NY. Entered the USMC Nov. 21, 1942. Stationed at Parris Island, SC; Hingham, MA NAD; Camp Lejeune, NC; Guadalcanal; Okinawa; Guam; Tsingtao, China.

Memorable experience was participating in the surrender ceremony of the Japanese military forces in Tsingtao, China, Oct. 25, 1945.

Awards/Medals: American Campaign Medal, Asiatic-Pacific Campaign Medal, WWII Victory Medal, Presidential Unit Citation, Purple Heart and the Good Conduct Medal. Achieved the rank of private first class and was discharged Feb. 12, 1946.

Married Renee Gushen on April 14, 1946 and has one child, Todd, married to Gail and a grandchild in May 1994.

Member of JWV Post 444, DAV Post 41, 6th Marine Division Association, China Marine Association, AmVets New Jersey Department.

Sokoloff is a retired accountant.

BENJAMIN SOLOMON, born on Aug. 8, 1919, Baltimore, MD. Inducted in the Army on May 13, 1941. Sent to Pine Camp, NY, and joined the formation of the 4th Armd. Div. Worked in regimental headquarters with then CPT Creighton Abrams (who became U.S. Chief of Staff).

After approximately one year, was transferred to the 8th Armd. Div., Ft. Knox, KY. Later sent to Camp Beale, CA; then Camp Bowie, TX. From there to the East Coast and shipped to Le Havre, France. Participated in battles up to Braunau, Austria.

Shipped back to the States and given a 30-day furlough. Afterwards he was sent to Camp Cooke, CA and received his first discharge in 1945 with the rank of first sergeant. He qualified as an expert on the machine gun and sharpshooter on the carbine.

Married in 1948 and has one daughter, one son and two grandsons. Worked in the field as a commercial interior designer. For over 18 years he was the owner of his own business. Many hospitals, hotels, motels, schools and ships were furnished and designed by him. He also was an advisor and consultant to one of the larger maritime unions in the U.S. doing custom design and installations. He traveled extensively the eastern part of the United States. Retired now and lives in Pompano Beach, FL.

CARL SOLOMON, born in New Brunswick, NJ, Aug. 20, 1917. Enlisted January 1942. Served with the USCGR, *Joseph T. Dickman,* APA troop transport ship.

Participated in the African Campaign, French Campaign, South Pacific, Italian Campaign for three and a half years.

Memorable experience was at his battle station when a bomb dropped and hit his sleeping quarters. He missed being killed by seconds.

Awards/Medals: American Campaign Medal, EAME Campaign Medal with three Bronze Stars, Asiatic-Pacific Campaign Medal, WWII Victory Medal, American Defense Service Medal, Coast Guard Good Conduct Medal. Medically discharged April 1945 as petty officer first class.

He belongs to JWV Post 133 NBNJ; DAV Post #17, Edison, NJ; VFW Post 10536 Highland Park, NJ.

Married Helen in 1945 and has a son, daughter and three grandchildren. Owned a trucking company for 25 years. Now in commercial real estate.

FREDRIC M. SOLOMON, born in the Bronx, Nov. 25, 1945. Attended Columbus High School, Bronx Community College and Buffalo State. Drafted Sept. 11, 1967. Received basic training at Ft. Jackson, SC; Ft. Lewis, WA, AIT. Arrived in Korea March 13, 1968. Assigned to C Co. 2/23 Inf. (M), DMZ duty.

Conducted security and counter espionage missions within the DMZ. On April 1, 1968 units along DMZ received hostile fire pay due to increased hostilities and firefights with the North Koreans.

Earned Imjim Scout Patch for DMZ duties.

Separated April 16, 1969. Married to Vicki and has daughters, Stacie and Cindy.

Currently a lieutenant with NYC Police Department's Narcotics Div. assigned to Manhattan North Narcotics.

IRVING SOLOMON, born Jan. 26, 1921, New York. Enlisted Oct. 16, 1942, in U.S. Army in Communications. Stationed at Ft. Dix, Ft. Bragg, Camp Kilmer and Casablanca, Africa. Saw action in Africa, Sicily, Italy, Anzio, Southern France, Germany and Austria.

Memorable experience was being the only Jew in his outfit, HQ&HQ Btry, 41st FA, 3rd Inf. Div. Outfit came from out west and made up of German farmers. All he heard from them was, "Hey Jew boy we are fighting for you Jews." In return he would holler, "Hey Albert I am killing your German brothers." This really got their goat.

Awards/Medals: Bronze Star, ETO, Good Conduct, seven Battle Stars, French Citation and Presidential Citation. Discharged Nov. 30, 1945, with the rank corporal.

He is a widower and has two sons. Retired and involved in many organizations.

LEON SOLOMON, born Hartford, CT, Oct. 19, 1920. Enlisted in the USN Seabees, EM2/c, 6th Seabee Bn. Stationed in Great Lakes, IL; Little Creek, VA; Gulfport, MS; Moffit Field, CA; New Hebrides, Guadalcanal; Auckland, NZ; New Caledonia. Participated in battles in Guadalcanal, Solomon Islands.

Memorable experience was Sept. 1, 1942, he was one of 200 sailors of the 6th Naval Construction Bn. landing on Guadalcanal. The 1st Mar. Div. had landed there Aug. 7, 1942, and moved from the beachhead past a dirt runway which was to become Henderson Air Field. Their job was to convert the dirt strip to a modern airstrip that could accommodate heavy bombers in all kinds of weather. This would be the jumping off point for the beginning of the Pacific offensive. With the Marines holding the perimeter, the Seabees were on the airstrip before daylight and stayed there until dark. Daily bombings and shellings slowed up their work, but when the airstrip was covered with steel landing mat, plane reinforcements came in off the aircraft carrier *Enterprise.* With their new air wing as protection they were able to rush completion of fighter strip one and then fighter strip two, and with this the Pacific offensive began.

Awards/Medals: Presidential Unit Citation, Pacific Theater, Good Conduct and WWII Victory. Discharged as EM2/c Dec. 22, 1945.

Married to Myriel and has one daughter, Barbara.

Solomon went back into construction after service and is now retired.

RICHARD F. SOLOMON, born in Far Rockaway, NY in 1923. Graduated from Far Rockaway High School in 1942, then enlisted in U.S. Army pilot training program. Upon graduation as a fighter pilot, he flew combat missions with the 356th Fighter Group, 8th AF over Germany until wars end.

Deactivated in 1946 and later recalled to active duty in 1950, he served in Korea, and Vietnam and was commanding officer of five USAF Air Defense Stations throughout the U.S. and overseas areas. He flew combat support missions to the besieged fortress at Khe San, Vietnam in 1968 before retiring from active duty in 1970.

Awards/Medals: USAF Commendation Medal, three Air Medals and numerous campaign ribbons and Battle Stars earned in three wars.

Married to his high school sweetheart, Rose, for 44 years; one daughter, Laurie.

Currently a jet pilot and manager of Florida Corporation. Member of Post 613 JWV.

VICTOR M. SOLOMON, COL, USAF, RET, born Dec. 13, 1928, Brooklyn, NY, BA from Yeshiva University, 1951. Ordained (Smicha), Rabbi Isaac Elchana Theological of Y.U., MA from Hunter College, STM, NY Theological Seminary, 1967. Certificate, Post Graduate Center for Mental Health, 1967, STD, Temple University, 1960. Ph.D, New York University, 1981. Ph.D, Florida Institute of Technology, 1982.

Entered USAAF, July 5, 1968. Assigned to 6100 Cbt. Spt. Gp, Tachikawa AB, Japan as chaplain. Served PACAF, 5th AF. Special assignments to 7th and 13th AFs covering Vietnam, Thailand, Korea, Okinawa, Philippines, Republic of China.

Professor and chairman of Psychology Department, Sophia University, Tokyo. Known as "Flying Rabbi of Far East." After four years extended active duty, was appointed associate director, JWB Commission of Jewish Chaplaincy, 1972. Reserves until retirement as full colonel, 1991. Last mission, Desert Shield/Storm.

Awards/Medals: 23 awards and medals, including Air Force Meritorious Service Medal with four OLCs, Korean Expeditionary Force Medal, Air Force Commendation Medal and Japanese Zenkokai Medal for Heroism.

Currently licensed clinical psychologist and director, Teaneck Counseling and Psychotherapy Center, and clinical assistant professor of psychiatry, University of Medicine and Dentistry/NJ Medical School.

Married to Marcia since 1953, four sons: Shmuel, Shimon, Yitzchak and Avi, and six grandchildren: Oren, Yaffa, Tzvi Hirsch, Kayla, Tzvi Gedalia and Tehila.

Memberships: JWV, USA, Commander JWV Post #554, American Legion. Active in professional, communal and religious organizations.

HENRY J. SOMMER, born December 1919 in Cologne, Germany. Adolf Hitler's becoming head of German nation coincided with Henry's Bar Mitzvah in January 1933. Fled Nazi Germany with parents in 1937.

Arrived on board USS *Washington* in New York Harbor on Nov. 11, 1937 (Armistice Day). Witnessed, standing on sundeck, Gen. John Pershing, ordering wreath to be lowered ████ ███ ██ ████ ██ ██ ████.

Volunteered for military service after Pearl Harbor. Basic training and regular duty with independent infantry regiment on special assignment in Washington, DC, followed by assignments at Infantry Officer's Training School at Ft. Benning, GA.

Later, shipped to North Africa and Italy. Assigned to Co. HQ as rifleman and interpreter in a rifle company of the 34th Inf. Div.

Near war's end, hospitalized due to concussion. Reassigned to Signal Intelligence Service where he translated intercepted enemy military radio traffic as well as captured classified enemy documents. Demobilized December 1945.

Battles: North Apennines, Rome Arno.

Awards/Medals: Combat Infantry Badge, American Service Medal, Good Conduct Medal, WWII Victory Medal, EAME Service Medal with two Battle Stars.

Married to Margot and has two daughters and four grandsons.

Retired horologist and a charter member and past commander of Post NR 769 JWV, life member of DAV. *Submitted by Henry J. Sommer.*

RICHARD SONDLER, born Oct. 2, 1924 in Providence, RI. Entered the Marine Corps March 1943 and served with 1st Marine Div. Stationed in Guadalcanal, Palau, Okinawa, China.

He was awarded two Purple Hearts, Silver Star, Presidential Unit Citation. Discharged November 1945. Achieved the rank of pharmacist mate, second class.

Self-employed entreprenuer. He is married and has three sons.

MORRIS M. SORITZ, born May 23, 1915. Worked at the Ford Plant until he enlisted in the USN, July 7, 1943. Served aboard the USS *Hornet* and participated in operations in Palau, Hollandia, Truk, Marianas, Bonins, Yap, Philippines, Ryukyus, Formosa, Luzon, Japan, China Sea.

Memorable experience was the typhoon over the Western Pacific on June 5. He staked his life against the fury to save an airplane which threshed loose from its moorings on the pitching flight deck of the *Hornet*. Adm. W.F. Halsey signed the Citation which commended S1/c Soritz for heroism.

Married in 1946, had two children. Was a member of Post 452 and past commander, 1951-1952. Passed away March 3, 1958.

ARTHUR A. SPARAGA

IRA SPEESLER, born in Baltimore, MD. Inducted July 9, 1943; classified as dental technician, special assignment. Served in Ft. Monroe Station Hospital, VA; Ft. Eustis, VA; Camp Ellis, IL. Assigned to 124th Gen. Hosp., Rolinson Barracks, Denbury, So. Devon, England; Glasenbach, Austria (Salzburg).

Memorable experience was October 1944 in London on R&R with a buddy and stayed at the Columbia Club Red Cross Hotel. They were both exhausted and slept soundly through the entire night. They arose early in the morning and were amazed to find the hotel and the street deserted. A London police officer showed them where a German V-2 rocket had struck during the night and destroyed every building on the block. The hotel had been evacuated and how lucky they were that the bomb did not strike that building.

Awards/Medals: the Good Conduct Medal, American Campaign, WWII, EAME Service Medal, Army of Occupation of Germany. Achieved the rank of staff sergeant.

Worked at a dental lab at the VA Hosp. in Lyons, NJ for 32 years. Retired Dec. 31, 1981. His wife is a retired registered nurse and they will celebrate their 50th wedding anniversary in November 1996.

Has two married sons and three grandchildren. Since retirement has been taking several college courses. He paints still-life, landscapes and wild life once a week at the Senior Citizens Center; volunteers one day a week at a local hospital; enjoys taking care of his vegetable and flower gardens at home; enjoys reading, concerts and theatre plays. He attends Elderhostal programs in various parts of the country and he enjoys vacationing in other states.

They are members of a conservative temple, Temple Beth Ahm, Springfield, NJ.

MORRIS SPEIGEL, served in the U.S. Army from Jan. 8, 1941-Nov. 17, 1945. Joined the infantry as a private at Ft. Dix, NJ, and remained there until 1942. Transferred to Ft. Meade, MD, in the infantry combat team and was there from May 15, 1944-June 1944. Prior to going to Ft. Meade, MD, Morris was attached to the same infantry stationed at Camp Pickett, NJ.

He left states with his outfit on the *Queen Elizabeth* from New York, and arrived at Scotland. Saw service in the ETO with the 28th Div. from July 1944-September 1944. Later transferred to the 9th Avn. Engrs. and served with them from March 1945-November 1945. He participated in the Normandy campaign, Northern France Campaign, Rhineland Campaign and the "Ardennes" Campaign in France. Visited many countries in Europe.

Awards/Medals: EAME Service Medal, Victory Medal, American Defense Service Medal, American Service Medal, Good Conduct Medal, Unit Citation, Presidential Citation, Infantry Combat Badge, Post Pearl Harbor Medal.

Returned to the States on the SS *West Point,* from Le Havre, France, and was discharged on Nov. 17, 1945, with the rank of corporal from Ft. Monmouth, NJ.

SAMUEL SPEIGEL, served in the Medical Corps of the U.S. Army from Dec. 26, 1942 until Feb. 17, 1946. His service began at Ft. Dix, NJ and he trained at the O'Reilly General Hospital from March 1943-June 1943. Was at Camp Shelby, MS with the Infantry Medical Unit from March 1944-November, 1944.

Served at Ft. Monmouth, NJ with the medical unit from January 1943-October 1943, and with the Coffeyville AAF with the medical unit there from November 1944-November 1945.

Awards/Medals: Good Conduct Medal in 1944 with clusters. The American Theatre of Operations Medal in 1945 and the Victory Medal in 1946. He was discharged in February 1946 with the rank of corporal.

Visited the Bartlesville and Independence in Kansas and Oklahoma, sometimes called the China, Burma, India of the middle west. He intends, sometime, to write his memoirs of his Army life or how to spend three years in a quandry. *Submitted by Max Sigal*

SIDNEY SPEIGEL, served in the U.S. Army from August 1942-Feb. 9, 1946. Entered the service at Ft. Dix, NJ with the rank of private first class.

Served in the Chemical Warfare Branch and took his Chemical Warfare Service training at Camp Siebert, AL from June 1944-November 1944.

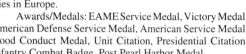

Went overseas from New Orleans, LA on the SS *Cuba* and arrived at Colon, Panama. He saw service with the Chemical Warfare Service in the Carribean Theatre from February 1945, to February 1946. *Submitted by Max Sigal*

MARTIN SPIER, born in Thannausen, Germany on July 11, 1925. Came to America in June of 1946 after several concentration camps, surviving Terezin, Auschwitz and Saxonhausen. He found his brother, Walter, and together they came to this country.

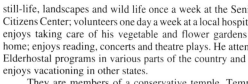

Served in the U.S. Army from Sept. 13, 1950-Sept. 15, 1952, Army Arty. Stationed at Ft. Devens, MA and Camp Stewart, GA. Also served in Southern Japan on the Korean border during the Korean War.

When he came out of the Army, he started his own business as a painting contractor where he works until today. Married to Monica (nee Baron) for 36 years, they live in Manhattan. Their daughter Jennifer and her husband, Neil, live in Yorktown, NY with their children: Benjamin, Katie, Rebecca and Jaime. Their daughter Audrey and her husband, Paul, live in Riverdale, NY with their daughters, Raquel and Nicole.

PHILIP SPINDEL, born Oct. 4, 1914, Clifton, NJ, USA. Inducted in the U.S. Army July 13, 1943. Served with 305th Army Signal Corps as private. Stationed in Ft. Dix, NJ; Camp Tocoa, GA; Atlanta Ordnance, GA; Camp Crowder, MO.

Served in England, France, Belgium and Germany and worked as a mechanic in motor pool.

Awarded four Bronze Stars, service in four battle zones, Good Conduct Medal. He was discharged as T/5, Oct. 11, 1945.

Married for 51 years and has two daughters and four grandchildren. Retired after 35 years as a Chevrolet parts manager.

Was sent home on R&R in the summer of 1945 when the atomic bomb was dropped on Japan. Released from Camp Cook, CA instead of going to the Pacific War Zone.

IRVING SPIVAK, born Oct. 20, 1917, in Syracuse, NY. Graduated from Central High School and Syracuse University.

Enlisted in the Navy on Dec. 7, 1942, as an aviation cadet.

Died Dec. 22, 1943, at the age of 26. Was awarded the rank of ensign posthumously.

MAURICE S. SPIVAK, Ph.D., P.E., ASCE, born in Medway, MA on Jan. 5, 1926. Enlisted in the U.S. Army on April 17, 1943. Served in Army Inf., 65th and 9th Divs. and the USA Counter Intelligence Corps.

Served in the ETO, participating in the famous Battle of the Bulge, battles in the Rhineland and others. During the latter part of WWII, he spent 13 days fighting as a machine gunner in the cellar of a bombed-out home in Saarlautern, Germany located near the Seigfried Line.

During a counter attack his unit was directed to pull out. Some of his comrades did not get word and did not escape the cellar. Spivak returned to the cellar and brought out a squad of men. He was honored with the Bronze Star Medal for this action. Other medals received include the Combat Infantry Badge, European Theater Medal, two Battle Stars, Cross de Guerre, etc. Discharged on May 26, 1946. He held a direct commission USNR.

A graduate of the military college of South Carolina, The Citadel. He holds graduate degrees in bio-chemistry and civil engineering. Dr. Spivak is proud of his association with arthritis research projects at Massachusetts General Hospital and his cancer research as a Worcester Foundation Fellow. He has presented professional/research papers nationwide; worked for DOD for 33 years, during which time he was instrumental in the relocation of Israeli airbases from the Sinai to the Negev following the Camp David Accords. He retired as chief of project management for Army Corps of Engineers.

Resides with his wife of 43 years, Annette "Honey," in Virginia Beach and is the father of three children: Michelle, Myra and Jonah, and has three grandchildren: David, Aaron and Emily.

SIDNEY STAHLER, M.D., born in Scranton, PA, Feb. 10, 1916. Enlisted in the U.S. Army July 30, 1943, as medical officer. Stationed Hammer Field, CA; March Field, CA; Chengtu, China (15 months) station hospitals.

Participated in battles in CBI (China, Burma, Indian Theatre of Operations).

Discharged as captain May 1946.

Married to Frances for 51 years and they have three children, and two grandchildren.

Stahler is a retired medical doctor.

RALPH STAT, joined the 83rd Div. in July 1944 as a replacement combat medic. He was fresh from the U.S. after a 30 day stay in one of England's Replacement Deports. The Battle of St. Lo had just ended and he was assigned to G Co. of the 329th Regt. He was placed in the 2nd Bn. and stationed in the 1st Plt. as company aidman.

His platoon became his new family and he was lucky enough to stay with them all through the rest periods and combats and reconnaissance. At the Battle of the Bulge, he was wounded in Petit Langlier, Belgium and sent to a recovery hospital in France.

Rejoined his outfit sometime in April 1945 when they were taking training in Holland. From then on it was Rag Tag Breakout through Germany to a few miles west of the Elbe River, when they met up with the Russians.

After discharge in December 1945, he returned to school and married his wife Sally. They were married in November 1946 and went into business together. They have two children, a daughter Susan and a son William.

He has been active in local community affairs such as Chamber of Commerce, Kiwanis Club and the local chapter of the JWV.

As a surprise for their 35th wedding anniversary, his wife, with the help of their Congressman, arranged to have an award presentation of his Silver Star Medal after a 37 year delay. It was a memorable occasion.

He can only thank God for having experienced and lived through the years of his association with the 83rd Div. during the war. It was one of the greatest experiences of his life.

BEATRICE (SEELAV, BENEDICK) STECHER, was born in New York City. Entered service July 1942 and served in WAAC, WAC, USAF. Stationed in New York City, Mitchell Field, NY, Pentagon, Frankfurt, Germany. Served as major in USAFR.

Memorable experience at Pentagon in charge of affidavits of American POWs for Japanese War Crime Trials in Manila; top secret officer in charge of couriers in Germany; in charge of DPs in German jails requesting repatriation, including Jewish personnel to Russia.

Discharged May 1948 with rank of major, in active reserves for three years until 1950 with rank of major. She received all the regular medals and occupation ribbons.

Divorced and has one daughter Jo, a senior nurse clinician at NYC Hospital in kidney and liver transplant, medical seminar speaker and active in city of Hope Research Center in California.

AGD, Personnel Air Force Public Relations at Pentagon, HQ 1st AF, 1st Fighter. Presently a part-time paralegal.

CHARLES STEIGLITZ, signed in second draft of 20 year olds and called to service March 21, 1942 to Ft. Jackson, SC. Assigned as a medical corpsman in Med. Detach., 307th Inf. Regt. of the New York area, Statue of Liberty, 77th Inf. Div.

Shipped to Oahu, HI May 1944 where the 77th Inf. Div. was trained for jungle warfare.

He took part in campaigns at Guam, Marianas Island Group; Leyte, Philippines Islands; Kerama Retto, Ie Shima, Okinawa, Ryukyu Islands; Cebu, Philippines where the war ended and Occupation Forces in Hokkaido, Japan for three weeks.

Shipped home from Yokohama to Tacoma, WA. Discharged Dec. 5, 1945, Ft. Dix, NJ. Received a Bronze Star for medical work on badly wounded men of a tank crew on Okinawa.

Married Pauline Weisberg in 1948 and has two sons, Scott (doctor) and Alan, five grandchildren and one great-grandson.

Is a draftsman and an estimator for the acoustical ceiling construction industry for 43 years. Today he is semi-retired, working two days per week. Member JWV J. George Fredman Post 76, North Bergen, NJ.

BEN STEIN, born in St. Paul, MN, Sept. 24, 1914. Entered service Aug. 23, 1943. Served with 12th Army Gp., Signal Corp, 3187th Sig. Svc. Bn., Co. C, as tech sergeant. Stationed at Central Signal Corp School, Camp Crowder, MO; Ft. Monmouth, NJ.

Participated in battles in Rhineland and Central Europe. Because of his superior organizational ability as chief instructor and coordinator of 20 cable splicing teams in France and Germany while under enemy artillery fire, extending beyond the call of duty, he was awarded the Bronze Star Medal and recommended for a direct commission as a 2nd lieutenant. However, after almost three years in the service, he declined the battlefield commission in order to come home.

Awards/Medals: Bronze Star Medal, American Theater Service Medal, EAME Service Medal and Good Conduct Medal. He was discharged April 13, 1946.

Married Molly and had two sons, one daughter and six grandchildren. He passed away Feb. 25, 1966.

DAVID STEIN, was born at Atlantic City Medical Center, A.C. Hospital June 1, 1928. Entered U.S. Army Jan. 11, 1951, and served as corporal in 7th Inf. Div., 7th Medical Bn. and was stationed in Korea.

Memorable experience includes division attack carried to 38th Parallel May 31, 1951; and working with MASH outfit.

Awards/Medals: Korean Service Medal with one Bronze Service Star and the United Nations Service Medal.

Discharged as corporal Jan. 11, 1953.

Retired from Superior Court. He has two daughters, Harriet and Nancy Stein. His mother, Dora Stein, is 101 years old.

MELVIN STEIN, departed Camp Upton for Laredo, TX. Unit consisted of all New York recruits, 25% were of the Hebrew faith. Originally all were to attend Officers Training School, only 10% achieved this distinction.

They were pressed into service as Military Police and shared duty with calvary with Southern Defense Command. Transferred to post of non-com supply officer attached to calvary. Transferred to post in north Texas, non-com in charge of ordnance for two army divisions.

Injured 1943 on patrol with Southern Defense Command. Operated on in 1944 for previous injury and operating surgeon petitioned for medical discharge which was turned down by headquarters. Placed on limited duty until his discharge in 1945.

Attended Counselor School in 1945 to assist with problems of veterans being discharged as to their rights of schooling and disability benefits.

SAM STEIN, born in St. Paul, MN Nov. 27, 1919. Enlisted in the USN Jan. 17, 1942. Received basic at Navy Pier Chicago, IL. Assigned to USS *South Dakota* (BB-57) for duration of war. The *South Dakota* shot down 32 Japanese planes.

Participated in Battles of Santa Cruz, Savo Island, Philippine Sea, six bombardments and 34 air strikes. Memorable experience was being one of first 500 men aboard when ship was built and put in service; was the only Jewish person aboard in crew of 4,500 men; and serving with Adm. Halsey, 3rd Fleet, while he was on board.

Awards/Medals: Navy Commendation for Battle of Santa Cruz and Savo Island plus 19 awards. He was discharged June 19, 1945, as coxswain.

After service he was a salesman selling candy. Married to Shirlee and has a son.

SAMUEL STEIN, born in Boston, MA, June 14, 1923. Graduated Boston Trade High School in the electrical department in 1942. World War II had started, so he enlisted in the USAAF on Oct. 19, 1942. He was transferred to Madison, WI and attended Radio School. He also attended Radar School in Boca Raton, FL.

While in Clovis, NM he was assigned to the 450th Bomb Gp. (H), 721st Sqdn. and sent to Alamogordo, NM for training on B-24 bombers. Afterwards, he was shipped overseas from the Port of Embarkation, Hampton Roads, VA aboard the Merchant Marine ship SS *Bret Harte.*

On Dec. 26, 1943 he arrived in Naples, Italy and proceeded to the base in Manduria, Italy. He was a member of the ground crew and participated in keeping the B-24 aircrafts radio and radar in good working order before the men went up on their missions.

The bombing areas covered by the 450th Bomb Gp. (H) "Cottontails" were Northern Italy, Yugoslavia, Greece, Albania, Bulgaria, Rumania, Czechoslovakia, Hungary, France, Austria and Germany. He was shipped back to the States on the USS *Wakefield* after one and a half years in Italy.

Coincidentally, before he went into the service, he worked on the USS *Wakefield* as an electrician's helper during its drydock in Boston. The other surprise was that the returning ship landed in Boston, his hometown.

After his furlough he returned to Clovis, NM to train on B-29 aircraft in preparation for the Pacific area of war. The war with Japan ended and he was discharged on Sept. 27, 1945, at Camp Chaffee, AR.

After the war, he received a degree in civil engineering and began working for the Commonwealth of Massachusetts, Department of Public Works for 42 years. He planned roads for state and federal highways throughout the state.

He has been happily married to the former Sylvia Fleshel for 45 years. They have two daughters, Ellen Rae who is a clinical psychologist and a registered nurse. She is married to Carl Lundin and they have two children, Julie Brook and Jay Alexander. His other daughter, Joan Carol, is a senior technical editor/writer for a large engineering firm.

Presently retired and active at the Synagogue in Stoughton, MA and also with the 450th Bombardment Group Association (H) "Cottontails." He is a member of the JWV, Dorchester Centre Post, No. 630.

PAUL S. STEINBAUM, born Jan. 18, 1915, in New York City, NY. Entered the Army June 22, 1942.

Stationed at 177th General Hospital in Le Mans, France; Regional Hospital; Carlisle Barracks, PA; Camp Pickett, VA; and Camp Shelby, MS.

Awards/Medals: European Campaign and American Campaign Medals. He was discharged March 11, 1946, with the rank of captain.

Retired from musical products

LEON L. STEINBERG, born in New York City, NY, June 17, 1922. Enlisted 245th CA, June 19, 1939, NYNG, a sea coast and antiaircraft artillery unit, federalized Sept. 16, 1940, and sent to Ft. Hancock, NJ; Camp Chaffee, AR; 416th FA GP HQ as heavy FA.

Left the States and landed in England. Assigned in France to 3rd Army, 20th Corps as army artillery. Entered Germany in Trier and the war ended in Passau, Baveria.

Memorable experience was seeing the devastation caused by war.

Awards/Medals: American Defense Service Medal, American Service Medal, Good Conduct Medal, EAME Service Medal, WWII Victory Medal, Army of Occupation and two Battle Stars. Discharged Dec. 6, 1945, as tech fifth grade.

Married Sally Pierce in 1954. They have two children, Richard and Faith, and two grandchildren, Joshau and Sara Rose.

Worked for the USN for 20 years and the city of New York as a carpenter. Now retired. Member of JWV Post No. 115, American Legion Post 1222, and Veterans Association 13th Rg. 59th AEF and 245th CA/NYNG.

MURRAY STEINBERG, born Feb. 16, 1924 in Utena, Lithuania. Entered service May 19, 1943. Received 13 weeks training as infantryman at Camp Wheeler, GA, then to Ft. Ord, CA and finally to Camp Stoneman, CA for shipment to Pacific.

Assigned to Co. A, 172nd Inf. Regt., 43rd Inf. Div. Saw action in Aitape, New Guinea, Hollandia, New Guinea and landed in Lingayen Gulf, Philippines with first wave. While in Philippines was assigned to I Corps and had the honor of being one of the infantrymen who was assigned to guard Gen Douglas MacArthur while he was visiting our headquarters at San Fabian, Philippines.

Was sent to Osara, Japan after their surrender and discharged Jan. 14, 1946, with rank of technical sergeant after 25 months overseas.

Awarded Combat Infantry Badge, Bronze Service Medal for meritorious achievement in ground combat against the enemy in Asiatic-Pacific Theater of Operation, Citation by Republic of Philippines, Presidential Citation, Asiatic-Pacific Campaign Ribbon with two Battle Stars, WII Victory Medal and Good Conduct Medal.

Married Ruth Kessler April 11, 1943. They just celebrated their 50th anniversary. Have four daughters: Cheryl, Sandra, Rhonda and Debra and four grandchildren: David, Amy, Jacob and Caleb Benjamin.

Past Commander of JWV, Post 32 of Worcester, MA.

SIGMUND STEINBERG, born Jan. 31, 1922 in Philadelphia, PA. Enlisted in Signal Corps Sept. 17, 1942. Basic and technical training Camp Crowder, MO. Shipped overseas to Australia June 12, 1943 heading 66 man platoon. Arrived Brisbane July 4, 1943. Traveled by narrow-gauge railroad to Cairns, Queensland where assigned to 2nd Engineer Amphibious Bde., 592nd Boat and Shore Regt., B Co. MOS placed him in signal group responsible for all electronic equipment.

Served in New Guinea, Bismark Archipelago, Southern Philippines and Luzon.

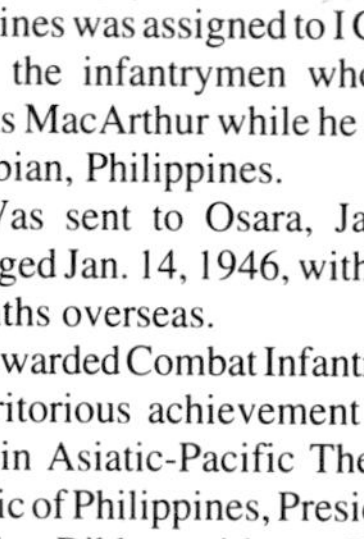

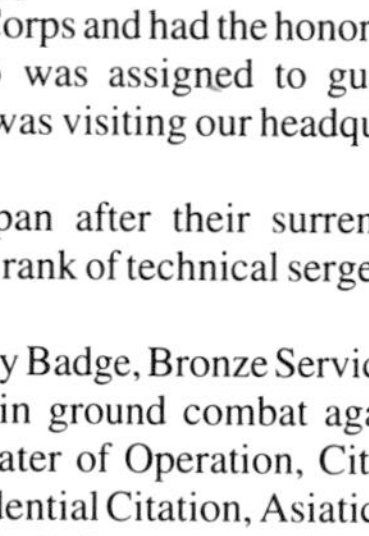

Will never forget sound of rain on corrugated metal roof when cured of deafening fungus in both ears. Applauded decision to drop atomic bomb, however terrifying, since it saved American lives, including mine, by cancelling imminent invasion of Japan.

Awards/Medals: Presidential Unit Citation (Corregidor), Philippine Liberation Medal with two Bronze Stars, Asiatic-Pacific Service Medal with four Bronze Stars and one Bronze Arrowhead and WWII Victory Medal.

Achieved the rank of staff sergeant and honorably discharged Nov. 13, 1945. Attended college under GI Bill. Married Judith Traurig Nov. 29, 1953, has a son, daughter and two grandchildren.

Retired from Dept. Army, ARDEC January 1987. Remain active in IES and Post 689 JWV. His hobbies include music and model building (aircraft and RR). He and Judy travel in their motor home from their Rockaway, NJ residence.

JERRY STEINMAN, born in Manhattan on Feb. 9, 1924. Majored in history at Ohio State University. Graduated May 1943. Entered the Army May 1943. Trained at Ft. Bragg, NC. Sent overseas to Europe in January 1944. Served in replacement depot headquarters in England, then France until December 1944.

Transferred to headquarters for southern France, then back to infantry training, then into the 106th Div. in artillery which went to the Lorient Submarine Base just before wars end.

Having been in war zones during the Bulge and in southern France HQ for January-February 1945 as well as at Lorient, he received three Battle Stars. After the Army, went to Columbia University, obtained a master's degree in history.

Married Irene Stephanie Dynenson Nov. 4, 1951. Member of JWV, and many other organizations. Presently publisher of Beer Marketer's *Insights.*

DEBRA H. LEIVES STERN, born in Brooklyn, NY, Jan. 21, 1924. Entered the service April 1944. Stationed at Ft. Ogelthorpe, GA; Camp Shanks, NY; Camp Kilmer, NJ. Served as WAC and received the rank of sergeant.

Memorable experience was after the war when the 82nd Paratroopers practiced before marching down 5th Avenue.

Awards/Medals: received first Purple Heart given out by President Roosevelt at Ft. Ogelthorpe, GA. Received quite a few awards but the most treasured is her Driver's Medal. Discharged April 1946.

Married Abraham Stern March 23, 1946, has three married sons and six grandchildren. She is active in JWV.

Her father, Max Lewis, and brother, Victor Lewis, served in WWII with her. Younger brother, Manuel J. Lewis, was a jet pilot during the Korean conflict.

Out of a family of five, only her mother, Rose Lewis, did not serve in uniform.

HARRY STERN, founded Action Manufacturing Company in 1946, following his graduation from Drexel University as a mechanical engineer and service in the USN during WWII. He is also founder of Action Arms Ltd., established in 1979. His extensive community involvement includes national board positions with the American Technion Society, American-Israel Chamber of Commerce, Shaare Zedek Hospital and the Ben-Gurion University. He also serves on the boards of the Solomon Schecter Day School, Akiba Hebrew Academy, Gratz College, the Middle East Council, and the Philadelphia Geriatric Center.

Among Mr. Stern's many awards are the Centennial Medal Award of the Jewish Theological Seminary of America, the Menachem Begin Award of the Shaare Zedek Center, and the Philadelphia Technion's Lifetime Achievement Award for his efforts to encourage the growth of Israel's economy through emphasis on technical education.

In 1991 and 1993 respectively, he was awarded honorary doctorates from Gratz College and the Israel Institute of Technology. Stern is a trustee of the former Congregation Emanu-El and Congregation Adath Jeshurun. He serves on the board of trustees of the Center for Judaic Studies of the University of Pennsylvania and is the founder and president of the Harry Stern Family Foundation, established to support a wide range of non-sectarian charities.

HERMAN STERN, born July 15, 1915, in New York City. Entered service October 1942. Stationed at Camp Croft, SC; Ft. Benning, GA; Officer Candidate School; ETO from Normandy through Belgium-Germany and Czechoslovakia. Served in the 2nd Inf. Div. Received the Indian Head Patch.

A memorable experience was in the Battle of the Bulge. Their division was in the Malmedy St. Vith area where German soldiers dressed in American uniforms, massacred his company cook and two other GIs in his company. Stern's life was probably saved by his machine gunner sergeant who protected their position and reportedly killed dozens of the enemy. He later was cited and received the country's highest military award (Congressional Medal of Honor) (his name Jose Lopez) was documented in Bill Moyer's TV special entitled *From D-Day to the Rhine."*

Achieved the rank of first lieutenant, infantry.

Now a CPA in practice for 55 years.

Married Selma, March 10, 1946. They have a son Dr. Robert A. Stern, Ph.D Astrophysicist daughter, Dr. Beverly Kingsley, Ph.D in Public Health, who has daughter Elizabeth and son Michael.

Stern is a member of JWV Yonkers Post 68.

HERMAN D. STERN, served from Aug. 25, 1943-Dec. 1, 1945. Went overseas to England with 79th Div., 3rd Bn. as T5 code clerk. Landed Normandy, Omaha Beach, D-6. Went inland to Ste Mere Eglise then up to Cherbourg the Division taking the ready surrender of thousands of conscripted non-German troops. Then South to reform at Avaranches, where, as part of Gen. Patton's Third Army, they participated in the breakthrough after the one thousand bomber air assault against the Nazis war "machine". The Division then "advanced" up to the little Maginot Line near the Belgium border.

At this point, due to severe systemic circulatory condition, he was reclassified to limited service; transferred to the Air Corps and assigned to HQ Co. MTO. at Caserta, Italy with promotions to staff sergeant Intelligence NCO.

Awards/Medals: Bronze Star Medal, three Battle Stars, Normandy, Northern France, Rhineland and the Combat Infantry Badge.

As a civilian, he re-entered U.S. Civil Service. Transferred from the Department of Justice Bureau of Prisons to the Disability Claims Section, Vets/Adm., New Jersey. Advanced to the Policy Staff, Department of Veterans' Benefits, Central Office, Washington, D.C. and retired 1973 as chief of staff for Policy and Legislation.

Now residing in a retirement community in Manchester, NJ.

JACK I. STERN, born in the Bronx, NY, on Aug. 31, 1927. Drafted on Feb. 8, 1946, he was a surgical technician at the 361st Station Hospital in Tokyo until discharged on April 28, 1947. Enlisting in the Air Force Reserve, he was called to active duty on Aug. 11, 1950, and served as personnel specialist in the 473th Troop Carrier Wing in Fukuoka, Japan,

He was separated as a staff sergeant on April 19, 1952. Received a direct commission as 2nd lieutenant on July 15, 1955, doing reserve duty as personnel programs staff officer for Air Force Systems Command at Andrews Air Force Base.

Retired from the Air Force Reserve as a lieutenant colonel on Aug. 13, 1983. In civilian life, Col. Stern retired as assistant personnel director for the city of New York. He now lives in Glen Ridge, NJ.

MARSHALL M. STERN, born April 27, 1946, to Sylvia (Goldstein) and Israel A. Stern. His father was a veteran of WWII and an active member of Malden Post 74 JWV until his death in October 1977.

After graduation from Northeastern University with a BS degree in civil engineering and having participated in Army ROTC, he was commissioned a 2nd lieutenant in the Transportation Corps and sent to Ft. Eustis, VA. The Army recognized that he had a degree in engineering and sent him to Harbor Craft Engine School. He spent a year in Ft. Eustis before being assigned to Vietnam.

When he left Vietnam in 1970 he was company commander of the 329th Transportation Co. (Heavy Boat).

Awards/Medals: Bronze Star Medal and Republic of Vietnam Honor Medal (First Class).

Honorably discharged from the Army, he attended and graduated from Northeastern University School of Law. He is a practicing attorney admitted to practice law in the states of Florida, Massachusetts, and New York. He is a partner in the firm of Pinks, Brooks, Stern and Arbeit, Hauppauge (Long Island), NY.

NATHAN L. (NAT) STERN, served in the USAF from December 1, 1942-January 6, 1945. Stationed at Alamogordo AAFB for a major portion of the time. He achieved the rank of corporal.

VIRGINIA MARIE STERN, born in Little Rock, AR. Joined the USN Nov. 9, 1942, trained at Iowa State Teachers College in Cedar Falls, IA and Naval Hospital in San Diego, CA. Assigned to Naval Hospital, Mare Island, CA and was the first woman from Arkansas to join the WAVES. She was in the first group of enlisted WAVES.

Spent 34 months in the service, working and teaching in laboratories. Received honorable discharge at Balboa Park, San Francisco, CA.

Studied biological sciences, chemistry and art in colleges. Worked in hospital laboratories for 27 years in New York City until she retired. Returned to Little Rock, AR, and joined the JWV, serving as QM of their post.

ISIDOR STERNBACH, born in New York City, 1926. Inducted into U.S. Army Infantry January 1944, Ft. Dix, NJ. Basic training was at Camp Croft, SC; jungle training at Camp Rucker, AL and embarkation from Ft. Ord, CA, to the Philippines.

Joined 32nd Inf. Div. during the Luzon Campaign in the Philippines. Attached to HQ Co., 128th Inf. Regt., Lingayen Gulf, where Gen. Yamashita surrendered his forces to their regiment. Later he was sent to Manila where he was tried and executed for his crimes.

After the atomic bombs were dropped on Hiroshima and Nagasaki in August 1945, their entire division prepared to invade the islands of Japan. As the "unconditional surrender" was being signed on the battleship *Missouri*. Their 32nd Inf. Div. with an armada of 20 ships, entered the ports of Kobe and Sasebo to occupy and normalize Japan in the areas of southern Honshu.

Returned to the States with a record of 654 consecutive days of combat, from Australia to Japan, transferred to the 25th Inf. Div. in Kyoto. Became Gen. Eisenhower's "Honor Guard" when he visited the headquarters of Gen. MacArthur in Tokyo.

Awards/Medals: Presidential Citation, Philippine Liberation, Asiatic-Pacific Campaign, WWII Victory Medal, Army of Occupation Medal and the Good Conduct Medal. He was discharged in November 1946 as T-5.

Employed primarily as an artist-display manager and advertising executive. Retired in 1991 and lives with his wife

Elizabeth in West Palm Beach, FL. Their son Richard and family live in East Stroudsburg, PA and their daughter, Elyse S. Maltz, and family live in the Mountain Lakes area, NJ.

LEONARD STERNE, born Oct. 23, 1918, New York City. Inducted Aug. 19, 1943, and did his basic at Ft. McClellan, AL. Was shipped to North Africa and went to Naples, Italy where he was assigned to HQ Co., 1st Bn., 349th Inf., Regt., 88th Div. in February 1944.

Awards/Medals: Bronze Star, Combat Infantry Badge, three Battle Stars, Presidential Unit Citation and Good Conduct Medal. He was discharges Nov. 9, 1945, from Ft. Dix with the rank of private first class.

Now semi-retired, living with his wife, Estelle. They've been married almost 55 years and are enjoying their children and grandchildren.

FRED STERNFELD, born April 7, 1896. Entered the U.S. Army Nov. 19, 1917, served with 303rd Engrs.

Awards/Medals: Great War of Civilization Medal, Victory Medal from state of New Jersey, Meuse and Argonne Defensive Sector, They did not pass, 1917-1918, from city of Elizabeth, NJ.

He was discharged from the service June 6, 1919.

Charter member of David Blick Post 63, Elizabeth, NJ. He died March 6, 1940.

ABRAHAM STETTNER, born in the country of Austria, Hungary in 1888. Came to the United States as a young boy.

Was in the U.S. Army Infantry from 1915-1918 with the rank of master sergeant.

MAX M. STETTNER, born and raised in New York City. He lived for 35 years in Lubbock, TX.

He was in the ROTC and went into the Air Corps in 1943. Served most of his time in China and India.

Was discharged in 1946, returned to school and became a doctor.

He died in March 1992.

BEN STEVENS, born in Toronto, Canada, June 4, 1919. Moved to Cleveland, OH in 1923. Graduated high school in 1937 and attended Cleveland College. Joined the Army in March 1942 and was activated in the new 82nd Inf. (later they were to become the 82nd and the 101st Airborne).

Made three cadres, helping to form the 98th Inf., 63rd Inf., and then the 1252nd Engr. Combat Bn. The last outfit trained at Camp Swift, TX, prior to shipping to the European Theatre in September 1944.

Attached to 3rd Army, trained in England and off to France through Calais. Participated in the Ardennes, Rhineland and Central Europe Campaigns. In Weimar their outfit helped liberate Buchenwald Concentration Camp on April 12, 1945

Left Army in December 1945 and back home to Cleveland to his wife Anne and daughter Natalie. He also has two sons Ralph and Mark. Moved to California in 1966.

RALPH STILLMAN

ALLEN D. STOLAR, born Dec. 3, 1924, in Washington DC. Inducted July 24, 1943, at Ft. Myers, VA and served wi

the Army Inf. as rifleman. Received basic training in Ft. Benning, GA. ASTP, Kentucky. Served with 106th Div., 424th Inf., I Co., Tennessee Maneuvers, then Camp Atterbury, IN.

Overseas to Replacement Camp, England; 44th Div., 71st Inf., A Co., France; and several Army hospitals for gunshot wound on Nov. 19, 1944, near Saarburg, France.

Memorable experience was landing at Omaha Beach in France October 1944; unloading from LST on LCT; bouncing up and down in 15' seas, then wading ashore, walking up narrow mine-cleared path to top of cliff and past temporary cemetery for those killed prior to his arrival as a replacement.

Awarded the Good Conduct Medal, WWII Victory Ribbon, Combat Infantry Badge, Purple Heart, European Theater Ribbon with one Bronze Star. Discharged March 8, 1946; Halloran General Hospital, Staten Island, NY. Achieved the rank of private first class.

His father, Harry Stolar, served in U.S. Army QM Corps in WWI, and was a member of JWV Post 58 in Washington, DC.

As a teenager he was in the Drum and Bugle Corps of Post 58 from 1940-1942. Has practiced law in Miami, FL from July 1951.

ANCHEL STOLZBERG, born Oct. 4, 1921, New York City. Enlisted February 1942 in U.S. Army. Spent three days at Ft. Dix, eight weeks at Ft. Bragg, NC, then to Kialua, Hawaii for jungle warfare training. Stationed at Guadalcanal; Vella Lavella, New Georgia Island; Luzon; Caraballo Mountains; Cagayan Valley; Pao San Manuel Santo Domingo.

Awards/Medals: Silver Star, two Bronze Stars, two Purple Hearts, Conspicuous Service Medal, Presidential Unit Citation, Asiatic-Pacific Medal, five Battle Stars, Military Merit, Soldier's Medal, Meritorious Service Medal and Marksman Medals (rifle and pistol).

Memorable experience was at reunion. Out of 3,000 men he was selected to present plaques to BG Fred C. Weyand and Maj. Gen. Claude M. Kicklighter. Honorable Medical Discharge, June 10, 1944.

Re-married to a wonderful lady, Victoria. In NYC was owner of a vending business, bar, telephone answering service and restaurant. Retired and sold everything in 1980. Moved to Las Vegas in 1993. Presently involved as actor in films, *Casino* and *Destiny*; radio and TV.

HARRIS B. STONE, born Oct. 16, 1923. Served in WWII July 28, 1943-Jan. 13, 1946; Korean War Jan. 18, 1952-March 5, 1953.

Entered the Signal Corps/Electronic Warfare. Discharged as 1st lieutenant.

National Commander of JWV 1979-1980; National Executive Director, 1980-1985.

Retired at highest rank for a civilian at Pentagon as the Director of the USN's Research, Development and Planning. He passed away June 17, 1993.

HERMAN STONE, born Aug. 22, 1925, Chicago, IL. Drafted March 10, 1944 in U.S. Army. Assigned to 8th Armd. Div., 49th AIB, Co. C. Stationed at Camp Blanding, FL; Camp Polk, LA; Tidworth Barracks, England; France; Belgium and Germany.

Joined the USAF January 1954. Stationed at Chanute AFB; O'Hara Field, Chicago; Lockborne AFB, OH; Castle AFB, CA; Armstrong, Ontario, Canada. Korea and Vietnam years were spent in the U.S., Canada and Wheelus AFB, Libya.

Entered ARNG Reserve 1980, retired 1990 as a lieutenant colonel at Los Alamitos, NG Base, CA.

Awards/Medals: Bronze Star, Air Force Commendation Medal, Army Good Conduct Medal, Air Force Good Conduct Medal, Occupation (Japan and Europe) Medal, Presidential Unit Citation. Retired November 1968, USAF, M/SGT.

Married Leah June 27, 1954. Has three sons and two grandchildren. Member JWV, American Legion, 32 degree Mason and Shriner and life member of DAV. From 1968-1991 worked for LA County, in California. Now a volunteer at hospital at Nellis AFB, NV.

JACK M. STONE, born Aug. 22, 1917, in Akron, OH. Received BS degree in accounting from Ohio State University, June 1939. Drafted Feb. 2, 1943. Sent to Finance Training School at Ft. Benjamin Harrison in Indiana.

Shipped overseas to Africa. Travelled the 1,600 mile trip from Casablanca to Bizerti via 40 and 8. It took 11 days and nights. Assigned to the 7th Army HQs Finance on invasion of Sicily in July 1943. Assigned to II Corps HQs Finance when II Corps traveled to Italy in September 1943. Assigned to 6th Corps HQs Finance when 6th Corps made the invasion at Anzio Beachhead in January 1944. After Rome captured in June 1944 he was assigned to the 88th Inf. Div. HQs, Finance. He was with the division until October 1945.

Returned to the States and was discharged on Nov. 11, 1945.

Awards/Medals: Bronze Star Medal for service at Anzio Beachhead along with five Campaign Stars. The highest rank he obtained was sergeant.

Passed the certified public accountants examination in 1950 and had his own practice until he retired in 1985.

Married to Rosalie 50 years on Dec. 24, 1989. They have five daughters, one of whom passed away on Jan. 29, 1990, and 11 grandchildren.

JOSEPH STONE

SANFORD B. STONE, born June 26, 1920 in New York City. Graduated from Case Western Reserve University in 1942, BS, DDS. Reported for active duty June 30, 1943, as a dental officer at Newport, RI Naval Training Station.

On Jan. 20, 1944, received orders to report to the USS *Tangier* (AV-8) which was to be the flagship for Commander Aircraft Southwest Pacific. In addition to his duties as dental officer, he was also the ship's welfare officer.

Participated in the Admiralty Islands, Halmahara Islands, New Guinea and Philippine Campaigns (Leyte and Lingayen Gulfs), and was awarded five Battle Stars.

In September 1945, he was assigned to be the dental officer at the Midshipman School, Columbia University. February 1946, transferred to the Naval Separation Center, Lido Beach, NY, where he served as dental officer until released from active duty, July 5, 1946.

During the summer of 1943 he had lunch with Capt. (Rabbi) Joshua Goldberg, the head of the USN Jewish

---

Chaplain Corps while he was inspecting the facilities for Jewish personnel at the Newport Naval Training Station. When he finished the inspection, Stone volunteered to drive him to the Newport bus station. The rabbi asked Stone if he would detour through nearby Ft. Adams. On exiting Ft. Adams, he said, "Now I will tell you why I wanted to visit Ft. Adams." Soon after I arrived in this country during WWI, I enlisted in the Army and was sent to Ft. Adams and assigned to KP duty peeling potatoes. So, I went from peeling potatoes in the Army in WWI to a captain (soon to be admiral) in the Navy in WWII".

Stone is married to Carolyn (Shapiro). They have two children, Dr. Joanne Wyman, married to Dr. Bruce Wyman and Gary Stone, married to Rosalie. They have four grandchildren, Jessica and David Wyman and Jacob and Samantha Stone.

BERNHARD STORCH, born Nov. 10, 1920, City Bochnia Poland. Entered Polish army November 1942, was discharged September 1945 with rank of sergeant. Served in the 1st Div. In May 1943 was assigned to join Non-Commissioned Academy.

First military action took place Oct. 10, 1943, near city of Smolensk, USSR, where he was awarded the Cross for Bravery.

After his discharge from the Field Hospital on Nov. 25, 1943, he was assigned to the 1st Arty. Regt., put in charge of a howitzer cannon, and fought through the entire center of White Russia, Central Poland, cities: Lublin, Warsau, Rivers Bug, Wisla, the entire East and West Pomeria to the Baltic Sea and rivers Oder and Spree.

Liberated concentration camp; Sobibor July 22, 1944; Majdanek July 23, 1944; Chelmno January 1945; Sachsenhausen April 19, 1945.

Fought in Berlin for 12 days and was involved bombarding the Reichstag. Ended the war May 2 at 2 a.m 1945.

He received three crosses, four medals, 11 campaign ribbons.

Left Poland the spring of 1946 and came to America, April 1947. Member of JWV. Served twice as commander of Post 756. Presently senior vice commander of Rockland-Orange District Council, and department executive committeeman. Storch is a retired designer of ladies clothes.

Married Ruth Nov. 18, 1945, and has one daughter, Gita, son Larry and three grandchildren.

SILVIN STORCK, born Aug. 27, 1920. Enlisted as aviation cadet, July 2, 1942. Served with 10th Fighter Sqdn., 50th Fighter Gp.

Overseas service in Normandy, Northern France, Ardennes, Rhineland, Central Europe, and air offensives of Europe.

His memorable experiences include the liberation of Paris and the liberation of Polish PW Camp.

Awards/Medals: EAME Service Ribbon with one Bronze and one Silver Star, Distinguished Unit Badge with one Bronze OLC, Good Conduct, two Presidential Unit Citations, Order of the Day, Belgium Army, Croix de Guerre, French army. He was discharged October 1945 as sergeant.

Graduated from Airplane Mechanics School and Instrument Specialist School, subsequently, assigned to 10th Fighter Sqdn. at Zephyr Hills, FL. Squadron sent overseas and prepared for the invasion of France. The 50th Fighter Gp. established first Air Field on the Normandy coast of France. A monument was erected by the French people commemorating the soldiers in their outfit who gave their lives. P-47 dive bombers closely supported Gen Patton's Army in France and Germany including the Battle of the Bulge.

Currently Storck is enjoying retirement along with his wife, three daughters and five grandchildren.

HAROLD STRASHUN, born Perth Amboy, NJ, Nov. 10, 1923. Graduated Perth Amboy High School, 1941. Enlisted in USN, V6 USNR, December 1942. Active duty Jan. 4, 1943.

Served at USNTS Great Lakes, IL, Great Lakes Hospital Corps School. Graduated July 1943 as HA2/c. USNH Great Lakes, NAS Pasco, WI-Acorn 57, AATD Port Hueneme, CA. RS Shoemaker, CA; USS *Rescue* (AH-18); RS Treasure Island, CA; USS LST 890.

Awards/Medals: Good Conduct Medal, Asiatic-Pacific Medal, American Campaign Medal and Victory Medal. He was honorably discharged March 12, 1946, PSC Lido Beach, Long Island, NY as PHM2/c.

Graduated from New York Hospital School of Radiography, Cornell Medical Center 1948. Began Radiography career with Radiology Group 1948. Retired from Group as chief technologist, 1993.

Married Ruth Sheinwald in Elizabeth, NJ Sept. 5, 1948. They have two sons Jeffrey M. (attorney-Union, NJ); Robert H. (pediatrician, St. Louis, MO). Two grandchildren, Daniel and Debra.

Member Post 63, JWV. Was also member of Post 43, JWV where his dad was a junior vice commander. Prior to WWII Strashun was a member of Sons of JWV. Member JWV Museum. Past Master Mt. Nebo Lodge #248 F&AM, Elizabeth, NJ. Member Masada Lodge #51 F&AM Union, NJ. Secretary of Cong. Bais Yitzchok Chevrathilim, Elizabeth, NJ since 1955. Member Board of Directors, Gomel Chesed Hebrew Cemetery Association, Elizabeth, NJ.

NATHAN STRAUSS, born in Wilmington, DE on May 23, 1922. Graduated from Wilmington High School in 1941. Enlisted in the Army in December 1942 with his older brother Charles Strauss and was stationed at Ft. Dix, NJ, and Camp Carson, CO, for engineering training. Nathan's sister, Freida, was in the WAVES in Washington, DC and brother-in-laws, Mack B. Mintz and Seymour Solomon were in the Navy and Army, respectively.

He was attached to the 1110th Cbt. Engr. Corps in England in 1943, hit Utah Beach, France, on June 16, 1944, Belgium, at the Battle of the Bulge and finally, Germany. 1110th was disbanded in October 1945 due to dwindling numbers. While stationed in England was able to see his brother Louis who had survived a torpedo attack.

Married in 1949 with two children, David and Andrea and now has three grandchildren: Mara, Martin and Ryan. Wife, Marion, passed away in 1976. Presently the proprietor of Red Star Wallpaper and Paint, established in 1911 by Nathan's father, Isadore Strauss.

PHILLIP STRAUSS, born April 22, 1921, New York, NY. Attended U.S. Merchant Marine Academy, Kings Point, NY as cadet midshipman, April 1942. Graduated as marine engineer, December 1943. Enlisted in the USN as ensign engineering officer and served until 1945 with a lieutenant (sg) commission.

From 1945-1948 served on various ships as first assistant engineer and chief engineer. Duty in the Atlantic, Pacific, England, Africa, China and Korea. Participated in Battle of Atlantic, Archange USSR (Myrmansk) RVN where 2/3 of convoy was sunk. Served in Israel, 1948-1949, and helped organize the Israeli navy

Discharged with the rank of lieutenant. He is late member and former commander of JWV Post 191, White Plains.

From 1949-1958 held various positions as handyman, plumber, electrician etc. In 1958 was appointed custodian engineer for NYC Board of Education. Presently at George Washington High School, Manhattan, NYC.

Married April 16, 1950, has three children: Ira, Daniel and Robin. Wife passed away in 1969. Married Ursula in October 1980.

KENNETH STREICHLER, born Sept. 14, 1945, Long Beach, NY. Enlisted in U.S. Army Sept. 24, 1967, 111th FA.

Commissioned Aug. 28, 1968. Achieved the rank of executive officer, Firing Btry., 104th FA. Discharged May 15, 1973.

Memorable experience was the honor of serving with some outstanding people.

He is currently a materials manager.

THEODORE R. STRUHL, M.D., born Jan. 5, 1917, Brooklyn, NY. Graduated high school in New York City, 1932. Graduated NYU, 1936. Graduated New York Medical College, 1942. Volunteered for the Medical Corps of the U.S. Army in 1941. Allowed to finish his medical training in 1942 and one year internship in 1943, and then went directly into the Army Medical Corps.

Initial training at Carlisle Barracks, PA, and from there to North Carolina Training Site, then overseas to the European Theatre. He was in the 35th Inf. Div., 110th Bn., attached to General Patton's 3rd Army. Served in the European Theatre from 1943 until almost 1946, then sent back to the States.

Started out as a first lieutenant in the Medical Corps, then promoted through the ranks to major in the Medical Corps.

Awards/Medals: EAME Service Medal, Combat Medic Medal, Unit Citation Medal, American Theatre Medal, WWII Victory Medal. He was honorably discharged in 1946.

Married to Ruth for almost 52 years. They have a son, Karsten, who is professor of philosophy in New York City, and a daughter, Wendy, who is a teacher in advance mathematics for advanced students in Oakland, CA.

A member of the JWV, American Legion, VFW and life member of the DAV.

At the present time he is in the full-time practice of surgery and is a senior surgeon at the Mount Sinai Medical Center in Miami Beach, FL. He does general surgery, gynecological surgery and gynecology, and sports medicine, all of which he is considered an expert.

SAM STULBERG, born in Marshall, MI Aug. 10, 1924. Entered military Dec. 10, 1943. Basic training (Coast Artillery) Camp Callan, CA, then assigned almost miraculously to same company as brother Morris in 97th Inf. at Ft. Leonard Wood, Mo. The 97th sent to San Luis Obispo, CA, then personnel sent to East Coast as replacements for European casualties.

Embarked Boston (Morris delayed for glasses, New York) debarked England and reunited briefly near Omaha Beach and at assembly area in France. Moved 15 men by plane to Pisa, Italy. (Sam direct/Morris via Paris & Lyon). Traveling separately, but meeting several times, both were assigned to 1st Sq, 1st Plt., K Co., 3rd Bn., 361st Inf., 91st Div. Now too close, Morris moved to 3rd Platoon. Fought to war's end and contact with Yugoslav Partisans in Goriza, Italy.

Decorations include: Combat Infantry Badge, Bronze Star Medal, Presidential Unit Citation. He was discharged May 1, 1946.

Married Sarah Weitzman 1962, children Adam Nathan and Minda Beth. Retired 1980 from U.S. Department of Interior (Geological Survey).

MARK S. SUGAR, was a general medical officer assigned to Ching Chuan Kang (CCK) Air Force Base in Taichung, Taiwan 1971-1973, the latter years of the Vietnam War. CCK was a C-130 cargo airlift unit that participated in air drops over Anloc and Kontum. He worked at the base hospital in Taichung and was also assigned TDY (temporary duty) to Shu Linko Air Station in Taipei which monitored activity on Quemoy and Matsu.

In his spare time he studied the Chinese language with the wife of a high ranking colonel in the ROC air force and enjoyed their friendship and hospitality during his tour of duty.

His fondest memories include medical volunteer work at the Maryknoll Clinic with the director "sister-doctor" treating many tropical diseases and working with the Aborigine mountain peoples in central Taiwan.

His most disturbing memories are his pilot friends who were shot down over Vietnam, never to return to Taiwan.

BERT SUGARMAN, born Sept. 4, 1921, in New York City, NY. Branch USAAC. Enlisted July 31, 1940. Radio operator, Gunner B-24, Liberators Topeka, KS; Casper, WY, Radio Operators School, Madison, WI; Control Tower Operator School, Chanute Field, Rantoul, IL; Halesworth, England; Galveston, TX.

Has 10 Battle Stars, 29 combat missions, Air Medal, Victory Medals. This is service during WWII. Served during Korean Conflict. Discharged August 1955. Attained rank of technical sergeant.

Married to Ruth and has children, Howard and James, and six grandchildren. Resides in San Francisco, CA. Department commander 1994-1995 Department of California.

Most memorable experience was visit to Matthausen and Ebemser Concentration Camps in 1945.

HARRY SUGARMAN, was born in London, England, June 25, 1891. Enlisted in the service May 1917. Served with 77th Div., 308th Inf., Co. B as corporal. Stationed in Camp Upton, NY.

Participated in battles at St. Mihiel, Argonne, and Beleau Woods. His memorable experiences includes killing the German that shot him.

Awards/Medals: WWI Victory Medal, Croix de Guerre with Palm and AEF Medal. Discharged January 1920 as corporal.

Married to Sylvia and had son Bert. Harry is deceased

LESTER L. SULLUM, was born in Scranton, PA, Feb. 12, 1915. Enlisted in service March 9, 1944, serving with Infantry, 1st Div. Stationed in Ft. McClellan, AL. Fought in the Battle of the Bulge.

Awards/Medals: two Purple Hearts, two Good Conduct Medals for bravery. Discharged Dec. 3, 1945 as private first class.

Retired from retail furniture business.

GEORGE SULMEYER, served in the U.S. Army Medical Corps from Dec. 11, 1943-Nov. 15, 1945. He entered the service with the rank of 1st lieutenant and held the rank of captain at time of discharge. He received his training at Carlisle Barracks, Carlisle, PA from Dec. 20, 1943 to Feb. 1, 1944 and at maneuvers at Louisiana with the 75th Inf. Div. until March 22, 1944 and was also with the 72nd Post Surgical Hospital at Camp Livingstone, IA from March 22, 1944 to July 4, 1944.

Sailed overseas from San Francisco, CA on the USS *Matsonia* arriving at Oro Bay, New Guinea and sailed from there on the USS *Joseph Reynolds* arriving at Lingayen Gulf Luzon from where he sailed on the USS *Natrona* arriving Nagoya, Honshu, Japan. He served in the Pacific Theatre Operations at New Guinea, Luzon and Japan with the 25

Inf. Div. and saw action in New Guinea, and the Luzon Campaigns.

Awards/Medals: several citations, decorations and promotions among them being two combat stars, assorted ribbons, Wolfhound Pins, Japanese Medal and Philippine Liberation Ribbon with star.

Promoted to the rank of captain on April 3, 1945. Visited the Manila, Batangas, Nagoya, Kyote, Isaka and many other places in the Far East. *Submitted by Max Sigal.*

LEON N. SUSSMAN, enlisted April 20, 1943, USN, MS. Served USN Hospital, Sampson AATB, Bizerte, Tunisia, USS LST 357; NOB Oran, Algeria; USN Det. Naples, Italy; USN Hospital Brooklyn, NY. Active duty from April 1943 to 1946. Reserve duty, July 1950 to 1967.

Awarded the EAME Service Medal with three stars, American Theatre, Purple Heart and Victory Medal. Discharged April 1946 as captain, USNR MC.

USN - Special (1) Established blood banking facility at Sampson USN Hospital; invasion of Salerno, Italy (USS LST 357); USN Hospital (operating base in Oran and Naples, Italy); USN Hospital Brooklyn, NY and St. Albans, LI.

Director of Hematology and Blood Bank at Beth Israel Medical Center in New York City 1946-1979; President, Medical Board BIMC 1970-1972; Clinical physician, Mt. Sinai School of Medicine, 1971.

Has published 107 medical journal articles; two books on blood testing for paternity.

ARNOLD D. SWARTZ, born March 14, 1916, Brockton, MA. Graduated Miami, Ohio University in 1937, commissioned 2nd lieutenant, USMCR. Active duty 1939 after Japanese code broken. Given regular commission 1940. Attached 3rd Defense Bn. shipped to Territory of Hawaii to set up defense of Midway.

October 26, 1941, married Rose Cetlin in Honolulu. After Hawaiian honeymoon, on detached duty Marine Barracks, Pearl Harbor, was Officer of the Day when Japanese attacked on December 7. Weeks later Rose was evacuated to Massachusetts and he returned to Midway and commanded antiaircraft battery when Japanese attacked.

Battalion was part of original attack on Solomon Islands. Served on Tulagi and Gavutu and Guadalcanal, his guns emplaced on Henderson Field runway. Tokyo Rose reported their destruction and his death frequently but falsely. After retirement owned a children's shop until 1951 when he became salesman and district manager for CPS-Ind.

Awards/Medals: Asiatic-Pacific Medal, WWII Victory Medal, Purple Heart, Silver Star and Certificate of Commendation. Swartz still works, gardens and golfs. He and wife, Rose, have a son, Jerry, and daughter, Janey, in Boca Raton, FL with grandchildren Lindsay and Daniel.

Member of Brockton Area of Retarded Citizens, Little Brothers Friend of the Elderly, Vice chairman, Brockton Library Foundation.

GEORGE SWARTZ, born in Boston in 1922. Enlisted in Navy right after Pearl Harbor and achieved chief petty officer rank aboard the *Susan B. Anthony,* a troop transport. Participated in the invasions of North Africa, Sicily and Normandy. Survived the sinking (by a German mine) of the *Anthony.*

Awards/Medals: EAME Ribbon with three Battle Stars, American Area Ribbon and WWII Victory Medal.

George was a member and commander of Post 193, Quincy, MA and the Hull, MA. American Legion Post. George was also very active in JWV National affairs. He founded Kenberma Products Company, now managed by son Alan. George succumbed to cancer in 1972. He was married to the late Ruth Fields. Has two sons, Alan and Jerry, a daughter, Dena, and six grandchildren: Melanie, April, Glenn, Jason, Gregory and Hillary.

HENRY D. SWARTZ, born in Boston, October 1925. Enlisted in Navy January, 1943. Basic training at Great Lakes Naval Center and University of Wisconsin's radio training courses. Assigned to Submarine Chaser #1307 as RDM2/c and 20mm gunner. Participated in North Atlantic patrols and Normandy invasion. SC #1307 sunk as result of landing craft barriers at Omaha Beach. Ship was salvaged, repaired and returned to duty.

Awards/Medals: EAME Ribbon with one Battle Star, American Area Ribbon and WWII Victory Medal. Honorably discharged in November 1945.

Married to Helen Simon with two children, Marcia and Jeffrey. Four grandchildren: Allison, Stacey, Rachel and Haley. He is a plastics engineer with 45 patents for inventions and founder of three plastics machinery companies. He is a member of Post #193, Quincy, MA.

NORMAN R. SWARTZ, was an art school graduate when in 1951, he enlisted in the USAAF. Completed basic training at Sampson, AFB, Finger Lakes Region, NY. Assigned to the training aids department of the navigator training section at Ellington, AFB outside of Houston, TX.

Went to Camp Stoneman, CA waiting disposition to the Far East.

Sent to Clark AFB, Luzon, Philippine Islands where he was assigned to the 581st Reproduction Sqdn. They designed and printed propaganda leaflets that were dropped over Korea.

With the end of the Korean War, he remained at Clark with the 2nd Air Rescue Gp. as a staff artist.

Upon his return stateside, he was assigned to a SAC facility, the 6th Bomb Wing at Walker, AFB, Roswell, NM.

In his tour with the 6th he went to Thule Greenland twice for their annual rotation.

He was discharged in 1955 with the rank of A/1c.

LEONARD E. SWEET, born Sept. 14, 1918, Madison, WI. Enlisted in the USN as engineering officer on LST, Feb. 9, 1943.

Great Lakes to Midshipman School to LST 667 in South Pacific.

Participated in: Tarakan, Visgyan Island; operated out of New Guinea and Sabre, Assault landings at Moratai, Leyte, Lingayen, Panay, Marivelas Bay and Corregidor.

Memorable experience was LST's small boat picking up MacArthur and taking him ashore after hitting the beach.

Awarded the Philippine Liberation, Philippine Unit Citation, American Campaign Medal, Asiatic-Pacific, WWII Victory and Navy Occupation Service.

Discharged as Lt (jg) USNR, April 15, 1946.

Married to Adelle and they have one son and three daughters.

Sweet is now retired in Appleton, WI.

MILTON SWEETWOOD, born April 19, 1917, in Newark, NJ. Drafted Feb. 20, 1941, and sent to 29th Inf. Regt.

attached to Infantry School, Ft. Benning, GA. OCS Class 74A, July 1942, commissioned 2nd lieutenant, Sept. 28, 1942, with TDY at Ft. Meade, MD. Assigned 3rd Div. in Casablanca, February 1943 and assisted in capturing Africa Corps in Tunisia.

Some Jews in the battalion requested to be allowed to go to Shul to celebrate either the Sabbath or Shavuos. Being the only Jewish officer in the battalion, he was assigned to take them to services in Tunis. With about a half dozen men he went to the Shul, where they were enthusiastically welcomed as saviours by the members. There were some French, English and South African Jewish soldiers there as well.

He was given the very great honor and Aliyah of carrying the Torah through the congregation. After services the members of the congregation insisted that they have dinner with them and they were allocated to different homes. Communications were difficult. They spoke neither English nor Yiddish, and Sweetwood spoke no French, their only language.

He has often wondered whether the great Aliyah did not go a long way toward saving his life, including some incidents little short of miraculous.

Awards/Medals: four Battle Stars, Infantryman's Badge and Purple Heart with cluster. He was separated from service Nov. 22, 1945 with the rank of 1st lieutenant.

A member of JWV Post 125, 7th Infantry Society, DAV and 3rd Division Society. He lives in Long Branch, NJ and has two children, Lori and Paul, and a wonderful wife, Hannelore.

BERNARD C. SYROP, born in Brooklyn, NY, Sept. 21, 1919. Drafted into the Army Oct. 7, 1941. Assigned to the horse calvary at Ft. Riley, KS, for basic training.

After entering the war, he went to Radar School in Drew Field, FL. Next destination by boat (60 days) to Karachi, India. Attached to 10th AF in Assam located at the base of the Naga Hills, head hunter country. The head hunters assisted them in setting up radar stations in the hills for spotting enemy aircraft.

Received his furlough overseas and spent it in the mountains near Tibet and visited many Lama temples.

After two and a half years overseas, troops were rotated and he returned to the states while the war was still going on. On the way home they stopped at New Guinea, Guadalcanal, New Zealand and Australia.

Awards/Medals: American Theater, EAME, Asiatic-Pacific with one Bronze Star, American Defense, Good Conduct and five Overseas Bands. Achieved the rank of corporal. Discharged October 1945.

Married Sylvia in 1946 and has two sons, Steven and Marc, and three grandsons.

Recently graduated Kingsborough Community College. Re-entered college to continue. Member of JWV Post 169.

A special memory was spending Rosh Hashanah in a foreign country. He was able to get a pass to Calcutta India to go to "Schul." He treated one and again the holiday with Indian Jews. It was quite an experience to learn how their customs were different from the American Jew, but the religion was exactly the same.

HERBERT TAFF, born in Jersey City, NJ, July 26, 1919. Graduated high school in 1938. Captained basketball team, played on the baseball and tennis teams.

Attended John Marshall College on a basketball scholarship. Attended Jersey City State Teachers College.

Entered service Jan. 16, 1941. Joined the Co. L, 39th Inf., 9th Inf. Div., Ft. Bragg, NC. Discharged June 26, 1945, with 130 points.

Participated in the landings of North Africa, invasion of Sicily. Trained in England for six months for the invasion of

France. Fought through France, Belgium, Ardennes, Battle of the Bulge, Germany.

Holder of the Silver Star, Bronze Star with OLC, Purple Heart and eight Battle Stars for campaigns in Algeria, French Morocco, Tunisia, Sicily, Normandy, Northern France, Ardennes, Rhineland and Central Europe.

Past New Jersey State Commander JWV of USA.

Resides in Ft. Lee, NJ and has two daughters and three grandchildren. Avid golfer; likes tennis, swimming and outdoors.

WALLACE TAFFET, born May 28, 1919, Nutley, NJ. Worked for Emerson Radio & TV Mfg. Corp. for five years, then for the U.S. War Dept. Signal Corps at Ft. Hancock, NJ. Came up with a solution to a transmission coil for radar and received the AF Civilian Medal for Defense of Washington, DC.

Entered the USN in 1944. Attended Intelligence Schools and subsequently invaded Japan Proper with Naval Amphibious Forces, 96th Div., 6th Army.

Memorable experience was typhoon in Okinawa, where they saved six crew members of PT boat and 36 crew members of yard minesweeper off reef in Buckner Bay.

Awards/Medals: WWII Victory Medal, American Area, Asiatic-Pacific Area and Good Conduct Medal. Discharged Feb. 10, 1946 with rank S1/c.

BS in education, CCNY and EE from Rutgers University. Partially owned and directed Metal Specialty Products Corp. and Taffet Electronics Corp, 1946-70. From 1971 was an instructor at various locations. Retired in 1989 from vocational education in NYS.

Happily married to second wife, Anne. He has a son David.

JOSEPH TANENBAUM, was born in Bayside, NY, Sept. 21, 1923. Enlisted April 23, 1943. Received infantry basic training at Camp Wheeler, GA. CBI, taught to be radio operator and was assigned to Chinese Artillery Btry. "Z" (Zee) Force, China.

His memorable experience includes his CO being captured by the Japanese. Became head of the team, sending information back to headquarters, including weather information for American planes to bomb and strafe the Japanese.

Awarded the Bronze Star and Special Breast Order Yun Hui from the Chinese Government. Tanenbaum was discharged October 1945 as T/5.

Married to Bernice and they have four sons and three grandchildren.

He is presently a lawyer, as are three of his sons. One son is a physician. Recently Chairman of Board, Flushing Hospital Medical Center, NY.

BORIS A. TARPELL (BORIS A. TOPOLSKY), was born Feb. 16, 1929, in Pittsburgh, PA. Joined the Pennsylvania National Guard, March 1948, 107th Field Arty. Bn. Btry. B 28th Inf. Div. in Ft. Indiantown Gap, PA 1948-1950. Camp Atterbury, IN 1950-1951; New Ulm, Germany 1951-1952.

His memorable experiences include his first experience with 987 Gentiles and found a great deal of anti-semitism.

Awards/Medals: Army of Occupation, WWII Victory, Unit Citation, Sharpshooters Medal and the Good Conduct Medal. He achieved the rank of staff sergeant, NG.

Married to Noreen Hershorin in 1951. They have two children Debra, born in 1956 and Alan born in 1957. Their grandchild Zachary Stavis was born in 1991.

Tarpell is currently retired.

ISIDORE L. TARSHIS, born July 8, 1915. Married and had a six month old daughter when he left home Dec. 23, 1943, to join the U.S. Army. Arrived at Ft. Dix, NJ; then sent to Ft. Bragg, NC, for 105 Howitzer basic training. Next was Camp Gruber, OK followed by POE, Ft. Lawton, WA.

Boarded the USS *General Breckenridge,* arriving in Hawaii 31 days later. They weren't allowed off the ship as President Roosevelt was visiting the island. It was off limits to all ships, so left for Guam where they stayed until he was discharged April 1946 with the rank of corporal.

Arrived home March 1946. Has wife, daughter, son, four grandsons and one granddaughter. Retired, but does volunteer for at the VA Lyons Hospital. He is member of JWV Post 536 Covered Bridge Post.

HAROLD TAUB, was born in Albany, NY on Oct. 16, 1925. He graduated Albany High School in 1943. Enlisted in the USN Dec. 1, 1943, and completed boot camp at Samson Naval Training Center. From Samson, he was sent to Electrician's Mate School at Purdue University.

Traveled to New Guinea aboard the SS *Sea Snipe;* he was subsequently stationed at submarine repair bases in Brisbane, Australia, Subic Bay, the Philippines, returning to the States in January, 1946.

Stationed briefly at Pier 92, New York City, then assigned to the USS *Houston.* He was discharged on May 21, 1946, at Lido Beach, NY with the rank of EM2.

In August, 1947, he married Leah Ann Jacobs of Springfield, MA. They have three daughters, three granddaughters and one grandson.

Harold retired from his business, Taub Heating and Plumbing, Inc. in December 1990. He enjoys playing golf and traveling, including three trips to Israel. He is a member of Albany Post 105.

ARTHUR D. TAUBER, born Aug. 4, 1920, The Bronx, NY. Attended Stuyvesant High School and graduated with BS in health, physical education safety and recreation from New York University, 1942.

Entered the U.S. Army in 1942, received basic training in the 397th Field Arty., 95th Inf. Div., Camp Swift, TX; jungle training in Camp Lejeune, LA; desert training in the Mojave Desert, CA, and amphibious training at Camp Pendleton, CA.

Transferred to USAAF and went to Denver University for basic pre-flight orientation. Returned to the ground forces and assigned to the 386th Inf. Regt., Co. D of the 97th Inf. Div. Went overseas to the ETO and saw action in the Rhineland.

When Germany surrendered, his division served as occupation forces, then returned stateside.

A brief furlough, then entire 97th Div. shipped to the Asiatic-Pacific Theater of Operations with staging area in the Philippines. When the atom bombs were dropped and Japan surrendered, the 97th entered Yokohama as occupation forces for the Tokyo area. Tauber served as recreation director of the Tokyo Golf Club for about three months before returning stateside.

Awards/Medals: Combat Infantry Badge, American Service Medal, EAME Campaign Medal, two Battle Stars, Asiatic-Pacific Service Medal, ETO Occupation, Japan Occupation Medal, WWII Victory Medal and the Good Conduct Medal.

Honorably discharged in 1946 with the rank of sergeant.

Returned to New York University Graduate School and recruited as a physical rehabilitation specialist at Halloran Army Hospital, Spinal Cord Injury Center, Staten Island, NY. Transferred to the Bronx VA Hospital in 1946, and became rehabilitation coordinator and administrator at New York, VA Hospital in 1955. Retired from the VA in 1975 and accepted a position at Yeshiva University, NY until 1986 when he retired and received professor emeritus status.

Married to Lenore C. Pomerantz for 51 years, Tauber has four grown children and 11 grandchildren.

LARRY S. TAYLOR, born March 28, 1941, New York, NY. Inducted into the USMC July 1, 1952.

He is currently major general, USMCR. His memorable experiences include 35 years service to Corps and country. Commanding general of 4th Marine Aircraft Wing.

BRUCE ELDRED TECLER, born June 17, 1927, Syracuse, NY. Attended Roosevelt Jr. High School. Graduated from Central High School in January, 1945. Employed with Sears-Roebuck Company. Enlisted in the USN on April 5, 1945. He died June 20, 1945, at the age of 18.

LOU R. TEEMAN, born on Oct. 29, 1920, Chicago, IL. Joined the Illinois Militia in 1941 and enlisted February 1942 in the USAAC. Sent to 8th AF, Savannah, GA AB and served 37 months overseas, including tours of duty in England and Russia. Honorably discharged and joined the USAFR at O'Hare Field, Chicago, IL.

Received direct commission from the ILNG while a member of the 698th AAA Gun Bn. in 1950 and first assignment as a platoon leader in the antiaircraft battery. Recalled into active federal service May 1951 and assigned XO of Co. B, 698th AAA Gun Bn. until May 1953.

Reverted back to the ILNG and served as battery commander until August 1956. Transferred to the USAR and assumed duty of the Bn. S-3 of a AAA Bn. Became adjutant in 1957 of the 85th Inf. Div. Arty. Has been an active reservist and served in an infantry training division, artillery brigade, transportation command and engineer command. Served as a company commander, battalion adjutant, battalion S-3, battalion executive officer, regimental adjutant, regimental S-3, battalion commander, division inspector general, chief of staff of a transportation command and assistant chief of staff of an engineer brigade.

Awards/Medals: U.S. Armed Forces Reserve Medal, Good Conduct with two clusters, National Defense Medal, WWII Medal, European Theatre of Operations with five Battle Stars, American Defense Medal and Air Force Reserve Medal.

Graduate of the Aeronautical University, has BA in aeronautical engineering. Studied at the Institute of Technology and University of Illinois in engineering and construction management. Graduate of the resident course of the United States Army Command and General College at Ft. Leavenworth, KS and was enrolled in the Industrial College of the Armed Forces Extension Courses at the time of retirement.

Retired from the USAR in 1977 as general and put on the Retired Officers Lists of the ILNG as a brigadier general with all the respects due this rank.

General Teeman is married to Gertrude Harriet Genow and has two sons. Presently retired from his own general contracting construction business and is a member of the Board of Directors of the ABC Industries of Chicago. Also a member of the Reserve Officers Association, JWV, American Legion, VFW and is a member of the professional engineering society.

SEVERYN TEIBLOOM, born March 31, 1920, in Warsaw, Poland. Entered the service Nov. 13, 1941. After basic training at Camp Croft, SC, assigned to 4th Div. at Camp Gordon, GA. Sent to Cornell University under the ASTP program. After nine months of intensive Russian language it was with the idea that they would be interpreters when the

American and Russian armies met. But instead, he went overseas as a replacement and was assigned to the 60th Inf. Regt. of the 9th Div.

He was discharged July 16, 1945, and 11 years later received a letter from the adjutant general's office that stated they had overlooked giving him the Bronze Star for "Meritorious Achievement against the enemy in the Rhineland Campaign."

Married and has three grown children and is the grandfather of five. In the insurance business for 46 years, he owns his own agency. Now semi-retired and enjoying life. He resides in Wilmette, IL.

MILTON TEICH, served in the U.S. Army and entered the Medical Department of the Army with the rank of private. *Submitted by Max Sigal.*

BERNARD L. TELL, born in West Brownsville, PA, Nov. 19, 1921. Moved in 1930 to Passaic, NJ. Entered the service November 1942 and was discharged in October 1945.

Staff sergeant with the 120th Regt. of the 30th Inf. Div. (Old Hickory).

Awards/Medals: Combat Infantryman's Badge, Bronze Star Medal, Good Conduct Medal, American Campaign Medal and Ribbon, WWII Victory Medal, EAME Campaign Medal and Service Ribbon with a Silver Service Star for Normandy, Northern France, Rhineland, Ardennes, and Central Europe Campaign, Distinguished Unit Citation and Emblem, Belgian Fourragere.

After discharge from service attended under graduate school at Rutgers University and the University of Maryland, received a Doctor of Dental Surgery degree. Will be married 50 years in June 1996 and has a son, daughter and two grandchildren. His son has taken over his practice, so now is enjoying a variety of activities.

LOUIS TENDLER, born Aug. 3, 1921, New Haven, CT. Joined the service Oct. 14, 1942, served as medical aidman.

Awards/Medals: five Battle Stars, Purple Heart with OLC, Silver Star with OLC, Combat Medical Badge, Bronze Star, Good Conduct Medal and EAME Theater Ribbon.

Discharged Oct. 22, 1945 with the rank PFC. He is retired and lives in Hamden, CT.

SIDNEY J. TENDLER, born in New York City, Sept. 9, 1921. Graduated James Monroe High School 1939. At age 21 enlisted in the USAAF, June 8, 1942.

Entered service as a aviation cadet but transferred to Radio-Radar School, Sioux Falls, SD, and Boca Raton, FL.

Taught electronics as an electronic instructor to the Emergency Rescue School in Biloxi, MS.

Subsequently flew overseas with the 7th Emergency Rescue Sqdn. and flew rescue missions from Okinawa to Japan. Flew missions as radio-radar operator with PBYs and B-17 rescue boat planes.

Discharged as a sergeant, Jan. 20, 1946.

Awards/Medals: American Service Medal, Asiatic-Pacific Service Medal, Philippine Liberation Ribbon and the WWII Victory Medal. Air Offensive Against Japan, Luzon and Western Pacific.

Married with two daughters and today very active as an advocate to seniors throughout Orange County, NY. Past Commander, Post #758 JWV, Monroe, NY. Two years Post Commander local American Legion Post and Life Member of local VFW Post. Member of Masonic War Veterans.

BERNARD TENGOOD, born in Eisenstadt, Austria on Jan. 22, 1919. After Hitler took over Austria in 1938, he left for Italy (six month stay) and then Denmark (one year). Arrived in the USA at the end of 1939, worked at Barnett Memorial Hospital in Paterson, NJ until he joined the military service in February 1941.

Received an honorable discharge March 1947. Worked for CIA for 28 years as a research analyst and translator for many languages. While working for CIA in Tehran (1961-1971), he was active in the Jewish community (conducting Friday night services and principal of a Sunday School for Iranian, Iraqi, Israeli and American Jews). Retired from CIA in December 1974 and currently working for the Keystone Shipping Co. in Philadelphia. He is happily married.

Statistical clerk, 9th Inf. HQ Ft. Sam Houston, TX (1941); instructor at Intelligence Training Center, Camp Ritchie, MD (1941-1943) and teaching German at Counter Intelligence School, Holabird, Baltimore, MD (1947). Prepared first handbook, *Identification of German Army*, 1942, a German language book for school in Holabird, and other intelligence.

His memorable experiences includes the reunion of his three brothers, (two of which were also in military service).

Awards/Medals: WWII Victory Medal, Good Conduct, American Service Medal, EAME Campaign Medal.

Participated in the Battles of the Bulge, Germany and France (1944-1945) on intelligence assignments. Last military post was at Oak Ridge, TN, as special agent for the Manhattan Project. His highest rank achieved was master sergeant. He is an active member of the JWV Post 791.

Married Selma M. Keystone after break up of family because of Hitler. Now works for a shipping company in Philadelphia.

BENNIE TICKOS, born March 15, 1918, Bronx, NY. Entered the U.S. Army at Camp Blanding, FL, March 5, 1941. Received basic training at Camp Blanding, FL. Maneuvers in Louisiana and North Carolina.

Foreign service, two years, 11 months, 20 days in England; Marseilles and Lyon, France; Oran, North Africa and Rome, Italy. Fought battles in Rhineland, WDGO 40-45, Rome-Arno WDGO 33-45.

Awards/Medals: American Defense Service Medal, Good Conduct Medal, EAME Service Medal. Honorably discharged, Sept. 20, 1945, 193rd MP Co. at Camp Blanding, FL.

Moved to Miami, FL in 1946 and continues to reside there in his retirement years.

JAMES S. TIERNEY, enlisted in the Navy in March 1944 from Miami, FL, age 17. Upon completion of boot camp was sent to Class "A" School, then to Basic Submarine School,

New London, CT. Progressed from apprentice seaman to chief yeoman. Was assigned to Staff Submarine School; USS *Odax* (SS-484); USS *Sea Cat* (SS-399); and Staff Commander Submarine Sqdn. 12.

Selected for commissioning, completed training in 1956, at Officer Candidate School, Newport, RI, and then assigned to USS *Norris* (DDE-859); Staff Commander Destroyer Sqdn. 14; Naval Postgraduate School, Monterey, CA; USS *Whitfield County* (LST-1169)l Staff Commander Cruiser Destroyer Force Atlantic; and command of USS *Traverse County* (LST-1160). Retired from Navy in 1967 as a lieutenant commander.

Entered the Navy with a high school education and left Navy with bachelor of science degree from Navy Postgraduate School and Master of Arts degree from George Washington University.

Presently commander, Department of Connecticut, JWV, and serving as vice chairman, National Centennial Committee. Previously commander Hartford Laurel Post #45.

Life member: Submarine Veterans of WWII; Veterans of Foreign Wars; The Retired Officers Association.

LEON D. TIKULSKI, had three years college ROTC at the University of Illinois. Inducted into the Army on June 19, 1943, and sent to Ft. Leonard Wood for basic training as a sergeant.

Returned to U. of Illinois on ASTP Program from late September 1943-March 1944. Sent to Ft. Belvoir, VA to OCS (did not graduate). Shipped to Camp Reynolds, PA as a private for additional basic.

Sent to Port Arthur, Canada and left there on the SS *Thompson*. Stopped at Dutch Harbor, Kodiak, and Kiska. Landed on Attu Dec. 24, 1944, and had KP on the 25th. Transferred to Shemya, a secret base, about a week later. All mail was censored until after he departed.

On Shemya he was post file clerk. Finally became a corporal in a staff sergeant's job. Advanced to post sergeant major and remained a corporal because the Alaskan Command froze all enlisted men's ranks about a week before he became sergeant major.

Shipped to Camp McCoy, WI for honorable discharge March 31, 1946.

BERNARD TILLIS, CPA, was born March 18, 1925, in Bayonne, NJ. Graduated Bayonne High School, June 1942; New York University, June 1948 (cum laude); and entered the Army July 17, 1943.

Received infantry basic training at Ft. Benning, GA, August-November 1943. ASTP (Army Specialized Training Program); basic engineering at St. John's University, Brooklyn, NY, November 1943-February 1944; 75th Inf. Div., Message Center (Courier), HQ Co., 290th Inf. Regt.; Camp Breckinridge, KY March-October 1944; ETO Nov. 1, 1944-Feb. 24, 1946.

Major campaigns participated in were: Battle of the Bulge (first action), Colmar Pocket, Ruhr Pocket.

The Division earned the nickname "Bulge Busters," Shrivenham American University, England, August and September 1945.

Memorable experiences: Seeing the regiment's first casualties at the aid station on Christmas Eve 1944 (Battle of the Bulge). Attending New Year's Eve Ball on Dec. 31, 1945, sponsored by the Paris Jewish newspaper at which several thousand Parisian Jews were present.

Awards/Medals: Bronze Star, Combat Infantry Badge, American Service Medal, EAME Campaign Medal, WWII Victory Medal.

Past Commander of JWV Post #125 - Still active. Past president of Shore Lodge 1685, Binai Brith. Received CPA Certificate in 1951.

Married to Dorothy Friedman June 5, 1949. They have a son, Robert and daughter Susan. They also have a grandson Ryan.

MORRIS TILLMAN, was born in Brooklyn, NY, Jan. 22, 1928. Enlisted in the service January 1953. Served in Finance Center; U.S. Army. Attended basic at Ft. Dix. Finance Center, Indianapolis and Finance, Pusan, Korea. Served in Korea immediately after truce was signed.

Honorably discharged October 1954 with the rank of corporal.

Has been a CPA from 1956 to present time. Still a partner in own firm in New Jersey. Served as president of Congregation Adas Israel in Passaic, NJ and its Men's Club and still serves on the congregation's executive board.

Married to Zelma since November 1954. He has two married sons and two grandchildren.

SANFORD TIMEN, born on April 7, 1914, Cleveland, OH. He was always in love with airplanes, built flying models as a youth and obtained his private license at Evansville College. Entered service, but was too old for Army pilot. The only position which called for a flying officer was flight engineer, so he set his goal for that.

After basic training, went to Airplane Mechanics School in Gulfport and became an instructor. Was joined by his wife Nettie, a former school teacher, who also became a flight instructor. Went to Lowry Field in Denver to attend Flight Engineer's School.

While in Denver, he became acquainted with their Jewish community whom he must laud for their treatment of the servicemen. They had Friday night services followed by an Oneg Shabbat. On Sunday mornings a breakfast was served to the servicemen at the Jewish center.

Joined crew in Walker Field, KS, and learned to fly the B-29s. His wife became Governor Man at the Sub Depot at Walker Field. She was in the propeller branch in Gulfport. After crew's transition on B-29s, they flew to their base on Guam with their own plane.

On one of their missions over Japan, their number three engine caught fire and had to be shut off. They dropped their bombs at a target of opportunity and set their power to maximum distance. By carefully nursing their fuel, they made it back to Guam where they were met by Gen. Hap Arnold who congratulated them on their feat. They were awarded the Distinguished Flying Cross for saving the plane and themselves.

At the end of the war, they were presented with the Air Medal with two OLCs and the Asian Campaign Medal with three stars.

He returned home to Columbus, OH, where he lost his wife to cancer. After his retirement he met Florence, a childhood sweetheart, in Florida. They were married and reside in Florida where they are very happy. Works as a security guard and also does volunteer work at Florida Medical Center.

EARL MELVIN TOBERMAN, born in Minneapolis, MN, March 20, 1920. Attended Minneapolis Public Schools; graduated North High School 1938; attended University of Minneapolis, graduating in 1942. Served in the U.S. Army. Stationed at Ft. Snelling, Camp Riley, POW Camp, Ripley, NE.

Awards/Medals: Good Conduct Medal, American Theater, WWII Victory, Sharpshooter. Discharged as staff sergeant March 1946.

Took over father-in-laws business. Later mobile home business with brother Gerald. Mason, Shriner, Adath Jeshuran Syn. B'nai B'rith. Boy Scout leader. Enjoyed bridge, gardening and fishing.

Met wife, Marion Tomsky, at University of Minneapolis, married November 1943 and had four children and three grandchildren. A very musical family. All four children played numerous instruments.

He is now deceased.

JOSEPH TODRES, born on March 9, 1918, in Newark, NJ. Entered the Army on April 16, 1943. Served in Army April 16, 1943-Nov. 30, 1945. Received basic training in the medics at Camp Pickett, VA.

Shipped to Camp Shelby, MS, received additional training in a station hospital, working in the Mess Department, preparing food for patients.

June 1944 shipped to Wrexham, England where a general hospital was formed, the 129th, and serviced severely wounded soldiers from the European War. Served abroad from June 27, 1944-July 30, 1945.

Awards/Medals: American Service Medal, EAME Campaign Medal, Victory Medal and the Good Conduct Medal. Discharged Nov. 30, 1945, at Ft. Dix as T-5.

Married to Claire for 53 years. Has a daughter Renee, son Allen, and two grandchildren, Matthew and Jennifer Schwartz.

He is now working in sales and semi-retired.

HOWARD R. TOLCHINSKY, DMD, born in Pittsburgh, PA, on July 18, 1942. Entered Army March 13, 1964; basic at Ft. Jackson. Served in Vietnam 1965 to 1966 with the 228th Signal Company at Cam Rahn Bay as a radio relay carrier operator, PFC.

Their unit was among the first in the area. They had only pup tents and cardboard boxes for shelter until larger tents arrived in about a month. He was so covered with mosquito bites the first night that he could not bend his fingers.

Married Linda Moughamer and graduated Doctor of Dental Medicine, University of Pittsburgh, 1973. He has his original short-timers calendar and many photographers to remind him of a place and time, far away and long ago. Member JWV.

RUBIN TOLVIN, born in Newark, NJ. Inducted into the USN Oct. 27, 1942. He was classified as seaman third class and served in the South Pacific.

Awards/Medals: two Purple Hearts, Good Conduct Medal, and Battle Stars. He achieved the rank of ship's cook second class.

Memorable experiences: Finishing basic training at Great Lakes Naval Base and going to Pearl Harbor where he boarded the USS *Helena*. Eight months and many battles later, she was sunk after being hit by Japanese torpedoes on July 5, 1943, in the Kula Gulf (Guadalcanal).

Many crew members were lost. He was one of the fortunate ones who, after spending five hours with his shipmates in what seemed a hopeless situation very near a Japanese occupied island (Vella LaVella), was among those rescued by crewmembers of the destroyer, USS *Radford*, a ship who returned from battle again and again against orders to save whoever remained in the water.

He was ordered to join the crew of the cruiser USS *Columbia,* and served until January 1945. During the invasion of the Philippines at Leyte Gulf, they were hit by Japanese kamikazes and many were killed. He was badly burned and spent one year at Ft. Eustis in the hospital. He again considered himself lucky.

Reading reunion notices in the DAV magazine 50 years later, July 1993, he learned that the USS *Radford* was looking for any *Helena* survivors to attend their reunion in Chicago. He and his wife did so and he was able to personally thank the actual men who pulled him to safety that night. They have since become friends and he and his wife have attended another reunion. Their third one is in Reno in October 1995 and they have reservations.

He is retired and proudly exhibits the *Helena, Columbia* and *Radford* on his den walls.

MERVIN B. TOMSKY, born in Minneapolis, MN, Oct. 6, 1925. Enlisted Feb. 22, 1944, and served in the Quartermaster Corps. Stationed in Assam, India—CBI Theater of War.

Memorable experiences include the six and a half weeks en route on troopship from Los Angeles to Calcutta; and serving as acting Jewish chaplain in addition to his regular duties.

Discharged May 26, 1996, as T-4.

Married to Helen Broude and they have three children. Conservative rabbi, retired and living in Sun Valley, CA.

PHILIP TOPIEL, born June 29, 1916, in New York City. Entered service Feb. 11, 1941, and was corporal of a searchlight squad stationed at Camp Pendleton, Virginia Beach. Transferred to Air Corps and graduated as pilot June 1943, from Luke Field Flying School, Phoenix, AZ.

Assigned to 451st Bomb Gp. and flew combat over Europe and Balkans. On 41st mission, was shot down by antiaircraft flak and held in German prison camp, Stalag Luft III for one year.

Awards/Medals: Air Medal with three OLCs and Presidential Citation with one OLC for participating in raids on Regensburg Aircraft Factory and Ploesti Oil Fields. Left Army August 1945.

Married to Rose and they have two children, Amy and Martin and four grandchildren, Scott, Jordan, Carrie and Benjamin, son-in-law Harry, daughter-in-law, Ellen. Member of JWV Post 550.

CYRUS TOPOL, born Boston, MA, Oct. 2, 1911. Graduated Dorchester High School 1929. Enlisted in USN March 1942 as SK3/c. Basic training Newport, NTS. Student and instructor GM School, Great Lakes NTS 1942-1943. Advanced Electric and Hydraulic School, Washington, DC, Navy Yard 1944.

Assigned USS *Missouri* pre-commissioning detail at Brooklyn Navy Yard. Commissioning ceremony June 1944 followed by months shakedown along East Coast. Then through Panama Canal to Hunter's Point, CA for a Pacific repaint job and on to Pearl Harbor arriving Christmas Day 1944.

Joined Pacific Fleet with Adm. Halsey and Adm. Spruance alternating as fleet admiral while onboard *Missouri*. Spent 1945 protecting invasions of Okinawa and Iwo Jima and fighting off kamikazes. Also 16" guns were used to knock out a steel mill on island of Hokkaido at 23 mile distance. *Missouri* was struck only once by exploding kamikaze at foot of Topol's 5" 38 enclosed twin antiaircraft gun. Sent all ammo below as smoke and fire raged on deck around his mount.

At official end of war *Missouri* chosen for site of Japanese surrender. On Sept. 2, 1945, he rose at sunrise, with his crew. They manned their guns and were all at battle stations all during the ceremony. He was a witness to it all from sunrise to sunset, from on top of his mount.

ROBERT A. TORNICK, born Aug. 28, 1921, Camden, NJ. Entered USMC April 6, 1943, discharged Feb. 23, 1946, with the rank of corporal. Basic training at Parris Island, SC, thence to Camp LeJeune, NC. Overseas assignment to Marine barracks, Pearl Harbor Oct. 16, 1943. Later, moved to Camp Catlin Tent City with the 6th Base Depot, thence to 7th Svc. Regt., Fleet Marine Force, Pacific, February 1945 heading for Saipan.

Left Saipan on the convoy for the invasion of Okinawa which took place Easter Sunday, April 1, 1945. Regiment informed that it has been awarded a Presidential Unit Citation for its action on Saipan.

October 1945: Regiment sent to Tientsin and Tsingtao China to repatriate the Japanese where it remained until February 1946.

Awards/Medals: WWII Victory Medal, Asiatic-Pacific, National Defense, Good Conduct Medal and a special "China Service" Medal by the Chinese Government.

The Regiment holds a reunion every two years; each time in a different part of the country.

In 1971 and 1972, long after the war, he earned a BS and MA from New York University. Presently: retired New York City teacher and guidance counselor. Member JWV Post 169, Brooklyn, NY and the China Marine Association.

Married to Irene, two sons, Barry and Michael, two grandchildren, Sharon and Jeffrey.

STEVEN TREATMAN, was born in Los Angeles, CA April 24, 1954. Enlisted Jan. 10, 1977 in USAF as TSG. Stationed at Pope AFB, NC; Webb AFB, TX; Fairchild AFB, WA; Kadena AB, Japan; Nellis AFB, NV; Ft. Bragg, NC.

Participated in Grenada, Operation Just Cause/Operation Urgent Fury; Operation Desert Shield/Desert Storm.

His memorable experiences include about 200 parajumps, supporting 82nd Airborne Div., Tac Air Control.

Awards/Medals: ARCOM with one device, AFCOM with two devices, Air Force Achievement Medal with three devices.

Still on active duty as TSG.

Married Jennifer Benjamin in 1992.

DAVID TROTINER, born April 6, 1923, Brooklyn, NY. Inducted in the service March 24, 1943, at New York City. Shipped to Ft. Dix, NJ, to a camp on Pacific Ocean near Watsonville, CA. After six weeks of basic training, he was ordered to Oklahoma A&M College, Stillwater, OK from June 1943-March 1944.

Received Certificate of Completion for two years basic engineering. Joined the 103rd Div., 409th Inf. Regt., 3rd Bn., Co. M at Camp Howze, TX, March 1944. Arrived in ETO with the 103rd Div. and was there from October 1944-August 1945.

Vividly recalls the liberation of concentration victims on or about April 30, 1945, on main road leading to Alps Mountains, in Bavaria, Germany. German guards had forced marched these people from Dachau, Germany concentration camp toward Austria. Most victims were Hungarian Jews, dressed in stripped light prisoner clothes.

Awards/Medals: WWII Victory Medal and EAME Theater Campaign Medal with two Battle Stars. Discharged at Ft. Dix, NJ, March 30, 1946 with the rank PFC.

Married Slyvia Anfang Dec. 25, 1947, they have two sons and three granddaughters.

Received BBA degree from Baruch School of Business Administration in New York City. Retired since 1985 as expert sales manager and contract administrator.

BERNARD TUCHINSKY, born Oct. 2, 1916. Enlisted in 1941. Served in the 37th Tank Bn., 4th Armd. Div., 3rd Army, in the ETO. On March 19, 1945, while in combat, Pvt. Tuchinsky was killed while operating the machine gun of his tank. His tank was hit three times by enemy armor piercing shells and was killed instantly.

He received the Purple Heart once in December 1944 and again in March 1945.

Buried in the U.S. Military Cemetery #1 at Stromberg, Germany. At present lies at rest in Brooklyn, NY. Survived by his father, Jacob, of New York and his mother, Rose.

He was married to Lena F. Chanchiske, daughter of Mr. and Mrs. Haskel Chanchiske of Syracuse, NY, in November 1943.

STANLEY L. TUCKER, born July 15, 1923, in Vineland, NJ. Joined the USN, Thanksgiving Day, Nov. 26, 1942, and reported to NTS Bainbridge, MD, Nov. 27, 1942. After boot training was sent to Little Creek, VA for amphibious training in LCVP, which were the first assault boats to take Army troops ashore.

Was aboard British LST with 110 Navy men and taken to Arzew, Tunisia, North Africa. After training was assigned to USS LST 350 in Oran, Tunisia. July 10, 1943 participated in the invasion of Sicily. In September was in the invasion of Salerno, Italy, then left for England. June 6, 1944 was in the invasion of Omaha Beach, Normandy, France.

Awards/Medals: American Area, EAME Campaign Medal with four stars, Victory Medal and Good Conduct Medal. Discharged March 17, 1946.

Married for 45 years, has two daughters, married and one granddaughter. He and his wife Esther are retired.

MYER S. TULKOFF, born Ashland, KY Oct. 24, 1927. Junior ROTC Ashland Senior High School. Entered U.S. Army Oct. 1, 1946. Basic at Aberdeen Proving Grounds, MD; Army of Occupation, Japan. Military policeman, 34th Inf., Kobe, Japan. Discharged Feb. 10, 1948 (T/5).

Army ROTC University of Kentucky (1950-1952); commanded outstanding drill company, 1952. Distinguished military graduate, ROTC; commissioned second lieutenant, May 30, 1952. Active duty July 1, 1952. Regimental headquarters Camp Breckinridge, KY 101st Abn. Div. Advanced training The Infantry School, Ft. Benning, GA, Korea, 1953. Released Dec. 26, 1953.

Joined civil affairs/military government Army Reserve unit 1955. Active reserve until retirement 1982 as colonel. Unit: HQ 353d Civil Affairs Command, New York Chief of Staff of unit.

Awards/Medals: WWII Victory Medal, Army of Occupation (Japan); Korean Service Medal; UN Service Medal; National Defense Service Medal, Army Reserve Medal and Meritorious Service Medal with OLC.

Married to Esther since 1954. Children: Donna Schwechter and Jonathan; three grandchildren: Daniel, Cary and Serena. Attorney in private practice. Member of JWV-Post 425.

BEN TUNIS, entered the Armed Forces in February 1943 at Camp Upton, NY, with the rank of private in the infantry. Received his basic training at Camp McCain, MS from February 1943-December 1943, and at Ft. Jackson, SC, from February, 1944-October 1944.

Sailed overseas on the HMS *Queen Elizabeth* out of New York City in October 1944, and landed in Glasgow, Scotland. He saw active service in the ETO with the 87th Inf. Div. from October 1944-July 1945.

Saw considerable action in France, Luxembourg, Belgium, Germany and Czechoslavakia. He visited many places in Europe among which were Paris, London and many other parts of England and Scotland.

Discharged with the rank of staff sergeant at Ft. Benning, GA. *Submitted by Max Sigal*

MANUEL TUNIS, served in the U.S. Army from Oct. 25, 1943-Dec. 11, 1945. Entered the service at Camp Upton, NY, with the grade of private. He received his basic training with the Coast Artillery at Ft. Terry, NY, from Nov. 14, 1943-Jan. 19, 1944 and other Coast Artillery training at Ft. Wright, NY, from January 1944-Dec. 4, 1945.

He saw no action but acted as columnist on the fort newspaper and acted as a Jewish chaplain for a while.

Awards/Medals: Good Conduct Medal, the Victory Medal and the American Theatre Campaign Ribbon.

He was discharged at Ft. Devens, MA with the grade of corporal.

He performed no heroic deeds and "had a dull, prosaic routine Army life." *Submitted by Max Sigal*

MARVIN TUNIS, served in the USN from Aug. 11, 1943-April 5, 1946. He entered the service in New York City with the rank of able-bodied seaman. He received his boot training at Sampson, NY from Aug. 18, 1943-October 1943 and also trained at Sonar School at Key West, FL, receiving Sonar training from October 1943-December 1943 and from December 1944-May, 1945.

Served aboard the USS *Excel* AM-94 doing minesweep duty and patrolling the waters off Portland, ME. Also served aboard the USS *Flicker* AM-70 with minesweep duties and patrolling in the North Atlantic area. He also served aboard the *Ware* DD-865.

Saw action with anti-submarine patrols and attacks in North Atlantic in 1944. Received promotions from AS to S2/c after boot training S1/c during sonarman training and SOM3/c in December 1944 after completion of training SOM2/c in December 1944.

His ship was one of the escorting destroyers with the USS *Midway* experimental run in the Arctic waters at Greenland in March, 1946. He held the rank of SOM2/c at the time of discharge on April 5, 1946. *Submitted by Max Sigal*

SAUL TUNIS

SIDNEY M. TURKEL, born Dec. 4, 1917, McKibben St., Brooklyn, NY. Entered U.S. Army April 23, 1942, at Camp Upton, NY. Served at Ft. D.A. Russell, Marfa, TX and Ft. Sam Houston, TX. Military Police and Signal Corps. Discharged Dec. 17, 1945.

Married to Livia (Shula) Rosenberg of Pulaski St. Brooklyn, NY.

Children: Dr. Elihu and Brenda Turkel of Kew Gardens Hills, NY and Beth and Benjamin Heller of Lawrence, NY. Six grandchildren: Joshua and Shira (twins) and Aliza Heller. Dahlia, Daniel and Yoie Turkel.

Employed by Filtered Water Service Corp. (Snowbird) for over 40 years. Member of Cohen-Lurie Post #120 Canarsie,

NY and Queens Jewish Center, NY, Rabbi Joseph Grunblatt, Forest Hills, NY.

NATHAN N. TYSON, born in Universal, PA Dec. 1, 1914. Enlisted Feb. 14, 1941, second lieutenant, USAF. Served with USAF, 22nd Observation Sqdn., navigator, observer, intelligence officer. Stationed at Brooks Field, TX training air to ground as observer, Marshall Field, Ft. Riley, KS (training with ground troops), (Desert Center, AZ training air to ground).

Participated in action against Japanese who finally gave up in Burma. CBI April 1943 to 1945 when war ended. Suffered severe jungle rot and weight loss and evacuated to USA two months before war ended.

His memorable experiences: liaison aircraft they ("L" 5's) used to rescue and picked up 24 rescues of downed airman in jungles of Burma from February 1943 to end of war.

Awards/Medals: Air Medal, Distinguished Flying Cross, Purple Heart. Discharged March 1946 after spending four months in hospital. He achieved the rank of major and is receiving 50% disability pay since end of the war.

His wife Geraldine died January 1990. He has three children, son Richard, presently medical doctor in Coral Springs, FL; son, Harvey and daughter.

Spends winter in Florida. Retired and active in local vet groups. Plays golf four days per week. Sold his successful business. (1946 through 1983).

IRV UDOFF, born March 31, 1926 in Baltimore, MD. Graduated Baltimore City College High School in 1944. Enlisted in the Navy, boot camp at Bainbridge, MD, then radar school in Virginia. In December 1944 joined USS *Bunker Hill* (CV-17) in radar - CIC Div., Rdm2/c. Became one of the editors of ship's newspaper, *The Monument.*

Participated in first carrier raid on Tokyo, Iwo Jima and Okinawa campaigns. On May 11, 1945 ship hit by kamikazes; 656 casualties, 392 killed. Trapped below decks, rescued and returned with ship to Bremerton, WA.

Awards/Medals: Pacific Theater Ribbon two stars, American Theater Ribbon, Victory Medal, Presidential Unit Citation with Bronze Star. He was discharged February 1946.

Attended University of Maryland, College Park, National Academy of Broadcasting, DC and University of Baltimore, BA degree. First 12 years worked as accountant for real estate development companies; past 26 years as an independent life insurance broker.

Married June 12, 1949, to Phyllis Joan Krauss. Reared three sons: Richard of Austin, TX; Howard of Livingston, NJ and Laurence, physician, Baltimore, MD in Oby-Gyn, infertility specialty. They have six grandchildren: Amanda Udoff, Eric, Marc and Jason Udoff, Pamela Rose and Geoffrey M. Udoff.

After five years, Udoff's book *The Bunker Hill Story* published by Turner Publishing Company in February 1995. Member Paul D. Savanuck Memorial Post No. 888.

GERALD F. ULLMAN, came originally from Europe to the U.S. in 1941, with his parents and aunt (now deceased). They left Germany, 1936 for Sweden, where they stayed in refuge for 4 1/2 years. They were harassed by the Nazi government of Germany in Sweden which was neutral. After Germany occupied Denmark, Norway and Finland they left Sweden via USSR for Japan. They were supposed to have gone, 1940-1941.

They arrived in the U.S. March 21, 1941. He entered high school in Los Angeles, CA May 1941. At first he was at Belmont High and moved over to Los Angeles High. Graduated January 1944 and entered the U.S. Army in 1943 with a deferment to February 1944. He was in the infantry and medics.

Discharged Jan. 1, 1945. A medical discharge was given to him on account of a perforated ear drum on both ears. The U.S. Government GI Bill of Rights of WWII gave him his chance.

He had various jobs, entered business with his father.

His father passed away in 1966. He married Edith E. Miller. They have one handicapped son, Marc Alan Ullman, who lives with them.

WILLIAM UNFANGER, born in Chicago, IL, Aug. 15, 1992, a retired attorney, over 50 years in practice, enlisted in Air Force June 1942, assigned to Army Airways Communications System (AACS), elite branch world wide service. Spent 180-days in Air Force hospital, all but 10 consecutive.

Stationed in El Geneina Anglo-Egyptian Sudan and duty in China Burma India Theater, (CBI) Kunyang, Yunnan province, set up two tents-two man radio homing beacon station over so-called Hump route over Himalayan mountains, threatened by raids from bandit forces and anti-Chinese government rebels. Initially they sort of lived off the land, being left canned GI provisions, hardly gourmet, and not enough, but not for long. They "bought" a cook. A Chinese army group stopped by, led by a somewhat English speaking officer who instead of confiscating their meager supplies, offered to buy a carton of cigarettes.

They traded cigarettes for a Chinese GI who could cook. Lee High took over the "household" chores and was happy, having been shanghaied off the streets and inducted forcibly into the Army without notice.

He dealt with villagers down in the valley, who had never before seen white people. It is believed to be the route originally taken by Marco Polo.

GILBERT UNGER, President, 90th Infantry Division Association 1994; President 537th AAA (AW) Battalion Association for life.

Publisher of 537th AAA Newsletter. Four issues each year since 1980.

Machine gunner on half-track, D-day plus eight to Czechoslovakia.

Awards/Medals: five Battle Stars and the Purple Heart (2).

SAMUEL R. UPIN, born in Seda, Lithuania, May 28, 1909. Inducted in the Army at Ft. Snelling, St. Paul, MN, as staff sergeant March 6, 1941. Received basic training at Camp Roberts, CA. Attached to Navy Medical Base. Stationed in New Hebrides in South Pacific on Efyte Island. He participated in no battles.

His memorable experience: Being on same Pacific Island for 34 months.

Awarded three non-combat awards. Discharged Sept. 11, 1945, as staff sergeant with one slash and five stripes.

He had two brothers, Charles and Otto Upin who served in WWI.

Married to Bernice Weinstein in St. Paul, MN 1949. They have two daughters and four grandchildren.

Retired from men's retail sales. Spends winter in Florida. He is a member of JWV Post 354.

JORDAN R. UTTAL, born on July 30, 1915, in New York City. Graduated from New York University in June 1935. Enlisted in Signal Corps/Air Corps on Dec. 29, 1941, as radar operator. As staff sergeant left for Air Corps OCS in August

1942, was transferred to Harvard Business School, and commissioned second lieutenant, statistical control officer Dec. 5, 1942.

Went overseas in May 1943 to 2nd BW HQ as assistant statistical control officer. In February 1944 was reassigned to become division photo officer. November 1944 with the rank of major he was reassigned as division statistical control officer.

He met and subsequently married the lovely British lady, Joyce Christie King, assistant to the Red Cross Field director at Horsham St. Faith.

Awards/Medals: Bronze Star, Croix de Guerre, EAME with six Campaign Stars, American Defense, Good Conduct, WWII Victory.

Returned to the States in August 1945 after 27 months overseas. Discharged November 1945 to resume career in food industry.

In 1948 he and six others founded 2nd Air Division Association and served two terms as president, and 17 years as a member of the Board of Governors of the Memorial Trust, 2nd Air Div. USAAF located in Norwich, England. In 1989, he was elected honorary president 2nd Air Division Association, and Honorary Life Governor of the Memorial Trust.

Member of JWV Post 256-Dallas, TX.

MAURICE VEGH, born 1930 in Rachov, Czechoslovakia. (Carpathian Mountains). At age 13, together with parents and sister, was sent to Aushwitz Concentration Camp, working for two years in coal mines, starving and witnessing horrifying atrocities. His family did not survive. Liberated 1945 from Buchenwald Concentration Camp, spent ensuing year in Scotland, four years in London prior to emigrating to U.S. in 1950.

Drafted into U.S. Army in 1952, basic training Ft. Dix, NJ. Sent as interpreter, due to knowledge of numerous Eastern European languages, to Headquarters, 63rd Signal Bn., Camp Truscott, Salzburg, Austria with rank of private first class.

Awards/Medals: Certificate for Administrative Work, Army Occupational Medal, Germany and National Defense Service Medal. Discharged 1954 at Camp Kilmer, NJ.

Married 1956 to British girlfriend, Phyllis, in London. Occupation: hairstylist. They have three sons: Warren, Robert and Darryl and four grandsons. Member of JWV Post 666, Long Beach.

LEROY VEGOTSKY, born in Trenton, NJ in July 1938. He graduated from Trenton Central High School in June 1956. Joined the National Guard in September 1955 and on July 7, 1965, he went on active duty. He was assigned to Ft. Sill, Artillery School, where he was admitted to OCS and graduated as a second lieutenant.

Assigned to the 24th Inf. Div. in Augsburg, Germany. After three months was ordered to Vietnam where he was assigned to the 34th Arty., 9th Div. at DongTam in the Mekong Delta. The 34th Arty. was part of the Mobile Riverine Force that operated throughout the Mekong Delta Region and other classified areas of Southeast Asia. He participated in the TET Offensive as well as Operation Junction City and Operation Coronado.

Awards/Medals: Silver Star, Bronze Star/2nd Award, Purple Heart/2nd award, and numerous other awards and citations. He was honorably discharged on April 9, 1968.

After discharge he attended Rider College, majoring in business. In 1986 he also became a paralegal and, at the present time, is still practicing in this field.

In 1970 he married Marie Ciliento who is a past department president of New Jersey. He had two children by his ex-wife: a son, Mark Howard, and a married daughter, Robyn Jill Kimura, both living in the San Francisco East Bay area.

GEORGE VICE, born in Newark, NJ, Oct. 21, 1923. Employed at Ft. Monmouth as a radio repairman with a deferment but enlisted into the Army Signal Corps November 1942, eager to serve his country, as did his father Henry Vice in WWI. He had extensive training at the Desert Training Center in California, Camp Shelby, MS, Ft. Benning, GA and Vint Hill Farms, VA. He was elevated to technical sergeant and acted as a drill sergeant when sent on cadre. His last two months were spent with the Alaskan Communication System and was discharged February 1946.

Married to Martha in 1947 and had children Alan and Sheryl. He has two grandchildren, Erin and Andrew. Martha died December 1988 and George remarried Mildred, March 1991. A life member of JWV, retired and soon to be department commander of New Jersey, June 1994.

LEONARD VICTOR, born in Chicago, IL on Sept. 1, 1927, and went to William Penn Grammar School and John Marshall High School. In the 1940s he tried to enlist in the Navy, however, he was turned down because he was too young (16 at the time). He joined the Merchant Marines and served 18 months.

Left the Merchant Marines and drafted in the Army in 1945. He had hoped to go in the Navy as he was already an able-bodied seaman but that was not the case. Basic training in field artillery at Ft. Sill, OK. Transferred to San Francisco, where he was transferred to the USAAC; then San Bernardino Army Depot to be trained in meteorology at San Bernardino Junior College. On completion of training he made corporal and was transferred to the 68th Bn., 101st Weather Reconnaissance where he served for two and one-half years. He served in the South Pacific and attained the rank of sergeant.

After he left the service he went to American School of Technology on the GI Bill and became an electronic engineer. He subsequently was hired by Lockheed Aircraft Company Missile Division in California and then went to Hughes Aircraft Corporation when Lockheed moved to Northern California. He was at Hughes for 15 years when he had to retired due to medical problems.

PRIVATE BENNIE VIENER, born in Saugus, Feb. 4, 1915. Moved to Millis at an early age and attended the Millis schools, graduating from Millis High in the class of 1933. After graduating he was engaged with his father in the poultry business.

He enlisted in April 1941, received training at Camp Edwards and in January was in the Southwest Pacific area. Viener was killed in action September 17 according to a telegram received by his parents from the Secretary of War. He was a member of Co. B, 101st Medical Regt. and was stationed in New Caledonia.

In addition to his parents he is survived by a brother, George, and three sisters, Mrs. Betty Baker of Brookline, Mrs. Celia Policow of Plymouth and Mrs. Elizabeth Tilson of Saugus.

ERNEST WACHTEL, born in Vienna, Austria and fled at the age of 14 upon Hitler's takeover of Austria. Coming by himself to the States, he lived with an uncle in New York City until the arrival of his parents, who ultimately were able to escape. They settled on a farm in New Jersey.

At the outbreak of WWII, he volunteered to serve in the U.S. Army despite the fact, that as a farmer he could have been exempted from the service. After basic combat training, he was sent to the Military Intelligence Training Camp, then shipped to England.

Several days after the invasion, was sent into France where he served as an Intelligence NCO in the G-2 Section of Patton's 3rd Army HQ, screening and interrogating German

prisoners. A day after the liberation of the infamous concentration camp, Dachau, he went to see for himself what he could do to help. He took several inmates and set them up in homes in Bad Toltz, Germany.

Was honorably discharged and returned to New Jersey. He raised a family of three daughters and has six grandchildren. He is still active in construction and real estate.

MAX M. WACHTEL, born Feb. 28, 1933, Danzig Free State1. Enlisted in the U.S. Army April 18, 1953, and stationed in Korea. He was discharged April 15, 1955, with the rank of corporal. He is retired.

HOWARD N. WAGNER, born in the Bronx, NY, June 13, 1960. Studied electrical engineering at Tufts University and attended Air Force ROTC cross-town at MIT. Worked as a civilian engineer until pilot training date came up, then off to the Air Force to pursue flying dreams.

After pilot training in Phoenix, remained for three years to teach and only got scared by students a couple of times. Next, off to the RF-4 reconnaissance aircraft for operational flying from Okinawa, Japan, Osan AB, Korea and Austin, TX.

Flew 25 combat missions in the Persian Gulf during Operation Desert Storm, earning three Air Medals. After nine and a half years in the Air Force, he traded in his flight suit for an airline pilot uniform.

Lives with his wife, Jan, in Austin, TX. No children at this point, just a lot of pets.

NORMAN WAGNER, born in Bronx, NY, Jan. 12, 1921. Majored in public administration at City College of New York. Called to active duty in March 1943 in the Army Enlisted Reserve Corps. Participated in the Army Specialized Training Program at Princeton University and in the Military Intelligence Training Program at Camp Ritchie, MD.

Served as staff sergeant in the ETO on POW Interrogation Team with the 75th Div. Participated in the Battle of the Bulge and Central Europe and Rhineland campaigns. During the Occupation of Germany, he was an interrogator assigned to Gen. Eisenhower's Army denazification program.

Discharged Feb. 17, 1946, he completed a master's in social work at Columbia University, later practiced in the rehabilitation, education and geriatric social work field.

Formerly married, has a son, Howard, a veteran of Operation Desert Storm, having served as an Air Force flight officer. Now semi-retired, he continues working as a P/T social work consultant, counselor and lecturer. Remains active in JWV Post 90 and various groups.

FRED WAHL, born in Poland, 1917. Joined the U.S. Army in 1942. Basic training at Ft. Belvoir, VA. Assigned to 850th Avn. Engrs., 8th AF. Spent six months in England, D-day + 6, landed in France, Omaha Beach.

Their task was to build and maintain emergency landing strips. In 1944 he was transferred to 12th Armd. Div., 23rd Tank Bn. He was a radio operator and translator in

German, Polish and Spanish. When they entered Austria in 1945, the war ended with Germany. Their job was to get all the German prisoners from railroad boxcars in trucks and to separation centers.

In May of 1945 they were on their way to Japan. Meanwhile Japan surrendered and they landed in Ft. Dix, NJ. He was discharged in December 1945. His awards include three Battle Stars.

He is also a survivor of the holocaust.

ALBERT L. WAKS, born 1905 in Warsaw, Poland and came to the USA in 1920 with his brothers and mother (his father came to America in 1913 to establish a livelihood for his family).

Graduated from the Institute of Photography and three years later, in 1928, became a naturalized American and member of a cavalry unit with the NYNG, 71st Regt., serving until 1934.

Inducted in the Army October 1942 and assigned to 1200th Svc. Unit, HQ&HQ Co., 2nd Svc. Cmd., ASF, stationed on Governor's Island, NY. Volunteered in 1944 for combat duty overseas and assigned to 165th Sig. Photo. Co., APO 230.

Stationed in Tidworth Park, England. With the onset of D-Day, embarked for France, landing on Utah Beach. Spent time in the field with American forces and the 2nd Free French Armd. Div., recording, in picture and on film, the events of Northern France and Germany campaigns.

He filmed and photographed for official Army records the liberation of Paris while sniper bullets were flying everywhere. Had many close calls, but sustained no injury.

Awards/Medals: Good Conduct Ribbon and Bronze Service Star. He was discharged with the rank of staff sergeant.

Resuming his private photography practice in civilian life, he also remained the official photographer for the New York 7th and 71st Regts. His photography and military career won him mention in: *Who's Who in the East* 1966-1967; *Dictionary of International Bibliography* (1967); *Royal Blue Book* (1969).

In his retirement, he became an enthusiastic pastoral landscape painter.

GEORGE J. WALD, born in Brooklyn, NY, Dec. 29, 1921. Enlisted in the USAR while a student at the University of Idaho where he was studying agriculture in the hope of becoming a veterinarian. Returned to Brooklyn and volunteered for active duty. Stationed at Camp Upton; Camp Wheeler, GA for infantry training; Camp Meade, MD, then shipped overseas.

During an enemy submarine attack in the crossing, he was pushed down a flight of stairs as the men rushed to their stations. His back was injured and he was transferred out of the infantry into a training school in England. Many transfers followed, London (where he met and married an English lady); Glasgow, Scotland; Bristol University, England (where he took a course in zoology).

After discharge he returned to the University of Idaho, receiving both BS and MS degrees in 1949. Plans to be a veterinary ended when his young wife died of polio on her 26th birthday, July 1949. With his young children, Carolyn (3) and Geoffrey (5 months), he returned to New York and obtained a teaching position in Michigan. Four years later became a teacher in Brooklyn and attended night school, receiving a doctor of chiropractic degree. Retired from teaching in 1987 and practiced chiropractic for nine years.

Remarried in 1957 to Sydney and had five children: Benay, Beth, Alison, Michael and Philip. In June 1993 he and his wife revisited England a gift from son Michael who accompanied them.

SAMUEL W. WALDMAN, born in Long Branch, NJ. Enlisted in the U.S. Army Dec. 28, 1942. Assigned to the

633rd Tank Bn., then transferred to 188th FA Band. Stationed at Ft. Dix; Ft. Lewis, WA; Mojave Desert Maneuvers and Camp Crowder, OK.

Memorable experience was being drafted after he was rejected for enlistment because of his eyes and flat feet. Also memorable was the band accompanying major Hollywood performers for shows.

Certified disability discharge on Oct. 16, 1943, with the rank private first class.

Married, widowed, has one daughter, grandson, a sister and parents. Stayed in Long Branch with family and friends. Retired from self-employment of 30 years, 11 years of civil service and part-time musician. He is past commander of JWV Post 316.

OTTO WALDMANN, born Jan. 19, 1926, in Wurzburg, Germany. Lived in Windsheim with his parents and brother and was arrested Kristallnacht Nov. 10, 1938, but released because of his young age. Immigrated to the US in January 1939 and lived in New York. On his 18th birthday he volunteered for the USN and after boot camp was assigned to the SeaBees at Camp Endicott, RI.

Volunteered for overseas duty after becoming a US citizen and assigned to the 83rd US NCB. Shipped out from Port Hueneme for Hawaii and the Philippines. Promoted to coxswain in May 1945. After end of war the 83rd Bn. was shipped to China to serve with 3rd Phib. Corps, USMC. Returned to the States in May 1946 for discharge.

Joined the organized Reserves and recalled to active duty in September 1950 and assigned to CB 105 (later to be known as ACB 2). Did amphibious landings with 2nd Marine Div. on the Atlantic coast and Caribbean islands. In June 1951 he left for three months to the Arctic in Operation Blue Jay where he was in charge of a barge which transferred cargo from ship to shore to build the air base in Thule, Greenland. Discharged as BM2/c.

Married Renate Katz and is the father of Karen Lynne and Kenneth Elliot. Lived in Syosset, Long Island for 39 years; widowed and remarried to Phyllis Hofman and currently resides in Chicago.

MILTON WASSER WALLACE, born Dec. 4, 1915, in Passaic, NJ. Parents: Chaim Wollach of Czernowitz, Austria, and Rose Wasser, of Galicia, Poland.

Entered U.S. Army in July 1942. Served as sergeant (cryptographer) with 7th Airways Communications Sqdn., Hickam Field, T.H., then as staff sergeant (special agent) with the Prov. Marshal General's Investigation Div., Pacific area.

Recalled in September 1960 as a first lieutenant (special agent) with the Counter Intelligence Corps during Korean conflict.

AB and JD from University of Michigan; LLM from New York University; MAT from Montclair State University.

Licensed attorney in Michigan, New Jersey and Territory of Hawaii; also merchant, stock broker and educator. Retired in 1989 as principal of the Passaic Public Schools Adult High School and Learning Center.

JULES WALLERSTEIN, born in Fuerth, Germany on March 21, 1927, where he resided. On May 13, 1939, his family and he boarded the ship *St. Louis* (for what was later called "The Voyage of the Damned") leaving for Cuba. Upon their arrival Cuba declared their visas were invalid and 937 passengers were to go back to Germany. Four European countries accepted them. His family settled in Brussels, Belgium and awaited passage to the U.S.

In May 1940 the Germans invaded Belgium. His father was interned and shipped to Camp Gurs, France. The only way to go to the USA was through the Free Zone to France. Wallerstein, his mother and sister smuggled their way to France and were interned at the Hotel Terminus in Marsailles. In December 1941 they left France and arrived in the USA in January 1942.

He was inducted in the U.S. Army in August 1945. Went to Ft. Knox, then shipped to Germany. Stationed in Frankfort/main and served with the 970th CIC as an investigator.

Interviewed Ilse Koch and her camp guard. She made lamp shades of prisoners skin who had unusual tattoos. Her husband was commander of Buchenwald.

Discharged in February 1947 as sergeant, he returned to New York. Has wife and two daughters. In 1967 they all moved to Norwalk, CT. Served in Norwalk as past commander of the JWV, chairman of the Allied Veterans Committee, member of the American Legion, and past grand chancellor of the Knights of Pythians.

SHELDON M. WALLERSTEIN, was born in Newark, NJ, Dec. 17, 1931. Enlisted in the U.S. Army July 24, 1955. Served with Military Police, 293rd and 298th MP Co., 5th Div.

Stationed in Ft. Gordon, GA; Ft. Ord, CA; Camp Desert Rock, NV. He was a so-called "Peace-time Vet."

Memorable experiences include being participant of atomic bomb tests (Operation "Plembbob") Nevada. Assistant confinement officer, Ft. Ord, CA; operations officer (MP) Camp Desert Rock, NV.

Discharged as first lieutenant July 23, 1957. Member of the National Association Atomic Vets, DAV, AMVETS, JWV.

Married to Loretta and has son, Seth; daughter, Gail; stepson, Thomas Allen; and step-daughter, Tammy Allen.

Vice-president of The Money Store Investment Corporation, Union, NJ (commercial mortgage lender.)

RONALD K. WALTEMEYER, was born in Baltimore, MD on Aug. 4, 1962. BS degree from Embry-Riddle Aeronautical University 1984. Graduate School at Embry-Riddle and Webster University. Entered Army in January 1985. Basic training at Ft. Lee, NJ. Upon graduating, entered Warrant Officer Entry Course (graduated June 1985) and Warrant Officer Flight School at Ft. Rucker, AL. Soloed TH-55 before proceeding to Ft. Lee, VA for Quartermaster Course. While in Virginia, he met his future wife, Maria. After graduation, assigned to Ft. Bliss, TX 6/3 ADA Patriot Bn. and later to the 507th Medevac Air Ambulance.

In 1987, accepted to attend OCS at Ft. Benning, GA. Graduated from OCS in October 1987. Second lieutenant bars pinned on by proud Mom! Immediately assigned to Airborne School and upon graduation, sent back to Ft. Bliss for ADA Officer Basic Course. After graduation, proceeded immediately to Ranger School at Ft. Benning. Graduated from Ranger School in August 1988. The next day, started studying Greek at Presidio of Monterey. Graduated one year later and then married a beautiful woman named Maria in July 1989. Sent overseas to Buedingen, Germany. Joined C 3-5 ADA as a platoon leader (Spearhead).

Traveled to Berlin from Nov. 9-12, 1989, for Veteran's Day Weekend and was caught in the midst of the excitement and history of seeing the "Fall of The Wall." Also enjoyed traveling in Europe with his wife, friends and soldiers. Participated in numerous combat runs, triathlons and soldiering events.

After the Fall of the Wall, the Army started downsizing units in Germany. Even in the midst of Saddam Hussein invading Kuwait, the unit was deactivated. Sent back to Ft. Bliss, TX, and trained reserve soldiers called back to active duty. Taught Aircraft Recognition, conducted Stinger Missile Range Training and other soldiering skills to soldiers who might be sent to Desert Storm or other missions. In addition, conducted training for ADA officers headed to Ranger School. Later became XO of the HQ Btry.

Left the military on May 31, 1992, despite being promoted to captain on May 1, 1992. Reason: To spend more time with family and friends. In seven and half years, he attended and graduated from some of the best military schools.

Started a second career with Merrill Lynch in June 1992 as a financial consultant.

The proud father of three children: Aaron, Rachel, and Rebekah.

He was awarded the Army Commendation, National Defense Service, Good Conduct, Army Achievement, Ranger Tab, Parachutist.

MILTON T. WALZER, born in Bronx, NY on Oct. 7, 1929. Graduated from CCNY School of Business (Baruch College) with BBA in accounting/economics in 1951.

June 1951, entered U.S. Army with rank of second lieutenant. Sent to Medical Field Service School, Fort Sam Houston, TX.

August 1951, arrived overseas at Japan Logistical Command, Fukuoka.

December 1951, joined 179th Inf. Regt., 45th (Oklahoma) Div. at Sapporo and sailed with convoy to Inchon, Korea, entering combat. Promoted to first lieutenant.

June 1952, awarded Bronze Star Medal "V", earned during Chinese counterattack.

September 1952, rotated back to U.S. Assigned as company commander, Medical Replacement Training Center, Camp Pickett, VA.

June 1953, separated from service. Later promoted to captain, USAR, Major, New York Guard.

Married to Virginia Urish. They have four children, Evelyn, Andrew, Susan, Robert and seven grandchildren.

Retired as president, Glo-Mark Products Co. Inc. Second career is accountant with New York State Department of Labor.

Currently, commander of JWV Post 731 South Orangetown, NY.

ROBERT WARREN, born in Brooklyn, NYC, NY, in 1947. Dropped out of college to enlist in U.S. Army. Assigned to a 105 howitzer unit (air mobile) in the 25th "Tropic Lightning" Inf. Div. Was in Tet Offensive and Tet Counteroffensive. Besides artillery crewman, an additional duty was to write articles for the Division newspaper (*Tropic Lightning News*).

Life member of JWV and past post commander of Newport News, VA.

Married to the former Susan Tse, with daughter Sharon receiving her Hebrew name at Commodore Levy Chapel, Naval Station Norfolk.

He has an international business practice specializing in foreign exchange repatriations. He is a member of the International Fraud Committee, Association of Certified Fraud Examiners. He is on the adjunct graduate faculty at Embry-Riddle Aeronautical University.

MAX WARSHAW, born Dec. 13, 1913, Kobrin, Poland. He emigrated to the U.S. with his parents in 1923. Joined the U.S. Army in March 1941; assigned to the 26th Inf. Regt., 1st Inf. Div.

The "Big Red One," as the division was nicknamed, sailed for North Africa shortly after the Japanese attack on

Pearl Harbor. Participated in seven major battles in Europe as an Army "medic" seeing action in Africa, Sicily, France, Belgium, Germany and landed with his unit at Omaha Beach on D-day in Normandy.

Taken prisoner in Germany by the Nazis Nov. 25, 1944. He was libeberated April 26, 1945.

Awards/Medals: two Silver Star Medals, three Bronze Star Medals, Purple Heart Medal, POW Medal, American Defense Medal, European Campaign Medal with seven Battle Stars, WWII Victory Medal, French Fourragere and the Combat Medic Badge. He was discharged Sept. 5, 1945, with the rank staff sergeant

He is member of the American Legion, Ex-POWs, 1st Inf. Div. Society, and life member and former commander of JWV of New York and New Jersey, past commander of VFW, Purple Heart Assoc. and DAV.

Married to Evelyn over 47 years. Retired since 1977 as a tractor trailer driver.

MURREY WASSER, served as a lieutenant in the Army Air Force as a combat pilot, ETO, was shot down over Germany, and became a POW.

SAMUEL WASSER, served as a private first class in the Infantry, AEF, during WWI.

SAUL WASSER, who volunteered for service immediately after Pearl Harbor. He was rejected by the Marine Corps, the Navy, and the Army, in that order. In 1942 he was drafted into the AUS, but was discharged when he applied for OCS and they discovered that he had only one eye. Subsequently he entered the Merchant Marine, where he served for the duration.

LEO S. WASSNER

MELVIN WAXMAN (MEL), born Baltimore, MD, March 12, 1920. Entered Army Nov. 9, 1942. Aberdeen, MD, Ord. School. Camp Santa Anita, CA, 462nd Ord. Evac. Co., England. Liaison for his company, prepared vehicles for invasion and was an ordnance radio operator attached to the infantry. After landing in Normandy D-day + 4, was selected to learn Morse Code on the battlefield.

Participated in action in Normandy, Northern France, liberating Paris, Ardennes, Rhineland and Central Europe, finally meeting up with the Russians at Torgau near the Elbe River.

Awards/Medals: American Theater Service Ribbon, EAME Service Ribbon, WWII Victory Ribbon. The "Certificate of Merit" was presented for outstanding performance of duty during the Battle of the Bulge in maintaining infantry and ordnance radio communications. Honorably discharged at Ft. Meade, MD 13 days after landing in the good old USA.

Married Florine Hornstein, Thanksgiving Day, Nov. 22, 1945. Built and operated one of the first modern Brunswick bowling lanes in Glen Burnie, MD, owned and operated a jewelry store, was an advertising and promotion consultant to the Sterling Silver Industry and fine stores throughout the country. Was a Kiwanian for 43 years as well as a Mason.

Has two sons, Ned and Jay, and two grandsons. Retired with his wife to Florida and enjoys boating and fishing.

SAM WAXMAN, born March 5, 1932, Brooklyn, NY. Served in the U.S. Army, assigned to 3rd Div., 65th Regt. as infantry rifle man. Stationed at Camp Breckinridge, KY and Korea. Saw action in the Chor Won Valley.

Memorable experience was capturing North Koreans with Russian equipment at the 38th Parallel.

Awards/Medals: Combat Infantry Badge, United Nations Medal, Korean Campaign with two Battle Stars, Good Conduct Medal and Syngman Rhee Citation. Dishcarged July 12, 1954, with the rank of corporal.

Married, has two sons and a granddaughter. Worked in wholesale plumbing business, retiring on March 4, 1994. He is proud to have helped create the future for a strong America.

HENRY A. WEDELL, born Aug. 15, 1917, Hannover, Germany. Joined the ILNG Aug. 15, 1941. Served with the Army Corps of Engineers stationed at Camps Grant, Ellis, Granite City, PTO: New Guinea, Philippines, Japan and island hopping.

Peace time service in Army Reserve Intel, 1945-1950. Re-enlisted Regular Army for Korean Service and served in Alaska, Germany, Korea, Vietnam.

Awards/Medals: Good Conduct, applicable service ribbons and Presidential Unit Citation. Retired Nov. 1, 1968, Ft. Bliss, TX with the rank of SDC E-7.

Married Irmgard E. Brinitzer, Neuman. They have seven living children, 14 grandchildren. Two sons served in they Army and one son served in Vietnam.

He was employed as telecommunications analyst with American Express Company 1969-1979. Retired from AMEX 1979.

Presently volunteer for VAMC Phoenix, AZ. Life member of JWV, DAV, VFW and member of American Legion, BPOE Elks. Active member JWV 194 QM, PPC; PDC; Past NEC.

ROBERT J. WEIL, born Oct. 5, 1913, Metz, France. Drafted April 11, 1941, in U.S. Army Infantry. Assigned to 13th Regt., 8th Inf. Div. as regimental switchboard operator. Stationed at Ft. Meade, MD, Ft. Leonard Wood, MO; Camp Forrest, TN; Camp Pendleton, VA; Camp Kilmer, NJ; Indiantown Gap, PA; Camp Laguna, AZ.

Saw action in France, Battle of the Bulge and Central Europe. Memorable experience was liberation of concentration camp in Germany.

Awards/Medals: Bronze Star with OLC, Infantry Combat Badge, Croix de Guerre and European Campaign Ribbon with four Battle Stars. He was discharged Sept. 18, 1945 as T-5.

His family all perished in Holocaust, he survived concentration camp. Retired in 1976 as clothing designer. Keeps active as tour director at Jewish Old Folks Home where he conducts Friday evening services and does volunteer work at the hospital, prison and talks to youngsters in the Philadelphia School District as well as all over the Delaware Valley.

GERALD WEINBERG, born April 24, 1921, St. Paul, MN. Graduated high school, 1939 and complete one year of a two year course in air conditioning at Dunwood Industrial Institute, Minneapolis. Schooling cut short as brother was inducted in the service and he took over management of hardware store.

When the store closed, he joined the Enlisted Reserve Corps, Aug. 27, 1942, in the Signal Corps. Trained as a radio

transmitter and receiver in Minneapolis and Chicago. Was rejected for active duty in Chicago because of bad eyesight. Returned to Ft. Snelling and memorized eye chart, then was inducted for active service May 24, 1943.

Basic training at Camp Kohler, June 7, 1943; overseas, Nov. 22, 1943, to New Guinea; then to the Philippines. Worked intercept stations for coded and uncoded messages both on land and ships. Most interesting operation was intercepting surrender conditions to Japanese as they were taking place.

Awards/Medals: Good Conduct Medal, Asiatic-Pacific Medal with three Bronze Stars, WWII Victory Medal, Philippine Liberation Ribbon, Honorable Service Lapel Button and Sharpshooter Badge with Carbine Bar. Honorable discharge Jan. 10, 1940, Camp McCoy, WI.

ROBERT E. WEINBERG, born New York City, May 21, 1923. Graduated Bayside High, Long Island, 1941. Enlisted Nov. 7, 1942.

Basic at Camp Crowder, MO. Was Morse Code instructor, Ft. Monmouth, NJ, 1943. Assigned to 293rd Joint Assault Sig. Co. Made three amphibious landings on North Coast of New Guinea, 1944. Went ashore on D-day morning at Lingayen Gulf, P.I. with the 3rd Bn., 20th Inf., Jan. 9, 1945.

Fought with 20th Inf. from landing until end of campaign at Manila with heavy fighting at Japanese strong point of "Munoz" In Japan after end of war, worked on Japanese radio equipment with 5250 Tech Intel. Co., some of the equipment was made in USA just before the war.

Awards/Medals: Asiatic-Pacific with two Bronze Stars and one Arrowhead, Philippine Liberation with one Bronze Star.

Honorably discharged Feb. 25, 1946, T-4 rating. Married to Marcia and has three children. Retired after 43 years in electronic repair business in Washington, DC area. Proud to be a veteran.

MARTIN I. WEINBERGER, born Nov. 28, 1923, Bayonne, NJ. Attended New York University prior to entering service and received an MBA after discharge. Completed ROTC training at NYU and Infantry OCS, Ft. Benning. Commissioned 2nd lieutenant in December 1943.

Service in Louisiana maneuver area with the 75th Div. Assigned to the 8th Div. in Normandy. Wounded in action in July 1944. Returned to duty to be wounded again in Hurtgen Forest, November 1944. Hospitalized at Lawson General Hospital in Atlanta from which retired for physical disability as a 1st lieutenant in June 1946.

Awards/Medals: Combat Infantry Badge, Bronze Star, Purple Heart with cluster, European Theater Ribbon with three Battle Stars.

Married 1947 to former Shirley Epstein of Bayonne (who died in 1994 after a three year battle with Lou Gehrig's disease). Raised two sons, Alan, a professor of law at St. Louis University, and Seth, an attorney in Chicago. Has four grandchildren.

Retired after a 42-year working career in the advertising agency business in New Jersey. Member of Bayonne Post 18 of JWV and National Amputation Chapter of the DAV.

WEINER FAMILY, Five sons and two in-laws of Anna Weiner, Cementon, NY, were all in the military service at the same time.

Ben Weiner, CPL, enlisted in the USAF at the time of Pearl Harbor, served at Patterson Field and in the Pacific as radio tech.

Alex Weiner, CPL, entered the Army in December 1942. Served in the QM Corps and was based in England.

Sam Weiner, S2/c, joined the USN in October, was based at Brooklyn Navy Yard.

Josephine Genevese Weiner, SGT, wife of Sam, enlisted in the Women's Army Corps in December 1942. Received basic training at Des Moines, IA and was stationed in Cleveland, OH.

Tony Weiner, T/CPL, enlisted in January 1942. Served in the USAAF at Patterson Field.

Julius Bricker, CPL, husband of Anna Weiner's daughter, Tillie, served in the U.S. Army.

Isadore Weiner, S2/c, served in the USN.

All the brothers were active at the Allentown Jewish Community Center before their military service.

EDWARD L. WEINER,
born Dec. 25, 1923 in Boston, MA. Enlisted in Army November 1942. Discharged December 1945. Served in ETOs 8th Armd. Div. Early 1945 was member of combat command liberating Nordhausen. He and Merle Dailey took prisoner a 1500-man Panzer Div. Bn., trapped in the Ruhr Pocket and anxious to give up, marching them to rear.

After Armistice, the 7th Armd. Inf. Bn., captured Gen. Kesselring's Nazi holdouts, the "Wherewolf Div.," in Germany's Hartz Mountains. Did occupation duty in Pilsen, Czechoslovakia.

Awards/Medals: Bronze Star, Combat Infantry Badge and three Battle Stars.

Completed college with BS in electrical engineering. Moved to California in 1956, leading team designing Thor IRBM Missile System. Retired from McDonnell Douglas and R&D as program manager in 1983.

With wife, Millie, raised three sons; Mark and twins, Jeff and Jim. Has wonderful grandkids, Gregory and Valerie (Jim) and Bryan and Kristi (Jeff).

Life member of DAV and active in JWV, publishing Post #595, *Sentinel*. Past commander, junior and senior vice commander and currently judge advocate.

SAMUEL WEINER,
born 1916, Syracuse, NY. Attended Jackson, Putnam and Vocational High Schools. Worked for the *Syracuse Herald-Journal* and Brown Lipe Chapin.

Entered the Army in 1942. Served in the 14th Inf. Div. Reported killed in the Battle of the Bulge in France in 1944 at the age of 28.

Survived by parents Mr. and Mrs. Louis Weiner.

WILLIAM E. WEINER,
born July 19, 1919, New Haven, CT. Graduated Hill House HS, 1937. Attended New York University in ROTC Program, graduated 1941 and commissioned 2nd lieutenant. June 1941 was assigned to Co. L, 18th Inf., 1st Div. October 1941, assigned to Co. M, 101st Inf., 26th Inf. Div.

Sent to China Burma Theater in late 1942 to facilitate the shipment of supplies on the famed Ledo Burma Road (from Ledo, India to Kunming, China). Memorable experience was meeting "Vinegar Joe" Stillwell and Frank Merrill, of Merrill's Marauders, in Burma. Also memorable was when Pat O'Brien and Paulette Goddard came to entertain the troops in Karachi, India.

Awards/Medals: American Campaign Medal, Asiatic-Pacific Medal and Victory Medal. Discharged in 1946.

Went into the tire business with his father, Jacob Weiner, became president in 1970 with his son, Scott, as vice president.

MATTHEW S. WEINGAST,
born Sept. 18, 1965, Queens, NY. Enrolled in Army ROTC at Georgetown University. Received commission in the Armor Branch in May 1987. Stationed at Ft. Knox, KY; Budigen, West Germany; SW Asia; Ft Huachuca, AZ; Ft. Meyer, VA. Served as cavalry platoon leader with 3rd Sqdn., 12th Cav. and as scout platoon leader with the 4th Sqdn., 7th Cav.

Participated in invasion of Iraq and liberation of Kuwait. The 4th Sqdn. 7th Cav. conducted numerous recon and security missions, including the Battle of 73 Easting.

Memorable experience was being part of a cavalry squadron during Desert Storm. The memory of witnessing acts of heroism and camaraderie of American soldiers in action during the spectacular violence and utter confusion stand out very strong in his mind.

Awards/Medals: Bronze Star Medal, Army Commendation Medal, Army Achievement Medal with three OLCs, SW Asia Service Medal with three Battle Stars, Liberation of Kuwait Medal, National Service Defense Medal, Overseas Service Ribbon, Army Service Ribbon and Air Assault Badge.

Married his college sweetheart, Nancy Koretz in April 1990. He is currently assigned to the Defense Intelligence Agency in Washington.

MAURICE WEINMAN,
born in New York City, 1921. Enlisted in service Nov. 18, 1942. Served with 78th Div., 10th Mountain Div., 9th AF, 479th Air Svc. Gp. in Camp Butner, NC; Ft. Hood, TX; Vineland AB, NJ; Charleville, France.

Participated in battles in Charleroi Belgium and Dinant, Belgium.

His memorable experience was crossing the English Channel on ship that had been sunk three times. Arrived in Le Havre France, after they had leveled the city only a few weeks before, and being warned that the natives were not friendly. Told not to leave bivouacked area.

Awards/Medals: American Campaign, EAME and WWII Victory Medal. Discharged Dec. 25, 1945, as private first class.

Married to Thelma in 1947. They have two daughters and three grandchildren.

Now retired and commander JWV Post 330 for the past 29 years. Past National Adjutant JWV.

TOBY WEINSHENKER,
COL, AUS, RET, enlisted as a private in the ILNG Nov. 2, 1939. Promoted to 1st lieutenant and served with 132nd Inf. Regt. as dental officer at battle of Guadalcanal. Returned to the U.S. and reassigned as corps dental officer with HQ XXI Corps, serving in the European Theatre until the end of the war.

Returned to ILNG eventually becoming commanding officer of the 108th Med. Bn. of the 33rd Inf. Div. Transferred to USAR where he completed his military career with 36 years service. His last assignment was as staff dental officer and inspector general of the 30th Hospital Center, USAR.

Awards/Medals: two Bronze Stars, Combat Medical Badge and Army Meritorious Service Medal. Promoted to brigadiere general in ILNG.

Father of two children, Eileen Goggin and Gary, a LTC, USAR. Also has seven grandchildren and five great-grandsons.

DAVID H. WEINSTEIN,
is a graduate of Hartford Public HS. Received a bachelor's and dental degree from Loyola University in Chicago in 1940. In 1941 he became the first dentist in Hartford to volunteer for the Army Dental Corps where he served for five years.

Participated in five major campaigns with the 1st Inf. Div. He was cited as probably being the first dental officer to

operate on patients in Germany, receiving the Bronze Star for skill, enthusiasm and uncompromising devotion to duty.

Discharged with the rank of captain in 1946. Stayed in the Reserves for 11 years.

Resides in West Hartford, CT with his wife, Mildred. They are members of Congregation Beth Israel where their five children were confirmed. Member of VFW and JWV Post 45.

HAROLD VICTOR WEINSTEIN,
born in Jamaica Plain, MA, Dec. 16, 1922. Enlisted Jan. 30, 1943. AUS, Air Corps, radar observer, Sea Search 866, air crew member. Stationed in Ft. Devens, Scott Field, IL; Boca Raton, FL; Tyndall Field, FL; Salina, KS; Hamilton Field, CA to Saipan.

Flew 30 combat missions and participated in Air Offensive Japan, Eastern Mandates and Western Pacific. His memorable experiences include the nameless faces that time has not erased of those that did not return from a mission.

Member of Combat Crew 13, 877th BS VH, 499th BG, 73rd BW, 20th AF, 21st Bomber Cmd., Station APO 237 (Saipan).

Awards/Medals: Asiatic-Pacific Theater Ribbon with three Bronze Stars, Air Medal with four OLCs, Good Conduct Medal and Distinguished Flying Cross.

Married Lorraine Foreman April 16, 1950, and has two daughters, Rhonda and Karen; son, Jack; and seven grandchildren. Retired in 1987 after 42 years as a plumber.

Charter member Milton, MA Post 696.

IRA P. WEINSTEIN,
born Chicago, IL, June 10, 1919. Entered the USAF as an aviation cadet in 1942. Trained at Ellington Field and graduated as a bombardier/navigator from Childress, TX.

Flew with the 445th BG, 702nd Sqdn. from Tibenham, England on all his missions until the last one, where he was shot down on the notorious Kassell raid on Sept. 27, 1944.

Parachuted from his plane, captured and taken to Dulag Luft at Oberusal, Germany. Interrogated and then sent to Stalag Luft I at Barth, Germany. Liberated by the Russians on May 11, 1945, and returned to the States in June 1945.

Awards/Medals: Distinguished Flying Cross, Purple Heart, Air Medal, Presidential Citation, POW Medal, American Campaign Medal, European Campaign Medal, WWII Victory Medal.

Memberships: 2nd Air Div. Assoc., Bombardiers, Inc., International B-24 Liberator Club, Caterpillar Assoc., JWV, and lifetime member of the Ex-POW Assoc. and 8th AF Historical Society.

Has been president of Schram Advertising Agency in Northbrook, IL since 1945.

JERRY BARROW WEINSTEIN,
born July 8, 1918, Baltimore, MD. Entered the U.S. Army April 26, 1943. Studied communications in the Replacement Training Center at Camp Wolters, TX and spent five months in regular rifle company work. Served as assistant regimental communications officer of the 106th Inf.

Participated in battles and campaigns in the Central Pacific, Eastern Mandates, Western Pacific and Ryukyus.

Awards/Medals: Asiatic-Pacific Service Ribbon and Medal, American Defense Service Ribbon, WWII Victory Medal and three Bronze Star.

Widowed after 40 years of marriage, has three daughters. He is retired.

LEONARD A. WEINSTEIN,
gave up occupational deferment and was inducted in 1943. Took basic training in the IRTC at Camp Blanding, FL. Served overseas in the 82nd Abn. Div. Participated in the Ardennes, Rhineland and Central Europe Campaigns.

His most terrifying memories are of fallen comrades. He recalls the confusion of that snowy winter. American troops had difficulty identifying the enemy, as the Germans used captured American tanks and uniforms. Allied planes unwittingly and relentlessly bombed and strafed GIs on the ground. Due to injuries, he was evacuated from the front and at war's end was stationed in occupied Berlin "in relative comfort" compared to the icy, bloody winter he had endured in the Ardennes.

Awards/Medals: Bronze Star, Belgian Fourragere, Presidential Unit Citation, Army of Occupation Medal (Berlin), Combat Infantry Badge and Glider Trooper Wings.

Past Department Commander (Ohio) and life member of JWV. A charter and life member of the 82nd Abn. Div. Assoc. He is now a major character in a book recounting the wartime experiences of GIs who fought in the Battle of the Bulge. The book *A Blood Dimmed Tide* by Gerald Astor is a compilation of personal stories of over 50 American and German eyewitnesses.

M. ARTHUR WEINSTEIN,
born Sept. 14, 1925, Brockton, MA. Entered the Army January 1944, 109th Inf. Regt., 28th Div., (Bloody Bucket), German-Blutiga Eimer.

Stationed in Ft. Eustis, VA; Camp Stewart, GA; Ft. Meade, MD; England, France; Belgium, Germany, Luxembourg.

Awards/Medals: Good Conduct, POW Medal, Combat Infantry Badge, ETO Ribbon with four Battle Stars and the Purple Heart. Discharged January 1946 as private first class.

Memorable experience when captured along wire patrol in Luxembourg with three buddies of Wire Section, one of whom was killed attempting to escape. Liberated by British led by Field Marshall Montgomery. Spent three weeks in British army and returned to England and finally turned over to American 7th General Hospital, fattened up and returned to USA, Lake Placid and Camp Shanks, NY. Discharged at Ft. Devens, MA.

Married to Barbara Warshauer, now deceased. They had two daughters. His father Samuel Weinstein was WWI Vet AEF; father-in-law Alex Warshauer was vet of WWI AEF.

Weinstein became first commander of JWV in Brockton, 15 years later he became commander of JWV 739.

SIDNEY WEINSTEIN,
LCDR, USN, RET, born Nov. 22, 1909, Buffalo, NY. Enlisted USN April 4, 1930, attended USNH Corps School with rate of hospital apprentice second class. Prior to war declaration served USS *Salt Lake City* (CVL-25) Naval Ammunition Depot, Iona Island, NY USS *Wyoming* (BB) Naval Hospital, Great Lakes, IL, 1st Med. Co., 2nd Mar. Bde, FMF Iceland, USS *Zeilin* (APA-3) commissioning.

USS *Zeilin,* participated initial Tulagi and Guadalcanal actions, to Long Beach Navy Yard for severe bomb damage repair. Transferred to Naval Hospital, San Diego May 1943. Transferred June 1944 to USS *Monterey* (CVL-26) with First Carrier Task Force, continuous action, severely damaged by

fire and storm of typhoon, to Bremerton for repairs, returned for Okinawa operation and Tokyo Bay surrender. Following war had many duty stations until retiring July 1, 1960 with rank of LCDR (MSC) USN.

Awards/Medals: Navy Unit Commendation, Good Conduct Medal, American Defense Medal with Fleet and Base Clasp, Asiatic-Pacific Campaign Medal with two Bronze Stars, WWII Victory Medal, Navy Occupation Service Medal, National Defense Service Medal, Philippine Liberation Ribbon with two Bronze Stars and American Campaign Medal.

After retirement was VP of large real estate corporation, retired 1973, various enterprises since. Married to Anne since March 1971, has four children, 14 grandchildren and three great-grandchildren. Resides in Palm Springs, CA. All children from previous marriage.

NAT R. WEINTRAUB (FRITZ/MATT),
born in Red Bank, NJ, in 1923. Inducted into the U.S. Army from Brighton Beach, in Brooklyn, NY, December 1943.

Assigned to a MP BN, at Camp Gordon, in Augusta, GA. In 1944, when Gen Eisenhower called for volunteers to replace the expected casualties from the invasion of Europe, he volunteered as an Infantry replacement and joined Co. A, 115th Inf. Regt., 29th Div.

Wounded on Dec. 20, 1944 in the left forearm.

Awards/Medals: Combat Infantry Badge, Bronze Star and Purple Heart.

RALPH M. WEISBARD,
tried to enlist with both the USN and Air Force but was rejected due to long term middle-ear infection and near-sightedness. Had his ear treated and eventually assigned to the Infantry and sent to Camp Shelby, MS, where he joined the 69th Inf. Div.

Onward to Europe, he joined the 7th Armd. Inf. Div., 48th Armd. Inf. Bn. Co. C. (a rifle company). Shortly before the German surrender he was offered a "Battlefield Commission" which he refused when told he would probably be sent to the Pacific Front.

Awards/Medals: Silver Star, Bronze Star, Purple Heart and Infantry Badge. With only one year of combat, he had 70 points and was discharged.

Finished college on the GI Bill. Retired from his CPA firm, he has wife, Ruth, two sons and a daughter.

EDWARD WEISBLOTT,
born May 13, 1931, Syracuse, NY. First enlistment was in the 249th FA, 27th Div., NYNG. At the start of the Korean War, he transferred to the Air Force and received his basic training at Sampson AFB, Geneva, NY. He was then stationed at the Training Command Base, Tindall Field, FL.

Volunteered for overseas duty and was shipped to the 51st Fighter Wing, K13, Suwon, Korea. Completing his overseas tour, was assigned to the 366th Fighter-Bomb Wing, Alexandria AFB, LA; and later to the 108th Aircraft and Control Flight, NYANG.

Awards/Medals: Korean Service Medal with one Battle Star, United Nations Service Medal, National Defense Service Medal. Honorable discharge at the rank of staff sergeant.

A member of Onondaga Post 131, JWV, VFW, Manlius Post 7872, Fayetteville, American Legion Post 369, and DAV Chapter 30.

Married to Jean Meltzer Weisblott, now deceased. Has a son, Robert, and a daughter, Fay. Retired from the USPS after 33 years of service.

HERMAN L. WEISEBERG,
born New York, NY, July 17, 1914. Entered the service January 1945. U.S. PHS, asst. surgeon, USCG, lieutenant (jg). Stationed in Chicago, New York, New Orleans, USS *Pasco,* USS *Topelo,* USS *Sterope.*

He was fortunate enough to be stationed stateside for several months. Went to sea June 1945, USS *Pasco,* Alaska, short stay (ships of that class given to USSR lend lease). USS *Tupelo* (Guam and Central Pacific), then USS *Sterope* (Guam, New Hebrides), then San Francisco and New York City.

Discharged July 1946. Achieved the rank of assistant surgeon, USCG, lieutenant (jg).

All members of his immediate family are deceased. Retired MD/family practice for 50 years.

ESTELLE WEISEL,
born Jan. 1, 1919, New York, NY. Entered the Navy Nurse Corps on Jan. 5, 1944. Served at the USNH, Oceanside, CA; USNH, Oahu, HI; USNH, Portsmouth, VA.

Discharged Nov. 23, 1946 as LTJG, USNR. She is now retired.

JACK WEISEL,
born in Bayonne, NJ, Jan. 27, 1922. Enlisted Dec. 8, 1941, in the 1st or 3rd Army, Btry. D, 453rd AAA Auto Weapons Bn.

Stationed with 122nd CA, Downey, CA; 453rd AAA, Fort Knox, KY; Btry D, 4537 AAA, Camp Davis, NC;

Participated in battles in Belgium, Battle of Bulge Germany under Gen Patton and Gen Eisenhower.

Discharged November 1945 as corporal.

He had one son ,Dr. Larry Weisel; daughter, Lori Fried; and five grandchildren. He passed away in 1992.

BARRETT WEISER,
born in Burbank, CA, Sept. 13, 1956. Joined the USN Nov. 18, 1974. Attended boot camp (CO 334), BE&E and EM "A" School in San Diego, CA. Graduated from Mare Island Naval Nuclear Power School, Class 7601 and S5G Prototype, reporting to first submarine September 1976.

Served aboard the USS *Lewis and Clarke* SSBN 644 (Gold), USS *Simon Bolivar* SSBN 641 (Gold) and USS *Sturgeon* SSN 637, completing nine FBN deterrent patrols, two overhauls and a shakedown trial. Also served as instructor at SUBTRAFAC, Charleston, SC. Completed 12 years of active duty in November 1986 and joined USNR in December 1986. Completed nine years in USNR most recently serving as the Reserve Command Senior Chief of the Naval Reserve Center, Philadelphia, PA.

His first submarine captain was Jewish. When he made chief petty officer (CPO) his father, S/Sgt Jack Weiser (WWII and Korea), assisted his wife, Colleen, in pinning on his anchors. It was his father's 63rd birthday. His wife and son, Nathan, pinned on his anchors when he made senior CPO.

Awards/Medals: Submarine Enlisted Dolphins and designation as a Navy Master Training Specialist, Navy Achievement, Good Conduct (three awards), Reserve Meritorious Service (two awards) and National Defense Medal.

He wears the Meritorious Unit Citation, Combat E and Sea Service Ribbons.

He works for the Department of Justice as a senior analyst. Has been married to Colleen for 15 years. They have one son, Nathan, and one child on the way, due in March 1996.

JACK WEISER, S/Sgt, born in Manhattan, NY, Sept. 25, 1920. Prior to WWII he was an aviation electrician at Lockheed Vega Company in California. Joining the USAAC, he left for basic training on his first wedding anniversary Jan. 24, 1943. He served in China, Burma, and India as a photo lab chief for two years.

As a combat aerial photographer and camera repair instructor, he had the privilege of teaching the black airmen of the 1st Bomb Gp. and support crews for the Tuskegee Airmen at Selfridge Field, MI and Godman Field (Fort Knox), KY, maintenance and repair of Combat Aircraft Cameras. He and his wife, Helene, helped establish and open Camp Springs, MD, which became Andrews Air Force Base, S/Sgt Weiser was honorably discharged in 1946.

Called to serve his country again during the Korean War, he was the photo lab chief for Hq Sqdn. 80th ABGP in French Morocco from 1951-1953. Honorably discharged in 1953 he used the GI Bill to complete a BS in finance from L.A. State College.

During his service he earned Combat Air Crew Wings and a Sharp Shooter Medal. He was awarded the Army Good Conduct, Asiatic-Pacific Service, WWII Victory, Korean War and National Defense Medals.

He and wife, Helene, have three children, Roberta, Evelyn and Barrett, and two grandchildren, Hilary and Nathan. One more grandchild is on the way. Staff Sergeant Jack Weiser reported for duty with the staff of the Eternal Commander on May 14, 1994.

MARTIN WEISER, born Dec. 5, 1912, Brooklyn, NY. Became a CPA in 1938. Graduated with BBA in 1940 from St. John's University. Entered the U.S. Army in December 1942. Served at Ft. Myers, VA, and HQ, Military District of Washington, Washington, DC.

Awards/Medals: Commendation for Meritorious Service Medal, WWII Victory Medal and American Campaign Medal. Discharged Aug. 2, 1946, as chief warrant officer.

Received his MA from New York University in 1952. A self-employed accountant, individual practitioner and taught a number of years as an instructor of accounting at a local city college. Retired, but still engages in part-time work. Member of Post 2 JWV.

Married Beatrice who passed away in 1968.

MOREY WEISMAN, born Oct. 24, 1916, New York City. Inducted into U.S. Army as private, June 1941. Volunteered as aviation cadet, started flight training May 1942 at 63rd USAAF Training Detachment, Douglas, GA; soloed after eight hours instruction. Graduated from Aviation Cadets, Class 43-A, AAF Advanced Flying School, George Field, Lawrenceville, IL. Commissioned 2nd lieutenant, USAAFR, January 1943. Assigned to B-25 Bomber Training School, 426th Sqdn., 309th BG, Columbia AAB, SC.

April 1943, ordered overseas aboard troop ship SS *Gatun;* appointed ship's chaplain and recreation officer. Their replacement group transferred to Army Transport Ship, *Clem,* in Trinidad; then crossed Equator, inducted as "Trusty Shellback" into "Ancient Order of the Deep".

Arrived at Ascension Island aboard *Clem,* July 1943. Joined 1st Composite Sqdn., Composite Force 8012. Assigned as co-pilot on B-25 Bomber, *Little Lulu.* In September,

just 15 minutes before take-off, was bumped from mission to allow co-pilot time for a new pilot; plane with entire crew lost at sea. Was promoted to first pilot and assigned to same mission, next day.

Rotation from overseas, April 1944, after 96 missions; assigned as test pilot with 2nd Electronics Experimental Squadron AAB, Fort Dix, NJ, flight testing radar (then top secret).

Promoted to 1st lieutenant July 1944. October 1944, assigned as chief test pilot in airborne electronic research and development for International Telephone and Telegraph Corporation at Westchester County (NY) Airport on detached duty; piloted plane at dedication ceremonies officially opening airport, February 1945. Ordered to inactive duty August 1945.

Type of aircraft piloted: PT-17, BT-13, AT-6, AT-9, AT-11, C-45, L-4, A-25, C-47 and B-25.

Awards/Medals: EAME Theatre Campaign Ribbon, American Theatre Campaign Ribbon, Air Medal, American Defense Service Medal.

Founder JWV Post at 92nd Street YMHA, New York City, 1946; served as post commander (post now consolidated in JWV Post #001, Manhattan, NYC). Served as chairman of Textile Veterans Association, New York City. Commended in 1989 by Secretary of USAF for developing and offering invention for Stealth Bomber technology.

In civilian life, spent over 50 years in textile and plastic fabrics industries, with several U.S. patents issued to him personally, others pending. Currently consultant commercializing own advanced technologies. Widowed in 1992; three sons, one grandchild.

SEYMOUR S. WEISMAN, born New York City, April 27, 1919. Education: BSS, City College of New York, 1939; masters, social work, Columbia University, 1947; Ph.D. Political Science, New York University, 1958.

Inducted April 1942. Sergeant, Weatherman. Air Corps, Rome, NY 1942-1943. Graduated Officer Candidate School, Radar and Searchlight Officer, Coast Arty., 1943; graduated Infantry Heavy Weapons School 1944; Company Commander (first lieutenant) replacement troops, Battle of the Bulge December 1945; Weapons platoon and executive officer, Co. E, 415th Inf., 104th Div., from January 1945 to V-E Day May 1945. Assigned as battalion adjutant, HQ Company Commander.

Awards/Medals: Bronze Star and Purple Heart. Discharged April 1946 with rank of captain.

JWV service at national headquarters: Membership and program director 1950-1951; Assistant National Executive Director 1952-55; National Consultant 1955-1995 except for 1974-1975 Acting National Executive Director; Executive Vice President, JWV National Memorial 1976-1976; Senior Fellow, National Museum, American Jewish Military History 1983-1995.

Other occupations: Adjunct Associate Professor of Political Science, City University of New York; Executive Vice President, City College of New York Alumni Association; Officer and Director, REDM Industries. Community Service: Member Board of Governors, United Service Organizations (USO) 1970-1980. Author of three books and numerous professional articles.

Married to former Betty Scott. Children Scott and Julie.

ABRAHAM L. WEISS, born July 4, 1924, New York, NY. Entered USN Jan. 26, 1943. Served at NRS, NY; CB NCTC WIM, VA; 69th NCB; 70th NCB, NCTC Davisville, RI; CB Maint. Unit 615; USN, PSC, Lido Beach, Long Island, NY.

Awards/Medals: American Theater, EAME with one star, Asiatic-Pacific with one star, Victory Ribbon, Expert Rifleman. Honorably discharged Dec. 27, 1945.

Married to Lillian and has two sons, Jerald and Daniel. The Weiss family are all JWV members. Abraham Weiss died May 12, 1994.

ALLEN WEISS, born July 11, 1918, Bronx, NY. BS (CCNY), 1937, MBA (NYU) 1939, CPA (NY). Served in USCG 1942-1946; Reserve Officers Training; District Clothing and Ship's Service Officer, member of Summary Court Board and occasional defense counsel, San Juan, PR; deck officer aboard cutter escorting merchant ships to Guantanamo Naval Base.

Had intensive training in radar/loran at Groton, CT, followed by assignment as electronic development engineering officer (Loran) at HQ, Washington, DC, until WWIIs end. Rank: lieutenant (sg).

His USCG experience was made memorable overall by the high professionalism and dedication of the senior officers he was privileged to serve with. They earned the men's gratitude.

His wife Florence died in 1955. He has daughter, Susan, son Robert and granddaughter Kelly Egan. Has been married to Enid since 1957.

Presently writing a business-oriented book. Published works: *The Organization Guerrilla (Atheneum); Write What You Mean (AMACOM).* JWV member. Listed in *Who's Who in the East.*

BERNARD L. WEISS, MAJ GEN, USAF, RET, served 32 years in the USAF. Born in the Bronx, NY, Sept. 9, 1933. Gen Weiss was a distinguished military graduate of AFROTC at New York University and was commissioned as a regular officer in 1955. Served in many contracting, weapon system development and logistic jobs. Was instrumental in developing the acquisition strategy for the F-16, F-15, B-1 and B-2 programs.

Retired in 1988 as commander, Air Force Contract Management Div., Kirtland AFB, New Mexico. Received MBA from Syracuse University in 1966 and an Advanced Management Certificate from the University of Michigan in 1978. Graduated from Industrial College of the Armed Forces in 1974. Gen. Weiss was awarded numerous medals and citations culminating with the Distinguished Service Medal with two OLCs.

After retirement he joined Sundstrand Corporation as a corporate officer, vice president and general manager. He worked with Sundstrand in both Rockford, IL and Redmond, WA. Upon the sale of Sundstrand Data Control which he managed, he retired in November, 1993.

He and his wife, Helene, reside in Naples, FL from where he operates as a consultant. They have three children and six grandchildren.

DANIEL WEISS, born Nov. 6, 1949, Bronx, NY, the son of Abraham and Lillian Weiss. Graduated high school in 1968; entered the USN April 1969 with basic training at Great Lakes. Assigned to USS *Shangri-La* and served in Vietnam from January 1970-January 1971.

"Join the Navy and see the world." This is a true statement because he did see the world. He came from a Navy family. His father was in the Navy during WWII and his brother Jerald retired from the Navy after 28 years. He and his brother both served in Vietnam but at different times.

Awarded the Republic of Vietnam and Vietnam Service Medals. He was discharged April 2, 1975 with the rank of E-3.

Worked as a workers compensation investigator and owned his own investigating business.

Married to Susan and has two children, Vincent and Ashley.

FRANKLN WEISS

SEYMOUR WEISS, was born in Brooklyn, New York and tried to enlist in the Army in 1948, but was turned down because of bad feet. When the Korean War broke out, he tried to enlist again, but was rejected again. Six months later, he received his draft notice.

This time, he was fine enough to be drafted. So on Sept. 19, 1951, he was inducted into the US Army and immediately sent to Camp Kilmer in New Jersey for processing and then onto the Aberdeen Proving Grounds in Maryland. He was assigned to the 696 Ordnance Ammunition Corp for 8 weeks of Basic Training and 10 weeks of school.

In April 1952, he started his trip to South Korea and finally arrived at Inchon May 10, 1952 and took a train to Seoul and then was sent to Uijongbu where he was stationed until Aug. 4, 1953. Afterwards, his journey home began and he was discharged Sept. 18, 1953 and he would love to hear from anyone who recognizes his picture.

GERALD N. WEISS, born in New Orleans, LA, June 14, 1923. Enlisted in the U.S. Army Aug. 1, 1942; stationed at Hot Springs, AR; San Antonio, TX; Sacramento, CA; Las Vegas, NV; Palm Beach, FL; Washington, DC; Shreveport, LA; Wichita Falls, TX; Oklahoma City, OK and Tokyo, Japan.

Memorable experiences include initial synagogue medical society meeting (first American-Japanese Military Medical Officers Meeting).

Awards/Medals: Air Force Longevity Service Ribbon with one OLC, Air Force Good Conduct Medal (Army), Air Force Training Ribbon, Air Force Overseas Long Tour Ribbon, WWII Victory Medal, American Campaign Medal, Air Force Commendation Medal, Meritorious Service Medal and Senior Physician Badge. Released from active duty June 30, 1948. He achieved the rank of lieutenant colonel.

Married and has three children. He is a semi-retired surgeon/administrator, medical director at Little Rock Plasma Alliance Center.

HYMEN H. WEISS, born in Detroit, MI, Aug. 27, 1914. Drafted April 30, 1941; assigned to the 60th Inf., 9th Inf. Div. and served at Ft. Bragg, NC; Camp Lee, VA; Camp Butner, NC; HQ Base "S" QM Section Army Forces Western Pacific; New Guinea; Bismark Archipelago and Southern Philippines.

Participated in the invasion of Morotai (Dutch Indies), invasion of CEBU and Philippines.

Memorable experiences include serving as special court prosecutor, building road with hand labor and fire in petroleum dump.

Awards/Medals: American Campaign Medal, Asiatic Campaign Medal, WWII Victory Medal and Philippine Liberation. Discharged Oct. 23, 1946, as captain QMC AUS; Reserve officer in 1950.

Married Rachel (deceased 1970); had daughter Jo Anne Boyd (deceased) and grandchildren, Deborah Rose and Fredrick Boyd. Married second to Iva.

He is a semi-retired leasing and commercial real estate broker.

JEROME WEISS, commander Post 533, born June 11, 1919, Providence, RI. Drafted into U.S. Army May 4, 1941. Basic training and Supply School at Camp Lee, VA then to Camp Livingston, LA.

Outfit alerted overseas 4 p.m. Dec. 7, 1941 (Pearl Harbor Day). Shipped out following day and spent 36 months in Panama Canal Zone.

Married 50 years to Elsie; children, Phyllis Kaye and her sons, Kristopher and Brad, Lake Alfred, FL; Robin Weiss, Cranston, RI; Fred Weiss, his wife Denise, and sons, Paul and David, Bedford Hills, NY.

Returned to the States and transferred to Ft. Lewis, WA. Last assignment was as supply sergeant to a WAC Detachment (which he didn't accept) in Camp Siebert, AL. Discharged Sept. 26, 1945.

Associated with the Weiss Stationery Co., Inc. over 50 years. Retired from the firm as president in 1984.

EDWIN M. WEISSLER, born in Chicago, IL, Feb. 3, 1932. Education: Crane Technical HS; Squadron Officer's School, March 1957; University of Illinois, Urbana, IL BSEE, 1961 and MSEE in 1971. Enlisted in the service in 1952.

Other military stations include: aviation cadet, radar, navigator and bombardier training; B-29 combat crew training; photo navigator, B-29, Forbes AFB, KS; pilot training, Spence AB, Georgia and Goodfellow AFB, TX.

B-26 pilot, 1739th Ferrying Sqdn. Amarillo, TX and C-124 pilot, 40th ATS, Dover, AFB, DE; electrical engineer, 6970th Spt. Gp., Ft. Meade, MD; C-124 pilot, 28th MAS, Hill AFB, UT; Group Plans Officer, 3rd Aerospace Rescue and Recovery Group, Tan Son Nhut AB, RVN; Office of the Inspector General, HQ AFSC, Washington, DC; commander, 1945th Communications Gp., Rhein-Main AB, Germany. From November 1974 to present, DCS/Plans and Requirements, HQ European Communications Area, Lindsey AS, Germany.

Awards/Medals: include the Legion of Merit, Bronze Star, Meritorious Service Medal, Air Force Outstanding Unit Award with one OLC, Vietnam Service Medal with four Bronze Service Stars, Vietnamese Cross of Gallantry, Republic of Vietnam Campaign Medal, Presidential Unit Citation in addition to five other medals or ribbons.

Married the former Carol Klein in July 1952. They have four children: Mark, Lisa, Paul and Lynn.

Colonel Weissler is active in the sport of Judo and holds a second degree Brown Belt. He has also been a student of Korean Karate and Tai Chi.

LEONARD WEISSMAN, born Aug. 22, 1922, in New York. Enlisted in the U.S. Army as a medical tech on Oct. 22, 1942. Military locations included Camp Grant, IL; Camp Cook, CA; and Ft. Ben Harrison-Indianapolis.

Participated in battles at Ardennes, Rhineland and Central Europe.

Many of his most memorable experiences occurred during his participation in the Battle of the Bulge. Through five days and nights of unbearable cold, he carried and treated wounded soldiers while on detached service to the 517th Cbt. Team of the 82nd Abn.

Awards/Medals: three Battle Stars, Good Conduct, Combat Medics Badge and Bronze Star. He was discharged on Dec. 2, 1945, with the rank private first class.

Weissman and his wife, Anita, live in Ft. Lauderdale, FL. They have a son, daughter and three grandchildren. He is the assistant manager of the cemetery at Menorah Gardens and Chapels, Ft. Lauderdale.

LEO WEISSMAN, born Newark, NJ on April 11, 1900. Enlisted in the U.S. Army on March 5, 1918.

Served in the French Mortar Battery Foreign Service from July 14, 1918 to March 15, 1919.

He was discharged April 8, 1919.

Married and has one child. He worked for E.I. DuPont for 33 years. He passed away in February 1950.

NAFTALI M. WEISSMAN (MARTY), born in Poland April 10, 1925. Arrived in the U.S. in 1948 on a Rabbinical Student Visa. Was drafted into the USMC in 1951 and shipped to Korea.

He was there two months when it was found that he had been drafted illegally. He was then sent to Japan and interviewed by a legal officer, and the information was sent to Washington. He was then sent back to the U.S. where they declared him a displaced person and sent him back to Korea.

After discharge from the USMC in 1953, he became a U.S. Citizen.

Married Helene Price, 1966, in New York. They have two sons, David in New York and Jeffrey and his wife, Terry, in Massachusetts. He owns a Kosher Butcher Shop in Cranston, RI and lives in Warwick, RI.

WILLIAM H. WEITZ, enlisted in the service Aug. 5, 1942. Active duty started March 26, 1943.

Served in the ETO with the 90th Chem. Mortar Bn. from October 1944 to July 1945.

He was discharged Jan. 24, 1946 with the rank of sergeant.

EDWARD S. WEITZLER, S/SGT, attended High Street Elementary School in West Medway and received his diploma from Medway High School in 1938. During his high school days he was an active participant in sports and was a highly regarded member of his class.

Enlisted in the U.S. Army June 12, 1942. Following his basic training at Ft. Meade, he was schooled and stationed at various other posts in the U.S.

He was killed March 31, 1945, in Germany, where he was serving with Gen. Patton's famed 3rd Army. According to the War Dept. "he laid down his life for a friend" when without thought of personal safety, he made a desperate but futile attempt to rescue a fallen comrade and was slain by a sniper's bullet.

Other than the Purple Heart which was awarded posthumously, he was decorated on numerous other occasions. The medals are now in his parents' possession.

Besides his parents he is survived by sister, Rhoda.

MARCELLA ETTINGER WEITZMAN, born in Millville, NJ on May 5, 1925. Graduated high school in 1941 and had to wait until she was old enough to join the USN in 1945. Worked at Millville Army Air Field after graduating high school and entered WAVES on May 30, 1945 from Philadelphia, PA.

Boot training was at Hunter College, NY. Stationed in Corpus Christi, TX with Pan American Ground Training Unit where she was in charge of paper work of all training activities. Pilots spoke Spanish and she learned to converse very well with them.

She was discharged Aug. 6, 1946, as Y3C.

After discharge went to Temple University in Philadelphia and majored in business. Met husband and was married for 30 years. Has one son, married and living in Doylestown, PA. She worked at NAS Willow Grove for eight years in Air Force Military Personnel and retired from civil service. Has been employed at Sears for 30 years part-time and going for 50.

Belongs to two women veteran organizations and is life member of Drizin Weiss Post 215 for three years where she is part of color guard.

GERTRUDE SUBINSKY WELLER, born in Miami, AZ. She was sworn into the WAACs in December 1942; basic training was in Ft. Des Moines, IA and study of Army administration at Russellville, AR.

Other military stations included Camp Polk, LA; Grenier Field, Manchester, NH; Bolling Field where she worked in the Weather Bureau, Pentagon.

When WAAC was changed to WAC, she re-enlisted. Was given records for 10 years of Japan weather and ordered to list the weather in five cities for the months of June, July and August.

Upon completion the records were taken to the chiefs of staff of the Army, Navy and Air Force. They suspected a landing date to be chosen, but much to their amazement, the atom bomb was released on Hiroshima.

Requested transfer for overseas duty at the war's end. Weather observers were among the personnel going over, but when she was advised that no one from the Pentagon would be sent overseas, she asked for a discharge which was granted Dec. 17, 1945, with the rank sergeant.

She is retired from business.

JULIUS WELLER, born April 9, 1917, New York City. Inducted in January 1942 at Camp Upton, NY. Shipped to Ft. Belvoir, VA February 4 for intensive eight week basic training course.

Shipped to Ft. Ord., CA April 14 to activate 341st Engr. Regt.; arrived May 1, Dawson Creek British, Columbia and started building the Alaska Military Highway.

Arrived Camp Sutton, NC, Aug. 1, 1943; landed at Cardiff, Wales, then to Devonshire, England, where in addition to more training, they converted some of the large gracious homes into livable quarters for those to come after them.

June 10, 1944, was part of an advance party sent to France to secure a campsite for their unit. They followed the 1st and 3rd Army through France, Belgium, Luxembourg, Holland and Germany. Was reassigned to the 51st Engrs. prior to being shipped home.

Discharged in October 1945 as private and has been a JWV member ever since.

Married to a WAC veteran and has two children and four grandchildren. He is retired.

J. SAMUEL WELTMANN, born May 9, 1909, Glen Lyon, PA. Graduated from Newport High School. Member of football, basketball teams and participated in other sports. In 1928 he moved to Syracuse and completed course of study at CCBI.

Married Belle Grossman in 1938 and had a daughter Terry. Worked in theaters in Utica and Syracuse and owned and operated a few neighborhood theaters in Syracuse.

Was active in the YMCA, YMHA, National Guard and won honors for sharpshooting and other sporting events. He was killed in action in Belgium on Nov. 4, 1944, at the age of 34.

Survived by his mother, Betty; brother, Norman; sisters, Regina Engel and Sylvia Joseph.

SAMUEL WERTH, born Norfolk, VA, Aug. 28, 1927. Entered active service March 14, 1951, Richmond, VA. Attended Leadership School, March 1951-June 1951; Army OCS, Ft. Riley, KS, July 1951-December 1951; Engineer School, Ft. Belvoir, VA, February-May 1952.

Worked on survey crews in Central and South America making topographic maps and laying out airfields. Served in Korea doing topographic surveys for ground control laying in field artillery and became commanding officer of the 25th Engr. Map Depot where he was responsible for the distribution of maps to all UN Forces in Korea. The 25th was directly under 8th Army HQ, Seoul, Korea from 1951-1953.

Awards/Medals: Korean Service Medal with two Bronze Stars, United Nations Service Medal, Meritorious Unit Commendations, and Commendation Ribbon with Medal Pendant.

Discharged Dec. 13, 1954, as second lieutenant from the U.S. Corps of Engrs., USAR.

HAROLD L. WERTHEIMER, born in Atlantic City, NJ, Feb. 10, 1908. Attended University of Pennsylvania, Wharton School of Commerce and Finance. Received degree of Juris Doctor from New Jersey Law School, now Rutgers University School of Law.

Entered the U.S. Army August 1942; assigned Southern New Jersey/Delaware Recruiting and Induction District HQ. Was station commander, Atlantic City, NJ Recruiting Station and later attached to Public Relations Branch, Second Service Command. Transferred Corps of Engineers, stationed Camp Sutton, NC and Ft. Lewis, WA. He was discharged September 1945.

Received reserve commission Judge Advocate General's Corps December 1948. Retired March 1967 with rank of lieutenant colonel.

Awards/Medals: American Theater Medal, WWII Victory Medal, Good Conduct Medal and Army Reserve Medal.

Was a practicing attorney for more than 60 years. Also served as attorney for U.S. Government, including legal counsel for Federal Aviation Administration Technical Center.

Member of JWV, American Legion and ROA. Married to Therese. He passed away April 1993.

LEROY WHITELAW, born May 24, 1896, Akron, OH. Inducted in September 1917, assigned to 78th Div. and had a year of active duty in France. He carried artillery and infantry ammunition to the front lines at night.

Memorable experience was attending a Yom Kippur service for Jewish soldiers in their area. The service was held in an old barn with about 30 men present and was a very solemn occasion as they were not sure if they would ever see another one.

Received honorable discharge and all the usual service awards.

Married to Louise for nearly 60 years and has three sons (he lives with the eldest, Philip), 10 grandchildren and six great-grandchildren.

STANLEY J. WIDES, enlisted in January 1942 into the Signal Corps. Basic training was at Camp Crowder, assigned to the 3111th Sign. Bn., Co. A and served in the ETO, England and France D-day plus two. Transferred to 24th Regulating Station.

He was discharged January 1946 with the rank tech third class. Awards include five Battle Stars and the Meritorious Service Award.

LEE WIEDER

EDWIN WIERNIK, resides in Kanski Court, Rahway, NJ. Served on light cruiser USS *Providence* for about one year. Did extensive traveling in the Caribbean. Was heading for Japan in August 1945 when Atomic bomb dropped and war ended.

Through Mediterranean countries as far as Istanbul, Turkey. Service time up, came home to New York on battleship *Missouri* visiting more countries.

Married almost 44 years to Elaine and has son, Gary, at home. Son, Allan, lives in condo in nearby Linden. Both are single. Sister, Estelle, her husband, Harold live in Bronx, NY.

PAUL WILDFOGEL, born in Manhattan, NY on Nov. 10, 1921. Joined the service Nov. 5, 1942, and served as medical tech 409 with the 391st Inf. Regt. Stationed at Ft. Dix, NJ; Camp Breckinridge, KY; Ft. Rucker, AL; Hawaii and Japan.

Memorable experiences include being selected by a two-star general while on maneuvers as an outstanding medic and promoted to T-5; meeting a childhood friend when stationed in Hawaii; traveling freely and touring Osaka, Kobe and Kyoto, Japan; and when invited to a Japanese home for dinner.

Awards/Medals: American Service Medal, WWII Victory Medal, Good Conduct Medal and Asiatic-Pacific Service Medal. He was discharged Feb. 1, 1946, as Tech-5.

Worked with sports people and business executives until retirement. He is active in JWV and the Knight of Pythias.

Married Sylvia Sobelman and has two sons: Dennis, a Ph.D. in mathematics and now working for Tandem Computers; and Jeff, Ph.D. in psychology and self-employed.

ABRAHAM WILENSKY (MICKEY), born Fargo, ND, June 14, 1920. Joined the U.S. Army June 14, 1920, serving in Light Ord. 27th Div. Stationed at Aberdeen Proving Grounds, MD, New Caledonia, New Zealand, Philippines, Luzon and Japan occupation.

Memorable experiences: using too many explosives to dig for a well and blew up camp tents and when driving a jeep through minefields.

Awards/Medals: Bronze Star, Markmanship, Occupation Medal and SE Theater.

Discharged Jan. 31, 1946, as staff sergeant.

Had wife, Mariam, and two daughter, Roberta and Barbara. He passed away May 17, 1986.

SIDNEY R. WILENSKY, born in Devils Lake, ND on Nov. 11, 1915. Drafted Oct. 2, 1941, and served in the Infantry, Reg. Supply, 3rd Inf., 7th Regt. He was stationed at Ft. Snelling, Camp Roberts, Ft. Lewis, Ft. Ord and Camp Pickett, VA.

Participated in the invasions of North Africa, Sicily and Italy.

With the help of a couple of friends (who found a boiler, pump, shower heads, etc. from buildings in towns and from an abandoned school) he made a rebuilt washer/drier "go in one end, come out the other, clean body, clean clothes." Word got around and a two-star general showed up looking for Wilensky. He didn't believe they could do all that just behind the front lines; but they did, and many other things too.

Awards/Medals: received all the usual ones, including some from France and Italy. Also put in for the Legion of Merit but never received it.

He was discharged July 15, 1945 as tech sergeant.

Married to Shirley and has one son, Howard. He is retired.

IRVING N. WILSON, born in Ross, Poland, March 21, 1921. Emigrated to U.S. Oct. 15, 1927. Graduated Morris High School, Bronx, City College, NY, Cum Laude 1942. Entered USAAC December 1942, assigned 2nd AF B-17 Heavy Bombardment.

Stationed Rapid City AB, SD where he was NCO of Transportation Office, supervised "nine beautiful civilian gals." Returned to Bronx for first furlough to marry pre-war sweetheart Bertie Rosenstein Aug. 6, 1944, and still married to her.

Overseas December 1944, assigned 8th FTRSQ, 49th FTRGP, P-38s. Communications staff sergeant handling combat mission reports, radio crystal bank and repairs, and secret IFF (Identification Friend or Foe) codes.

Stationed New Guinea, Leyte, Mindoro, Luzon, Okinawa and Atsugi Airdrome, Japan. Was scheduled for invasion of Japan in unarmed glider, Nov. 1, 1945, to land at Atsugi Kamikazi Training Base, "fortunately the Atom Bomb saved his life."

Awards/Decorations: Asiatic-Pacific Medal with three Battle Stars, Philippine Liberation with two stars, Occupation Japan, Presidential Unit Citation with cluster, Philippine Independence and Philippine Presidential Unit Citation. He was discharged Jan. 6, 1946.

Owned own export/import business, automotive franchises and automotive service center. Life member and post commander JWV, AMVETS, VFW. Commander and national executive commander for Department of Texas, JWV.

Has daughter, Laura, VP Nations Bank, Dallas; grandson, Steven; and son, Bill.

ALBERT I. WINER, born Lowell, MA on Dec. 19, 1932. Enlisted in the USAF Oct. 12, 1951, Administrative NCOIC, U.S. Air Forces, Europe, Wiesbaden, Germany, Sampson AFB, Geneva, New York, Air Training Command, Europe, Wiesbaden, Germany.

Was in communications in Germany for three and a half years. His memorable experience was running teletype classified documents between Washington, DC; Bonn, W. Germany; Moscow, USSR.

Awards/Medals: Army of Occupation, Germany, Good Conduct Medal, Meritorious Service Medal, other misc. (11 ribbons in all). He was discharged Oct. 11, 1959, as airman first class/buck sergeant. Retired Dec. 19, 1992, USAR, SCM E 9.

Worked as Army Reserve tech., completed Army Reserve service as SGM E-9, 33 years of civil service and retired July 2, 1993. He is member of JWV, Post 31, Lynn, MA.

Married with two sons, two daughters and eight grandchildren.

LLOYD B. WINICK, served in the U.S. Army from Jan. 8, 1942-Nov. 18, 1945. Entered the service at Boston, MA; basic training consisted of engineering training at Westover Field, MA from Jan. 12, 1942-Oct. 1, 1944, when he received infantry training at Camp Gordon, GA until Oct. 14, 1944.

Served with the Medical Dept. at Westover Field, MA, also with the AITC at Camp Gordon, GA during October 1944 and with the Evac. Hosp. at Ft. Jackson, SC during November 1944.

Sailed overseas from Boston, MA on the SS *James Parker* and arrived at Le Havre, France; sailed from Marseilles on the SS *John Squire* and arrived at Newport News, VA. Served with the 136th Evac. Hosp. in the ETO from March 18, 1945-Sept. 2, 1945, and saw action during the Battle of the Bulge in Belgium and the Battle of Germany, crossing the Rhine River there.

Received several promotions and was a staff sergeant when discharged. Among the many places he visited overseas were Paris, Cologne, Germany, Metz, France, Lyons, France, Saarbrucken, Germany and the Riviera. *Submitted by Max Sigal.*

MELVIN WINICK, entered the USN April 24, 1943, as apprentice seaman and discharged as torpedoman first class. Received his recruit training at the USN Training Station at Newport, RI as well as the Torpedo Station at Newport, RI; Torpedo Station at Montauk, Long Island; mine demolition at Solomons, MD; bomb disposal, Washington, DC; Submarine School, New London, CT; minesweeping at Solomons, MD and Mine Depot at Yorktown, VA.

Sailed with the Atlantic and Pacific Fleets and sailed on the USS *Nevada* from Honolulu to San Pedro, CA. Saw action in the North Atlantic Theater, South Atlantic Theater with the Atlantic Fleet and in the North and South Pacific with the Pacific Fleet, having been attached to Naval Intelligence, he was unable to divulge any action that he had seen, but it is reported that some of his work consisted of mine demolitions.

Received the Presidential Citation and a Letter of Commendation. He visited practically the entire world from Nova Scotia to North Africa, to Hawaii, to Japan, and many other places. He participated in the atomic bomb experimentation's in 1946 in the Pacific. *Submitted by Max Sigal.*

SAMUEL WINIK, born in Baltimore, MD, April 2, 1924. Served in the ETO with the U.S. Army and participated in the Normandy, Northern France, Ardennes, Rhineland and Central Europe campaigns.

Decorations include the Good Conduct Medal, American Theater Ribbon, EAME Ribbon and WWII Victory Ribbon. He was honorably discharged in December 1945 as tech third grade.

 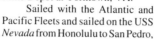

Was co-founder of Haar-Win Parking Co. and retired at age 44. Tiring of retirement in 1983, he came back and currently serves as parking consultant and director of research and development to Quille Parking Co. and Quille/Crown Parking. He is tireless in his commitment to civic and philanthropic endeavors.

A life member of Maryland Free State Post 167, JWV and awarded "The Commodore Uriah P. Levy" Leadership Award Nov. 3, 1985, and on July 27, 1986, was named "Honorary Colonel" by the Ft. McHenry Guard Units.

Married to Debbie and has two sons, Steven Bruce and Jay Leslie, stepdaughter Martha L. Himes; and three grandchildren: Nicole Faith, Shelby Renee and Laura Beth Winik.

MARTIN H. WINN, born in Chicago, IL on Nov. 4, 1915. Inducted May 1943 and assigned to the USAAC, Amarillo, TX for basic training. Attended Photo School, Lowry Field, Denver, CO, then assigned to 102nd Photo Sqdn., 3rd AF, Alexandria, LA. Transferred to Will Rogers Air Field, OK first to the 30th Ftr. Sqdn. then to the 11th Cbt. Mapping Sqdn.

While in training at Will Rogers Field, Oklahoma City, he injured his leg and was transferred to the 11th Cbt. Sqdn. The unit he transferred from was shipped overseas and the ship was lost; only the pilots who flew over made it.

Overseas training was at Greensboro, NC, transferred to POE at Newport News, VA for overseas duty. Arrived at Naples, Italy, assigned to the 3rd Photo Tech Sqdn. and

advanced to Florence, Italy. Participated in Rome-Arno, Northern Apennines, Po Valley and Southern France campaigns.

Awards/Medals: American Theater Ribbon, EAME with four Bronze Stars, Good Conduct Medal, Victory Medal and the Presidential Unit Citation. He was discharged Nov. 14, 1945, with the rank private first class.

Graduated from Chicago City College. Today he is retired and a member of JWV Post 396, American Legion and VFW. Also president of the Troupers Inc.

Has wife, Mary; two daughters, Ilene and Alice; three grandsons: Joshua, Ira and Gabriel.

LEONARD WINOGRAD, born Nov. 14, 1922, Pittsburgh, PA, son of Emil and Bess Winograd who were in the vaudeville business. Enlisted in the USAAC and graduated from San Marcos, TX Navigation School.

Flew out of Italy with 376th BG. On 43rd mission, parachuted into Yugoslavia, captured after three days in the snow and taken into Germany as a POW.

Awards/Medals: ETO Medal with five Battle Stars, Air Medal with three OLCs, WWII Victory Medal, POW Medal and Greek Air Medal.

Attended University of Pittsburgh after discharge for BS in business administration (1946); Hebrew Union College-Jewish Institute of Religion, Cincinnati, BHL (1956), MAHL (1958), Rabbinical ordination (1958), Doctor of Hebrew Letters (1967) and Doctor of Divinity (Honorary) (1973).

Worked in family motion picture business until 1954, then studied for the rabbinate. Was rabbi of a conservative congregation and served a reform congregation in McKeesport; was part-time Jewish Chaplain of the State Mental Hospital in Somerset, PA; assistant professor of psychology at Mt. Aloysious College, Cresson, PA and taught at both St. Francis Seminary, Loretto, PA and Westmoreland County Community College.

He served as president/chairman of Teen Canteen, Human Relations Advisory Council, Tri-State Zionist region, Greater Pittsburgh Rabbinic Fellowship and served on the National Executive Council of the ZOA.

Was national chaplain of American POWs, served on the national board of the Central Conference of American Rabbis, was co-founder of Pittsburgh Voice for Soviet Jewry, the Community Day School, the Jewish Congregation Basketball League of Greater Pittsburgh and co-ordinator of the Greater McKeesport Interfaith Clergy Dialogue.

Married Pescha Cooper; children: Emil, Harry, Michael and Ethan; seven grandchildren: Andrea, Max, Paul, Samuel, Jeffrey, Joseph and Moe. Has one sister, Selma Cohen, and one brother, Kenneth, both of Pittsburgh.

Retirement followed a stroke which left his left side paralyzed. He has written a syndicated column for the Jewish Telegraphic Agency, worked as national membership consultant and has published three books.

WILLIAM KENNETH WINOGRAD, born in Rochester, PA on May 13, 1930, to the late Emil and Bess Winograd of the motion picture theater family. Worked at the Majestic and Oriental Theaters while attending Geneva College where he earned a BA degree.

During the Korean War he served in the U.S. Army in the Coast Artillery on Okinawa and Korea.

Returned to Rochester as an executive with the Rochester Amusement Co. and took over the management of the Rialto and State Theatres of Beaver Falls and the Hi Way 51 Drive-In Theater. Became a full-time director of a home for the Lintz Sheltered Workshop for handicapped and retarded.

in the horse cavalry. Entered the service as private in the Armd. Force. Basic training then OCS, he served in the 23rd Cav. Recon. Sqdn. (mechanized).

Volunteered for parachute duty and sent to Ft. Benning for training. Went overseas to join H Co., 3rd Bn., 513th PIR and was in the Hüertgen Forest Campaign.

Was a platoon leader in the largest airborne invasion in history, Operation Varsity. Jumped east of the Rhine, then joined the British Guards Armd. Bde. Attached to the coldstream guards they formed a flying column, driving towards Muenster.

Awards/Medals: Bronze Star and Purple Heart.

He was discharged in April of 1946 as 1st lieutenant.

Moved to Miami, FL and entered the life insurance profession. Served as president of the Million Dollar Round Table and the Association for Advanced Life Underwriting. Has given over 3,000 speeches and seminars in 16 countries and at 36 universities. Biography is in *Who's Who in America* and *Who's Who in the World* and *Who's Who in Finance and Industry*.

SHELDON WOLPIN, born in Lakewood, NJ on April 6, 1923. Entered active service Jan. 23, 1943, USNTC, Camp Peary, VA; Seabee boot camp; 12th Construction Bn. on Adak where the only action he saw was Jap Zeros flying over them. They landed on Attu later, only to find the Japanese had "departed." Other stations were Camp Parks, CA and Puget Sound Navy Yard, Bremerton, WA.

Awards/Medals: Asiatic-Pacific, American Theater and Victory Medal. He was discharged Dec. 5, 1945, joined the USNR, attained rank lieutenant junior grade.

Attended DePauw Univ. V-12 Program, Supply Corps Midshipman School, Post Graduate School of Business Administration, Harvard Univ., Boston, MA.

Owner/operator of Wolpin's Furniture House and then Wolpin's Ethan Allen Gallery, 1945-1979, and is now retired.

Served on boards of Congregation Sons of Israel, B'nai B'rith, Judean Unit; active in Robbins-Feldstein JWV, Lakewood; Ocean County Jewish Federation; American Legion and several professional affiliations.

Married Oct. 30, 1949, and has four children: Ellen, Marilyn, Stewart and Richard.

WANDA C. WOOD, COL, born in Nettleton, MS in 1946. Earned a bachelor's degree from University of Southern Mississippi in 1968; master's degree from Sul Ross State University, Alpine, TX in 1976.

Completed Squadron Officer School in 1974, Armed Forces Staff College in 1980 and Air War College in 1989.

Stationed at Maxwell AFB; 1971-72, chief of data control section at Udorn Royal Thai AFB, Thailand; staff personnel officer at HQ AF Security Svc., Kelly AFB, TX; AF Military Personnel Ctr., Randolph AFB, TX in 1973; Webb AFB, TX in 1975; chief of Consolidated Base Personnel Office at Myrtle Beach AFB, SC in 1976.

In 1981 she was assigned as the director of personnel, 81st Tactical Fighter Wing at RAF Bentwaters, United Kingdom. She returned to the U.S. in 1984 to serve as the director of AF Personnel at the National Security Agency, Ft. Meade, MD. In 1989 she assumed command of the 66th Cbt. Spt. Gp., Sembach AB, Germany. In 1993 she became commander of the U.S. Military Entrance Processing Command, Great Lakes, IL.

Awards include the Legion of Merit, Defense Meritorious Service Medal, Meritorious Service Medal with two OLCs, AF Commendation Medal with three OLCs and the German Army Honor Cross in Silver.

She is married to Lt. Col. Leslie Wood, USAF (RET).

ALLEN WOROB, served in the U.S. Army with the amphibious engineers. Entered the service with the rank of private on March 8, 1943, at Newark, NJ. Received his basic training at Camp Lee, VA from March 19, 1943-October 1943 and at Ft. Warren, WY from October 1943-January 1944.

His unit sailed overseas on the HMS *Mauratania* from New York and arrived at Liverpool, England. He saw duty in the ETO from March 1944-November 1945. Participated in the D-day Normandy Invasion June 6, 1944, and the Battle of the Bulge in December 1944.

He visited many outstanding places among which were the Castle of King John in England; the Tintern Abbey, England; Switzerland; The Spa in Belgium and he played golf in Waterloo.

Awards/Medals: received many citations, decorations and promotions, among which were the EAME Service Medals, Good Conduct Medal, Victory Medal, four Battle Stars, Invasion Spearhead and Belgian Ribbon. He was discharged in Newark, NJ on Nov. 27, 1945, with the rank of sergeant. *Submitted by Max Sigal.*

EDWARD L. WURZBERG, born New York City, Nov. 18, 1922. Enlisted April 1, 1943 in the U.S. Army and trained with the 783rd MP BN, then as a MOS 622, Finance 1st 3rd grades.

Awards/Medals: American Theater of Operations, M1 Rifle Expert, Victory Medal and Good Conduct Medal. He was discharged March 28, 1946, as staff sergeant.

Married Mildred Kotick in 1952 and has two daughters and two grandsons.

Retired from sporting goods business and shares time between Boynton Beach, FL and Lincoln Park, NJ.

MICHAEL S. WYSOR, born in Manhattan on May 8, 1949. Graduated from Cornell University in 1971, Dept. of Pharmacology, Cornell Univ. Med. College, 1971-1972; Dept. of Preventive Medicine (parasitology and tropical diseases) New York Univ, Med. School and MS, 1974; Dept. of Histology, New York Univ. School of Medicine, Ph.D., 1978.

Direct commission as 1st lieutenant Med. Svc. Corps, U.S. Army, 1978. Basic training at Ft. Sam Houston, San Antonio, TX, 1978. Assigned to Special Studies Sect., Dept. of Parasitology, Division of Experimental Therapeutics, Walter Reed Army Institute of Research, Washington, DC.

Promoted to captain 1980. Walter Reed Army Institute Certificate of Achievement, for research into the chemotherapy of tropical diseases. U.S. Army Med. Research Institute of Infectious Diseases, Ft. Detrick, Frederick, M.D. and Armed Forces Med. Intel. Ctr.

He received honorable service connected disability on Nov. 30, 1987.

Married Wanda June Drinnon May 5, 1990. Graduated Mount Sinai Med. School in 1992; internship at Cabrini Med. Ctr., NYC; presently in residency, Division of Radiation Oncology, NY University School of Medicine, NYC. He is member of JWV.

ASHER YAFFEE, served in WWI as a bugler and runner. He enlisted at the age of 17 and was killed in action at the age of 18. He is survived by brothers: Hyman, Morris, Sam and Albert, and sisters, Ceil and Kate.

HYMAN YAGODA, deceased, was in the Army Infantry and served in the European Theater. He had a serious service connected spine injury. Unfortunately, nothing else is known about his military career. *Submitted by brother-in-law of Irving Hauptman.*

STEVEN YAGODA, nephew of Irving Hauptman, enlisted in the Army and served from February 1966 to December 1968. He served in Virginia and Alaska Army Transportation Corps as a 1st lieutenant.

ISIDORE YANCO, born in New York City, Dec. 27, 1914. He then relocated to Medway, MA in 1921, graduated from Medway High School as an honor student in 1932. He returned to New York after graduation and became food service manager for a large restaurant chain. He entered the U.S. Army in 1943.

After completion of boot camp at Aberdeen Proving Grounds, MD, his Co. B, 1st Bn. was assigned to the Quartermaster School, Camp Lee, VA for advanced food service technician courses. In 1944 he was assigned to a base in Hawaii and then on to serve in the Korean War. He returned in 1954 to the U.S. and became senior instructor at Ft. Devens, Ayer, MA, where he was originally inducted, and was responsible as a commandant of the 1st Army Food Service School, as well as a food service overseer for the entire base. His expertise and responsibility in its entire facet gave him the title of "Mr. Food Service."

Isidore Yanco received Masonic membership in the Caleb Butler Lodge AF&AM in Ayer, MA. In a very short time, he was promoted to the rank of master sergeant. M/Sgt. Yanco's authorized awards were: Good Conduct Medal, American Campaign Medal, Korean Campaign Medal, 1st OLC Medal and many other numerous awards and citations. He was a 21-year veteran and a member in good standing with the JWV. He was honorably discharged from the U.S. Army on July 31, 1964, and was then employed as a supervisor for a large oil company until his death in June of 1966.

Unmarried, he was able to dedicate his entire life to his God, his country, his parents, his family and his friends. He will never be forgotten. His great-nephew served in the Persian Gulf, and is presently serving in the U.S. Army, stationed in Germany, assigned to Patriot Missile Operations.

NATHAN YANCO, born in Medway, MA, April 10, 1930. Graduated from Medway High School in 1947 and attended Suffolk University, Boston, MA. He was placed on active duty with the Air Force during the Korean War in May 1951 with the 89th Troop Carrier Wing stationed at Bedford AFB, MA. Transferred to the 131st Fighter Wing at Bergstrom AFB, Austin, TX. Eventually, his outfit was transferred to George AFB, Victorville, CA. He was discharged from the Air Force in October 1952 due to a truce agreement between North and South Korea.

Yanco was employed for a large petroleum firm, then started his own successful petroleum business in 1969, which he is still president of and active in to this day.

Married Elaine Grover of Brookline, MA, Oct. 24, 1954. They have four lovely children and seven beautiful grandchildren: Daniel, Steven, Elizabeth, Samantha, Gary, Lee and Esty. Their son Eric is currently employed in the retail division and daughter Rhonda is employed in an administrative position of their father's oil business. Son Jeffrey is involved in the computer field and occasionally does consulting for the oil company and son Glen is an attorney and also general counsel for Yanco's company. The children all reside in Peabody, MA, where Yanco still resides since moving there with his family in 1962 from Brookline, MA.

He is member in good standing of the Commanders Club DAV; American Legion; JWV Post 220, Peabody, MA; Jewish Federation of Men's Clubs; Temple Ner Tamid, Peabody, MA; and numerous other civic organizations.

IRVING J. YAROCK, born in Worcester, MA, Sept. 25, 1916. He graduated from Rhode Island State College in 1939 with a BS degree and a commission as a 2nd lieutenant, Infantry.

Called to active duty in July of 1941 and assigned to the 18th Inf., 1st Inf. Div. He participated in the landing in North Africa and served in Algeria and Tunisia, where he was captured at Longstop Hill by the African Corps. He spent 27 months in and out of Italian and German prison camps, finally being liberated by the 14th Armd. Div.

He remained with the Reserve in ever increasing levels of command and retired as a colonel with the Combat Infantry Badge, Bronze Star, European Campaign Ribbon with Invasion Arrow and four Battle Stars, American Theater, Commendation Ribbon with OLC, WWII Victory Ribbon and 30 Year Reserve Ribbon.

Yarock served three terms as commander of JWV Post 32, and has been their quartermaster for several years. Also a member of the American Legion, MOWW, DAV, ROA, TROA, the Association of the U.S. Army and the National Association of Uniformed Services.

He is now retired.

NORMAN L. YEAMANS, born in Richmond (Staten Island), NY Jan. 27, 1927. Enlisted May 30, 1945, in the U.S. Army and completed Infantry Signal Basic training at Camp Blanding, FL. He served as studio and master control engineer with the Armed Forces Radio Network, 6800th HQ Co. USFET in Munich and Frankfurt, Germany.

Awards/Medals: Army of Occupation Medal, EAME Campaign Medal, Good Conduct Medal and WWII Victory Medal. He was discharged Oct. 29, 1946, as tech 3rd grade.

Founding member of Temple Beth Torah Ocean, NJ and held many board positions. Retired from civilian position with Dept. of the Army Aug. 31, 1974. Awarded Research and Development Achievement Award for Technical Achievement in 1972. Founded NY Limo Service in Ocean, NJ and presently training recent Russian immigrant to take over the business. Life member of Post 125.

Married Blossom Littenberg Dec. 21, 1953, and they have three children: Jack, Dan and Bonnie. Dan served in the USAF seven years and flew supply missions for Desert Shield and Desert Storm as aircraft commander of C-141. He has two children and is a life member of Post 125.

STANLEY N. YEAMANS, born Nov. 2, 1919, Richmond (Staten Island), NY and is a brother to Norman Yeaman. Enlisted Sept. 24, 1942 in the Army, served in HQ&HQ Co., 474th Inf. Military locations: Scotland, England and Norway.

Memorable experiences were the V-2 rocket attacks in London at close range.

Awards/Medals: EAME Service Medal and the Good Conduct Medal. He was discharged Nov. 6, 1945, as private first class.

Employed by Dept. of Buildings, city of New York. Was member of team that rewrote New York State Building and Fire Prevention Code. He is a member of Post 550.

Married twice, Blanche Jacobson and Ruth Bennett, and widowed twice. Two children by first wife, Bruce (a doctor in family practice) has three daughters and Leslie (vice president of computer firm) has three sons).

MILTON YOCHEL, born New York, NY (eastside), Jan. 26, 1923. He moved to Williamsburg, Benson Hurst and Sheeps Head Bay, Brooklyn. Graduated from Sethlow Jr. HS and Strauben Mueller Textile HS (what is now Fashion Institute).

Married Leonora Ehrlich in November 1948 and they have four daughters: Karyn, Scarlett, Marsha and Cindy. Divorced June 1978 and became very active in Parents Without Partners. Was on their board as director of new and potential members; was also vice president of Public Relations. Married Patrica Masdian in 1984, mother of three daughters: Susan, Stephanie and Stacie. He is grandfather to Christopher, Joey, Danny, Crystal and Sal.

Retired in 1977 from DCASR, DLA as a quality assurance specialist. Worked on Apollo 11, Special Satellite, EA6B, B-1 and various other programs. Belongs to JWV Post 50, American Legion Post 1786 (was vice commander of Post 1766), AF Association, Queens Sqdn. and a loyal Order of the Moose Lodge 518.

Joined the USAAF Oct. 28, 1942. Received indoctrination at Camp Upton, NY. Went to Miami Beach for basic training, then to Truax Field, Madison, WI for Radio School and advanced basic training. Sent to Salinas and Great Bend, KS for crew member training. Sent to Camp Patrick Henry, VA for overseas preparation.

Boarded liberty ship SS *Smith and Johnson* to Casablanca, North Africa. Flew and landed across each North African country. Flew from Cairo, Egypt to Karachi, India. Trucked from there to Charrah and Dudkundi, India where the first B-29 bases began with the 20th AF, 58th BW, 444th BG and ended in 676th BS as a radar mech 867.

From there had a great memorable experience as a radar OBS Mech. Bomb 2867. Flew the Hump (over the Himalayas) to advance bases, A1 and A2, in Chengtu and Kwnehan, China in B-29 Furar and aborted numerous enemy primary missions due to engine and various other problems. Twice, he almost had to bail out of B-29.

As a secondary mission they left their two bomb bay gas tanks each time for the rest of their outfit to utilize. Later on, assigned as crew chief to maintain the radar equipment and install camera on their planes.

Shipped out on Navy APA USS *General* to Tinian in the Marianas in West Pacific, where they continued fighting the enemy. As a participant in the air offensive of Japan, Burma, Central Burma and China, he received the Asiatic-Pacific Service Medal with four Bronze Stars and the Distinguished Unit Badge with two OLCs. Was also awarded the American Service, WWII Victory and Good Conduct Medals. Received the Sharpshooter Badge for use of the Carbine M1.

When the war was over, sent home to a camp in San Francisco, CA, then he was discharged at Ft. Dix, NJ on Nov. 23, 1945.

LAWRENCE K. YORN, born in Newark, NJ, Jan. 12, 1937. Joined the U.S. Army in July 1962, served with the 4th Armd. Div., 46th Med. Bn. and was stationed at Heilbronn, Germany.

He was honorably discharged in June 1964 with the rank of captain.

Yorn is a dentist.

SAMUEL G. YOUNG, bombardier/navigator, on the famous B-17G, *The E-Rat-I-Cator*, the only original plane of the 452nd BG to survive the war. He won his first and only lottery in 1940, in which he was inducted into the U.S. Army for one year. Two years later, his request to join the USAC arrived and he left the 9th Inf. Div. to become a bombardier.

Graduated Bombardier School as second lieutenant, March 11, 1943, Big Springs, TX (Class 43-4). Graduated Navigation School in San Marcos, TX. He then left for England with his original crew and original plane and saw combat with the 452nd BG stationed at Deopham Green.

He was on the first three missions that hit "Big B" (Berlin) and after 13 missions, he was grounded with a ruptured intestine and assigned as a personnel equipment officer after attending school at Cheddington, England. He was assigned to teaching parachute survival, dingy ditching and equipment handling.

Awards/Medals: European Theater Campaign with six Battle Stars, Air Medal with cluster, WWII Victory Medal, American Defense Service Medal and Distinguished Unit Citation.

Young was discharged as first lieutenant October 1945. He married Ruth in 1946. Retired from the contracting business in New Jersey after 20 years and moved to California in 1965, where he was the West Coast director for an entertainment publication until 1988. He retired again to a life of golf and indulging his three wonderful children and six grandsons.

He did a bit of combat photography, a few of which can be seen in Martin Bowman's *Castles in the Air*. The story of the B-17 Flying Fortress crews of the 8th Air Force.

He is a member of DAV, Bombardiers Inc., 8th Air Force Historical Society and past commander of JWV Roselle-Linden Post #437 and a past president of the New Jersey Home Improvement Contractors Association.

LEON YOUNGER, born in London, England Nov. 17, 1917. A member of JWV Post 718, Pittsburgh; DAV conscripted 1940 left Liverpool, England on winnie special convoy No. 3, *Athlone Castle,* with 10,000 troops for Bombay, India 1941 from Bombay to Calcutta by train. Now in British 14th Army. Went to Siri Lanka for jungle training. Fought rear action, chased back to India from Burma by the Japs.

Volunteered and flown in as a replacement for Gen. Wingate's Chindits behind the enemy lines in Burma being captured by Japs but escaping after a half hour through the tall grass. Helped by friendly Burmese crossing the deadly and disease ridden Valadan Valley. On one side the East Mayu Range of hills, on the other the West Mayu Range. Controlled by the Japs finally reaching Chittergong, India. Sick with malaria, into rest camp, then posted back to 37th Field Regt., 25th Indian Div. to the Arravan Burma. Four landings along coast of Burma, wounded at Kangaw. Back to England 1946. Decorations: 39/45 Star Burma Star, Victory Medal, War Medal and Wound Stripe.

ALAN YURMAN, born in Kearny, NJ, July 3, 1942 (3rd generation Yurman). Received a 2nd lieutenant's commission after completing ROTC at Texas University, July 1966. Assigned to Armor School at Ft. Knox, and later transferred to Flight School at Ft. Wolters, TX. Went to Ft. Rucker, AL and completed helicopter training.

He was sent overseas in November 1967 and assigned to the 240th Heli. Co. in Vietnam. A command pilot, he saw active combat during the Tet Offensive of 1968. It was a time of extreme danger with long combat flying time. Shot down once and lost a number of helicopters in his command group.

Awards/Medals: Bronze Star, Purple Heart, Air Medal with V, Air Medal with 30 clusters, Army Commendation and area campaign ribbons.

Stayed in Reserves from 1971 to 1978 and was honorably discharged as a major in 1983. He presently works for the National Safety Transportation Board as an aviation investigator.

BENJAMIN YURMAN, born in New York City, Oct. 14, 1914. Enlisted Feb. 2, 1944, in the U.S. Army and was stationed at Ft. Dix, Camp Upton, Camp Gordon, San Francisco and the Philippine Island of Leyte.

After a week in San Francisco, they were sent to California and given summer clothes. Spent a week in the Pacific Ocean and finally landed on Leyte Island. There were still plenty of Japanese on the island, but eventually they got rid of them.

Awards/Medals: WWII Victory Medal, Bronze Service Star, American Campaign Medal, Asiatic-Pacific Campaign Medal, Good Conduct Medal and Philippine Liberation Ribbon.

Served with the 3484th Ord. Maint. Co., Luzon. Discharged as tech five. Retired.

MAX YURMAN, JR., born in New York City, Jan. 1, 1921 (2nd generation Yurman). Joined the USN on Oct. 16, 1942, and stationed at Naval Operating Base, Northern Ireland.

Memorable experience was defeating the submarine wolf packs in the battles of the Atlantic and the initial landing of Marines in Japan.

Last ship he served in was the USS *Waukesha* (AKA-84), an attack cargo ship. Their ship participated in the Pacific bringing cargo and Marines to the beaches of the Philippines, Okinawa and Japan.

Stayed in the Reserves as a shipfitter first class petty officer for 10 years and was honorably discharged the second time in 1955.

Medals/Awards: European Theater, Asiatic-Pacific, Philippine Liberation, American Theater, Navy Occupation, WWII Victory, and the Good Conduct Medal.

A graduate engineer from the State University of New York and has a MA degree from Rutgers Univ. Presently, works for the state of New Jersey with the Dept. of Labor as an employment counselor. He is a past department commander of New Jersey and has served all echelons in post, county and state.

Married to Ruth Lernor on June 14, 1941, has two children, Alan and Lois (deceased May 15, 1991), and one step-grandson, Louis, a lawyer. Yurman and his son, Alan, both belong to the Sanford L. Kahn Post #538, Kearney, NJ.

MAX YURMAN, SR., served in the U.S. Army enlisting on Feb. 22, 1916 (1st generation Yurman) Served in the Horse Cavalry under Gen. J.J. Pershing's command on the Mexican Border.

When the U.S. entered WWI, he went overseas with the American Expeditionary Forces in the 1st Div. His assignment was with the Signal Corps in the 2nd Field Bn., Co. B as a motorcycle courier.

Received Commendation for four major campaigns: Monriddier-Noyon Defensive, June 9-13, 1918; Aisne-Marne Offensive, July 18-Aug. 6, 1918; Saint Mihiel Offensive, Sept. 12-16, 1918; Meuse-Argonne Offensive, Sept. 26-Nov. 11, 1918.

He was with the occupation troops in Germany and returned to the States where he was honorably discharged on June 28, 1919, as private first class.

Joined the Furrier Worker's Union as a union organizer and was shot by a New York Policeman on July 27, 1920, during a labor dispute. He died at age 22.

MURRAY ZAGORSKI, born in Chrzanow, Poland, May 28, 1926. In March 1941, was taken to a concentration camp in various places in Germany and liberated on May 5, 1945. A Holocaust survivor, he came to the U.S. in 1947 and moved to Nutley, NJ with his sister (also a survivor). They were all that remained from his family of six.

Joined the U.S. Army in 1950 at the beginning of the Korean War. Trained at the 3rd Armd. Cav. Regt. at Ft. George G. Meade, MD, as a tank commander for scouting and patrolling.

Because of his foreign language knowledge, he was put into Army Intelligence and sent to Germany with the 317th MI Svc. His prime mission was to interrogate prisoners or illegal border crossings from the occupied Soviet Union. He was honorably discharged in 1956.

Married in 1959 and later divorced, has one daughter, Ann, and two granddaughters, Emily Rose and Allison Celia Kaplan.

ABRAHAM S. ZAKAR, born in Corfu, Greece, May 3, 1912. Inducted March 26, 1942, Camp Upton, NY. Basic training at Ft. Eustis, VA, Antiaircraft Training Ctr. Other military locations included: Camp Stewart, GA; Camp Campbell, KY; Liverpool, England; France and Germany.

After the armistice, served with Occupation Forces until September 1945.

Awards/Medals: Bronze Star, American Service Medal, European-Africa Medal, Central Europe, Rhineland, Good Conduct Medal, WWII Victory Medal, three Battle Star Citations, Unit Combat Citations and Carbine MM Marksman Medal.

Returned to States on USS *Warren* and was honorably discharged Dec. 11, 1945.

Attended City College of New York, Pratt Institute, Pace Univ., College of the Desert, Cal-Poly Univ. (Pamona, CA) and Cal State University in San Bernadino. BA in accounting and paralegal studies, Associate of Arts in real estate and business administration and Master of public administration. Served as treasurer and controller of Davis & Warshow, Inc. in Maspeth, NY from 1961 until retirement in 1978. Presently, commissioner, city of Palm Springs; business counselor, SBA-SCORE; volunteer AARP senior tax preparation program and accounting and financial consulting services.

Member of National Assoc. of Public Accountants, San Diego Jewish Genealogical Society and Service Corps of Retired Executives.

Married Betty R. Yohai, March 29, 1941; children: Stuart Steven, Gary Ira and Rayna Joyce, and grandchildren, Alexandra and Julian.

MYRON ZALEON, born Syracuse, NY, Nov. 6, 1921. Graduated from Nottingham High School and attended Syracuse University.

Left Syracuse University in July 1942 and joined the USAAF. Trained at Lincoln, NE and Atlantic City. Served overseas and was killed in a plane crash in India Jan. 2, 1944, at the age of 22.

NATHAN ZANKEL, born in New York City, Aug. 16, 1928. Joined the USNR, December 1951. Attended Supply Officers School and served in the USS *Kermit Roosevelt* (ARG-16).

Received honorable discharge October 1964 as lieutenant colonel. Awards/Medals include the Korean Campaign and two Battle Stars.

Employed with CED Manufacturing Company.

NATHAN ZARUCHES, born in Chicago, IL Nov. 4, 1922. Enlisted in the USN October 1941. Basic training at Great Lakes Naval Training Station. Graduated New London Submarine School, assigned as an instructor on the school submarine USS 0-3. Requested overseas assignment. Transferred to the USS *Barb* (SS-220) and USS *Griffin* (AS-13). Duty stations included Panama Canal; Pearl Harbor; Midway Island; Subic Bay, P.I.; Brisbane, Australia; Submarine Squadron 12, Fremantle, Australia; and senior electrician on Kwajalein Atoll during Operation Crossroads, the Atomic Bomb Test.

Received an honorable discharge from the USN, November 1946. Recalled during the Korean Conflict. Received an honorable discharge from the USNR, November 1951.

Awards/Medals: American Theater, Asiatic-Pacific, Submarine Combat Dolphin, Philippine Liberation Medal, Good Conduct Medal, WWII Victory Medal.

PC JWV Post 389. Employed by IRS from September 1956 to November 1987. Received mid-level management training, University of Chicago, top-level management training, University of Michigan, retired as senior regional analyst.

LEONARD ZATZ is a teacher of Distributive Education and has performed excellently. He has been aggressive and efficient in seeking out business opportunities for Distributive Education students.

He has exercised leadership nation-wide in sponsoring DECA programs. Students and faculty, hold him in high regard.

LEWIS B. ZIMAN, born in Scranton, PA Sept. 20, 1919. Enlisted in the service July 7, 1941, and served in the Medical ASF Regional Hosp. at Camp Lee, VA.

Spent four years and five months at Camp Lee, three years as hospital sergeant major. He was discharged Dec. 14, 1945 as master sergeant.

Married with three daughters and nine grandchildren. Currently, he is a funeral director. A member of JWV Post 165.

HARRY LOUIS ZIMMERMAN, born in San Antonio, TX, Aug. 9, 1942. Enlisted July 1967 in the Army Special Forces. Served in Ft. Bragg, NC and the Republic of Vietnam.

On the night of Aug. 17-18, 1968, when Camp Loc Ninh was attacked and mortared by VC, Capt. Zimmerman combined with the VNSF personnel to direct his men in antifire to stop the VC human wave assaults. He contacted the plane for flare drop and accurate artillery fire causing the VC withdrawal, leaving behind 20 dead and eight assorted weapons.

Awards/Medals: National Defense Service Medal, Vietnam Jump Wings, Purple Heart, Vietnam Commendation Medal, Silver Star, Vietnam Service Medal, Meritorious Unit Citation, Soldiers Medal, Army Commendation Medal, Bronze Star Medal and the Vietnam Cross of Gallantry with Silver Star. He was discharged in July 1969.

Married Betty Goodman July 1970. They have two daughters, Carrie and Cecelia. He is a criminal defense attorney.

JACK B. ZIMMERMANN, Colonel, USMCR, born May 11, 1942, San Antonio, TX. Graduated from USNA, Annapolis, MD and commissioned a USMC 2nd lieutenant, June 3, 1964. Served two tours in Vietnam as an artillery officer, including command of two batteries.

Received two Bronze Stars for heroism, and was wounded at the Rockpile, near the DMZ. Was one of very few Jewish USMC combat commanders in Vietnam. Served as a staff officer at a joint command and at HQ USMC.

Earned a master's degree in management, Purdue University. Graduated from law school at the University of Texas and served as judge advocate. Served 14 years active duty and 16 years as drilling Reservist. Commanded a reserve infantry battalion and later an Inspector Detachment of Division Headquarters. Served as senior staff officer at Aircraft Wing and Force Service Support Group. Final tour as a general court-martial judge.

Decorations include Joint Service Commendation Medal, Navy Commendation Medal with Combat V, Combat Action Ribbon and numerous meritorious and service ribbons.

A nationally known civilian criminal defense attorney, he has been married to the former Ilene Marcia Weinberger since 1964, and has a daughter, Terri Raye Jacobs, and a son, David Wayne, both of whom are officers in the USMC.

ARTHUR S. ZINSTEIN, Lieutenant, born Paterson, NJ, Nov. 19, 1918. Educated in Paterson and Jersey City, NJ. Entered the U.S. Army January 1940 and attached to the 44th Div. Med. Corps, Ft. Dix, NJ.

Later entered the USAF, attended Flying School at Victorville, CA and graduated in top 10 with rank of lieutenant. Received his navigation wings, then went to Flying School to receive Bombardier Wings and awarded both ranks.

Stationed at Biloxi, MS, then transferred to Pratt, KS. After visit from Gen. Arnold with well wishes, he flew command ship of 315th BG (first B-29s out of U.S.) and directed them to safe landing in India in 1944.

Memorable experience was when reunited with his younger brother, Hobart, for a brief one day session, after four years. He made several strikes on Japanese targets and died in action June 5, 1944.

HOBART ZINSTEIN, born Paterson, NJ, January 1943. Educated and graduated in Jersey City, NJ. Enlisted in the Armed Forces November 1942, assigned to 31st Hvy. Constr. Bn., USA Sig. Corps. and trained in Indiana.

Shipped to North Africa 1943, then to China Burma India to install communication on Burma Road from Assam to Chungking, China. Traveled Burma Road between these points bringing supplies as battalion supply sergeant.

Crossed Himalayas and survived three monsoon seasons in that time. Biggest thrill was meeting his older brother in India in 1944. This will remain with him forever.

He was discharged November 1945 and joined JWV Lt. Grover Post 10 as a charter member and is still a member. Carried first Israeli flag on Veterans Day 1948 as color guard.

Retired, he resides in Wayne, NJ with his wife, June. They have three children and two grandchildren

ABE ZITREN, born Sept. 29, 1923, New York City, NY. Entered the U.S. Army on Nov. 14, 1942. Served with the 310th Sig. OPN BN (9th Army) and was stationed at England, France, Belgium, Holland and Germany (including the Battle of the Bulge).

Discharged Oct. 30, 1945, as sergeant. Awards/Medals: Good Conduct, American Campaign, ETO with two stars, WWII Victory, Army of Occupation with clasp (Germany).

Married 50 years to Mildred and has two daughters and four grandchildren.

SIMON ZIVIN, born Jan. 5, 1918, Chicago, IL. Joined the USAR in 1938 and was inducted into the service in August 1943. Upon completion of Medical School training, University of Illinois, College of Medicine, Chicago, IL in 1942, he entered the Medical Corps of the U.S. Army as a 1st lieutenant.

Served at several camps in the U.S., mainly Camp Callan, CA and Ft. Knox, KY. In August 1944 was sent to the ETO as a member of the 5th Auxiliary Surgical Group attached to the 3rd and 9th Armies and served in England, France, Belgium, Holland and Germany.

Primary duty was anesthesiologist attached to several Evacuation Hospitals. In addition to the European Campaign Medal with four Battle Stars, received the Unit Citation Award as well as the Victory Medal. His most memorable remembrances are the Liberation of Paris, Battle of the Bulge and crossing the Rhine River into Germany over the Remagen Bridge.

In November 1945 he was separated from active service with the rank of captain. With the outbreak of the Korean Conflict in 1951, he was recalled to serve on the interim basis as chief of medicine at the Valley Forge Hospital, Phoenixville, PA.

Practicing internal medicine for 45 years in the Chicago, IL area. His family consists of wife, Mabel (married in 1942); two sons, Justin (M.D.) and Martin; two daughters, Nadine (died in 1945 while he was overseas) and Linda. His twin brother, Israel, was a lieutenant colonel in the Army Medical Corps and passed away in 1984.

PAUL S. ZONDERMAN, born in Boston, MA on March 10, 1939. Enlisted in the USMC with active duty from 1965-1967. Stationed at Quantico, VA; Newport, RI; and 29 Palms, CA. Served with HQ Bn. 3rd Mar. Div. in Da Nang and Phu Bai, Vietnam in 1967.

Memorable experience was meeting his daughter Lauren, who was born while he was in Vietnam, for the first time when she was six months old.

Awards/Medals: National Defense Service Medal, Vietnam Service Medal with one star, Presidential Unit Citation and Vietnam Campaign Medal with device. Was released from active duty in December 1967 and achieved the rank of captain in the USMCR.

Married to Ann R., has daughter, Lauren, and son, Jeffrey. He is an attorney in Schenectady, NY.

MERTON L. ZUBRES, born Albany, NY, Aug. 17, 1913. Attended Albany public schools, Union College at Schenectady, NY and graduated from Albany Law School in June of 1937. Commissioned 2nd lieutenant, QM Corps, Nov. 30, 1940, USMA, West Point. Ordered to active duty April 21, 1941 and activated 2nd Bn., 54th QM Regt., Camp Lee, VA, May 15, 1941.

Military Stations/Locations: Ft. Dix, NJ; Ord. School, APG, MD; Camp Brandford, VA; Liverpool where assigned to Ord Depot 0-614 at East Harling near Norfolk; Depot 0-646, Rushden, Northants; Sept. 8, 1944, ordered to Southampton for crossing English Channel to France.

Memorable Experiences: transferring troops from LCT 199 to 206 on English Channel without losing a single member of Army or Navy personnel; attending commanding officers conference in Paris to review movies of German surrender and the liberation of concentration camps; and the joy and celebration of the French people in Paris after surrender of Germany and their liberation.

Medals/Awards: American Defense Medal and Ribbon, EAME Medal and Ribbon with two Bronze Stars, Northern France Campaign Medal with Ribbon and two Bronze Stars, Rhineland Campaign Medal and Ribbon with Bronze Star, German Campaign Medal with Ribbon and WWII Victory Medal with Ribbon.

July 25, 1947, appointed CO of 333rd Ord. Bn., Reserve, with HQ in Albany. On Sept. 1, 1950, two companies assigned to the 333rd for training at Pine Camp, NY and were ordered to active duty to participate in the Korean Conflict. Was relieved from active status and transferred to Retired Reserve Dec. 30, 1954, with the rank of lieutenant colonel.

Married Dorris Fleishman June 22, 1947, has three sons: Mark, Barry and Richard. Retired Dec. 31, 1987, from practice of law and became Domiciliary of Florida, living at Boca Raton. Was commander of JWV Albany Post 105 in 1947.

SANFORD B. ZISKIND, joined the service in August 1943 and served with the 4th Div. Inf. in the ETO.

Memorable experience was D-day with Tank Battalion. After 31 months, he was discharged in March 1946.

LEONARD ZVIBLEMAN, born Jan. 12, 1919, in St. Louis, MO. Shipped to McClennend Field, Sacramento, CA, June 9, 1941, and became part of the 7th Sqdn., 62nd Troop Carrier Group. After 11 months in California, the entire group transferred to England, September 1942.

As aerial engineer in unarmed C-47 (the work horse of the Air Force), he towed gliders, dropped Paratroops, hauled wounded and supplies in Sicilian, Naples-Foggia, Tunisan, North Apennines, Rome-Arno, Southern France, Po Valley, Balkans and Greece campaigns.

Awards/Medals: eight Bronze Stars for above campaigns, Air Medal with two clusters, Good Conduct Medal and is entitled to wear the American Defense Service Ribbon, EAME Campaign with five OLCs. Received honorable discharge September 1945 with the rank of tech sergeant.

Married to Elma Lerner and has two married daughters and two grandchildren. Retired after 32 years of self-employment in an auto-parts business.

STANLEY N. ZWAIK, born Aug. 4, 1918, Jamaica, NY. Served in the Army Military Police and was stationed at Ft. Riley, KS; OCS, Ft. Oglethorpe, GA; 801st MP BN, New Zealand; Sydney, Australia; Milne Bay, New Guinea; and Manila, Philippines.

Memorable experience was meeting his brother by accident in the New Guinea jungles.

Awards/Medals: Asiatic-Pacific Medal with two stars, WWII Victory Medal and the Philippine Liberation Medal. He retired in 1963 as lieutenant colonel.

Married to Anne and has two daughters, Jodi and Steffi, and four grandchildren. An attorney since November 1942 and still practicing law.

JWV Experiences: commander, Queens County, NY, 1956-1957; commander, Dept. of New York, 1968-1969; past national commander, 1982-1983 and held many other elected and appointed positions.

ALICE H. ZWEIMAN, born Brooklyn, NY, Sept. 22, 1922. Enlisted Aug. 10, 1943, USN. Attended USN Training Schools (aircraft instruments) in Bronx, NY and Chicago, IL.

Served at Naval Air Station, San Diego, CA and worked on Norden Bombsight (repaired and installed) and worked on inspectroscope.

Discharged Nov. 25, 1945, as aviation machinist mate 2/c.

LEOPOLD J. ZWEIMAN, entered the U.S. Army Aug. 4, 1941, Ft. Dix, NJ. Basic training at Camp Lee, VA; served with Medical Corps August 1941-November 1941.

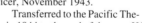

Military locations/stations include Kelly Field, TX, November 1941, Medical Corps; Eglin AFB, FL, April 1942, Medical Corps; OCS, Gainesville, FL, April 1943; 712th MP BN, Attica, NY, April 1943; Camp Upton, NY, police and prison officer, November 1943.

Transferred to the Pacific Theater in 1944 to the end of the war, HQ company commander. Discharged at Ft. Dix in February 1945.

MITCHELL M. ZWEIMAN (MICKEY), born West New York, NJ, March 13, 1919. Inducted Aug. 3, 1942, entered active service Aug. 17, 1942, Newark, NJ, mess sergeant.

Participated in action in Rome-Arno and Naples-Foggia.

Received the EAME Service Medal and the Good Conduct Medal. He was honorably discharged Nov. 7, 1945 as staff sergeant.

He passed away March 18, 1989. He had one son (deceased) and is survived by his wife.

ROBERT M. ZWEIMAN, born New York City, Nov. 9, 1927. Graduated New York University School of Commerce, Accounts and Finance with a BS in accounting in 1945 and from the New York University School of Law with a J.D. in law in 1949.

Enlisted U.S. Army on April 24, 1946; basic training in the mechanized cavalry at Ft. Knox, KY, then service as a tech 5 grade in the Army Finance Dept. at two replacement and disposition centers in the Philippines. He was discharged on July 25, 1947, and awarded the WWII Victory Medal.

Admitted to practice of law in New York in 1952 and in New Jersey in 1962. Engaged in the practice of law until 1991.

Commander of North Hudson J. George Fredman Post 76, 1954-56; the Hudson County Council, NJ, 1960-61; the Dept. of New Jersey, 1967-68 and was national commander from 1981-82. Also served as a post, county, department and national judge advocate, national executive committee chairman, international liaison officer, national foreign affairs committee chairman, national resolutions committee chairman, coordinating committee chairman and presently serves as the national centennial chairman. Developed programs and policies as the managerial coordination of the JWV and NMI, Manual of Ceremonies revision, Allied Veteran Missions to Israel and JWV Direct Mail fund-raising campaigns.

As a JWV representative, he was elected to two terms, 1967-1969, as the national chairman of the All-American Conference to combat communism. The conference was an umbrella organization composed of the national representatives of 38 national civic, veteran, fraternal and service organizations. He also served on the Executive Committee of the AIPAC, NJCRAC, Conference of the Presidents of Major Jewish Organizations. Served as the president of the National Museum of American Jewish Military History from 1988-90.

Married in 1956 to Geraldine Scotti, a learning disabilities teacher-consultant.

WILLIAM ZWEIMAN, born Jan. 30, 1890, Zdollinous, Russia. Enlisted in the U.S. Army in 1917, served in HQ Co., 48th Inf. and was stationed in Newport News, VA.

Discharged April 13, 1918, as private. He married Marie Fernand Diska and had three sons: Leopold J., Mitchell M. and Robert M.

A member of North Hudson Post 76, he passed away Oct. 13, 1955.

NORMAN ZWERLING, born July 7, 1922, Philadelphia, PA. Graduated from high school in 1940 and enlisted in the USN in 1942. Basic training at Bainbridge, MD.

As pharmacist mate, he was shipped to 6th Beach Bn. One of the first medics to hit Omaha Beach on D-day, H-hour. Was hit by shrapnel on the second day and was the first wounded to be evacuated.

Transferred to USS *Rudderrow* (DE-224) and survived typhoon off Okinawa. Went up the line on promotions.

Medals/Awards: Presidential Citation, French Croix de Guerre, Bronze Star, Purple Heart, American Campaign, Asiatic-Pacific; European North Africa Campaign with two Bronze Stars, Philippine Liberation, Good Conduct, American Defense, USN Exp., Normandy Invasion from France. Honorably discharged in 1945.

Married to Gertrude and has two sons, Jerry A., Arthur J. and four grandchildren: Debbie, Barry and twins Aaron and Robert.

Life member of DAV. He owned a towing service and retired from city of Philadelphia in 1979.

Robert M. Zweiman, JWV Past National Commander and National Centennial Chairman acted as Master of Ceremonies at the March, 1996 Centennial Gala. National Commander Neil Goldman cuts the official 100th anniversary cake.

Some of the proud and dedicated members of JWV and JWVA enjoying JWV's Festival 100.

JEWISH WAR VETERANS INDEX

The biographies are not included in the index since they appear in alphabetical order in the book.